THE CAMBRIDGE HANDBOOK OF
CONSTITUTIONAL THEORY

This Handbook brings together contributions from leading scholars of constitutional theory, with backgrounds in law, philosophy and political science. Its sixty chapters not only offer an exceptional survey of the field but also provide a major contribution to it. The book explores three main areas. First, the values upheld by a constitution, including rights, freedom, equality, dignity and well-being. Second, the modalities of a constitutional system, such as the separation of powers, democratic representation and the rule of law. Finally, the institutions through which it operates, both legal and political, including courts, elections, parliaments and international organisations. It also considers the challenges confronting constitutional arrangements from growing inequality, populism, climate change and migration.

Richard Bellamy is a Professor of Political Science at University College London (UCL), and a Fellow of the British Academy. He is the author of eleven monographs, including *Political Constitutionalism: A Republican Defence of the Constitutionality of Democracy* (Cambridge University Press, 2007).

Jeff King is a Professor of Law at University College London (UCL), and was previously a Fellow and Tutor in Law at Balliol College, Oxford. His other works include *Judging Social Rights* (Cambridge University Press, 2012). From 2019 to 2021, he was Legal Adviser to the UK House of Lords Constitution Committee.

The Cambridge Handbook of Constitutional Theory

Edited by

RICHARD BELLAMY

University College London

JEFF KING

University College London

Shaftesbury Road, Cambridge CB2 8EA, United Kingdom

One Liberty Plaza, 20th Floor, New York, NY 10006, USA

477 Williamstown Road, Port Melbourne, VIC 3207, Australia

314–321, 3rd Floor, Plot 3, Splendor Forum, Jasola District Centre, New Delhi – 110025, India

103 Penang Road, #05–06/07, Visioncrest Commercial, Singapore 238467

Cambridge University Press is part of Cambridge University Press & Assessment, a department of the University of Cambridge.

We share the University's mission to contribute to society through the pursuit of education, learning and research at the highest international levels of excellence.

www.cambridge.org
Information on this title: www.cambridge.org/9781108491310

DOI: 10.1017/9781108868143

© Cambridge University Press & Assessment 2025

This publication is in copyright. Subject to statutory exception and to the provisions of relevant collective licensing agreements, no reproduction of any part may take place without the written permission of Cambridge University Press & Assessment.

First published 2025

Printed in the United Kingdom by CPI Group Ltd, Croydon CR0 4YY

A catalogue record for this publication is available from the British Library

A Cataloging-in-Publication data record for this book is available from the Library of Congress

ISBN 978-1-108-49131-0 Hardback

Cambridge University Press & Assessment has no responsibility for the persistence or accuracy of URLs for external or third-party internet websites referred to in this publication and does not guarantee that any content on such websites is, or will remain, accurate or appropriate.

Contents

List of Figures		*page* xi
List of Contributors		xiii
Preface and Acknowledgements		xix
1	**Introduction: Of Constitutions and Constitutional Theory** *Richard Bellamy and Jeff King*	1

PART I VALUES

2	**Human Dignity** *Jeremy Waldron*	23
3	**Rights** *Rowan Cruft*	38
4	**Equality** *Annabelle Lever*	56
5	**Liberty** *Philip Pettit*	71
6	**Well-Being** *Sarah Conly*	88
7	**Self-Government** *Thomas Christiano*	102
8	**Justice: Procedural and Substantive** *Rainer Forst*	121
9	**Recognition** *Helder De Schutter*	136

PART II MODALITIES

10	**Impartiality** *Matthew H. Kramer*	157
11	**Constitutional Legitimacy** *Nomi Claire Lazar*	176
12	**Sovereignty** *David Dyzenhaus*	192
13	**Constituent Power** *Martin Loughlin*	208
14	**Representation** *Nadia Urbinati*	225
15	**Deliberation** *Simone Chambers*	246
16	**Opposition** *Grégoire Webber*	262
17	**The Separation of Powers** *Jacob T. Levy*	279
18	**The Rule of Law** *Jeff King*	297
19	**Constitutional Conventions** *Jon Elster*	316
20	**Secularism** *Cécile Laborde*	333
21	**Constitutional Review** *Christoph Möllers*	343
22	**Constitutional Interpretation** *Timothy Endicott*	361
23	**Proportionality** *George Letsas*	378
24	**Civil Disobedience** *Candice Delmas*	397

25	**Constitutional Entrenchment** *N. W. Barber*	417
26	**Emergency Powers** *Karin Loevy*	433
27	**Regulation** *Julia Black*	451
28	**Cost–Benefit Analysis** *Matthew Adler*	470
29	**Revolution** *Nimer Sultany*	491

PART III INSTITUTIONS

A The State

30	**The State** *Anna-Bettina Kaiser*	523
31	**The Material Constitution** *Marco Goldoni*	537
32	**Federalism** *Stephen Tierney*	553
33	**Consociationalism** *Joseph Lacey and Nenad Stojanović*	568
34	**Corporatism** *Steven Klein*	585
35	**Guarantor (or the So-called "Fourth Branch") Institutions** *Tarunabh Khaitan*	603
36	**Central Banks** *Jens van 't Klooster*	622

B The Executive

37	**Presidentialism, Parliamentarism, and Their Hybrids** *Steffen Ganghof*	640
38	**Prerogative** *Thomas Poole*	656

39	The Administrative State *Blake Emerson*	678
40	Executive Rulemaking *Susan Rose-Ackerman*	698

C The Democratic System

41	Constituent Assemblies *Joel Colón-Ríos*	721
42	Citizenship *Elizabeth F. Cohen and Cyril Ghosh*	736
43	Elections *Daniel Weinstock*	753
44	Political Parties *Jonathan White and Lea Ypi*	776
45	Legislatures *Richard Ekins*	792
46	Referendums *Silvia Suteu*	810
47	Citizens' Juries/Minipublics *Cristina Lafont*	829

D The Legal System

48	Constitutional Courts and Supreme Courts *Christine Landfried*	848
49	Judicial Independence *David Kosař and Samuel Spáč*	867
50	Bills of Rights *Richard Bellamy*	884
51	Administrative Law *Farrah Ahmed*	902
52	Horizontal Effect *Oliver Gerstenberg*	917

E The Global System

53 **Global and National Constitutionalism** 938
    Carmen E. Pavel

54 **Regional Integration** 955
    Turkuler Isiksel

55 **International Organisations** 974
    Anne Peters

PART IV CHALLENGES FOR CONSTITUTIONAL DEMOCRACY

56 **Inequality** 997
    Roberto Gargarella

57 **Populism** 1015
    Paul Blokker

58 **Climate Change** 1034
    Jocelyn Stacey

59 **Migration** 1053
    Sarah Song

60 **Constitutional Hardball** 1070
    Mark Tushnet

Bibliography 1089
Index 1211

Figures

27.1	Regulatory systems – an analytical framework	*page* 454
36.1	Four steps in the interpretation of a central bank mandate	627
37.1	Six basic forms of government	642
48.1	The preconditions for legitimate and effective constitutional review by courts	854
49.1	Judicial independence formula	871

Contributors

Matthew Adler, Richard A. Horvitz Professor of Law and Professor of Economics, Philosophy and Public Policy, Duke University

Farrah Ahmed, Professor, Melbourne Law School, University of Melbourne

N. W. Barber, Professor of Constitutional Law and Theory, Trinity College, University of Oxford

Richard Bellamy, Professor of Political Science, University College London (UCL)

Julia Black, Professor of Law and Regulation at Oxford University and a Visiting Professor of Law at the London School of Economics and Political Science

Paul Blokker, Professor of Political Sociology, Bologna University

Simone Chambers, Professor of Political Science, University of California, Irvine

Thomas Christiano, Professor and Head of Philosophy, University of Arizona

Elizabeth F. Cohen, Maxwell Professor of United States Citizenship, Department of Political Science, Boston University

Joel Colón-Ríos, Professor of Law, University of Essex; Adjunct Professor, Te Herenga Waka - Victoria University of Wellington

Sarah Conly, Professor Emerita of Philosophy, Bowdoin College

Rowan Cruft, Professor of Philosophy, University of Stirling

Candice Delmas, Associate Professor of Philosophy and Political Science, Northeastern University

Helder De Schutter, Professor of Social and Political Philosophy, KU Leuven.

David Dyzenhaus, Professor of Law and Philosophy and Albert Abel Chair, University of Toronto

Richard Ekins, Professor of Law and Constitutional Government, University of Oxford

Jon Elster, Robert K. Merton Professor Emeritus of the Social Sciences, Columbia University

Blake Emerson, Professor of Law, UC Los Angeles School of Law

Timothy Endicott, Vinerian Professor of English Law, University of Oxford

Rainer Forst, Professor of Political Theory and Philosophy, Goethe University Frankfurt

Steffen Ganghof, Professor of Comparative Politics, University of Potsdam

Roberto Gargarella, Senior Researcher (CONICET/Argentina), Univ. Pompeu Fabra (Barcelona)

Oliver Gerstenberg, Senior Lecturer in Law, Faculty of Laws, UCL

Cyril Ghosh, Lloyd B. Politsch '33 Chair in Law & Associate Professor of Political Science, Clark University

Marco Goldoni, Professor of Philosophy of Law, University of Glasgow

Turkuler Isiksel, Associate Professor, Department of Political Science, Columbia University

Anna-Bettina Kaiser, Professor of Public Law and the Foundations of Law, Humboldt University of Berlin

Tarunabh Khaitan, Professor of Public Law, London School of Economics and Political Science; Honorary Professorial Fellow, Melbourne Law School

Jeff King, Professor of Law, Faculty of Laws, UCL

Steven Klein, Senior Lecturer in Political Theory, King's College London

David Kosař, Professor of Constitutional Law and Co-Director of the Judicial Studies Institute, Masaryk University

Matthew H. Kramer, Professor of Legal and Political Philosophy, University of Cambridge

Cécile Laborde, Professor of Political Theory, Nuffield Chair of Political Theory, University of Oxford

Joseph Lacey, Associate Professor of Political Theory, School of Politics and International Relations, University College Dublin

Cristina Lafont, Harold H. and Virginia Anderson Professor of Philosophy, Northwestern University

List of Contributors   xv

Christine Landfried, Professor Emerita of Political Science, University of Hamburg

Nomi Claire Lazar, Professor, Graduate School of Public and International Affairs, University of Ottawa

George Letsas, Professor of the Philosophy of Law, Faculty of Laws, UCL

Annabelle Lever, Professor of Political Philosophy, Sciences Po, Paris (IEP, Paris); Permanent Researcher at CEVIPOF

Jacob T. Levy, Tomlinson Professor of Political Theory, Chair of the Department of Political Science, and Coordinator of the Research Group on Constitutional Studies, McGill University

Karin Loevy, JSD Program Manager, Researcher, Institute for International Law and Justice, New York University School of Law.; Kathleen Fitzpatrick Postdoctoral Visiting Fellow with the Laureate Program in International Law, Melbourne Law School

Martin Loughlin, Professor of Public Law, LSE

Christoph Möllers, Chair in Public Law and Legal Philosophy, Humboldt University of Berlin

Carmen E. Pavel, Reader in Politics, Philosophy, and Economics, Department of Political Economy, King's College London

Anne Peters, Director, Max Planck Institute for Comparative Public Law and International Law, Heidelberg; Professor of Law, Universities of Heidelberg, FU Berlin and Basel; L. Bates Lea Global Law Professor, University of Michigan

Philip Pettit, L. S. Rockefeller University Professor of Human Values, Princeton University; Distinguished Professor of Philosophy, Australian National University

Thomas Poole, Professor of Law, LSE

Susan Rose-Ackerman, Henry R. Luce Professor Emeritus of Jurisprudence, Law School and Department of Political Science, Yale University, and Professorial Lecturer in Law, Yale Law School

Sarah Song, Professor of Law, Philosophy, and Political Science, University of California, Berkeley

Samuel Spáč, Assistant Professor of Political Science, Comenius University; Senior Researcher, Judicial Studies Institute, Masaryk University

Jocelyn Stacey, Associate Professor, Peter A. Allard School of Law, University of British Columbia

Nenad Stojanović, Professor of Political Science, University of Geneva

Nimer Sultany, Reader in Public Law, School of Oriental and African Studies

Silvia Suteu, Professor of Law, European University Institute

Stephen Tierney, Professor of Constitutional Theory, University of Edinburgh

Mark Tushnet, William Nelson Cromwell Professor of Law, Emeritus, Harvard Law School

Nadia Urbinati, Kyriakos Tsakopoulos Professor of Political Theory, Columbia University

Jens van 't Klooster, Assistant Professor of Political Economy, Department of Political Science, Amsterdam University

Jeremy Waldron, University Professor and Professor of Law, New York University

Grégoire Webber, Canada Research Chair in Public Law and Philosophy of Law, Queen's University

Daniel Weinstock, Katharine A. Pearson Chair in Civil Society and Public Policy, Faculty of Law, McGill University

Jonathan White, Professor of Politics, European Institute, LSE

Lea Ypi, Professor in Political Theory, LSE

Bentham House Conference, 'Foundational Concepts in Constitutional Theory' held at the Faculty of Laws, University College London, 10–12 July 2019.

From Left to Right:

Front row: Jacob Levy, Nadia Urbinati, Helen Brown Coverdale, Lea Ypi, David Dyzenhaus.

Second row: Candice Delmas, Amanda Greene, Nomi Claire Lazar, Kimberley Brownlee, Simone Chambers, Philip Pettit, Carmen Pavel, TRS Allan, Jeff King, Oliver Gerstenberg.

Final row: Matthew Kramer, Matthew Adler, Richard Bellamy, Timothy Endicott, Thomas Christiano, Jonathan White, Daniel Weinstock, George Letsas, Jeremy Waldron, Adam Swift, Helder de Schutter, Rainer Forst, Jon Elster, Rowan Cruft, Martin Loughlin.

Preface and Acknowledgements

Scholarly and political reflection on constitutions and constitutionalism has undergone considerable upheaval in recent decades. Following the rights revolution in the early 1990s, faith in judicially enforced constitutional rights became widespread. Often regarded as the crowning achievement of liberal democratic government, this faith wavered as judicial review came in for trenchant and sometimes familiar critique. At the same time, various testing political storms were brewing or in full swing. These included rapid globalisation, new theatres for terrorism, worsening economic inequality, the advent of post-liberal political populism and well-founded fears about the consequences of climate and technological changes. In the midst of these developments, a tremendous amount of scholarly work has been done on the meaning and implications of a broader range of constitutional values, concepts and institutions. The preoccupation with rights and judicial review has become less all-consuming than it was, and work by constitutional lawyers has begun to tilt towards the more political features of constitutional orders. At the same time, increasingly specialised work in political theory and political science has resulted in a new degree of depth that such hedgehog-like concentration necessarily produces.

This Handbook is the result of a discussion between us that there was a need for a compendious exploration of the central and foundational concepts in constitutional government. It should reflect the broad view of the values, principles and institutions linked to constitutional government, as well as the disciplinary ecumenism that characterises our own interests. And it should be guided by the kind of intellectual openness that underlines the collaboration, given the differences between our views. Our hope is that such a Handbook will prove resourceful to students and to scholars interested in diverse and sometimes remote areas of constitutional theory. To give effect to the idea, we hatched plans for convening a gathering of an improbably high-quality group of constitutional theorists at the Faculty of Laws, UCL, for a Bentham House Conference. Held in July 2019, most of the scholars with chapters in Parts I and II of the Handbook attended, and the papers were subject to scrutiny not only by the other contributors and panellists but also by a range of other theorists based at UCL at the time. Alas, our plans to host further conferences for authors contributing to Parts III and IV were trounced by the advent in March 2020 of the COVID-19 pandemic. That pandemic also resulted in delays in finalising the manuscript(s) for various contributors and us editors, particularly those with school-aged children. Despite the inauspicious timing, we are immensely proud of the result. Our editorial approach was time-consuming but rewarding. We each read and commented individually on the chapters before meeting to discuss them for an hour, and later returning to authors jointly composed comments. We feel the approach helped to contribute to a very high quality volume, which we are pleased to shepherd to publication.

We owe deep debts to various persons who helped bring the project to fruition and to a close. Karolina Kopcyznska-Grobelny provided outstanding research assistance in the first two years of the project, helping us keep track of the paper flow. Ashley Denny Petch of the UCL Laws events team allowed us to hold an outstandingly well-organised conference at which everything was in good working order. We are highly indebted to colleagues at the UCL Faculty of Laws, and in particular to those who awarded us the privilege of hosting the Bentham House Conference on this topic. Their judicious advice on the application was instrumental to how the process was carried out. We would also like to thank the team at Cambridge University Press, including Finola O'Sullivan, who was our original editor for the project but who had moved on at the time the book went to press. Marianne Nield was very helpful at every stage of the process, and we appreciate the flexibility shown about the inevitable delays resulting from the COVID-19 pandemic.

We would also like to thank the scholars who participated in the July 2019 Bentham House Conference but who did not contribute chapters to the volume. These persons chaired sessions or commented on papers by contributing authors. They include T. R. S. Allan, Kimberlee Brownlee, Helen Coverdale, Amanda Greene, Jeffrey Howard, Prince Saprai, Adam Swift, Kevin Toh, Paul Tucker and Albert Weale. They were a vital part of the brain trust for those crucial two days.

We single out in particular the extraordinary contribution of Cosmin Vraciu, whose assistance in the second half of the project was crucial for moving it forwards and getting it over the line. He copy-edited every chapter in the volume and made dozens of valuable observations and suggestions which only the most discerning reader would notice. The precise form of the final volume depends, in no small part, on his rare combination of critical judgment and tireless attention to detail.

Jeff King would like to thank the Leverhulme Trust, whose Philip Leverhulme Prize funded teaching relief that was critical in completing this volume; the UCL Faculty of Laws for a relevant period of sabbatical leave, and for its superb collegiality and support for parents; and in particular his wife and eternal collaborator Julika Erfurt, whose wisdom guides any of his successful pursuits. He offers no apologies to his children for suffering his absence, because they rightly suffered none. Richard Bellamy thanks both the European University Institute, where he was Director of the Max Weber Programme at the time of the Bentham Conference, and the Political Science department at UCL, for providing funds for both the conference and for research assistance with the volume. He is also grateful as ever to Sandra Kröger for her forbearance and intellectual and emotional support over the course of the editorial marathon required to bring this project to fruition.

Richard Bellamy & Jeff King
London, October 2023

1

Introduction

Of Constitutions and Constitutional Theory

Richard Bellamy and Jeff King

The late Joseph Raz once remarked that 'the writings on constitutional theory fill libraries' (Raz 1998, p. 152). Whether true or not, the present volume assembles a mini library of essays by some of the leading scholars in the field with the ambitious goal of covering a broad range of the central topics of contemporary constitutional theory. In doing so, we have sought not only to survey but also to help define the topography of the subject by elaborating an innovative conceptual scheme for this book. This scheme consists of four parts: values (I), modalities (II), institutions (III) and challenges (IV). The topics proceed from the abstract to the more concrete. In this scheme, values specify those attributes, conditions or norms, all – or some – of which, most constitutional theorists consider to be of fundamental moral worth (e.g., dignity, liberty, equality, welfare and self-government). Though there are disagreements as to how these values are to be understood, at least some subset of them is widely regarded as foundational to the normative justification of any constitutional order, with many theorists considering most or all of them as intrinsically valuable. As such, these values serve to anchor normative arguments about the appropriate ends and means of constitutional law and politics. The modalities relate to arrangements, processes or principles that, while also abstract, are somewhat more complex, institution-dependent and invariably of instrumental worth (e.g., the separation of powers, the rule of law and political representation). Although these are often deployed as self-evidently worthwhile, they are ultimately judged by how well they serve deeper values. The contributions to this Handbook tend to elucidate these connections. The category of institutions is broad, encompassing concrete institutions, offices and political arrangements (e.g., the state, electoral systems, administration, government, legislatures, referendums and central banking). The chapters discussing these institutions often offer a normative account of their ideal role alongside a quite contextualised account of their functioning (and weaknesses) in one or more constitutional orders. We consider the inclusion of these essays as one of the major contributions of this Handbook and the more intensely institutional focus should be seen as major domain for future constitutional theorising (Waldron 2016d). Lastly, the category of challenges encompasses theoretical discussion of certain social, political or environmental problems that have a profound impact on constitutional government. Inequality, climate change, populism, migration and 'hardball' tactics come in for constitutionally specific analysis.

While the editors asked the authors to contribute a sketch of the field, they also invited them to advocate their own distinctive views of the topic in question. However, the reader will be able easily to distinguish where the authors' accounts of 'the field' leave off and their own distinctive views commence. Each chapter also comes with a selection of recommended readings, allowing readers to further develop their own distinctive views.

Any attempt to provide a topical summary of such a broad landscape risks proving both controversial and incomplete. Instead, this Introduction aims to explore those issues that remain important to all the essays but are not the focus of any. Among them is the very definition of constitutional theory itself, as well as the definitions of constitutions, constitutional rules and norms, and constitutionalism. These tasks occupy the remainder of this introduction.

I CONSTITUTIONAL THEORY

There is no widely adopted definition of 'constitutional theory'. Nevertheless, at its most basic, descriptive, level, constitutional theory can be regarded as theoretical argument or reflection about the role, nature or practice of public constitutional arrangements, both legal and political, in one or more countries. Such argument or reflection can be carried out in three distinguishable ways, which we call normative, conceptual and positive constitutional theory.

Normative constitutional theory consists chiefly of normative arguments in favour of particular constitutional arrangements or practices. It is a branch of applied political theory. It is *constitutional* theory because the arguments usually offer a closer attention to constitutional institutional detail than is commonly observed in political theory.[1] It is constitutional *theory* because the normative arguments frequently seek to transcend particular political orders (i.e., the arguments aspire to agent-neutrality). In that sense, normative constitutional theory is distinct from familiar arguments in constitutional law and politics, which contend for specific outcomes – such as how a particular case should be decided – in particular constitutional orders that are densely structured by settled norms, principles and usage.

Conceptual constitutional theory presents arguments about the deep nature of constitutional features, institutions and ideas, typically put across as conceptual or explanatory truths rather than normative arguments. What is the nature of sovereignty, and how does it relate to the nature of law? What is a state? In what sense is constitutional law 'higher law'? What are the essential characteristics of

---

[1] However, Waldron's (2016d) *Political Political Theory* is an effort to make more political theorists do what we here call normative constitutional theory.

legislatures, governments and the judiciary? What is constituent power and what is its connection to what is sometimes called ordinary and higher-law making? Martin Loughlin exemplifies this understanding of constitutional theory when he writes that '[i]f constitutional theory is to form a distinct inquiry, it must aim to identify the character of actually existing constitutional arrangements' (Loughlin 2005, p. 186). Loughlin does not mean, however, the character of arrangements in a particular country He means to refer to constitutional arrangements across at least a broad set of countries whose political arrangements differ fundamentally (Loughlin 2005, p. 186).[2] His endeavour is comparable to that of H. L. A. Hart's *Concept of Law* (1961), which the author famously described as an exercise in 'descriptive sociology' (Hart 1994 [1961], p. v). Loughlin considers the role of constitutional theory as being to 'identify a system of postulates' or 'a set of concepts' such as powers, rights, sovereignty, state, liberties and so on. It is 'the job of the theorist to … offer an explanation of the character of the practice' (Loughlin 2005, p. 186). Though this approach purports to be explanatory, we refer to it as conceptual. The 'explanations' are neither sociological nor empirical in any rigorous sense. Yet there is a long history of often excellent work in this vein. To take two old foes, Hans Kelsen's (1967 [1960], pp. 286–320) definition of the state as entirely subsumed within and at one with the legal order is a fine example of conceptual constitutional theory. Likewise, so is Carl Schmitt's (2008 [1928], pp. 75–82) rival attempt to describe the relationship between sovereignty and constituted law-making power. In this volume, the chapters on constituent power, the material constitution and federalism can be regarded as fine examples of what we consider to be conceptual constitutional theory. Such accounts are conceptual because the authors contend the concepts embody certain inherent meanings, such that usage of these terms in ways that are inconsistent with their alleged postulates are not simply unsound normatively but represent a misunderstanding that could be equated logically with a basic category mistake.

Positive constitutional theory consists of theoretical accounts of particular constitutional orders (or sets of constitutional orders). Sometimes described as 'self-understandings', or social theory, such accounts aim to indicate the attitudinal presuppositions of constitutional actors (persons, institutions and commentators) toward the principles and practices that animate the constitutional order and provide guidance on how controversies are settled within it. For example, Bruce Ackerman's *We the People* sets out to describe and theorise a 'dualist' democracy, whose essence turns on the distinction between normal (legislative) and higher (constitutional) law-making (Ackerman 1991, chap. 1). He distinguishes such a democracy from a rights-foundational constitutional order and a monistic constitutional order. He associates dualism with the United States, rights-foundationalism with post-war Germany and monism with the UK. In so doing, he indicates a positive constitutional theory

---

[2] 'Constitutional theory must acknowledge the nature of the activity that lies at the heart of all political constitutions' (Loughlin 2005, p. 186).

associated with each. John Hart Ely's *Democracy and Distrust* provides a theory of judicial review but offers it as an interpretation of the US Constitution that is concerned with 'process writ-large' (Ely 1980, chap. 4). As such, it has quite limited interpretive application to other constitutional orders such as the German post-war Basic Law. J. A. G. Griffith's famous essay on the political constitution contended aphoristically that the constitution is '[e]verything that happens', while noting that 'if nothing happened that would be constitutional also' (Griffith 1979, p. 19). This argument sought to describe the workings of the peculiarly political British constitution; it was not a discourse on the nature of constitutions more generally.[3]

Positive constitutional theory is not limited to particular legal orders. It can extend to families of legal orders of a given type as well, as when grouping countries under 'aversive' or 'transformative' (Klare 1998; Hailbronner 2017), or 'Commonwealth' (Gardbaum 2013) models of constitutionalism. Positive constitutional theory can often be ambiguous about the extent to which it is descriptive or normative. This is a difficulty that is inherent more generally in what Ronald Dworkin (1986, chap. 2) calls the 'interpretive attitude' or, and more plainly, in what Habermas (1996, chaps. 3 & 4; Gaus 1996) refers to as 'rational reconstruction'.[4] All the theories indicated earlier entail both description and normative theorising. Most of them have been widely received as normative (sometimes polemical) arguments, on occasion with questionable historical work behind them. While positive constitutional theory aims to take history seriously – as it must – it will inherently risk oversimplifying and idealising historical events and narratives in order to produce a unified account in the service of the author's preferred normative theory. This is a common issue among historians as well, including constitutional historians. In his classic critique, Herbert Butterfield (1951, p. v) castigated the Whig constitutional historian's tendency 'to emphasise certain principles of progress in the past and to produce a story which is the ratification if not the glorification of the present'. Nevertheless, at its best (and Griffith is a good specimen), positive constitutional theory exhibits a subtle attention to how power has shaped current constitutional institutions, norms and practices, and it offers powerful explanatory clarity of both a retrospective and prospective kind. Other examples of good positive constitutional theory include work on global constitutionalism and many interesting contributions to the theories animating the European Union.

The scheme of the present volume indicates a clear preference on our part for normative constitutional theory. This choice reflects a mild measure of scepticism about the lasting value of conceptual and positive constitutional theory, and of the comparative importance of normative constitutional theory. With the former,

---

[3] However, see Bellamy (2007), which draws on Griffith to construct a full normative theory of constitutionalism.
[4] According to Pedersen (2008, p. 458), 'Habermas seeks to combine an interpretative and explanatory approach to reality, but this approach must be descriptive as well as normative simultaneously.'

our scepticism is in part motivated by a long-standing suspicion of the capacity of conceptual argument to shed deep light (see Marglos and Laurence 2019, esp. sect. 5.2). Conceptual definitions can often be based on muted normative arguments or can obscure relevant moral issues by suggesting that they are conceptually irrelevant. One example is the idea of constituent power. The potentially dangerous idea that constituent power must of conceptual necessity be 'unbound' – and thus free of any legal restraint whatsoever – is a salient example with real-world purchase of conceptual reasoning determining a crucial normative issue. That issue is whether a constituted legislature should be able to set binding limits on the mandate of a constituent assembly. Another issue for conceptual constitutional theory is the unstable status of facts. The tradition trades on real-world examples and can at times be dismissive of normative arguments as ungrounded in reality. Yet, when historical counter-examples or contrasting accounts of the same events are offered, they can be dismissed as irrelevant to the concept or as what a theorist such as John Finnis (2011 [1980], pp. 9–11) would describe as a 'non-central case'. Positive constitutional theory, as noted in our brief discussion earlier, runs the risk of conflating description with normative argument (of being, in other words, 'bad history').

We must make clear, nonetheless, that our scepticism is mild and easily rebutted – and rebutted without exception in all the specimen contributions to this volume. Conceptual analysis, provided it is not extravagant in its claims, has a role in helping advance understanding not only in constitutional theory but also throughout the social sciences. And positive constitutional theory can shed great light on the ideas that animate constitutional orders, just as models do in sociology and political science. There is also a scepticism to be faced with our own emphasis on normative constitutional theory. One legitimate protest is that the very idea of normative constitutional theory risks allowing the subject to be 'completely absorbed into political philosophy' (Loughlin 2005, p. 186). Yet we are not disturbed by this overlap. Normative constitutional theory is to political theory what bioethics (or applied ethics in general) is to ethics. It is unnecessary to draw a clear line between them. The distinction is rather one of family resemblance, where writings cluster at one or the other end. The ends are typically distinguishable depending on the extent to which institutional detail plays a significant role in the discussion.

Whichever mode of constitutional theorising one adopts, however, one needs to have some view of what a constitution is, what constitutional norms are and what constitutionalism is. It is to these issues that we now turn.

II DEFINING CONSTITUTIONS: CONCEPT AND CONCEPTIONS

Notwithstanding our mild scepticism of conceptual reasoning, for the purposes of this volume it remains necessary to postulate a working definition of 'constitution' and relate it to different views of the idea. In doing so, it is helpful to distinguish between what John Rawls calls a concept and its various conceptions.

Rawls (1999a, p. 5) views the basic concept as 'specified' by the common 'role' it plays in different accounts or conceptions of it. As such, the concept operates at a more abstract level than any of the related conceptions. Most commentators on constitutions make a distinction similar to Rawls' by distinguishing between more basic and more elaborate definitions of a constitution. For example, Anthony King makes a distinction between a small 'c' and a capital 'C' constitution. He defines the former as 'the set of the most important rules and common understandings in any given country that regulate the relations among the country's governing institutions and also the relations between that country's governing institutions and the people of that country' (King 2009, p. 3). In a parallel manner, Kenneth Wheare distinguishes between 'constitution' in the broad and in the narrower sense. He defines the former as a way of describing 'the collection of rules which establish and regulate or govern the country, the government', noting that these rules 'are partly legal … and partly non-legal or extra-legal, taking the form of usages, understandings, customs or conventions' (Wheare 1951, pp. 2–3). He contends that 'in most countries of the world … it is possible to speak of this collection of rules as 'the Constitution'' (Wheare 1951, p. 1).

Lest King's and Wheare's analysis seem too parochially (and idiosyncratically) British, as, for example, Giovanni Sartori believed (Sartori 1962, pp. 853–857), consider Hans Kelsen's distinction between the 'material' and the 'formal' constitution. On Kelsen's account, '[t]he constitution in the material sense consists of those rules which regulate the creation of the general legal norms, in particular the creation of statutes' (Kelsen 1946a, p. 124), whereas the constitution in the formal sense is 'a solemn document' which contains the rules of the material constitution (though it may also contain other rules) and which is adopted and modified only under special procedures – which makes the formal constitution more difficult to amend than the ordinary law (Kelsen 1946a, p. 124). The constitution in either the material or the formal sense can claim to be '[t]he basis of the national legal order' (Kelsen 1946a, p. 258) and as such 'the highest level within national law' (Kelsen 1946a, p. 124). On Kelsen's view, therefore, the UK can be regarded as having a material constitution, which consists of the statutory and customary law regulating the making of the law, but not a formal constitution. So Kelsen's distinction between formal and material seems to approximate both King's distinction between capital 'C' and small 'c' constitutions, and Wheare's distinction between constitutions in the broad and in the narrow sense. The difference is that Kelsen takes the material constitution to concern only the rules for making rules (a view, as we see later, that is echoed by Rawls and Hayek), and not also the organisation of other public authorities, such as the executive or the judiciary, as King and Wheare (and Ivor Jennings 1963, pp. 33–34) do. However, he acknowledges that we may use the notion of a constitution in a 'political' as opposed to the 'legal' sense, in which case the constitution refers not only to the regulation of law-making but also to the regulation of the other branches of government, such as the executive or the judiciary (see Kelsen 1946a, pp. 258 sqq).

King's small 'c' constitution, Wheare's 'broad sense', Kelsen's 'material' constitution and, as we note below, what Raz calls the 'thin sense' of a constitution can all be viewed as attempts to delineate something like Rawls' notion of a basic concept of the constitution. That is, these definitions seek to generalise the properties of any conception of the constitution. Yet they perhaps fail to abstract sufficiently from actual constitutions. We suggest the following as a more abstracted account of the basic concept:

> A constitution is the collection of norms that are recognised and applied by public officials (and citizens) in a given political order, and that specify (i) which persons or institutions possess the authority to govern; (ii) the most basic substantive norms that distribute, guide and regulate the scope and exercise of that authority; and (iii) the conditions under which valid law is made and applied.

As King notes, a definition of this kind 'may strike some readers as uncontroversial, even platitudinous, but in fact such a definition, however innocent-seeming, carries a number of important implications'. In particular, it offers a definition that 'is wholly neutral in moral and political terms' (King 2009, p. 3). To say a country has a constitution is not *ipso facto* to say it has a 'good' constitution. Nor is it to say that its constitution takes a particular form, such as being codified. The norms it serves and the form it takes belong to different conceptions of a constitution.

No system of governance is likely to be able to operate in an entirely ad hoc way, especially if it applies to a society of any size, diversity and complexity. There will need to be a number of shared understandings among both rulers and ruled regarding how power is allocated between the different persons and institutions of the political system, so all know who can govern, with regard to which issues, where and over whom, in what ways and when. Even an authoritarian system of an absolutist kind will be unable to subsist on the basis of coercion alone. It will need to involve some widely acknowledged (if not necessarily widely approved) specification of who holds power, a designation of that power as binding over all matters for the inhabitants of a given territory, and an indication of how it can be delegated and exercised by the agents of the holder of power. Without such rules, there can be no continuity of the state and legal authority (Hart 1994 [1961], chap. 2).

Consequently, all political systems of any complexity will have a small 'c' constitution in the 'broad' or 'material' sense, consisting of a set of legal and non-legal norms of the kind described above. As we note in Section III, these norms, both formal and informal, operate in a largely analogous way to what Hart termed the 'secondary rules' inherent in any organised exercise of power (Hart 1994 [1961], pp. 95–96; Gardner 2011, p. 162). That is, they designate who has the right to rule and how that rule may be rightfully exercised. As such, they provide what Rawls describes as 'the highest system of social rules for making rules' (Rawls 1999a, p. 195, and see p. 197 and Rawls 2005, p. 448). In a similar spirit, and with a direct reference to Hart (Hayek 1973, p. 135), Hayek considers a constitution as a 'superstructure' consisting of 'all those rules of the allocation and limitation of the powers of government' (Hayek 1973, p. 134). That said, Hayek's definition seems over capacious since it would make by-laws mandating procedures for rubbish collection constitutional.

Just as the existence of such rules does not per se determine the type of government – so that in this sense, a dictatorship may be as constitutional as a democracy, so too they need not take on any particular canonical form. A small 'c' constitution need not take on the shape of a capital 'C' codified constitution, to employ King's terminology. These norms may be conventions or law; they may be codified as a set of non-legal guidelines, be enacted as ordinary law or have the status of law by dint of their recognition as such by legal and other officials; and they can be either changed easily or entrenched to varying degrees of inflexibility. They can be also changed by unconstitutional revolution, where there is a dramatic breach in legal continuity between two legal orders within the same state. To some extent, a constitution, and its history, will involve elements of some (and in many cases all) of these formulations. In the United States, for instance, there is much discussion of unwritten constitutional norms (Amar 2012) and supra-textual constitutional amendment (Ackerman 1991).

Raz seeks to address the difference between a constitution and a form of constitutional government by distinguishing between 'the notion of "a Constitution" ... in a thin sense and ... a variety of thicker senses' (Raz 1998, p. 153). The thin sense amounts to his version of the basic concept, whereby a constitution 'is simply the law that establishes and regulates the main organs of government, their constitution and powers, and ipso facto it includes law that establishes the general principles under which the country is governed' (Raz 1998, p. 153). The 'thicker sense' involves his preferred conception and refers to the 'canonical formulation' as 'superior law' of the legal rules that are 'constitutive' of the legal and political structure of a system of governance. He observes that a 'thick' constitution typically involves much more than its being written down and granted the status of superior law. It also entails 'judicial procedures to implement the superiority of the constitution' and 'legal procedures' that entrench it by making constitutional reform harder than ordinary legislative change and seek to ensure its durability and stability. Finally, it often enshrines 'principles of government', such as basic civil and political rights, 'that are generally held to express the common beliefs of the population about the way their society should be governed' (Raz 1998, pp. 153–154). However, one should avoid reifying such empirical features of certain existing constitutions as conceptually necessary. As Raz acknowledges, these seven features define only one of many possible 'thick' views of the constitution and each of them is 'vague' in its application (Raz 1998, p. 154).

Certainly, constitutional theorists cannot avoid empirically examining and normatively assessing a range of different 'thick' constitutional mechanisms, as our contributors have done in this Handbook. Yet these thick 'conceptions' inevitably remain parasitic upon a more basic or 'thin' concept, as Raz recognised. However, although Raz considers the 'thin' sense of a constitution to be clearer and less contestable, he regards it as simply 'tautological', 'for in that sense the constitution is simply the law that establishes and regulates the main organs of government, their constitution and powers' (Raz 1998, p. 153). As we show later, his statement that the constitution is law is mistaken and it is further mistaken to think that the constitution must establish the organs of government, rather than recognise and regulate the operations of those who have the right to govern. Our focus for the moment is nevertheless upon the similarities between Raz's thin notion of constitution and King's equation of a small 'c' constitution with J. G. A. Griffith's famous dictum regarding the British constitution, quoted in Section I, that the constitution is 'everything that happens' (or does not happen) (King 2009, p. 4). Sartori (1962, p. 857) went so far as to decry any such 'formal' definition of a constitution as 'banal and uninteresting', at best offering 'a shorthand report which may describe – assuming the constitution in question is applied – the formalization of the power structure of the given country'. However, a little bit more is involved. For these rules need to be structured in a way that reflects 'the general principles under which the country is governed' (Raz 1998, p. 153), whether they be autocratic or democratic.

Our view, which shapes the organisation of this volume, even if not all contributors necessarily agree with this point, is that even constitutions in the thin sense will possess three different, if related, features that structure the claim to possess and exercise authority. As we specified above, the basic concept of a constitution concerns the effective norms specifying the right to govern, the distribution and regulation of that governing power, and the ways valid law is made and applied. In a political system of any complexity, we believe that these norms will typically be structured in the following way. First, there will be a constitutional set of values reflecting the substantive standards or ends that the particular constitutional configuration is understood to realise. These do not need to be normatively appealing values, though the ruling classes will invariably affirm their constitutional values as being so. They may be theocratic, totalitarian, traditional or transformative. They will often be found in constitutional preambles (S. Levinson 2011), and increasingly in the diverse programmatic or 'mission statement' features of constitutions (King 2013), referred to as 'state-goal specification' (*Staatszielbestimmung*) in German constitutional law (Sommermann 1997). Yet, in many constitutional orders such goals will be implicit rather than stated explicitly. Second, there will be a set of constitutional *modalities* consisting of certain intermediary norms, often processual, whose recognition by the institutions of the state will be necessary for the constitutional system to realise its substantive values. In some systems, this may mean deference to divine authority or holy scripture. In others, it may mean a radically democratic distribution of authority or a potent recognition of the separation of powers, political representation, or judicial review. Finally, there will be constitutional *institutions* that form the public political infrastructure tasked with the delivery or implementation of the substantive constitutional goals. Institutions are the contact point between citizens and those wielding political power.

As we insisted above, this explanatory scheme is not committed to any particular normative programme. So, absolutism may have as its justifying value the divine right of kings, with hereditary succession a modality for ensuring its transmission, that is then realised through the institution of a hierarchical system of oaths of allegiance. In other words, our understanding of the 'concept' of a constitution is that it consists of the formally or informally articulated understandings of the substantive values, processual modalities, and legal and political institutions that constitute any mode of governance. Yet this basic concept can take very different forms and relate to very different regimes. It can be 'thickened', in Raz's terminology, or 'narrowed' in Wheare's, in numerous ways. In other words, the concept of a constitution is consistent with very different conceptions of constitutionalism.

As we noted in Section I, these different conceptions can be treated analytically and descriptively. That may allow them to be classified in various ways – as autocratic or democratic, for example, and enable the interactions and relations between agents and institutions to be examined and possibly explained in terms of certain causal chains. Yet, such analytical or descriptive taxonomies will not in and of themselves indicate which form of constitution is desirable and ought to be adopted. As we have suggested, that choice will ultimately be normative and follow from the nature of the values we seek to instantiate through certain modalities and institutional arrangements. Constitutional theory of the conceptual and positive kind can help us see how far those values can be credibly realised through particular legal and political modalities and institutions. However, the choice between different narrow or thick forms of constitutionalism cannot escape being grounded ultimately in a normative assessment of the justification and legitimacy of the values those forms seek to realise (Sartori 1962, pp. 857–858).

So far as the present Handbook is concerned, the chapters aim to expound the constitutional theory that is associated with a very broad range of contemporary governments whose constitutional orders are nominally committed to democracy and respect for basic human rights. However, we have not assumed that such a normative commitment can only be realised in terms of a single canonical set of constitutional arrangements, such as those stipulated in Raz's 'thick' conception. Our contributors hold both different conceptions of the constitutional values associated with a democracy committed to rights, equality and dignity, and of the various modalities and institutions through which these values might be realised.

III CONSTITUTIONAL NORMS: WRITTEN, UNWRITTEN, LEGAL AND POLITICAL

Section II addressed the very idea of a constitution. Here, we turn to address the nature of the constitutional norms through which any constitutional order needs to operate – whatever narrow or thick form it may take, and be it authoritarian or democratic, although – as we noted – our focus is on the latter. We begin by distinguishing between norms, on the one side, and usage, habits, or practice, on the other, before turning to two abstract types of norms: rules and principles.

Finally, we address differences between legal and non-legal norms, both written and conventional.

While usage and habits are an important part of concrete political arrangements, we would hesitate to consider them constitutional. This stems from our view that constitutions are normative in character, generative of obligations and rules, and not just a report of the way decisions happen to be taken at a given point in time. We accept that this view is not universally shared. We of course recognise that usage, habit and practices can be important, not least because over time they can evolve into conventions, particularly when they become the basis for reciprocal or legitimate expectations about the conduct of public officials and institutions.[5] Yet, we find it difficult to base a *right* to govern on the basis of habit, usage or practice alone, and still less a set of norms designating the distribution and limits of powers, and the sources of law-making authority. Constitutions ordinarily imply a basic scheme for putting the norms into relation to one another – for example, by determining their relative status in situations of conflict – and for distinguishing between norms internal and those external to a particular constitutional order.

We consider constitutional norms to comprise at the most abstract level rules and principles that are each both legal and non-legal. On the distinction between rules and principles, we generally follow the analysis of Dworkin (1977, chap. 2), which is amenable to legal positivist understandings of the nature of law (Hart 1995, Postscript; Patterson 2021, esp. pp. 678–679; cf. Raz 1972). Rules have an on-off or binary character in the sense that they are breached or not. This arises mainly from their greater clarity or specificity (e.g. quorum rules, term limits). Principles in this context include both what we have termed values, such as dignity and equality, and modalities, such as the separation of powers, rule of law, and good administration. Such principles have the dimension of weight and importance, and are typically more general and often normative or appraisive in character. Consequently, their application to concrete disputes is liable to more disagreement. Rules can be legal or non-legal. Legal typically means amenability to judicial enforcement, and this possibility can arise either through the application of primary or secondary (executive) legislation or through the application of judicially recognised customary rules. When non-legal, rules typically take the form of constitutional conventions. Conventions are usually rule-like because they are founded on concrete previous practices that serve as a reference point when considering whether an official is bound by them.[6] The consequences for breach of such rules are political rather than legal.

---

[5] An excellent example of which can be found in *Erkine May's Treatise on the Law, Privileges, Proceedings and Usage of Parliament* (25th ed., 2019). First published in 1844, it is known as the 'Bible of parliamentary procedure' in the UK Parliament, though Parliament itself only began to publish it online in 2019.

[6] However, as Ivor Jennings (1963, p. 135) famously observed in setting out what became the judicially noticed 'Jennings Test' for the existence of constitutional conventions, we can ask what are the precedents?; did the actors feel bound?; and, crucially here, what is the reason for the precedent? Here,

Constitutional principles can be likewise legal and non-legal in form. Principles such as the rule of law, the separation of powers, and the principle of democratic accountability are frequently recognised in judicial decisions across the world. They may be based on an explicit constitutional text, be found to be implicit in the constitutional text or constitutional arrangements, or be judicially recognised as part of the common law or *droit commun* in that broader legal order. These possibilities exist in both common law and civil law legal traditions, and in municipal and international legal orders. Importantly, however, constitutional principles can be and are recognised in the political or non-legal order, by political actors, the public administration, and civil society. For instance, the principles of public accountability, of transparency, of the (perhaps internal) self-determination of national minorities, of democratic accountability, the separation of powers and also the rule of law can found powerful political arguments by persons who have no ambition to have the principle vindicated in judicial proceedings. At the same time, the breach of such principles is regarded by those who use them in argument as *more* than an immoral or unjust act. For example, the invocation of the political constitutional principle that it is wrong for a parliamentarian to lie to parliament is to claim that the person has violated a positively recognised political principle that lies at the foundations of the political order that exists in that country. Such is the work done by the term 'constitutional' when paired with the word 'principle' in that mode of argument. This point raises the question of what gives such norms real political authority in a given system. There are deep disagreements in jurisprudence about the nature of law and how judges and other officials should recognise what constitutes law in a given order (Hart 1994 [1961]; and Dworkin 1986, chap. 2). Our view is that what makes norms effective as genuinely constitutional norms, and not merely as political values, is their positive recognition and affirmation in the statements and behaviour of public officials together with a general practice of compliance. In that regard, we follow the legal positivist view in grounding the positive authority of constitutional norms in social practice (Hart 1994 [1961], chap. 6; and cf. Kelsen 1946a, pp. 41–42, 118–119). There is nothing in that position that denies the hugely significant role for interpretation of constitutional norms, which can extend, elaborate or even reform the understanding of a given norm, consistently with what is typically its deeply appraisive character. Indeed, much of the most interesting activity in arguing about the requirements of positive or actual constitutions is to be found in offering competing conceptions of constitutional concepts (or what we have called values and modalities).

This analysis also raises the question of the relationship between formal codification and the idea of a constitution. As we saw in Section II, Wheare contends that a constitution in the broad sense is made up of a variety of different sorts of rules and

---

Jennings places the question of the justification for the practice at the heart of determining what a convention at the present time may require.

principles – from written laws to unwritten conventions, some in a codified text and others in aspects of the common law, and still others in features of the prevailing political arrangements, such as the sovereignty of the King in parliament. However, this argument has been controversial. Thomas Paine famously contended that to be a constitution it needed to be codified. As he put it: 'A constitution is not a thing in name only, but in fact. It has not an ideal, but a real existence; and wherever it cannot be produced in a visible form, there is none' (Paine 1995 [1791], p. 122). In a rhetorical challenge to Edmund Burke, he demanded, 'Can then Mr Burke produce the English Constitution? If he cannot, we may fairly conclude, that though it has been so much talked about, no such thing as a constitution exists, or ever did exist, and consequently that the people have yet a constitution to form' (Paine 1995 [1791], p. 123).

Powerfully stated and much quoted though it may be (see McIlwain 1940, pp. 2, 9), Paine's critique nevertheless proves doubly flawed. First, much of the English constitution is written in the form of ordinary statutes: such constitutional legislation includes the Act of Settlement 1701, that established the independence of the judiciary; the Representation of the People Acts 1832–1928, that turned the UK into a representative democracy; and the Human Rights Act 1998, that incorporated the European Convention on Human Rights into UK law (King 2009, pp. 5–6; Gardner 2011, pp. 163–164). Still, there is also much that is unwritten – neither the role of the Prime Minister nor that of the cabinet are provided for by statute (King 2009, pp. 6–7). Meanwhile, as Paine noted with regard to the Septennial Act, such legislation is not entrenched. He also denies its constitutionality on the grounds that it is not 'a thing *antecedent* to government', that is 'not the act of its government, but of the people constituting a government' (Paine 1995 [1791], p. 122). However, that also is not entirely true. Paine here offers a normative argument in the language of a conceptual truth about constitutions. Were it true, much of what has historically been discussed as constitutional and most of the world's constitutions today could not be seen as constitutions. Elected governments with a popular mandate frequently make constitutional reform legislation and only a fraction of written constitutions have issued from a constituent assembly of any truly egalitarian democratic pedigree. More importantly, even codified constitutions need supplementing by legislation, conventions and both judicial and executive interpretation that over time accretes new constitutional meanings of undoubted authority. Indeed, as King notes, what they leave out often proves of greater constitutional importance than what they include, much of which can 'border on the comic' (King 2009, p. 5).[7] For example, he remarks how very few capital-'C' Constitutions provide 'for one of the most significant features of any constitutional order: the country's electoral system'.

---

[7] His favourite example is the description of the coat of arms of the republic of Austria in the Austrian Constitution, an 'inconsequential' provision 'which might well have been drawn from an operetta libretto' (King 2009, p. 7).

Thus, there is no provision in the US Constitution for the plurality-first past the post system used almost universally in the United States. That Constitution also nowhere explicitly provides for what has come to be regarded as one of its chief features – the empowerment of US courts to strike down federal statutes and government acts on the grounds that they are 'unconstitutional' as opposed to merely illegal (King 2009, p. 7). Indeed, as Dicey noted (1915, pp. 28–29), conventions can often govern what is written down as well as serve for what is not. Looking at the US electoral college, for example, Dicey pronounced that the 'understanding that an elector is not really to elect, has now become so firmly established, that for him to exercise his legal power of choice is considered a breach of political honour too gross to be committed by the most unscrupulous of politicians' (Dicey 1915, pp. 29–30). Perhaps – though it appears that former President Donald Trump was sufficiently unscrupulous to risk such a breach, much as President Franklin Delano Roosevelt would breach what Dicey also considered an unassailable 'conventional limit' on a President being re-elected more than once (Dicey 1915, p. 29). As occurred with this latter example, it may always be possible to revise the constitution to include the convention. However, it is almost impossible for any document, no matter how detailed, not to rely on some conventions as to how to interpret those provisions it does contain and to stand in for those it does not.[8] The role for a written constitution, if any, is specified by a political argument and does not flow from the very concept of a constitution (see, e.g. King 2019b).

Of course, the same goes for non-codified, small 'c', constitutions – the very view that certain statutes might be constitutional in nature 'comes of the unwritten law of the law-applying officials who subsequently treat them as having that status' (Gardner 2011, p. 165). As John Gardner (2011) has remarked, as important a question as 'should a constitution be written and entrenched?' is the question of whether it can ever be fully written at all? Judges and other law-applying officials mediate the application of constitutional norms. In judicial practice, the practice of desuetude can operate where judges refuse to apply a statutory provision that has a record of non-enforcement by the executive or courts (Bickel 1962, pp. 143–156; Kelsen 1946a, pp. 119–120). Even constitutional provisions can be amended or lose their force by operation of desuetude (Albert 2014a). At the most radical end, revolutions can occur where legal officials cease to recognise older constitutional norms and begin recognising new ones. For all these reasons, Gardner observes that many legal theorists consider 'it is part of the nature of a constitution that it is unwritten, and that its so-called written parts are only parts of it because of their reception into the unwritten law that is made by the customs and decisions of the courts and other

---

[8] That is not to deny that a newly founded state could adopt a constitution and proceed afresh. It could borrow norms from other jurisdictions but as it was freshly founded one would not say it was relying on conventions. However, whereas Conventions bind, foreign precedents simply serve as menus of options during interpretation.

law-applying officials' (Gardner 2011, p. 170). Although Gardner disputed this view, that was only because he considered all possible interpretations that might be given to written constitutions as 'part of their meaning *qua* written' (Gardner 2011, p. 194). The very nature of his argument illustrates how odd the proposition is that constitutions can *only* consist of written norms.

The view that constitutions must be written is also at odds with the widely recognised role of constitutional conventions. Dicey distinguished 'the conventions of the constitution' from 'the law of the constitution'. He thought the former 'are not enforced or recognised by the Courts' and that they 'make up a body not of laws, but of constitutional or political ethics' (Dicey 1915, p. xiv). To some that stance has seemed at odds with Dicey's own acceptance that much of the English constitution results not from statute law but the decisions made by courts with respect to the rights of individuals under common law (Jennings 1963, pp. 69–71). Yet, the line between law and convention is not always stable, and sometimes, political conventions can arguably emerge as the basis for legal decisions. A sometimes controversial example of that might be the UK's *Miller* 2 case, in which the Supreme Court held that the attempt by Prime Minister Boris Johnson to prorogue Parliament for an unusually long period at the height of the UK's withdrawal negotiations with the European Union amounted to an unlawful stifling of parliamentary accountability.[9] The idea that ministers are accountable to Parliament lies at the core of the UK's political constitution, but the claim that a legal remedy could lie for the Prime Minister's interference with that process was novel. For some commentators, the case merely vindicates that, contra Dicey, courts can and do sometimes recognise and enforce constitutional conventions (see further, Barber 2010, chap 6).[10]

As Sartori notes, there is a tendency among British commentators, that he puts down to the 'British habit (and perhaps coquetry) of understatement', to describe the British constitution in such 'thin' or 'broad' terms as to make it seem that nothing stands in the way of an executive possessing a parliamentary majority doing whatever it wishes, including abolishing parliament itself. Indulging a certain coquetry of his own, Sartori likens Jennings' classic text as being as useful a guide to the UK's constitutional arrangements as Vishinsky's 1952 apologia was for the Stalinist constitution of Soviet Russia. Yet, as he remarks, this approach fails to take the principle of parliamentary sovereignty seriously. For, if it means anything, it surely suggests that the prerogatives of the Crown are ultimately subject to the authority of Parliament, and in particular to the elected chamber therein (Sartori 1962, p. 854). As he concludes, if so then it would be wrong – contrary to what many British scholars aver – that parliamentary sovereignty contradicts the very idea of a 'higher law', such that a parliamentary majority could pass '*any* law whatsoever', including abolishing itself.

---

[9] *R (on the application of Miller and another) v The Prime Minister* [2019] UKSC 41.
[10] A view decisively rejected by the UK Supreme Court: *R (on the application of Miller and another) v Secretary of State for Exiting the European Union* [2017] UKSC 5 [136]–[151].

That said, as commentators on Sartori's article pointed out, it equally shows that the form of government provides as much of a constitutional check and balance on how power is exercised as a written document – one that constrains how governments act rather than simply what they can do, as the *garantiste*, limited government, conception of constitutionalism favoured by Sartori tends to do (see Morris-Jones 1965; Maddox 1982, 1984). Constitutions are plainly political as well as legal (Bellamy 2007).

IV CONSTITUTIONALISM

When describing the basic concept of a constitution in Section II, we deliberately did so in relation to a type of regime – that of an authoritarian dictator or absolutist monarch – many might deem unconstitutional. However, we noted that such an assessment of these regimes derives not from a different account of the concept of a constitution so much as a different conception, one that reflects a view of the purpose of a constitution as being to hinder rather than facilitate authoritarian rule. Such a conception involves associating the constitution with a different set of values and, as a result, of modalities and institutions as well, to those associated with an authoritarian regime.

Section III, on norms, also called into question a further assumption about the very concept of a constitution – one most clearly expressed by Paine: namely, that a constitution must take a certain canonical written form, the writing of which logically (and temporally) precedes government, be superior law, be upheld by certain judicial procedures, be relatively entrenched, and reflect an actual or hypothetical constitutive act of the people, to the extent that it forms a plausible common ideology among those subject to it. Though Raz (1998, pp. 153–154) – like others who follow Paine (e.g., McIlwain 1940, p. 9; Grimm 2019a, p. 25) – sees these as fundamental substantive elements of a 'thick' constitution, none of them seem necessary aspects of a constitution *per se*. They may or may not be desirable, but they can all be matters of debate, reflecting not only normative choices governing the values a constitution ideally exists to uphold, but also both normative and empirical matters concerning how those values might be most appropriately and effectively upheld in reality.

Different thick conceptions of the constitution, therefore, give rise to different – and often divergent – conceptions of constitutionalism, where 'constitutionalism' is understood as an ideology of the nature of constitutional government. That there can be different conceptions of constitutionalism arises from the fact that the key components of the concept of a constitution can be regarded as being 'essentially contested' in the manner classically identified by W. B. Gallie (1956). Gallie ascribed such contestation to five features of many legal and political concepts: namely, that the concept is (1) evaluative – reflecting particular ideologies or normative programmes, (2) internally complex, (3) possesses constituent elements that are variously describable and capable of being ascribed different weights, and (4) is open-ended – capable of being modified in unpredictable ways in the light of changing circumstances. Finally, (5) 'each party recognizes the fact that its own use of it is contested by those of other parties, and that each party must have at least some appreciation of the different criteria in the light of which the other parties claim to be applying the concept in question' (Gallie 1956, pp. 171–172). It is not just that a constitution designed to realise the authoritarian norms associated with the *Führerprinzip* clearly has a different evaluative stance to one grounded in democratic norms associated with the principle of accountability, but also that understandings of these norms and the values and modalities involved may differ, as may their relationship to other norms. After all, each of these norms is evaluative and complex in itself, and their respective constituent elements can be given different weights – as can each value and modality in relation to other values and modalities. Meanwhile, constitutions are not just ideal, purely theoretical, constructs; they exist in the real world in part to address non-ideal problems, such as a lack of agreement on, or full compliance with, moral and legal norms. Even when there is agreement at the level of values, views on the modalities and institutions can reflect differences over the likelihood and character of the problems their realisation may encounter.

Thus, many differences among those holding similar values can arise from their having differing expectations about human motivation – for example, as to whether or not one should assume, as Hume suggested, that all individuals are 'knaves' with 'no other end … than private interest', and if so what that entails for obtaining the collective action needed to promote public goods, avoid public bads and deal with emergencies and crises (Hume 1985 [1742], p. 42). That assumption led the Federalist advocates of the US Constitution to consider that virtue must lie in institutions rather than human beings, and involve a form of checks and balances in which 'ambition must be made to counteract ambition' (Hamilton, Madison, and Jay 2003 [1787–1788], p. 252). Yet, a belief in universal knavery may prove self-defeating, with measures aimed at countering it producing unexpected and perverse results – such as the political deadlock created by the US system of checks and balances, or the short-termism and influence of funders created by biannual elections, both constitutional flaws that bedevil US politics. So, along with disagreements at the level of values can go disagreements relating to the ways empirical evidence and assumptions get incorporated in a given constitutional theory and the modalities and institutional arrangements it advocates. Yet, the need to take such evidence and assumptions into account prompts a further novel feature of this volume – the mix of philosophers, legal scholars and political scientists among our contributors, several of whom draw on each other's work to varying degrees.

As we remarked above, all of the contributors to this volume hold a broadly democratic view of constitutionalism, that treats equality and freedom as core constitutional values. However, they understand them differently – both in themselves and in their relations to other values, as well as holding different empirical assumptions regarding the real conditions likely to inhibit or facilitate their realisation. As a result, their views of modalities and institutions may also differ. Take, for example, the common view of a constitutionalism as a form of 'limited' government (Waluchow and Kyritsis 2023), what Sartori calls a constitution in the *garantiste* sense, from the French notion of 'garantisme' (Sartori 1962, p. 855). Jeremy Waldron (2016b, pp. 30–32) has noted how a number of analytically distinct understandings have been associated with the idea of limitations, some more restrictive of the scope and exercise of governmental authority than others. At the most restrictive end of the scale, constitutional limits are associated with a minimal view of the state and hence less government, with constitutional protection given to property rights, freedom of contract and the laxly regulated laissez faire workings of an allegedly free market. These are economic liberal (or neoliberal) constraints associated with a narrowly negative conception of liberty, especially the economic liberty to produce and trade goods and services. They potentially constrain many democratic demands for state intervention to improve working conditions, such as an expansive view of the scope of the right to strike to secure such improvements; calls to provide better public services – such as more extensive welfare, health and education systems; appeals to enhance environmental protections; or a desire to upgrade and expand public infrastructure. These demands become liable to challenge not only as misguided from a given neoliberal economic standpoint, but also – and more far reaching – as legally and politically illegitimate. Less restrictive is the idea of restraint, as in prohibitions on torture, detention without trial or interference with religious belief. These might be regarded as ethical liberal constraints, concerned to ensure relations of equal respect among citizens and individuals more generally. Finally, at the least restrictive end of the scale, limitation can mean control. As Waldron notes, this need not be a purely negative notion. A driver controls a car not only in the sense that she can prevent it leaving the road and crashing, but also in being able to direct it toward certain destinations by a given route and at a given speed. Government regulation to implement the democratic demands mentioned earlier could be consistent with control in this sense, with citizens being placed in the driving seat through the electoral process. Indeed, most of the world's constitutions concede the Habermasian argument that for citizens to be able to exercise control assumes constitutional protection of a series of enabling rights to welfare, education and so forth (Habermas 1996, chap. 3; King 2012, chap. 1). The point applies equally to other constitutional provisions and concepts, as has been noted often (e.g. King 2013, 2022). Thus, the very goods economic liberals seek to constitutionally limit the state from enacting, can be seen by others as requiring constitutional protection to enable the democratic control of the state as well as the realisation of an egalitarian form of liberty. Likewise, while some might argue that political equality requires constitutional judicial review to uphold equal political rights (Ely 1980; Habermas 1996), others contend that such equality is only consistent with 'weak' forms of review and requires a system where the constitution itself is open to relatively easy democratic change and renewal.

On this latter account, the democratic process is not simply instrumentally valuable for, and limitable by, its capacity to realise certain constitutional values. The process itself may be viewed as intrinsically valuable and inherently constitutional (Waldron 1999a; Bellamy 2007).

There is no agreement among contributors as to the balance between what might be called the negative and positive features of constitutionalism (Barber 2018, pp. 2–9), or on the degree to which democracy embodies constitutional values and modalities or may require legal restriction to abide by them. To this extent, democracy, like constitutionalism, is essentially contested by the contributors. However, in line with Gallie's fifth criteria, all recognise the fact of such contestation, and so endeavour to defend their view. As Gallie's essay took pains to point out, argument over the merits of different conceptions of essentially contested concepts (like constitutionalism) can be expected to shed important light on the concept at issue.

CONCLUSION

This volume explores what might be regarded by some as a Western model of constitutionalism. Yet, it is a model that has been globally diffused and developed, much like the ideas of democracy and human rights. It is an ironic form of hubris to believe that Western and especially European thinkers are in any way the owners and custodians of such concepts. Indeed, this volume includes a number of examples of authors from the global south who provide critical insights on the topic they are considering that draw on their non-Western backgrounds. This is not to deny the existence or importance of alternative models of constitutionalism. Yet, even a volume as large as this cannot be comprehensive in scope of all things constitutional. To chart these different traditions and compare and contrast them with the model explored here requires other volumes. Our attempt has merely been to offer an overview of the values, modalities, and institutions of those forms of constitutionalism that are broadly aligned to the political and legal systems of contemporary democratic systems, and to highlight some of the contemporary challenges they confront and the ways these systems might be adapted or reformed in the light of them. As we have noted, even within that narrow focus there are broad disagreements, sufficient to fill a very large volume.

RECOMMENDED READING

Alexander, L., ed. (2001). *Constitutionalism: Philosophical Foundations*, Cambridge: Cambridge University Press.
Baines, B., Barak-Erez, D., & Kahana, T., eds. (2012). *Feminist Constitutionalism: Global Perspectives*. Cambridge: Cambridge University Press.
Barber, N. (2018). *The Principles of Constitutionalism*, Oxford: Oxford University Press.

Gardner, J. (2011). Can There Be a Written Constitution? In L. Green and B. Leiter, eds., *Oxford Studies in Philosophy of Law*. Oxford: Oxford University Press, pp. 162–194.

Gaus, D. (2013). Rational Reconstruction as a Method of Political Theory between Social Critique and Empirical Political Science. *Constellations*, 20 (4), 553–570.

Grimm, D. (2016). *Constitutionalism: Past, Present and Future*, Oxford: Oxford University Press.

Hailbronner, M. (2017). Transformative Constitutionalism: Not Only in the Global South. *The American Journal of Comparative Law*, 65 (3), 527–565.

Kelsen, H. (1946a). *A General Theory of Law and State*. Translated by Anders Wedberg. Cambridge, MA: Harvard University Press.

Loughlin, M. (2010). *Foundations of Public Law*. Oxford: Oxford University Press.

Maddox, G. (1982). A Note on the Meaning of "Constitution". *American Political Science Review*, 76 (4), 805–809.

Maddox, G. (1984). Communication: On Constitutionalism. *American Political Science Review*, 78 (4), 1070–1071.

McIlwain, C. H. (2008). *Constitutionalism: Ancient and Modern*. rev. ed, Indianapolis, IN: Liberty Fund Inc.

Morris-Jones, W. H. (1965). Communication: On Constitutionalism. *American Political Science Review*, 59 (2), 439–440.

Sartori, G. (1962). Constitutionalism: A Preliminary Discussion. *American Political Science Review*, 56 (4), 853–864.

Waldron, J. (2016b). Constitutionalism: A Skeptical View. In J. Waldron, *Political Political Theory: Essays on Institutions*. Cambridge, MA: Harvard University Press, pp. 23–44.

Waluchow, W. & Kyritsis, D. (2023). Constitutionalism. *The Stanford Encyclopaedia of Philosophy*. Available from: https://plato.stanford.edu/entries/constitutionalism/.

PART I

Values

2

Human Dignity

Jeremy Waldron

My task is to consider the role of human dignity in constitutional law. Here is a suggestion I would like to offer about the work that it does. Human dignity serves not only as the content of certain rights or as a ground or foundation for human rights in general, but also as a basis on which fundamental rights are interpreted and applied. Indeed, not only that: I think human dignity works as an integrating idea across the whole range of constitutional considerations – structural as well as rights-based, empowering as well as constraining. The idea of human dignity is indispensable not only to our sense of the constitutional protections that we need, but also to our whole sense of the underlying status and authority of the ordinary human persons for whose sake constitutions are framed and their provisions upheld.

I HUMAN DIGNITY IN CONSTITUTIONAL AND HUMAN RIGHTS LAW

Though human dignity is an ancient idea and though it played a significant role in late Enlightenment moral philosophy and in nineteenth-century Roman Catholic moral theology as well, it really did not surface in constitutional texts and in modern constitutional jurisprudence until the second half of the twentieth century. There were a few exceptions. The 1919 Constitution of Finland, Article 1(1), undertook to "guarantee the inviolability of human dignity."[1] And the preamble to the Irish Constitution of 1937 said that the document sought "to promote the common good, with due observance of Prudence, Justice and Charity, so that the dignity and freedom of the individual may be assured…."

At the end of the Second World War, and in revulsion against the horrors of Nazism and other forms of fascism, references to human dignity became more common and more insistent in charters of fundamental rights (Habermas, 2010, pp. 465–6). The Charter of the United Nations said in its preamble that the peoples of the world were determined "to reaffirm faith in fundamental human rights, in the

---

[1] For this reference, I am grateful to Barak 2015.

dignity and worth of the human person." In 1948 the Basic Law of Germany made dignity a supreme principle of governance: "Human dignity shall be inviolable," said its opening provision and, in the years that followed, the Federal Constitutional Court of Germany insisted that this means all other laws and all other rights have to be understood through a dignitarian lens.[2] In the same year, 1948, the Universal Declaration of Human Rights (UDHR) made dignity fundamental among the principles it set out. In its preamble the UDHR proclaimed that

> recognition of the inherent dignity and of the equal and inalienable rights of all members of the human family is the foundation of freedom, justice and peace in the world, ... [and that] the peoples of the United Nations have in the Charter reaffirmed their faith in fundamental human rights, [and] in the dignity and worth of the human person....

Article 1 of the UDHR announced, "All human beings are born free and equal in dignity and rights." And its socio-economic provisions held that everyone who works is entitled to "to just and favourable remuneration ensuring for himself and his family an existence worthy of human dignity" (UDHR, Article 23).[3] Now, the UDHR is not law, let alone constitutional law. But it has provided both inspiration and template for the use of dignity in the constitutions of the nations of the world. And the various functions it assigns to dignity in the syntax of human rights – sometimes foundational, sometimes to help specify the content of an enumerated right – have been important, as we shall see, for its constitutional role.

Today, more than 150 nations invoke dignity in their constitutional jurisprudence or in their bodies of Basic Law, though admittedly in some of them it is not much more than a passing reference. In one or two countries, the place of human dignity is secured by court-made doctrines rather than constitutional text. In Canada, for example, there is no mention of dignity in the Charter of Rights and Freedoms, but it has had a major presence nonetheless in the interpretation of rights to equality and in end-of-life issues such as assisted suicide.[4] So too in the United States: there the Supreme Court, without benefit of any mention of human dignity in the text of the U.S. Constitution,[5] has repeatedly invoked it as a concept necessary for making sense of the Eighth Amendment – a role best known from debates about capital punishment in the 1970s.[6]

---

[2] See, for example, the German Air Safety case: Feb. 15, 2006, 115 BVerfGE 118 (FCC).
[3] See also UDHR Article 22 for reference to "the economic, social and cultural rights indispensable for [each person's] dignity and the free development of his personality."
[4] For the equality case-law, see *Law v. Canada (Minister of Employment and Immigration)*, [1999] 1 S.C.R. 497. For the use of human dignity in an end-of-life case, see, e.g., *Carter v. Canada (Attorney-General)*, 2015 SCC 5, [2015] 1 S.C.R. 331.
[5] But dignity is referred to in the text of some of the US state constitutions – in Article II.4 of the Constitution of Montana, for example.
[6] See *Furman v. Georgia* 408 U.S. 238 (1972), at 270–81. But see also the use of human dignity in the jurisprudence of the Fourth Amendment on reasonable searches and seizures (*Rochin v. California*, 342 U.S.

Some have seen, in dignity's appearing in constitutional jurisprudence all over the world, a sort of signal from each constitutional community to the others that they are willing to learn from one another in the elaboration of this and allied ideas (McCrudden 2008, pp. 694–7).[7] It is also a signal that the constitutional communities in question take seriously the relation between constitutional rights and human rights. Each body of jurisprudence is supposed to inform the other, and since the human rights material is, as it were, held in common, national discussions of human dignity can be seen as allusions to this commonality.

II THE SYNTAX OF DIGNITY

We saw that, in the UDHR, human dignity operates at a number of different levels. In the preamble it seems to have a foundational presence – a role also made explicit in the International Covenant on Civil and Political Rights (ICCPR), whose preamble says that "rights derive from the inherent dignity of the human person." In Article 23 of the UDHR, by contrast, dignity helps determine a benchmark for social and economic rights.

Some countries in their constitutions indicate a similar variety of roles for human dignity. The best example is the 1996 Constitution of South Africa (CSA), which both uses dignity as a benchmark for conditions of detention[8] and cites respect for and protection of inherent dignity as something to which people have a fundamental right.[9] As well as those two quite different uses, the CSA (in section 1) also sets out dignity as a constitutional value, standing alongside other values like equality, non-racialism, non-sexism, the rule of law, and democracy. The CSA's Bill of Rights, we are told in Section VII, is a way of affirming those values, and subsequent provisions assign specific roles for these constitutional values in interpretation (section 39) and in regard to the limitation of rights (section 36).

These different types and levels of operations – e.g., dignity as one specific right among others and dignity as the basis of all rights – are all too often dismissed as

---

165 (1952), at 174), the Fifth Amendment on self-incrimination (*Miranda v. Arizona* 384 US 436 (1966), at 457), and substantive due process in the Fourteenth Amendment (*Planned Parenthood v. Casey* 505 US 833 (1992), at 851). There are good overall surveys in Goodman 2005–6 and Neuman 2000.

[7] McCrudden 2008, p. 695 quotes Justice O'Connor as saying, in her dissenting opinion in *Roper v. Simmons* 543 U.S. 551 (2005) at 605 that Americans' "evolving understanding of human dignity certainly is neither wholly isolated from, nor inherently at odds with, the values prevailing in other countries. On the contrary, we should not be surprised to find congruence between domestic and international values, especially where the international community has reached clear agreement ... that a particular form of punishment is inconsistent with fundamental human rights."

[8] CSA, section 35: "Everyone who is detained, including every sentenced prisoner, has the right ... to conditions of detention that are consistent with human dignity, including at least exercise and the provision, at state expense, of adequate accommodation, nutrition, reading material and medical treatment...."

[9] CSA, section 10: "Everyone has inherent dignity and the right to have their dignity respected and protected."

evidences of confusion. Luis Roberto Barroso, of the Brazilian Constitutional Court, has argued that it is "contradictory to make human dignity a right in its own, however, because it is regarded as the foundation for all truly fundamental rights and the source of at least part of their core content" (Barroso 2012, p. 357). But I actually do not think it is contradictory.[10]

Suppose dignity *is* the foundation of our rights; then the role of particular rights-claims is to point out what this foundational consideration requires in particular areas (speech, worship, privacy, health care, and so on.) For some of these particular areas, it may be well known that dignity requires φ (say, freedom of worship or freedom from torture) and so we may talk directly of a right to φ without mentioning dignity. In other areas, there may be no independently familiar benchmark, so we refer to dignity itself as the criterion of what is required: that is what seems to be going on in the UDHR's insistence in Article 23 on "remuneration ensuring...an existence worthy of human dignity." We do not say what the required level of remuneration is: but we say that questions are to be asked about human dignity as a way of pinning it down. There is no contradiction here and we have not had to assign different meanings to different occurrences of "human dignity," as Michael Rosen has suggested, in order to prevent a contradiction from arising (Rosen 2012, pp. 59–60).

What about the distinction between human dignity as a right (whether it is general or specific) and human dignity as a constitutional value? The deontic syntax of dignity has always been a little unclear. Kant famously described it as a species of value – value beyond price – in the *Groundwork of the Metaphysics of Morals*:

> In the kingdom of ends everything has either a price or a dignity. What has a price can be replaced by something else as its equivalent; what, on the other hand, is raised above all price and therefore admits of no equivalent has a dignity.
> (Kant 2012 [1785], p. 42)

But, as Stephen Darwall notes (2006, pp. 132–8), Kant in his later work also presents dignity as a sort of *commanding* value – it is the basis on which each of us "exacts respect for himself from all other rational beings in the world" (Kant, 2017 [1797], p. 201). This gives dignity a more direct and compelling normativity than that associated with values generally. (It makes it more like the rights-based edge of a principle.) Either way the understanding of dignity as a non-fungible value certainly affects how policy calculations are to be made. Consider, for example, the way in which the lens of human dignity in Germany's Basic Law refracted the government's appeal to the right to life in the *Air Safety Case* and sustained a refusal by the Federal Constitutional Court to countenance trade-offs among different quantities of human lives.[11]

Aharon Barak (2015, pp. 49 ff.) points out that "human dignity" does different work as a constitutional right than it does as a constitutional value. A right to dignity

---

[10] The argument that follows is adapted from Waldron 2012b, pp. 18–19.
[11] The German Air Safety case is cited in footnote 2 above.

(like a right to anything else) is supposed to operate insistently in the form of an uncompromising principled demand, and though of course there are always questions to be asked about the interpretation of its content, answers to those questions are to be laid out on the deontic matrix of a compelling normative claim. But if human dignity is a constitutional value, then it also makes itself available as an idea to guide the interpretation of all rights provisions, even those that are not explicitly rights *to* dignity in either a general or a particular sense. Plus, dignity as a value may also be involved in forms of constitutional jurisprudence that identify new rights as implicit in what is regarded as a living constitutional text. It features in the purposive aspect of such judicial extrapolations. We see this happening in American constitutional jurisprudence, in the line of cases addressing the question of which liberties are to be treated as particularly importance in substantive due process analysis.[12]

One or two U.S. scholars have argued that the use of dignity as a constitutional value along these lines is incompatible with the spirit of constitutional rights in the American tradition. They see it as introducing "a values-centered constitutionalism, one that emphasizes the needs of the community over the individual, and that protects rights, but only alongside other interests and values" (Rao 2008, p. 255). The reference here seems to be to the role dignity plays in proportionality analysis and in determining possible limitations upon rights, as in the South African provisions mentioned above. However, it is probably better to associate the reference to dignity with one strand among others in U.S. constitutional controversy, rather than to call it un-American. And certainly, it is wrong to say that the dignitarian approach involves tainting individual rights with communitarianism. Even if there is a communitarian element in the very idea of limitations upon rights, the fact that such limitations must be shown to be acceptable in a society based on human dignity, actually reintroduces an individualist constraint into the limitation equation.

III THE FOUNDATION OF RIGHTS

Unlike the UDHR and the ICCPR, national constitutions mostly do not make grand proclamations about the foundation of the rights they protect. They just stipulate what the rights are and state that they must be upheld. So, for example, there is a contrast between the Bill of Rights associated with the U.S. Constitution and the opening lines of the 1776 Declaration of Independence: "We hold these truths to be self-evident, that all men are created equal, that they are endowed by their Creator with certain unalienable Rights...."[13] Still people find it natural to see dignity as foundational for rights in constitutional law as well as for those laid down in human rights documents.

---

[12] See, e.g., *Planned Parenthood v. Casey* 505 US 833 (1992), at 851 and *Lawrence et al. v. Texas*, 539 U.S. 558 (2003) at 567.
[13] For the connection between the two, see Black 1997, p. 22.

We should be careful, however, in our understanding of "foundations." The ICCPR formulation – that "rights derive from the inherent dignity of the human person" – suggests that human dignity is a sort of major premise and that sufficient knowledge of it will enable us to deduce the rights that it entails (rights as conclusions of a syllogism); or it suggests that human dignity is the telos of rights, and conclusions about particular rights can be inferred on the basis of instrumentalist reasoning (rights as a means to an end). I have come to see these understandings of foundationalism as unhelpful (Waldron 2015). Instead, we may think of human dignity as, so to speak, the *flavor* of certain constitutional rights, as a way of making sense of them and establishing their significance.

To firm this up: We may want to try thinking of human dignity as a *status*-idea, under the auspices of which we range a number of different rights and other normative elements. A legal status sums up the whole normative situation of a person in certain conditions, such as bankruptcy or infancy. Human dignity does this with regard to the default status, so to speak, of a human individual. It draws attention to the rights, duties, powers, and immunities that attach to the human person as such. Now, this is a technical point, but we can hardly treat human dignity as a foundation of rights if, as a status term, it functions primarily as a container or covering term for some given array of individual rights. Still, there is something like a foundational element present in this analysis: A status term is not just an abbreviation for the elements ranged under it; it makes sense of their being grouped together in terms of what Jeremy Bentham (1834) calls "*une base idéale*," an underlying reason.[14] And in the case of human dignity that underlying reason seems to be the special and momentous significance of the ordinary individual human person. I will say more about this in Section IV.

Before I get to that, however, let me say a word about the positive law and the suprapositive aspects of human dignity. Constitutional rights exist, in the first instance, as black-letter positive law; they are framed and enacted by human lawmakers. And for some rights there may not be much else to be said about them. Americans have the right to bear arms, for example, or the right to trial by jury in common law suits where a sum greater than twenty dollars is at stake because that is what a bunch of people decided in the late eighteenth century. But certain other rights – to free speech and freedom of worship, the right not to be subject to cruel punishment, the right to the equal protection of the law – are usually taken to point beyond their black-letter formulations and beyond the contingent decisions of their framers to a source for their standing among us that transcends positive law and legitimates and compels their observance. They are understood to have what is sometimes called a "suprapositive aspect" (Neuman 2003, pp. 1866–7).

A number of scholars treat general references to dignity in human rights law and in some constitutions as references to the objective character of this suprapositive

---

[14] Note, however, that John Austin (1885, vol. II, pp. 687–8) disagreed with Bentham over this view of status-terms; Austin held a pure abbreviation view of status terms.

aspect. Klaus Dicke (2002, p. 114) says that dignity conveys the point that we are required to *recognize* certain facts about human beings as the basis of their rights; our attitude towards them is not just constructive; we don't just make them up.[15] Christopher McCrudden (2008, p. 679) says something similar: it is part of the core meaning of "human dignity," he says, that it conveys this ontological content. There is something about humans – their dignity – that commands or requires our recognition; it is not just the registering of some way we have decided to behave towards one another. And everyone who uses the term "human dignity" makes an implicit promise to give an account of that something.

IV SACREDNESS

Should we think of human dignity as a religious idea, attesting non-negotiably to the *sacredness* of the human person? Some theorists worry that human dignity might operate as a sort of Trojan horse for the infiltration of religiously-loaded content into moral and political theory.

It may be helpful, however, to put the point the other way round (Gushee 2013). We know that, historically, the richest and most powerful accounts of the commanding value of individual personality were articulated in the context of religious world-views.[16] Now, beginning with the Enlightenment, there have been attempts to develop secular accounts of this – accounts that might capture a sense of the sacred that is secular on the one hand but avoids a sort of bland utilitarianism on the other. Kantian moral philosophy is one such attempt; Ronald Dworkin's late work on religion is another (Dworkin 2013); George Kateb (2014) is a third. Even though everyone knows that the idea of human dignity comes trailing a religious as well as philosophical heritage, still talk of dignity in modern jurisprudence represents an attempt to see whether moral and political ideas can be extricated from those foundations, without abandoning the key insights of respect for personhood. This remains a work-in-progress: Dignitarian jurisprudence is one of the sites where we are trying to figure out whether a sense of the momentous importance to be attached to every human individual can be expressed altogether in purely secular terms.

This process is undertaken more or less tolerantly, or more or less aggressively. Many philosophers think of themselves as engaged in a systematic endeavor to construct a frame of moral analysis that simply excludes the influence of what they

---

[15] See also Schachter (1983), p. 853.
[16] For a fifteenth century example, see Della Mirandolla (1996). Human dignity also occupies an important role in modern Catholic moral theology, connecting with ideas about the image of God in every human being. In John Paul II (1995), the encyclical *Evangelium Vitae* (EV), we are told of "the almost divine dignity of every human being" (EV §25):

> [M]an, although formed from the dust of the earth ... is a manifestation of God in the world, a sign of his presence, a trace of his glory. ... Man has been given a sublime dignity, based on the intimate bond which unites him to his Creator: in man there shines forth a reflection of God himself. (EV, § 34)

call "irrational religious ideas." They worry that the term "human dignity," even when it is used by secular thinkers, retains many of the characteristics of religious discourse – pomposity, a lurch toward transcendence, lack of definitional clarity, grand-sounding equivocation, a shrinking from rigor and so on.

Others, less exercised by these worries, are determined to remain alert to all the various ways in which the momentous significance of the human individual can be accounted for. I think Christopher McCrudden (2008, pp. 675–8) intended to sound cynical when he said that the statesmen framing the UDHR used the phrase "human dignity," whenever they wanted to sound grand and transcendent but couldn't agree on what to say. But their perseverance with this can also be seen as a tribute to the as-yet-untapped resources available in various religious traditions for making sense of the supreme importance to be accorded to each individual in modern jurisprudence and political morality.

V IS DIGNITY REDUNDANT?

It is sometimes said that the idea of human dignity is redundant, since whatever is of value in its application can be captured by other, better-understood concepts.

Plainly, human dignity has important resonances with equality and liberty, and these are more familiar values. Some theorists (Macklin 2003; Pinker 2008) wonder whether "dignity" could not be replaced with "autonomy," for the latter has in their eyes a relatively straightforward meaning and a clear connection with a liberal privileging of choice in the living of a human life. But we may need both: Dignity is used in constitutional analysis to discern the sort of choices that are of particular importance in the constitutional value of autonomy or ordered liberty;[17] to do that, something more than the bare idea of liberty is necessary (Taylor 2006, p. 150).

Dignity is also important in capturing concerns associated with degradation – even degradation that is the upshot of choice and consent. The issue of dwarf-tossing illustrates these concerns. In 1995 the French *Conseil d'État* recognized that the protection of dignity may appropriately be invoked by police authorities in shutting down sports that involve the manipulation of disabled persons "presented as such" for public entertainment.[18] Does this mean that talk of dignity imports a moralistic element into a field previously dominated by autonomy-values? Some have said so (Hennette-Vauchez 2011): they worry that human dignity will be cited as a ground for upholding sexual orthodoxy. But does this mean we should abandon any notion of treatment or behavior unworthy of a human being? Maybe that would be too hasty. Our experience in the law relating to the mistreatment of detainees has shown that we definitely do need a concept of degradation with which to condemn certain modes of detention and interrogation, and that the key to that concept is not the

---

[17] See, e.g., *Planned Parenthood v. Casey* 505 US 833 (1992).
[18] CE, Ass., 27 Octobre 1995, 372: *Commune de Morsang-sur-Orge*.

involuntariness of the treatment, but the contempt that bestial degradation shows for the dignity of human nature. We must hang on to that as a distinctive value, even if we want to question its deployment in other cases that involve sexual misconduct. Dignity has the advantage of bringing together concerns about freedom and non-degradation in a way that autonomy, as it is popularly understood, does not.[19]

VI DIGNITY ACROSS THE FULL RANGE OF CONSTITUTIONAL PROVISIONS

So far, we have been concentrating on the role of human dignity as an organizing idea in regard to the rights element of a modern constitution. I mentioned the important distinction between (i) dignity as a right and (ii) dignity as a constitutional value (Barak 2015). But though dignity as a constitutional value helps inform our interpretation of constitutional rights, it can also serve as a value that informs the constitution as a whole. It can work as an integrating value for the entire constitutional edifice.

So, extending its ambit out from the content of particular rights, we find that dignity is also used to capture the importance of citizenship and what judges and scholars have called "the right to have rights" (Arendt 1973). In the United States, when Chief Justice Warren said in *Trop v. Dulles* 356 U.S. 86 (1958) that "[t]he basic concept underlying the Eighth Amendment is nothing less than the dignity of man," he associated human dignity with precisely this element. The case was about the use of denationalization as a punishment. Determining that denationalization was an unconstitutional punishment, the Chief Justice argued that

> [t]here may be involved no physical mistreatment, no primitive torture. There is instead the total destruction of the individual's status in organized society. It is a form of punishment more primitive than torture, for it destroys for the individual the political existence that was centuries in the development. The punishment strips the citizen of his status in the national and international political community. His very existence is at the sufferance of the country in which he happens to find himself. While any one country may accord him some rights, and presumably as long as he remained in this country he would enjoy the limited rights of an alien, no country need do so because he is stateless. Furthermore, his enjoyment of even the limited rights of an alien might be subject to termination at any time by reason of deportation. In short, the expatriate has lost the right to have rights.[20]

This association of human dignity with political status is important. I have argued elsewhere (Waldron 2012b, p. 73) that human dignity is itself a status concept: I talked about this in Section III above. It is a status concept under which we range and rationalize a number of different elements, explaining their significance jointly

---

[19] But for a more refined understanding of autonomy, see Raz 1986.
[20] *Trop v. Dulles* 356 U.S. 86, at 101–2 (1958).

and severally in terms of a single organizing idea. In moral theory, that organizing idea is (as we have seen) the momentous considerability of the human person. In constitutional jurisprudence, it is the notion that republican political arrangements are made for the benefit and empowerment of ordinary members of the public.

"Dignity" used to be deployed as a term for high office: the dignity of a king or the dignity of a judge. This is how "*dignitas*" was used by Roman statesmen, to mark out special status or high authority (Hennette-Vauchez 2011). I have found it useful to consider that this hierarchical notion of dignity has not been abandoned, but in a sense reversed. We are now *all* possessed of high-status dignity: perhaps we always were. That's what conceptions of human dignity have to justify: the high status of all human beings (Waldron 2007).

Some of this may be captured in the special role of citizenship (Waldron 2013). In republican political theory, the dignity of citizenship is not just the status of a passive beneficiary of our constitutional arrangements, but that of an active and empowered participant.[21] This is particularly important in the constitution of a republic, whose fundamental norm is political equality. Gerald Neuman points out that "the entire edifice of U.S. constitutional law is built on a vision of human dignity, as reflected in popular sovereignty, representative government and entrenched individual rights" (Neuman 2000, p. 251).[22] But it is not just the United States. Constitutional government everywhere is about recognition and empowerment of ordinary people. Human dignity makes sense of our active political equality in democratic and electoral arrangements, our empowerment as participants and our standing to demand accountability (Waldron 2016a). It is our status as members of the popular sovereign – each of us as a person in "We the people" – in whose name the constitution is constructed. Even at ground-zero of the elaboration of human dignity in moral philosophy, Kant (2012 [1785], pp. 42–5) found it necessary to invoke a political image – the image of each person as (like) a legislator in the kingdom of ends (actually "republic of ends" is a better translation).[23] We are like lawmakers, not just subjects in the moral enterprise. In Kantian moral philosophy, that's a metaphor. But it takes on direct and literal importance in constitutional jurisprudence. We – all of us – are credited as makers of the constitutional structures that protect us and empower us.

Beyond that, whatever constitutions do in the way of establishing and maintaining democracy and in protecting the integrity of electoral and representative institutions is also in large part a reflection of dignitarian ideas. We will miss this if we associate the dignitarian aspect of a constitution with the upholding of rights *against* democracy. Human dignity most definitely *is* engaged on the side of such rights

---

[21] See also Kant (2017 [1797], p. 113): "Certainly no human being can be without any dignity, since he has at least the dignity of a citizen."
[22] On the other hand, see Neuman (2000, pp. 251–2), for failures of universalism in US constitutional law.
[23] See also the discussion of Kant's conception of the kingdom of ends in Waldron 2018.

against the majority, but it is engaged too on the side of democratic empowerment. Many jurists see constitutionalism as just a limitation on majority rule (Sajó 1999). But constitutions have to empower as well as constrain, and the constitution of a democracy involves the difficult task of empowering those who would otherwise be powerless for the purposes of ordinary political decision-making (Waldron 2016b, pp. 36–8). The man whom Colonel Rainsborough referred to in the 1647 Putney Debates as "the poorest he that is in England" is the hardest man to empower, because if things are left to themselves he will have no political power at all (Sharp 1998, p. 103). If he is empowered and if his empowerment is secured, it is the affirmative achievement of a democratic constitution that has had to go out of its way to ensure that he has and keeps as much formal political authority as "the greatest he." And this too is motivated by our conception of his human dignity and his entitlement to be treated as an equal in the political process.

What I am trying to show, in other words, is that dignity has work to do in almost every aspect of constitutionalism. It motivates and informs rights-based constraints, democratic ideals, and many of the structural principles that constitutionalism insists on: for example, the separation of powers, bicameralism, federalism – all of which are ways of designing government to respect the dignity of ordinary people and to prevent it from riding over them roughshod.

Even a constitutional principle like the rule of law conveys the importance of human dignity. We respect dignity, when we insist that law must provide a stable framework for action.

> To embark on the enterprise of subjecting human conduct to rules involves of necessity a commitment to the view that man is, or can become, a responsible agent, capable of understanding and following rules, and answerable for his defaults. Every departure from the principles of law's inner morality is an affront to man's dignity as a responsible agent. To judge his actions by unpublished or retrospective laws, or to order him to do an act that is impossible, is to convey to him your indifference to his powers of self-determination.
>
> (Fuller 1969, p. 162)

As Raz (1979b) has pointed out, dignity is what is at stake in the formal requirements of the rule of law such as clarity, stability, and prospectivity. "[O]bservance of the rule of law is necessary if the law is to respect human dignity," states Raz and also, "Respecting human dignity entails treating humans as persons capable of planning and plotting their future." It requires that our rulers act as though the lives and the plans of ordinary people are important and that our rulers foster an environment friendly to such planning, a predictable environment at least so far as the demands of political power are concerned. The due process aspect of the rule of law also picks up the dignitarian theme: we empower people as participants in the legal process and sponsor and structure the making of arguments. As I have said elsewhere (Waldron 2012c, p. 210),

Applying a norm to a human individual is not like deciding what to do about a rabid animal or a dilapidated house. It involves paying attention to a point of view and respecting the personality of the entity one is dealing with. As such it embodies a crucial dignitarian idea – respecting the dignity of those to whom the norms are applied as beings capable of explaining themselves.

Put all this together, and we see human dignity operating as a wide-ranging constitution value, picking up and gathering together a whole array of ideas – an array of protections, benefits, structures, empowerments, entitlements, institutions, forms of respect, and equalizations going well beyond a list of individual rights.

VII SKEPTICISM ABOUT MEANING

I believe the pervasiveness of human dignity as I have just explained can help us with some of the skepticism that is sometimes expressed about the vagueness and malleability of the concept. For one hears a steady drum-beat of suspicion about human dignity in the philosophical literature, especially among those moral philosophers who take part of their job to be the maintenance of intellectual hygiene (see Pritchard 1972). Ronald Dworkin, who actually wanted to deploy the idea, says that "[t]he idea of dignity has been stained by overuse and misuse" (2011, p. 204).[24] There is considerable unease about an idea that seems vulnerable to overuse because of its chameleon-like character; it is all things to all people; it is a purely decorative device; "nothing but a phrase" (Beitz 2013). Sixty years ago, Bertram Morris (1946, p. 57) observed that "[f]ew expressions call forth the nod of assent and put an end to analysis as readily as 'the dignity of man.'" It doesn't help, say the skeptics, that official use of this concept in constitutions and international charters of rights is still uncontaminated by any authoritative definition. A respected human rights jurist, Oscar Schachter once observed of "human dignity" that "[i]ts intrinsic meaning has been left to intuitive understanding," and he worried that "[w]ithout a reasonably clear general idea of its meaning, we cannot easily draw specific implications for relevant conduct" (1983, p. 849).

In my view, these concerns are overblown. As many jurists have pointed out, lots of value-terms do their work in constitutional jurisprudence without the benefit of simplistic definitions.[25] Not all definitions in law come in the form of a checklist of necessary and sufficient conditions. Instead a thick value term like "dignity" serves as a catalyst for thinking; and the heritage it trails is an invitation to reflect on the application of that thinking to the case at hand. "Human dignity" may not have a ready-made definition, but it refers to the history of our attempts over the centuries to say what is special and worthy of respect in the human individual. That this use

---

[24] Still, when he introduced the term he said that "it would be a shame to surrender an important idea or even a familiar name to this corruption" (Dworkin 2011, p. 204).

[25] See generally, H.L.A. Hart, *Definition and Theory in Jurisprudence*.

of it may be challenging or difficult for lawyers doing advocates' work should not be – as the Supreme Court of Canada seems to think it is[26] – a disqualifying factor. We sometimes need concepts in law that challenge the demands of technical advocacy and that invite serious normative reflection, ideas whose elaboration involves continual argument about their proper application (Gallie 1956). It would be a mistake to filter out of the law all concepts of this kind for the sake of spurious clarity.

Moreover, we must expect – what we have seen already in some of this discussion – that a concept as wide-ranging as dignity will not always give us easy and unequivocal solutions in constitutional argument. American constitutional jurisprudence is replete with examples of human dignity being cited on both sides of a given issue – on both sides of an argument about gun rights, for example, or *pro se* representation in court.[27] In the latter case, Justice Breyer said that "a right of self-representation at trial will not 'affirm the dignity' of a defendant who lacks the mental capacity to conduct his defense without the assistance of counsel," while Justice Scalia said (in dissent) that "the loss of 'dignity' the right is designed to prevent is not the defendant's making a fool of himself by presenting an amateurish or even incoherent defense. Rather, the dignity at issue is the supreme human dignity of being master of one's fate rather than a ward of the State—the dignity of individual choice."[28] These two opinions do not cancel each other out. Rather, in each case, the appeal to dignity enriches the sense of what is at stake on both sides of a given issue. It shows that the concept is, as Roberto Barroso (2012) argues, "multi-faceted." Different uses and the generation of different insights is not the same as different and equivocal meanings. Human dignity has work to do all over our constitutional jurisprudence, and it is no surprise that the work it does should crop up sometimes in ways that disconcert those who are looking for easy arguments.

VIII A CONSTITUTION AS A WHOLE

A constitution is not just a "heap" of provisions, each separate from the others, which we are supposed to mine for particular texts or doctrines that may be used as the basis of "slam-dunk" arguments in court. It is supposed to make sense as a whole – both as a machine whose moving parts work together (Kammen 2006), and as something with normative integrity along the lines of Ronald Dworkin's conception in *Law's Empire* (1986). The integrity component means paying attention to what different provisions and doctrines, in what appear to be different areas of

---

[26] *R. v Kapp* 2008 SCC 41 at § 22: "[A]s critics have pointed out, human dignity is an abstract and subjective notion that ... cannot only become confusing and difficult to apply; it has also proven to be an *additional* burden on equality claimants, rather than the philosophical enhancement it was intended to be."

[27] See, e.g., *McDonald v. Chicago*, 561 U.S. 742 (2010) on gun rights, and *Indiana v. Edwards*, 554 U.S. 164 (2008) on pro se representation.

[28] *Indiana v. Edwards*, 554 U.S. 164 (2008), 176 (Breyer J. for the Court) and 186–87 (Scalia J., dissenting).

constitutional concern, have in common. We are familiar with this in colloquial terms when we assume that the US Constitution, for example, is pervaded by a commitment to freedom, and that unless we can see what is in common between (say) freedom as upheld by the First Amendment, freedom as reinforced in the voting rights provisions, and freedom as embodied in various structural checks and balances, then we don't really understand it.

The burden of my argument in this paper is that "human dignity" performs a similarly pervasive and uniting function within many liberal/democratic constitutions. It has particular work to do when it figures in the content of some particular right, but, beyond that, it helps mark out the point of the whole enterprise. We, the nominal authors of such a constitution, attribute human dignity to one another. We insist on being treated by our government with that dignity and on the protections that are necessary to ensure that. Indeed, we insist as a matter of dignity that the government is ours and for us to control; its accountability to us, through established political mechanisms, is a matter of the tribute that agents must pay to the dignity of those who employ them (Waldron 2016a). By insisting on the rule of law, we maintain that we are to be treated with dignity even when it is a question of coercing us. Our well-being is to be regarded as that of individuals with dignity and not as the well-being of cattle who graze for their masters' benefit. All these constitutional uses of dignity – and more – are united in a common conception that, I think, is pervasive and indispensable in modern constitutionalism.

RECOMMENDED READING

Barak, A. (2015). *Human Dignity: The Constitutional Value and the Constitutional Right*, Cambridge: Cambridge University Press.

Beitz, C. (2013). Human Dignity in the Theory of Human Rights: Nothing but a Phrase? *Philosophy and Public Affairs*, 41(3), 259–90.

Dicke, K. (2002). The Founding Function of Human Dignity in the Universal Declaration of Human Rights. In D. Kretzmer and E. Klein, eds., *The Concept of Dignity in Human Rights Discourse*. The Hague: Kluwer Law International, pp. 111–20.

Habermas, J. (2010). The Concept of Human Dignity and the Realistic Utopia of Human Rights. *Metaphilosophy*, 41(4), 464–80.

Hennette-Vauchez, S. (2011). A Human *Dignitas*: Remnants of the Ancient Legal Concept in Contemporary Dignity Jurisprudence. *International Journal of Constitutional Law*, 9(1), 32–57.

McCrudden, C. (2008). Human Dignity in Human Rights Interpretation. *European Journal of International Law*, 19(4), 655–724.

Neuman, G. (2000). Human Dignity in United States Constitutional Law. In D. Simon and M. Weiss, eds., *Zur Autonomie des Individuums: Liber Amicorum Spiros Simitis*. Baden-Baden: Nomos Verlagsgesellschaft, pp. 249–71.

Rao, N. (2008). On the Use and Abuse of Dignity in Constitutional Law. *Columbia Journal of European Law*, 14(2), 201–55.

Rosen, M. (2012). *Dignity: its History and Meaning*, Cambridge, MA: Harvard University Press.

Sharp, A. (2001). *The English Levellers*, Cambridge: Cambridge University Press.
Waldron, J. (2012a). *Dignity, Rank and Rights*, New York: Oxford University Press.
Waldron, J. (2012b). How Law Protects Dignity, *Cambridge Law Journal*, 71(1), 200–22.
Waldron, J. (2013). Citizenship and Dignity. In C. McCrudden ed., *Understanding Human Dignity*. London: The British Academy, pp. 327–43.
Waldron, J. (2015). Is Dignity the Foundation of Human Rights? In M. Liao, M. Renzo, & R. Cruft, eds., *The Philosophical Foundations of Human Rights*. Oxford: Oxford University Press, pp. 117–37.

3

Rights

Rowan Cruft

This chapter attempts two tasks, conceptual and normative.[1] Firstly, I argue that constitutions need not include rights as a matter of logic: it is possible for a set of laws and conventions to qualify as a genuine constitution of a state or legal system even if they do not contain any rights – or *almost* none.[2] Nonetheless, secondly, I argue that rights-free constitutions miss out on something valuable: it is hard to see non-rights constitutions as intended to serve citizens qua individuals. In particular, I argue that there are strong reasons in favour of constitutional rights on both natural rights and democratic grounds. I end by explaining the way in which rights function as *limits* on government power: we will see that they need not be the limits that constitutional*ists* endorse.

I THE NATURE OF RIGHTS AND THE POSSIBILITY OF NON-RIGHTS CONSTITUTIONS

Like Gardner, I take it that 'in every legal system there are rules that specify the major institutions and officials of government, and determine which of them is to do what, and how they are to interact, and how their membership or succession is to be determined, and so forth. [...] These rules without which there would be no legal system (or some of them, invariably in combination with some other rules) make up the constitution of that system' (Gardner 2011, p. 162). In Gardner's view, constitutional law regulates institutions of inherent power, where this means institutions whose power is irrevocable, even if 'irrevocably delegated' (ibid., p. 181).

I also follow Gardner (2011), with Bellamy (2007), in assuming that constitutions need not be purely legal. They are, rather, the rules and practices that constitute a system of political power (including law) as the system it is: the rules and practices which, if changed or continually violated or ignored, should lead us to conclude not

---

[1] For their patient, insightful help and comments, many thanks to Richard Bellamy, Jeff King, Cosmin Vraciu and participants at the Bentham House conference from which this volume emerged.
[2] For the exceptional case, power-rights, see later in this section.

that there has been a change within the system of political power and law, but rather that that system has ceased to be, perhaps instead being replaced with an alternative system or overturned. Finally, I will also assume that constitutions need not take written form, though of course some do.

Must constitutions so understood include individual rights? Many do, especially written or proclaimed constiutions: consider the role of the Bill of Rights in the US constitution, or the role of the 'Declaration of the Rights of Man and of the Citizen' in the French constitution. Are there conceptual reasons why any genuine constitution must include rights – that is, why any system of law and power must have rights at its core? Some theorists might answer: clearly not, because there are historical and counterfactual examples of rights-free constitutions, that is, of systems of political and legal power that do not fundamentally confer rights. The proponent of this answer might refer to debates about whether Confucian systems of power involve individual rights at all, or about whether the ancient Romans and ancient Greeks had the concept.[3] Or they might refer to the possibility of Feinberg's (1970) imagined 'Nowheresville', in which everyone is subject to the duties we all recognise at present, but none of these duties correlate with rights.

With one notable exception, I will agree that the rules and practices constituting a system of political and legal power – the rules and practices without which the system would not be the system it is – need not include rights: legal-political *duties or rules* are enough on their own to be the constitution of a system of power. Respect for these normative forms is enough to make such a system, without respect for norms-taking-the-form-of-rights – bar one exception noted below. But we cannot simply refer to the examples of the previous paragraph in order to establish this. Norms that are not *framed* in rights terms could still be rights even if they are not described or conceived explicitly using the concept. For example, constitutional duties to *allow* citizens to travel freely within the state's territory guarantee that citizens are subject to no legal duty to refrain from traveling within the territory. Rights theory – to be explained in a moment – tells us that such constitutional guarantees qualify as citizens' Hohfeldian privilege-rights or liberty-rights: privilege-rights of freedom of movement. Similarly, constitutional rules vesting a body (e.g. Parliament) with the capacity to create new duties qualify – says rights theory – as Hohfeldian power-rights for that body. Thus, constitutions – written or unwritten – that eschew the word 'rights' but still introduce the relevant privileges or powers will end up including rights in this sense, even though they are not framed in rights terms (Hohfeld 1964).

What this reveals is that to know whether constitutions can really eschew rights, we need to know what exactly rights are. And for that we need to enter rights theory. The previous paragraph shows us that the absence of the word 'a right' need not prove that a constitution lacks rights. Perhaps, indeed any system of rules must,

---

[3] On whether Confucianism involves rights, see Ihara (2004) and Rosemont (2004); on whether the Ancients had the concept, see F. Miller (1995), Garnsey (2007, chap. 7).

as a matter of logic, include such a concept. A right confers a normative status that highlights the right-holder in a way that is in some sense positive for them. Hohfeld (1964) famously distinguishes four types of rights:

- A has a claim-right that B do PHI iff B is under a duty to A to do PHI.
- A has a privilege-right against B to do PHI iff A is under no duty to B not to do PHI.
- A has a power-right over B iff A has the normative ability to create or remove some duty (or other Hohfeldian normative position) of B's.
- A has an immunity-right against B iff B lacks a normative ability to create or remove some right (or other Hohfeldian normative position) of A's.

With this taxonomy at hand, we can see that almost any possible constitution will need to include some power-rights. If a constitution is to allow that the political-legal system it constitutes can change – e.g., if it is to allow that new laws can be created – then whichever body or person is empowered to make this change, therefore, holds a Hohfeldian power-right. As Wenar (2020, sect. 3) says, 'even the most rudimentary human communities must have rules specifying that some are entitled to tell others what they must do. Such rules ascribe rights'. Perhaps a political-legal system that makes no provision for any changes within it is a logical possibility, but it is not a live one. Any real constitution must contain power-rights, giving some parties power to adjust some of the rules within the system.[4]

But in my view, that is all. The other Hohfeldian positions are not essential components of constitutions. Any *liberal* constitution will need to include some privilege-rights: permissions that are irrevocably protected within the political-legal system that they constitute, specifying actions that constitutionally cannot be forbidden. But a constitution in which any action could potentially be able to be forbidden by the authorities seems a live – if illiberal – possibility. And such a constitution will not contain constitutional privilege-rights.

A particularly interesting question is whether some constitutional duties must necessarily be *owed to* citizens as their Hohfeldian claim-rights, even if they are not so framed in the constitution. For Hohfeld, A has a claim-right that B do something PHI iff B owes a duty to A to do PHI (Hohfeld 1964, pp. 36–38). Hohfeldian claim-rights have several distinctive features that are central to rights' role in the popular imagination: First, the claim-right is the only *violable* Hohfeldian position: it is the only Hohfeldian position that specifies a particular act whose non-performance qualifies as the right's violation (see Cruft 2019, pp. 83–84). Secondly, the Hohfeldian claim-right highlights a particular party as *the wronged victim* when

---

[4] This does not mean that any constitution must confer power-rights that would enable *the constitution itself* to change. Unalterable constitutions seem like a live possibility. But a constitution enabling *no legal-political change whatsoever* does not – and that is why inclusion of some power-rights seems inevitable for any constitution.

a duty is violated, the party *to whom* reparations or apology are owed, the party who can, potentially, forgive or waive in their own name.[5] Thirdly, because claim-rights entail duties (or, I would controversially say, are themselves a species of duty), they inherit the distinguishing features of duties – namely, a conceptual relationship to importance and force.[6]

Standard theories say the same thing about claim-rights that I have said about privilege-rights and power-rights: such theories maintain that a constitution could contain claim-rights without being framed in these terms, so long as it contained constitutional duties that were genuinely owed to a particular party as her rights. But what is this 'owed to' or 'directed duty' idea? This is an area of live, difficult debate. Current theories of the nature of claim-rights include the following:

Interest or Benefit Theory

(i) *Justificatory variant*: The duty to PHI is owed to A (as A's claim-right) iff A's interests ground the duty (Raz 1986, p. 166).
(ii) *Necessary connection variant*: The duty to PHI is owed to A (as A's claim-right) iff PHI-ing would necessarily place A in a position typically beneficial for a human (or where relevant, animal or group) to be placed in (MacCormick 1982; Kramer 1998 and 2010).

Will, Control, or Demand Theory

(i) *Will/control variant*: The duty to PHI is owed to A (as A's claim-right) iff A holds certain powers over the duty (e.g. to waive, enforce, resent, forgive it) (Hart 1955; Steiner 1994; see also Darwall 2012).
(ii) *Demand variant*: The duty to PHI is owed to A (as A's claim-right) iff A is specially placed to demand it (Feinberg 1970; Gilbert 2018).

Hybrid Theory (Sreenivasan 2005; McBride 2021): The duty to PHI is owed to A (as A's claim-right) iff A's interests ground or are tracked by A's level of power or control over that duty.

Each of these theories has famous problems. For example, the Interest Theory struggles to accommodate legal claim-rights that do not serve right-holders' interests, such as useless property rights. And the Will Theory struggles to accommodate

---

[5] See Thompson (2004) for a good articulation of this view. Cornell challenges the assumption that being owed a duty and being wronged by its violation stand and fall together (Cornell 2015).
[6] Some characterise duties as practical reasons that are 'categorical' – holding 'irrespective of the duty-bearer's prevailing personal goals at the time when it comes to be performed' – and 'exclusionary' (or as Gardner puts it, 'required') – so that 'some or all of the valid reasons *not* to do the required thing are to be discounted' (Gardner 2018, pp. 21–22). Others characterise duties as reasons that are demandable or enforceable (see Gilbert (2018) for this claim regarding rights-correlative directed duties). My current view – influenced by discussion with Kieran Setiya – is that duties are reasons in relation to which *the duty-bearer's will not to do what the duties ask* gives others no reason not to make the duty-bearer perform them.

unwaiveable claim-rights and claim-rights of animals and babies.[7] In response, theorists have recently tried new approaches:

> Kind-Desire Theory (Wenar 2013): The duty to PHI is owed to A (as A's claim-right) iff (i) PHI is to be 'done to' A, and (ii) parties of A's kind desire to be PHI'ed, in virtue of their kind, and (iii) the duty is permissibly enforceable.
>
> Addressive Theory (Cruft 2019): The duty to PHI is owed to A iff because of the duty's form, PHI is canonically conceived second-personally by the duty-bearer as to be 'done to you, A', and (if A is a capable party) PHI is canonically conceived first-personally by A as to be 'done to me'.

All but the last of these theories – with its non-reductive reference in the analysans to a duty's 'form' as directed or undirected – implies that just as a constitution may contain Hohfeldian privilege-rights or power-rights without being framed in rights terms or 'directed duty' terms, so it might contain claim-rights without using that concept. For example, a constitution might place the state under constitutional duties to ensure that citizens can vote. If these duties are justified by citizens' interests in voting, then the Justificatory Interest Theory tells us that the relevant constitutional duties are citizens' constitutional claim-rights whether or not they are described in rights terms. Similarly, a constitution might vest citizens with control over other citizens' duties not to assault or touch them. The Will Theory tells us that the relevant constitutional duties qualify as citizens' constitutional claim-rights not to be assaulted – whether or not they are so described in the constitution.

I have some doubts about any theory of claim-rights that works like this, ascribing claim-rights where lawmakers and wider society do not conceive them as claim-rights. I have said that constitutions allowing change *must* include some power-rights, and hence, even social-legal systems of rules whose makers and inhabitants do not think in rights terms must contain such power-rights. But I think we should be very wary of finding rights too often in systems whose members do not use the concept. The Interest and Will Theories would both find rights in Feinberg's *Nowheresville*: any duty over which someone had control, or that was grounded on or necessarily served someone's interests, would turn out to be that person's right even though the Nowheresvilleans do not so conceive it. Similarly, the theories would find rights in Confucian systems or Ancient systems whose members do not use the concept. This worries me. If authoritative parties (including everyday people living under a system) assert that their legal system does not involve rights, it is prima facie problematic to insist – on the basis of theory – that they must misunderstand their own system by failing to have spotted the rights within it.

For some contentions – e.g., the assertion that wolves are extinct in a territory – people from outside the system have equal epistemic authority to those within the system: if I see wolves when glancing over the border into your territory, I can readily

---

[7] See e.g. MacCormick 1982.

contend that you have failed to spot them. Matters seem different with created normative artefacts like legal or conventional rights, including constitutional rights. Regarding their existence, the participants in the relevant created system have a certain epistemic authority. If they lack the very concept of rights, then it seems (other things being equal) problematic to find such things within their system. If they have the concept, but deny that their system contains rights, then again I think we have some (defeasible) reason to be wary of finding rights within their system. At least, some explanation is needed for why those within the system erroneously failed to notice the rights constituting their system. My complaint with most theories of claim-rights is that they prompt the need for such an explanation too frequently.

This is one count against most of the theories of claim-rights listed. Relatedly, we might worry about the conceptual limit these theories impose on the ability of lawmakers – including constitution-makers – to make rights at will, independently of the location of interests or powers, desires or demands. While legislatures can create duties with almost any content they wish, borne by almost any party they specify,[8] they seem – according to the theories listed – to be more conceptually limited in the duties they can deem to correlate with claim-rights: Will Theory famously disallows unwaivable duties to be rights, and the other theories impose similar limits: for example, Interest Theory is unable to make duties that necessarily serve or are grounded by someone's interests avoid being rights for that person. Now, of course, there will be some conceptual limits on the rights we can create: it seems conceptually impossible for rights to be held by the colour blue or the discipline of mathematics, and conceptually impossible for rights to be things which consume food or have a physical size. But the theories listed impose much more restrictive limits on the *rights* legislatures can create than on their creation of *duties*.

On the basis of these arguments, I favour my Addressive Account of claim-rights, though I must refer the reader to Cruft (2019) for more details. On this account, there is no necessity for a constitution to contain claim-rights: whether it contains claim-rights depends on whether duties in the constitution specify action that should given the duties' form be conceived in relevant first- and second-personal ways. A constitution need not contain duties formally requiring such conceptions of action – though we will see in the next two sections that it would be good if it did! But Feinberg's Nowheresvillle could, on this account, have a constitution that contains almost no rights – none other than those power-rights specifying the possibility of change. An unchangeable constitution need contain no rights whatsoever. This seems the correct result to me, allowing us to avoid having to read rights anachronistically back into all systems of power that were not conceived in rights terms. (Of course, there will be some systems that are likely to contain rights even though people didn't realise this. But that requires a special explanation.)

---

[8] Note the 'almost' and see some exceptions just below.

In this first Section, I have argued that it is not conceptually necessary that legal constitutions contain claim-rights or privilege-rights – though any must contain some power-rights specifying who can change the system. And any *liberal* constitution must contain privilege rights. In the next two sections, I argue that any *democratic* constitution must also contain claim-rights. But first a further question: must constitutions contain *duties*, where this means legal-political reasons for action that the agent should heed independently of whether she wants to or decides not to, and that can potentially prompt enforcement independently of the agent's wishes? In my view, to qualify as a legal system, a system of norms must include duties. But I am not sure that duties must be present in the system's *constitution* – that is, its irrevocable parts without which it would not be the system it is – if it is to qualify as a legal system. I can imagine systems of power and law whose governing, defining norms are simply goals or high-weight values.[9] In such cases, for the relevant goal or value to qualify as constitutional, it is perhaps necessary that *government officials* are subject to legal duties to maintain the relevant goal or value as *a goal or value of the system*. And I have said that the system itself must contain duties. But I doubt its constitution must, as a matter of logic.

II THE VALUE OF CONSTITUTIONAL RIGHTS: NATURAL RIGHTS AND HUMAN RIGHTS

Even if, as Section I argues, constitutions are not *logically* required to contain rights (or, at most, must contain power-rights enabling change), I believe there are still good moral reasons for us to choose to institute a range of rights within our constitutions, including claim-rights and privilege-rights. In the current Section and the following one, I outline two related moral reasons in favour of constitutional rights: one based on the importance of natural or human rights, and one based on the values of democracy. Both sets of pro-rights reasons spring from the fact that the inclusion of rights within a constitution stands in a supportive relationship with the idea that the purpose of government and law is to serve the people who are subject to it.

Suppose one important purpose of government and law is to serve the people who are subject to it. This view is central to most modern conceptions of state authority, including liberal and many non-liberal conceptions. My Addressive Theory says that constitutional claim-rights are constitutional provisions whose form requires the state to regard citizens second-personally as 'you, to whom this action (required by constitutional duty) is done'. Such a second-personal conception of citizens, by government and law, coheres closely with conceiving government's ultimate purpose as the serving of its citizens. If people are *not* conceptualised in this second-personal

---

[9] See Nickel's discussion of the Sustainable Development Goals (Nickel 2013). If they are not in some sense enforceable limits, these goals will not be duties. Yet they could still constrain government decisions.

way by their state, government and law – e.g., if constitutional rules are simply taken as rules to be respected by the state and its officials, *without* the state and its officials being required by the rules' form to think of what the rules require as actions 'to be done to you, citizens' – then, it is harder for the state and officials to remember that their institutions' purpose is to serve citizens.

How institutions conceive those over whom they exercise power is important both instrumentally and in principle. Instrumentally, requiring officials and their institutions to recognise those over whom they wield power as right-holders can have important beneficial effects, making it harder for the relevant people to be thought of as subhuman, as nuisances that do not deserve respect.[10] But recognition by institutions of people as rights-holders is also important in principle, independently of its effects. Carter (2011) argues that equal respect for citizens requires that the state not delve nosily into the details of its citizens' lives and abilities, even if this would be instrumentally beneficial. Similarly, I think it is non-instrumentally important that the state conceive its citizens as parties that it acts on second-personally in fulfilling its constitutional duties, and hence, as parties that it wrongs when it violates constitutional rules. The same non-instrumental value attaches to enabling citizens to demand fulfilment of some constitutional provisions not just on behalf of *the legal community in the abstract*, but on behalf of *themselves qua right-holders*. Further, it seems important that the system of law and power build in this focus on the individual citizen at its roots – where this means in its constitution, in the form of the rules which, if changed, stop it being the system it is. Only if the constitution contains claim-rights does a system's very nature reflect its being there for the sake of individual citizens.

Yet, even if this is correct, one could achieve these aims – of making those subject to the state's power *wronged* by violation of constitutional rules – by including *some* legal claim-rights-held-by-individuals in the constitution. This point does not tell us which constitutional provisions should be claim-rights. On this issue, there are two sources of guidance. First, we should look to any rights that exist independently of their social recognition, as human rights or natural rights. Second, there is also a conceptual link between democracy and many rights. I examine the first of these approaches in the current section, and the second in the next.

Recognition-independent rights are constituted by Hohfeldian positions – claim-rights, privilege-rights, power-rights, immunity-rights – that people hold whether or not they or anyone else ever thinks that they hold them, and hence, whether or not they are institutionalised in law or convention. Human rights are conceived in this way by 'naturalistic' theories, which maintain that they are the rights a person holds simply in virtue of being human, whether or not this is recognised in law

---

[10] See the empirical work in Simmons (2012). See also Gaita's reflections on the grip of the idea of a 'common humanity' (2001).

or elsewhere.[11] There is a clear historical parallel with the idea of 'natural rights', though I resist the approach which defines these as rights that would be held in an asocial 'state of nature'. For I resist the idea that such an asocial state would involve anything like humans as we know them. 'Natural' rights on my account are simply rights whose existence does not depend on people's recognition or social construction of them.

In other work, I have defended the possibility of recognition-independent or natural human rights: in my view, Raz's Justificatory Interest Theory of rights is best conceived as an account specifically of recognition-independent natural moral claim-rights rather than of claim-rights in general (Cruft 2019, chaps. 1–4). On this view, a natural claim-right exists when a particular party's good is of sufficient moral importance on its own to place others under duties to serve that good. In such a scenario, I argue that when considering what their duties require, the relevant 'others' need to think second-personally about the party whose good morally grounds their duties – if they are properly to recognise that these duties are morally grounded by the good of a party with subjectivity. The central thought is that when a party (i) with a good (e.g., with well-being, interests, needs, projects, for whom possession of freedom, agency, capabilities, wisdom or perhaps other things are good) and (ii) with natural first-personality (unlike, say, 'Siri', Microsoft, or a car or other artefact that can nonetheless do 'better' or 'worse') is such that an action's being good for that party naturally makes someone morally duty-bound to perform that action, then the moral duty in question must carry the second-personal (and, where applicable, first-personal) requirements that make it owed to the party whose good makes it exist (ibid., chap. 7).[12]

Consider your claim-right not to be tortured: your interest or need not to be tortured is sufficiently morally important on its own to make it the case that I have a duty not to torture you; my duty is generated by your interest or need largely independently of whether it serves others beyond you.[13] The central moral role played by your interest or need not to be tortured in grounding my duty not to torture

---

[11] For this naturalistic view, see Griffin (2008), Tasioulas (2015), Cruft (2019); for the rival 'political' view which defines human rights by their relation to state sovereignty, as rights that are of concern to the international community, see Beitz (2009), Lafont (2012), Rawls (1999b), Raz (2015); for the legal view that human rights are fundamentally a set of international, regional and constitutional legal institutions, documents and practices, see Buchanan (2013). For argument broadly consonant with that of the current section *from* natural moral rights to constitutional rights, see Fabre (2000).

[12] I draw on this chapter in my discussion here.

[13] This point can seem especially plausible when we note that the duty in question might in extreme cases be justifiably infringeable. In the case of torture I doubt that is ever true, but for other rights it might be. It is the existence of the duty, rather than respect for it, that is groundable largely by the right-holder's own interest. Further, a moral duty can be groundable in this way – by the right-holder's good working largely on its own – while also being groundable in other ways, for example by how it serves the common good. The hallmark of natural rights is that they protect duties groundable primarily by the right-holder's own good; this leaves open the possibility that they are also groundable in other ways (Cruft 2019, pp. 124–5)

you – the interest or need of you, an addressable site of subjectivity – is registered by the duty's formally requiring me to conceive you second-personally as not-tortured by me, rather than simply requiring me not to engage in the act of torturing you.

If there are such natural moral claim-rights – duties that are naturally owed to particular parties because they exist for the sake of those parties – then there is defeasible reason for systems of power and law to enshrine these rights, and indeed a strong reason for any *constitution existing for the sake of the people* to enshrine them. Or at least, this is true of those natural moral claim-rights that are of public moral importance, unlike, say, a right to fidelity within friendships or romantic relationships. Elsewhere, I outline the relevant form of 'public importance' as involving a right's being morally permissibly claimable on the right-holder's behalf by anyone; there are several ways to interpret this notion of human rights as 'everyone's business'.[14] But the key point here is that natural claim-rights with some such public importance deserve both strong protection and symbolic reflection in positive law and power – and further, they deserve this protection in the system's core purposes, reflected in the rules of the constitutional institutions that make the system what it is. This need not mean 'direct translation' into constitutional law, but some formal recognition of their existence and importance.

In particular contexts, this reasoning can be defeated, for example, if constitutionalising certain important natural rights has counter-productive effects, perversely incentivising rights violations or creating war or riots. But a default in favour of constitutional protection or recognition of some sort seems justified to me, given the special moral importance of respect for the individual, an importance reflected in the existence of natural rights. (This is not to rule out in addition the inclusion of other rights – beyond 'natural human rights' – in constitutions.)[15]

III THE VALUE OF CONSTITUTIONAL RIGHTS: DEMOCRACY AND CLAIM-RIGHTS

The simple argument of the previous section – from the public importance of certain natural human rights to their recognition in a constitution – should be supplemented by a conceptual argument about the relationship between democracy and constitutional rights. I take democracy to be more than simply the idea that a state's purpose is to serve those subjected to its power. Democracy includes the idea that ultimate power should lie with those subjected to the state's power, and should lie with each

---

[14] Cruft (2019, chap. 10).
[15] It is notable that even theorists like Buchanan, who are sceptical of the idea that most human rights in positive law are founded on natural rights, allows that if there *are* such natural rights and they are of public importance, then human rights law should reflect them. His main worry is simply that there are not enough natural rights to justify the full range of human rights law we need (Buchanan 2013, pp. 58–64; note also his plausible claim that some natural rights lack the public importance to be enshrined in international law (pp. 56–7)).

of them equally.[16] I can see some attraction to the controversial view that this requires not only claim- and privilege-rights to equal suffrage and equal rights of participation in public deliberation, but something like the full panoply of natural human rights. Only with this full range secured, including claim-rights to justice under the law (habeas corpus, fair trials etc.), and claim-rights to food, housing, healthcare and education, will each who is subject to political power hold a genuine opportunity (not equal, but equal enough) to participate in political decision-making. Even rights that are frequent targets of sceptical criticism, such as the human right to holidays with pay, seem to me necessary for democracy. Citizens in a democracy need the thought and reflection made possible by some affordable time away from work. If this is only available to some, then the society in question is not truly democratic.[17]

I recognise that the thesis of the previous paragraph is highly controversial, especially if taken as an argument for *constitutionalising* a wide range of claim-rights including welfare rights. Rather than press this controversial claim here, I will restrict my argument to the thesis that whether one favours a *wide* range of protections of the individual participant as necessary for genuine democracy, or whether one believes democracy favours only a *narrower* range (perhaps simply rules enabling all participants an equal say in the public sphere and an equal vote), it is important that the rules identified as strictly necessary for democracy take the form of constitutional claim-rights. That is, it is important that whatever are identified as essential democratic needs – certainly including equal suffrage and equal opportunities for participation, but perhaps also including much more – be secured by *rights*, rather than non-rights rules. And it is also important that they be *constitutionalised*.

Taking the latter first: *constitutionalising* democratic rights is non-contingently required for democracy. Recall Gardner's characterisation of constitutional rules as governing institutions whose power is irrevocable within the system (2011, p. 181): rules that I characterised as those which if changed or continually violated mean an overthrow of the system, rather than a change within it. The character of these rules plays an especially important role in determining the character of the system. Now there might be systems whose constitutional rules confer claim-rights only on the monarch, or confer no claim-rights at all (see Section I), but which nonetheless give citizens *non-constitutional* democratic claim-rights of participation, perhaps including the wide range of welfare rights that are arguably necessary for democracy. Such a system would be democratic in one sense, but in my view it would not be truly or fully democratic. This is because were its democratic aspects to be removed, the system would by hypothesis still be the same system, as its constitutional rules (involving claim-rights for the monarch or no claim-rights at all) are separate from and can survive independently of its democratic components.

---

[16] See e.g. Christiano (2008), Kolodny (2014).
[17] Compare Waldron (1993a, pp. 12–13) on the right to holidays with pay. On the range of rights required for democratic equality, see Christiano (2008).

Now imagine a system whose constitutional rules include democratic elements, but these do not take the form of claim-rights for each citizen: this system might include a rule requiring that each person have the power to vote, and that each person be able to participate equally in the public sphere. It might even include the wider welfare rules that are perhaps further necessary for democracy. Nonetheless (and this is key), suppose these constitutional rules *do not take the form of claim-rights for individual citizens*. If this state fails to empower some to vote or participate, it does wrong, violating its own constitutional rules; if these requirements are overthrown it stops being the system it is. Yet, if this state fails to empower some to vote or participate, it does not necessarily thereby wrong individual citizens – because the constitutional requirement of democratic empowerment is not an individual participatory claim-right within the system. Even this seemingly democratic system is therefore, in my view, not truly or fully democratic. This is because I see the idea of self-government, government by the people, as central to democracy. And a system which need not count as *wronging a citizen* when it excludes them from participation in government does not genuinely embody self-government by the people. Such a constitution would not be truly democratic, because its democratic features – its inclusion of all citizens in the creation of law and policy – could not plausibly be seen as existing for the sake of the citizens. Simply requiring people to be able to participate, even as a matter of constitutional law, is not enough. This requirement of potential participation must take the form of a claim-right for each person, if they are to have status as a proper member within the self-governing polity.

If this is correct, the value of democracy gives powerful reasons in favour of constitutional claim-rights. Systems whose constitutions lack claim-rights might still contain democratic elements, and they might still enable universal participation in self-government. But such democratic features will not be essential to the system, reflecting its point as governed by and there to serve its citizens. If we are serious about being a democracy, constitutional claim-rights are what we need – though these might not take the form of an explicit, written constitution with a bill of rights.[18]

IV RIGHTS, CONSTITUTIONALISM, AND INDIVIDUALISM

I argued in Section I that constitutions need not contain rights as a matter of logic (except, perhaps, the power-right to institute changes). Sections II and III went on to argue that there are nonetheless strong moral reasons in favour of constitutional

---

[18] Furthermore, we need a constitution that offers official public avenues for individual citizens to contest the democratic credentials of proposed laws or policies. Here I follow Lafont's argument in favour of constitutional judicial review, as central to citizens' democratic ability to contest their state's democratic credentials: As Lafont puts it, 'the right to legal contestation guarantees all citizens that their communicative power, their ability to trigger political deliberation on issues of fundamental rights and freedoms, won't fall below some unacceptable deliberative minimum regardless of how unpopular or idiosyncratic their views may seem to other citizens' (2020, p. 232).

rights: as a way of enshrining natural human rights and democratic values. In particular, any system of power and law whose purpose includes serving the individual citizens who live under it should include claim-rights within its constitution.

In the current section, I explain how these points relate to constitutional*ism* as a doctrine of limited government. Many see constitutions as impediments to democracy – perhaps impediments in the name of justice, but impediments nonetheless, which prevent majorities from interpreting rights as they wish, and indeed from adopting rights-violating policies.[19] Whether this is correct depends on the constitution in question, and on what form of majority rule is truly democratic. My view is that political decisions made by a majority some of whose members have been deliberately misled by others, and some of whom justifiably fear others' power, will not carry democratic legitimacy. I believe this line of thought can be developed to support the conclusion that a wide range of human rights should be respected if a system is to be genuinely democratic. But, as noted above, I will not pursue this argument here. Instead, my aim in the current section is to clarify the relationship between constitutional *rights* and constitutional*ism*. I will argue that a constitution's containing rights need not in itself imply that the system governed by the constitution must be a constitutional*ist* system of 'limited government'. We will see that there is a form of individualism implied by the inclusion of rights within a constitution, but this individualism is compatible with a range of political positions from left to right, positions in which government is relatively limited *or* relatively unconstrained and empowered.

My point builds on Waldron's observation that constitutions and the rights therein can empower and require action from government as much as they can limit: it all depends on the constitution in question. As Waldron (2016b, p. 33) puts it,

> Legal control of government, subjection of government decisions to the constraint of overarching law, can either limit or expand what the government is doing. Consider for example Section 26 of the Constitution of South Africa, which requires the state to take reasonable legislative and other measures to achieve progressive realization of the right to adequate housing. If the government escapes legal control, it might neglect this priority and devote resources to a more limited agenda. A government under law, however, is required to expand its agenda to include housing among its high priorities, and that is what the South African Constitutional Court decided in the *Grootboom* case.

As this example makes clear, the inclusion of *rights* within a constitution need not point in a 'limited government' direction. It depends what rights are included. Rights to housing, health and welfare provision will demand a lot from government. I am sympathetic to the thought that such rights should be constitutionalised on the grounds outlined in Sections II and III above. Libertarians and right-liberals will

---

[19] For doubts especially about judicial review, see Bellamy (2007), Waldron (2006).

favour less demanding rights, and will thereby in my view fail fully to uphold human rights and democracy – but they will, of course, think differently.

In the current section, I prescind from this debate and instead outline a rather different way in which the inclusion of any individual rights within a constitution gives the system of power it governs a distinctive character that might seem to be a 'limit': the system will be inherently focused on the individual. I have presented this as a positive feature of rights constitutions (Sections II and III), but some might disagree. For example, in arguing that democratic constitutions should include rights, have I ruled out the possibility of democracy for people committed to non-individualistic moralities?[20] We have seen that claim-rights focus duties on particular individuals (the rights-holders); and we have seen in Section I that constitutions are logically not required to contain rights. Must non-individualistic moral conceptions favour non-rights constitutions, and hence be undemocratic? In the current section, I argue that the answer to this question varies for different forms of non-individualism.

One important, commonly asserted thesis in this area notes that among the individual human's goods which can ground her constitutional, legal and moral rights are socially shaped interests and interests in living a socially embedded life. These include interests far more extensive than those the individual would hold in an asocial 'state of nature': for example, interests in loving relationships, in social play, in speaking one's native language, in forming a trade union, in doing one's duty by one's various communities including friends and family, in many further forms of political and wider social participation. One way to interpret some communitarian or non-individualistic claims is as a reminder that (almost?) all our interests are socially shaped and embedded in this way.[21] Constitutions containing rights can readily accommodate this point, by including protection for rights grounded on these social interests. Rights-containing constitutions are perfectly compatible with this sort of communitarian or non-individualistic insight. (This not to deny that there might be tensions within such constitutions, for example, in their handling of the relationship between individual claims to property and indigenous property rights. The point is just that the individualism of the rights concept is compatible with rights protecting fundamentally social interests.)

Nonetheless Section II's defence of constitutional rights as reflecting natural or moral human rights presupposes that we can distinguish *a party's good* (the rightholder's) from *the good of the group or of others*, and isolate that party's good as the predominant ground of a natural duty. This is the basis of natural human rights: duties that exist for the sake of a particular party. Can we really isolate a party's good

---

[20] Compare Buchanan (2013, chap. 7).
[21] On the social shaping of the interests or needs that ground our rights, see Nickel (2007) and Griffin (2008), and more explicitly in Gould (2004, p. 63 and pp. 94–102); Parekh (2004, chap. 4), Nussbaum (2011), Gould (2014) and Brownlee (2020). See also my Cruft (2019, p. 126), on which I draw here.

in this way? Some non-individualistic or communitarian theorists might disagree.[22] Such views are harder to fit with my argument for constitutional rights. If the individual's interests either cannot be conceptually isolated at all from the interests of the wider group, or if so isolated they cannot function naturally to ground duties or rights, then the natural rights argument for rights-containing constitutions that I defended in Section II will be mistaken. For if such conceptual isolation of the individual's interest is not really possible, or if when so isolated individual goods cannot on their own play a major part in grounding natural duties, then I am wrong to claim that there are natural moral human rights.

Suppose this concern is correct. We might still think there could be reasons to create legal and conventional rights – including constitutional rights. But the reasons for doing this are fairly weak, in the absence of natural moral rights to which legal-conventional institutions might give institutional form. We might think there are no natural moral rights but nonetheless include rights in our constitution in order to affirm that its purpose is to serve citizens qua individuals. But it is unclear why we would do this if we did not think that an individual's good can sometimes be sufficient on its own morally to ground duties that will thereby qualify as the individual's natural moral rights. Thus, one central reason for including rights in a constitution – that the constitution thereby wears on its face its purpose in serving citizens qua individuals – should lead the theorist to favour the natural rights argument sketched in Section II.

Might there be alternative reasons to include rights in a constitution, reasons that do not lead to the duty-grounding importance of the individual's good? One might favour rights as means to achieve aggregated or collective goods. This seems plausible as a defence of Hohfeldian liberties and powers: for example, liberties and powers are necessary components of markets, defensible in terms of the efficiency they achieve for the aggregate.[23] Such instrumental arguments seem less effective in support of Hohfeldian *claim-rights*, given that 'undirected' duties without correlative claim-rights, or duties owed to the collective as their collective right, can do the same work by demanding the same actions as those demanded by individual rights. Perhaps people better police duties that serve the collective if they think of the duties in question as correlating with their own individual rights, but this strikes me as dependent on highly contingent features of our psychology.[24]

---

[22] I am not sure which views would generate this disagreement: various forms of communitarianism are possible, and only some would deny that we can distinguish the individual's good from the community's good in the necessary way. Possibly relevant views include Taylor's (1985) rejection of 'atomistic' views of the self, some forms of Confucian view (see Ihara 2004; and Wong 2004), and Mbiti's analysis of African conceptions of the self in which 'Whatever happens to the individual happens to the whole group, and whatever happens to the whole group happens to the individual. The individual can only say "I am, because we are; and since we are, therefore I am"' (1970, p. 141 – compare Menkiti 1984, p. 171).

[23] Compare the efficiency arguments for the market in Hume (1978 [1739–40]) and Smith (1976 [1776]) – see the useful summary in Buchanan (1988, chap. 2).

[24] For fuller development of these doubts about the success of non-individualistic arguments for rights, see Cruft (2019, chap. 13).

One might favour *democracy* for fundamentally non-individualistic reasons, and haven't I argued that democracy requires constitutional claim-rights (Section III)? For example, one might argue from the 'democratic peace thesis' to the conclusion that states should become democracies, then draw on Section III's argument to say that this requires rights-based constitutions. Or one might make a similar argument from the epistemic benefits of democracy.[25] To assess either argument, we need to examine how far the instrumental and epistemic benefits of democracies depend on their being full democracies in the manner outlined in Section III where this involves individual constitutional rights: that is, how far valuable results like peace and non-famine, or the epistemic benefits of well-informed political decisions, depend on citizens being able to make claims against each other and their government or state *in their own name*. I can imagine a non-individualistic theorist claiming that the relevant benefits (peace, non-famine, epistemic well-informedness) can be achieved by enabling citizens to make claims against their government or state, but not in their own name, rather in the name of citizens at large. Such a system would need constitutional rights held by the citizenry as a group, rights that any citizen can claim on behalf of the group. But it is not clear that such a system needs rights held by individual citizens. Perhaps such individual rights are instrumentally beneficial, but it is unclear how much good turns simply on being able to make a claim *in one's own name as right-holder*, as opposed to being able to make exactly the same claim (to be allowed to vote, to press one's views in public debate) *in the name of the wider community*, or *in relation to an undirected constitutional duty*. The instrumental benefits of democracy seem to depend on people being able to press claims to participate in the political process. Being able do this *in one's own name as an individual right-holder* does not seem very necessary to the delivery of the instrumental benefits: these seem to depend primarily on ensuring that everyone can participate, rather than ensuring that they do so in their own name. To deliver a strong case for individual rights in the constitution, I think we need a commitment to democracy that is not just instrumental or epistemic: something more like the premise in Sections II and III about the importance of the state's purpose being ultimately to serve each individual.

Either a 'democratic' constitution without individual rights, or a constitution that includes such rights but purely for instrumental reasons, misses out something important: such constitutions fail to recognise and institutionalise the duty-grounding importance of each individual's good, what Rawls (1971, p. 27) calls the 'separateness of persons'. There is nothing incoherent in failing to recognise this, as Section I showed. So non-individualistic theorists that take routes like this can be logically impeccable. But in order to adopt Section II's and III's approach, such theorists need to recognise the duty-grounding importance of each individual's good. This is compatible with the

---

[25] For the epistemic benefits of democracy, see Estlund (2008) and Peter (2009).

insight that (almost?) all individual goods causally and constitutively require social interaction. But it is incompatible with the view that the very idea of 'my' good cannot be conceptually distinguished from the wider community's good.

Where does this leave debates about constitutional*ism* as a doctrine of 'limited government'? It implies that political power constrained by constitutions containing rights is *not* thereby necessarily 'limited' in any particular direction. The workings and direction of such 'limits' will depend on the particular rights the constitution contains, as Waldron highlighted. Further 'limits' on how the government's relation to those it governs can be conceived will turn on whether the inclusion of rights in the constitution is for instrumental or more principled (e.g., natural rights) reasons. Natural-rights-based constitutions – as argued for in Section II – are 'limited' to a certain conception of the individual as themself a ground of duties. Constitutions that contain rights for democratic reasons, and that are not only instrumentally or epistemically committed to democracy, will be similarly 'limited' to viewing their purpose as to serve their individual members as self-governing – as argued for in Section III. The precise 'limits' imposed depend on what is required for democracy. This will certainly include requiring governments to uphold fair and equal participation in public debate and voting, but could involve much more extensive positive requirements.

CONCLUSION

In Section I, I argued that constitutions need not contain rights as a matter of logic, even though they might sometimes do so without being framed in rights terms. I went on in Sections II and III to defend rights constitutions as morally necessary if a state is to be genuinely democratic, and genuinely to recognise each individual on their own as a source of moral duties. In Section IV, I noted that while Section II's defence of rights constitutions is compatible with recognising the wide range of socially shaped human goods, it is not compatible with views that wholly deny that we can conceptually separate an individual's good from that of the wider community. In this narrow sense, constitutional rights defended on Section II's and Section III's grounds are a 'limit' on government – one that forces systems of power to exist for the sake of the individual humans they govern, to recognise the moral force of individual interests. But this 'limit' is compatible with – indeed I think probably requires – demanding government welfare programmes.

RECOMMENDED READING

Cruft, R. (2019). *Human Rights, Ownership, and the Individual*, Oxford: Oxford University Press.

Cruft, R., Matthew Liao, S., & Renzo, M., eds. (2015). *Philosophical Foundations of Human Rights*, Oxford: Oxford University Press.

Fabre, C. (2000). *Social Rights under the Constitution: Government and the Decent Life*, Oxford: Oxford University Press.

Feinberg, J. (1970). The Nature and Value of Rights. *The Journal of Value Inquiry*, 4 (4), 243–257.

Gardner, J. (2011). Can There be a Written Constitution? In L. Green and B. Leiter, eds., *Oxford Studies in Philosophy of Law*. Oxford: Oxford University Press, pp. 162–194.

Gilbert, M. (2018). *Rights and Demands*, Oxford: Oxford University Press.

Gould, C. (1988). *Rethinking Democracy: Freedom and social cooperation in politics, economy, and society*, Cambridge: Cambridge University Press.

Hohfeld, W. N. (1964). *Fundamental Legal Conceptions as Applied in Judicial Reasoning and Other Legal Essays*, New Haven: Yale University Press.

Ihara, C. K. (2004). Are Individual Rights Necessary? A Confucian Perspective. In K.-L. Shun and D. B. Wong, eds., *Confucian Ethics: A Comparative Study of Self, Autonomy, and Community*. Cambridge: Cambridge University Press, pp. 11–30.

Jones, P. (1994). *Rights*, Basingstoke: Macmillan.

Kramer, M., Simmonds, N. E., & Steiner, H. (1998). *A Debate Over Rights: Philosophical Enquiries*, Oxford: Oxford University Press.

Neuman, G. (2003). Human Rights and Constitutional Rights: Harmony and Dissonance. *Stanford Law Review*, 55 (5), 1863–1900.

Raz, J. (1986). *The Morality of Freedom*, Oxford: Oxford University Press.

Shute, S., & Hurley, S. (1993). *On Human Rights: The Oxford Amnesty Lectures 1993*, Oxford: Oxford University Press.

Thomson, J. (1990). *The Realm of Rights*, Cambridge, MA: Harvard University Press.

Waldron, J., ed. (1984). *Theories of Rights*, Oxford: Oxford University Press.

Waldron, J. (2016b). Constitutionalism: A Skeptical View. In J. Waldron, ed., *Political Political Theory: Essays on Institutions*. Cambridge, MA: Harvard University Press, pp. 23–44.

4

Equality

Annabelle Lever

What does it mean to treat people as equals when the legacies of feudalism, religious persecution, and of authoritarian and oligarchic governments have shaped the landscape within which we must construct something better? This question has come to dominate much constitutional practice as well as philosophical inquiry in the past fifty years. The combination of Second Wave Feminism with the continuing struggle for racial equality in the 1970s brought into sharp relief a variety of ways in which people can be treated unequally, while respecting the formalities of constitutional government. Most obviously, the content of laws can mistreat them by wrongfully assuming that they are either threats to others or, like children, need to be protected from harm through paternalistic limitations on their freedom of action. Or, as those concerned with class inequality have long noted, formal equality can create legal requirements, permissions, and prohibitions whose burden falls predictably, and often solely, on groups who are already marginalised, and most in need of state protection (Kairys 1990).

Above all, what these two great political movements made plain, is that a concern for *group inequality* and specifically, *group injustice*, must figure in the formulation and adjudication of individual rights, if legal protections for equality are adequately to combat the causes of inequality. Getting to grips with *that* challenge, it became clear, required going beyond the familiar analyses of inequality inherited from Liberalism and Marxism, given the many different ways in which people can be equal or unequal (Hackett and Haslanger 2006, pp. 3–15).

In the first part of this chapter, I will seek to illustrate these claims, by focusing on efforts to reframe the theory and practice of constitutional equality given demands for sexual and racial equality. I will then show that analytic philosophy has also come to recognise the various non-reducible dimensions of equality in ways that reinforce the claims of critical legal theory, even as philosophers highlight their disconcerting consequences. If equality has multiple irreducible dimensions, conflicts amongst the legitimate demands of equality are unavoidable features of law and politics, even in the best possible world, and are likely to be particularly painful when set against a background of historical injustice. The chapter concludes with the challenge to democratic constitutionalism, and the scope for constructive responses to those challenges, which the rapprochement between critical and analytic thinking on equality suggests.

For the purposes of this chapter, I will use the terms legal and constitutional equality interchangeably, on the assumption that the core idea of constitutional government is government limited by law and, whatever its form, open to legal challenge. A constitutional government, sometimes, presupposes the existence of a distinctive set of legal norms, called constitutional norms, that provide the standard by which the legitimacy of other laws can be challenged or justified. Likewise, while the values held to prove that the government is, or is not, constitutional can be extensive and diverse, I assume that the treatment of people as equal is one of them. Finally, I assume that we are concerned with the challenges of reconciling equality and constitutionality in a government animated by the democratic ideal that people be able to authorise the laws under which they live. I will focus on issues of sexual and racial equality and especially on efforts to highlight the legal significance of their structural dimensions, not because these are the only interesting issues of constitutional equality, but because their extent and significance shape the way that other issues of equality are approached.

I TREATING PEOPLE AS EQUALS

Second Wave Feminism and the struggle for racial equality highlighted the many ways in which apparently constitutional democratic government can coexist with, and even justify, extensive inequalities of rights, liberties, and opportunities, as well as unjust differences in income, wealth, and status (Rhode 1991; Minow 1990). Above all, what these two great movements made plain is that efforts to counter inequality amongst individuals need to attend to the role of law in replicating and justifying inequality amongst groups, inequalities that certainly have economic consequences, but cannot be reduced to issues of class or unequal income and wealth. For example, sexual and racial inequality cannot be divorced from violence, and the patterned nature of that violence cannot be explained adequately by class differentials or class conflict. Most violence against women, including rape, happens to them through men they know, including men with whom they live. Similarly, lynching cannot sensibly be understood in terms of class conflict, rather than as efforts to maintain and enforce racial segregation and hierarchy (Lyons 2013, pp. 19–46; Rosenberg 2004). Hence, the 1980s and 1990s led to new ways of thinking about the relationship between constitutionality and equality conceptually, morally, and empirically, even if those innovations were, and remain, contested.

To understand these developments, it helps to remember that by the 1970s American women had been entitled to vote since the beginning of the twentieth century, and in Europe since the end of the Second World War at least -with the exception of Switzerland, where women had to wait until 1971 to vote in Federal elections. Yet, they commonly laboured under a mass of disabilities that were humiliating and constraining – when not actively exploitative, coercive, and impoverishing. If they were married, they could not open a bank account in their own name without their husband's consent, let alone take out a loan for their professional or personal use; they could be required to give up paid work on marrying and were constrained in the work that they could apply for, even when single; above all, family law assumed that men were the head of the household – be they fathers or husbands – and did little to recognise or protect women's claims, as distinct from their husbands, in the sexual and reproductive relations (Cretney 1998). On the contrary, the idea that rape in marriage is a contradiction in terms encapsulated the idea that, once married, women's status and rights are replaced by those of their husband. Political parties of the right were, characteristically, wedded to upholding such norms on religious grounds, or because they were familiar, traditional, or 'natural'. Parties of the left typically supposed that women's demands could be reduced to those of male workers for better pay, conditions of work, or recognition, and, if not, should take a back seat to them. Hence, feminist approaches to the law and, particularly, to constitutional law in the US were motivated by the urgency of moving beyond piecemeal efforts at the reform or enforcement of particular laws, and towards a wholesale challenge to the sexually inegalitarian assumptions and ideals that they appeared to share.

So, too, with the fight against racial inequality. On the one hand, it required fighting legal segregation in schools, on public transport, hotels, restaurants, and the like. On the other, it meant challenging apparently race-neutral laws and practices – such as the reliance on local property taxes to fund public schooling or literacy requirements for voting – whose burdens fell disproportionately on members of racial minorities (Freeman 1990). As with laws that disadvantaged women generally, or in sex-specific social roles such as 'wife' and 'mother', combatting racial segregation depended on showing that racial equality simply could not be held consistent with laws and customs that systematically demeaned, coerced, or restricted people who were held not to be white. Hence, it required an analysis of the *group wrongs* created by such laws and practices, even if those wrongs presented themselves to a Court in the form of an individual plaintiff, often supported by organisations such as the National Association for the Advancement of Colored People (NAACP) and the American Civil Liberties Union (ACLU).

For these challenges to succeed, it had to be clear that the intention to discriminate is not a necessary part of a successful claim against inequality in general, or wrongful discrimination, in particular. That is, a successful legal challenge to practices like firing married women who do not voluntarily leave their jobs, not hiring women because they might become pregnant, or not hiring or promoting black workers to 'front of house' jobs, could not depend on showing that employers hold some special animus against women as distinct from men, or against black people, as distinct from those considered white. Custom, habit, nature, expense, customer choice, and inconvenience could all be cited to explain and justify such behaviour and, therefore, to rebut the claim of personal prejudice or ill-will on the part of a particular employer (Dworkin 1994; Law 1984; Olsen 1995; Rhode 1991).

For feminists, then, it was necessary to challenge the idea that marriage can legitimately entail a series of disabilities for women as wives from which men as husbands do not suffer. Indeed, it was necessary to show that those laws and customs constitute unjust forms of discrimination and reproduce unjust sexual hierarchies, even if some women might not wish or need to work once married, might not desire to open a separate bank account, and might be ready for sexual intercourse whenever their husband wanted. Similarly, challenging racially discriminatory practices meant opening up the most prestigious educational, occupational, and recreational establishments, even though their appeal might be limited. It also meant insisting that police harassment of racial minorities is not just a matter of individual bad-luck, or of the odd 'bad-cop' but can be common, even systemic, with racial minorities being routinely treated with a violence and contempt from which the white majority rarely suffer (Engel and Swartz 2014; Harris 2003; Lever 2005; Zack 2015).

In short, egalitarian legal theory and practice since the 1970s has been concerned with the way that inequalities can be reproduced independently of the intentions of actors. An important aspect of that demonstration – with relevance to constitutional thought and practice in other domains – has been the insistence that we cannot treat people as equals while supposing that they must think, feel, or behave alike (hooks 2000; Rich 1980). It is therefore no rebuttal to a charge of sexual harassment that other women haven't complained, any more than it would be a charge of racial discrimination that you were the only one to challenge poor pay and safety at work. Group-based egalitarian arguments, in other words, need not founder on unreasonable demands for unanimity or, even of majority agreement; however, desirable unanimity or consensus might be morally or politically (Karlan and Cole 2020). Of course, the effects of structural injustice can promote a sense of collective identity, despite significant disagreements about its nature, content, and political significance (McPherson and Shelby 2004). However, the ability to identify group-based obstacles to individual rights turns on the choices or actions that individuals are legally permitted, required, or forbidden to make (and the penalties attached to their options), and not on how many people want or expect to make those choices now in the future (see Pettit, in this volume; Wolff and de-Shalit 2007).

However, if sexual equality meant women should be able to differ from each other without suffering collective disadvantage as compared to men, it seemed absurd to suppose that women must systematically compare themselves to men for legal claims of sexual inequality to stick. That, indeed, was the problem with the justly ridiculed US Supreme Court decision in *Geduldig v Aiello* (417 U.S. 484 [1974]). Faced with the question of whether it is sexually discriminatory for health insurance to exclude the costs of pregnancy and childbirth from its coverage, the US Supreme Court concluded that there was no injustice to 'pregnant persons' – as though all that mattered to equality is that women, like some men, do not want to have children, and not the fact that it is women, and not men, who become pregnant and give birth. (However, see Perreau (2021) for the ways that technology and politics have complicated these issues recently.)

Even where biological difference is not at issue, it is unclear why men should provide the standard that women must meet in order to successfully compete for income, scarce opportunities, or to have their claims to respect and freedom recognised. Thus, in an influential essay on 'equality and difference', Catherine MacKinnon summarised the dilemma facing feminist efforts to use the law to protest sexual inequality (MacKinnon 1987, pp. 32–35). She noted that the idea of equality as similar treatment – an ideal identified with liberal, or 'sameness' feminism – predictably reproduces, even exacerbates, substantive inequalities of rights and opportunities in a world where women have been deprived of income, wealth, opportunity, and rights because they are women, rather than men. Efforts to challenge sexual discrimination at work frequently fail because women look less qualified than men, because of the time they spent raising children and doing the lion's share of unpaid domestic tasks that could have been shared with men, even though they are demonstrably capable of meeting the requirements of a given job. But nor will it do, MacKinnon argues, to say that sexual equality requires legal recognition and protection for women's differences from men, as 'difference feminism' suggests (see Hackett and Haslanger 2006; Minow 1990). Certainly, some of those differences reflect attributes, such as the disposition and ability to care for others, that are valuable, that women often display, and with which they often identify. Hence, seeing them purely as the product of oppression, because women are habitually valued for the care they provide, would be wrong.

Equality for women requires reconsidering the social value and respect accorded to female activities, attributes, and dispositions, as 'difference feminists' insist, just as 'sameness' feminists are right to demand that women, like men, should be able to share in, and compete for, the good things in life. However, instead of trying to choose between these contrasting, and partly persuasive views of sexual equality, MacKinnon (1987, pp. 32–45) argues that we should place questions about sexual equality in their proper political context. The way in which men and women differ from each other are not reducible to natural facts, arising independently from politics (Mill 1969). Hence, MacKinnon (1987, pp. 32–45) claimed, the test of sexual equality is whether a given law or practice subordinates women to men, rather than whether it justifies that subordination on the grounds that women are, or are not, like men. Biology, like other natural facts – or, indeed, like custom and personal preference – may have a legitimate place in legal arguments about equality. But that role, if any, requires legal argument and justification because law, no more than philosophy, is required to 'mirror nature' (see also Rorty 1979; Karlan and Cole 2020; Taub and Schneider 1990).

MacKinnon's critique of legal theory and practice helps to highlight two distinctive elements in contemporary reflection on equality and law that transcend her understanding of the causes of sexual inequality, or of the best way to remedy them. The first is the insistence that problems of inequality are best understood as problems of *subordination* or *unequal power*, rather than of arbitrary *differences* between people who should really be treated the same. As feminists have insisted, 'an equal opportunity harasser' – or a boss who sexually harasses male as well as female employees – does not make sexual harassment okay. Nor, importantly, does it alter the reasons to consider sexual harassment by bosses or their fellow employees a threat to equality of opportunity because of its consequences for the stability of women's employment, their prospects of promotion, and their willingness and ability to compete for otherwise desirable forms of work (MacKinnon 1979); The second element highlighted by MacKinnon's 'subordination' approach to equality, is that unless one adopts an explicitly political and critical perspective on the social world, one will consistently fail to recognise inequality for what it is, and will therefore be blind to, or actively support, laws that permit coercion, exploitation, marginalization, and impoverishment because one sees them as the legally permitted consequences of morally permissible choices, or the unchangeable expression of 'natural' differences (Haslanger 2012). For example, the staggering differences in wealth between white and black people in the contemporary US are often seen and justified as the outcomes of individual choice, luck and/or differences of character and talent, rather than as the result of slavery, segregation, and of post-war government subsidies for home ownership, from which black people were deliberately excluded (Hamilton and Darity 2010; King 1997; Rothstein 2017). Likewise, the 'feminisation of poverty', remarked in many countries since the 1980s, is treated as the natural consequence of more liberal conditions of divorce, and not of the way that legislatures, employers, and courts value women's time, activities, opportunities, and security, including their access to adequate pensions in old age (Glendon 1991; Okin 1989; Pateman 1988).

Taken together, these two elements in contemporary reflections on equality and law draw our attention to the epistemology of injustice. Specifically, they force us to reflect on the ways that apparently rational, empirically well-supported and impartial claims about people's circumstances and actions require scrutiny, given our habituation to injustice and difficulty in recognising it for what it is. The literature, in this respect, is now enormous, but it can be helpful to look at Kimberlé Crenshaw's important critique of American discrimination law, and its failure to recognise the way that racial and sexual injustice intersect, in order to grasp the epistemic problem and its relationship to legal practice (Crenshaw 1994; Kairys 1990; Collins 2008; Perreau 2021; Mercat-Bruns 2015, 2016, 2018, 2021).

The practical, legal problem that forms the subjects of Crenshaw's paper is this: that an otherwise attractive and fair rule, 'last hired, last fired', which seeks to protect older and more expensive workers from being replaced by younger and cheaper ones, will predictably have unfair consequences for black women, given that racial and sexual discrimination meant that they were less likely to be hired for attractive jobs than white men and women, or black men (Crenshaw 1994, p. 41). However, those unfair consequences will not look unfair if legal protections against sex discrimination assume that sex discrimination is the *only* form of discrimination from which its victims suffer, and that victims of race discrimination would have done just fine were it not for the racial discrimination to which they fell victim. Such 'but for' analyses of discrimination (Crenshaw 1994, p. 45) have the unfortunate effect of taking white women as the paradigmatic victims of sex discrimination (Crenshaw 1994, p. 42). They, therefore, make it seem that if black women are hired later than white women and men, and therefore, fired before white women and men, the harm they have suffered, if there is one, cannot be one of sex discrimination but of *racial* discrimination. Yet, as women, black women like white women will have been hired after white men and will therefore be vulnerable to being fired before white men. Conversely, these 'but for' models of race discrimination have the unfortunate effect of suggesting that the firing of black women cannot be a form of *race* discrimination, because if they are fired when black men are not fired, what they must be suffering from sex is *sex* discrimination and not *race* discrimination. Yet, this is to ignore the fact that black women, like black men, were unable to be hired when white men and, subsequently, white women were hired, because they were black. Despite laws meant to protect them from racial and sexual discrimination, then, black women can find themselves in a situation where they are held to have been treated equally although sexual and racial discrimination are both operative and hamper their life chances. As Crenshaw (1994) concludes, unless one recognises that sex discrimination happens to black women as well as white women and that it may operate in a different way in the two cases, one will blind oneself to what sex discrimination looks like. Worse, one will not only fail to remedy it, but will replicate and justify it in ways that confuse freedom for black women with what, for everyone else, would be understood as unjustified constraint; and will confuse equality for black women with what, for everyone else, would be understood as failures of recognition, protection, and remedial action. Similarly, unless one recognises that racial discrimination happens to black women as well as black men, and that they may take different forms and have different effects, one will fail to see rape, murder, harassment, exploitation, silencing, and stereotyping as forms of racism, and will suppose that brutal, degrading, invasive, and coercive treatment are an appropriate reflection of their needs and deserts (Roberts 1997).

II THE DIFFERENT DIMENSIONS OF EQUALITY AND CONTEMPORARY ANALYTIC PHILOSOPHY

These important and influential claims about equality and constitutionality now find an echo in some parts of analytic philosophy. Indeed, analytic debates about equality, although often frustratingly abstract, hypothetical, and idealised for those used to critical theory, reinforce, and sometimes, supplement these ideas of equality.

For example, Thomas Scanlon emphasises the *comparative* dimension of claims to equality, and argues that 'People have good reason to object to stigmatizing differences in status, to objectionable forms of control, and to social institutions that are unfair, even if eliminating these things would not increase their welfare' (Scanlon 2018, pp. 6–7). And, like Young, Scanlon insists that, '[r]ecognizing the diversity of the reasons for objecting to inequality is important ... because it helps us to understand the differences between the kinds of inequality we face.... These different forms of inequality are subject to different combinations of moral objection' (Scanlon 2018, p. 4).

Hence, Scanlon's analysis of equality emphasises the multiple dimensions of inequality, and suggests ways of distinguishing claims to equality, which in their nature are comparative, from humanitarian, prioritarian, and sufficientarian concerns, which need not be (Scanlon 2018, pp. 1–3, 29–32, 154). Our objections to inequality may not be egalitarian 'all the way down', Scanlon emphasises, in that our reasons to care about equality may be consequentialist, rather than based on the thought that there is something intrinsically objectionable to people being unequal. But in so far as they are concerned with people's *comparative* standing, treatment, and situation, they will be egalitarian. As Martin O'Neill summarises Scanlon's ideas, 'We don't just want to see equal distribution of some *thing*. We want to live together on terms of equal recognition, in ways that avoid interpersonal domination, prevent the emergence of stigmatizing differences in status, allow people to retain the self-respect that comes with seeing themselves as equal to others, and preserve the kind of background equality that can be a precondition for fair competition in the political and economic domains.' (O'Neill 2016; see also Anderson 2010; Lippert-Rasmussen 2018).

In short, despite the different forms that equality can take, and the different reasons to care about it, Scanlon insists that objections to inequality can be logically coherent, morally justified, and perfectly reasonable. Just as analytic philosophy in the 1970s and 1980s highlighted the conceptual and moral complexity of claims to 'liberty', and of the legal relations which might instantiate that ideal, so analytic philosophy since the 1980s has come to recognise the moral and conceptual complexity of claims to equality. Admittedly, the process has proceeded in fits and starts, as efforts to bring conceptual clarity to claims about equality and justice led some analytic philosophers into a debate about 'the metric' of equality, as though liberties, opportunities, income, wealth, and the 'social bases of self-respect' must be seen as equalising people along one dimension of life (Dworkin 2000; Cohen 2008). However, as Rawls argued, liberties are not fully fungible, so that trading off freedom of religion for political freedom does not protect some core thing, 'liberty', while (re)distributing it across different pots, as though it were water. Nor can we treat people as equals, given reasonable disagreement about facts and values, and suppose that one primary good, or essential all-purpose good, can be traded off against another – as though some given amount of income or wealth might make up for racial, religious, or sexual discrimination and harassment (Rawls 1971; Dworkin 1977; Walzer 1983; Wolff and de-Shalit 2007). Hence, while analytic philosophers are still concerned carefully to distinguish between various consequentialist and non-consequentialist conceptions of equality, and to clarify the ways in which luck might reflect or undermine it, they have tended to show that, as with 'liberty', 'property', 'wellbeing', and 'rights', what looks at first sight like a simple noun – 'equality' – is best thought of as short-hand for a variety of concerns with the things that people are able to have and to be, and with the ways that they relate to each other, and to the non-human world.

Indeed, the implication of Iris Marion Young's dissection of the different faces of structural injustice is that opposition to subordination, no more than opposition to domination or oppression, relieves us of the need to distinguish the different dimensions of equality for philosophical and practical purposes (see Hackett and Haslanger 2006, pp. 3–16). Unfortunately, not only does that mean that it is often far more difficult to tell how unequal people are than we might have thought (or hoped), it is also the case that alleviating one form of inequality might exacerbate another or use resources for one group that might have benefited another (Wolff and de-Shalit 2007). Hence, while there is something satisfying, as well as reassuring, in the way that analytic and critical thinkers have come to stress the different dimensions of equality, their agreement on this point forces us to confront an often unpalatable truth: that a commitment to equality is intensely political not merely because it requires us to reject political forms and ideals that presuppose the justice of hierarchical arrangements, but also because it forces us to confront serious conflicts of interest, need, and right between people whose claims may be genuinely compelling. In short, the unfortunate consequence of agreement on the multiple dimensions of equality is that we can no longer pretend that conflicts amongst the deserving are merely an artefact of questionable methodological assumptions – too individualist, sexist, capitalist, racist, say – or of questionable philosophical or political methods that are too analytic, empirical, idealised, realist. Instead, one must confront the fact that in theory, as well as in practice, conflicting demands for equality are as important as conflicts between equality and life, liberty, happiness, and solidarity.

III DEMOCRACY AND CONSTITUTIONALITY

Democratic government is meant to enable people to address their conflicting claims in ways that reflect the value of constitutional government, and itself to instantiate a compelling conception of people as equals, that can be used to determine whether some people are wrongly subordinated to others. However, this picture of democracy is clearly too simple given what we have learned about the way that sexual and racial inequality are replicated and justified. Just as law cannot be seen as an apolitical realm of expert and principled judgment, to be distinguished from politics as an unappetising mix of arm-twisting, back-scratching, and number-counting (Dworkin 1985; Waldron 1999b), so democratic politics cannot be seen as a realm of free collective expression and deliberation, contrasted with the expensive, individualised, often technocratic sphere of legal judgments and reasoning. As feminist and critical race theorists have shown, without specific efforts to address the problem, representative democracy is as likely to reproduce and justify, as to overturn, individual disadvantages based on ascriptive group inequalities (Guinier 1994; Williams 1998). In such circumstances, democratic elections – and the legislative bodies that they constitute – become the means by which power is transferred from one sphere of life to another, and imposed upon unwilling, or largely helpless, individuals.

To see the problem, and its relevance to constitutional government, it helps to understand the limitations of influential and attractive conceptions of pluralist democracy, such as those of Robert Dahl, or John Hart Ely (Ely 1980; Cohen 2009; Dahl 1998; Guinier 1994; Williams 1998; Mansbridge 1999; Phillips 1995; Lukes 2005). Against a background of civil and political rights and freedoms, Dahl hoped that individuals would be able to form and join political parties, unions, interest groups, and other associations to advance their interests as they see them. Universal suffrage, equally weighted votes, and majority rule would then work to ensure that political competition was fairly decided, in ways that would have normative force for political losers, as well as for political winners. Hence, Ely (1980) and Dahl (1998) supposed, the justification for removing decisions from the ordinary democratic process – whether to have them adjudicated by constitutional courts or by special super-majoritarian political procedures – is that core rights of political choice and equality are at stake in ways that would call into question the legitimacy of political procedures and, therefore, of political results.

However, the ability to form, join, and leave a political association is no real protection against forms of oppression based on people's ascriptive, rather than voluntary, ties, and the problem is exacerbated by the ways that our ascriptive ties – ties of sex, race, disability, and, in many ways, also of class and religion – reflect longstanding hierarchies of power and status. Hence, political theorists of representation have argued forcefully that democratic forms of representation must accommodate forms of group rights that liberal and pluralist views of democracy prevent. They must do so not because groups are more important than individuals, or that it is groups *rather than* individuals who are properly seen as the bearers of moral or legal rights, but because in political, as in legal fora, we cannot protect the rights of individuals if we ignore the groups to which they belong (see Guinier 1994; Mansbridge 1999; Phillips 1995; Williams 1998).

Once one recognises that problems of inequality often present themselves very similarly in legal and political settings and in ways that are mutually reinforcing, it becomes clear that our understanding of constitutionality, as of equality, simply cannot depend on sharp distinctions between law and politics. Specifically, failures adequately to include and represent disadvantaged groups in democratic decisions often call into question the *constitutionality*, not just the *democratic quality*, of the decisions that have been made (Williams 1998, pp. 193–194). For example, where representatives are overwhelmingly male, and drawn from socially advantaged groups, the laws that they pass will frequently not bind them substantively, in that their ability to pursue their own interests will be unconstrained, unharmed, and at no risk from the law, even if it is misconceived or flawed. Men passing restrictive abortion laws, that necessarily affect women in the first instance, is an obvious example of the problem (Roberts 1997; Schwartz 2020). Likewise, if wealthy legislators pass legislation on poverty-relief, or the terms of welfare and income support, it is most unlikely that they will suffer if their legislation is callous, arbitrary, or driven by sexual, racial, religious, and class prejudice (King 1995; Pateman 1998). In such circumstances, where the ruler and the ruled constitute two different and, sometimes, opposed, social groups, it is difficult to distinguish constitutional government from the pervasive, albeit ceremonial, imposition of the wills of some people on those less fortunate than them.

Inadequate forms of political representation, then, not only threaten the ideal of democratic government, but of constitutional government as well. The use of law as a medium of government is not the prerogative of constitutional governments; and absolute monarchs may well abide by the laws that they pass. The trouble is that their subjects have no means to ensure that their legitimate interests figure in the content and justification of laws, and also to ensure that laws will not be changed simply because they have become an inconvenience to their rulers. In short, if the aim of constitutional government is not simply to ensure that laws are fairly applied, but to prevent capricious, ill-informed, selfish, corrupt, and cruel legislation (Waldron 2016e), then failures of democratic representation erode the differences between constitutional and unconstitutional governments. Constitutional equality, then, cannot be divorced from the degree to which democratic forms of inclusion and participation structure social relations, however important it may be to be able to distinguish undemocratic governments by the degree to which they recognise, respect, and support the rule of law. Our ability to distinguish constitutional from absolute government, however benevolent, depends on our ability to see law-making, interpretation, and execution as expressions of citizens' political *agency* and not merely a reflection of their legitimate *interests* (Zurn 2007). Hence, norms of constitutional equality, as well as of democracy, can motivate efforts better to include citizens – especially those from disadvantaged groups – in the different phases of making, interpreting, judging, and implementing law (Cohen and Sabel 1997; White 2020).

For example, democratic constitutionalism means that members of historically disadvantaged groups should be able to advance their interests *as a matter of course* within the political process and be seen as fully representative of citizens' entitlements to rule as those from more advantaged backgrounds. There are a variety of measures through which this might be realised, including the promotion of more descriptively representative elected legislatures, the greater use of sortition, citizen-initiated referenda, special efforts to support participation by the electorally marginalised, as well as the more effective insulation of electoral competition from disparities in income and wealth (Cohen 2009; Cagé 2020; White 2020; Zurn 2007).

However, the differences between an absolute government and a democratic government are not reducible to the character of the legislature they produce. Where undemocratic governments can, quite coherently, see citizens simply as the objects of law, to be organised, pacified, argued over by legal and political professionals, democracy demands respect for people's judicial, as well as legislative, capacities, and for their interest in defending their rights, and those of others. Of course, democratic principles are scarcely so transparent or specific as to preclude ongoing debate about the justification of strong forms of judicial review, or the relative merits of adversarial and non-adversarial legal systems (Lever 2009; Waldron 2006). Indeed, it is doubtful that democratic principles can be specified with such precision and certainty as to preclude significant differences in legal or political institutions; and their application, one might suppose, must be context-dependent and, at least in part, reflective of the people whose institutions they are to be.

One need not, then, assume that democracies must use lay judges and juries to recognise their democratic appeal, and their significance for democratic norms of constitutional government (Dzur 2012; Lever 2009; Schwartzberg 2018). The case for lay juries as instruments of democratic constitutionalism is not that citizens are epistemically better judges of facts and law than professional judges, nor is it that they are the most convenient way of doing justice, either. Such empirical claims may or may not be true, although where professional lawyers are scarce, citizen juries may, indeed, be an effective way of resolving disputes, and the diversity of citizens chosen by lot may have epistemic benefits that legal professionals lack (Lever 2017; Schwartzberg 2018). The point, rather, is that citizens are entitled to share, as equals, in the government of their country; and interpreting and applying law is an important aspect of governing.

Thus, a concern for constitutional government, not merely for democracy, can underpin efforts to institutionalise lay participation in the judicial as well as legislative and executive aspects of politics, and might support Dzur's lament about the increasing marginalisation of lay juries, even in countries famed for their use (Dzur 2013). Moreover, as legalised forms of judgment are not the prerogative of the criminal law, but inherent to the modern administrative state, some forms of direct citizen presence, participation, and oversight in legal matters will likely apply to the processes by which social security, employment, health, housing, and other benefits are routinely granted or denied to individuals. So far, philosophers have paid relatively little attention to the different forms that such citizen presence might take in the administrative and executive aspects of government. But that is beginning to change, as political philosophers recognise that democratic equality means treating citizens as rule-makers or rulers, and not just as the beneficiaries or victims of decisions made by others (Brown 2017; Cohen and Sabel 1997; Heath 2020; Fung and Wright 2003; Fung 2004).

CONCLUSION

In a world deeply scarred by injustice, it has often seemed that a commitment to equality puts us on a collision course with constitutional government, because the substantive demands of the former conflict with the formal demands of the latter. We have also seen that the challenges of reconciling equality and constitutionalism do not vanish once we accept the legitimacy of democratic government. On the contrary, the extent and severity of those challenges become all too apparent, because democratic elections, by themselves, are an insufficient remedy for the inequalities which undemocratic governments authored and allowed.

Social movements – and the philosophical, legal, and political reflection which they have inspired – highlight the urgency of democratising our legal practices and institutions, and their critique of current practices can suggest ways in which we might do so. They have also highlighted the inadequacy of the ways we think about, and practice, democracy. At one time, it may have seemed that there was some special type of democracy we could embrace to make our laws more consistent with people's claims to equality. But given how little we know about the differences between democratic and undemocratic governments, and how imperfect are the forms of democracy with which we are familiar, such hopes seem misplaced. Rather, it seems that we must negotiate our way amongst competing, if plausible, conceptions of democracy, each with their own advantages and disadvantages, based on what we learn about the causes and consequences of inequality as we go.

There is, then, something utopian about democratic ideals of constitutionalism. We may hope, with Rawls (1993), that democratic constitutionalism is realistically utopian, even if our realities and utopias are different from his. More optimistically, we might hope that conflicts between constitutionalism and democracy are less inevitable than they might seem when legal equality is reduced to treating 'like cases alike'. Such a conception of equality, indeed, appears to limit the appeal of constitutional government and to set it on a collision course with democratic politics. But, as we have seen, while equality is an inherently comparative ideal, its content and justification require philosophical, empirical, as well as legal reflection, to determine the relevant basis for comparison, and what it is that a concern for equality requires us to compare.

Although legal reflection and judgment are often contrasted with their political equivalents, politics can inspire and motivate legal progress because of the knowledge and epistemic reflection which social movements mobilise, not simply the political and legal challenges which they generate. Moreover, as we have seen, an analysis of inequality suggests that failures of constitutionalism and democracy often have a common cause and may be susceptible to common remedies. These commonalities become apparent when we supplement ideals of equality as similar treatment with attention to the ways that people are socially differentiated, of the role of politics in creating and justifying that differentiation, and of enabling people to treat each other as co-authors of the laws under which we live. Thus, democratic constitutionalism permits and often requires efforts to make our legal and political institutions more inclusive than they are at present, while supporting more expansive and less institutionally differentiated conceptions of politics and law. So, while it would be foolish to suppose that conflicts between constitutionalism and democracy are impossible, or that they can leave the practice of equality untouched, we have reasons to think that constitutional democracy is realistically utopian, and that the forms of equality which it requires are amenable to, and deserve, our best efforts.

ACKNOWLEDGMENTS

Many thanks to Richard Bellamy and Jeff King for inviting me to write this chapter; and for carefully editing it for me. Many thanks to Chiara Destri, Valeria Ottonelli, Attila Mraz, Melissa Williams, and Stuart White for helping me to clarify my ideas and to avoid pitfalls into which I was about to land. Bruno Perreau and Marie Mercat-Brun helped me with references to French and European cases. Finally, a thank you to Lea Ypi for comments on an early draft, which made me think about the utopian elements of democratic constitutionalism.

RECOMMENDED READING

Anthony, L. & Witt, C. (2001). *A Mind of One's Own: Feminist Essays on Reason and Objectivity*, Boulder, Co: Westview Press.
Cagé, J. (2020). *The Price of Democracy: How Money Shapes Politics and What to Do About It*, Cambridge, MA: Harvard University Press.
Cohen, J. (2009). *Philosophy, Politics, Democracy: Selected Essays*, Cambridge, MA: Harvard University Press. pp 154–180.
Collins, P. H. (2008). *Black Feminist Thought: Knowledge, Consciousness, and the Politics of Empowerment*, New York: Routledge.
Dworkin, R. (2000). *Sovereign Virtue: The Theory and Practice of Equality*, Cambridge, MA: Harvard University Press.
Ely, J. H. (1980). *Democracy and Distrust*, Cambridge, MA: Harvard University Press.
Hackett, E. & Haslanger, S., eds. (2006). *Theorizing Feminisms: A Reader*, Oxford: Oxford University Press.
hooks, bell, (2000). *Feminist Theory: From Margin to Center*, London: Pluto Press.
Kairys, D., ed. (1990). *The Politics of Law: A Progressive Critique*, New York: Pantheon Books.
Lyons, D. (2013). *Confronting Injustice: Moral History and Political Theory*, Oxford: Oxford University Press.
MacKinnon, C. A. (1979). *The Sexual Harassment of Working Women: A Case of Sex Discrimination*, New Jersey: Yale University Press.

MacKinnon, C. A. (1987). *Feminism Unmodified: Discourses on Life and Law*, Cambridge, Mass.: Harvard University Press.
Mercat-Bruns, M. (2016). *Discrimination at Work: Comparing European, French, and American Law*, Oakland: University of California Press. Available at: https://doi.org/10.1525/luminos.11.
Morrison, T. (1992). *Race-ing Justice, En-gendering Power: Essays on Anita Hill, Clarence Thomas, and the Construction of Social Reality*, New York: Pantheon Books.
Olsen, F., ed. (1995). *Feminist Legal Theory*. 2 vols. New York: New York University Press.
Pateman, C. (1988). 'The Patriarchal Welfare State', in ed Amy Gutmann, *Democracy and the Welfare State*, New Jersey: Princeton University Press, pp 231–260.
Roberts, D. (1997). *Killing the Black Body: Race, Reproduction, and the Meaning of Liberty*, New York: Pantheon Books.
Rothstein, R. (2017). *The Color of Law: A Forgotten History of How Our Government Segregated America*, Norton.
Scanlon, T. (2018). *Why Does Inequality Matter?* Oxford: Oxford University Press.
Waldron, J. (1993). *Liberal Rights: Collected Essays 1981–1991*, Cambridge: Cambridge University Press.
Williams, M. (1998). *Voice, Trust, and Memory: Marginalized Groups and the Failings of Liberal Representation*, Princeton, NJ: Princeton University Press.
Wolff, J. & de-Shalit, A. (2007). *Disadvantage*, Oxford: Oxford University Press.

5

Liberty

Philip Pettit

The idea of liberty or freedom is predicated of different subjects, as in talk of free choices, free persons, and free societies. We will take the primary subject of freedom here, as it is probably most often taken, to be the free choice. The view of free choice that is sketched later enables us, as we shall see, to give an account also of what it is for a person and a society to be free; indeed, any plausible view of free choice is likely to make a similar extension of the freedom concept possible.[1]

I ANALYTICALLY ACCEPTABLE THEORIES OF FREE CHOICE

A choice in the sense in which we take it here consists in a set of mutually exclusive and jointly exhaustive options facing an agent, where one or another of those alternatives will be realized, depending on the agent's wish. A choice in this sense will be free – it will be a free choice for that agent – insofar as the options are not subject to relevant hindrances and are suitably accessible to the agent.

Free choices in the sense addressed must be free, period, not just free under one or another aspect. Thus, you might be legally or formally free to choose A or B and yet, given my opposition, not enjoy a free choice between those options. You might not be subject to a legal hindrance to choosing as you wish – you might have the legal freedom to choose – but you would still be subject to the hindrance that I put in your way. Thus, you would not be really or effectively free in the choice.

What sorts of hindrances are relevant in reducing or removing the freedom of a choice in our sense? In line with most approaches to the topic, although not with all, we shall assume here that hindrances will be capable of reducing the freedom of a choice only if they meet three conditions. Any would-be account of freedom of choice that did not require the absence of all and only those hindrances would

---

[1] We also speak of free actions, where these do not necessarily presuppose free choices in the sense relevant here; they are actions that are willingly or voluntarily chosen, and not chosen just because of the comparative unacceptability, as at least it seems, of alternatives. We speak too of a free world but this is naturally taken to be a world of free societies.

remain a merely would-be account under this approach. The account might purport to target freedom of choice but it would not offer a theory of what we would count as a free choice; it would change the subject along the way.

The first of these conditions is that freedom-reducing hindrances in our sense must be externally sourced, not the sorts of hindrances associated with internal inability or inhibition; someone can enjoy freedom of choice, after all, even if they are psychologically unable to make full use of it. By contrast, those who espouse positive freedom, as it is sometimes called (Berlin 1969), require the absence, not just of external hindrances, but also of various forms of internal incompetences.

The second condition is that hindrances, as they are understood here, must be unintentionally endured if they are to reduce the agent's freedom of choice. *Injuria non fit volenti*, as an old legal saw has it: no wrong is done to a consenting person. To adapt the tag to our case, no loss of freedom is imposed by a hindrance that an agent chooses to undergo.

Taking up the third condition, hindrances in the sense employed here do not have to be in any independent sense wrong or unjust in order to reduce someone's freedom in a choice. Even if it is justifiable for some individual or agency to impose on an agent in the exercise of a certain choice – justifiable, say, because of the need to protect others – the hindrance is still a hindrance and it still reduces the agent's freedom of choice. Those who reject this view are often said to adopt a moralized conception of freedom (Bader 2018).

Our assumption, then, is that ordinary ways of speaking about freedom in choice – and certainly the way of speaking adopted here – make it plausible to hold that hindrances that reduce such freedom must be externally sourced, unintentionally endured, and liable to be just or unjust. But introducing those restrictions still leaves room for many different accounts of what freedom of choice requires. These accounts may claim to be broadly faithful to our talk of free choice and to be acceptable as analyses of the concept. But even if they are all treated as analytically acceptable in that sense, they still differ on a crucial, substantive issue. They identify competing properties as the referents of the concept. They offer rival stories as to what freedom of choice, understood in our sense, actually consists in (Pettit 2019).

How to choose between such theories? That is going to depend on the use to which we want to put it. The assumption here is that we want a theory of freedom – a theory of freedom in choices, persons and societies – that can serve us well in thinking about how political systems, in particular constitutional orders, should be organized. We want it to play a role in an overall theory of constitutional and political justice that gives support, perhaps after some adjustment, to our considered judgments about matters of justice, and about related issues. Such a theory would enjoy what John Rawls (1971) calls reflective equilibrium: an equilibrium, achieved after some reflective adjustments, with judgments that we are independently disposed to uphold.

II MODES OF DIVERGENCE BETWEEN THEORIES

Rival, analytically acceptable accounts of freedom diverge, broadly, on four significant fronts. The first divide stems from a division about what it is to hinder someone's choice. On one approach, I will hinder your choice iff I actually check you, imposing a constraint of some kind on your options. On another, I will hinder it iff I control your choice in some degree: I have the discretionary power of imposing one or another constraint on your options, should I wish to influence your choice. While checking and controlling often go together, they need not do so. I may control your choice without actually checking it, as when I would impose a constraint, and thereby check it, if I wanted to influence your choice but am actually willing to let you choose as you wish. And I may check a choice without controlling it, as when I impose the constraint unwillingly – say, under coercion – or even do so unintentionally: in this case, I would constrain it in the way that any natural obstacle might do so.

The second way in which rival accounts may divide turns on the nature of the constraints that are imposed in checking someone's choice and imposed or at least available to be imposed in controlling it. They may be or may not be required to originate with human beings in an intentional and willing manner: to spring from the will of others. It is hard, though perhaps not impossible, to imagine control without taking the controller to be a human agent imposing their will. But, the checking of a choice might presumably occur as a result of natural obstacles or hurdles.

The third way in which rival accounts diverge arises also from a difference about the nature of the constraints involved in checking or controlling. We may hold that a constraint does not affect a choice and reduce the agent's freedom unless it is preventive in character: unless its imposition makes it impossible for the agent to choose the affected option. Or, rejecting that line, we may take constraints in a more inclusive way to cover not just preventive obstacles but any factors that change the options, say by imposing a cost on some options or by making it difficult to identify or understand them. Thus, I might check your choice in this sense, not by removing an option in a manner that prevents you from choosing it, but by replacing it by a penalized counterpart or by misrepresenting it to you in deception or manipulation.

Now, about the fourth way in which rival accounts may divide. Whether the hindering of a choice requires check or control, and whether it involves a willed or unwilled, preventive or non-preventive constraint, it may or may not be required to frustrate the agent. I will frustrate you in the relevant sense only if I hinder your choice of preferred option; only if, in that sense, I reduce your likely preference-satisfaction. Freedom might be thought to require nothing more than non-frustration: the unconstrained ability to choose what you actually prefer. Or it might be taken to require the unconstrained ability to choose whatever you might prefer: the ability to choose any option, whether it is the one you actually prefer or not.

In order to affect the freedom of someone's choice, then, a hindrance

1. may check the choice, imposing a constraint on one or another option, OR may control it on the basis of a discretionary power to impose a constraint.
2. may OR may not require the relevant constraint to originate in the will of another human being.
3. may OR may not require the constraint, willed or unwilled, to be preventive: that is, to make it impossible for the agent to choose the option affected.
4. may OR may not require the constraint to affect the agent's preferred option: that is, to frustrate the agent by reducing preference-satisfaction.

These variables allow us to construct a variety of theories about what constitutes freedom of choice in our sense. Three families of theories stand out in the history of thought (Pettit 2014): the Hobbesian notion of freedom as non-frustration, Berlin's concept of freedom as non-interference, and the republican ideal of freedom as non-domination. They hold respectively that it is essential and enough for freedom of choice, first, that you escape all preventive checks and get what you actually prefer: you are not frustrated; second, that however checked by natural factors, none of your options is willfully checked, whether preventively or non-preventively: you do not suffer interference with any of them; and, third, that you are not subject to control or domination by another in exercising the choice: you avoid interference and avoid it regardless of whether others are friendly or hostile.

These three theories can be mapped in the following matrix. I ignore the variations possible within each of the three as well as the other mappings and the other theories that are in principle possible. Here is the mapping:

	Check/control	Willful?	Preventive?	Of preferred?
Non-frustration	No checking	by any means	that prevents	a preferred option
Non-interference	No checking	by another	that changes	any option
Non-domination	No control	by another	that changes	any option

III FREEDOM AS NON-FRUSTRATION

The paradigmatic representative of the non-frustration theory is Thomas Hobbes (1994, 21.2). He holds that a person will enjoy freedom in a choice just insofar as 'he is not hindered to do what he has a will to': that is, he is not hindered from doing what he prefers to do. On this account it does not matter that the agent would be hindered from taking another option, had they preferred it instead; all that matters is that the agent gets what they want. Hobbes holds that the only sort of hindrance that counts as relevant in the reduction of freedom, at least in the proper sense of freedom, is the prevention of a choice, and that this may originate in any external force, human or non-human, willing or unwilling, intentional or unintentional.

Whether we interpret freedom as non-frustration in the strict Hobbesian way or in a looser manner, it falls to a critique developed by Isaiah Berlin (1969) in his 1958 lecture on 'Two Concepts of Liberty'. Suppose that you are unfree in a choice between A and B because, first, A is subject to hindrance, B is not; second, you happen to prefer A; and, third, you therefore suffer frustration. Berlin points out that in that case you can escape frustration and make yourself free by adapting your preferences and coming to prefer B instead. Suppose you are incarcerated for three months, for example, and yearn to live outside. If you can get yourself to savor being in jail for that period, say by thinking of the benefits – a roof over your head, assured access to meals, tolerable heating – then on this conception you will be able to make yourself free.

The idea that you might be able to make yourself free in this way is inconsistent with the common judgment that it takes more than psychological accommodation for someone to achieve liberation. 'To teach a man that, if he cannot get what he wants, he must learn to want only what he can get may contribute to his happiness or his security; but it will not increase his civil or political freedom' (Berlin 1969, p. xxxix). The failure of the approach on this count suggests that freedom as non-frustration is unlikely to play a role in a reflectively equilibrated theory of justice. The failure is so great, indeed, that contrary to the line taken earlier, we might not treat the approach as offering us even an analytically acceptable theory.

Although freedom as non-frustration is an implausible theory, it may still appeal, since people often equate freedom with preference-satisfaction. An equation of that sort is implied in economic theories that associate welfare with getting what you want and represent getting what you want as enjoying freedom. But the equation is not often explicitly defended, at least not in the contemporary literature, partly as a result of points made with force by Amartya Sen (1993, p. 39). Those points are broadly in line with Berlin's criticism of the theory.

IV FREEDOM AS NON-INTERFERENCE

According to the theory of freedom as non-frustration, all that is needed for freedom is that the option you prefer should be an open door: push on it, and you will get through. What Berlin proposes instead is that all the doors in a choice should be open, not just the door you actually push on; all the options, even those the agent finds unappealing, should be available. This open-doors view of freedom equates a free choice with one where none of the agent's options is subject to interference: none is interfered with in advance of choice and none would be interfered with, if the agent happened to choose it.

Freedom as non-interference assumes that interference need not be preventive. It acknowledges that there are many ways of disrupting an agent's choice, short of actually making the choice of a certain option impossible. Thus, I will interfere with your choice between certain options if, rather than preventing any option by removing it from the choice, I replace one or more options by penalized alternatives: I impose a penalty or cost on your choosing such an option. And I will interfere with your choice if I misrepresent one or more options to you: I deceive you about the options – I might do this in making a credible, bluff threat to penalize an option – or I manipulate your perception and understanding of them (Pettit 2014).

But, Berlin not only takes interference in the broad sense, allowing it to assume the form of removing, replacing or misrepresenting an option; for reasons he does not fully explain – see (Van Parijs 1995) for a critique – he also limits relevant forms of interference to those that are sourced in the intentional and, it appears, willing actions of human beings. This limitation makes sense, as we shall see, on the view that equates freedom of choice with non-domination. But it is hard to see why it is required on the view of freedom as non-interference, notwithstanding the number of people who follow Berlin (Lawless 2018).

Some recent thinkers who are in broad agreement with Berlin on the other points, break with him in arguing in favor of the view that interference must involve prevention: the removal of an option from a choice (Carter 1999; Kramer 2003). They hold that penalizing an option X, or perhaps misrepresenting it, may also be bad but deny that it reduces the freedom of the agent in an affected choice, say between doing X and doing Y. It is bad, roughly, insofar as it means that the agent would have been prevented from choosing according to their wishes in a possible choice that, unlike the actual choice, involves the options of doing X without-penalty-or-misrepresentation and doing Y. To suffer prevention in such a possible choice, it is said, is to suffer a loss in 'overall freedom'. Notwithstanding this move it is at least counterintuitive to deny that the agent's freedom in the X-Y choice itself is reduced by another's penalizing or misrepresenting an option to the agent (but see debates in (Laborde and Maynor 2007)). And so, we may return to Berlin.

Is Berlin's open-doors conception of freedom of choice likely to appeal? It is not exposed to the dramatic sort of objection that holds against freedom as non-frustration. But there are two grounds for thinking that it is unlikely to figure, or at least figure centrally, in a reflectively equilibrated theory of justice.

One is that for all that the theory says, it will not matter that the absence of interference that you enjoy in a choice is wholly fortuitous, being contingent on someone else's goodwill: say, on my being happy to let you choose as you will. Do you enjoy freedom in a particular choice between A and B when it is up to me whether or not to allow you the latitude to make the choice? Do you enjoy freedom in a general type of choice, say between speaking your mind and not speaking your mind, when you can make such a choice only so long as I permit it? The issue raised in these questions is whether it is enough for freedom in a choice to be able to act as you will, even when you depend on the acquiescence of another for enjoying that ability, even when it is the will of that other that is ultimately in charge. Does freedom in a choice, or type of choice, require 'independency upon the will of another', in an old republican phrase (Sidney 1990, p. 17)?

Plausibly, freedom in a choice does require this sort of independence: a form of entrenchment against others which means that in the choice at issue it is your will that is in ultimate charge. Opponents may argue that the theory of freedom as non-interference can also indict your exposure to the unexercised power of another, since the existence of that power will make interference likely (Goodin and Jackson 2007). But what if it doesn't make interference likely? What in particular, if it doesn't make it likely, because you are astute enough to keep the other sweet, relying on the effect of fawning or flattery to achieve that effect? Surely in that case, there is still reason to think that the non-interference you enjoy is not enough for freedom, the latitude you achieve not enough for liberty (Pettit 2008).

The second ground for questioning the theory of freedom as non-interference is that it makes the interference of a democratically controlled state just as inimical to freedom as the interference of an unconstrained agent, whether that be a private offender or a public dictator. However democratically controlled – and however such control is desirable on other grounds – the interference will still constitute interference and will still reduce the freedom of those it affects. Berlin (1969, pp. 130–31) registers this when he says that the 'connection between democracy and individual liberty is a good deal more tenuous than it <has> seemed to many advocates of both'.

The idea here was already endorsed by Jeremy Bentham (1843a, p. 503), an early defender of the equation between freedom and non-interference. 'All coercive laws', he says, '… and in particular all laws creative of liberty, are, as far as they go, abrogative of liberty'. Bentham would argue that such laws might reduce the level of interference overall, perpetrating less interference than they prevent. But whether or not they do this is independent of whether they are democratically controlled. Bentham's fellow utilitarian, William Paley (2002, p. 314) put the point sharply when he argued that, if it imposes the same laws, then 'an absolute form of government <will> be no less free than the purest democracy'.

The first of these two problems is that freedom as non-interference is socially non-demanding: it offers no ground for complaining about someone's being under a power of interference on the part of others, provided that power is not actually exercised. The second is that the theory is politically non-directive: it offers no ground, or at least no principled ground, for supporting democratic restrictions on the state's power of interfering in the lives of its citizens.

V FREEDOM AS NON-DOMINATION

These two problems with freedom as non-interference provide a cue for introducing the idea of freedom as non-domination, which has been closely associated with the long republican tradition of thought (Pettit 1996, 1997; Skinner 1998; Lovett and Sellers 2025). This theory argues that it is essential in a free choice, not just that all doors should be open, but also that there should be no door-keeper in a position to close a door at will in the face of the agent. Within the relevant area of choice, there should be no *dominus* or master who holds a power of interfering at will in the agent's decision.

On this account, you will not be free to speak your mind or not to speak your mind – you will not have freedom of speech – if I am positioned to interfere in the choice, should I wish: if, to that extent, I enjoy *dominatio* or domination over you (Lovett 2010, Appendix). Even if you enjoy the latitude to speak your mind or not, you will enjoy it only because it accords with my wishes: only because I permit it. Your will is going to be subject, in other words, to my discretion or will: your ability to speak as you wish is going to be contingent on my continuing to be happy to grant you that ability.

Thus, you may fail to enjoy freedom in a choice – freedom as non-domination – even in the absence of any actual interference. That possibility relates to the first complaint made about freedom as non-interference. It means that unlike freedom in that sense, freedom as non-domination is socially demanding. It offers a basis on which to complain about any situation in which some people are subject to a discretionary power of interference on the part of others, even a power that others do not choose to exercise.

But as the theory of freedom as non-domination scores in that social respect over its rival, so it scores also in a political respect. It offers a ground for arguing in favor of democratic controls over the power of interference that the state enjoys in relation to its citizens.

At least it offers ground for arguing in support of this conclusion, granted a number of plausible assumptions (Pettit 2012, 2023). First, that the state is an inescapable reality in a world exhausted by states, where no regime could resign or abdicate without inviting another state to take over its territory and people. Second, that the job of the state is to impose laws under which people can live in relative peace – and, ideally, freedom – with one another. Third, that the state has to impose laws coercively on would-be offenders in order to keep them in line, and to assure others of protection against offenders. And, fourth, that the state's laws must be imposed coercively on all, if only because it would be infeasible to single out the would-be offenders who need to be kept in line.

That the state coercively imposes laws on its subjects does not mean that it can decide as it will about which laws to impose: that it can decide to impose laws that unnecessarily restrict everyone's freedom of choice, for example; or that it can decide to impose laws that do not treat or respect its subjects as equals. Did the state have the discretionary power – in republican terms, the arbitrary power – of deciding on what laws to impose, thereby interfering with its subjects, then it would certainly control and dominate them.

At this point, the connection to democracy becomes salient. Insofar as the state is democratically constrained by a system of control to which its subjects have equal access – insofar as it has to operate on terms dictated under that system – then to that extent its power over subjects, however inescapable, will not be dominating.

The state will not relate to subjects as a master to servants but, ideally, as a servant to its masters.

This observation shows that unlike freedom as non-interference, freedom in this third construal is not only socially demanding, but is also politically directive. Let domination be the enemy of freedom in choice, and it will not just follow that freedom requires people to be guarded against even an unexercised power of interference on the part of others. It will also follow that they ought to live under a state that has to impose its laws on terms dictated by its subjects: it has to formulate, administer and adjudicate those laws under pressures and procedures that its subjects dictate.

Once we equate freedom with non-domination, then, we can recognize that there are two dangers of domination against which we will want to protect people. First, there is the danger of private domination that materializes when other people have a power of discretionary interference in someone's life. And second there is the danger of public domination that arises if the laws imposed by the state, however effective they may be in guarding people, even guarding them against private domination, are imposed on a discretionary basis and give a dominating power to those in government. We now look at what freedom as non-domination requires in each of those areas, arguing that unlike the rival theories, it supports a theory of justice that plausibly satisfies the test of reflective equilibrium.

VI GUARDING AGAINST PRIVATE DOMINATION

Let us assume that freedom as non-domination is an ideal that all are meant to be able to enjoy equally and enjoy in the highest degree across the widest range. This assumption implies that people should be able to enjoy freedom in as many choices as possible, consistently with other individuals – or at least other adult, able-minded individuals – enjoying the same freedom; we may describe those choices as the basic liberties. And it means that they should be able to enjoy freedom in those basic liberties with the greatest assurance that is possible, consistently with others enjoying at least that same level of assurance.

How are people to be enabled to enjoy such equal freedom in relation to one another? How else but by means of laws, together with the supportive norms and structures that suitable laws presuppose or elicit? The ideal of guarding people against one another's power is essentially an ideal for shaping the laws under which they are to live.

Broadly, there are three roles law must play if it is to enable people to enjoy equal freedom as non-domination in relation to one another, combating the danger of private domination. It will have to identify the basic liberties that people can each enjoy; it will have to protect people generally against interference in the exercise of those choices; and it will have to secure them against misfortunes that would be likely to expose them to private domination.

The basic liberties that the law identifies, to take up the first role, will have to be choices such that all can exercise them, and all can enjoy exercising them, at one and the same time as others (Pettit 2014). They will not include essentially competitive choices, as when each seeks an advantageous position. They will not include choices that inflict harm on innocent parties, as when each tries to bully others. They will not include collectively self-defeating choices such that everyone is worse off for everyone's exercising them. And so on.

Such choices may have to be carved out by the law. Not everyone can choose to drive as they wish on the road; but everyone can choose to drive on the left or the right. Not everyone can address a crowd at once, at least not in a way that they can each enjoy; but everyone can address a crowd under Robert's rules of order (Hart 1973). And not everyone can use things as they wish; but everyone can use things more or less as they wish, if they own them under local property laws – property laws, presumably, that do not restrict the enjoyment of such choices to a rich elite. How exactly the basic liberties should be specified, however, is a matter of controversy and will require determination by the state in any society.

The second role of law must be to protect individuals in the exercise of such liberties. But how much protection should it provide? How far should the law go in providing safeguards for people against one another's domination? A natural suggestion is that they should be safeguarded to the point where, by the most stringent local criteria, they can look one another in the eye without reason for fear or deference. If they can pass this eyeball test, as we may call it, then, absent excessive timidity, they will be able to live and relate to one another as their own men and women. They may enter relations of mutual dependency, as in love and friendship and solidarity, but they will each do so from a position of strength that is ensured under local law and norm.

There are four areas, broadly, in which the law should provide such protection for people against the danger that some of them may be dominated by other individuals or by the corporate bodies' individuals form: churches, corporations, associations, and the like. The four types of protection the law should provide against that danger are: general, direct protection; general, indirect protection; specific, direct protection; and specific, indirect protection. The exact specification of these protections is bound to be a matter of controversy but the broad outline is clear.

The law will provide a general, direct form of protection of people insofar as it criminalizes various offences against basic liberties, regulates activities that may jeopardize the enjoyment of those liberties and guards against possibilities of discrimination that may undermine it. The law will provide a general, indirect sort of protection insofar as it enables people to charge others with breaches of tort or contract law that affect their basic liberties. The law will provide a specific, direct form of protection insofar as it gives status rights to those in vulnerable positions vis-à-vis others, whether as spouses, workers or consumers. And the law will provide a specific, indirect form of protection insofar as it gives certain powers of self-protection to such people, say by enabling spouses to seek divorce, workers to unionize and consumers to bring class actions in defense of their rights.

Apart from providing such protections for people's enjoyment of their basic liberties, the law should play a third role in providing security against dangers that would make domination possible and likely; again, it would ideally provide for security up to a level dictated by the eyeball test. It should provide for the social security of all, since those who are homeless or hungry, or in urgent medical need, will have to depend on the philanthropic or exploitative offers of others, and will be thereby exposed to domination. It should also provide for people's informational security, ensuring access to a basic education, to re-training in new essential skills, and of course to reliable information about the society and state. And it should provide for judicial security, with access to reliable counsel in the event of being charged with crimes or having to defend against civil charges, as well as in the event of having justiciable complaints against others.

These observations indicate that the ideal of freedom as non-domination, unlike freedom as non-frustration or non-interference, supports a rich set of demands on the laws under which people live. To that extent it holds out an ideal of justice that is likely to satisfy the test of reflective equilibrium. Specifically, it holds out an ideal of social justice: that is, of justice in people's relationships with one another. But, as we shall now see, freedom as non-domination also holds out an ideal of political justice: that is, of justice in people's relationship with the state that imposes laws upon them. It does this insofar as it calls for measures to guard against public as well as private domination.

VII GUARDING AGAINST PUBLIC DOMINATION

If the laws that give people freedom as non-domination in relation to one another were to depend on the discretionary will of some individual or body – say, the will of an absolute monarch, a privileged elite, or a colonial power – then they would expose people to public domination. People would be dominated by the unconstrained will at the source of the law and would live at the mercy of whatever their *dominus* chose to do. They would suffer, not the private domination against which the laws can protect and empower, but the public domination associated with being collectively and individually exposed to the will of a master.

The laws that guard individuals against one another might be described as decision-taker laws, since they constrain the subjects of the state in dealing with one another. In order to guard individuals against the state itself, however, in particular against it's having discretionary power in choosing the decision-taker laws to impose, authorities in the state must be subject to a distinct, although perhaps overlapping body of decision-maker laws (Pettit 2023).

These laws would create pressures and procedures that force those who run the state to impose only laws of a kind endorsed broadly by subjects. They would allow the authorities to impose law, as is required in any state and in that sense to interfere in people's lives. But suitable decision-maker laws would deprive the authorities of the ability to impose law at their own discretion; it would make their interference non-dominating.

The eyeball test provides a benchmark for determining whether decision-taker laws guard people adequately against private domination: it requires those laws to enable people to look one another in the eye without reason for fear or deference. A parallel test would provide a similar benchmark for determining whether decision-maker laws guard people against public domination. We may call it the tough-luck test.

Whatever decision-taker laws are imposed by the state, they are always going to be unwelcome in one or another sector of the society: this is because people differ in their interests and in their views of what form the laws should take. Decision-maker laws would presumably guard against public domination if they ensured that even those who find a decision-taker law unwelcome, as some always will, can view it without the resentment or indignation associated with seeing it as the intrusion of an independent will in their lives (Strawson 1962).

What decision-maker laws – what constraints on the power of decision-makers – would enable those who are disappointed about a law that the state imposes to view the imposition without resentment or indignation? Presumably, laws that deprived the decision-makers of discretionary power, forcing them to impose laws under a system of control in which citizens share equally with others. We may assume that no one can resent having to live on equal terms with others. If decision-makers were subject to such control, then those opposed to any law would have to recognize that it emerged – unluckily for them – under a system of control that gave them an equal say with others. They would have to see it as just tough luck that the law selected on such terms happened to frustrate their personal plans, to impact on those in their sector of society, or to jar with their personal sense of justice.

Decision-maker laws will guard against public domination, then, and satisfy the tough-luck test, if they are designed to give people an equally shared form of control over the decisions taken by the authorities in the name of the state. But how in practice might they do this? Plausibly, they would have to give people at least three forms of control over public decision-making, including the decision-making involved in the imposition of decision-maker laws themselves. They would have to enable people to share equally in framework control over the institutions dictating how they are governed; operational control over how those in government, running the state, behave in imposing laws; and selectional control over how those in government are appointed.[2]

Take framework control first. Whatever the divisions of interest and opinion within a state, it must act under a framework for decision-making that is accepted

---

[2] For a different view of how popular control might be achieved, see Ingham (2019).

on all sides; otherwise, politics would be indistinguishable from war. This broad framework, perhaps supported by custom as much as by any written text, should be subject to a system of popular control to which individuals have equal access. While it may not have been selected by a popular vote, say in a previous generation, it should be subject to amendment by popular referendum in any generation. The only limit to amendment ought to be this: that, short of an agreed secession, no referendum should be allowed to limit those protected by the laws or to give some more protection than others.

But decision-maker laws must also give people operational control over those in power. A constitution that is subject to popular amendment and control might actually impose few constraints on government; it might even establish an absolute monarch. Thus, the framework established or maintained by people on an equal basis should force officials in government to operate in ways that guard against the discriminatory restriction of some section of the people or that impose an unnecessary restriction on all: a restriction will be unnecessary to the extent that it plays no role in enhancing people's enjoyment of freedom as non-domination.

These operational controls would include containment devices such as a rule of law, a rule of checks and balances, a rule of entrenched rights and a rule of common reasons akin to Rawls's (1993) rule of public reason. But operational controls would also include arrangements for forcing government to consult people on various issues – say, by means of a citizen assembly (Perse and Warren 2007) – as well as arrangements that enable citizens individually or in public-interest bodies to invigilate and if necessary, contest what government is doing.

The rule of common reasons is perhaps the most contentious of these proposed devices. It would require the measures taken in making, administering and adjudicating law – and indeed also in contesting law – to be justified by reference to considerations that are considered relevant on all sides; and, where rival candidates score equally well on that score, to be adopted under tie-breaking procedures supported by such considerations (Forst 2012). Common reasons will often derive their omni-lateral relevance from the fact of reflecting elements in the popularly maintained framework: say, a presumption of inclusion in recognizing citizens, and a presumption of equality in their claims on the state. But they may also appear as relative novelties in the course of democratic debate and decision: this, for example, in the assumption that the state should play a role in establishing public health measures or in compensating the victims of natural catastrophe.

The third requirement that decision-maker laws must satisfy if they are to have any hope of enabling popular control of government, would give selectional control over who is to govern them to ordinary people. A lottocratic arrangement might claim to do this (Guerrero 2014). But the more regular arrangement would allow for the popular election of domain-general authorities, legislative and perhaps administrative, and for the appointment under suitable constraints of transparency and accountability of domain-specific authorities. Such domain-specific authorities will be required to ensure the reliability of public data and information; to monitor and review domain-general authorities, and indeed one another, for conformity to financial, legal and ethical guidelines; and to discharge roles where election is likely to create a conflict of interest: these include regular judicial office, the organization and scrutiny of elections and the determination of interest rates.

The reason for preferring the election of domain-general authorities to their appointment by lottery, or indeed any other mechanism, is not necessarily that election will identify the best candidates for office; it may do only moderately well on that count. Rather, it is that the ritual of regular elections is crucial for reaffirming and reinforcing people's common interest in freedom of information, freedom of speech and freedom of association (Schumpeter 1984). These are all freedoms that need to be recognized, celebrated and entrenched in an effective democracy; let them be compromised and people are likely to lose much of their control over government, whether of a framework, operational or selectional kind.

As the demands of freedom as non-domination on the private front direct us to a plausible theory of social justice, we now see that its demands on the public front directs us to a plausible theory of political justice. Which form of justice is the more important? Equivalently, which danger is greater: that of private domination against which social justice guards or that of public domination against which political justice serves?

The question is not likely to be pressing, if only because of the overlap in the two bodies of law. But on the face of it, guarding against public domination has priority (Pettit 2015). If people control government then any failure of government to guard against private domination can in principle be rectified. If people do not control government then, no matter how well government – say, a benign dictatorial or colonial power – does in supporting private non-domination, what it does will never be enough and will always be fragile. It will not be enough, since people will depend on the goodwill of the government for maintaining this support; it will always be fragile, since any change in the personnel or the will of government may remove that support.

VIII LAW AND LIBERTY

On our understanding of freedom as non-domination, laws obviously play an absolutely crucial role. Decision-taker laws define the choices in which people are to enjoy freedom. They provide for the protections needed to enable people to exercise those choices, and empower people in securities essential for those in vulnerable positions. Decision-maker laws are necessary, on the other side, if the state that establishes decision-taker (and decision-maker) laws is not itself to be a dominating power in people's lives. Those laws must put the common framework of government in people's hands; they must impose operational constraints on those in government; and they must ensure that the selection of the authorities in government is grounded in popular, electoral choice or conducted under popular scrutiny and constraint (Pettit 2023).

Far from law being itself a challenge to freedom, then, as under the non-interference approach, this theory recruits the law to the task of making freedom possible. It makes it possible for people to enjoy private freedom as non-domination in their relationships with one another and public freedom as non-domination in their relationships with the state. It makes it possible, not just to determine when choices are free, but to determine when persons are free and when societies are free. The free person will be the person who is equally protected with others against the danger of private and public domination. The free society will be the society in which persons are free in that double sense.

The relation between law and freedom is instrumental, on this approach, not definitional. What it means to be a free person is to be your own man or woman, not living under the private or public power of another, and law is the instrumental means whereby people can attain that status, ideally in an equal way. But the instrumental relationship of law to freedom is constitutive, not causal (Pettit 1997, chap. 3). It's not as if, with laws in place, we have to wait and see whether people will gain freedom as a downstream, causal effect. The relationship between laws and the freedom of subjects is like the relationship between the antibodies in your blood and the immunity they give you against disease. The existence of a suitable set of decision-taker and decision-maker laws constitutively guarantees or helps to guarantee people's freedom just as the presence of a suitable suite of antibodies constitutively guarantees or helps to guarantee your immunity.

IX CONSTITUTIONALIZING THE LAW?

How far should the law that enables freedom be constitutional and how far may it have just the character of statutory or common or customary law? Almost all constitutions, written or unwritten, have provisions that establish operational and selectional constraints determining who is to hold public office and how they are to behave in exercising that office. But many constitutions also have provisions guarding against private as much as public domination: they constrain decision-takers as well as decision-makers. Constitutions often entrench and protect certain freedoms, such as the freedom of speech or religion, and they sometimes require the state to support certain forms of security, as when the US Constitution requires 'a criminal defendant to have the Assistance of Counsel for his defense'.

To entrench a law constitutionally is to ensure that it cannot be changed by a legislative majority, whether or not it can be changed by a popular majority. There is serious reason for entrenching a decision-maker arrangement when it is likely that one or another side in politics, should it achieve a comfortable legislative majority, will be tempted for party-political reasons to try to change it.

People may control government cooperatively in seeking to maintain a common framework for dictating the operation and selection of government. But their cooperation is like the cooperation of tennis-players in abiding by agreed rules. It presupposes an intense competition between different sides, whether at the polls, in the parliament, in the courts, in the media or on the streets. The competitive desire of each side to win power under such a framework can make the framework itself unstable – and can endanger the cooperation that distinguishes politics from war – if it is possible for a legislative majority to change it.

This argues for the abstract principle that laws establishing measures that may attract opportunistic, partisan opposition should be constitutionalized and thereby stabilized. But it is bound to be hard to apply this principle in concrete practice, for circumstances may dictate different applications. In some circumstances, indeed, constitutionalizing an element in the framework may actually be counterproductive; it may stir up feelings for or against the arrangement that make for instability rather than stability.

If an element in the framework is constitutionalized, should it be capable of amendment in a popular, majoritarian vote? Again, this is a difficult issue that may call to be resolved in different ways under different circumstances. Perhaps only two observations can be made with any confidence.

The first is that there should be protections against allowing a measure to become such a mark of tribal fidelity to one or another side of politics that rational debate recedes. A super-majoritarian requirement might serve this role, as might a requirement that any proposal be first adjudicated in a citizens' assembly. The second observation that can be made with confidence, however, is that however protected against majoritarian decision, amendment should not be so difficult that it makes the framework effectively canonical and unchangeable: it makes it into a *fait accompli* that effectively disempowers ordinary people.

This second observation is particularly important, when the judicial review of legislation for whether it conforms to the constitution is put in the hands of a court that is non-rotating, politicized and powerful, in the manner of the U.S. Supreme Court. But this is not the place to run a critique of such a model of judicial review, nor to outline an alternative.[3] Suffice it to note that if a constitution makes amendment realistically available, then that in itself will deny any judicial, reviewing body the sort of power that would make it democratically questionable.

ACKNOWLEDGMENTS

I am grateful to Richard Bellamy and Jeff King for comments on an earlier version, and to Nicolas Coté for a discussion of many of the issues the topic raises.

---

[3] For some recent contributions to this debate see Waldron (1999a), Bellamy (2007, 2019), Hickey (2019).

RECOMMENDED READING

Berlin, I. (2002). *Liberty: Incorporating Four Essays on Liberty*. Edited by H. Hardy and I. Harris. Oxford: Oxford University Press.
Carter, I. (1999). *A Measure of Freedom*, Oxford: Oxford University Press.
Hayek, F. A. (1960). *The Constitution of Liberty*, Chicago: University of Chicago Press.
Hirschmann, N. J. (2003). *The Subject of Liberty: Towards a Feminist Theory of Freedom*, Princeton: Princeton University Press.
Kramer, M. H. (2003). *The Quality of Freedom*, Oxford: Oxford University Press.
Laborde, C. & Maynor, J., eds. (2007). *Republicanism and Political Theory*. Oxford: Blackwell.
Lovett, F. (2010). *A General Theory of Domination and Justice*, Oxford: Oxford University Press.
Lovett, F and Sellers, M.N.S. (2025). Handbook of Republicanism, Oxford: Oxford University Press.
MacCallum, G. C. (1967). Negative and Positive Freedom. *Philosophical Review*, 76 (3), 312–34.
Patterson, O. (1991). *Freedom in the Making of Western Culture*, New York: Basic Books.
Pettit, P. (1997). *Republicanism: A Theory of Freedom and Government*, Oxford: Oxford University Press.
Pettit, P. (2014). *Just Freedom: A Moral Compass for a Complex World*, New York: W.W. Norton and Co.
Pettit, P. (2023). The State, Princeton, NJ: Princeton University Press.
Raz, J. (1986). *The Morality of Freedom*, Oxford: Oxford University Press.
Ripstein, A. (2009). *Force and Freedom: Kant's Legal and Political Philosophy*, Cambridge, MA: Harvard University Press.
Sen, A. (2002). *Freedom and Justice*, Cambridge, MA: Harvard University Press.
Skinner, Q. (1998). *Liberty before Liberalism*, Cambridge: Cambridge University Press.
Swanton, C. (1992). *Freedom: A Coherence Theory*, Indianapolis: Hackett.

6

Well-Being

Sarah Conly

The primary goal of a benevolent state is to promote the well-being of its citizens. We create governments, and tolerate their existence, because having a government makes us better off than we would be without one. Thus, a state should be so constituted as to make us better off, and insofar as a state has an articulated constitution – a set of goals, methods, and limitations by which the state should abide – these should be framed in terms of citizens' well-being.

Of course, there may be a state which doesn't hold its citizens as the primary goal. This is a position that is not logically inconsistent. Such a state would not, however, be desirable. We generally think that secular states should be attuned to welfare. Indeed, even religious states may be oriented to what makes us better off, even if that is in the afterlife. If a thing is not wanted or valued by people, and doesn't make them better off in any other sense, insisting on its adoption seems dictatorial. State policies that make people worse off in the short and the long run are, to say the least, difficult to justify, and it is unlikely that this a state any populace would want to endorse.

Two questions naturally arise, given this: first, what does well-being consist of? Second, what efforts to enhance well-being can a state make without those steps actually undercutting well-being? Insofar as state efforts constrain action for the sake of well-being, there is a danger that these constraints will limit liberty in a way that actually undercuts the individual achievement of well-being. The question is whether and how personal liberty plays a significant role in well-being. If we limit liberty in order to bring us to one desirable state (say, good health) that doesn't necessarily increase well-being if the loss of liberty in itself diminishes well-being.

Philosophers have given a fair amount of thought to well-being. As is their want, however, philosophers have by no means reached a consensus on this. The most popular theories of well-being are three: hedonism, where well-being is a function of how much pleasure a person feels over her life; desire-satisfaction, where well-being is a function of what the person wants actually being obtained (whether or not that yields pleasure); and what are known as objective list theories, where well-being consists of some specific states or activities being engaged in by the individual. The first two of these are considered subjective theories of well-being, in that whether a person is well off is a function of that agent's own feelings or her own attitudes: she is well off if she feels a certain degree of pleasure, for the hedonist, or, on the second view, to the extent that gets what she wants. Objective list theories are, as the name suggests, considered objective theories of well-being, because whether the person is well off is determined by something other than her own attitudes: even if she experiences a lot of pleasure in life and attains all her goals, her life might still be judged lacking on this account if, for example, her only goal, and the source of her extreme pleasure, lies in something that, according to those who hold this view, does not have value. At the same time, on this view, something she takes no pleasure in and does not want might nonetheless make the person better off when included in her life. John Rawls introduced the successful counting of blades of grass as something which would not enhance well-being, even if it gave the individual more pleasure than anything else and was what she most wanted to do (Rawls 1971). On the other hand, things like fruitful social relations, knowledge, and creative activity do tend to make the list of those who propose this sort of objective view.

In many ways these theories overlap in their specifics – getting what we desire often results in pleasure, and objective lists theorists often endorse activities or states that as a matter of fact yield pleasure or satisfy desires. What, however, should we actually do to promote our own or others' welfare? Here, the differences between the theories become more apparent, especially when it comes to permissible government schemes for advancing welfare. While there are certainly aspects of welfare that are not affected by state policies, these are likely, in the modern world, to be very few. I may think it is simply between me and my self-help book if I follow its recommendation and derive joy from the simple things in life like looking at wildflowers, but will there be wildflowers for me to look at? That depends on climate change, urbanization, policies as to parks or transportation into the country, etc. To make a long story short, the possibility of most goods will be affected by governmental policy. And as Cass Sunstein has pointed out, what we value is itself affected by government policies: "Whether people have a preference for a commodity, a right, or anything else is in part a function of whether the government has allocated it to them in the first instance." (Sunstein 1993b, p. 199). There was a time, no doubt, when this was not true, when individuals roamed through a sparsely-populated world gleaning or not gleaning well-being from their natural surroundings without being affected by state institutions, but those times are gone. Thus, the constitution of the state is a large determinant of whether and how a person can achieve well-being.

So, what should the state do? How should individual interests inform its constitution? There is widespread agreement that a good state would enact regulations to prevent people harming one another in serious ways. Being assaulted clearly has a negative impact on our well-being, and we are agreed at this point in time that there should be state measures to prevent this, or at least to discourage it. While preventing others from doing us serious harm is good, however, and should normally be the priority when it comes to government policies, it will not be sufficient, in many cases, for the achievement of an individual's welfare. In the modern world much of the harm to our welfare comes from our own actions, or from our own failure to act. The controversy lies in what states should be designed to do when it comes to interfering with our choices as to what to do to ourselves. This is not entirely unconnected to others' actions, of course. Requiring that people wear seat belts means requiring that car makers install seat belts and that the police incentivize seat belt wearing with fines for those who don't wear them. Banning smoking means forbidding others from producing or selling cigarettes. These restrictions are different from restrictions on assault, however, because they are geared towards protecting an individual from doing something he would do voluntarily, something that in some sense he wants to do. The idea, of course, is that the state would introduce such restrictions with an eye to promoting the individual's welfare, but would such restrictions actually be self-defeating, undercutting the welfare they are designed to augment? To answer this question, I will look at each of the three major theories of well-being. I will conclude that no matter which type of theory is considered, there is nothing about losing (some) personal liberties that is inimical to well-being, and much about losing liberties that will make us better off.

I PLEASURE AND STATE INTERFERENCE

The hedonistic view of well-being says that well-being is a function of the pleasure a person feels in her life. Pleasure, and only pleasure, makes a life good, and pain, only pain, makes a life bad. If we accept this view, what sort of role should we recommend that the state take toward its citizens? What role does the liberty to act play in the actual acquisition of pleasure? Do we gain great enjoyment from being free to make choices, either for the sake of that freedom itself or in the places we end up when we choose, or do we get more pleasure when government curtails some activities and interferes to promote some others? The answer, naturally, is that it all depends on what interference the state sanctions, but on the whole, there is nothing antithetical about robust state controls and hedonistic well-being.

Presumably, we all, at times, have experienced displeasure when we have been frustrated by state regulations. In those cases we dislike having our ability to act curtailed, and on this view that in itself detracts from our welfare. However, frustration has many sources other than state regulations. Not being able to send my child to the best university he could get into because I can't pay the huge tuition bill is painfully frustrating. Not being able to get home quickly because traffic is terrible is also frustrating. In these cases, government measures might actually eliminate frustration. If we tax fuel enough there should be less traffic, and thus less frustration. If governments require the creation of relatively cheap public universities, I am more likely to be able to send my child to college. And so forth. To object to government actions that remove liberties – by, for example, requiring taxes on gas or more taxes on income to fund public universities – doesn't make sense if those actions actually alleviate other frustrations, unless there is something particularly distasteful, in terms of our affect, about constraints that arise from the government. Do government constraints feel worse, do they make us feel less happy, than do other constraints, simply by nature of being government constraints?

They may, to begin with. This will depend in part on the ideology of the individual who is constrained by the government to pay taxes to support the public university, or to slow down on the highways, or to give up smoking. And regardless of ideology, there are some who react to each new regulation – if they notice it – with a special feeling of resentment. Still, there are two things to note here. First, even the intense displeasure introduced in some by a state regulation may be outweighed by the pleasure that regulation may make possible. So, people may feel anger, frustration, and other such painful feelings when confronted by a ban on cigarettes, but may still end up with more pleasure – and thus, on this view, greater welfare – if that ban is in place. Since they will generally be more fit, less diseased, and with more money to spend, they end up better off, even if irritated at the government's paternalistic action. Second, people become less irritated as they get used to many constraints, especially when the end result of that constraint is increased welfare. Sometimes, this revision of preferences – the change in what one wants or likes because of constraint on getting what one previously wanted or liked – is referred to as the formation of adaptive preferences (Elster 1983). Some people think that adaptive preferences are irrational, and to that extent bad. I think there is a sense of practical rationality in which revising one's tastes in light of what is actually achievable is quite rational. Indeed, we frown, for example, on people who cannot get over their failed career hopes and develop an interest in something else. If the adaptation makes one worse off on the whole, then of course it may be deplored: we do not want people to adapt to oppression when there are alternatives that would make them better off. Generally, though, developing a preference for something that is more beneficial seems to be something we do and should encourage, even when that change comes about because external agents have removed the option to pursue the less beneficial alternative. People in the US greatly resented both seatbelt laws and drunk driving laws when those were introduced, but at this point, most people take them for granted and, while they may certainly be made unhappy if they are actually given a ticket for a violation, no longer experience dissatisfaction at the mere knowledge that such laws exist. And they are furthermore less likely to die or kill someone else in a car accident, which seems to be a result to be lauded.

Thus, if we accept a view of welfare wherein a life is well lived insofar as it includes felt pleasure and avoids felt pain, there is no argument against government constraints on liberty as long as those constraints are well designed. We already accept a loss of liberty when allowing certain liberties that would harm others. Paternalistic constraints can be as productive of welfare as the constraints we normally accept in our treatment of other people.

II DESIRE-SATISFACTION AND STATE INTERFERENCE

Desire satisfaction theories hold that a person is well off to the extent that her desires are fulfilled. This is different from hedonism because fulfilling a desire may not be what gives you the most pleasure: fulfilling your desire to discover the cure for cancer might lead you into a lonely and in many ways disappointed life, capped only at the end by a few short minutes of knowing that your goal was met before your fall to the floor in a fatal heart attack. For many people, though, the fulfillment of desire is more intuitively acceptable as a criterion of welfare than mere pleasure, since it allows the agent to choose what a well-lived life will be about for her.

Such theories are more complex in some ways than hedonism, however. Desire satisfaction theories must, to be coherent, have a way of prioritizing desires. For one thing, some desires are for inconsistent outcomes (Jane wants to raise children, and at the same time wants to live a life unencumbered by responsibility) and when both goals cannot be reached we need to know which counts more toward well-being, assuming that they don't both count to the same degree. Even without inconsistent objects, it is simply the case that there won't be the time or the resources to satisfy all the desires a person has in her life, unless she is unnaturally narrow in her range of wants. We tend, then, to categorize some desires as more central than others, so that their satisfaction should be prioritized.

Some feel that whether a desire's achievement contributes to well-being depends on whether that desire fits some sort of evaluational criterion, and not necessarily that of the agent who holds it. For example, it has been argued that only the fulfillment of rational desires contributes to welfare, or that only the satisfaction of desires for what is truly valuable should count as contributing to welfare (Scanlon 1998; Wolf 1998). Obviously, such theories lead to questions as to what desires are rational and what ends are truly of value. In introducing these criteria external to the agent's own motivational set these theories are less subjective in their evaluation of welfare, since rationality and value on this account tend to have objective criteria., even though the range of acceptable desires is fairly wide. A more pure desire-satisfaction account will take the agent's own desires as the sole determinants of that agent's well-being, so that if Mephistopheles believes that for him it is better to reign in hell than serve in heaven he achieves well-being when he successfully sets up a demonic kingdom. Simon Keller has argued that the achievement of the agent's goals, whether those be taking over Middle Earth, counting blades of grass, or engaging in the metaphysics of actions, should be the determinants of well-being, and I have found that argument persuasive (Keller 2004; 2009). I will, then, discuss whether there is a conflict between what Keller calls the unrestricted view desire-satisfaction theory of welfare and restrictions on liberty. Views about the objective value of liberty will be discussed below when I look at the Objective List accounts of well-being.

Could a desire-satisfaction theory of welfare be incompatible with state-sponsored restrictions on liberty? Well, no doubt it could. It all depends on what people desire, and, where there are conflicts between desires, what things they desire most. However, I think we can see that in terms of actual psychology, most people do not want most, or centrally, to control choice where choice makes it more likely that they would end up worse off.

This may seem unlikely. Consider again tobacco: as far as I know, it is legal in every country except Bhutan.[1] Of course, its use is often greatly disincentivized by taxes, which can bring the price of a pack of cigarettes to more than $10. And within many countries it is illegal to smoke in certain locations, and while the rationale for that is that second-hand smoke is harmful to other people, it certainly makes smoking more difficult for the actual smoker, who may be sent to the Siberia of a far-away parking lot in the depths of January. Yet, smoking remains legal, so there is evidence that we do want the freedom to choose to smoke, even though smoking makes us more likely to suffer disease and early death.

Let us leave aside the fact that in many places tobacco companies are probably the determinants of tobacco policy more than the actual citizens of the country. It is still true that there are people who want the liberty to choose to smoke. However, this is a case where we need to consider what desires are most important to a person, so that we may favor the more central desire in cases of conflict. As said above, we have many, many desires and it is impossible to fulfill them all, so we need, whether as an individual deciding what to do or a polity determining a legal regulation, a way to choose the most significant. Granted, how exactly to determine which desires should be favored over others is difficult. Should it be the desire we endorse, that is, the desire we approve of ourselves having? Should it be the desire we feel most strongly at a given instant? Should it be the desire we feel over the longest period of time? Should it be the desire whose satisfaction is most linked to the satisfaction of other desires? This is a difficult question.

I think, though, that at least two things are true. First, for most people, the desire to have a long and healthy life is more central on any of these criteria than are temporary and minor satisfactions. While not everyone who smokes becomes sick or dies early, smoking over the course of a life significantly increases the likelihood of those things. This is presumably why, according at least to US statistics, most people who smoke want to quit; the majority of them try to quit, and the majority (61%, as of 2018) do indeed eventually quit. Indeed, since quitting is very difficult, they try to quit over and over, which suggests that the transitory pleasure of smoking is not seen even by the smoker as being worth the price that is paid.[2] So, it looks as though while cigarettes remain legal, most people would certainly rather not smoke, and that includes those that do currently smoke. This does not, of course, mean that

---

[1] Tobacco Control Act of Bhutan 2010. Available online from: https://web.archive.org/web/20110706162944/http://www.nab.gov.bt/downloadsact/Dz076.pdf.
[2] Center for Disease Control, "Smoking and Tobacco Use," www.cdc.gov/tobacco/data_statistics/fact_sheets/cessation/smoking-cessation-fast-facts/index.html, accessed July 15, 2021.

they wouldn't prefer the liberty to smoke, simply on the grounds that they like to have options. It suggests, though, that even that liberty is less significant to people than the desire to live a long and healthy life. We have gotten used to other restrictions that eliminate many options before we have a chance to know about them. We welcome the Food and Drug Administration, the Medicine and Healthcare Products Regulatory Agency, the European Medicines Agency, etc., even while we may object to some of their individual decisions. We are used to the fact that they eliminate many dangerous options, and we don't want those liberties back given their too-often calamitous results.

What liberties should and which should not be restricted if we accept a desire-satisfaction account of welfare is naturally an empirical question – we need to know what citizens desire, and what they desire most – but there is nothing in the nature of the desires that most people feel that would lead us to think that benevolent interference in many liberties would detract from welfare. Here, as in all cases, a proponent of the desire-satisfaction view of welfare needs to consider what and how strong our desires are, but there is nothing special about the desire for liberty of action per se.

III OBJECTIVE LIST ACCOUNTS OF WELFARE AND STATE INTERFERENCE

The theory that might most obviously be incompatible with robust state interference is the objective list theory. As I have said, there are different lists that are suggested as comprising criteria for well-being. While some objective lists include either pleasure or (at least some) desire-satisfaction on their lists, for these theories neither the experience of pleasure nor desire-satisfaction are sufficient for well-being. Thus, a person who believes in objective criteria for well-being may well believe that even if it results in pain, and even if it is not what we most want, we must have liberty if we are to live well. If we cannot act (sufficiently) freely, we cannot be well-off.

Why? One possibility is that liberty is a good means to achieving something that is a component of welfare. Anything that is valuable merely as a means to something else, though, is in principle eliminable without loss. My car is valuable to me merely as a means to getting places I want to go; if I could simply beam there my car would no longer be of any value to me. If liberty is only valuable because it provides a pathway to something else, it is, in theory at least, something we might do without. If we are to include certain liberties from state interference as parts of a good life, such that their loss is *always* per se a diminishment of well-being, we need to consider liberty as something which in itself contributes to our welfare. For example, Christopher Rice writes"Many people value loving relationships, meaningful knowledge, autonomy, or achievement without thinking of these things as mere instances of desire-satisfaction or as mere means to other goods" (Rice 2013, p. 202). If autonomy, which here may be construed as personal liberty, is a constituent of welfare, then its loss would be a diminishment of welfare. If it is an essential constituent, its loss would mean the absolute loss of welfare – a person without it cannot be well off.

Is personal liberty in this sense a constituent of welfare? Does it make us better off just by our having it? And if so, is it an essential component? While an advocate of any particular item on the objective list may, at some point, have to say "because it just is" to justify a claim about something's value for human welfare, there are sometimes defenses available in the way of further explanation.

For example, a number of people have defended the importance of personal liberty on the grounds that it is a necessary component of personhood. If it is essential to personhood, it is essential to a person's welfare. If we seek the well-being of persons, as opposed to the well-being of toucans or petunias, we obviously do not want to eliminate their personhood in the pursuit of making them better off. Gerald Dworkin took something like this position: "[A]utonomy is a capacity that is (partly) constitutive of what it is to be an agent. It is a capacity that we have a responsibility to exercise and that grounds our notion of having a character." (Dworkin 1988, p. 32)

I have avoided the term "autonomy" thus far because it has different uses both in philosophy and without. In some cases, it refers to an internal quality, roughly the ability to make rational evaluations. Whether we can truly resist irrational thinking is difficult to know, but that is not my concern here. My concern is with the ability to *act* on one's decisions.

The two are quite distinct. If a being were truly unable to reflect and evaluate choices, that is, unable to practice internal autonomy, it does seem plausible to say that that being was not a person. We do think of our intelligence in general, and our ability to evaluate and decide in accordance with that evaluation in particular, as necessary for being a person, and possibly sufficient. But being restrained from acting on a choice is a very different thing from being unable to think and evaluate. As we have just seen, no one objects to restraining liberty of action when the action would unjustly harm another. The person can exercise his reflective capacities and decide to do something bad, and we can handcuff him to prevent his succeeding in his assault. Do we feel that when we restrain a potential criminal, we make him less of a person? Surely not. And while we think that restraining people entirely – making them slaves – is reprehensible, do we think that slaves aren't persons? No, they are persons who are being used horrifically. Being a person is simply not a function of being able to act as one wants.

It is true that frustrating someone's desire to act will lead to negative subjective states, as we saw above. It will make the person unhappy, which could make him worse off on the hedonistic view of welfare, and it is by definition a failure of a person to act on his desire, which could make him worse off on the desire-satisfaction theory of welfare. As we saw above, though, these losses will be, if the policy is good, offset by positive gains to pleasure and/or the satisfaction of desires, so it won't make people worse off in that respect. If a particular restriction of liberty does not on net make a person worse off on either the hedonistic or desire-satisfaction views of welfare, what else about it could be considered a diminishment of well-being?

One answer lies in what might be called the construction of state control in its underlying assumptions and effects. As noted above, there are many institutions, individuals, and circumstances that prevent me from doing things I choose to do. The cost of real estate prevents me from buying my dream house; the traffic on the road keeps me from getting home on time. While most of us may care more about these disappointments and annoyances than we do about many state restrictions on what we do – wearing seat belts is not an irritant for most of us – state restrictions are more frequently the target of those who complain about incursions on their personal liberty. And while one might think that the inequality present in some of these merely social restrictions (the fact that I can't buy my dream home, but Donald Trump can) would excite resentment, on the whole it does not seem to as much as new state regulations do. Some of this might arise from the belief that social restrictions – an economy that prevents me from buying my dream home, traffic that swallows hours of my day – are avoidable, where state restrictions are not. While this might explain the difference in how much resentment we feel at the two kinds of restrictions, it is based on an error: while it is true that in theory our economic structure allows any individual to build his dream home, most of us will never be able to. Traffic, similarly, might be avoided if we could somehow all live and work away from urban centers, but again, that is not realistic. State restrictions, though, can and do change, because we have a relatively accessible formal mechanism for that.

The problem for those who especially resent state restrictions, then, is not that we are stuck with state restrictions more than with other practices that limit our options. There is a relevant difference between restrictions that arise from general social institutions and those that derive directly from the state, however, that may influence us. It might be argued that state restrictions diminish our welfare more than others do because state restrictions are intentional. Whatever way wealth distribution or traffic patterns were developed, it wasn't from a committee of people who sat down and decided that some of us should be stuck for hours on the highway. State regulations, however, develop in just that way. Some set of people decides that our behavior needs to be regulated, and then they set about to regulate it, meaning they purposefully interfere in what we do in order to make us do (or at least, strongly incentivize us to do) what they think is best, not what we would otherwise choose to do. Thus, they substitute their judgment for our judgment.

In cases requiring expertise we might think that it is reasonable for the experts to substitute their judgment for ours. That is why we build a bridge the way the engineers say it should be built, not the way we think would be prettier. When it comes to more general rules about living, such as whether or not to smoke, however, people tend to think their own opinion is as good as another's. For one group to override the opinion of others suggests that the former doesn't share this estimation – those in the group think their own judgment is superior. This, in turn, is taken to mean that they lack respect for those whose liberty they curtail.

To be disrespected might be taken to remove an element of well-being. This may depend on the reasons for which we are disrespected. If a person disrespects, in the sense that they disparage, for example, my ability to play basketball, I may lose something, but that is no big deal. For one thing, I can't play basketball, so their assessment is accurate rather than one that maligns me. Furthermore, having my ability to play basketball disrespected is to be disrespected in a way that is peripheral rather than central. I suppose I'd rather be good at basketball than not, but it doesn't mean a whole lot to me because I don't think of myself primarily as a basketball player. If we are disrespected by the state, however, that may suggest that we are disrespected as persons, since they disrespect our ability to evaluate and make good decisions, and as we saw above, the ability to evaluate well may be taken as an essential property of being a person. To be disrespected as a person, moreover, is to be given an unequal status, and that makes us worse off. Being properly respected and equal in status to our fellows is, on this account, one constituent of well-being. Elizabeth Anderson, for example, in discussing equality, has argued that the point of egalitarian justice is to "to create a community in which people stand in relations of equality to others." (Anderson 1999, pp. 288–289). Inequality in our status as persons may seem to make some worse off than others, even if those latter do not suffer in material ways.

This is not an implausible story. However, it isn't actually correct. For one thing, it is not clear that being disrespected in itself makes a person worse off. Let us say that somewhere in the world very far away there is someone who for some reason has heard of me and knows a bit about me. Let us say he regards me as inferior to himself because I am a woman. Am I worse off than I otherwise would have been? This unenlightened fellow would likely be a pain to be around and any women in his orbit would very likely suffer from that. Let us imagine, however, that he lives in such isolation that he cannot communicate or act on his disrespect. It exists, but it is never manifested. I don't know about it, and thus am not bothered by it. How am I worse off? His is a false belief and very likely a blameworthy belief, but the existence of the belief in itself does not in itself affect my well-being. It is simply an attitude in his head. It's as if a madman in Siberia thought I was an invader from Mars, but never communicated that idea to anyone in any way that could affect me. It just would make no difference to me. Being disrespected as a person does not in itself make the object of that disrespect worse off.

And, in fact, restrictions on liberty that are benign and beneficent need not be disrespectful. Anderson argued that the point of equality is to "assert the equal moral worth of persons." (Anderson 1999, p. 312). Whether or not it is the point of equality, that the state should regard people as having equal moral worth is certainly a desirable thing, and we would not want a government that regarded people as unequal in moral worth. However, there is nothing about restricting personal liberty that means some people think they are superior to others. As has been manifestly demonstrated through empirical literature (Kahneman and Tversky 2000; Kahneman 2011), we are all prone to certain mistakes when we make decisions. To acknowledge this is no more disrespectful than is putting up guard rails on dangerous curves. Those who put up the guard rails are not asserting that they themselves are superior drivers. They are acknowledging that we are all prone to misjudge our speed at times, and that if we go off the road we are all liable to great suffering. Thus, protecting us all from foreseeable error is only rational. Sometimes, the best way to do that is to restrict our liberty of choice.

A distinct concern, however, is that freedom of choice is inextricably linked to the internal evaluative capacities that are thought to be essential of personhood. For example, Griffin writes: "And having chosen, one must then be able to act; that is, one must have at least the minimum provision of resources and capabilities that it takes (call all of this 'minimum provision'). And none of this is any good if someone then blocks one; so ... others must also not forcibly stop one from pursuing what one sees as a worthwhile life (call this 'liberty'). Because we attach such high value to our individual personhood, we see its domain of exercise as privileged and protected." (Griffin 2008, p. 33) Without freedom of choice, we cannot really be agents: "To be an agent, in the fullest sense of which we are capable, one must first choose one's own path through life—that is, not to be dominated or controlled by someone or something else (call it 'autonomy')." (Griffin 2008, p. 33). So, apparently, Griffin believes that freedom of action must accompany the ability to evaluate. But this supposed connection of the internal process of evaluation and decision and the external ability to implement one's choices is, to say the least, vastly overstated. Why should we think it is true? We frequently evaluate and make decisions and find ourselves unable to act on those. It is true that this can be frustrating, as discussed above, but how does it directly reduce the value of the evaluative capacities that make me a person?

It is possible that the argument is that without being able to choose according to one's own evaluation one will simply lose interest in evaluating things. That is certainly something that happens in some contexts: while I might occasionally think of what I would do with a million dollars in spending money, that doesn't interest me a lot because I don't have and will never have that much to spend. But this doesn't mean that I have lost any abilities. It might be thought to be different if the intervention comes from the intentional action of the state rather than simply a concatenation of impersonal circumstances such as economic class, but again we should consider why. Let us imagine that I trust the state, as so many manifestly do not. Will I allow my evaluative capacity to fall into general disuse because I trust the state in many cases to decide what is right?

There is no reason to think that having laws that curtail freedom of action will cause the ability to evaluate to atrophy. It is worthy of note that no one seems to worry about this when it comes to criminal laws. There is no argument that we should allow murder to be legal so that people may learn to evaluate for themselves whether killing an innocent person is right or wrong. No one seems to think that we should do away with laws that punish theft and leave it up to the individual to consider the morality of it for himself, lest we diminish agency. We do want people to understand the wrongness of murder and theft, but we do not think we need to allow them the option to murder or steal in order for them to think about that. Indeed, it seems quite possible that having laws in place actually helps people correctly evaluate the moral worth of actions and the moral worth of other persons. We are social creatures, after all, and while deviating from a social norm is certainly possible and is sometimes a very good thing, our evaluations are always influenced by the people and institutions around us. Thus, good institutions can encourage good values. This doesn't need to consist of unthinking adherence to legal codes no matter what they are. A law tells us that a certain number of people believe strongly in a certain social value, like the moral worth of all persons, and that is part of the education process needed for an agent to evaluate well. A breakdown of law and order is not normally seen as promising an advanced stage of moral reflection, but rather an insensitivity to moral value and a stunted ability to reflect and evaluate.

Why, then, should other restrictions, done for the sake of the individual herself, prevent a person from considering what is truly of value or any other operation of serious reflection? It is true that if a state were to deprive its agents of all freedoms, if it put them in jail or marched them along without any opportunity for choice they might lose interest in choice, but this is not what is envisaged by state restrictions on choice that are done for the sake of welfare. Typically, a restriction on a person's liberty is done to benefit others, or, in the case of paternalistic restrictions, for the good of the individual being constrained. All reasonable deprivations of liberty are done after a review, either implicit or explicit, of the costs and the benefits which result from the restriction. Measures that would intrude into the life of the individual so much as to deprive them of an interest in life and in the reflective capacities that guide that life would not be in the interest of the individual, and thus, not the goal of the well-constituted state.

IV CAVEATS

The Slippery Slope

It may be that when people worry about the loss of liberty, they are worried that while creating a state that has the power to take away liberties to personal choice need not diminish welfare, it could result in such a loss – it all depends on what liberties are taken away. If we give government this power, it will probably be used badly.

One scenario is that government may be run by evil-doers who want only to increase their own power, even if they do that under the guise of benevolent concern for the citizenry. On the one hand, evil-doers are real and guarding them against them should be a priority. On the other hand, this isn't a problem peculiar to laws that infringe on personal liberty. All sorts of law can be misused. As we know, we generally accept laws that keep a person from significantly hurting someone else. A government of evil-doers could use these other-regarding laws to solidify their control. Many things can be criminalized on the grounds that they present a danger to others, even when they don't: consider making criticism of the government illegal on the grounds that it endangers national security. This doesn't mean we shouldn't have any laws. It just means that bad governments can use any means to control the populace, and that we need to guard against bad government by paying attention, voting, etc.

A more subtle danger may be genuinely benevolent governments who interfere with personal liberty in order to impose their own vision of welfare. They want to promote their citizenry's well-being, but their view of what well-being consists in is peculiar or simply wrong. When they impose it, they make people worse off, not better off.

This, too, is quite possible. It is perhaps a practical reason to oppose the adoption of objective list views by the state. Since objective views do not depend on the endorsement or positive view of the individuals whose welfare they describe, they may more easily reflect the idiosyncratic ideas of those in power. Consider a religious government, for example, which considers that people are genuinely better off if they practice Catholicism whether they like it or not, and thus, burn Protestants at the stake. Subjective views, however, by their nature have to refer either to what pleases the citizenry or to what they desire, and this is a check on what sorts of things can be imposed upon them. Granted, mistakes can be made here as in any sort of legislation, but the principle is one that has inherent regard for the wishes of the populace.

Instrumental Value

A second legitimate concern we may have arises from the fact that even if a liberty does not per se augment the welfare of an individual, many liberties are important instrumentally. In the first Section, I said that when a liberty is important merely as a means to some other good it is in principle eliminable: if we can reach that good through some other means, we no longer need that means. This is true. However, if we have no other way to reach that desired good, the means necessary to achieve it are, in actual fact, not eliminable. The liberty to self-govern might be like this: whether or not it is a source of pleasure, and whether or not it's what we really desire, it seems to be better than alternative forms of government at generally leading to sources of pleasure, to the satisfaction of desires, and to most goods placed on any plausible list of objective goods. So, in point of fact, we need to retain many liberties as means to welfare-enhancing ends. None of this, however, means that all liberties are important.

CONCLUSION

Sometimes, liberties make us better off, but it depends on the specific liberty and what it contributes. There is nothing about loss of liberty per se that does us any harm.

RECOMMENDED READING

Anderson, E. (1999). What is the Point of Equality? *Ethics*, 109 (2), 287–337.
Bradley, B. (2009). *Well-Being and Death*, Oxford: Oxford University Press.
Bradley, B. (2014). Objective Theories of Well-being. In B. Eggleston and D. Miller, eds., *The Cambridge Companion to Utilitarianism*. Cambridge: Cambridge University Press, pp. 220–238.
Conly, S. (2013). *Against Autonomy*. Cambridge: Cambridge University Press.
Conly, S. (2016). Autonomy and Well-Being. In G. Fletcher, ed., *The Routledge Handbook of Well-Being*. London, New York: Routledge, pp. 439–449
Dworkin, G. (1988). *The Theory and Practice of Autonomy*, Cambridge: Cambridge University Press.
Fletcher, G. (2013). A Fresh Start for the Objective-List Theory of Well-Being. *Utilitas*, 25 (2), 206–220.
Griffin, J. (2008). *On Human Rights*, Oxford: Oxford University Press.
Heathwood, C. (2014). Subjective Theories of Wellbeing. In B. Eggleston and D. Miller, eds., *The Cambridge Companion to Utilitarianism*. Cambridge: Cambridge University Press, pp. 199–219.
Keller, S. (2004). Welfare and the Achievement of Goals. *Philosophical Studies*, 121 (1), 27–41.
Keller, S. (2009). Welfare as Success. *Noûs*, 43 (4), 656–683.
Mill, J. S. (1978). *On Liberty*, Indianapolis: Hackett.
Mill, J. S. (2017). *Utilitarianism*, Indianapolis: Hackett.
Rawls, J. (1971). *A Theory of Justice*, Cambridge, MA: Belknap Press.
Raz, J. (1986). *The Morality of Freedom*, Oxford: Oxford University Press.
Rice, C. (2013). Defending the Objective List Theory of Well-Being. *Ratio*, 26 (2), 196–211.
Sumner, L. W. (1995). The Subjectivity of Welfare. *Ethics*, 105 (4), 764–790.
Thaler, R. & Sunstein, C. (2008). *Nudge*, New Haven: Yale University Press.
Wolf, S. (1997). Happiness and Meaning: Two Aspects of the Good Life. *Social Philosophy and Policy*, 14 (1), 207–225.

7

Self-Government

Thomas Christiano

I WHAT IS SELF-GOVERNMENT?

In this paper I outline a conception of self-government that is deflationary but nevertheless quite demanding. I argue that attention to the conditions necessary to the achievement of self-government of an egalitarian sort may influence how we are to think of the proper aims of constitutional institutions.

I start by discussing popular-will conceptions of self-government and argue that they are fatally flawed. Then I discuss some deflationary accounts of self-government (that do not rely on a substantive conception of popular will) and I argue for an account that includes concern for procedure and outcomes. I end by discussing a massively underdiscussed part of democratic theory, which is essential to the idea of self-government, and that is the role of information in citizenship and the conditions under which we can hope equality can be realized. I argue that a proper appreciation of these conditions should influence how we think about what a constitution of a self-governing society should be doing.

II POPULAR WILL CONCEPTIONS OF SELF-GOVERNMENT

The popular-will approach understands collective self-government as occurring when the activity of a society is regulated by the popular will of its members. The popular will is understood as the product of a function from the individual wills of its members. In the early modern version, it understands the popular will and the common good in terms of the interests of the members seen as free and equal persons (Rousseau 1997 [1762]). This gives us a very natural reading of the idea of self-government: the people ruling itself. There is, on this view, a strong analogy between individual self-government and collective self-government. Self-government can be connected intrinsically to democracy or republican rule or it can be understood in a way more contingently connected to popular participation.

In the first instance, a self-governing society is a society that effectively pursues the common good predominantly through popular participation. Here, free and equal citizens, for the most part understanding what the common good is, deliberate and vote in favor of policies that accord with the common good. Rousseau allows for individual mistakes concerning the common good but requires that most people are likely to have a correct understanding of the common good.

Rousseau thought that this state of affairs was likely to arise only in small communities of virtuous persons. But modern thinkers have argued that some version of this can obtain in large and very diverse communities. Robert Goodin and Christian List have argued that one can apply the Condorcet Jury Theorem, which formalizes Rousseau's insight. In large societies, when each member of the society has, on average, a better than even chance of apprehending the correct answer, majorities are highly likely to arrive at the correct answer; and that likelihood increases as the size of the society increases (List and Goodin 2001). Others have argued that one can apply the idea of the wisdom of the crowd to large scale societies (Surowiecki 2004). And some have argued that the "diversity trumps ability" theorem of Lu Hong and Scott Page can be applied to large scale collective decision-making settings (Hong and Page 2004; Landemore 2013).

These latter accounts argue that, given certain assumptions about voters, the majority is highly likely to arrive at the right answer as between alternative courses of action. First, what the right answer consists in is left obscure. Is it the common good? Is it justice? What is the standard of correctness in the first place?

Second, the assumptions are rarely if ever satisfied. The assumption of independence, which requires that voters arrive at their conceptions independently from one another, cannot hold in modern societies. This assumption is necessary for the Jury Theorem and the Wisdom of the Crowds idea because they both rely on statistical claims about large numbers of trials. In the Jury Theorem, the law of large numbers guarantees that the majority of decision makers, if each member is more likely to be right than wrong, will be highly likely to be correct. The Wisdom of the Crowds thesis is that large numbers of voters will be randomly connected with the truth and so the errors will cancel each other out and only the right answers will prevail. But this assumption of independence simply doesn't hold normally in large societies.

The other assumption is that voters will get the right answer (in an as yet unspecified sense) more often than not. But, it is not clear what the expression "better than random" means here. Does it mean a better than random chance of getting the right answer, given all the possible outcomes? Or does it mean a better than random chance at getting the right answer among any two or three randomly selected alternatives? If "better than random" means better than a random chance at getting at the truth among all possible alternatives, it is not a very heartening thought and will not be sufficient to establish the majority result. And better than random in the sense of among any two or three possible alternatives makes the collective decision maker the hostage of the agenda setter, for which there are no similar results. Furthermore, if there is significant disagreement on values and social science, there is likely to be disagreement on whether people are better than random at getting at the truth, however we understand that notion. So, if one disagrees with a majority outcome, one can just as easily revise one's estimate of the quality of voters by thinking that perhaps they were not, on average, better than random (Estlund 2008).

The Hong-Page result depends crucially on the idea that we are engaged in problem solving, and thus, that everyone will end up recognizing the solution to the problem when it is arrived at. Otherwise, there is no clear way in which the best outcome will be arrived at. This is the assumption of Oracle (Landemore and Page 2015). This assumption makes sense for problems that are relatively simple and do not involve significant disagreements about value; it is hard to know how it can help solve the issues of modern democratic societies in which there is an enormous amount of disagreement both in terms of values and in terms of the understanding that is necessary to realize those values (Stich 2014).

These latter views all attempt to establish an a priori basis for the thesis that broad and equal participation will tend to have good results. They argue that popular participation is desirable because it tends to produce the right answers to the key questions of politics. The importance of broad and equal participation is essentially instrumental. And the principle is that procedures of a certain sort will likely have certain good outcomes.

To be sure, the traditional view of political philosophers has been that people are not equally endowed with abilities to understand the common good and how to achieve it. And traditional approaches to self-government have tended to be non-egalitarian in that they accorded greater weight to the participation of some individuals and a lesser, if any, weight to that of others. So, the traditional republican approach to self-government permitted a great deal of inequality. And societies that have been republican have tended to endorse quite strong forms of inequality of political status even among those who are permitted to participate in politics. The Roman Republic made political status and participation depend on whether one was a member of the aristocracy, the landed gentry, the plebs or slaves just to name some of the broad categories (Cicero 2017). Modern republics recognized a number of distinctions of political status between those who own property, those who own no property, slaves, and women. They gave lesser or no rights to those who owned no property. And this was partly on the purported grounds that property holders were wiser and that they held a greater stake in the republic (Foner 2019).

The idea that these societies could express a popular will is a bit foreign to us since we don't see how one can express a popular will when large numbers are excluded or have lower political status. But we should remember here that we do not include children or severely mentally disabled persons even though they are a part of the people and their good is part of the common good. The reason for this exclusion is a sense of lesser cognitive ability, but that was certainly part of the purported reason behind the exclusion of the propertyless and women. The significance of this exclusion is mitigated for children since they grow up to become full participants normally and everyone is a child during her life. So, there is a kind of equality in terms of lifetime participation in politics. But this does not hold for the severely mentally disabled.

III CRITIQUE OF POPULAR WILL ACCOUNTS OF SELF-GOVERNMENT

Probably, the most powerful challenge to the idea that the popular will substantively can regulate a society comes from social choice theory. Arrow's Impossibility Theorem asserts that it is always possible that a society can fail to develop a minimally consistent popular will out of the diverse preferences of the membership. That is, there is always some profile of individual preferences (that is a distribution of preferences among persons) in a community that is such that the community cannot be said to have a social preference that is transitive and respects certain very elementary requirements that most would agree ought to regulate a conception of popular will. This suggests that there may be no popular will or at least no rational popular will in many circumstances (Riker 1982).

There are a number of possible responses defenders of a substantive conception of the popular will could give. The first, ably defended by Gerry Mackie, argues that the empirical evidence suggests that in fact the profiles of preferences that arise in modern societies tend not to issue in the kinds of problems the theorem points to. So, though an unlimited domain of preferences can generate social preferences with problematic properties, the normal situation is not one of unlimited domain but much more narrowly curtailed profiles of preferences. These profiles do not often generate problematic social preferences (Mackie 2004).

Mackie's argument has been rejected in recent work on the grounds that the empirical evidence for Mackie's claim is pretty slim and mostly goes from evidence about what people say they will vote for. Moreover, given the amount of disagreement we see in modern societies, it is argued that it is highly improbable that that disagreement will be sufficiently tame to avoid the problems of social choice because, as long as we see disagreement on more than one dimension, we are likely to see the kinds of preference profiles that lead to problematic social preferences (Ingham 2019). Often, people think of disagreement in politics as on a unidimensional left-right spectrum. This would tame individual preferences in a way that leads to rational social preferences, but it is not clear that political disagreement is like this in modern democracies. In the United States, for example, we can see different dimensions of disagreement: disagreements about the degree of desirable government intervention in the economy, disagreements on the extent of civil rights, disagreements on questions of war and peace, disagreements on international trade and other economic institutions, disagreements on immigration, just to name a few.

Riker also argues that the results of social choice theory impugn the fairness of democratic processes. The theory suggests that outcomes of decision making are indeterminate for any particular social choice function. But recent work has argued that fairness can be preserved once we take into account the intensity of preference. Ingham has shown that there can be determinacy once we see that majorities with more intense preferences can win in contests with other majorities even when there are cycles. Equality can be understood as groups having equal abilities for success when they are the same size and have equally intense preferences. (Ingham 2019)

IV DEFLATIONARY ACCOUNTS OF SELF-GOVERNMENT

The analogy between individual self-government and collective self-government breaks down once there is no clear way to aggregate individual preferences into a social preference. A deflationary account of collective self-government avoids an appeal to a substantive notion of popular will or even a full-dress notion of the common good. It is skeptical about the idea of a substantive conception of a people as an agent that makes decisions in accordance with its will.[1] The deflationary approach to self-government is motivated by the reality of disagreement among citizens, and the consequent unlikelihood that there is consensus or even always a majority winner among citizens, along with the desirability of respect for different people's judgments. The contemporary idea of collective self-government does require that all minimally competent adult residents can participate effectively, and as equals, in the making of law and policy, but the ideal of self-government on the deflationary view is not understood in terms of the realization of a popular will in a substantive sense. Self-government involves the participation of citizens according to a principle of justice.

One extreme version of this is to say that self-government requires only procedures and processes to be reasonably democratic. That is, they implement some rough approximation of equal access to political influence or power. This procedural approach eschews appeal to outcomes altogether. Hence, self-government no longer appeals to the idea that the common good is promoted by the procedures because there is too much disagreement on what the common good consists in (Waldron 1999a). Alternatively, we could simply define the common good in terms of the outcome of a reasonably fair democratic process, with the same result.

The troubles with the purely procedural approach to the deflationary account of self-government are: one, it presupposes, without acknowledging as such, that democracy works reasonably well for all the participants. Two, it is not a stable account of the value of self-government. Three, this approach to self-government

---

[1] This is not incompatible with David Miller's view that a sense of common identity among members may enhance the quality of decision making in a democratic society. Miller agrees that common identity is not necessary to effective and equitable democratic decision making (Miller 2020, p. 57). Furthermore, a sense of common identity is fully compatible with multidimensional disagreement among members and the consequent absence of a rational social preference.

seems to ignore the fact that the aims of all the participants are for it to work well, for themselves and for the society as a whole.

The first difficulty is that a purely procedural approach sounds like a good idea but only because our experiences of the democratic process and procedure have been, on the whole, quite good for almost everyone in the society, as I will argue in what follows, certainly in comparison with various forms of authoritarian rule. If our experience of democracy had been quite generally very bad, I am not sure we would be enthusiastic about it. So, democracy has to have some kind of important instrumental value for its members for it to be a success. And the value must be such that it advances the interests of everyone to some significant extent. This is in no way incompatible with saying that democracy also has intrinsic value. Indeed, it is a condition of the intrinsic value of democracy that the possession of power is useful to people. What democracy does, on the view I am suggesting and will develop more in what follows, is distribute instrumentally useful power quite widely. And the value of this wide and perhaps egalitarian distribution of power depends on the value of the power itself. If people could make very little use of such power or its use turned out to be counterproductive, then we would not and should not be concerned that it be distributed equally.[2]

Second, the purely procedural approach is puzzling because the very same values that undergird democratic procedures also support equal basic liberal rights and perhaps even economic rights. If one says that one disagrees about these other values, one can say the same about the value of democratic procedures.

The third concern about the procedural approach is that it fails to account for the importance that citizens attach to having a political system that has just and good outcomes. Each citizen is duty bound to pursue justice and the common good and each has a right to promote and protect her interests in this pursuit. Citizens argue for and reject policy and law, or candidates that promote them, on the grounds that the law or policy is unjust, partial to the interests of a select group or simply ineffective. It would be paradoxical to say to these citizens that they should pursue these aims in a society structured in a way that is likely to defeat those aims. And yet the procedural approach would seem to recommend this in those circumstances in which democracy is completely counterproductive.

What I would like to present here is a deflationary account of the meaning and value of self-government in politics that combines both instrumental and intrinsic value. It combines both a concern for good outcomes and a concern for the intrinsic importance of equality.

---

[2] This is a general requirement of a principle of equality, in my view. Equality is only valuable to the extent that it is equality of goods of which more is better than less (or vice versa). Equality, say, in the number of letters in people's names is of no significance because there is no value in having more or less letters in one's name (within limits). This conception of equality is inherently opposed to leveling down. I have argued this with Will Braynen in Christiano and Braynen (2008).

V IMPORTANCE OF POLITICAL EQUALITY

A society is self-governing when its collective decision making is regulated by a principle of political equality. The ideal of political equality implies a realization of equal political power over collective decision making, limited by a set of equal fundamental political and liberal rights. The opportunity to influence outcomes of collective decision making is made equal ideally speaking when only the greater willingness to engage in political activity and the force of the better argument can make one person more influential than others. The principle of equal opportunity for influence has been the driving force behind the inclusion of the working class, minorities and women in the political process. It has also animated the calls for equal sized electoral districts and for rectifying gerrymandered electoral districts designed to exclude minorities. It has been at the basis of efforts to limit the influence of inequality of wealth and income on electoral campaigns either through public finance of campaigns and limitations on expenditures and contributions to campaigns and/or by means of limiting the most expensive part of campaigning: television advertising.

The ideal of political equality, while remaining a stimulus to political reform in many societies, is rarely fulfilled. There is, however, a kind of minimally egalitarian form of democracy which makes an appreciable difference to all the members of society. This form of democracy realizes equality of opportunity of influence in a more formal sense. It gives members equal rights to vote and the right to run for office, the rights freely to form and participate in political associations and express political opinions, rights to participate in political discussion and propose political solutions to problems. Political equality gives one a right to access to political power to exercise one's rights effectively. It gives one a right to compete on free and fair terms for offices and for influence over people's opinions. Minimally egalitarian democracies are all at least partially committed to realizing the stronger ideal and so they have made some efforts toward limiting the influence of economic inequality on collective decision-making.

I want to sketch out an argument here for the principle of political equality as an ideal and minimum threshold. The first part of the argument is that the wide distribution of power over collective decision-making, given by minimally egalitarian democracy, is a great benefit to all the members. It is important that there is empirical support for the idea that the disadvantaged do normally have a good sense of how to advance their interests when they get the vote. There is a strong relationship between the rise of universal manhood suffrage by the end of the nineteenth century and the era of progressive reform in the United States and Europe culminating, after the extension of the suffrage to women, in the creation of the modern welfare state. The welfare state results in protection of unions, workers, the elderly and many others and leads to high rates of economic growth and increased economic equality in the second half of the twentieth century (Acemoglu and Robinson 2009, pp. 58–64). Granted there may be disagreement on these matters, there is certainly a sufficiently large body of economic opinion that favors the development of the welfare state to suggest that reasonable people disagree here. It is hard to deny that the disadvantaged have known how to promote plausible conceptions of their interests. Another interesting piece of data in support of this view is the recent work of economic historian Gavin Wright arguing that the Voting Rights Act of 1965 played a major role in boosting the economic fortunes of African Americans in the South as well as those of poor whites (many of whom were also burdened by the literacy tests and poll taxes). Wright argues that we can see that Black disenfranchisement after the end of Reconstruction led to a precipitous loss in educational resources as well as other state resources previously devoted to African Americans and poor whites. And these resources were significantly restored fairly soon after the passage of the Voting Rights Act (Wright 2013).

When we add to these observations the more general findings that minimally egalitarian democracies tend not to go to war with one another, protect basic human rights much better than non-democracies, produce public goods on a much greater scale, avoid famine in areas previously plagued by it, and many other results (Christiano 2011), it is really hard to argue that the disadvantaged are not getting some significant bang for their votes.

The wide distribution of political power is a great boon to all those who share in it. The recognition that only when people have power, whether it be liberal power or political power, are their interests advanced, is the first fundamental idea of liberal and democratic thought. It is the idea that animates the drive for the inclusion of the working class, women, and minorities. The wide distribution of power can be supported instrumentally because we have rough measures that are sufficiently clear of the great goods that are advanced by it and the great evils that are avoided. Those measures are rough and any more precise or refined measure of quality of performance is the subject of controversy and conflict.

The argument for the intrinsic value of democracy starts with the importance of the possession of power to the advancement of interests. Democracy is the equal distribution of this instrumental good of political power. It is the equality of distribution that has the intrinsic merit. But, it can only have that intrinsic value because the thing being distributed is of great value to the people who possess it.

What is the argument for having equal distribution of power rather than merely a wide distribution of power? It starts with the fact that societies find themselves in circumstances of disagreement, cognitive bias and conflicts of fundamental interests over collective decisions. There is extensive disagreement on issues of the justice of legislation and the common good, which must be negotiated in the process of collective decision making. We recognize, in addition, that in any moderately complex society there are many conflicts of interests among the members. And we can see that, given limited and fallible cognitive abilities, each person is cognitively biased towards their own interests and experiences even if they are being conscientious in trying to understand the common good.

It is in the light of this pervasive disagreement, cognitive bias and conflict of fundamental interests combined with the importance of power in advancing interests as well as the equal importance of everyone's interests that the argument for the intrinsic value of political equality arises. The reality of disagreement makes it the case that outcome standards beyond the rough ones employed to support the wide distribution of power, are controversial and uncertain. Persons and groups within society have their own distinctive outcome standards by which to assess law and policy and in terms of which they argue for or against candidates and parties.

The reality of conflict of interests and cognitive bias makes it the case that these outcome standards reflect the particular interests and backgrounds of the groups who have them. As a consequence, any use of an outcome standard for assessing political outcomes, beyond the standards used to justify the wide distribution of power, must be seen by citizens as working to the special advantage of some of the citizens. It must be seen as violating the ideal of equality of advancement of interests and, therefore, the equal status of all citizens.

The principle of political equality is a principle that is justified from a public standpoint, that is, a standpoint in which all citizens can plausibly see that they are treated as equals. This is the standpoint from which the intrinsic value of political equality can be appreciated. From this standpoint, no outcome standard beyond that sufficient to justify the wide distribution of power, can be employed to justify the rules of the political game because they are all controversial. Here, the only standard for justifying political rule is the principle of equality itself understood as regulating the distribution of political power. Hence, the need to make decisions collectively suggests that equal political power over the collective decisions is one necessary component to treating persons publicly as equals. That distribution reflects the perspective of the whole society on the interests of each person (again, given the background conditions of disagreement, conflict and bias). It realizes the equal importance of each person's interests in a way that each person can see this to be the case. Therefore, it realizes public equality.

Minimally egalitarian democracy realizes this public equality in some minimal though very important way. The principle of political equality is what animates the efforts more fully to realize equality in the political process so as to achieve something closer to the ideal of political equality.

The egalitarian conception of self-government sketched here suggests a limitation to an alternative way of thinking about self-government. Republican conceptions of self-government put the emphasis on the avoidance of domination by others or anti-power (Pettit 2012). But, there are two problems with this approach from a modern standpoint. One, people want positive power to determine the collective features of their society, not merely the avoidance of power. They want such power because it is essential to satisfying their natural duties of justice and to shaping some of the basic features of their societies. To be sure, that power must be constrained by egalitarian basic liberties and economic rights and we expect that power to be exercised with the aim of promoting the common good, but it is a positive form of power we are concerned with. Two, as we noted earlier, classical republican approaches like Cicero's are deeply opposed to equality, yet they do propose systems of anti-power. They make everyone accountable to everyone else. Yet, something important is missing and that is equality. But once we understand the ideal of equality of political power properly exercised and constrained, then we have all we need to understand the foundations of democracy.

To be clear, what citizens ought to be aiming at in participation is the common good and justice. Within the context of a publicly equal system of collective decision-making, the bases of their rights to participate are the interests advanced in participation because their conceptions of the common good are normally heavily skewed toward their own interests and experiences, not by design, but because of the ordinary limitations of human cognitive functioning. To be sure, in a society with a lot of injustice, oppressed groups permissibly focus on advancing their own fundamental interests that have been unfairly neglected by the larger society. This focus is consonant with a concern for the common good when the neglect has been sufficiently serious.

Given the classical republican espousal of inequality, it is worth exploring the grounds of equality of political status. The basic status is grounded in an effective and adequate ability to reflect on and advance a conception of justice and an ability to advance one's interests. The basic idea is that one has a right to form one's own judgments on what good policy is and one has a right to power to advance those judgments.

Probably, the most basic argument for equal status is the long history of failures of governments in which some have taken more power than others on the basis of an asserted superior ability to rule. That thesis has been systematically taken apart by the observation of the beneficial consequences of including previously excluded groups.

To be clear, equal political status does not rest on a judgment that persons have equal abilities for good political or moral judgment. It explicitly avoids comparative assessment of ability for political judgment and rests only on a minimum standard (Rawls 1971; Christiano 2008). Equal political status is founded on the idea articulated above that there is a deep disagreement among persons about the good and justice. A normal concomitant to such disagreement is that each one of us finds some people less reliable sources of the truth on these matters than some others, but there is a great deal of disagreement as to who these people are and what the relevant criteria for choosing them are. The standards by which one might judge some people more capable than others are inevitably controversial. They reflect the interests and backgrounds of those who promote them (Christiano 2008).

So, the idea is that society sets aside judgments of superiority, inferiority or equality in deciding on the basic rights and gives persons equal political, economic and liberal rights to figure out for themselves who they trust or believe and who not.

For example, even in cases where people properly defer to the judgments of other persons, we still leave it in significant part to the non-experts to determine who they will trust and who they will not trust to do a good job. If we were to distribute rights to make these decisions (about who to trust and defer to) unequally, that would be a publicly clear way of treating people as unequals.

To be sure, in economic exchange we impose some limits on who is permitted to offer certain services. We impose licensing requirements on doctors, engineers, lawyers and plumbers. In some cases, this limits the freedom of each person, to some degree, to choose the kind of person from whom to receive certain services. At the same time, each person may seek out advice from anyone she pleases and may refuse any service from a qualified professional.

We do not impose even such minimal requirements on politicians, party officials or opinion leaders. This is because political competition for votes tends to be much more about the basic aims, values and other aspirations politicians aim at, and the degree of disagreement on these issues is normally greater than the degree of disagreement on medicine or plumbing.

VI PARTICIPATION AND INSTITUTIONS

Self-government in politics relies on the effective participation of citizens in the process of collective decision-making. Citizens must be able to participate in a way that can be said plausibly to promote the common good while defending their interests. But, we need a clear understanding of how citizens can do this. In particular, we need an understanding of the conditions under which citizens can participate effectively and as equals. This will help us think about some constitutional features of democracy. To make progress here, we must develop the micro-theory of democratic participation.

Information is a central element in our understanding of how democracy works and of how political equality should be understood. Political power in a minimally egalitarian democracy comes in two very different dimensions: brute power and informational power. Brute power takes the form of voting power, in which I include both the power of having a vote and the power one's vote has through a scheme of voting rules and representation.[3] This is power to achieve what one wants merely by acting. This is power to achieve results after the activity of persuasion is exhausted.

The second dimension of power is the informational. In my view, once we have achieved minimally egalitarian democracy, this is the most important dimension of political power. But let us be clear about what it is. By "information" I mean to

---

[3] Within brute power there is also the power to make the society pay for a collective decision that one does not like. An example of this is the power of capitalists to withdraw investment from an area on which the government has imposed regulation or the power of unions to go on strike to achieve political aims. I leave this important dimension to the side for this chapter.

include all values and beliefs that are important to making a decision. This involves understanding the nature of one's interests and the common good. It involves understanding the relation between policy and one's interests, and the common good. And it involves beliefs about the relation between policy and politicians. The two key elements of this dimension of power are the power to transmit information to others through the media and the power to receive and comprehend information in a way that relates interests and concerns to policy and politicians.

We usually think of political equality in terms of equal votes and other resources that enable us to achieve outcomes. But in fact, in a minimally egalitarian democracy, the most important sources of inequality of power derive from inequalities in the information system of democracy. Once persons have equal votes and there are free and fair elections, the big question is how people use their votes, which is determined by what information they have about their interests, policy and politicians. To see this, imagine a world in which every person has highly reflective conceptions of their interests and the common good, and is fully informed about policies' effects on them and their society, and politicians' dispositions toward policies. In such a world, a minimally egalitarian democracy would be a fully egalitarian democracy. Electoral campaigns would consist solely of announcements as to who will run. Politicians would simply be chosen on the basis of who does better in satisfying citizens' preferences. This is the world of the spatial theory of voting in political science. And this equality would hold regardless of inequality in wealth in the society.

The problem in our world is that we are at best only modestly informed about our societies and it is costly to become better informed. It is costly to transmit information. It is also costly to receive information: one needs the tools to understand the communications one receives in such a way that one can effectively participate. The tools are costly, and it takes time, labor and money to think about and discuss information and to pursue more of it.

Minimally egalitarian democracy and significant inequality of wealth can give rise to political inequality because some have much more resources to finance transmission and reception of information. Politicians pay much more attention to those who are well informed because they know that they can lose their votes if they choose policies the informed voters don't like. Politicians do not have to worry about this as much with uninformed citizens. The uninformed, if they vote, will tend to vote on cues that are less reliable indicators of policy such as party identification, personality or even half-truths and fabrications. The consequence is that politicians tend to be more responsive to those who are well informed than to those who are not. Hence, access to information and the tools for understanding it are essential to political power.

Politicians must also pay attention to those who have the power to transmit information to others since this influences the beliefs and values of others. This occurs in a number of ways. The media generates information that influences the development of preferences and beliefs in citizens. Political campaigns and other independent political advertising enable politicians and parties to get their views broadcast. And interest group lobbying provides politicians with information to craft legislation. Since the affluent are much more likely to be able to finance these activities, there is likely to be a kind of bias in the direction of the preferences of the affluent. In part, this is because there are significant differences in values between the affluent and the poor; for example, the poor tend to prefer more redistribution while the affluent do not. So, if the affluent are financing most of the transmission of information then there is likely to be some significant bias against redistribution (Erikson 2015). Of course, this is by no means complete since we see that all modern liberal democracies have created powerful welfare state apparatuses since the advent of universal suffrage (Elkjaer and Iverson 2020).[4]

VII THE MODEL OF CITIZENSHIP

With this idea in mind, I now develop a conception of the informational environments that citizens find themselves in in modern democracies. I focus on the element of the power to receive information primarily. I start by articulating a crude version of the Downsian picture of citizenship (Downs 1957). Then, I will show how this view needs to be improved into a more sophisticated Downsian view and suggest how difficulties can arise if we understand citizens in these terms and how we can solve these problems.

Suppose we think of a citizen as a rational agent in traditional economic terms. The agent wants to maximize utility through her actions, where utility is defined in terms of her preferences, whether self-interested or not. Political activity involves voting, arguing with people about policy and trying to persuade them to change their minds. It involves organizing with other people to get one's point of view articulated in the larger society. All of this requires action, and it requires becoming informed about what actions best pursue one's aims.

At the same time, each person is one among many. Each voter in the United States is about one in over a hundred and fifty million or so in a presidential contest. And each person can estimate the value of his vote as the product of the difference between the various candidates at issue and the probability that he makes a pivotal difference to the outcome (by determining victory and by determining a visible difference of the margin of victory [or loss] of his candidate).

No matter how we conceive of this product, the chances of making a significant difference to the outcome are extremely small for each citizen. If we evaluate the

---

[4] There is a raging debate among political scientists about the effect of economic inequality on political equality. Some are skeptical that there are strong effects such as Elkjaer and Iverson (2020), and Guntermann (2020), while others are quite certain that there is an extremely strong effect such as Bartels (2008), Gilens (2010), Solt (2008), and Schlozman, Brady and Verba (2018). I have steered a middle course in this essay, which is articulated by Erikson (2015).

activities above of voting, persuading, and organizing in these terms, the expected utility of any one of these actions is going to be very small, considering one's own well-being alone or even including the well-being of friends and family. On the other hand, if one considers everyone's well-being in one's decision, one might get an expected utility that approximates the effect of one's decisions in non-political matters.

If we think of citizens as predominantly self-interested, they will be almost completely rationally ignorant of politics, because citizens collect information up to the point where the marginal benefit of an additional amount of information is equal to the marginal cost of collecting it. Since the marginal expected benefit to the primarily self-interested voter is extremely small, virtually any marginal cost will be too high to justify collecting information. Hence, the prediction of this crude version of the model of citizenship is that citizens will know next to nothing about politics as a general rule. There is some empirical evidence that appears to bear this out in the results of large election surveys that seem to show that people are not very well informed about politics (American National Election Studies 2020).

This model, if correct in the main, would appear to undercut the claim of democracies to be self-governing. The idea of self-government may not require the existence of a popular will in any substantive sense, but it does require that each group of citizens exercises some degree of control over the direction of policy in proportion to its size and the extent that the policy matters to them as a group. This is not a sufficient condition, but it is a necessary one. The situation of citizens in the crude version of the Downsian model is like that of small children trying to drive a car by turning the driving wheel and pushing the accelerator and brakes but without knowing about how these actions affect the movement of the car. They have some power, but they have no understanding of how to use it. The car does not contribute to the child's individual self-government. The vote and the rights of citizenship do not contribute to the self-government of citizens on this model. Some people who assert that this model is correct encourage us to reject democracy as we know it as a form of rule or at least to curtail its activities in significant ways (Somin 2014; Brennan 2016). Others think that it shows that democracy does not embody self-government, though they do think that democracy can help avoid the worst disasters (Schumpeter 1958; Hardin 1999).

VIII A MORE SOPHISTICATED MODEL OF CITIZENSHIP

The crude model has many problems. First, it does not predict very well. It appears that the wealthy and the well-educated are pretty well informed about politics, while others are less so (Erikson 2015, p. 21). The model should predict that they are no better informed. Second, it is hard to square the model with the evidence that every part of the society seems to do significantly better when it gets the vote, as we observed above. Third, the model relies on conceptions of practical knowledge and political motivation that appear to be unfounded. The main evidence adduced in favor of the model is that people do not answer questions very well around election time about basic matters of politics, but how much does this tell us?

This last point is important for our understanding of self-government and constitutionalism. We make use all the time of an extensive epistemic division of labor in the decisions we make in economic life as well as in private life and in politics. The information on which we act is distributed among many individuals (Hutchins 1995). The society would ground to a halt if we did not do this. From the fact that I cannot tell you how the engine in my car works you cannot infer that I do not act on good information when I take my car out. As long as my mechanic gives the car a good bill of health, I act on good information when I take it out. The same goes for my own body and my reliance on my doctor's opinion. Hence, I can and do act on good information even if I am not able to present you with that information when asked. This suggests that the ability to answer questions about politics may not give us a reasonable conception of citizen competence (Lupia 2016). To be sure, if there is a problem with this division of labor (that is, if doctors, financial advisors or mechanics are corrupt), we may end up acting very badly because the other parts are not performing their epistemic functions.

In addition, the crude Downsian view relies on an excessively narrow conception of human motivation. Though people often act from narrowly self-interested motivations, there are also clearly other kinds of motives such as motivations connected with fair sharing of burdens and altruistic motivations (Mansbridge 1990; Fehr and Fischbacher 2006). Citizens generally report that concerns for the common good play a significant role in their political participation (Mackie 2012). Furthermore, persons are often willing to put in their fair share of a larger project even when doing so does not make much of an independent difference. We see this in recycling efforts and abstaining from littering and many other aspects of social life (Bowles 2016); voting in an informed way seems like a natural circumstance in which this willingness to make a small contribution to a large effort plays a role.

There is another way that the division of labor influences how well-informed people are. If we take seriously the economic idea that people collect information up to the point where the marginal benefit of collecting it is equal to the marginal cost, we have to ask the question: how do they determine what the marginal costs and benefits of information are? Downs argues that people determine these from participating in what he calls the "free information system." Information is free only relative to the purpose one is pursuing. For Downs, free information with regard to politics involves information one receives in other activities. For instance, an owner of a firm gathers information about law and policy regarding the activities of her firm, in order to run the firm properly. Lawyers seek information about the law in order to exercise their professions properly. Other sources of free information are informal conversations with friends, co-workers, family and others. One may also get free information in church. And, of course, education is a source of free information.

They are free with respect to politics to the extent that one acquires the information for other purposes, but one can make use of them in thinking about politics.

It is from this base of education, conversations, and information from work that one gets a sense of what other information one needs to determine whether and how to participate in politics. With a weak source of free information, one may start with a poor basis for determining how and where to acquire further information. Downs illustrates this with an example of a dishwasher in a non-union restaurant, who does not receive a high-quality education, or much information about law or politics at work or from friends and family or co-workers, assuming they have similar jobs and similar educations. A good source will do the opposite. Professionals, businesspersons receive a lot of information about politics at work and from similarly placed friends and family and are usually the recipients of high-quality education. Downs argues that this plays a role in explaining the greater political power of the wealthy and educated in the political system. They benefit from better free information and as a result acquire higher quality information with which to participate. It is important to note here that the difference in free information and the subsequent differential effect on the informedness of the dishwasher and the lawyer has nothing to do with any difference in innate capacity. It has everything to do with different places in the division of labor.

The greater amount of information one acquires freely then enables people to make politicians more responsive to them. Politicians pay a lot of attention to those who pay attention to them. The less informed can be more easily satisfied with party identification or a nice personality. We do have evidence both that the affluent tend to be better informed and that politicians tend to be more responsive to the opinions of the affluent (Bartels 2008; Gilens 2010). We have a bit of evidence that suggests that these two facts are connected but there is more empirical work to be done (Erikson 2015).

But this suggests an important role for the division of labor in influencing the distribution of power in a political society. A division of labor that puts some people in the position of power in economic life and puts others in positions of very little power is likely to affect the distribution of political power among those persons, because of the differences in the free information streams people experience in different parts of the division of labor. These differences lead to differences in access to information. One place where we have some evidence of this is in the role that unions play in enhancing the power of lower middle class and working-class people. In districts in the US where there is high union density, politicians tend to be significantly more responsive to lower income persons, bucking the kind of tendency noted before of the strong bias of the political system toward the interests of the wealthy (Flavin 2016; Becher and Stegmuller 2021). Furthermore, members of unions tend to be better informed and take more nuanced positions than non-members (Kim and Margalit 2017). Hence, it makes sense to say that unions enhance the political power of working-class persons by enhancing their access to understanding politics.

This conception of the dependence of persons on the division of labor in the performance of their political duties has a couple of different dimensions. First, there is, as we have noted, the dependence of the amount and quality of free information on the division of labor in society. Second, there is a dependence of persons on a division of labor in political decision-making. We normally rely on cues from our friends and co-workers as well as opinion leaders to determine how we should vote and participate more generally. This is very similar to the cues we rely on in economic life. If I can rely on my friends and co-workers to be informed about various important matters, this can help me make good decisions even if I do not possess all or even much of their knowledge. And they can do the same with me. In addition, we rely on associations such as political parties, unions and other secondary associations to direct us to politicians and policies that are desirable. Unions, for example, aggregate information and resources and are thereby able to transmit information that is to the benefit of workers and lower income people.

IX DIVISION OF LABOR, CONSTITUTIONALISM AND SELF-GOVERNMENT

Hence, it appears that both the distribution of wealth as well as the distribution of power in an economic system may play a significant role in affecting the distribution of power in the political system. The distribution of wealth influences the distribution of political power because the wealthy subsidize the transmission of information and must inevitably do so with some bias towards their own interests. And the wealthy have more resources with which to become well informed. The distribution of economic power influences the degree to which persons are recipients of high-quality free information and, therefore, influences the distribution of access to information. We can call this a kind of complementarity of the political and the economic institutions.

To the extent that the ideal of self-government implies an equal distribution of political power, and the economic division of labor and distribution of wealth play an important role in determining the distribution of political power, constitutionalism ought to take this into account, because one of the basic functions of a constitution is to make self-government possible. Given the embeddedness of access to information in the economic system, constitutional thinking ought to move past a preoccupation with the formal structure of minimally egalitarian democracy and attempt to shape the informal structures that determine the distribution of informational power in political society. We see efforts at moving past defining constitutions merely in terms of rights against the state and toward including social rights (King 2018); this argument pushes that agenda further with a grounding in the centrality of certain rights to the maintenance of self-government.

There are three areas in which constitutional theory can help advance self-government. First, constitutions must have provisions ensuring that electoral contests are fair. This requires provisions that detach the distribution of power in electoral contests from the distribution of wealth. This can be done either by making campaigns less expensive, say, by forbidding television advertisements or by limiting the amount of funds that can be privately devoted to electoral campaigns. Otherwise, the expense of the transmission of information ensures that the affluent have a dominant role in selecting candidates for election and advancing their prospects. Second, constitutions must promote the capacities of persons to receive political information and process it. They must ensure that each person in a society receives an education that prepares them for citizenship. And, given the complementarity of economic and political institutions, they must promote economic institutions that ensure that all persons have the kind of economic power that connects them with the political system and thereby enables them to participate effectively in the political system. The right to join a union and to strike are two important institutional supports, but I recommend taking a broadly promotive stance toward unions and other means of worker participation in firms (O'Neill and White 2018; Bogg and Estlund 2018). Third, constitutions must enable an economically broad-based system of secondary institutions such as trade unions and other organizations that are able to inform citizens of their interests and concerns on an ongoing basis and are also able to play a role in crafting legislation. This role is essential for the transmission of information over the long term to citizens in the society as well as the transmission of information to legislators. Without support for associations for poorer citizens and working-class citizens, the transmission of information in society at large and in legislative assemblies is dominated by affluent citizens and this defeats the aim of self-government.

CONCLUSION

In this short piece, I have attempted to lay out the foundations of self-government. I have argued against some prominent versions of this notion and replaced them with an egalitarian conception. I have ended with focus on the definition of the role of citizens within a self-governing society and the conditions that enable citizens to fulfill their roles in a properly constructed constitutional system.[5]

RECOMMENDED READING

Anderson, E. (2006). The Epistemology of Democracy. *Episteme: A Journal of Social Epistemology*, 3 (1–2), 8–22.

Christiano, T. (2008). *The Constitution of Equality: Democratic Authority and Its Limits*, Oxford: Oxford University Press.

Cohen, J. (2009). *Philosophy, Politics, Democracy: Selected Essays*, Cambridge, MA: Harvard University Press.

---

[5] Funding from the ANR Labex-IAST is gratefully acknowledged.

Downs, A. (1957). *An Economic Theory of Democracy*, New York: Harper Books.
Estlund, D. (2008). *Democratic Authority*, Princeton: Princeton University Press.
Hardin, R. (2000). *Constitutionalism, Liberalism and Democracy*, Oxford: Oxford University Press.
Locke, J. (1988). Second Treatise on Civil Government. In *Two Treatises on Government*. Edited by P. Laslett. Cambridge: Cambridge University Press.
Mill, J. S. (1991). *Considerations on Representative Government*, Amherst, NY: Prometheus Books.
Pettit, P. (2012). *Republicanism: A Theory of Freedom and Government*, Oxford: Oxford University Press.
Riker, W. H. (1982). *Liberalism Against Populism: A Confrontation Between the Theory of Democracy and the Theory of Social Choice*, San Francisco: Waveland Press.
Rousseau, J.-J. (1973). *The Social Contract*. Translated by G. D. H. Cole. London: J. M. Dent & Sons.
Schumpeter, J. (1958). *Capitalism, Socialism and Democracy*, New York: Harper and Row.
Somin, I. (2014). *Democracy and Political Ignorance: Why Smaller Government is Smarter*, Stanford, CA: Stanford University Press.
Waldron, J. (1999). *Law and Disagreement*, Oxford: Oxford University Press.

8

Justice

Procedural and Substantive

Rainer Forst

I THE PRIORITY OF JUSTICE

It is a commonplace in political philosophy that, when it comes to the question of the good (or best possible) social and political order, we have to assume a plurality of relevant values. In Isaiah Berlin's famous argument for the value of liberty as non-interference, for example, he lists justice, equality and fraternity among "many other values" as rival goals to be realized in collective political life (Berlin 1969, p. 161). Pluralists like Berlin do not provide a higher-order value that can establish normative priorities among these values; justice is just one value among many (Berlin 2013, p. 12).

I believe that this is the wrong starting point. Like John Rawls (1999a, p. 3), I consider justice to be "the first virtue of social institutions." This means that a conception of justice must provide reasons concerning the kind and degree of, say, liberty that members of a normative order can *justifiably* and *justly* claim and demand of each other, just as it must provide reasons concerning the kind and degree of equality, solidarity, welfare, security, tolerance and so on. Justice is a normative concept that does not compete with these other values on the same level; rather, it is situated at a normative and justificatory level above such values and, therefore, can neither be based on them nor be subordinated to them. In this sense, it is morally autonomous and defines these values with respect to what a just order requires and, if necessary, it sets corresponding constraints on them.

This does not mean that these values can be reduced to justice or that justice is the only "real value." It means that justice is an independent normative concept for determining what these other values mean within the framework of a normative order which claims to be just – that is an order that determines the basic standing of persons within a political and social structural framework. Justice needs to be spelled out by higher-order *principles* that determine the place and implications of various *values* within such a context. This is a conceptual as well as a normative, deontological statement, not an ontological one; it does not take any stance on the objectivity of values but it needs to take a stance on the special validity of principles of justice.

In what follows, I will begin by unpacking these claims, before going on to argue for a particular conception of political and social justice and, finally, showing how on this conception procedural and substantive aspects of justice are related. I call this conception *justice as justification*.

II JUSTICE AND THE CONSTITUTION

My argument operates primarily at the level of political-philosophical reflection without starting from an analysis of existing constitutions. However, I do want what I say to be understood as following a method that Jürgen Habermas (1996, chap. 3) calls "rational reconstruction" of the basic principles of a just social and political order, and that includes a just constitutional order, whether the constitution is written or unwritten. Such a reconstruction seeks to uncover the normative logic implicit in a just constitutional order and thus has explanatory value with respect to existing orders, although its basic character is a normative one; in this way, it also allows for an important critical distance to be maintained toward existing constitutions. Its normativity is not of a purely external nature, however, since the tradition of democratic and liberal constitutionalism reflects basic principles of justice, although often it realizes them only imperfectly. At the same time, the normative force of the principles of justice is not based on historical or actual realities, for then the conception of justice could not be autonomous in the sense emphasized earlier. When it comes to basic principles of justice, history does not ground normativity; yet, history places these principles within particular contexts and traditions that matter for the realization of justice (Forst 2002, 2019).

There is nothing paradoxical in arguing, on the one hand, that a political constitution should be defined as a legal and political framework for the authorized construction of norms that can claim to be just – and thus, that it must be grounded in basic principles of justice, which may be substantive or procedural – and, on the other hand, that the concept of justice hardly ever features as an explicit constitutional principle or norm, whereas constitutions regularly contain references to liberty, equality or democracy. If my general thesis about the priority and autonomy of justice is correct, then justice determines the form that liberty, equality and so on justifiably and justly will have, and thus it can be seen as the implicit core of a justifiable constitutional order. This core becomes explicit when certain realizations of or constraints on liberty or equality or democracy are criticized as "unjust," and such criticism must be answered with appropriate justice-based reasons.

III REASONABLE DISAGREEMENT

There is another reason for regarding justice as an autonomous, higher-order concept that orders other values within a normative framework of social and political life – namely, the fact that in modern political communities there are major disagreements about these values, their priorities and their interpretation, and that a stable and well-ordered political community is in need of basic principles that can regulate such disagreements justly and lead to legitimate forms of decision-making. As Jeremy Waldron (2016c, p. 7) argues with regard to the abovementioned value pluralism: "The fact is that whether these values are objective or not, we have disagreements about them; people who are thoroughly committed to their objectivity disagree about them."

Rawls concludes from this that a conception of justice must have a normative standing beyond such disagreements, although here I cannot go into detail about how Rawls justified a conception of justice beyond what he called "reasonable disagreement" (see Forst 2017b). But the logic of his argument requires a justification of a "moral" (Rawls 2005, p. 11), "freestanding" conception of justice that is not the object of reasonable ethical disagreement between "comprehensive doctrines" of the good.

Waldron's argument raises doubts about such a strategy. For according to him, the fact of deep disagreement also reaches to the level of justice, both in its concrete application and its basic principles and foundations. Why would justice, apart from all other values and doctrines, be exempt from such disagreement? And whence would it derive its normative power to be the umpire for deciding whether a disagreement is *reasonable* or *unreasonable*? Is there a non-reasonably rejectable notion of justice (based on reason) on which such a decision could be grounded? For those who believe that justice has the priority I mentioned and that it is not based on mere social compromise or convention, there obviously has to be such a notion.

Some, like Stuart Hampshire (2000, p. 53), believe that this makes the case for a rationally grounded conception of *procedural* justice: "Fairness and justice in procedure are the only virtues that can reasonably be considered as setting norms to be universally respected. The claim to universal respect is founded upon the antecedent claim of rationality to universal respect; and this claim in turn is founded on, and is supported by, a universal feature of human behavior: the habit of adversary reasoning in conditions of uncertainty, the equal attention to arguments pro and con before a conclusion is accepted."

Hampshire's approach places a great deal of weight on what he calls "the norm of rationality in argument" (ibid., p. 53), and subsequently I will suggest a way to make good on such claims. Suffice it to say here that we need to be aware that the thesis outlined earlier, that justice takes priority over other values and orders them normatively, calls for a normative, rational justification for the asserted priority. Whether that grounds a purely procedural notion of justice (as Hampshire thinks) or also a substantive one must be established in what follows.

IV REALISM

Still, in the eyes of so-called realists, we may seem to have lost track of the realities of political life. As Bernard Williams (2005, p. 2) argued, we should not consider the realm of politics as one of "applied morality," because it follows its own dynamics and no demigod exists who could legitimately "apply" morality to the unruly realities of political life. Williams directs our attention to the "first" Hobbesian political question "as the securing of order, protection, safety, trust, and the conditions of cooperation" (ibid., p. 3). Justice, we may infer, comes later. Thus, there are other political values to take care of first. But Williams goes on to explain that the first political question really is the question of legitimacy, or of basic legitimacy, such that "the state has to offer a justification of its power *to each subject*" (ibid., p. 4). And he goes further, because he does not want to consider "successful domination" (ibid., p. 5) as fulfilling the basic legitimation demand, hence, the acceptance of a power situation based on fear or on ideological delusion ought to be ruled out. And so Williams defines what he calls "the critical theory principle" (based on Habermas's (1975) notion of counterfactual, non-dominated discourse) as the right principle for solving the first political question. The principle states that "the acceptance of a justification does not count if the acceptance itself is produced by the coercive power which is supposedly being justified" (Williams 2005, p. 6).

If that is the principle suggested by realism as a principle of legitimacy, it is safe to say that my following argument is also situated within the realm of realism, because I regard the critical theory principle as a basic principle of justice based on the reflexive human capacity of critical, reasonable justification. Unlike Williams, I think that the concept of legitimacy cannot ground such a critical content, as it is a normatively dependent concept that needs to be substantiated by independent terms like, first and foremost, justice (Forst 2017a, chap. 8). What is required is a critical conception of justice that does not reproduce social power asymmetries.

V TWO WAYS OF THINKING ABOUT JUSTICE

It is time we defined the concept of justice. But here, we must take note of a fundamental difference between two paradigmatic ways of thinking about political and social justice (see Forst 2014, chap. 1). The first, and in my view deficient, one is the result of a particular interpretation of the ancient principle *suum cuique*, which is taken to mean that the primary issue of justice is what goods individuals justly receive or deserve – in other words, who "gets" what. This then leads either to comparisons between people's sets of goods, and thus to relative conclusions, or to the question of whether individuals have "enough" of the essential goods, regardless of comparative considerations. Such goods-and distribution-centered, *recipient-oriented* points of view are held by so-called "luck egalitarians" (Arneson 2004; G. A. Cohen 2011a), for example, but also by "sufficientarians" (Frankfurt 1997; Parfit 1997) as well as theorists who argue on the basis of certain fundamental human needs or capabilities that need to be realized. Martha Nussbaum (2006, p. 82) expresses this latter view as follows: "Justice is in the outcome, and the procedure is a good one to the extent that it promotes this outcome."

Rawls holds the opposite view, which he calls "pure procedural justice." It obtains "when there is no independent criterion for the right result: instead there is a correct or fair procedure such that the outcome is likewise correct or fair, whatever it is, provided that the procedure has been properly followed" (Rawls 1999a, p. 75). This presupposes that the procedure truly exhibits the virtues of fairness and impartiality, and Rawls's theory, starting from an "original position" of strict impartiality and leading to two principles of justice for a social basic structure, develops such an ideal.

There are many aspects of the debate between outcome-oriented and procedural views, and I cannot go into them in greater detail here. But I think that underlying this debate are different views of what constitutes a just social order, one which focuses on individuals as receivers of certain goods and thus presupposes an independently valid "metric" of just distributions, while the other focuses on the political structures of constructing social justice by joint action and discourse under the right conditions. Justice is something citizens create or construct together, not something they receive.

Seen from the latter, constructivist view, recipient-focused conceptions neglect the *political* question of who determines the basic structures governing the production and distribution of goods and in what ways, as if there could be a great distribution machine – a neutral "distributor" (G. A. Cohen 2011b, p. 61) – that only needed to be programmed correctly using the right account of justice outcomes. But, according to a more consistently political understanding of justice, it is essential that such a machine should not exist, because this would mean that justice could no longer be understood as a political accomplishment of the subjects themselves but would rather turn them into passive recipients of goods (cf. Young 1990). This is a point where the frequently made distinction between "pure" distributive, outcome-focused, substantive justice and procedural political justice (Caney 2014) has to be problematized, for according to the second, constructivist paradigm of justice that is closer to Rawls's view or to discourse theory, social, distributive justice can only come about through political institutions that are politically just. Accordingly, a benevolent distributive dictator could not establish distributive justice, even if he or she used the "right metric" (assuming there could be such a thing), for justice is about the standing you enjoy within the institutional scheme to which you are subject, which necessarily includes your standing as a politically autonomous member who co-determines the basic structure of society, to use Rawls's (1999a, p. 6) term.

Secondly, the goods-oriented view also neglects the fact that justified claims to goods do not simply "exist" in such a way that they could be known by a "distributor," but can be arrived at only through political discourse in the context of corresponding procedures of justification in which – and this is the fundamental requirement of political as well as social justice, as I will point out – all can, in principle, participate as free and equal individuals. This is a point stressed by discourse theorists, and it is in part an epistemic and in part a moral point (Habermas 1995). There are no uncontested criteria of justice apart from those that are required for the practice of the autonomous collective determination of justice under the right conditions. Once that kind of *fundamental* justice has been established, the debate between competing views of achieving *full* justice will have to be a public, democratic debate (which will properly be called democratic given the critical theory principle mentioned earlier).

Finally, in the third place, the goods-fixated view of justice largely leaves the question of injustice out of account; for, by concentrating on overcoming deficiencies in the distribution of goods, it deems someone – to use a highly abstract alternative without further conditions like a shared basic structure, for example – who suffers want as a result of a natural catastrophe to be equivalent to someone who suffers want as a result of economic or political exploitation. Although it is correct that assistance is morally required in both cases, it is required in the one case, according to a certain understanding of the grammar of justice (and absent further social and political conditions), as an act of *moral solidarity*, but in the other as an act of *justice* conditioned by the nature of one's involvement in relations of exploitation and injustice and of the specific wrong in question. Ignoring this difference can lead to a situation in which what is actually a requirement of justice is misinterpreted instead as an act of generous assistance or "aid."

For these reasons, it is especially important when dealing with questions of *distributive* justice to recognize the *political* point of justice. On the second, constructivist paradigm, justice must be geared to *intersubjective structural relations*, not to *subjective* or *putatively objective states* of the provision of goods or of well-being. Only in this way, by taking into consideration the *first question of justice* – namely, the question of the justifiability of social relations and, correspondingly, how much "justification power" individuals or groups have in a political context – can a critical conception of justice be developed, one which gets at the roots of relations of injustice.

This is why I disagree with G. A. Cohen's view that the core idea of (distributive) justice is "that an unequal distribution whose inequality cannot be vindicated by some choice or fault or desert on the part of (some of) the relevant affected agents is unfair, and therefore, *pro tanto*, unjust, and that nothing can remove that particular injustice" (Cohen 2008, p. 7). Like Rawls (1999a, chap. 5), I do not hold the general belief that "wrong" choices of individuals vindicate certain inequalities, because the distinction between choice and circumstance is hard to draw in the first place when judging complex life situations and is also not one that would be available to any imaginable justice administration. And even if we could use it, it would lead to a social system of control and punishment for "wrong" choices that appears unjust and cruel (Forst 2020a).

VI THE AUTHORITY OF JUSTICE AND THE CONCEPTION OF JUSTICE AS JUSTIFICATION

When it comes to deciding between the two rival paradigms, we need to take our orientation from the *concept* of justice itself. Rawls's original definition, which states that institutions are just when "no arbitrary distinctions are made between persons in the assigning of basic rights and duties and when the rules determine a proper balance between competing claims to the advantages of social life" (Rawls 1999a, p. 5), is helpful in this regard. Arbitrariness should be understood in a social and political sense, that is, it assumes the form of *arbitrary rule* by individuals or by a part of the community (for example, a class) over others, or of the acceptance of social contingencies that lead to social subordination and domination. The term "domination" is important in this context because it signifies the arbitrary rule of some over others, that is rule without proper reasons and justifications and (as a higher-order form of domination) without there being proper structures of justification in the first place (Forst 2017a, ch. 10).

According to this concept, justice as a virtue in a general moral sense implies that human beings should not subject others to arbitrary actions and decisions, where "arbitrary" means "not justifiable with good reasons between the subject and object of action." Hence, *political and social justice* refers to the legitimate claim, or the basic right, of each person not to be subjected to a set of institutions, formal or informal, to rules and structures of action in an arbitrary way, such as when the powerful impose an order on the less powerful, as in Thrasymachus's famous provocative definition of what justice means (Plato 2000, book 1). Again, the meaning of arbitrariness is "without good reasons." But, as we noted earlier, what counts as a good reason here is a highly contested matter: Does one accord priority to the most talented, to those who are ethically deserving, the needy, the industrious, those who choose wisely, or to all equally?

At this point, we must take a *reflexive* turn and work our way up from the core concept of justice to a conception of justice as containing a *practice* of public justification. If we aim to overcome arbitrary social and political relations and institutions (and also exclude arbitrary justifications for such relations and institutions), and if we have no "natural" or objective candidate for what "non-arbitrary" means, then we must take the principle of justification, understood as a principle of reason (defined as the faculty of justification), as the core of the conception of justice – let us call it a conception of *justice as justification* (Forst 2012). According to the principle of reasonable justification, those justifications for social relations and institutions are free from arbitrariness that can withstand the discursive test of reciprocal and general justification among free and equal persons. We arrive at the principle of reciprocal and general justification by a reflexive and recursive (O'Neill 1989) consideration of the validity claim (Habermas 1990) of social and political justice norms to be reciprocally and generally binding on all those who are part of a normative order.

Hence, a conception of justice as justification relies on just those principles that are implicit in the very claim to justifiability which characterizes justice norms. This is a Kantian, discourse-theoretical interpretation of Hampshire's thought cited above.

The criteria of reciprocity and generality imply that one may not make a claim on others within a context of justice that one is not willing to grant all others (reciprocity of claims); and they mean, furthermore, that the justification of such claims has to be conducted in a normative language that is open to all and is not determined by just one party (for example, by a religious majority) and that no party may impose its own contestable notion of justified needs or interests on others who could reasonably reject it (reciprocity of reasons). Generality requires that no one who is subject to a normative order may be excluded from participating in the discourse through which it is justified.

According to this discursive conception, the proper authority for determining what justice means is the subjects who participate in a normative order *themselves*, while empirically speaking they are not generally equals but find themselves in very different situations of power. Thus, struggles for justice within such a scheme aim first and foremost to achieve a higher level of justificatory *quality* and *equality*, that is, to realize a higher level of political justification and to secure a better legal, political and social standing for groups who have been marginalized and are struggling to become equal subjects of justification.

The question of the *authority of justice* is essential for understanding the conception of justice as justification. According to it, the determination of justice is a matter for the participants themselves, but in a manner that excludes justificatory arbitrariness, according to the critical theory principle that Williams, following Habermas, stresses. So, the authority of justice is *their* authority, if properly exercised on the basis of the principle of reciprocal and general justification. This is the rational core of a conception of justice as justifiability that is not reasonable to reject because it is itself based on the principle of reasonable justification.

Hence, the need in practice for a *basic structure of justification* that overcomes the danger that social forces and privileges are merely reproducing themselves within asymmetrical and dominating discursive relations. This is what fundamental justice aims to achieve, and this has a number of *substantive* as well as *procedural* implications. The authority to define justice rests with those who are subjected to a normative order; but they must be, and respect each other as, *equal* justificatory authorities if such justification is to be authoritative. Otherwise, it might just be another form of social domination. If fundamental justice was achieved, the discursive, democratic construction of legal and political norms of justice would aim at establishing what I call full justice, i.e. a *fully justified basic structure*.

The normative groundwork on which this conception rests is based on a fundamental moral claim of free and equal persons to be respected as autonomous normative authorities when it comes to the normative orders to which they are subject. This is my version of the Kantian idea of respecting others as "ends in themselves."

Their "dignity," to use an important foundational concept often cited in constitutional texts (Waldron 2017), means that they *are* such justificatory authorities, and it implies a basic moral *right to justification* (Forst 2012). The conception of justice as justification spells out what this basic right implies in contexts of political and social justice.

VII SUBSTANTIVE PROCEDURALISM

The task of a constitution is to lay down the norms of fundamental justice so that subjects of a normative order possess a basic standing as non-dominated equals; in that sense, a constitution is a justified framework of justification, and there are certain substantive and procedural presuppositions of justice that must be fulfilled if such a framework is to be able to generate norms of justice in a democratic manner. If these are secured, a constitution is a proper mechanism for the authorized construction of justice. A just constitution models the authority to determine justice in the right way (Forst 2020b).

In that sense, my view is close to Richard Bellamy's notion of "political constitutionalism" according to which a constitution "represents a fundamental structure for reaching collective decisions about social arrangements in a democratic way" (Bellamy 2007, p. 4). However, I consider democracy to be the political form of justice as justification, and since justice as justification is wedded to the moral-political notion of persons as non-dominated equals and as not being subject to norms that cannot be reciprocally and generally justified, I believe that my view combines aspects of substantive and procedural justice in a particular way that need not be hostile to certain legal forms designed to secure basic rights such as constitutional review, *pace* Bellamy's view.

I distinguish three aspects in which my view is substantive and procedural at the same time. *First*, this is a substantive moral view insofar as the conception of justice is grounded in a notion of the right to justification and of the autonomy of persons as equal agents of justification. It is not a view based on some ethical notion of the good life, but one that regards humans as autonomous law-givers in the realm of norms, who are only bound by certain principles and criteria of practical reason. So, there is *one* substantive source of all aspects of justice relevant to justice as justification, whether substantive or procedural, distributive or political. This is a version of the "equiprimordiality" of basic subjective rights and democracy for which Habermas (1996, chap. 3) argues; but it differs from his conception, since he sees two sources at work (the discourse principle and the legal form) whereas I think there is only one, namely, the principle and right to justification (Forst 2016).

Second, the notion of fundamental justice contains substantive as well as procedural norms of non-dominated legal, political and social standing that have to be secured in a fundamentally just normative order. The means for securing them range from subjective rights to certain legal procedures as well as democratic procedures;

yet, whatever form this takes, the aim can be traced back to a single root: to realize the status of persons as free from domination and as being able to be an agent of justification to overcome or avoid domination and to establish terms of justified rule. Viewed in this way, basic rights, such as those enshrined in certain constitutions, are not grounded in supposedly non-democratic values like liberty that compete with and constrain democracy; rather, rights raise the threshold of justification when there is a danger of existing forms of justification failing to live up to certain justifiable standards of reciprocal and general justification.

Note that "justification" operates in this formulation on two levels: there are established processes of justification, whether political or legal (as in court proceedings), and there are certain forms of respect whose violation cannot be justified reciprocally and generally. I hesitate to call this "real" versus "ideal" justification, because my main point is to bring the two together by way of constitutional design; still, whatever form real justification takes, the counterfactual question of whether a norm *could* be justified between justificatory equals always remains in place. The art of crafting a constitution is to find ways of improving existing forms of justification so that they better realize the force of and *toward* the better, i.e., reciprocally and generally non-rejectable, argument in legal and political procedures.

The *third* connection I see between substantive and procedural justice is based on a reflection on their institutional interconnectedness. Every basic right requires a substantive justification for why it cannot be rejected between normative equals, while the criteria for that argument are those of reciprocity and generality, which cut through the values used to justify unrestricted liberty, for example. These criteria are used to question and expose unjustifiable interpretations of certain values that benefit only some. Thus, a right to freedom of religion is justified among equals who differ concerning their views of the true religion, in the knowledge of the dangers of religious domination; but the extent and limits of this right must be determined between normative equals without privileging religious views even if held by majorities or large parts of the population.

Even if there is a good justification for such a right, it cannot exist without clear and appropriate procedures for securing it and for interpreting its scope and limits. Thus, political procedural justice must be in place in order to secure and interpret that right, and institutions of legal procedural justice must be in place if the right has been violated either by lawmakers (who, for example, agreed by majority or referendum that Muslims may build mosques but not minarets) or by other institutions or private actors. Viewed in that way, basic rights are not extra-political, preformatted moral constraints on democratic procedures; rather, they rest on justifications that stress certain standards of respect which must be institutionally and procedurally safeguarded. This does not predetermine the institutional form, whether political or legal, in which this is achieved.

In a nutshell, to return to the contrast between Nussbaum and Rawls mentioned earlier, does this approach allow for independent criteria for judging the outcomes of political decision-making? Yes, in a number of ways it does. Can these criteria be traced back to some other source than the right to be respected as an equal agent and authority of justification? No, they cannot. Does this mean that democratic procedures, if they violate well-justified and justifiable standards of respect, have failed to be properly democratic? Yes, it does. That is why the remedies for such substantive injustices have to be sought in democratic modes of self-correction, which must always be accountable to public justification and be fed back into it. There are no authorized "guardians" of substantive justice who can correct or constrain democracy; there can only be democratically authorized, reflexive political and legal procedures to correct unjustifiable forms and outcomes of public, political justification in a publicly justifiable way. A constitution, as the institutionalization of rule by reciprocal and general justification, must install such corrective mechanisms. These can take the form of courts, of the separation of legislative powers into several chambers, possibly additional forms of representation for the underrepresented with veto rights in particular areas, a publicly funded party system, using lotteries to balance certain forms of public power, creating deliberative fora to debate public issues and so on. Again, the institutional forms of self-correcting procedures of justification can vary, and coming up with new ones is a task for our constitutional imagination. Enhancing minority representation and voice is not antidemocratic insofar as it is designed to overcome the danger of majorities dominating smaller groups. A failure of adequate justification is a failure of democracy as a practice of justice, both substantively and procedurally.

Thus, it is mistaken to say that a critique of such failures of justification if, for example, pointed out by a constitutional court, involves using substantive justice to correct procedural justice called democracy. For if a majority overpowered a minority, questioning basic rights implied by fundamental justice (as in the minaret case, or in denying essential social security resources), the failure is one of substantive as well as procedural justice, because the demand of reciprocal and general justification was violated. Certain ways of correcting such decisions harbor authoritarian dangers, as Bellamy and Waldron rightly point out, but they are not in principle undemocratic. They remind democracy of its task, namely to honour and raise the threshold of justification. In a just constitutional order, the authority of justice can neither be usurped by majorities who dominate minorities nor by Platonic legal-moral guardians who are not bound by the requirements of public justification and impose unjustifiable views on a political community. In a normative order aiming at justice, the criteria of the *quality* and the *equality* of justification form a unity.

VIII RIGHTS AND JUSTICE

I will explain my view about the intertwinement of procedural and substantive justice with reference to the question of rights, which is one of the most important means for realizing both aspects of justice. Basic rights are reciprocally and generally valid – i.e., mutually justifiable – claims on others (agents or institutions) that they should do or refrain from doing certain things determined by the content of these rights. We call these rights basic or fundamental because they define the status of persons as full members of a normative order in such a way that they provide protection from severe forms of legal, political and social domination that endanger equal membership.

Basic rights should be regarded as expressing *congealed and solidified justifications* that establish the status of moral equals in the legal, political and social world as free from domination. The justification of each individual right, despite the general moral background, is a "grounded" and contextual exercise, since a number of historical normative experiences and justifications are sedimented in such basic rights as freedom of religion, political participation or access to education. To claim such rights means to use these congealed justifications as *normative powers*. They provide a safe and secure status or standing in the social world. The basic right to justification enables individuals to take ownership of these justifications, as it were, and to use them to ward off illegitimate power claims – but also to contest these justifications when they are open to the suspicion of being one-sided or narrow. The right to justification, as a "veto right" against false justifications, as a particular, higher-order normative power not just to use but also to co-determine rights, is always in place, whereas the content of basic rights is fixed to some extent but is still open to being questioned.

There are two levels on which one can argue for basic rights. On the first level, a *status-based argument* shows how certain basic rights are necessary to institutionalize and secure the very status of being a justificatory equal who is free from legal, political or social domination. On a second level, a *reciprocity-based argument* shows how further rights claims cannot be reciprocally and generally rejected among equal justificatory authorities. The second characterization is broader than the first, because in this case arguments do not point directly to the status-implications of certain rights as does the first justificatory strategy. Examples for the first group of rights are basic rights to life, bodily integrity, personal liberty, equality before the law and a fair trial, gender equality, non-discrimination, freedom of expression, freedom of collective action including political protest, freedom of political participation as an equal, freedom of movement, the right to citizenship, to means of social subsistence and a minimum standard of social life, and to protection against cruel punishment. Examples of the second group are rights to religious liberty (of belief and practice), freedom of the press, to artistic expression and scientific inquiry, to educate one's children and to education more generally, to privacy, to work and exercise an occupation, and to personal property. Neither group of rights includes any "absolutes" but only specific rights within the bounds of reciprocity and generality; for example, there is no absolute right to personal liberty at the expense of the non-domination rights of others, nor is there any prior or "natural" definition of the right to property and what it entails. Every right in the abstract and in its concrete form needs to be justified as a claim that cannot be denied between justificatory equals who aim to establish a status of legal, political and social non-domination by way of basic rights (as part of a basic structure of justice more generally). Thus, these rights constitute an important part of fundamental justice.

I cannot discuss the full list of rights at this point, so a few examples will have to suffice. The right to individual liberty – or, as the German Basic Law puts it, the *"freie Entfaltung der Persönlichkeit,"* i.e., the free development and expression of one's personality – is non-rejectable between persons who respect each other as justificatory equals and independent authorities in the realm of reasons, or, in Rawls's terminology, as "self-authenticating sources of valid claims" (Rawls 2005, p. 72). Contrary to what many liberal theories argue, this does not presuppose that such liberty is a precondition for a good life based on self-reflection and self-determination. Rather, individual liberty is justified by the basic respect for others as normative equals who would be subjected to domination if some members of society were in a position to define the liberty of others in terms of reasons that can be reciprocally and generally rejected, for example, in terms of religious reasons that are not sharable or paternalist considerations that purport to reflect the "true interests" of others who do not share them. Such forms of respect resonate with a certain notion of human dignity as a justificatory authority equal to others, and the justifications congealed in basic liberty rights that contest restrictions on individual liberty involving domination express this status. These justifications do not exclude legitimate reasons for restricting such liberty or freedom; the German Basic Law, for example, adds that the right to personal liberty presupposes that one does not violate the rights of others. There are no fixed "natural" basic rights apart from the fundamental rights claim to all of the rights that can be reciprocally and generally justified.

The right to political participation, to take another example, is of special importance in a just and democratic order. For it expresses our standing as normative equals and authorities in the space of social reasons in a particular way: it is an expression of that dignity and confers a higher-order normative power on persons as coauthors of the law, thereby generating the demand within a normative order to make its institutions of participation and decision-making more inclusive and effective. The normative power of political autonomy is of a higher order than the Hohfeldian normative power to change other persons' legal powers by selling them an object I own, for example (Hohfeld 1919, p. 52). For it is the normative power to co-determine the framework within which such lower-order changes in power occur.

Social rights as rights to participate in social institutions, from the workplace to educational systems and other areas of life, finally, are not justified in instrumental terms as being required to realize the "worth of liberty" (Rawls 1999a, p. 179). Rather, they are intrinsically justified as rights to prevent social domination and to be a social equal in fundamental respects. Domination assumes many forms, and being easy prey to economic exploitation is a clear and long-standing danger to which a definition of basic rights must respond. Again, there is no notion of the minimally good life at work here. Rather, the main reason for such rights is to endow every person with a basic standing that provides them with protection against different forms of social domination, ranging from economic exploitation to oppression within familial structures (J. King 2012). Then the right to social goods such as food, housing, education and medicine is no longer primarily a right to certain means of subsistence, but is instead a right to a social standing as a full member of society.

In addition, it must be emphasized that such rights are far from being the only means of furthering social justice; the economic order, as an important part of the normative order, ought to be fully subject to processes of political justification, and the criteria of reciprocity and generality give each person, including the worst off, a *veto right* against unjustifiable economic arrangements. This, it seems to me, is the correct political reading of Rawls's difference principle. Rather than reading it as an "end-state" or "patterned" (Nozick 1974, chap. 7) outcome-oriented principle, we should understand it as endowing the worst-off groups in society with a right to justification that trumps violations of reciprocal and general justification. This is what Rawls says when he explains the conditions under which social inequalities can be justifiable: "Because the parties start from an equal division of all social primary goods, those who benefit least have, so to speak, a veto. Thus, we arrive at the difference principle. Taking equality as the basis of comparison, those who have gained more must do so on terms that are justifiable to those who have gained the least." (Rawls 1999a, p. 131)

If my argument in this chapter is correct, then a just constitutional order must find ways to legally and politically institutionalize such veto possibilities. And the correct response to the question of whether this is a point made by substantive or by procedural justice is to reject the "or."

ACKNOWLEDGMENTS

I am indebted to the participants of the conference at University College London that Richard Bellamy and Jeff King organized in June 2019 and where I could present a draft of this text. The probing comments and questions by Richard and Jeff helped me enormously to improve my arguments, and I am truly grateful for that. Special thanks also to Adam Swift (continuing a long-standing exchange) and Helder de Schutter for their great commentaries, and to Cécile Laborde, Lea Ypi and Philip Pettit for enlightening follow-up discussions. I also benefitted from a presentation of this text at the University of Michigan while I was the Sunderland Faculty Fellow at their Law School in the fall of 2019, with special thanks to Daniel Halberstam, Scott Hershovitz, Don Herzog, Gabriel Mendlow, Steve Ratner, Don Regan and Mathias Reimann for inspiring discussions. In addition, I greatly benefitted from discussions of a revised version of this paper at a seminar in Berlin conducted by Mattias Kumm and Stefan Gosepath (in 2021) and at a workshop at the University of Notre Dame organized by Paul Weithman (in 2022). At that occasion, Robert Audi was so kind to send me extremely valuable written comments. I also thank Ciaran Cronin, Felix Kämper and Amadeus Ulrich for their help in preparing this text.

RECOMMENDED READING

Cohen, G. A. (2008). *Rescuing Justice and Equality*, Cambridge, MA: Harvard University Press.
Dworkin, R. (2011). *Justice for Hedgehogs*, Cambridge, MA: Harvard University Press.
Habermas, J. (1996). *Between Facts and Norms. Contributions to a Discourse Theory of Law and Democracy*, Translated by W. Rehg. Cambridge, MA: MIT Press.
Hampshire, S. (2000). *Justice is Conflict*, Princeton: Princeton University Press.
Miller, D. (1999). *Principles of Social Justice*, Cambridge, MA: Harvard University Press.
Nozick, R. (1974). *Anarchy, State, and Utopia*, New York: Basic Books.
Nussbaum, M. C. (2006). *Frontiers of Justice. Disability, Nationality, Species Membership*, Cambridge, MA: Harvard University Press.
Parfit, D. (1997). Equality and Priority. *Ratio*, 10 (3), 202–21.
Rawls, J. (1999a). *A Theory of Justice*, rev. edn, Cambridge, MA: Harvard University Press.
Rawls, J. (2005). *Political Liberalism*, exp. edn, New York: Columbia University Press.
Sen, A. (2009). *The Idea of Justice*, Cambridge, MA: Harvard University Press.
Waldron, J. (2016). *Political Political Theory. Essays on Institutions*, Cambridge, MA: Harvard University Press.
Walzer, M. (1983). *Spheres of Justice. A Defense of Pluralism and Equality*, New York: Basic Books.
Young, I. M. (1990). *Justice and the Politics of Difference*, Princeton: Princeton University Press.

9

Recognition

Helder De Schutter

One of the most intense discussions in political and legal theory in the past few decades concerns the moral desirability of recognition granted by the state to the national, cultural, and linguistic identities of its citizens (I. M. Young 1990; Taylor 1995; Honneth 1995; Kymlicka 1995; Fraser and Honneth 2003; Gutmann 2003; Van Parijs 2011; Patten 2014; Tamir 2019). With over 7100 languages spread over less than 200 countries, 51 violent conflicts or wars over autonomy or secession (Heidelberg Institute for International Conflict Research 2021, p. 19) and on-going armed conflicts over self-determination and autonomy in 2020 in 17 countries (Minority Rights Groups International 2021), an important task for political and legal theory is to figure out the grounds of recognition of sub-state national, cultural, and language identities, and the manner in which these identities, if deemed recognition-worthy, are to be recognized.

In this Chapter, I articulate a framework for normatively understanding and evaluating claims for cultural and linguistic recognition, and outline and defend one recognitional regime within that framework. The framework is triadic: the conceptual map of normative discussions over recognition, I claim, can be divided in three parts: nonrecognitionalism (Section I), monorecognitionalism (Section II) and recognitional pluralism (Section III). My goal is to stake out and defend a conception of recognitional pluralism. To do so I need to show, against nonrecognitionalism, that the relevant identities are recognition-worthy (Section I), and, against monorecognitionalism, that recognition ought to be distributed in an equal and pluralistic fashion (Section II). In Section III, I defend one member of the family of recognitional-pluralist conceptions of recognition, the *equal services* account, according to which the state should provide equal services to each of the identities making up the state, from which individuals can then tap at will to construct their own individual identity.

I will in what follows distinguish between *recognition-worthiness* and *material recognition*. When I say that an identity (e.g., as a speaker of a language, or as a member of two national cultures at once) is recognition-worthy, I mean that the interest in the identity is important enough for the state to seek to protect or satisfy it.

By material recognition, I mean the actual (state) support granted to identity-related features of groups.[1] This state support can be included in the constitution. Examples of constitutional accommodations of recognition include: a reference in the constitution to the essential multinational or multilingual make-up of the population and the need to reflect this diversity in the policies the state pursues, a constitutionally provided right to forms of national political autonomy (all the way up to the addition of a secession clause, as the Ethiopian constitution does), and a constitutional rule that involves sub-state national-cultural groups in the processes required to amend the constitution. But in addition to, or instead of the constitution, also more downstream policies pursued in accordance with those constitutional principles can realize recognition. These more downstream policies include subsidies for national-cultural festivals; rights to (state-subsidized) schools, universities, courts and state agencies functioning solely or also in the group's language; rights to distinct official holidays for minority members or for a more minority-friendly reform of the official holidays calendar for all; and exemptions from existing laws (see Levy 2000, pp. 125–160 for a helpful classification of claims).

The distinction between recognition-worthiness and material recognition is relevant because, as I will argue, the case for material recognition does not necessarily follow from an affirmation of recognition-worthiness. And conversely, it is not because the state grants an identity actual benefits that it deems the identity recognition-worthy. The link between the two must be argued for.

My particular concern is with the appropriate form of the state's *legal* recognition of sub-state *national, cultural, and linguistic identities*. I, therefore, leave non-legal areas of recognition – in particular the recognitional spheres of love and esteem (Honneth 1995) – to one side. And while I think that both the framework and the position I defend are extendable for other types of identities, including in particular religious identities, I will limit myself to claims by long-settled groups for the recognition of national-cultural and/or language identity, which can be found, for example, in Catalonia in Spain, Québec and indigenous peoples in Canada, Tigray in Ethiopia, Iraqi Kurdistan, Flanders in Belgium, the Tamil and Sinhalese in Sri Lanka, speakers of Sámi and Swedish in Finland, the thirty-six official indigenous language groups in Bolivia, Welsh in the UK, etc.

I AGAINST NONRECOGNITIONALISM: TWO INTERESTS

A normative theory of recognition, I hold, requires two steps. Step 1 identifies a set of interests in recognition; step 2 articulates a principle of distribution of those interests. This first section concerns the interest in recognition. We need an account of this interest in order to combat nonrecognitionalism, the first of the triadic

---

[1] In defining material recognition in this way, I broadly follow Alan Patten's definition of recognition (Patten 2014, pp. 156–160).

normative map of positions vis-à-vis recognition. Nonrecognitionalism is the view that the relevant identities are not recognition-worthy. When designing state policy we do not take identity on board as an interest to be satisfied. We should just work out whatever needs to be done without reference to the value of identity or recognition. Nonrecognitionalists may seek to further any goal or interest except the satisfaction of identity interests for reasons of recognition-worthiness – identities are simply not recognition-worthy.

This view has one interesting complication: the nonrecognitionalist rejection of the recognition-worthiness of identity is compatible with policies or state structures that do end up granting material recognition. The nonrecognitionalist is indifferent to whether or not a particular identity receives material recognition, as long as the interests she cares about – non-identity interests – are satisfied or maximized. She could select any particular non-identity interest, such as communicative efficiency, deliberative democracy, state cohesion, or equality of opportunity, and then recommend pursuing whatever policy serves that non-identity interest or goal best, even if that policy creates material-recognitional benefits for some group.[2]

Such nonrecognitionalist positions often end up arguing for forms of national and linguistic homogeneity. Take for instance the interest in democracy. Many have argued that democracy requires a shared language. This was one of the central arguments appealed to in French revolutionary language policy proposals, such as in the plans by Bertrand Barère (1794) and Henri Grégoire (1794), both approved by the French Assemblée Nationale. While despotic monarchs do not need to pay attention to the linguistic make-up of society, says Barère, in a democracy citizens need to surveil each other and public officials, and to do so a shared language is needed (Barère 2002 [1794], pp. 327–328). Similar arguments can be found in Grégoire, who associates linguistic diversity with aristocracy, and democracy with unilingualism (Grégoire 2002 [1794], pp. 335–336). Today, along lines akin to the revolutionary justification of this democracy interest, Daniel Weinstock has argued that we should impose the majority language in so far as (and no further than) that imposition is "required in order for the state to be able to communicate effectively with its citizens" (Weinstock 2003, p. 267). This language policy will in most cases "advantage the language of the majority. But it will do so for pragmatic reasons to do with the organization of a functioning democracy, rather than because the majority linguistic community in question is seen as bearing 'intrinsic' value, or (…) because the defence of the language of the majority is uniquely just (…)" (Weinstock 2003, p. 269). Similarly, Brian Barry has argued that "[w]e can negotiate across language barriers but we cannot deliberate together about the way in which our common life is to be conducted unless we share a language" (Barry 2001, p. 227). Therefore, "democratic states that still have an open future (with regard to the possible development

---

[2] In what follows, I extend to questions of national-cultural recognition a frame I have developed before for issues of linguistic justice (see e.g. De Schutter 2022).

of distinct linguistic communities) have every reason for pursuing the course that leads to a linguistically homogeneous polity" (p. 228).

Or take the equality of opportunity interest. Grégoire put the link between linguistic diversity and the *inégalité des conditions* at the heart of his proposal to annihilate the *patois* on French territory (2002, p. 350). The basic motivation for his proposal – that minorities must be enabled to speak a language of wider opportunities – is also present in several otherwise far more liberal proposals of contemporary linguistic justice theorists. For example, it drives Thomas Pogge's argument that the interest of Hispanic children in learning English in the US trumps the Hispanic group's interest in preservation and recognition of Spanish in case these two interests clash. On this basis, he explores an *English-First* principle (though not an *English-only* principle, the analogue of the French-only view of Grégoire), according to which "the most important linguistic competence for children now growing up in the US is the ability to communicate in English; and the language of instruction in public schools in the US should therefore be chosen by reference to the goal of effectively helping pupils develop fluency in English" (Pogge 2003, pp. 118–119).[3]

The resulting policy recommendation of nonrecognitionalism is similar in both cases: pick the policy that realizes the favored non-identity outcome. If the successful realization of weighty goals like deliberative democracy or equality of opportunity depends on or is significantly furthered by the sharing of a language or a national culture, then policymakers should pursue that shared language or culture, even if that means that no, or more limited, material recognition is granted to other groups.

But, while nonrecognitionalism often supports homogeneity-inducing policies, it can also side with heterogeneity. This is the case when the desired non-identity outcomes are furthered by granting material recognition to identity groups. For example, Lord Acton argued that a diversity of nations within the same state can act as a bulwark against the power of the state (Acton 1862). Similarly, James Buchanan has supported federalism in Europe on the basis of the argument that state power in federations is weaker than in unitary constellations (Buchanan 1995–1996). On different grounds, Jacob Levy has defended forms of multicultural accommodation as a means of avoiding political and ethnic violence, state-based cruelty to ethnic minorities, and civil war (Levy 2000).

In short, nonrecognitionalism seeks to bring about or maximize non-identity interests. The interest in identity is not worthy of recognition. In order to contest nonrecognitionalism, then, we need to build a convincing normative case for the recognition-worthiness of certain identity interests.

One might think this step is not necessary. It does not matter which interests in identity are recognition-worthy, one might hold; what matters is only the fact that

---

[3] Pogge's position creates space for *some* Spanish recognition. He just argues that the non-identity interest in the education that is best for each child overrides the identity interest. As such he is not a pure nonrecognitionalist, who would reject the recognition-worthiness of identity.

people *desire* recognition. For example, Alan Patten has suggested that the fact itself that multiple groups desire a certain good is sufficient to ground a claim for the equal distribution of that good (Patten 2002, p. 567, n. 23). What gets this argument underway is the sheer desire for the good; no underlying account of the value of the good is required.

However, without an underlying account of the interests served by recognition and their moral significance, the case for recognition runs the risk of being thought of as simply not very important, or as being easily overridable when conflicts with other values and interests present themselves. Such an account is particularly needed if we want to give recognition of the national/language/cultural identities some form of constitutional status, as I think we should, and as many states in the world do: think for example of Ethiopia's recognition of states, nations and peoples in its Constitution, Canada's constitutional recognition of indigenous rights, Belgium's constitutionally guaranteed official multilingualism, or South Africa's constitutional clause that all of its eleven official languages are to enjoy "parity of esteem."

Thus, the case for recognition must be grounded in underlying interests weighty enough to warrant recognition. These interests will in some cases need to be balanced against other, non-identity interests, but they are necessary ingredients of that balancing project. What are these interests in identity that warrant recognition? I will now articulate and defend my own versions of what I think of as the two most persuasive interests that have come to us, both in the history of political thought and in the contemporary debate over these issues. I call them life-world access and dignity.

> LIFE-WORLD ACCESS: Co-linguals and co-nationals share a mental world of cultural and linguistic references. Because access to this shared mental world constitutes a fundamental interest, we should pursue a policy or state structure that grants people access to their own language and national culture.

Language proficiency is a key to a room: only the speakers have direct access to whatever is discussed in the room (see also De Schutter 2016, p. 44). And growing up in that room – i.e. in a language community – surrounds people with particular sets of information and opportunities: children are made familiar with the literature of that language, with shared cultural references, specific and often ritualized catchphrases in the public sphere, language-specific proverbs and metaphors, shared ways of formulating and balancing arguments, and so on. In this way, each language discloses and structures what we can call a "life-world", which "supplies members with unproblematic, common, background convictions that are assumed to be guaranteed" (Habermas 1984, p. 125). A life-world comprises shared presuppositions about the world and about our identity, beliefs, and value systems. Language co constitutes this life-world and is part of the things that give access to it. In this way, we can say that language has a *world-disclosing* function. Language discloses a world of specific meanings and ways of conceptualizing the world. Language is only in part a tool for inter-individual communication between fully constituted people. It also shapes people, by inculcating them in a specific cognitive community (see De Schutter 2016: 52).

This is true also for the national culture one belongs to: just by virtue of frequent interaction, co-nationals are familiar with national-cultural ways of framing and responding to events, and being reasonable and persuasive. Surely, language and national culture are not the only features that constitute the life-world. States do so as well: they co-shape our expectations, our outlook on life, our rights, and our opportunities. Climates do so too, by enabling and limiting certain of our options. So do our socio-economic conditions, the physical architecture of our cities, or the natural landscapes of our surroundings. All these things co-structure our life-world, and language in itself is not sufficient to mark off a distinct life-world. But language, and the national culture in which it is often embedded, are a crucial part of the mix of things that shape a life-world: the language one speaks determines to a large extent the novels one has read and believes one should read, the ideas one has heard, and the evidence with which certain assumptions are held.

Because language discloses the world in a situated way, speakers who have no or only partial access to their linguistic and cultural horizon can experience disruptions in their ability to realize their selves in the world. They may face disorientation in the world, or *anomie* (Merton 1938, p. 682; see also Cairns 2000, pp. 87, 109; and Carens 2000, p. 246 for an application to indigenous communities). Indeed, cultural and linguistic assimilation without continued integration within one's original community may increase feelings of isolation and alienation, and has been associated with an increased suicide risk (Wadsworth and Kubrin 2007, pp. 1877–1879). For immigrant minorities, for example, bilingualism in both the host society's dominant language and the immigrant group's original language has been shown to be associated with greater psychological and economic benefits than full assimilation into the dominant language (Portes and Hao 2002; Agirdag 2014, p. 450).

Moreover, in settings where minority members live in a society structured around the majority's cultural life-world, interactions between minority and majority members will often be characterized by further disadvantages that result from unequal life-world access. In particular, minority members may be perceived by the majority as less credible or intelligent. Minority members may in this way become victims of forms of epistemic injustice. These can result from negative associations with particular accents or with lack of fluency in the dominant language. They can also ensue from difficulties in understanding someone due to different ways of conceptualizing the world in different languages (Peled 2018, pp. 4–5; Fricker 2007).

This interest in life-world access has historically come to us via Herder and the German Romanticism that developed in its wake. While French revolutionary figures such as Grégoire were also centrally concerned with national-cultural and language policy, they denied the recognition-worthiness of access to language and culture. Interestingly, they did agree on the role of language and peoplehood for individual and collective mindsets – they affirmed the life-world function of language and culture (Grégoire 2002, pp. 336–348) – but they did not see any value in *protecting* access to one's own life-world. In fact, they did the opposite: they argued for the eradication of minority languages and *patois* on French territory, and for their assimilation into French. What made Herder stand out here was the way he turned the life-world argument into an argument for resisting assimilation and colonialism, and for recognizing people's own identities. This Herderian line has been shared by an impressive lineage of likeminded "romantic" scholars from Hamann over Humboldt to Gadamer, Taylor, Tamir, and Kymlicka today. They have stressed the importance of linguistic life-worlds to identity and shared the normative conclusion that languages rights are justified. In doing so, some of these scholars have tied the interest in life-world to liberalism's core premises. In the theory of Will Kymlicka (1995), an advocate of this line of argument, the interest in culture is woven into the quintessentially liberal value of autonomy, thus instantiating a liberal linguistic turn (De Schutter 2016). Extended to national identity, this argument is also a pillar of contemporary liberal nationalism, as in the theory of Yael Tamir (2019: 45).

> DIGNITY: The dignity of a group is affected by the status publicly accorded to it. To further this interest, states with multiple groups who hold their language or national culture in comparably high regard should recognize the concerned identities equally.[4]

Social institutions should support the goods of dignity and self-respect because these are essential to living a full life (see e.g., Rawls 1993, p. 319; 1999a, p. 386; Margalit 1996). But dignity and self-respect have cultural-recognitional preconditions. Social institutions should avoid publicly disaffirming certain cultures and languages. This has absolute dimensions: the state should not publicly denounce a particular national minority, for example, by labeling it as backward or unwanted. But there are also relative preconditions of dignity. When there are several groups in a state, all of whom value their national culture and their language comparably strongly, but the language and culture of some groups are receive material recognition whereas those of others do not, or those of others receive significantly less extended forms of recognition, then this can be reasonably felt as a violation of the equal dignity of the lesser-recognized languages' cultures. If the groups are not equally respected, then the state confers a message of lesser status to these groups, negatively affecting the dignity of their members (see also Van Parijs 2008).

This concern with linguistic and cultural dignity is older than the romantic interest in life-world protection. Its history as an argument for cultural-linguistic

---

[4] This section of the paper is based on my more elaborate analysis of the dignity argument for multiculturalism in De Schutter 2023.

recognition goes back to the defense of European vernaculars and local nationhood in the Renaissance. Fifteenth and sixteenth century "vernacular humanists" used the values of dignity and honor in their arguments for the vernacular (see Gravelle 1988; Patten 2006). On this view, it is important not to live in humiliation and shame. We are to be proud and honorable citizens. Yet this importance of dignity has cultural and linguistic preconditions: we should not bow linguistically and symbolically to other languages and peoples, as if they have superior status. Instead, we should use and cultivate our own vernacular, and speak it with eloquence, and without loanwords. This view was born in Italy, and spread throughout Europe. Its advocates included Pietro Bembo, Lorenzo de Medici, and Trissino in Italy, Joachim du Bellay in France, and Coornhert in the Low Countries.

Compared with the life-world view, this dignity case for recognition has less clearly been the subject of a historically continuous tradition. But it has resurfaced as a grounding principle for contemporary linguistic justice, for instance, in the work of several republican theorists emphasizing linguistic non-domination (Banai 2013; Morales-Gálvez 2017), by French scholars in their opposition to the invasion of English (see Serres and Polacco 2018), and also by liberals such as Van Parijs (2011), who rests his theory of linguistic justice on the interest in part on "equal dignity" or "parity of esteem."

This tradition has historically emphasized dignity but not necessarily *equal* dignity. Many vernacular humanists insisted on the *unique* dignity that their own vernacular provided. Examples include Simon Stevin's assertion that Dutch was the language of Paradise (Stevin 1955 [1586]) or Machiavelli's attempt to show that Florentine is superior to all other Italian dialects (2005, p. 139).

Yet, if this tradition can give rise to demands of unequal dignity, is it then not an important objection to the dignity argument that dignity claims often are unreasonable, claiming entitltements to a greater share than one is actually entitled to (see e.g., Stilz 2015 for this objection)? And does that not show that the dignity case for recognition fails?

It is true that demands made in the name of dignity may be unreasonable. But the unreasonableness of a particular dignity claim does not undermine the protection-worthiness of dignity; it only invalidates the proposed distribution of its protection (De Schutter 2023, p. 34). Consider other examples of unreasonable demands. Elsa and Anna have to divide a cake. Elsa claims the full cake; Anna claims half the cake. All else being equal, Anna's demand is more reasonable. But the unreasonableness of Elsa's claim to the full cake does not invalidate her entitlement to a share of the cake; it only invalidates her particular distributive claim. Applied to recognition: the unreasonable claim that, say, Dutch deserves superior recognition does not affect the reasonability of granting recognition for Dutch, along with equal recognition for other languages. Both Elsa and Dutch are entitled to equal shares. So we can preserve the language of dignity without also taking its inegalitarian history on board. As Jeremy Waldron put this point based on Gregory Vlastos: we should be like a "caste society with just one caste (and a very high caste at that). Every man a Brahmin" (Waldron 2012b, p. 34).[5]

The two interests I have defended – in life-world access and in dignity – call for different recognitional measures. The life-world interest is realised by policies that enable groups to grant their members life-world access, such as through publicly-subsidized mother-tongue education, state funding for cultural associations, and the promotion of group-specific media such as public radio and television stations. This realisation of the life-world access interest does not of itself demand *equal* recognition; only sufficient access is required. This is different for the dignity interest: beyond some minimal absolute measures (such as the absence of public denouncements of the identity), dignity in itself mandates equality: what is required is the same level of recognition enjoyed by other groups with similar dignity interests. Indeed, granting one group a higher status makes all the others experience second-class status.

At the same time, there are many cases where the life-world and the dignity interest mutually reinforce each other. If one group receives subsidized mother-tongue education in order to realize access to a linguistic tradition for its speakers, another group may see it as an insult to their equal status and dignity if they do not also receive the same benefit. Here, the dignity case for equal treatment provides support for the satisfaction of the life-world interest. Conversely, the life-world case for such mother-tongue education also provides independent support for those groups who already see it as a matter of honor and equal respect that they are also, just like the other groups, granted the right to mother-tongue education.

II AGAINST MONORECOGNITION: EQUALITY

Having identified two interests in recognition, I now turn to the manner in which these interests are to be distributed. I submit that, if the proposed distribution of identity interest satisfaction is to qualify as just, it will need to meet a standard of equality. In particular, members from different language groups must be treated with equal concern: if two groups have reasonable demands in order to satisfy fundamental interests, then what is given to the members of one group must be equally given to the members of the other group. If material recognition is to be politically provided, it has to be equally provided for all, not only for some and not more for some than for others.

Two types of theories do not belong to the family of equal recognition theories (Section III will specify and defend one member within that family): nonrecognition theories (which hold that identity is not recognition-worthy) and non-egalitarian recognition theories. The former was addressed in the previous section. My target

---

[5] For a fuller analysis of why the unreasonability of dignity claims does not invalidate the dignity interest, see De Schutter (2023).

now is recognitional non-egalitarianism or monorecognitionism: the view that we ought to recognize the identity interests of some more than those of others.

Such non-egalitarian distribution of recognition gives rise to the recognitional injustice of misrecognition. Misrecognition can come in two forms (see De Schutter 2014). *Intergroup misrecognition* occurs when one group's recognitional stakes get priority over those of other groups. *Intragroup misrecognition* occurs when the recognitional interests of some members of a group get priority over those of other members of the same group.

An example of an *intergroup misrecognition* is the recognition of language groups in linguistically mixed areas through the "linguistic territoriality principle" (LTP). The LTP prescribes territorially demarcating zones within which language recognition is to be restricted. On the strong version of the LTP, each territorial unit should extend material recognition to just one language in public education, political institutions, civil administration, and the legal system. Speakers from other languages cannot receive public support for their language. On a weaker version, some recognition can be extended to those other languages, but one local language receives the lion's share of the recognition and functions with the borders of the territory as its "queen" (Van Parijs 2011, p. 147).

The strong version of the LTP is the foundational pillar of the language policy regimes of Belgium and Switzerland. It is also seen as an ideal by several linguistic justice advocates in Québec and Catalonia, where weaker versions of the LTP exist. If such a strong implementation was successful, the Anglophones and Spanish speakers would be stripped of their language rights in Québec and Catalonia respectively.

The problem with the LTP in both versions lies in the fact that the nature of linguistic heterogeneity in the current world makes it impossible to draw or redraw borders such that unilingual zones are the result. When neighborhoods, streets, or even apartments contain members of both groups, as is the case in almost all instances where linguistic justice is a very salient issue and where the LTP is considered or implemented, then any LTP-instantiation will imply a state-backed priority in recognition of the identity interests of some group(s) over the recognition of the interests of minorities, who are then recognitionally treated as second-class citizens. Doing so in my view clashes with the ideal of equal recognition: it sees the interests of some as more important or recognition-worthy than those of others.

Van Parijs, who defends the LTP as a measure of linguistic justice, acknowledges the problem for those who are left on the wrong side of the border after the implementation of the LTP, and argues for extending temporary language rights to such minorities, such as "native" francophones in Flanders. "They can make use of this possibility until they die or move away, without this possibility being extended to any newly born or newly arriving resident" (Van Parijs 2011, p. 167).

But this solution essentially tells the minority that, while they can stay, they will never enjoy a status equal to those of other citizens, because the life-world access and the dignity of the other group(s) are prioritized. For that reason, I see the LTP as an instance of intergroup misrecognition.

Charles Taylor argues, with respect to the goal of granting recognition to a national group: "In the modern world it will always be the case that not all those living as citizens under a certain jurisdiction will belong to the national group thus favored." (1995, p. 244). But while Taylor defends such favoritist measures, distinguishing between fundamental liberties that can never be restricted and "privileges and immunities" that can be granted to particular groups (1995, p. 247); on my argument a theory of recognitional justice should reject them because they fall outside of the scope of equal recognition.

Let us move on to the second category. *Intragroup misrecognition*[6] occurs often when group members implement measures to ensure the survival of a group's language or culture on a given territorial unit but thereby restrict the language entitlements of some. A controversial example is Québec's Loi 101/Bill 101, which seeks to prevent children from French-speaking families from attending English-medium public schools in Québec – essentially by restricting access to those schools to children who have at least one parent who was educated in English in Canada. The bill's purpose is to ensure the survival of the French language in Québec.

From the point of view of the fair provision of recognition, the problem with a survivalist defense of policies of monorecognition is that the protection of the identity interests of the pro-surivalists requires the restriction of the interests of those who shift or assimilate (De Schutter 2014, p. 1042). As long as there are no changers, there is no reason to recognize the other language. Yet the very moment people start shifting, it is no longer fair to restrict all or most public recognition to the stayers, because if we are interested in legitimate language recognition, the language recognition of all must count. In such cases, people make different choices out of the available linguistic options, and there are *stayers* and *changers* (De Schutter 2014, p. 1044). Equal recognition implies that stayers and changers are equally recognition-worthy; it is incompatible with giving stayers priority. In fact, when some members of a group change their language identity, the language recognition argument tracks them and supports recognizing their new language identities, while providing support for the language identity interests for the stayers as well.

Charles Taylor argues that societies ought not to be "neutral between those who value remaining true to the culture of our ancestors and those who might want to cut

---

[6] My use of this concept is indebted to what Kymlicka calls "internal restrictions." Kymlicka and I reject internal restrictions. But Kymlicka appears to limit this concept to measures that seek to protect "the *historical customs or religious character* of an ethnic or national group through limitations on the basic civil liberties of its members" (1995, p. 44, see also 1995, p. 152 and 2001, p. 60; italics mine). What I call intragroup misrecognition is broader: it is not limited to intragroup measures that protect the cultural character, but includes measures that protect the existence of the group as a distinct group through limiting the choices of those who would want to assimilate to another language or culture.

loose in the name of some individual goal of self-development" (1995, p. 246). But I think not attempting to maintain such neutrality in the domain of language policy is an example of intragroup misrecognition. Pluralistic societies should in my view set out to do what Taylor rejects: to uphold a form of identitarian proceduralism such that each citizen can compose her own identity structure from the available material recognition granted by the state to the various identity groups.

III RECOGNITION PLURALISM: THE EQUAL SERVICES ACCOUNT

I hope to have made it credible that there is a case for accepting a pluralism of identity interests that should be equally recognized. What does equal identity recognition amount to?

It is important to distinguish two different modes of equal identity recognition, the basic logic of which I derive from Charles Taylor (1995, p. 248) and Alan Patten (2014, pp. 119–123). I call them generic and group-specific recognition. Generic recognition realizes identical treatment through material recognitional disestablishment. This approach confers equal recognition-worthiness to all, by conferring zero material recognition. The state keeps it hands off cultural policies: it is culturally and linguistically "neutral" in the disestablished sense of the term.[7] Indeed, both life-world benefits and dignity are equally distributed by the state when it grants material recognition to no group. For example, in a society where some people prefer blue shirts and others prefer yellow shirts, constitutional neutrality over shirt color standards is fair to all: all else being equal, everyone can access or exhibit their own preferred color identity and no status priority occurs.

The second mode is to hand out portions of material recognition to each of the groups through group-specific measures. Group-specific recognition can realize equal recognition through such things as subsidized mother-tongue education or healthcare, the requirement on behalf of supreme court judges to be proficient in the constitutive languages of the state, or the redrawing of internal state boundaries in order to provide distinct sub-state nations with self-government.

Where it is possible, mode one is often to be preferred, as the default mode of dealing with diversity. But from the point of view of recognitional equality, there are two conditions under which there is a case for switching from mode one to mode two. Firstly, there are many dimensions of state policy that cannot be culturally disestablished. The state "cannot help but give at least partial establishment to a culture when it decides which language is to be used in public schooling, or in the provision of state services" (Kymlicka 1995, p. 111). When the state cannot

---

[7] In a similar analysis, Alan Patten calls this neutrality as disestablishment *privatization*. Privatization is one of the forms that his preferred "neutrality of treatment" can take; another is evenhandedness (Patten 2014, pp. 119–121).

be disestablished for the policies it wants[8] to pursue, the best means of granting equal status to all is to provide evenhanded portions of material recognition.[9] When Singapore makes the Chinese language a part of public education, it should also do so for the languages Tamil and Malay (which it does). If the state symbolically mentions one of South Africa's languages in the constitution, it should mention all the languages. If the identity is strongly felt, and if the state cannot avoid to or chooses to distribute recognition, it must do so evenhandedly (Carens 2000).

The second condition is instantiated by the life-world access interest. Even in policy domains or situations where disestablishment is possible, the interest in cultural and linguistic life-world access mandates stepping out of generic recognition in order to give special material recognition to minority groups whose members risk losing access to their cultural and linguistic life-world due to, for example, market forces or the strong assimilationist pull of another culture.

For these reasons, we should in many cases grant material recognition to identity groups. And we should avoid doing so in a way that realizes recognitional injustice by instantiating monorecognition either through intergroup or intragroup misrecognition. Instead we should distribute recognition pluralistically, granting equal portions of material recognition to all.

To do so, recognitional pluralism needs a principle of equality. Consider the following two candidate principles: the *equal services* principle and the *equal per capita principle*. I see these as two members of the family of equal recognition theories. Of these two I defend the first.[10]

The equal services principle holds that (roughly) equal public services must be provided in the state's official languages. These are the languages in which the state speaks, in its constitution, during official ceremonies, when its anthem is sung, when organizing public education (either through bilingual schools or unilingual schools in the various languages), and in the schoolbooks it subsidizes, when its policy interacts with citizens, when the prime minister addresses the population, when citizens address its civil servants for administrative issues, in the funding of its hospitals (either through requiring bilingualism among hospital personnel or buy providing multiple unilingual hospitals), and so on. It does so in principle without regard to the actual number of speakers: if a language is an official language, then the relevant service will be delivered in it, even if that group is significantly smaller in size than a majority group or experiences strong assimilationist pull from another language.

---

[8] In many cases, disestablishment is possible (by avoiding policymaking altogether) but not preferable. The state could for instance choose not to provide public education. But once the state does provide education, it is subject to the demands of recognitional justice, including the linguistic justice claims on the part of minorities for mother-tongue education, for example.

[9] See Joseph Carens for this conception of justice as evenhandedness (2000).

[10] Here I follow and extend the argument developed in De Schutter 2017.

Here is one practical example: the principles behind the language policy model instantiated in the Belgian capital region of Brussels embody this equal services account. French dwarfs the Dutch in Brussels in terms of numbers of speakers, but public services are provided in both languages. So the language policy principle of Brussels is the opposite of the LTP; it aims to provide comparable services to both language groups. Healthcare, administration, education, and museums can be accessed in both languages. Judges and police officers are legally expected to be bilingual. Official documents (the voting ballot, the tax form etc.) are produced in both languages.

The second, equal per capita principle of equal recognition holds that equal per-capita shares of public assistance are to be allocated to both groups (Patten 2014; see for a similar proposal Gans 2016). In Patten's version, we imagine granting everyone equal-per-capita portions of the available budget for language recognition. Since each citizen can be expected to donate their portion toward the support their own language identity, the majority language will receive more portions than minority languages. This may be suboptimal from the point of view of the minority but it is the result of a fair distribution. As a result of this fair distribution, "a more restricted set of public services may be offered in less widely spoken languages, or speakers of such languages might be expected to travel farther to find services in their own language, or the eligibility of such people to receive services in their own language may be constrained by a 'where numbers warrant' proviso" (2014, p. 200). For this reason, the per-capita conception of equality can also be called arithmetic or numerical equality (Gans 2016, p. 98).

Because of their higher numbers, majorities have scale advantages in the organization of public services. For example, the printing cost of schoolbooks, city renovation brochures, or voting instructions will be lower per page in the majority language. But due to such scale advantages, a per capita system may render it impossible for the speakers of different language groups to enjoy roughly equivalent services. To correct for this, the equal services approach will typically grant a higher-than-per-capita portion of the available recognition to the minority, so comparable services can be offered to both groups. In such cases, the equal-services approach takes equal interest recognition to imply giving more absolute material recognition (in the form of a higher than per capita share of available resources) to the minority language group. This results in a form of *inverse* per-capita distribution (De Schutter 2017, p. 78): the lower the number, the higher the resources per capita.

To be clear, the equal services approach does not in and of itself mandate inverse per-capita prorating. It just stipulates that comparable services must be offered to both groups, and that whatever recognitional budgetary distributions are required to make these possible must be in place. This will often amount to higher per capita shares for the minority but other divisions may be mandated as well. For instance, particular geographical obstacles may drive up the costs of language provision for the majority: if the area where the majority members live is very thinly populated or is hard to reach whereas the minority does not have these disadvantages, it can be equally or even more expensive per capita to realize similar services for the majority than for the minority. In such cases, a per capita division or inverse pro-rating to the benefit of the majority is what is called for by the equal services principle.

How can this equal services view be justified? I think fairness speaks in its favor. The parties in a hypothetical original position who know they are members of an existing national-cultural-linguistic group in society but not of *which* group, have good reasons to ensure that, in the linguistic social contract they are asked to provide and agree to, public institutions enable life-world access and express equal dignity for all groups, including the minority. Since under a per capita division life-world access and dignity will be in many cases not or unequally realized, it is irrational for the parties to the linguistic contract to agree to such a per capita regime. Doing so would mean that, in the original position, they take the gamble that they will be majority language speakers, and thereby put their life-world access and dignity up for grabs in the event they speak a minority language (De Schutter 2017, p. 84). Instead, their most rational solution is a principle of recognitional parity entailing – in most cases – more funding for linguistically needy groups, with the aim to enable more or less comparable services for all.

Many of my examples have so far come from the field of language policy, but recognitional pluralism and its equal services account can be applied to other domains of national-cultural identity as well, such as to official national holidays, the protection of holy sites, and the inclusion of cultural symbols in official speeches and the constitution. An additional important domain of application is the distribution of self-government in multinational states. In multinational states, recognitional pluralism can be realized through multinational federalism, as I will now argue.

Multinational federations such as Belgium, Canada, and Spain (a quasi-federation) grant portions of self-government to multiple national-cultural units, while also retaining an overarching form of state-wide self-government. In multinational states, federalism is in my view justified because it instantiates recognitional fairness. It does so in two ways: by realizing intergroup and intragroup recognitional fairness.[11]

Firstly, multinational federations realize *intergroup* fairness because they distribute evenhanded portions of material recognition (in the form of self-government rights) to multiple national-cultural groups, giving sub-state nations such as the Flemish, the Québécois, and the Catalans partial self-government. And they often do so in ways that give more per capita recognition to smaller segments than to bigger ones, for example, through over-representation instead of equal per capita numbers per province in the federal Senate in Canada (where, for example, British

---

[11] I have argued for this conception of federalism as fairness at greater length in De Schutter 2011, which I here reinterpret from the point of view of the distinction between intragroup and intergroup recognition.

Columbia has an equal amount of six seats as Newfoundland and Labrador, despite being ten times as populated), or through other majority-limiting measures such as parity requirements between members of the two main language groups in the government in Belgium. Refusing such partial national autonomy is an instance of monorecognition in the form of *intergroup misrecognition*: it grants all the self-government to the majority nation, thereby realizing a non-egalitarian distribution of recognition.[12] Federalism, instead, installs measure of recognitional fairness.

But secondly, federalism is also well-equipped to realize *intragroup* fairness, because federalism fairly distributes national-cultural recognition in cases where not all identity preferences can get their way, as when groups are internally divided about national identity. In multinational settings, we often find empirical instances of intragroup identity pluralism, with some members of the component nation (e.g., Flanders or Catalonia) referring to the sub-state nation (Flanders, Catalonia) and others to the state-wide nation (Belgium, Spain) as their sole or primary form of national-cultural identity, while still others claim dual identities to both nations (Swyngedouw et al. 2015 for Belgium; Garcia et al. 2017 for Spain; Bilodeau 2015 et al. for Canada). In such settings, federalism can in my view be seen as an evenhanded solution to the identity pluralism that exists among the citizens of the sub-state units. Federalism is then justified as a fair compromise between those in Flanders who claim that Flanders is their primary national identity source and those in Flanders who refer to Belgium as their primary national identity context. As a result, both Flemish secession and Belgian unitarism would compel some to experience *intragroup misrecognition*: secession would be great for those with a Flemish-only identity but bad for those with a Belgian-only identity; a non-federal unitary Belgian state would be great for the latter but bad for the former. Federalism, instead, offers a fair solution in such cases, by the avoiding the conferral of all material recognition to a particular national subgroup.

One note before concluding. I have argued for equal recognition of national-cultural identity *interests*. Equal *interest* recognition does not necessarily imply equal *language* recognition or equal recognition of *national cultures*; sometimes, unequal recognition of a language best serves the individuals' identity structure. For example, some people with dual identities have lower identity stakes in one of their identities: less in their Flemish than in their Belgian national identity, for instance (or vice versa), or less in their dialect than in the standard language. We therefore do not need to give lower-stake national identities or dialects *equal* recognition. What we need is equal recognition of the overall identity interests, not necessarily equal recognition of nations or languages. This means that some form of *subordinate recognition* for one of the nested nationalities or for the dialect can be consistent

---

[12] Unitarism in multinational states can also result from a *nonrecognitionalist* stance, when the state rejects the recognition-worthiness of sub-state nations for reasons of, say, efficiency, democracy, or equality.

with equal identity recognition. Also the recognition of immigrant languages and cultures can be thought of in this vein: the non-identity and identity interests that immigrants have in their heritage language typically deserve recognition but the mode of immigrant language recognition can often legitimately be subordinate to the recognition enjoyed by the majority language.[13]

CONCLUSION

I have discerned three ways of responding to national-cultural and linguistic diversity: (1) no recognition-worthiness, (2) recognitional priority to one identity, and (3) recognitional pluralism guided by a principle of equal recognition. Within the family of equal recognition theories, I have defended the equal services account and I applied it to language policy and multinational federalism. In closing I would like to respond to one possible objection.

The objection is that not all identities are recognition-worthy. Take unreasonable identity claims, such as claims by racist or manifestly illiberal groups. These too may uphold a life-world or express demands of dignity. We could solve this problem in two ways, corresponding to two ways in which these identities are problematic. Firstly, we might identify a liberal-democratic filter for any recognitional demands of identity. Only demands that the filter allows are recognition-worthy candidates for material recognition. In a similar way, Honneth argues that only recognitional demands that increase individuality and social inclusion are legitimate (Fraser and Honneth 2003, p. 187). Secondly, my theory makes a distinction between the interest in identity and the distribution of the satisfaction of these interests. For the latter, I appeal to a principle of equality. Unreasonable identity claims, such as those that seek to privilege one group's identity over all others are explicitly ruled out by this equality principle. They yield misrecognition.

ACKNOWLEDGEMENTS

I am grateful to Richard Bellamy, Simone Chambers, Jacob Levy, and Jeff King for many helpful comments and suggestions.

RECOMMENDED READING

De Schutter, H. (2011). Federalism as fairness, The Journal of Political Philosophy 19(2), 167–189.
De Schutter, H. (2014). Testing for Linguistic Injustice: territoriality and pluralism. *Nationalities Papers*, 42:6, 1034–1052.
De Schutter, H. (2017). Two principles of equal language recognition. *Critical Review of International Social and Political Philosophy*, 20:1, 75–87.

---

[13] I cannot make the full case for this claim here. See De Schutter (2022) for my account of linguistic justice for immigrants.

De Schutter, H. (2020). Intralinguistic Justice. In Y. Peled and D. Weinstock (eds.) *Language Ethics*. McGill University Press, 146–177.

Fraser, N. & Honneth, A. (2003). *Redistribution or Recognition? A Political- Philosophical Exchange*, London: Verso.

Habermas, J. (1994). Struggles for Recognition in the Democratic Constitutional State. In A. Gutmann, ed., *Multiculturalism: Examining the Politics of Recognition*. Princeton: Princeton University Press, pp. 107–148.

Honneth, A. (1995). *The Struggle for Recognition: The Moral Grammar of Social Conflicts*, Cambridge: Polity Press.

Machiavelli, N. (2005). 'A Discourse or Dialogue Concerning Our Language' (ed. and tr. W. J. Landon), In. Landon, W. J., Politics, Patriotism, and Language : Niccolò Machiavelli's "secular patria" and the Creation of an Italian National Identity. New York: Peter Lang, pp. 129–142.

Markell, P. (2003). *Bound by Recognition*, Princeton: Princeton University Press.

Okin, S. M. (1999). *Is Multiculturalism Bad for Women?* Edited by J. Cohen, J. Howard and M. Nussbaum. Princeton: Princeton University Press.

Patten, A. (2014). *Equal Recognition: The Moral Foundations of Minority Rights*, Princeton: Princeton University Press.

Philips, A. (2007). *Multiculturalism without Culture*, Princeton: Princeton University Press.

Tamir, Y. (2019). *Why Nationalism*, Princeton: Princeton University Press.

Taylor, C. (1994). The Politics of Recognition. In A. Gutmann, ed., *Multiculturalism: Examining the Politics of Recognition*. Princeton: Princeton University Press, pp. 25–74.

Tully, J. (1995). *Strange Multiplicity: Constitutionalism in an Age of Diversity*, Cambridge: Cambridge University Press.

Young, I. M. (1990). *Justice and the Politics of Difference*, Princeton: Princeton University Press.

PART II

Modalities

10

Impartiality

Matthew H. Kramer

Impartiality as a property of government is central to many of the major constitutional concerns of liberal democracy. This essay will tersely consider the nature and implications of impartiality in three main areas that are of particular constitutional significance: the rule of law; the distinction between the right and the good; and freedom of expression. Because of constraints of space, each of the discussions below is no more than a sketch of the complex matters that are at issue in debates over impartiality.

I IMPARTIALITY AS A DIMENSION OF THE RULE OF LAW

As an aspect of the objectivity of law, impartiality consists of disinterestedness and open-mindedness.[1] So construed, it can also be designated as "detachedness" or "impersonality." It is to be contrasted with bias and partisanship, but also with impetuousness and whimsicalness (though sometimes not with genuine randomness). This dimension of legal objectivity, which is central to any constitutional guarantee of due process of law, pertains above all to the judgments and procedures through which laws are given effect. Like some other aspects of the objectivity of law, it is a scalar property rather than an all-or-nothing property; it is realized to varying degrees.

Impartiality is, obviously, a lack of partiality. Among the things essential to it is either the absence of any known personal stake in one's decision or an ability to let one's decision be unaffected by one's awareness that one has a stake therein. Somebody usually has a personal stake in a decision if he himself or a close relative or friend stands to benefit significantly in the event that the decision goes in some direction(s) rather than in some contrary direction(s). To be sure, such a stake is not present if a person has a close relative or friend on each side of the issue under consideration. For example, when a parent has to decide which of her two children should be allowed to play with a certain toy, her impartiality is not undermined by

---

[1] In this section, I draw intermittently on some portions of Kramer (2007, pp. 53–68).

the fact that she has two close relatives who each hope to benefit from her decision. Precisely because the personal stake of each of those relatives is offset by that of the other, the parent's impartiality is unimpaired. When there is not an even balance of this sort on each side of an issue, however, a decision-maker's impartiality is tarnished by her knowing that the fortunes of a close relative or friend will be significantly affected by the upshot of her deliberations.

Impartiality is strongest only if there is no personal stake on the part of anyone who renders a judgment on some matter. However, especially in connection with the creation of laws but even sometimes in connection with the administration of them, the avoidance of a personal stake for each decision-maker is not altogether possible. Consider, for example, the legislators who have to vote on a bill that will affect the distribution of the burdens of taxation among people with differing levels of income. If the proposed bill will be sweeping in its effects, then every legislator will to some degree have a personal stake in the outcome of the vote. Much the same can be said about judges and administrators who have to interpret central provisions of the bill or who have to arrive at other determinations that will significantly bear on the distribution of the burdens of taxation. If the absence of any personal stakes in these legislative and judicial and administrative decisions were prerequisite to the impartiality of the processes through which the decisions are reached, then those processes could not be impartial. Every legislator or judge or administrator will have a personal stake in the aforementioned decisions (and in a number of other determinations that have to be rendered in the course of anyone's fulfillment of legislative or judicial or administrative responsibilities). We should not conclude, however, that impartiality concerning these matters is impossible. In regard to any decision for which the avoidance of a direct personal stake on the part of the decision-maker(s) is not feasible – because every legal official will have such a stake – each official involved should strive for impartiality by seeking to prescind from his personal prospects as he arrives at the decision in question. There are no grounds for thinking that people are incapable of mentally stepping back from their personal fortunes in order to arrive at disinterested perspectives on matters with which they have to deal. Efforts to attain to such perspectives may fail quite frequently, but they are not inevitably doomed to failure.

Like disinterestedness, open-mindedness is an essential component of impartiality as a dimension of legal objectivity. One evident ingredient of open-mindedness is the absence of prejudice and favoritism. If some person P harbors special animosity or special fondness toward certain people – particularly on grounds such as race and religion and ethnicity, which are unrelated to people's merits and probity – then P lacks the open-mindedness that is essential for reaching impartial decisions on matters that pit such people against other people. To be sure, P might still be able to render impartial judgments on matters that involve only the sorts of people toward whom she feels peculiar antipathy or affection. If P is biased in favor of Hispanic people, for instance, she might nevertheless be suitably impartial when passing judgment on a contract-law dispute between two Hispanic businessmen. However, insofar as her prejudices do bear on an issue which she is called upon to resolve – and, thus, insofar as those prejudices are likely to inflect her stance on that issue – her perspective is not open-minded and is therefore not impartial.

Another central constituent of open-mindedness (and thus of impartiality) is the absence of whimsicalness and impetuosity. Someone who plunges ahead without attending to the actualities of a situation is failing to display open-mindedness, just as dramatically as someone whose prejudices blind him to those actualities. To be open-minded in addressing some problem is in part to be scrupulously ready to learn of the sundry facts from which the problem arises. Albeit somebody who proceeds on the basis of caprices and conjectures might fortuitously arrive at a correct decision in any particular context – as might somebody who proceeds on the basis of prejudices – the outcome will not have been reached through a process that is designed to avoid favoring or disfavoring anyone arbitrarily.

In a system of law, judges and other legal officials need to become acquainted with all the reasonably ascertainable facts that bear upon the legal questions which they have to answer. This requirement of official open-mindedness can of course be satisfied through more than one set of techniques for the gathering of information. While the adversarial structure of disputes and prosecutions in Anglo-American law involves one such set of techniques, the very different structure of disputes and prosecutions in many civil-law countries involves a different set of information-gathering techniques that can be just as fitting. Whatever may be the exact procedures that are employed, legal officials will not be performing their roles in an open-minded manner unless they do their best to attune themselves to the specificities of the situations on which they are passing judgment. For that purpose, it is crucial that each party to a legal dispute be allowed to participate in the information-gathering processes – whether those processes are adversarial or inquisitorial. Since some key aspects of the relevant facts may be missed if the parties do not have opportunities to express their views, the provision of such opportunities is indispensable for the impartiality of a legal system's workings. In the absence of such opportunities, those workings may be placing certain parties at a disadvantage simply because the legal officials are being kept ignorant of vital information. Also indispensable, clearly, are opportunities for participation by witnesses or by other people who are in possession of germane information. If such sources of information are excluded from the processes by which legal officials determine the jural consequences of people's conduct, those processes will be conjectural rather than open-mindedly sensitive to complexities. Officials who rely on surmises are hardly doing their best to avoid arbitrariness.

A caveat should be entered here. Although impartiality does consist in detachedness, it does not in any way entail a lack of empathetic understanding of human actions and intentions. Legal-governmental officials who have to pass judgment on countless instances of the conduct of others will frequently not be able to perform their functions adequately unless they grasp the typical mainsprings of human behavior and the specific mainsprings of the behavior of particular individuals (Nussbaum 1995). They have to be able to identify themselves with other people sufficiently to fathom why those people have acted in certain ways. Such identification does not constitute approval, and therefore does not constitute a departure from impartiality. Though officials may well countenance some of the motivational patterns which they encounter, they may well deplore other such patterns; the sheer feat of gaining an empathetic understanding of those patterns, a feat that can take place in response to evil conduct as well as in response to laudable conduct, is per se neither a condonation nor a condemnation. It is fully consistent with impartiality. It is indeed often essential for impartiality, since officials cannot guard against arbitrariness unless they base their decisions on all reasonably accessible information that is both accurate and relevant. In many contexts, that information squarely includes what can be gleaned through empathetic understanding. (Given the importance of empathy in adjudicative and administrative settings, the importance of including people from diverse backgrounds throughout the ranks of adjudicators and administrators is equally great.)

Impartiality to quite a high degree is a feature of every legal system of governance, regardless of whether the system is liberal-democratic or malignly repressive (or something in between). In liberal-democratic systems of governance, however, the property of impartiality also serves to encapsulate certain moral ideals. One strand of those ideals is directly tied to the epistemic reliability of impartiality. That is, insofar as decision-making is not swayed by self-interested motivations or skewed by prejudices or clouded by ignorance, it is considerably more likely to yield determinately correct results. When legal officials are called upon to reach decisions and to answer legal questions, they are endeavoring – or should be endeavoring, at least in a liberal-democratic system of law – to render the decisions and answers prescribed by the applicable legal norms. They are seeking to construe and effectuate those norms in accordance with the terms thereof. For that end, a posture of impartiality is crucial. If legal officials allow their deliberations to be inflected by their own selfish interests or by invidious biases or by uninformed impulses, they are substantially reducing the probability that those deliberations will culminate in correct decisions. They are thereby shirking their legal responsibility to give effect to the laws of their system and to foster the values embodied in those laws. Because the laws of a liberal-democratic system of governance are benign, the officials are likewise shirking their moral responsibilities.

Note that these observations about the epistemic reliability of impartial decision-making do not overlook the fact that the officials in virtually any system of law will be legally empowered and permitted to exercise discretion in some of their law-effectuating activities. Whether the norms of the system which confer the discretionary authority on the officials are explicitly formulated or not, they exist as second-order norms with legally dispositive force. As such, they themselves have to be construed and applied by the officials along with the other laws of the system. If the approach of the officials to those norms is marred by departures from impartiality, then the likelihood of incorrect applications of the norms is greatly increased. Engaging in such departures, the officials are heightening the risk that the manner or the occasion of some exercise of discretion will not be in keeping with what they have been authorized to do. Impartiality, in short, is as important for the epistemic and ethical reliability of officials' discretionary decisions as it is for the epistemic and ethical reliability of their other legal decisions.

One major ethical reason for insisting on legal officials' impartiality, then, is focused on the outcomes of their processes of decision-making. Impartiality markedly increases the probability that those outcomes in a liberal-democratic system of governance will be ethically correct. Another major consideration in favor of impartiality is focused on the processes of decision-making themselves. While helping to ensure that legal norms take effect in accordance with their terms, the impartiality of officials additionally helps to ensure that the operations of a legal system are fair and are perceived as fair. Their impartiality is not a sufficient condition for the fairness of those operations, of course, but it is a necessary condition. When a decision-making procedure lacks impartiality, it is doubly injurious to every person D who is disadvantaged by the upshot of the procedure. It is injurious because the upshot itself is of course detrimental to D's interests, but also because the whole procedure bespeaks contempt – or, at the very least, a dearth of respect – for D. That second type of harm would have been present even if the outcome of the procedure had fortuitously gone in D's favor.[2] If the absence of impartiality stems from the dominance of self-seeking motivations on the part of the officials involved, then their pursuit of their own interests at the expense of D is a cavalier devaluation of him. That devaluation is an ignominious slight, quite apart from the disadvantageousness of the officials' ultimate decision. If the absence of impartiality is due to prejudice against D, then the indignity inflicted upon him is even more noxious and palpable. If the absence of impartiality resides in a state of uninformedness that could have been overcome without unreasonable difficulty, then the officials are displaying the meagerness of their concern to do justice to D.

Whenever officials stray from the ideal of impartiality, they derogate from the objectivity of their legal system by overweeningly infusing its operations with elements of their own outlooks. They skew those operations as they let their decisions be shaped by their selfish interests or their prejudices and predilections or their impulses and conjectures. They thereby deviate from their responsibility to gauge

---

[2] Although an aleatory procedure for decision-making has sometimes been commended as impartial, and although it can indeed be impartial in some contexts – such as the selection of people for jury duty (Duxbury 1999, pp. 74–81) – it lacks impartiality in the contexts of law-application which I am discussing here. In those latter contexts, an unweighted aleatory procedure will be heavily biased against any party to a legal proceeding whose case (on the merits and on the available evidence) is stronger than the case of the rival party or parties in that legal proceeding. Even more important, an aleatory procedure of any kind will bespeak the contempt or disrespect to which I refer in the text.

the legal consequences of people's conduct by reference to the terms of the applicable legal norms. The officials gauge those consequences instead by reference to aspects of themselves. In so doing, they increase the likelihood of their arriving at morally inappropriate outcomes, and they diminish the procedural fairness of their legal system's workings. They evince disrespect for the people who are subject to their rule, and they hazard the risk that those people will develop a commensurate sense of disrespect for them.

II IMPARTIALITY AS LIBERAL NEUTRALITY

In liberal political philosophy during the past several decades, the ideal of impartiality as neutrality among reasonable conceptions of the good has loomed large.[3] Although that ideal for a system of governance was given voice in various forms by classical exponents of liberal democracy such as John Stuart Mill, its present-day prominence is due chiefly to the writings of John Rawls and Ronald Dworkin. Rawlsians in particular have laid stress on the proposition that every system of governance is morally forbidden to show partiality toward some reasonable conceptions of the good over others.

Reasonable Conceptions of the Good

Conceptions of the good are accounts of what is valuable or worthwhile or excellent or conducive to human flourishing. Such conceptions are differentiated from conceptions of justice; that is, ideas about the good are differentiated from ideas about the right. Thus, when Rawlsians and others maintain that governments are morally obligated to remain neutral among reasonable conceptions of the good, they are contending that governments are morally obligated to remain neutral among reasonable theses about the good that are not equivalent to doctrines of justice (though those theses might be combined with principles of justice in comprehensive creeds such as religions or wide-ranging ethical codes).

Whereas a theory of justice distinguishes between right and wrong by articulating standards that prescribe what is morally required or morally forbidden, a conception of the good distinguishes between good and bad by articulating standards that prescribe what is valuable or worthwhile or outstanding. Conceptions of the good specify virtues or modes of excellence or grounds for commendation. They are chiefly evaluative in their tenor, though of course their evaluations are characteristically associated with normative conclusions.

Naturally, Rawlsians and Dworkinians do not hold that systems of governance are morally required to remain neutral among all conceptions of the good. Rather, they hold that such systems are morally required to remain neutral among all *reasonable*

---

[3] I have warily explored this ideal at great length in Kramer (2017).

conceptions of the good. Indeed, their neutralism would be utterly implausible if it were not qualified in that fashion, since nobody could credibly submit that governments are morally required to remain neutral in relation to the conceptions of the good respectively harbored by sadists and racists and paedophiles. Such a qualification, however, gives rise to a need for an explication of the property of reasonableness.

Rawls took the property of reasonableness to consist in an embrace of basic tenets of liberalism and in a disposition toward liberal tolerance. A conception of the good is reasonable if and only if it is consistent with those tenets and with such tolerance. Hence, a reasonable person (in the Rawlsian sense) accepts that other adults of sound mind in her society are free and equal, and she likewise accepts that a political society is properly understood and arranged as a system of fair cooperation for the benefit of everyone. Adults of sound mind are equal in that there are no natural hierarchies among them that can appositely be translated into political hierarchies. People are of course endowed unequally with attributes such as strength and agility and intelligence, but each adult of sound mind is endowed with two basic moral powers: a capacity for a sense of justice and a capacity for a conception of the good. By dint of possessing these two moral powers, every adult of sound mind is free. Moreover, although those powers are themselves possessed unequally among people, all adults of sound mind are endowed with them "to the requisite minimum degree to be fully cooperating members of society" (Rawls 1993, p. 19). In that fundamental respect, all adults of sound mind are equal. The deliberative and cooperative faculties that make persons free are also what make them equal to one another.

Free and equal persons are to interact with one another in a society that is a fair scheme of cooperation for the benefit of each of them. Anyone who is reasonable will recognize that her own status as a free person is paralleled by that of every one of her fellow citizens.[4] She will thus recognize that any scheme of social cooperation is illegitimate unless its operations are fair not only to her but also to every one of those fellow citizens. As a reasonable person, furthermore, she is disposed to participate in such a scheme and to abide by its norms – provided, naturally, that others will similarly comply with those norms.

Of course, even though every reasonable person grasps that other adults of sound mind are likewise free and equal persons and that any system of societal interaction will therefore be illegitimate unless its workings are fair to everyone, there is no basis for supposing that all such persons will converge on a single set of principles of justice in their views of what their system of societal interaction should be. Whatever Rawls may have thought during the early stages of his career, he was well aware in *Political Liberalism* that there is room for reasonable disagreement over the specifics of principles of justice (1993, p. 226). Hence, the reasonableness of a

---

[4] Like Rawls, I use the term "citizen" to designate everyone who is "a normal and fully cooperating member of society over a complete life" (Rawls 1993, p. 18).

conception of the good does not depend on the congruence of that conception with some particular set of principles of justice. Rather, it depends on the congruence of that conception with the broader axioms of liberalism that have been recounted here. A conception of the good is reasonable only if it allows that all adults of sound mind are free and equal persons and that the basic institutions which structure the interaction of such persons are illegitimate unless they are fair to everyone.

Closely related to what has just been said about the multiplicity of reasonable standards of justice is the second main aspect of Rawlsian reasonableness. Rawls observed that, in any society where extreme manipulation and oppression are not wielded, certain features of human beings and of the complicated ethical issues which they have to address are such as to ensure that people will disagree intractably over those issues even after careful reflection thereon. Those convergence-thwarting features are what Rawls called "the burdens of judgment" (1993, pp. 54–8). A reasonable person understands that the burdens of judgment are operative in human intercourse, and is disposed to be tolerant in recognition of them. A reasonable conception of the good is consistent with such understanding and tolerance.

Because of the burdens of judgment which Rawls recounted at some length, tenacious wrangling over sundry ethical questions is not only possible but also very likely – even among people who are all reasonable. Any reasonable person will recognize the general import of the burdens of judgment, even though of course not every such person will enumerate and formulate those burdens in Rawls's exact wording. That is, any reasonable person will recognize that "many of our most important judgments are made under conditions where it is not to be expected that conscientious persons with full powers of reason, even after free discussion, will all arrive at the same conclusion" (Rawls 1993, p. 58). Apprehending as much, and apprehending that the use of force to suppress reasonable doctrines is itself unreasonable, any reasonable person will be disposed to tolerate numerous conceptions of the good – all reasonable conceptions of the good – espoused by her fellow citizens.

Liberal Neutrality

Rawlsians and other liberal neutralists submit that any system of governance is morally required to maintain a relationship of neutrality between itself and all reasonable conceptions of the good. Having glanced at the general nature of the relata (the reasonable conceptions of the good), we should now ponder the general nature of the relationship. What is the relationship of neutrality which Rawlsians believe to be morally obligatory?

Outside the debates between Rawlsians and their opponents, one of the most common understandings of neutrality pertains to the effects of any policy or decision or law. In the context of those debates, neutrality of effect would consist in leaving unchanged the relative levels of difficulty with which any reasonable conceptions of the good can be realized. That is, a policy or decision or law is neutral in its effect if it does not impede (or facilitate) the fulfillment of any particular reasonable conception of the good to a greater degree than it impedes (or facilitates) the fulfillment of any other reasonable conceptions of the good. Given the relative levels of difficulty with which any reasonable conceptions of the good can be realized in the absence of some policy or decision or law, that same balance of levels of difficulty among the different conceptions will obtain in the presence of the policy or decision or law if the ideal of neutrality of effect has been achieved.

As most participants in the disputation between Rawlsians and their opponents have recognized, the ideal of neutrality of effect across all reasonable conceptions of the good is absurdly infeasible. Virtually every law or policy of any significance – and of impeccable legitimacy – will differentially affect the realizability of reasonable conceptions of the good. A system of governance as a whole will produce differential effects on a vast scale. Even if those multitudinous effects could all be known and charted (*mirabile dictu*), there would be no way of offsetting the differential impacts that would not produce further such effects. As an ideal of political morality, neutrality of effect is a disastrous non-starter. Accordingly, Rawlsians and Dworkinians are not talking about neutrality of effect when they insist that systems of governance should remain neutral among reasonable conceptions of the good. As Rawls himself declared: "Neutrality of effect or influence political liberalism abandons as impracticable" (1993, p. 194).

Whereas hardly any Rawlsians have subscribed to the ideal of neutrality of effect, nearly all of them do espouse the ideal of neutrality of justification. In other words, they believe that the neutrality of any law or policy hinges on the rationale that underlies it. Suppose that some law L, if adopted and implemented, would promote the realization of a reasonable conception of the good CG. Can L's tendency to further the realization of CG be legitimately invoked by the proponents of L as a justification for it? Can such a justification be sufficient to render the adoption of L morally legitimate? Rawlsians answer the second of these questions negatively. They believe that the tendency of L to advance CG is never in itself sufficient to vindicate morally the adoption and implementation of L. Though such a tendency can legitimately be invoked as an ancillary factor in support of L by the proponents thereof, it is only an ancillary factor. Unless those proponents also credibly maintain that some justice-related considerations are sufficient to vindicate morally the exertions of governmental power involved in the implementation of L, their adoption of such a law is non-neutral and is thus morally impermissible. So the Rawlsians contend, with a focus on neutrality of justification.

Unlike the ideal of neutrality of effect, the ideal of neutrality of justification is not outlandishly unattainable. Indeed, the feasibility of gauging the neutrality or non-neutrality of the justifications that underlie laws or policies is the paramount factor that has led most Rawlsians and their allies to favor this conception of neutrality over neutrality of effect. Nonetheless, the ideal of neutrality of justification is unsatisfactory *sans plus* for any liberal neutralists. Its test will fail to disallow a multitude of laws that are non-neutral by any liberal reckoning. Let us consider here one example that can serve to illustrate why neutrality of justification is inadequate as a touchstone for liberal legitimacy. Suppose that the population of a certain country Placatia is divided approximately equally among adherents of the Green religion, the Blue religion, and the Gray religion. Suppose further that a significant number of extreme Bluists are inclined to resort to violence or other forms of abusive behavior if their religion is not treated preferentially by being officially designated as the established faith – with the privileges that are appurtenant to such a status – in Placatia. By contrast, any fanatics among the Greenists and Grayists are too few in number to pose any serious danger of civil unrest. Although the Placatian legal-governmental officials do their best to deal with the specter of violence by improving their operations of policing and by endeavoring to inculcate an ethos of tolerance and mutual respect through their educational system, they eventually conclude that the best way of ensuring civil harmony is to designate Bluism as the established religion within their society. They place Bluism in that favored status not because they believe that its doctrines are true; on the contrary, a majority of the officials are not Bluists, and quite a few of them are not religiously observant at all. Their rationale for elevating Bluism to a special status is focused solely on the preservation of civil order and on the consequent securing of conditions for the prosperity and stability of Placatia.

In these circumstances, the justification that underlies the Placatians' conferral of a privileged position on Bluism is impeccably neutral. Hence, if neutrality of justification is the touchstone for determining whether any law or policy satisfies the constraint of neutrality, the Rawlsians will have to conclude that the designation of Bluism as the established religion of Placatia does indeed satisfy that constraint. To be sure, such a conclusion would not commit the Rawlsians to the further proposition that the establishment of Bluism as the officially endorsed faith in Placatia is morally legitimate. They could maintain that, despite the neutrality of the law under which Bluism has become endowed with a specially privileged status, the assignment of that status to any religion is morally illegitimate in a heterogeneous country like Placatia. Nevertheless, although the Rawlsians in being guided by the principle of neutrality of justification as their lodestar have not ipso facto committed themselves to approving the Placatian policy, they have committed themselves to classifying that policy as unexceptionably neutral. Such a verdict of unexceptionable neutrality is overwhelmingly dubious, for the chief vice of the Placatian policy is that it so grossly favors one reasonable conception of the good – one reasonable comprehensive doctrine – over other such conceptions that are widely endorsed in Placatia. Despite the neutrality of the justification that underlies it, the policy is manifestly non-neutral. (Note that the point made by this example does not hinge on the fact that the situation therein involves non-ideal circumstances in which a government is responding to unjust threats. Elsewhere – in Kramer 2017, pp. 23–4 – I have presented an example that does not involve such circumstances.)

Thus, if we are to fix upon a conception of neutrality that is fully suitable for understanding the debates between Rawlsians and their opponents, we have to move beyond neutrality of justification. To say as much is not to say that the principle of neutrality of justification – like the principle of neutrality of effect – should be jettisoned. It is fine as far as it goes, but it does not go far enough. We need to come up with a conception of neutrality which encompasses neutrality of justification but which also extends more broadly.

To grasp what is at stake in the controversies between liberal neutralists and their opponents, we should attribute to the neutralists a concern not only with the underlying objectives of anyone but also with the means that have been selected for the attainment of those objectives. If a person P deliberately performs an action or brings about a state of affairs as a means of attaining some end, then both the end and the means are intended by P. P has aimed to perform the action or to bring about the state of affairs, just as he has aimed to attain the desired end by means of the action or the state of affairs. A principle of neutrality of means and ends, then, comprises not only a principle of neutrality of justification but also a requirement of neutrality in relation to each of the steps chosen for the furtherance of any goals. By the reckoning of neutralists, a government proceeds illegitimately unless its actions are neutral both in the ends for which they are undertaken and in the means through which the government seeks to fulfill those ends.[5] Let us return here to the scenario of Placatia. Although the establishment of Bluism as the officially recognized and privileged religion in Placatia is neutral in the end which it aims to advance, it is decidedly not neutral in the means chosen for the realization of that end. To further the objective of promoting civil peace and stability – an objective that is neutral among reasonable conceptions of the good – the legal-governmental officials in Placatia have markedly favored one reasonable comprehensive doctrine over others. Thus, although the government's bestowal of a privileged status on Bluism satisfies the constraint of neutrality of justification, it does not satisfy the more demanding constraint of neutrality of means and ends. That more demanding constraint is what Rawlsians and other neutralists should be insisting upon.

Having singled out the conception of neutrality that should be espoused by Rawlsians and Dworkinians, we should now ruminate briefly on the range of the decisions and actions to which the constraint of neutrality applies. This question has divided Rawlsians (and other neutralists) amongst one another. Rawls himself in his later work – with some hesitance, but with moderate clarity – took the view that the requirement of neutrality covers only constitutional essentials and basic matters of justice. He understood the constitutional essentials as the fundamental

---

[5] Note that the neutrality or non-neutrality of the ends and means adopted by legal-governmental officials is not determined by the officials' beliefs (if any) about the neutrality or non-neutrality of those ends and means. Non-neutral ends or means are scarcely rendered neutral through being incorrectly perceived as neutral by the officials who embrace them.

structure and operating principles of a society's legal-governmental system, and he understood the basic matters of justice as the fundamental rights and liberties of citizenship that are comprehended by his first principle of justice (1993, p. 227). At a number of junctures in *Political Liberalism*, Rawls suggested pretty clearly that the constraint of neutrality is applicable only to these constitutional essentials and basic matters of justice. Let us look at only one passage, where Rawls was mulling over the calls of some environmentalists for a fundamental reorientation of the relationship between humanity and the ecosystems of the natural world. He wrote that "the status of the natural world and our proper relation to it is not a constitutional essential or a basic question of justice, as these questions have been specified.... It is a matter in regard to which citizens can vote their nonpolitical values and try to convince other citizens accordingly. The limits of public reason do not apply" (1993, p. 246).

Quite a few liberal neutralists have sided with Rawls on this point, but resistance has been mounted by some other Rawlsians. Jonathan Quong, for example, has argued more sustainedly and forcefully than anyone else against Rawls's stance on the scope of the constraint of neutrality. In the ninth chapter of his 2011 book *Liberalism without Perfection*, Quong engages in a systematic critique of Rawls's stance. Near the outset of that chapter, he announces the conclusion which he will be seeking to vindicate in opposition to Rawls: "I argue, contra Rawls, that the idea of public reason [with its constraint of neutrality] ought to have a much broader scope – that it should regulate all the political decisions in a liberal democratic society" (Quong 2011, p. 258). Quong advances several lines of reasoning in support of his conclusion, but his central point is that the requirement of neutrality among reasonable conceptions of the good is derivative of the general principle that political power cannot legitimately be exercised unless the exertion of such power is fair to everybody affected by it. Quong argues that this general rationale for the requirement of neutrality does not cease to be applicable when the exertions of a government's power pertain to ordinary political matters rather than to constitutional issues or basic questions of justice. Hence, even if Rawls's distinction between the ordinary and the constitutional/basic could be drawn unproblematically, it would not furnish any grounds for confining the reach of the constraint of neutrality. So Quong forcefully contends.

This sketch of liberal neutralism has omitted countless far-reaching complexities that have to be taken into account by any satisfactory investigation of the matter. Having pursued such an investigation at great length elsewhere (Kramer 2017), and having there embraced some major aspects of neutralism while rejecting or transforming some other major aspects, I should here simply emphasize that impartiality in the form of liberal neutralism is one of the most oft-discussed foci of contemporary political philosophy. An acquaintance with debates over impartiality in that guise is unforgoable for anyone who seeks to engage seriously with the fundaments of modern liberal democracy.

III IMPARTIALITY AS FREEDOM OF EXPRESSION

One further area in which the ideal of impartiality has been especially salient in the controversies among philosophers for the past few centuries is that of freedom of expression.[6] Developed most sophisticatedly in the theoretical literature that has arisen from the famous First Amendment to the U.S. Constitution, arguments in favor of freedom of expression have distilled several ways in which any system of governance should be impartial with regard to communicative activities. Because those arguments are usually framed in terms of "neutrality" rather than in terms of "impartiality," I will chiefly use the former terminology here.

The moral principle of freedom of expression as I understand it here is as follows. No system of governance can ever legitimately subject anyone to sanctions or other disadvantages for engaging in communicative conduct, where the rationale for the sanctions or disadvantages is focused on the communicative tenor of the conduct. Every system of governance is morally obligated to refrain from penalizing any communicative activities qua communicative activities. In other words, any restrictions imposed by a system of governance on some communicative activity are morally legitimate only if they have been imposed not because the activity is communicative but instead because it instantiates a type of misconduct whose wrongness is not distinctively communicative.

Communication-Neutrality

The most general respect in which a system of governance should strive to uphold the ideal of freedom of expression is to refrain from disadvantaging communicative activity qua communicative activity. In other words, if any restrictions imposed by a system of governance on some communicative activity are to be legitimate, they must be imposed not because the activity is communicative but instead because it constitutes a type of wrongdoing that is communication-independent in that the wrongdoing can be perpetrated either through communicative conduct or through non-communicative conduct. In precisely this respect, the purposes of any legitimate restrictions are communication-neutral. Let us briefly ponder here Oliver Wendell Holmes's famous example of a man who maliciously shouts "Fire" in a crowded theater. Although such an action is communicative, the prohibition of it is morally legitimate because the action constitutes a type of wrongdoing that can be perpetrated either through communicative conduct or through non-communicative conduct. That is, the shouting is an attempt to induce serious public disorder in circumstances where the disorder is very likely to result in deaths or injuries and damage to property. Such an attempt could have been undertaken through non-communicative conduct such as the firing

---

[6] For a much longer treatment of the matters discussed in this section, see Chapter 2 of Kramer (2021).

of a gun or (for that matter) the ignition of a fire. Hence, the proscription of such misconduct can be – and almost always will be – communication-neutral in its purpose.

An insistence on communication-neutrality has given rise to some of the most famous doctrines in American First Amendment jurisprudence. Let us glance here at the distinction between advocacy and incitement, as it has been drawn by the U.S. Supreme Court in the celebrated 1969 case of *Brandenburg v Ohio*. When somebody's utterances incite other people to engage in serious criminality, her statements are aimed at bringing about some major wrongdoing in circumstances where the imminent occurrence of the wrongdoing is highly probable as a result of the statements. That is, a communication that amounts to incitement is characterized by three main elements: the intendedness of the link between the communication and some serious misconduct, the imminence of the misconduct, and the likelihood of the occurrence of the misconduct. By contrast, when somebody advocates the perpetration of misconduct but does not commit incitement, at least one of the three elements just specified is missing.

A classic example of incitement is John Stuart Mill's scenario of a fiery speaker who rails against the iniquity of corn-dealers while addressing a mob of angry people who have gathered outside the home of a local corn-dealer (Mill 1956, pp. 67–8). In Mill's scenario, and in other cases of incitement, the utterance of inflammatory statements by a speaker is constitutive of the speaker's participation in the serious and imminent misconduct which the statements are designed and likely to bring about. Because of the proximity between the inciting utterances and the imminent criminality which they are intended to produce, the utterances are subsumed into the criminality as some of the initial stages thereof. Consequently, the imposition of sanctions on Mill's fiery speaker can unequivocally be consistent with the principle of freedom of expression. Punishment should be administered not because of the communicative character of the speaker's fulminations, but because of their having constituted his direct and deliberate involvement in the perpetration of a lynching. Accordingly, that punishment can be communication-neutral.

What the *Brandenburg* criterion for incitement enables us to do, in any context where somebody (like Mill's rabble-rouser) has exhorted people to commit violence or other serious wrongdoing, is to determine whether the exhortations can be penalized in a communication-neutral manner or not. If the utterances in question do meet the *Brandenburg* test for incitement, then a relevant communication-neutral legal prohibition – a prohibition on rioting or vandalism or murder or arson, for example – can be applied to those utterances in a communication-neutral fashion. Contrariwise, if the speaker's declamations do not meet the *Brandenburg* test and are therefore properly classifiable as mere advocacy rather than as incitement, then any sanctions imposed in response to them are not communication-neutral. Even if the legal prohibition that provides for the sanctions is itself communication-neutral (like the prohibition on rioting or vandalism or murder or arson), any application of it to an act of mere advocacy is not communication-neutral. Unlike incitement, mere advocacy is not subsumed into the misconduct for which it calls; it is not sufficiently proximate to that misconduct to be so subsumed. Hence, if it is subjected to legal sanctions, it is subjected as an act of communication rather than as one of the opening stages of the communication-independent misconduct. Administered in such circumstances, the sanctions are not communication-neutral and are thus in violation of the principle of freedom of expression.

Content-Neutrality

Another type of impartiality required under the principle of freedom of expression is that of content-neutrality, which obtains in two main varieties: neutrality of subject matter and neutrality of viewpoint. A system of governance that is impartial in abiding by the constraint of neutrality of subject matter does not differentiate among the topics that can be broached whenever communicative activity is permitted. Helpful here will be an example. Suppose that a local ordinance permits the placement of advertisements (in return for set fees) on the sides and backs of municipal buses, and suppose that the ordinance excludes from this arrangement any advertisements that address politically sensitive topics. That exclusion does not discriminate among viewpoints at all; it applies to any political advertisements irrespective of the points on the political spectrum whence they emanate. Nonetheless, it plainly does discriminate on the basis of subject matter. With regard to a prominent public setting, its purpose is to delimit the range of topics that can be raised by potential communicators and pondered by potential addressees of the communications. Such a content-specific restriction contravenes the principle of freedom of expression, even though a municipal government could legitimately exclude advertisements altogether from the sides and backs of its buses. What contravenes the principle of freedom of expression is not the extent of the restriction but its fine-grainedness. Of course, that feature of the restriction could have been accentuated. For example, instead of excluding all political advertisements, the ordinance might have excluded only advertisements pertaining to abortion or only advertisements pertaining to matters of immigration. Either of those exclusions would have been less wide-ranging than the exclusion of all politically sensitive topics, but – precisely for that reason – either of them would have been more fine-grained as an effort to direct the flow of public discourse in a prominent public setting. Selectivity can be as problematically inimical to freedom of expression as is overinclusiveness.[7]

Arguably even more important than neutrality of subject matter, as an aspect of impartiality in the domain of freedom of expression, is neutrality of viewpoint. Suppose that, instead of excluding all political advertisements from the sides and backs of municipal buses, a local ordinance were to exclude all advertisements that

---

[7] For an illuminating exploration of this point, see Kagan 1992 (a few portions of which are superseded by Kagan 1996).

express opposition to the policies of the United Kingdom's Labour Party. Or suppose that, instead of excluding all advertisements that pertain to the matter of abortion, a local ordinance were to exclude all advertisements that call for the outlawing of the practice of abortion. Neither of these examples involves a restriction on the range of topics that can permissibly be addressed in a prominent public setting, but each of them involves a restriction on the range of viewpoints that can permissibly be espoused within that setting. Opponents of the Labour Party or of abortion are not allowed to proclaim their views in the form of advertisements on public buses, whereas admirers of the Labour Party and proponents of the "pro-choice" side in controversies over abortion are allowed to proclaim their views in such a fashion. Once again, what makes the exclusions objectionable is their selectivity. A municipal government is not morally obligated to make the sides and backs of public buses available as spaces for advertising, but a policy in favor of making them available as such spaces (in return for paid fees) cannot legitimately discriminate with reference to the viewpoints of would-be advertisers.

Speaker-Neutrality

A further type of governmental impartiality required under the principle of freedom of expression is speaker-neutrality. Although this kind of neutrality is closely related to neutrality of viewpoint, the two are not equivalent. For example, a particular person might be legally prohibited from speaking publicly on a certain issue, even though others who share that person's position on the issue are legally permitted to speak publicly about it. Indeed, a particular person might be legally prohibited from speaking publicly about some matter, even though other people are legally permitted to appear on radio or television to articulate that very person's pronouncements on the matter. Just such a situation obtained in the United Kingdom from 1988 to 1994, when broadcasters throughout the country were legally banned from airing the voices of members of Northern Irish terrorist groups – and members of the political party Sinn Féin – on radio or television (Donohue 2008, pp. 293–4). British broadcasters during that period were legally permitted to employ actors to read out the words that had been uttered by the members of those groups in interviews or in other public statements. Consequently, everything said by the terrorists and their political comrades could legally be aired on radio or television in the United Kingdom, provided that the voices of the terrorists or their comrades were replaced with actors' voices. In such a situation, there was no transgression of content-neutrality by the British system of governance, but there was an obvious transgression of speaker-neutrality.

A point to be emphasized here about speaker-neutrality is that it forbids not only the identity-based disadvantaging of a speaker but also any identity-based preferential treatment. This point has sometimes been overlooked even by eminent champions of the values of liberal democracy. For instance, when writing about the egregiously unjust U.S. Supreme Court case in which the Court upheld the conviction of Eugene Debs for speaking against the role of the United States in the First World War, Rawls lamented that the Court was "little troubled by the constitutional question raised in *Debs*, even though the case involves a leader of a political party, already four times its candidate for the presidency" (1993, p. 351). Rawls was right to be indignant about the Supreme Court's judgment in the *Debs* case, but he erred in suggesting that the stature of Debs as a politician was a factor which militated against that judgment. The stature of Debs as a politician was irrelevant; no preferential treatment of his utterances was warranted on that ground. Decisive instead was the fact that his orations did not give rise to any clear and present danger of serious misconduct. They did not constitute any participation on his part in such misconduct. This communication-neutral ground for acquitting Debs is also straightforwardly speaker-neutral. It applies to the orations of Debs the same standard – the *Brandenburg* Court's version of the clear-and-present-danger standard – that is applicable to the orations of any other speaker.

The Upshot of Neutrality

If and only if a legal mandate partakes of each type of neutrality that has just been adumbrated, it is in conformity with the requirements laid down by the principle of freedom of expression. Though some types or instances of communicative conduct might be prohibited by a mandate that is in conformity with that principle, they are not prohibited because of their distinctively communicative character or contents or because of the identities of the people who engage in them. Instead of being prohibited qua acts of communication, those types or instances of conduct are prohibited because they are constitutive of some communication-independent misdeeds. Communication-neutrality and subject-neutrality and viewpoint-neutrality and speaker-neutrality, then, are the hallmarks of laws enacted by a system of governance that exerts the self-restraint involved in the realization of freedom of expression.

Of course, the foregoing types of neutrality are crucial not only in connection with the terms and purposes of the laws that have been enacted by a system of governance, but also in connection with the processes whereby those laws are implemented through the decisions and actions of administrative and adjudicative officials. Even if a statute or some other law is itself impeccably in compliance with the principle of freedom of expression, it might be applied selectively by administrative officials or adjudicative officials in contravention of that principle. Hence, the foregoing types of neutrality are required (under the principle of freedom of expression) in processes of administration and adjudication as well as in the outputs of legislation. In relation to any law or policy that is adopted by a system of governance, the principle of freedom of expression is fulfilled only insofar as both the law or policy itself and the implementation of it are characterized by all of the aforementioned types of neutrality.

Impartiality construed as these several types of governmental neutrality in the domain of freedom of expression is clearly in need of justification. After all, a stance of blanket neutrality will carry with it some significant drawbacks in a number of instances. For example, let us briefly contemplate again a municipal ordinance that excludes certain viewpoints from being expressed on the sides and backs of public buses. If every such ordinance is disallowed, and if strict viewpoint-neutrality is insisted upon, the municipal government may sometimes find itself presented with applications for advertisements from odious groups. Why should the local officials have to choose between allowing no advertisements to be placed on buses and leaving open the possibility of occasional advertisements placed by such groups?

A satisfactory answer to this question – and a satisfactory answer to any cognate question about any of the other types of neutrality required in the domain of freedom of expression – would amount to a full-scale justification of the principle of freedom of expression. Such an endeavor is of course far beyond the scope of this essay.[8] However, we can gain a rough sense of the appropriate focus of that endeavor if we reflect afresh on what has already been said about the difference between the extent of a restriction and the selectivity of a restriction.

If the best justification for freedom of expression were to be centered on the provision of opportunities for speakers (and writers and composers and artists) to articulate their ideas and sentiments, we would be hard pressed to explain why selective restrictions on freedom of expression are frequently more problematic than wholesale restrictions. After all, the latter restrictions curtail the opportunities for expression that are available to speakers (and writers and composers and artists) far more extensively than do the former restrictions. We would face comparable difficulties if the best justification for freedom of expression were instead centered on ensuring that potential listeners and readers and viewers enjoy ample access to the articulated ideas and feelings and hopes of other people. Selective restrictions impinge on such access less severely than do sweeping restrictions.

Nor will we be able to account for the moral disparity between selective curbs and blanket curbs if we try to vindicate the principle of freedom of expression by concentrating on a societal desideratum such as the promotion of knowledge. Though the pursuit of such a desideratum would typically be badly hampered by any wide-ranging curbs on communicative activities, it could typically be furthered rather than hampered by some suitably selective curbs. Thus, like a focus on opportunities for self-expression or on access to other people's articulations of their ideas and sentiments, a focus on a societal desideratum such as the growth of knowledge will not enable us to explain why selective restrictions on freedom of expression are especially objectionable.

---

[8] I present a full-scale justification in Chapter 4 of Kramer (2021). In so doing, I build on some of the ideas elaborated in Kramer (2017).

To come up with a suitable explanation, we need to train our attention instead on the relationship between a system of governance and the society over which that system presides. When such a system imposes selective constraints on freedom of expression, the control which it exerts over central aspects of people's lives is particularly fine-grained. For reasons that can only be mentioned fleetingly here, the minuteness of that control is both overweening and degrading. It is overweening because it assigns to governmental officials a decisive say over the specificities of communicative interaction qua communicative interaction,[9] and it is degrading because it makes the success of a system of governance partly dependent on the non-occurrence of modes of expression which an ethically more robust system of governance could tolerate. Toleration is of course not equivalent to condonation; a key aspect of the ethical robustness of a system of governance is the extent to which its operations avert any untoward effects that might ensue from the modes of expression which it leaves legally unrestricted. Consequently, one decisive measure of the ethical health of a system of governance is its ability to sustain the self-restraint that is constitutive of freedom of expression. We are helped to recognize as much through a focus on the requirements of impartiality in the domain of communicative interaction.

RECOMMENDED READING

Barry, B. (1995). *Justice as Impartiality*, Oxford: Oxford University Press.
Duxbury, N. (1999). *Random Justice*, Oxford: Oxford University Press.
Greenawalt, K. (1992). *Law and Objectivity*, Oxford: Oxford University Press.
Kagan, E. (1992). The Changing Faces of First Amendment Neutrality: R.A.V. v St Paul, Rust v Sullivan, and the Problem of Content-Based Underinclusion. *Supreme Court Review*, 1992, pp. 29–77.
Kramer, M. (2007). *Objectivity and the Rule of Law*, Cambridge: Cambridge University Press.
Kramer, M. (2017). *Liberalism with Excellence*, Oxford: Oxford University Press.
Kramer, M. (2021). *Freedom of Expression as Self-Restraint*, Oxford: Oxford University Press.
Mendus, S. (2002). *Impartiality in Moral and Political Philosophy*, Oxford: Oxford University Press.
Mill, J. S. (1956). *On Liberty*. Edited by Currin Shields. Indianapolis, IN: Bobbs-Merrill. Originally published in 1859.
Nagel, T. (1991). *Equality and Partiality*, Oxford: Oxford University Press.
Nussbaum, M. (1995). *Poetic Justice*, Boston, MA: Beacon Press.
Quong, J. (2011). *Liberalism without Perfection*, Oxford: Oxford University Press.
Rawls, J. (1993). *Political Liberalism*, New York: Columbia University Press.

---

[9] Let us recall that an utterance is unprotected by the principle of freedom of expression if it constitutes serious wrongdoing that can be perpetrated either through communicative conduct or through non-communicative conduct.

11

Constitutional Legitimacy[*]

Nomi Claire Lazar

If the fundamental political problem is establishing and maintaining "order, protection, safety, trust, and the conditions of cooperation," then, as Bernard Williams (2005, pp. 3, 5) notes, "something has to be said to explain ... what the difference is between the solution [i.e., state power] and the problem." That something is legitimacy and it is a key role of constitutions to bolster it.

Power is legitimate when justified, and justification rests on reasons. The reasons we give for calling power legitimate tend to take two forms: Power justified by conformity with existing norms yields 'order-based' legitimacy. Power justified by the promise of good outcomes yields 'performance-based' legitimacy. Because constitutions are themselves systems of rules against which we assess the legitimate use of power, it may seem that constitutional legitimacy is straightforward: play by the rules is legitimate play. Yet, not just any rules will do. Only a legitimate constitution can legitimate, and how did legitimacy get into the constitution in the first place? Moreover, since rules require interpretation, they can't legitimate action directly. That is, it is not obvious how legitimacy gets out of a constitution either. Legitimacy, then, sits at a mysterious nexus of normative statecraft.

To investigate, Section I explores key empirical and normative approaches to the study of constitutional legitimacy. Aspects of these substantive models have intuitive power, yet strain to explain legitimacy's puzzles. Section II suggests a focus on legitimacy's function, not its substance. Political legitimacy from this vantage, seems functionally akin to currency, and constitutions to the banks that store it. Constitutions draw legitimacy from diverse substantive order- and performance-based sources, which explains the combination of intuitive plausibility and inadequacy of the accounts in Section I: from consent procedures, appeals to tradition, to right, to God, and to noble sentiments, from the promise of effective institutions and the fear of vicious ones, leaders build up a constitution's stores of legitimacy at the outset. These diverse sources are transformed into an exchangeable 'stuff', a

---

[*] An earlier version of this argument appears in *Review of Constitutional Studies* 26(2) and is republished here with kind permission of the editors.

currency, which constitutions then store for later use. Just as market factors impact the functional worth of stored currency, diverse political and social factors may bolster or reduce a constitution's legitimacy over time. The fluctuating value of these legitimacy-stores impact political opportunities and agents' power to seize them. This functional model, in drawing attention to what legitimacy does not what it is, better illuminates constitutions' complex and dynamic role in mediating the entente between power and people. Empirically, legitimacy is dynamic and in flux. And this, normatively, is exactly as it should be.

I EMPIRICAL AND NORMATIVE APPROACHES TO LEGITIMACY

Scholarly approaches to legitimacy may be normative or empirical. The first seeks morally necessary and sufficient conditions for legitimacy. The second asks what actually brings people to accept power's legitimacy. Both normative and empirical accounts of legitimacy can be performance- or order-based (Lazar 2019), as is depicted in the matrix below.

	Normative	Empirical
Performance-Based	"A legitimate government serves the people."	"When leaders work in the people's interest, people tend to accept their power as legitimate."
Order-Based	"Only a rule of law regime that protects rights is legitimate."	"People accept a monarch's power if she is the rightful heir."

Ordering frameworks that, empirically & normatively, seem to ground legitimacy are diverse. In Max Weber's empirical account of legitimate domination, two types are order-based (Weber 1978, pp. 212 ff). The first, tradition, describes culturally entrenched rules and procedures for granting and accepting power, whether election, succession, or religious sanction (such as with the selection of a Dalai Lama). Tradition, like unwritten constitutional conventions, reflects power's appropriate exercise 'around here.' That we have long done things this way is an independent reason to continue. Weber's second type, legal-rationality, marks order in black letters: in constitutions, laws, and administrative regulations. Legal-rational orders generate, through conformity with bureaucratic norms and procedures, what some call procedural or input legitimacy (Scharpf 1999).

Empirically, constitutions may lend order-based legitimacy to political action, while tradition and procedure can serve as order-based justifications for a constitution's own legitimacy. Commonly, when constitutions are made, constitutional conventions, plebiscites and referenda lend the document procedural sanction.

These diverse modes of justifying authority may ground legitimate power through conformity with diverse perceptions of right rule or rightly constituted order.

Regardless of power's conformity to order, empirically, people expect power to serve their interests. This is called 'performance legitimacy,' and is associated with Confucian-influenced regimes like those in China and Singapore, where leaders commonly, explicitly justify power on the grounds of good results (Morgenbesser 2017; Zhao 2009). But performance legitimacy is evident everywhere. Warlords and extremists in weak states use performance to build legitimacy too: prioritizing social and justice services, keeping order, then use this performative capacity to justify their power. And Scharpf (1999) has shown the key importance of good performance to European Union legitimacy, calling performance 'output' legitimacy. If people lead better lives through good policy and its effective execution, then, leaders claim, power deployed to those ends is justified. In democracies, performance failures can be placed or displaced onto leaders or parties, buffering regime legitimacy, and increasing stability. Where it becomes obvious the constitution itself has failed, this failure, beyond justice considerations, can ground calls for constitutional reform (Levinson 2008).

Weber's third type of legitimate domination, charisma, draws on performance too. Charismatic leaders insinuate a connection with God. But it is not just divine connection that gives a charismatic figure their power, but the promise of capacity: 'God is with us; we cannot fail.' This illuminates why charismatic leaders often challenge sitting power: a touch of divinity unsettles tradition and normative order, undermining order-legitimacy. And belief in a leader's superhuman capacity is reassuring, when facing Goliath. Charisma is a promise of imminent performance.

Empirically, people use order- and performance-based criteria to impute and assess constitutional legitimacy. But this contradictory and relativistic mishmash of empirical reasons cannot satisfy normative demands. People may believe a charismatic leader can cleanse the world of corruption but does that belief actually render her legitimate? And what of laws that conform with wicked constitutions, made by wicked regimes? Law may conform, but is this real legitimacy? An empirical description of how people assess constitutional legitimacy generates puzzles, because legitimacy is intuitively normative. From where, then, do constitutions draw the normative authority they lend?

Scholars take two types of normative approach to address this. They make arguments that the content of a constitution is right and good, or else that the procedure for making the constitution was right and good, regardless of the content (Michelman 2003b, pp. 125–127). Both kinds of arguments have order- and performance-based versions.

Since the seventeenth century, procedure-centric accounts of normative constitutional legitimacy have tended to focus on consent. As Grotius (1901, Bk 1.3.8) argued, a nation may choose "what form of government she pleases. Nor is this right to be measured by the excellence of this or that form of government, on which there may be varieties of opinion, but by the will of the people."

Consent transfers the people's sovereign power, along with fiduciary responsibility, to an agent or body that works on their behalf. Consent theories thus rest on a substantive normative claim: that we are entitled to rule over ourselves, and that consent is necessary for self-rule.

Empirically, states make rhetorical use of this normative claim to promote buy-in for a new or amended constitution. They engage in what might be termed 'consent theater'. Where liberal individualist assumptions prevail – that there are discrete persons whose individual wills together form the people's will – this may take the form of a constitutional convention, or public input gathering process. More seriously, constitutions are sometimes formally ratified through referenda. Even in populist or authoritarian contexts, a leader may claim to be the people's avatar with the constitution serving as an expression of their true will. Thus, there is consent theater around even China's constitutions. Even in theocracies, such as Iran and the United Arab Emirates, popular sovereignty figures prominently in constitutional preambles alongside divine sovereignty as a legitimating claim. Consent theater works only through consent's moral force. Why make a show of it otherwise?

Yet, if consent really is the normative ground of constitutional legitimacy, does this not uncomfortably imply that a vast majority of people have lived under illegitimate government. Few, including in modern liberal democracies, have actually consented to the constitution that governs them. 'We the People' is a fiction (Barnett 2003). Many constitutions are older than their subjects and citizens. And most states also have stateless and refugee denizens who acknowledge the state's legitimate power regardless of any right or opportunity for consent. If one argues that, by dwelling in the state, these and citizen-denizens give tacit consent, two replies present. Those who are stateless or refugees may have no safe alternative: consent or die is not consent. Those who are citizens may well ask on what authority the state may demand they consent or leave. Does the state not need authority in the first place in order to justly make this demand? But is not this territorial authority precisely what begs justification (Brilmayer 1989)? Furthermore, some regimes have very high empirical legitimacy markers despite authoritarian or authoritative form, even where there has been a paucity of opportunities for consent (Gilley 2006). And historically, few regimes had consent procedures[1]: were all these really illegitimate?

Even existing opportunities for procedural voice – a plebiscite or referendum – offer limited or binary choice. By what authority was the range of choice and procedure for choice instituted in the first place? Any earlier procedure-choosing-procedure will face the same trouble, ad infinitum (Barnett 2004; Zurn 2010, pp. 215–216). Furthermore, even were every choice on the table, and everyone a choosing participant, decision rules are laden with their own normative

---

[1] Some notable exceptions include parts of sub-Saharan Africa, some indigenous North American nations and confederations, and the pre-Genghis Steppe Mongols. Here, as likely elsewhere, consensus and voting procedures were at times the norm (Gomez 2018; Fenton 1998; Morgan 2007).

assumptions: Majoritarianism or unanimity? Democratic deliberation or technocratic expertise? These normative assumptions make the options on the table either too thick to garner genuine agreement, or too thin to make clear to what people are agreeing. At no point along the regress of norms and procedures does this cease to be a problem. That a 'no' in a constitution-making setting may prolong chaos or violence, as in the wake of civil war, makes the whole process look more like coercion, further straining the notion of consent.

It is also worth noting that constitutions are often elite bargains that solidify power relations of a moment (Hardin 2013), and not all elite aims align with popular aims. Regardless of the procedure that brought negotiators to the table, they will likely seek to preserve not just state stability, but their own interests too. Certainly, there will be compromises with weaker parties, but these secure buy-in to prevent future threats to a favorable status quo. Wherever someone claims to speak on behalf of the multitude, there, as Sanford Levinson (2011, p. 158) has noted, the 'We' of 'We the People' could ultimately be understood as an act of violence, silencing diversity. Claims of consent are ideological from this perspective. With their aid, winners may assert moral sanction for unequal configurations of power.

If these empirical factors make genuine consent rare, then if consent grounds constitutional legitimacy, either few or no constitutions are actually legitimate, at least through time.

Yet the idea of consent seems nonetheless normatively powerful and intuitive. What should we make of this? Is legitimacy all show? Even if consent were robust and substantive, it would capture only the imperative of self-rule. Is that enough? What if people consented to rule by a wicked regime (Dyzenhaus 2010)? Would we, then, say the regime is legitimate but also evil?

For those who would respond in the negative, legitimacy may rely on a constitution's moral content. A constitution, on this view, is legitimate only if its contents meet a justice threshold (Buchanan 2003, p. 432). This approach faces its own difficulties.

For instance, who decides the justice threshold, a philosopher? What entitles her? The force of reason? Some, following Rawls, suggest hypothetical consent may provide a solution to this dilemma. That is, a constitution may be legitimate if its essential contents are such that "all citizens as free and equal may reasonably be expected to endorse [them] in the light of principles and ideals acceptable to their common human reason" (Rawls 1993, p. 137). These essentials are then defined in terms of core political rights and freedoms, which are given priority over other goods, and which all are reasonably able to exercise. Yet, would all endorse a constitution that puts the right before the good? Reasonably, whether or not wrongly, some thinkers argue this approach is not just wrong in itself, but has harmful consequences for human well-being (Vermeule 2022). To lower the bar and say "most citizens would endorse" means returning to the procedure problem, who lowers the bar? Who decides the threshold? And who decides who?

And there are other worries: might a Rawlsian standard of reasonableness favour preservation of the status quo? And is any of us anyway reasonable, given the countless cognitive biases that cloud our thinking? Reasonableness is, if not an unreasonable standard, certainly a fraught one.

So, we arrive at this concerning tentative conclusion: Even on the basis of some objectively just principles and procedures, it remains mysterious how legitimacy 'gets into' a constitution, a legitimacy from which political leaders must be able to draw for political power going forward. That the ruled consented to power captures one powerful intuition. That a constitution has just content seems to matter too. But push either approach, and we fall into infinite regress. It seems we need some procedure to settle on principle, but some principle to settle on procedure. Push a little, and it appears there is no coherent, compelling discrete set of moral criteria that might give substance to 'legitimacy'.

Nor do these difficulties stop once a constitution is settled. I suggested above that constitutions serve as ordering frameworks that bestow legitimacy on political action and law. Yet, constitutions cannot legitimate just by virtue of their status as ordering frameworks, for rules require judgment and are not self-interpreting. Who decides the correct mode (Bork 1971; Scalia 1997; Barnett 2004; Solum 2008; Strauss 2010; Waluchow 2007)? Some, like William Rehnquist (1976, p. 693), argue that a constitution must be interpreted in accordance with the original intentions of founders. But for older constitutions in particular, how could we know what these intentions were? And is it reasonable to expect intentions were uniform (Brest 1980, p. 214)? What if intentions were perverse? For example, there is evidence Representative Howard Smith introduced sex discrimination as an element of Title VII in the United States "not necessarily because he was interested in rooting out sex discrimination in all its forms, but because he may have hoped to scuttle the whole Civil Rights Act and thought that adding language covering sex discrimination would serve as a poison pill."[2]

Politics and procedure mean "legislative preferences do not pass unfiltered into legislation" and these processes are "too complex, too path dependent, and too opaque to allow judges to reconstruct whether Congress would have resolved any particular question differently from the way the clear statutory text resolves that question" (Manning 2003, pp. 2390, 2410). This has led constitutional scholars and United States Supreme Court Justices, notably Scalia and Gorsuch, to argue that legal texts "mean what they conveyed to reasonable people at the time" (Scalia and Garner 2012, p. 16). Yet, language is often vague, ambiguous, and always contextual, and interpretation would then frequently require heroic efforts at historical-linguistic reconstruction. When the textualist recommends we then resort to framers' intent, this returns us to the problem inherent in intent-based interpretation. Worse,

---

[2] Bostock v. Clayton County Georgia, 590 U.S._ (2020), 29. The Court cites Whalen C. and Whalen B. (1989) *The Longest Debate: A Legislative History of the 1964 Civil Rights Act*. pp. 115–118.

ambiguity and absurdity may require judicial discretion to locate, not just interpret, because they are not always obvious (Dougherty 1994).

Yet another puzzle: if rules maintain their original meaning through time, and are stable in this way, have they not, by virtue of the contextual nature of language and meaning, in fact changed their sense, once socio-political context shifts (Brest 1980, p. 234)? It is precisely this puzzle that animates the fearsome dissents to the US Supreme Court's textualist ruling in *Bostock v. Clayton County* (590 U.S._ [2020]).[3]

In other jurisdictions, the development of socio-political context is part of the tradition of interpretation. *Edwards v. Canada* (1928) considered Section 24 of the Constitution Act (1867), which states that the Governor General may summon "qualified Persons" to the Senate of Canada.[4] The Supreme Court had ruled that 'Persons' could not be understood to have included women when the Act came into force, and therefore, that women could not serve in the Senate. But on appeal this was overturned by the Privy Council of the United Kingdom, holding that regardless of whether the word 'Persons' included women in its original sense, the moderns of 1928 would surely include them. The Privy Council argued that a constitution should be understood to be "a living tree capable of growth and expansion within its natural limits," and hence, that if women were, in 1928, considered Persons in the relevant sense, the constitution should be understood in this light. Language develops with society, and a constitution must be allowed to change in this changing socio-political soil.

But to accept this school of interpretation concedes that much stronger power to the interpreter. Does the interpreter not come to form part of the 'rule' in its actualization? Of course, this activity of interpreting is clothed in procedure and reason, often sanctioned by public values (Sunstein 2009) and can still be understood as legal-rational in this respect. It is certainly not arbitrary. But constitutional rules are no longer 'the legitimating authority' of themselves. Rather, from this perspective, legitimacy stems from interpretative acts of contextual fitting in light of overarching principles, themselves chosen and defended on the basis of substantive judgments. Constitutions are at once 'the last word' while their every word relies on a shifting range of interpreters whose own legitimacy may ebb and flow (Gibson & Caldeira 2009). Constitutional rules confer legitimacy on political action only to the extent that they are appropriately interpreted and situated.

Rules need interpretation to confer legitimacy, and interpretation involves interplay of power, normativity, and processes of reason-giving. Interpretation and judgment mediate constitutions and their legitimating force in other ways too. For example, many constitutions explicitly provide for, or conventionally tolerate, their own limitation, derogation or suspension. Section I of the Canadian Charter of

---

[3] It is one absurd consequence of the textualist reasoning of this case that while gay and transgender people now have Title VII protection, bisexual people apparently do not.
[4] Edwards v. A.G. of Canada, 1930 AC 124, [1929] UKPC 86.

Rights and Freedoms, for example, allows for limits on rights which a free and democratic society might deem reasonable. And some emergency power provisions provide near carte-blanche for emergency legislation. These features suggest constitutions can legitimate action in part through enabling the non-enforcement of normal rules (Lazar 2009). This in turn suggests that constitutional legitimacy draws from multiple sources and confers legitimacy from multiple streams: perhaps natural law, extra-legal normativity, and, notably, performance.

Performance is substantive – we really want a state order to serve the public good – but it is symbolic too. Attitudes toward the interpretation and enforcement of constitutions in diverse regimes suggest symbolic communication of moral identity is important, for example, a fact which helps account for the otherwise puzzling role of constitutions in non-rule of law regimes. In states such as China, the constitution matters even when leaders only selectively enforce its provisions. The idea of the constitution matters alongside its content. Public attitudes and the fact that political leaders amend or replace constitutions, from time to time (Gilley 2006), support this.

The United States, too, provides evidence that a constitution's legitimacy, and capacity to legitimate is partly its symbolic, identity communicating function. For evidence: the American inclination toward the most charitable possible interpretation of their constitution, where charitable means, for each person, most in line with their pre-existing moral understanding of the idea of America (Michelman 2003a, p. 364). Where the US constitution exhibits moral failings and where judges' rulings seem to justify a constitutional vision that diverges from a citizen's moral priors, Americans sometimes interpret these as judicial mistakes, kinks to be ironed out, rather than evidence of moral incoherence or disrespectability (Graber 2010). Americans want their constitution to be legitimate 'deep down', worth venerating, regardless of what it actually says and does. Over time, the constitution achieves its 'correct' form: that form which captures some normative idea embodied in peoples' pre-existing conception of their homeland (Balkin 2011, Scheingold 2004).

All this suggests a constitution's power to legitimate rests on diverse moral resources, beyond interpretation, because these precede and provide the lens through which activities of interpretation take place. Respect for a governmental system of which a constitution forms a part is partly prior to the activity of interpretation. The constitution becomes a symbol of, not just a source of legitimacy.

It follows, then, that legitimacy does not flow directly from conformity with constitutional rules. The constitution's legitimating capacity stems from the interplay of rules with power and principles. Power flows around and through rules, and action is justified not solely with reference to rules but to varying interpretations of the public good.

So, we have reached a seeming impasse. There is – and can be – no single, clear normative source for a constitution's legitimacy. And there is – and can be – no direct legitimating power that a constitution can confer. What's more, the strict distinction between empirical and normative approaches to legitimacy, seems markedly clouded, as scholars have noted in other contexts. On any strict normative conception, no constitution in the world is legitimate, notes Habermas (1979, p. 205). And Beetham has noted that we don't think constitutions are legitimate because (empirically) people believe them to be, but rather their legitimacy is justified in terms of peoples' broadly normative beliefs (1991, p. 11). Engaging the normative character of consent earlier, it seemed to matter whether anyone actually consented. And conversely, empirical evidence of consent seemed insufficient to satisfy normative quandaries. And evidently, constitutional norms respond to, make sense within, and in turn give rise to empirical contexts. Hence, any strict separation of empirical and normative studies of legitimacy is bound to be somewhat artificial and obfuscating.

Once it is clear that legitimacy embraces diverse normative and empirical features, then the salience of empirical elements suggests one final difficulty with our typical ways of approaching constitutional legitimacy: this difficulty is time. Over time, the empirical conditions of life, and of political life change. So, in time, normative evaluations of constitutions and their legitimacy tend to change. This suggests a constitution which holds normative legitimacy at one point may lose it later, whether suddenly or slowly, without the text of the constitution changing at all. Conversely, over time, a people may grow accustomed to and embrace a constitution that was controversial or had no consent procedure at the outset. We know this to be so empirically – constitutions do sometimes come to seem illegitimate. And it makes sense normatively: if it matters that a constitution works, if performance matters, and if it matters that a constitution is just, then novel empirical conditions or moral insights may call for novel provisions. It is thus necessary that any account of constitutional legitimacy take account of its *dynamism*.

How, then, ought we to think about constitutional legitimacy?

II LEGITIMACY AS CURRENCY

It may be that there are no necessary and sufficient criteria that could automatically switch on legitimacy for a constitution, absent empirical context. And it may be that, while conformity with constitutional rules matters for political legitimacy, judgment and power always mediate. Laws never rule on their own. And yet, there is something powerfully intuitive about the roles of consent, of justice, and of the substantive – not just symbolic – power of the constitutional text.

Hence, for insight into the legitimacy of constitutions, I propose we consider a model that captures these peculiar features – the overlapping and sometimes conflicting moral criteria, the intertwining of the empirical and normative, and legitimacy's dynamism. In place of an attempt to model legitimacy – both of the constitution itself and of the legitimacy a constitution confers – substantively, consider instead a functional model.

By a substantive model, I mean one which aims to capture the essence of legitimacy, the criteria for calling a constitution 'legitimate'. By a functional model I mean one which illustrates how legitimacy does its normative work. The functional model I shall now present makes use of an analogy to currency and banks.

Like a currency, legitimacy can be drawn from a range of normative and performative sources, held as a generic, commensurable stuff, then 'spent' to support diverse powers and actions. Like a currency, levels of legitimacy are dynamic, and can fluctuate across time, in response to events. Those fluctuations track the interplay of events, actions and rhetorics deployed by political leaders, together with peoples' situation-specific willingness to, so to speak, buy it. Peoples' willingness may depend in turn on individual character, circumstances, fears, and aspirations. And, like a currency, whatever cultural elaborations develop around it, a constitution's worth is ultimately defined by a core function: legitimate constitutions protect stability. When legitimacy is overdrawn, constitutions come to seem illegitimate. They call out for amendment, replacement, even revolution. Let us consider how well this functional analogy between constitutions and banks, legitimacy, and currency, illuminates the phenomena, beginning with the problem of power and stability.

Power is an abstract potential that manifests in concrete, particular acts – political acts – the legitimacy of which is the ultimate (though not exclusive) object of our interest. This is because it is through acts that power touches us. Leaders work for public acceptance of actions, laws or projects, particularly where these involve a major policy shift or social or fiscal cost. To persuade, a leader may argue for some intrinsic quality of the proposal with reference to a normative frame or promised outcome. But it would be impossibly inefficient to engage in such efforts in support of every or even many political actions. For this reason, many exercises of power are accepted on the grounds that the active person or organization is entitled to decide and act – up to a point. That is, a person holds power as a capacity, a potential, and an elastic entente about this potential obtains between them and the subject people. Such political actors have a store of legitimacy to 'spend' on political actions. Here is the first move: from the legitimacy of the act to the legitimacy of the power to act.

Where do an agent's stores of legitimacy come from? There may be tradition and normative order-based considerations: the person came to power in the correct way (e.g., election, succession, appointment). And there are certainly performance-based considerations: Perhaps she has already proved herself effective and principled. Perhaps a leader is particularly charismatic or holds a powerful form of technocratic expertise: both are proxies of capacity and promise future performance. Then, as actions are in fact successful, this yields legitimacy dividends. Where they are unsuccessful, legitimacy is lost. A person's stores of legitimacy – performance- and order-based – fluctuate. But where they meet a critical threshold, a leader can act politically, with less need to justify any specific act.

But while this stockpiling of legitimacy in an individual is more efficient than case-by-case deliberation, it is precarious. Individuals are mortal, after all. And the dispensability of individuals bolsters state stability: short-term performance failures can be displaced onto individuals who are then ejected from power, e.g., through elections, preserving institutional legitimacy. For these reasons, it is better – more efficient, more stable – to principally (though not exclusively) stockpile legitimacy not in a person, but in a constitution, written or otherwise.

Max Weber (1978, pp. 246 ff.) famously made this point: stability requires that charismatic power be institutionalized. But this is not solely on account of the rational-legal form of a constitution. After all, rules, as we've seen, don't rule on their own, but require interpretation to actualize, authority to command obedience, and performative success to endure. Rather, a constitution's capacity to stabilize power stems from its capacity to serve as a bank for stockpiling and withdrawing diversely sourced legitimacy, including, but not limited to legal-rationality.

What sources are these? From where can this currency be gathered? Just as with legitimacy claims for actions and political leaders, claims of legitimacy for constitutions tend to be made on grounds of correspondence with backgrounded or self-justifying conceptions of order or else with claims of performative capacity. Indeed, all claims, normative or descriptive, invoke some justification from existing ordering frameworks and maintain their power to the extent they perform as good heuristics in the world. That is, we accept claims partly on the basis of their correspondence with a broader set of often unexamined, ontological, and epistemological assumptions and partly on the basis of apparent correspondence with reality, i.e., performance. These ordering frames form a conflicting multiplicity both across and within cultures and individuals. They are constituted partly by substantive facts about the world, and partly by assumptions about the way the world works. They can reflect tacit theories of causality, whether scientific or related to fate, fortune, predestination, etc. They may involve assumptions about temporality: whether events move in time in great cycles, in progressive or eschatological lines, etc. And they may be animated by normative heuristics: perhaps utilitarian or deontological or grounded in a religious creed. A claim of legitimacy for, or on the basis of, a constitution will, like any other legitimacy claim, rely implicitly or explicitly on ordering frames. Since diverse frames will resonate with diverse constituents, political leaders may appeal to several, as they work to bank legitimacy in a new or amended constitution.

Tradition (including of the common law variety), consent procedures, and the substantive correspondence of constitutional principles with norms or ideology are examples of order-based sources of legitimacy that can be stored in a constitution. Leaders may claim a constitution better conforms to natural law, tradition, justice, the true soul of the nation, or the people's will, whether expressed through some symbolic or substantive consent-procedure or through the insight of a vanguard or, in populist regimes, a people's avatar. The constitution, leaders may claim, seeks to institute the 'Right Kind of Regime' with respect to adherence of its substantive contents to abstract normative principles: liberal, democratic, theocratic, etc. Leaders may emphasize that the new constitution rights old wrongs or restores national sovereignty. Regardless of its substantive content, the very fact of constitution making may serve as a means of symbolically rejecting the past, or restoring just order (Landau 2018). Here, the South African Constitution serves as an emblematic example.

New constitutions also shore up stores of legitimacy at the outset through a promise of performance. People accept power only where that power, on balance and over time, works more or less to their advantage. So technocratic claims about effective institutional design, checks and balances, power-sharing mechanisms among ethnic, linguistic, or other factions etc. matter for legitimacy too. As Hardin (1999) has argued, a key function of written constitutions is to solve dangerous coordination problems, and they are legitimate partly on these grounds alone.

A leader may also attempt to store, in a new constitution, legitimacy sourced in their personal charisma, such as was perhaps the case with France's 1958 Gaullist constitution. Charisma is often a proxy for capacity, a promise of future performance. A leader may claim special insight into the times, a sort of kairotic power to see the true cause of national decline, for instance, and the knowledge to correct it, alter the flow of time, and by means of a new constitution restore a golden age. That it is *their* constitution adds to its power. The constitution becomes an extension and enabler of a claimed capacity to act for the people. Hungary's 2012 Basic Law spearheaded by the populist leader Viktor Orbán is a fine example here. A constitution stores and secures leaders' charismatic power, their promised capacity.

Leaders may also source legitimacy for a new constitution through a claim that it embodies the true spirit of a people. It becomes a national symbol, an element of identity over and above a tradition of adherence. The symbolic power of belonging means that creating a new or destroying a corrupt old constitution, or genuflecting to the simple power of a constitution's very existence creates authority through a claim of symbolic representation of a collective self (Schmitt 2008 [1928]).

At the point of declaration, at the 'now' and 'hereby' named in many constitutional preambles, the constitution will have as much legitimacy stockpiled as its promulgators have successfully drawn from these wells of normative order and promises of performance. But constitutional legitimacy is neither binary nor static. It is highly dynamic: generated, preserved, and depleted through its interplay with power and political practice. As a constitution's stores of legitimacy fluctuate, its status as a normative order from which law and power can draw legitimacy for political action fluctuates too.

When those in power show respect for a constitution and adhere to its norms, the constitution's stock of legitimacy is normally reinforced. Conversely, where a constitution is regularly ignored or circumscribed, its stock of legitimacy will likely diminish. But this is not uniformly the case. Sometimes, constitutional constraints may prevent government from effectively performing fundamental functions, as when checks and balances, and rights provisions impact speed and effectiveness in response to a crisis. Where there are no provisions for flexibility and this results in performance failure, respecting the constitutional order could actually diminish a constitution's legitimacy.

And in some regimes, the constitution may take on a semiotic power that allows the document to become self-bolstering. Over time, a constitution may seem more and more self-evident, as is arguably the case in the United States and, until recently, the United Kingdom. It becomes part of the furniture of the world, one of the background ordering conditions of day-to-day life. In such regimes, the idea of the constitution may come to have a pseudo-mystical expressive power, beyond any of its provisions. Those with a stake in the constitutional order can use a variety of means – education, propaganda – to bolster this effect. Increasing the constitution's symbolic resources increases legitimacy dividends too.

Conversely, the longer the time elapsed since a constitution came into force, the greater the likelihood that normative and cultural frames have shifted, frames which may have originally been important sources of legitimacy. As such conditions change, so might the relative contribution of one frame or another to the constitution's legitimacy account. When normative frames become particularly disjointed and begin to break down, the webs of justification that steadied constitutions are cut. Then constitutions are likely to be at their most fragile, their stocks of legitimacy depleted. This generates moments of uncertainty that may constitute ripe conditions for amendment. This was true of Canada in the lead up to the 1982 Charter of Rights and Freedoms, and perhaps of the United States at the time of the 13–15th Amendments. Where amendment is not viable, constitutions at such times may have little power to steady a regime unless legitimacy can be replenished from an alternative source: perhaps a novel normative framework, if some suitable one can be found. And in fact, despite our sense that constitutions are stalwart, as Elkins, Ginsburg, and Melton (2009) have shown, constitutions last on average for only nineteen years.

Alternatively, at such critical junctures, stocks of legitimacy may be bolstered by underlining past performance or asserting claims of future capacity. What will count as good political performance varies somewhat from place to place, time to time, and person to person, but at a minimum will probably include a justice infrastructure, and some basic level of economic, food, and physical security (Sheridan 1975; Jackson 2003; Peake 2003; Marten 2007; Roy 2011; La Serna 2012; Darag 2016). When these core elements of performance are consistently demonstrated, this increases stores of legitimacy and may substitute – temporarily at least – for shaky normative frameworks. Where they are absent or severely threatened over time, this impacts perception of political legitimacy, regardless of the normative characteristics of the regime and its constitution. A regime that is liberal, but where citizens live without hope, in poverty or fear, may struggle. That is, government – no matter how closely it conforms to normative order – bleeds legitimacy when it consistently or else suddenly and spectacularly, fails to perform. Regimes need to perform, and they need to communicate that performance not only with respect to past achievement but also with respect to capacity going forward. Regardless of procedure, some past consent-event, or the normative bona fides of a constitution, the legitimacy banked in a constitution will fluctuate in its ability to support political action, in part with its capacity to perform and in part with its capacity to adapt to shifting normative (ordering) conditions.

Because performance failures form a particular threat to legitimacy, the institutions set out in a constitution not only sanction power but often provide mechanisms for managing failure. For example, elections provide a means of displacing performance failure in the short and medium terms away from regime type. One party may be thrown out in favor of another, one candidate or representative in favor of another, and within political parties, leaders may resign or be ejected to preserve the legitimacy of a platform. In this fashion, a constitution's legitimacy stores are partially preserved from the negative effects of a regime's performance failure by the institutions they set out. This is so even when that failure might be reasonably if partially attributed to flaws in the design of those very institutions.

Notably, political leaders may use obverse techniques to try to prevent or displace their own failures and shore up their personal legitimacy. On one hand, this explains some leaders' tendency to overreact to public threats, even at the expense of respect for a constitution. A failure to manage the threat or prevent it from coming to pass impacts legitimacy. On the other, it explains how a populist leader may succeed in displacing responsibility for public suffering onto a regime and away from personal failures or global complexities beyond her control. This creates opportunities to concentrate and solidify power. Such rhetorical tactics, relying as they do on the gathering and spending of performance legitimacy, can facilitate the stealthy replacement of a democratic constitution with one that concentrates nationalist or authoritarian power (Landau 2018, p. 534). Attention to these tactics helps illuminate mechanisms of democratic deconsolidation when the stability of the constitutional status quo is, from the perspective of a political leader, undesirable.

Consider how much better this functional model of legitimacy reflects lived political and normative experience, both among leaders and citizens, whose support for a regime and its constitution may be articulated and may fluctuate on the basis of a whole range of considerations. Such considerations and the reasons they generate may be individual or collective, robustly normative or brutally utilitarian. They are normally multiple, overlapping, and contested. Like norms more broadly, they may conflict, or compel differentially in different circumstances or for different people of different temperaments at different times. The model is culturally elastic, reflecting the possibility of strength and stretch but also its dynamic and tentative shape. A commitment to power's legitimacy can be active, exuberant and explicit or grudging, and tentative. An entente may last for a long time, crumble gradually, or fall apart in a moment. Constitutional legitimacy is dynamic and complex, not static and binary. For reasoning, whether implicit or explicit, about constitutional legitimacy rests on factors which are necessarily dynamic, because they are political. A constitution acts as a bank in which these various kinds of claims can be converted to this commensurable currency: when a constitution holds enough, it serves the function of dramatically slowing political dynamism and increasing political stability.

I have now made three key claims. First, I have been sketching a conception of legitimacy as a dynamic force, a political currency that can be stored in and withdrawn from a constitution. Second, I have claimed constitutions contribute to political stability in part because they serve as legitimacy banks. And finally, I have illustrated that the sources of this currency and the draws upon it are diverse. These claims suggest a model of constitutional legitimacy with several advantages over a consent-binary conception or a model grounded in the meeting of or conferring of a set of normative qualifications. The currency model helps explain why leaders and denizens of authoritarian and authoritative regimes take constitutions seriously enough to amend or replace them, even when the institutions and constraints they describe do not clearly map onto practice. And, it helps explain why leaders bother to make constitutions with little consultation and notably absent consent procedures. Once we have accepted that legitimacy has diverse sources and confers diverse benefits, the political value of a constitution as a legitimacy bank in such regimes is evident despite the consent-gap. A constitution can help create consent because it holds legitimacy, rather than becoming legitimate on the basis of consent.

This model better explains why people in regimes like the United Kingdom or the United States revere constitutions grounded as much in tradition as in consent, even when consent forms a dominant political norm, and even where, as in the United States, the optimal performance (or even continued rationality) of the constitution may be in question. The model allows for both a constitution's semiotic power and the relationship of legitimacy to performance, which a rational-legal model reliant on consent cannot.

And this model better captures legitimacy's dynamism. Over time, a constitution may be more or less revered, more or less authoritative and this model provides a means of capturing, and perhaps even measuring this (Gilley 2006; von Haldenwang 2016). From this vantage, the people have a continuous role in demanding and recognizing constitutional legitimacy on normative grounds, well beyond consent's binary moment.

Finally, the model respects and encourages a range of questions about why people accept power. It is on the basis of dynamic, but broadly normative reasons that people judge a constitution's legitimacy. Where there are opportunities for explicit consent, it marks a judgment on the basis of moral reasons. People give or withhold their consent because they have already deemed power and its use acceptable. It is appropriate that they do so on diverse grounds, because political normativity is foundationally dependent on reason giving, not final determination. Thus, the empirical character of debates over legitimacy is also robustly normative. A constitution sits at the nexus of these empirically occurring and recurring robust normative debates. In drawing from, holding, and conferring the stores of legitimacy that result, constitutions are normatively engaged actively and continuously with power.

RECOMMENDED READING

Barnett, R. (2003). Constitutional Legitimacy. *Columbia Law Review*, 103 (1), 111–148.
Beetham, D. (1991). *The Legitimation of Power*, London: Macmillan.
Brilmayer, L. (1989). Consent, Contract, and Territory. *Minnesota Law Review*, 74 (1), 1–35.
Dyzenhaus, D. (2010). *Hard Cases in Wicked Legal Systems*, Oxford: Oxford University Press.
Gilley, B. (2006). The Meaning and Measure of State Legitimacy: Results for 72 Countries. *European Journal of Political Research*, 45 (3), 499–525.
Hardin, R. (2003). *Liberalism, Constitutionalism, and Democracy*, Oxford: Oxford University Press.
Michelman, F. I. (2003b). Is the Constitution a Contract for Legitimacy? *Review of Constitutional Studies*, 8 (2), 101–128.
Rawls, J. (1993). *Political Liberalism*, New York: Columbia University Press.
Scharpf, F. (1999). *Governing in Europe: Effective or Democratic?* Oxford: Oxford University Press.
Vermeule, A. (2022). *Common Good Constitutionalism*, Boston: Polity.
Weber, M. (1978). *Economy and Society: An Outline of Interpretive Sociology*. Edited by G. Roth and C. Wittich. Berkeley: University of California Press.
Zurn, C. (2010). The Logic of Legitimacy: Bootstrapping Paradoxes of Constitutional Democracy. *Legal Theory*, 16 (3), 191–227.

12

Sovereignty

David Dyzenhaus

In *Leviathan*, Hobbes posed for modernity what we can think of as the puzzle – even the paradox – of sovereignty for constitutional theory. The sovereign of a particular polity is the person or body who wields ultimate authority to make law. It follows, he claimed, that the sovereign is legally unlimited (Hobbes 1991 [1651], p. 184). This 'ultimacy mark' of sovereignty has implicit within it another element, the 'independence mark': the sovereign cannot be subject to – is independent from – all other sovereigns, as Hobbes sets out in his regress argument that to suppose that the sovereign is subject to law is to suppose another sovereign to whom the sovereign is subject, and so on (Hobbes 1991 [1651], p. 224).

The puzzle is commonly supposed to arise because an absolute, i.e. legally unlimited, sovereign is able to make any law it pleases, including a law limiting its authority. But in fact, the problem is deeper. For Hobbes, like Bodin before him, the sovereign is the one who makes law (Bodin 1992 [1576], p. 56). Since the sovereign is the law-giver, its will is identified by subjects when a law is made for them. Put differently, to make its will known, the sovereign must comply with whatever criteria of validity are publicly recognized in that society for the making of law. Any sovereign is then legally constituted, even if not limited, in that it must comply with a further mark of sovereignty – the 'validity mark'. Legal change, including change to the validity mark (or marks), must happen in accordance with the criteria of validity. Hobbes's sovereign is the legal sovereign.

There is one further mark. Hobbes, again like Bodin before him, insisted that while the sovereign's authority is absolute, it is subject to the laws of nature, of which Hobbes has an extensive list (Hobbes 1991, p. 224; Bodin 1992, pp. 31–2). This is so for Hobbes even in the domain of international affairs. While a sovereign will solve the problem of the state of nature for any particular society, Hobbes claimed that in international affairs there will always be a state of nature between the plurality of states. But such states are subject to the laws of nature in their dealings with each other (Hobbes 1991, pp. 90, 244). I will call this 'the fundamental legality mark' in order to distinguish it from the more formalistic validity mark: To count as an act of sovereign will a law must be consistent with the laws of nature, in more contemporary terms with the fundamental legal commitments of the legal order.

It is at this point that the idea of legal sovereignty may seem to unravel. Hobbes was clear that, just like human individuals in their state of nature, states in the international state of nature get to interpret what the laws of nature require, which boils down to doing what it takes to ensuring their survival. But if that's what sovereign subjection to the laws of nature means in international affairs, it must mean the same in domestic affairs. The sovereign – the person at the apex of legal authority, gets to interpret the limits of its authority. It has, as the Germans say, *Kompetenz-Kompetenz*, jurisdiction to determine its jurisdiction.

It may thus seem unsurprising, then, that Rousseau, five years after he had set out his own theory of legal sovereignty in *The Social Contract*, suggested that the only solution to the 'great problem of Politics' of subjecting the sovereign to law is to 'establish a despotism that is arbitrary and indeed the most arbitrary possible'; a solution which amounts, despite his own scorn of both Bodin and Hobbes for having put forward (or so he supposes) just that view, to 'the most perfect Hobbism' (Rousseau 2004, p. 268).

This figure of the not only legally unlimited but also unlimitable sovereign haunts political and constitutional theory, particularly in our illiberal era of 'America First' and 'Get Brexit Done!'. It animates what I will call for the sake of contrast, and because it is still widely considered the solution to the problem of how to achieve political order, the 'political idea of sovereignty'. I will argue that in order to properly oppose this troubling figure, one needs to have in place not only all four marks of sovereignty, but also a political theory of their value. There is a politics to the legal idea of sovereignty.

I TWO-SIDED STATE

In the nineteenth century, sovereignty remained one of the main organizing ideas of constitutional and legal theory. The sixth and best-known lecture of John Austin's *Lectures on Jurisprudence* (Austin 1861), first delivered in 1828, is devoted to the topic, as are Lectures II, III, and VII of A. V. Dicey's 1885 *The Law of the Constitution* (Dicey 1915), still the leading text on the UK constitution. Sovereignty remained a preoccupation of jurists in the first half of the twentieth century, especially between the wars. After World War II, it retained a central place in theories of public international law until the 1990s. But then it more or less vanished from view in constitutional theory, as is evidenced by the fact that it was not on the first list of topics for this comprehensive Handbook.

Sovereignty did not vanish all of a sudden. In 1961 HLA Hart devoted Chapter 4 of *The Concept of Law* to the topic because he thought it necessary to loosen the grip of Austin's command theory of law on legal theory before he could move on to providing his own account, built on his exposure of Austin's errors (Hart 1994). In addition, it returned as a topic briefly in his discussion of 'parliamentary sovereignty' (Hart 1994, pp. 148–52) and more prominently in the last chapter on international law, which (as many have noted) seems more of an afterthought that an integral part of the text.

If we distinguish between the external face of sovereignty – the face the state presents to other states – and the internal face – the face presented to the state's officials and subjects – we can say that the internal face vanishes while the external face remains in view. That sovereignty did not disappear from public international law theory, and only reappeared in legal theory when legal philosophers began in this century to take international law as worthy of inquiry, testifies to the resilience of the political idea of sovereignty in any discussion of the interaction of states. For in international space, there is no legislature and the international courts and arbitral bodies that exist have jurisdiction only with consent of the parties. In this space, states are taken to face each other as independent, autonomous constitutional actors, with the executive of each state as their sole representative.

The executive thus strode the international stage as the only constitutional actor. It was subject to the contingencies of power politics, but not to any legal constraints, except those to which it had consented. In contrast, within states the executive seemed to be just one item of the complex constitutional furniture of the state, subject to the control of both parliament and the courts. Put differently, within the state the executive had been brought under the control of the law and the rule of law, as well as under the control of fundamental constitutional principles as seemed self-evidently the case if such principles were set out in an entrenched constitution and was arguably the case even in jurisdictions where the constitution was said to be unwritten.

Austin helps us to understand both sovereignty's disappearance in the public law theory of the modern legal state and its recent reappearance. In his legal theory, law is the commands of a legally unlimited sovereign, identified as such by the habit of obedience of those subject to his power, who motivates obedience by attaching sanctions to his commands. Since constitutional law would bind the sovereign internally and international law would bind it externally, Austin concluded that constitutional and international law are not law 'properly so called' – legally binding rules – but rules of conventional morality (Austin 1861, pp. 177, 204).

Austin's idea of sovereignty is thus political rather than legal. The sovereign is a pre-legal political entity that stands outside of the legal order made up of its commands, the products of sovereign will. Since what it wills is the law, it cannot be both sovereign and subject to any other entity's will. He located sovereignty in the 'numerous body of the *commons* … as share the sovereignty with the king and the peers, and elect the members of the commons' house' (Austin 1861, p. 245). This complex sovereign delegated to Parliament its powers not absolutely, but in terms of an implicit trust that the Parliament would not use the powers in violation of the trust; for example, it would not attempt 'to annihilate the actual constitution of the supreme government.' The trust was enforced by constitutional law, which is to say enforced by mere 'moral sanctions'; though Austin hastened to add that all 'constitutional law, in every country whatever, is, as against the sovereign, in that predicament' (Austin 1861, pp. 246–7).

Dicey pointed out that Austin seemed to have offered two different definitions of sovereignty: the political definition – sovereignty resides in the electorate, the king and the peers; and the legal definition – Parliament effectively wields sovereignty because during its lifetime it can make any law that it likes, including one that annihilates the constitution (Dicey 1915, pp. 68–72). From the legal perspective, Dicey suggested, it would be more accurate to use 'sovereignty' in the Austinian sense as 'simply the power of law-making unrestricted by any legal limit' (Dicey 1915, p. 70). The political sovereign is, as Austin saw, the body the 'will of which is ultimately obeyed by the citizens of the state', though Dicey suggested that it was the will of the electorate that was more important than the electorate combined with the Lords and the Crown (Dicey 1915, pp. 71–2).

On this view, there are two ideas of sovereignty. From the legal perspective, one understands sovereignty from the inside, which involves adopting the perspective of a judge – of the public official who makes final determinations on what counts as a legal act. From the political perspective, one will be concerned with the preconditions of legal order, and thus with such issues as identifying the people who ultimately decide on whether to support the legal order. Such support is necessary for any legal order to exist, so that we might say that any legal order must be considered legitimate, or at least not worth rebelling against, by at least some significant segment of the population subject to it. But why that segment has that view, or the precise content of the view, is not a matter for legal science; it is the proper study of social or political science.

It is striking that German legal theory reached basically the same set of conclusions at more or less the same point in time. The main figure in German constitutional theory at the end of the nineteenth century was Georg Jellinek, who developed a 'two-sided' theory of the state in an attempt to explain how a sovereign could be bound by both constitutional law and international law (Jellinek 1905). Jellinek belonged to the school of 'statutory positivism', which was not unlike Austin's command theory of law in that its legal theory was built on the idea of the primacy of statute law made by a legally unlimited, and thus, sovereign state. His predecessor in this tradition was Paul Laband who presented a legal theory that justified constitutional monarchism – the constitutional order of the late nineteenth century Prussian state – at the same time as insisting on the exclusion of politics from legal science (Caldwell 1997, pp. 13–39).

Laband and other statutory positivists argued that the state ruled comprehensively through primary legislation, faithfully implemented by the administration, with judicial review for the constitutionality of statutes prohibited, and review for the legality of official action under the law confined to seeing whether the officials had kept within the letter of the law. The legal order was thus understood as a 'closed positive system of laws deriving from a sovereign source (the state)' (Caldwell 1997, p. 34). Individuals had only those rights that the state had seen fit to grant them in its legislation. This apparently authoritarian theory is tempered by the fact that the public officials may exercise power against individuals only when authorized to do so by statute, and the enactment of statutes is the preserve of the legislature.

Unlike Austin, Laband did not deny the existence of international law. Rather, he saw it as the product of treaties between states, enforceable as such by the states, and capable of becoming part of domestic law if the public law institutions of the state enacted international law provisions into domestic instruments (Koskenniemi 2001, p. 185). However, he, like others in his school, had no way of explaining how, as a juridical matter, either domestic constitutional law or international law could be understood as legally binding on the sovereign. Both kinds of law were recognized as existing in fact, though how the 'ought' of legal authority could be derived from the 'is' of these facts was beyond the reach of legal theory, as one might think Austin more frankly recognized when it came to the command theory of law.

But Austinian frankness comes at a revealing cost – of denying that both international law and domestic constitutional law are laws, which makes the project of subjecting political power to the rule of law futile. As I have already indicated in respect of Laband, his legal theory, despite his claims as to its scientific nature, was an attempt to develop an account of the *Rechtsstaat* – the rule-of-law state – which would explain the *juridical* nature of *constitutional* monarchy. That is, it would explain how political decision-making in such a system is not arbitrary because all decisions require prior legal authorization. It was against these backdrops that Kelsen in the 1920s and Hart in the late 1950s resurrected the legal idea of sovereignty.

II BASIC NORM AND THE RULE OF RECOGNITION

In *The Concept of Law*, Hart's ground-clearing task was to argue that Austin was wrong that the sovereign is legally unlimited because in the modern legal state there are secondary legal rules, of which the 'ultimate' rule is the 'rule of recognition' which will 'specify some feature or features possession of which by a suggested rule is taken as a conclusive affirmative indication that it is a rule of the group to be supported by the local pressure it exerts' (Hart 1994, p. 94). But, as Hart acknowledged, the ground for a juridical conception of sovereignty had already been amply laid in England by work in public law by William Wade and R. T. E Latham (Wade 1955; Latham 1949). Even more significant, as Hart also recognized, is that Kelsen had in the 1920s developed a full juridical account of sovereignty, which was in fact the basis for Latham's work on Commonwealth constitutional law (Hart 1994, pp. 292–3). According to Kelsen, at the base of every legal order is a *Grundnorm* or basic norm that must be hypothesized in order to make sense of the idea that there is a unified normative order. The *Grundnorm* tells the officials and subjects of the order that the constitutional norms of that order – from which all other norms derive their validity – must be obeyed (Kelsen 1992 [1934], pp. 54–5).

Hart argued that his rule-of-recognition analysis was superior to Kelsen's *Grundnorm* because the idea that there is a basic norm that tells officials to obey the constitutional norms of their legal order is redundant. All one needs to understand the juridical nature of sovereignty is the existence of the official practice which makes up the rule of recognition, which can be observed externally as a matter of fact – what officials actually do in applying its criteria – though which from the official perspective must be understood in terms of their voluntary acceptance (Hart 1994, pp. 292–3). But he shared with Kelsen the claim that sovereignty – in the sense of the independent and ultimate lawmaking power of a society – is a juridical idea which must be explained as a matter of the exercise of a legally constituted authority, not in terms of an exercise of sheer unmediated coercive power. It could even be said that they argued that legal theory should rid itself to the greatest extent possible of the concept of sovereignty because in political and legal thought it is so bound up with the idea of a legally unlimited political entity. As Kelsen said at the end of his 1920 major work on sovereignty, the 'concept of sovereignty should be radically supressed' (Kelsen 1981, p. 320). And he and Hart succeeded in that the legal idea of sovereignty dominated discussion of the internal legal order to the extent that sovereignty ceased to be its organizing idea, replaced by either one of two fundamental constitutional ideas – the basic norm or the rule of recognition – both of which seek to explain why the marks of sovereignty are not only ultimacy and independence but also validity; that is, the sovereign is not only ultimate and independent, but also is legally constituted.

But legally constituted in this sense does not mean more than the imperative for a sovereign to observe formal criteria of validity in order to express its will. It does not, that is, reach the mark of fundamental legality or compliance with the fundamental commitments of legal order. Nevertheless, the replacement opened up the possibility of reconceiving the fundamental constitutional idea as substantive or moral fundamental legal principles, most prominently in Dworkin's legal theory (Dworkin 1996c). Sovereignty could then either be not used at all or used as an empty placeholder to designate which institution should have the 'last word' when it comes to the interpretation of constitutional law, understood in this way. Thus, Jeffrey Goldsworthy's *The Sovereignty of Parliament* (1999) argued for parliament as the ultimate guardian of the constitution, while T. R. S. Allan's *The Sovereignty of Law* (2013) argued for judges as the ultimate interpreters of constitutional principle, and thus also of the law that constrains parliament.

While this debate was often cast by the parliamentary side as one between 'political' and 'legal' 'constitutionalists', this characterization is misleading. One could say that both sides adopt the slogan: Sovereign is he who decides on the law; and at this point the positions may seem to unravel, just as we saw in Hobbes. For this provocative claim aligns their position with Carl Schmitt's claim in Weimar that 'Sovereign is he who decides on the state of exception', with the only difference that Schmitt regarded the executive as the body that should have the last word because, in his theory, the executive is the guardian of the constitution (Schmitt 2005 [1922], p. 5).

Schmitt presented his argument that in the state of exception – an existential situation in which the identity of a political community is at stake – as a legal argument about the appropriate place of a strong, unitary executive in the Weimar constitutional order. He therefore presented himself as the saviour of not only Germany's constitution but also of democracy itself. His position is most explicit in his 1931 argument that the president is the guardian of the constitution, so that when it comes to the limits on executive power under Article 48 – the emergency powers provision of the Weimar Constitution – it is for the executive itself to determine these, not judges. This is because Schmitt's theory of the judicial role supposes that a judge adjudicates properly only when he subsumes the facts of a case to the determinate content of a statute. The independence of judges depends on such a role being available to them and so they are incapable of resolving the political disputes that face the guardian of the constitution (Schmitt 2015, p. 125). Such disputes have, Schmitt asserted, to be resolved not by a higher authority but by a 'neutral third', in his view, the president of the Reich because he alone can take political decisions in the name of the 'whole of the political unity' of the German people. On this point, Schmitt rested his final claim that the president has a democratic legitimacy that judges lack (Schmitt 2015, pp. 168–75).

Kelsen responded that the issue is first and foremost a normative one about the demand for constitutional institutions that control the behaviour of other constitutional institutions, a demand which 'expresses a requirement of the rule of law, namely the requirement that the exercise of the state's functions be as lawful as possible' (Kelsen 2015, p. 235). He pointed out that Schmitt's conception of democracy has nothing to do with the political system in which an elected parliament is the ultimate law maker, and in which all executive decisions require an ultimate warrant in a legislative source. Rather, the democratic bond is one forged between the executive and the people, on the basis of a vision articulated by the executive of the identity of a homogeneous political community, which requires a clear distinction to be made between friend and enemy. Parliamentary government is part of the problem; hence, as soon as its slow and cumbersome mechanisms of debate and attempts to find a compromise between conflicting interests are marginalized or even eradicated, the better for democracy. Kelsen's focus throughout is on the fact that Schmitt's argument is an ideological one against both parliamentary democracy and the institution of a constitutional court, which has the right to test the validity of acts of state for their constitutionality. He therefore accused Schmitt of disguising a political argument that sought to find in the executive's bond with the people a surrogate for the divine right of the monarch under claims about what sovereignty is and what the Weimar Constitution required (Kelsen 2015, pp. 177–81). Thus, Kelsen suggested that making sense of the legal idea of sovereignty and disentangling constitutional issues from normative argument about the desired nature of political community would clarify the terms of the political debate of the time (Dyzenhaus 1997).

It is Kelsen's position that makes best – in my view, the only – sense of a 'political constitutionalist' stance if such a stance is supposed to indicate a fundamental difference between itself and a *legal* constitutionalism'. For political constitutionalism, at least as proposed by most of its proponents, the stance boils down to a combination of two claims: first, the debate about the appropriate design of constitutional order cannot be settled within legal theory since it is a debate about political legitimacy; second, the best design is one in which parliament, rather than judges, has the last word on the interpretation of constitutional principles.

But to take just Dworkin's interpretive theory, the most prominent example of a legal constitutionalist position, the first claim is one that he advanced throughout his career in even more radical form since he thought it applied to legal theory in general, not merely to theories of constitutional design. And the second claim, as he never tired of pointing out, is an internal interpretivist one about how best to take forward what we can think of as the rule-of-law project of rendering political power non-arbitrary by requiring that it be exercised only on the basis of a legal warrant (Dworkin 1978). In brief, most political constitutionalists are no less legal than their foil. Together they suppose that the sovereign is a juridical body which makes the final decision, not against the law, but on what the law requires.

An authentic political constitutionalist is, then, one who adopts Schmittean, anti-juridical logic in the service of a political end – the establishment of the identity of a homogeneous political community. But while this position in its most explicit form is deeply unattractive to anyone committed to democracy, the rule of law, and constitutionalism, it is not so easy to reject, especially if one accepts the terms of the debate as one in which the issue is which institution should have the last word.

First, in any concrete situation there will be conflicting decisions about what the law requires, which, if the disfavoured institution prevails, will be regarded as a decision against the law. Second, this point holds even if the constitution of a legal order makes it clear that judges are guardians of the constitution in which case there may seem to be no question in a concrete case of conflict between the legislature and the judiciary since the legal order has pre-committed to final judicial decision. For these conflicts can still arise through claims about the 'political questions doctrine', 'non-justiciability' or deference to the legislative delegation of authority to the executive in sensitive areas like national security and immigration. If it seems appropriate in this second kind of case that the executive should have the last word, Schmitt's argument finds the toehold that it needs.

Put differently, if:

1. the major issue in constitutional theory is which institution should have the last word; and
2. the executive seems to be the appropriate candidate in this second kind of case even in what we might regard as a fully constitutionalized legal order, one in which there is judicial review of legislation; since
3. these cases are ones that the executive must resolve because they are mini states of exception, situations in which at the margins the political identity of the community is at stake; then,
4. when the situation moves from the margins of legal order to the centre the executive's role as guardian of the constitution is inescapably writ large. Further,
5. since at stake is the community's political identity, the success of any executive decision will depend on whether the executive makes the friend/enemy distinction in a way that can appeal to a substantial segment of the population. Finally,
6. since a decision will fail that perpetuates the situation of fractious pluralism that led to the state of exception, the mark of a successful decision is that it appeals to a substantively homogeneous segment of the population.

This is a political rather than a legal logic. But it is legal in so far as it begins in argument about concrete legal problems that require a resolution. As such it has a worrying salience in contemporary debates.[1]

III THE EXTERNAL SOVEREIGN

As Austin, Schmitt and Kelsen clearly saw, one must have a consistent view in this regard: either the political idea or the legal idea of sovereignty both externally and internally. Any attempt at combining the two is radically unstable.

Kelsen's solution was to maintain the legal idea of sovereignty in both spaces via his fundamental constitutional idea – the basic norm. For Kelsen, a 'primitive' society has a legal order so long as its members both accept the norms as binding and seek to understand each norm as part of a meaningful unity, thus presupposing the basic norm. Similarly, so long as one can hypothesize a basic norm for the norms of

---

[1] For example, it is the logic that explains the otherwise strange displacement in the 'Brexit debates' from assertions about the loss of sovereignty evidenced in the fact that Parliament was no longer the supreme legal authority in some respects to assertions that the attempt by Parliament to take control of the Brexit process was an unconstitutional usurpation of the place of the executive as guardian of both the constitution and democracy. As Tom Poole has argued, the issue is not whether the lawyers making these arguments had read Schmitt's work, but that they embraced a Schmittean logic. He has presented this position in a number of blog posts, for example, 'The Executive Power Project', Poole 2019, the title of which is a riposte to the title of the website which is the vehicle for these arguments: https://judicialpowerproject.org.uk. For the extended argument, see Poole 2020.

international law, there is in place a legal order, and one that demands obedience from all those subject to it. In the international legal order, as in a primitive society, the subjects – states in the former and individuals in the latter – are at the same time the officials, responsible as they are for interpreting as well as enforcing the public norms of their order.

It is this conception of legal order that leads to Kelsen's opposition to dualism about the relationship between the space of public international law, on the one hand, and that of domestic constitutional law, on the other. But, he pointed out, one could explain the relationship between national law and public international law from two different monistic perspectives, which I will call 'national law monism' and 'international law monism'. The former insists that only one national legal order exists so that valid legal norms are only those norms that can trace their validity to its basic norm. In contrast, the latter states that there are many valid national legal orders, but they are all part of the international legal order and so trace the validity of their norms back to the ultimate basic norm of the international order. From this perspective, the independence of states from each other is made possible by a kind of dependence, i.e. the fact that international law has delegated to them the authority to make binding law within their jurisdiction (Kelsen 1992, pp. 107–25).

At times, Kelsen suggests that his choice for international law monism is determined not by legal theory but by a political preference for cosmopolitanism over nationalistic imperialism. But early in his thought on this topic he insisted that national law monism was an incoherent stance, at odds with both the fact that there is a plurality of independent states and with the binding nature of international law, which he explains in terms of the ethical value of the basic norm of international law. As he puts it in his book on sovereignty of 1920:

> There is a generally accepted understanding of the nature and concept of international law that it constitutes a community of states with equal rights. The proposition of the coexistence of a multiplicity of communities, which despite their actual differences in size, population, and effective means of exercising power are legally of equal value and, when it comes to their mutually delimited spheres of power, bound in a higher community is an eminently ethical idea and one of the few really valuable and uncontested components of contemporary cultural consciousness. But this proposition is only possible with the help of a juristic hypothesis: that above the communities understood as states stands a legal order that mutually delimits the spheres of validity of the individual states in that it hinders incursions by one into the sphere of the others, or at least subjects them all to equal conditions for such incursions (Kelsen 1981, p. 204).

He concluded that 'when the primacy of international law fulfils this function, the concept of law is simultaneously perfected in a formal and substantive sense. The law attains the organization of humanity and thereby a unity with the highest ethical idea' (Kelsen 1981, p. 205).

In addition, Kelsen ended one of his discussions of the international/domestic relationship by saying that it 'is by juristic interpretation that the legal material is transformed into a legal system' (Kelsen 1946a, p. 375). His emphasis on the role of juristic interpretation in making an order legal is significant. Like Hart, he did not offer a theory of adjudication since such a theory was, he thought, a political theory beyond the scope of legal science. He also emphasized that at each of the levels of legal activity below the level of legislation there is an irreducible moment of judicial or official creativity.

But, unlike Hart and his followers, Kelsen denied that there are gaps in the legal order (Kelsen 1967, pp. 245–50). In this respect, Kelsen's legal theory is closer to Dworkin than to Hart as, in his view, a legal order provides seamlessly for an authorized official to solve by a legal procedure any problem raised within the legal order (Honoré 1994, pp. 109–12). Indeed, his legal theory goes further than Dworkin's since it rejects a distinction that Dworkin relies on between legislation – the instrument of policy and the province of the legislature – and adjudication – the realm of principle and the province of the judiciary (Dworkin 1978). For Kelsen, the moment of creativity in legislation is much more heightened than in adjudication, but it is quantitatively rather than qualitatively different. Legislation is a legally authorized act that must respect the constitutional norms that govern its production.

In setting out this position, Kelsen, was primarily concerned with explaining legal order from the perspective of one who accepts that the norms of that order are binding, not because of any threat of force, but because they are part of an authoritative order. For if one adopts what Hart was to call the 'internal point of view', one assumes that the answer to any legal question will be produced by legal procedures and will make sense of that individual's subjection to the material and formal norms of the legal order by displaying them as a unity (Hart 1994, p. 89).

Kelsen was thus mostly concerned to answer questions about what makes an order legal: a polity governed in accordance with the rule of law in the sense that law regulates its own production and all legal problems are solved in a dynamic process of norm application by legal procedures. Moreover, as we can see from the long quotation above, in his early work he accepted that the assumption of the unity of legal order introduced a natural law element to his legal theory, thus transcending the limits of a 'strict positivism' (Kelsen, 1946b, p. 437). He recognized that the same point had to apply to the assumption when it was made about the international legal order. 'In this sense', he said 'there is absolutely no contradiction between natural law and positive law' (Kelsen 1981, p. 252.)

Hart's view is different. Like Kelsen, he diagnosed the situation of law before the advent of the modern legal state as 'primitive' and applied the same label to the situation of international law. His reason for the diagnosis is also the same – the lack of adjudicative institutions. But because the lack of adjudicative institutions shows there is no rule of recognition, it followed for Hart that there is in these spaces no legal order. Yet while he was rather ambiguous about whether there is law properly so called in the pre-modern space, he did think that there is law in the international space, but only in the sense that there are primary rules which states regard as binding (Hart 1994, pp. 232–7).

Hart could not, however, offer any account of how international law binds. As I have argued elsewhere, his critique of Kelsen seems to assume that a norm of one legal order enters the space of another legal order only if the rule of recognition of the latter validates a law that imports the norm. That assumption commits him on theoretical grounds to dualism and so he elides a distinction between dualism as a description of actual state practice and dualism as a theory of international law (Dyzenhaus 2020).

Dualism as a theoretical position is an attempt to make sense of international law as law properly so called, which makes international norms effective within the domestic legal order conditional on legislative incorporation. But that leaves it uneasily perched between a conception of sovereignty as both political and thus legally unlimited, as in Austin or Schmitt, and a conception in which sovereignty is understood to be legally constituted by one's candidate for the fundamental constitutional idea. This is not to say that states cannot be more or less dualist in practice, if all that is meant by this label is that states will have different ways of giving shape to their relationship with the order of public international law. From a theoretical perspective that seeks to understand law's normativity, however, this is not dualism because international law monism is the theory that explains why states are under a prior obligation to give shape to that relationship. States can do a better or worse job of this, just as they can do a better or worse job of arranging their national constitution.

That dualism as a theoretical position collapses into national law monism – a claim about the primacy of the national state – and that national law monism is incoherent as a juridical theory does not however mean that it is wrong. It might, that is, tell us, as Rousseau suggested, that a legal or juridical idea of sovereignty can't be had and so one has to resort to what he called a 'complete Hobbism' – the location of ultimate law-making authority in one legally unlimited institution. The only marks of sovereignty are then ultimacy and independence. It goes without saying that fundamental legality is no longer a mark, but neither is validity since the latter is subject to sovereign prerogative. The sovereign can change the criteria of validity at will, including by implication, that is, by an act of will that does not comply with the criteria. The executive is the only candidate for such an institution, as Schmitt argued, and it strides the national stage much as it is taken by many to stride the international. As I will now argue, in order for the legal idea of sovereignty to properly oppose the political idea, it has to reveal the politics of his idea by completing the package of the marks of sovereignty with the fourth mark of fundamental legality.

IV PRIMACY OF THE STATE?

The fact that it is up to states how to manage their relationship with international law implies a kind of primacy when it comes to the internal face of sovereignty.

Hence, the debate in international law between the 'declaratory theory', which argues that recognition of an entity as a state merely confirms its legal status, and the 'constitutive theory', which argues that an entity that aspires to legal statehood, requires the recognition of other states. The debate replays that over sovereignty in general. Legalists like Kelsen tend to argue that the legal idea of sovereignty requires the constitutive theory. In contrast, those who assert the primacy of a political conception of sovereignty will usually adopt the declaratory theory, and consequently the view that the decision by states to recognize an entity as a state is a political act. But in fact, most positions end up with some mix of declaratory and constitutive elements.

So much was recognized by Hermann Heller, who, while largely forgotten today, was one of the most important legal and public law theorists of Weimar. In his 1927 monograph on sovereignty, Heller argued for the primacy of the internal face, which meant that he proclaimed his allegiance to the declaratory theory, but also recognized that any theory has to have elements of both. Like Kelsen, he argued for the legal idea of sovereignty, but, like Schmitt, he argued that all fundamental juridical ideas are political. Put differently, Heller advanced a legal idea of sovereignty but regarded that idea as nested in a wider political theory of the modern legal state. In this way, he sought to combine the two sides of Jellinek's theory in one unified state theory (Heller 2019 [1927]).

To suppose that it is for the executive to decide the existential questions of the day is to put forward, as Heller said of Schmitt, a theory not of sovereignty but of 'organ sovereignty', that is, a theory in which one institutional actor is taken to speak for the legal order as a whole (Heller 2019, pp. 101–4). Moreover, the precise location in the executive can only mean, as Heller warned of Schmitt, setting in motion the argument outlined above which ends with the executive freed of legal constraints and held out as the guardian of both the constitution and democracy.

Heller was in 1927 even more concerned by what he saw as the emptiness of Kelsen's theory in which sovereignty is so radically repressed that the sovereign actor may seem to disappear. This occurs when one reduces legality to the validity mark, thus eliminating the mark of fundamental principles of legality. He argued that more than the fundamental principles are eliminated in making the sovereign subject to positive law alone. For a sovereign that is utterly subject to positive law, and to positive law alone, becomes identical with positive law. In other words, sovereignty itself is eliminated and in this way the dream is achieved of the *Rechtsstaat* – of the elimination of arbitrariness from political life through putting in place the impersonal rule of law. But that achievement is only theoretical. In practice, the moment cannot be eliminated when some person or institution must make a concrete, final decision, so sovereignty will constantly assert itself. Indeed, in *Sovereignty* Heller detailed many instances where Kelsen and others who would eliminate sovereignty recognized the futility of this task; and he took Schmitt's signal but only service to legal theory to be his argument that the deciding sovereign must be brought back into the centre of legal theory. It is Schmitt's only service, because for the sovereign properly to re-enter legal theory, he must come accompanied by the fundamental legal principles, which it is his job to concretize and which make sense of the idea that sovereign power is ultimate legal power (Heller 2019, pp. 101–4).

With Kelsen, Heller thus regarded as crucially important to legal order the juristic assumption that a legal order is autonomous, that is, a closed or gap-free system of norms. But unlike Kelsen, for whom the assumption is an epistemological requirement, Heller saw it as a political and ethical precondition of legal order. It makes it possible to order a society along legal lines; in particular it makes possible constitutional legal order, an order which binds the powerful to the rule of law (Heller 2019, pp. 118–21).

On the one hand, Heller emphasized what he called the law-formative character of power: legal order secures and even increases the resources of the powerful. On the other hand, he emphasized that increased and more stable power comes at a price: the powerful perforce finds themselves constrained by the legal order. This aspect of the *Rechtsstaat* Heller called the power-formative aspect of law. What connects these two aspects, establishing a dialectical relationship between law and power, is ethics, more precisely the ethical fundamental principles of law. The function of the assumption is to serve legal order conceived as a dialectical unity of law, power, and ethics (Heller 1996 [1934], pp. 1179–81).

The assumption does this service by enabling an interpretation of the law, in particular of the law of the constitution, which strips the law of its quality of temporality in order to help ensure its historical continuity. The law is necessarily temporal, in a state of flux because it is but part of an ever-changing, overarching political and social order. The role of law in that overarching order is to give the order some relative stability and that requires the jurist to ignore the flux for the purposes of stability-enhancing interpretation. The jurist must interpret the law as if it were autonomous to facilitate the endeavour of the *Rechtsstaat* in achieving an aim which in reality can never be achieved. That aim is to ensure that the whole of the state organization will function in compliance with norms (Heller 1996, pp. 1189–90).

In his posthumously published *Staatslehre*, Heller distinguished more clearly between 'ethical fundamental' and 'logical fundamental' principles. The latter are formal, in the sense that all law must observe requirements of legality. But it is the ethical fundamental principles, prominently the principle of equality, which the positive law must seek to express. The substance of the rule of law is derived from these ethical fundamental principles, by contrast with the formal *Rechtsstaat*, which will be in place wherever there is the form of law. In Heller's view, it is their very lack of determinate content that permits ethical fundamental principles of law to stabilize a constitution. They are supra-positive in that they are beyond positive law, though not supra-cultural as they formulate values already embedded in our cultural practices. That they are based in cultural practices, does not, however, mean that they are culturally determined (Heller 1996, pp. 1191–5).

V POLITICAL LEGAL THEORY

As I have indicated, the terms of the debate between political and legal constitutionalists invite Schmittian theories through accepting that the main issue in constitutional design is who should have the last word, i.e. by proposing different versions of organ sovereignty. But that these two camps locate sovereignty in juridical institutions which are in a symbiotic relationship makes a big difference. If one locates sovereignty in a supreme parliament, one presupposes judges who will enforce parliament's law, otherwise parliament's supremacy cannot be maintained. And if one locates sovereignty in the law as interpreted by judges, unless one lives in some fantasy world in which there is only common law, one presupposes a body of enacted law. Both are, as I suggested, versions of legal constitutionalism and differ only in their views as to the best design of the legal constitution, much as one can design a state's reception of international law differently. In contrast, to locate sovereignty in the executive, as Schmitt's example shows, is to adopt an anti-juridical logic that presupposes the political idea of sovereignty.

We are now in a position to see why positions in debates about sovereignty form a complex whole in which claims made about the nature of political community are linked to both claims made about the concept of sovereignty and claims about what the constitution requires. The legal idea of sovereignty requires that a political community be understood as a jural community, one in which the relationship between individuals and the state (as well as many important relationships between individuals) are mediated by law. As Heller formulated this part of the position, it follows Hobbes's precise 'juristic' formulation in arguing that to say that 'a people' 'wills' something is to say that the state wills it, that is, the collection of institutions that make up the legal state. In expressing this will, the state performs the act of representation that follows from the assumption that each legal subject had agreed with every other legal subject that 'on matters essential to the common peace', the unitary expression of state will must be accepted as the will 'of all and each' (Heller 2019, pp. 107–8). It is political because it opposes the conception of the political advanced by Schmitt which seeks to reduce the essence of politics to an existential, extra-legal decision. It does so by elaborating a theory in which politics involves the renunciation of anarchic violence and a commitment to working out conflicts within the framework of the law. It is with the establishment of such a framework that sovereignty in the primary legal sense is achieved – that a legal state comes into existence (Heller 2019, pp. 104–9; Dyzenhaus 2019, pp. 45–6). And within that framework, the executive is subject to law, both internally and externally (McLachlan 2020).

RECOMMENDED READING

Allan, T. R. S. (2013). *The Sovereignty of Law: Freedom, Constitution, and Common Law*, Oxford: Oxford University Press.

Arato, A. (2016). *Post Sovereign Constitution Making: Learning and Legitimacy*, Oxford: Oxford University Press.

Bodin, J. (1992). *On Sovereignty*, Cambridge: Cambridge University Press.

Bourke, R. & Skinner, Q., eds. (2016). *Popular Sovereignty in Historical Perspective*, Cambridge: Cambridge University Press.

Caldwell, P. C. (1997). *Popular Sovereignty and the Crisis of German Constitutional Law: The Theory and Practice of Weimar Constitutionalism*, Durham: Duke University Press.

Cohen, J. L. (2012). *Globalization and Sovereignty: Rethinking Legality, Legitimacy and Constitutionalism*, Cambridge: Cambridge University Press.

Goldsworthy, J. (1999). *The Sovereignty of Parliament: History and Philosophy*, Oxford: Clarendon Press.

Grimm, G. (2009). *Sovereignty: The Origin and Future of a Political and Legal Concept*, New York: Columbia University Press.

Heller, H. (2019). *Sovereignty: A Contribution to the Theory of Public and International Law*, Oxford: Oxford University Press.

Krasner, S. D. (1999). *Sovereignty: Organized Hypocrisy*, Princeton: Princeton University Press.

Lee, D. (2016). *Popular Sovereignty in Early Modern Thought*, Oxford: Oxford University Press.

MacCormick, N. (2001). *Questioning Sovereignty: Law, State, and Nation in the European Commonwealth*, Oxford: Oxford University Press.

Pavel, C. (2015). *Divided Sovereignty: International Institutions and the Limits of State Authority*, New York: Oxford University Press.

Rawlings, R., Leyland, P., & Young, A. L., eds. (2013). *Sovereignty and the Law: Domestic, European, and International Experiences*, Oxford: Oxford University Press.

Schmitt, C. (2005). *Political Theology: Four Chapters on the Concept of Sovereignty*. Chicago: University of Chicago Press.

Walker, N., ed. (2003). *Sovereignty in Transition*, Oxford: Hart Publishing.

13

Constituent Power

Martin Loughlin[*]

The concept of constituent power emerges alongside that of the modern idea of the constitution. In modern understanding, the constitution is a document that defines the powers of the main institutions of government, determines their relations, and regulates the relation between those institutions and the citizens of the state. The authority of this constitution rests on the conviction that, having been drafted in the name of 'the people' through an exercise of their constitution-making power, the people are conceived as authors of that constitution. The concept of constituent power enables us to present the constitution as an expression of collective self-government. It can therefore be seen to be closely associated with the idea of popular sovereignty.

This chapter examines how the concept of constituent power emerged in modern thought, explains its original meaning, sketches its subsequent evolution in thought, and evaluates the role it continues to play in contemporary constitutional discourse.

I ORIGINS

The concept of constituent power was first formulated with precision during the late-eighteenth century American and French revolutions, but its origins can be traced to developments in early-modern thought and especially to Calvinist reinterpretations of Bodin's pioneering work. In *Les six livres de la république* (1576), Bodin outlined the modern framework of public law founded on the concept of sovereignty. This foundation was subsequently radicalised by such Calvinist jurists as Beza, Althusius, Lawson, and Locke who claimed the state is based on what they called a 'double sovereignty'. Accepting that 'personal' sovereignty (*majestas personalis*) is held by the prince, they maintained that nevertheless 'real' sovereignty (*majestas realis*) vests in the people (Lawson 1992 [1678], p. 47). It is from

---

[*] This chapter is a revised and expanded version of chapter 5 of AGAINST CONSTITUTIONALISM by Martin Loughlin, Cambridge, MA: Harvard University Press, Copyright © 2022 by the President and Fellows of Harvard College. Used by permission. All rights reserved.

this partition between 'personal' and 'real' sovereignty that a distinction is drawn between the constituted power of the office of government and the constituent power of the people to establish that office.

This distinction was adopted by reformers caught up in the European political and religious conflicts of the sixteenth to eighteenth centuries. It can be seen clearly expressed in the writings of the English Levellers. In *A Remonstrance of Many Thousand Citizens, and Other Free-born People of England, to their own House of Commons* of 1646, they claimed that 'we the people' choose our representatives to the Parliament, that the power vested in these representatives is merely a 'power of trust – which is ever revocable' because 'we are your principals and you our agents', and that since only the Commons 'are chosen by us the people' neither the King nor the Lords possess political authority (Levellers 1967, pp. 113, 115). Governing authority, they have asserted, is not conferred from above by God; it is acquired from below by the people. Such claims coalesced in the idea of the sovereign people, which became formalised in the doctrine of popular sovereignty (Franklin 1978; Morgan 1988).

The core elements of popular sovereignty were presented in Locke's *Second Treatise of Government*. Locke maintained that political society is created as an original compact entered into by a freely consenting people whose main reason for doing so was to establish a fixed system of government that will guarantee protection of their property. He also argued that, if ever the government breaches the terms of this compact, they put themselves in 'a state of War with the People', who possess 'a Right to resume their original Liberty, and, by the Establishment of a new Legislative (such as they shall think fit) provide for their own Safety and Security' (Locke 1988 [1689], § 222). Locke may not have used the phrase 'constituent power' but he most surely founds his scheme of government on its foundation. Franklin (1978, p. 124) thus argues that Locke resolved the problem of resistance in a mixed constitution by introducing 'a clear and consistent distinction between constituent and ordinary power', a distinction which in one form or another 'is now accepted in all constitutionalist systems'.

Over the course of the following century, American colonists sought to break from the British crown. Their Declaration of Independence is assumed to have been drafted by Jefferson, but the words used are those of Locke. The preamble to the Declaration first states that 'to secure these [unalienable] rights [of life, liberty and the pursuit of happiness], governments are instituted among men, deriving their just powers from the consent of the governed'. And it continues that 'whenever any form of government becomes destructive to these ends, it is the right of the people to alter or to abolish it, and to institute new government, laying its foundation on such principles and organizing its powers in such form, as to them shall seem most likely to effect their safety and happiness'. Through an exercise of constituent power, the American colonists asserted their right to break the original compact with the British crown and establish a new type of government. This new type of government was established by the US Federal Constitution of 1787, the world's first modern written constitution.

II CONSTITUENT POWER FORMULATED

Similar ideas shaped the course of the French Revolution. The Revolution, 'the most important single event in the entire history of government' (Finer 1999, p. 1517), might be said to have commenced on 17 June 1789, the date on which the meeting of the Third Estate declared itself to be the National Assembly. That momentous declaration had been drafted by Emmanuel-Joseph Sieyès who, in his pamphlet *What is the Third Estate?* proceeded to explain its significance.

Faced with the imminent bankruptcy of the state, in 1789 the King convened a meeting of the Estates-General. Sieyès argued that these conditions were symptomatic of a deeper bankruptcy of the entire political order and that instead of convening this advisory assembly, a constituent assembly authorised to address the case for fundamental constitutional reform should have been established. Claiming that the *ancien régime* had lost its authority, Sieyès maintained that prime responsibility for this lay with the nobility. Far from being producers of the nation's resources, they had become its most avaricious consumers. They had ceased to be an aristocracy charged with the affairs of governing and had become a caste who maintained privileges without corresponding duties. In effect, they had seceded from the nation and become its enemies.

Sieyès's pamphlet proclaimed the third estate as the nation and, reformulating the meeting as the national assembly, demanded that sovereign authority be transferred from the king to that body. This initiated a political and legal revolution. On 4 August 1789, the newly established National (Constituent) Assembly removed the privileges of the nobles and the clergy, thereby abolishing feudalism and establishing the principle of equality before the law. The Assembly then established a committee to prepare a draft constitution and, as an intended preamble to that constitution, on 26 August adopted a *Declaration of the Rights of Man and the Citizen*. This proclaimed that 'men are born and remain free and equal in rights' (art 1), that the aim of 'political association is the preservation of the natural and imprescriptible rights of man' (art 2), that 'sovereignty resides essentially in the nation' (art 3), that law is 'the expression of the general will' (art 6) and that, without a defined separation of powers, a society 'has no constitution at all' (art 16).

Sieyès explained that the nation originates in a social contract which transforms an aggregate of individuals into a unified body politic possessed of a single common will: 'The nation exists prior to everything; it is the origin of everything. Its will is always legal. It is the law itself' (Sieyès 2003 [1789], p. 136). The nation therefore exists prior to the constitution and the government established by a constitution serves only at the pleasure of the nation's will. It follows that the nation is not bound by any prior constitution since it 'cannot alienate or prohibit its right to will' (ibid., p. 137). The nation as the bearer of constituent power determines the constitutional form of the state.

It is today an orthodox tenet of legal thought that constitutional law is fundamental law. The point Sieyès makes is that while the law of the constitution may take effect as fundamental law with respect to the institutions of government, the constitution is established by the higher authority of the nation. Constitutional law is fundamental law with respect to the office of the government, but the constitution is itself the product of a higher law, that of the constituent power of the nation.

Sieyès was undoubtedly influenced by Rousseau, but he deviates from him in crucial aspects. The most important aspects concern the formation of the national will. Rousseau had argued that sovereignty cannot be represented and the moment a people gives itself representatives it is no longer free. Sieyès, by contrast, argues that a constitution can only be made by representatives. In contrast to the constitutions of the ancient republics that Rousseau extolled, some political division of labour was necessary in a modern state. For Sieyès, the basic law is not an idealised 'general will': it is formulated by representatives as a 'common will'. And, once ratified by the people, that common will is as valid as that of the nation itself. These precepts reveal the significance of the concept of constituent power that Sieyès formulates.

Sieyès' concept of constituent power 'is an account of people's power according to which the supreme political authority ... entails *exclusively* the power to authorize the creation of the political order through the writing of a Constitution' (Rubinelli 2019b, p. 51). Rubinelli also argues that once the constitution has been established, 'the people's constituent power is present only indirectly, as expressed and enforced through the rules established in the constitution' (ibid.). That is, Sieyès had devised the concept of constituent power not as an expression of popular sovereignty but as a modification of it. Concerned that sovereignty implied an absolute power which when transferred from the king to the people exposed real dangers of its despotic abuse, he posited the people's constituent power as an extraordinary power, to be exercised only at founding moments, by which the people are able to freely establish the constitutional order under which all might live.

This point is reinforced with respect to Sieyès' treatment of representation. Although the nation is the bearer of constituent power, he argues that 'a great nation cannot in real terms assemble every time that extraordinary circumstances may require'; it must therefore entrust this power to a body of 'extraordinary representatives' who act as 'a surrogate for an assembly of that nation' (Sieyès 2003, p. 139). This body of extraordinary representatives must be distinguished from the ordinary representatives of the people who are 'entrusted with exercising, according to constitutional forms, that portion of the common will that is necessary for good social administration' (ibid.). There may be nothing special about the membership of these different representative groups; they might even comprise the same individuals. But they are distinct because their powers are distinct: one acts as an ordinary legislature whereas the other deliberates 'as would the nation itself' to establish a constitution (ibid., p. 140). The former is a constituted power exercising the function of legislating, the latter is exercising constituent power.

Considered in this light, Sieyès may indeed provide 'the key to the French Revolution' (Bredin 1988), but his account was designed to appeal to the bourgeoisie who, it was anticipated, would become 'the natural governing class' of the commercial society that was emerging (Sewell 1994, p. 39). Since this commercial society is founded on productive work and the division of labour, Sieyès extends those characteristics to the political domain through the principle of representation: the legislative task is to be exercised by the people's ordinary representatives, the people's constituent power is to be exercised by a body of extraordinary representatives, and responsibility for ensuring that legislators act within their constitutional powers is to be given to a 'constitutional jury' (Goldoni 2012). Sieyès formulates an account of constituent power that comes to play a central role in the establishment of modern constitutional democracy.

The character of modern constitutional democracy is further elucidated once it is noted that, having excluded the nobility from the nation, Sieyès maintains that the political nation does not include women, beggars, vagabonds, domestic servants, or anyone dependent on a master (Sieyès 2003, p. 107). The nation's representatives must be limited to the 'available' classes within the third estate: 'those with the kind of ease that enables a man to be given a liberal education, to cultivate his reason, and to take an interest in public affairs' (ibid., p. 110). Sieyès therefore argues first 'that the Third Estate is the entire nation because its members do all the useful work of society and that the nobility is alien to the nation because of its idleness' but then argues that the legitimate representatives of the people are 'those classes of the Third Estate whose wealth frees them from the daily press of labor and gives them sufficient leisure to concern themselves with public affairs' (Sewell 1994, p. 152). The concept of constituent power he invokes is designed to justify the transfer of political power from the aristocracy to the bourgeoisie.

Sieyès presents a concept of constituent power for a modern world of liberal and constrained constitutional democracy. His account jettisons the language of sovereignty, replacing it with a scheme in which ultimate power vests in 'the nation' who exercise their power only at certain critical founding moments. At those moments, the nation's main task is to appoint extraordinary representatives to a constituent assembly charged with the responsibility of devising a constitution. The distinction between constituent and constituted power becomes his chosen method of justifying modern governmental authority.

III CONSTITUENT POWER AND CONSTITUTIONALISM

After the late-eighteenth century revolutionary movements, nation-states at critical moments in their histories adopted modern constitutions. When doing so, they generally worked with an understanding of the hierarchical relationship between ordinary law, constitutional law, and constituent power. But once the authority of this written constitution had been consolidated and states were faced with fewer potentially destabilising 'founding moments', constituent power was destined to become a marginal, if not redundant, concept. Since provision for change was incorporated within the constitution, there could be no reason to fall back on the potentially unruly idea that the authority of government rests on the will of the multitude.

Accordingly, the concept of constituent power was retained but it was reformulated by constitutional lawyers as a doctrine concerning the powers of special assemblies charged with the tasks of constitutional amendment or revision (Rubinelli 2020, chap. 2). As the French jurist Raymond Carré de Malberg (2004, p. 504) explained, 'constituent power can be conceived as an essentially legal power only so long as it has its origin in an anterior statutory order and is exercised in accordance with that pre-existing order'. Constitutional lawyers sought to tame the idea of constituent power by re-interpreting it as a principle of constitutionalism.

As the French experience exemplifies, this ambition to transform constituent power into a special category of constituted power could not easily be realised in practice. Despite claims to have invented the concept, the French had great difficulty in establishing a stable constitution that could halt its Revolution (Furet 1981). It was also not apparent that, despite its accepted understanding by constitutional lawyers (Möllers 2011b, pp. 171–172), the concept was available only for liberal purposes. Ernst-Wolfgang Böckenförde (2017b, p. 172) suggested that constituent power 'was not transferrable to the monarch, because his position of power ... stood within an entirely different legitimatory context'. But others have argued that constituent power is simply as an expression of the political will that is able to establish a constitution. It was in this sense that Napoleon (1910 [1804], p. 182) could assert that 'I am the constituent power'. And in the period after 1815, French constitutional development was driven by 'the clash between monarchy and popular sovereignty as two formative political principles' and in this dispute 'the monarch also laid claim to the constituent power' (Böckenförde 2017b, p. 173).

But the most important reason why constituent power could not be absorbed into constitutionalism is because of ambiguities that were latent in Sieyès' account. Maintaining that constituent power vests in 'the nation', Sieyès used the latter term in two distinct senses. Initially, he presented it in an idealised sense: 'a body of associates living under a common law' and which is 'the origin of everything' (Sieyès 2003, pp. 97, 136). But he also gave it a concrete meaning, suggesting that it is the group that controls the forces of production in society. The differences between the abstract and concrete meanings of 'the nation' has been utilised by constitutional scholars to present different understandings of the concept's meaning.

These differences are bolstered by the concept continuing to be entangled with controversies over the meaning of sovereignty. Sieyès believed that constituent power could replace sovereignty in modern constitutional thought. In this respect he was unsuccessful. One reason why constituent power has remained a contested concept in constitutional thought is that its meaning has become inextricably bound-up with different conceptions of sovereignty. It is to these that I now turn.

IV CONSTITUENT POWER AS SOVEREIGN POWER

Controversies over the meaning of constituent power shaped nineteenth-century French debates, but in the early twentieth century they acquired a general European significance. After the First World War, monarchies were toppled and republics established. Nowhere were the resulting constitutional controversies more intense than in Germany. The German Revolution of 1918 transferred authority from the Kaiser to the people, a change symbolised by the Declaration in Article 1 of the 1919 Constitution that 'the political power (*die Staatsgewalt*) derives from the people'. But thereafter many issues concerning the legitimacy of the new constitutional order remained in a state of irresolution. Seeking guidance, many constitutional scholars returned to the debates over the French Revolution.

Faced with the task of giving an account of the legitimacy of this modern democratic state, Weimar jurists reflected on the meaning and status of constituent power (Zweig 1909; Redslob 1912) and focused in particular on the question of whether and how constituent power could be represented. The most systematic, and the most controversial, account was given by Carl Schmitt. For Schmitt, the constitution was the circumstantial product of particular historical conditions; it was established by virtue of a specific political decision which is given jural form as the constituent power.

Schmitt's account of constituent power must be situated in his general account of state and constitution. He maintains that the state is 'the political unity of the people' (Schmitt 2008 [1928], p. 59). This is not an abstract idea: the state comes into existence through an actual historical process and as an expression of the relative homogeneity of a people. And just as the 'concept of the state presupposes the concept of the political' (Schmitt 1996 [1932], p. 19), so the formal written constitution presupposes the existence of the state (Schmitt 2008, p. 76). The constitution is the outcome of a decision of sovereign will, an exercise of constituent power. Rival jurists such as Hans Kelsen, presupposing the autonomy of law, equated the state with the legal order and regarded the state's authority as a presupposition of legal thought. In doing so they eliminated constituent power as a category of legal thought. Schmitt, by contrast, maintains that any attempt to sever the norms of legal order from the facts of political existence distorts both legal knowledge and the nature of constitutional arrangements.

Schmitt argues further that the formal constitution must be distinguished from the constitution of the state. The latter is not a mere formal unity; it is not found in norms but in a substantial sense of the political existence of the state. The state is the concrete condition of political unity. Recognising that there are likely to be various competing interests within the state, Schmitt argues that unity is maintained only if some means of overcoming conflict can be devised. This is achieved by way of a sovereign power able to impose its will in response to any threat to political unity. In normal times, the sovereign may be masked: formal constitutional mechanisms are sufficient to resolve disputes. But the sovereign must always remain, not least because the issues that might threaten unity can never be predicted in advance. For Schmitt, the sovereign is the agent that identifies the situation in which unity is threatened and acts to resolve that threat. In this situation, the law – including constitutional law – may recede, but the state – the condition of political unity – remains (Schmitt 2005 [1922], p. 12). This is sovereign power as constituent power.

For Schmitt, then, constituent power is the political will that determines the institutional form of the state. It establishes the constitution but, contrary to Sieyès, it is a power that continues to exist in order to maintain the authority of the constitution. Who, then, is the bearer of constituent power? That is a circumstantial question. Constituent power is evidently exercised in the name of the people, but since 'the people' can exercise that power only through representatives, the question becomes: who is best able to represent the people? In Weimar Germany, Schmitt argued that the President, being directly elected by the people, is the republican version of the monarch and the bearer of constituent power. He brings formal legal analysis to bear on that argument but recognises that the president is more than a mere creature of the formal written constitution. The president is the agent that is able to act to maintain unity and safeguard the 'substance' of the constitution.

This concrete conception of constituent power thus expresses both the political will that makes the formal constitution and the will that maintains the constitution of the state. It is most commonly expressed as the will of the people, in whose name this constitution is established. But this answer does not resolve the issue of who is able to speak in the name of the people. When Schmitt (2005, p. 5) argues that 'sovereign is he who decides on the exception', he is identifying the person or office that bears the constituent power.

In this realist analysis, Schmitt rejects any abstract conception of sovereignty. For him sovereignty is simply 'the highest, legally independent, underived power' (Schmitt 2005, p. 17). Sovereignty is assumed to be an expression of the power exercised by a sovereign; the abstract collapses into the concrete. It follows that for Schmitt constituent power similarly is an expression of the 'highest, legally independent' political will. It provides the essential foundation of legal normativity, is the product of 'actual interests', and it functions both to establish a formal constitution and to maintain that sense of continuing unity through time, a role that may require action which is not strictly in accordance with the formal written constitution. Although drawing on Sieyès' analysis, Schmitt extends the concept far beyond the limits Sieyès imposed.

V SOVEREIGNTY AND CONSTITUENT POWER

In the Weimar debates on state and constitution, Hermann Heller sided with Schmitt against Kelsen in accepting the distinction between the formal and substantive – the abstract and the concrete – senses of constitution. Like Schmitt, Heller relativised the formal concept but he criticised Schmitt's way of polarising the dichotomy. 'Every theory beginning with the alternatives, law or power, norm or will, objectivity or subjectivity', Heller states, 'fails to recognize the dialectical construction of the reality of the state and goes wrong at its very starting point' (Heller 1996 [1934], p. 1214). The constitution as normative construction and political reality must be distinguished but because law has a 'power-forming quality' the constitution can never be adequately expressed as the decision of a norm-less power. Whether the bearer of constituent power is the prince or the people, the power they exercise is not acquired existentially; it must have been generated by some sense of the normative order of that state. Heller's critique of the positions of Kelsen and Schmitt reveals an alternative conception of constituent power.

The alternative conception is explained by reference to Schmitt's account of sovereignty. Schmitt identifies the source of the term 'sovereignty' in the figure of the sovereign, but thereafter skates over the subsequent dialectical development. The term 'sovereign' was originally coined to denote the office of the ruler who was not legally obligated to any other power. The ruler's 'sovereignty' thus signified the absolute quality of the legal relationship between the ruler and the subject. But even in the early-modern period it was recognised that the ruler holds a representative office, and therefore, whatever deference might be paid to the king's majesty, the ruler does not exercise a personal power. This recognition came about in a circuitous manner, in that first the monarchical image of the sovereign ruler was idealised ('the king can do no wrong'), which opened up the possibility of institutionalising 'the king's will'. Once institutionalised, the sovereign could be conceived as a corporate office. Through internal differentiation, the 'sovereign' powers of government no longer inhered in the person of the ruler: they came to be exercised variously through the king-in-parliament, the king-in-council, the king's ministers, and the king's courts. Sovereignty thus expressed the absolute legal authority of the ruling power in its corporate capacity.

That marked only the first stage of its dialectical development. Through institutionalisation, internal differentiation and corporatisation of the office of the sovereign a distinction could be drawn between the sovereign powers of rule and the concept of sovereignty. Specifically, the powers of rule could be divided, but sovereignty – expressing the absolute authority of the ruling power – could not. This point had already been clearly understood by Bodin. Schmitt (2005, pp. 8–9) claimed that Bodin was the first to identify the sovereign as an entity able to determine the exception, but he overlooked the fact that Bodin also was the first to appreciate that a distinction must be made between sovereignty and the sovereign powers of government.

This Bodinian distinction between sovereignty and government is of particular significance once we follow through Schmitt's argument. In *Political Theology*, Schmitt (2005, p. 36) declares that 'all significant concepts of the modern theory of the state are secularized theological concepts'. While we can appreciate the point, the dialectic changes once sovereign power is seen to be conferred from below by 'the people' rather than being bestowed from above by God. It also becomes complicated because, despite claims made for 'popular sovereignty', the fact is that 'the people' exist *qua* people only once the 'sovereign' office of government has been established. The statement that 'the people is sovereign' is therefore thoroughly ambiguous. Any attempt to specify the sovereign of Schmitt's definition – the entity possessing 'the highest, legally independent, underived power' – in the modern world remains contentious. But uncertainty over identification of the sovereign does not indicate uncertainty about sovereignty.

The way out of the paradoxical status of the people was to change the basis of the argument. This can be seen in the way Rousseau reworks the question of ultimate authority from a historical investigation into a thought experiment. He treats the originating source not as a historical event but as a virtual act. This act, the social contract, is a symbolic expression of the passage from natural to civil existence. And once its virtual character is acknowledged, then, other than in a symbolic sense, power is not delegated from the people (the multitude) to their governors (Rousseau 1997 [1762], p. 71). But this formulation puts the concept of constituent power in question. The answer seems to run as follows. The political is a world in which we imagine ourselves as citizens impressed with powers and rights and able to reflect on the terms by which the collective association – the state – is organised. Within this worldview, no entity, whether the people or the prince, can be said to possess 'legally independent, underived power' and the status of sovereign remains unsettled. Yet the concept of sovereignty is not: sovereignty is an expression of the power and authority created through the formation of that worldview. Sovereignty vests neither in the ruler, nor in the office of government, nor in the people but in the set of relations created through the establishment of these practices. But what then of constituent power?

In Locke's scheme, the concept conferred a right of rebellion: if the constituted authority breaches the terms of trust, power as of right reverts to the people. Constituent power here expresses more than a de facto power relationship: it is a relationship of right which rests on the distinction between the right of the constituted authority to make (positive) law and the right by which this power to make law is conferred. This latter right is best conceived as 'political right' in the sense employed by Rousseau in *Du Contrat Social*, whose subtitle reads: *les principes du droit politique*. In this worldview, constituent power is more precisely termed 'constituent right'. Constituent right expresses not just founding aspirations but the intrinsically dynamic aspect of constitutional ordering.

The significance of Rousseau's formulation is clarified once placed in a more general political context. That is, once it is accepted, first, that the political is a domain of indeterminacy, secondly, that since the constitution of the state expresses a way of political being, a gulf will always exist between the norm (the written constitution) and the actuality (the way of being) and, thirdly, that this gulf is filled by the activity of governing. Constituent right expresses in constitutional language the way we understand how that gulf is negotiated. Rejecting Schmitt's claim that it can signify an existential unity of the people that precedes the formation of a constitution, constituent right expresses a dialectical relation between 'the nation' posited for the purpose of self-constitution and the constitutional form through which the nation speaks authoritatively. Consequently, the notion of sovereign decision that Schmitt postulates can never mark an 'absolute beginning' or spring from 'normative nothingness'. Action always entails reaction; constituent power always refers back to constituted power. Founding ideals can only be understood normatively, but their purpose is to set the framework for an actually existing political association.

Although the political domain is sometimes conceived normatively as one of freedom ('absolute beginning'), it can be maintained only through the establishment of governing institutions. The founding moment is often messy: the break may take place through an act of violence (war, conquest, revolution, secession, etc.) and, containing no 'natural' community, the territorial dimension of the state invariably has a certain arbitrariness. An intrinsic tension is established between the sovereign (the office of government) and sovereignty (the authority of the set of relations established in the political domain). This generates a dialectical engagement between the institutional arrangements established and contestations of their role and purpose according to the ideals of their constitution.

In this worldview, constituent power cannot mean, as adherents of popular sovereignty maintain, that authority is located in the people (*qua* the multitude). Nor is it a redundant category as contended by those who would absorb these political ideals into a rarefied exercise of legal constitutionalism. Constituent power is best conceived as an expression of the continuing political activity that is undertaken to challenge the failures of the institutionalised form of constituted authority to live up to the founding principles (e.g., liberty, equality, solidarity) of that constitution. The concept of constituent power enables us to explain how the constitution changes through time in the face of the constitutional document remaining unchanged (see, e.g., Ackerman 1991, 1998, 2014).

This conception of constituent power depends on acknowledging the distinctive nature of political power. Political power derives its character from the paradoxical nature of the foundation. It is generated through a symbolic act in which a multitude of people recognise themselves as forming a unity, a collective singular: *we the people*. But that act cannot remain only in the realm of belief. It must also have actual effects. And this will generally involve the use of force, not least because what some celebrate as liberation in the founding act, others experience as defeat. To manage such tensions, an institutional framework is needed. Consequently, 'the people' *do ordain and establish a system of government.*

The enacted constitution vests authority in the constituted authorities to legislate, adjudicate and govern in the interests of the collective association. By limiting, channelling and formalising these competences, the constitution becomes a medium of power-generation. This follows from a nostrum bequeathed by Bodin and repeated many times since: 'the less the power of the sovereignty is (the true marks of majesty thereunto still reserved), the more it is assured' (Bodin 1962 [1576], p. 517). Otherwise put, political power is restrained in order that constitutional authority is enhanced. But the constituted authorities retain extensive discretionary powers, which reflects the gulf between the constitutionally prescribed arrangement (an expression of sovereignty) and the decisional capacity of governmental institutions (an expression of sovereign authority). Political power is *generated* through symbolic representation of foundation/constitution (as *potestas*) and is then *applied* through the action of government (as *potentia*).

The meaning and purpose of constituent power within this worldview can now be more precisely specified: it expresses the generative aspect of the political power relationship. Contrary to the concrete versions presented by Schmitt (2005) or Negri (2009), constituent power does not equate to the material power of a multitude. This is the materialist fallacy, which reduces constituent power to fact. Constituent power exists only when that multitude can project itself not just as the expression of the many (a majority) but – in some senses at least – of all (a unity). Without this symbolic representation, there is no constituent power. But constituent power similarly cannot entirely be absorbed into the constituted order and equated with some founding norm. Were this to be the case, the tension that gives the political domain – and constitutional discourse – its open and provisional quality would be eliminated. This is the normativist fallacy and its realisation would not lead to 'the rule of law' (an impossible dream), but it would surely destroy political freedom.

VI CONTEMPORARY CONSTITUTIONAL DISCOURSE

Sieyès may have deployed constituent power in place of sovereignty, but it evidently has remained bound up with that concept. Sovereignty has evolved along two tracks, the concrete and the abstract, each of which identifies constituent power not just as the power that makes the constitution but also as the power that maintains governmental authority through continuing constitutional development. But these two tracks express different understandings of sovereignty and draw on different conceptions of law. The concrete, treating sovereignty simply as the power of a sovereign, presents law as *voluntas* (will). The abstract treats sovereignty as the expression of a set of politico-legal relations and conceives law as *ratio* and specifically as *ratio status* (political reason).

This modern evolution creates a situation of such complexity that some might wish that Sieyès' ambition had been realised. Yet, instead of moves to abandon the concept, we see in contemporary scholarship a proliferation of novel conceptions of the term. These innovations include the claim that constitutional courts are becoming the primary bearers of constituent power (Kahn 2011, p. 9), that constituent power must be reformulated to address the issue of legitimacy in global governance (Habermas 2012, pp. 28–37; Patberg 2016), that in the postnational order *pouvoir constituant* is being transformed into *pouvoir irritant* (Krisch 2016), that constituent power must now be reformulated in system theoretical language as the code of intersecting national and transnational regimes (Thornhill 2012, 2013) and that its emancipatory potential is now exhausted and must be replaced with a power of resistance called 'destituent power' (Agamben 2014). Rather than evaluating these initiatives, I propose to consider how recent governmental developments have had an influence on conceptualisation along these two tracks of sovereignty. They are addressed in post-sovereign and post-sovereignty conceptions of constituent power.

Post-sovereign Constituent Power

The case for post-sovereign constituent power has been made in two recent books by Andrew Arato (2016, 2017), whose main target is Schmitt's account of constituent power as sovereign power. Arato (2017, p. 31) argues that sovereign constitution-making 'involves the making of the constitution by a constitutionally unbound, sovereign constituent power, instituted in an organ of government, that at the time of this making unites in itself all of the formal powers of the state, a process that is legitimated by reference to supposedly unified, pre-existing popular sovereignty'. This, he maintains, places too much power in constituent assemblies and, as the history of modern revolutions shows, the idea of 'sovereign constitution-making' tends to lead to dictatorship (Arato 2016, pp. 26–28).

In its place, Arato makes the case for establishing a 'new paradigm' of post-sovereign constitution-making. This evolves from practice that was first instituted in Spain during the 1970s, was then extended in post-communist Central Europe and reached its most developed forms in post-apartheid constitution-making in South Africa. He calls the practice 'post-sovereign' because in the transition to a new constitutional order no single agency can claim to embody the constituent power of the people. Constitutional renewal is treated as a multi-stage process reflecting a 'post-revolutionary' understanding of change. And this post-sovereign conception of constituent power, he claims, is more likely to ensure the establishment of a stable constitutional democracy (Arato 2017, chap. 5).

Highlighting the dangers of presenting 'the people' as a collective unity, Arato seeks to de-mystify the subject by presenting the people as an irreducible plurality and showing how constituent power must be similarly differentiated. Constitution-making tasks are therefore allocated among a variety of institutions none of which can claim to hold sovereign power. Post-sovereign constitution-making stresses the importance of treating the exercise as an on-going process of constitutional learning which makes use of such techniques as round tables, extensive participation exercises, the adoption of an interim constitution and the establishment of flexible amendment procedures.

Arato's thesis on post-sovereign constitution-making can be read as an attempt to restore Sieyès' original intention of employing constituent power as a replacement for the concept of sovereignty. Highlighting Schmitt's misappropriation of Sieyès' analysis, Arato extends Sieyès' differentiation between ordinary and extraordinary representatives by de-mystifying the abstraction of 'the nation' and dispersing these powers among a variety of institutions. This is a valuable corrective, but it avoids any consideration of the juristic foundations of constitutional order. Rejecting Bodin's distinction between sovereignty and government, Arato (2016, pp. 275–281) collapses sovereignty into government and abandons the political metaphysics through which political jurisprudence is able to carry on its work.

Post-sovereignty

Post-sovereignty jurists make more radical claims about constituent power. They assert that sovereignty and constituent power are concepts founded on the modern idea of the state and have now been superseded in the contemporary post-national, post-state world. Promoting a conception of legality as a moral practice that evolves according its own unique criteria of integrity, they maintain that the distinction between domestic and international legal orders has now been eroded and with it the entire modern panoply of state-based concepts, such as sovereignty, constituent power and the hierarchical ordering of documentary constitutions.

The implications for constituent power are cogently presented by David Dyzenhaus. Dyzenhaus (2012a, p. 231) argues that modern constitutional thought wrongly assumes that authority 'inheres not in the kind of authority that the decision instituted … but in that the decision was taken by the nation'. Once the authority of law is properly grasped, he suggests, the concept of constituent power is rendered superfluous. He maintains that legal order is 'best understood from the inside', that 'legal order has intrinsic qualities that help to sustain an attractive and viable conception of political community' and that it is 'those intrinsic qualities that give law its authority' (ibid., 233). Dyzenhaus rejects constituent power as the source of a regime's authority in favour of an account of authority derived from the intrinsic quality of an abstract conception of legality. The modern constituent claim founded in democracy and representation is supplanted by a claim about the rule of law.

Rejecting the authority of positive law enacted in accordance with a constitution established through an exercise of constituent power, Dyzenhaus (2012a, p. 244) argues for the authority of a concept of legality that 'amounts to a constitutional *morality* underpinning all legal orders'. This concept of legality evidently promotes equal concern and respect for the individual and upholds such abstract principles as rationality, proportionality and subsidiarity, but beyond this it remains unpacked. We should, he says, 'think of things in terms of an unfinished and unfinishable project' (ibid., p. 257). But he is adamant 'that the idea of constituent power is at best a distraction for legal theory, at worst, when it is deployed by the likes of Schmitt, subversive of the very ideals professed by those who invoke it to understand constitutionalism' (ibid.).

Dyzenhaus' account reinforces the post-positivist, normativist, cosmopolitan claims that have been advanced by Mattias Kumm. In a series of papers, Kumm (2009, 2010a, 2013) has argued that the modern account of constitutionalism, based on what he calls 'democratic statism', is outmoded and is now ripe for replacement by a method that conceives of constitutionalism as an evolving practice through which all claims to authority are to be justified by reference to such basic principles as legality, rationality, proportionality and subsidiarity. In the paradigm shift Kumm envisages, constituent power – the archetypal 'democratic statist' concept – evidently has no place.

But Kumm has recently modified his argument. Following Habermas (2012), he now seeks to reformulate rather than abolish the concept. Claiming that constituent power is not just situated domestically as 'we the people', he asserts that it can also be found located in 'the international community' (Kumm 2016, p. 698). He justifies this on the basis that constituent power 'is not foundational and uncircumscribed but grounded in, constrained, and guided by the idea of a community of free and equal persons governing itself through the medium of the law as part of an international community' (ibid.). Stripping constituent power of any decisionist, collectivist or foundational authority, he reinterprets it as an expression of the idea of a global community of free and equal individuals. The concept is thus reconceived as an expression of virtual representation in a world beyond sovereignty. But is such an amorphous entity as 'the international community' capable of yielding a sufficiently robust account of post-national collective self-identification? In the words of Neil Walker (2016, p. 910), it seems obvious that 'scattered in various fragments, the postnational institutional configuration lacks the constitutive unity to provide an anchoring identity'.

What ultimately unites the arguments of Dyzenhaus and Kumm is their belief that political authority can be grounded in an evolving moral practice of justification. Whether advanced in the language of legality or constitutionality, the claim being made is that the political worldview, advanced by an abstract concept of sovereignty as an expression of the authority of a set of political relations, must be rejected. Political reason is to be replaced by the unfolding of universal moral reason.

CONCLUSION

The concept of constituent power was formulated in the late-eighteenth century as part of a modern movement that sought to jettison the absolutist connotations of the language of sovereignty and replace it with the power of extraordinary representatives of the people to draft a written constitution that would define the legitimate powers and duties of governing institutions. It was a key component of a liberal progressive movement that envisaged a shift from ancient to modern in thought, from feudalism to capitalism in society, from aristocracy to the bourgeoisie as ruling power, and from traditional to legal-rational claims to authority. The movement saw its endpoint in the establishment of modern constitutional democracy.

The problem is that constitutions are not self-enforcing documents. In seeking to establish an authoritative framework through which political power is both generated and constrained, the question of sovereignty could not be ignored. It is for this reason that a conception of constituent power that acts only at the moment of constitutional enactment and thereafter is converted into a type of constituted power could not displace the question of sovereignty. Constituent power continued to be tied to contested conceptions of sovereignty.

I have suggested that in this transition sovereignty is not overcome but does change its meaning. Sovereignty in modern understanding is an expression of the power and authority created through the political worldview. Conceived as such, the concrete sense of 'sovereign' must be differentiated from the abstract quality of 'sovereignty'. This differentiation between sovereign and sovereignty has significant implications for understanding constituent power today. Given that the establishment of a documentary constitution cannot be assumed to have eliminated sovereign power to the extent that all political relations are refracted through the formal structures of the written constitution, it cannot be assumed that the constitution adequately reflects the way in which the state is actually constituted. Constituent power may therefore be understood not just to express the power that establishes the constitution but also as that which preserves the constitution of the state in ways not clearly contemplated in the constitutional text.

This claim is assumed to be controversial because Schmitt defines this aspect of constituent power as a 'legally independent, underived power'. But his argument can now be glossed. He himself recognises that it is not 'the adequate expression of a reality, but a formula, a sign, a signal' and that 'in political reality, there is no irresistible highest or greatest power' (Schmitt 2005, p. 17). In the period since Schmitt wrote, the influence of constitutions in regulating political life has in most parts of the world significantly increased. To the extent that it has, this aspect of constituent power has been subject to a much greater degree of institutional restraint but, as even Arato (2016, chap. 4) is obliged to acknowledge, it cannot be said to have been entirely overcome.

Constituent power performs an even more important role when considered through the lens of sovereignty. The ambition of constitutionalism to establish a regime in which all political relations are refracted through the formal structures of the written constitution can be advanced only if that constitutional framework is flexible enough to remain open to radically different interpretations. Constitutions are fixed only because they are capable of changing their meaning. And they change their meaning as a consequence of changes in the constitution of the state. Constituent power, re-interpreted as 'constituent right' (*droit politique*), undertakes the work of adapting the formal 'constitution of government' to the constantly changing meaning of the 'constitution of the state'.

To realise this aspiration, constituent power gives rise to a new species of law, that of 'constitutional legality' (Loughlin 2017, chap. 8). Its character is revealed once

Schmitt's claims are construed in the light of Heller's work. Schmitt's reference to constituent power as 'legally independent' power means only that it operates not strictly in accordance with positive law, and when he writes that in exceptional circumstances 'the law recedes but the state remains', this means that positive law must be re-interpreted according to the working of political right. This new species of constitutional legality has evolved only in the last fifty or so years. It evolves because of a growing institutionalisation of political reason (aka, reason of state), which in turns leads to the politicisation of legal reason. Government according to law – constitutional government – no longer means governing in accordance with the written rules; it signifies governing according to certain abstract principles of legality whose explication (*pace* Dyzenhaus, Kumm and liberal normativists) is as much the consequence of political as legal reason. The workings of constituent power – constituent right – continues to have value as an expression of the driver of this development.

RECOMMENDED READING

Arato, A. (2017). *The Adventures of the Constituent Power: Beyond Revolutions?* Cambridge: Cambridge University Press.

Böckenförde, E.-W. (2017). The Constituent Power of the People: A Liminal Concept of Constitutional Law. In his *Constitutional and Political Theory*. Edited by M. Künkler and T. Stein. Oxford: Oxford University Press, pp. 168–185.

Bodin, J. (1576). *Les six livres de la république*. Paris: Jacques du Puis.

Dyzenhaus, D. (2012). Constitutionalism in an old key: legality and constituent power. *Global Constitutionalism*, 1 (2), pp. 229–260.

Loughlin, M. (2003). *The Idea of Public Law*, Oxford: Oxford University Press, chap. 6.

Loughlin, M. & Walker, N. (2007). *The Paradox of Constitutionalism: Constituent Power and Constitutional Form*, Oxford: Oxford University Press.

Napoleon, I. (1910). *The Corsican: A Diary of Napoleon's Life in His Own Words [1804]* R. M. Johnston ed. Boston: Houghton Mifflin Co.

Negri, A. (1999). *Insurgencies: Constituent Power and the Modern State*. Translated by M. Boscagli. Minneapolis: University of Minnesota Press.

Rubinelli, L. (2019). How to think beyond sovereignty: one Sieyès and constituent power. *European Journal of Political Theory*, 18 (1), 47–67.

Rubinelli, L. (2020). *Constituent Power: A History*. Cambridge: Cambridge University Press.

Sieyès, E.-J. (2003 [1789]). What is the Third Estate? In *Political Writings*. Translated by M. Sonenscher. Indianapolis: Hackett, pp. 92–162.

14

Representation

Nadia Urbinati

Representation, a Latin word with no Greek equivalent, designates a delegated action on the part of someone on behalf of someone else. It has no conceptual link with democracy, a Greek word with no Latin equivalent. As political historians have copiously demonstrated, the public usage of representation emerged in the Middle Ages within the juristic tradition dealing with conflicts between central and local authorities, imperial and religious (Clarke 1964; Keane 2009). Its genesis accounts for its mix of private (legal representation in court) and political (representation in government) elements (Pitkin 1967). Thus, on one hand, representation conveys the idea of somebody being authorized to act or speak for somebody else (the Latin word *re-presentare* means to make something, such as the will of the sovereign, manifest or present). On the other hand, it conveys the idea of the representative forming a unitary will that did not exist before: for example, this is the way Thomas Hobbes employed it to construct the sovereign (Skinner 2002, pp. 177–208). Historically, that mixture opened the avenue to the most important transformation of political authority in modernity: the construction of "representative government," a government based on the electoral selection of lawmakers and the limitation and separation of state powers. Historically, representative government enabled a constitutionalization of politics. This transformation started with the English, American and French revolutions of the seventeenth and the eighteenth centuries. The subsequent democratization of a representative government was neither easy and peaceful nor quick; in many western countries, it stabilized only after World War II. The inclusion of large numbers of citizens in the process of opinion and will formation through universal suffrage was the main problem that representative government had to solve. In many countries, a written constitution helped that solution along with the stabilization of party pluralism and the acceptance of organized oppositions. Political representation achieved a democratic character when suffrage stopped being a function for the protection of social interests and groups and became an individual right connected to other rights, such as freedom of speech and of association. Today, societies are democratic "not simply because they have free elections and the choice of more than one political party, but because they permit effective political competition and debate" (Hirst 1990, pp. 33–34).

Representative democracy has four main features: (a) the sovereignty of the people expressed in the cyclical electoral appointment (generally a few years) of the representatives; (b) representation as a free and mandate relation; (c) electoral mechanisms to ensure at least some responsiveness from the representatives to the people in whose name they speak and act; and (d) the universal franchise, which grounds representation on an important element of political equality (Urbinati and Warren 2008, p. 387). Within this government, representation is both an institution that is directly associated with lawmaking (parliament or congress) and a form of participation. Indeed, its foundation in regular and periodical elections makes legitimation by consent a condition that transcends institutions and involves citizens' public judgment of politicians and government. This reveals the dual character of representation – passive and active – and the relation of *interdependence* it designates, such that "the *persona repraesentata* is only the person represented, and yet the representative, who is exercising the former's right, is dependent on him" or her (Gadamer 2004, p. 141, note 250). Representation brings a novel kind of freedom to the fore, one that does not need to be associated with the citizen's direct action or presence in the place where decisions are made, as is the case in direct democracy. It enlarges the space and meaning of politics in ways that cannot easily be reduced to electoral authorization, and it invariably connects with both the lawmaking institution and the citizens' voluntary participation, their equal right to claim, vindicate, and monitor. The implications of the mixture of representation and democracy in contemporary politics are the issues of this chapter.

The first section analyzes representation in relation to the constituent power. Since representative democracy is first and foremost the name of a form of government, reference to people's sovereignty, the constitution and electoral authorization is not accessory (Habermas 1996, pp. 462–515). The starting point for any understanding of the function and role of representation in modern democracy is first of all the shift in the location of sovereignty from an individual (the monarch) to a collective that is made of individual citizens (the people), not corporate groups or estates. As this section argues, that shift marked a revolutionary motion in which representation played the crucial role of unifying the constituent power of the collective (the citizens) by creating its institutional order around lawmaking – which relies essentially, although not exclusively, on representation through elections. In modernity, the ancient principle of democracy as 'giving laws to oneself' returned to life thanks to representation.

The second section analyzes the impact elections have on the interdependent character of representation. Although it starts with the equal distribution of voting rights among individual citizens, representation is not reducible to "a static fact of electoral politics" (Saward 2010, p. 3). A means capable of unifying a number of citizens by constructing their claims and giving them a unitary voice (constituency), representation can be implemented in various ways, and at least three: as political mandate, as pure delegation, and as embodiment. My thesis is that the first one is more receptive to the interdependent character of representation than the other two because it keeps the institutional order in communication with the represented without aiming to close the gap that differentiates them. In a government whose source of legitimacy is election, representative political mandate is an unavoidable conundrum because while representation claims to speak for the whole (the parliament is the organ of the sovereign), it is rooted in a dense web of social interests and passions that demand to be translated into political projects (and are the true competitors in elections). Equal as electors, citizens are unequal and different on several accounts, and their differences surface when they form opinions and vote. How is it possible that pluralism translates into decision (the law) without the violation of social diversity and the free expression of ideas? The political mandate solves this problem more consistently than pure delegation and embodiment, which are alternative attempts to represent the people. Political groups or associations give citizens' voices power, which allows political conflict while stabilizing society. In addition, they exalt political representation's distinctiveness as a function that can hardly be judged like any other profession and evaluated based on a tangible output because voters do not vote or judge their representatives based on a single claim, issue, or request.

This brings us to the third section, on the way the gap between represented and representatives (or citizens and parliament/congress) is managed in a society that wants representative democracy to approximate the democratic principle of self-government. Communication between state institutions and extra-institutional life is one key function here. It is performed by several intermediary means, including political parties, civil associations, movements, the media, and now also the Internet. Thanks to them, citizens try to give their political presence an effective and persistent character through time. Their strength and social rootedness signal the strength of democratic representation insofar as they allow decision-makers to always be in relation with (and inspected by) those who receive laws and are both the main source of inspiration for representatives and the public tribunal that judges them (Mill 1977 [1861]; Plotke 1997; Warren 2018). However, communication is not a final remedy, because although it manages the gap, it also injects citizens' dissatisfaction with the elected organ (Mansbridge 2020; Rosanvallon 2006). Furthermore, communication can hardly avoid partiality in judgment. Thus, while the collective sovereign wants the law to be the will of the whole, electoral representation fragments that will and subjects lawmaking to partisanship and compromising practices. It makes it impossible to insulate the law from society's divided interests and partisan politics (Waldron 1999b, pp. 4–5). Communication makes a lawmaking assembly the echo chamber of society's passions and interests; the side effects of parliamentary politics (party divisions, unfulfilled promises, bargaining, compromise and the lack of transparency) also make the assembly the target of citizens' distress. Distrust in representatives reverberates on the practice of lawmaking, which wrecks the aura of rationality and impartiality traditionally ascribed to the law.

The last section brings to an end the analysis of the ambiguities of communication and discusses some of the themes in the contemporary discourse on the "crisis of democracy." Communication provokes two uneven trends: it provides information and counters the risk government work becoming an opaque process; but it cannot guarantee that certain citizens and social groups will not hold more influence than others over political institutions and the practice of lawmaking. Recently, populist critiques of the establishment have targeted the first of these two trends and proposed forms of representation that aim to overcome the gap between institutions and society. As to the second trend, representation has recently been put on trial by a rich corpus of political analysis with the goal of restituting power to the citizens over their representatives through horizontal processes of communication that rely on social media and digital devises.

In conclusion, in contemporary democracy, political representation is a terrain of participation and controversies, as the issues and claims and proposals it unfurls are the means by which citizens construct and challenge the political direction of their country. It is thus reasonable to say that representation gives the name to both a form of government and a process of participation that citizens animate in order to influence the elected and approximate self-government. Its democratic character nourishes the citizens' suspicion that the elected neglect their claims and savor the oligarchic air surrounding institutions; that suspicion mobilizes two contrary impulses: managing the gap between representatives and the represented or closing it instead.

I THE DEMOCRATIC REPRESENTATIVE CONSTITUTIVE MOMENT

Representative government had a revolutionary history that officially started with the Glorious Revolution in England in the seventeenth century, when the call for legitimacy by electoral consent translated into anti-absolutism. The democratic implications of representation erupted in the eighteenth century, with the American revolution of 1776 and the French one of 1789, where written constitutions were made by the revolutionaries through *ad hoc* elected assemblies that did not intend to be representative in the ordinary lawmaking sense as parliaments. The "one off" nature of constitutional conventions created originally in the United States was meant to state the sovereign will in its foundational intention and be representative of the whole people, not just its parts, and theoretically forever, not for a limited period. (Pitkin 1967, pp. 144–145). It was also meant to draw a common grammar regulating political rivalry for achieving representative seats and the majority without the latter changing the rules of the game and taking the place of the sovereign power (Urbinati 2019, p. 102). Those conventions showed by default the unavoidable partiality implied in the retrospective relation of accountability that ordinary elections for representatives establish (Dunn 1999). Indeed, "one off" elections for constitutional conventions were meant to break the logic of short-term interests attached to elections and the logic of reward by reelection. They were an acknowledgment of the partisan and conflicting nature of representative politics (Rosenblum 2008). What is more, they revealed the revolutionary nature of the constituent power of the collective when the latter wants to give itself laws and constructs its polity's institutional order, which are nothing more than the rules managing the future process of approximating politics to the principle of self-government. In this regard, the European revolutions of 1848–1849 marked a watershed innovation because they showed also with their dramatic conclusions, the difference between conceded constitutions and self-proclaimed constitutions. On the one hand, *constitutions octroyées* were charters that monarchs conceded paternalistically to their subjects under the pressure of tumults; sovereignty remained above the subjects and treated them as recipients of its benevolent concessions, which some jurists translated into the language of public law.[1] On the other hand, when democratic tumults succeeded either in dethroning monarchs or subjecting them to constitutional limitations, ordinary people declared themselves to be the only sovereign and wrote down their intents, procedures and institutions, thus subverting prior hierarchical relations of power; the role of jurists was played by constituent assemblies. Although the 1848–1849 revolutions ended with repression (and in France, with the coinage of Bonapartism as a new form of plebiscitary dictatorship or Caesarism) and failed, and although "pure" *ad hoc* conventions "are in a minority" historically (Elster 2017, p. 81), when we approach the issue of democratic representation we presume *ideally* that kind of impulse toward a collective declaration of self-government and the rejection of external sources of legitimacy. Democratic constitutions are not *octroyées* and are sovereign all the way through. They are a political pact that citizens make while assuming their differences and foreseeing their future disagreements, compromises, and lawmaking (Bellamy 2007, pp. 4–5). The immanent legitimacy of democratic sovereignty is actualized through suffrage and representation, the twinset institutions and practices that designate the mediated and compromissory modality of politics in modern democracies. Representation is thus more than simply a technique of power. Its appearance in modern history marked the emancipation of political power from patrimonialism and paternalism and, moreover, created a practice of decision-making base on criteria that are autonomous from those which shape other domains (like the economy, religion, and the family) and are consistent with the principles of self-government. Thus, Claude Lefort defined the sovereign power in representative democracies as a *modus operandi* that proceduralizes and de-substantializes power (2007, p. 114).

---

[1] The French Charter of 1814, the archetype of all *octroyed* constitutions, contains the following royal statement in its preamble: 'We have voluntarily and by the free exercise of our royal authority granted, and grant, made concession to our subjects, both for us and for our successors and forever, the constitutional charter that follows' (my translation); see Jackson 2012; and Klein and Sajó 2012.

II POLITICAL MANDATE, DELEGATION, AND EMBODIMENT

In contemporary democracies, representation originates in free and regular elections based on universal suffrage and terminates in lawmaking; like with ancient direct democracy, it is ingrained in the principle of equality by law and under the law (*isonomia*) and the right to talk in public and dissent (*isegoria*), two procedural kinds of equality, not social or substantive, that translates into civil and political freedom. Representation that originates in elections means 'to act in the name of the people' never replace them or dispossess them of their equal freedom. Elections defeat blind deference and set the tone of the relationship between citizens and the elected as one of trust and distrust at the same time. They actualize a political mandate that makes representation different from pure delegation and from embodiment, the other two forms representation can take. To grasp the differences among them we have to silhouette the nature of representation. Headed its etymological meaning, to represent means to present again or make present someone or something that is absent (a guardian representing the interests of a minor or an attorney representing a client in court are forms of representation). Starting from this non-political definition, there are three directions that representation can take: as *legal mandate*, that is, delegation in the juridical sense of principal-agent relationship (pure delegation with imperative mandate); as *representativeness*, that is, sociological likeness that transcends all volitional choice of electors and aims at representing an empirical sameness that embodies the society; and as *responsibility* or *political mandate* of those chosen toward the choosers, which belongs properly to electoral representation actualized through political parties. Of the three directions, the sociological one is the most unpolitical as is meant to careful reproduce the characteristics of a group or class or a population without any intentional effort to translate those characteristics in political proposals. Representation disconnected from competitive elections can be sociological likeness as with statistical samples or can be unification of the virtual people through a plebiscitary leader who claims to represent the whole above its parts. In sociological representation, what matters is not the procedure that can best guarantee the coincidence of opinions between representative and represented because this coincidence is assumed to exist already. If representation is defined as a state of similarity of social status and coincidence of opinions, other method of selection can do, for instance lottery or acclamation. This is opposite to political representation, which is concerned with precisely the way to ensure the relation between represented and representatives. But political representation is also different from pure delegation: "representing my constituency" in the parliament is never an absolute act of devotion to my constituency's desires nor can it ever be (this is what pure delegation wants to be); it entails instead that I (the representative) judge the claims of my constituency according to both the principles of our democratic community, particularly equal political equality, and the proposals and positions that qualify my constituency. In political representation, both the public and my constituency retain their freedom to criticize me and eventually discontinue their trust in me. What makes representation democratic is that it is generative of political decisions and founded upon the rights citizens have to participate in the making of those decisions through voting and informal participation in the public sphere of opinion formation: by electing we do not accept to be ruled but we participate in the selection of the political direction of our country we prefer by choosing one part rather than others. Within this context that is made of motivational judgments and partisan interpretations, representation tends to create a surplus of political action and contestation that divides the people into parts (this is what representation as sociological sameness and as embodiment oppose). While a monarchical sovereign "cannot disagree with himself, out of envy, or interest," an "Assembly may" and does so systematically (Hobbes 1991 [1651], p. 132); this makes a democratic society look like a permanent battlefield whose powerful weapons are words and votes. No decision is sheltered from people's judgment and inspection, and therefore, attaining the unity of decision in a collective body made of representatives is a symbolic task at most. Although the multitudes remain outside and excluded in their "collective capacity" of lawmaking (Federalist No. 63), their exclusion is apparent because the same forces of dissent and disagreement that linger in society also cross into the assembly (Waldron 1999b, pp. 31–32).

This osmotic nature of representative politics marks the limit of the representatives' power and enlarges the space and meaning of politics as we said at the start. For this reason, divorcing the outside and the inside of the state from each other, or trying to insulate lawmaking from partisan politics and social pressures, would be tantamount to impoverishing democracy and representation. Yet some insulation is needed. Above all, if we consider that democracy does not contemplate full equality, but only basic political and legal equality, communication between society and lawmakers might have to circumscribe the influence of tolerated forms of inequality. Democratic constitutions are conceived so as to neutralize the power of the wealthier few to influence lawmaking; to that end, they either include norms that *insulate* institutions from special interests or incorporate demands that the state actively *counteract* social inequality in order to pre-empt possibilities for unequal political influence. A minimal conception of democracy is more consistent with the former option; a social conception is more consistent with the latter. Whatever road they take, democracies must ensure that equal political power is permanently reproduced, because it is only on this condition that political representation is democratically legitimate. Democrats have to establish and preserve equilibrium between potential candidates so that they can compete on a fair basis, while providing voters with a chance to enter the competition, if they so choose, and to make their voices heard (Beitz 1989, pp. 194–195). Democracy seems to work better in societies where economic inequality is contained and constantly kept in check; conversely, it is often toothless in societies where economic resources for political participation are left to the market and electoral campaigns depend largely on private donors (Piketty 2018). Representative democracy does not prescribe that government abstain from intervening with positive policies in order to protect its foundational principles (Schlozman, Page, Verba, and Fiorina 2005, pp. 19–87).

This comprehensive form of political freedom gives representative democracy a dual feature or a diarchy of will (decision-making) and public judgment (opinion formation and expression). This feature makes political representation different from the other kinds of representation we mentioned, as we shall see more diffusely below. Moreover, the diarchic link between 'decision' and 'opinion' throws into doubt the legalistic rendering of political mandates that has inspired critics of representative democracy in the name of direct participation. As argued by Hanna Pitkin, in relation to the democratic sovereign, the classical etymology of re-presentation as "to make present or manifest or to present again" through a sort of contract of pure delegation (Pitkin 1967, pp. 8–10) is problematic for two reasons.

The first reason is that it presumes a pre-political entity, waiting to be made manifest and, moreover, to be manifest in a monistic and not pluralistic way. This conception can hardly work with constructed collective bodies, constituencies and parliaments. A version of it can be detected in today's populist rhetoric of electoral victory as an act of "taking the people back," as if the people existed before representation, or they were not represented before that victory, or perhaps that previous majorities were not truly legitimate (Urbinati 2019). Political representation plays a de-substantializing and de-personifying function in two ways: it shows that there is no people that pre-dates it; and it makes the fully-fledged political appearance of claimants in their plural voices possible (Saward 2010, p. 42). Thus, although elections have been considered an aristocratic institution, in modern states the electoral process engendered two developments that became crucial to the birth of democracy. On the one hand, it touched off a separation between society and politics, or better said a transition from *symbiotic* relationships between the delegates and their communities (as in the ancient regime, when the subjects were represented as members of the estate they belonged to by birth) to forms of adhesion that were thoroughly *politically constructed* by electors and citizens and thus *symbolic*. On the other hand, the disassociation of candidates from their social niches foregrounded the role of speech and ideas in politics and transformed representation into a process of construction of claims through partisan discourses and with a view to making political decisions. Hence George W. F. Hegel could write that representation brings dissent into politics because in politicizing society it carries the plurality of interests and difference of visions into the public, and Max Weber could accentuate the notion that the political aspect of voting lies in citizens' ability to transcend their social being *by their own doing*, that is to say, to act independently of their social identity and become themselves representatives of their interests and political community (Hegel 1967 [1821], § 311; Weber 1994 [1919], pp. 57–59). The political dialectics that representation generates translates into a form of political mandate that activates partisan groups and manages conflict – when we vote for representatives we do not vote for rulers or individual officers with some specific administrative functions (and skills) but we vote for a collective body that is made of representatives of our political proposals.

This brings us to the second way in which pure delegation is inadequate. Reasoning from the perspective of the paradigm of principal/agent relation, Jean-Jacques Rousseau correctly thought that political freedom precludes the reduction of the citizens-state relation to a private contract of alienation (2003 [1762], bk. 3, chap. 15). If representative government were a system in which the will of an agent (the representative assembly) were the will of the principal (the people) in a juridical sense, Rousseau's sarcastic references to the fictitiously free and *de facto* slave Britons would be legitimate ("The people of England regards itself as free; but it is grossly mistaken; it is free only during the election of members of parliament. As soon as they are elected, slavery overtakes it, and it is nothing" – Rousseau 2003, p. 66). As Hans Kelsen would argue, in the absence of an imperative mandate, delegation would be a pure and simple transfer of sovereign power from the people to their representatives (1992, pp. 290–291). However, Rousseau's sarcasm adds up to a caricature rather than a description of a representative assembly which is not, nor can be, rendered in juridical terms – either as an act of transfer or as its opposite, strict delegation. The novelty of political mandate based on elections escapes theories of sovereignty as a monistic act of the will and thus also the identification of representation as a contract of transfer of that will.

Historically, the transition from a private relation of advocacy (agent/principal relation) to a public relation of advocacy (political mandate) was achieved with the revolutions that gave birth to elected parliaments. It marked the diarchic transformation of sovereignty, a process in which several agents – some formal, like parliaments, some informal, like opinion makers and parties – participate and none can claim to represent sovereign power alone. Within that diarchic political context, representation entails both claim-making outside the state and decision-making through the organs of the state. Emmanuel-Joseph Sieyès and Immanuel Kant translated the fact of representative government that emerged in their times into a theory that posited representation as the legitimate form of political presence consistent with a practice that pertained to all social relations insofar as they were artificially constructed and not owned by anyone (Urbinati 2006, chaps. 4 and 5). Representation became the name of a process for making collective subjects, at the very same time unifying citizens according to interpreted and chosen issues and pluralizing their belongings and partisan sidings. Hence, Lisa Disch makes constructivism start with the representative turn of the eighteenth century, a revolutionary shift from "topographical [social] categories" to representation as a grand process by means of which the identity of the represented is wholly made by the citizens in their political struggle for power (2015, p. 490). The switch from individual to collective sovereignty corresponded with this switch in representation from mirroring (social sectors or estates) to constructing constituencies, from pure delegation (person-to-person relation between elector and elected) to a political mandate.

The effects of these changes were paramount for democratization, as they marked the transition from the above-mentioned sociological representation as giving "presence" (*being like*) to representation as promoting "activity" (*acting with and speaking for*) (Gauchet 1995, p. 48). This kind of "activity" includes the means by which citizens vindicate their interests, seek advocates to promote them, and aspire to a kind of representative adhesion that augments the chances of seeing their claims fulfilled. This adhesion is the face of partisan siding, predicated on the assumption that competent lawmaking requires social knowledge enriched with a passion for the cause to be advocated. Yet the question is not one of "proximity to the people," as in the conception of embodiment, which we will soon analyze (Müller 2016, p. 43; Ankersmit 2002). Representation in the assembly requires "passionate" and "intelligent" advocates, who are neither blind partisans nor bureaucratic placeholders (Mill 1977, p. 432). It makes partisanship a help rather than hindrance to competent deliberation (White and Ypi 2016). This proposition is congruent with the fact that "legislation is associated with democracy" and legislatures are "mostly elective and accountable bodies" (Waldron 2016e, p. 125).

Thus conceived, political representation is far more than a system of division of labor or a state institution. It is the name of a complex political process that activates the sovereign well beyond the formal act of electoral authorization, that transforms its presence into political influence, that unifies and connects the "fluctuating" "atomic units" of equal citizens by projecting them into a future-oriented perspective (Hegel 1967, pp. 200–201). Representation confers an unavoidable ideological dimension on politics, because constituencies are forged by "action-related systems of ideas" – ideas that seek effectiveness as they filter and interpret information in the process of putting them into practice – and not information per se (Friedrich 1963, pp. 88–89). In this sense, representation is prompted by an aspirational ideal of communication (Mansbridge 2020), although it is more than a quest for listening and responding because it takes part in constructing the very claims that ask for voice and attention. Representation makes modern democratic society resemble a vast and webbed forum in which, to paraphrase Kant, no deed or issue remains unheard and cast away from peoples' eyes and judgment. It can thus never be truly descriptive of social segmentations because of its unavoidable inclination to transcend the photographic "here" and "now" and to project instead a future perspective to be actualized or achieved that translates almost naturally into advocacy and vindication. This premise is paramount to understanding the meaning of representation as political mandate versus two other meanings mentioned above: delegation and embodiment.

Delegation originates in the contractual/private domain of principal/agent relations. At first glance, a principal/agent relation, or the relation between a lawyer or a broker and her clients, and that between electors and their political representatives, show some semblance. A broker is an advocate of my financial interests and I delegate to her the care of them; as with a political representative I vote for, our interaction generates a trust whose strength reflects my satisfaction with and positive judgment of her service. Reappointment is in both cases a reward and a sign of trust. Yet, despite this phenomenological and linguistic similarity, political representation belongs in a thoroughly different genre and cannot be identified with a private contract of delegation, although historically, it started in the contractual domain (Gierke 1958, p. 61). A few years ago, a body of work by feminists and scholars of minority issues explicitly linked political exclusion to the standard model of representation based on the individualistic principal/agent scheme (Guinier 1994; Williams 1998). It is reasonable to say that calls for the principal/agent scheme testify to a society whose cleavages are so deep as to fragment the collective sovereign into homogenous groups, each of which seeks a lawyer-kind of delegate. The principal/agent relation of delegation is normatively in contradiction with a democratic conception of the sovereign as a collective made of free and equal citizens whose voting power is individual and absolutely identical in weight; reclaiming it would be in and by itself the admission that society is made of unequal groups rather than citizens, with grave violation of legal and political equality. Historically, the emancipation of political representation from the principal/agent contract was paramount for the system of representative democracy to acquire legitimacy and for representation to emancipate itself from social niches or estates and the paradigm of person-to-person relations. It happened thanks to the acquisition of the principle of equal power by each elector and the right to suffrage. This political innovation, which can be traced to the Levellers, was a watershed in the normative codification of the system of selection of representatives by elections, and in the practice of electoral competition among equal agents with the public working as a surveillance eye, communication network, and judgmental tribunal (Kishlansky 1986).

Although they are a form of authorization, elections are not at all like a sovereign's signature on a contract of transfer. Rather, they are a method of choice for the formation of a collective organ (the parliament or the congress) that makes laws which have a hold on all subjects, and whose validity does not depend on the output they deliver to each elector. Elections' validity rests on the general compliance with the rules and norms that define their performance and in relation to which the entire process of political participation occurs. Hence, to develop this analysis of the concept of delegation further, while social or corporate representation is tailored to the specific set of functions that pertain only to a given corporation's or society's members, political representation is linked to the making of decisions that apply to all persons who live under the jurisdiction of the state (even those who choose not to vote and those who are not yet or not at all citizens), as well as the members of those corporate entities. Technically speaking, whereas the former relation is one of delegation (mostly with direct recall as the delegate is judged based on her fulfillment of the goal she was selected to achieve), the latter is one of free mandate (not only for practical reasons, as the implications involved in a law are too many and complex to be simplified in a single issue or interest, but also for normative reasons as the parliament or the congress is representative of the *whole* people, not only of the electors who voted for its members). In the corporate domain, decisions are tailored to the specific interests of corporate members only – they aim at particular persons (*ad personam*). This was, for instance, the structure of medieval guilds or of corporatism in fascist regimes. But lawmaking by parliaments applies to all kinds of people without naming anyone in particular, even if their decisions have been made by partisan groups and passed by majority – they aim at everyone (*erga omnes*). This makes sense simultaneously of the political and the democratic nature of electoral representation. *Inclusion* in the demos and *political equality in power* of the included are the two indivisible principles contained in the switch from individual to collective sovereignty, which is in all respects the starting point of both democracy and representation as a political mandate that citizens manage by associating in political groups and creating claims and proposals.

However, although formally identical as electors, citizens are diverse in many respects in their social life and in relation to many things that contribute to form their minds and political desiderata. Representation renders social richness and plurality into political programs that are inclusive of many claims, yet not all, and are capable of creating a collective subject acting with one will (the parliament or congress), although the many wills composing it are never erased and although it does not have the ambition of replacing the whole (Rosenblum 2008). The trick is that while an election's legitimacy is translatable into quantitative outcomes (votes to be counted), representation remains in the terrain of opinion and feelings, ideological justifications and partisan identifications (Morgan 1988, pp. 67–71). Political representation entails a kind of mandate that is not legal or juristic but is essentially political and permanently reconstructed and corroborated, based on a circular relation of opinions and judgments between state and society, citizens and representatives. The kind of equality it relies upon is not arithmetical – as with elections – because the right to free speech, freedom of association and the public expression of dissent or opinions activate "political influence" or a kind of power that is largely informal, hard to assess with precision, unequally performed and not directly effectual. Thus, *while elections make representatives, they do not make representation*, which takes place in the extra-state domain through parties, political associations and the media in a permanent attempt to control and monitor the gap that separates citizens from their institutions (Urbinati 2006, chap. 1).

This mix of pluralism and unity in the domain of influence and decision-making also makes representation as a political mandate far apart from representation as an embodiment. Embodiment shares with pure delegation the ambition of filling the gap between representatives and represented; and it shares with sociological reproduction the ambition of giving a face to persons or groups that are already there. In addition, it aims at overcoming pluralism within the citizenry and representing the unity of the whole above its parts. Its goal is to translate proximity into unison and pass from communication to fusion. Its ambition is not to represent citizens' claims and give them passionate advocates but to restate the identity of the collective body above its parts and under a symbolic unifier (Sintomer 2013). Whereas "speaking for" and "acting for" are the characteristics of a political mandate, "stand for" and talking and acting "as if" the representative were the people is the character of embodiment, whose task is not making citizens partake in the political action of the government but rather overcoming pluralism, conflict and dissent. "If the main goal to be achieved is the welding of the nation into a unified whole … then it is tempting to conclude that a single dramatic symbol can achieve this much more effectively than a whole legislature of representatives" (Pitkin 1967, pp. 106–107). This form of representation has become a prominent reaction to party politics and liberal democracy.[2] The goal of embodying the whole is, in effect, to overcome the political mandate through parties and parliamentary politics and to restore the unity of intent and the will that the monarchical sovereign had before the parliamentary regime supplanted it. Thus, while applicable to a representative and symbolic figure of the nation (like an elected president or a constitutional monarch), embodiment is hardly consistent with political representation in parliaments. Representation as embodiment tends toward an *irresponsible leader* who bypasses accountability through a quest of faith in his person, independent of (and at the given time against) the limits that institutional checks impose on him (Urbinati 2019, chap. 3). When and if this applies to lawmaking, the risk is to have it overflow from constitutional democracy into the promotion of an authoritarian regime. In representation as embodiment, we see the anxiety associated with the loss of unity of the will following the transformation of the sovereign power from individual to a never fully homogeneous and harmonious collective, and the anxiety generated by political conflict that the pluralism of competing partisan forces generates. Representation as embodiment is the sign of a society impatient with democracy's cacophony; although it erupts as radical antagonism of "we" versus "them," its ambition is the achievement of a society structurally unified and not plagued by political conflict.

In ancient popular governments, the *capopopolo* – made up of the tribune, the *dux*, and the demagogue – was the forerunner of the charismatic leader in modern mass democracy. The Caesarean implication of representation as embodiment when applied to political decision-making power is far from imaginary. Theodor Mommsen's depiction of Julius Caesar as the chief of the "new monarchy," who put an end to the corrupt republic and the misery of conflict, inspired both Max Weber and Carl Schmitt (the theorists who contributed most to the advancement of a plebiscitary and populist rendition of democracy) (Urbinati 2014, chap. 4). Schmitt's conception of representation as embodiment targeted the very notion that parliaments might be authorized through elections, a secret ballot and individual suffrage. He instead advanced the idea of a populist leader who would save society from the trap

---

[2] "The notion that 'the people' are one; that divisions among them are not genuine conflicts of interests but are merely self-serving factions; and that the people will be best looked after by a single unpolitical leadership that will put their interests first – these ideas are *anti*political, but they are nevertheless essential elements in a political strategy that has often been used to gain power" (Canovan 2005, p. 87).

of accountability and party advocacy by using elections as acclamation of the people against its minority parts. But a populist leader "has the confidence of the entire people not mediated by the medium of a parliament splintered into parties. This confidence, rather, is directly united in his person" (Schmitt 2008 [1928], p. 370).

III PARLIAMENT, POLITICAL PARTIES, AND THE PERMANENT CRISIS OF DEMOCRACY

I said at the start that political representation is at the heart of modern democracy. It was not always like that. The rise of parliamentary government started in the nondemocratic age of liberal constitutionalism. In the nineteenth century, it was popular to argue that democracy would weaken the role of legislative power in favor of the executive. The association of democracy with plebiscitary leadership and the power of the masses can be found in the work of authors as diverse as John Stuart Mill, James Bryce and Max Weber (Selinger 2019, pp. 194–199). Such views persisted until after the victory of Fascism and Nazism. An echo of that belief can be found in the coinage of terms (still successful in contemporary politics) such as "mass democracy," "totalitarian democracy," "illiberal democracy," and "authoritarian democracy." But Mill, Bryce and more explicitly Weber and Gaetano Mosca paved the way for an encounter of democracy with liberal politics and pluralism (Bellamy 2014a). They connected a representative government with elections and the tribunal of public opinion, and deemed the representative assembly a deliberative body relying upon free and frank discussion of ideas among competent orators. Listening to electors' voices and interests was the condition for achieving the general interest thanks to wise representatives. Jeremy Bentham had given this theory a successful rendering when he defined the place of judgment in deliberation.

We have to consider the proposition that judgment and deliberation are not necessarily democratic and their utility in understanding the interests of the many is conditional on the information and knowledge that decision-makers gather from society. Based on this, we can explain Bentham's maxim that each individual is the best judge although not the best actor of her own interest. While a pass to equality and publicity, that maxim was not yet a pass to democracy. The idea that only the wearer can tell if her shoe pinches does not yet entail a claim for equal power as knowing where my shoe pinches does not make me know how to fix it. Bentham's maxim was meant to counter aristocratic (i.e., unelected) government, not to argue for democracy. It was meant to prove that only getting information from the public would allow the pursuing of the "universal interest" and reveal the damage caused by "sinister interests" (Bentham 1843b, pp. 33, 455). Bentham's maxim entails that the recipients of political decisions – the subjects to the law – are always the best judge and *this* fact alone makes them non-subjected; yet they do not need to be able to partake in decisions. Being a competent judge of one's interests and being a competent agent are two different things: politics entails professional competence and divisions of labor, which is what elections allow. Thus, representative government belongs to popular (versus aristocratic) government because all that lawmakers need in order to perform in the general interest comes from their recipients: the information on the pinching shoe, the authorization to make decisions, and a verdict on their service. Although Bentham subscribed only to a "formalistic" notion of representation as "standing for," the place he gave to the authority of citizens' judgment opened the floor to the idea that "acting for someone else independently and with discretion is not possible" (Pitkin 1967, p. 199). Thus, while reference to judgment was also central in the works of James Madison and Edmund Burke, it was with the English Utilitarians, and Bentham in particular, that judgment came to be understood as the preserve of each person, as the other leg of sovereignty along with the will: communication between institutions and society was the spirit of representative politics although not contemplated in any rule and procedure. This was the premise that consolidated the appreciation of parliamentary politics in the liberal age.

Representation, competent orators, and the public were three basic components of representative government in the liberal age that both its supporters (Bentham, Mill, Bryce and Weber) and its critics (Schmitt) assumed. Representative politics was made of the following triangulation: a deliberative conception of the parliament as an *agora* (this was Mill's analogy) hosting speakers advocating pro or contra certain proposals; an idea of representation as a mirror of ideas and interests embedded in society and seeking a *point d'appui* in the parliament; and good orators, who advocated not as delegates of partial interests but as prudent speakers who translated the claims they advocated for into policies in the service of the general interest. In his *Considerations on Representative Government* (1861), Mill proposed Themistocles and Washington as models of speakers in the House; in his essay on "Parliament and Government in Germany" (1919), Weber praised Pericles and Caesar as demagogues who achieved civil unity in a climate of division and contestation. Although they were mistrustful of the plebiscitary implication of mass democracy and aware of the risks of demagoguery, Mill and Weber both deeply appreciated parliamentary rhetoric and did not dream of making politics an art of truth seeking. It was actually Weber who revealed, much more explicitly than Mill, the existing of an unavoidable tension between the deliberative function of the representative assembly and the anti-deliberative implications that demagoguery would entail. In his 1919 essay, Weber was inspired by Gladstone and the American presidents whose leadership above parts and parties was capable of awakening Parliament and Congress, respectively, from their routinized processes, while exposing the representative assembly to the influence of charismatic leaders. To Weber, bringing democracy to parliamentary politics would require combining deliberative representation with passionate rhetoric. It would entail making the parliament look like a *forum*, in which orators performed in order to captivate the audience, and not merely or even primarily to produce laws (a task better served by the deliberative parliament). With Weber, communication between state and society took the form of a true performative and constructive discourse and was not simply the gathering of information and judgment (Bentham), but also the door to the advancing of progressive causes through purposive rhetoric (Mill). But whereas in Mill's view, parliamentary orators interacted essentially with their peers in the House and aimed, all of them, for reasonable lawmaking, in Weber's case, demagogues in the parliament interacted not solely with their peers but above all with the citizens and the media outside, which were in fact their most important reference point. The public tribunal (Bentham) and the agora (Mill) gave away to the forum (Weber) in which the role of the public was not mediated by prudent and virtuous orators but was in direct communication with the emotions of the audience.

Representation as mirroring social ideas and interests featured in the deliberative assembly of a liberal parliament thanks to two interrelated factors: suffrage as a function of the few for the protection of their interests rather than a right; and virtuous representatives. According to Madison, representing pluralism required competent leaders (Hamilton, Jay and Madison 1961, no. 10). In the age of liberal representation, a free mandate did not raise serious problems of legitimacy because the elected and their electors belonged to the same privileged class: the enfranchised. The liberal parliament appeared as a version of direct democracy of the few over a population that remained deprived of sovereignty and whose interests were included in those of the represented. Before democracy, the parliament resembled an agora in all respects, where the heat of emotions was a performative condition of deliberation with a public of likeminded people as its judge. Democracy changed all of that.

The extension of suffrage put representation on trial in the name of the two functions that had energized the liberal parliament: representativeness and advocacy (Urbinati 2006, chap. 1). The expansion of the suffrage and its identification with a fundamental right of the citizen, no longer a function for the protection of property interests, made the communication of the parliament with society a source of permanent conflict. The idealized image of lawmaking, ridiculed by Schmitt, as a deliberative exercise performed by virtuous representatives, clashed against a society that was made of citizens who were unequal in many respects and seldom associated according to class interests. The triangulation of the agora-model (deliberative assembly, free public speech and virtuous rhetoricians) was shown to have quite opposite implications once the electorate was made of such diverse and even opposite interests. Mirroring society would entail fragmenting the collective sovereign. Relying upon good rhetoricians was a meager prospect.

Rather than individual rhetoricians, collective actors were needed as agents of representative politics, partisanship identification and propagation of their ideas. The identity and character of these collective actors was one of the most debated topics in the twentieth century. Living in a time and country that witnessed the suffocation of the liberal parliament by a one-party-regime (fascism), Antonio Gramsci named the party in mass democracy a "New Prince" (1989) because in his mind, it formed a collective that acted as one leader and was capable of unifying a plurality of social interests without falling under the opposing extremes of either a quarreling party pluralism (as in liberal parliamentarianism) or a Caesarean regime (as with fascism). Organization was paramount, as it made the party capable of selecting and forming candidates for electoral competitions and state administration, of promoting participation by motivating the militants through a system of values and interpretative shortcuts (ideology) that infused emotional identification with a cause, and of expanding influence in society and achieving a majority. With mass parties, rhetoric changed its meaning and location: it was no longer associated with the skill of a leader and confined to an individual's parliamentary performances as in the liberal age. According to some of their early visionary critics, mass parties would actually change the nature of liberal democracy by subjecting electors and public opinion to the exigencies devised by the party machineries (Ostrogorski 1902; Weil 2013 [1950]). Yet organized parties became the protagonists of the renaissance of democracy after World War II, as collective rhetoricians that set communication and representative claim-making in motion. Since then, the destiny of representative politics has been (and still is) deeply connected to the question of parties' moral legitimacy.

Already in 1911, Robert Michels revealed the conundrum of representative democracy: organization "is the weapon of the weak in their struggle with the strong" and yet is also the gateway to bureaucracy, power concentration and verticalization – which is to say, to oligarchy (1962 [1911], p. 61). Michels made it clear that representative democracy could not escape the dilemma of creating undemocratic groups (parties) in order to perform well in elections. Today, critics of parties follow Michels' track when they oppose direct constituent-representative communication and objective information against partisan siding (Rosenblum 2008). Yet, it was party pluralism and the emancipation of parties from factions that helped stabilize representative democracy in the age of the active role of society and the audience (Mair 2013). Hence, while the age of liberal parliaments was marked by the dismissal of political parties, the age of democratic parliaments coincided with their acceptance and praise (Kelsen 2013 [1929]; Schattschneider 2009). The old liberal triangulation was replaced with this new one: *parliament, parties and the public*. In democracy, representation becomes the picture of an enlarged electorate constructed through interpretations and ideological assumptions that political parties carry out, not individual orators or parliaments of notables.

With democracy, representation drops any pretense of mirroring society and proposes itself as a constructivist project that transforms society into a battlefield of organized interests, in which parties lead the conflicts and define the limits of compromises and alliances: parties more than parliaments perform de facto lawmaking. And whereas in the liberal age, the free mandate was the condition for virtuous representatives to state their responsibility before the electors, in the democratic age, it is a legal proviso that has no strength to resist the power of the party to impose its line of behavior on its parliamentary arm. The power of the party over representatives restituted power to the citizens against the elected but at the cost of subjecting them (although with their consent) to the party; the decline of the party would thus fatally translate into a decline of democratic representation.

According to Elmer E. Schattschneider, "party government" brought to the fore the difference (and superiority) of political versus legal constitutionalism, insofar as parties operate in "a legal no man's land" and do a job the law cannot do and yet a representative democracy needs (2009, p. 12). Parties could guarantee limitations of power (the main goal of legal constitutionalism) and strengthen the institutional order by precisely doing what the law could not: guarding the political mandate of the elected. While the law cannot take liberty away from representatives, parties can. This renders the paradox of representative democracy quite well: it is an institutional order whose strength is proportional to the strength of bodies (parties) that internally are not truly democratic (Rosenbluth and Shapiro 2018). Finally, parties' interest in enlarging electoral consent is an "engine for expanding the scale of conflict" and making democracy capable of resisting pressure groups (parties' true rivals), whose goal is instead that of narrowing the pool of participants (Schattschneider 1988, p. 12).

Returning to the distinction between forms of representation we have illustrated in the previous section, we may conclude that what gives representation a democratic character is the fact that suffrage is a right of the citizen. The problem is that the institutions of individual suffrage and free mandate weaken the power of the individual elector; hence, democracy requires complementing suffrage with a complex system of rights that animate citizens' participation well beyond the election day and animate parties and movements (Brito Vieira and Runciman 2008, pp. 55–62). Thus, citizens in contemporary democracies have two equally important powers: free and regular elections for choosing among more than one options and the right to free speech and association in order to effectively participate in political competition, opinion formation and debate.

IV BEYOND REPRESENTATION?

Representative democracies are losing perceived legitimacy all over the world. To explain the recent explosion of talks and writings on the "crisis of democracy," scholars have called into question representative institutions and interpreted the decline of "voter turnout, party membership, trust in politicians, and interest in politics" as symptoms of electoral representation's agony (Tormey 2014, p. 105). In a 2004 article on the uneasy alliance of representation and democracy, Pitkin wrote that although it "is not exactly false" to state that representation has made democracy possible in modern states, this assumption is "profoundly misleading" if it is used to hide the fact that the legitimacy citizens ascribe to representation is contingent upon the circumstances in which it functions (2004, p. 336). The recent decline of democracy's perceived legitimacy tells us that the problems faced by representation in today's democracies come from ways that representatives have begun to operate in and the way the public functions. As to the former, elected politicians are immersed in practices that favor political corruption instead of preventing or combatting it; this perversion comes primarily from the flow of private money in electoral campaigns, yet it also emerges from the weakness of parties relative to their organizational and symbolic strength. As to the public, the media system feels the allure of the audience as much as politicians do and tends to become an organ of entertainment that ceases to check the government and the elected and often become promoters of leaders. Thanks to the oligarchic ownership and control of the means of communication, citizens with greater economic power have more chances to elect the representatives they prefer and, thus, facilitate laws that favor their interests (Baker 2007). This infringement of equality is primed to jeopardize democratic procedures regulating access to representation by lowering the barriers against arbitrariness (Winters 2011). All in all, the combination of private money and opinion formation turns into a new oligarchic violation of equal opportunity to effectively exercise political rights (Dawood 2006).

Democracy is not leaderless; however, it requires a broad competition for selection of leaders and the circulation of leaders. Democracy opposes the formation of a separate class that splits the collective sovereign into two groups, the rulers and the ruled. As we said above, the democratic character of representation consists in that it activates a circular current of judgment that keeps institutions under people's eye and imposes power limitation on the elected. In ancient direct democracies, this goal was fulfilled by using a lottery to select jurors and administrators, while citizens retained lawmaking power in the Assembly. Under a system of representative democracy, this goal is fulfilled by regular and free elections with short-term tenure and the limitation of re-election. In almost all contemporary democracies these controlling devices have fallen into disuse. The system regulating the selection of candidates adds to this problem both when it relies on party cooptation and when it is based on primaries in which citizens end up voting on candidates they never helped scout. Although they take different forms in different countries, these circumstances of corruption invariably exacerbate the oligarchical potentials of elections. The nexus of wealth-power is the source of one of the most daunting problems, and in two senses: first, because wealth can be used to elect reliable representatives (although buying a large assembly is hard and although we cannot state a linear causal relation between influencing deliberation and determining decisions); second, because wealth can be used to manipulate a free mandate, the central requirement of political representation. This manipulation can take different forms; in the United States, for instance, lobbyists monitor congressional votes taken by representatives who may well have been elected thanks to private donors whom lobbyists represent.

To preserve democracy, power must circulate and never be captured by any single person or section of society. Democracy does not demand full equality, only legal and political equality. Nor does democracy necessarily require the gap between state and society to be closed; rather, it wants permanent communication that allows for surveillance, control and renewal of the elected. But, as we saw at the start, that gap is open to cockeyed potentials, for while it stimulates countless forms of participation and contestation, it also allows factional interests to participate in the game of political influence. The need to keep the system open and power circulating imposes permanent maintenance work on democrats. The matter of "how to impede the oligarchic transmutation of representative democracy" is the object of a rich corpus of research and constitutional designs, which hope to contain the elite's power and block the translation of economic power into political power (McCormick 2011). This brings us back to the two humors of representative democracy, one that wants to close the gap between citizens and institutions and one that wants to manage the gap instead. The former deems representative democracy as a second best while the latter deems it a good system because of its capacity to create a web of indirectness and intermediation that takes possession and absoluteness away from power while guarantees pluralism and freedom. Accordingly, reforms or changes should aim at keeping the representative system open to renewal and the citizens' voice strong enough to never be ignored by representatives.

Those who blame our current malaise on ideological manipulation and parties hope to restore citizens' democratic power by forging new norms on transparency that impose, for instance, open voting in the parliament or the congress (D'Angelo and Ranalli 2019). On the same track are those who relate the possibility of restoring democracy to the belief that the intermediary role of parties can be overcome through forms of digital interaction between citizens and representatives that might produce de facto imperative mandates. The drive behind these proposals is a desire to close the gap between government and civil society, and a wish to make transparency the mark of a direct representative relationship. According to this view, visual inspection and raw information, free of ideology and partisan interpretations, are seen as the key for overcoming parties, which are accused of having primary responsibility for representative politics' perceived decline of legitimacy (Casaleggio and Grillo 2011). This is the common denominator of several proposals, all of which hope to replace party democracy and electoral representation with digital direct representation and selection by lottery (Landemore 2019). Recent experimentations of lawmaking and even constitution making with a mix of digital/direct democracy and elections have rekindled traditional discontent with political mandates. The calls for transparency and closing the gap between representatives and the represented resonates with the call for authenticity, an argument that reasserts mirror representation (*being like*) against representation as *claiming and acting for*.

The Internet promises citizens the ability to practice self-government, ease the process of voting (creating the prospect of more referenda), advance law-making initiatives and send instructions to the elected. Direct interaction that digitalization allows seems capable of narrowing the gap in which special interests maneuver the system. I have elsewhere detected and critically analyzed this new phenomenon as "direct representation" versus political mandate representation (Urbinati 2019). Direct representation is the terrain upon which newly born digital movement parties operate in several democratic countries; they claim it is possible to bypass old party organization (and its unavoidable oligarchic structure) altogether by activating direct channels of horizontal interaction between leaders and citizens. The paradox is that these digital movements inaugurate forms of plebiscitary democracy based on an audience and marked by strong vertical leadership that aggregates followers in a void of organization (Gerbaudo 2019). At times, the revisions of the political mandate system may take a yet different road and aim at representation as embodiment with the goal of unifying claims and claimants under the figure of a leader who makes parties useless (Laclau 2005). Representation as delegation and representation as embodiment are thus back and they ally against political mandate and party politics. The crisis of and opposition against parties, therefore, appear to be feeding into a crisis of political representation (Merkel 2014). This is the circumstance of politics that should attract our attention when we complain about today's decline of the democratic tenor of representation.

RECOMMENDED READING

Ankersmit, F. (2002). *Political Representation*, Stanford: Stanford University Press.
Brito Vieira, M. & Runciman, D. (2008). *Representation*, London: Polity Press.
Disch, L., de Sande, M., Urbinati, U., eds. (2019). *The Constructivist Turn in Political Representation*, Edinburgh: Edinburg University Press.
Gerbaudo, P. (2019). *The Digital Party: Political Organization and Online Democracy*, London: Pluto Press.
Hamilton, A., J. Jay, J. Madison (1987 [1787]). *The Federalist. A Commentary on The Constitution of the United States*, Edited E. M. Earl, New York: The Modern Library.
Kelsen, H. (1992). *Introduction to the Problems of Legal Theory: A Translation of the First Edition of the Reine Rechtslehre*, Oxford: Clarendon Press.
Kelsen, H. (1999 [1945]). *General Theory of Law and State*, Translated by A. Wedberg, Union, NJ: The Lawbook Exchange.
Kelsen, H. (2013 [1929]). *The Essence and Value of Democracy*, Edited by N. Urbinati and C. Invernizzi Accetti, Lanham: Rowman & Littlefield.
Mair, P. (2013). *Ruling the Void: The Hollowing of Western Democracy*, London: Verso.
Manin, B. (1997). *The Principles of Representative Government*, Cambridge: Cambridge University Press.
Mansbridge, J. (2003). Rethinking Representation. *American Political Science Review*, 97 (4), 515–528.
Pitkin, H. F. (1967). *The Concept of Representation*, Berkeley: University of California Press.
Pitkin, H. F. (2004). Representation and Democracy: Uneasy Alliance. *Scandinavian Political Studies*, 27 (2004), 335–342.
Plotke, D. (1997). Representation is Democracy. *Constellations*, 4 (1), 19–34.
Saward, M. (2010). *The Representative Claim*, Cambridge: Cambridge University Press.
Sintomer. Y. (2013). The Meanings of Political Representation: Uses and Misuses of a Notion. *Raisons Politiques*, 50 (2), 13–34.
Urbinati, N. (2006). *Representative Democracy: Principles and Genealogy*, London and Chicago: The University of Chicago Press.
Urbinati, N. (2014). *Democracy Disfigured: Opinion, Truth and The People*, Cambridge, MA: Harvard University Press.
Urbinati, N. & Warren, M. (2008). The concept of Representation in Contemporary Political Theory. *Annual Review of Political Science*, 11 (1), 387–412.
Waldron, J. (1999). *Law and Disagreement*, Oxford: Oxford University Press.

15

Deliberation

Simone Chambers

Constitutions structure, protect, and promote many different types of deliberation in liberal democracies. Reversing this relationship, we can also say that many types of deliberation are involved in making, changing, and interpreting constitutions. In this chapter I do not survey all these potential sites and roles of deliberation in constitutional theory and practice. Instead, I focus on the interventions of deliberative democratic theory into constitutional theory.

I begin Section I with a brief discussion of what is deliberation. Although, like all interesting political concepts, deliberation is a contested concept, it is by now a familiar concept not really in need of much introduction. But for the purposes of the typology and analysis I develop in this chapter it is important to clarify what I mean by deliberation and how I am using the term. The take-home message here is that I understand deliberation first and foremost as a normative theoretical standard and not an empirical practice although many empirical practices can be evaluated using the deliberative standard.

In theorizing about constitutions this normative standard is introduced at different levels of analysis and has different functions in different theories. Section II begins with the most abstract and what might be called the foundational employment of deliberation. Here we see constitutions as being created and legitimized through democratic deliberation as well as essentially functioning as guarantors of that deliberation. These theories are what I call deliberative constitutionalism. From those foundational views that employ deliberation as a framework to reconstruct constitutionalism as such, I turn, in Section III, to theories that are interested in delineating how we ought to be deliberating about constitutions within established liberal democratic orders. This moves the discussion from a constituent function of deliberation to a constituted function and role. A powerful and influential answer to the 'how' question appeals to public reason. While some contributors to this debate argue that public reason is a defining feature of constitutional deliberation, others question its plausibility. The question of how we should be deliberating about constitutional essentials naturally leads to the question of who should be deliberating about constitutional essentials in Section IV.

There are three natural answers to this question: courts, legislatures, and citizens. Within deliberative democracy theory the answer is often a combination of these three but there are important variations. I look at arguments that claim that courts have a very special role in constitutional deliberation, arguments that focus on the legislature in distinction to courts, and then arguments that look to citizens either in the broad informal public sphere or in structured citizen forums. With some recent deliberative developments in citizen constitution-making we return to questions of constituent power in Section V. Here, I argue that deliberative constitutionalism offers a view of democratic constitutionalism that stresses the role of inclusive and robust public debate in the creation of a popular will with the legitimate authority to exercise constituent power.

I WHAT IS DELIBERATION?

Very generally I take deliberation to mean the weighing of reasons or considerations in light of practical decisions about what to do. Deliberation in this practical sense is obviously important for law and politics. Every regime, political leader, decision maker, engages in deliberation. Political philosophers from Aristotle to Hobbes have spent a good deal of time thinking about deliberation, what it entails, and how to do it well. There is also quite a lot of scholarly work that looks at and analyses deliberation about constitutions, for example, how do judges decide cases. In the contemporary context of political philosophy and constitutional theory, however, deliberation is usually not a neutral purely descriptive term; rather it is a term most often connected to some idea of deliberative democracy or democratic deliberation. Adding democracy or democratic to deliberation introduces a number of normative (and sometimes epistemic) qualifiers to deliberation. The weighing of reasons or considerations in light of a practical decision about what to do takes place *between equals* or is the appropriate sort of deliberation for or about people considered as free and equal. The between people part implies that deliberation is intersubjective. It can go on in your head but it involves a plurality of views.

Pluralism and the challenges pluralism poses for collective decision-making among equals is the background assumption of all conceptions of deliberation in this tradition. The intersubjective nature of deliberation also means that deliberation is not simply about *weighing* reasons, it is also and for some essentially about *giving and receiving* reasons. The people giving and receiving the reasons to be weighed must have some fundamental or initial equal standing. This does not mean that all views and claims are equally valid or strong. It means all participants in the process are to be considered to have an equal dialogic right to make a claim or argument and that the persuasiveness of the claim or argument must reside in the merits of the argument not the standing of the arguer. The deliberative ideal models the idea of free and equal citizens in a dynamic process of persuasion in which citizens exhibit respect for each other through offering justifications and reasons as they collectively problem solve public policy questions.

Deliberation in this democratic sense is the process of exchanging and weighing reasons or considerations in view of a collective practical decision to be taken by free and equal persons. Deliberation is not strictly speaking a *decision rule*, if by decision rule we mean how and when we stop deliberation and act on some chosen principle, policy, or practical conclusion. Deliberation is decision-oriented in that it is *about* taking a practical decision but it is not obviously a decision rule that dictates when a group has closure on a question and indeed many of our most important deliberations are about what rule we will choose to take various types of decisions. The most common decision-rule within democratic deliberation is majority voting. Thus, it would be a mistake to think of deliberation and voting as two competing procedures of democratic decision-making. Voting is not a way to decide how to vote, and deliberation, I want to insist, has no default decision rule attached to it. In democracies, most deliberation will need a vote to be decisive and, for deliberative democrats, most votes need deliberation to be legitimate (Manin 1987).

Deliberative democracy both as a model of face-to-face practice, say in a mini public or citizens' assembly, as well as a broad paradigm to understand a full democratic system has no problem with counting votes or with majority rule. Deliberative democracy's issue with aggregation is not an objection to voting or counting votes; it is an objection to democratic *theory* that focuses exclusively on the vote, says nothing about the opinion and will formation that precedes the vote, and invests aggregation with the full weight of democratic legitimacy. Thus, it is not the practice of voting but the normative weight and role of voting that is the target.

Now, it might be thought that consensus is the default decision rule for deliberation. The thought here is that if the essential driving force of deliberation is the persuasiveness of arguments then the natural end of this sort of activity would be when everyone was persuaded or everyone was in agreement. There is a great deal of debate within deliberative democracy theory about whether consensus is the proper end or telos of deliberation with a number of theorists abandoning the ideal (Elstub and McLaverty 2014). But even for theorists who retain consensus as the telos of deliberation this is understood as a regulative ideal that does not translate into either a default empirical decision rule nor a requirement that all participants take consensus as their subjective goal in real empirical encounters (Neblo 2007).

Deliberation is compatible with and sometimes enhanced by many different sorts of decision rules, the most common being majority voting (Moore and O'Doherty 2014). One-person one-vote is a principle that recognizes the essential equality of all citizens and there are good reasons to endorse a majority rule (rather than say super majority or unanimity) as the decision procedure that best instantiates that equality (Schwartzberg 2013). Thus, for pragmatic as well as moral reasons deliberative democrats endorse majority rule as a democratically appropriate way to take decisions.

What is important for the deliberative democrat, however, are the reasons, justifications, and discussion that backup a decision as well as the conditions under which that political communication takes place, not simply the number of votes that support a decision. This relationship between deliberation and voting translates into a democratic theory in which the procedures that constitute a democratic regime are expanded beyond free and fair elections and majority decision-making to encompass a robust theory of opinion and will formation as well as multiple and various institutional mechanisms through which that opinion and will impacts, determines, and shapes public policy decisions – voting being only one such mechanism. In the final section of this chapter, I introduce a brief example of what such an expanded view of democratic legitimacy might look like in the real world.

The addition of democracy to deliberation introduces a normative dimension or framework to the study of deliberation. We are not simply describing the deliberation that goes on in liberal democracies, there is also always a sense that deliberating in this democratic way is right, appropriate, or good. Why it is right, appropriate, or good varies a great deal across theorists. But generally, there are procedural and/or outcome-based reasons for valuing deliberation. Procedural reasons are almost always moral and involve some claim that reason-giving under conditions of pluralism and equality is a way to treat one's fellow citizen as free and equal and deserving of respect. Reasons here can have a very particular meaning, for example, Rawls' idea of public reasons or a very lose meaning signifying, for example, arguments rather than threats or genuine attempts at persuasion rather than strategic attempts to manipulate. Outcome-based reasons for valuing deliberation can be moral and/or epistemic. Moral outcome-based views suggest that deliberation can lead to outcomes that are legitimate or right; epistemic outcome-based views claim that deliberation can lead to epistemically better or more truth apt outcomes than other procedures.

Finally, deliberation as I am using it in this chapter, is first and foremost a normative theoretical standard and not a particular empirical practice. Some face-to-face highly structured mini publics, for example, look like they are clear exemplars of a democratic form of deliberation. And they very well might be, but particular context-specific institutions are exemplars only to the extent that they more or less live up to the normative standard and no one institution or practice can ever fully capture that standard. Some Constitutional Court deliberations, for example, might also live up to a deliberative democratic standard (Mendes 2013). As a normative standard, deliberation can be used to evaluate many different sorts of phenomena not only or exclusively face-to-face practices of deliberative decision-making. For example, one might want to ask in relation to constitutional matters, what sorts of reasons for or against the right to marriage equality are circulating in the broad informal public sphere. Or that standard might apply to a democracy as a whole. So, although I will be talking about institutions, I do not take deliberation to be identified with any one practice or institution.

II DELIBERATIVE CONSTITUTIONALISM

Deliberative constitutionalism is a term that has been gaining usage (Kong and Levy 2018; Elstub and Pomatto 2018). It points to the intersection between deliberative democracy and constitutional theory. But this could mean many things as deliberative democracy is now a broad paradigm encompassing lots of variation and disagreement (Levy et al. 2018). I employ the term rather narrowly to refer to constitutional theory that uses a conception of deliberation to either reconstruct, justify, or elucidate constitutionalism as such. Thus, deliberation is foundational to the constitutional theory and not simply an important modality among others within a constitutional order. Jürgen Habermas' discourse theory of law and democracy is the most prominent version of deliberative constitutionalism but I would also include Carlos Santiago Nino, Bruce Ackerman, Frank Michelman, and Andrew Arato (among others) in this list, all of whom have significantly different views of constitutionalism to Habermas (Ackerman 1991; Arato 2016; Michelman 1999; Nino 1997).

Habermas begins his deliberative constitutionalism with a co-originality thesis that postulates that liberal rights and democratic self-determination are fundamentally interdependent. Liberal democracy developed over time in a bootstrapping historical process that saw, on the one hand, the constitutional rights first articulated in the eighteenth century gaining traction, and on the other hand, the justification of those constitutional rights relying more and more on claims that they are or would be the outcome of some form of popular willing, choice, or contract. 'We the people' supplants God, Nature, abstract rationality, or tradition as the ultimate source of constitutional authorization and authority, but "We the people" is morally authoritative only to the extent that it speaks under conditions of freedom and equality.

The historical learning process that Habermas charts is given philosophical anchorage by the introduction of discourse theory. The interdependence between rights and democracy is mediated by a deliberative theory of validity and justification. This is the discourse principle (D): "Just those action norms are valid to which all possible affected persons could agree as participants in rational discourse" (Habermas 1996, p. 107). Habermas argues that in our modern world, substantive sources of justification such as God or natural law can no longer perform the function of justifying collective norms. The combination of disagreement about these substantive sources and a respect for the free and equal status of fellow citizens undermines the possibility of having a clear buck-stopper that can serve as a foundational justification for collective norms. Under modern conditions of pluralism, we fall back on the conditions of justification as such. Rational discourse is the technical term for a form of communication where only justification goes on. Here we conceive of the conditions of this conversation in such a way as to ensure that only "the unforced force of the better argument" has sway (Habermas 1996, p. 306). For this to happen each participant should have "an equal opportunity to be heard, to introduce topics, to make contributions, to suggest and criticize proposals"

(Habermas 1996, p. 305). A rational discourse is not an empirically observable conversation but rather a philosophical device (a reconstruction) to give us a sense of the general conditions of justification and validity. The general conditions of justification and validity are a form of democratic deliberation where all participants are free and equal co-deliberators in the process of establishing justified norms.

If we think of the (D) principle in terms of the validity of law, we are led to the conclusion that citizens need to be in a basic relation of equality with one another to be able to collectively validate law. The validation of law is analogous to the justification of a norm. The discourse theory explains why collective willing (if undertaken under conditions of equality and freedom) could generate legitimate outcomes rather than simply random and arbitrary outcomes. This basic relation of equality is then understood in terms of rights: "the system (of rights) should contain precisely the basic rights that citizens must mutually grant one another if they want to legitimately regulate their life in common by means of positive law" (Habermas 1996, p. 118). These basic rights divide into 5 categories (Habermas 1996, pp. 122–123). The first three refer to basic liberties of the individual and would include such things as freedom of speech and religion, freedom of association, and due process. The fourth category covers citizenship rights and guaranties "equal opportunity to participate in processes of opinion-and-will-formation" (Habermas 1996, p. 123). The final category encompasses rights to the social and environmental conditions that would be required to adequately exercise 1–4.[1]

A system of rights then is a precondition of valid law making; citizens must be in a relation of equality with one another to make valid law.[2] But this appears to place rights prior to democracy and undermine the co-originality thesis. Habermas denies this. First, he has not deduced any specific rights but only the need for certain categories of rights. Specific rights, like freedom of religion, for example, need to be enacted and made into positive law in real political communities with real constitutions and enforcement (Habermas 1996, p. 125). Each legal, political, and national context will vary and so each system of positive rights (each constitution) will differ. Thus, rights as legal instruments are justified as outcomes of discursive processes and not as prerequisites. The philosopher can reconstruct the general idea of and need for a system of rights, but they are not really rights at all until they are enacted into a constitution in the name of the people. Furthermore, the philosophical reconstruction is only possible as an adjunct to the historical and empirical process of bootstrapping: "'the' system of rights does not exist in transcendental

---

[1] While this view of the justification of rights appears to be similar to Ely's famous argument justifying constitutionally enforced rights as the necessary condition of democratic procedures (Ely 1980), Habermas' co-originality view justifies a wider and deeper set of important constitutional rights than Ely and also insists that democratic procedures do not have priority over rights.

[2] Carlos Santiago Nino offers a very similar view: constitutional rights are derived from and "based on the principles of autonomy, inviolability, and dignity of the person and are derived from the assumptions of the social practice of moral discourse" (Nino 1997, p. 63).

purity. But two hundred years of European constitutional law have provided us with sufficient number of models. These can instruct a generalized reconstruction of the intuitions that guide the intersubjective practice of self-legislation in the medium of positive law" (Habermas 1996, p. 129).

The self-reflective feedback loop of deliberative bootstrapping that is the core of the co-originality thesis appears to undercut the legitimacy of founding moments: the people have to be under a constitution to legitimately make a constitution. On this view, foundings do have a legitimacy deficit; they are in essence 'groundless' if seen as an isolated event that can generate legitimacy ex nihilo. As Habermas puts it, "we understand the regress itself as the understandable expression of the future-oriented character, or openness, of the democratic constitution…. [T]his fallible continuation of the founding event can break out of the circle of a polity's groundless discursive self-constitution only if this process – which is not immune to contingent interruptions and historical regressions – can be understood in the long run as a self-correcting learning process" (2001, p. 774).

Deliberative constitutionalism reimagines the exercise of constituent power as a disaggregated deliberative democratic process over time. Although this process may bear a procedural resemblance to deliberative democratic ideals of (ordinary) self-government, Habermas, Ackerman, Michelman, and Nino, all embrace a dualism that insists on a distinction between higher law-making from ordinary law-making. The line is quite bright in Ackerman (less so in Habermas), who seems to have a rather pessimistic view of the deliberative potential of ordinary law-making but an uplifting narrative about constituent power exercised over time and through history in extraordinary moments of constitutional mobilization (Ackerman 1991; see also Vargova 2005). At these moments one sees the "mobilized deliberation" of engaged and self-conscious publics undertake the transformative politics of reinterpreting the constitution (Ackerman 1991, p. 290).

The picture of deliberative constitution-making briefly sketched here suggests a shift away from the classic readings of the modern constitution that stress, on the one hand, foundings, documents, and births of constitutional orders in voluntarist acts of rational agency or collective willing, and on the other hand, constitutionally established amending procedures for changing the constitution post-founding. Constitution-making and amending is understood instead as a disaggregated deliberative process over time that could have any number of institutional homes and legal venues including "landmark" legislation, referendums, constituent assemblies, on-line crowd sourcing, roundtable conferences, and court decisions. What is important is that a certain type of public inclusive discourse is generated.

Deliberative constitutionalism, as I have defined it here, not only understands the exercise of constituent power in deliberative terms but also the fundamental justification of modern constitutionalism as such in deliberative terms. I now turn to deliberation within a constituted order, and more particularly to the question of how we should be deliberating about constitutions and who should be doing the deliberation. In what follows, I pay particular attention to Rawls' theory of public reason. But it might be worth pausing and asking why I have not included Rawls in my category of deliberative constitutionalism despite the fact that he fully endorsed the idea of deliberative democracy as well as an idea of co-originality in which democracy and liberal constitutions are interdependent. It seems to me that discourse and deliberation play a deeper constituent role in Habermas' constitutional theory than public reason does in Rawls' theory. Public reason proceeds from shared ideas of justice rather than being constitutive of those principle. But more importantly public reason is not a theory of democracy but a moral constraint on reasongiving in liberal societies. The deliberative constitutionalists I include here all take up and elaborate the question of how and why citizens should be understood as the creators of constitutions at the same time as bound by those constitutions. It is not that Rawls would disagree with deliberate constitutionalism, it is that he did not elaborate a theory of deliberative constitutionalism in this sense.

III PUBLIC REASON AND CONSTITUTIONAL DELIBERATION

Public reason theory focuses precisely on the question of how we should be deliberating about constitutional essentials. Public reason is the reason, reasoning, or reasons that are morally appropriate for the public justification of laws and policy agendas (especially when these touch on constitutional essentials) within liberal democratic constitutional orders.

The pivotal role of public justification in contemporary ideas of legitimacy is rooted in respect for the deep pluralism that characterizes modern polities as well as the recognition of the free and equal status of each citizen. Although there are many competing ideas of public reason, some of which challenge Rawls' particular version, almost all of them start with something like Rawls' liberal principle of legitimacy: "Our exercise of political power is proper and hence justifiable only when it is exercised in accordance with a constitution the essentials of which all citizens may reasonable be expected to endorse in light of principles and ideals acceptable to them as reasonable and rational" (2005, p. 217).

The challenge in fulfilling this idea of legitimacy is that people disagree at a very deep level about fundamental principles and conceptions of truth and the good. Public reason envisions a solution to this problem by introducing a constraint on the sorts of reasons that one can appeal to in justifying a political order. Rather than seek consent for our proposals, we instead seek (or we ought to seek) to fold the fact of pluralism into our very reasoning and deliberative processes by only appealing to reasons that our fellow citizens could share or accept. Deliberation about constitutional essentials is especially subject to this moral constraint.

Public reason seeks to identify a set of reasons or a type of reason that could be shared or acceptable to all. This naturally leads to the question of whether there are any such reasons and if there are what would they look like? Rawls' answer to this question evolved over his career as he sought to identify and describe reasons that were both neutral towards all (reasonable) competing ideas of the good as well as treated those ideas and the people who held them fairly and inclusively in public discourse (2005, pp. 435–490). The core feature of his conception was the exclusion of appeal to comprehensive ideas of truth and good. The focus of much of this debate has been religious reasons as paradigmatic examples of comprehensive views and their place in public justification and by extension the equal place of religious citizens in deliberations about constitutional essentials (Neufeld 2015; Quong 2011). I do not take up this debate or pursue questions about specific conceptions of public reasons as this would take us far afield. Instead, I focus on the more generic claim that we ought to be seeking public reasons (whatever they may be) in deliberation about constitutions.

Deliberation is about reason-given and public reason is about the reasons we should be giving in deliberation so there is an obvious affinity between these two concepts but there is also some ambiguity between public reason theory and deliberative democracy theory. First, not all public reason/public justification theory does in fact endorse deliberation. Sometimes, public justification is fully severed from deliberation and democracy as, for example, in the convergence theory of justification (Gaus and Vallier 2009). What is important in this view is that individuals (especially individuals who make coercive law), have sufficient (public) reasons for what they do. It is not required and is sometimes thought to be counterproductive to give or exchange those reasons with others (Vallier 2015). Second, much of the public reason literature, while often offering a generic endorsement of deliberative democracy, has very little to say about democratic theory per se, as it focuses on analytic, epistemic, or moral puzzles of public reason and not the process of exchanging such reasons, and sometimes suggests that deliberative democracy just is a theory of public reason (Freeman 2000).

On the side of deliberative democracy theory, we see a divide between people who think that public reason is a defining feature of deliberative democracy (Lafont 2020; Cohen 1996; Gutmann and Thompson 1996) and those who question whether there are such things as public reasons (Waldron 1999a) and eschew any moral constraints on reasons within deliberation. Others in the deliberative democracy camp take a fully institutional view of deliberation and so are also uninterested in the moral constraints on reasons (Fishkin 2018) or suggest that deliberative democracy should approach the question of public reason procedurally rather than substantively. For example, Habermas criticized Rawls for stipulating the substantive content of reasons within deliberation rather than the procedural rules that guarantee inclusion and equality (Habermas 1995). Public justification for Habermas is "ultimately based only on reasons that withstand objections under demanding conditions of communication" (2008, p. 49).[3] This is not (in the case of Habermas)

---

[3] Habermas does exclude religious reasons (but not comprehensive reasons) from legislative deliberation, and this certainly looks like a public reason constraint (2008, p. 128).

because there is no hope of agreement or finding reasons we share but because shared reasons need to be constructed in the procedure itself and we cannot always predict what these may be.

The question of the place and or strength of a public reason constraint in deliberation often plays itself out in debates about who should be deliberating about the constitution. It is no accident that the stronger one's endorsement of the possibility of public reason, the more likely one is to endorse constitutional courts as the place were the best and most important constitutional deliberation takes place.

IV COURTS, PARLIAMENTS, AND CITIZENS

John Rawls famously suggested that supreme or constitutional courts are exemplars of public reason. Supreme courts are the institutions whose deliberation is exclusively within the limits of public reason which is to say that "public reason is the reason of (the) supreme court" (2005, p. 231). Although Rawls notes that legislators and ordinary citizens are under some obligation to appeal to public reason, he also acknowledges that both these groups are faced with many political questions for which more partisan, interested, or comprehensive forms of reasoning may very well be appropriate. A supreme court by contrast is tasked with impartiality and neutrality of a special kind. As an exemplar, the court's reasoning is one we should seek to emulate: "to check whether we are following public reason we might ask: how would our arguments strike us presented in the form of a Supreme Court opinion?" (Rawls 2005, p. 254). Finally, courts fulfill their role as exemplar when they "give public reason vividness and vitality in the public forum."

To the extent that one thinks that democratic deliberation is under a public reason constraint the more likely one is to think that a constitutional or supreme court has a special perhaps exclusive role in constitutional deliberation. This brings up the question of judicial review. This is not the place to canvas the broad and lively debate about judicial review and its relation to democracy. Instead I only look at arguments that base the support for or criticism of judicial review on the grounds of the quality and character of the deliberation of a constitutional court. There are three main grounds for supporting judicial review from a deliberative perspective. The first, and the one most indebted to Rawls, is that court deliberations embody a form of ideal democratic deliberation especially when looked at in comparison with the deliberation in legislative assemblies or even worse the public sphere.

John Ferejohn and Pasquale Pasquino present an empirical study of European and American high courts where deliberation is synonymous with public reason and the exclusive purview of courts. "John Rawls described courts as exemplary deliberative institutions – forums in which reasons, explanations, and justifications are both expected and offered for coercive state policies" (Ferejohn and Pasquino 2002, p. 22). They argue that deliberative expectations diminish as one moves from courts to public agencies, legislators, and then finally voters. The ballot box is a "reason-free zone" where citizens do not have to have nor are they expected to give reasons for the votes (2002, p. 26; see Mendes 2013, p. 93). Ferejohn has also noted that "deliberative expectations are inversely correlated with democratic pedigree" (2008, p. 206). But this has missed an important element of Rawls' idea of exemplar. Rawls argues that citizens too are bound by a duty of civility. Just because the act of voting does come with a requirement to justify one's vote or even the fact that public opinion might show that many citizens would have a hard time justifying how they vote, these empirical observations do not undermine the normative claim that citizens ought to have such reasons especially when they are voting about important questions of basic justice.

Christopher Eisgruber makes an even stronger argument that the Supreme Court "is a kind of representative institution well-shaped to speak on behalf of the people about questions of moral and political principle" (Eisgruber 2001, p. 35; see also Alexy 2005). Both Ferejohn and Eisgruber base their argument (to some extent) on a negative assessment of legislative debate. Elected legislatures often fail to live up to a high bar of public reason neutrality and are pushed by electoral pressures in many non-deliberative ways. In a critical assessment of court-centered views of deliberation, Christopher Zurn describes these views this way: "Constitutional courts then because they speak in the language of the people's public reason and because they are the institutional representations of the people's public reason, are in fact eminently democratic actors, even when they are legislating new constitutional content" (2020, p. 326). A supreme court is "uniquely qualified to represent the people's principles because of its specially heightened capacities for reasoned deliberation about fundamental moral-political matters" (Zurn 2020, p. 335). Zurn suggests that if we take a look at how courts actually deliberate and the reasons they actually give we see that very little public reason and principled deliberation goes on. He does not argue that courts violate public reason constraints so much as that those constraints are irrelevant because court decisions are overwhelmingly taken up with narrow legal questions of precedence and procedure; they rarely introduce the sort of principled moral arguments that might "give public reason vividness and vitality in the public forum."

Zurn is surely right about this but the argument does not fully demolish the claim that courts can give public reason vividness and vitality. That role perhaps requires that the core moral claims embedded in the decisions be taken up in the public sphere by public sphere actors. Thus, it is not the written decisions that we should be looking at but rather the public debate that these decisions spark (Mendes 2013).

The second strategy to defend judicial review from a deliberative point of view argues that these courts have a special task of facilitating and protecting deliberation. Rather than focusing on slapping down substantive outcomes that violate the constitution and so setting themselves against democratic self-government, this view sees a special role for the court to facilitate citizen deliberation and exercises of democracy both at the broad participatory level as well as the level of representative legislatures. Habermas notes, "a rather bold constitutional adjudication is even required in cases that concern the implementation of democratic procedures and the deliberative form of political opinion-and will-formation" (1996, pp. 279–280; Zurn 2007 also endorses this view). Courts do not speak for the people; courts and judicial review are essential to allow the people to speak for themselves. This argument is careful not to overstate the role of the courts *vis a vis* legislatures and is not premised on the argument that legislatures are poor and untrustworthy deliberators.

There is a third argument, most recently put forward by Christina Lafont, in defense of judicial review on deliberative grounds. While it might appear that legal activism takes questions out of the public political sphere and sequesters them in the closed halls of Supreme Court adjudication, Lafont argues that this is a mistaken picture. "In constitutional democracies with judicial review, the right to legal contestation guarantees that all citizens can, on their own initiative, open and reopen a deliberative process in which reasons and justifications aimed at showing the constitutionality of a contested policy are made publically available, such that they can be scrutinized and challenged with counter arguments that might lead public opinion to be transformed and prior decisions overturned." (2020 pp. 212–213). Lafont's argument does not explicitly rely on the claim that legislative deliberation falls below a deliberative threshold but it does so implicitly. For Lafont deliberation is defined by public reason. The way to get public reason into public political deliberation is to frame questions as constitutional rights questions. Thus, constitutional legal challenge is how we kick start high-quality deliberation; debates focused on ordinary legislation do not appear to be able to achieve this goal.

Arguments against judicial review and in favor of parliamentary or political constitutionalism depend heavily on claims about the undemocratic nature of courts. But sometimes the issue is also about deliberation. There are two main deliberation-based arguments. The first argument questions the claim that only courts (and rarely legislatures) can be home to principled reason-giving and suggests that this claim is often based on an assessment of legislatures that draws on empirical observation of pathologies. But just because some legislatures have not lived up to high standards of deliberation does not mean that they can't live up to those standards and sometimes they in fact do live up to these standards. Courts too have a very spotty empirical record on this matter (Waldron 1999a).

The second argument is that strong judicial review is often connected to a public reason claim and for political constitutionalism, public reason is an unattainable ideal. Public reason theorists are wrong to think that while citizens disagree deeply about conceptions of the good they can find shared starting points regarding right and justice (Bellamy 2007; Waldron 2006). Citizens disagree just as much about right and justice as about conceptions of the good. Thus, the aspirations of public justification are at best unattainable and at worst simply dress up particular partial interests in the guise of shared principles. If disagreement goes all the way down, then there is no deliberative short cut. We must rely on a strict proceduralism of one-person one-vote and majoritarianism. This view often places some emphasis on deliberation in the public sphere and in legislatures but with the overriding role of majority rule, these views often clash with deliberative democracy theories.

V DELIBERATIVE CONSTITUTION-MAKING IN PRACTICE

In this final Section, I return to the question of the exercise of constituent authority in making and changing constitutions. I suggest that deliberative constitutionalism offers a normative standard through which to assess and compare the popular and elite deliberative processes undertaken to affect constitutional change.

Deliberative constitutionalism is a form of popular or democratic constitutionalism that insists on citizen-participation in constitution-making and changing. Although that participation will often involve voting, popular sovereignty is understood to be invested in processes of collective egalitarian discourse that precedes and informs voting. This introduces a proceduralized and disaggregated understanding of the people as the agent of popular sovereignty and wielder of constituent authority. The people is always a work-in-progress over time. This perspective downplays singular, decisive, irreversible founding moments and stresses that constitutional politics, while still higher law-making, is ongoing. The assessment of whether the democratic system does a fair job in facilitating, channeling, and empowering popular opinion and will formation in processes of constitution-making cannot be reduced to a single vote outcome or majoritarian decision but must be assessed on the procedural elements that shape and determine the discourse (broadly understood). Votes are only as good as the procedural/discursive context in which they take place. Although akin to the idea that only *free and fair* elections count as democratic, a deliberative view insists that the democratic legitimacy of outcomes must also rest on an assessment of the conditions of public debate and communication. On this view then, constitutional referendums where freedom of the press is severely curtailed would lose a significant amount of democratic legitimacy. But, so would constitutional referendums where there was a great deal of misinformation or significant sectors of the population were excluded from having their views aired or the process was rushed and superficial.

What would this view of constitution-making look like in practice? Deliberative constitutionalism suggests certain institutional innovations, but there is no one institutional blueprint that would fit every case. It is both a critical yardstick to retrospectively assess constitutional reform procedures as well as an ideal that might inspire institutional design. Let me end with a brief illustration.[4]

---

[4] There are other interesting cases of citizen participation in constitutional reform, for example Iceland, Estonia, and Luxemburg, that I do not have time to discuss (Reuchamps and Suiter 2016).

The year 2012 saw the establishment of the Irish Convention set up to review the existing Constitution and advise on reform (Suiter, Farrell and Harris 2016). The Convention had 100 members: one chair, sixty-six randomly selected ordinary citizens, and thirty-three places reserved for legislators allocated proportionate to each party's seats in Parliament. This composition was an innovative departure from other citizens' assemblies in bringing together ordinary citizens with the expertise and perspective of law-makers across the ideological and partisan spectrum. The Convention began with a remit to review and consider a number of constitutional questions which the Convention expanded on in its first meeting thus establishing its power as an agenda setter. After much deliberation, consultation with civil society, and input from citizens at large, the Convention submitted 40 recommendations to the government for consideration, a number of which would require a constitutional referendum to enact. Three have subsequently gone to a referendum the most significant of which was the marriage equality referendum of 2015.[5] A number of scholars as well as public intellectuals have dubbed this process a success along with the 2018 referendum on abortion that followed a second 2016 citizens' assembly this one composed of 100% randomly selected citizens. (Farrell, Suiter and Harris 2019; Suiter et al. 2016). The differing makeup of the 2012 and 2016 citizens' constitutional assemblies is also a good illustration of the way different institutional designs might fit with different issues and questions. The first assembly was tasked with a major overhaul of the full constitution and benefited from the expertise of law-makers. The second citizens' assembly while taking up five constitutional questions, focused much of its time on abortion, and here party partisan position might have had a negative effect on achieving a non-partisan deliberation within the assembly as well as the role of the assembly in facilitating and creating trust among citizen a large.[6]

The 2012–2014 constitutional process is a good illustration of how to think about the popular exercise of constituent power in deliberative terms. The process was drawn out over 3 years and appears to have been designed to initiate an inclusive public dialogue or national conversation. Thus, there was a sense that citizens needed to work through the issues, especially the marriage equality issue, in a collective public communicative process before any question was put to a vote. Popular opinion and will formation took place through the triangulation of three institutions mediated by an open, free, and critical public sphere: a democratically elected Parliament, a special Convention on the Constitution with a significant citizen component, and a popular referendum process. None of these institutions

---

[5] The other question on the 2015 ballot was to reduce the age of candidacy for the President from 35 to 21 and then in October 26, 2018 to repeal the law against blasphemy.

[6] The other questions addressed by the 2016 citizens' assembly were not all clearly constitutional questions and add up to a bit of a grab bag. They were, i) how to respond to an aging population, ii) how to respond to climate change, iii) the manner in which referendums are held, and iv) fixed terms for parliaments (Farrell et al. 2019)

alone represent the definitive exercise of popular sovereignty; the people exercising constituent authority can be seen in a retrospective assessment of the deliberative quality, inclusiveness, and fairness of the process as whole. The mediation of the public sphere is all important as it allowed for a national conversation over time that gave the final vote its democratic credentials.

Deliberative constitutionalism suggests an evaluative normative framework that can be applied to actual constitutional reform processes in order to gauge the quality, quantity, inclusiveness, and impact of public debate both inside and outside formal institutions.[7] Deliberative constitutionalism can also inform institutional design going forward. For example, as Scotland moves forward to have a second referendum on independence, there is a commitment to establish a citizens' assembly as well as number of other institutional innovations to engage citizens in a public debate about the future of Scotland.[8] The need to design the process to promote a national conversation and not just a national decision is an explicit topic of that very conversation (McKerrell 2019). Deliberative constitutionalism offers a theoretic framework to understand the ideal of constituent authority underpinning that need.

CONCLUSION

Deliberation has always played an important role in modern constitutionalism. Indeed, one could think of the modern written constitution as the deliberated constitution in contrast to Aristotle's descriptive view of constitutions or McIlwain's practice-based view of the ancient constitution (McIlwain 2008). Modern liberal democratic constitutions are the product of conscious design within deliberative bodies. Contemporary deliberative democracy theory unpacks and makes explicit the normative ideal of deliberation and the ways that good deliberation mirrors values central to constitutionalism. In particular, equality, autonomy, respect, and inclusiveness are all modeled within deliberation. For this reason, we are seeing the growing place of deliberation within constitutional theory.

RECOMMENDED READING

Ackerman, B. (1991). *We the People: Foundations*, Cambridge, MA: Harvard University Press.
Arato, A. (2016). *Post Sovereign Constitution Making: Learning and Legitimacy*, Oxford: Oxford University Press.
Bächtiger, A., Dryzek, J., Mansbridge, J. & Warren, M., eds. (2018). *The Oxford Handbook of Deliberative Democracy*, Oxford: Oxford University Press.
Contiades, X. & Fotiadou, A. eds. (2017). *Participatory Constitutional Change: The People as Amenders of the Constitution*, New York: Routledge.

---

[7] For a comparison of democratic constitutional reform from this perspective in Turkey, Hungary, Poland, Venezuela, Ireland, and Scotland, see Chambers 2019.
[8] www.citizensassembly.scot/

Chambers, S. (2019). Democracy and constitutional reform: Deliberative versus populist constitutionalism. *Philosophy and Social Criticism*, 45 (9–10), 1116–1131.

Habermas, J. (1996). *Between Facts and Norms. Contributions to a Discourse Theory of Law and Democracy*. Translated by William Rehg, Cambridge: MIT Press.

Habermas, J. (2001). Constitutional democracy: A paradoxical union of contradictory principles? *Political Theory*, 29 (6), 766–781.

Lafont, C. (2020). *Democracy without Shortcuts: A Participatory Conception of Deliberative Democracy*, Oxford: Oxford University Press.

Levy, R., Kong, H., Orr. G., & King, J., eds. (2018). *The Cambridge Handbook of Deliberative Constitutionalism*, Cambridge: Cambridge University Press.

Mendes, C. H. (2013). *Constitutional Courts and Deliberative Democracy*, Oxford: Oxford University Press.

Neblo, M. (2007). Family disputes: Diversity in defining and measuring deliberation. *Swiss Political Science Review*, 13 (4), 527–557.

Nino, C. S. (1997). *The Constitution of Deliberative Democracy*, New Haven: Yale University Press.

Rawls, J. (2005). *Political Liberalism. Expanded Edition*, New York: Columbia University Press.

Reuchamps, M. & Suiter, J., eds. (2016). *Constitutional Deliberative Democracy in Europe*, Colchester: ECPR Press.

Waldron, J. (1999). *Law and Disagreement*, Oxford: Oxford University Press.

Zurn, C. F. (2007). *Deliberative Democracy and the Institution of Judicial Review*, Cambridge: Cambridge University Press.

16

Opposition

Grégoire Webber[*]

I FRIEND AND ENEMY

For things said and done in the House of Commons on 2 March 1629, Sir John Eliot, John Selden, and others were denounced by Charles I as 'vipers' for their 'undutiful and seditious carriage' and sent to the Tower of London (Gregg 1984, pp. 179–186; Thrush and Ferris 2010, p. lvi). The King's Bench denied that the privilege of Parliament extended to seditious speeches and affirmed their sentence in the Tower at the King's pleasure.[1] Eliot would die there in 1632, becoming a martyr to the freedom of parliamentary speech later awarded constitutional recognition in Article 9 of the Bill of Rights 1689. That privilege of Parliament is today given a more encompassing affirmation in the freedom of expression recognised in all free and democratic societies, one purpose of which is to secure a measure of participation in political decision-making and self-government. No society can be free or democratic if its rulers look upon all who dissent as enemies of the state. And so, it is not without some irony that, in the storied affair of Eliot and others who risked their freedom and more to affirm the right of Parliament to disagree with the King, they themselves appealed to accusations of treason. The three protestation resolutions by Eliot and others regarding the Church of England and the levying of subsidies without parliamentary approval – all recited in the Commons as the Speaker was held down in his chair and the door of the chamber was locked from royal interference – each affirmed that those who would defy the resolutions' edicts would be judged 'a capital enemy to the Kingdom and Commonwealth' (Gardiner 1906, pp. 82–83).

It is an achievement in human affairs when those who disagree with each other on matters of state and government can look upon each other as political adversaries rather than as enemies in a civil war. An adversary is to be defeated in argument and vote; an enemy is to be defeated more conclusively. Such a distinction between

---

[*] For comments and discussion, I thank the Editors, Richard Bellamy and Jeff King, and several colleagues.
[1] *R v Eliot, Holles and Valentine*, [1629] 3 St Tr 293–336 (King's Bench).

political adversary and enemy is evocative of Schmitt's criterion of the political, according to which a political enemy is 'the other, the stranger' and 'something different and alien, so that in the extreme case [existential] conflicts with him are possible' (Schmitt 1996 [1932], p. 27). Without in any way endorsing or sharing Schmitt's criterion, we can appreciate how claims from rulers past and present that those who protest against measures and who dissent against governments are treasonous and subversive highlight the special challenge raised by the idea of opposition: that one may look upon the other with whom one disagrees over the direction of public affairs not as an enemy, but as one's political friend. Such a possibility is ready at hand in private affairs, where two friends may agree to disagree peacefully on all manner of topics. But in public affairs, where decisions are momentous and sometimes secured against the recalcitrant by recourse to coercive measures, the idea of opposition is more trying. Viewing one's adversary in argument and outcome as one's political friend invites the thought that a political community may combine unity with division and cooperation with dissent. It is a thought that emphasises that even though there is political disagreement, such disagreement does not dissolve a political community.

It would be a long march from Eliot's conviction for sedition to Sir John Cam Hobhouse's quip, in Commons debate two centuries later, that those who spoke in opposition to a measure proposed by His Majesty's Government could be referred to as 'His Majesty's Opposition' (Parl. Deb., vol 15, col. 135, 10 April 1826). From this rhetorical flourish in 1826, to which we owe the now settled practice in Commonwealth parliaments to designate His Majesty's Loyal Opposition, it would be only a matter of years before, in the general election of 1841, Sir Robert Peel's Tory Opposition would return more members to the Commons than his Liberal opponents and, on this basis, be invited by Queen Victoria to replace those Liberal members in government (see Webber 2017, pp. 361–366). This is credited as the first instance when a political formation in opposition to government was invited to assume the responsibilities of government. The swing of the pendulum between the government and opposition benches in elections that followed helped to establish the understanding that the Loyal Opposition is the Government-in-waiting and that, in turn – though it is not often put this way – the Government is the Loyal Opposition-in-waiting.

In the many years between the reigns of Charles I and Queen Victoria, the sovereign's management of government affairs yielded to the cabinet and the sovereign's selection of cabinet atrophied to a formality, with the real power of selection residing in the Prime Minister and the composition of the Commons (Bagehot 2001, p. 100). Such evolution may suggest that opposition flourished only with the decline of monarchical rule, such that it became possible to claim that neither those in nor those out of government were 'more or less the Queen's Friends than the other' (Potter 1966, p. 7). There is truth in this claim, but it is a truth that invites reflection on different modalities of opposition. One may make known one's opposition to specific measures and one may make known one's opposition to those who hold the office of government (Sections II–III). While opposition to those who rule may safely be pursued only in constitutional arrangements that contemplate changes in government, the freedom to make known one's opposition to measures may be secured even absent such democratic arrangements. These two different modalities of opposition – to measures and to governments – draw on a reciprocal understanding that those who oppose and those who rule are both committed to the political community and to realising the requirements of justice, freedom, and well-being (Section IV). Depending on the design of its system of government, a constitution may enable or empower opposition, with the parliamentary form of government differing in important respects from the presidential (Section V). Some constitutional arrangements and proposals award to opposition members in legislatures and elsewhere some degree of authority in exercising the office of government. There are important merits to such coalition or consensus arrangements and proposals, but they change the function of opposition, for when those who oppose begin to govern, a version of the question *quis custodiet ipsos custodes* (who guards the guardians) arises: who stands in opposition to the opposition (Section VI)?

II MODALITIES OF OPPOSITION: MEASURES

Serious questions invite serious interrogation and the future direction of a political community – what ought to be permitted, prohibited, and required by some or all – are among the most serious of questions. The burdens of judgment should humble anyone resistant to an open mind. The 'hazards involved in the correct (and conscientious) exercise of our powers of reason and judgment in the ordinary course of political life' are many, said Rawls (2005, pp. 56–57), and involve imperfect access to conflicting and complex empirical and scientific evidence, difficult and imprecise weightings of competing considerations, varying epistemic and experiential access to evaluations of moral and political value, and incommensurabilities in comparisons. In Rawls' introduction to the burdens of judgment, these hazards illuminate the reasonableness of disagreements *between* persons, but the challenges to the sound exercise of reason and judgment highlight how *each one of us* will have reason to favour open inquiry and to entertain a measure of doubt with respect to our own conclusions. We – each one of us – have reason to abide by Cromwell's prayer: 'I beseech you, in the bowels of Christ, think it possible that you may be mistaken' (Carlyle 1845, p. 448).

Given the burdens of judgment and the likely numerous reasonable alternatives from among which a selection must be made in public affairs, it will be 'unrealistic ... to suppose that all our differences are rooted solely in ignorance and perversity, or else in the rivalries for power, status, or economic gain' (Rawls 2005, p. 58). Thus, even without assuming anything about the democratic possibility that those in government may be removed from office in favour of others, there is reason to favour the freedom to make known a plurality of opinions, including those in opposition to measures proposed or selected by those in authority. Such opposition is justified by Kant on the basis that, assuming good will by the ruler but without assuming 'that the head of state can neither make mistakes nor be ignorant of anything', the freedom to make known 'error' or 'ignorance of certain possible consequences of the laws' (1991, p. 84) can help a ruler correct the injustice of measures. Without such freedom and its commitment to publicity, which Kant channelled via the freedom of the pen, the ruler will be deprived of 'all knowledge of those matters which, if he knew about them, he would himself rectify' (1991, p. 85).

For a ruler to fear such freedom on the basis that it 'might cause political unrest' would be, for Kant, 'tantamount to making [the ruler] distrust his own power and feel hatred towards his people' (Kant 1991, p. 85). Such distrust and hatred may reveal much about the rulers of times past and present that entertain no patience for opposition to measures. At least up to the time of Eliot's death, no parliamentarian could 'presume with safety' to criticise on those great matters of state that were reserved to the exercise of the royal prerogative (Hockin 1971, p. 52; Webber 2017, pp. 361–362). One could seek redress on matters local and private, but such matters were not 'in opposition to' the Crown's measures, which attended to weightier matters (Hockin 1971, pp. 55–56). On those weightier matters of state – royal succession, the church, and foreign policy – there was no freedom to make known 'error' or 'ignorance of certain possible consequences'.

Though not the basis for Kant's commitment to the freedom of the pen, one may relate the modality of opposition to measures to the idea of reciprocity. It obtains when there is a shared understanding between ruler and ruled that, though those in authority have the responsibility to decide, both ruler and ruled are committed to the requirements of justice, freedom and well-being and may make known their reasons for and against measures by appeal to such. This shared commitment and the necessary open inquiry to inform one's understanding of the requirements of a just society serve 'an important function regardless of whether the political structure of a nation is democratic or not' (Emerson 1963, p. 883). The open inquiry that allows for all things to be said for and against a measure strengthens one's understanding of the complexities of pursuing a just society. Opposition, thus understood, is directed to making a stronger appeal to justice, freedom and well-being than the appeal of those who support the measure. It is targeted and not *ad hominem*: on this modality of opposition, one makes the case against the measure, not against the ruler.

This modality of opposition may be channelled via voice and word, rather than via disobedience, resistance and rebellion, if the ruler receives the arguments of those in opposition in the spirit of Socrates' instruction that to be defeated in argument is a benefit to be welcomed, not a burden to be avoided, for one is relieved of error (Plato 1997, pp. 457c–458b). Such openness to the possible instruction of arguments formulated in opposition to measures holds no matter how popular a measure and so awards even the lone dissenter a voice to make known disagreement: *etiam si omnes, ego non* (even if all others, not I). With a shared commitment to a just society, '[e]verybody sees that wholesome political changes are prepared, matured, and promoted by public discussion' and that 'a weak minority, when it has reason on its side, is enabled, by the exercise of this right, to grow in time into a strong minority, and finally to become a majority' (Anon 1855, p. 2).

On this understanding of reciprocity, the thought that one may view one's adversary in argument and outcome as one's political friend is not difficult to grasp. With the benefit of a shared commitment to realising a just society, the focus of opposition is on measures, not persons, even if one opposes the actions of persons with authority to rule. Such opposition is justified by the burdens of judgment, by the need to correct error and ignorance and by the public instruction on the complexities of justice, freedom and well-being enabled by free and open inquiry. The alternative is to abandon a shared commitment to political friendship, such that the ruler governs not openly and honestly, ready to meet criticism with the better argument, but by suppressing 'all manifestation of opinion adverse to their acts and policy' (Anon 1855, p. 1). There is, in such circumstances, no permission for 'unfavourable criticism' and the ruled 'must simulate approbation, or at least they must suppress disapprobation' (Anon 1855, p. 1; de Jouvenel 1966). Such are the conditions of despotism.

The freedom that stands opposed to such despotism need not be all-encompassing, but it does require the freedom to oppose measures. No political community can be free without free discussion, but free discussion on measures is not the whole of political freedom. No political community can be free *and democratic* without extending free discussion to the question of who should rule.

III MODALITIES OF OPPOSITION: GOVERNMENT

In his many constitution studies, the great student of the British constitution Ivor Jennings paired the idea of opposition with democracy and with the freedom that only democratic government can provide: 'If there be no Opposition, there is no democracy' (1959, p. 16); 'The symbol of liberty is Her Majesty's Opposition' (1961, p. 209); 'opposition is an essential part of democratic government' (1969, pp. 82, 158); 'The test of a free country is to examine the status of the body that corresponds to Her Majesty's Opposition' (1963, p. 62). Freedom is here understood to encompass the freedom to oppose not only measures, but also the authors of those measures. With such freedom emerges the possibility of organised opposition – capital 'O' Opposition – which seeks to replace the rulers and assume their office. This modality of opposition – opposition to government – invites a different question for a political community. Can one be political friends with those whose opposition is *ad hominem*, directed not to this or that measure, but more systematically to oneself as the author of those measures?

One is a 'citizen of excellence', a 'good citizen', says Aristotle, if one knows both 'how to rule and how to obey' (1996, Bk III, ch 4, 1277a25). This idea invites a thicker understanding of reciprocity than that required for opposition to measures. Under the first modality of opposition, reciprocity is understood as a mutual acknowledgement that adversaries in argument are devoted to realising a just society when advocating for or against measures. Such reciprocal understanding need not extend beyond measures to the question of who should rule. When such a question is live, however, then the contest for who should rule expands the scope for open inquiry to making known reasons for and against different contenders for office.

Such free discussion brings within the range of inquiry reasons that find no home in the open inquiry about measures: reasons that are *ad hominem*, speaking to a ruler's experience, judgment, and wisdom as someone who is competent, trustworthy, honest or not. The question of political friendship takes on a new dimension when one is being accused of being an incompetent manager of public affairs, corruptible, weak or worse. In turn, the question of political friendship can also be examined from the point of view of one who opposes, by asking after one's willingness to obey measures proposed and adopted by those whose character one judges to be a disqualification from office.

The idea of standing opposition to those in office is a recent development in the history of human affairs. Before the rise of party in the British House of Commons, it was thought to be unparliamentary to prejudge the government's measures by being a 'party man'. The good parliamentarian, the 'man with no faction sworn', would exercise judgment on measures and on select ministers, evaluating their respective merits as propositions and as stewards of public affairs, but would not surrender that judgment to indiscriminate opposition to the government as a whole (Hockin 1971, p. 61; Webber 2017, p. 364). To do so would be to abandon one's responsibility for open inquiry and would weaken the bonds of reciprocity that such requires.

When one opposes a government promiscuously, debates over measures become an opportunity not only to explore the requirements of a just society, but also to mount opposition to the government. The clever oppositionists will be familiar with the burdens of judgment and the complexities of public affairs, and will readily find grounds for criticising every proposed measure, reserving judgment only on 'by what arguments, in what manner, at what time, and to what extent' the case against should be mounted (Anon 1855, p. 8). They may target their opposition 'to the person by whom, the time when, the manner in which, the extent to which, the proposition is made' (Anon 1855, p. 11). They may say that 'the measure is desirable in itself', but that 'it is poisoned by the source from which it comes' (Anon 1855, p. 11). They may, in turn, 'object to the degree: it is not enough; it is a miserable fragment, a pitiful abortion: or it is too much; it spoils a sound principle by carrying it too far' (Anon 1855, p. 11). They may focus on the category of time, condemning a measure as 'too late', saying the 'proper time is past', or condemn a measure as 'premature', having been proposed prior to due consideration, inquiry and ascertainment of facts (Anon 1855, p. 11). The clever oppositionists may, 'by a slight deflexion of the ethical nomenclature', 'invest good qualities with unfavourable associations', showing a prudent course of action to be lacking in resolve, a confident course to be arrogant, a bold act to be rash, a cautious approach to be lacking in conviction, an act of principle to be uncompromising, a compromise to be unprincipled (Anon 1855, p. 9).

Under this modality of opposition, no thesis escapes a counter-thesis, no action a reaction – everything done and not done is liable to the worst construction by those who are opposed to those in government. And yet, there are good reasons to be political friends with another whose antipathy is liable to put the worst construction on one's measures and character.

Although the modality of opposition to government is different in orientation, it is not so different in substance to the modality of opposition to measures. That latter modality appeals to the requirements of a just society in argument for or against a measure. Those same appeals animate *ad hominem* opposition in three ways. First, not all *ad hominem* opposition is, in truth, *ad hominem*: some opposition against a ruler is grounded in the measures that the ruler proposes to realise or repeal. Opposition to a ruler is premised not only on the promise that the 'outs' might one day be 'in' – that would be pure *ad hominem* opposition – but rather on the promise of a different programme of government: the one favoured by those now in opposition to the ruler. On this understanding, opposition to a ruler may be motivated by opposition to the ruler's programme of measures new and old and, so, also be sourced in the same appeals to the requirements of justice, freedom, and well-being that characterise opposition to measures.

Second, some *ad hominem* opposition is itself grounded in an appeal to the truth that a community will not thrive and its future will be in jeopardy if its rulers are incompetent, dishonest, corruptible, or weak. Good government is itself a public good, not least because the capacity of measures to realise a just society assumes that those responsible for the management of public affairs are of good will and have the talent to see those measures through.

Third, a standing opposition to those in office, no matter the merits of their measures or the soundness of their management of public affairs, 'has great and real advantages' for it serves the political community to have 'close and jealous scrutiny' of all that government does and fails to do (Anon 1855, p. 14). It is a familiar idea that the merits of a proposal are least tested when the proposal enjoys the broadest support: mistakes are more likely where there is ready agreement and no searching inquiry. On the understanding that the political community is well served by disputation, one should recognise the merits of there being dedicated persons who, even when their criticism is artificial and exaggerated, fulfil the promise of *audi alterum partem* (hear the other side) and *disputatio in utramque partem* (dispute each side). The public accountability of rulers that accompanies determined disputation by the opposition is a solid foundation for acknowledging the merits of political friendship with those who seek to remove one from office.

IV RECIPROCITY AND RESPONSIBILITY

On 5 October 1970, the British Trade Commissioner was kidnapped in Montreal by members of the Front de libération du Québec (FLQ), a militant group advocating for an independent Quebec. Five days later, the Deputy Premier of Quebec was taken by the FLQ. On 16 October, the Government of Canada invoked the War Measures Act, pronouncing a state of 'apprehended insurrection' in the province of Quebec and declaring the FLQ an 'unlawful association' (Canada 1970a, 1970b). In the days that followed, the Deputy Premier was killed, the Canadian Forces were deployed to Montreal, and nearly 500 people were detained without *habeas corpus* in a period of Canadian history known as the October Crisis (Tetley 2014).

By contrast, the creation in 1968 of the Parti Québécois, a political party devoted to securing Quebec's independence from Canada by democratic means, was welcomed by the Prime Minister of Canada on the basis that it 'made it possible to have a fight out in the open in a democratic forum, instead of having to deal with all these malcontents mouthing off about independence and setting off bombs' (Trudeau 1993, pp. 240–241). The 'fight' in contemplation did not involve civil war or force, but argument and vote. Less than a decade after joining the opposition benches in the Quebec legislature, the Parti Québécois assumed office in 1976 and, four years later, put the question of Quebec's future to a vote in a referendum.

The different strategies of the FLQ and the Parti Québécois invite reflection on how far political opposition should carry out its disputation of measures and governments. The bounds of reciprocity and political friendship between those who rule and those who oppose may vary in intensity and will inform the political strategies of those in opposition. Where the bounds are strong, an opposition will criticise and dissent and seek, in time, to replace the government, but will not seek out revolutionary changes in government (Webber 2017, pp. 378–380). That is not to say that there are no grounds for civil disobedience or rebellion or revolution – there are many, as world affairs, past and present, regularly highlight – but they signal a weakening of the bounds of reciprocity and political friendship. When the bounds are strong, a political opposition makes use of two tools of opposition: argument and time (Webber 2017, pp. 375–378).

The tool of argument has already been explored: it is by appeal to the better argument that those in opposition can be effective in opposing measures, proposing changes, and recommending new officeholders. Time, however, is a less obvious tool of opposition. Where terms in government are fixed by custom or by law, time may seem an inapposite tool in relation to the modality of opposition to government; in turn, time may seem at best ineffectual in relation to the modality of opposition to measures as it appears to achieve no more than a delay to the inevitable enactment of a contested measure.

Yet, the tool of time is inherent in the very idea of opposition for it compels government to answer argument with argument, the case against with the case for.

Defending the government's measures and character against opposition claims is a time-consuming exercise. It delays the work of government even when government has the better argument and its management of public affairs is competent and sound. The work of government is regularly delayed for longer periods of time when the better argument or sound management is lacking, for the government will be called on to answer more questions and defend itself more fully. In this way, even if opposition does no more than delay the inevitable adoption of *this* measure, the tool of time will delay a whole suite of *other* measures, effectively defeating those that are not pursued at all due to lack of time before the next election or because the government has lost political capital.

Within the bounds of reciprocity, time and argument can be formidable tools, but they are not, save exceptionally, tools to defeat measures or governments. Those in opposition to measures and governments know that the responsibility to govern falls to others, at least for now, and those others will know to hear criticism and dissent and will yield to the delay that all open inquiry and free discussion requires. Such mutual understanding helps inform the idea awarded special prominence in the customary designation of the Official Opposition in Commonwealth parliaments as a *loyal* opposition.

Many who investigate the idea of loyal opposition search out an answer to the question: to what subject matter or to which person is the opposition loyal? Such investigation rightly situates loyalty 'in the context of associational ties', but may wrongly assume that loyalty 'discourage[s] questioning and dissent' (Kleinig 2014, pp. 2, 109). Accepting that a loyal opposition is not loyal to the measures or to the government being opposed, some have sought out other subject matters of loyalty, such that one can reconcile loyalty with opposition. Rawls points to 'the basic features of the Constitution' or 'constitutional essentials' (2001, p. 49), which echoes Kant's injunction that the freedom of the pen be exercised within 'the bounds of respect and devotion towards the existing constitution' (1991, p. 85). Others suggest that those in opposition may be loyal to 'the institutions of the state' (Lowell 1920, p. 451), 'the established constitutional framework' (Punnett 1973, p. 13; Rose 1984, p. 23), 'parliamentary democracy' (Brazier 1999, p. 167), or, simply, 'the rules of the game' (Smith 2013, p. 6; Wheare 1967, p. 80). Yet others suggest that 'the Crown' is the beneficiary of opposition's loyalty (Jennings 1959, pp. 363–364; Punnett 1973, p. 399).

All of these suggestions interrogate what is *owed by* those who oppose: loyalty to some subject matter or person. Yet, as highlighted by the evolution from King Charles I's disposition to view opposition as sedition and treason to Queen Victoria's invitation to the Tory opposition to form a government, the idea of loyal opposition may signal more about the other half of the associational tie: namely, about what is *owed to* those who oppose (Webber 2017, p. 367). Of course, the dispositions of those who oppose matter: are they to carry out their opposition within bounds, with the tools of argument and time, and in the spirit of political friendship, or are they to have recourse to kidnappings and bombs? But the history of the customary designation of a Commonwealth parliamentary opposition as a Loyal Opposition suggests that it signals a course correction against the now dated readiness to label opposition to the King's measures as seditious, treasonous, and *disloyal* (Waldron 2016d, p. 122; Webber 2017, p. 367). It signals that there need be no absence of political friendship between those who disagree on the merits of measures and rulers and that 'loyalty may not only be compatible with dissent, criticism, and even opposition, but be manifested best through them' (Kleinig 2014, p. 111). An opposition is loyal, on this understanding, insofar as those in government recognise that opposition to measures and governments is not an act of treason, but an act of political friendship called for by a shared commitment to the political community. In turn, loyal opposition warrants such recognition when it acts within the bounds of this shared commitment.

V THE *ALTERA PARS* OF GOVERNMENT

Despite the importance for a free and democratic society of opposition to measures and to rulers, the place of opposition within a constitution – whether it is empowered and facilitated or not – is often an afterthought in constitutional design, rather than an organising one. It is regularly the consequence of the design of government: opposition is said to be a 'dependent concept', such that 'the character of the opposition is tied to the character of the government' (Blondel 1997, p. 463). It is the alter ego or '*altera pars* of government' (Ionescu and de Madariaga 1972, p. 10; see also Helms 2004). To explore the thought that the place of opposition changes in important ways across different systems of government, the parliamentary and presidential systems may be compared, drawing on the United Kingdom and the United States as their respective exemplars.

Though less the product of design and more the result of 'historical accidents' and 'happy experience' (Bagehot 2001, pp. 11, 13), the British parliamentary system combines 'the close union, the nearly complete fusion, of the executive and legislative powers' together with the institutional recognition, visibility, and public standing of His Majesty's Loyal Opposition. The parliamentary system, combined with an electoral system that favours single-party governments, favours strong government and a strong opposition.

By convention and law in the United Kingdom, the political formation designated as the Official Opposition is 'the party in opposition to Her Majesty's Government having the greatest numerical strength in the House of Commons' (Ministerial and Other Salaries Act 1975, s. 2). The Leader of the Opposition is the leader of that party and the Leader and party will receive financial assistance from the public purse to carry out their critical functions. The Leader receives a salary on a par with ministers of the Crown and the Opposition as a whole will receive monies for research and staff and for the development of a political programme to compete for office in the next election (Kelly 2020; Ministerial and Other Salaries Act 1975, s. 2; Political Parties, Elections and Referendums Act 2000, s. 12).

It is to the Loyal Opposition and other opposition parties that now falls the greater part of what was, historically, the responsibility of the House of Commons as a whole to hold to account a government external to the chamber (Amery 1964, p. 31; Wheare 1967, p. 79). The balance of the constitution between the three estates of the realm – monarchy, aristocracy, and commons – was replaced in time with a balance internal to the House of Commons between Government and Opposition. By custom of the House, the Speaker will alternate between government and opposition members in debates, such that '[t]he nation is forced to hear two sides – all the sides, perhaps, of that which most concerns it' (Bagehot 2001, p. 17). Key tools of political opposition are at the ready in Commons debate: the better argument can be made in the study of government measures and administration and, even if subject to the Government's greater control over the parliamentary calendar, the Opposition can delay the passage of a great many measures and upset the Government's timetable.

That said, the Opposition's strategy is not to make use of the tools of opposition with a view only 'to oppose everything and propose nothing', as Sir George Tierney is said to have recommended (Jennings 1969, p. 167). Rather, the Opposition's pursuit of office tempers any criticism that tends towards excess, for the Opposition will lose credibility as a contender for office if it is unreasonable in its disputations or obstructive in the management of Parliament. By attempting to relate public opinion outside Parliament to political criticism inside, the Opposition seeks to make the better claim to represent the electorate. Through debate between Government and Opposition in the chamber, 'the appeal to the people is not an occasional ceremony, but a process which goes on daily and hourly in the parliamentary session' (Jennings 1961, p. 88).

The Leader of the Opposition makes claim to be the next Prime Minister and designates certain members of the opposition caucus as members of a shadow cabinet with the critical responsibilities of shadow ministers (Punnett 1973, p. 36; Webber 2017, p. 380). In presenting to the public an alternative government, the Opposition vies for office not only at every election, but at every debate in the Commons. At every moment, the public has before it an alternative political formation ready to assume the responsibilities of office at the next constitutional opportunity and, so, '[t]he nation knows it can be governed by different people with different policies: *there they are*, designated as such, present and recognized within the legislative institutions' (Waldron 2016d, p. 103). So central is this aspect of the Opposition in the parliamentary tradition that, when Prime Minister Churchill formed a wartime coalition cabinet in 1940, the Speaker ruled that there was no official Opposition to be recognised by the House because it could not be said there was 'a party in Opposition to the Government from which an alternative Government could be formed' (Hansard, HC, vol. 361 col. 27, 21 May 1940).

In contrast to the 'hyphen which joins', the 'buckle which fastens' the executive to the legislative branch in a parliamentary system, the US President and members of his cabinet are not drawn from Congress and are constitutionally disqualified from being members of two branches at once (U.S. Const. art I, § 6, cl 2; art II, § 2, cl 1). The president, unlike the prime minister, does not require continued congressional support to remain in office. Unlike the balance between Government and Opposition in a parliamentary system, the checks and balances in a presidential system are between, rather than within, institutions (see Bellamy 2007, pp. 195–207). The constitutional relationship between the president and Congress was framed on the conviction that '[a]mbition must be made to counteract ambition', in part by 'divid[ing] and arrang[ing] the several offices in such a manner as that each may be a check on the other' (Hamilton, Madison & Jay 2008 [1787/88], no. 51). The role of opposition here was to be assumed by each institution: each institution, when it governed, would face opposition from the others just as, when any of these other institutions governed, they would face opposition from the others, so that all exercises of all power would be checked and made accountable.

Whereas the rise of party helped to institutionalise the role of the opposition in a parliamentary system, the rise of party challenged the framework envisaged by the framers of the US Constitution. With the allegiance of members of Congress now shared between their constitutional position and their political formation, the incentives of congressional members to hold the president to account will 'vary significantly, and may all but disappear, depending on whether the House, Senate, and presidency are divided or unified by political party' (Levinson and Pildes 2006, p. 2315). The result is that the separation of powers model under the US Constitution is at least two models. There is a 'party-divided' separation of powers and a 'party-unified' separation of powers, depending on which party holds the presidency and whether that same party holds a majority in Congress. Where the two Houses of Congress are themselves divided, with one party holding a majority in one chamber and the other in the other chamber, Congress is neither exclusively divided against nor united with the president along party lines.

Within the House of Representatives, the Speaker is selected from the party with the majority in the chamber, as is the designated majority leader, who ranks behind the Speaker within the party leadership. Unlike the Speaker in the parliamentary tradition, who is convention-bound to abandon partisan favour and to preside over the chamber as a neutral arbiter, the Speaker in the House of Representatives leads the majority party and acts accordingly. In turn, there is a designated minority leader from the party with the minority of seats in the chamber. The Senate is also organised into majority and minority offices on the basis of party composition in that chamber, with the exception of the role of Speaker, which the Constitution awards to the Vice President and, in her absence, a President Pro Tempore. Although the US Constitution has always contemplated that each House shall choose its 'officers' (art I, § 2, cl 5 and § 3, cl 5), the practice of awarding offices according to party standing arose nearly a century later in the House of Representatives and two decades after that in the Senate (Ripley 1967). The party leadership receives a salary without distinction between their majority and minority status, with the exception of the Speaker of the House of Representatives, whose salary is near that of the Vice President (Brudnick 2018).

In the 'party-united' separation of powers, the Speaker and majority leaders will be of the same political formation as the President. In some ways, this resembles the parliamentary system of government when the political formation in government holds a majority in the Commons. However, unlike a parliamentary system, where the leader of the majority in the Commons is also the prime minister, the presidential system assigns three officeholders to the parliamentary one: the Speaker and majority leader in the House of Representatives and the President. (There is also the majority leader in the Senate who, unlike the Leader of the House of Lords, is not convention bound to moderate the upper chamber's legislative role.) Also unlike a parliamentary system, where the Leader of the Opposition has standing, by custom and by the swing of the pendulum, as the prime minister-in-waiting, neither the minority leader in the House of Representatives nor the minority leader in the Senate is presumed by their political formation or the greater public to be the president-in-waiting.

In the 'party-divided' separation of powers, the party in opposition to the president will exercise far more institutional authority than the official opposition in a parliamentary system. The party in opposition to the president will hold the offices of speaker in the House of Representatives and majority leader in both chambers and so may do more than appeal to the tools of argument and time; by virtue of their congressional offices, these three actors may, by relying on the votes of their political caucus, defeat measures favoured by the President[2] and introduce and enact their own measures, subject to the President's veto, which is itself subject to congressional override (US Constitution, art I, § 7). Yet, in defeating measures favoured by the president and in enacting their own measures, the speaker, majority leaders, and their political caucus are not exercising the function of an opposition: they are exercising the authority of Congress and, in so doing, are governing. In this way, their authority is greater than that of the Leader of the Opposition in a parliamentary system who – even when the Prime Minister's political formation does not hold a majority in the Commons – would be very much surprised if the Government were to lose a vote on a measure. The difference turns on the institutional role of the Official Opposition in a parliamentary system: it is a critical role, unlike the institutional role of the majority leadership in Congress, which is to lead the House in exercising its legislative responsibilities (Ekins 2012, pp. 169–173; Ekins this volume).

---

[2] The expression 'measures favoured by the President' communicates the idea that, though the President cannot introduce legislation in Congress, the President's party colleagues in the House and Senate may do so on the President's behalf.

In another way, however, the standing of the majority leadership in the 'party-divided' separation of powers is lesser than that of the Leader of the Opposition, for no member of the majority leadership in Congress can claim to be the president-in-waiting by virtue of that office. Neither the law nor the custom of the US Constitution recognises an Official Opposition that is office-seeking. Of course, the opposition in Congress is office-seeking in the sense that members of the House of Representatives and senators seek re-election every two or six years. But the majority leadership in a 'party-divided' separation of powers and the minority leadership in a 'party-united' separation of powers are not the presumptive government-in-waiting. This changes the dynamics of opposition, for even excessive criticism and obstruction does not easily translate into a loss of credibility for that party formation to contend for the office of president. The coordinator of opposition stratagems in Congress is not, by virtue of that role, the party's candidate for president at the next election.

Though there is 'plenty of opposition' to the US Government and 'plenty of people leading and anxious to lead this opposition', 'there is no one official Leader of the Opposition' (Wheare 1967, p. 81; Polsby 1997). Except for the great contest for the office of president every four years, the US president, unlike a prime minister, does not compete on a day-to-day basis with another of comparable rank. The loser in that great contest disappears from view after the electors have cast their ballots for president (U.S. Const. art XII). (It was not always so. Prior to the Twelfth Amendment, the US Constitution provided that the office of Vice President would be awarded to the person who secured the second highest number of electors for the presidency (U.S. Const. art II, § 1).) A government that loses a vote of confidence in the Commons may, on that same day or after an election, see the Leader of the Opposition become the prime minister, but the impeachment of a President will not return to that office anyone other than the Vice President (US Constitution, art II, § 1, cl 6; Amendment XXV).

VI OPPOSITION IN GOVERNMENT?

Comparisons between the place awarded to opposition within parliamentary and presidential systems of government are not all-things-considered evaluations of the merits of those two systems. But such comparisons do highlight how constitutional design may empower and facilitate opposition to measures and to governments. For this reason, it is welcome to note that some constitutional arrangements and some proposals for new arrangements seek expressly to empower the opposition.

One such proposal recommends awarding some of the 'winner's powers' – the powers to govern, including 'the power to legislate and to coerce' and 'to command and control' – to the 'losers', being those in opposition (Fontana 2009, p. 556). The opposition, on this proposal, would do more than 'prevent the exercise of winners' powers' (Fontana 2009, p. 556); they would also be awarded 'real decision authority' to legislate, to be appointed to an executive office, or to appoint judges (Fontana 2009, pp. 565 n. 38, 571–581).

The overall merits of proposals to substitute the 'exclusive, competitive, and adversarial' majoritarian model of government with a measure of consensual government distinguished by 'inclusiveness, bargaining, and compromise' is not our present focus (Lijphart 2012). Our focus is instead to question whether awarding 'winner's powers' to 'losers' is compatible with the latter's opposition to measures and rulers. There is reason here for caution. The idea of 'opposition in government' is better captured by abandoning the idea of 'opposition', for the responsibilities of government and opposition are precisely opposite. Those in opposition cease to be in opposition when they begin to exercise the responsibilities of government. If one governs, then one does not oppose those who govern; in turn, if one opposes measures or governments, then one is not proposing the measures or in government.

The high drama in the Westminster Parliament in September 2019 illustrates the challenges of conceiving of the opposition *as an opposition* when it exercises the responsibilities of government. The policy of Her Majesty's Government was for the United Kingdom to leave the European Union on 31 October 2019 and not to apply for any extension beyond this date. Her Majesty's Loyal Opposition and other opposition parties in the Commons did not support the Government's policy. The Government's policy was also opposed by a number of government backbenchers who, together with official and other opposition parties, secured a majority of votes to adopt the European Union (Withdrawal) (No. 2) Act in a single sitting on 4 September. After passing the Lords, the Act received royal assent on 9 September and required the Prime Minister to ask the European Union for an extension and set out the form of letter that the Prime Minister was to send to the European Council.

This episode draws attention to how, when the opposition to the government begins to govern, it is no longer fulfilling the function of an opposition. Form and function may come apart. Throughout the parliamentary consideration of the European Union (Withdrawal) (No. 2) Act, the Government found itself playing the role of opposition, criticising and disputing the measure favoured by the Loyal Opposition and its majority in the Commons. Such majority was secured by a coalition of different parties in the Commons, including members of the Government's caucus. This example of coalition, consensus, or consociational governing may be celebrated as an example of cross-party compromise and collaboration over the more competitive and adversarial to-and-fro-ing between Government and Opposition. Yet, it remains that, by divorcing form and function, the parliamentary episode in September 2019 upset the constitutional understandings of government accountability and responsibility.

Within the bounds of reciprocity, a political opposition generally recognises its station as otherwise than in government. Its station is all-important for a free and democratic society, for it compels accountability. In this respect, opposition can be said to contribute to government, for it contributes to good government. But such contribution is valuable precisely because of its critical function, a function that is otherwise than the function of governing itself. This critical function is secured in part by awarding those in opposition with authority and special powers in and over committees of the legislature. The critical function of those in opposition is also promoted by 'the authority to compel information' from government and to designate 'opposition days' in the parliamentary calendar (Fontana 2009, p. 574). The power of committees to compel openness in government measures and administration, the power to compel disclosure of information, and the power to debate matters of the opposition's choosing are all of constitutional significance, but their significance is precisely that of empowering the opposition to hold to account those who exercise the winners' powers. These opposition powers are not *winners' powers* awarded to those who are not the winners. They are powers that facilitate and empower the opposition to act as an opposition rather than as a government.

CONCLUSION

Political friend and enemy. King Charles and Queen Victoria. Measures and governments. Reciprocity and responsibility. Time and argument. Constitutional design and dependency. Prime Minister and Opposition Leader. Party-divided and party-unified. Speaker and President. Majority leader and minority leader. Winners and losers. These are but some of the pairings of ideas explored in this chapter. As pairings, all play on the idea of opposition, which is to make the case against the case for, to hear the other side, to dispute the way forward.

In political affairs, opposition to measures and to governments can sometimes be, like politics itself, an 'unpleasing spectacle': '[t]he obscurity, the muddle, the excess, the counterfeit piety, the moralism and the immorality, the corruption, the intrigue, the negligence, the meddlesomeness, the vanity, the self-deception, and finally the futility ... offend most of our rational and all of our artistic susceptibilities' (Oakeshott 1996, p. 19). But, in 'modifying the reign of arbitrary violence in human affairs', the freedom to be in opposition to measures and governments is an achievement in the course of human history and a major contribution to the pursuit of good government in human communities. In the face of too much constitutional and democratic backsliding today, wherein governments warn of the enemy within and label criticism and dissent subversive and seditious, there is every reason to be reminded that political friendship not only tolerates, but facilitates, encourages, finances, and even institutionalises opposition to measures and to governments.

RECOMMENDED READING

Applbaum, A. I. (1999). *Ethics for Adversaries*, Princeton: Princeton University Press.
Dahl, R. A., ed. (1966). *Political Opposition in Western Democracies*, New Haven: Yale University Press.
Fontana, D. (2009). Government in Opposition. *Yale Law Journal*, 119 (3), 548–623.

Jennings, I. W. (1969). *Parliament*. 2nd edn, Cambridge: Cambridge University Press.
Johnson, N. (1997). Opposition in the British Political System. *Government and Opposition*, 32 (4), 487–510.
King, A. (1976). Modes of Executive-Legislative Relations: Great Britain, France, and West Germany. *Legislative Studies Quarterly*, 1 (1), 11–36.
Kleinig, J. (2014). *On Loyalty and Loyalties: The Contours of a Problematic Virtue*, Oxford: Oxford University Press.
Laski, H. (1944). The Parliamentary and Presidential Systems. *Public Administration Review*, 4 (4), 347–359.
Levinson, D. J. & Pildes, R. H. (2006). Separation of Parties, Not Powers. *Harvard Law Review*, 119 (8), 2311–2386.
Punnett, R. M. (1973). *Front-Bench Opposition: The Role of the Leader of the Opposition, the Shadow Cabinet and Shadow Government in British Politics*. London: Heinemann.
UK Parliament, (1940). House of Commons, Hansard.
UK Parliament, (1975). Ministerial and Other Salaries Act.
UK Parliament, (2000). Political Parties, Elections and Referendums Act.
Waldron, J. (2016). *Political Political Theory*, Cambridge, MA: Harvard University Press.
Webber, G. (2016). Loyal Opposition and the Political Constitution. *Oxford Journal of Legal Studies*, 37 (2), 357–382.

17

The Separation of Powers

Jacob T. Levy

What a constitutional monarchy has in common with a constitutional democracy, and what sets them apart from *other* monarchies or democracies, is not a bill of rights or even a written constitutional charter; the UK, Canada, and New Zealand at various times were constitutional states without one or both of these. If charters are not necessary, they're also famously not sufficient: neither a text that announces the overriding principle that the state is subject to direction by an unreviewable party or religious body, nor a text that is a mere sham, will make a state constitutional.

Instead, it seems to me that we begin to identify historical monarchies as constitutional from the time when they adopted a separation of powers; and we worry that a democracy is abandoning constitutionalism today when the separation of powers is eroded or eliminated (see Ginsburg and Huq 2018). Both a legislature that at least sometimes acts as something other than the instrument of the head of executive government and an independent judiciary seem to be necessary features of constitutional government. This is, after all, what Montesquieu (1989[1748]) maintained when first articulating the idea of the separation of powers as we understand it; he identified the presence or absence of the separation of powers as a, and perhaps *the*, key difference between moderate governments and lawless despotism. In this chapter I will elaborate on what I take to be Montesquieu's position and the good reasons for it: that the separation of powers distinguishes constitutional from other governments by institutionalizing the rule of law in a particular way. It joins the basic legalistic impulse of distinguishing prior rule-making from subsequent rule-application and rule-enforcement to inherited practices shaped by the mixed government tradition of giving powerful social and political interests distinct political institutions. The combined result is an articulated multi-stage process of lawmaking, adjudication, and enforcement that runs through distinct institutions staffed by separate personnel, with a particular eye on protecting a secure liberty against the armed branch of the state that we have come to identify as the executive. These norms and practices have a great deal to recommend them, but thinking through their logic and history in this way will also highlight some areas of fragility and incompleteness that I will discuss at the end of the chapter.

The idea that the separation of powers is the *sine qua non* of constitutional government represents a disagreement with an influential tradition of thought that treats the core of constitutionalism as substantive countermajoritarian protection of rights. Walter Murphy, for example, held that "constitutionalism is a normative political creed that endorses a special kind of political order, one whose principal tenet is as follows: although government is necessary to a life that is truly human, every exercise of governmental power should be subject to important *substantive* limitations and obligations" (2007, p. 6; compare 1988, p. 6).

In one sense this is much too restrictive, demanding that constitutionalism as a concept be limited to those authority structures that openly fly the flag of moral realism. Here I follow Waldron (1999a) in thinking that, in the absence of implausibly strong shared epistemic access to moral truth, moral realism is a red herring, and that our political condition is one of perpetual at-least-partial disagreement with our fellow subjects about serious normative questions (see also Levy 2016). On the other hand, I think it is in a curious way not restrictive enough, allowing as it does for those "substantive limits" to exist mainly or entirely *outside* the governing institutional structure. The believing Christian might endorse the claim about substantive limits and advise the absolute king to heed those limits on peril of his immortal soul, but that is unreasonably far afield from what "constitutionalism" refers to.

But the conclusion that constitutionalism is crucially institutional, not moral, and that the core constitutional institution is a separation of powers, does not get us very far by itself. Scholars who agree that the separation of powers is central to constitutionalism do not agree on quite what it *means*. McIlwain (1940) conceived the essence of modern constitutionalism to be the subjection of governmental action to restriction by law, which depends on an independent judiciary standing apart from the ordinary government. Gordon, by contrast, thinks of that as almost paradoxical, and considers checks and balances, countervailing power, to be constitutionalism's core idea. McIlwain in turn disdained "checks and balances." This opposition is symptomatic of the fact noted by Waldron (2016f) that the separation of powers is an especially undertheorized concept in the tradition of constitutional theory.

Countervailance by itself isn't particularly normatively interesting. Despite the fantasies of unitary will found in early modern monarchical absolutism or the imagined construct of Oriental despotism, competing power centers are probably inevitable in any organization large enough to manage the government of a state. North, Wallis, and Weingast (2009) help us to think about premodern states as always *coalitions* of rent-seeking elites, unified in their effort to extract resources from those they rule, but internally characterized by multiple power centers and shifting alliances. Even totalitarian states saw meaningful contestation between the armed services, the secret police, and the party apparatus, among others. We might even describe them as having checked and balanced; the ambition of the KGB sometimes counteracted the ambition of the Red Army. But this basic organizational fact is, at most, the raw material out of which a constitutionalist understanding of the separation of powers could be built. One particular constellation of competing power centers did evolve into the institutional arrangements that we now think of as legislative and executive, but Gordon goes seriously wrong by therefore collapsing constitutionalism into countervailance.

The rule of law and the distinction between law and governance, by contrast, *are* normatively important, and they are coherent aspirations outside the particular institutional setting of a separation of powers; but they are fragile. Consider Fuller's (1969) parable of King Rex, who failed to make law eight different ways, through the absence of generalized rules, of prospective rules, of promulgated rules, of rules that were possible to follow, and so on. Fuller never says that the aspiration to be a king who is simultaneously a legislator and a judge of cases *itself* will necessarily lead to a failure to make law. The separation of powers is absent from his analysis altogether; the parable is built on Rex's intellectual mistakes about law, not any institutional incapacity. But the eighth of his failures does arise from his combination of roles: the rules he promulgates and the cases he decides fail to correspond to each other. Rex-as-judge doesn't feel accountable to Rex-as-legislator, and doesn't notice the inconsistency. Fuller's interest is in the formal fact that the rules aren't effective in guiding the outcome of cases, and so Rex's subjects can't use them as a basis for plans. But the example nicely encourages the idea that the rule of law is bolstered by putting rule-making and case-decision not just into sequential chronological moments but also into the hands of distinct actors. And this is even before taking account of Rex-as-*king*, an executive ruler with political interests and command of the armed force of the state, an actor with political enemies and not just juridical critics. (We will return to the importance of that kind of executive power.)

McIlwain's and Gordon's accounts are thus symmetrically incomplete, both capturing a necessary part of the story. The separation of powers is where those two ideas meet and merge. It is, again, the rule of law institutionalized as a separation of stages in the process of rule-making and rule-enforcement, with each stage housed in a distinct institution with distinct personnel. It is, as we will see below, an attempt to bring the legalistic principle that no one should be judge in their own case into political life. Waldron (2016f, p. 46) has helpfully described this as an:

> articulated, as opposed to undifferentiated, [mode] of governance. The idea is that instead of just an undifferentiated political decision *to do something about person* X, there is an insistence that anything we do to X or about X must be preceded by an exercise of legislative power that lays down a general rule applying to everyone and not just X, a judicial proceeding that makes a determination that X's conduct in particular falls within the ambit of that rule and so on.

While I have some disagreements of detail with Waldron, and I will push this idea in directions with which he would probably disagree, this concept of articulated governance is right and I will follow him in using it. And in thinking about the purpose and justification of the separation of powers, it will help to keep in mind that *to do something about person* X includes (though of course is not exhausted by) imprisoning, punishing, exiling, or executing them, and that the governing officials in control of the armed force of the state are traditionally all too eager to do those *somethings* to political rivals, dissidents, those who fall into their personal disfavor, useful scapegoats, and so on. The insistence on prior rulemaking and adjudication by actors not under the direct control of those with the power to imprison or execute thus not only protects the liberty of ordinary individual persons, but also transforms politics.

This means the separation of powers not only bridges both McIlwain's rule of law with Gordon's countervailance, it also bridges many of the familiar divisions in the broader literature about constitutionalism: that between political and legal constitutionalism, as well as that between the *constitution*, that is creation and positing, of political power, and a power-constraining ideology of *constitutionalism*.

It also, I think, bridges many versions of the division between liberalism and republicanism (a distinction I think is overdrawn in general). The liberty that the separation of powers protects is both non-interference – I may not be thrown into a cage or killed – and non-domination: I will not live in submissive fear of such punishment, and will therefore be able to take a more active part in politics. In constraining a politics of domineering, politicized violence, in insisting on the value of impartial and impersonal rulemaking and adjudication, the separation of powers makes possible a positive vision of politics with widespread participation in practices of argument and reasoning. That is not to deny that there are different emphases between avowedly liberal and republican accounts of the separation of powers, or that there are liberal and republican accounts that veer away from this shared core conception: liberal arguments that overemphasize mere countervailance and veto points, or democratic-republican accounts that prioritize an executive embodying a unified democratic will (Rosanvallon 2011a, 2018; contrast Abizadeh 2021a). But this core idea of the separation of powers finds complementary, not contradictory, justifications in liberal and republican vocabularies.

Barber (2018) criticizes liberty-centered accounts of the separation of powers in favor of an account of state efficiency that emphasizes differing institutional competences: it is useful for the legislative power to be vested in a large, discussion-based assembly, for example. Barber contrasts this with a simple model of the separation of powers as enhancing liberty based on friction, a version of the brute-force checks and balances. He is right to say that mere institutional conflict need not enhance liberty; but mere institutional *difference*, with various specializations, is not a separation of powers. A legislature is organized differently from a court and both are different from a chief executive. A central bank is also organized differently from an army; the different functions demand different forms. An account of liberty, the rule of law differentiation of rulemaking and rule-enforcement, and constraint on the executive – none of which is a blunt checks-and-balances doctrine – motivates the particular attention to legislation, judging, and enforcement that we single out under the name of the separation of powers.

The separation of powers so understood is a general feature of constitutional systems, including all constitutional democracies. That is to say, it is not unique to presidential systems in which the head of executive government is elected independently from the legislature. It also exists in parliamentary systems with responsible ministerial government. Its meaning is of course slightly complicated when members of the ministerial cabinet are also members of parliament. But its meaning is also slightly complicated when, say, a president exercises the legislative power of vetoing legislation, or when a house of a bicameral legislature sits as a court in impeachment. That is to say, as Publius argued, we should not exaggerate the sharpness of the separations of personnel or functions required to give the separation of powers effect.

Like, I think, many other basic concepts of modern constitutionalism, the idea of the separation of powers emerged as an explanation and rationalization of existing practices, then became a norm that shaped future decisions about institutional design. In this chapter, I will also suggest that it is a concept in need of updating. But I do think it is theoretically tractable and historically comprehensible as it is, and that its core meaning is recognizably crucial for constitutionalism.

I MEDIEVAL ORIGINS

The Rule of Law

Genealogically, we should distinguish the two ancestral strains of the separation of powers: the one McIlwain saw from the one Gordon saw.

The rule of law as a procedural matter and the idea of fundamental law that shapes and defines the business of government are both ancient ideas, but the ancient understandings of them were not tied up with an institutionalized and independent judiciary. When Aristotle distinguishes between regimes that rule according to law and those that do not, there is no implication that the latter are *illegal*, or that there could be an actor or institution within the regime with the authority to declare them so. The identification of such fundamental lawfulness with a particular institution was made possible through the medieval development of legal codes and systems not primarily legislated by political authorities, and adjudicated by a class of professional jurists (Berman 1983; Brundage 2008). This took a number of forms: canon law that was promulgated by the Church; the recovered Roman civil law that did not owe its authority to any then-extant ruler, and that was developed more in the universities that trained lawyers to practice across Catholic Europe than it was by rulers; and, of course, the English common law, and systems of courts of law and of equity. All of these allowed for at least the *possibility* of a conflict between law and politics, one in which some actor held authority to speak on law's behalf. Although early modern critics of absolutism exaggerated the relevant medieval history, discerning a clearer legal check on royal or parliamentary power than had ever stably existed, they at least built their myths out of intellectual and institutional materials medieval jurisprudence really had left behind. By Hobbes' time, it was clearly possible to see challenges to sovereign legal capacity from the various *other* claimants to jurisprudential authority, and he aimed to rebut them all.

The seventeenth-century abolition of the Star Chamber and the formalization of the principle that *habeas corpus* could be asserted even against detention by order of the king were crucial developments in turning ancient constitutionalist legend into real English law. The holder of supreme political power was *not* immune to the demands of law; and criminal punishment demanded legal process, not mere political enmity. This is, I think, the core of the idea of the rule of law that becomes in turn central to both liberalism and constitutionalism in later modernity, in a way that we perhaps lose track when our attention is wholly consumed by the question of the judicial review *of legislation*. And it is one part of the core of the separation of powers: a distinction between political authority and the power to legally punish, made institutionally real by putting them into different hands.

Consider Coke's opinion in *Doctor Bonham's Case* (*Bonham v College of Physicians*, 1610), the object of some fascination in the twentieth century (and in particular in the United States) because of its status as a possible origin for the judicial review of legislation: "in many cases, the common law will control Acts of Parliament, and sometimes adjudge them to be utterly void: for when an act of parliament is against common right and reason, or repugnant, or impossible to be performed, the common law will controul it, and adjudge such act to be void." Less attention has been paid to the particular violation of common right at stake. Immediately before that sentence, Coke identified it: "The Censors cannot be Judges, Ministers, and parties; Judges, to give sentence or judgment; Ministers to make summons; and Parties, to have the moiety of the forfeiture, *quia aliquis non debet esse Judex in propria causa*" – that is, no one may be judge in their own case. The College of Physicians that found Bonham guilty of violating its chartered monopoly on the practice of medicine within seven miles of London was not only the beneficiary of the monopoly but also the beneficiary of the fines it assessed on pain of an imprisonment it carried out. The separation of judge and minister is not just the same principle as the separation of judge and party to the case, though as we will see Montesquieu also noted the connection between them. Coke treats them both, however, as fundamental principles of the rule of law, of common right – and the demand to separate the roles is, almost explicitly, an early separation of powers doctrine.

Governing Powers

The idea of checks and balances among opposed powers is more straightforwardly ancient. The Classical Greek understanding of a mixed constitution or *politea* might not always have imagined institutional separation among the one, the few, and the many; that era's discussions of the idea that the best constitution might be found by blending the three standard forms were typically more suggestive than detailed. But the Hellenistic and Roman understanding of the same idea, articulated most memorably by Polybius, certainly did: The Assembly, the Senate, and the Consuls were institutionally distinct.

Mixture is not separation, and the impulse behind the mixed constitution was typically to encourage the inclusion and participation of different classes, allowing to each a share in power and increasing perceived legitimacy. But distinct institutions that could naysay each other provided the typical shape. The way the *populus* and the Senate or, later, the Commons and the Lords could both feel securely included was to prevent either from being able to govern without the other. The possibility of vetoes compelled cooperation. The mixed constitution so routinely celebrated in medieval and modern European thought was thus not a simple *blending* of classes or forms of government; it was a multiplication of institutions. The systems of estates across medieval Europe developed out of practical considerations about who held military and fiscal power, not out of conscious applications of Roman republicanism, but the institutional similarity arose out of similar needs. Medieval government by estates and the ancient idea of mixed constitutionalism had obvious affinities, and early modern anti-absolutists drew freely on both.

Government by estates did not necessarily involve any clear separation of governing functions; its clearest contemporary descendant is the bicameral legislature, whether the upper house is called by the Roman name of Senate or the Gothic name of "House of Lords." The Westminster system, for example, vests ultimate authority in "the Queen (or King) in Parliament." The one, the few, and the many each have a distinct (though not equal) say in the exercise of a *shared* sovereign legislative authority, and countervailance takes the form of demanding the consent or assent of each actor to use that shared authority.

On the other hand, the tradition of government by estates *did* help shape the eventual distinction between legislative and executive power: the latter calling for the decisiveness, unity of will, and speed of action one man might exercise in particular cases, the former better suited for deliberation and debate about general rules. Here again the medieval and early modern practice echoed the Roman, with kings taking the place of consuls. This distinction between legislative and executive authority was primary for the first of the canonical articulations of the idea of the separation of powers in modern political thought, John Locke's.

II EARLY MODERN TRANSFORMATIONS

Locke

Out of the raw materials of the long seventeenth-century conflict between the Parliament and the Crown, Locke (1988 [1689]) built a theory specifying the duties and mutual accountability of both in a way that would not have been quite recognized by the traditional partisans of either. Locke's account of the "subordination" of powers infused the central conflict of government by estates with juridical normative content, and helped develop a norm of separation that later generations would take as valuable in its own right even when it did *not* map onto preexisting patterns of power.

Locke distinguished among a supreme legislative, and subordinate executive and *federative* powers – the last referring to control over military and foreign affairs, almost invariably vested in the same office as the executive power, but distinguished from it by a more attenuated relationship to law and legislation. In retrospect, this is an interesting path not taken. Executive power and federative power are not parts of an articulated process with different steps happening in different institutions staffed by different personnel; they are different kinds of activity engaged in by the same institution staffed by the same personnel. We recognize the distinction mainly in the negative today: the constitutional constraints on domestic police that don't apply to the armed forces or border police, or martial "law" as the substitution of the federative power for domestic constitutional government. But it's still all too common for agencies to justify expansions of *executive* power with reference to the needs of *federative* power, and it might do us good to return to Locke's sharp distinction between the two.[1]

To contemporary eyes, of course, the more striking thing about Locke's account is the absence of the judicial power. He kept his intellectual distance from the ancient constitutionalism associated with Coke, common lawyers, and the Magna Carta, uncharacteristically so for his political circles. His original compact is presented as an alternative to the ancient constitution, not, as was common among other Whigs, a paraphrase of it. The downplaying of the judiciary compared with our expectations might simply be a side effect of his skepticism of the conservatism of the common law judiciary. But I think there is a more theoretically substantial reason. In his account, the whole of civil government has juridical purposes; the legislature is always in the business of specifying rights, and the executive inherits the dispute-resolution function that we all give up when we renounce being judge in our own cases. If all of civil government is fundamentally judicial, identifying judicial authority with the particular institution of the courts would have been too narrow.

In any case, the core of his theory was neither the inclusion of the federative power nor the omission of the judiciary; it was the careful and complicated analysis

---

[1] On the other hand, Locke's distinction also carries the risk of treating foreign and defense policy as *entirely* extralegal and immune to legislative and judicial oversight. And here I don't only mean that federative power must be exercised in accordance with *international* law. As Zeisberg (2013) has shown in her superb study of the separation of powers in practice, there is good reason to want legislative participation in the setting of the broad outlines of foreign and defense policy, as well as legislative oversight of the ways that those policies are implemented. The too-sharp distinction between intrinsically lawless federative power and lawful domestic executive power can be seen not only in the existence of extraterritorial lawless prisons such as Guantanamo Bay but also in the abusive conduct of immigration and border controls around the world – and the tendency of those abuses to creep inward from the borders, in the expanding hunt for those subject to deportation.

of relations between the holders of legislative and executive power. The *Second Treatise* takes a clear side in the constitutional disputes that had marked English politics for decades: both taxation and legislation belong straightforwardly to Parliament, and the legislative authority it wields is the primary authority of government. In a theory of government resting as Locke's does on lawfulness and the rights of the people, the legislative clarification and specification of rights is fundamental – more fundamental than one might have imagined from the scarcity of actual statutory legislation in the era. Most of Locke's examples of tyranny that justify resistance are examples of the executive impinging on the legislature, not directly on the rights of private citizens; infringing on the legislature *just is* a violation of the rights of the people at large. And yet the real need for executive prerogative power to act outside the law calls that practical effect of legislative supremacy into doubt. Locke not only recognizes the need for laws to be executed, he also recognizes the need for decisive and rapid extralegal action that promotes the public good. And indeed he recognizes legitimate executive authority over the legislature itself on such questions as the times of its meeting, while recognizing that the authority might be abused.

The omission of the judiciary might make a kind of intuitive sense to us still. At a certain level of abstraction, it seems that the crucial separation is that between the rule and its application to a particular case, that is, between the work of the legislature on one hand and, on the other, that of judging and executing, understood jointly. In Locke's state of nature, where legislation as such is absent since the law of nature governs directly, the obstacle to peace is that each man is *judge and executioner* of that law, both. In entering civil society, each man surrenders that combined power. It's an embarrassment for a certain kind of ordinary language treatment of the separation of powers that it seems so much as if *courts* "execute" the laws by applying them to particular cases. If most important distinction is between rule-making and application to cases, then the separation of judicial and executive power seems minor if not genuinely odd.

Montesquieu

What we find in Montesquieu's *Spirit of the Laws* sixty years later is, however, quite the reverse. In his statement of a doctrine of the separation of powers in what became its canonical categorization of legislative, executive, and *judicial*, the separation between the last two of those emerges as fundamental.

Montesquieu added to Locke's concern for the separation of general rule-making from decisions about particulars a more direct attention to due process and criminal justice, and so engaged in his famous act of re- (or mis-) description of the English constitution as being committed to clear separations among executive, legislative, *and judicial* power. The combination of legislative and executive power was bad, and England stood out as the state that properly distinguished them; but moderate European states in general were distinguished from despotisms by the separateness of the judiciary. Bourbon kings had absorbed most of the legislative power of the estates, and the Estates-General had not met in decades; but France was still not *quite* a despotism even after Louis XIV, because the nobility-staffed *parlements* still tried cases, acted as repositories of laws, and judged whether royal decrees conformed to the laws and constitution of the kingdom.

In the most substantial recent study of the separation of powers in political theory, Waldron (2016f, pp. 59–61) comments that "Montesquieu provides next to nothing in the way of a tissue of argument for the separation of powers in the most famous passages devoted to the subject ... Montesquieu said very little ... Often, Montesquieu offered little more than tautologies.... It is time we acknowledged Montesquieu's failure to provide us with arguments explaining in detail why the separation of powers is necessary for liberty." He concludes "I am a devotee of *The Spirit of the Laws*, but I learn from what is hinted at rather than articulated in its assertions."

There is a little bit of truth to this, but it is easily exaggerated. The truth in it applies to the explicit treatment of the separation of powers in the study of the constitution of England in Book 11 by itself. It doesn't apply to the large parts of the book devoted to judicial process, criminal law, and punishment – particularly Book 6, in which magistrates, legislators, and monarchs are sharply distinguished as Montesquieu elaborates and defends a vision of due process of law, legal formalities, and institutions of judgment.

> In despotic governments, the prince himself can judge. He cannot judge in monarchies; the constitution would be destroyed and the intermediate dependent powers reduced to nothing; one would see all the formalities of judgments cease; fear would invade all spirits.... In monarchical states, the prince is the party who pursues those who are accused and has them punished or acquitted; if he himself judged, he would be both judge and party. In these same states, the prince often receives what is confiscated; if he judged the crimes, he would again be both judge and party. (p. 78)

Similarly, Montesquieu holds that the king's ministers should not also act as judges (p. 80), due to the necessary conflict between judicial neutrality and the vigorous pursuit of the king's business.

The opposition between despotism and all of the moderate forms of government is fundamental to *The Spirit of the Laws*, and explicitly turns on liberty *and* on the separation of the sovereign from judging. What connects those? Recall that Montesquieu defines liberty both as security with its accompanying tranquility of mind (the opposite of "fear [taking] possession of the people's minds"), and as the freedom to do what the law allows. The latter has confused some commentators, giving rise to the false idea that Montesquieu was a theorist of positive liberty. But if I am free to do what the law allows, then *I must not be punished if I have not violated the law*, with a reasonably robust rule-of-law understanding of what it means to have violated a law and to be convicted of it. My opinion of my security follows. I know that if I follow the law I am not vulnerable to *lettres de cachet*, being grabbed on the streets or from my bed by the king's guards or the secret police, being haled before the Star Chamber, being singled out by a bill of attainder or subject to *ex post facto* punishment, being prosecuted for the kinds of alleged crimes for which convictions can never rest on an adequate evidentiary basis (witchcraft and sodomy are Montesquieu's examples), or being punished on trumped-up charges of treason. I benefit from that tranquility and knowledge of my security rather than suffering from the fear that characterizes despotism (Compare Shklar 1989; Kateb 1992).

Adam Smith, who followed Montesquieu closely enough in many respects that I think we can treat him as an expositor of these connections among liberty, security, and the separation of powers, argued that the "separation of the province of distributing Justice between man and man from that of conducting publick affairs and leading Armies is the great advantage which modern times have over antient, and the foundation of that greater Security which we now enjoy both with regard to Liberty, property, and Life" (Smith 1985 [1762–3], p. 203).

His later rephrasing of the idea in the *Wealth of Nations* used language that makes Montesquieu's idea of security-liberty perhaps even more accessible to contemporary readers. "When the judicial is united with the executive power, it is scarce possible that justice should not frequently be sacrificed to, what is vulgarly called, politics. The persons entrusted with the great interests of the state may, even without any corrupt views, sometimes imagine it necessary to sacrifice to those interests the rights of a private man. But upon the impartial administration of justice depends the liberty of every individual, the sense which he has of his own security. In order to make every individual feel himself perfectly secure in the possession of every right which belongs to him, it is not only necessary that the judicial should be separated from the executive power, but that it should be rendered as much as possible independent of that power" (Smith 1981 [1776], pp. 722–723).

With all of this in mind, I think Montesquieu's account of the separation of powers becomes much less mysterious, and Montesquieu's reasons for departing from Locke in distinguishing the judicial power from the others become clear. While he has a great deal to say about better and worse laws and approaches to legislation, he does not center his analysis of the problem of liberty under government on acts of general legislation that restrict more than they should. Rather, he focuses on the risk of *lawless* state action, and the unfreedom (through fear) it *necessarily* creates.

These are the normative commitments Montesquieu aims to infuse into the legal process articulated through multiple separate powers. But Montesquieu was an ancient constitutionalist with government by estates always in mind, and he doubted the stability of institutional divisions that did not rest on social facts. He argued that the separation of powers is harder to sustain in republics than in moderate monarchies with an aristocracy and intermediate powers. And so, his account of the judiciary is a curious one. The very important class of professional judges and jurists more or less disappeared from his celebration of the English jury system. Even when he praises the system of precedent characteristic of common law, he does not mention the professional judges who did the real work of propagating and following precedent.

Instead, he devoted apparently disproportionate attention to the judicial functions of the House of Lords. These were real enough: The House of Lords was the court of highest appeal, as well as being the jury of "peers," in both senses, who could hear trials of members of the nobility, and the site of impeachment trials. It did not wield ordinary judicial power; however, the extraordinary judicial power it held (while also acting as a house of the legislature) was constitutionally significant. The impeachment power subjected even the king's ministers to the law, while the sole right to try the nobility protected a class of political elites from direct royal retribution. This treatment of the House of Lords served to remind French readers of his treatment elsewhere in the book of the *parlements*, and more generally of the nobility as a bulwark of legal constraints on monarchical power. The reader of *The Spirit of the Laws* interested in French rather than English constitutional debates would come away with an appreciation for a separation of powers motivated by normative commitments to liberty and the rule of law, and stabilized by founding the separate powers on distinct bases of social power and group loyalty (See Levy 2015, 2021).

I have said above that I would amend the idea that the separation of powers is to be understood as the rule of law institutionalized through an articulated process, with each step of rulemaking, rule-adjudication, and rule-enforcement housed in a distinct institution with distinct personnel. We have now reached the amendment. Formal procedures that fit that description can be embedded in the law, but the law cannot guarantee its own stability or supremacy. Either a legislature or an executive, but most standardly an executive, can use its powers in ways that subvert the system as a whole. It might be illegal for an executive to rule by decree or to punish opponents without trial, but the executive's command of the armed forces and police forces calls into question whether that law will bind. The secret police can *in fact* seize and imprison dissidents; the army can *in fact* storm the legislature and declare it dissolved. So, the separation of powers as a practice typically involves putting political weight behind the institutional separations, and particularly behind the other two branches' freedom from the executive force: allowing the independently powerful nobility to impeach ministers of the king, forbidding the prosecution of members of the legislature for their speech within that body, requiring the military to depend on the legislature for regular appropriations. These aren't strictly part of the articulated rule of law process, but neither are they brute-force countervailance and balancing. They politically bolster that legal process.

Publius

The American constitutional founders followed Montesquieu in his conviction that the separation of powers was crucial to liberty and the rule of law; "the accumulation of all powers, legislative, executive, and judiciary, in the same hands, whether of one, a few, or many, and whether hereditary, self-appointed, or elective, may justly be pronounced the very definition of tyranny" (Hamilton, Madison, and Jay 2003 [1787–1788], p. 292). Federalist 47 affirms Publius' adherence to Montesquieu's doctrine, and insists against opponents of the new federal constitution that it is compatible with the separation of powers. This is in large part a matter of showing that the separateness of powers should not be absolute. An executive veto, a Senate conducting impeachment trials, and so on allowed the three branches to meaningfully constitutionally limit each other, just as in the English constitution Montesquieu had celebrated. It is in Federalist 51 that Publius modifies the doctrine, adjusting it in light of the challenge of institutionalizing it without a monarchy or a nobility.

By 1787, any residual American belief that the Senates in their bicameral state legislatures should emulate the House of Lords in the representation of a distinct social class was fading fast. There wasn't an aristocratic class to be found, and there was no appetite to create one (Wood 1969). The idea formulated by Publius that took hold in the American constitutional imagination was that the virtues of the British constitution as reimagined by Montesquieu could be recreated *without* the underlying class distinctions among commoners, peers, and royals. Ambition counteracting ambition among officeholders, acting with jealousy of their institutional rights and privileges, would suffice: members of Congress, judges, and the president (and, presumably, their state-level counterparts) could be trusted to stand up to each other simply because their institutional interests were in tension with each other. The new constitution included the power and authority to bolster and secure the core rule of law element of the separation of powers, allowing each branch to prevent the others from acting unlawfully. The interests and ambitions of the office-holders would, it was hoped, provide them with the motives and incentive to *use* that power.

III RECOVERING AND CHALLENGING THE TRADITION

This understanding of the separation of powers still has real theoretical force. The dangers of lawless executive power that animate it are very much still with us, and the holders of executive power are today perversely eager to dress up their immunity from oversight or interference in the language of the separation of powers. A clear understanding of the normative commitments animating the idea might help us see through that kind of thing.

But the model of the separation of powers that Montesquieu and the American framers canonized faces genuine institutional and intellectual challenges in contemporary applications as well. Taking the underlying idea of the separation of powers seriously may require rethinking it in light of changes Montesquieu and Publius could not have anticipated.

Parties and Responsible Government

The theory of the separation of powers as worked out in the eighteenth century, particularly the separation of executive from legislative power, faced probably its most substantial challenge from the rise of *partisan* democracy. On the one hand, we might imagine parties as supplying in a democratic and egalitarian age what social class no longer could: an animating reason for those who occupy different offices to really check each other rather than cartelizing and cooperating (Levinson and Pildes 2006). Something like this might animate the folk theory of divided government that seems to be a part of American political culture: many American voters consistently say they prefer the presidency and Congress to be controlled by different parties. If at least some of them act on that preference, it could partly explain the regular swing to the party that does not control the White House in midterm Congressional elections.

On the other hand, the primacy of partisanship can mean that the separation of powers loses much of its imagined effectiveness. The American presidential system tends to leave the executive free from constraint when the same party controls the executive and the legislature; and during divided government, oversight and investigation by the legislature is widely regarded as (and often may well be!) mere opposition-partisan posturing. Nineteenth-century parliamentarist constitutionalists developed a model of executive responsibility to, rather than separation from, the legislature, a model that depends on rather than ignoring parties (Selinger 2019). But that model shows signs of its own of trending toward executive dominance of a legislature whose plurality or majority party the executive leads (Poguntke and Webb 2005). Political theory is in shockingly early days when it comes to thinking about parties and partisanship (but see Muirhead and Rosenblum 2020); one effect of this is that the separation of powers hasn't been properly re-understood in light of the centrality of parties to democratic government. The questions of whether parties can satisfactorily substitute for the social classes imagined by Montesquieu as bolstering the separation of powers, and of whether they cripple the jealousy of office vision offered by Publius, remain seriously understudied (Levy 2021).

The Administrative State

The separation of legislative authority and executive personnel, and sometimes of the judicial function as well, is widely taken to have become impossible with the growth of the modern administrative and regulatory state, another topic that is as yet not taken seriously enough in the political theory literature (but see Heath 2020). Legislatures could not write regulatory rules in sufficient detail as to be reliable guides for action, and could not revise them often enough to allow them the needed flexibility, and so they of necessity delegate rule-making authority to executive agencies within broad purposive limits. Moreover, the expertise required to judge cases under the resulting complex regulatory regimes is best found in those agencies themselves and not in judges (to say nothing of juries), so the agencies will often act as quasi-judicial rule-enforcers as well as quasi-legislative rule-makers. Finally, because the rules need to be responsive to unpredictable fact patterns and opportunism on the part of those trying to dodge regulation, the agencies will often need to specify rules only in the moment of applying them. The traditional concerns about *ex post facto* legislation and the rule of law that animated interest in the separation of powers in the first place will more or less necessarily give way. (See, among many others, Fuller 1969; Hamburger 2014; Ginsburg and Menashi 2010; Posner and Vermeule 2010; Sunstein and Vermeule 2017).

Now, I think these arguments often overstate the strict *necessity* of some particular institutional shape of regulatory agencies. At the cost of some duplication there could be *distinct* rule-making and rule-enforcing regulatory agencies covering the same subject matter. At the cost of some delay, agencies' proposed new or revised rules might be treated as expertly drafted proposed legislation, with a routine legislative practice of passing those rules into law in an omnibus measure. I am inclined to doubt that the institutional shape administrative agencies happened to take in western democracies in the early twentieth century – an era of unusually high confidence in technocratic expertise and unusually low confidence in either democratically elected legislatures or rule-of-law-oriented judiciaries – is their only possible functional shape. And there is more variation in those institutional practices– cross-nationally but also within any one system – than the debates sometimes let on.

In any case, a usable theory of the separation of powers today will have to come to terms with the reality of the administrative state, and will have to find a path besides the two that seem to be available in the American nondelegation debates: abandoning separation of powers reasoning as anachronistic, and abolishing the administrative state as unconstitutional and incompatible with the rule of law.

How Many "Powers"?

Similarly, but more broadly, the precise division of governing power into three by Montesquieu that was subsequently enshrined by the US Constitution is probably overdue for reconsideration. For all of Montesquieu's attention to the dangers of executive power, what we think of as "the executive branch" in the eighteenth century was tiny and simple compared with what it is in all modern states today.

For separation of powers-like reasons – protecting the rule of law, distinguishing rule-making from rule-application, and constraining the capacity for the self-serving, corrupt, politicized, and abusive use of discretionary powers – there is good reason for many of those executive powers to be separated *from one another*. In functioning constitutional democracies this has been done in practice, mostly as a matter of convention and practice rather than law. But it hasn't been incorporated into the theoretical understanding of the separation of powers itself. And sometimes when theory doesn't keep up with practice, the normative value of the practice is underappreciated, and the practice itself is left vulnerable.

Within what we're used to treating as "the executive," constitutional democracies have a variety of separation-of-powers-like norms and conventions. Final civilian authority over the military combined with a substantial insulation of the military from partisan politics is very much that kind of norm. So is the combination of a professional civil service that works to implement policies set by the political executive while remaining insulated from partisan politics (Heath 2020). The professional civil service ought to be impartial in implementing regulatory policy, and ought not to be used as a partisan tool to harass the opponents of the current political executive. The prosecutorial and police forces, the armed forces, and the agencies overseeing elections themselves are particularly critical in this regard, but insofar as all administrative agencies have a kind of prosecutorial character, the problem extends broadly. Politically selective enforcement by tax agencies, for example, can easily become an abusive tool in the hands of the political executive.

We don't notice the separation of political executive from military or from the civil service and administrative state as "separation of powers" problems, because we are too used to treating all of those together as "the executive." But they're vital for the robustness and stability of constitutional government as we now understand it, and call on the same kinds of reasons as traditional separation-of-powers arguments, particularly the need to prevent the highest political officials from abusing governing authority to punish their opponents.

I don't think it will do as a reply to say that neither the military nor the civil service can be a "power" in its own right because of their ultimate responsibility to the authority of the political executive. The military mustn't decide what wars to fight; the career civil servants of the administrative state depend on policy direction being set by ministers or presidents who face democratic political accountability, within the broad boundaries of statutes passed by legislatures who do too. Neither the military nor the civil service is supposed to decide the major questions about what aims to pursue. But we can find parallel thoughts throughout traditional separation-of-powers arguments. After all, the executive does not determine the laws it is told to execute, nor the judiciary the laws under which it judges cases. The traditional theory held that those fundamental decisions were left to the legislature. But this did not reduce the executive or the judiciary to being simple subordinates of the legislature, Locke notwithstanding. Their work was insulated from its work in important ways. The legislature set the fundamental principles but did *not* command their applications to particular cases. The structure of authority between the political executive and the administrative state is not identical to that, but is similar enough to let us recognize a relationship of kind.

It is worth noticing that this understanding of an internally-separated executive relies in part on the recognition that it is normal and legitimate for the political executive to be *political*; it is appropriately partisan. Treating partisanship as pathological, invisible, or simply external to the basic constitutional order is a serious obstacle to clear understanding here, and here again we see that a viable theory of the separation of powers is entangled with an understanding of partisan contestation.

This division of the executive into three might seem to echo the tripartite structure of the traditional model: political executive in place of policy-setting legislature, administrative state as the judiciary applying rules to particular cases, standing army and police as the executive sword. I don't mean it that way and don't consider three to be a particularly important number. The evolved practices of constitutional democracies include practices of separation that we should probably keep analytically distinct from each other. For example, independent central banks look like executive agencies according to the traditional division, but their status is defined by separation-of-powers-like norms and rules that make them less accountable to the political executive than cabinet ministries. Agencies that have authority over criminal investigations and prosecutions are importantly distinct from the political executive and from the military, but aren't quite like the rest of the civil service either. In some ways this arm of the executive may be especially independent. It is common for there to be conventions that treat the minister of justice or attorney general as somewhat less political than other ministers, somewhat more insulated from daily questions of partisan advantage or loyalty to the head of government. We also frequently find offices charged with enforcing laws and ethics regulations on members of the government itself, offices that are necessarily somewhat protected from the officials they monitor. And yet there is reason for these executive agencies to be especially constrained, too. Investigative and prosecutorial agencies wield considerable power to begin with; within the civilian domestic state, they are perhaps the most frighteningly powerful state agents. Together with the prison system, they hold precisely the power that we saw animating concerns about executive authority in traditional theories in the first place. While one core worry of constitutionalism is political officials using criminal investigation and law enforcement to harry their opponents, there's no more reason to feel sanguine about those agencies becoming supreme powers themselves, uncontrollable and unaccountable. The investigative and prosecutorial agencies have too much power and discretion to be left as independent as the judiciary, and yet politicizing them undermines the impartiality of law in a way that resembles a politicized judiciary. So, the developed practice of distinguishing the investigative and prosecutorial agencies from the rest of the civil service seems right, and the familiar ongoing struggles about how much independence and how much accountability these agencies should have reflect real problems that differ from those that apply to the regular civil service. The Montesquieuian rule of law reasons for special attention to the executive's control over the violence of the criminal law apply within the disaggregated executive, too.

RECOMMENDED READING

Ackerman, B. (2000). The New Separation of Powers. *Harvard Law Review*, 113 (3), 633–729.
Barber, N. (2018). *The Principles of Constitutionalism: A Republican Defense of the Constitutionality of Democracy*, Oxford: Oxford University Press.
Bellamy, R. (2007). *Political Constitutionalism*, Cambridge: Cambridge University Press.
Bonham v College of Physicians (1610) 8 Co Rep 107.
Gordon, S. (1999). *Controlling the State: Constitutionalism from Ancient Athens to Today*, Cambridge: Harvard University Press.
Hamilton, A., Madison, J., & Jay, J. (2003[1788]). *The Federalist: With Letters of Brutus*. Edited by Terence Ball. Cambridge: Cambridge University Press.
Hayek, F. A. (1973). *Law, Legislation, and Liberty, vol. 1: Rules and Order*, Chicago: University of Chicago Press.
McIlwain, C. H. (1940). *Constitutionalism Ancient and Modern*, Ithaca NY: Cornell University Press.
Montesquieu. (1989 [1748]). *The Spirit of the Laws*. Edited by A. Cohler, B. C. Miller, and H. S. Stone. Cambridge: Cambridge University Press.
Pettit, P. (2012). *On the People's Terms: A Republican Theory and Model of Democracy*, Cambridge: Cambridge University Press.
Poguntke, T. & Webb, P., eds. (2005). *The Presidentialization of Politics: A Comparative Study of Modern Democracies*, Oxford: Oxford University Press.
Vile, M. J. C. (2012 [1967]). *Constitutionalism and the Separation of Powers*, Indianapolis: Liberty Fund.
Waldron, J. (2016). *Political Political Theory: Essays on Institutions*, Cambridge: Harvard University Press.

18

The Rule of Law

Jeff King[*]

The rule of law is a normative ideal specifying how law and legal institutions should operate in any political order. It is of interest to lawyers, political theorists and political scientists alike (Shapiro 1994; Fleming 2011). The concept is recognised extensively in the positive law of many legal orders, including constitutions, in international law, the decisions of law courts, and in their constitutional customs and practices. There is also significant disagreement over the meaning of the idea, which can be enlightening (Waldron 2002). It has been common to identify conceptions of the rule of law as being either formal or substantive (Craig 1997; Tamanaha 2004, chaps. 7, 8). This distinction helps to sort theories neatly along lines dictated by how ambitious the rule of law desiderata (requirements) are, and in particular if the conception requires the observance of human rights or democracy. Yet the distinction is less precise about illuminating the theoretical underpinnings of contrasting conceptions. I will therefore distinguish between two other important ways of thinking about the rule of law in twentieth-century thought. I will describe the first as the legal essentialist approach. It defines the rule of law by reference to a theory of the essence of legality. Those following this approach often (but not always) identify the formal features that a legal system must possess if law is to be able to function *as law*. The other approach is the limited government approach. It presents the rule of law as a political ideal motivated by the role of law in protecting liberty. It defines the rule of law as the legal negation of an important aspect of arbitrary coercive

---

[*] Professor of Law, University College London; Director of Research, Bingham Centre of the Rule of Law. The ideas in this chapter date to an Alexander von Humboldt Foundation funded visit to the Humboldt University of Berlin, hosted by Professor Christoph Möllers, subsequently developed during leave provided by the Philip Leverhulme Prize (2017) and through formal visits at the University of New South Wales (2019), the University of Toronto (2020) and workshops at Harvard (2019), the University of Ottawa (2020), and Erasmus University (2020). In particular the author thanks Nick Barber, Richard Bellamy, Paul Burgess, Vincent Chiao, Conor Crummey, Yasmin Dawood, Hasan Dindjer, David Dyzenhaus, Timothy Endicott, Evan Fox-Decent, Amanda Greene, Vicki Jackson, Ronald Janse, Martin Krygier, George Letsas, Christoph Möllers, Martin Loughlin, Peter Oliver, Julian Sempill, Kevin Toh, Grégoire Webber and Robin West for extensive feedback on previous drafts.

power. The limited government approach sees the concept as a component of political theory, whereas the legal essentialist approach presents it as a specification of legal excellence and hence an outworking of the concept of law.

In this chapter, I will briefly present both approaches, before arguing that the legal essentialist approach fails to solve three puzzles that the limited government approach fares better at answering. I nevertheless take the answers the limited government approach gives as a departure for presenting a brief sketch of a regulatory conception of the rule of law. As with the limited government approach, this conception posits legal regulation as a key legal part of the solution to the problem of arbitrary power. Yet departing from most versions of that approach, the regulatory conception recognises private arbitrary power as an antagonist or damaging to the rule of law and ultimately argues for a significant social dimension of the rule of law. That dimension entails a duty founded upon the rule of law ideal to legally regulate private arbitrary powers whose exercise allows some to impose coercion as well as non-consensual exploitation on others. Through meaningful regulation, such power becomes non-arbitrary, which is not to say that it becomes just. On this view, which departs from some deep libertarian traditions in the limited government approach to the rule of law, the rule of law and the welfare state can be seen as complementary rather than antagonistic.

I LEGAL ESSENTIALIST APPROACHES

Formal Conceptions and the Essence of Legality

Most of the post-WWII accounts of the rule of law given by legal theorists adopt a predominantly formal idea of what the rule of law requires, one which John Rawls (1999a, pp. 206–213) refers to as 'justice as regularity'. At its core, it requires open, clear, stable, coherent and prospective rules amenable to enforcement by independent and impartial judges who listen and respond to the parties of the legal dispute. Lon Fuller and Joseph Raz each offer such accounts and derive them from different accounts of the nature of law. Fuller espoused a theory of the 'inner morality of law' that was procedural in outline, one which is 'concerned, not with substantive aims of legal rules, but with ways in which a system of rules for governing human conduct must be constructed and administered if it is to be efficacious and at the same time remain what it purports to be' (Fuller 1969, chaps. 2, 4 and pp. 97, 153). Fuller's work more broadly was concerned with distinguishing between different forms of social ordering, including managerial discretion and market mechanisms (Rundle 2012), while identifying the distinctiveness of legal ordering. Fuller proceeds from the allegory of the King, Rex, who cannot effectively guide his subjects without respecting eight criteria of generality, publicity, prospectivity, intelligibility, consistency, practicability, stability and congruence (Fuller 1969, chap. 2). These ultimately amount to his desiderata of the rule of law. He argues that a 'total failure' of any of the desiderata he outlines 'results in something that is not properly called a legal system at all' (Fuller 1969, p. 39).

In 'The Rule of Law and its Virtue', Joseph Raz is critical of the 'promiscuous' use of the rule of law concept, which he felt led to its 'perversion' (Raz 1979b.) In seeking to avoid these problems, he outlines the bedrock of his approach to defining the rule of law:

> [I]f the law is to be obeyed *it must be capable of guiding the behaviour of its subjects.* It must be such that they can find out what it is and act on it. This is the basic intuition from which the doctrine of the rule of law derives (Raz 1979b, p. 214).

For Raz, '[i]t is of the *essence of law* to guide behaviour through rules and courts in charge of their application.' (Raz 1979b, p. 225, emphasis added). He thus pares back the rule of law concept to two basic aspects: '(1) that people should be ruled by law and obey it; and (2) that the law should be such that people will be able to be guided by it.' (Raz 1979b, p. 213). The first of these he refers to as the 'law and order' idea of the rule of law, upon which he does not elaborate. The second aspect is the principle that generates his well-known features or 'desiderata' of the rule of law (Raz 1979b, pp. 214–219):

1. All laws should be prospective, open and clear.
2. Laws should be relatively stable.
3. The making of particular laws should be guided by open, stable and clear rules.
4. The independence of the judiciary must be guaranteed.
5. The principles of natural justice must be observed.
6. The courts should have review powers.
7. The courts should be easily accessible.
8. The discretion of crime prevention agencies should not be allowed to pervert the law.

Raz distinguishes clearly (though perhaps artificially) between the rule of law – *what it is* – and its virtue, or, *what it can do* (see similarly Lovett 2016, pp. 100 ff). That separation differs sharply from the limited government approach, which is not essentialist, and derives an account of the rule of law from a normatively posited rather than conceptually derived function for law.

Both Fuller and Raz adopt formal conceptions from different standpoints about the nature of law and its relationship to social practice on the one hand and morality on the other. John Finnis' natural law account, which adopts broadly the same list of features as do Raz and Fuller, also refers to the rule of law as 'the specific virtue of legal systems' or, 'a state of affairs in which a legal system is in legally good shape' (Finnis 2011 [1980], p. 270). All such accounts view the rule of law as derived from an account of the essence of legality rather than from a political theory of law's substantive aims. Jeremy Waldron has gone furthest in expounding the grounds for this deep connection between the concept of law and the rule of law – although in his account, the idea of the rule of law serves to inform that of the concept of law as much as the other way around (Waldron 2008–2009). He argues that 'casual positivism' such as Raz's tends to put undue emphasis on the importance of determinate rules and sublimates the importance of courts, procedure, and that it has a very spare conception of what a legal system is (though in my view the criticism bites on Fuller's account more than Raz's). Waldron details the basic elements of a legal system which he believes the rule of law requires and which the very concept of law requires (i.e., courts, public norms, positive enactment, orientation to the public good, and systematicity). Immanent in several of these is the importance of procedure, of giving persons affected by decisions a suite of contestatory rights in legal proceedings, a list he considers quite different from the "formal" list of desiderata (Waldron 2011b, pp. 5–7).

Separation Anxiety

The approaches outlined above leave open a troubling question: why seek to define what is by all accounts a *normative political ideal*, and one as important as the rule of law, by deriving it from an essentialist account of the nature of law and the legal system? If one's theory of law binds the nature of law closely together with justice, as does that of Ronald Dworkin (1985, chap. 2; 1986), TRS Allan (1994, 2003, 2013), or the later writings of FA Hayek (1973, 1976), then one can have a good answer to that question. But that answer comes at the high price of making an account of the rule of law dependent on the acceptance of a thick natural law theory, which for many distracts unhelpfully from the question of the meaning of the rule of law value.

The emphasis on the essence of legality is doubtless linked to the view that one obviously cannot have an account of the rule of law without an account of what law is. But that is not obvious. The limited government approach of the rule of law can and has historically been a thoroughly normative account of what law should do and how legal systems should be shaped. The legal essentialist approach anyway needs to bring into the account some theory of why the essential features of the legal system are normatively appealing. The form of argument would be revealed as absurd if the function of legal systems in market economies were shown to be that it assists propertied classes in exploiting labour (cf. Kennedy 1997; Unger 1976).

What all of the accounts above do is connect the idea of behaviour guidance and predictability with the idea of autonomy. The idea is roughly that such rules are important because they enable people to fashion and direct the course of their own lives, treating them as responsible agents. This is a theme running through the accounts of Fuller (on which see especially Rundle 2012), Raz, and greatly emphasised by Waldron, Finnis, and Hayek. This is what provides a superficial link between the formal theories and the liberal tradition, and gives them moral appeal. But the link is superficial in some of these accounts (though not in Hayek) because it emphasises behaviour guidance and choice, while excluding other features of that tradition, such as the other elements of liberty, democracy, rights and non-domination. Furthermore, the emphasis on self-guiding autonomous action presupposes that the value of the rule of law is aimed chiefly at the rationally autonomous and well-informed users of legal systems, who seek out adjudicatory resolution of their rights. That is unfortunately a very small percentage of the beneficiaries of the rule of law. Many possess neither the know-how, the language skills, the capital, and in many cases not even the mental capacity of self-direction to capitalise on those kinds of participatory benefits. And many of those that have all the above lack the time to engage. If the rule of law is important for these kinds of reasons, it would be critically vulnerable to the left-critique that it is a bourgeois value.

Ultimately, the most compelling argument and consistently advocated defence of the formal conceptions of the rule of law is one of conceptual parsimony. Raz sets out the argument:

> If the rule of law is the rule of the good law then to explain its nature is to propound a complete social philosophy. But if so the term lacks any useful function. (Raz 1979b, p. 211)

The attractiveness of this particular argument is that it is not parasitic upon legal essentialism. Anyone can invoke this rationale and simply stipulate to a formal definition for those reasons. Waldron restates the argument as the 'separation thesis': '[w]e are better off arguing for the Rule of Law in the respects in which the Rule of Law's concerns cannot be duplicated under the auspices of any other ideal' (Waldron 2012d, p. 75). But it is not obvious why this austere segmentation should apply here. Many mid-level political ideas, such as human rights, exploitation, discrimination, access to justice, the separation of powers and democracy will be composites of more fundamental values, and reducible thereto over extended discussions. Yet they each have a social function. The rule of law's social function is to set out an institutionally sophisticated account of the role of appropriate legal protections.

A second argument put by Waldron is that thicker, substantive understandings would lead to 'a general decline in political articulacy, as people struggle to use the same term to express different ideals' (Waldron 2012d, p. 48). Though this is a widely shared concern among legal theorists, the (professedly practical) problem seems exaggerated as a matter of practice. Richly substantive definitions are adopted not only by the late Lord Bingham (2010), Britain's wisest judge in a generation, but also by the European Commission for Democracy through Law, and the United Nations.[1] They are also employed by the leading rule of law indices used worldwide (not to underrate the methodological problems attendant thereto) (Møller and

---

[1] European Commission for Democracy Through Law, 'Report on the Rule of Law' CDL-AD(2011)003rev; United Nations Security Council, 'The rule of law and transitional justice in conflict and post-conflict societies: Report of the Secretary-General' (2004) UN Doc S/2004/616.

Svend-Erik Skanning 2014; Versteeg and Ginsgburg 2016). These persons and institutions are at the business end of rule of law application. The rule of law value has never been in such wide currency or degree of articulacy or study.

Another and even better argument of Waldron is that a capacious view of the concept could be mischievous rather than confusing:

> [W]e should not try to trick people into exaggerating the importance of any particular value or ideal by insinuating it into the fabric of our other ideals, or by using it to colonize the ideals that are best stated (at least in the first instance) without reference to it (Waldron 2012d, pp. 100–111).

In setting out this concern, Waldron is in the main concerned about those who may seek to 'hijack the less controversial character' of the rule of law in order to advance a more controversial value such as property rights (Waldron 2012d, p. 111).

This is the best exposition of a concern that is raised frequently, and in particular against the social dimension I draw attention to below. In form, however, it is a collateral attack on the argument, sometimes even an *ad hominem* challenge. Is it right to assume sleight of hand among those who argue for a connection between the rule of law and property, or social justice? Hayek was stridently clear and had a very well-worked out theory for the link between the value of property and the rule of law. The same could be said of the role of property rights in the nineteenth century liberal or 'bourgeois *Rechtsstaat*' ideal in Germany, one that was criticised by Carl Schmitt:

> the principles of the modern, bourgeois-*Rechtsstaat* constitution correspond to the constitutional ideal of bourgeois individualism.... [T]his constitution contains a decision in the sense of bourgeois freedom: personal freedom, private property, contractual liberty, and freedom of commerce and profession. The state appears as the strictly regulated servant of society (Schmitt 2008 [1928], p. 169).

The connection between liberalism, property and the *Rechtsstaat*[2] was evident in Immanuel Kant's *Doctrine of Right* (*Rechtslehre*) (Kant 2017 [1797]). As a leading commentary indicates, Kant is recognised as having 'fathered the idea of a juridical state, which in German is called the *Rechtsstaat*...' (Byrd and Hruschka 2010, p. 1). The juridical state in that work is an instrument giving protection to the 'axiom of external freedom,' and the legal protection of contract and property rights are the principal subjects of Part I of *The Doctrine of Right*. There was and is nothing duplicitous about the mode of argument, which has also been restated in a more contemporary form (Ripstein 2009, chap. 4). The pedigree of the property argument is quite proper in fact.

---

[2] I have excluded systematic comparison between *Rechtsstaat* and the rule of law due to the ongoing debate about the differences between them. I believe in common with MacCormick (1989) and Hayek (1960, chap. 13, see esp. note 32) and official translations of the German Basic Law that the differences are greatly exaggerated. (For a strongly contrasting view see Meierhenrich 2021).

Yet for some this kind of response may simply refute the idea of insinuation at the expense of confirming deep suspicions about the endgame of the concept and its use. In that connection it bears mentioning that the neoliberal conception of the rule of law has been largely justified under a formal model of the rule of law. Legal certainty, stability, predictability, and the ability to plan were the features emphasised by Hayek, and recall that Raz claimed he was 'following in the footsteps of Hayek and many others who understood "the rule of law" in similar ways'. (Raz 1979b, p. 211). With Hayek (see further below), the emphasis on planning and predictability naturally leads to the emphasis on enforcement of contracts, protection of property rights, subdued regulation and at the most drastic levels the relinquishment of legal sovereignty over investment arrangements. In other words, there is good reason to think the formal approach if anything courts rather than prevents the insinuation of ideals like neoliberalism, and has in concrete practice been a Trojan horse for them (Nader and Mattei 2008). This is seen clearly in the German concept of the *Rechtsstaat*, which Schmitt's critique cited above exposes. In 1934, at the height of the popularity of the so-called 'formal' and positivist conception of the *Rechtsstaat* (Böckenförde 1987, chap. 3), Franz Neumann observed that '[t]he idea of *Rechtsstaat* only develops clearly if it is considered in the context of the economic, political and philosophical system of liberalism,' adding later that '[t]he *Rechtsstaat* has the sole and exclusive aim of securing freedom and property, which are seen as inviolable liberties anterior to the state…' (Neumann 1987 [1934]). Beyond the problem of neoliberal conceptions of the rule of law, there is also the very real problem of formal conceptions being used to shore up the legitimacy of authoritarian legalism (Rathja 2012; Cheesman 2014).

The better response to Hayek and the libertarian, anti-regulatory conception of the rule of law is not to dismiss the value outright, or reject the attempt to link liberty and the rule of law, but rather to show that the conception of liberty guiding their theories of the rule of law is flawed (e.g., Plant 2010; MacCormick 1989). A similar strategy was adopted by advocates of the 'new liberalism' and Progressivism in response to the failings of classical liberalism, which led to huge changes to social policy in Britain and America (Weiler 1982; Ryan 1982, pp. 89–99; see also Pettit 1997).

Three Puzzles for the Legal Essentialist View

Beyond the issues surveyed above, there are three other difficulties or puzzles that the legal essentialist approaches, particularly the formalist ones, do not seem to resolve.

The first is how it responds to the intuitive idea that anarchy is incompatible with the rule of law. Raz mentions the idea of law and order as part of what the rule of law means, but puts it aside. Fuller admits that the very first kind of failure of the rule of law is 'the failure to achieve rules at all' (Fuller 1969, p. 39). Yet while neither denies that rules are needed under the rule of law, they do not adequately explain *why* the rule of law idea requires rules or *what* should be covered by such rules (cf. Finnis 2011 [1980], p. 252; Lovett 2016, pp. 9 ff, 21 ff). The omission is problematic because plainly not all areas of social life should be regulated under law, so a simple postulate such as "there must be rules" is inadequate. That simply invites the question – 'rules *for what*, precisely, and what does that answer say about the rule of law value?' The limited government approach has a clear answer here. Raz compounds the mistake by saying that the rule of law is a negative virtue, in that it is 'merely designed to minimize the harm to freedom and dignity which the law may cause' (Raz 1979b, p. 228). As Martin Krygier has noted, this 'negative' conception of the rule of law is at odds with the older tradition's concern with quintessentially *unlawful* arbitrary *power* (Krygier 2012b; see also Krygier 2011). It was a protest about the absence of law, not its evils.

The second puzzle is the failure to give a satisfactory account of the relationship between the rule of law and administrative discretion, most notably the welfare and regulatory state (Davis 1969, chap. 1). Sir Edward Coke admonished government to '[l]eave all causes to be measured by the golden and straight mete-wand of the law, and not to the incertain and crooked cord of discretion.' (Coke, cited in Hayek 1960, p. 147). Fuller (1969, pp. 64–65) credits Hayek's critique of regulation and suggests more work needs to be done on reconciling vague regulatory standards in legislation and rule of law values. Raz is more committal. He accepts Hayek's argument that the rule of law conflicts with the welfare state, but adds that '[c]onflict between the rule of law and other values is just what is to be expected.' (Raz 1979b, p. 228). He argued that Hayek's mistake was to give 'overriding importance' to the rule of law. Yet this approach fails to systematically integrate the co-existence of two fundamentally important political values and institutions. With no suggestion about how to resolve such conflicts, the approach is liable to weaken respect for one or the other. It is akin to announcing that one accepts the conflict between human rights and democracy with equanimity. Lovett (2016) is a critic of theories that focus on the essence of *legal systems*, but from similar motivations he does derive an account of the rule of law from a positivist conception of law as a social practice (Lovett 2016, pp. 9 ff; Part II). Contrary to Raz, he offers an excellent example of reconciling discretion and regulation (Lovett 2016, pp. 192–200). He contends that *strong discretion* and *accountability discretion* each violate rule of law standards but that *rule-implementing discretion* does not. He also proposes non-domination as a metric for evaluating whether departures from the rule of law are justified (Lovett 2016, pp. 124–125). While these refinements improve on Raz's claim (and in the context of a quite different theory), I will argue below that the issue is more persuasively addressed after recognising the social dimension of the rule of law that Lovett denies.

A third and final puzzle is to explain how the legal essentialist conceptions relate to historical thinking about the rule of law in modern politics. Fuller makes no real effort to relate his inner morality of law to the existing writings about the rule of law. Though Raz positions himself as the defender of orthodoxy, he departs from the tradition of defining the rule of law in opposition to a politicised notion of arbitrary power, as expounded in the work of Hayek and many others. For instance, AV Dicey, the great Victorian jurist who remains a leading authority on the British constitution, and widely viewed as the proto-formalist, was clear about the connection. He argued that the rule of law entails the 'absolute supremacy or predominance of regular law as opposed to the influence of arbitrary power, and [it] excludes the existence of arbitrariness, or prerogative, or even of wide discretionary authority on the part of the government' (Dicey 1915, chap. IV). While Waldron's work exhibits careful attention to (if selective deployment of) the major historical canons, Raz, Fuller and Finnis are indifferent to them, as is to an important extent Lovett. This is plainly not a conceptual error, but it is to some extent a weakness. The rule of law concept is embedded in a wide range of concrete legal practices as well as broader political usage. For instance, Brian Tamanaha's superb monograph (2004) on the history, politics and theory of the rule of law only arrives in Chapter 7 at discussing formal theories of the sort addressed in this section. It is that background which largely explains the diffusion of the value and its positive recognition, of how the idea has entered the semantics of Western political and juristic thought. Theorists are obviously welcome to develop new accounts or even to stipulate definitions. It would nevertheless be better all things considered to engage with and criticise, reform or repudiate those approaches rather than to ignore them altogether.

II THE LIMITED GOVERNMENT APPROACH

Arbitrary Power

Under the limited government approach, the rule of law comprises a set of normative claims about the role of legal regulation in constraining the arbitrary power of public officials. It sets out conditions under which the law and legal system can play a role in constraining arbitrary power. This approach builds on a rich history of liberal and republican theorising about the role of law in constraining executive power. Indeed, the history extends back well before liberalism. In 1656, James Harrington invokes Aristotle's claim that 'the rule of law, it is argued, is better than that of any man...' (Aristotle 1996, p. 78) when he reasons that '[t]he art whereby a civil society is instituted and preserved upon the foundations of common rights and interest ... [is], to follow Aristotle and Livy, the empire of laws, not of men' (Harrington 1992 [1656], p. 8).

Julian Sempill has written an excellent exposition of the limited government approach's thinking about the rule of law (Sempill 2018a). Within this, the rule of law is contrasted with arbitrary power, namely with being under the controlling, uncertain and unaccountable will of another:

The essence of the charge is that, in wielding power over one or more others, a power-holder has disrespected something that ought to have been respected, in particular, an interest, expectation, or right that is a genuinely "respect-worthy thing." (Sempill 2018a, p. 367)

Martin Krygier (2011, p. 175) contends that the main idea of the rule of law is that it would 'involve legal reduction of the possibility of arbitrary exercise of power by those in a position to wield significant power'. He takes 'opposition to the exercise of arbitrary power' as the key ideal defining the rule of law (Krygier 2014, p. 89). He adopts Philip Pettit's definition of arbitrary power, namely, that '[a]n act is perpetrated on an arbitrary basis, we can say, if it is subject just to the arbitrium, the decision or judgment, of the agent[…] that it is chosen or rejected without reference to the interests or the opinions, of those affected.' (Pettit 1997, p. 55). Krygier (2017) expands this idea with the metaphor of 'tempering power' (King 2019a for discussion). Gerald Postema has provided what is now the most sophisticated restatement of the rule of law ideal in this approach, developing significantly Krygier's notion of tempering power. He articulates the core idea of the rule of law in the following way:

> The rule of law imposes a moral demand upon political communities and their governments. It demands that they be structured in such a way that those who are subject to power, from whatever quarter, are provided protection and recourse against its arbitrary exercise though the law's distinctive features, tools, and modes of operation. In sum, when law rules in a political community, it *provides protection and recourse against the arbitrary exercise of power through law's distinctive tools*. (Postema 2022, p. 62)

Postema is clear that law's distinctive tools are only one way to reduce arbitrary power. He is also clear that the rule of law is a moral ideal, 'a component of a good, decent and just community' and hence not a derivation from essentialist legal theory (Postema 2022, p. 63). The reduction of 'arbitrary power' through law is not merely the consequence of observing the rule of law, as with Raz, but the normative political demand for it is what generates the rule of law desiderata.

Postema develops an account of both power and of arbitrariness. There is power of position (where one's position entitles one to privileges even if these are not used to command others to do something (e.g., bribe taking)) and the power of one agent over another (Postema 2022, p. 28). The power is arbitrary when it is *unilateral* and *unaccountable*. It is unilateral when '[t]he wielder's perspective on the action is the only relevant deliberative perspective; no other side or perspective is considered.' (Postema 2022, p. 29). The idea is that one person is subordinated to the will of another. I think Postema is basically though not exactly right here. A decision-maker could act arbitrarily while taking good faith council with a range of others – as did monarchs acting under theories of divine right. A similar issue also applies to Raz's somewhat curious *a priori* definition of arbitrary power under which the act was arbitrary 'if it was done either with indifference to whether it will serve the purposes which alone could justify the use of that power or with the belief that it will not serve them' (Raz 1979b, p. 219). A decision-maker can scrupulously seek to abide by a strict religious code or personal credo that they in good faith believe justifies their power, as did James I in England (Hart 2003, p. 57; Williams 2021). Indeed, the maxims derived from Roman law, of *legibus solutus* (that the King is 'released from the laws') and *quod placuit principi, habet vigorem legis* ('what pleases the prince has the power of law') enjoyed a rich theoretical justification in medieval natural law theory (Skinner 1978, pp. 178–184, cf. pp. 117–134). We can nevertheless continue with Postema's basic framework if we maintain that power over others is arbitrary if it is either (a) neither norm-governed nor accountable, or, (b) it is norm-governed but unaccountable to the subject of the power for the interpretation and application of those norms. One can see here how if this form of arbitrary power is the evil, law provides a distinctive remedy. Respect for the traditional formal desiderata of the rule of law follows from this basic set of ideas. Excessively vague laws or capricious executive acts are a form of power that is not norm-governed. And power will only rarely be accountable for the interpretation and application of such norms if there is no fair process of adjudication available.

The Liberal and Republican Traditions

This approach is deeply connected to the liberal and republican tradition of respecting the value of liberty and autonomy. In this limited government approach, law is represented as a positive regulatory value rather than a 'negative virtue' of any sort. Locke's *Second Treatise on Government* discusses the problem of arbitrary power extensively, contrasting it with government under law (Locke 1988 [1689]). His positive understanding of the role of law, noticed and expounded by Philip Pettit (1997, p. 37), is that it could be *constitutive* of liberty rather than the negation of liberty as in the account provided by Raz and more famously by Hobbes. For instance, Locke wrote,

> [T]*he end of law is not to abolish or restrain*, but to *preserve and enlarge freedom*: for in all the states of created beings capable of laws, *where there is no law, there is no freedom*: for liberty is, to be free from restraint and violence from others; which cannot be, where there is no law: but freedom is not, as we are told, *a liberty for every man to do what he lists*: (for who could be free when every other man's humour might domineer over him?) but a *liberty* to dispose, and order as he lists, his person, actions, possessions, and his whole property, within the allowance of those laws under which he is, and therein not to be subject to the arbitrary will of another, but freely follow his own. (Locke 1988 [1689], § 57)

This passage speaks not only to the intimate relationship, in this approach, between the law and liberty, but also to how the aim of law is to protect against 'every other man's humour' as much as it is the state itself (the latter being the principal concern in Locke's subsequent discussion of the relationship between law and tyranny). Locke's famous expression 'where law ends, tyranny begins' (Locke 1988 [1689], § 202) adorns the entrance of the US Department of Justice.

The association of the limited government approach with the rule of law is doubtlessly the inspiration for Judith Shklar's famous observation that much of the writing about the rule of law appears like 'a football in a game between friends and enemies of free market liberalism' (Shklar 1987). This owes much to the work of FA Hayek. Hayek's understanding of the rule of law was decisively influential in the founding of the Mount Pelerin Society, the intellectual engine of contemporary neoliberalism, which contains clear commitments to the rule of law in its statement of aims.[3] His rule of law views were complex and evolved. In *The Constitution of Liberty*, he follows the limited government approach by considering the rule of law value as a purely normative ideal (Hayek 1960). While Raz announced a similarity between his own approach and that of Hayek, in reality the latter's earlier account was plainly substantive. Hayek engages extensively with the origins of the term and philosophy of the rule of law – taking the Locke quote I have reproduced above as the leading quotation for his chapter on 'the origins of the rule of law' (Hayek 1960, chap. 11). He also explores its relationship to the *Rechtsstaat* concept, its role in American constitutionalism, and he then proceeds, in light of his investigation, to enumerate the 'essential factors which together make up the rule of law' (Hayek 1960, chaps. 13, 14). Here, he confirms that '[t]he rule of law is ... not a rule of the law, but a rule concerning what the law ought to be, a meta-legal doctrine or political ideal.' (Hayek 1960, p. 181). In terms of substance, which Hayek outlines in the chapter entitled 'The Safeguards for Individual Liberty' (Hayek 1960, chap. 14), he specifies that the rule of law requires a written constitution, intensive substantive review of administrative discretion, and most notably, the legal protection of rights under a bill of rights (Hayek 1960, pp. 187–190).

As it happens, I believe that Hayek adopted the right approach – let's say methodology – to defining the rule of law. I say so because unlike quibbling with the legal essentialists about what the nature of a legal system is, we can directly and profitably challenge Hayek's conception of liberty and substitute a better one (Plant 2010; MacCormick 1989). That conception of liberty is more systematically worked out in Hayek's *Law, Legislation and Liberty*, which also becomes more of a natural law legal essentialist tract than his earlier work was. In this book, he sets out the idea that law (*nomos*) is by its nature (or 'purpose') concerned to protect liberty by 'facilitat[ing] that matching or tallying of the expectations on which the plans of the individuals depend for their success' (Hayek 1973, chap. 5, pp. 93–94; and see pp. 107 ff.). He also argues that 'the maximal coincidence of expectations is achieved

---

[3] Available at www.montpelerin.org.

by the delimination of protected domains', namely, through the protection of property rights (Hayek 1973, pp. 101 ff.). As explained by Raymond Plant (2010), the law in Hayek's scheme must be *nomocratic* rather than *teleocratic* – that is, concerned with norms and not with ends (cf. Hayek 1973, chaps. 5, 6). But the obvious flaw with this conception of liberty is the thought that liberty and autonomy could be satisfied by a robust legal scheme of contract and property rights protection without regard for the inequalities of wealth and power that suffuse it and are exacerbated by it. As Rawls would put it, '[b]ackground fairness is lacking' (Rawls 1999a, p. 243). Also unpersuasive was Hayek's critique of teleological forms of law-making, which maintained that the application of human judgments about redistribution, planning and regulation entailed the imposition of conceptions of the good in substitution for self-determined answers to those same questions. One can doubt both whether the justice of Hayek's anti-perfectionist scheme is viable (cf. Raz 1986, chaps. 5 and 6; Plant 2010), and the idea that legislatively guided regulatory welfare capitalism cannot be accounted for within anti-perfectionist accounts of liberalism (Rawls 1999a, chap. 5; Dworkin 2000, chap. 2).

Respect for Human Rights

It is from this limited government approach emerging from liberal and republican political thought that some leading institutionalised accounts emerge, including Tom Bingham's widely read and politically-embraced definition of the rule of law:

> all persons and authorities within the state, whether public or private, should be bound by and entitled to the benefit of laws publicly and prospectively promulgated and publicly administered in the courts (Bingham 2010, p. 69)

This definition updates the classical liberal conception insofar as it is more explicit in recognising that the rule of law creates obligations that apply to private persons as well as public officials. Lord Bingham's desiderata of the rule of law also famously includes the following: 'The law must afford adequate protection of fundamental human rights.' On both points, it is broadly consistent with the definition of the rule of law adopted by the United Nations Secretary General.

> [t]he rule of law is a principle of governance in which all persons, institutions and entities, public and private, including the State itself, are accountable to laws that are publicly promulgated, equally enforced and independently adjudicated, and which are consistent with international human rights norms and standards.[4]

Similarly, the post-Second World War German conception of the material *Rechtsstaat* is marked by its inclusion not only of the procedural and formal features

---

[4] See www.un.org/ruleoflaw/what-is-the-rule-of-law/ and United Nations Security Council, 'The rule of law and transitional justice in conflict and post-conflict societies: Report of the Secretary-General' (2004) UN Doc S/2004/616.

of the formal *Rechtsstaat*, but also by its requirements that legislative power is bound by higher law and that all power respects fundamental rights (Schmidt-Assman, p. 552; see further Böckenförde 1991).

These claims understandably give commentators discomfort (Tamanaha 2004, chap. 8). The scope of international human rights law is extremely broad, and includes (to take one example from article 12 of the International Covenant on Economic, Social and Cultural Rights) a right to 'the highest attainable standard of health'. Few could expect that a failure to fulfil this norm would in itself amount to a breach of rule of law values. The limited government approach has thus far largely assumed that human rights meant a small sphere of civil and political rights. Even if it were, the form of argument is somewhat unclear – though sophisticated exceptions certainly exist (Fox-Decent 2008). While it is easy to show that the violation of human rights is a failure to treat persons with respect, and so too is the exercise of arbitrary power over them, it is quite another thing to deduce a requirement to comply with human rights norms from a rigorous account of arbitrariness such as that given by Postema above. For that very reason, Postema does not embrace that claim, and rather concludes that the rule of law and respect for human rights 'are distinct values, although they are complementary and intertwined' (Postema 2022, p. 109; and see chap. 5 generally). While I basically agree, I will return to this theme further below, in the effort of offering an improved account of the relationship between human rights and the rule of law.

The Limited Government Approach and the Three Puzzles

I have suggested above that the legal essentialist approach gave unsatisfactory answers to three puzzles. The limited government approach does a far better but not perfect job of responding to each. We can begin by acknowledging that the third puzzle – the failure to take the rule of law idea's historical background seriously – is taken incredibly seriously under this approach, and sometimes brilliantly (Hayek 1960, chaps. 11–14; Heuschling 2002; Sempill 2018a; Postema 2022). Let's then consider the other two puzzles. Regarding the explanation of the incompatibility of anarchy and the rule of law, the limited government approach has always had a plain answer to 'what' must be covered by law – arbitrary power. However, the traditional concern has been *coercion by the state*. This is made most explicit in Hayek's analysis, but was implicit in most others. Hence, if there is no arbitrary *state power* to limit – in a state of anarchy – it seems to follow that there is no rule of law concern. Recent accounts have consolidated a move towards recognising the application of rule of law norms to private power (e.g., Lovett 2016), but stop short of elaborating upon the social dimension of the rule of law, as I illustrate subsequently.

The second puzzle was how to explain the co-existence and reconciliation of the rule of law and the welfare state. Many writers working expressly or implicitly in the limited government approach have great sympathy for the welfare state, Lord Bingham most certainly included. They often marginalise the tension that exists here. As argued earlier, it is not credible to deny that any tension exists here, nor as I argued above to simply accept the basic incompatibility without seeking mutual accommodation. Let me thus address another two attempted strategies for reconciling the two, from within the limited government approach. One is to deny that there is a problem with regulatory power if it is founded on clear rules conferring the power and the discretion is suitably structured (Davis 1969; Lovett 2016, pp. 192–200). The difficulty with this line of argument on its own is that the residual scope of executive discretion and interpretive latitude remains huge. It is implausible to deny it. The unanswered deep question is whether an admittedly large amount of executive discretion is compatible with rule of law values and if so why. The other answer the limited government approach offers is that extensive administrative discretion is only acceptable when accompanied by extensive judicial control. The latter is seen as a curative to the ills generated by the former. Here too there is an important element of truth. However, if it is admitted that extensive and legally unregulated state power is a source of arbitrariness, and if it is accepted, as it must be, that courts are emanations of the state, then we seem forced to admit that extensive judicial power may itself be a rule of law problem (Tamanaha 2004, pp. 124–125). That is the source of rule of law-based conservative and frequently progressive arguments against judicial power. It is also the subject of tens of thousands of pages of administrative law writing about the appropriate role for judges in the modern administrative state (see, e.g., Mashaw 1983).

III THE SOCIAL DIMENSION OF THE RULE OF LAW

The best response to these two defects of the limited government approach is to conceive the rule of law as a regulatory ideal that extends to private and not just public power. Just these tendencies have begun to emerge in recent years, and find fine exposition in Postema's work. We can start by recognising that the significance of the problem of private power. As Sabeel Rahman clarifies in his important study, the Progressive Era thinkers like Louis Brandeis and John Dewey phrased their critique of the market economy as a problem of 'the accumulation of arbitrary, unchecked power over others' (2016, p. 13). While one response to this was democratisation, another was regulation (often by experts) through agency rule-making. Sociologist Philip Selznick was among the first to recognise and apply rule of law values to industrial relations within firms, recognising the quasi-governmental character of the relationship between employer and employee (Krygier 2012a, chaps. 7 and 8). Decades later, Elizabeth Anderson would pick up the same theme in her book *Private Government* (2017), followed soon after by Chiara Cordelli's neo-Kantian critique of privatised state functions as arbitrary (2021). In responding to Waldron's essay on the importance of procedure to the rule of law, Robin West, an important feminist jurist, argues that his and other more formal accounts 'ignore the ways in which the law expresses the will of the state to protect weaker parties harmed not by the state but by stronger private entities' (West 2011, p. 35; West 2003). Julian Sempill (2017, 2018b) has done the most recent systematic work at exploring the implications of the limited government approach for the workplace in particular. I follow the insights of each of these studies. And they occur as other theorists of the rule of law and both essentialist and limited governments recognise that the ideal applies to the private sphere (Austin and Klimchuk 2014; Lovett 2016). Postema's account in *Laws' Rule* (2022) now systematically develops that view and applies in particular to digital regulation.

I would argue in favour of a social dimension of the rule of law that would differ from most of these accounts, thus far, in two main ways. First, I avoid the expression 'private government' because I think it trades on the unfortunate stigmatisation of government in the American and classical liberal political discourse. I rather see government as an engine of democratic expression and enabler of egalitarian forms of liberty and opportunity. Second, these approaches have not, at least not until the recent publication of Gerald Postema's book, integrated these intuitive insights into a more systematic theory. I will thus outline some steps towards setting out a regulatory conception of the rule of law that entails an important social dimension (see also King 2022). This account builds on and was inspired by the still incompletely developed German concept of the social rule of law state (*sozialer Rechtsstaat*) and social state principle (*Sozialstaatsprinzip*) (Heller 1987 [1930]; Abendroth 1968; Kirschheimer and Neumann 1987, chaps. 1 and 3).

First, the rule of law is best understood as a *regulatory* ideal that requires proactive legal regulation rather than only governmental restraint. It can be contrasted with an ideal which is in indifferent or silent about *whether* there is legal regulation and is only concerned with what *form* any *given* legal regulation takes (see further Postema 2022, pp. 32–35). Second, the preoccupation with the regulation of *arbitrary power* in the limited government approach to the rule of law is based on a deep concern about the role of law in protecting freedom, and, historically, with addressing the use of *coercion* by public officials. Third, the reasons justifying a liberal rule of law concern for the legal regulation of public coercion apply equally to (a) the use of *private coercion* such as sexual assault, domestic violence, robbery, paramilitary activity and criminal racketeering, and (b) the resort to *private non-consensual exploitation* in which persons are wronged and have no choice but to consent to the wrongdoing. These two claims in particular address what can be called the social dimension of the rule of law. Fourth, the social dimension of the rule of law is best understood as a state duty to provide legal regulation of non-consensual coercion and exploitation, with a view to its elimination. Non-consensual exploitation, building on the *non*-Marxist analysis of it by Bob Goodin (1988, chap. 5) and Alan Wertheimer (1996), as well as Joel Feinberg (1988, chap. 31, pp. 177 ff.; 1986, chap. 24), involves transactions in which a person takes unfair advantage of another, and that other person has no choice but to consent. Both unfair advantage and defect of consent in this sense are notoriously difficult to define, but that both are systemic social problems is equally hard to deny. Due to the difficulty of specification, and the unsuitability of adjudication for determining answers in a casuistic way, the social dimension of the rule of law could not in the first instance rely upon judicial enforcement as the mode of protection. Instead, it calls for the enactment of bespoke regulatory regimes in exploitative fields of social interaction. These would at a minimum comprise family law, employment law (including health and safety regulation), landlord-tenant law, anti-discrimination law, consumer protection law, and various other areas in which private power is exercised over individuals. Such regimes must furnish frameworks, grounding individual rights and duties that are enforceable in accessible courts and tribunals, and which are proactively enforced along with other regulatory laws. It is that last quality – the form of protection it demands – that truly makes appropriate the ideal as a rule of law conception.

If we reconsider the three puzzles, we can see that this regulatory conception addresses them. The connection to history is clear. Though this regulatory conception transforms the classical liberal ideal, the development is if anything incremental in light of recent writings on the rule of law within the approach. It fully explains the relationship of the rule of law to what must be regulated, and it specifies how it is to be regulated – the role of statute and accessible tribunals becomes prominent in this conception. And on the relationship between law and the welfare state, this account transforms it from antagonistic to harmonious. There is a complex story to be told but the important move in the argument is that administrative discretion plays a *positive* rule-of-law role in the same way that police power or judicial power plays a positive rule-of-law role in the classical liberal conception of the rule of law. Every libertarian accepts the need for police powers in order to keep property safe. And every egalitarian should and does accept the need for administrative discretion (and judicial discretion) to prevent and address concentrations of power and exploitation in market and other private relations. Those are explanations *internal* to a theory of the rule of law, because it is likely that the regulatory state is ordinarily less arbitrarily empowered than is the private person who is sought to be regulated. We can accrete to this picture the existence of a densely structured normative framework of legal structuring, democratic and public law accountability, and constitutional principles relating to the separation of powers, including principles of judicial restraint.

Readers may well be concerned that it is implausible to argue that any failure to eliminate non-consensual exploitation is a failure of the rule of law. However, that is not the argument. It is rather that the rule of law requires that such powers be legally regulated. The key claim is that one cannot simply leave the law out of it. Perhaps that seems like a limited achievement, and it is here that the rule of law's limited virtue does find appropriate expression. But the conception is still robust in particular ways. It would reject the older common law rule that an employer has complete and arbitrary discretion to terminate an employment relationship at any time for any reason, and support its abolition.[5] Another example is the failure to provide any legislative framework for dealing with rape or spousal abuse, leaving it to the general criminal law. It would call for a bespoke regime for dealing with sexual offenses and domestic abuse (e.g., the UK's Domestic Abuse Act 2021). The rule of law principle is admittedly a demand for good faith rather than just any legal regulation, but that does not mean that any failure of that regulation to eliminate the exploitation or coercion is a failure of the rule of law. The proper object of the rule of law demand is the existence of an appropriate scheme of regulation, rather than the substantive justifiability of every measure within it.

Human Rights and Democracy Reconsidered

We can here consider again the claim set out in substantive conceptions of the rule of law, that the rule of law requires the protection of fundamental rights. In my contention we should read the demand to mean 'adequate *legal* protection' of fundamental rights, and hence that a legal order must provide meaningful legal recourse for those whose rights are violated. On this view, the rule of law does not dictate or micromanage the substance of human rights adjudication, but it does require that there be a legal procedure for raising and taking seriously complaints about them. It does so because human rights interests are a highly sensitive area of power relations where arbitrary public and private power is acutely in play. Hence, a regulatory conception of the rule of law principle can legitimately require a statutory regime of equality law, or a statutory or constitutional bill of rights. That does not entail that every violation of the norms contained within such schemes are violations of the rule of law.

We can lastly observe that the social dimension of the rule of law does not assimilate the whole of good social policy with the rule of law. The state could rather use anti-trust regulation, or confer universal benefits or a basic income that could conceivably eliminate the need for complex legal regulation. In practice, however, all worlds of welfare capitalism have opted for delivering such schemes through complex legal regulation, in the form both of market regulation and in the provision of legally enforceable social security benefits (Esping-Anderson 1990, chap. 2). In addition to labour law, landlord/tenant law, family law, and consumer protection law, all such regimes provide extensive and legally enforceable social security benefits whose function is to allow persons to 'decommodify' themselves in the job market.

A final key question concerns the relationship between democracy and the rule of law, which is complex (Postema 2022, chap. 5). Why should law be the answer to arbitrary power rather than democracy? In my view, democracy and law provide

---

[5] See the *Report of the Royal Commission on Trade Unions and Employers Association (the Donovan Commission)* (Cmnd 3623, 1968), ch IX, and esp 142–143 for the core rationale.

alternative ways of controlling the exercise of arbitrary political power. They are intimately connected insofar as a democratic system cannot function without a legal order giving reliable effect to past collective political decisions or ensuring the executive is held to account for day-to-day administration. And it is hard to conceive of a non-democratic polity in which the rule of law is respected – though an occupying power or democracy on a restricted franchise could conceivably offer it. More importantly, arbitrary power can be accountable both legally and politically. Where the political control of arbitrary power is present and robust (e.g., over a party's manifesto promises to the electorate), the claim to the existence of arbitrary public power is weak, and case for legal control under the rule of law banner thus is also weakened or defeated. This is why I do not think the rule of law (necessarily) entails the judicial review of statutes, and why judicial restraint on democratic grounds is valid (King 2008). But where political accountability is in fact weak, for example, where the issue lacks political salience or where the person or group at issue is distinctly vulnerable to a majoritarian bias or neglect within the system (King 2012, chap. 6), the normative political demand for legal accountability is much firmer.

RECOMMENDED READING

Anderson, E. (2017). *Private Government: How Employers Rule Our Lives (and Why we Don't Talk about It)*, Princeton: Princeton University Press.

Craig, P. (1997). Formal and Substantive Conceptions of the Rule of Law. *Public Law*, 467–487.

Fleming, J. ed. (2011). *Getting to the Rule of Law: NOMOS L*, New York: New York University Press, pp. 64–104.

Fuller, L. L. (1969). *The Morality of Law*, rev. edn, New Haven: Yale University Press.

Krygier, M. (2017). Tempering Power. In M. Adams et al., eds, *Constitutionalism and the Rule of Law: Bridging Ideas and Realism*. Cambridge: Cambridge University Press, pp. 34–59.

Lovett, F. (2016). *A Republic of Law*, Cambridge: Cambridge University Press.

Meierhenrich, J. & Loughlin, M. eds. (2021). *The Cambridge Companion to the Rule of Law*, Cambridge: Cambridge University Press, pp. 39–67.

Postema, G. (2022). *Law's Rule: The Nature, Value, and Viability of the Rule of Law*, Oxford: Oxford University Press.

Raz, J. (1979b). The Rule of Law and its Virtue. In J. Raz (Ed), *The Authority of Law: Essays in Legal Philosophy*. Oxford: Clarendon Press, pp. 210–229.

Sempill, J. (2018a). Ruler's Sword, Citizen's Shield: The Rule of Law and the Constitution of Power. *Journal of Law & Politics*, 31 (3), 333–415.

Tamanaha, B. (2004). *On the Rule of Law: History, Politics, Theory*, Cambridge: Cambridge University Press.

Waldron, J. (2008–2009). The Concept and the Rule of Law. *Georgia Law Review*, 43 (1), 1–61.

19

Constitutional Conventions

Jon Elster

INTRODUCTION

The scholarly debate on constitutional conventions deals almost exclusively with the United Kingdom and other Westminster systems in the British Commonwealth, including provincial systems[1]. The present paper includes other democracies (the United States, Norway, contemporary France) and one non-democratic system (the French *ancien régime*). Including the last reflects my stipulative decision to include the unwritten political norms in non-democratic regimes among constitutional conventions. At this stage I shall not try to characterize them, except to say that Constitutional Conventions (CC) are *political norms that have causal efficacy but are not judicially enforceable*. The main aim of the article is to identify the sources of this efficacy.

My interest is positive or explanatory, to discuss how CCs arise and evolve and the mechanisms by which they influence decision-makers. By and large, I shall assume that they are not made intentionally, but grow "as do lilies in the field," an expression that has been applied to medieval institutions as distinct from modern, planned statecraft (Knorr 1944, p. 24). It follows that CCs "have no unifying feature and so form merely a 'discrete unconnected set'" (Munro 1975, pp. 232–233). They have no "official hierarchy" (Barry and Miragliotta 2015, p. 206) that would allow one convention to trump another.

The claim that CCs *emerge* but are *not made* requires modification. Perry and Tucker (2018) argue for the existence of "top-down" CC, while also arguing that they are parasitic (my word) on the bottom-up variety. The recent tendency in Westminster systems to codify and sometimes modify CCs by issuing Cabinet Manuals (Blick 2012) illustrates the point. I shall mostly ignore this development, not because it is unimportant, but because it is shrouded in a cloud of conceptual

---

[1] The present paper is a highly revised version of Elster 2007, informed by the publication of Galligan and Brenton, eds. (2015) as well as by several other recent papers and by some older papers that had not come to my attention at the time, notably Morton (1991–92). I am indebted to Fredrik Sejersted for comments on an earlier version of the present paper. Unless otherwise noted, italics are mine.

uncertainty (see for instance Aroney 2015, p. 32). Although a similar cloud surrounds bottom-up CCs, whose very existence may sometimes be questioned, they have a more robust status.

In what follows I draw on examples of CCs in Westminster systems, the United States, Norway, contemporary France, and the *ancien régime*, to discuss the characterization, existence, emergence, and modus operandi of CCs.[2]

I CHARACTERIZING CCs

I start with some general observations about CCs. Consider first their subject matter. With virtually no exception, they regulate the "machinery of government," that is, the relation between the main branches of the government, their prerogatives, and the limitations on their powers. None of them address issues of individual rights.

In countries that have both a written constitution and CCs, the latter fall in three groups. Some turn clauses of the written constitution into dead letters, notably in Westminster countries with a written constitution where clauses that allocate powers to the governor-general or the upper house have largely fallen into disuse. The abdication by the American Congress of the right to regulate the jurisdiction of the Supreme Court also falls in this category. A second group are prima facie violations of clauses of the written constitution. Examples include voting by proxy and the amendment of the constitution by referendum in the Fifth French Republic. The largest category is made up of freestanding CCs that neither muzzle nor violate clauses of the written constitution.

We can also classify CCs with regard to federalism, separation of powers, and checks and balances. Federalism is at stake in the Canadian CCs that regulate representation of the provinces in the Cabinet and in the Supreme Court. Separation of powers is at stake in the CC that the British Cabinet cannot instruct the Attorney General, and in the CC that Congress cannot use its power to limit the jurisdiction of the Supreme Court. Checks and balances are at stake in the Canadian CC that the committee overseeing public accounts is chaired by a member of the opposition, in analogous CCs in Norway and France, and in the CC that the American Congress cannot "pack the court."

The *modal* nature of CC has been subject to controversy. On one view, they always operate by creating *obligations* to act or to refrain from acting. On another

---

[2] I shall not address, except in passing, an issue not much discussed in literature: the *disappearance* of a CC (as distinct from the discovery of its non-existence, as took place in Iceland in 2013). Although the loss of prerogative powers through desuetude (Jaconelli 2005, p. 154, note 18) may seem to be an example, the CC may just be dormant rather than dead (Perry and Tucker 2018, p. 783). It may be premature to assert that the decision by the Supreme Court on September 24, 2019 declaring unlawful the prorogation of Parliament by royal prerogative, on the advice of the Prime Minister, caused this CC to disappear.

view, they may also confer *entitlements* to act (Marshall 1986, pp. 7–8). The CC that entitled deputies of the Fifth French Republic to vote by proxy falls in the latter category, as does the CC allowing the constitution of the Fifth Republic to be changed by referendum. In Norway, it has been debated whether parliament under certain conditions has a right or a duty to initiate impeachments and a right or a duty to review the protocols of cabinet meetings.

For the UK, Jaconelli (2005, p. 19) argues that some alleged "entitlement-conferring" CCs are better seen as reflecting the fact that CCs typically allow for exceptions. "As an instance of [entitlement-conferring conventions] he refers to the point that the Monarch is entitled, in certain circumstances, to reject a request of the Prime Minister that Parliament be dissolved. But this situation may be more neatly categorized as an *exception* to the convention that the Queen is to exercise her legal powers on ministerial advice." Along similar lines, he asks whether the American convention against a third-term presidency was "one which limited the President to two terms in *all* circumstances" or "a rule that applied only in relatively limited settings, being inapplicable in times of economic stress and with rumours of war abroad" (Jaconelli 1999, p. 33). CCs may have different "degrees of bindingness" (Heard 1989) that affect their causal efficacy.

The static and dynamic relations among statutes, written constitutions, and CCs vary. They can both *trump* each other and *replace* each other.

Consider first relations at a given point in time. In the UK, an explicit statute (almost) always trumps a CC, since the sovereignty of parliament knows (virtually) no limits. In such cases, the violation of the CC may show that it is already dead (Morton 1991–92, p. 138). If a country has a written constitution, it trumps statute by definition. Even if (as in France before 1974) the constitution does not provide judicial review to override the statute, its priority may be enforced by *higher-order CCs*, "maxims of political morality" (Dicey 1915, p. 70) or "moral and political sanctions" (*ibid*., p. 87). As shown by the Fifth French Republic, a CC may trump the written constitution. A CC may also *circumvent* the written constitution without violating it. In the United States, a CC emerged to elect senators by direct popular vote even before the constitution was amended to this effect, when state legislators were chosen with a view to whom they would elect to the Senate (Horwill 1925, p. 204; Bryce 1995, pp. 90–91). In addition, a CC may block *excessively frequent* changes of the constitution (Andenæs 2003, p. 14).

There is similar variation in the dynamic relations. A CC can be replaced by statute, as happened in 1986 when the New Zealand CC that only persons who hold seats in parliament could be ministers was enacted as statute (Blick 2015, p. 255). A CC can also be replaced by a constitutional amendment, as happened when the United States enacted the 22nd amendment to replace the two-term presidency CC after Roosevelt violated it. In the United States, replacement of statute by a constitutional amendment occurred in 1919 when advocates of prohibition used the constitution to entrench the ban (Horwill 1925, p. 15).

II THE EXISTENCE OF CCs

There is general agreement that the *existence* of a CC is closely linked to a widespread *belief* in its existence. Some actors will *refrain from violating* a CC only if they believe it exists. Others will *sanction violations* of a CC only if they believe it exists. "If one key actor feels not bound by what others regard as the rule, the convention ceases to do its work, and in fact ceases to exist" (Russell 2015, p. 240).

Consider the seemingly paradoxical decision by the Canadian Supreme Court in the Patriation case. When only six out of nine judges said that the CC in question existed, doesn't that prove that it didn't? And what if it had been a five to four decision? The case is inconclusive, however, since the judges were not *actors* – neither *violators* not potential *sanctioners of violations*, two groups that presumably make up Russell's category of "key actors." If both sets of actors believe that the CC exists, it does. If neither believes that the CC doesn't exist, it doesn't. What if one of them does but the other doesn't? For more than a century, American Presidents acted on the belief that there existed a CC requiring them to address Congress in writing rather than orally. When Woodrow Wilson showed up in person in 1920, nobody objected. As the belief in the CC had *guided the behavior* of his predecessors, I nevertheless conclude that it existed in their time. The statement that *"breaches […] provide the acid test of the efficacy of the [CC]"* (Morton 1991–92, p. 139) ignores the fact that *false beliefs can have causal efficacy*.

Conversely, if potential sanctioners believe in the existence of a CC but potential violators don't, the latter may violate it and discover that they were wrong. However, they also may not. Suppose that all potential sanctioners – the voters, for instance – *share the belief* in the existence of a CC, but that *the sharing itself is not shared*. In an extreme case, each voter may believe that she is the only one to believe in the existence of the CC (pluralistic ignorance). If it is violated, she may not be motivated to seek out fellow citizens to march in the streets. The violators will feel confirmed in their belief that the CC did not exist, or, if they never considered the issue, persist in ignoring it.

One "acid test" for the existence of a CC, then, is the fact that potential violators *abstain from violating it* because they *believe* that doing so would trigger sanctions, regardless of the accuracy of the belief. In many cases, it may not be possible to verify the requisite mental states. Yet we know that when Ulysses Grant and Grover Cleveland failed to run for a third presidential term, it was because they or their entourage had internalized the two-term CC (Jaconelli 1999, 32 note 22). Also, some incumbent governments clearly pull their punches because of a caretaker CC. "For example, in New Zealand restraints have tended to be applied from approximately three months before the general election is due" (Menzies and Tiernan 2015, p. 100).

Another acid test is when *a violation occurs and is sanctioned*. The 27th Amendment to the American Constitution states that "no law, varying the compensation for the services of the Senators and Representatives, shall take effect, until an election of Representatives shall have intervened." A CC to the same effect existed long before the passage of the amendment: there was such a high "degree of citizen indignation when legislators voted themselves a pay increase in 1816 that almost two thirds of them failed to return to Capitol Hill after the next election" (Young 1986, p. 59). The 1993 Canadian election involved "the signing of a contract to privatize the Pearson airport. If signed, it would bind future governments to a fifty-seven-year lease. [...] The signing of the contract was an obvious breach of the caretaker [CC] [...] Public unease regarding signing of the contract likely contributed to the significant defeat the Progressive Conservative party faced [which lost all but 2 of 156 seats] at the election" (Menzies and Tiernan 2015, pp. 104–105).[3]

III THE EMERGENCE OF CCs

Written constitutions are *made*; unwritten CCs *evolve* or *emerge*. It is hard to quarrel with the first part of this conventional wisdom, but the second requires some elaboration.

It is commonly asserted that CCs are created by *precedents*. In some cases, this process will be "the gradual hardening of usages over a period of time" (Morton 1991–92, pp. 125–126). For an illustration, consider the seating arrangements at a scientific conference. On the first day, the participants seat themselves more or less at random. On the second day, the arrangements of the first day emerge as a convention that facilitates the allocation of seats. On the third day, the convention has hardened into a feeling of entitlement and a sense of obligation to respect it on the part of others. If a newcomer tries to take "my" seat, I feel a pang of irritation (Isaac, Mathieu and Zajac 1991, p. 342). Seating arrangements in assemblies can generate similar feelings of entitlement and obligation. One might think that they do not qualify as CCs, as they belong to *customs* that have no intrinsic political importance (Banfield 2015, p. 190). In some cases, however, seating conventions do have political implications (Bailly 1804, vol. 1, p. 330: Aulard 1882, p. 60; Nethercote 2015, pp. 150–151).

---

[3] These two acid tests rely on *actual* decisions: decisions to abstain from violating a perceived CC and decisions to violate a CC, followed by sanctions. Could one show the existence of a CC by referring to *counterfactual* decisions? Suppose that a certain behavior falls outside written as well as unwritten norms, because nobody has practiced or even envisaged it. One might still argue that there is and always has been a CC against it if at any given time in the past a violation, had it occurred, *would have been* sanctioned. The disposition to react might be "latent or subconscious but *would be activated* if [the politicians] were confronted by a situation involving the choice of whether to act consistently or inconsistently with the convention, or another's choice to act inconsistently" (Sampford 1987, p. 376). Arguably, political life has many invisible CCs of this kind. The "spirit of the constitution" might prevent certain proposals from even coming to anyone's mind. As an example, "a Prime Minister [of Canada] must not recommend him or herself to be appointed Governor General" (Heard 1991, p. 12). Although no substantial issues are involved, I prefer actual decisions as criteria for the existence of CCs.

More central cases of gradual evolution include the following. In the first edition of *The American Commonwealth* Bryce (1888, p. 519), doubted there was a CC obligating the House of Lords to accept a bill passed by the Commons in two successive parliaments; two decades later Horwill (1908, p. 100) asserted that there was. Later, Bryce (1915, p. 350) moderated his statement. In Great Britain, "the conventional nature of cabinet [...] emerged slowly as the monarch ceased to turn up to meetings of his key council and as ministers became more answerable to the parliament than to the King" (Weller 2015, p. 73). Ivor Jennings (1963, p. 101) claimed to observe a CC in statu nascendi – "an administrative practice slowly changing into a convention" – viz. that "in framing social legislation the appropriate department must consult the appropriate outside 'interests'." In the United States, "Congress slowly created a convention against using impeachment for purely political reasons" (Wilson 1992, p. 700). Although it may be "impossible to fix precisely the date at which the [American] Electors ceased to exercise an independent judgment" (Horwill 1925, p. 46), the emergence of this CC was an inevitable consequence of the rise of political parties.

More generally, and more intangibly, in Westminster systems the secular trend toward democratic and popular government has created CCs depriving the monarch (or the governors-general) and the House of Lords (and other upper houses) of their veto power over legislation. This gradual process, which can be compared to the incremental extensions of the suffrage, did not depend on the accumulation of precedents but on the broader extra-parliamentary balance of social forces. The details of the emergence and evolution of these CCs depend on context and accident, but the overall development of Western political systems – whether written or unwritten – leaves no doubt that they were embedded in a larger social context. As Phillipson (2019) observes, there is a sharp contrast between the democratic *substance* of many CCs and the non-democratic *process* that led to their adoption. He writes, for instance, that "What we know as the famous Salisbury-Addison convention (that the Lords will not oppose 'manifesto Bills') came about as a result of an agreement between two unelected peers." Perhaps they saw the writing on the wall and wanted to defuse the class struggle and prevent social unrest?

In some cases, we can identify specific events that, in retrospect, appear to have created a CC. The no-third-term presidency CC can be traced back to Washington's refusal to stand for a third term – for who could imagine themselves superior to him?[4] The British CC that if a government is defeated in an election, it should resign immediately rather than wait for the meeting of Parliament arose when Disraeli resigned after his defeat in 1868. The CC of senatorial courtesy can be traced back to successful objections by the two senators from Georgia to a nomination by Washington to a confirmable post in that state (Horwill 1925, p. 128). The British CC that the Cabinet

---

[4] It might not have taken hold, however, but for the similar refusals of Jefferson in 1808 and Jackson in 1836 (Horwill 1925, p. 128).

cannot instruct the Attorney General dates from 1924, when MacDonald's government was defeated after the Attorney General had withdrawn a criminal prosecution after the Prime Minister intervened (Marshall 1986, p. 113).

None of these events involved an *intentional* attempt to create a CC. In recent times, however, "the [...] emergence of the Sewel convention in the United Kingdom, which requires that Westminster 'will not normally legislate with regard to devolved matters except with the agreement of the devolved legislature', supports [the] idea of a deliberately created convention" (Aroney 2015, p. 32; see also Hazell 2015, p. 174 on the "instant creation" of this CC). In such cases, it remains to be seen if the convention *sticks*. The adoption of a law and the declaration of a convention differ in that non-compliance with the former does not destroy it. A case in which non-compliance with the latter did destroy it was the failure of an attempt to change "the role of the [Canadian] Senate by changing the conventions surrounding appointments [by pledging 'to appoint as senators those who had been elected by special elections held in those provinces that agreed to hold such elections'] rather than through constitutional change. Unfortunately, there was no suggestion that [Prime Minister] Harper was interested in a bipartisan Senate" (Sharman 2015, pp. 168–169).

The role of elections and referenda in sustaining, creating or destroying CCs is complex, since a vote for or against a given proposal can often be interpreted in several ways. After the French referendum in 1962 on direct election of the president, the positive vote was interpreted in three ways: as an approval of direct election, as an approval of amending the constitution by referendum, and as an expression of confidence in de Gaulle. Conversely, when the 1969 referendum on reform of the Senate resulted in 52% negative votes, it not only implied the defeat of the proposal and de Gaulle's instant retirement from office, but was also seen by some as "neutralizing" the precedent that had been created in 1962. Although to my knowledge there is no evidence that any No-voters were in fact motivated by the constitutional issue, some have interpreted the vote as a *referendum on referendums*. The case is not unique. In 1975, the Australian Labor government had a majority in the lower House, while the Liberals and their allies from the Country Party had a majority in the Senate. When the Senate delayed its vote on supply, the Governor General called for elections, which resulted in a Liberal landslide. Again, the outcome could be interpreted in more than one way.

Hume observed that voters may not *care* that much about procedural matters (Hume 1983, p. 482). In a systematic analysis, with many examples, Schauer (2009–10, p. 795), writes that "if the suspicions about the less-than-often-assumed effect of law on official decisions that I have offered in this Article are sound, then officials who correctly assess public support for their actions on first-order moral, political, policy, and prudential grounds will rarely suffer if those publicly supported first-order decisions happen to violate the law." I return to the question in the next Section.[5]

---

[5] One may speculate about how a counterfactual event might have created or blocked a CC. It has been argued, for example, that if the impeachment of President Andrew Johnson had led to a conviction, as

I want to warn, finally, against *functionalist explanations* of the emergence of CCs. According to Blick (2015, p. 259), "if experiments in the codification and enforcement of conventions become too successful, it might prove necessary to evolve [sic] another set of tacit, more malleable conventions, the observance of which would depend on self-restraint more than formal external mechanisms, for the system to function satisfactorily." Yet needs do not create their own satisfaction. If they did, Rome would have developed a Salic Law.

IV THE CAUSAL EFFICACY OF CCs

One can distinguish four ways in which CCs affect the behavior of politicians, officials, and voters.

(1) *CCs as coordination equilibria*. The feature of games with a coordination equilibrium is that (unlike games with a cooperation equilibrium) no actor has an incentive to deviate unilaterally from the strategy that is best for all if chosen by all. Consider a standard example of a convention in the sense of David Lewis (1969), the rule that when a telephone conversation is interrupted for some reason, the one who made the call in the first place should call up again. Although there are other conventions that could serve the same purpose – preventing that both or neither call up again – this one stands out on efficiency grounds, since it is more likely that the person who first called up knows which number to call.

The Salic law is a Lewisian convention. Abstractly speaking, there are several rules that might serve to decide what happens upon the death of a monarch. One might use the Salic law, or allow for male succession through the female line, or allow for female succession. Each of these procedures is as good as the others, just as driving on the left hand of the road is as acceptable as driving on the right. What matters is that there is a consensus on one of them. On the road, lack of consensus may create a collision; in politics, it may create civil war. In Lewis's telephone example, one convention emerged because it was more efficient than the alternatives. In the choice among laws of succession, one of them is singled out because it is the status quo. All expect and expect others to expect that the Salic rule will continue to be used, because, as Pascal wrote, "Civil war is the greatest of evils."

On one occasion this argument probably influenced the choice between royal pretenders. When Napoleon was about to capitulate before the Allied (English, Austrian, Russian, and Prussian) forces in March 1814, the nature of the successor

---

it failed to do by one vote, the United States would have turned into a parliamentary regime where the president could be deposed on political grounds (Schlesinger 1973, pp. 74–5). Another counterfactual is that if 2 % of the voters in the 1962 French referendum had switched from Yes to No, leaving the sum of negative votes and abstentions superior to the positive votes, de Gaulle would have left office and the use of referendum would not have set a precedent for a CC (Vedel 1985, p. 163). In these cases, a small change might have tipped the constitutional balance.

regime was wide open. Tsar Alexander strongly opposed the return of the Bourbons. Wellington was discreetly in favor of this option, but did not press it. Other options included the regency of the Empress Marie-Louise and conferring the throne to Bernadotte or to the Duc d'Orléans. In the end, Talleyrand served as a kingmaker, when he persuaded Alexander that only a restoration of the monarchy had the focal-point quality necessary for a stable regime. As Talleyrand (1967, vol. 2, p. 165) wrote in his *Memoirs*, "An imposed King would be the result of force or intrigue; either would be insufficient. To establish a durable system that will be accepted without opposition, one must act on a principle. […] And *there is only one principle*: Louis XVIII is a principle, he is the legitimate King of France."[6]

(2) *CCs as cooperation equilibria*. I now turn to CC as cooperation equilibria, which can emerge when political actors have the occasion to interact over some period of time and are restrained from deviating from the mutually beneficial strategy by fear of subsequent defection by others. An example from Hume (1978, pp. 520–521) shows the difficulty:

> Your corn is ripe [in August]; mine will be so [in September]. It is profitable for us both, that I should labour with you [in August], and that you should aid me [in September]. I have no kindness for you, and know you have as little for me. I will not, therefore, take any pains upon your account; and should I labour with you upon my own account, in expectation of a return, I know I should be disappointed, and that I should in vain depend upon your gratitude. Here then I leave you to labour alone: You treat me in the same manner. The seasons change; and both of us lose our harvests for want of mutual confidence and security.

I have substituted "August" and "September" for Hume's "today" and "tomorrow" in order to point to a way out of the predicament of the farmers. I have an incentive to cooperate with you in August 2020, because I know that your desire to receive my cooperation in August 2021 will make you keep your promise to help me in September 2020. For this mechanism to generate cooperation, four conditions have to be satisfied: the first mover cooperates in the initial interaction; the interaction has no known terminal date; the actors do not discount the future heavily; and the reward parameters fall in a given range that does not generate a temptation to defect (Luce and Raiffa 1957, chap. 5).

Applied to the politics of CC, we may distinguish two cases.

In *intra-legislature* (or intra-cabinet) situations, logrolling can induce cooperation. This practice is observed in the American Senate ("Senatorial Courtesy"). "If you help me to get the appointments I want in my state, I will help you get the

---

[6] The principle that "the King can do no wrong" can also be understood as a coordination equilibrium. Although partly rooted in an older tradition, a more important source was "the pragmatic experience that royal responsibility was *liable to cause successor struggles and civil war* […] and the recognition that 'the remedy would be worse than the disease'. The irresponsibility of the King was above all a stabilizing mechanism in society" (Sejersted 2002, p. 172).

appointments you want in your state" (Horwill 1925, pp. 128–129; see also Gerhardt 2000, pp. 64, 143–144). In the British Cabinet, "Measures low in controversy may be settled by bilateral discussions between two ministries, with the object of producing an agreement that will be formally ratified by the Cabinet. Ministers who have not been involved in negotiations prefer to let recommendations pass without question, in the expectation that their bargains will similarly be approved when they appear on the cabinet agenda" (Turpin 2002, p. 229). The practice of *pairing* also falls in this category.

The last example can serve to illustrate the fragility of cooperation equilibria. In Canada, "sometimes the temptation to catch the other side off-guard is too strong. A notorious example occurred in the 1926 vote of no-confidence, where the single vote from a broken pair tipped the balance to bring own the short-lived Meighen government" (Heard 1991, p. 79). An article in *The Economist* from 18 Dec 2018 deplores the weakening of the unwritten norms that have guided British politics for a long time, and cites as one of many examples the breakdown of pairing arrangements. In 2018 a Tory MP voted even though his Lib Dem "pair" was on maternity leave.

When a cooperation equilibrium is broken by the government, the opposition can adopt the same behavior if it comes to power in the next legislature (see below). Alternatively, the current legislature may censor the government. In Great Britain, Australia and Canada, the government abstains from using its legal powers to reap the "spoils of office," sharing at least some of them, such as membership or chairmanship of parliamentary committees, with the opposition. When two members of the opposition in the British parliament "were excluded [from their committees] seemingly for the vigour with which they had performed their function of scrutiny, the House of Commons delivered a rare cross-party rebuke to government in voting to restore the two members to their places on the committees" (Turpin 2002, p. 486).

Inter-legislature cases arise from alternations in power. The formal structure of this case differs from the previous one, since in each legislature only one actor – the governing party – has a choice to make, for example, whether or not to respect the debts incurred by its predecessor. The temptation to "defect" (go for short-term gain) may then be restrained by the thought, "What we do to them today, they may and probably will do to us if they accede to power in the next legislature." Again, the reward parameters as well as the rate of time discounting will determine whether a cooperative equilibrium exists. Moreover, as I discuss below, the choice by the government may also affect the likelihood of an alternation in power.

This is an age-old idea in elective political systems.[7] Among recent cases, I first cite an episode from 1926, when the Norwegian parliament was discussing whether

---

[7] The first case I've come across dates from 1565, and involves a conflict between Protestants and Catholics in Lyon during the wars of religion: "The accounting of the disastrous financial inheritance

to impeach former Prime Minister Berge. Members of his government argued that he had not been able to consult with parliament because he did not know whether the deputies from the Labor party could be trusted. "This provoked the majority in the protocol committee so strongly that it was used as a main argument for impeachment: 'This reasoning leads us beyond the limits of the existing constitutional system. This time it was a 'bourgeois' government that did not trust parliament because it included representatives for the labor party. If a labor government were to be formed, as we have seen in Sweden, Denmark and England, *that* government might not trust the *bourgeois* representatives. The majority believes that it is the duty of [the lower house] to make it impossible to draw this consequence for the future.'" (Sejersted 2002, p. 246). The CC in question is the norm that the government must provide information to all parties impartially. It was violated in 1948, when the Communists were excluded from a committee on security matters (*ibid.*, p. 252), certainly because they were not seen as trustworthy, but perhaps also because there was no risk that they would ever form the government in the future.

Consider now the CC that governments should not open the papers of their predecessors (Hylland 2007). A plausible reason for this convention is that "a Minister who wants to be protected in the future would see to it that former Ministers are likewise protected" (Cooray 1979, p. 73; also Jaconelli 2005, p. 172, note 80). To explore this argument, we may assume that the objective function of government includes its own reelection as well as the general interest. The two are intertwined, since economic growth, for example, can enhance the prospects of reelection. Yet the public interest can also serve as an end in itself, as shown by the fact that some governments are committed to the reduction of global warming, despite the lack of any electoral payoff. The government can also try to ensure reelection by spreading false or true rumors about the opposition, playing dirty tricks of various kinds, and so on. At the same time, the government may deliberately refrain from using such tactics, out of concern for the general interest. During the presidential campaign of 1965, de Gaulle's advisors suggested he use the incriminating past of his opponent, François Mitterand, against him. In spite of his personal animosity towards Mitterand, de Gaulle refused to use these tactics. "One must not do anything that would damage the presidency, if he should one day come to occupy it" (Peyrefitte

---

from the war years divided the city council, with the Catholics refusing to assume the debts contracted during the troubles by the council at the time, which was Protestant. The Protestant council members who were still in place, notably Pierre Sève, contested this disavowal and reminded the council 'that one has never had the custom of disavowing the officials' and that one risked creating a dangerous precedent which would be contrary to the interests of the city as a juridical person and as a political body: '*if we start disavowing our predecessors, the same could happen to us*' warned Pierre Sève in the session of July 10 1565" (Christin 1997, pp. 117–18). This restraint was not opportunistic behavior on Sève's part, since in the session on July 19 he abstained from using the politics of the empty chair to paralyze the council. "In both cases, he put the institutional and juridical continuity of the city ahead of confessional discord" (*ibid.*, p. 120).

1997, p. 75). Also, if the government expects that the opening of the archives at time t will lead its successor to open its archives at some time t + n, it has an incentive to commit as little as possible to paper and rely instead on oral communications and "walks in the park," to the detriment of good policy making. At the same time, its reelection prospect may benefit.

The determination of which party shall form the government in period t +1 is obviously endogenous, depending in part on the actions taken by the government in period t. Thus, if the government in period t decides to open the archives of its predecessor (currently in the minority), it may discover unsavory facts about the opponent that can help it win the next election. If its decision to open the archives becomes public knowledge, however, it may suffer the "blame and shame" from violating a convention. The government may also be deterred from opening the archives if (as suggested earlier) this action would have a negative impact on efficiency and if efficiency affects the chances of reelection. Although it is difficult to model these more complicated effects, I conjecture that the self-limitations we observe can, to some extent, be attributed to the thought that "If we do this to them, they will do this to us."

In the United States, the reason why Congress abstains from using its power to limit the jurisdiction of the Supreme Court may be that "once one political faction uses certain means that threaten judicial independence, *other factions will be more willing to use those devices in the future*. The long-term stability of the system, including the doctrine of separation of powers, is undermined by such unconventional tactics" (Wilson 1992, p. 693). This line of reasoning suggests that even if it has the requisite majority, one party in Congress will not pass "a statute preventing all federal courts, including the Supreme Court, from reviewing a congressional statute outlawing the burning of the American flag" (*ibid.*, p. 689), fearing a tit-for-tat if the other party were to come into power. In other cases, such as a Republican majority not using its power to prevent the court from reviewing anti-abortion legislation in the states, it may abstain out of fear of defeat at the polls.

Before turning to this mechanism, I shall exhibit two examples of the *breakdown* of CCs based on tit-for-tat. The Detainee Training Act of 2005, was aimed at stripping federal courts of jurisdiction to consider habeas corpus petitions filed by prisoners in Guantanamo. Congress had never tried to use this power, and even then the attempt failed (Calabresi and Lawson 2007). In Australia, there is a CC limiting the access of a government to the papers of its predecessors. "Access to those records requires the approval of the leader of the party that had held government. That was the 'rule'. But in 2014 the Australian government released some cabinet records of its predecessor to a royal commission without asking approval. There was nothing the former government could do to prevent it" (Weller 2015, p. 87).

(3) *CCs maintained by fear of sanctions*. Bentham (1999, p. 149) saw "the grand antiseptic effect of publicity" as the main control on deputies, operating through the "dread of shame" and, more important, "the fear of being removed in an assembly liable to change" (*ibid.*, p. 30). Although Bentham did not explicitly refer to pressure

to conform to unwritten norms, Dicey (1915, p. cxlii note 15) took a step in that direction. In addition to his (almost universally rejected) idea that some CCs are maintained because they "could not be violated without bringing a stop to the course of orderly and pacific government," he asserts that "others might be violated without any other consequence than that of exposing the Minister or other person by whom they were broken to *blame or unpopularity*" (*ibid.*). Marshall (1986, p. 17), finally, is fully explicit: The "remedy for alleged convention-breaking is generally recognized to be, in the main, political. *Either* the government can be shamed by publicity and political debate into conceding error or changing its course of action, *or* its misdeeds can be made the subject of argument at the next General Election."

This argument is not inconsistent with the one set out in (2). In Hume's example, a farmer who fails to reciprocate the assistance of another might be ostracized by his neighbors. Similarly, a government that opens the papers of its predecessors because it is not sensitive to "the shadow of the future" might be punished by the voters. The argument is also consistent with the one set out in (1). Although the coordination equilibrium of driving on the left side of the road is basically sustained by self-interest, it can be reinforced by social norms that make other drivers express their disapproval of those who move into the other lane to get ahead. The principle that the King can do no wrong is reinforced by the cult of royalty that grows up around it and the punishments meted out to detractors.[8]

In a passage written much later than the one just cited, Bentham (1990, p. 63) also suggests that by losing the estimation of the Public Tribunal an offender might "be deprived [...] of their good offices and upon occasion even be exposed to [...] positive ill offices at their hand." That is, a *revolution* no less than non-reelection can serve as a sanction on the violation of a CC. In a given situation, "the country would [...] enforce the morality of the constitution by placing before any Minister who defied its precepts the alternative of resignation or revolution" (Dicey 1915, p. 302). Pincus (2009, p. 17) cites a pamphleteer (with whom he disagrees) who wrote that the principle of the Glorious Revolution was to destroy a "mad bigot" who violated the ancient constitution and that there was "no evidence to suggest that the revolutionaries had any intention of increasing the power of the people."

Violations of a CC can cause popular sanctions at the urns, as in the United States in 1816, in Canada in 1993, and more controversially in France in 1969. In a few cases, violations may have caused physical violence. When Theodore Roosevelt stood for a third term after a split in the Republican Party, which had failed to nominate him, feelings ran high. "While on one of his speech-making tours, Mr. Roosevelt was shot at by a man of unbalanced mind, who said: 'I shot Theodore Roosevelt because he was a menace to the country. He should not have a third term. I shot him as a warning that men must not try to have more than two terms as

---

[8] Strictly speaking, punishments are not required. The *mere knowledge that others disapprove*, or might disapprove, of what one is doing can affect behavior (Dana, Cain, and Dawes 2006).

President.'" (Horwell 1925, p. 95). In the sixteenth and seventeenth-century France, it was sometimes argued that regicide was admissible against kings who violated the fundamental laws of the kingdom (Jouanna 1998, pp. 217–218).

Conversely, *fear of sanctions can prevent violations*. Banfield (2015, p. 191) writes that "no [Canadian] prime minister who wished to be reelected would consider using the power [to disallow provincial legislation]." In New Zealand, "[t]he driving force for both continuity and change [of CCs] has ultimately been the political parties' fear of voters' displeasure at the ballot box" (Duncan 2015, p. 219; see also pp. 223, 225). In a more general statement, Blick (2012, pp. 197–198) writes that "[f]or those directly involved in working the constitution […], a judgement of what is the prevailing public interpretation – or to put it in another way, *what can and cannot be got away with* – is likely to be important." In the United States, fear of physical violence rather than electoral defeat may have deterred violations of the CC that all members of a state delegation to the Electoral College vote for the candidate who received most votes in their state.[9]

On two occasions, in 1972 and in 1994, the Norwegian parliament acted on a CC to the effect that it had to respect the outcome of a referendum, even though it was only a consultative one. Before Iceland held a similarly consultative referendum on a draft constitution in 2011, the author predicted on Icelandic TV that if the people approved the draft, parliament would feel obliged by a similar CC to approve it too. He was proven wrong: the draft was approved by a large popular majority, but parliament shelved it (see Elster 2016 for details). Since there was no popular outcry or electoral consequences for the deputies, we can infer that the CC did not exist. Politicians acted as if it did not, and the people did not care very much.

(4) *CCs as self-denying ordinances*. While acknowledging that violations of a CC can trigger sanctions, Morton (1991–92, p. 141) argues that these are essentially epiphenomena:

> [T]he unconstitutional act, the failure to comply with conventions, will quite naturally be regarded as undermining or eroding a commitment to a basic set of ideals; as weakening the foundations of a non-partisan value system. In view of the profound respect in which the principles of democratic legitimacy are held, it is entirely predictable that acts which are perceived to undermine them […] will

---

[9] "There has been no instance within living memory of any failure to obey the party's behest, but everyone is agreed that, if such a thing happened, the culprit, however technically innocent of any violation of the law, would suffer severe penalties. According to Professor J. A. Woodburn, any Presidential Elector who voted independently for a candidate of his own choice 'would probably not find it comfortable to return home.' He 'would be ostracized and despised and would be visited with the social condemnation and contempt due to one who had been guilty of an infamous betrayal of public trust; and a Presidential candidate elected by such betrayal would probably not accept the office.' Benjamin Harrison, indeed, goes so far as to predict that 'an Elector who failed to vote for the nominee of his party would be the object of execration, and in times of very high excitement might be the subject of a lynching'" (Horwill 1925, pp. 37–8).

generate serious corrective action. [...] *But it would be wrong to suppose that it is these 'political sanctions' which provide the explanation of the normative force of conventions.*

Other authors also argue that some CCs owe their existence to their democratic legitimacy, referring to them as *self-denying ordinances*. According to Hazell (2015, p. 174),

"In all cases conventions [in the United Kingdom] are a *code of self-restraint*: about not exercising powers to the full, not abusing power and respecting the constitutional role and functions of the other branches of government." So to take just four examples ..., there are conventions limiting the Monarch's choice of prime minister, conventions restraining the prime minister's power to make war, conventions constraining the Westminster parliament's exercise of its legislative power, and conventions regulating the conduct of the judiciary. In most cases conventions have been developed as a *self-denying ordinance* by one branch of government to *restrain its own behavior.*

Perry and Tucker (2018, p. 778) note that "[I]n 1932 the Treasury and the House of Commons Public Accounts committee agreed that, in general, authority for expenditures ought to flow from a specific statute rather than from an Appropriations Act. In the words of the Constitution committee [of 2012–13], the '1932 concordat amounts to a *self-denying ordinance by the Treasury*', which would be respected 'in the interests of constitutional propriety'." In a discussion of Australian caretaker CCs, Nethercote (2015, p. 141) writes, "Although [conventions are] very much the means by which administrators strive to regulate (restrain) the behavior of incumbent ministers in an election period, inasmuch as they have ministerial authorization, it is as *self-denying ordinances.*" He also argues that the refusal by the leader of the opposition to tolerate refusal of supply by the Senate, which was controlled by the opposition, "could be regarded as a *convention of the self-denying type*, and some have seen it as such; but it *also represents prudence* – oppositions too hungry for office do not readily win, and may quickly lose, the regard of voters" (*ibid.*, p. 146). In this case, self-denial and self-interest suggest the same behavior. In other cases, they don't.[10]

Many explanations in categories (1), (2) and (3) of the modus operandi of CCs rely implicitly on the premise that "the non-justiciable quality of conventions

---

[10] "[T]he most important factor explaining the abolition of Canadian provincial upper houses [...] was the appointed nature of their membership which simultaneously denied any democratic legitimacy to the chambers and made them the object of patronage appointments. It is possible that *a self-denying government might have aimed to create some partisan balance in the chamber*, but the temptation to use a place in the legislative council [the Senate] to *accommodate powerful political interests and to reward partisan benefactors* proved hard to resist. In other words, successive governments had no interest in establishing conventions for appointments that maintained a partisan balance or that furthered the parliamentary function of the upper house" (Sharman 2015, pp. 161–2).

renders their observance dependent on the continuing cooperation and perceptions of *self-interest* of those who command them" (Barry and Miragliotta 2015, p. 205). If the courts can't enforce the CCs, they have to be maintained by the self-interest of the "key actors." This claim is implausible for electoral sanctions of violations. Even if *politicians* may abide by the CC out of a self-interested desire to be reelected, it makes little sense to say that the American *voters* in 1816 or the Canadian ones in 1993 acted in their self-interest when they refused to return politicians because they had violated a CC. The voters punished politicians because they judged their actions to be *wrong*. As for politicians, some are highly principled and others are not, or less so. Some seek to promote the public interest with little regard to their self-interest (understood as including party interest). Even those who are mainly motivated by the latter pay lip-service to the public interest, and in doing so may actually be led to promote it (Elster 2018, p. 212).

For Morton, CCs are justified only by the democratic values that sustain them. What he calls "footpath conventions" do not rise to the level of CCs. "[T]hey may be the result of compromises, ways of getting things done, as agreed methods for avoiding disorder and surmounting obstacles. More importantly, footpath conventions have no democratic pretensions; no necessary links with legitimacy. They can conduce to order and efficiency in repressive regimes as well as in those in which freedom is valued. It is salutary to be reminded that long term systematic corruption in public life notoriously generates its own established practices and understandings" (Morton 1991–92, pp. 126–127). Although there is no quarrel with definitions, I believe the Salic Law did more than "avoiding disorder." It was not a political traffic rule, but a vastly benign superstition.

As noted, Barry and Tucker (2018, p. 782) observe that CCs are not made intentionally. Hence, they argue, "The risk that they will be used to create damaging, self-interested rules is attenuated" (*ibid*.). Moreover, the fact that they are flexible "is important because it is much harder to bind your successors to an undesirable, self-interested rule if you cannot fix the rule in a canonical formulation" (*ibid*.). Conversely, to the extent that CCs are becoming codified in Cabinet Manuals, self-interest gains some purchase. Commenting on executive dominance of the Manual, Blick (2012, p. 203) writes,

> In the UK the lack of a fully codified constitution renders conventions exceptionally important as a means of limiting government. [...] Should the executive be producing a document such as the manual which wields influence [...] over the nature of the constraints on itself, particularly given that in some areas such a text is likely to be partial? [...] There is no reference [in the 2011 Manual] for instance, to a convention some believe to exist that ministers should not publicly criticize judges and particular judicial decisions. [...] Furthermore, it is arguably inappropriate for a document approved by the Cabinet to play a part in determining the procedures for government formation following general elections, since any given Cabinet is an interested party.

In conclusion, CCs can regulate the relations between pretenders to a throne, between political parties, between political institutions, between successive governments, and between politicians and citizens. In all these capacities, they have causal efficacy. They do so by different motivational and cognitive mechanisms that resist easy summary.

RECOMMENDED READING

Avril, P. (1997). *Les conventions de la constitution*, Paris: Presses Universitaires de France.
Blick, A. (2015). Constitutional Reform. In B. Galligan, & S. Brenton, eds., *Constitutional Conventions in Westminster Systems*. Cambridge: Cambridge University Press, pp. 249–260.
Bryce, J. (1915). *The American Commonwealth*, reprint Indiana: Indianapolis: Liberty Fund 1995.
Cooray, L. J. M. (1979). *Conventions. The Australian Constitution and the Future*, Sydney: Legal Books.
Dicey, A. V. (1915). *Introduction to the study of the law of the constitution*, 8th edn., London: Macmillan and Co.
Heard, A. (1989). Recognizing the Variety Among Constitutional Conventions. *Canadian Journal of Political Science*, 22 (1), 63–82.
Luce, R. & Raiffa, H. (1957). *Games and Decisions*, New York: Wiley.
Marshall, G. (1986). *Constitutional Conventions*, Oxford: Oxford University Press.

20

Secularism

Cécile Laborde

A basic idea of church-state separation seems central to the tradition of liberal democratic constitutionalism. At the very least, a liberal democratic state does not rest its political sovereignty on religious authority. Beyond this basic separation, however, it is unclear whether, and which secularism is required by liberal-democratic ideals.

This chapter puts forward the view that liberal democratic states must meet the standards of *minimal secularism*. The three (jointly necessary and sufficient) standards of minimal secularism are: personal liberty, equal inclusion and public justification. Each targets one discrete feature of religion; and there is no need further to separate state and religion, once the standards are met.

Minimal secularism is a distinctive theory of liberal legitimacy, in two ways. First, it is compatible with a plurality of permissible models of state-religion relationships, beyond US- or French-style separation. Second, it does not single out religion as uniquely special, but instead connects liberal legitimacy to discrete features of religion (that are shared with non-religious beliefs and practices). The plural standards of liberal legitimacy require that religion be *disaggregated*.

Minimal secularism fares well in relation to two critiques of, or alternatives to, secularism. First, it is not vulnerable to the claim that secularism is hostile to religion, marked by an ethnocentric legacy of church-state separation, or committed to a Christian, and specifically Protestant conception of religion. Second, it is more structured and precise than theories of state neutrality towards the good. Or so I shall argue.

The chapter is organised as follows. The first section introduces some challenges to secularism; the second develops the neutralist response to them; and the third introduces minimal secularism as a more robust and fuller response.

I SECULARISM AND ITS CRITICS

Preliminary Definition

This chapter focuses on political, not ethical secularism. Ethical secularism denotes a comprehensive worldview, typically an atheistic or anti-religious outlook that defines the goods of human life and flourishing without reference to divine or otherworldly values. Political secularism merely refers to the idea that a principled distance should be maintained between the state and religion (Bhargava 1998).

We find an early intimation of this idea in John Locke. Religion, Locke thought, is about the aspirations to salvation of the individual soul. The state has no authority to shape or control such aspirations: it cannot effectively compel inward belief, nor does it have the competence and wisdom to distinguish true from false belief. The state should, therefore, adopt a policy of toleration of religious beliefs. Its role is limited to the care and protection of 'outward things, such as money, land, houses, furniture, and the like'. In such domains, churches are in turn incompetent, and should not meddle with the business of government. What is 'above all things necessary', Locke famously wrote, is 'to distinguish exactly the business of civil government from that of religion, and to settle the just bounds that lie between the one and the other' (Locke 1991, p. 17. Cf Forst 2017c).

Roughly speaking, the state is a temporal authority, concerned with the provision of temporal goods; and it should leave the management of spiritual affairs to religious institutions, or individuals themselves. Such differentiation is one of the defining features of the secular age (Taylor 2017). In contemporary liberalism, this basic intuition has evolved into what has been called 'two-way protection': protection of religion from the state, and protection of the state from religion (Gutmann 2000, 2003). These two ideas are paradigmatically expressed by the two Religion Clauses of the US First Amendment: the Free Exercise clause, and the Establishment clause.

Empirically, political secularism does not presuppose or require social secularisation. Pervasively religious societies, such as the United States and India, have secular states. Philosophically, political secularism does not take a stance about the truth of religion: it is an answer to the distinctively political question of how to live together in societies marked by a reasonable pluralism of beliefs and worldviews. Political secularism bears affinities to what John Rawls called 'political' liberalism as opposed to 'comprehensive' liberalism (Rawls 1993; Waldron 2004).

Criticisms

Political secularism, briefly sketched here, has been subjected to three chief criticisms.

1 Dogmatic Separation

According to this first charge, advocates of two-way protection often end up advocating strict separation between state and religion. Yet this is a dogmatic view. Two main (mostly empirical) arguments have been presented. First, many existing liberal states have regimes of religious establishment. Institutional separation is an exception rather than the norm worldwide. The First Amendment to the Constitution of the United States, as well as the French *laïcité* laws of 1905, stipulate that the state must neither establish any particular religion nor publicly endorse or support any particular faith. By this definition, however, many liberal democracies would not qualify as secular, since regimes of 'weak' or 'moderate' establishment' remain common, and their liberal credentials are not contestable, including by contrast to openly secular, separationist regimes (Modood 2016). Second, legal and political separation is also the exception rather than the norm. All states are in fact actively involved in defining, regulating and controlling religion. Critics have shown that secular states such as the United States, France and Turkey ride roughshod over any principle of separationism and tightly control or manage religion, often in the name of public order and security (Sullivan 2005; Agrama 2012; Asad 2012; Shakman-Hurd 2015). The very project of separating the temporal authority of the state and the spiritual authority of religious institutions has proved to be, in Stanley Fish's memorable words, 'mission impossible' (Fish 2000).

2 Arbitrary Singling Out

According to the second charge, secularism arbitrarily singles out religion. It subjects religion to a uniquely special, exorbitant system of both protections (religious exemptions from laws) and restraints (ban on state endorsement of religion). Yet it is difficult to see what justifies such an exorbitant regime in contemporary pluralistic societies. First, the uniquely special protection of religion is not warranted. There is nothing special about religious beliefs, such that they deserve special exemptions from general laws (Barry 2001; Nickel 2005; Leiter 2013; Dworkin 2013). Whatever feature is singled out as protection-worthy (conscience, depth of commitment, cultural tradition) can be found in other identities, beliefs and commitments. Furthermore, whatever feature is singled out, it is not clear why it deserves special protection under conditions of ethical pluralism. Second, the uniquely special containment of religion is not warranted either. While anti-religion sceptics worry about the special protection of religion under free exercise, pro-religion advocates worry about the special containment of religion under the establishment clause (and similar provisions in western constitutions). Why single out religion as particularly problematic, while making no special provision against state endorsement of secular ideologies such as atheism, libertarianism, or nationalism?

3 Protestantised Religion

This critique shifts attention to the conception of religion that secularism relies upon. First, it conceives religion mostly as an expression of belief. The problem here is that, as a result, secular law is biased towards individualistic, belief-based religions. Religious rituals and practices were seen by Locke to require merely bodily acts, and therefore, as not essential to religion. Religion is supposed to be about mind, belief and thought, rather than constituting an activity in the world. Religion, on this modern Protestant reading, is private, voluntary, individual, textual, about obligation, and about belief (Sandel 1998; Asad 2012; Mahmood 2005, 2009; Shakman Hurd 2015;

Spinner-Halev 2005; Sullivan 2005; Sullivan, Hurd, Mahmood, & Danchin, 2015; White 1998). As Saba Mahmood and others have shown, however, a great deal of religious practice – ritual observance, dietary habits, dress and bodily behaviour – are not best described through the Protestant categories of belief, sincerity, or choice (Mahmood 2005). In Judaism, Islam, Hinduism, aboriginal religions, as well as many forms of Christianity, practices and community are more important than belief and individuality. Second, secularism construes religion as its dangerous, absolutist, violent 'Other'. Theorists tend to describe the 'problem' of religion as one of deep, intractable conflict rooted in doctrinal dogmatism. This is a clear legacy of the European wars of religion, which connected fanaticism and violence (Cavanaugh 2009). Yet this obscures the militancy of secularism itself: authoritarian and totalitarian regimes in the twentieth century have mostly been secular states. It also erases the fact that lived religion is not typically about doctrine and belief: religion is more often experienced as a mode of social identity, one similar to culture, ethnicity, or nationality.

II NEUTRALIST SECULARISM

Our first response to this set of challenges is to point out that separationism holds a more limited place in political liberal philosophy than critics assume. This is because most liberal philosophers, in the broadly Rawlsian tradition, are committed to a version of what can be called neutralist secularism. Neutralist secularism is not committed to separation as a normative ideal. Nor does it hold that religion is uniquely special. As a result, it is not vulnerable to the criticisms of secularism canvassed in the previous section.

Liberal Justice and Neutrality

We first need to clarify the relationship between liberalism and the contested term of neutrality. A liberal state is not neutral towards liberal moral principles such as human rights and non-discrimination. It is not neutral about liberal justice. As a result, there is no paradox of state interference with religion. Religion is not a naturalised sphere of human activity that is immune from political regulation. Liberal states should only protect justice-respecting conceptions of the good, not conceptions of the good *simpliciter*. In addition, neutrality requires that the state not side with or favour *any* (justice-respecting) conception of the good, whether religious or not. This conception of liberal neutrality provides a preliminary answer to the three challenges set out above.

1 Dogmatic Separation

Neutralist secularism is not vulnerable to the first charge, because separation is at most a derivative, not an intrinsic, requirement of neutrality. Critics mistakenly equate practices of church-state separation with political secularism. Yet practices of separation between state and religion are only valuable as *means* to specifically liberal *ends*: they are not ends in themselves. Metaphors and slogans about 'walls' and 'separation' do not provide a sensible conceptual apparatus for the analysis of religious liberty (Eisgruber & Sager 2007). Plainly, not all secular regimes or policies are liberal, as the example of communist atheist states demonstrates. Nor should the separation doctrine be zealously defended at the expense of freedom of conscience, as the Islamic veiling controversies in France and Quebec illustrate (Laborde 2008; Maclure & Taylor 2011). In practice, state regulation of religion can be justified by good reasons (protection of basic rights) as well as bad reasons (majoritarian conceptions of public order, religious animus). Neutralist secularism provides critical tools to assess practices of existing states: critics exaggerate the gap between ideal and critical approaches to secularism.

The ideal of separation, then, has a limited place in neutralist secularism. As a downstream principle, neutrality can demand either even-handed impartiality (similar level of support) or hands-off abstention (separation proper). State abstention from religious and cultural affairs is only one possible instantiation of liberal neutrality (Patten 2014). Generally, it is a mistake to take separationist policies as the litmus test for secularism (Bhargava 1998; Modood 2016; Maclure & Tayor 2011; Laborde 2013).

2 Arbitrary Singling Out

Liberal neutrality does not single out religion as uniquely special: it demands equal respect for religious and non-religious conceptions of the good. (Dworkin 2013; Eisgruber & Sager 2007; Taylor & Maclure 2011; Schwartzman 2012). Religion is only one of the conceptions of the good life that make up the reasonable pluralism of contemporary societies. What is called neutrality in contemporary liberal philosophy is a generalisation of the classical ideal of disestablishment and religious toleration. The liberal state is required to be neutral between religions; and also between all aspects of its citizens' conceptions of the good, whether these are religious or non-religious. Liberal neutrality seeks to extend and generalise the protections (and burdens) traditionally associated with religion to a broader category of what Rawls called 'conceptions of the good' (Rawls 1971, 1993).

The upshot is that the liberal state does not single out religious views and conceptions as uniquely problematic. It does not separate itself uniquely from religion but, rather, refrains from endorsing or promoting any controversial or comprehensive conception of the good. Neutralist liberalism, therefore, has been called an *egalitarian* theory of religious freedom (Schwartzman 2012; Laborde 2014). Religious freedom is only one instantiation of a more basic right: a right to personal freedom or ethical independence, which is also at stake in other controversies around conscience, sexuality and abortion. There is nothing special about religion that would warrant that religious citizens should receive uniquely privileged treatment in the law – say, in the form of exclusive exemptions on the ground of religious belief.

As philosophers such as Rawls and Ronald Dworkin have argued, it is the human capacity for moral or spiritual agency, not for leading good lives with a determinate, perhaps religious, content, which should ground the respect that the state owes to persons *qua* persons. In their book, *Religious Freedom and the Constitution*, US constitutionalists Christopher Eisgruber and Lawrence Sager argue that religion should be treated as no worse, but also no better, than other forms of human experience (Eisgruber & Sager 2007). For example, the doctrine of humanist atheism should not be 'established' by the state. However, secular conscience – for example, mandating objection to military service – deserves as much respect as religious conscience.

3 Protestantised Belief

Liberal egalitarians have generalised the notion of 'religion' to a broader, vaguer, and therefore, less ethnocentric and biased category. Religion is morally and politically salient as one of the conceptions of the good, ethical worldviews and ways of life that make up the pluralism of contemporary societies. The state is not secular but rather *neutral* about the good. As a result, religious believers and groups neither enjoy nor suffer exclusively special legal treatment; they are treated under a broader regime of equality. The upshot is that neutralists are not guilty of working with the wrong conception of religion. They need not take a stance on whether 'real' religion is belief-based/Protestant.

Neutralist secularism is a plausible first answer to the criticisms of secularism. Yet it suffers from a disabling ambiguity. In brief: what it means to treat religion and 'non-religion' equally is unclear. Theorists should ask deeper questions about which relevant feature religious and non-religious conceptions share, such that they should be treated equally. The much-used Rawlsian phrase, 'conception of the good', is too vague to do the work that egalitarian liberals intend. Consider how the slogans of neutrality and equality fail to provide much guidance in many of the most salient controversies about the public role of religion. Are state-sponsored religious symbols analogous to cultural symbols? Should fashion hats as well as Muslim hijabs be exempted from regulations about workplace uniforms? Should Intelligent Design theories be taught on a par with Darwinism in schools? Is criticising a religion the same thing as criticising a race? Should disadvantaged religious minorities benefit from positive discrimination policies? Should the state offer equal support to leisure, educational, and religious activities?

In all these (and related) controversies, the idea of a simple analogy between religion and non-religion is of limited use, and neutrality plays a diminishing, almost evanescent role (Laborde 2017b). As critics of secularism have pointed out, the term 'religion' has a multiplicity of meanings and referents, and it resists the simple 'analogising' strategy of neutralist theorists. In practice neutralist theorists have singled out specific features of 'religion' or 'conceptions of the good', depending on which normative question they ask. They have intimated – yet not developed – the crucial insight that the concepts of religion and the good should be analytically disaggregated (Laborde 2017a). Furthermore, the boundary between justice and the good is often precisely what is at issue in controversies about the public place of religion, and therefore, the domain of neutrality (where neutrality applies) remains unclear. The idea of secularism-as-neutrality is inconclusive or indeterminate about what justice demands in key controversies about justice. We need to provide a more fine-grained, but also a more modest, account of the proper relationship between secularism and liberalism.

III MINIMAL SECULARISM

Minimal secularism is a deliberately incomplete theory, because secularism is a theory of liberal legitimacy, not of full liberal justice. It does not deliver conclusive solutions to all controversies about the place of religion in the constitution and laws of liberal states. Yet it identifies the minimum standards that have to be met for states to achieve liberal legitimacy. In particular, it is able to explain the sense in which most states that have been called 'constitutional theocracies' (Hirschl 2010) are straightforwardly in violation of liberalism. Another crucial contribution of minimal secularism is that it disaggregates religion to bring out different modes of ethical salience of religion. It does not assume that religion is simply a Rawlsian conception of the good. Instead, it picks out a plurality of relevantly salient dimensions of religion, which are shared by non-religious conceptions, identities and beliefs. On the theory I defend, a state holds liberal legitimacy if it meets the three standards of minimal secularism, which each pick out a different feature of disaggregated religion: personal liberty, equal inclusion and public justification (Laborde 2017a). Let us analyse them in turn.

The State must Protect and Promote Personal Liberty

Historically, the disestablishment of religion disentangled state law from traditional religious moralities, so as to open a sphere of individual self-determination in ethical matters. The first principle of minimal secularism is that the state should not enforce matters of comprehensive ethics, which include, among others, sexuality, family arrangements, eating codes, work, and dress, on its citizens (as long as they do not infringe the rights of others). The liberal state should not enforce matters of comprehensive ethics because they often go to the core of people's sense of *integrity*, of living up to their own ethical commitments and projects. Since most religions have clear codes governing these matters, this is an ethically significant feature of religions that determines how religious beliefs and practices must be treated by the liberal state.

Here the ethical *salience* of religion is that it is a personal conception of comprehensive ethics. A secular state is a state that does not enforce a religious ethical code: it does not limit personal liberty by enforcing its own code of ethics. This first principle of minimal secularism generates mostly negative duties (respect of freedom of conscience and religion). It explains why the state should secure basic integrity-based liberties (such as religious freedom) over non-basic liberties (freedoms that are less connected to people's integrity, such as the freedom to wear a fashion hat or – in Charles Taylor's famous example – to move unimpeded by traffic lights) (Taylor 2006). It also generates positive duties (e.g., special exemptions from general laws; substantive rights of exit from all-encompassing, comprehensive institutions such as traditionalist religious communities).

Religion is not uniquely special. The first principle protects *not only* religion (there are secular systems of comprehensive ethics, such as veganism or humanist pacifism) and *not always* religion (religion is not always a system of comprehensive ethics: some of its prescriptions and precepts have been both thinned out and culturalised, such that they are not objectionable impositions of comprehensive, integrated ethical systems – cf. the institution of marriage; Sunday laws; *halal* and *kosher* meat).

The State must Guarantee the Equal Inclusion of all Citizens

Historically, the disestablishment of religion from the state helped secure equal status of vulnerable and marginalised religious minorities. The second principle of minimal secularism is that a secular state must be *inclusive*. It must grant its members equal status or standing, and avoid communicating the message that some citizens have greater civic standing than others. Here, the ethical salience of religion is that religious affiliation often works as a marker for either vulnerable or divisive (or both) social identities. A secular state is a state that guarantees the equal inclusion of all citizens, either through equal individual rights (e.g., Jews in revolutionary France) or through forms of differentiated citizenship (e.g., personal law systems in South Africa or India). And crucially, it is a state that does not equate citizenship with membership of any one religion: it is a state that eschews religious nationalism.

Religion, again, is not uniquely special. The second principle of minimal secularism applies *not only* to religion (ethnic nationalism and religious nationalism are problematic for the same reason) and *not always* to religion (in contexts where religious affiliation is not divisive or subordinating – when it is more like sporting allegiance – some forms of benign and symbolic official religious recognition are permissible).

The State must Offer Public Justifications

Historically, the disestablishment of religion from the state coincided with the gradual substitution of secular reasons for religious argument in public discourse. The third principle of minimal secularism is that a liberal state must be justifiable to those over whom it exercises its authority. In contemporary political philosophy, this principle is defended as a principle of liberal public reason (Eberle & Cuneo, 2015;

Quong 2017). Minimal secularism proposes a permissive principle of public reason as *accessible* reason. A state is secular, on this view, when its officials justify laws and policies by reference to reasons whose force can be understood and democratically debated by citizens: accessible reasons.

Here, the ethical salience of religion is that religious worldviews are partly epistemically closed, such that they rely on beliefs (concerning, for example, the existence of God) that may be intelligible but are not accessible in public reason. The third principle of minimal secularism, then, is that the liberal state must eschew appeals to inaccessible reasons when justifying laws and policies. By contrast, individuals and civil society groups can bring up any argument they think relevant to public debate. In a minimally secular state, it is the state, not the citizens, that is expected to be secular. This principle explains the widely shared intuition that the state cannot coerce all citizens in the name of inaccessible reasons, such as the will of god or scriptures of a sacred text.

Religion, here again, is not uniquely special. The third principle applies *not only* to religion (there are inaccessible secular beliefs and references, such as appeal to purely personal experiences) and *not always* to religion (some religious references are accessible, when they are factual or ethical instead of openly metaphysical). Of course, the principle of accessible public justification is only a necessary, not a sufficient, criterion of liberal permissibility. For an institution, law or policy to be compatible with minimal secularism, it must, in addition, meet the two principles of personal liberty and equal inclusiveness mentioned above.

In sum, there is no single property of religion that justifies the complex set of policies a legitimate liberal state must adopt towards religious beliefs and practices. There are a number of different features of religion (integrity-related beliefs and practices, vulnerable social identities, inaccessibility of reasons) that become ethically salient in different political contexts and call for forms of *restricted* state neutrality, and sometimes, legal protections and exemptions. The upshot is that states can associate themselves with religious institutions, ideas and symbols *when these are not comprehensive, divisive or inaccessible*. Minimal secularism is more determinate than neutralist secularism because it specifies when – and why – religious establishment is – or is not – problematic at the bar of liberal legitimacy. As a result, it allows us to offer a better answer to the three challenges posed by critics of secularism, as follows:

Dogmatic separation: Unlike neutralists, minimal secularists can explain *when* state official recognition and endorsement of religion is permissible. A state may be non-neutral but still respect personal liberty, equal status, and public justification.

Arbitrary singling out: Unlike neutralists, minimal secularists do not deploy a vague category of 'conception of the good', but explore the multiple currencies of equality that are relevant to liberal legitimacy.

Protestantised religion: Unlike neutralists, minimal secularists take seriously the plurality of religious experiences beyond 'belief-based' and 'doctrinal' paradigms.

To conclude, minimal secularism offers a trans-national standard of liberal legitimacy, relevant to countries with non-Christian religions and no tradition of church-state separation. It offers a framework for a normative comparative secularism. The upshot is that US- or French-style separationism is not the golden standard of liberal constitutionalism. Constitutions that give a greater place to religion, either through formal yet vestigial establishment (England) or through the positive recognition of minority religious identities (India) might do as well at the bar of minimal secularism. Yet most states which Ran Hirshl has called 'constitutional theocracies' (Hirschl 2010) will fail to meet the criteria of minimal secularism (and therefore liberal legitimacy), because they typically do not achieve sufficient standards of personal liberty, equal inclusion and public justification.

Minimal secularism does not only provide a general test of the all-things-considered liberal permissibility of particular *constitutions*, however. Its multi-criterial theory, and its sensitivity to different meanings and salience of religion in different contexts, also offers fine-grained evaluations of the permissibility of particular *laws and policies*. It is important to be clear, however, about the limits of the normative ambition of minimal secularism. It is not designed to provide conclusive solutions to all controversies about the place of religion in liberal states. It only delivers minimal standards, leaving more substantive resolutions to the interplay of political, legal, and constitutional mechanisms in particular societies. There is no single secular solution to all the debates about the relationship between religion and state.

RECOMMENDED READING

Asad, T. (2012). Thinking about Religious Belief and Politics. In R. Orsi, ed., *Cambridge Companion to Religious Studies*. New York: Cambridge University Press, pp. 36–57.

Bhargava, R., ed. (1998). *Secularism and its Critics*, New Delhi: Oxford University Press.

Eisgruber, C. & Sager, L. (2007). *Religious Freedom and the Constitution*, Cambridge, MA: Harvard University Press.

Gutmann, A. (2010). Religion and State in the United States: A Defense of Two-Way Protection. In N. Rosenblum, ed., *Obligations of Citizenship and the Demands of Faith*. Princeton: Princeton University Press, pp. 127–164.

Hirschl, Ran, 2010, *Constitutional Theocracy*, Cambridge, MA: Harvard University Press.

Laborde, C. (2008). *Critical Republicanism. The Hijab Controversy and Political Philosophy*, Oxford: Oxford University Press.

Laborde, C. (2017a). *Liberalism's Religion*, Cambridge, MA: Harvard University Press.

Leiter, B. (2013). *Why Tolerate Religion?*, Cambridge, MA: Harvard University Press.

Maclure, J., Taylor, C. (2011). *Secularism and Freedom of Conscience*, Cambridge, MA: Harvard University Press.

Mahmood, S. (2005). *Politics of Piety: The Islamic Revival and the Feminist Subject*, Princeton University Press.

Taylor, C. (2017). *A Secular Age*, Cambridge, MA: Harvard University Press.

21

Constitutional Review

Christoph Möllers

INTRODUCTION

There is nothing self-evident in the conjunction of the terms "constitution" and "review" or in a connection between "constitutional review" and the judiciary. Still, the proliferation, justification and critique of constitutional courts has been the most debated issue in constitutional theory over the past decades. This paper tries to take a step back and reflect upon the theoretical foundations and, somewhat unavoidably, the historical and institutional contexts this debate rests upon. Its aim is neither to criticize nor to justify any form of constitutional review as such. It will rather develop a more specific argument trying to undermine the assumption that there is much to be said in general, that is, across different jurisdictions, about these questions. At least, my argument against a misleading generality is in itself a general argument. I will proceed in three steps. After a quick conceptual introduction into some of the terms in Section I, I will give a necessarily short overview over the past and current debates. Section II will lead to two negative results: a critique of the still current Americocentrism in constitutional scholarship and a critique of analytic arguments that operate with excessively generalized assumptions. In Section III, I will then develop an approach toward a meaningful comparison and critique of constitutional courts and other bodies tasked with constitutional review. In the context of a Handbook of constitutional *theory*, the reader ought to keep in mind that the set of arguments discussed here is less clearly "theoretical" and much more intertwined with historical path dependencies and institutional technicalities than is the case with other topics like "dignity", "freedom" or "democracy".

I CONCEPTUAL PRELIMINARIES

Today, we associate the notion of "constitutional review" with the idea of a court that takes a constitutional text as the standard for the review of legislation. But in order to get from the idea of a constitution to its review through a judicial body, some steps have to be taken, steps that are not systematically necessary, but are historically contingent paths without any convincing claim for institutional progress.[1] First of all, "constitutions" are not necessarily norms in an emphatic sense. They constitute a political community, that is, they ground an institution in certain social facts.[2] Whether this counts as a normative enterprise is up to debate. But even if it did, it would not necessarily follow that the constitutional norm becomes a point of reference for a review of the non-constitutional legal order. This requires a hierarchy of norms that is historically not a necessary feature of a constitution. Finally, even if there is an established hierarchy of norms, this does not necessarily imply its review by specialized organs or even courts.[3]

To illustrate these distinctions through constitutional phenomena: We might wonder if the English "ancient constitution" (Pocock 1987) is a norm or just a more or less comprehensive description of the habits of the English political system. Most nineteenth century European constitutions have no concept of constitutional supremacy; they are just specific statutes that set up the organization of the state,[4] as is still the case with the so called "constitutions" of International Organizations (Klabbers 2009, pp. 74–92). Finally, there are still many constitutional orders that do not use centralized or generalized constitutional review by courts or even explicitly exclude it like the Dutch constitution. Some of them may have parliamentary chambers to apply constitutional standards, some of them, like Sweden or the UK, entrust parliamentary commissions with the review of the constitution.[5] Many systems of judicial constitutional review are distributed over the whole judiciary, mostly working under an apex institution, a supreme court (Landfried, this volume). Even this enumeration is not complete, ignoring special institutions that do not perfectly fit the type of a constitutional court like the French *Conseil Constitutionnel* (Rousseau, Gahdoun & Bonnet 2016, pp. 67 et seq.)[6] and international courts like the European Court of Human Rights[7] or the Inter-American Court of Human Rights (Davidson 1992).

II DEBATES ON CONSTITUTIONAL REVIEW: A SHORT OVERVIEW

Continental European Debates

1 Republican Tradition and European Practice

The critique of courts is as old as modern constitutionalism. We find it in the French revolution, which also produced one of the first relevant proposals to introduce

---

[1] There are many progressive narratives present in the debate on constitutional review, in Germany the story of the constitutional court as the "final stone in the building of the Rechtsstaat" metaphor: Thoma 1953/2008, p. 541.
[2] The more recent philosophical debate on constitution and constituting as might become interesting for lawyers and political scientists: Epstein 2015.
[3] Nino 1996, pp. 187 et seq. (in particular p. 196).
[4] For Germany: Wahl 1981, p. 495; for France: Troper 1973.
[5] For the Commonwealth tradition, especially with regard to New Zealand: Gardbaum 2013.
[6] For a critical assessment from inside: Schnapper 2010.
[7] The ECtHR explicitly claims not to practice constitutional review, esp. in inter-state conflicts, but see Bellamy 2014, p. 1037.

constitutional review (Siéyès 1795, p. 5).[8] Politically, the debate was split between liberals, who endorse moderation through courts (Gauchet 1995, p. 18), and radical republicans, who want to see the work of the legislature and the executive undisturbed by other institutions.[9] Two basic arguments are already developed in this early context. From an institutional point of view, courts show a tendency to privilege the rights of parties at the cost of general citizenship and its democratic expression in the form of general laws. This point is made against the French "parlements" even before the revolution. From the perspective of democratic theory, courts lack accountability, more so if the applied concept of democracy rejects representation. The independence of courts prevents their democratic accountability. Both arguments are still in use and still worth being considered (see infra, IV), they remain practically powerful not only in their country of origin but also in other nations.

Constitutional review was not only a problematic institution from a radical republican point of view, but also remained practically rare in the common context of constitutional monarchy that dominated at least European constitutionalism before World War I. This shows that doubts about a judiciary that could check political decisions did not remain limited to democratic politics. Practically, constitutional review in nineteenth century Europe is mostly understood as the possibility to prosecute executive office-holders, cabinet members, in courts that were not responsible to parliament.[10] There is basically no constitutional court of the modern form in continental Europe before 1918/19.[11] Even federal systems like Germany or Switzerland only created a type of Federal Supreme Court without developing a strong doctrine of federal constitutional supremacy.[12] While these courts guarantee the unified application of federal statutes, they do not guard the competences between political levels. Before World War I, there was no European *McCulloch v. Maryland*.[13] Outside of Europe and the U.S., it is Latin-America that provides us in this epoch with further examples of constitutional review (Gargarella 2013, p. 37).

2 Kelsen

Hans Kelsen gave the first more or less analytical argument for constitutional review (Kelsen 1929, pp. 51 et seq).[14] In context of the German debate of the Weimar Republic

---

[8] It is, albeit, quite contested in how far it is appropriate to read this as a precursor for modern constitutional review: pro Roubier 1929, p. 465; contra Troper 1973, p. 59.
[9] But as a matter of fact, many radicals endorsed some form of check upon the legislature: Fioravanti 2007, p. 91.
[10] We still find considerable traces of that in the French system: Beaud 1999, pp. 80–85. And in the American impeachment procedure, in which the Senate functions like a court: Gerhardt 2019, pp. 33 et seq.
[11] For the early Czechoslovakian case: Osterkamp 2009, p. 11; for Colombia: Espinosa & Landau 2017, p. 2.
[12] For the federal origins of constitutional review: Beaud 2005, pp. 49 et seq.; Schönberger 2011, pp. 385 et seq.
[13] McCulloch v. Maryland, 17 U.S. 316 (1819).
[14] The best account of the debate in German still is Wendenburg 1984, pp. 43 et seq.; for the political context Caldwell 1997.

and with the important background of his personal experience as a constitutional judge in Austria in the 1920s, it becomes weighted. Kelsen derives his argument from his[15] concept of hierarchy of norms (*Stufenbau*) and also from the necessity to establish an independent control of the legality of all kinds of law-making (Kelsen 1929, pp. 35 et seq.). For Kelsen, a legal system can only be closed when its supreme norm is reviewed by a legal mechanism. While it is difficult to accept his claim that there is a necessary connection between constitutional supremacy and constitutional review through courts,[16] it is important to see that Kelsen was not blind to the disadvantages of such an institution and that he named at least two important limits to the action of constitutional courts:

Firstly, his ideal was a court that provided a merely procedural review. He was explicitly critical of vague substantial constitutional norms which he deemed to be a considerable risk for an open democratic process. One of his own examples for a vague unreviewable norm is "freedom" (Kelsen 1929, pp. 69–70). That means that Kelsen did not want to provide any justification for substantial rights review. Secondly, he defines review as "negative legislation" (Kelsen 1929, p. 56). The formula does not claim any form of government by judges.[17] The "negative" part is more important: all claims by courts to define the duties of the legislator or other procedural forms of judicial activism go against Kelsen's preference for a purely reactive court that can neither pick cases nor instigate state action.

3 Post-War Developments

The proliferation of strong constitutional review through courts after World War II and, again, after 1989 all over the world, has not necessarily been accompanied by a lot of theoretical reflection. Countries that introduced strong specialized constitutional courts like Italy, Germany, South Africa or Taiwan did also produce some scholarship on the topic (Bryde 1982, pp. 147 et seq.; Roux 2015; Troper 2008), but the subject was by no means as central in the academic or political debate there as it was and is in the United States. Decisions by such courts produced political frictions, in Germany, for example, in the early 1950s and the 1990s (Collings 2015, pp. 38, 232), but this never led to a serious institutional debate on the merits of the court as such. In countries with a strong parliamentary or republican tradition like France, Great Britain or Switzerland and the Commonwealth countries, and also in other liberal-democratic monarchies like Denmark or Sweden and in further countries like Estonia, the review of rights was mainly introduced through the European Convention of Human Rights. This provoked questions about the relationship between national and international law

---

[15] The first to develop the concept is Merkl 1927, p. 172.
[16] Nino 1996.
[17] This formula is from Alexis de Tocqueville.

with arguably different institutional problems than the one raised by what one may call the "republican problem".

Provincializing the U.S.: The Counter-Majoritarian Difficulty

While the American debate on judicial review has been influential all over the word, doubts about its relevance are growing (Robertson 2018, p. 192). The U.S. Supreme Court seems too particular an institution for more general insights, and even theoretical contributions which are framed in a more abstract or universalist semantic owe too much to their specifically American institutional and historical origins. For two reasons, there may be little to be learned from framing our problem in the form of the so-called "counter-majoritarian difficulty" (Bickel 1986, p. 16).

The first reason refers to the uncertain origins of the review powers of the U.S. Supreme Court. Without going into any details, they are historically contested, and at least partly the result of an act of self-empowerment by the Court (Kahn 2003, pp. 2686, 2696; Kramer 2004, p. 115). This makes the American case attractive as a point of reference for similar developments, namely the case of the Supreme Court of Israel (Friedman 2016, p. 54), maybe the European Court of Justice,[18] but much less so for constitutional orders with an explicit review mandate.

The second reason comes from the way theoretical argument and institutional context are connected. Let me mention just one example: John H. Ely's concept of representation reinforcement (Ely 1980, pp. 87 et seq.) that has been adopted by authors outside the U.S. (Habermas 1996, pp. 257 et seq.). On an abstract level, the justification of constitutional review as an instrument to empower democratic processes may seem sound. We will come back to it. But the way Ely makes this idea operational, addressing the problem of "discrete and insular minorities"[19] and their representation in Congress (Ely 1980, pp. 73 et seq., for a critique Ackerman 1991, pp. 3–33) is very specific: it works under particular social conditions with regard to the size and status of minorities and it only works in a majority voting system.

All in all, there seem to be many very particular issues about the American constitutional system: its degree of open politicization in the appointment process and voting behavior of the justices,[20] the lack of internal deliberation between them, the general distrust of formal arguments after legal realism and critical legal studies, the extreme rigidity of the amendment procedure, the counter-majoritarian character of the legislative process, and the aforementioned unclear constitutional basis for

---

[18] See for instance the case of van Gend en Loos in 1962, where the court developed the direct effect of European Union law: European Court of Justice, 5th February 1963, Van Gend en Loos, 26/62, EU:C:1963:1; Azoulai & Rasnača 2016, p. 171.

[19] United States v. Carolene Products Company, 304 U.S. 144 (1938).

[20] For the appointment process in the United States: Nemacheck 2017; for an overview on studies on voting behavior and partisanship on the U.S. Supreme Court see D'Elia-Kueper & Segal 2017; for comparable research on the German court with weaker results: Engst et al. 2017.

judicial review powers. Waldron's statement that the justification of constitutional review may only work for specific deficiencies of the American legislative process (Waldron 2006, p. 1403) may cut both ways. The critique of judicial review may also only be valid with regard to the deficiencies of the American judicial process. All in all, the Anglo-American debate suffers from the fact that many of its participants (often due to a lack of knowledge of foreign languages) have primary access only to systems without constitutional review or to the U.S. system with its very particular and long constitutional history, maybe missing some of the institutional nuances of specialized constitutional review. Despite the fact that comparative constitutional law has become truly global on many levels, from a constitutional duty to look at foreign constitutions in the South-African constitution to actively comparing international courts like the ECtHR to a globalized academic discourse, it still seems to be a fact that the arguments exchanged with regard to the legitimacy of constitutional review mostly stem from Anglo-America, either from the U.S.-American experience or from a Commonwealth reading of political constitutionalism.

Analytic Arguments: Pros and Cons

1 The Core of the Critique

Waldron's piece on the "Core of the Critique" is the attempt to extract the general analytic point out of the old republican and the new American critique of constitutional review: Under democratic conditions, legislatures are a more egalitarian forum for settling constitutional conflicts on rights than courts are. Legislatures are thus more democratically legitimate, and there is no proof that could back the assumption that courts are more likely to produce more rights-friendly outcomes (Waldron 2006, pp. 1389–1395). Under constitutional review, cases are already formatted as a general political conflict, and there is no relevant distinction in the way courts and legislatures reason. It is important to keep in mind that Waldron's argument is only applied to the review of *rights*. The core of Waldron's case then claims that constitutional courts and democratic legislatures fulfil the same function, the authoritative settlement of a contested rights issue, under different legitimation conditions, so that only these conditions are relevant for the question of who should decide upon the settlement.

2 Conventional Wisdoms: Weak Cases from Constitutionalism, Separation of Powers and Rights

Before we come back to Waldron's point, it is important to see that it puts considerable pressure on many arguments in favor of constitutional review. Claims that judicial review procedures strengthen "rights",[21] or "separation of powers" (Saunders

---

[21] See the references in Waldron 2006.

2018, p. 72; differently Möllers 2013, pp. 16–50), "constitutionalism" (Vile 1967, pp. 173 et seq.), or even "reason" (Rawls 1993, p. 231) mostly do not bother to explain how exactly this happens, but rather insinuate that all of these values would be better protected by a constitutional court than by a political organ. They take a close relationship between courts and these values for granted. Their argument is often based on either a general suspicion of democratic politics, or a conception of constitutionalism in general or separation of powers in particular that ignores the political side of both principles: by understanding constitutionalism just as the containment of politics through means of law and by taking separation of powers not as a form to organize political power, but as a safeguard to keep it at bay. This line of argument is often accompanied by a strong moral idealization of legal reasoning in court. A very short look at two of these arguments may be helpful.

The argument that a constitutional complaint in court may give the democratic community a pause to reflect upon the specific rights perspective of the plaintiff that had not been debated or could not have been anticipated in the democratic process is plausible (Lafont 2016, pp. 272–275). But it does not justify the power to strike down the statute in question, it is, as an argument *from* institutional reflexivity, also one *for* institutional reflexivity, but not for the ultimate political power that may strike down a political decision made by a democratic majority. Therefore, it only justifies weak judicial review that proposes a change to the legislator. It is, then, no accident that representatives of political constitutionalism like Bellamy and Waldron can also endorse weak judicial review just because this form of reflexivity does not give any hard power to judicial institutions.

The more general point, made by Rawls (Rawls 1993, p. 234), would be that politically independent courts are a place of public reason in that they can deliberate important questions independently from any political and social pressures. Rawls' idea has found many followers in liberal political theory (Lafont 2016, pp. 271–272). As generators of justification, constitutional courts seem to be promising candidates for the position of guardian of the "rationality" of political action. But apart from the practical question whether constitutional courts, especially those which do not deliberate like the American one, do live up to these normative expectations, and apart from the theoretical question whether we should understand democratic politics as a form of rational deliberation,[22] the argument seems quite unspecific. Should we just put some people into a room, aloof from politics and social contexts, and let them decide important questions, or do we need some more concrete institutional precautions like political representation, and if we opt for the former, how are these people specifically connected to any idea of public reason?

---

[22] This leads us deeply into debates between liberals and realists in political theory. For a realist critique see Geuss 2008.

3 Jurisprudential Background Questions

One of the problems of this debate lies in the fact that it is heavily dependent on more fundamental questions concerning the relation between law, politics and morality. Kelsen is an unusual case in that he is often seen as a central figure of both democratic constitutionalism, that emphasizes the importance of legislation, and a promoter of constitutional review by courts. More typical is an elective affinity between certain camps in constitutional theory and analytic jurisprudence. On the one hand, strong models of a necessary moral content of legal arguments, like Dworkin's, tend to affirm a strong conception of judicial review, most notoriously in his formula of the Herculean judge (Dworkin 1986, p. 239).[23] On the other hand, we see that an understanding of law as a mere social fact will often tend to affirm the role of the legislator.[24] This latter line of argument extends all the way from Bentham's critique of the Common Law courts to today's political constitutionalism. This is not the place to reconstruct the highly contested relation between constitutional and jurisprudential arguments, but it seems at least necessary to warn against too easy connections between both levels of discourse. As we will see in the critique of Waldron's argument, there is no necessary democratic case against courts if they act in a certain institutional manner, namely "as courts". Likewise, it is not entirely clear why a possible moral content of "the law" should be better located in the hands of judges than in the hands of parliamentarians. Therefore, there may be a case for undermining the academic frontlines, as Kelsen did, and there may be a form of political constitutionalism which accepts at least some form of constitutional review by courts as legitimate.

III LEGITIMACY OF CONSTITUTIONAL REVIEW: A RE-CONSTRUCTION

Taking up Waldron's core case, the two central questions are: first, is there a relevant difference between courts and legislatures with regard to their democratic legitimacy; and second, is there a relevant difference in their procedure? Critics of constitutional review will usually answer the first question in the affirmative, and the second in the negative, while I would take the justificatory differences to be smaller and the procedural ones to be bigger. But irrespective of which answer one may give, the problem looks different with regard to federalism and separation of powers and for deficient democratic governance.

---

[23] For a nuanced interpretation of this figure: Shapiro 2011, pp. 307 et seq.
[24] For example, Shapiro (2011, pp. 177 et seq.) combines his jurisprudential argument for a purely social understanding of law with the idea of a "plan", arguably a legislative task, certainly not a judicial one.

The Normative Claim of Justificatory Arguments or the Political Foundation of Judicial Review

The question what is actually claimed by making a justificatory argument in constitutional theory for or against constitutional review is rarely asked. It might sound meaningless for a political philosopher who wants to make a point about the normative qualities of an institutional set-up. Still, such an argument resonates differently in different constitutional orders. The more a constitutional review is formally entrenched, the less relevant the theoretical debate seems. This is one reason why the critique of counter-majoritarianism resonated, for example, in Israel, but not in Germany (Möllers 2014, pp. 16–18). As a matter of fact, we already noticed the limited relevance of the critique of judicial review in many constitutional orders, and one decisive limit is the state of the law in a given political community.[25]

Does this observation have any normative value of its own beyond positive law? I believe it does for the following reasons: The relation between a democratic decision and a normative philosophical case against judicial review seems to become more difficult if there is an explicit democratic decision for judicial review. Let us assume that there is a democratic community that lives up to Waldron's criteria. But in this community, there is also a permanent hyper-majority for the constitutional review of parliamentary majority decisions through a non-majoritarian constitutional court. Are we allowed to ignore this hyper-majority in the name of the democratic legitimacy of majoritarian institutions? Or wouldn't we rather have to accept that there is a majority that favors an institutional set-up in which even the settled decisions of its own majoritarian institutions could be set aside by a court as long as the decisions of other majorities are treated in the same manner? I would choose the second option and accept that we may deal with a democratic community that wants to be under a certain form of judicial review.

Still, one might wonder how far this argument can take us. On the one hand, it should certainly make a difference if there is a decision of the constitution-maker to institutionalize constitutional review, and on the other, it is obvious that not every institution is evenly legitimate because it has been created in a democratic procedure,[26] a problem we know well from the debate on the limits of delegation and the legitimacy of independent agencies.

Therefore, qualifications seem necessary: Firstly, some democratic mandate for constitutional review is a necessary condition for its justification, not a sufficient one. Still, it takes some of the counter-majoritarian argument's bite. Secondly, we need safeguards to keep the democratic mandate of the court active. The most basic

---

[25] One may see the state of the law as an expression of a bourgeois liberal position, as Hirschl (2004, p. 46) does; but this again seems over-general when we look at the role of constitutional courts with regard to welfare rights, for example, in Latin America, India and Continental Europe.

[26] Central Banks come to mind as a comparable institution: Tucker 2018, pp. 147–194.

is that the decision for review as well as the standards it applies should be subject to democratic revision. This sounds like a trivial requirement, yet given the widespread review of constitutional amendments on a standard that is not-amendable, it is not (Roznai 2017, pp. 212–225). In order to keep constitutional review politically responsive, we also have to think about the degree of entrenchment of constitutional procedures. Given the status quo affinity of qualified majority rules[27] there is a case for a simple statutory basis of procedural rules even if the court itself is constitutionally entrenched. To strengthen the political plurality on the court, there may be a case for an appointment procedure that requires a compromise between political camps, but these are already relatively specific issues. The general point so far is that we should treat constitutional review as a specific form of democratic delegation that has to be checked upon, but that is not undemocratic per se, at least as long as the way courts act can be distinguished from the legislative process (infra 2. a).

The bigger point behind this argument is an ambiguity in the debate between political, legal and moral constitutionalisms. One may understand the critique of constitutional review as a core topic of political constitutionalism, a model that emphasizes that constitutions are not merely supreme statutes, but political documents, that do not limit, but *constitute* a political process, and whose interpretation is not just the business of lawyers and legal institutions, but of the political branches and the people they represent (Bellamy 2007, pp. 176–208; Waldron 1999a, pp. 86–88). But given the fact that the constitution-giving and constitution-amending assembly is itself a political organ, it is far from clear how far this general point can lead. It may well be the case that a political community makes a political decision in favor of legal constitutionalism. Constitutions, then, become constitutional law, and this law is not the product of public reason, but of a political congregation. This means that the democratic core of the case against judicial review might not be as democratic as it seems and that the case of political constitutionalism against courts might be less of a political one than philosophical, second-guessing a democratic decision in favor of judicial review with a non-political argument that triggers the question of its own legitimacy (Rorty 2012, p. 175).

To be sure, my argument only raises the possibility that there is a majoritarian mandate for judicial constitutional review (Gargarella 2013, pp. 161–162). It neither claims that there ought to be such a mandate, just because we observe constitutional review in a given community, nor does it claim that, if there was such a mandate, the question of the legitimacy of constitutional review would simply be resolved. The fact that the decision for constitutional review was taken in a democratic procedure cannot justify constitutional review as such, yet it seems equally problematic to assume that this fact should be irrelevant. Still, the question remains why the democratic constitution-maker should make such a choice.

---

[27] The case for simple majority rules is not only based on equal treatment of the group that makes the decision, but also on equal treatment of the alternatives it may decide upon: May 1952, pp. 681 et seq. Generally: Sunstein 1993d, pp. 124–133.

Procedure Revisited: Constitutional Courts as Hybrid Entities

1 If it were Just a Court…

The second central question then concerns the differences between legislative and judicial review procedures. Most of the critical literature claims that differences between both are not relevant. But the intellectual effort invested into this point is conspicuously modest (Tushnet 1999, pp. 54–71; Waldron 2006, pp. 1349 et seq.). To make a sufficient claim, it would be necessary to do much more empirical and conceptual work, and it is not probable that this would produce the same or similar results in different legal orders.

Let us assume constitutional review was carried out by "real courts", that is, by politically independent institutions that decide conflicts between parties on a case-by-case basis through the application of meaningful rules that are set by a democratic constitution-maker. The decision would be prepared by an oral argument in which parties would present their case. The court would not be able to choose cases, its reasoning could not simply be traced back to political contestation, the justices would be selected in a manner that would make it difficult to identify them with a political orientation. Would there be any problem with its legitimacy, if all of this was backed by a political majority?

The fact that the court could strike down a legislative decision in an explicitly non-representative procedure could be seen as problematic, but the fact that the process is politically backed and that it would be considerably different from the legislative process seem to be able to mitigate the problem. Now, it is clear that most forms of constitutional review are different. We will look at two issues, the question of courts deciding "cases" and the way courts reason.

2 "Settlements" and Cases

Waldron argues that at least under contemporary U.S.-American conditions, there is no relevant difference between a constitutional "settlement" of a rights case by Congress or by the Supreme Court (Waldron 2006, pp. 1376–1378). My claim would be that even in the U.S., this is only true for a very selected class of cases, for cases that address general human rights issues, like the right to marriage for homosexual couples. When we look at a wider class of cases, even of rights cases, it is not clear which form a "settlement" issued by Congress could assume: How would Congress or any other parliament have settled, for example, New York Times v. Sullivan[28] or the similar Lüth-case?[29] Both deliver a specific holding with regard to the relation between free speech and private law remedies that is very much dependent on factual constellations. It is not clear how to put the holdings of these and many other

---

[28] The New York Times Co. v. Sullivan, 376 U.S. 254.
[29] BVerfGE (Collection of Decisions of the Federal Constitutional Court) 7, 198.

cases into a constitutional amendment because they are so intertwined with the facts of a specific case. Even if there was a strong case against constitutional review, and even if it was possible to design an ex ante review through parliamentary committees, it is hard to deny that this would yield a different form of "settlement" than a court procedure. The distinction between rules and judgments, made invisible through the notion of a "settlement", does not evaporate in constitutional review. The problem is perhaps less a normative one, not one of voices not being heard, but rather a cognitive one of concerns that are too specific to find their way into the forms of legislative decision-making. Judicial techniques like the interpretation of a statute in accordance with the constitution or the cassation of extreme cases of police action are not simply open to the form of a constitutional amendment that requires a certain degree of semantic generality.

The normative flipside of this observation would be a plea for judicial minimalism that has already been developed for different constitutional orders (Lepsius, in Jestaedt et al. 2020; Sunstein 1999, pp. 61 et seq., 259 et seq.). This minimalism, the need to decide only specific cases with specific holdings, should be prescribed by parliamentary statutes, not by constitutional courts themselves. One important remedy for the whole problem of constitutional review, which Bickel already saw (Bickel 1986, pp. 228–234), is procedural law. To be sure, this is not a general solution for the problem of justification, but it illustrates that one core element of critique – the similarity between legislative and judicial decisions – stands on a feeble basis. It seems that the philosophical critique suffers from a certain ignorance of institutional forms and may be too strongly fixated on big cases.

3 Legal Reasoning and Deliberation

A similar point can be made with regard to the way constitutional courts reason. Liberal endorsers and political critics of constitutional review seem to share the vision of an idealized philosophical rights reasoning as standard for constitutional review, either to find it realized or to be disappointed by its lacking. Though the claim that the "reasoning" (better: the reason-giving) of a court is not better than a debate in parliament, but just adds "legalisms" (Waldron 2006, p. 1386) may be perfectly fine from a philosophical point of view, it misses the political (!) character of legal (!) institutions. The fact that a legal argument is, arguably, an argument that operates under certain constraints, that is, the "law", is itself a political fact. At least under ideal conditions, the restrictions or shortcomings of a legal argument are produced by a democratic constitution-making body. The reasoning of a court, therefore, does not have to be better or equally good as a parliamentary debate, it has to be different in its reference to constitutional constraints.

Even if constitutional reasoning was closer to political philosophy than reasoning in civil law (Robertson 2010, pp. 347 et seq.) it would be important that, for political reasons, concepts like dignity, democracy or liberty do have distinctively different meanings in different constitutional orders. It would miss the political particularity of constitutional law to ignore these differences, to treat them as a deficiency or to review them according to a general standard derived from political philosophy. Arguments from constitutional law are arguments that are developed in and by a political community which may take up universal concepts, but not without giving them a meaning that is shaped by the community's institutional and doctrinal peculiarities. It is no accident that constitutional reasoning looks quite different from political theory, it is the only way constitutional law can operate. Again, this is no general justification for the way constitutional courts argue, but it is a refutation of the idea that they argue deficiently because they argue in a legal form.

A fatal counter-argument could claim that the reasoning of courts is just a camouflage of political preferences of the judges. To be sure, this is a legitimate line of critique, especially if courts are split into two stable political factions as seems to be the case with the U.S. Supreme Court. But as long as this is not the case with all or most constitutional courts, this remains an empirical observation without any general claim.

An important institutional feature to be observed in this context is the practice of deliberation, because deliberation may serve as an instrument to push existing preferences into the background. We know that there are considerable differences between courts in this regard,[30] and although it seems not only improbable but also undesirable that the deliberation should follow ideal Habermasian standards, which would never lead to any decision, it is enough that judges modify their preferences in a deliberation to have doubts about the assumption that the procedure is just a political epiphenomenon. Again, this does not mean that there are not completely politicized courts in countries like Hungary, Russia or Venezuela. Such courts exist, just as there are parliaments without democratic legitimacy in these or other countries.

Beyond Rights: Federalism and Separation of Powers Under Review

The Anglo-American debate on constitutional review is widely centered around the protection of rights though much political contestation appears in cases about federalism or separation of powers. But even if we accept a framework of political constitutionalism that requires some majoritarian mandate for constitutional review, the question of legitimacy of this review may change its meaning with regard to such cases.

One might argue that a court case concerning the distribution of federal powers in which the court reviews a statute just functions like a rights case: an undemocratic institution controls a democratic vote. But the fact that in a federal constitutional

---

[30] For Brazil: Afonso Da Silva 2013, pp. 557–584; Hübner Mendes 2013; for Germany: Kranenpohl 2010, in particular pp. 81–252; for France: Schnapper 2010, pp. 127–135, 274–277; for Italy: Cassese 2015.

system there are two political communities with two democratic constituencies makes this analysis less convincing. The question which of the federal levels is empowered to act implies, at least in a democratic federation, the question which of the two possible majorities is the relevant one (Möllers 2011a, pp. 258 et seq.). Neither a federal legislature that acts against the will of the majority in one of its sub-states nor a sub-state legislature that acts against the will of the overall federal majority can use their majority as a convincing democratic justification. They need a rule that decides which majority is politically in charge or a substantial argument about the externalities of this decision (Tiebout 1956, p. 423). Does that mean that there is no problem with the constitutional review of federal powers? No, there are many reasons why it does not. But it is important that these reasons are, on the one hand, practically relevant, but, on the other, do not share the strong normative claim of democratic legitimacy, but are rather prudential. Let us just mention some of them. Firstly, in many constitutional orders[31] the distribution of powers between the federal levels is no politically innocent question: empowering the federal level in the U.S., the European level in the EU or the Eidgenossenschaft in Switzerland is a politically contested project. Deciding such cases is easily interpreted as taking sides in a political conflict. Secondly, the strict review of federal powers has a tendency to halt and stall political reactions to social developments. There may be a particular need for an open interpretation of such norms in constitutional orders that are difficult or almost impossible to amend like one of the U.S. or the European Union. Thirdly, one may argue that the content of federal norms is normally not as easy to review because they are often explicitly discretionary like "necessary and proper" (Amar 1999, 755 et seq.) or comparable clauses.[32] Therefore, there is a case in favor of an interpretation of such norms that gives some leeway to the political process, but then again, to which one, the central or the sub-federal? And on the other hand, there is a traditionally strong case for the protection of unity and integrity within a federal order as famously expressed by Holmes' dictum: "I do not think the United States would come to an end if we lost our power to declare an Act of Congress void. I do think the Union would be imperiled if we could not make that declaration as to the laws of the several States." (Holmes 1913/1920, pp. 295–296).

Where does that leave us? It leaves us with an even messier and less clear-cut problem to which strong normative reasons hardly apply, but where other rather institutional arguments may speak against a strong constitutional review.

A comparable situation can be observed with regard to separation of powers. Conflicts between political organs, between government and parliament, do not suffer from the counter-majoritarian problem when both parties of the conflict enjoy political legitimacy. Still, there may be institutional reasons to be careful to define the institutional relations between political organs by means of strictly reviewable

---

[31] Germany seems to be an interesting exception.
[32] For example, the notoriously judicially underenforced notion of subsidiarity in the EU Treaty.

legal norms. If a political process is about the organization of will-formation, of collective judgment in an Arendtian sense, we may be careful not to put too many procedural constraints on it (Möllers 2013, pp. 110–111). Still, questions such as whether parliament gets access to governmental information, whether the decision to send troops abroad needs parliamentary consent or whether government may use emergency powers to get financial resources beyond the parliamentary budget, could need framing through formal rules. Even if courts refused to review them, they would give, through their refusal, a meaningful answer to the problem. For reasons of mere institutional power, such a refusal will regularly privilege the executive branch. One may argue that such questions even need a specific constitutional procedure.[33]

Again, the counter-majoritarian argument does not really fit the point, but that does not mean that constitutional review is necessarily a useful or legitimate tool. Still, if we accept that institutional conflicts between the branches may be solved on a rule-based basis and if we observe that the absence of formal reviewable procedures may privilege the stronger actors, that is, the executive, there may be a case for specialized constitutional review.

Beyond Functioning Democracies

Finally, a totally different justification of judicial review would remind us of the fact that there are many semi-functional democratic systems in which constitutional courts may play a different role. Obviously, it is not the case that constitutional review can just compensate deficiencies of a given political system. To the contrary, in many cases courts will just share deficiencies of the general constitutional system. Rule of law institutions are not self-sufficient, they need the majoritarian basis which they are called to check upon (Gargarella 2013, pp. 161–162; Przeworski 2019, pp. 5–7). But on the other hand, there may be cases in which the concrete possibility for a constitutional court to mitigate institutional reasons provides a substantial reason of justification to step in. One example would be the suo moto cases of the Supreme Court of India in which the court tried to protect the rights of persons who had no possibility to sue themselves (Pillay 2019, pp. 162–164). Another example shows the case of the South-African constitutional court (Roux 2015, pp. 15 et seq.). Such and comparable cases in other jurisdictions are often messy. They may be justified in their concrete context, but they do not provide the basis for a general theory of judicial intervention.

Therefore, the hope that constitutional courts are generally successful or even necessary for stopping democratic orders from becoming authoritarian is unwarranted (Huq 2019; Tushnet 2018b, pp. 330 et seq.). Courts may slow down such a development, but we also see courts as agents of authoritarianism. Above all, it is important

---

[33] So as critique of American constitutional procedure: Greene 2011, p. 129.

to see that specialized constitutional courts can easily be packed and serve afterwards as a formidable instrument for political control of the whole judiciary. Decentralized constitutional review could be the more resistant institutional set-up.

Challenges from Empirical Research

The most dramatic change in the academic description of constitutional courts will come from new methods of empirical legal research. So far, we can see different approaches that look for causal explanations for the decisions constitutional courts make as well as for the decision to introduce constitutional review as such.[34] Much of this research takes constitutional jurisprudence to be the result of political influences, be it the specific political attitudes of concrete judges, a general tendency of constitutional courts and their political backers to protect a certain set of liberal values, or simply property rights (Hirschl 2004, pp. 146–148), or to entrench political decisions by a political majority at the brink of losing their political lead (Ginsburg & Versteeg 2013, pp. 606 et seq.). Such research is a welcome antidote against the self-sufficiency of general theories and against too strong normative claims of courts and their academic justification. Yet, the assumption that constitutional jurisprudence is driven by political forces can finally only be proved by a convincing prognostic success or by a systematic empirical comparison between legal arguments on the one hand, and such external factors on the other, as explanations for concrete decisions. The latter seems fraught with methodological difficulties. It is easier to explain constitutional reasoning away in a kind of Marxian model of basis and superstructure than to take it empirically into account. But this may change with the rise of better models of quantitative text analysis that take reasons seriously. A move to what has been called in another context "quantitative formalism" (Moretti 2015) could be helpful. And again, it is not entirely clear if such research will lead to meaningful general results that claim to describe all constitutional orders or if it would be more promising to accept path dependencies and to look at certain clusters of constitutional systems to get meaningful results.[35] It is fair to say that this kind of empirical constitutionalism has so far not been achieved (and would not necessarily be accepted by) other more advanced strands of empirical political sciences, but this is not an argument against its further pursuit.

How to Assess the Legitimacy of Constitutional Review

If we accept the democratic decision to introduce constitutional review as a legitimate move and if we also accept that this decision may have its democratic costs

---

[34] For an example of the former using regression analysis, see Kantorowicz & Garoupa 2016; for an example of the latter using delegation theory, see Dyevre 2015.
[35] As the Varieties of Capitalism approach proposes for political economy, cf. Hall & Soskice 2001, pp. 2–68.

(Scharpf 1970, pp. 46 et seq.), then the way we assess the legitimacy of constitutional review shifts from the grand argument between political and legal constitutionalism to the large area of procedural and organizational detail. Under these conditions, it does not make sense to second-guess an explicit constitutional mandate for constitutional review as such, nor should we conflate the question of a court's legitimacy with the substantial outcome of its decisions (Möllers 2013, p. 139).

If constitutional courts should be obliged to decide in a more or less judicial procedure, this could have many implications. To name just three of them: courts should have little control over the cases they decide upon, they should be reluctant to impose positive duties of state action, and they should see themselves bound by their own case law. There may be counter arguments against these results, but more important than the normative claims is the descriptive attention that should be shifted to such questions. Again, this should not lead us to the fruitless distinction between "activist" and other courts that does not describe anything. But the perspective on procedural law helps to assess the legitimacy of court action under its own normative conditions and not just against an abstract normative model (Möllers, in Jestaedt et al. 2020, pp. 131–196).

The same is true for the organizational substructure of constitutional courts, a notoriously underrated topic. Every organization has its internal politics and in the case of constitutional courts it may be especially interesting to connect this with its macro-political environment. Questions like the role of a court's president, the procedure in which they are created and the role they play in the assignment of cases may often explain much of a court's decisions-making practice. It may help to analyze how the court is connected to or immunized from external political influence. A court in which justices become political icons with their own constituency, but do rather not deliberate with each other, may resonate differently with the general political process than a court whose justices are more or less publicly unknown, but heavily dependent on ongoing internal consensus-building.

IV OUTLOOK: A PLEA FOR CONTEXTUALISM

It makes sense to get a perspective on constitutional review beyond the interpretation of a given constitution, a perspective that looks at justification and legitimacy. To take such a perspective is nothing specific to constitutional review, we do it as political and constitutional theorists with parliaments, governments, administrative agencies and ordinary courts. A certain fixation on constitutional review in constitutional theory (and a certain ignorance especially of the legislative process) is probably better explained through a disciplinary bias of lawyers toward courts than through the fact that constitutional review is as such either a good or a problematic institution. To be sure, there are specific problems with constitutional review, but they are so specific that one has to be careful with general theories. Such problems are better defined immanently through a look at the normative assumptions, the political and historical motives for them and the institutional culture behind them in a given constitutional order.

The perspective on the organization may also lead us to accept that many constitutional courts are not well described as "courts", but rather look like hybrid semi-political institutions. This seems, at first glance, a point that brings home Waldron's critical argument, but at a closer look it does not necessarily do so. The fact that constitutional courts are different from other courts and that they act in a more political fashion does not mean that they are like parliaments. If they operate like parliaments by replicating a party conflict they are surely dysfunctional, and Waldron's argument works in this context. But if they are courts with political appointees, which get public attention and receive political critique, then they function in a manner that sets them apart from both legislatures and ordinary courts. This also means that the way we assess their legitimacy must be different from both the way we assess normal courts and the way we assess parliaments.

RECOMMENDED READING

Bellamy, R. (2007). *Political Constitutionalism*, Cambridge: Cambridge University Press.
Bellamy, R. (2014). The Democratic Legitimacy of International Human Rights Conventions: Political Constitutionalism and the European Convention on Human Rights. *European Journal of International Law*, 25 (4), 1019–1042.
Bickel, A. (1986). *The Least Dangerous Branch*, New Haven: Yale University Press.
Espionosa, M. J. & Landau, D. (2017). *Colombian Constitutional Law*, Oxford: Oxford University Press.
Gargarella, R. (2013). *Latin American Constitutionalism, 1810–2010*, Oxford: Oxford University Press.
Hirschl, R. (2004). *Towards Juristocracy*, Cambridge, MA: Harvard University Press.
Jestaedt, M. et al. (2020). *The German Federal Constitutional Court*, Oxford: Oxford University Press.
Kelsen, H. (2013 [1929]). *The Essence and Value of Democracy*. Edited by N. Urbinati and C. Invernizzi-Accetti. Lanham, MD: Rowman & Littlefield.
Möllers, C. (2011). Multi-Level Democracy. *Ratio Juris*, 24 (3), 247–367.
Nino, C. S. (1996). *The Constitution of Deliberative Democracy*, New Haven: Yale University Press.
Robertson, D. (2018). The Counter-Majoritan Thesis. In G. Jacobson, M. Schor, eds., *Comparative Constitutional Theory*. Cheltenham: Edward Elgar, pp. 189–207.
Waldron, J. (1999). *The Dignity of Legislation*, Cambridge: Cambridge University Press.
Waldron, J. (2006). The Core of the Case Against Judicial Review. *The Yale Law Journal*, 115 (6), 1346–1406.

22

Constitutional Interpretation

*Timothy Endicott**

The Constitution of India, adopted by the Constituent Assembly in 1950, provides that 'the Constitution shall stand amended' if a bill to amend it is passed in each house of the parliament by not less than two-thirds of the votes (Article 368). But on the Supreme Court of India's interpretation, the Constitution shall *not* stand amended if such a bill would alter 'the basic structure' of the Constitution.[1]

The Constitution of India provides that Supreme Court judges 'shall be appointed by the President ... after consultation' with 'such of the Judges ... as the President may deem necessary' (Article 124(2)). But the judges have interpreted the Constitution to require that the President must appoint as judges those selected by a 'collegium' of judges, membership of the collegium being specified by the judges.[2]

And then the judges held that a constitutional amendment to establish a broad-based judicial appointments commission was unlawful under the 'basic structure' doctrine, on the ground that judicial primacy in the appointment of judges is part of the basic structure of the Constitution.[3]

Indian constitutional law offers a paradigm of constitutional interpretation that departs from the arrangements laid down in a written constitution; we could offer examples from many countries. How can judges understand such constitutional departures as *interpretations*?

The answer, I will argue, is given by a general equivocation about interpretation, and a specific tension between constitutional law and constitutional justice. Interpretation ascribes meaning to its object, and we equivocate between meaning

---

[*] Vinerian Professor of English Law, University of Oxford. I am very grateful for comments from Trevor Allan, Raquel Barradas de Freitas, Luís Duarte d'Almeida, and David Dyzenhaus.

[1] *Kesavananda Bharati v State of Kerala* (1973) 4 SCC 225. See the reasons of Chief Justice Sikri at paragraphs 13–15, presenting the doctrine as the judges' interpretation. Krishnaswamy (2009), a wide-ranging and penetrating study of the doctrine, argues that 'the constitutional changes through which the basic structure doctrine originated and developed satisfy the criteria of constitutional interpretation' (188).

[2] *Supreme Court Advocates-on-Record Association v Union of India* (1993) 4 SCC 441, *In re Presidential Reference*, [1998] Supp 2 SCR 400, AIR 1999 SC 1. See Sengupta (2019), chapter 2.

[3] *Supreme Court Advocates-on-Record Association v Union of India* (2016) 5 SCC 1. See Bhatia (2018).

as significance and meaning as signification. The boundaries of constitutional interpretation are put in question by that equivocation, and by the tension between the rule of constitutional law, and the demands of constitutional justice.

I INTRODUCTION

Constitutional interpretation is *constitutional* because it is done to determine what the constitution requires and what it permits. It is *interpretation* because it is the activity of working out the meaning of an object. I will focus on the constitutions of nation states, and on the role of constitutional interpretation in courts of law.

The charm of interpretation puts constitutional law under strain. The charm of interpretation is the attraction that inclines all of us to understand the conclusions we wish to reach as interpretations. It is a feature of law in general (Endicott 2012), and it is an engine of constitutional change. It pulls against the constitutional imperative of the rule of law. Yet, ironically, the charm of interpretation is an inherently conservative urge: no one would feel it, if they felt free to act on a whim. The resultant tension between interpretive conservatism and creativity – between the rule of constitutional law and the say-so of an interpreter – becomes the captivating focus of constitutional adjudication. It will be the focus of this chapter.

It is so difficult to give a satisfactory general account of the distinction between identifying the requirements of the constitution through interpretation, and merely saying that whatever you wish the constitution to require is your interpretation. It is impossible to draw that distinction in a way that will attract consensus. But we have to work at drawing it: in the decision making of state officials who are bound by the constitution, it is a crucial element in the broader distinction between responsible government, and government by their arbitrary fiat. I will call it the distinction between interpretation and say-so. Every new interpretation has an inventive element. But some inventions are *not* interpretations; by speaking of the distinction between interpretation and say-so, I am referring to the distinction between inventions that are and are not interpretations.

Part of the agenda of this chapter will be to warn against judges engaging in arbitrary government, ascribing their decisions to 'interpretation' when they are flouting their constitution, or making up new constitutional norms. But if you favour judicial innovation in constitutional law, I hope to take you with me quite a long way. You need the distinction between interpretation and say-so. For if we cannot draw it, we will have to be sceptics about interpretation.[4] The coherence of the notion of interpretation depends on the possibility that judges might misrepresent or misconceive their decisions as 'interpretive'.

---

[4] Pierluigi Chiassoni (2019) makes a plea for healthy scepticism about interpretation; see especially pp. 1–8. And see Guastini (2019, p. 13) and Barradas de Freitas (2016).

II MEANING: AN EQUIVOCATION BETWEEN SIGNIFICANCE AND SIGNIFICATION

Constitutional interpretation is the process of working out the meaning of constitution-making acts. And what is meaning? In respect of a language, it is what we share that makes it possible for us to disagree with each other. A word means what people understand it to mean; we do not ordinarily disagree about it.[5] Agreement about the meaning of words facilitates the deep and important disagreements, as to what an utterance means, if anything, and as to whether it is true, if it asserts a fact, or whether to go along with it, if it asserts a norm. Our agreement about the meaning of words does not answer those questions.

Infants can grasp that an utterance is significant – they can tell that it is important to a speaker that she is speaking, and speaking *to someone*. They can grasp that a way of speaking *means* that the speaker is angry, or delighted. Significance of that kind is the sort of meaning that can be ascribed to a tone of voice or to a change in the colour of the speaker's face.

The difference between an infant and a child is that the child has learned not simply that the colour of the speaker's face may mean that she is angry, but that when she says, 'I am angry', *she means* that she is angry; for her to say something is for her to use language that signifies. A tone of voice can be significant, but it has signification only insofar as the speaker is using it for a communicative purpose. Words are signifiers; an utterance is the use of signifiers to say something. Think about the difference between the meaning of the colour of the speaker's face, and the meaning of the utterance; the latter is *what she means*. Understanding the utterance means understanding a person.

For the child, learning to understand words and to understand utterances means learning to understand persons. And that is how she learns to engage in the process of reasoning that may be needed to work out what the utterance means (what the speaker is referring to, whether she is teasing…). That process is interpretation, and its result is an interpretation: an understanding that can only be gained by creative reasoning. By creative reasoning, I mean reasoning that uses a sensitive grasp of the speaker and of the situation to provide premises that support a conclusion as to the meaning of the utterance – that is, what the utterer signified.

Meaning in the sense of signification – unlike meaning in the sense of significance – offers the possibility that an agent may order relations by signifying that relations are to be ordered in this way, rather than that. Propositionality in the meaning of linguistic utterances is the most terrific facility. It is not essential to the ordering of relations. We can order relations with a tone of voice, or by picking up a child and sitting her on her chair at the table. But the facility is just so useful for the articulate

---

[5] We might do so. You might think that 'disinterested' is so generally understood to mean 'uninterested' that it means 'uninterested', while I think that understanding it in that way is a very popular mistake.

and intentional ordering of relations among persons, that in a political community – where ordering relations is difficult and complicated – it becomes a practical necessity for governance according to law. It is essential because it is the only way to order things if you have to deal with people.

A constitution is an ordering that establishes a political community and enables us to be members of it. When it comes to our constitution, our aspirations are wrapped up with its meaning, in the sense of its significance. Meaning as signification and meaning as significance are intertwined in all orderings of relations by the use of language. That is because orderings of relations can be just or unjust, and because they instantiate power relations. When a mother tells a child what to do, what the mother signifies is interwoven with the significance of the fact that it is she who is saying it (and, therefore, with the whole complex significance of their relationship). The true significance of an ordering of relations – its proper purposes – can be fulfilled more or less or not at all by an articulate exercise of power. In law making, legal signification is often very usefully demarcated from the rights and wrongs of the relationships involved. When a buyer signifies acceptance of the seller's price for a new car, for example, an understanding of the *significance* of the transaction and of the relationship justifies treating the buyer as having an obligation to pay the price *signified* in the offer, and the signification of a price is not coloured by the significance of the transaction. Power relations are rendered colourless by the law's purpose of enabling the two parties to bind themselves to an agreement. They, too, may be subject to the charm of interpretation, but it does not generally colour their understanding of the price.

What the makers of a constitution have signified is not generally demarcated so neatly from the significance of the constitution-making transaction. The significance of a constitution has a particular force that affects our grasp of the signification of the actions by which it was made and by which it is sustained and developed. It can become an article of faith, a matter of respect for our community, that our constitution is to be understood as a good one, requiring and permitting what it ought to require and to permit. It can come to seem like a sort of insult to our shared identity, to understand those acts of constitution making as signifying an arrangement that is unjust, or that is ineffective for the public good. More in constitutional interpretation than in any other area of law, what is signified by the law maker becomes interwoven with the significance of the transaction. All our presumptions of political morality shape the meaning-as-significance of constitution-making acts, and then those presumptions take on the aspect of the meaning-as-signification of those acts. They become the drivers of innovative interpretations. Interpretations ascribe *meaning* in both of its equivocal senses. There may be nothing signifying that the constitution requires some conduct that it ought to require, and yet the demands of constitutional justice seem to have this result: that it is a matter of the meaning of our constitution (in the sense of its significance – its point, its proper purposes, its value and its values) that it must require that conduct. The Indian Supreme Court's basic structure doctrine is a paradigm of the colouring of constitutional interpretation by the significance of the constitution-making act: the judges see themselves as responsible for determining the meaning of the Constitution, and their views as to its significance are, in a certain sense, views as to its meaning.

The significance of a constitution puts a strain on constitutional interpretation. It generates a destabilising presumption that can lead to the overinterpretation and the underinterpretation of the arrangements that the constitution makers signified. Interpretation is the nexus between the factual aspect of constitutional law (in the case of India, the fact that the Constituent Assembly adopted the Constitution that it adopted, along with all the facts as to the establishment of the Assembly and its composition and operation, and the nature of the power allocated to it, and the context in which it acted), and its normative aspect (constitutional rights and powers, duties and liabilities in Indian law).

To interpret a law-making act is, primarily, to ascribe a meaning to the action of the law maker in signifying (in the way and in the context in which the law maker did so), *that it is to be the law that* [and then you could quote the words of the instrument to finish the statement of the object of interpretation]. The primary object of Indian constitutional interpretation is the act of the Constituent Assembly in adopting the Constitution of India in 1950.[6] It was the Assembly and not the Court that decided what the content of the Constitution was to be. The Assembly decided that there would be a federal structure, a bill of rights, a bicameral legislature, a President, directive principles of state policy, and so on. The primary purpose of constitutional interpretation is to determine what the Assembly did, in the exercise of its power.

That object and that purpose are primary because, as the rest of this chapter will argue, a court must treat the act of the Constituent Assembly as the object of constitutional interpretation, and must give effect to that act in accordance with its true signification, if India is to have a constitution – that is, a framework of government, enduring across time, and binding public authorities including the courts.[7] The court's commitment to that pursuit (which I will call the 'primary mode of interpretation') is essential, if the Assembly's adoption of the Constitution is to have legal effect today. And there is no other way on offer for India to have a constitution at all. The judges' approach to interpretation must give effect to the allocation of constitution-making power to the Assembly. The ascription of meaning to the Assembly's action is what it takes to

---

[6] I will use 'Constitution' with a capital 'C' for an instrument by which a constitution was established for a state (as in India), so that the act of adopting the instrument is the primary object of constitutional interpretation. In respect of India, that instrument can be amended; the object of constitutional interpretation has come to include the actions of federal and state institutions in making more than one hundred amendments. Can judicial decisions also become objects of interpretation in constitutional law? See Section VII, 'Other objects of constitutional interpretation'.

[7] For an alternative approach (in which the object of constitutional interpretation is not any act in the exercise of a law-making power, but the whole pattern of the community's constitutional history, and the purpose is not to give effect to an exercise of power, but to construct a set of principles that honours the community's history), see Dworkin (1985, 2006). For a very useful survey of other alternatives, see Waluchow and Kyritsis (2023).

make it true – from day to day, 70 years and more after Indian independence – that the constitution-making act of the Constituent Assembly has effect (and, therefore, that the Constitution of India *is* the Constitution of India). The interpretive nexus between the factual and the normative aspects of the law lies in the interpreter's commitment to decide the meaning of that object – that act – in accordance with the principles of interpretation. As Richard Ekins wrote, the object of constitutional interpretation is 'the Constitution, which is an intentional lawmaking act rather than a text floating free in the world' (Ekins 2017b, p. 1). In Ekins' view, 'the point of such interpretation is primarily to understand the meaning that those who made the Constitution intended to convey by promulgating the text in question' (p. 1). I agree with Ekins' account of what it is that an interpreter ought to interpret, but I think that the point of constitutional interpretation is to understand the meaning *that the Constituent Assembly conveyed*, rather than the meaning *that they intended to convey* (see Section IX).

III THE RULE OF LAW AND CONSTITUTIONAL INTERPRETATION

Legal stability is a requirement of the rule of law, and constitutional stability is a requirement of constitutionalism. In fact, constitutional stability is essential for a good political community, which means that it is a requirement of constitutional justice. Without stability, the constitution cannot fulfil its central role of providing a bearable framework of government for people who cannot agree as to what is the best framework of government. That achievement – settlement of the terms of governance – depends on a very great, artificial stability in the existence and operation of institutions established by the constitution, and on a political culture of inertia in accepting the authority of those institutions, and on adherence to norms that the Constitution imposes on institutions and officials. If a constitution is too easily changed, or is not regularly adhered to, then the form of government will be perpetually unsettled. A constitution is a solution to a huge coordination problem – how is the political community to be governed? Civil peace depends on the solution to that problem. It is a coordination problem because although a good constitution will secure a *just* settlement, the need *for a settlement* is itself highly exigent, and is partly independent of the justice of the settlement. We can say of a stable constitution that – regardless to some extent of constitutional justice – it is a solution to a problem that needed a solution.

For these reasons, the approaches to constitutional interpretation that people call 'living tree'[8] or 'evolutive' (Letsas 2007[9]) patently involve dangers to constitutional stability, and to the good of the political community. But as with so many issues of political and

---

[8] *Edwards v Attorney General of Canada* [1930] AC 124 (PC) 136: 'The British North America Act planted in Canada a living tree capable of growth and expansion within its natural limits.'

[9] The Strasbourg Court's interpretive role is very closely analogous to the interpretive role of a domestic constitutional court, as Letsas makes clear in his defence of evolutive interpretation.

legal morality, it would be a mistake to overgeneralise. From the need for constitutional stability, it does not follow that the constitution ought not to change. Likewise, it does not follow from the general rule-of-law requirement of stability that the law should not change. Stability is a crucial but vague desideratum for the rule of law in general, and for the rule of constitutional law most especially. The criterion for meeting it is whether the change in question would make it harder for the law to serve its purposes.

Gifted lawyers and judges deal imaginatively with the tantalising distinction between giving effect to the constitution and changing it. Their assertions of the requirements of constitutional law may be a pretence for advocating or making arbitrary changes. Or their constitutional ingenuity may result in wise and responsible change to the constitution.

The constitution has changed if it requires today what it did not require yesterday (or a century ago). In 1765, Lord Camden made new constitutional law in the great English case of *Entick v Carrington*, establishing that a warrant from the Secretary of State did not lawfully authorise the search and seizure of property on suspicion of seditious libel. He made new law without claiming to change the law; on the contrary, he appealed to the ancient constitution. Responding to the defendant's argument that the use of such warrants had been the practice since the Glorious Revolution of 1689, he wrote:

> [T]he common law did not begin with the Revolution; the ancient constitution which had been almost overthrown and destroyed, was then repaired and revived; the Revolution added a new buttress to the ancient venerable edifice.
> (1765) 2 Wils KB 275, 292.

So far as metaphors go, I think that building renovation is more apt, as a portrayal of constitutional interpretation, than the popular metaphor of a living tree. A living tree provides a good metaphor in a way, since it is a reminder of the need for stability; a tree needs some very significant rigidity in order to be a healthy specimen. Yet it is a poor metaphor insofar as it suggests that changes to a constitution are endogenous and organic, and represent in themselves the fulfilment of the organism's destiny. The living tree metaphor tends to obscure a crucial fact: that the changes are crafted by interpreters.

The changes that result to a constitution from the practice of its interpretation are more like renovations to a building, than they are like the growth of a tree. Builders who are *renovating* do not tear down the building and put up a new and different one. After a good renovation, the building will have been made more beautiful and suitable for the present day and for the future, but it will be the same ancient venerable edifice. That is why some buildings – and doubtless some constitutions – ought to be demolished, rather than renovated.

Good renovation will depend on the renovators' own present-day architectural brilliance, of course, and also on their sensitive grasp of whatever genius lay behind the original construction of the ancient venerable edifice, and behind the changes that have been made to it since. The renovators may well need to remedy failures of the original builders, or the botched work of other renovators. But comity toward those initial builders and earlier renovators – that is, respect for their craft – is generally a virtue in renovating an ancient venerable edifice. And constitutional interpretation, likewise, generally calls for an attitude of comity toward the framers and amenders – that is, respect for their craft.

But good renovators do, after all, have to be good designers (and not mere imitators of their forebears). And good constitutional judges must seek to do justice, or a certain constitutional form of justice which ought to be explained.

IV CONSTITUTIONAL JUSTICE

If the death penalty is unjust, that does not mean that the constitution must prohibit it. There may be no need for a prohibition. It may be the case that no one would think of proposing such a thing. Representative politics or international pressure may prevent advocates of the death penalty from getting the death penalty enacted as law. Then, constitutional justice may not demand a constitutional prohibition of the death penalty. The United Kingdom constitution does not prohibit it, and the UK is as just, in this respect, as Germany or Iceland. For a contrary view see Weinrib (2016), arguing that a constitution is morally flawed if it does not secure 'human dignity, conceived in terms of the right of each person to equal freedom' (p. 3) against infringement by the state, and even against the juridical possibility of amendment of the constitution to allow infringement. On that theory, if the death penalty does not respect dignity, it is not enough if there is no prospect that persons will be subject to it, or threatened with it; their dignity is infringed if the constitution does not provide a non-amendable justiciable guarantee against it. But in my view, if persons in countries such as the UK and Canada are secure against the imposition of a death penalty, there is no insult to their dignity in the fact that it is not the law that gives them that security.

By 'constitutional justice', I mean those aspects of justice that the constitution must secure. It depends on what the community needs its constitution to require or to permit, in order for it to be a just community. Judicial primacy in the appointment of judges is a demand of constitutional justice in India, if the Indian state cannot be a just state unless the constitution protects judicial primacy.

No doubt, mistakes are made in constitutional adjudication when judges and others succumb to the lure of what we could call the fallacy of constitutional justice: the assumption that if a form of state action is wrong, then justice demands that the constitution must prohibit it. It would be a fallacy of political morality to think that a constitution is morally deficient if it does not prohibit all injustices. It would be a fallacy of political metaphysics to think that a constitution necessarily does prohibit all injustices. These fallacies can become drivers for government by the say-so of the interpreters of a constitution.

Even though the demands of constitutional justice depend fairly radically on political, economic, social and cultural conditions in different communities, I do not suppose that there is any country in which the constitution could legitimately prohibit all unjust schemes of taxation. Constitutional law must not to do so if its mechanisms (such as making the prohibition justiciable in a court) are inept for restraining the potential injustice (as they may be if the court is incompetent to identify injustice in public finance). And it is unnecessary, if there are other techniques for fighting the potential injustice.

Partisan gerrymandering of districts for election to a legislature is a political injustice. That does not mean that it is a constitutional injustice. It becomes a constitutional injustice only if the community needs its constitution to prohibit partisan gerrymandering – as it may do if, for example, the capacity of the legislature itself to right the injustice is corrupted by the gerrymandering, and there is no other constitutional technique to prevent the abuse of power. *Then*, partisan gerrymandering is a constitutional injustice.

And in that case, is the Constitution to be interpreted as prohibiting partisan gerrymandering? In the primary mode of interpretation, the answer is: only if the makers of the Constitution prohibited it by the act of adopting the Constitution. And that is not a question of constitutional justice. Even if you do not agree about the primary mode of interpretation, perhaps you can agree on the following principle: to insist that the Constitution *must* be interpreted as prohibiting partisan gerrymandering is to *abolish* constitutional interpretation, and to authorise the interpreters of the Constitution to implement constitutional justice.

And now, supposing that the Constitution cannot be understood as prohibiting partisan gerrymandering, is it illegitimate for a court to hold partisan gerrymandering to be unconstitutional? That does not follow; it is an open question as to whether improving the constitution in this respect is something that the court can responsibly do. Remedying a constitutional injustice is, *prima facie*, a gift to the nation. But then, departing from the constitution is *prima facie* wrong for an institution charged with giving effect to the constitution as it is. That is how the jurisdiction of a constitutional court is different from an amending formula. Just as there are some gifts that you have no right to give me, it is possible to imagine circumstances in which it would be unjustifiable for judges to remedy a constitutional injustice (as, e.g., when doing so would operate as a precedent for a destabilising practice of judicial constitutional reform that the judges cannot trust themselves or their successors to engage in responsibly). These questions are not questions of law, but of the probity and the morality of a judicial assumption of an authority that no constitution-making act has ever conferred on them. It is part of the standard ideology of constitutionalism that judges should not assume powers that have not been conferred on them. That adds to the charm of constitutional interpretation: constitutional court judges long to see their own action as based on constitutional interpretation.

The rule of law is itself a requirement of constitutional justice because if you or I are acting in a public capacity, we owe a duty of responsible government – instead of arbitrary government – to the community (and, often, to particular individuals or groups). The rule of law may seem to require constitutional courts not to change the constitution. The ideology of constitutionalism deploys the notion of interpretation to portray actions of a constitutional court as identifying the constitution as it is (through interpretation), and not as changing it. The double irony of this incoherent ideology is that interpretations do change the constitution, and that judicial changes to the constitution are not necessarily illegitimate (whether they are or are not based on interpretation). The rule of law does not require courts not to make changes; however, it requires them not to make arbitrary changes. For them to make law legitimately by their say-so, there has to be something that makes it non-arbitrary to do so.

Here, then, is a proposal for a theorem of morality in constitution-making by *any* agency: for anyone's say-so to count as a legitimate ground for a constitutional norm, there must be reasons for that agency to exercise constitution-making authority. The Indian Constituent Assembly's say-so is a legitimate ground of constitutional norms today because of the law initially establishing it, and the politics of Indian independence, and the reasons that the country has even today to count the Constituent Assembly's work in another era as genuinely establishing a constitution for the nation. That is why the Constituent Assembly's say-so quite rightly counts as a source of constitutional law today.

Why does the say-so of the Supreme Court of India count as a source of constitutional law? Not because it was authorised to make constitutional law, but because of a combination of particular constitutional needs of the political community (in particular, the constitutional need for resolution of disputes as to the constitution), and the Court's unique opportunity to meet such needs. Those needs and that opportunity may give it reason to exercise constitution-making authority, even if no one authorised it to do so.

V CONSTITUTIONAL CHANGE

The principle of constitutional stability requires that every constitutional amending formula should be constrained. That proposition could serve as an element in the definition of a constitution: nothing would count as a constitution, if it could be amended as easily as the fee for a driver's licence can be amended. If there is any good rationale for the Supreme Court of India's basic structure doctrine, perhaps it is that the Constituent Assembly made it too easy to amend the Constitution (Article 368), and that only the judges of the Supreme Court could meet a constitutional need for constraint on amendments.

Constitutional interpretation, as it is practised in many present-day states, has the effect of an amending process that is constrained only by the costs and the adventitious nature of litigation, the interpretive doctrines of the courts, the self-restraint of the judges, and whatever political pressures they may be under not to go too far. You may say that this is an insufficient constraint on constitutional change, when the notion of interpretation is so radically flexible. And that is the danger of constitutional change by judicial decision – such as the development of India's basic structure doctrine. It is very easy to imagine a polity in which the judges do as they wish, call it 'constitutional interpretation', and thereby abandon constitutionalism. Judges have acted with abandon at particular points in the actual constitutional practice of India, the U.S., the U.K., and other countries.

Yet in those constitutional states, the forces of political culture restraining the judges can be very strong in some respects, although those forces are not rule-governed, and they may leave scope for opportunism. Even in the Supreme Court of India, the judges do not exactly treat the constitution as their plaything. Consider this recent statement of the form of constraint:

> 'The need of the present has to be served with the interpretative process of law. However, it is to be seen how much strength and sanction can be drawn from the Constitution to consummate the changing ideology and convert it into a reality. The immediate needs are required to be addressed through the process of interpretation by the Court unless the same totally falls outside the constitutional framework or the constitutional interpretation fails to recognise such dynamism.'[10]

This is a vague statement of the pressure under which Indian judges operate in constitutional adjudication. It is accurate because it is vague. Their freedom is equivocal: 'it is to be seen' what they can do. In that context of decision, the central constraint on judicial change is the judges' need to present it (to themselves, and to their community) as interpretation.

VI CONSTITUTIONAL ADJUDICATION WITHOUT INTERPRETATION

The charm of interpretation can make it look as if *all* issues in constitutional adjudication are to be answered by an interpretation, so that a court can only decide in favour of a claimant if the best interpretation vindicates the claim. But many issues in constitutional disputes are not interpretive issues. I will briefly address three important sorts of decisions, in giving effect to a constitution, that are not interpretive: applying abstract evaluative standards, resolving indeterminacies, and acting equitably.

If a Constitution bans 'cruel' punishments, a court may very well have an interpretive task to carry out, in working out what the adoption of the provision signified. The court may need to work out whether the term 'cruel' is to be understood in some special sense that could be stated in different, clearer and more articulate terms, as the result of a good interpretation.

---

[10] *Common Cause v Union of India* (2018) 5 SCC 1 [160], Deepak Misra CJI.

But what if the best conclusion as to the meaning of the provision, understood in its context, is simply the presumably obvious: that the utterance is to be understood as banning cruel punishments? Then, if the issue before the court is whether a particular punishment is cruel, there is *nothing interpretive* in the court's responsibility to decide whether the punishment in question is unconstitutional. Not that the task is not important or demanding; perhaps the task is more important and demanding than interpretation. The task calls for practical wisdom, which requires sensitivity to the position of the offender, to the purpose and the effects of the punishment, to the viable alternatives, and so on. The issue may call on the court to articulate or to elaborate a conception of the dignity of the human person. That is not a matter of constitutional interpretation in the primary mode. If the Constitution outlawed cruel punishments, it conferred on the court – assuming the justiciability of the issue – the remarkable, open-ended authority that goes with the responsibility for giving effect to the provision. The court has authority to articulate or to elaborate a conception of the dignity of the human person that is to be treated as the community's conception. It is a law-making authority if there is a doctrine of precedent. It is a very important function of constitutional courts. It encompasses much of the reasoning of constitutional rights adjudication.

But lawyers and judges tend to call the exercise of such forms of authority 'interpretation', and of course they are not misusing the English language; it *is* interpretation in an extended sense – it gives meaning to the constitution. But it is not interpretation in the primary mode. It does not reach its conclusion by working out the meaning of the Constitution. In the primary sense of 'interpretation', the role of deciding what counts as a cruel punishment is fundamentally non-interpretive.

You could say the same of the role of a court in resolving indeterminacies in the constitution arising from vagueness, or from the characteristic incompleteness of Constitutions as instruments for the creation of a framework of government. Consider disputes about the effect of a will or a contract. It may seem that the court's role is just to decide whether there is a valid will or contract, to interpret it, and then to apply it. But the court also has to be ready to complete an incomplete contract or will (where it can do so responsibly), by adopting any measure, not repugnant to what the parties have actually done, that will make it possible to give effect to their purpose of making a will or a contract. That may be the court's job, for example, in deciding when a delay in delivery of goods counts as a breach, if the contract (in the sense of the instrument by which the parties made the contract) says nothing about time of delivery. To justify such a measure, it is not necessary for the court's resolution to be based on an interpretive judgment – that is, a judgment as to the meaning of the contract. It is very common in private law for courts to seek to do what they can so that such an instrument may have effect, rather than fail. And how much more important it is that a Constitution should have effect, rather than fail. A court can hold that there *was no* contract if the agreement is too incomplete (e.g., if a purported contract for the sale of goods states no price). The court cannot hold that an incomplete constitution is no constitution.

In addition to resolving disputes in ways that make the requirements of a constitution more complete, it can be legitimate for a court to depart from a general rule of a constitution on grounds of equity. We tend these days not to think of courts as exercising an equitable jurisdiction to dispense from statutes, let alone from constitutions. But why shouldn't a judge exercise such a jurisdiction? You may say, 'because the judge must adhere to the Constitution, of course, rather than depart from it!' But then you are begging the question, which is, whether the judge must adhere to the general rules of the Constitution. And although an equitable constitutional jurisdiction (i.e., an authority to depart from the Constitution on grounds of justice) is patently a jurisdiction that can lend itself to judicial waywardness, it is not inherently more dangerous – or more in tension with the ideal of the rule of law – than a judicial power of constitutional interpretation.

The fundamental duty of courts is not to interpret, but to provide resolution according to law. The duty to interpret arises where interpretation is necessary to work out the meaning of an object in order to decide the case. In constitutional cases, adopting a resolution is in itself a step toward making political community bearable and therefore sustainable, and worth sustaining. It is a solution to a coordination problem – a specific instance of the overall coordination problem I mentioned earlier, of how we are to be governed. There is value in the judicial capacity to deliver a resolution. Although it should always be done in a way that is compatible with the best interpretation of the Constitution, the value of resolution does not depend on interpretation.

Here, too, I hasten to add that if judges describe everything they do in identifying the law of the constitution as 'constitutional interpretation', we do not yet have any reason to think that there is anything wrong with the results, or the process. They are misdescribing what they are doing. They may be succumbing to the charm of interpretation. Yet there may even be value in their incomplete self-understanding (when we might find a more accurate explanation of what they are doing). That self-understanding may contribute to a culture of constraint in their exercise of the creative role that the constitution gives them.

VII OTHER OBJECTS OF CONSTITUTIONAL INTERPRETATION

The adoption of an instrument titled 'Constitution' is, of course, not the only way of making constitutional law. The common law provides another way, through the effect that it gives to judicial decisions. In a system with a doctrine of precedent, a court deciding a new constitutional case must treat the decisions of the courts in previous constitutional cases as objects of constitutional interpretation. That practice makes judicial decisions into sources of constitutional law.

It may seem that decisions interpreting a Constitution ought not to be treated as precedents. You might say that fidelity to the 1950 Constitution requires Indian courts to treat it as the one and only object of interpretation. Treating anything else as an object of constitutional interpretation can only result in deviation from the Constitution.

But the Indian Supreme Court uses a strong form of *stare decisis* in constitutional cases; that is what makes the 'basic structure' doctrine into a rule in Indian constitutional law (rather than a particular idea that the Court acted on once, and may or may not act on again). And *stare decisis* is justifiable as a matter of principle, in spite of the value of treating the act of the Constituent Assembly as a constitution-making act. Fidelity to the Constitution is at the centre of constitutional law, but (1) there is no reason to think that fidelity is better attained if each court in a new case must rethink what the Constitution requires, and (2) fidelity is not the only value. The doctrine of precedent equips constitutional law with a reflexively ordered technique of self-regulation. That is, it subjects constitutional law to the rule of law, with the potential for gains in stability and consistency. And it enables the Supreme Court of India to meet needs of the community for the future (see, Section IV), and not only to meet the need for resolution of particular disputes.

Even apart from interpretation of a written Constitution, all common law systems have inherited norms of constitutional law that developed through judicial reasoning at common law. Adjudication over *habeas corpus* often involves constitutional interpretation – interpretation of the practice of judges over centuries in issuing the writ. The legal effect of that practice is one striking feature of an unwritten constitution like that of the UK. And a second is that an unwritten constitution (at least, in the case of the UK) enables changes to the framework of government by ordinary legislation. As a result, it may seem infinitely flexible. But by the same token you might say that it is infinitely inflexible, because it offers no technique for entrenchment of constitutional rules, *except* that it allows for something akin to entrenchment through the development of judicial doctrine. And in particular, it gives constitutional significance to techniques of statutory interpretation: constitutional principles become presumptions (sometimes irrebuttable!) in statutory interpretation. So the UK courts have decided that decisions of any executive agency can be quashed for error of law, even if Parliament has enacted that the agency's decisions shall not be questioned in a court.[11] And they have, in effect, overruled a statute authorising a minister to prevent disclosure of government information, after a tribunal has ordered disclosure.[12] The judges tend to see these constitution-making interferences with statute *as interpretation*. The concept of interpretation comes under the same strain here, as in the interpretation of a Constitution.

VIII WHY SHOULD CONSTITUTIONAL INTERPRETATION BE DONE BY COURTS?

I have addressed the role of courts because I think that there are pressing reasons, generalisable across quite diverse constitutions and political traditions, for elements of the meaning of a Constitution to be justiciable. Those reasons are that:

---

[11] *R (Privacy International) v Investigatory Powers Tribunal* [2019] UKSC 22.
[12] *R (Evans) v Attorney General* [2015] UKSC 21.

(1) Coordination is valuable in some constitutional arrangements (Section III), and courts have the capacity to impose coordination. That value explains why it is a lapse in constitutionalism, if it becomes politically feasible for other agencies to ignore judicial rulings.
(2) The independence of judges from some aspects of political life may protect the exercise of the interpretive power from certain forms of abuse.

It is rash to generalise, but we can say that it is generally valuable for a constitution to have a balance between representative and independent decision-making institutions, and to make various corresponding separations of powers. The independence of judges is both a form of separation of power, and a protection for other constitutional separations of power (see Jacob Levy's chapter in this book, on the separation of powers).

And how good it will be for the political community, if the judges are wise. But the pressing reasons for constitutional adjudication – coordination and separation of power – do not depend on their wisdom. The task of constitutional courts is, as Dieter Grimm has put it, 'to decide cases and not to develop a constitutional or methodological theory' (Grimm 2016, p. 167). I think that a court would not be better if the judges shared a theory of constitutional interpretation. In fact, I think it is valuable if they do not do so. There can be a benefit to the community if each judge always feels somewhat defensive about their own approach, and feels a need to implement it in ways that will make their theory – if they have one – look acceptable to others. The results (and therefore the development of constitutional law) will sometimes go one way and sometimes another; some amount of controversy and disarray in the courts' methodology and theory will tend to act as another (somewhat inchoate, unofficial, non-rule-governed) form of constitutional constraint.

CONCLUSION: SHOULD WE TALK ABOUT THE INTENTIONS OF THE FRAMERS?

Indian law secures aspects of constitutional justice by conferring law-making power on a democratic Parliament, and protecting freedom of speech, and committing the institutions of government to pursue certain aspects of social justice. But you might say that there is no moral force, today, in the sheer fact that some movers and shakers decided in 1949 that it should be so. Indians owe much admiration and a debt of gratitude to Dr Ambedkar and the members of the Constituent Assembly, but they do not owe a duty of obedience to those people. And yet, the value of constitutional stability creates a very pressing need for the people of India today to treat the Constituent Assembly as having made a Constitution for the country, by an action they took 70 years ago. It endures today as they intended it to endure, but the reason for Indians to sustain it now is the need of the political community, today and for the future. The primary mode of interpretation is primary because it involves an attitude to interpretation that the interpreters of the Constitution must take, if they are to treat the Constituent Assembly's adoption of the Constitution of India as effective.

It is a standard tenet of the ideology of constitutionalism in states with constitutional courts that the judges must only interpret, and not depart from the constitution. If, in the practice of 'interpretation', the judges are actually renovating the ancient venerable edifice, the reality is not in accord with that ideology. Judges on a constitutional court may change the constitution more or less arbitrarily if they succumb to the charm of interpretation, and view all their constitutional preferences as interpretations of the Constitution. On the other hand, the idea that judges must only interpret can stand in the way of constitutional change that could legitimately be undertaken by judges. I have argued that not everything the judges can legitimately do in determining disputes as to constitutional law is interpretation, and that judicial change to the constitution is not in principle contrary to the ideals of constitutionalism.

But judicial change must be constrained in the interests of constitutional stability. Our equivocations over the nature of meaning make the idea of constitutional interpretation very flexible, so that it can operate as a facility for constitutional change. Like a process for amending a Constitution, that facility for constitutional change needs to operate with constraint and circumspection; ironically, it is possible that the practice of changing the constitution through adjudication may acquire some of the much-needed constraint if the judges have to present such changes – to the community, and to themselves – as a matter of interpretation.

I have not delved into the debates between theorists and judges who attack or defend the notion that the point of interpretation is to identify intentions of the authors of a Constitution. Those debates, of course, get their poignancy from the strain that I have discussed. Debates over the intention of the framers are debates over the tension between the desiderata of constitutional stability and constitutional justice. Richard Ekins has developed a powerful argument that the point of constitutional interpretation 'is primarily to understand the meaning that those who make the Constitution intended to convey by promulgating the text in question' (Ekins 2017b, p. 1, and see generally Ekins 2012; contrast the views defended in Waluchow 2014, chap. 3.9.2; and Kavanagh 2002). The crucial point in law making (including the making of a Constitution) is what a law maker lawfully conveys. This is why I have proposed that the primary mode of interpretation is the ascription of meaning to the fact that a law maker did what it did in the exercise of a law-making power. The law is, after all, what the law maker makes (whether the law maker is a constituent assembly, or a court, or the institutions authorised to amend a Constitution). The whole point of the empowerment of persons or other agencies to make a Constitution or a statute or a will or a contract, of course, is to enable them to make the law that they intend to make. But it is their action, and not their intention, that makes the law.

I should add that it seems to me that the strain that I have been exploring in this chapter – and the risk of unconstrained constitutional change – can arise notwithstanding the results of (some of) the debates over the intention of the makers of a Constitution. For the strain has the result that lawyers and judges who agree with Richard Ekins may well find themselves imputing to the constitution makers the intention to establish constitutional justice, and ascribing to their acts a meaning that accords with constitutional justice. For them, it is the same as for proponents of 'living tree' interpretations: sometimes, constitutional interpretation is the tribute that caprice pays to the rule of law.

RECOMMENDED READING

Balkin, J. M. (2016). The Framework Model and Constitutional Interpretation. In D. Dyzenhaus and M. Thorburn, eds., *Philosophical Foundations of Constitutional Law.* Oxford: Oxford University Press, pp. 241–264.

Bobbit, P. (1991). *Constitutional Interpretation*, Oxford: Blackwell.

Dworkin, R. (1996). *Freedom's Law: The Moral Reading of the American Constitution*, Cambridge, MA: Harvard University Press.

Fallon, R. (1987). A Constructivist Coherence Theory of Constitutional Interpretation. *Harvard Law Review*, 100 (6), 1189–1286.

Goldsworthy, J. (2006). *Interpreting Constitutions, A Comparative Study*, Oxford: Oxford University Press.

Kavanagh, A. (2002). Original Intention, Enacted Text, and Constitutional Interpretation. *American Journal of Jurisprudence*, 47 (1), 255–298.

Raz, J. (1999). On the Authority and Interpretation of Constitutions: Some Preliminaries. In L. Alexander, ed., *Constitutionalism: Philosophical Foundations*. Cambridge: Cambridge University Press, pp. 152–193.

Roznai, Y. (2017). *Unconstitutional Constitutional Amendments*, Oxford: Oxford University Press.

Stone, A. (2009). Comparativism in Constitutional Interpretation. *New Zealand Law Review*, 2009 (1), 45–68.

Waluchow, W. & D. Kyritsis (2023). Constitutionalism. In E. Zalta, ed., *The Stanford Encyclopedia of Philosophy*, Stanford: Stanford University. Available from: https://plato.stanford.edu/archives/spr2018/entries/constitutionalism/; see Section 7, 'Constitutional Interpretation'

23

Proportionality

George Letsas

I WHAT IS PROPORTIONALITY?

Proportionality figures prominently in the text of many constitutions. Constitutional lawyers usually refer to it as a principle pertaining to the interpretation of fundamental constitutional rights. Its nature as a constitutional doctrine, however, is ambiguous. It is not clear whether it picks out a self-standing moral principle, or whether it serves as an umbrella doctrinal term, attached to a multiplicity of underlying principles that are jurisdiction-specific. If the former, philosophical accounts of proportionality can be *wholesale*, applying universally across constitutional orders. If the latter, then accounts of proportionality should be *retail*, confined to specific constitutions.

The concept of proportionality is relational in two ways (Letsas 2015a). First, it requires that a property of a given act (e.g., the severity of punishment) stand in proportion to a property of another act (e.g., the gravity of a committed wrong). Proportionality ties together properties of different acts, such that a change in the property of one act (e.g., the pettiness of a theft) should bring about a change in the property of the other (e.g., the leniency of punishment). Second, the relevant act must generally be *other*-regarding, governing the interaction between two moral agents (e.g., the punishing agent and the wrongdoer) and having an impact on someone's interests. One might say that the amount of money one pays for a gym subscription is disproportionate to how many times one uses it. But this statement does not engage any moral principle, because going to the gym is not an *other*-regarding act. Leaving aside the question of whether there can be moral duties to oneself, the main subject-matter of morality is interpersonal interactions. Proportionality as a moral principle should therefore be distinguished from the general ethical injunction, familiar from Aristotle, to avoid extremes ("the golden mean") (Aristotle 1975).

The use of proportionality in most constitutional orders seems, on its face, to meet both these conditions of relationality. According to its orthodox understanding, proportionality requires that when government acts in a way that interferes with individuals' constitutional rights, that the interference be proportionate to a legitimate public interest. It is also *other*-regarding, in that it governs the interaction between state authorities and individuals. The requirement is imposed by courts, when interpreting constitutional rights, and it is sometimes stated explicitly in the text of the constitution, alongside the enumerated constitutional right. When, for instance, the police are engaged in surveillance, they interfere with the right to private life of criminal suspects, with a view to preventing crime – a legitimate public interest. The constitutional requirement is that the interference with the right to private life be proportionate to the aim of preventing crime. If it is not, then the police are acting unconstitutionally, in virtue of breaching the principle of proportionality.

The question of how governmental action impacts on individual rights raises questions of universal significance, regardless of the specificities of particular constitutional orders. Proportionality assessment requires looking at a property of governmental action (promotion of public interest) and a property of individuals (their status as right-holders). How these properties should be understood and what relation should hold between them is, however, a contested philosophical issue. It is not clear, for instance, whether we should understand the relation between public interest and rights in purely welfarist terms, or whether it is some quality of the interfering state act which matters. Can relatives of a criminal suspect, for example, be subject to minor surveillance in order to prevent a serious crime? Or does the fact that they are not suspected of a criminal offence make even minor governmental intrusion into their privacy disproportionate and regardless of the threatened harm?

To motivate proportionality, as a fundamental constitutional issue, we need to make further assumptions. A constitution may fail to contain a list of fundamental rights; or it may enshrine morally dubious rights, such as the right to bear arms (U.S. Const. amend. II 1791), or morally dubious aims, such as the protection of public morals (ECHR Arts. 8–11 1971). If proportionality as a constitutional doctrine has an inherent moral dimension, it must ride on the back of genuine moral norms that govern political action. There are three premises on which wholesale accounts of proportionality are typically built. Together, they form part of the political ideal that is usually referred to as *constitutionalism*.

First, constitutional rights, as found nowadays in most constitutions, are not just creatures of the law, but mirror fundamental moral rights – such as the right to life, or the right not to be tortured – which individuals have independently of the law. These rights serve as high-order constitutional norms even in the absence of a written constitution, or a bill of rights (Allan 2013).

Second, government is in principle permitted to interfere with individual liberty through coercive means, such as police action, threat of a criminal conviction, or enforcement of civil liability. Moreover, the promotion of public interest is a core function of government; it may require action that restricts individual liberty, such as imposing lockdowns to fight a pandemic, so long as it does not violate fundamental rights.

Third, protection of fundamental individual rights should, as a matter of ideal political morality, be a core constitutional issue. Rights should enjoy special legal protection, typically in the form of judicial review. It is a core function of courts, when applying the constitution, to engage in an assessment of whether interference with individual freedom amounts to a violation of a fundamental right.

Each of the above three premises can be contested. Some moral theories, such as utilitarianism, do not recognize individual rights as fundamental moral norms. And some political theories dispute that state authority is ever legitimate (Wolff 1998), or assign minimal content to forms of public interest that can justify interference with liberty (Nozick 1974). Finally, some hold that the primacy of rights as moral/constitutional norms does not necessarily entail that they should be protected by courts, through judicial review (Bellamy 2007; Waldron 1993c). Here, I will assume the truth of the first two premises and explore how different accounts of proportionality might affect the arguments for and against the third premise. I will give an account of the main positions in the literature and propose an alternative account, which I call proportionality as fittingness.

II A DIVERSITY OF METHOD

The distinction between proportionality as a self-standing moral principle and proportionality as an umbrella term, largely tracks a divide in the methodology employed by constitutional lawyers who write about proportionality. One approach is to engage in *bottom-up* accounts of proportionality, seeking to analyze and critically assess how proportionality operates within specific constitutional settings, such as Europe, Canada, Israel or South Africa. Proportionality travels well as a constitutional doctrine, figuring in most constitutional regimes. But the significance of its constitutional role varies. In the USA, for instance, its presence is much less central, being largely contained to matters of criminal punishment, and the interpretation of the 8th Amendment (Sullivan and Frase 2008). Bottom-up accounts begin with the relevant provisions of a given constitution, then move on to an analysis of the relevant case law that interprets those provisions, and – at final instance – they evaluate the moral relevance and significance of the legal role of proportionality, that is, the role it has been given to play by constitutional drafters and/or courts, within a given jurisdiction. Bottom-up accounts target whichever modes of judicial analysis and argumentation operate under that label.

The bottom-up approach leaves open the possibility that the legal concept of proportionality might be a mere homonym of proportionality as a moral principle. Some scholars, for instance, who employ the bottom-up approach, argue that proportionality is morally unjustified because its use by courts has undermined the liberal principles underlying fundamental rights (Tsakyrakis 2009). This critique is directed against the practice that operates under the heading of proportionality, rather than a particular conception of its moral value.

A top-down approach differs. It begins with seeking to identify whether proportionality-type reasoning in constitutional law tracks some moral concern that exists independently of positive law. This is plausibly the case with judgments of proportionality in self-defense and punishment. For example, it would be wrong to kill someone in self-defense when the nature of the threat the attacker poses is minor (e.g., a bruise), even in the absence of constitutions, courts or governments. The constitutional rights protected around the world tend to include rights similar to those protected by criminal law and to track the rights of interpersonal morality to life, bodily integrity, not to be tortured, and so on. It is not an accident, for instance, that proportionality figures in the criminal law of self-defense in similar ways to the law of the use of lethal force by state agents such as the police (Hurka 2005, p. 38). That is not to say of course that there might not be rights one has specifically against the government, which do not directly track rights of interpersonal morality. Equality-based arguments of constitutional rights link their normative content to the right to be treated with *equal respect and concern* by one's government (Dworkin 1996c). Some accounts of proportionality seek to trace the philosophical origins of the concept to ideas of equality, both distributive and corrective, going as far back as Plato (Lever 2020; Poole 2010). The classical idea that justice is about giving people their *due*, ties the concept of proportionality to the value of equality.

A second methodological divide, which cuts across the first one, is between institutional and non-institutional approaches. Institutional approaches to proportionality locate its normative significance on the question of how courts should go about reviewing the action of the other branches of government. It can be argued, for example, that proportionality is an institutional device that is used to structure the division of power between courts and the other two branches of government (Kyritsis 2014). On this view, an action of public authorities may be deemed proportionate, not because it does not violate a constitutional right (it may do), but because courts, when exercising powers of judicial review, may have to defer to the judgment of the political branches of government, including on the basis of *non-rights-based* considerations. If that is true, ideas of judicial deference, or self-restraint become central to an account of proportionality (King 2008). They are deployed in defense of legal doctrines, such as the *margin of appreciation* (Benvenisti 1999; Letsas 2006), which human rights courts use when reviewing state action.

Others, such as Arthur Ripstein, take proportionality to speak to the question of what means of institutional enforcement should be available when one's moral rights have been violated (Ripstein 2016). For Ripstein, the morality underlying individual rights does not settle questions about how to act when one's rights are violated. It takes institutional action by public officials to determine what is a permissible form of responding to rights violations. Finally, some treat proportionality as giving institutional effect to a moral right, the right to demand and to be given a justification when one is affected by the actions of governmental authorities (Dyzenhaus 2014; Kumm 2010b; Moller 2019).

What is common to institutional approaches is that they do not take proportionality to speak exclusively to the content of the individual rights protected by the constitution. Non-institutional approaches, by contrast, take proportionality to be a determinant of rights. The precise way in which proportionality serves this role depends on one's underlying theory about the nature of rights. Proportionality can be a determinant of rights externally, by allowing non-rights-based considerations to *defeat* the right (*externalism*); or it can do so internally, by allowing certain considerations to *qualify* what the right is (*internalism*). Let us stipulate, for instance, that "stop and search" operations by the police constitute a proportionate interference with the right to private life. We can say that proportionality determines that one's moral right to private life is defeated by the normative significance of preventing crime. The individual right here is infringed, which is a moral loss and cause for regret. Alternatively, we might say that proportionality qualifies the scope of one's moral right to private life so that it does not cover the freedom not to be stopped and searched by the police. Both *internalism* and *externalism* have to explain the conditions under which proportionality allows certain considerations to serve as defeaters, or qualifiers. Externalism need not deny, of course, that institutional considerations have an inherent normative link to matter of rights. For instance, they might hold that, as a matter of political morality, legislatures are better suited to make decisions in conditions of epistemic uncertainty about rights. All that they deny is that proportionality covers exclusively first-order questions about the morality of individual rights.

Finally, it can be argued that the whole idea of proportionality as a constitutional principle should be debunked: it is merely a heuristic device used by courts to engage in the epistemic task of identifying what rights people have and whether they have been violated, under a specificationist account of rights (Landau 1995; Letsas 2015a; Webber 2014). From an objective perspective, according to this view, proportionality neither defeats, nor qualifies, the relevant right. A constitutional order can, without any loss to the task of accurately determining fundamental rights, do away with proportionality-talk altogether. This is compatible with arguing that there might be instrumental reasons for courts to use a test that is structured in the way the test of proportionality is.

III PROBLEMS WITH INSTITUTIONAL APPROACHES TO PROPORTIONALITY

One objection to institutional approaches is that they are both over- and under-inclusive. Consider the view that proportionality is a judicial means to give effect to the moral right to demand a heightened justification when public authorities interfere with one's freedom. Mattias Kumm takes proportionality to be an institutionalized form of what he calls "Socratic contestation." There seem to be cases however where authorities are in a position to provide a heightened form of justification, yet their actions are still disproportionate. In the case of *E.B. v France*, the applicant, a lesbian woman, was found by the French authorities to be ineligible as a potential adoptive parent, on two grounds: first, because of the lack of a paternal referent in the household of the applicant and, second, because of the attitude of the applicant's homosexual partner who expressed no commitment to the adoption plans. Both these grounds were found to be legitimate and applicable in this case. However, the European Court of Human Rights (ECtHR) found that there was a disproportionate interference with the applicant's right to family life because there was some evidence that the first ground was used, in the circumstances of the case, as a pretext and that it was the applicant's homosexuality that served, implicitly, as a decisive factor (the Court said that the implicit use of that factor "contaminated" the decision of the authorities). Here, it appears that a valid justification was given but it was insufficient to make the interference proportionate.

On the other hand, there might be cases where no justification is given, yet the actions of public authorities are not disproportionate. Consider, for instance, manifestly ill-founded applications for judicial review, or cases in which the applicant has suffered no significant disadvantage and raises no issue of constitutional principle. Given concerns about judicial workload, several constitutional or human rights courts reject such applications without giving any reasons. There is here an interference with the right to fair trial (or due process), which is in tension with the right to be given a justification, but one which many jurisdictions, quite plausibly, take to be proportionate given the scarcity of judicial resources.

The claim that proportionality analysis serves to structure institutionally the duty to justify governmental interference with liberty might be assessed at a more abstract level. In democratic states, citizens get to hold the government into account periodically, through elections. Legislators, representing their constituents, debate publicly the merits of draft bills, before they become law. Yet such forms of accountability and justification do not extend to providing a concrete explanation *to* a particular person as to why *their* liberty was restricted. The need for an individualized justification might seem particularly important in modern times, with the growth of the executive branch and delegated legislation. The problem however with viewing the principle of proportionality in this light is that proportionality far from exhausts the possible grounds for justifying state action. Not all unlawful state action amounts to a violation of a constitutional right. Government may act illegitimately in ways that do not engage constitutional rights. It may act *ultra vires*, interfering with a person's liberty in ways not prescribed by law, or it may breach a legal right that is granted through ordinary legislation. Ordinary courts provide avenues for individuals to challenge restrictions on liberty as unlawful, and demand a legal justification, without invoking a constitutional right. Their role is to uphold all legal rights and provide litigants with a normative justification for their decision, drawing on objective legal principles (Dworkin 1981).

It is true, of course, that individuals and their lawyers have strong incentives to present any legal claim as a breach of a constitutional right. And some courts have been welcoming, lowering the threshold of admissibility, or expanding the scope of what falls within a protected right (Gerrards & Senden 2009). This has created the illusion that any restriction of liberty is justiciable as a matter of constitutional rights. Yet we must not conflate a trend in litigation with the character of constitutional adjudication, as a forum dedicated to the foundational legal principles of a polity. Proportionality, as a constitutional principle, relates to restrictions on fundamental rights, such as the right to life, freedom of expression, and freedom of conscience. These rights are normative pre-conditions for a meaningful democratic governance and express core commitments of the political morality that underpins the constitution. My right not to be persecuted for my religious or political beliefs is not on a par with my liberty not to be disturbed at night by airplane noise.[1] By treating proportionality as an open-ended institutional avenue for challenging any kind of restriction on liberty, one downplays the significance of constitutional rights and devalues their political significance. The role of constitutional courts is not just to ensure that there is a valid justification for restricting liberty, but to ensure that the restriction does not violate a set of particularly weighty reasons that apply to government, such as the duty to treat individuals as free, equal and autonomous agents.

Objections can also be raised against the view, put forward by Ripstein, that proportionality speaks to the enforcement of our moral rights, as opposed to their normative content. Proportionality arguably has a place in rights-reasoning outside the context of institutional enforcement. Consider this example. Suppose that your partner threatens to pinch your cheek softly, against your will. You can prevent them from doing so by threatening to reveal a lie they have said at work. We can still ask whether this means of defending your right to bodily integrity is proportionate, even though the defensive act falls outside the means public officials may use in coercively enforcing our rights. In arguing that such a threat would be disproportionate, and hence wrong to issue, we would appeal to the fact that the threat is out of place in the context of an intimate relationship (Letsas 2017). Proportionality appears to have a place in determining the scope of interpersonal rights and not just their institutional enforcement. If that is true, at least some judgments of proportionality in constitutional adjudication track questions of what rights individuals have, as opposed to how much deference or self-restraint courts should show in enforcing them. One could further argue that these cases are central and that cases of deference or self-restraint are marginal, or even judicial mistakes (Letsas 2018b).

Finally, the debunking view faces the objection that, outside constitutional adjudication, it is undeniable that proportionality has a moral dimension and plays a role in identifying the content and scope of rights, as in self-defense and the use of lethal force. Moreover, the view has the difficulty of explaining away the enduring

---

[1] *Hatton v United Kingdom* (Application no. 36022/97) [2003] ECHR 338 (8 July 2003); Letsas 2007.

and prominent presence of proportionality in constitutional law. If proportionality does no normative work in determining outcomes in rights-reasoning, why haven't generations of judges and constitutional lawyers realized its vacuity? These are not, of course, conclusive arguments against the debunking view. A positive case must be made for the moral dimension of proportionality.

IV THE PROPORTIONALITY PUZZLE

Non-institutional approaches take proportionality to be a determinant of constitutional rights, either externally, or internally. It is a contested issue, however, how proportionality serves this normative function. In some jurisdictions, influenced mainly by the German constitutional practice, proportionality is said to do so through a *balancing* exercise. In German constitutional theory, the test of proportionality has three prongs:

(i) Is the impugned measure rationally connected to the pursuit of a legitimate aim (the "*suitability*" test)?
(ii) Is the measure necessary for the pursuit of that aim (the "*necessity*" test)?
(iii) Is the seriousness of the interference with the applicant's right proportionate to the benefits gained in pursuit of the legitimate aim in question ("proportionality in the *narrow sense*," or "*balancing*")?

The last prong is supposed to capture the core of the constitutional function of proportionality. Here is how Judge Barak (2012, p. 340), a former judge of the Supreme Court of Israel, describes this part of the orthodox test in his book on proportionality:

> The last test of proportionality is the "proportional result" or "proportionality *stricto sensu*" (*Verhaltnismassigkeit im engeren Sinne*).... [A]ccording to proportionality stricto sensu, in order to justify a limitation on a constitutional right, a proper relation ("proportional in the narrow sense of the term"), should exist between the benefits gained by fulfilling the purpose and the harm caused to the constitutional right from obtaining that purpose. This test requires a balancing of the benefits gained by the public and the harm caused to the constitutional right through the use of the means selected by law to obtain the proper purpose. Accordingly, this is a test balancing benefits and harm.

Balancing here is a form of *externalism*, assessing whether the benefits gained by third-parties defeat one's right. If the cost of interfering with someone's right is minor and the benefits to others are huge, then the right may be lawfully infringed. But if the cost to the right-holder is high, and the benefits to others are minor, then the right should be upheld. In either case, the aim of balancing is a form of cost-benefit analysis, in that it sacrifices the liberty of a person (the right-holder) in order to increase the amount of liberty enjoyed by others.

This understanding of balancing invites the objection that it consists in a form of consequentialist reasoning, which is incompatible with the deontological nature of rights. It appears, for instance, to allow the punishing of innocent persons for minor offenses, when doing so confers a major benefit to public interest; or the banning of a religious practice, when doing so reduces the risk of large-scale atrocities committed by religious fanatics. Some court judgments seem to succumb to this type of consequentialist reasoning. In the case of *I.A. v. Turkey*, the ECtHR found that imposing a minor fine for a religiously offensive publication is a proportionate interference with the right to freedom of speech. Such cases motivate *bottom-up* accounts which condemn proportionality altogether as an assault on human rights (Tsakyrakis 2009).

In response to such worries, some have sought to provide an account of balancing that escapes its consequentialist implications. Robert Alexy (2002) has argued that the constitutional rights of the German Constitution are principles, rather than rules, and that principles are *optimization* requirements. He writes (Alexy (2002), p. 67):

> Principles are optimization requirements relative to what is legally and factually possible. The *principle of proportionality in its narrow sense*, that is, the requirement of balancing, derives from its relation to the *legally* possible.... [T]he *principle of proportionality in its narrow sense* follows from the fact that principles are optimization requirements relative to what is legally possible.

Alexy's optimization requirement is constrained by a proviso about what is "legally possible." But this proviso is ambiguous. Understood to mean what is legally *permissible* the proviso seems circular. Proportionality as a legal principle is meant to determine what the constitution permits and we cannot define it in terms of what is legally permissible. If, on the other hand, Alexy's proviso means what is permissible under other areas of law (say criminal law, or administrative law, or tort law) then it seems wrong: constitutional law, *qua* higher-order law, is used to judge the lawfulness of other areas of law. We cannot assume that what these areas require is lawful and hence to be optimized. Suppose that a human rights challenge is launched against a criminal statute that prohibits blasphemous remarks made about the dominant religion. Is the task of optimizing the constitutional principle of free speech constrained by what that criminal statute requires, such that we should try to make some space for a prohibition on blasphemy (say in the form of a minor offence)? The opposite seems to be the case: the constitutional right to free speech should direct the court to strike down the criminal prohibition and assign no weight to it. Perhaps Alexy might reply that, in this example, legal principles are optimized by ignoring the criminal statute. Such a reply however would entail that the conception of balancing as optimization does little, or no work. It simply stands for the proposition that courts, in making proportionality judgments, must apply the correct legal principles.

If we accept that the concept of balancing necessarily involves trade-offs between rights and public interest, we are led to a puzzle: how is it that government may permissibly infringe fundamental moral rights, so long as it does so proportionately? Rights, at least on a deontological moral outlook, are supposed to resist trade-offs, acting as *side-constraints* (Nozick 1974) or *trump cards* (Dworkin 1977) held by individuals against government. Trade-offs between one's rights and public interest raise doubts about whether constitutional rights are genuine moral rights in the first place. The puzzle is further complicated by the fact that not all constitutional rights are subject to balancing. Examples include the right not to be tortured, the prohibition of slavery, or the right not to be subject to retrospective punishment. Constitutional lawyers distinguish between absolute constitutional rights, which are not subject to proportionality analysis, and so-called "qualified" rights, which do. Yet shouldn't all constitutional rights operate similarly, if they mirror fundamental moral rights?

Concerns about how constitutional limitations to rights can be squared with assigning rights primacy *qua* moral norms drives a significant number of philosophical inquiries into proportionality. Some accounts of proportionality track traditional debates about the merits of deontology and the limits to consequentialist reasoning (Kumm & Walen 2014). We may put the worry that balancing raises in the form of an inconsistent triad:

(a) The rights protected in constitutions mirror fundamental moral rights of the individual (*the stringency of rights thesis*).
(b) Proportionality is essential to the determination of constitutional rights (*the necessity of proportionality thesis*).
(c) Proportionality reasoning involves the balancing of rights against other considerations (*the balancing thesis*).

Asserting all three propositions commits us to an inconsistency. If one accepts that rights are stringent deontological norms, then one cannot accept both that proportionality involves trade-offs with non-rights-based considerations *and* that it is essential to the determination of rights. A useful typology of proportionality theories is between the three possible combinations of propositions in this triad. Consequentialists reject (a) but accept (b and c). They treat constitutional rights as posited legal rules whose aim is to maximize utility. Debunking views and bottom-up criticisms of proportionality, on the other hand, reject (b) but accept (a and c). They accept that rights resist trade-offs and that proportionality assessment necessarily involves balancing but reject that proportionality should have any place in constitutional adjudication. I propose instead to reject (c) and accept (a and b), defending the idea of proportionality without balancing. This may initially sound counter-intuitive, given the prominence of balancing in constitutional practice. But the other two theses in the triad (the stringency of rights and the necessity of proportionality) are no less prominent in constitutional practice and, as theorists, our task is to provide the most coherent account possible of that practice.

V INCOMMENSURABILITY AND BALANCING

An account of the role of proportionality within a constitutional scheme inevitably makes assumptions about the nature of individual rights, *qua* moral rights. Within academic debates about proportionality, the common assumption is that rights protect important aspects of well-being (Raz 1986). Freedom from pain and suffering, ability to express oneself freely and to form intimate relations, freedom from arbitrary state interference and religious or other persecution, are all essential to individual flourishing. Balancing is viewed as a way to handle conflicts between competing interests, either between those of the right-holder and the public, or between those of two right-holders. A person's interest in their real property may come into conflict with the interest of others in having schools, or hospitals built instead in their plot of land. A person's interest in satirical speech may come into conflict with the interest of religious believers not to have their symbols disparaged.

The idea of balancing assumes that there is a way to quantify the significance of the competing interests, and to allow minor or moderate restrictions on one's rights, when gains to the well-being of others are substantial enough. This does not necessarily mean that the numbers of those whose interests are affected matter, as consequentialism holds. Let us suppose that encountering blasphemous speech has a mild impact on the interest one has in practicing their religion. Criminal prohibition of blasphemy, on the other hand, is a severe restriction of freedom of expression. If numbers count, one would find the prohibition proportionate when the blasphemers are few and the offended believers are millions. But if numbers do not count, one might find that the interest in avoiding blasphemous speech is not as significant as the interest in expressing religious satire without being imprisoned. Assuming this welfarist account of rights, we might think of the wording of constitutional rights as a preliminary ordering of interests. With respect to absolute constitutional rights, the drafters did not consider that the interest in avoiding torture or slavery could ever be outweighed by other interests. But with respect to the so-called qualified rights, they thought that the interest in free expression or privacy may well give way to more weighty interests, justifying restrictions to the corresponding constitutional right.

Some constitutional scholars who endorse a welfarist picture of rights, however, do not think that balancing is always possible. They hold that interests of well-being may be incommensurable, making comparisons between them in case of conflict impossible (Raz 1986). It might not be possible, for instance, to compare whether an immigrant's interest in their family life is less, equal or more significant than the interest in controlling a state's borders and deporting non-nationals (Endicott 2014). The idea of incommensurability, in turn, bolsters claims that courts must show deference or self-restraint in making proportionality assessments (Urbina 2017). If there is no right answer to the question of whether an immigrant's interest in family life is more weighty than national security interests, then it is not obvious why courts, rather than legislatures, should make the choice between the two. As the choice is in essence arbitrary, the elected branch of government might be considered a more legitimate body to make decisions when incommensurable interests conflict.

An interest-based theory of rights, and its corollary doctrine of incommensurability, permits a skeptical view about judicial review and the adjudication of constitutional rights. It shifts the emphasis away from the question of what rights individuals have, to the question of whether courts should be involved in balancing acts that admit of no right answer. If, for instance, there is no right answer to whether free speech is weightier than freedom of religion, then arguably constitutional courts should not use their power to impose their preferred choice on everyone else. Judicial deference, or self-restraint become ways to allow people (though not non-nationals) to make that choice collectively, through their elected representatives. It does not follow of course that an interest-based theory necessarily entails skepticism towards judicial review or that there are no other arguments against judicial review. It is only that the worry about incommensurability presupposes this picture of rights.

In the remaining of this chapter, I shall put forward an alternative picture of rights and, in turn, an alternative model of what the proper role of proportionality within constitutional adjudication is. The picture has its roots in the deontological tradition and the view, familiar from Kantian philosophy, that the right is to be defined independently of the good. The dialectic of the argument is this: by abandoning an interest-based theory of rights, one avoids the need to balance interests, and – in turn – the threat that incommensurability poses to judicial review and proportionality reasoning by judges.

VI REASON-BASED THEORIES OF CONSTITUTIONAL RIGHTS

Interest-based theories of rights locate the illegitimacy of an interference with individual liberty on the impact it has on the right-holder's interests. What makes it wrong to censor speech, for example, is the impact it has on individuals' ability to express themselves, impart and access information, form independent judgments and the like. The point of protecting these interests against harm is ultimately to allow individuals to lead a flourishing life. This familiar view of rights has dominated philosophical thinking about constitutional rights and judicial review. But it has obscured an alternative way of understanding rights, particularly rights held against government. The view I have in mind is non-teleological, in that it does not seek to explain the wrongfulness of interfering with liberty solely in terms of the interests of well-being that it harms. It underpins a family of theories about moral rights that is sometimes referred to as "status-based" theories (Nagel 1995). The implications this view has for constitutional rights and judicial reasoning have not been fully fleshed-out in the relevant literature. Yet, properly understood, it underpins central cases decided by courts under proportionality reasoning. What follows is not a defense of status-based theories of rights, but an account of what they entail for proportionality assessment by constitutional courts.

In his early view on free speech T. M. Scanlon drew a distinction between two different ways of explaining violations of the right to freedom of expression (Scanlon 1972). The distinction is between theories that assess the illegitimacy of a restriction and those that assess the illegitimacy of the *reason* or *justification* for a restriction. The former theories look at the character of the acts which are restricted and whether the restriction harms important interests of well-being. The latter theories, by contrast, look at what a given restriction is trying to achieve. Consider bans on blasphemy. We can look at the harm done to the interest of speakers in blaspheming and then balance it against the harm blasphemous speech causes to the interests of those who practice the dominant religion. Alternatively, we can look at what the rationale for such a ban might be. Suppose the reason is best understood as a way to curb the spread of heretical views. Such reason is illegitimate because it is premised on the idea that people should be prevented from having false beliefs about religion. As Scanlon explains, the government cannot act on this reason compatibly with treating individuals as free and autonomous agents. The justification imputed to the ban violates the liberal principle that government has a duty to treat individuals as having a particular *status*, namely being autonomous agents who are responsible to form their own beliefs about religious matters.

Scanlon's distinction corresponds to two different conceptions of constitutional rights. On one conception, which we may call the *recipient*-oriented approach, it is something about the liberty of the individual affected by state interference that makes a moral difference. On the competing conception, which we may call an *actor*-oriented approach, it is something about the attitude expressed by the government when interfering with individual liberty that makes a moral difference. The contrast between the two conceptions is manifested in how harmful consequences are taken into account. On an *actor*-oriented approach, it is irrelevant that harm occurs if the reason or justification for state interference is illegitimate. For example, a person has a constitutional right to express heretical views, even if – as a result of that expression – people will form dangerous beliefs that will lead to harm. Such harm is not balanced against the right to freedom of expression; it is discounted instead, since a ban on heretical speech, which would have prevented the harm, violates a core duty of government. On a *recipient*-oriented approach, by contrast, a person's constitutional right to express heretical views is constrained by the harm it causes on its recipients. It would be relevant, for instance, that followers of the dominant religion are offended by heretical speech. Whether the constitutional right to express heretical views should prevail depends on balancing all the relevant harms against the interest in expressing one's religious views.

The distinctive aspect of an *actor*-oriented approach is the emphasis it places on the reason or justification imputed to governmental action. This is not a matter of seeking to uncover the subjective motivations of state officials, such that the very same restriction will be constitutionally lawful if taken with good motives, but unlawful if taken with bad motives. Rather, it is an interpretive question about how, as an objective matter, we should understand state restrictions and what attitude they manifest on the part of the government. The government is bound by reasons that pertain to its coercive role, most importantly the duty to treat citizens as free, autonomous and equal moral agents. The *actor*-oriented approach does not presuppose that all or most individuals have good rational faculties of judgment, or that it is always good for individuals to exercise their autonomous judgment. It is not an approach based on the importance of the interest in autonomy, as it is often assumed (Howard 2019; Simpson 2013). Scanlon remarks in this respect that there is nothing wrong about individuals voluntarily deferring their judgment to experts with respect to truth and falsity. What is morally objectionable is for the government to force individuals coercively to trust its own view on truth and falsity. The legitimacy of state coercion depends on respecting the status of individuals as autonomous agents, however good or poor their judgment is, and regardless of whether they exercise their autonomy or not. Crucially, the illegitimacy lies in the attitude of government, not the impact in has on the autonomy of individuals. Bans on hate speech, for example, beneficial as they might be, prevent coercively everyone from receiving such forms of speech, including individuals who can judge well hatefulness and would never endorse, or act on them (Dworkin 1996c). The ban is incompatible with the government's reason not to force individuals to trust its own view on truth and falsity about moral matters.

The view that we should look at the legitimacy of the *reasons* for restricting liberty, rather than the legitimacy of the restriction itself, underpins the very influential theory of constitutional rights put forward by Ronald Dworkin. In Dworkin's famous metaphor, rights are "trump" cards held by individuals against the government, when its action is based on a category of reasons, particularly reasons that offend its duty of equal respect and concern. The point of constitutional rights is to block or exclude such reasons, in a way that certain cards trump all others in familiar card games. His theory, initially developed in the context of the US Constitution, assigns to constitutional rights a robust role, and rules out the possibility of any balancing. The government's duty to treat individual with equal respect and concern is not to be balanced against other considerations. It is a necessary condition for the legitimacy of state coercion. What is absolute is not the significance of individual interests protected by rights, but the blocking of reasons or justifications that are incompatible with the coercive role of government.

Perhaps the best illustration of Dworkin's reason-based approach is his account of abortion and euthanasia (Dworkin 1994). The traditional way to tackle these thorny moral issues is through the balancing of the interests involved: the interest of women in controlling their body, the interests of the unborn fetus, the interests of terminally ill patients not to suffer, or the interests of vulnerable patients not to be put under pressure to end their lives. This interest-based analysis leads to intractable questions about whether fetuses have an interest in life and, if so, whether it can be balanced against the interest of women to control their own body. Similarly, it is not clear how to balance the interest of terminally ill patients not to suffer a terrible death against the risk that legalization of euthanasia poses to vulnerable patients (Dorf 2008). Dworkin's approach, by contrast, is radically different, eschewing discussion of interests. His starting point is that the value of human life is not derivative from the interest of a person to be alive but is instead detached, having intrinsic value, or sanctity. We can understand, for instance, the statement that something of value is lost, even when it is in the best interest of a person in a permanent vegetative state to have their life ended; the value of life is not derivative from the interest in being alive. Building on this premise, Dworkin argues that decisions about when life begins and ends involve deeply ethical questions about the sanctity of life, similar to questions raised by religion. It is therefore impermissible for the government to coerce individuals, through a legal ban, into accepting its own view about truth and falsity with respect to such ethical decision. His defense of the right to abortion and euthanasia is premised, not on the interests of women and terminally ill patients, but on what counts as an illegitimate justification on the part of the government when regulating coercively individual choices. The defense of these constitutional rights does not presuppose, nor depends on, the balancing of any interests of well-being.

VII PROPORTIONALITY WITHOUT BALANCING

Can a reason-blocking theory of rights be reconciled with the idea of proportionality? At first glance, it might be thought that if the theory is incompatible with balancing, it is also incompatible with proportionality. Recall that, at an abstract level, proportionality reasoning is relational, comparing two properties (e.g., the gravity of the wrong and the severity of punishment), in the context of an *other*-regarding action. One way to unpack this relationality in constitutional law is in terms of the following two properties: the interests of the right-holder, on one hand, and public interest on the other. But this is just one way. An alternative way is to compare the reasons that apply to the acting agent with the character of the action they take. Suppose that a teacher disciplines an unruly pupil by forcing them to recite a religious prayer. We may call this punishment disproportionate because it does not fit the reasons that apply to the role of a teacher. Teachers are not allowed to use their powers of discipline with a view to forcing a religious education on pupils. They must respect pupils' autonomy to choose their own religious beliefs. This is so even if this method of punishment is efficient, serving the interests of the pupils in an orderly learning environment. The role of a school teacher here differs from say, the role of an abbot in a convent that one has voluntarily joined. An abbot ordering a monk to recite a religious prayer would not count as disproportionate punishment.

It may be objected at this point that actions whose character does not fit the reasons of the acting agent are not disproportionate, but simply inappropriate. Proportionality, the objection goes, is only relevant when the action taken is appropriate, yet excessive in some sense. Suppose the teacher expels a student. Expulsion is considered an appropriate or just form of punishment, which would be proportionate for a severe offence, but disproportionate for a minor offence. The answer to this objection is that it is only by knowing all the reasons which apply to an acting agent that we can know what counts as the right proportion of any act. An act can only be excessive relative to a reason. Consider life-tariffs in criminal sentencing. Imprisonment is thought of as an acceptable form of punishment and life tariffs are considered proportionate punishment for serious offences, such as murder. But what if the life tariff imposed is not reviewable by a judicial body? The ECtHR has held that prisoners serving life sentences must have a possibility of release and their sentence should be subject to a review through a dedicated mechanism. The European Court opined:

> [I]f such a prisoner is incarcerated without any prospect of release and without the possibility of having his life sentence reviewed, there is the risk that he can never atone for his offence: whatever the prisoner does in prison, however exceptional his progress towards rehabilitation, his punishment remains fixed and unreviewable. If anything, the punishment becomes greater with time: the longer the prisoner lives, the longer his sentence. Thus, even when a whole life sentence is condign punishment at the time of its imposition, with the passage of time it becomes – to paraphrase Lord Justice Laws in *Wellington* – a poor guarantee of just and proportionate punishment.[2]

The thought here is that the gravity of the offence is not the only consideration that matters to punishment. Atonement and rehabilitation are also relevant considerations to sentencing and they control the appropriate proportion of imprisonment. The length of imprisonment is not in itself a crucial factor but a proxy for how all the relevant justifications for criminal punishment play out in a particular case. A punishment might be thought as just and proportionate taking into account only one factor (gravity of the offence), but unjust and disproportionate taking into account other relevant factors (rehabilitation). Assessing the proportionality of punishment requires taking into account all relevant reasons that apply to state authorities, and philosophers sometimes distinguish between wide and narrow proportionality (Hurka 2005; Kamm 2013; McMahan 2005).

Assessing whether the action of state officials fits the reasons that apply to their role differs fundamentally from balancing goods and harms to affected interests. An unrepentant offender may derive no benefit from having their life sentence reviewed by a judicial body. The duty of the state to provide for review is not grounded on the potential good it will have for prisoners' interests. It is instead grounded on the duty of the government to treat individuals as responsible moral agents who can atone for their wrongs, however atrocious. Furthermore, the potential harm that review of

---

[2] Vinter *and others* v United Kingdom (Application nos. 66069/09, 130/10 and 3896/10) [2016] III ECHR 317 [112]

life sentences might cause to public safety (say, because of recidivism) is not a relevant consideration, to be balanced against the duty to treat offenders as responsible moral agents. The same logic applies to the doctrine of the presumption of innocence. The state's duty is not based on a calculation that the benefit to defendants' interests outweighs the harm caused to public interest by acquitting guilty offenders (false negatives). Even if it can be shown that the harm caused by the doctrine of the presumption of innocence is substantial, we would have no less reason to presume the defendants to be innocent. This is because the justification for the doctrine lies in the demand for fairness in the criminal process: the state yields an extraordinary amount of power in this domain (powers of arrest, detention, prosecution, handling evidence) and it would be unfair if individuals did not possess an arsenal of judicial safeguards. The duty of the state is to conduct a *fair* trial, not an efficient or a cost-effective one.

The reason-based theory of rights conceives of proportionality as the requirement that the action of state officials *fit* or *match* the set of reasons that apply to their distinctive role. It is an internalist account of proportionality since it takes the principle to cover only first-order questions about individual rights. We may call this the *fittingness* conception of proportionality (Letsas 2018a). These reasons, being *actor*-oriented, are not in competition or conflict in the way interests of individuals are. Recall that harms occurring when state authorities act on sound reasons are discounted. The harm occurring by allowing people to express heretical or hate speech, or allowing wrongdoers to walk free from the criminal justice system, is not a reason that competes with the duty not to censor speech on the basis of its merits, or the duty to uphold the presumption of innocence.

Does this fittingness notion of proportionality find ground in judicial practice? It is true that courts often follow Aharon Barak's account in describing proportionality as the relation between the cost to one's right and the benefit to public interest. Yet, on closer inspection, the reasoning of courts focuses on the reasons which underpin governmental action and eschew any balancing of interests. Consider the landmark case of *Niemietz v Germany* (1993).[3] The authorities in this case searched the law office of Mr. Niemietz while investigating an anonymous hostile letter sent to a judge, alleging that he had abused his office in order to persecute critics of the Church. Mr. Niemietz was identified as the author of the letter and was charged with criminal offence of "insulting behavior." The doctrinal construction followed by the European Court was seemingly one of balancing the right to private life of the applicant against the legitimate aim of preventing crime and protecting the judiciary. The Court held that the search engaged aspects of the applicant's private life and that it was disproportionate to the aim for which it was undertaken. Yet this conclusion could not have been reached on the balancing model of proportionality. If the question was whether the benefit to solving crimes was higher than the

[3] *Niemietz v Germany* (A/251-B) (1993) 16 E.H.R.R. 9.

cost of the interference with the applicant's privacy, then the search would have been proportionate: it was the only way to determine who the author of the letter was and it had little impact on the applicant's privacy. It was after all his office, not his home that was searched. But if the question is whether being an atheist who criticizes church tax is a valid reason or justification for using the executive powers of criminal law, then the answer is different. The fact that state officials disagree with a citizen's philosophical or political beliefs are impermissible grounds for issuing search warrants. It became clear from the facts of the case that the authorities had used their powers of criminal law (prosecution for insulting behavior, investigation, searches) in a vindictive way, targeting an anti-clerical protester. The Court blocked this reason, ruling the interference with the applicant's right disproportionate.

A defense of proportionality as fittingness does not assume that all judicial decisions are best explained as giving effect to a reason-blocking theory of rights. But this is true of course of any theory of proportionality. Some decisions will count as outliers or mistakes, otherwise the theory would lack a critical edge. In so far as accounts of proportionality are bottom-up, seeking to gain support from practice, the question is whether decisions reached by courts can be justified under a balancing model. The fittingness conception denies that this is possible, and offers an alternative explanation of judicial outcomes.

CONCLUSION

One thing constitutions do is to set out fundamental principles of political morality that bind institutional action and assign strong political rights to individuals. At surface level, the principle of proportionality operates as a doctrinal heading under which courts scrutinize state interference with individual liberty and assess the scope of their own institutional authority. I have argued however that in substance proportionality is best understood as concerning the normative foundations of constitutional rights and the duty of courts to pursue, through principled legal reasoning, the moral truth about them. The balancing model of proportionality, and the idea of judicial self-restraint, presuppose a contested conception of what these fundamental constitutional rights are. But if we take seriously both the idea of fundamental rights and the principle of proportionality, we must abandon the misleading metaphor of balancing and the problems of incommensurability and judicial skepticism to which it inevitably leads.

RECOMMENDED READING

Alexy, R. (2002). *A Theory of Constitutional Rights*, Oxford: Oxford University Press.
Barak, A. (2012). *Proportionality*, Cambridge: Cambridge University Press.
Dworkin, R. (1981). Is there a Right to Pornography? *Oxford Journal of Legal Studies*, 1(2), 177–212.

Huscroft, G., Miller, B. W., & Webber, G. eds., (2014). *Proportionality and the Rule of Law*, Cambridge: Cambridge University Press.
Jackson, V. & Tushnet, M. (2017). *Proportionality: New Frontiers, New Challenges*, Cambridge: Cambridge University Press.
Klatt, M. & Meister M., (2012). *The Constitutional Structure of Proportionality*, Oxford: Oxford University Press.
Kumm, M. (2010). The Idea of Socratic Contestation and the Right to Justification: The Point of Rights-Based Proportionality Review. *Law and Ethics of Human Rights*, 4(2), 142–175.
Letsas, G. (2015). Rescuing Proportionality. In R. Cruft, S. Liao, M. Renzo, eds., *Philosophical Foundations of Human Rights*. Oxford: Oxford University Press.
Letsas, G. (2018). Proportionality as Fittingness. *Current Legal Problems*, 71(1), 53–86.
Lever, A. (2020). A Sense of Proportion: Some Thoughts on Equality, Security and Justice. *Res Publica*, 26(4), 357–371.
Möller, Kai. (2012). *The Global Model of Constitutional Rights*, Oxford: Oxford University Press.
Nagel, T. (1995). Personal Rights and Public Space. *Philosophy and Public Affairs*, 24(2), 83–107.
Poole, T. (2010). Proportionality in Perspective. *New Zealand Law Review*, 2010 (2), 369–391.
Ripstein, A. (2016). Reclaiming Proportionality. *Journal of Applied Philosophy*, 22(2), 24–31.
Tsakyrakis, S. (2009). Proportionality: An Assault on Human Rights? *International Journal of Constitutional Law*, 7(3), 468–493.
Urbina, F. (2017). *A Critique of Proportionality and Balancing*, Cambridge: Cambridge University Press.

24

Civil Disobedience

Candice Delmas

How societies treat their dissidents is a test of how liberal they are. According to the standard dichotomy between liberal and illiberal societies, the latter arrest, jail, torture, and even murder dissidents, while the former defends freedom of expression and welcomes dissent. Constitutional governments, which rule through law, protect citizens' basic rights of free speech and assembly. However, they are not bound to tolerate civil disobedience, that is, principled, public, and nonviolent act of *lawbreaking* undertaken by an agent willing to accept legal sanctions in order to protest a law, policy, or institution. Martha Nussbaum (2019, p. 178), for instance, insists that it is "irresponsible" to "confuse … civil disobedience … with protected free speech." On her view, which represents many officials' and laypersons' view, the civil disobedient must be willing to bear the burden of violating the law without trying to claim constitutional protection. But this begs the question: How should a constitutional state – one that respects subjects' basic rights – treat civil disobedients? This chapter presents and critically engages with some of the most prominent answers legal scholars, political theorists, and philosophers have given to this question.

On what I'll call punitive approaches, which I present in Section I, civil disobedience is first and foremost an act of resistance that threatens the constitutional order, and thus a public wrong worthy of punishment. Theorists of civil disobedience have challenged this approach since the 1960s, especially by conceiving of civil disobedience as a kind of dissent, which liberal democratic societies ought to and can "make room" for. Sections II and III examine these "constitutionalizing" approaches, with Section II focusing on the case for leniency, and Section III on the case for broad accommodation. Section IV examines the costs of constitutionalizing approaches and reclaims the understanding of civil disobedience as a kind of resistance, alongside its uncivil counterparts, that is sometimes justified and even necessary in constitutional democracies.

I PUNISHING CIVIL DISOBEDIENCE

Why should the state punish civil disobedience? The punitive approach offers two related answers. According to a first general answer, lawbreaking or disobedience, be it criminal or civil, is wrong and cannot be tolerated because it impedes states' mission to establish law and order; it undermines the rule of law; and it destabilizes society, both through example, by signaling to others that anyone can disobey if they feel the urge, and in principle, by expressing disrespect for law's authority. The principled character of civil disobedience does not preclude its destabilizing tendency. On the contrary, if every conscientious person were to violate the law each time they find it unjust, society would be thrown into a disorder akin to the Hobbesian state of nature. Disobedience, including civil disobedience, is thus conceived as a public wrong that must be punished – a type of conduct to be condemned and deterred in the interest of protecting the legal and social order.

According to the second answer, civil disobedience in particular is a proper object of punishment because of its anti-democratic nature: it openly flouts democratic decision-making processes, and involves agents putting themselves above the law. Some philosophers (C. Cohen 1971, pp. 138–145; Weinstock 2016, p. 709; Dworkin 1985, p. 112) see in it a violation of reciprocity, a kind of civil "blackmail," and a sign of "moral self-indulgence," insofar as a minority, whose views didn't prevail, disregards democratic processes and imposes on the majority its own view of the good and just. U.S. Supreme Court Justice John Paul Stevens wrote in a 1971 case involving the religiously motivated burning of draft cards in protest against the Vietnam War:

> One who elects to serve mankind by taking the law into his own hands thereby demonstrates his conviction that his own ability to determine policy is superior to democratic decisionmaking. Appellant's professed unselfish motivation, rather than a justification, actually identifies a form of arrogance which organized society cannot tolerate.[1]

On this view, civilly disobedient agents, as they self-appoint "to serve mankind," accord themselves a larger say in public matters, objectionably making themselves an exception to prevailing rules. Civil disobedience appears like an assertion of moral superiority and misplaced sense of entitlement, a way to say, "I know better than everyone else what is right and wrong." It is wrong, and deserves punishment, because it neglects both the constitutional ideal of the rule of law and the democratic ideal of lawmaking as a collective enterprise.

This last argument only arises in liberal democracies, which both make decisions through democratic procedures and provide citizens with meaningful opportunities to dissent when they oppose particular outcomes. Thus, in Joseph Raz's view (1979a chap. 14), civil disobedience is morally permissible only in illiberal states that fail to recognize subjects' right to dissent and deprive them of lawful channels to air their grievances. But where citizens can vote, organize, demonstrate, run for office, petition their government, appeal in court, submit constitutional

---

[1] United States v. Cullen, 454 F.2d 386, 392 (7th Cir. 1971).

challenges, and so on, civil disobedience is morally and legally impermissible, because it consists of unlawful and objectionable attempts to bypass and frustrate the democratic process.

A proponent of the punitive approach does not have to deny the social value and moral justification of *some* acts of civil disobedience in order to maintain a punitive stance toward civil disobedience in general. Justice Abe Fortas wrote (1968, p. 9):

> I am a man of law…. But if I had lived in Germany in Hitler's days, I hope I would have refused to wear an armband, to Heil Hitler, to submit to genocide…. If I had been a Negro living in Birmingham or Little Rock or Plaquemines Parish, Louisiana, I hope I would have disobeyed the state law that said I might not enter the public waiting room reserved for "Whites"…. I hope I would have had the courage to disobey, although the segregation ordinances were presumably law until they were declared unconstitutional.

Fortas doesn't advocate blind obedience to law. He admires the courage of those who refuse to comply with gravely unjust law and even deems disobedience a moral duty.

His goal in *Concerning Dissent and Civil Disobedience* is to reconcile the state's need of every subject's obedience to law (for its rights-preserving function) with the "equally basic need to disobey" unjust laws in the interest of justice (Fortas 1968, p. 10). Disobeying unjust law is a *moral* obligation, while complying with the law is our primary *legal* obligation. Fortas claims that the two obligations can be reconciled through the agent's acceptance of punishment, which marks her respect for the rule of law, where her disobedience otherwise suggests contempt for the rule of law. I dub the requirement that agents willingly accept arrest, prosecution, and punishment "non-evasion" for short.[2]

As Terrance Sandalow (1969) argued in his review of Fortas's book, the thesis that non-evasion successfully reconciles these moral and legal obligations is on shaky ground, given the deep tension, if not outright inconsistency, between the justification of particular acts of civil disobedience and the legitimacy of punishing those. First, Sandalow noted, the conflict is not between a moral and a legal obligation but between two moral duties: the duty to obey the law is conceived as a moral requirement, not a merely legal one, and Fortas himself views disobedience to unjust law as a moral duty. Second, through punishment, the state communicates that the civil disobedient ought not to have disobeyed. But if the balance of moral reasons weighs in favor of disobeying rather than obeying the law, then there is nothing to condemn and the state ought not to punish her. Punishing justified civil disobedience thus raises a serious moral problem.

---

[2] The vast majority of legal theorists defend non-evasion as a requirement of civil disobedience. They usually mean one or more of four attitudes: (i) willing submission to arrest and prosecution, (ii) guilty plea in court, (iii) no appeal to criminal defenses, and (iv) no complaint for the punishment received. See Delmas (2019) for an analysis and critique.

Champions of the punitive approach respond that even if particular acts of civil disobedience can sometimes be morally justified, the state ought to punish agents, who in turn ought to accept punishment. U.S. Solicitor General Erwin Griswold (1968, p. 10074) put it thusly:

> [I]t is of the essence of law that it is equally applied to all, that it binds all alike, irrespective of personal motive. For this reason, one who contemplates civil disobedience out of moral conviction should not be surprised and must not be bitter if a criminal conviction ensues…. [O]rganized society cannot endure on any other basis.

Griswold grounds the duty of non-evasion on the destabilizing potential of civil disobedience. On his view, the distinction between criminal and civil disobedience does not constitute a morally relevant difference as far as the law is concerned. Thus, courts need not and shouldn't assess "personal motive." In turn, civil disobedients cannot ask for special treatment; they must demonstrate their respect for law by accepting arrest and punishment without complaint.

Non-evasion is to civil disobedients what impartiality is to the courts: a rule-of-law-based imperative. A constitutional government must apply the law impartially and treat like cases alike. Judges commonly stress that courts' proper function excludes attempting to distinguish between justified and unjustified acts of civil disobedience. In that spirit, one wrote: "We deal with legal rights and established law. From these we cannot depart, without a violation of our duty."[3] In short, impartiality demands courts' neutrality, and neutrality requires punishing all civil disobedience.

But judges' professions of neutrality can hide problematic partiality. The case I just mentioned regarded abolitionist disobedience to slavery laws. As Matthew Lippman (1994, p. 324) has shown, "despite their protestations of neutrality, the federal judiciary was the central force behind the enforcement of the Fugitive Slave Act," rarely acquitting abolitionist defendants and harshly punishing captured fugitive slaves. The judiciary "was quick to stress that no state can 'defeat or obstruct' the right of slave owners, but remained mute concerning the plight of the enslaved and indentured," he noted (ibid.). Judges concealed their promotion of ruling-class interests behind the language of law's impartiality and judicial neutrality.

A historical pattern of judicial bias doesn't refute the claim that judges should be impartial. Indeed, they should be impartial. But it doesn't follow that they can't or shouldn't inquire into disobedient agents' principled motivations. Griswold's declaration that the law "binds all alike, irrespective of personal motive" is equivocal: in order to treat like cases alike, judges often examine defendants' personal motives, as when assessing criminal defenses. Treating like cases alike demands treating civil disobedients as civil disobedients rather than as garden-variety criminals and doesn't clearly (let alone a priori) rule out examining agents' purported justifications for their actions.

---

[3] Driskill v. Parrish, 7 F. Cas. 1100 (C.C.D. Ohio, 1845) (No. 4,089).

II CONSTITUTIONALIZING CIVIL DISOBEDIENCE (TAKE 1): LENIENCY

On a Saturday in March 1964, Henry Brown and four other African American members of Congress of Racial Equality (CORE) entered the whites-only Audubon Regional Library in Clinton, Louisiana. Brown requested to borrow a Booker T. Washington book. After the librarian informed Brown that the book was not available at this branch, the men sat down in silence and refused to leave when asked to. The five men were arrested and found guilty of breach of peace. The Louisiana Supreme Court refused to hear the men's legal appeals, so the case went all the way to the U.S. Supreme Court, which reversed the convictions in 1966.

Writing for the majority, Justice Fortas stressed that First Amendment rights "are not confined to verbal expression, but embrace other types of expression, including appropriate silent and reproachful presence, such as petitioners used here".[4] The state's interference with this right to peaceable and orderly protest, he noted, was "intolerable under our Constitution." The *Brown v. Louisiana* Court reaffirmed what the Civil Rights Act of 1964 had already established: that all individuals had the right to equal use of public facilities with no discrimination on the basis of race. What was groundbreaking, however, was the notion that sit-ins were a kind of protected speech that the government ought not to unduly interfere with.

Until then, sit-ins had been construed as a tactic of economic coercion, not a peaceful mode of persuasion. Sit-ins were central to labor strikes in the early twentieth century. The United Auto Workers adopted the tactic in the 1930s, following the example set by the International Workers of the World, and shut down big factories in Flint, Michigan, and elsewhere (see Meyer 2007). Activists from the labor movement brought the sit-in over to the Civil Rights Movement after World War II, particularly via the Highlander Institute. In 1960, when more than 70,000 civil rights activists participated in sit-ins of whites-only lunch counters and picket lines, many of those arrested were charged with loitering and picketing, under antilabor legislation, as well as serious crimes like "intimidation," "conspiracy," and "fomenting anarchy" (which earlier labor activists had also been convicted of) (see Fairclough 1987, p. 60).

Philosophers, including Hugo Bedau (1961), Carl Cohen (1971), Ronald Dworkin (1978 [1977], 1985), John Rawls (1999a [1971]), Peter Singer (1973), and Jürgen Habermas (1985), also began conceptualizing civil disobedience as dissent, rather than coercion or resistance.[5] This reconceptualization, combined with the tripartite distinction between civil, criminal, and revolutionary disobedience, opened a space

---

[4] Brown v. Louisiana, 383 U.S. 131 (1966).
[5] Michael Walzer (1970) and Howard Zinn (2002) constituted notable exceptions to this trend of conceptualizing civil disobedience as speech.

for civil disobedience in constitutional liberal democracy, thus paving the way for constitutionalizing approaches' pleas for leniency (examined in this section) and accommodation (Section III).

The punitive approach construes civil disobedience as an act of resistance, meant to frustrate the workings of the system, a threat to the rule of law, and a public wrong. Proponents of constitutionalizing approaches changed this understanding of civil disobedience by depicting it as essentially symbolic speech, in contradistinction with criminal and revolutionary disobedience. Whereas criminals typically break the law covertly and for self-interested reasons, civil disobedients break the law publicly and openly, in order to persuade the public to change certain laws or policies. Their disobedience is public in another, special sense: it makes an appeal to widely endorsed constitutional principles, not private interests or conceptions of the good (Rawls 1999a, p. 321; Habermas 1985, pp. 103–104). In addition, civil disobedients are committed to nonviolence (as a requirement of communicative expression) and willing to accept punishment, in contrast to revolutionaries and criminals who are willing to use violence and evade punishment.

Rawls (1999, p. 322) captured the importance of these self-restraints – publicity, nonviolence, and non-evasion, which together mark the disobedient act's civility – by stressing that civil disobedients act "within the limits of fidelity to law," and hence neither necessarily undermine the rule of law nor flout democratic ideals. For Dworkin (1985, p. 105), civil disobedients "accept the fundamental legitimacy of both government and community"; and on Habermas's view, agents undertaking civil disobedience "recognize the democratic legality of the existing order," whereas rebels, who are engaged in "resistance proper," do not (1985, p. 103). Civil disobedience, for Habermas, exists within the space between legitimacy and legality: it targets particular illegitimate laws while maintaining "wholly intact" the constitutional state and its legal order (ibid.). Because of these attitudes and constraints, civil disobedience, and only civil disobedience can have a place in society.

Dispelling the concerns about the dangers of civil disobedience by highlighting its civility was just the first step in the argument. In order to constitutionalize civil disobedience, theorists also had to establish its contribution to constitutional democracy. They did so by conceiving of civil disobedience as a symbolic form of public argumentation, directed at the majority and intended to bring about reform. Rawls (1999a, p. 320) defined it as an act by which "one addresses the sense of justice of the majority of the community." Singer (1991) called it "a plea for reconsideration." For Habermas (1985, p. 99), it is a "symbolic ... appeal to the capacity for reason and sense of justice of the majority."

The justification of civil disobedience further articulates the conditions for its effective role in constitutional democratic society. Both Rawls and Habermas required acts of civil disobedience target serious and long-standing injustice, be undertaken as a last resort, and appeal to widely endorsed constitutional principles.[6] Far from undermining the rule of law or destabilizing society, civil disobedience could then strengthen the social and legal order. Rawls (1999a, p. 336) stressed the justice-enhancing value of civil disobedience, noting that "it serves to inhibit departures from justice and to correct them when they occur," while Habermas (1985, p. 103) conceived of civil disobedience as "the guardian of legitimacy." Habermas (1985, p. 99) even took the state's treatment of civil disobedience as a "litmus test" of the maturity of the political culture of a constitutional democracy: "Every constitutional democracy that is sure of itself considers civil disobedience as a normalized – because necessary – component of its political culture."

Where Rawls and Habermas saw civil disobedients as citizens engaged in political arguments, Dworkin analogized them to Supreme Court Justices engaged in constitutional disputes. When the law's validity is doubtful, civil disobedience is constitutionally acceptable – even welcome – and may in fact not involve lawbreaking at all (given the law's possible unconstitutionality). The paradigm of civil disobedience, on this view, is the constitutional test case, where one directly breaks and protests an unjust law, such as a racial segregation statute, and challenges the law in question as unconstitutional.[7] Like Supreme Court Justices, civil disobedients weigh in on disputes over how best to interpret and apply certain constitutional principles and contribute in that way to "law's integrity."[8] Dworkin (1985, pp. 104–116) labeled this kind of civil disobedience, which articulates constitutional rights claims, "justice-based," in contradistinction to "integrity-based" disobedience, undertaken when the law requires doing something one's conscience forbids, and "policy-based" disobedience, which targets a program deemed "unwise, stupid, and dangerous" but not unjust. Dworkin's example of justice-based civil disobedience is the Civil Rights Movement's activities; assisting escaped slaves in violation of the Fugitive Slave Law illustrates integrity-based civil disobedience; and anti-nuclear protests exemplify policy-based civil disobedience.

---

[6] Rawls also required civil disobedients coordinate their protests with other minority groups with similar grievances, in order to minimize the disruption, while Dworkin added "consequentialist caution" – the idea that "an actor must take consequences into account and not break the law if the likely result will be to make the situation not better but worse according to his own lights" (Dworkin 1985, p. 108).

[7] Indirect civil disobedience, in contrast, involves breaking an unobjectionable law, say, against trespass, in order to protest another unjust law or policy, such as nuclear armament. Only agents engaged in direct civil disobedience may contend that they are not really breaking the law, given its doubtful validity. Early theorists of civil disobedience generally found direct civil disobedience more readily justifiable than its indirect counterpart, although neither Rawls nor Habermas thought that justified civil disobedience didn't really involve lawbreaking.

[8] Dworkin's theory of law demands judges articulate the best justification of their community's legal practices. Law as integrity, the particular theory that fits the U.S. legal system, requires constructing an interpretation of law as structured by a coherent set of principles of justice and fairness. See Dworkin (1986).

This tripartite typology traces the kinds of convictions that form the basis of the act of civil disobedience in question. Both integrity- and justice-based civil disobedience involve "convictions of principle" (regarding the law's wrongness and the demands of one's conscience, respectively), while policy-based civil disobedience stems from "judgments of policy" having to do with the common interest (Dworkin 1985, p. 107). Dworkin justified integrity-based and justice-based civil disobedience, but not their policy-based cousin, which, he thought, violates the democratic principle of majority rule, insofar as matters of policy (unlike matters of justice) must be left to the majority. Civil disobedience is justified by its contribution to the constitutional order: it yields better, more just outcomes over time.

Dworkin (1978, p. 251) insisted on the breadth of the constitutional opening for civil disobedience:

> Doubtful law is by no means special or exotic in cases of civil disobedience. On the contrary. In the United States, at least, almost any law which a significant number of people would be tempted to disobey on moral grounds would be doubtful – if not clearly invalid – on constitutional grounds as well.[9]

Civil disobedients, then, do what judges do, but from below: they challenge the constitutional validity of unjust law. For instance, Dworkin (1978, pp. 252–253) encouraged observers – lawyers, officials, the media, and the public – to reconstruct anti-Vietnam War resistance (which involved both integrity- and justice-based civil disobedience) through a legal and constitutional lens, as arguing: that the declaration of war did not pass constitutional muster; that the U.S. government was committing war crimes in Vietnam; that the draft discriminated against the economically underprivileged by exempting college students; and that laws that made it a crime to counsel draft resistance abridged freedom of speech. Challenges like these are not only constitutionally permitted, but also invited, since they help make law more faithful to the principles of justice and fairness that justify it (on Dworkin's theory of law).

Many theorists accept the value of constitutional challenges but argue that once the law is found constitutional by a high court and their initial conviction is upheld, civil disobedients have a duty to accept their punishment and recognize the law's validity. For instance, Nussbaum (2019, p. 177) argues that while Paul O'Brien and other dissidents, in 1966, may have believed in good faith that their First Amendment rights protected their right to burn their Selective Service registration cards in protest against the Vietnam war, they could no longer make this case once the Supreme Court had settled the question negatively in *U.S. v. O'Brien*.[10] In

---

[9] Dworkin's account of civil disobedience in 1968 and 1970 (in essays for *The New York Review of Books* which were reprinted in *Taking Rights Seriously*, chaps. 4 and 5) does not cross over with his account in 1985, which lays out the tripartite distinction.
[10] United States v. O'Brien, 391 U.S. 367, 382 (1968).

contrast, Dworkin argued that forcing citizens to obey court decisions – including the Supreme Court's – would mean forcing them to do something their conscience forbids them to do, which is too much to ask.

Dworkin refused to make the constitutional buck stop at the Supreme Court, in light of: (i) the instrumental value of constitutional disputes; (ii) courts' fallibility – the simple idea that judges can be wrong about the law; and (iii) the constitutional imperative, entrenched in the First Amendment and rooted in dignity, to respect individuals' "right to conscience." In his view, citizens should continue to follow their own judgment about doubtful law, regardless of higher courts' decisions about the matter. To the charge that such course of conduct would violate the rules of the democratic game, as proponents of the punitive approach contend, Dworkin's response was twofold. First, he insisted that civil disobedients can "appeal to a standing and well-understood exception to the majority-rule principle," the same that judges appeal to when they review, and void, democratically enacted laws that "outrage the principles of justice embedded in the Constitution" (Dworkin 1985, p. 111). Second, Dworkin argues that requiring people to obey the law against their moral conscience would impose an undue burden on them – a point that applies especially to integrity-based civil disobedience. Existing conscientious objection exemptions for religious pacifists recognized this burden, although legislators and judges had failed to realize that the same burden weighed on those who conscientiously objected to the Vietnam War in particular rather than to all wars, and on moral and political rather than religious grounds.

The right to conscience, for Dworkin (1978, pp. 228–237), thus grounds a weak "right to break the law." It is a right in the sense that one "does the right thing to break the law, so that we should all respect" the agent when she follows her conscientious judgment about doubtful law and when she refuses to comply with a law that requires her to do what her conscience forbids, but not in the strong sense that the government would do wrong to stop her. Despite his critique of the punitive arguments, then, Dworkin deemed the right to disobedience compatible with the state's right to punish. Contra C. Cohen (1966, p. 6), Rawls (1999a, p. 322), and others, however, Dworkin did not defend agents' moral duty to accept punishment (1985, pp. 114–115). He considered non-evasion a good strategy for justice- and policy-based civil disobedience but denied it was a conceptual, moral, or tactical requirement for integrity-based civil disobedience. Dworkin argued that utilitarian reasons for punishing civil disobedients should be weighed against the fact that the accused acted out of principled convictions, and that the balance should generally favor leniency.

Indeed, more important than the state's right to punish is its "special responsibility to try to protect him [the citizen who follows his own judgment in the face of doubtful law], and soften his predicament, whenever it can do so without great damage to other policies" (Dworkin 1978, p. 260). The government can exercise its responsibility of leniency by *not* prosecuting civil disobedience at all, depending on the balance of reasons, including individual rights, state interests, social costs, and constitutional benefits. Reasons for prosecuting in any particular case are "practical," not intrinsic or deontological ones, and always potentially defeasible. In general, prosecutors should not charge disobedients with the most serious offenses applicable and judges should give them light sentences. Leniency seems to contravene the demand for impartiality and judicial neutrality we discussed earlier. But on Dworkin's theory of legal interpretation, judges cannot avoid making normative judgments about the law when deciding cases and they must do so to treat like cases alike. Leniency follows from the recognition of the special constitutional status of civil disobedience. Rawls and Habermas explicitly endorsed Dworkin's arguments for leniency.

Finally, constitutional governments' duty to protect freedom of speech forbids them from curtailing the latter even for the sake of the "general interest" (Dworkin 1978, p. 231). That is, a government can never make it illegal for people to speak their mind. Dworkin thus argued that Vietnam War dissidents had a moral right to break the laws banning draft resistance advocacy, because they retained their right to free speech, in contravention of the law. Contra Nussbaum, then, dissidents whose rights to free speech are curtailed, may rightfully disobey these restrictive laws, mount constitutional test cases against these, and present their civil disobedience as constitutionally protected speech.

This is how early constitutionalizing approaches like Dworkin's, Rawls's, and Habermas's brought civil disobedience within the constitutional framework, rebranding it as a type of dissent that appeals to constitutional principles and can enhance laws' justice and legitimacy. Dworkin further supplemented the instrumental case for civil disobedience, given its role in supporting law's integrity, with a noninstrumental defense grounded in the imperative to respect individuals' basic right to conscience. These constitutionalizing arguments support the state's responsibility of leniency toward civil disobedients – but not yet the case for accommodation. To this next step we now turn.

III CONSTITUTIONALIZING CIVIL DISOBEDIENCE (TAKE 2): ACCOMMODATION

It is almost an article of faith that civil disobedience cannot be legalized. Legalizing civil disobedience seems, first of all, like a contradiction in terms: how could there be civil *disobedience* if civil disobedience is legal? Second, legalization would take away the visibility that civil disobedients seek to attract through their arrest and prosecution. Third, it would take away agents' opportunity to demonstrate their sincere commitment and respect for law through their willing acceptance of civil disobedience's costs. Fourth, it would lead to chaos, both through proliferation of civil disobedience and by inviting frivolous and excessively disruptive protests. Fifth, civil disobedience cannot be legislated because of its doubly "savage" or "wild" nature, in Albert Ogien's phrase (2015, p. 592): "it is designed to expose democracy's limitations, spontaneously, under emotional impulse and in an uncontrolled way." Therefore, to legalize civil disobedience would be to eliminate the conditions for its possibility (per the first and fifth arguments) or effectiveness (second through fourth arguments).

However, what some theorists have come to advocate is not legalization of civil disobedience in the sense of providing civil disobedients with complete immunity to arrest and prosecution. Rather, they seek to *legally recognize* civil disobedience as a special category of conscientious expression or political speech. They defend on this basis a general (defeasible) presumption against punishment of, and in favor of communicative engagement with, civil disobedients.

David Lefkowitz (2007), Kimberley Brownlee (2012, chap. 4), and William Smith (2013, chap. 4) are the most prominent champions of the moral right to civil disobedience, conceived as a liberal right of conduct. Just as the right of free speech protects illiberal and offensive speech, not just "good" speech, so the right to civil disobedience protects civil disobedients who pursue illiberal, undemocratic or otherwise problematic causes from punishment (within limits), and not only those engaged in justified civil disobedience. This right to civil disobedience entails a presumptive claim-right against censure and punishment, which means there may be weighty countervailing reasons to punish or penalize civil disobedience.

Lefkowitz and Smith conceive of the moral right to civil disobedience as a right to political participation. Lefkowitz argues that, well understood, the right to political participation extends beyond legal methods, given the way democratic politics works: on the one hand, there is the need for collective action, which entails that, at some point, the debate must stop and a vote must be taken; on the other hand, democratic losers "may justifiably complain that, had there been further time for debate and deliberation, or had they enjoyed greater resources for the dissemination of their arguments, their own (reasonable) views might have won majority support" (Lefkowitz 2007, p. 213). This is why the moral right to political participation is not limited to the right to participate in the decision-making process by voting, but further includes "a right to continue to contest the decision reached by such a process after the fact by a variety of means, including suitably constrained civil disobedience" (ibid.). The right to civil disobedience is embedded in Lefkowitz's conception of political obligation as a disjunctive "duty to obey the law or engage in civil disobedience" (Lefkowitz 2007, p. 215).

Brownlee, for her part, expands on the understanding of civil disobedience as conscientious expression by grounding the right to civil disobedience in the "principle of humanism," according to which "society has a duty to honor the fact that we are reasoning and feeling beings capable of forming deep moral commitments" (Brownlee 2012, p. 7). Society ought to allow persons who find themselves burdened by law's demands to freely disobey on the basis of their conscientious convictions. Liberal societies already do this to varying degrees for the benefit of conscientious objectors, who are often exempt from complying with rules and orders that conflict with their moral (especially religious) conscience. For instance, most countries that provide reproductive healthcare services such as contraception and abortion have enacted "conscience clauses" to grant healthcare professionals the right to conscientiously refuse to provide such services. Forty-eight states in the U.S. permit parents to refuse to immunize their children for "nonmedical" reasons, on the basis of religious belief; and twenty states among those permit exemptions based on nonreligious personal convictions, such as anti-vaxxers' pseudoscientific (and demonstrably false) belief that vaccination causes autism. This kind of deference toward conscientious objection – and indeed this loose and permissive understanding of conscientious objection itself – is usually justified within a constitutional framework by appeal to the respect owed to individuals' conscientiousness and the recognition of the moral and psychic burdens of complying with law that goes against one's beliefs.

Brownlee's central argument in *Conscience and Conviction* is that civil disobedience is in fact more conscientious than conscientious objection, given the features that make conscientious acts of disobedience worthy of protection. She understands conscientiousness or "conviction" as a descriptive property that designates sincerely held, though possibly erroneous, "communicative" moral commitment. When we have a conscientious conviction that something is wrong, on Brownlee's view (Brownlee 2012, chap. 1), we must (a) avoid the conduct in question to the best extent that we are able; (b) judge such conduct in others to be wrong as well; (c) be willing to bear the risks of honoring our conviction; and (d) be willing to communicate the reasons that we think justify our conviction to others. Civil disobedients, who disobey publicly and seek to persuade others to join them, more readily exemplify these four elements than conscientious objectors, who often disobey privately. To that extent, civil disobedience deserves *more* constitutional protection than conscientious objection.

Lefkowitz and Brownlee argue that the state has a presumptive duty not to punish civil disobedients, and that agents should enjoy presumptive immunity from punishment. While Lefkowitz defends a claim-right against punishment but not against penalty (e.g., fines), Brownlee argues it protects against *all* forms of state interference. Since this right is presumptive, countervailing reasons to punish or penalize civil disobedience may outweigh it. But she contends that even when judges are justified to punish civil disobedients, they ought to apologize to the latter for infringing upon their rights (Brownlee 2012, p. 251). Lefkowitz and Brownlee constitutionalize civil disobedience by revealing its basis in fundamental rights and showing how constitutional governments can accommodate it. They build on and expand the case for leniency, urging officials at all levels to use their discretion to *not* sanction civil disobedients.

Philosophers have focused on the question how courts should treat civil disobedients, while neglecting to apply the question to law enforcement. Yet the police have much discretion in how to deal with civil disobedients. In particular, they have no obligation to arrest protesters when they commit minor violations of the law such as traffic obstruction: accommodation of and communication with protesters is something they can but all too rarely decide to do. Instead, many governments practice militarized repression of protests. Local police departments in the U.S. often respond to demonstrations with riot gear and other military equipment.[11] The British government has sought to strengthen public order laws and secure new police powers to crack down on Extinction Rebellion (XR), the global environmental movement whose street protests, die-ins, and roadblocks for climate justice have brought cities to a standstill.

One notable exception to the theoretical neglect of law enforcement is William Smith's (2013, chap. 5) articulation of a "policing philosophy" that orientates policing strategies toward accommodation, rather than prevention, of civil disobedience. On Smith's view (2013, p. 111), "the police should, where possible, cooperate with civilly disobedient activists in order to assist in their commission of a protest that is effective as an expression of their grievance against law or policy." Accommodation requires communication channels between police and activists and involves strategies such as pre-negotiated arrests.[12] While the U.S. implements punitive and strong-handed law enforcement strategies, the United Kingdom's current goal, according to one senior police source, is to develop "move forward" – proactive and preventive – tactics that are designed to clear the streets of XR demonstrators (Dodd *et al.* 2019). Neither approach respects the right to civil disobedience.

A constitutional government committed to recognizing the right to civil disobedience would also have to reform part of its criminal laws and make available certain defenses. Brownlee proposes two. First, disobedients should have access to a "demands-of-conviction," excusatory defense to point to the deep and sincere reasons they had for believing they were justified in acting the way they did (Brownlee 2012, chap. 5). Second, Brownlee argues that states should accept necessity as a justificatory defense for civil disobedience undertaken as a reasonable and parsimonious response to violations of and threats to non-contingent basic needs (Brownlee 2012, chap. 6).[13] As these defenses suggest, constitutionally recognizing civil disobedience does not mean making civil disobedience legal. Civil disobedients would still be arrested and prosecuted, but they would get to explain and justify their actions in court. They would be heard.

---

[11] The tendency has been even more pronounced after Donald Trump took office and issued an executive order providing local law enforcement with military gear and weaponry. See Presidential executive order on restoring state, tribal, and local law enforcement's access to life-saving equipment and resources. *Federal Register* 82, 168, Executive Order 13809 of August 28 (2017).

[12] A number of police forces in democratic states pursue accommodation with protesters. See Della Porta et al. 2006.

[13] Non-contingent basic needs are needs that the being must have for continued survival as the kind of being it is. Brownlee adopts a pluralistic approach to necessity that goes beyond the usual standard of imminent danger.

Hannah Arendt (1970) goes the furthest in this direction by conceiving of civil disobedients as lobbyists for the people, whose appeals legislators should listen to in a forum specially designed for that purpose. Habermas calls for leniency toward civil disobedience, but, contra Arendt, denies that it can be *institutionalized*, that is, established as a conventional, structurally organized practice. Civil disobedience brings to the fore public arguments articulated by spontaneously emerging associations – fluid, overlapping, subcultural, "wild" publics, that inform and invigorate civil society and are thus essential for democracy (Habermas 1996). For Habermas, civil disobedience must remain outside institutionalized processes of decision making in order to preserve its radical energy, which organization would otherwise corrupt (see Çıdam 2017).

Let's take stock of how these constitutionalizing arguments face up to the objections that opened this section. As we saw, accommodating civil disobedience doesn't remove the conditions for its possibility; it neither makes civil disobedience legal nor invites its uncontrolled proliferation. But it is true that accommodation would significantly reduce the costs associated with civil disobedience. And if civil disobedience derives its effectiveness from agents' absorption of brutal police repression and acceptance of prosecution and harsh punishment, then accommodation hinders this particular mechanism of persuasion. It is nonetheless implausible to deplore this prospective loss. Civil disobedience might just have to change in the process (within or without institutionalized processes, pace Habermas) – to rely less on the communicative power of suffering endured and to imagine a new aesthetic of persuasion.

What are we to make of Ogien's point that civil disobedience cannot be legislated because it consists in essence of an extra-legal, unexpected, impulsive, and "wild" usage of the law to express grievances and articulate political claims? First-person testimonies by practitioners, especially activists trained in nonviolence, refute his depiction of civil disobedience as undertaken "unexpectedly [*à l'improviste*], in the grip of an emotion, in a wild manner." It is inaccurate and misleading to deny the extensive practical and moral deliberations that go into civil disobedience actions. Further, the point of the civility of civil disobedience is precisely to neutralize accusations of "wildness" or rebellious lawlessness.

Ogien does not make any reference to Habermas's conception of civil disobedience as belonging to the "wild" public sphere. As far as I can tell, his distinction between "civilized" and "wild" uses of the law simply maps onto the more pedestrian distinction between lawful and unlawful dissent. Civil disobedience is "wild," in his view, because it "forces judicial intervention in a process of public reevaluation of a legal duty that is deemed unjust, disgraceful, dangerous or illegitimate" (Ogien 2015, p. 582). Ogien doesn't explain why the state couldn't legally recognize and accommodate activists' desire to set in motion this process. Champions of constitutionalizing approaches to civil disobedience have shown that the state could in fact do this.

But there is a grain of truth in Ogien's analysis: to constitutionalize or legally accommodate civil disobedience as conscientious speech is to domesticate or "declaw" it, to extend the metaphor of wildness. In the final section, I examine the limits and costs of constitutionalizing civil disobedience and reclaim the understanding of civil disobedience as resistance.

IV COSTS OF CONSTITUTIONALIZING APPROACHES

The liberal democracies we live in, for the most part, have not constitutionalized civil disobedience. Few show frequent leniency toward civil disobedience; most only do so occasionally at best. Constitutional democracies as well as authoritarian states (albeit to different degrees) tend to dissuade civil disobedience through antiprotest legislation, police repression, and harsh punishment. Constitutionalizing approaches offer crucial resources to critique this tendency. But in this final section, I want to highlight these approaches' costs and limits, especially the ways in which they end up deterring resistance against injustice, first, by misrepresenting civil disobedience, second, by excluding other kinds of principled disobedience.

The issue of misrepresentation unfolds in various ways. The understanding of civil disobedience as a means to bring constitutional test cases is especially problematic. As Frances Olsen (2005, p. 225) has shown, constitutional litigation invites but also limits civil disobedience: "It may encourage violations of the law that 'fit' constitutional challenges while also channeling protest in those directions." It isn't enough to civilly disobey a law that one deems unjust and unconstitutional: activists must follow lawyers' guidance to plan a successful test case – one that presents a clean fact pattern and an "appealing" individual defendant. Thus, constitutional litigation through test cases, Olsen notes, "may encourage thinking in terms of rights in an abstract and individualistic way and correspondingly discourage thinking in terms of power, politics and organization," which is how grassroot social movements operate (ibid.). The effect is to deter civil disobedience that isn't geared towards constitutional litigation.

Although Rawls and Dworkin didn't reduce civil disobedience to its role in setting up tests cases for constitutional litigation, they discouraged disobedient protest over matters other than basic questions of justice and the constitutional principles that bear on them. Rawls (1999a, p. 327) argued that certain issues of justice, such as economic inequalities, were not appropriate targets of civil disobedience, because they would not be widely seen as clear and blatant injustices (unlike, say, racial segregation). Dworkin (1985, pp. 111–112), for his part, found antinuclear protest unjustifiable to the extent that it turned on judgments of policy instead of appealing to fundamental principles of political morality.

In addition, constitutionalizing approaches misrepresent civil disobedience by expecting agents to endorse the legitimacy of, and show their respect for, the political and legal system. In fact, civil disobedients often contest the state's legitimacy and reject its claim to their obedience, even when they otherwise try to communicate a forward-looking commitment to fidelity to law. By making the acceptance of the system's legitimacy a necessary condition for, and the basis of, special protection claims, constitutionalizing approaches deradicalize civil disobedience.

Constitutionalizing approaches that center on individual conscience further moralize and subjectivize civil disobedience. Dworkin's and Brownlee's accounts epitomize this issue. Dworkin defends a weak, and Brownlee a weighty, right to break the law, on the basis of the right to conscience. Both argue that requiring individuals to obey the law when it conflicts with their deep moral commitments – whatever these may be – would impose an excessive burden on them. As Robert Jubb (2019, p. 962) has noted, Brownlee fails to explain "why individual conscience should weigh so heavily against the decided will of a majority, even in cases where the majority is right." Indeed, disobedience may undermine the equal civil standing of certain groups, as in cases of conscientious refusal to comply with antidiscrimination laws.

The conscience-centered model also makes the burdens of legal compliance a subjective matter. In doing so, it ignores the objective oppressive harms of certain unjust laws, policies, and institutions, which may be such that *everyone ought to resist* the injustice in question and refuse to comply with the laws that sustain it (Delmas 2018). Thoreau's call (1974, p. 73) to "[l]et your life be a counter friction to stop the machine [of an unjust government]," Gandhi's (1923, p. 215) declaration that one has a "duty to withdraw his support" from a government that "hurt[s] him or his nation," and King's (1963) insistence that "one has a moral responsibility to disobey unjust laws" and promote justice, model this understanding of the duty to resist. In short, by focusing on the burdens of law on conscientious individuals, the constitutionalizing approach misses the burdens of oppression that general compliance with unjust laws may generate, even in democratic contexts. And by conceiving of civil disobedience as conscientious dissent first and foremost, constitutionalizing approaches also miss the noncommunicative goals of much civil disobedience. Agents often seek to frustrate ongoing wrongs, prevent harms, and resist injustice – not merely speak against it – and see this work as their and everyone else's responsibility.

Turning to the second issue, constitutionalizing approaches that conceptualize civil disobedience narrowly – as public, nonviolent, and non-evasive – distort political action by excluding all sorts of non-civil principled disobedience from the realm of justifiable lawbreaking. Indeed, they wrongly suggest that disobedience that isn't civil is ipso facto criminal or revolutionary. Covert, violent, and evasive acts of disobedience are thus out of bounds for these constitutionalizing approaches, but not for "inclusive" accounts of civil disobedience, which have relaxed or abandoned the criteria of civility (e.g., Brownlee 2012; Milligan 2013; Celikates 2016; Scheuerman 2018). However, these accounts jettison the very point of civility, which is to adhere to a given script in order to demonstrate (at least forward-looking) respect for law. They further miss practitioners' deliberate departures from this script: *not* engaging in civil disobedience is sometimes the activists' point, as in the 2019–20 pro-democracy protests in Hong Kong (Delmas 2020). In these ways, inclusive accounts lump together, while narrow accounts exclude, distinct types of principled disobedience.

I propose instead to conceptualize "uncivil disobedience" – a cluster concept that covers various, disparate types of unlawful resistance that only have in common to violate the marks of civility. Agents of uncivil disobedience act covertly by concealing their identities; violently, against persons or property; or evasively, by avoiding arrest and prosecution. Examples of uncivil disobedience include leaks of classified information, guerrilla protests, distributed-denial-of-service attacks, hunger strikes, ecotage, and animal rescue. Instrumental and non-instrumental reasons can sometimes support covertness, violence, and evasion in principled disobedience (Delmas 2018).

Covertness and evasion may help realize certain worthwhile ends. Covertness is key to members of the Sanctuary movement in Europe, for instance, and to moving unauthorized immigrants from dangerous areas to safer ones along the new "underground railroad" in North America. Pro-immigrant rights activists also engage in lawful advocacy and civil disobedience to draw attention to their cause, but public and open disobedience in the direct assistance effort would doom it to failure and put in jeopardy the immigration prospects of those it purports to help. The same goes with evasion, since arrest and imprisonment would hinder the possibility of aiding persons in need.

There can also be non-instrumental reasons to evade law enforcement or refuse to accept punishment. To the extent that civil disobedience is taken as a signal of fidelity to law, flouting it can express distrust of and disrespect toward the legal system. When this disrespect is well grounded, that is, based on facts about the system's unjust and unfair treatment of some members, agents have reasons to express their attitude through evasion. Militant suffragists in the U.K. and the U.S., anti-apartheid activists in South Africa, and African Americans under Jim Crow, among many others, expressed warranted distrust of the legal system. Many groups of people, such as Native Americans under North American settler colonialism and low-income communities of color in the U.S., still have reason to distrust the state and can be justified in expressing their disrespect through evasive principled disobedience. Even if evasion is counterproductive to the ultimate goal, then, it is important to highlight its intrinsic aptness.

Use of force may also help achieve valuable ends, such as defense of self and others. Sea Shepherd, who illegally harass and sometimes damage whaling fleet, estimate that their interventions between 2002 and 2017 saved over 6,000 whales and helped bring about the end of whaling in the Southern Ocean (Sea Shepherd 2018; but see McKie 2017). For another example, the Deacons for Defense and Justice formed under Jim Crow as an armed group to protect CORE members from Ku Klux

Klan violence, and soon extended their activities to civil rights work such as organizing and voter registration. Self-defensive force against immediate threats to one's life is lawful, but the Deacons made a point of publicly displaying their force, sometimes in violation of local gun laws. Similarly, the Black Panthers publicly carried loaded firearms, first legally then illegally after the 1967 Mulford Act, which was crafted in response to Black Panthers' armed patrolling of Oakland, California. These groups' uncivil threats of violence were essential to their mission – collective self-defense against white supremacist violence. They could of course have registered their grievances through lawful and civil ways (and did, also), calling for better protection of their communities and denouncing systematic police brutality. But collective self-defense in the Jim Crow context primarily required the threat or use of force.

So: How should a constitutional democracy treat civil disobedients in its midst? Proponents of the punitive approach correctly appreciate the disruptive effects of principled disobedience but fail to appreciate the essential role of civil disobedience in constitutional democracy and its stabilizing powers. Liberal philosophers defend the state's responsibility to treat leniently and even accommodate civil disobedients in order to respect their freedom of conscience and right to dissent. However, they tend to distort civil disobedience and exclude other kinds of justifiable principled disobedience. Civil disobedience should be situated on a repertoire of resistance (rather than mere dissent or political argument), alongside its uncivil counterparts. Does my analysis suggest we should de-constitutionalize civil disobedience? Or constitutionalize uncivil disobedience?

On the one hand, one might seek to extend the constitutional protections advocated in favor of civil disobedience to some forms of uncivil disobedience, such as unauthorized government whistleblowing, which is often grounded in constitutional principles (Snowden 2019), and animal rescue operations, which can easily be interpreted as political dissent or conscientious expression. Most states nonetheless refuse to see these actions as speech. While some animal rights activists have been permitted to justify their actions in courts (usually to little avail), government whistleblowers charged under the Espionage Act in the U.S. are legally barred from defending their disclosures of classified information. In any case, conceiving of uncivil disobedience as conscientious speech would also misrepresent their activities, as I suggested earlier.

On the other hand, if we deny that civil disobedience should be conceived as a kind of dissent, we remove it from the realm of constitutionally protected speech, and thereby lose some crucial resources to shelter civil disobedients from the brunt of the law. Perhaps we also make it less likely that the public will hear them out, since de-constitutionalizing seems to amount to an "ousting" from constitutional democracy.

Solving this aporia requires answering a more fundamental question than the one this chapter sought to answer: how we should think about constitutionalism? My intuition here is that extra-constitutional challenges to the constitutional order may be integrated in, and contribute to strengthening, a radical constitutionalism. Critical Race Theory scholars like Mari Matsuda (1987) have defended dual interpretations of constitutionalism, and the rights rhetoric that characterizes it, as both an instrument of domination in the hands of the powerful and a potentially powerful weapon for emancipation. Matsuda describes Frederick Douglass's and Martin Luther King, Jr.'s "radical constitutionalism" as an adoption and transformation of mainstream consciousness of law from the bottom, by those victimized by it. She proposes a doctrine of Reparations as her contribution to radical constitutionalism. A doctrine of Disobedience, centered on the basic right to resist oppression (rather than freedom of speech and conscience), could be another. It remains to be developed.

ACKNOWLEDGMENTS

Previous versions of this chapter were presented at the Ohio State University Political Theory Workshop, the UCL Bentham House Conference on Foundational Concepts in Constitutional Theory, the Nuffield College Political Theory Seminar, the Edinburgh Political Theory Seminar, and the Edinburgh Legal Theory Seminar. I am very grateful to the organizers and participants at these events for stimulating conversations and helpful suggestions. Special thanks to Richard Bellamy, Helen Brown Coverdale, Kim Brownlee, Philip Cook, Dana Howard, Don Hubin, Jeff King, Cécile Laborde, Joaquín Reyes Barros, and Marc Spindelman.

RECOMMENDED READING

Bedau, H. A., ed. (1991). *Civil Disobedience in Focus*, London: Routledge.
Brownlee, K. (2012). *Conscience and Conviction: The Case for Civil Disobedience*, Oxford: Oxford University Press.
Çıdam, Ç., Scheuerman, W. E., Delmas, C. et al. (2020). Theorizing the politics of protest: Contemporary debates on civil disobedience. *Contemporary Political Theory*. Available from: https://doi.org/10.1057/s41296-020-00392-7
Delmas, C. (2018). *A Duty to Resist: When Disobedience Should Be Uncivil*, New York: Oxford University Press.
Dworkin, R. (1978 [1977]). *Taking Rights Seriously*, 5th edn, Cambridge, MA: Harvard University Press.
Habermas, J. (1985). Civil disobedience: Litmus test for the democratic constitutional state. Translated by J. Torpey. *Berkeley Journal of Sociology*, 30, 95–116.
Milligan, T. (2013). *Civil disobedience: Protest, Justification and the Law*, London: Bloomsbury Academic.
Rawls, J. (1999a [1971]). *A Theory of Justice*, rev. edn, Cambridge, MA: The Belknap Press of Harvard University Press.
Raz, J. (1979). *The Authority of Law: Essays on Law and Morality*, Oxford: Oxford University Press.
Scheuerman, W. E. (2018). *Civil Disobedience*, Cambridge, UK, Medford, MA: Polity Press.

Schwartzberg, M., ed. (2020). *NOMOS LXII: Protest and Dissent*, New York: New York University Press.
Smith, W. (2013). *Civil Disobedience and Deliberative Democracy*, Cambridge, UK: Routledge.
Walzer, M. (1970). *Obligations: Essays on Disobedience, War, and Citizenship*, Cambridge, MA: Harvard University Press.
Zinn, H. (2002 [1968]). *Disobedience and Democracy: Nine Fallacies of Law and Order*, Cambridge, MA: South End Press.

25

Constitutional Entrenchment

N. W. Barber[*]

Most of the time the rules that determine the process by which an institution makes law are constant across the range of its law-making activities. Among other things, these rules set the quorum for the body, the number of times it must consider and vote on a proposal, and the number of office-holders in the institution who must approve the measure before it becomes law. Though the body may make decisions on many different areas of law, these procedural rules – what we might describe as the institution's default rules – remain constant. This chapter considers one form of departure from these default rules: those situations in which law-making has been rendered harder through the entrenchment of an area of law. In these areas, the institution must engage in a special and more arduous process to change the law.

Entrenchment comes in a number of different forms, and there are a number of different reasons why we might want to entrench areas of law. This chapter argues that entrenchment rules are at their most attractive when there is a connection between the reason for entrenchment, the manner of entrenchment adopted, and the area of law entrenched. When these three elements connect, a strong case for entrenchment can be made. When they come apart it is harder – though not necessarily impossible – to defend entrenchment.

The chapter identifies three groups of types of entrenchment: those rules that require a rule altering the law to take a certain form, those rules that require the institution to spend extra time considering the alteration to the law, and, finally, those rules that expand the unit that must approve the change. Crosscutting these distinctions are three further variables. First, entrenchment rules can be self-imposed – the institution making it harder for its future incarnations to alter the law in an area – or imposed on that institution by another constitutional body. Second, the entrenching rule may, itself, be entrenched (it is "self-embracing") or the institution may be competent to alter the entrenching rule using its default process for legal change.

---

[*] A version of this paper was originally published as 'Why Entrench?' in (2016) 14 *International Journal of Constitutional Law* 325, and I am grateful for the permission of the journal to reprint it in this form. The original article is longer and includes examples omitted here.

Finally, the entrenching rule may automatically apply in a given area or it may empower some other group or institution to render it harder for the institution to alter the law: the entrenchment may be "triggered" by this other party.

The chapter then examines the arguments that should inform constitutional actors considering making use of entrenchment. These arguments area illuminated by the typology of entrenchment: entrenchment is at its most attractive when the form of entrenchment and the reasons for using this constitutional device are aligned. Advocates of entrenchment need to explain why the default rules of legal change should be departed from in a particular area, and why this particular type of entrenchment should be adopted.

I A TYPOLOGY OF ENTRENCHMENT

There is no consensus among lawyers and political scientists about the nature of entrenchment. At its most general, entrenchment has been used to describe any rule that is difficult to alter (Levinson 2011, p. 672; Schwartzberg 2007, chap. 1). There is a sense in which we could talk of the rules that constitute the British National Health Service (NHS) as being politically entrenched; while the NHS is established through ordinary statute law, it enjoys strong support from the public and it is virtually impossible to imagine any political party campaigning for its removal. Taken this broadly, all legal rules are entrenched to some degree. At the other extreme, Eric Posner and Adrian Vermeule provide a sharp, legal, definition of entrenchment (Posner and Vermeule 2002, p. 1667). On their account, entrenchment exists when a legislative body passes a rule that binds its future incarnations. The Canadian Bill of Rights is an example of a piece of legislation of this type: the statute was passed by the Canadian Parliament, and purports to constrain that institution. Vermeule and Posner's model of entrenchment would not extend to limitations on an institution that have been imposed by another constitutional body.

This chapter charts a middle course. It takes entrenchment to signify a legal rule that makes it more difficult for a body to change the law in an area that, but for the entrenching rule, would fall within its jurisdiction, and be alterable under the default rules of legal change. We can distinguish between the entrenching rule – the legal rule that renders change harder in a specified area – and the legal rules that are entrenched – those rules that are within the area specified by the entrenching rule. This account of entrenchment is narrower than the political scientists' understanding, but broader than Posner and Vermeule's interpretation. It does not encompass political entrenchment; just because a rule is practically or politically hard to alter does not render it entrenched on this account. On the other hand, while this understanding of entrenchment includes all the examples that fall within Posner and Vermeule's category, it also includes some limits that are imposed on an institution by another body. So, a rule of a written constitution which imposed, in certain areas, a requirement of a supermajority on the legislature would amount to entrenchment on this account, but would fall outside of Posner and Vermeule's definition.

While this chapter concentrates exclusively on legal entrenchment, the divide between legal and political entrenchment is a fine one. Sometimes political entrenchment can be effected by convention, that is, brought about by a non-legal constitutional rule (Barber 2010, chaps. 5–6). Many of the entrenchment rules discussed in this article could be grounded in a non-legal constitutional rule. Conventions could require that a referendum be held before a particular element of law is altered (Qvortrup 2006), or could require a federal level of government to secure the agreement of the states or provinces before changing the constitutional balance between the center and the regions (Marshall 1987, Chapter 11). Much of the discussion of legal entrenchment found in this article will also be applicable to the attractions and functioning of these non-legal, political, conventions.

When entrenchment is discussed the subject of the entrenchment is normally – perhaps almost invariably – a legislature. That legislatures are ordinarily central to the topic is unsurprising: on the common understanding of the separation of powers it is legislatures, rather than other branches of the constitution, that change the law. But few modern scholars would accept this simplistic account of legal change. Other bodies – in particular, the courts – also have the power to make law and can also be the subjects of entrenchment rules.

Though courts and legislatures make law in different ways, similar questions can be raised about the process through which the power is exercised. As with legislatures, the legal system specifies a set of default rules though which courts can effect legal change. The default rules of the court are rarely discussed in constitutional scholarship, but they embody choices that have been made within the system (Waldron 2014a; Shugerman 2002–2003). Some systems, for example, require decisions to be made unanimously – all the judges on the court must agree before the case is resolved – whereas others are satisfied by a majority decision. Given that judges make law, and given that they are empowered to do so under a default rule, it is possible that courts could be the subjects of entrenchment in a similar manner to legislatures. It could be argued, for example, that the courts' power to strike down statutes as unconstitutional should be exercised only when a supermajority of judges concur (Caminker 2003). Although the remainder of this chapter will focus on entrenchment as a limit on legislatures, many of the claims it makes could be applied, with a little caution, to other types of constitutional institution.

Types of Entrenchment: Form

Perhaps the most limited form of entrenchment is the requirement that a measure to alter the law must be expressed in a certain way; the body can alter the law, but must do so through a prescribed form. This may simply require that the new rule explicitly repeals the old – the court will not accept repeal by implication – or the body may have to adopt a prescribed form of words to effect the alteration.

The requirement of express repeal modifies the rule that resolves conflicts between legal instruments. In many systems, when two statutes from the same level of constitutional hierarchy conflict, precedence is given to the latter (Young 2008, Chapter 2). Even if the more recent act does not expressly repeal the earlier, it is taken to have been impliedly repealed. One, very limited, form of entrenchment removes the operation of implied repeal in an area of law: now the legislature must expressly repeal the earlier rule. This form of entrenchment can be seen in some statutes, such as America's Administrative Procedure Act, that exclude the doctrine of implied repeal: these rules can be altered, but they must be altered expressly.[1]

A second set of entrenching rules demand that the repealing law adopt a specified form of words. Section II of the Canadian Bill of Rights 1960 provides that the laws of Canada should be read and applied in conformity to that statute, unless "it is expressly declared by an Act of the Parliament of Canada that it shall operate notwithstanding the Canadian Bill of Rights." (Sossin 2004; Erdos 2010, chap. 4).[2] Once again, the entrenching rule requires the legislature to make it plain that the more recent statute stands irrespective of the earlier statute, but the example differs from those of the previous paragraphs in that the statute specifies a form of words that the legislature must use to signify its intention. The form of words required by the entrenching statute might, sometimes, serve to make it harder for the later body to escape the constraint. The entrenching body can specify the reason for the entrenchment in the form of words that the amending body is required to use when altering the law. The entrenchment rule can serve to "frame" the later debate around alteration, forcing the body to address the original reasons for the measure, perhaps compelling it to express the alteration in a politically unattractive manner.

Types of Entrenchment: Time

A second form of entrenchment requires that a body spend longer than normal deliberating the amendment of a measure, slowing the process of legal change in a given area (Albert 2014a). It may require that the legislature wait for a certain period between initial consideration of a measure and a final vote on the proposal, either by determining that a set period of time must elapse between the proposal and decision, or the rule could slow deliberation by requiring that the body consult with other institutions before reaching a decision about the alteration of the law.

---

[1] Administrative Procedure Act, 5 U.S.C. § 559. *See also* South Africa's Promotion of Equality and Prevention of Unfair Discrimination Act 2000, § 5

[2] Canadian Bill of Rights 1960, § 2. *See also* the Victorian Charter of Human Rights and Responsibilities Act 2006, § 31.

Entrenching rules that slow the process of legal change may hope to encourage careful deliberation by prolonging the process of debate, but, sometimes, the delay also requires that the deliberation spans an election: one manifestation of a legislature may propose the alteration, but it is a later manifestation that will make the decision to change the law. This allows the electorate to have some involvement in the process: at the very least, unpopular alterations can be debated during the election campaign (Dinan 2006, pp. 55–57, 310–311; Comella 2013, pp. 55–62; Elkins, Ginsburg and Melton 2009, pp. 167–171; Albert 2014).

Types of Entrenchment: Voting Units

A further form of entrenchment expands the group required to vote for the measure (Lijphart 2012, pp. 207–219). Such expansion can take two forms. It can be internal, either by requiring a supermajority of those entitled to vote or by requiring a specified level of support from sections of that institution, or it can be external, requiring the support of another constitutional body.

Perhaps the most common form of entrenchment is the supermajority (Schwartzberg 2013). Whereas most institutions' default rule for making law is simple majority, requiring that over half of those voting support the change, a supermajority demands that the change receive a greater level of support. Alternatively, internal entrenchment may empower specific groups within the legislature by requiring the support of designated groups within the chamber: some consociational mechanisms could be interpreted as forms of entrenchment (Lijphart 1977, Chapter 2).

Entrenchment can also expand the voting unit beyond the body that would, under the default rule, make the decision. Perhaps the most common instance of this is a requirement to hold a referendum before the decision is made. Often, the demand for a referendum protects fundamental features of the constitution, but sometimes the range of rules covered can be surprising: in Australia, for example, it seems that the national flag may only be changed after such a vote.[3] A further form of external expansion draws other constitutional institutions into the decision. In some federal systems the agreement of regional assemblies is needed before the balance between a regional and national government is altered.[4]

Some of the instances of entrenchment discussed in the earlier section on delaying rules require reconsideration here. Where the delay is caused by an obligation to consult another body or by the requirement that the decision-making process span an election, these rules will also serve to draw an external group into the decision-making process. They do not expand the voting unit, though, as the groups they include do not have the legal capacity to veto the proposal. Even where the decision crosses an election, there is no requirement – as there would be if a referendum

---

[3] Flags Act 1953, as amended by Flags Amendment Act 1998.
[4] *See, for example,* Canada's Constitution Act 1982, § 38.

were needed – that the electorate agrees to the change. Nevertheless, delaying rules of this type do provide a formal constitutional mechanism through which parties outside the voting unit can participate in the deliberations surrounding the change and can seek to influence the decision.

Crosscutting Distinctions: Self-imposed Entrenchment

Most entrenching rules are imposed on the institution by another body; often, they are imposed by a body higher up in the constitutional order. This may be the body that authored the state's constitution or, less commonly, the legislature that established the institution – as with the entrenchment rules that constrain the Northern Ireland Assembly. More rarely, the entrenchment rule is imposed on the institution by a body outside of this chain of constitutional hierarchy. The courts have the capacity to impose such constraints on legislatures in some instances, as is the case with the possible emergence of entrenchment in the British system (Ahmed and Perry 2014) and Israel (Weill 2012). Yaniv Roznai has recently argued that courts should effectively entrench aspects of constitutions: judges would assess the fundamentality of proposed constitutional changes and gauge the legitimacy of the proposed mode of change, testing the balance of these two factors (Roznai 2017, pp. 228–230). If Roznai's proposal were adopted, aspects of the constitution would be entrenched, but the extent of the entrenchment would not be known until after the judges had spoken.

Although most instances of entrenchment are imposed on the body from outside, there are a number of instances in which institutions have sought to impose constraints upon themselves. As the composition of institutions changes over time – new legislators are voted in and older legislators step down – self-imposed entrenchment rules are normally attempts by one group of office-holders to impose constraints on their successors (Holmes 2012). This cross-generational institutional constraint can prove controversial: why should a past set of office-holders place limits on the actions of the present set (Rubenfeld 2001, chap. 2)? Such constraints may be especially problematic if the rules establishing entrenchment do not, themselves, meet the standards of the entrenchment rules they enact: it may, for instance, be hard to defend a rule requiring a supermajority passed by a simple majority (Roszkowski and Goldsworthy 2012).[5]

Crosscutting Distinctions: Self-embracing Entrenchment Rules

Self-imposed entrenchment rules can sometimes be removed using the default process for legal change. It is arguable, for instance, that the Australian Flags Act lacks any special legal protection: whilst the statute requires a referendum before the flag

---

[5] See the discussion in *McGinty v Western Australia* (1996) 186 CLR 140, per Gummo J, at 297.

is redrawn, this requirement is, itself, alterable under the full range of the default rules for legal change (Williams, Brennan, and Lynch 2014, p. 758; Carney 1989, p. 93). On other occasions, the entrenching statute may be alterable through some of the default processes of legal change but protected from other aspects of those rules: so, as was discussed earlier, the legislature may be able to expressly repeal the entrenching statute, but may not be able to do so by mere implication. It might be argued that there is little point in imposing a constraint on a body that it is free to remove: why require a special process to change an area of law, but allow that constraint to be removed through the default process of law-making (Roberts and Chemerinsky 2003; Albert 2015)? This may be a little pessimistic. Entrenching rules that can be altered through the normal process of legal change provide, at the very least, an argument that can be raised during the process of deliberation; it requires that the body seeking to alter the entrenching rule overcome the limitation and, in so doing, address the reasons that lay behind the original decision to entrench.

Fear of the alteration of the entrenching rule through the default process of legal change may lead the body to entrench the entrenching rule itself (Weill 2014, pp. 141–150). The Israeli Basic Law: The Knesset is an instrument of this type. Not only does the law entrench key legal elements of the democratic structure of the state, requiring an absolute rather than a simple majority for change, it also entrenches the rule that entrenches these features (Weill 2012; Saunders 2011, p. 51).

Crosscutting Distinctions: Entrenchment Rules Triggered by Another Body

Most entrenchment rules are triggered when a body decides to alter a particular area of law but sometimes another group or institution is empowered to trigger entrenchment. In the American Senate, the filibuster rule enables two-fifths of Senators to impose a requirement that a bill gain the support of three-fifths of the Senate to pass through that institution. Similarly, in the Northern Ireland Assembly, thirty members can present a "petition of concern" in response to a bill put before the Assembly; this triggers a requirement that the bill receive cross-community support before enactment.[6]

II WHEN IS ENTRENCHMENT DESIRABLE?

Arguments for entrenchment can be divided into two groups: the general and the particular. General arguments for entrenchment are those that apply to any set of rules, and the two most important turn on stability and identity. Entrenchment can make an area of law more stable by making it harder to change. It can also indicate areas of law that the state regards as essential to its identity: entrenchment acts as a signal of the importance of the rules. In these instances, the aim of entrenchment is simply to

---

[6] Northern Ireland Act 1998, s.42.

make the law harder to change, using this additional difficulty to enhance the stability of the law or to indicate the special importance of the rules protected. Particular arguments for entrenchment, in contrast, rest on the claim that the default rule for legal change is, in an area, inappropriate, and altering the process by which the law is changed can cure or mitigate the problem. The objective of particular arguments for entrenchment is the modification of the normal process of legal change to remedy a problem with the default rules. In so doing, legal change is made harder, but the imposition of this additional difficulty is not the point of the entrenching rule but rather a side-effect of the use of entrenchment to remedy a deficiency found in the operation of the default rules. For instance, an entrenchment rule that sought to protect the position of regional legislatures by requiring their consent to laws that alter their jurisdiction would provide a clear example of this. There is a reason for entrenchment (protection of regional legislatures from decisions made at the national level) that connects to the scope of rules that are entrenched (those setting the jurisdiction of the legislatures) and to the type of entrenchment adopted (their agreement is required before their jurisdiction can be altered).

General Argument for Entrenchment: Stability

Stability is a desirable – and, to a degree, a necessary – quality of a legal order. One of the defining objectives of law is that it guides conduct, and, all else being equal, stable law guides conduct more successfully than unstable law. Though the stability of a law does not speak directly to its moral value (an evil law could be as stable as a good law), when stability is found within the context of a functioning legal order it allows people to predict how power will be exercised over them; when there is a functioning legal order, even the worst sort of state sees its range of action constrained, and some freedom, however minimal, is left to its people (Barber 2018, chap. 4). Of course, most real-world legal orders are a mix of the good and bad, and then the merits of stability reach beyond this minimalist account. Now the law helps people to live valuable lives, creating possibilities for their interaction. Not only can people predict how the state will exercise its coercive power over them, they can rely on the state to help them pursue projects and collaborations. Instability in the law can threaten the law's capacity to play this constructive role.

There is, then, a general argument for entrenchment: any type of entrenchment makes legal rules harder to change and so enhances their legal stability and can raise confidence in the legal system. But the stability brought by entrenchment is *legal* stability: by definition, entrenchment makes it harder to change the law. It need not follow that entrenchment produces *political* stability; indeed, it may be that entrenchment increases the political volatility of an issue by making it harder for the law to be altered through the normal processes of legal change (Holmes 1993, pp. 50–52). Cass Sunstein's claim that entrenchment can facilitate the workings of a constitution by removing a divisive issue from political debate, allowing law-makers to concentrate on other areas in which consensus can be reached, may sometimes be correct (Sunstein 1991). But one of the examples he gives – the right to abortion in American law – shows how contentious an issue can remain, even if entrenchment makes it legally hard to reopen the issue. The law surrounding abortion in America may be relatively stable – the rules are hard to alter – but the politics surrounding abortion are febrile, and entrenchment may have played a part in raising the temperature of the debate. Legal stability may have been bought at the price of political instability.

A General Argument for Entrenchment: Identity

A second, and common, argument for entrenchment comes from the identity of the state. It is sometimes claimed that certain rules are so important, so essential to constitutional identity, that their change would challenge the very continuation of the state. This might explain why, for some, entrenchment determines the content of the constitution: these are the rules that are fundamental to the identity of the state (Alexander 2009). It has been argued that constitutional devices may modify the constitution, but they should not be permitted to destroy it: some core aspects of the state's constitution are, or should be, beyond the reach of constitutional change (Jacobson 2010, chap. 2; Schwartzberg 2007, pp. 169–184; Schmitt 2008 [1928], pp. 75–88; Albert 2010, pp. 678–685). Sometimes states put those rules they regard as essential to their identity beyond legal change – and these unalterable rules fall outside of the scope of this chapter – but sometimes these rules are protected by a form of entrenchment: they are made harder to alter, but change remains possible.

Though popular, the argument for entrenchment from identity is weak. The argument embodies a doubtful descriptive claim coupled with a problematic normative assertion. The doubtful descriptive claim relates to the identity of the state. When discussing the identity and continuity of the state there is a tendency to seek the single thing, the golden thread, that confers identity on the state and the preservation of which establishes the continuity of that institution. But the state is made up of a number of elements – territory, members, institutions, and the rules that constitute and connect them (Barber 2010, chap. 8). Rather than a golden thread, the identity and continuity of the state should be imagined as a rope, in which many threads are entwined. Even radical change to the constitution, such as the replacement of one written constitution with a wholly new document, does not necessarily break the continuity of the state.

The normative basis of the argument from identity also merits examination. Even if it is accepted that the alteration of the rule would amount to an alteration of the identity of the state, or the effective destruction of the constitution, it is far from clear why this should, in itself, be considered a bad thing. There is no inherent value in constitutional continuity: that a state has this or that necessary characteristic does not, by itself, render the characteristic valuable. If the objection to an alteration to the constitutional order is, simply, that it amounts to a radical change, this is not, in itself, a powerful argument against the shift.

There is a more modest version of the argument from identity that might occasionally justify entrenchment. Sometimes, entrenchment acts as a signal of importance, a public declaration that the state regards a rule as being of especial value or significance (Albert 2010, pp. 685–693; Sunstein 1996). In a community that regards entrenchment in this way, entrenchment can be used as a device to pick out certain features of the constitution as having special significance. It can have an educative function, bringing forward these key features, and, in so doing, can help members of the state understand and identify with the constitution.

Particular Arguments for Entrenchment: Reminding the Body of Reasons Relevant to the Alteration of the Law

The last section concluded with the observation that there may sometimes be an educative value in entrenchment; a similar, narrower, argument for entrenchment turns on its capacity to act as an *aide-mémoire*, reminding the institution of the reasons relating to the laws protected by the entrenching rule (Albert 2013, p. 229; Winterton 1980, pp. 170–172).

Some entrenchment rules allow the legislature to alter the protected area of law relatively easily, but require it to acknowledge the reasons for entrenchment. Entrenchment rules that specify a required form for the alteration of the law often play this function. For instance, in Canada, the legislature can legislate contrary to the Bill of Rights, but only if it declares its willingness for the law to operate notwithstanding that document. The entrenchment rule appears relatively weak – it can easily be satisfied – but the legislature is compelled to address the reason animating the original entrenchment. It could be that being forced to address these issues will, by itself, deter the legislature from acting; it is reminded of reasons bearing on the legislative decision it might otherwise have forgotten.

The use of entrenchment as an *aide-mémoire* links most cleanly to formal types of entrenchment. Here the reason for entrenchment (reminding the legislature of a relevant consideration) connects to the rules that are entrenched (those where that consideration is relevant) and to the manner of entrenchment (the legislature is compelled to address this consideration). Given that this type of entrenchment serves only to present the law-maker with reasons that – the entrenching body believes – are relevant to the decision, it is easy to justify this set of entrenchment rules. If the original act of entrenchment was a mistake, or if the reasons it sought to bring to the attention of the law-making body are no longer relevant, the constraint the entrenching statute places on the legislature will be limited: the legislature can acknowledge the reasons animating the entrenching statute, but, having acknowledged these reasons, continue to alter the law.

The capacity of entrenchment rules to compel, or induce, legislatures to reflect on considerations that they might otherwise ignore, also helps explain the potential value of entrenchment rules that can be removed using the default process of legal change. A legislature that is considering overturning the entrenchment rule is led to consider the reasons for the original decision to entrench: not only should it consider whether the rules protected by the entrenchment rules should be changed, it should also consider the further, and distinct, question of whether the entrenchment rule itself should be altered.

Particular Arguments for Entrenchment: Protecting Groups within the Legislature

Most of the time legislative decisions turn on simple majority votes: if more than half of those voting support a measure, the measure is successful. The losing minority rarely has reason to complain about their defeat under the default rule; after all, if we give equal weight to the worth of all legislators, we should ascribe equal significance to their votes, and a vote against a measure should count for no more than a vote that supports it. The argument from the equal status of legislators is normally sufficient to defend a default majority rule. But there are some situations in which the constitutional role of the legislature may require a departure from this rule, and require a form of entrenchment.

The job of a legislature is not simply to vote on legislation; it should also deliberate prior to its vote. This deliberation should be directed towards the common good, identifying ends that benefit the community, and determining a rational scheme for pursuing these goals (Ekins 2012, chapter 5; Barber 2018, chapter 6). In a well-functioning legislature all of the representatives should be included in this deliberative aspect of the legislative function – even those who end up on the losing side. They can challenge and refine the legislature's conception of the common good, and debate the means selected by the legislature to pursue those ends. The minority also have a representative role to play: making sure that the views and interests of their constituents are heard in the Chamber. In short, it would be a mistake to think that the justification for the default rule for legislative decision-making also justifies the exclusion of the losing minority from legislative deliberation.

There are at least two groups of situations that can arise in which the tasks of a legislature may require a departure from the default rule to protect the losing minority group and provide a potential justification for a form of entrenchment.

First, in some polities the parties within the legislature are not oriented towards the common good of the community, but rather towards the good of a portion of that community. In such societies politics is sectarian rather than ideological, with the parties fighting to protect and advance the interests of their groups. This type of politics is sometimes found in societies that are characterized by a deep ethnic or religious divide. Strict adherence to a simple majority default rule in these instances is likely to result in one sectarian group using the power of the legislature for its exclusive advantage or, worse still, to the disadvantage of the other group.

Second, where the majority group of representatives is able to push through its policies it may come to undervalue the contribution of minority representatives to the deliberative aspect of legislating. This pathology will often accompany the first – where a group of legislators fails to value the well-being of a portion of the citizenry it will also fail to respect the contributions of legislators who are drawn from that group – but it can arise independently. In a polity that is characterized by ideological disagreement – in which the legislators agree that legislation should be oriented towards the common good, but disagree over the content of that good – the majority group of representatives may show insufficient consideration towards their opponents. Their capacity to win votes under the default rule without the support of some legislators may lead them to undervalue the contributions of those legislators to debates, perhaps manipulating or shaping procedural rules to exclude them from the deliberative process.

In each of these instances, entrenchment can play a role in mitigating the deficiencies of the legislative process. By requiring a supermajority for certain decisions, an entrenching rule can protect the minority group, either by preventing the majority from overriding the minority or, more subtly, by requiring the majority to negotiate with the minority before the law can be changed.

Particular Arguments for Entrenchment: Protecting Regions

In the previous section the entrenchment rule had the effect of widening the group within the legislature who needed to reach agreement before a decision could be reached. These rules could serve to protect minorities in the legislature. A further analogous argument for entrenchment turns on its capacity to protect regions from decisions made at the national level by including, in some way, these regions within the decision to change rules relating to the constitutional balance between the national level of the government and the regions. This type of entrenchment expands the voting unit outwards: bodies outside the national legislature are given a say in the decision to alter the law.

Particular Arguments for Entrenchment: Protecting Institutions in the Constitution

The previous sections considered the role that entrenchment can play in protecting minority groups within the legislature and regions within the state. One of the ways that it achieved this was by incorporating these bodies within the decision-making process. A similar device could be used to protect other institutions within the constitution: in principle, an entrenchment rule could incorporate any institution into the decision. Even the courts could be included in the process: perhaps the agreement of the Supreme Court should be required before the legislature passes a law that restricts the power of that institution. The institution that is most commonly protected by entrenchment, though, is the citizenry: the broad mass of the electorate who vote for the legislature and constitute the political community that the legislature serves. The citizenry can be incorporated into the legislative decision by requiring the support of the electorate through a referendum before the change in the law is permitted. Where the proposed change radically alters the democratic structures of the state, there is a strong argument that the alterations should be submitted to the people; their role in the constitutional order is being changed, and they should be directly involved in this decision (Shu 2008).

Particular Arguments for Entrenchment: Guarding against Moral Panics

A common argument for constraining legislatures, often heard in debates over bills of rights, warns of the dangers of legislation passed during a moral panic (S. Cohen 2011). Moral panics are periods of temporary, widespread irrationality, during which a polity forgets the fundamental moral beliefs on which its constitution rests, and rushes to make changes that it will later regret. Entrenchment rules can help protect against moral panics in two ways: by forcing the law-maker to address the earlier constitutional commitments that are being overturned during the panic, and, second, by slowing the process of legal change.

The capacity of entrenchment to act as an *aide-mémoire* was discussed earlier in this chapter, but it is worth noting that entrenching rules requiring a particular form may prove especially useful as a guard against moral panics. It is of the nature of moral panics that they are moments of forgetting: the deeper commitments of the polity are overlooked in a time of crisis, an omission that is later regretted. Entrenchment rules that require legislation that deviates from a Bill of Rights to make that deviation explicit, at least compel the legislature to address the gap between the considered values of the polity and the new legislation.

A stronger defense against moral panics slows the process by which the legislature can alter the law. Moral panics are – by definition – transitory. Compelling a legislature to consider a change to the law over an extended period increases the chances that the panic will subside – and, if the opinion of the legislature remains consistent over this time, makes it less likely that the decision to alter the law was caused by a panic.

III WHAT IS WRONG WITH ENTRENCHMENT?

The default rules that govern legal change should have been chosen for good reason; those determining the law-making power of the institution should have selected rules that enable the body to fulfill its constitutional role within the state, rules that neither make the process of legal change too hard nor too easy. Consequently, entrenching rules always require justification: because they add an extra burden to the process of legal change specified by the default rules, that extra burden, to be defensible, must have been imposed for good reason. The onus of argument lies on those advocating entrenchment to explain why it is desirable, rather than on those who oppose it.

The presumption against entrenchment requires those who argue for the rule to demonstrate its value. But once it has been shown that there is some merit to the rule, the arguments against entrenchment must also be assessed: the good reasons for entrenching may be outweighed by reasons against. These arguments will, of course, depend very much on the particular context and nature of the proposed rule, but there are two broad groups of arguments that ordinarily weigh against entrenchment. First, that entrenchment rules make it excessively hard to change the law, making it difficult for institutions to respond to the needs and wishes of the citizenry, and making it harder to hold law-makers accountable for their decisions. Second, entrenchment rules may create friction between institutions within the constitution, either by enabling one institution to limit another or by encouraging institutions to attempt to circumvent these limits.

Entrenchment Leading to Inflexibility in the Law

A defining feature of an entrenchment rule is that it makes some parts of the law harder to change than would otherwise be the case. As Jon Elster has observed, the usual purpose of constitutional rules is to bind others in the future: it is one generation seeking to place limits on its successors (Elster 2000). This can present a number of dangers. Most plainly, it may inhibit the capacity of law-makers to respond to changes in their community: a rule that seemed valuable and sensible at one point in time may seem misguided later. Or it could be that something that once seemed important comes to be regarded as an unnecessary constraint on the evolution of the state. By making legal change harder, entrenchment can raise concerns that go beyond the problems caused by inflexibility. Making it harder to change the law can also inhibit democratic government and blur accountability for political decisions. Democracy requires, in part, that a legislature be effective, that it be capable of enacting laws. By making it harder to change the law entrenchment may sometimes run against democracy, preventing the legislature from pursuing the wishes and interests of its electorate (Albert 2010, pp. 676–679).

More specifically, entrenchment may make it harder to apportion responsibility for decisions within the constitutional structures of the state. Where the entrenching rule was drawn up some time ago, it may be impossible to hold the authors of the rule accountable for the limitations it imposes on contemporary institutions.

Where an institution places constraints upon itself, should a future manifestation of that institution be regarded as responsible for these limitations?

Creating Tension between Institutions

Entrenchment can create tension between institutions in a number of ways. First, and most obviously, entrenchment often requires the involvement of another body – normally the courts – to make it effective. There are a range of questions that the courts may be asked, or required, to answer. The most basic relate to the justiciability of the entrenchment rule: the court must decide whether this is the type of rule that falls within its jurisdiction to apply and interpret. If it is within jurisdiction, the court may then be required to interpret the rule and adjudicate on its breach (Schwartzberg 2007, pp. 184–189). Finally, the court must decide on the consequences of the breach: does it render the apparently enacted statute invalid, or should the court confine itself to declaring that the statute was enacted unconstitutionally? Consideration of the role of the court in entrenchment underlines its potential to generate tensions between institutions (Goldsworthy 2010). The body subject to entrenchment may have a different answer to these questions than that given by the court. The court may be compelled to pick sides in a constitutional dispute: there may be rival understandings of the entrenchment rule within the legislature, or, perhaps, the court must choose between the arguments of the national legislature and other constitutional institutions.

The previous paragraph considered the tension that might be caused when the court seeks to uphold the entrenchment rule. A further, and less obvious, source of tension may arise when the court seeks to, or is encouraged to, circumvent the entrenchment rule (Eule 1987, pp. 387–388). This could be regarded as a power-grab, an ambitious court stepping into the space left by the legislature, but it could also be an instance in which necessity compels judicial intervention. If the legislature is unable to respond to changing social needs because of entrenchment, the court may be required to supplement the omission. Such innovation, whether necessary or not, can come at a cost. The fairy-tale that the courts invariably declare, rather than make, the law may be one of the sources of the courts' perceived legitimacy: people may accept the decisions of the courts because they think that judges apply pre-existing law, determined by the legislature. Radical decisions, or decisions that are contested by other constitutional institutions, can serve to expose the fairy-tale, and weaken the authority of the court.

A final danger brought by some forms of entrenchment is the risk of tit-for-tat behavior. Where an institution starts to engage in self-entrenchment, placing limits on its future incarnations, there is a chance that entrenchment will become a tool of party politics (Williams, Brennan, and Lynch 2014, p. 737). When one political group controls the legislature it may seek to entrench its political objectives to prevent its decisions being overturned after an election. When control of the chamber shifts, the incoming party may have little hesitation in using the same device against its rivals.

CONCLUSION

This chapter has argued that entrenchment should be seen as a constitutional tool, a device, or set of devices, that can be used to solve certain problems: the temptation to regard entrenchment as unequivocally good, or invariably bad, should be resisted. While a badly crafted entrenchment rule may be better than nothing, entrenchment is at its most attractive when the reason for departing from the default rule informs the type of entrenchment adopted and the area of laws entrenched. Reflection on these three elements should guide those considering using entrenchment and, also, those who interpret and apply the entrenchment rules.

RECOMMENDED READING

Albert, R. (2010). Constitutional Handcuffs. *Arizona State Law Review*, 42 (3), 664–716.
Albert, R. (2014). The Structure of Constitutional Amendment Rules. *Wake Forest L. R.*, 49, 913.
Elster, J. (2002). *Ulysses Unbound*, Cambridge: Cambridge University Press.
Eule, J. N. (1987). Temporal Limits on the Legislative Mandate: Entrenchment and Retroactivity. *Law and Social Enquiry*, 12 (2–3), 381–459.
Levinson, D. J. (2011). Parchment and Politics: The Positive Puzzle of Constitutional Commitment. *Harvard Law Review*, 124 (3), 657–746.
Marshall, G. (1987). *Constitutional Conventions*, Oxford: Oxford University Press.
Posner, E. & Vermeule, A. (2002). Legislative Entrenchment: A Reappraisal. *Yale Law Journal*, 111 (7), 1165–1706.
Schwartzberg, M. (2014). *Counting the Many: The Origins and Limits of the Supermajority Rule*, Cambridge: Cambridge University Press.

26

Emergency Powers

Karin Loevy

Emergencies are famously described as the limit of legality, the place where law ends and something else begins, sovereign decision, politics, arbitrary rule, violence; something else that is an exception to normal law, to normal order, to normal institutions. This was the starting point for much of the post-9/11 (mainly North American) debates in constitutional and legal theory about the place of emergency powers in public law and it is also the message that resonates (somewhat artificially) in emergency powers debates in Covid-19 contexts. Such debates are often jump-started by reference to either an American constitutional tradition going back to the Federalist papers envisioning a pragmatic tension between constitutional norms and factual necessities (Hamilton 1961b [1787], Federalist No. 23; Jefferson 1905 [1810]) or to a European tradition of liberal-sceptic political theory envisioning emergencies as an existential paradox inherent to liberal law (Schmitt 2005 [1922]; Agamben 1998, 2005). But these persistent sources and the constant tendency to rely on them in thinking about emergencies as "exceptions" are quite misleading as they serve to hide and obscure a most prevalent characteristic of contemporary emergencies. Rather than sudden and unexpected events they occur against the background of long-term and prevailing processes where "law" appears in its most dynamic, mobilized, productive form. Emergency law, its practices and doctrines, and the institutions that regularly deal with threats are constantly developing in every jurisdiction as well as in international and transnational legal complexes. But the theory that critiques emergency law and evaluates its consequences perpetuates a static dichotomy between "norm" and "exception."

To show why and how emergencies are opportunities for legal, institutional and normative mobilization rather than occasions where law "stands still" in the face of a need for decision, the rest of this chapter will lay out the field's basic areas of concern, the large and formative questions that have been, and still are, at the heart of discussions about emergency powers in constitutional theory and in the day-to-day politics of its practice.

The first and most fundamental question that underlies the field of emergency powers in public law is whether law can, and whether it should constrain public officials in their response to emergencies. In western constitutional and political theory this question is traditionally answered within one of three models: the extra-legal model, inspired by John Locke's discussion of the Prerogative, the neo-Roman model, based on Machiavelli's interpretation of the Roman institution of dictatorship, and the legality model which in recent years have been significantly theorized by David Dyzenhaus. The first section of this chapter will outline these responses and argue that while very different in their theoretical underpinnings, they share a strong common purpose, they are all attempts to solve the problem of containment of emergencies – largely defined as unexpected threats – within a particular legal and political order. This is one reason why in emergencies law is especially mobilized – because the legal and political theory of emergency is constantly focused on containment.

In the second section of this Chapter 1 move to the more practical problems that are at the forefront of the day to day politics of emergencies in public law: the problem of *definitions*, the problem of *authorization*, the problem of *temporality* and the problem of *jurisdiction*. These problems, or "sets of questions," stem from what Bernard Manin identified as the *paradigm* or *doctrine* of emergency powers, a universally applied doctrine underlying emergency legal mechanisms from martial law in the British Empire to the French state of siege and the German state of exception to today's emergency declarations and derogations (Manin 2008). According to the doctrine, under certain conditions defined as an emergency (*definition*), deviations from norms may be authorized (*authorization*), for *a limited period of time* (temporality), within a particular jurisdiction (*jurisdiction*). After presenting the doctrine I will show how each of its features - definitions, authorizations, temporality, and jurisdiction – opens up a host of opportunities for actors to mobilize normative, legal and institutional change.

This insight leads, in the final section of the chapter to the question of constitutional change and continuity in emergencies. If the timeframes of emergency are long and flexible, multiple and overlapping rather than "exceptional," then law in emergencies is a constantly shifting space of opportunity in which normatively charged political projects can be manifested. If we want to design legal and constitutional mechanisms that will better respond to threats, we should acknowledge emergency beyond "the exception," as a dynamic field of legal and normative mobilization and productivity.

I CAN LAW CONSTRAIN EMERGENCY POWERS?

The impact of the two quite different traditions mentioned above – the federalist tradition of pragmatic exception and the critical tradition of existential exception – is felt in the persistent unrest and often-artificial air of many emergency powers debates. Both formulations draw liberal thinkers to at least two existential difficulties in the jurisprudence of emergency powers. The first concerns law's ability to effectively contain threat and crisis; the second concerns law's ability to effectively contain power. Under *pragmatic intuitions*, a reality of unexpected and extreme danger requires some degree of accommodation to provide for the extensive power necessary to handle and contain it. The worry is, on the one hand, that constrained government will be too slow or inhibited to allow such accommodation and, on the other, that when allowed, it will damage, corrupt or impinge on the much-cherished political order for the preservation and continuity of which it is permitted. Under *critical intuitions*, such accommodations are either naïve or fraudulent. Exceptional measures to handle the exceptional case, whether necessary or abused, expose the fact that sheer power lies under the veil of liberal rule.

What both traditions share is a structural and political concern about the sources of legitimate power to respond to threats. Can law, and should law, constrain officials in response to an unexpected threat? – Ask pragmatists and neo realists, and they engage in institutional analysis and design to solve the pragmatic tension between necessity and law. Can law, and should law, constrain emergency powers? – Ask critics of power in the liberal state, and they engage in unmasking the authoritarian premise of absolute sovereignty behind the façade of liberal constitutionalism. The integrity, legitimacy and stability of political arrangements are seen by both traditions to be reflected in their response to external threats.

The Post 9/11 Emergency Powers Debate

Since both issues – unconstrained power and unconstrained threat – seemed especially pressing around the turn of the last century, a wave of scholarly work focused on the question of the "state of exception" as the limit of law (see overview in Scheuerman 2006). Critical theory authors embraced Carl Schmitt's analysis of emergency powers as a way of pursuing a radical critique of the oppressive histories, logical structures and epistemologies of modern liberal law (Agamben 1998, 2005; Hussain 2003; Sarat, Douglas & Umphrey 2005). Law, described Giorgio Agamben, in a much cited work, neglects "living beings" by excluding them internally, confining them in zones of exception within, but simultaneously expelled from, the legal order (Agamben 1998; more in Witt 2007; Benton 2006).

In contrast, legal (and mostly north American) theorists in the post 9/11 debate were largely committed to preserving a liberal rule of law and offered grounds to reconstruct emergency laws and policies. Oren Gross, for example, in his vast neo-realist study of the history and politics of emergency powers, accepted Carl Schmitt's proposition that law cannot accommodate emergencies (Gross 2003; Gross & Ni Aolain 2006; Gross 2008). Confronted by extreme anxiety, general norms will fail to respond effectively. The legal order will either try to accommodate the exception or act as if it doesn't (legally) exist; both approaches risk seepage of the exceptional response into the normal order. In the name of securing a liberal democratic rule of law in view of this contamination, Gross denies the legal basis of emergency conduct and places it normatively in the extra-legal sphere. Provided that state officials will publicly and transparently admit their extralegal conduct and succumb to ex-post checks, Gross believes or hopes that their harmful effect will be restrained (Gross 2008).

Gross' "extralegal model" for dealing with emergencies has been subject to considerable criticism (Dyzenhaus 2005, 2006a; Posner and Vermeule 2005, p. 55), the strongest of which turns practically and theoretically against his sharp distinction between extralegal emergency and legal normalcy. If indeed an emergency cannot be legally contained, how can it be contained extra-legally? Not only is it not realistic to expect that officials will admit the "extralegality" of their conduct, there is also no reason to believe that extralegal action will not "seep" into the legal order just as legal conduct does. Still, other theorists were attracted to Gross' logic of the extra-legality of emergency response. Mark Tushnet, for example, agreed with Gross (and Schmitt) that emergency acts disguised as limited by the rule of law are often actually unlimited state power. But he denied Gross' restraining retrospective legal mechanisms. Only public action, through the institutions of "ordinary politics," and not legal responses, can prevent the abuse of emergency powers. Tushnet argued that a political constitution, one that is based on a mobilized citizenry, is the normatively correct response to law's admitted inability to restrain emergencies (Tushnet 2005a, 2008a; Honig 2009).

While Tushnet's proposal moved the debate further away from legality, toward a vision of democratic politics, David Dyzenhaus steered it back to it. Only the principle of legality, he argued, confronting Schmitt's (and Gross') legal skepticism, can (and must) constrain emergency. According to Dyzenhaus, by creative institutional experiments, moral resources and law's authority can be maintained even under great stress, provided that there is a willingness to loosen some formalistic doctrines such as the separation of powers (Dyzenhaus 2005, 2006a, 2007a, 2007b, 2008).

Alongside these highly theoretical debates there were many accounts that went beyond the question of law's limits and tried to deal with the more practical questions at the legal foreground. Acting on the assumption that the rule of law must be preserved under extreme political peril, they asked: what kind of institutional structures might better preserve the rule of law in such conditions? Are ex-post measures like judicial review better than ex-ante legislative (and specifically constitutional) redress? What are the right balancing norms and mechanisms between security and human rights? Are there non-derogable rights even in emergency situations? (Ackerman 2004; Cole 2003, 2004; Ferejohn & Pasquino 2004; Tribe & Gudridge 2004; Dyzenhaus 2007b)

As the initial shock of the terrorist attacks on the United States waned and the Bush administration's legal and political position became increasingly unpopular, the debates over emergency measures gradually moved away from the question of the possibility and the desirability of a legal constraint of emergency powers. The Obama administration tied its position on security to a commitment to legality as a mirror image of its predecessor (but see: Greenwald 2011, Ackerman 2011,

Morrison 2011). Meanwhile, Donald Trump's uses of emergency declarations were seen widely as sham and therefore they did not spark renewed theoretical debates about what type of legal response true emergencies require (but see Goitein, 2020). Still, it is hardly a baseless prediction that visions of emergency as the existential exception will resurface in the occasion of future national catastrophes.[1] The two distinct formulations that underlie intuitions about the limit of law in the context of emergencies will certainly not fade away.

It is therefore useful to reveal the paradigmatic responses to the question of law's role in crisis in western legal and political theory. There are three broad structures that attempt to explain and solve the emergency paradox (or tension): the extralegal Lockean model of prerogative, the model of legality and the Neo-Roman model of dictatorship. It is important to note that these are very broad, archetypal analytical models that imply different ways of thinking about the connection between the "core" meaning of liberal politics and liberal law and the "marginal," "contingent," need to overcome it. They all attempt to account not only for the technical problem of constraint, but also for its connection to the political stability of a modern collectivity.[2] Eventually, the three archetypical and seemingly conflicting models have much more in common than is acknowledged by current scholarship. Not only are they all echoed, confusingly, in the classic mechanisms of emergency powers, but also, more importantly, they all reflect a strong commitment in the liberal tradition to engineer solutions to the problem of containment. These models should be seen, I claim, not as justifications for the creation of "exceptions" to the legal and political order, but rather as theoretical projects in liberal imagination – imagining the possibility of containing threats within a specific (often, wished for) legal and political order.

---

[1] It is striking how many voices in the American debate rely on the assumption that exceptional powers in exceptional times are an inevitable reality that is here to stay. From Clinton Rossiter's stating in 1948: "That constitutional dictatorship does have a future in the United States is hardly a matter for discussion" (Rossiter 2002 [1948], p. 306) to Samuel Issacharoff and Richard Pildes pointing to the historical inevitability of legal change towards less emphasis on individual rights in dangerous times (Issacharoff & Pildes 2004, p. 161).

[2] There are alternative mappings of existing legal and political theories for dealing with an emergency. Jules Lobel's influential article from 1989 distinguishes between **"absolutist" "relativist" and "liberal"** frameworks (Lobel 1989); Scheuerman distinguishes between **Schmittian and non-Schmittian** theories and between **democratic formalists' procedural and liberal lawyers' substantial answers** (Scheuerman 2006). Ferejohn and Pasquino distinguish between **monistic and dualistic** models and within the dualistic model they distinguish between **constitutional and legislative models** (Ferejohn & Pasquino 2004). Gross distinguishes between **models of accommodation, "business as usual" models and the extralegal model** (Gross 2003). Dyzenhaus' notes the models I propose here but his analysis of the different positions seems to suggest that he distinguishes only between two models – those who acknowledge an extralegal space and those who deny it (Dyzenhaus 2006b). The map that I suggest below relies on distinguishing the source of political power to deal with the threat. I propose it in order to outline structural and political answers to liberal concerns about the effective containment of a crisis and power. The question is, as I argued above, not only about the means for handling exigency but also about the sources and structure of legitimate political power.

The Extralegal Lockean Model of Prerogative – An Authority Residing Outside the Law

Going completely outside the law in appropriate cases preserves, rather than undermines, the rule of law in a way that bending the law to accommodate for catastrophes does not (Gross 2004, p. 240).

This model denies not only the possibility of legal containment but also regards its absence as desirable (Gross 2003, 2008; Tushnet 2005a, 2008a; Posner 2003, pp. 292–321). In a crisis, legal norms are either sacrificed or manipulated. It is the political sphere – neither law nor legality – that should be trusted to deal with both a crisis and its normative consequences. Following the logic of Locke's prerogative power, this model locates at least part of this political power in a pre-legal context – at the historical moment of society's creation when the prerogative originated (Locke 1980 [1689], § 159–168, 162). Law was created to limit only the harmful use of this prerogative authority but it did not and should not limit the power itself, which is rooted in the relation between the people and the king as one of trust (Pasquino 1998). Legitimate political order is possible in a rule of law state provided that the political power to overcome the law for the common good is always present. While Locke's prerogative power, wide and pragmatic, was limited only by an appeal to heaven (Locke's code for the right to resist [Locke 1980 [1689], §168]), recent advocates of this model in the post 9/11 emergency powers debates have imagined a somewhat limited version. They emphasized the expectancy of ex-post political or legal ratification of the extralegal action. The official who performs extra-legally in an extreme condition must do so publicly and transparently and agree to accept democratic ratification or vetting in the aftermath (Gross 2003, p. 1023; for more on the Lockean prerogative see: Medina 2002; Fatovic 2004, 2009; Casson 2008; de Wilde 2010, Fatovic & Kleinerman 2013).

The Legality Model – Law's Authority Manifested under Crisis

We cannot understand law itself unless we see law as a project which aspires to realize the values of the rule of law (Dyzenhaus 2006a, p. 231).

This model denies the existence of a legal or moral exception claiming that law's resources can and should accommodate any crisis. It is often described as a "monistic," "legalistic" stand in favor of pure containment through pure legality, naïve at best and hypocritical at worst (Gross & Ni Aolain 2006, p. 94; Zuckermann 2006, p. 522). This criticism does not take seriously enough the model's internal answer to the problem of containment. According to the legality model's recent theoretical presentations (Dyzenhaus, 2005, 2006a, 2007a, 2008, Tribe & Gudridge 2004), law is neither a procedural requirement nor an inspirational principle. It is a political project with a practical aim – to make real the idea of law, the idea that rule is politically justified only if it is governed by law. Each one of the participants in the project – the judiciary as well as the legislature and the executive – have an equally important role, they don't compete over power; they must all cooperate under a regulative assumption that each legal decision taken by another participant is in compliance with the project (Dyzenhaus 2006a, p. 147). The rule of law, therefore, is not a theoretical concept to aspire to. It is both existentially constitutive, forming the conditions of "being an authority" (Dyzenhaus 2006a, p. 12) and regulative as it governs the interpretation of the decisions of all institutional actors (Ibid., p. 147).

Emergency situations are in this model opportunities for law to play out, to show its "real" face, to be realized. The legality model ties any official response to an emergency to a legal distinction replacing any other type of distinction (specifically: the normal/extra-normal distinction that the other models assume). "Law" remains intact not because it is "all resilient" but because it is nothing but a political "project" tying all official responders to an emergency to a political commitment to the rule of law. But what is this "project?" It is not merely an activity of "protection" or "preservation" of legal institutions and legal norms. Instead it is in itself a somewhat revolutionary activity of "bringing law to the world," of "constitutionalism." As Chief Justice Charles Evan Hughes declared in *Blaisdell*: "The constitution was adopted in a period of great emergency. Its grants of power to the Federal government were determined in the light of emergency and they are not altered by emergency."[3] This is at the heart of the original legacy of "our constitution" that emergency measures are its subject just as much as normal time measures.

The Neo-Roman Model of Dictatorship – A Mixed Regime

(N)o Republic will be perfect, unless it has provided for everything with laws, and provided a remedy for every incident, and fixed the method of governing it. And therefore concluding I say, that those Republics which in urgent perils do not have resort either to a Dictatorship or a similar authority, will always be ruined in grave incidents. (Machiavelli 1965 [1517], 1.34)

This model traced back to the Roman institution of dictatorship or more accurately to its early modern celebrators (Manin 2008, pp. 139–143), is arguably the most common in the western emergency powers tradition (Ferejohn & Pasquino 2004, p. 239). It assumes a duality of normal and exceptional situations which can be detected mechanistically or by an authorized organ. This division is the basis for acknowledging a legal place for an exceptional government that is authorized to deal with emergency situations conservatively – that is, with the sole task of returning as soon as possible to normal government. A declared existence of an exception (as a special threat to a specific political order of a given political community) triggers and justifies exceptional government which is preservative or conservative in that it functions to reestablish the regular government (Ibid.). This model is theoretically

---

[3] Home Building & Loan Assn. v. Blaisdell, 290 U.S. 398 (1934).

connected to the institution of Roman dictatorship (Machiavelli 1965 [1517], 1.34) and its neo-Roman adaptations (e.g., Blackstone 1979 [1765–1769], p. 132). It is distinguished from the extralegal model in that it envisages the move between the normal and the exceptional situations as technically (and often constitutionally) constructed. The distinction itself, the creation of exceptional powers to determine and respond to emergencies, is engineered for the sake of the protection of the normal order from which they emerge.

But the mechanics of duality are not only conservative of the normal order, they are also constitutive of its very being. For Machiavelli dictatorship is an important aspect of the strength of the City because of the ways in which it figured as a regular feature of its historical evolution. The dictatorship was one of the "usual remedies" that Romans created for overcoming "urgent" and "imminent" threats from its warring neighbors. Their attacks, Machiavelli says, did only harm for those neighbors – in fact, it was these acts that caused Romans to create the useful institution which served to strengthen Rome. In other words, Rome's neighbors' attempts to destroy her actually strengthened her resilience, made her think of a method, a way, to handle future dangers: thus, the institution of dictatorship (Machiavelli 1965 [1517], 1.33).

And so – emergency government is, for Machiavelli, not only a flexible solution for assuring continuity in view of imminent threats to its conservation – it is also seen as an intrinsic part of the process of the Republic becoming stronger to handle threats. A mechanism is created not strictly because of Roman cleverness but also because of its neighbors' foolishness – the institution itself is a part of the evolution of Rome's greatness. Dictatorship as an institutional genius is an intrinsic part of Rome's becoming what it was (Machiavelli 1965 [1517], 1.34, 1.30).

This regularity is stressed by Machiavelli not only as an attribute of the institution (that it is reliable because it is based on its own rules and limitations) but also in relation to the problem which it intended to solve – that of "extraordinary hazards." The problem is that customary government is too slow for handling urgent threats (Machiavelli 1965 [1517], 1.34), but also that response to urgent threats is often as dangerous or even more dangerous than the threat itself: "remedies are most dangerous when they have to apply to some situation which cannot await time" (Ibid.). In other words – the regularity of the institution is required not only to avert the danger of its misuse but even more to correspond to the type of threats envisioned – that they may create further risks.

Therefore, an institution must be established in any Republic to prevent it from using "extraordinary methods" in time of need. "For although the extraordinary method would do well at that time, none the less the example does evil, for if a usage is established of breaking institutions for good objectives, then under the pretext they will be broken for evil ones" (Machiavelli 1965 [1517], 1.34).

To sum up – the Neo Roman model of dictatorship emphasizes regularity and constraint in the institutional mechanism for handling emergencies. This is mainly what accounts for the swift shift from regular to irregular government and back. But this regularity is not only a technical solution to the problem of sudden, threatening change. In fact, it is connected to the evolution of a stable political system. It is born from threats and dangers that the system had to deal with and it is a regular feature of every political system that it has to deal with threats. The Neo-Roman model in Machiavelli's account depicts continuity and change in the state's institutional capability to handle its actual threats. As long as these capabilities are intact, and as long as the move on the "irregular-regular" axis is possible, the political entity may be "perfect."

II THE EMERGENCY POWERS DOCTRINE

Not surprisingly, the liberal resources of crisis management, the "extralegal," the "legal" and the ideal institution of "dictatorship," are deeply entrenched in the classic mechanisms and institutions of emergency powers. However, it would be a mistake to confound any existing mechanism with any specific justificatory model. The ideas, stories and justifications that are spelled out or implied in the archetypical models can be seen to exist, albeit confusingly, in the constitutional arrangements that were historically put in place to contain crises. What follows is not an attempt to map the legal techniques of emergency measures and compare them but only to show why it would be impossible to map the archetypical models above on to the diverse reality of existing mechanisms. Instead, historical examples have inherent in them something of each of the models.

First, on dictatorship: "Dictatorship" was referred to above as an archetypical model, not because of its historical antiquity but because of the type of inspirational shadow it had cast on the neo-Roman and republican thought of emergency law through Machiavelli's account (but also Montesquieu, Harrington and Rousseau, see in Manin 2008, pp. 3–7). This is an account of a customary (or constitutionally) entrenched institution, conservative and preservative in function and in purpose. In times of crisis, the Senate names a person who then steps in to restore order. While holding absolute power (the dictator's measures were subject to no veto or appeal) his mission was limited to six months or to its completion (Mommsen 1952, p. 168). While this historical depiction fits the neo-Roman model, it also has some essential features of the two other models. First, the institution is entrenched in constitutional custom (de Wilde 2012), used regularly as oppose to "occasionally" (Manin 2008, p. 7), and is aimed at the preservation of the constitution – these are features of the legality model. On the other hand, the "absolute" power to take any measure necessary with no accountability is a feature of the extra-legal model. And so the historical dictatorship is seen to be not simply a conservative mechanism for the move back and forth from regular to irregular reality and government but also, and most importantly, one that is legally entrenched and at the same time free of any constraint.

From prerogative to martial law and suspension acts in the common law tradition although the extralegal idea of prerogative was a central subject in common law during the seventeenth and eighteenth centuries it was controversial and a case for conflict between King and Parliament (Pasquino 1998, pp. 198–199). In 1689, the year Locke published the Two Treaties, parliament began passing annual mutiny acts creating a separate branch of military law and attempting to bind the king's action in times of crisis. By the end of the eighteenth century the king's prerogative was bent before parliamentary sovereignty on the question who could authorize and maintain martial law, as it had to be derived from civil authorization. Courts had already stepped in to determine that the King could only declare martial law under the authority of the annual mutiny acts (see Grant v Gould 1792, 126 E.R. 434). Locke's prerogative found its "judge on earth" as martial law was already governed within the norms of law making. Around the same time, acts suspending habeas corpus were also recognized as emergency institutions in common law. The first such act was passed in 1689 shortly after William and Mary's accession to the Crown to prevent the return of James II.[4] This act was the precedent of all subsequent suspensions (Crawford 1915). However, the recognition of this practice as an emergency institution clearly locates it in the neo-Roman tradition – evidenced by the fact that both Montesquieu and Blackstone share an understanding of a conservative legally entrenched and temporarily limited mechanism to suspend the law "in order to preserve it forever."[5] And so, common law emergency mechanisms, influenced by the theory of prerogative, are also infused by ideas from the other models: Inspired by the idea of the mechanistic management of the move from regular to irregular realities and back, martial law was also already understood as necessarily bound by positive regular law and judicial doctrine (for a fascinating account of rule of law infused debates in the context of the imperial exercise of martial law, see Kostal 2005).

The State of Siege in the French Constitution – On July 1791, in the midst of the French Revolution, the Constituent Assembly issued a legislative decree establishing the *l'état de siège*, to be distinguished from a state of peace (when normal law applies) and a state of war (when civil authorities are still responsible for the domestic order with security matters allow them to take special measures; [Svensen & McCarthy 1998, pp. 36–37]). In a state of siege, the civil authorities would be replaced by military authorities "when there was a serious threat of attack or

---

[4] "An Act for Impowering His Majestie to Apprehend and Detaine such persons as He shall finde just Cause to Suspect are conspiring against the Government," 1 William & Mary, c. 2, Statutes of the Realme, vi 24.

[5] Blackstone, echoing Montesquieu: "if the legislative power believed itself endangered by some secret conspiracy against the State or by some correspondence with its enemies on the outside, it could, for a brief and limited time, permit the executive power to arrest suspected citizens who would lose their liberty for a while only so as to preserve it for ever" [qui *ne perdraient leur liberté pour un temps que pour la conserver toujours*] (Montesquieu 1989 [1748], XI, ch. 6). Following exactly the same wording and connecting it to the Roman institution, Blackstone writes on the suspension of habeas corpus in English constitutional law: "As the senate of Rome was wont to have recourse to a dictator, a magistrate of absolute authority, when they judged the republic in any imminent danger.... In like manner **this experiment ought only to be tried in cases of extreme emergency; and in these the nation parts with its liberty for a while in order to preserve it forever**" (Blackstone 1979 [1765–1769], p. 132).

rebellion" (Ibid.). This was designed as a form of dictatorship – a suspension of the normal law while its conditions are regulated by law. By 1815 a law of siege authorized the executive to declare a state of siege at his discretion and two different types of siege were acknowledged – the "actual state of siege" prompted by an external military threat challenging the state and a "constructive state of siege" occasioned by internal dissent to the regime (Radin 1942; Manin 2008, p. 17). In 1849 a new state of siege law gave parliament alone the right to declare a state of siege and in 1878, in response to further abuse, only when there was "imminent peril," for a limited time and physical territory (Svensen & McCarthy 1998, p. 39). Explicitly, the State of Siege doctrine reflected a commitment as in the Roman dictatorship to a preservative legally entrenched institution for the temporary suspension of law. French jurists argued that constitutional government, confronted with crisis, must be able to respond and curtail rights but that it is possible to regulate such response in advance so to achieve non-arbitrary response that is better than ad hoc crisis legislation (Reinach 1885, pp. 272–275; Romain 1918, pp. 16–19, 482–483; Manin 2008, p. 16). The aim was, again, preventing arbitrariness but with ex ante regulation, rather than ex-post accountability. While the function of maintaining public order passed to the military and these authorities were granted powers to infringe specified rights, the law explicitly provided that citizens enjoy their other rights.[6] Also, while military courts were to assume jurisdiction over all crimes and offences against the security of the Republic, the constitution and public safety and order (Ibid., art. 8), French courts had often refused to recognize the judgments of such tribunals (Scheppele 2008, p. 170). Finally, the evolution of the doctrine from the revolutionary decree to the 1849 law and then to the 1878 law reflected a sensitivity to its abuse (Manin 2008, pp. 16–20; Scheppele 2008, pp. 169–170). Whereas, for example, the 1849 law had no mention of duration, the 1878 statute[7] provided that the state of siege "shall set the period of its duration" and added "at the expiration of this period, the state of siege shall cease automatically unless a new law should prolong it" (Art 1 cl.3, 4, in Manin 2008, p. 20). And so, here too, we see that the historical institution is infused, not to say confused, by the different justificatory frameworks of emergency containment – on the one hand it is a mechanism that enables flexibility to resist a range of threats; on the other, its development is one of specifically legalistic sensitivity to abuse.

The German constitutional tradition of the State of Exception – the first constitution of unified Germany, the Imperial Constitution of 1871 granted the Kaiser sole power to declare war and to exercise exclusive powers necessary for conducting war (Article 68). This was based on a post-1848 Prussian law of June 4, 1851, concerning the state of siege, according to which a military commander could take direct control of any civilian administration in his jurisdiction (Caldwell 1997, pp. 54–55). Going further to legality, the 1919 Weimar Constitution put restrictions on the ability of the President

---

[6] Law of August 9, 1849, *Le Moniteur*, 12 août 1849, art. 9–11.
[7] Law of April 4, 1878, *Journal Officiel de la République Française*, 4 avril 1878.

to declare an emergency and handle it. Article 48 (2) permitted the President, when "public safety is seriously threatened or disturbed" to use any measures necessary, including to use the armed forces and suspend many rights, in order to restore law and order. The Reichstag had the authority to require the President to cease such measures on demand (article 48(3)). However, the President had the power to dissolve the Reichstag (article 25). The politics of the late uses of Article 48 on the way to Weimar's collapse, was infused with the Reichstag dissolution following its resistance to declarations of state of exception and emergency decrees (see Winkler 2006, chap. 7). This politics was informed by the theoretical debates of the era regarding the appropriate interpretation of presidential powers in the "state of exception" in which legalism (under Kelsen's account, Kelsen 1932) and extra-legalism (under Schmitt's account, Schmitt 2005 [1922], pp. 85–94; see Vinx 2015) were juxtaposed in the interpretation of a mechanism that was arranged according, arguably, to the model of dictatorship. This confusion is reflected in the way that the shadow of the catastrophic failure of the Weimar democracy informs the discussions about emergency powers in the latter part of the twentieth century and until today. Was the tragic destiny of article 48 a proof of the failure of legalized emergency institutions? Was it a proof of the failure of mechanistic constitutional solutions to a crisis? Or was it that article 48 served to allow the extralegal abuse of grand prerogative powers? The German state of exception's shaky theoretical basis is resonant in the interpretation of the source of its failure.

Can the variety of terms and institutions and the fact that none can be traced back to one conclusive theoretical model teach us anything about the operation of this field, or is it just an indication of its sheer unruliness? In the next pages I will argue that there is more commonality between the three models than their confused appearances in historical legal instruments of emergency management suggests. In fact, it is no surprise to see traces of the different liberal theory responses to the problem of containment in actual emergency instruments – as all of these instruments, just as the models justifying them, have a common functional structure: a legal doctrine that resolves to contain exigencies within a given legal and political order.

From Mechanisms to the Emergency Doctrine

Bernard Manin has claimed, on the basis of his study of three historical emergency institutions (the Roman dictatorship, common law's martial law and the French state of siege) that the three cases, and indeed – historical emergency institutions across legal and constitutional traditions share a common, three-featured structure that he has called "the emergency paradigm":

> It is striking to find in the theory and practice of emergency institutions across a variety of contexts the three elements forming this structure: (1) Authorized deviating from higher order norms as reflected in the constitution; (2) Special conditions designed to make sure that circumstances necessitate (1); (3) Temporal limitations on (1). (Manin 2008, p. 23)

These three features – *authorized, circumstantially defined*, and *temporal* deviating measures – are present in the classic historical emergency institutions, although each is differently specified and emphasized.

For example, in the constitutional custom of the *Roman dictatorship*, Manin explains, an external single magistrate is appointed by the Consuls after the Senate had decided a dictator was required (*authorization*); to respond to threats of war or civil dissension (*definition*); to act as necessary with no veto, appeal and with legal immunity, for a period of six months or to step down as soon as he had fulfilled his task (*temporality*). In *common law's martial law*, military officials and martial courts are authorized by parliament (*authorization*); when ordinary courts are closed (*definition*); for as long as the conditions hold (*temporality*). In the *French state of siege*, military officials are authorized in ex ante legislation (*authorization*); to handle law enforcement and maintain public order and to infringe on specified rights, in conditions of "imminent danger resulting from foreign war or armed insurrection" (*definition*); for a period that according to the 1848 law is to be set in the law declaring the state of siege and automatically cease (*temporality*). The same structure may be applied to the *German state of exception*. Here it is the President who is authorized, by ex-ante legislation (*authorization*) to take the measures necessary to restore order with the help of the military and to infringe on specified right, "when public safety is seriously threatened or disturbed" (*definition*), these measures must be suspended immediately when the Reichstag so demands (*temporality*).

But the differentiation is not strictly a formal matter, restricting and permitting departures from constitutional norms. As Manin describes each of the institutions, he shows that the specified emphasis in each of them (and in the jurisprudential discussions about them) on these different features has a very particular and often contested meaning within the given constitutional order.

For example, on the issue of temporality there is a great divergence not only in the formal structure of the limitation (six months, one year, and so on) but also, and most importantly, in its function. For example, Cicero described the significance of the time limit in the Roman dictatorship not as a limitation on the unconstrained powers granted to the dictator, but as a way to highlight the difference between a dictator and a king, to show that dictatorship is consistent with the Republic as a form of government. "While the dictator would hold twice as much power as each consul thus getting perilously close to monarchy, he would be kept within republican limits by holding such power for only half of the consuls' term" (Cicero 2017 [52BC], III, 3; Manin 2008, p. 6).

In sharp contrast, when Blackstone and Montesquieu describe the suspension of habeas corpus acts they both refer to temporality as a classic liberal sensitivity: if the legislature, believed itself endangered, it could, for *"a brief and limited time,"* permit the executive power to arrest suspected citizens who *"would lose their liberty for a while only so as to preserve it for ever"* (Montesquieu 1989 [1748], XI, ch. 6; Blackstone 1979 [1765–1769], p. 132). The principle of liberty may be restricted only for the sake of liberty, not for any common good. The short duration of the measures is supported on modern liberal grounds, "just as it had been supported earlier ... on republican grounds" (Manin 2008, p. 9).

And so, although the reference to the Roman institution represents a self-aware continuity in tradition it is most interesting to see that the basic features of the doctrine reflect a deep connection between specific constitutional facts and the specific form that the emergency doctrine takes according to its interpreters. "Time limits" – as other features of the emergency paradigm – are not neutral "restrictions" over excessive power. They are connected in important and conflicted ways to the political values and the deep tensions and contestations of the constitutional order which the emergency institution is meant to preserve. They are therefore important keys, though not easy to decode, to the self-understanding of what it is to be preserved.

A fascinating example of the way that the features of the doctrine are contested even within one institution is shown in AV Dicey's analysis of habeas suspension acts. Contrary to Blackstone, Dicey does not emphasize an ex-ante vision of temporality. What is important for Dicey is not the promise that the time restricted suspension of liberty safeguards a future of liberty, but the promise of ex-post accountability that the limitation entails – not the fact that temporal suspension is limited by the specified duration (usually one year) after which liberty is restored, but that as soon as the suspension expires officials who broke the law become liable to indictment for the illegal conduct during the time of the suspension. The acts of suspension mean only that remedies for wrongful arrests are denied *for the moment* and for the specified time, it is not *a license* to make such wrongful arrests (A. V. Dicey 1915, pp. 140–141). The point here is not that the loss of liberty is worthwhile because it is brief, as Blackstone implies. The time limit is commendable because it allows for accountability for illegal and wrongful acts (Ibid., 142–143). Still another way to put it is that for Dicey, the short duration does not serve to justify the suspension but to indicate that remedy and accountability is a constitutional requirement (Dyzenhaus 2009b, pp. 35–36).

The same idea on the importance of ex-post evaluation is seen in Dicey's analysis of martial law: "One should always bear in mind that the question whether the force employed was necessary or excessive will, especially where death has ensued, be ultimately determined by a judge and jury, and that the estimate of what constitutes necessary force formed by a judge and jury, sitting in quiet and safety after the suppression of the riot, may differ considerably from the judgment formed by a general or magistrate, who is surrounded by armed rioters" (Dicey 1915, p. 185). Here it is not only the question of time limit that is being invoked but that of definitions or conditions for the use of force. Dicey insisted that this is "a question of fact to be determined in any case by the Courts in the same way as any other question" (Ibid., Appendix X, p. 404). As soon as the Courts sat again, they could determine not only whether an individual was wronged but also whether martial law has been properly employed, namely in the right conditions (Ibid., 406–407). The same temporal limitation, in the same legal instrument, may be interpreted and applied differently in the context of contested views over the political value of the rule that is to be preserved. For Blackstone it is a rule that is grounded in a political ideal of liberty. For Dicey, in a political ideal of legality.

CONCLUSION: THE LEGAL POLITICS OF CONTAINMENT

The specific ways in which threat is being managed and controlled within a specific political order is deeply connected to stability and legitimacy. Martial law was an arena for contestation about the value of normal law in the context of empire. Dictatorship was not only a mechanism designed to allow deviation but an important aspect of the Roman constitution, a part of its political identity. The Emergency doctrine's constant substantive feature is a commitment to the containment of exigency, not as a universal feature but as a politically defined and contested feature of a given legal and political order.

This insight into the politically differentiated significance of the legal doctrine of emergency powers, also leads us from the background theoretical problem of containment and constraint – to the more practical problems that constitute day-to-day practice in the field. Each aspect of the "emergency doctrine" – *definitions, authorizations, temporality* (and *jurisdiction*, since every emergency mechanism assumes operation within a jurisdiction rather than universally) – is also a particular tension area which generates much productive normative and institutional mobilization in specific cases of legally managing threats. Each of these tension areas has been problematized in the history of emergency jurisprudence in a way that strongly adheres to the master narrative of exceptional deviations for exceptional circumstances:

The assumption about the *problem of definitions* is that emergencies are particularly and inherently hard to define, at least in advance. The task is therefore limited to naming the agent (the executive) who will identify and declare the emergency. On the *problem of authorization* it is that emergencies require "unlimited powers" that must also be "constrained"; With the focus on "powers" vs. "constraints" the paradox is overwhelming – how can necessary "unlimited powers" also be "constrained?" The *problem of temporality* is commonly understood as a problem of "no time": emergencies require an immediate, ad hoc response – but this must be limited "in time." And finally, the *problem of jurisdiction* is portrayed as inherently a problem of sovereignty: because sovereigns decide that there is an emergency and what to do about it within their separate jurisdictions.

These assumptions are dominant in positive law and in common attitudes across jurisdictions, but they serve to obscure the complexity of the questions that are raised in emergencies in relation to each of the doctrine's features. For example: While emergencies are often defined as "impossible to define," "undefinable": a situation "the details of which cannot be anticipated ... the elimination of which cannot be spelled out" (Schmitt 2005 [1922], pp. 6–7), a term "inherently open-ended and manipulable," which may "defy precise definitions" (Gross & Ni Aolain 2006, pp. 5–6); a thing "that does not permit of any exact definition"[8] – in real cases there are genuine and meaningful contestations about a host of complex *definition questions* and problems. Not only questions about what should count as an emergency, but about the methods and procedures of defining and identifying threats, about the standards of evidence required, and the importance of improving conditions for contestation over the government's claim that there is an emergency. There are crucial practical reasons for us to acknowledge this broad and rich complex of definition questions because if you allow to claim that there is an emergency without check you don't only allow abuse, but you risk that mistakes of identification continue into the horizon of future responses disguised as positive legal doctrines.

And this is true also regarding *problems of authorization*. Persistent theories of exception maintain that in emergencies "the preconditions and the content of jurisdictional competence are necessarily unlimited" (Schmitt 2005 [1922], p. 6) or that "(n)o constitutional shackles can wisely be imposed on the power to which the care of it (cf. of exigency) is committed" (Hamilton 1961b [1787], Federalist No. 23). Emergency powers theory that rigidly juxtaposes "powers" vs. "constraints" – construes the problem of authorization in emergencies in the form of the question how to allow necessarily unlimited "powers" to respond to unknown threats that will also be constitutionally, legally, culturally or politically – "constrained." This emphasis conceals a reality in which response powers never simply exist outside of complex institutional environments. Since we are worried so much about "constraint" of unlimited "powers" we on the one hand construct extremely complex constitutional and institutional power relations and on the other, ignore the effects that these relations have on actual response environments – the complex institutional context in which such decisions are made must not be overshadowed by outdated fantasies of unlimited powers.

And on the *problem of temporality*: in traditional emergency theory "time" is a basic point of concern; under emergency conditions there is "no time" to apply cumbersome legal procedures. Special emergency mechanisms, therefore, allow application of urgent, ad hoc measures, provided that they are temporarily restricted. *The problem of no-time* is solved by the assurance of temporality. For Locke for example the prerogative power arises when the lawmaking power is "too numerous and too slow for the dispatch requisite for execution (Locke 1980 [1689], §160) and only until" the legislator can conveniently be assembled to provide for it (Locke 1980 [1689], §159); And in Montesquieu "…it could for a limited time, permit the executive power to arrest suspected citizens…" (Montesquieu 1989 [1748], p. 159). But emergency time is a much more flexible and complex issue than the "no time" exceptional depictions. First the more typical timeline of emergency management practices is a circular one. Emergencies are hardly concise in one moment but on

---

[8] Bhagat Singh and Others v. The King Emperor, [1931] LR. 58 Ind. App. 169, para. 3

a continuous loop from ex-ante anticipation, prevention and preparation to real time response and to ex-post recovery and mitigation in preparation to the next occurrence. Second – the "no time" structure obscures the many and multilayered other "time frames" that the legal management of emergencies entail. For example, while the "ticking bomb scenario" is the prototypical exceptional emergency time framework, it conceals many other timeframes that regulate the use of force in security interrogations such as ongoing national security timeframes of prolonged emergency management, administrative law timeframes of ex-ante authorization, criminal law time frames of ex-post liability, ambivalent bureaucratic timeframes in the interrogation room, and more.

The traditional understanding of the problem of exceptional time, or "no time" dramatically overshadows the politics generated by these other "time frames" that are legally significant and politically mobilizing. We can hardly see the outcome of this politics, the mundane but multiple and proliferating politics of emergency management if we stick to a theory of emergency time as exceptional time.

Finally, problems of jurisdiction are also subject to the adverse consequences of the theory of exception. Scholars of emergency powers theory describe emergencies as belonging to sovereigns who decide on the measures to address them. The sovereign's control over borders is assumed and jurisdictional problems are acknowledged when threats come from outside those borders or when an attempt to handle them from outside those borders arises. But sovereignty obscures the reality of multiplicity of jurisdictional claims in emergencies which provide opportunities for different actors, inside and outside sovereign jurisdictions to express their unique capabilities and to effectively and legitimately solve them.

If we want to imagine and design better emergency response systems they must have the flexibility, the openness and the sensitivity for the experiential learning processes that emergencies require.

They must have spaces and procedures for contestation over the identification of emergencies, and the definition of what counts as an emergency.

They must take seriously the complex institutional context in which emergencies are handled, and the impact of the distribution of powers on response environments so that the wide range of actors involved in managing emergencies will be prepared to take part in these processes.

They must be open to the possibility that strict jurisdictional separations may be challenged in order to effectively and legitimately respond to emergencies.

They must properly acknowledge that the management of emergencies takes place on a long term, partly circular timeline from preparation to response and recovery and not in an exceptional time frame outside of regular timelines.

They must acknowledge that emergencies are dynamic processes of learning by which environments of response may improve their response capabilities rather than momentary constitutive and dramatic occasions in which law is either "broken" or "preserved."

RECOMMENDED READING

Agamben, G. (1998). *Homo Sacre: Sovereign Power and Bare Life*. Translated by D. Heller-Roazen. Redwood City, CA: Stanford University Press.

Dyzenhaus, D. (1997). *Legality and Legitimacy: Carl Schmitt, Hans Kelsen, Hermann Heller*, Oxford: Clarendon Press.

Dyzenhaus, D. (2006a). *The Constitution of Law: Legality in a Time of Emergency*, Cambridge: Cambridge University Press.

Feldman, L. (2010). The Banality of Emergency. In A. Sarat, ed., *Sovereignty, Emergency, Legality*. New York: Cambridge University Press, pp. 136–164.

Ferejohn, J. & Pasquino, P. (2004). The Law of the Exception: A Typology of Emergency Powers. *International Journal of Constitutional Law*, 2 (2), 210–239.

Gross, O. & Ni Aolain, F. (2006). *Law in Times of Crisis: Emergency Powers in Theory and Practice*, Cambridge, UK: Cambridge University Press.

Honig, B. (2009). *Emergency Politics*, Princeton, NJ: Princeton University Press.

Hussain, N. (2003). *The Jurisprudence of Emergency: Colonialism and The Rule of Law*, Ann Arbor: University of Michigan Press.

Kostal, R. (2005). *A Jurisprudence of Power: Victorian Empire and the Rule of Law*, Oxford: Oxford University Press.

Lazar, N. (2009). *States of Emergency in Liberal Democracies*, New York: Cambridge University Press.

Locke, J. (1980 [1689]). *Second Treatise of Government*. Edited by C. B. Macpherson. Indianapolis and Cambridge: Hackett Publishing Company

Machiavelli. (1965 [1517]). Discourses on the First Decade of Titus Livius. In *Machiavelli: The Chief Works and Others*. Volume 1. Translated by A. Gilbert. Durham: Duke University Press, pp. 175–532.

Manin, B. (2008). The Emergency Paradigm and the New Terrorism: What If the End of Terrorism Was Not in Sight? In S. Baume, B. Fontana, eds., *Les usages de la s'eparation des pouvoirs*, Paris: Michel Houdiard, pp. 136–171 (also available from: http://as.nyu.edu/docs/IO/2792/emerg.pdf).

Montesquieu. (1989 [1748]). *The Spirit of the Laws*. Edited by A. Cohler, B. C. Miller, & H. S. Stone. Cambridge: Cambridge University Press.

Scarry, E. (2011). *Thinking in an Emergency*, New York, NY: W.W. Norton & Company Inc.

Scheppele, K. L. (2008). Legal and Extralegal Emergencies, In K. E. Whittington, R. D. Kelemen, G. A. Caldeira, eds., *The Oxford Handbook of Law and Politics*, Oxford: Oxford University Press, pp. 164–188.

Scheuerman, W. E. (2006). Survey Article: Emergency Powers and the Rule of Law After 9/11 *The Journal of Political Philosophy*, 14 (1), 61–84.

Schmitt, C. (2005 [1922]). *Political Theology: Four Chapters on the Theory of Sovereignty*. Translated by G. Schwab. Chicago: University of Chicago Press.

27

Regulation

*Julia Black**

One of the features, and for some the frustrations, of modern democratic states is the need to delegate day-to-day responsibility for the myriad of activities the state has taken on. These functional pressures led first to the growth of the administrative state, and latterly to its close cousin, the regulatory state (see e.g., Majone 1994; Gilardi et al. 2006). Consequently, greater attention has been paid to the role of regulators in constituting, not just administering, the regulatory systems which govern the activities of both public and private actors. For constitutional scholars, regulatory agencies can have the disadvantage of blurring the separation of powers, acting as both rulemaker and executive decision maker, and sometimes, enforcer as well. Self-regulatory and transnational regulatory bodies, lacking such legislative mandate, pose further challenges. Mistrust in regulators is increased in an era of populism and rejection of experts. So in democratic states, at least, there is a continual debate as to how much power regulators should be allowed to wield, and how to ensure that regulators are acting in line with constitutional norms and values, that is, are 'constitutionalised'.

This chapter explores this question. The first part provides a model of polycentric regulatory systems, setting out their key elements and some of the underlying assumptions on which the model is based. Although the focus here is on constitutionalising state-based regulatory systems, the polycentric model applies equally to non-state, international and transnational systems. The second part of the chapter argues that the task of 'constitutionalising' regulatory systems is itself a regulatory task, one which includes but goes beyond the function of calling regulators to account. Thus, it follows that the same polycentric model can be used to analyse constitutional systems, at least those parts which are performing that regulatory role. This analysis is undertaken in the third part, which further argues that whilst structures are important, it is the nature of the relationships within and between the constitutional and regulatory systems which is key to understanding the dynamics of constitutionalisation. As key constitutional actors, notably the executive and the

---

* Professor of Law, London School of Economics and Political Science.

legislature, are also political actors, their own behaviours may not always be in line with the norms and/or spirit of the constitution. As such, there is always a question as to whether, in their relationships with regulators, they are seeking to constitutionalise them or politicise them, and also the extent to which politicisation is acceptable within the constitutional framework. Finally, it is suggested that although, or indeed because, state-based regulatory systems are embedded in the state's constitutional order, constitutionalisation may be necessary but not sufficient for a regulatory system to be seen as trustworthy and legitimate.

I THE POLYCENTRIC MODEL OF REGULATORY GOVERNANCE

Regulation, or regulatory governance, is understood here as a series of intentional, sustained and focused attempts to change the behaviour of others in order to pursue a collective purpose, using a range of techniques which often, but not always, include a combination of rules or norms and some means for their implementation and enforcement (Black 2001; Koop and Lodge 2017). Regulation can focus on any area of social or natural activity, from how wars are conducted to how buildings are constructed. Regulation may involve a high degree of state involvement, or none at all, or involve both state and non-state actors in various ways, each of whom may use legal and/or non-legal norms. Thus, regulation is a mode of governance not just of government, and the terms 'regulatory system' and 'regulatory governance system' will be used interchangeably.

Regulation is an activity which can be performed by a range of individuals and organisations. Those participating in that common regulatory project may be sufficiently interrelated to form a system, regime or network, the boundaries of which are delineated by the definition of the project which they are engaged in pursuing, and which has some continuity over time. Regulatory systems can range in their polycentricity, that is, in the degree of dispersal and fragmentation of actors in the system (regulators, regulatees, intermediaries, etc.), in their degree of internal coherence and connectivity, and in the extent to which they are clearly delineated. Importantly, both state-based and non-state-based systems are all polycentric to varying degrees – it is not the case that 'centric = state', and 'polycentric = non-state'. They also vary in their relationships with other systems, with which they may compete, coordinate, cohabit, clash or simply ignore (Eberlein et al. 2014).

Further, those participating in, and thus constituting regulatory systems (as individuals or organisations) are independent agents, each with their own normative or value frameworks. They also have different cognitive frameworks, they rely on different sources of knowledge, have different capacities for action, have different sources of social, political, legal and economic capital, and, relatedly, different degrees of power and/or authority, all of which can affect their behaviours, roles, interests or views, and their interactions with others.

Regulatory systems are dynamic, continuously evolving, and through reflexive interactions and feedback loops are constantly being reconstituted, redesigned and reformulated in the process of their performance. Regulators, including state-based ones, are active not passive participants in the system's evolution, or indeed its creation or amendment. Indeed, putative or existing regulators (as individuals and as organisations) may actively seek to shape the rules which confer new powers on them, or adjust their existing powers and remit. Further, regulatory systems are embedded in different social, cultural, technical, political, legal, economic and market systems with which they interact, and as such are characterised by complex internal and external interactions and interdependencies both within themselves and with other regulatory systems. Finally, in order to function effectively, all regulators, even state-based ones, have actively to create their own legitimacy and trustworthiness, an important point to which we will return.

Analysing Regulatory Governance Systems

As the foregoing suggests, regulatory systems can be difficult to navigate both for participants and observers. Further, although regulation itself is an intentional and purposive activity and as such involves an element of design, regulatory systems are living social systems in the broadest sense, with inevitable limits to the extent to which they will function over time and space in the way either their designers or participants anticipate. So, the question is, how can we analyse a dynamic regulatory system, either 'objectively' from the external standpoint of an observer, or interpretively from the 'internal' viewpoint of different participants?

Building out from the above, I suggest we should think of regulatory systems as a particular form of social system with six key elements, all of which constantly interact to produce a dynamic system (Figure 27.1).

Goals, Purposes and Values

A logical starting point is with *goals, purposes and values* – what is the common project the regulatory system is trying to achieve, and which values is it trying to attain or uphold in the pursuit of that project? Regulation is an inherently purposive activity, and as the goals are likely to be contested, it is also an inherently political one. Since the 1980s, the standard economic justification for state-based regulation in liberal democracies such as the US and the UK has been that the purpose of regulation is to correct market failures in order to achieve a particular model of economic efficiency. However, although the 'market perfecting' justification is influential, the purposes of regulation have historically always been more extensive (for review, see Baldwin, Cave and Lodge 2012). They include managing risks to health, safety, or the environment, facilitating coordination, or managing scarce resources. Regulation can also be aimed at controlling the power of particular social, political

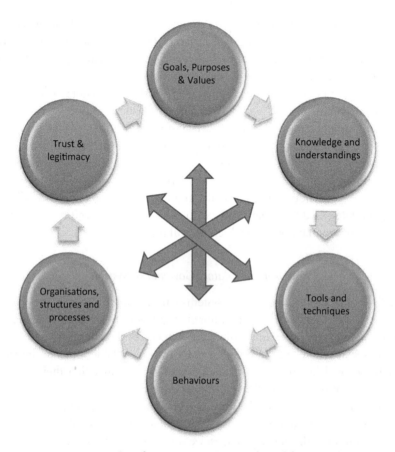

FIGURE 27.1 Regulatory systems – an analytical framework

or economic groups, and at upholding rights and values such as principles of equality, freedom of speech, privacy, or the rule of law. Moreover, the purposes and values of any regulatory system may, and likely will, morph over time as governing parties come and go. They may be in tension, or be strategically uncertain and inchoate to facilitate the agreement of a political bargain, or left open as a matter of design, to enable more experimentalist forms of governance (Sabel and Zeitlin 2008).

Knowledge and Understandings

The second element of any regulatory system is the *knowledge and understandings* of actors within it, particularly but not exclusively those who are influential in shaping its design and operation, whether as regulators or otherwise. It is their cognitive frameworks and their epistemologies: how they perceive and interpret the world around them; which sources of knowledge they see as valid and relevant, and so draw on in constructing and reinforcing those cognitive frameworks (see e.g., J. C.

Scott 1999; Jasanoff et al. 2001; Black 2013a). It is also their ideas of the purposes they are meant to be achieving, of the dynamics of the area of social life in which they are intervening (e.g., markets, organisations, individuals), of the physical or material properties of things and the interaction of humans with them (e.g., the natural environment, digital technology), and indeed of the properties of the regulatory system itself, including of the calculative techniques being used (see below).

The importance of analysing knowledge and understandings is particularly evident in the regulation of risks. There is often significant contestation as to whether a risk exists and, if so, of what nature and scale (see e.g., Beck 1992). The highly differential national and regional responses to the continually emerging risks of Covid-19 provide a good example. The genome sequence of Covid-19 was made available globally by China in mid-January 2020. Faced with the same data, countries which had experienced SARS, such as China and South Korea, concluded Covid-19 was similar to SARS; in contrast, countries which were more familiar with flu, such as the UK, concluded it would be similar to flu. The same data was interpreted very differently. It was a classic example of the 'duck/rabbit' illusion – a drawing which to some looks like a rabbit, to others like a duck (www.illusionsindex.org/i/duck-rabbit). There are myriad of reasons for why countries responded so differently to Covid-19, particularly in the early days, but the differential interpretations of the same data is a key factor.

Risk tolerances are also important. Where the impacts and/or probabilities of risks are relatively unknown policy makers and regulators face a dilemma: should they adopt a precautionary approach, prohibiting or closely regulating a product or activity until there is a certain level of understanding of the risks, or should they be 'pro-producer' or 'pro-innovation', regulating the product or activity only lightly, if at all, and relying on an ability to remediate any damage that may be done if the risk crystallises? Often, these questions involve highly technical and scientific assessments, but the dominance of a scientific cognitive framework can exclude other cognitive frameworks or values, such as those of ethics (see e.g., Nuffield Council on Bioethics 2016). The dominance of a particular model of scientific epistemology, along with power structures, can also exclude those who are not part of the accepted scientific community in the determinations (political or otherwise) of what constitutes 'valid' knowledge. As a result, multiple proposals have been made for how to include a wider set of knowledge, perspectives and experiences in how regulation is framed and performed (see e.g., Brown 2009; Jasanoff 2017).

Regulatory Techniques

How those involved in the design and performance of regulatory systems perceive the world they operate in and the problems they have to address (and the acceptability of any solutions they may devise) is fundamental to the third element of regulatory governance systems: the design and operation of *regulatory techniques, or technologies of regulation*. There is a myriad of forms and combinations of regulatory techniques, giving rise to multiple categorisations. Thus, for example, 'command and control' styles (detailed legal rules backed by legal sanctions) are contrasted with other 'new governance' forms of regulation: principles-based, outcomes-focused, risk based, management-based, process-based, experimentalist, anticipatory, responsive and so forth (for review see Baldwin, Cave and Lodge 2010 and 2012).

In essence, the broad suite of regulatory techniques includes but is not limited to legal or non-legal norms (principles, standards, codes, guidance and so forth); methods for detecting, monitoring, auditing and certifying; liability rules for those causing harm; and sanctions for non-compliance. It includes calculative models (e.g., for calculating prices, the spread of diseases, assessing risks, and increasingly for analysing data through techniques such as AI and machine learning (see e.g., Callon and Muniesa 2005; P. Miller 2001)). It also includes architecture (both hard architecture of the built environment and 'soft' architectures of codes or algorithms (Lessig 2009; Yeung 2018)); 'technology' including digitally enabled techniques such as smart contracting or smart rules; information and communication, and techniques for 'nudging' behaviours as well as for directing them (Thaler and Sunstein 2021). Moreover, methods of regulation can also be objects of regulation. So, for example, regulation can be focused on market or organisational structures and processes as well as on individual behaviours, and regulators can use each of these as techniques to pursue the regulatory project.

The debates on regulatory techniques are important for understanding how effectively regulation can achieve its goals, but focusing on techniques to the exclusion of the other dimensions of a regulatory system risks over-simplifying the challenges of achieving those goals, over-looking the politics involved in their selection, design and implementation, and under-playing the normative goals of regulation and its need for trust and legitimacy.

Organisational Dynamics, Structures and Processes

The fourth element of the framework is comprised of the structures, processes, capacities and motivations or cultures of the *organisational actors* within the regulatory system, relationships between those organisations (see e.g., Powell 1990), and relationships between systems themselves (see e.g., Eberlein et al. 2014; Wood et al. 2019). Understanding the interaction of institutional structures with behaviours, and organisational behaviour more generally, are sub-disciplines in their own right (see e.g., Knudsen and Tsoukas 2009; Greenwood et al. 2017). Much of the regulatory research to date has focused on the interactions between regulators and regulatees in the context of compliance and enforcement, and on how firms respond to regulation (Ayres and Braithwaite 1992; for review see Gunningham 2010). The internal dynamics of regulators are just as important, including how they are funded, organised and how they prioritise (see e.g., Black and Baldwin 2010). Furthermore, multiple other actors can be involved in the interactions and 'regulatory conversations' which play an important role in constituting regulatory systems, including intermediaries such as certifiers, insurers, auditors, and consultants. Those undertaking any regulatory functions require the capacities and associated resources necessary to undertake those functions, both material and human (funding, expertise, organisational systems and processes, the ability to learn), as well as legal, social and political capacity. Organisational actors also need the motivation or internal culture to use those capacities to further the goals of the regulatory system, which may not necessarily align with their own interests (C. Scott 2001; Black 2003).

Further, as noted above, the design of organisational structures and processes can itself be a regulatory technique, for example, by requiring certain structures of corporate governance, or the allocation of certain regulatory responsibilities to clearly identified individuals, or the adherence to certain safety procedures, as can the design and operation of the institutional architecture of a regulatory system (e.g., Sabel and Zeitlin 2008; Godwin and Schmulow 2021).

Behaviours

The operation of regulatory systems is also fundamentally dependent on the behaviours of those constituting them or interacting with them, and have been the subject of the compliance and enforcement literature for some time. For example, how does the compliance function gain influence over the business; when are safety officers' concerns overridden in pursuit of 'getting the job done'; and what role does leadership play in driving the adoption of regulation (see e.g., Gunningham 2010).

Regulators' own perceptions of how people will respond to regulatory interventions, whether they are firms, consumers or others, is also significant, and depends on their own cognitive frameworks for analysing behaviour. Over the last twenty years or so, the economic model of the rational actor has gradually given way to more nuanced understandings of behaviour, and behavioural psychologists and anthropologists are increasingly being called on by regulators seeking to understand the different behaviours of people in both market and non-market contexts (OECD 2017).

The behaviour of regulators themselves is also a critical factor. Again the rational actor model has been influential in the regulatory literature, with the assumption that all regulators will be seeking to pursue their own preferences (e.g., Levine and Forrence 1990). In contrast, more sociologically rooted analyses adopt a less transactional and more relational approach. Research into the interactions of regulators, regulatees and various intermediaries within the regulatory system, such as consultants and legal advisors, shows how the regulatory system is constituted and co-created through those interactions, or 'regulatory conversations', in the processes of interpreting, implementing and negotiating compliance with regulatory rules (e.g., Black 2002, 2003; Gray and Silbey 2014; Abbott, Levi-Faur and Snidal 2017).

Cognitive psychology is also introducing a deeper understanding of behavioural biases which can be relevant in the regulatory context (see e.g., Khaneman et al. 1982; Jansen and Aelen 2015).

Trust and Legitimacy

The final, and most important, element of any regulatory system is *trust and legitimacy*. Whether and how trust and legitimacy are bestowed and by whom are some of the foundational questions of political and constitutional theory, but they also have a sociological dimension. Legitimacy, in the sociological sense, means having one's right to govern accepted, that is, perceived as legitimate, by those who are being governed or on whose behalf one is purporting to do so (Beetham 1991; Suchman 1995). State-based regulators derive their legal right to govern from their legal mandates. But whilst a legal mandate may be necessary, it may not be sufficient for a regulatory system to be trusted. Any regulatory system, and the myriad of organisations within it, needs to be trusted and perceived as legitimate by a critical number of legitimacy communities in order for it to function, even if it is not universally seen as legitimate (Black 2008). Legitimacy communities include those who are relying on the regulatory system to protect or support them, for example, as producers, citizens or consumers, as well as those it is seeking to regulate.

In democratic systems, there are generally four broad sets of core legitimacy and accountability demands which are usually made by such legitimacy communities, in different combinations (Black 2008). First, claims based on what may be loosely termed 'constitutional values', such as the rule of law, procedural fairness, and accountability. Second, claims based on normative values, aligned with the goals the regulatory system is trying to achieve, such as the attainment of justice, ethics, environmental sustainability or the management of risks. Third, claims based on democratic values, such as dialogue, participation, representation, and – again – accountability either directly to the *demos* or to those who have been elected to act on its behalf. Finally, core legitimacy and accountability demands can be claims based on functional performance such as effectiveness, expertise, and efficiency. It is important to note that these demands can be made of both state and non-state regulators. Further, in each case, the demands of each group or legitimacy community can pull in different directions. So, maintaining trust and legitimacy is an ongoing task requiring transparency and continual engagement, and it is a particularly difficult one in the context of managing risks, as has been illustrated by the Covid-19 pandemic.

It is perhaps not surprising, therefore, that regulators act positively to demonstrate their own trustworthiness, to create their own legitimacy, in order to meet the claims of these multiple communities. Just as regulatees can 'go beyond compliance', regulators can act in ways which go beyond the formal requirements of accountability placed on them. They can engage in informal as well as formal consultations, adopt greater degrees of transparency and reporting than may be required, have regular stakeholder engagement meetings, as well as a range of other measures (e.g., Thatcher 2002; Black 2013b). However, regulators may need for the purposes of their own survival and functional effectiveness to pay attention to some legitimacy communities more than others, which again raises issues of exclusion of less powerful groups.

Summary

Separating out the different elements of a regulatory system for independent analysis is of course artificial as in practice they interact in important and complex ways. Cross cutting dynamics of power, discourse and time also pervade these different elements and their interactions. Often, an analysis of any particular regulatory system will focus on one or two elements. Whilst that is a practical approach – not every analysis of regulatory systems has to cover every element – it does need to be cognisant of their existence and relevance. For if we are really to understand the dynamics of any regulatory system as a whole we have to look at each element in the context of its interaction with the others. Concomitantly, we cannot extrapolate from an analysis of one element how the dynamics of the whole system do or are likely to operate. Further, as noted, regulatory systems also often interact with other systems in important and complex ways. The analytical framework provided here enables us to understand the dynamics of regulatory governance systems, both as observers and as participants. It can also help us to analyse deep-rooted causes of failures and to think through the potential impacts of changes in any part of the system. Critically for this discussion, it provides the groundwork for the next stage of the analysis.

II CONSTITUTIONAL SYSTEMS AS REGULATORY SYSTEMS

Given their complexity, trying to ensure that regulatory systems operate in line with constitutional precepts and values is inevitably challenging. In essence, constitutional actors are trying to influence regulatory systems just as regulators are trying to influence the social and economic systems they regulate. Most importantly for debates in public law, the argument here is that constitutional actors are doing far more than trying to call regulators to account; in the hard-worn phrase, they are trying to 'regulate the regulators'. To analyse how they do so, it is suggested that we should 'flip' the perspective – not simply look 'down' on regulatory systems from the perspective of constitutions and constitutional actors, but also look 'up' at the latter through the lens of regulatory systems. In so doing, we see that constitutional governance systems can be as polycentric as regulatory governance systems, and their interactions with their respective sets of regulatees just as complex. Each is trying to regulate the dynamics of complex, polycentric systems over time and at a distance, whilst themselves operating within a complex, polycentric system.

Using the polycentric model to analyse constitutional systems assumes a particular conception of constitutions. It sees them as dynamic and evolving sets of norms, values and practices (even if their written texts remain unchanged) which express the constitutive and the regulative aspects of the relationship between the governing and the governed (see also Loughlin 2003). Their participants, as individuals and organisations, are active in the constitution's evolution. Constitutions are thus reflexive: they are being constantly interpreted, constituted and altered by the practices of those occupying the institutions they create, whose actions they shape but by whose actions they are in turn shaped as well. Moreover, as some of the core constitutional actors (notably the executive and legislature) are explicitly political actors, there is thus necessarily a sense in which constitutional dynamics are at once legal and political (Gee and Webber 2010).

The institutional architecture of the state, too, will vary in its polycentricity, that is, in the degree of dispersal and fragmentation of actors in the system, in their degree of internal coherence, and in the extent to which their roles are clearly delineated. Those participating will also have different normative or value frameworks, cognitive frameworks, different capacities for action, and different degrees of power and/or authority, all of which can affect their behaviours and their interactions with others. Finally, all those entities comprising and participating in the constitutional system have actively to maintain their legitimacy for the system to survive and function effectively.

Hence, in the discussion which follows, the polycentric model will be used to explore how constitutional systems may or can interact with state-based regulatory systems in an attempt to constitutionalise them. Note that in most cases, the main 'target' of constitutionalisation is usually a regulatory agency created by legislation. Even though in practice a regulatory regime will be constituted by a number of agencies and/or others interacting in various ways, it is challenging for the 'system' as a whole to be the target for those seeking to constitutionalise it, so in practice, attention is more often focused on regulatory agencies as singular actors. Constitutionalising non-state actors who participate, or indeed are key actors, in either state or non-state based regulatory regimes, poses additional conceptual and functional challenges which are not explored here.

The subsections below look at the relationship between constitutional systems and regulatory systems, using the polycentric model set out above. It looks at different elements of the constitutional system involved in the activity of 'constitutionalising' the regulatory system, and which element of the regulatory system is being constitutionalised. For reasons of presentation and brevity, each element of the constitutional and regulatory system is discussed simultaneously, but there is no exclusive relationship between an element in one system and its 'twin' in the other. So regulatory organisations can be constitutionalised not just by constitutional organisations but also by various constitutionalising techniques, and so forth. Further, it is not necessarily the case that the regulatory system is passive in the relationship; it is possible for the two systems to have a reflexive relationship in which each shapes the other and is shaped by it in turn, though whether and how they do so is an empirical question.

One of the complicating factors, however, in considering the relationship between constitutional and regulatory systems is that key actors, particularly the constitutional system, are also political actors. Thus, as we will see subsequently, there is a constant issue as to when the political constitutional actors are using their powers over regulators for political rather than constitutional ends, and to what extent that is a legitimate use of such powers.

We can start the analysis at any point in the framework, but for the sake of symmetry with the exposition above, the same ordering is used here.

III CONSTITUTIONALISING REGULATORS THROUGH CONSTITUTIONAL GOVERNANCE

Constitutionalising Goals, Purposes and Values

In principle the barest definition of a constitution is to provide an allocation of powers and functions to different institutions of the state, and to provide the rules which both constitute those institutions and set the parameters for how they operate (Raz 1998). For some, it is additionally to encode or otherwise express norms and values which those institutions must observe in the exercise of their powers and functions. Those norms may or may not be included in the written text of the document or documents comprising the constitution, may be derived from the wider legal system in which the constitution is embedded, or may be generated endogenously through the practices of the institutions of the state and those who occupy them. For others, constitutions provide the framework of relations between those in pursuit of a commonly shared enterprise (see e.g., Dyzenhaus and Thorburn 2016). Constitutions may also be the outcomes of bargains between powerful political actors, and their function includes providing a coordinating device for those political bargains to be upheld, and a stabilisation mechanism which enables them to become self-enforcing (Elkins et al. 2009).

Even as outcomes of political bargains, constitutional systems can seek to ensure that in the conduct of governance certain values are upheld by the institutions of the state, including but not limited to rights of individuals and groups. Of central relevance to the project of constitutionalising regulatory systems, at least in democratic societies, are the principles of the rule of law and, for some, the need for law (and constitutions) to secure the rightful conditions under which each can pursue their own ends compatibly with others being able to do the same (Fuller 1969; Craig 2017; Allan 2013; King, this volume).

Constitutional values can also be generated endogenously through the practices of the institutions of the state and those who occupy them. They may be values which are essential to the prudent and peaceful running of the state in a way which contains political conflicts and to ensure the maintenance of the public realm, the state, as an autonomous entity (Loughlin 2003). Principles of public law, such as rationality, proportionality, necessity, or propriety, can derive from the practical, political reasoning based on prudential considerations and the need constantly to reconcile competing conceptions of the role of the state (ibid). Others have argued that the social and economic purposes of regulatory law and regulatory rules should be recognised in the interpretation which courts and others give to such rules, drawing on principles embedded in the constitutional settlement (Sunstein 1990).

Whilst constitutions set out norms and values, the question of which norms and values in fact underpin, constrain, enable and are expressed in the practices of those who govern is clearly an empirical question. That is fairly obvious. But what is less often noted is the relationship of the goals and values of the constitution – both as written and as performed – to the cognitive frameworks and epistemologies of those writing and performing it.

Constitutionalising Cognitive Frameworks and Epistemologies

In the context of constitutional systems, cognitive frameworks are the understandings of its purposes and how it operates (or should operate) of those who create the constitution (if there is a single moment of creation), and of those who 'perform' it, that is, continuously develop and enact constitutional practices over time. Epistemologies are the sources of knowledge which were drawn on in its creation, and importantly those which are drawn on during its day-to-day performance and evolution and which may change over time, just as for regulatory governance systems. They may be expressed in the text or sources of the constitution, or in written conventions, but they can only ever be partially inscribed.

The preoccupation of Anglo-American constitutional writing with the US and British constitutions can blind us to the fact that around the rest of the world, constitutions can have a remarkably short life – few are more than fifty years old (Elkins et al. 2009). Accounts of the creation of other constitutions, particularly to resolve situations of violence or conflict, can provide fascinating insights into how the issues of cognitive framing and sources of knowledge, as well as power, impact on the drafting of a constitution (though this is not to argue for a particular approach to interpreting constitutional texts). The post-second world war constitutions of Germany, Italy, and Japan, for example, bear the marks of the constitutional upheaval which preceded them. The negotiation of the constitution in South Africa from 1993–1996, provides a further example. In drafting the new South African constitution, one of the core questions was which was the biggest problem which the state, and thus the constitution, needed to address: ethnic conflict or social and political inequality? For those leaning towards the former, the constitution should adopt a consociational model, with emphasis on managing conflict through a carefully crafted balance of powers between ethnic and/or regional groups with the state playing the role of a mediator. For those leaning towards the latter, the constitution should adopt a justice model with an emphasis on individual civil, political and socio-economic rights, enacted by a strong central state operating through majoritarian decision making, and upheld by the courts. The constitution which emerged was a product of many factors, but not least of these different understandings of its role and purpose in the particular context of the time (Ebrahim 1999).

Focusing on the relationship of the constitutional system to the regulatory systems of the state, how the latter are perceived from a constitutional perspective goes to the core of two fundamental questions in constitutional theory: the source of constitutional authority, and the role of the state. The distinctions can be overstated, but it is useful to draw out in simple terms the different ways in which answers to these questions frame how regulatory agencies in particular are viewed from a constitutional perspective.

As Martin Loughlin clearly articulates, there are competing conceptions of the source of the state's authority and its role: as an agent of the individuals comprising the polity, whose role it is to protect the rights and autonomy of those individuals to pursue their own conceptions of the good life (the state as *societas*); and as a 'pastor' or guardian whose role it is to enable the collective well-being of the community, providing for each the opportunities to fulfil their potential for the benefit of all (the state as *universitas*) – though there are many variants in between (Loughlin 2003).

For who see the state as *societas*, anything other than minimal interference in their lives by a democratically elected official is constitutionally offensive (see e.g., Harlow and Rawlings 2009). Independent regulatory agencies, which are usually key actors in the regulatory system, are even more problematic. Not only may they breach the doctrine of separation of powers by combining executive, rule-making and judicial functions (see e.g., Gilardi et al. 2006), but they may also have quite broad mandates to act independently of elected politicians. Moreover, for yet others, they are problematic as they are staffed by unelected technocrats whose narrow epistemologies and cognitive frameworks unjustifiably exclude the experiences, views and values of those who are not part of the same technocratic or scientific elite. Their distance from the democratic polity may be a functional necessity but it is one to be regretted and calls into question their legitimacy.

However, from the perspective of the state as *universitas*, in which the state is a pastor, or guardian, whose role is to act prudently for the collective good of the people, regulatory institutions can be seen as an essential part of the government; if not as partners in a common enterprise, then at least as agents in its pursuit. Extrapolating further, in the perspective of the state as *universitas*, the functional efficacy of regulatory agencies is critical to the attainment of the overall project. The problem is not that regulators may have too much independence but they may have too little, and are insufficiently insulated from political overseers to be able act as the technocratic experts they need to be to function effectively and consistently over time. Additionally, from an economic perspective, regulators need to be able to make time consistent 'credible commitments' to provide certainty and confidence for private industry, which can only be done by embedding the regulatory regime in such a way that it is difficult for a new governing party or coalition to revoke it (e.g., Gilardi 2009). Their political independence is the solution to the problem of political interference and a critical feature of their ability to function and thus, for some, for their legitimacy.

The distinction between the two positions is drawn starkly here to emphasise a point, and views can obviously be more nuanced. Moreover, the challenge of how to ensure that regulatory agencies act in accordance with their mandates and wider constitutional norms and values is common to both. The problem is often conceptualised in terms of a classic principal-agent relationship. The people, through democratic elections, delegate to the executive and legislature the right to govern them; in turn, the executive and legislature delegate to a range of regulatory organisations and individuals the powers to address particular problems or attain particular goals. The challenge is then to ensure the agent does not deviate from the precepts of their constitutional, and political, principals. In the public interest theory of regulation, those political principals are acting in the public interest (and implicitly, in line with constitutional values). The challenge of 'regulatory drift' is seen in terms of preventing 'regulatory capture', in which the regulator starts to act instead in favour of the interests of the industry they are regulating. In contrast, public choice theorists do not assume politicians are acting in a broader public interest (or indeed in line with constitutional values), unless it suits them to do so. Instead, they argue that elected politicians treat regulatory laws as goods which can be traded in the electoral marketplace, with favourable laws being 'sold' to the highest bidder (Mueller 2003). The problem is seen still ensuring regulatory agencies do not defect or drift away from the will of the enacting coalition (McCubbins et al. 1989), but for political reasons, rather than any great concern with the need to uphold the public interest or constitutional values.

It is the dual nature of the executive and the legislature as both political and constitutional principles which make the debate on what *should* be their relationship with regulatory bodies so contested, especially when some degree of regulatory independence is enshrined in legislation. What for some is an entirely justifiable exercise of powers by democratically elected actors is for others an unwarranted political interference in the functioning of a legally independent body. And if elected politicians stretch the constitution to its limits in pursuit of their political agendas, then a further argument may come into play: that independence of regulatory agencies is a constitutional necessity. In other words, regulatory independence enables not just credible, technically expert, and time-consistent decisions to be made but constitutional values to be realised, especially when those values are being challenged, or indeed flouted, by those in the political institutions of the executive and/or legislature. Conventionally, it is argued that it is elected politicians who take strategic benefit from this 'independence buffer', as they use it in 'blame games' to distance themselves from regulators in times of crisis. But it can also be argued that independence protects the regulatory part of the state from the pernicious and polarising effects of politics. For example, Michael Lewis's account of the Trump administration suggests that the structurally closer those agencies were to the state the more they were vulnerable to the damaging effects of highly partisan politics on their operation (Lewis 2018). Though of course the haven, such as it may be, is fragile: it will last only as long as political constitutional actors allow.

Constitutionalising Techniques

The methods or techniques used by constitutional systems to try to manage regulatory systems are themselves tools of regulatory governance. They may apply ex ante, to day-to-day operations, and/or operate as ex post accountability arrangements. They include all those techniques noted above, such as legal and non-legal norms governing behaviours, the design of organisational structures and processes, the management of regulatory capacities, including staffing and budgets, requirements for monitoring, audit and reporting, and the imposition of consequences, if not always sanctions per se.

Inevitably the main actors in constitutional systems cannot easily monitor the day-to-day decisions of the regulators, just as regulators cannot monitor the day-to-day activities of those they regulate. And, as the regulatory state has grown in size and complexity and regulatory technologies have become more diverse, so the range of constitutionalising techniques itself becomes more varied, and arguably more juridified. Clearly, the regulators' legal mandate is a key tool for determining what powers regulators will have and setting the framework for how they will be used. However, as noted above, the legally defined goals and purposes of a regulator, and the matters to which they have to 'have regard' may be multiple, inchoate and/or conflicting, sometimes deliberately so (e.g., *Deep Water, the Gulf Oil Disaster and the Future of Offshore Drilling* 2011), confounding the constitutionalising challenge.

There can be a plethora of legal and non-legal codes which set out how regulators should develop, implement and enforce regulatory requirements. These include requirements to consult on new regulatory proposals, to conduct cost benefit analysis and/or regulatory impact assessments, to act in a manner which is transparent, efficient, targeted and proportionate, or pursue wider goals such as economic growth or (more recently) net zero emissions and biodiversity. They may also include post-implementation reviews or sunset clauses, though the latter are less common (OECD 2018).

But legal rules are never sufficient (or even necessary) to determine how people, organisations or systems will respond. So other constitutionalising methods focus on structures, such as the design of regulatory organisations, and/or people through the appointment of key personnel by the executive and/or legislature. Funding can also be used as a political as well as a constitutional tool of control (Hood 1983). Indeed, the degree to which regulators are bounded in practice can have much more to do with executive control over budgets and staffing than with the definition of their formal legal powers – and it can become a matter of real constitutional debate if the executive or legislature seeks to truncate the capacity of regulators to fulfil their roles through such indirect means, rather than through legislative changes to their purpose and scope (see e.g., Lin 2019).

Constitutionalising Organisations

As noted earlier, the structures, processes, capacities, motivations and cultures of organisations within the regulatory system are key to its dynamics; by the analogy pursued here, the same is true for constitutional systems. Also, as noted, a complicating factor in analysing the dynamics of the legislature and executive in particular is that they are both constitutional and political actors. Analysing their dynamics, and indeed those of other constitutional actors such as the courts, are subjects in their own right, but it is the relationship between constitutional actors and regulatory governance systems that is in focus here.

The courts are in the front line of efforts to constitutionalise not just regulatory agencies but their relationship with other branches of government as well, and so it is not surprising that most legal debates on constitutionalising regulatory systems revolve around competing theories of judicial review (Harlow and Rawlings 2009). Broadly speaking, those who advocate for a rights-based conception of the constitution, particularly if the sources of those rights are found in common law (in common law systems), argue for a more interventionist role for the judiciary to ensure that those rights are upheld by the state and individuals are protected from unwarranted state intervention. In contrast, those who advocate for a functionalist conception of the constitution, and a 'guardianship' role of the state as leader and governor of the common enterprise, argue for a less interventionist role. They favour a greater margin of discretion for regulatory actors, arguing that their technical expertise and decision processes are more suited to making the multiple trade-offs, which are often involved in regulatory decisions where competing goals have to be pursued (ibid).

Turning to the relationship of the legislature and executive with regulatory systems, observing that there is a tension between the independence of regulators and their accountability is neither new nor surprising. Some constitutional governance arrangements are also more accommodating of independent regulatory agencies than others. There have been attempts to 'score' the independence of different regulators by focusing on their formal powers and accountability requirements (e.g., Hanretty and Koop 2011). In practice, however, navigating the boundaries of those critical relationships is complex, and is being constantly negotiated in the day-to-day performance of any regulatory regime through the formal and informal interactions of regulators and their political overseers. As the head of any regulatory organisation knows, independence is as much a state of mind as it is a series of formal legal or even political arrangements.

Furthermore, the executive and legislature can find it hard to organise themselves in such a way as to 'regulate the regulators' effectively, particularly as the complexity of the regulatory landscape and the technical nature of the regulatory functions increase. Hence, the creation of a plethora of other organisations which are charged with constitutionalising regulatory systems, either through ex ante controls or more usually ex post accountability arrangements. The extended 'intra-state' regulatory apparatus may include central 'better regulation' units, national auditors or equivalent bodies who seek to regulate and/or evaluate regulators' performance (see e.g., C. Scott 2001). They can include ombudsmen or other complaints bodies in addition to courts or specialist tribunals. *Ad hoc* inquiries may be appointed to investigate regulatory failures. There may also be extra-national bodies involved in overseeing state-based regulators and holding them to account within particular regulatory domains, on a legal or non-legal basis, as in the EU systems of regulation.

But the ability of any other organisations, whether national or extra-national, to play a role in constitutionalising regulatory systems is dependent on their own powers, capacities, resources and motivations. And those are in turn dependent on the willingness of constitutional/political actors to enable those organisations be effective. Here again the political character of the executive and legislature may be in tension with their constitutionalising role. The executive or legislature may deliberately deprive 'intra-state' actors of the ability to act as effective 'regulators of the regulators' by denying them adequate resources or information, or refusing to cede much effective power to them. And, of course, their effectiveness is always limited by the manner and extent to which those in the regulatory system respond.

Constitutionalising Behaviours

Behaviours are a key element of any social (including legal, economic or political) system, whether of organisations or individuals. As noted above, constitutional systems can use a range of regulatory governance techniques for monitoring and sanctioning regulators' and regulatory bodies' behaviour. Rules targeted at individuals can include provisions on conflicts of interest, lobbying, and limits on 'revolving door' appointments. More generally, regulatory organisations are likely to be subject to requirements for transparency and reporting, including protections for whistleblowers. They are usually monitored through audits, inquiries, and performance evaluations. As noted, they may be required to have complaints and dispute resolution procedures, including ombudsmen and dedicated compensation systems. Sanctions on individuals vary and may include dismissal, and for a regulatory organisation the ultimate sanction is abolition.

But no rule is self-enforcing and, from a constitutional perspective, the behaviours of regulators and regulatory bodies are often problematised in terms of how to manage their inevitable discretion. The potential for regulators to 'drift' from their mandates or be 'captured' by industry interests has been noted above. Cognitive psychology has long drawn attention to decision-making biases, particularly in situations of risk and uncertainty (Kahneman et al. 1982). More recently, attention has been drawn to the potential for 'cognitive capture': that regulators may regulate in favour of regulatees because they share a common cognitive framework and rely on the same sources of knowledge to inform their decisions (Black 2013a). Ultimately, understanding the behaviours of those in the regulatory system requires close engagement with their day-to-day decision making. It also requires deep theoretical understanding of the interactions of institutional structures and processes with organisational and individual behaviours, and there is a wealth of literature (outside legal scholarship) which explores the behaviour of individuals and organisations, including those of rational, sociological or historical institutionalism on which legal scholars could profitably draw (on which see e.g., Black 1997; W. R. Scott 2001; Powell and di Maggio 1992; Greenwood et al. 2017).

It should not be assumed that it is only regulators who may act in tension with accepted constitutional norms. Highly partisan politics can put constitutional settlements under strain, and constitutional actors can play 'constitutional hardball' by acting within the letter but not the spirit of the constitution, pushing their constitutional powers to their limits rather than acting with tolerance and restraint. As Levitsky and Ziblatt argue in the context of the US: 'When partisan hatred trumps politicians' commitment to the spirit of the Constitution, a system of checks and balances risks being subverted in two ways…. Under divided government … legislative and judicial watchdogs become partisan attack dogs…. Under unified government, [they can transform] from watchdog into lapdog', paving the way for authoritarian rule' (Levitsky and Ziblatt 2018, p. 126).

Building Trust and Legitimacy through Constitutionalisation

In turning to consider the element of trust and legitimacy in regulatory systems we come full circle, back to constitutional norms and values. From a constitutional perspective, whether or not regulators are (or should be) trusted and seen as legitimate, depends on the extent to which their existence and actions are seen to be in line with constitutional norms and values, that is, constitutionalised. The assessment can be made on the basis of the values of the constitutional system in which they are embedded, or on the basis of separate, normative constitutional theories.

One of the key mechanisms to build trust and legitimacy in a regulatory system, from a constitutional standpoint, is through systems of accountability. 'Looking down' on regulatory systems from a constitutional perspective, accountability is usually framed in terms of how to manage the tension between regulatory independence and legal and political control. There will never be a 'right' answer to that question in the abstract. The trade-offs that will inevitably have to be made between delegation and control are too complex, the dynamics of the relationship between regulatory and constitutional/political actors too dynamic, and the demands of different legitimacy communities too diverse for that to be so; instead relationships will have to be continuously re-evaluated against contested democratic, functional, normative and constitutional criteria.

Ultimately, considerations of trust and legitimacy bring us back to the intrinsically embedded position of state-based regulatory systems in the constitutional order. State-based regulatory systems can draw on the legitimacy of their constitutional system if they are perceived, and trusted, to be acting consistently with it. But acting constitutionally may be necessary but not sufficient for regulators to be perceived as trustworthy and legitimate by different legitimacy communities, hence their active attempts to create their own legitimacy. And if the state, or some of its core constitutional actors, are not trusted and seen as legitimate by those on whose behalf they purport to govern, then it is unlikely that its regulators will be either, no matter how hard they try. In such situations, perhaps paradoxically, it is those furthest from the state which are seen as the more legitimate, and perhaps even the more constitutionalised.

RECOMMENDED READING

Baldwin, R., Cave, M., & Lodge, M. (2010). *Oxford Handbook of Regulation*, Oxford: Oxford University Press.

Baldwin, R., Cave, M., & Lodge, M. (2012). *Understanding Regulation: Theory, Strategy, and Practice*, Oxford: Oxford University Press.

Harlow, C. & Rawlings, R. (2021). *Law and Administration*, Cambridge: Cambridge University Press.

Jordana, J., & Levi-Faur, D., eds. (2004). *The Politics of Regulation: Institutions and Regulatory Reforms for the Age of Governance*, Cheltenham: Edward Elgar Publishing.

Levitsky, S. & Ziblatt, D. (2018). *How Democracies Die*, New York: Broadway Books.

Lewis, M. (2018). *The Fifth Risk: Undoing Democracy*, UK: Penguin.

Majone, G. (1994). The Rise of the Regulatory State in Europe. *West European Politics*, 17 (3), 77–101.

OECD (2018). *Regulatory Policy Review*, Paris: OECD.

Scott, J. C. (1999). *Seeing Like a State: How Certain Schemes to Improve the Human Condition Have Failed*, New Haven: Yale University Press.

Scott, W. R. (2001). *Institutions and Organizations*, 2nd edn, London: Sage Publications.

Suchman, M. C. (1995). Managing Legitimacy: Strategic and Institutional Approaches. *The Academy of Management Review*, 20 (3), 571–610.

28

Cost–Benefit Analysis

Matthew Adler

This chapter will address the place of cost–benefit analysis (CBA) in constitutional law, by way of a case study. I'll describe, and puzzle over, CBA's absence from most U.S. constitutional doctrines, notwithstanding its major role in U.S. administrative law. The general questions that I seek to illuminate are by no means limited to the U.S. How might CBA figure within the tests that constitutional courts use to adjudicate alleged violations of constitutional rights? How might it serve to determine the structure of constitutional institutions? Would it be justified for CBA to play these doctrinal roles? But these general questions are fruitfully addressed in the context of a specific legal system – here, the U.S. legal system.[1]

I MODERATE WELFARISM AND CBA

Let's start by getting clear about some central concepts: moderate welfarism, quantitative CBA, and qualitative CBA.

Welfarism

By "moderate welfarism" I mean the family of ethical views that (1) are *welfarist* in their outcome ranking, and (2) make the welfarist outcome ranking a significant determinant of the ethical status of choices.

An outcome ranking stipulates how possible outcomes compare to each other (for any two outcomes, the first is ranked as better, worse, or equally good as the second), and does so in a transitive fashion.[2] An outcome ranking is *welfarist* if it hinges on individual well-being in the sense of satisfying the Pareto principle, which has two

---

[1] A natural way to extend this case study beyond the U.S. would be to assess whether proportionality analysis (used in many countries' systems of constitutional adjudication, [Stone Sweet & Mathews 2019], although not the U.S.) is in practice a form of CBA, and to evaluate whether it should be.

[2] Transitivity: If one outcome is at least as good as a second, in turn at least as good as a third, then the first is at least as good as the third.

parts: (1) if each person is equally well off in outcome *x* as she is in *y*, then the two outcomes are equally good; and (2) if at least one person is better off in *x* than *y*, and everyone is at least as well off in *x*, then *x* is better than *y*[3] (Adler 2012, chap. 1.).

Philosophers debate whether well-being consists in preference satisfaction, the occurrence of certain mental states (e.g., hedonic states), the realization of various objective goods, or some hybrid of these (Adler 2012, chap. 3). Moderate welfarism, as I mean to define it, is agnostic on this issue.

A wide variety of outcome rankings satisfy the Pareto principle and thus count as welfarist. I will use "overall welfare" as shorthand for any plausible welfarist outcome ranking. This includes not merely the familiar utilitarian ranking (outcome *x* at least as good as *y* if and only if the sum total of well-being in *x* is at least as large as the sum total in *y*) but also the other plausible welfarist outcome rankings discussed in the philosophical literature: prioritarianism, leximin, egalitarianism, and sufficientism (Adler 2019).

Consider now the role of the outcome ranking with respect to the ethical status of choices. An ethical view is consequentialist if the ethical status of a given (individual or governmental) choice, relative to a set of available choices, is *wholly determined* by the outcome ranking. The details of this determination are complex. Roughly, we can say that each choice corresponds to a probability distribution across outcomes. Whether one choice is better than, worse than, or equally good as a second depends upon the outcome probabilities for each choice, plus the outcome ranking (Adler 2019, chaps. 3, 4). An ethical view is *welfare-consequentialist* if the ethical status of choices is wholly determined by the outcome ranking *and* that ranking is welfarist.

My definition of "moderate welfarism" includes, but is not limited to, welfare consequentialism. It also encompasses ethical accounts that determine the ethical status of choices in light of *both* a welfarist outcome ranking *and* non-consequentialist factors. A paradigmatic such view is one that hybridizes overall well-being and deontological constraints (Kagan 1998). A constraint is an absolute or defeasible ethical norm against certain actions (e.g., killing), even if the action has good consequences. According to a hybrid view, actions that violate constraints are impermissible. As between permissible choices, one choice is better than a second if better in light of overall well-being.

Quantitative CBA

"CBA" is used in this chapter to mean a whole class of assessment methodologies – namely, those that assess choices (in particular, governmental choices, also referred to here as "policies") in light of some welfarist outcome ranking. CBA (of some sort) is justified by moderate welfarism. Any version of moderate welfarism posits *some* welfarist outcome ranking R^w, and then supposes that the ethical status of choices

---

[3] These are sufficient, not necessary conditions.

in a given choice set $\{a, b, c \ldots\}$ depends, in significant part, on how those choices compare in light of R^w. It will therefore be useful, according to this version of moderate welfarism, to have a methodology for evaluating choices in light of R^w. Such methodology is a type of CBA.

CBA, in its most rigorous form, is quantitative – in the sense that it measures well-being on some numerical scale. The form of quantitative CBA that predominates in governmental practice is "money-metric" CBA (Adler 2019). This technique measures well-being impacts on a monetary scale and aggregates.

Money-metric CBA is best justified as a rough proxy for the sum total of well-being (Adler & Posner 2006). The fact that policy a has a greater money-metric value than a^* indicates – although not with perfect accuracy – that a yields a greater sum total of well-being. Money-metric CBA fails to be a *perfect* indicator of this sum total because of the diminishing marginal utility of money.

In short, money-metric CBA is an imperfect tool for implementing the utilitarian outcome ranking. A better tool would be a utilitarian social welfare function (SWF). The SWF format quantifies individual well-being using an interpersonally comparable indicator of well-being, rather than by translating well-being changes into monetary equivalents. This methodology is a type of quantitative CBA that – like money-metric CBA – is very well developed in the academic literature. Different functional forms for the SWF correspond to the various species of welfarist outcome ranking. The utilitarian SWF orders policies in light of the sum total of well-being. We can also construct prioritarian, egalitarian, sufficientist, and leximin SWFs (Adler 2019).

Qualitative CBA

Qualitative CBA is a less structured counterpart to quantitative CBA. It is *less* structured than quantitative CBA – not wholly unstructured. Both versions of CBA begin by identifying the major well-being dimensions affected by the governmental policies under consideration, and then proceed to characterize the effect of each policy on those dimensions. An individual's well-being depends upon many different aspects of her life. CBA, to be practicable, cannot take full account of these aspects. Rather, it must focus on a relatively small list of welfare-relevant attributes, such as longevity, health, income, leisure, environmental quality, and so forth. The appropriate list will depend upon the type of policy at stake; for example, the assessment of public health policies may differentiate individuals by longevity, health, and income, while the assessment of tax policies (as per the standard approach in the academic literature on taxation) may ignore individuals' longevity and health, and instead focus on their income and leisure attributes.

Both versions of CBA then proceed to describe policy impacts on the types of well-being attributes (the "dimensions") singled out for consideration. This stage of the assessment, in a well-conducted CBA – qualitative or quantitative – will require numerical data. For example, in evaluating a public health policy, we'll need to estimate the number of premature fatalities avoided, the reduction in non-fatal health conditions, and the cost in reduced income.

The critical difference between qualitative CBA and its quantitative counterparts, what makes it "qualitative," is how it proceeds *after* the characterization step – how it aggregates information about the policy's effect on each dimension (income, health, longevity, leisure, etc.). These multidimensional impacts are not commensurated on a single scale of individual well-being, be it money (money-metric CBA) or an interpersonally comparable non-monetary scale of well-being (the SWF format). Instead, the analyst at this stage is asked to make an intuitive judgment about the policy's effect on overall welfare.

II CBA IN NON-CONSTITUTIONAL U.S. PUBLIC LAW

CBA currently plays a key role in the decisions of administrative agencies in the U.S. federal government, and in judicial review of federal administrative action. It would be incorrect to describe this role as merely the exercise of policy discretion by agencies. Rather, CBA now has a central place in U.S. administrative *law*.[4]

CBA enters into U.S. administrative law in three different ways. First, all so-called executive agencies (those whose heads are removable at will by the President) are required, by Presidential directive ("executive order"), to use CBA in issuing regulations (Renda 2011, Sunstein 2018b). This mandate was put in place by President Ronald Reagan in 1981, and has remained in force (in one form or the other) since then.[5] The requirement placed on agencies under the current CBA executive order (E.O. 12866, 3 C.F.R. 638 (1994)), is twofold. Substantively, agencies are required to conform to a CBA test in issuing regulations, if CBA is permitted by the underlying statute that the agency is implementing. In other words, CBA is made the master criterion for executive agency rulemaking, up to the limits of statutory constraint. Procedurally, agencies are required to prepare a written document, setting forth in detail the costs and benefits of each proposed regulation, for "significant" regulations (in particular, those anticipated to have at least $100 million of compliance costs). These documents, typically quite voluminous, are reviewed by a powerful oversight body (Office of Information and Regulatory Affairs, OIRA) within the federal Office of Management and Budget. The proposed regulation cannot be issued until OIRA approves it (or the President intervenes to settle a dispute between the agency and OIRA).

---

[4] "Administrative law" here is shorthand for *non-constitutional* administrative law. CBA is not seen to be constitutionally mandated for agencies. Rather, as we'll now see, it enters administrative law via non-constitutional routes.

[5] This chapter was drafted during the Trump administration and finalized (December 2022) during the Biden administration. President Trump did not repeal Executive Order 12866, and – as of December 2022 – President Biden has not done so either.

The CBA order itself does not expressly mandate quantitative rather than qualitative CBA. However, OIRA in an authoritative guidance document (Circular A4, Sept. 17, 2003), and in its oversight practices, instructs agencies to measure well-being impacts using a money metric as far as possible.

The CBA executive order is a legal text; it is legally binding on the agencies subject to it. Although the order is not directly judicially enforced, it *is* enforced by OIRA and treated as binding by executive agencies. Moreover, the order has major indirect effects on judicial decision, as we'll see momentarily.

The second route of CBA into U.S. administrative law is via statutory interpretation. Although a few statutes explicitly require CBA, this is unusual. Much more common is statutory language that invites but does not require CBA, or language that might well be taken to discourage or preclude it. Nonetheless, courts increasingly read statutes as permitting or even requiring CBA (Masur & Posner 2018).

This trend can be seen not merely at the court-of-appeals level, but in the Supreme Court's decisions. *Whitman v. American Trucking Associations*, 531 U.S. 457 (2001), was not receptive to CBA. Section 109 of the Clean Air Act directs the Environmental Protection Agency (EPA) to set national air quality standards at a level "requisite to protect the public health" with an "adequate margin of safety." The Court held that this language precluded the EPA from taking into consideration compliance costs. CBA was not even permitted by the statute, let alone required.

Since *American Trucking*, however, the Supreme Court has warmed considerably to CBA. In *Entergy v. Riverkeeper*, 556 U.S. 208 (2009), the EPA had used CBA in specifying cooling-water-intake structures for power plants. The relevant language of the Clean Water Act hardly encouraged CBA. It stipulated that the regulation of the intake structures should "reflect the best technology available for minimizing adverse environmental impact." Still, the Court read this language as permitting (although not requiring) the use of CBA.

EPA v. EME Home City Generation, 572 U.S. 489 (2014), involved the cross-state pollution provision of the Clean Air Act, requiring states to prohibit pollution that would travel across state lines and "contribute significantly" to diminished air quality in other states. It would seem that whether pollution "contributes significantly" to diminished air quality is independent of the cost of pollution control. Still, as in *Entergy*, the Court held that the EPA was permitted to use CBA.

Michigan v. EPA, 135 S. Ct. 2699 (2015), is the Court's most recent statutory interpretation case regarding CBA (as of the drafting of this chapter), and the most hospitable to the technique. Here, the EPA had *declined* to use CBA in slating power plants for regulation under Section 7412 of the Clean Air Act. The Court overturned the EPA's decision, holding that the "appropriate and necessary" language of the statutory provision *required* CBA (at least qualitative CBA). The Court stated, "No regulation is 'appropriate' if it does significantly more harm than good" (*id.* at 2707), and elaborated:

The Agency must consider cost – including, most importantly, cost of compliance – before deciding whether regulation is appropriate and necessary. We need not and do not hold that the law unambiguously required the Agency ... to conduct a formal cost-benefit analysis in which each advantage and disadvantage is assigned a monetary value. *Id.* at 2711.

The third channel by which CBA enters U.S. administrative law is section 706(2)(a) of the Administrative Procedure Act, 5 U.S.C. sec. 706(2)(A), which requires that the agency's reasoning process not be "arbitrary" or "capricious." This requirement has (evidently) very wide scope, and figures very frequently in judicial review of agency action (Pierce, Shapiro & Verkuil 2014, pp. 282–287, 340–345). It has become the legal basis for judicial oversight of the details of agency CBA. Agency CBA documents, whether prepared in order to comply with the CBA executive order (in the case of executive agencies) or otherwise, may well enter the record for judicial review that courts examine in adjudicating an arbitrary-and-capricious challenge under sec. 706(2)(A). How the CBA has been performed is then grist for the mill of the court's arbitrariness assessment (Cecot and Viscusi 2015; Sunstein 2017). Cecot and Viscusi (2015) find that courts often give close consideration to the details of an agency's CBA and with some regularity reject a CBA as inadequate.

III CBA IN U.S. CONSTITUTIONAL LAW: RIGHTS

The U.S. Supreme Court, in its case law, has set forth a dense and varied body of doctrines protecting individual rights – applying both to the federal government and to the states, and safeguarding a wide swath of rights, including free speech, free exercise of religion, the right to bear arms, freedom from unreasonable arrest or search, protection for private property, guarantees of adequate process both in criminal cases and in non-criminal adjudications, a right against "cruel and unusual" punishment, fundamental personal liberties, and a right to equal treatment.[6]

In addition, the Court applies a default standard to all state and federal lawmaking, grounded in both the Due Process and Equal Protection Clauses: so-called rational basis review (RBR). Every law is *at least* subject to RBR. It may also or instead trigger some right that yields heightened scrutiny (by which I mean any form of judicial scrutiny more demanding than RBR). The RBR requirement is that the law be rationally related to a legitimate governmental purpose. This default standard is applied quite deferentially by the courts, but it is not entirely toothless.

All the doctrines just mentioned are the Court's "first-order" doctrines: they are the rules that the Court uses, and instructs lower courts to use, in adjudicating challenges to state and federal governmental action. I'll now review the place of CBA in these first-order constitutional doctrines. CBA as a second-order judicial

---

[6] Chemerinsky (2019) is an excellent treatise reviewing much of U.S. constitutional rights doctrine.

methodology – as a tool that the Court employs in deciding what the first-order doctrines should be – is addressed subsequently, in Part V.

CBA rarely appears in this body of first-order doctrine. The biggest exception is procedural due process doctrine, governing the structure of non-criminal adjudications. (Criminal adjudications are covered by more specific constitutional guarantees). The Due Process Clause prohibits the deprivation of "life, liberty or property" without "due process of law," and thus the claimant must first show that at least one such protected interest of hers is implicated by the adjudicatory process that she challenges. If so, the court moves on to determine whether constitutionally sufficient process has been afforded, and does so using the test set forth in *Mathews v. Eldridge*, 424 U.S. 319 (1976).

> [I]dentification of the specific dictates of due process generally requires consideration of three distinct factors: First, the private interest that will be affected by the official action; second, the risk of an erroneous deprivation of such interest through the procedures used, and the probable value, if any, of additional or substitute procedural safeguards; and, finally, the Government's interest, including the function involved and the fiscal and administrative burdens that the additional or substitute procedural requirement would entail. *Id.* at 335.

This test directs the court to determine whether additional procedures are constitutionally required (beyond those already afforded to individuals by statute or regulation) by considering the benefit of additional procedure in reducing adjudicatory error, and then balancing that error-reduction benefit against the cost of additional procedure (here taking into account the importance to the individual of the benefit or burden at stake in the adjudication). In short, *Mathews* tells courts to test the constitutional sufficiency of adjudicatory procedures by using qualitative CBA.

CBA also enters into the Court's Fourth Amendment jurisprudence, prohibiting "unreasonable searches and seizures." The role of CBA in the Fourth Amendment case law is complex. Certain types of searches or arrests cannot be undertaken by law enforcement without a warrant from a neutral magistrate, obtained on a showing of probable cause. In other contexts, however, the Court may engage in a qualitative CBA. For example, it does so in evaluating Fourth Amendment excessive force claims. See, for example, *Graham v. Connor*, 490 U.S. 386, 396 (1989).

Finally, as of the drafting of this chapter, CBA had recently appeared within the constitutional case law governing abortion rights. For three decades following the decision in *Planned Parenthood v. Casey*, 505 U.S. 833 (1992), the Court followed the "undue burden" framework, which evaluated restrictions on pre-viability abortion by asking whether the restriction had the purpose or effect of placing a "substantial obstacle" in the path of the abortion right. In *Whole Woman's Health v. Hellerstedt*, 136 S.Ct. 2292 (2016), which struck down a state law imposing stringent safety requirements on abortion facilities and providers, the Court (per Justice Breyer, generally a proponent of CBA) clarified that the undue burden test involved a qualitative CBA: courts should "consider the burdens a law imposes on abortion access together with the benefits those laws confer." *Id.* at 2309. Performing a qualitative CBA, the court found that the law would not significantly increase abortion safety, but would force many existing facilities to close and thereby reduce women's access to abortion.

In June 2022, subsequent to the drafting of this chapter, the Court in *Dobbs v. Jackson Women's Health Organization*, 142 S.Ct. 2228 (2022), overruled *Casey* and *Roe v. Wade*, 410 U.S. 113 (1973), and held that the Constitution does not protect a right to abortion.

With these three (now two) exceptions, CBA is absent from the Court's rights doctrines. To be clear, by CBA I mean something more specific than a multi-factor balancing test. Constitutional scholars often use "balancing" to mean a quite general class of right doctrines, whereby rights are defeasible by countervailing considerations, or multiple factors are weighed against each other (Aleinikoff 1987; Gardbaum 2010). By CBA, I mean either (a) quantitative CBA (in fact, constitutional doctrine never requires courts to use this type of CBA) or (b) qualitative CBA, in which a law's various impacts are informally balanced *as a matter of overall welfare*. Qualitative CBA tells the court that the weight (informally) assigned to a given impact should be its *welfare* weight: the difference it makes to overall well-being. Very few rights doctrines are plausibly interpreted as instructing courts to do this.

The reader might object that even the doctrines I've singled out as embodying qualitative CBA are *best* interpreted not as that, but as multifactor balancing of some other sort. Perhaps – but if so, this simply underscores my main point, that CBA plays little role in constitutional rights doctrine.

It's worth noting that in *District of Columbia v. Heller*, 554 U.S. 570 (2008) (holding that the Second Amendment confers a personal right to firearms), Justice Scalia writing for the majority rejected Justice Breyer's proposal to resolve Second Amendment challenges via CBA.

> He proposes ... none of the traditionally expressed levels [of scrutiny] (strict scrutiny, intermediate scrutiny, rational basis), but rather a judge-empowering "interest-balancing inquiry" that "asks whether the statute burdens a protected interest in a way or to an extent that is out of proportion to the statute's salutary effects upon other important governmental interests." ... We know of no other enumerated constitutional right whose core protection has been subjected to a freestanding "interest-balancing" approach. *Id.* at 634.

Scalia's claim that CBA (interest balancing) *never* appears in constitutional rights doctrine is overstated, but not by much.

Note that Scalia in this quotation distinguishes between CBA and the tiers of scrutiny. This is a correct, and significant, distinction. The tiers of scrutiny have the structure of means-end tests, *not* CBA. Rational basis review (RBR), a default level of scrutiny for all laws absent a right that triggers heightened scrutiny, was mentioned above. To repeat: it asks whether the law is rationally related to a legitimate governmental purpose. Strict scrutiny is the most stringent of the three tiers. It is used in many different areas of rights doctrine: for example, to evaluate equal protection challenges to racially discriminatory laws; to assess free-speech challenges to "content-based" laws restricting speech; and to adjudicate restrictions on certain fundamental liberties, such as the liberty of contraception. If strict scrutiny is triggered, the law will be struck down unless narrowly tailored to a compelling governmental interest. Intermediate scrutiny also figures repeatedly in judicial doctrine. For example, it is the standard for equal-protection challenges to gender discrimination and for free-speech challenges to the regulation of commercial speech, and is employed by the court for some fundamental liberties not covered by strict scrutiny (such as marriage, parenting, and familial association). Intermediate scrutiny asks whether the law is substantially related to an important governmental interest (Chemerinsky 2019; Fallon 2019).

Clearly, RBR is not CBA. RBR asks merely that the government identify some legitimate purpose; this could be a purpose to advance some dimension of well-being (health, safety, longevity, environmental quality, income …), but it need not be. Further, RBR doesn't instruct the court to balance the law's benefit – be it a welfare benefit, in advancing some well-being dimension, or a non-welfare "benefit," in pursuing some non-welfare goal – against the law's costs. As long as the law plausibly achieves some benefit, it passes the rational basis test.

It might be objected that CBA, if incorporated into judicial doctrine, should build in a significant measure of judicial deference to legislatures. But RBR is different from deferential CBA, which would ask something like: was it rational for the legislature to believe that the benefits of the law outweighed the costs? Such a test takes account not only of plausible benefits but also of plausible costs; by contrast, RBR is purely benefit-focused.

Intermediate and strict scrutiny, too, are not CBA. They remain benefit-focused, with the twist that the benefit must be graded as "important" (intermediate scrutiny) or "compelling" (strict scrutiny). Here, it might be objected that each test could be understood as asking the judge to engage in a kind of category-level CBA. Specifically, the intermediate scrutiny test could be construed as telling the judge the following: "Imagine, in a qualitative way, the average cost of laws that trigger intermediate scrutiny. Now, categorize an interest as 'important' for purposes of intermediate scrutiny if and only if the average benefit of laws advancing that interest is greater than this average cost." A parallel interpretation could be given of strict scrutiny.

But category-level CBA is not the same as a CBA of each law. It is much cruder – permitting laws that would fail law-by-law CBA, and vice versa. Let C^{int} be the average cost of laws that trigger intermediate scrutiny. Assume that a law advances some interest which is "important" in the proposed sense, namely that the average benefit of laws advancing that interest is B^*, with $B^* > C^{int}$. Let C be the cost of the specific law, and B the benefit. It could be the case that $B < C$ even though $B^* > C^{int}$.

Conversely, it might well be that the law passes law-by-law CBA (B > C) even though it fails intermediate scrutiny (the average benefit of laws advancing the type of interest advanced by this law is $B^+ < C^{int}$). A parallel critique applies, of course, to strict scrutiny understood as category-level CBA.

See generally Kaplow (2019a, 2019b), analyzing the difference between CBA and "structured decision procedures."

IV CBA IN U.S. CONSTITUTIONAL LAW: STRUCTURE

The U.S. Constitution doesn't merely protect individual rights, but also constrains the institutional structure of the federal government, and divides power between the federal government and the states, and between the states.

Federal Government Institutions

CBA plays no role in the Court's doctrines governing the institutional structure of the federal government: the "separation of powers" and other such doctrines. This is *not* because the Constitution's text in this domain is invariably so clear as to preclude CBA. On a number of issues, the text is quite vague. For example, it anticipates that there will be officials tasked with implementing the law other than the President, but says little about how these officials will be removed, how the President will oversee them, and what oversight role Congress can have.

Moreover, on issues where the text is unclear, the Court sometimes uses functional tests. For example, the test that was articulated in *Morrison v. Olson*, 487 U.S. 654, 691 (1988), for the constitutionality of statutory restrictions on the President's authority to remove subordinate officials, is "whether the removal restrictions are of such a nature that they impede the President's ability to perform his constitutional duty, and the functions of the officials in question must be analyzed in that light." "Impede" seems to anticipate some kind of balancing of the reasons for and against limiting Presidential removal power. However, the Court in *Morrison* gave no indication that this balancing should take the form of CBA, that is, asking whether restricting removal is likely to increase or reduce overall welfare.[7]

Federalism: Scope of Federal Power

Under the doctrine of enumerated powers, each provision in a federal statute must fall within at least one of the powers explicitly granted by the Constitution. The Supreme Court doesn't rely on CBA in construing the scope of the enumerated powers. I'll illustrate by discussing the Court's doctrines regarding the Commerce

---

[7] In *Seila Law v. CFPB*, 140 S.Ct. 2183 (2020), the Court abandoned the *Morrison* balancing without overturning the specific result in *Morrison*.

Clause – the power "[t]o regulate Commerce ... among the several States" – which is the chief source of federal regulatory power.

Modern (post-1937) Commerce Clause doctrine is quite expansive – authorizing Congress to regulate not only interstate activities, but also intrastate activities that "substantially affect" interstate commerce [Chemerinsky (2019) reviews this case law]. Using this formulation, the Court has upheld federal wage and hour requirements applied to firms that ship only a portion of their supplies interstate; a wheat production quota applied to a small dairy farmer; the regulation of strip mining; a criminal prohibition on loan sharking; a prohibition on race discrimination in public accommodations; and a ban on marijuana cultivation or possession applied to individuals growing marijuana at home for medical use. Still, modern understanding of the Commerce Clause is not limitless. For example, in *NFIB v. Sebelius*, 567 U.S. 519 (2012), five justices (without agreeing on a single majority opinion) found the individual-mandate provision of the Affordable Care Act – requiring each individual to maintain health insurance coverage – to be beyond the scope of the Commerce Clause.

Beginning with Tiebout (1956), economists have theorized about the welfare-maximizing allocation of governmental authority in a federal system. A striking feature of the Court's Commerce Clause jurisprudence is that the Court *lacks* any such theory. The "substantial effects" case law *doesn't* ask whether it would be better, on balance, for the type of activity at issue in a given case to be allocated to federal or state authority. Instead, the Court focuses on the *causal* impact of intrastate activity. Justices who favor federal authority over some activity argue that there is a clear causal nexus between the activity and out-of-state harms; justices who reject federal authority argue that this nexus is attenuated. This approach ignores, first, that in-state activities causing significant out-of-state harms might also cause significant in-state harms. Unless the pattern of out-of-state harms and benefits is quite different from the pattern of in-state harms and benefits, the welfare case for federal intervention is not established. Conversely, states might generally face a collective-action problem in regulating activity by mobile actors (who can threaten to move away from a jurisdiction that regulates stringently), even if the activity has largely in-state causal effects.

As a consequence of the Court's failure to engage in any kind of CBA regarding the appropriate location of regulatory power, the pattern of Commerce Clause decisions appears haphazard from the point of view of overall national welfare. For example, in *Gonzales v. Raich*, 545 U.S. 1 (2005), the marijuana-ban case, the Court reasoned that home-grown marijuana could, in the aggregate, affect the volume and price of marijuana sold in the interstate market. By contrast, in *Sebelius*, the five justices who rejected Congressional authority to enact the individual-mandate provision of the Affordable Care Act reasoned that the mandate was a regulation of *inaction* rather than *action*, and hence especially inapt to satisfy the substantial-effect test (construed causally).

But, clearly, there is a very strong overall-welfare case in favor of allowing Congress to regulate the health insurance market, rather than leaving it within exclusive state jurisdiction. Individual states might well hesitate to impose an individual insurance-purchase mandate or concomitant requirements on health insurers (such as the Affordable Care Act's requirement that insurers not exclude or price discriminate against those with preexisting conditions) – fearing that healthy individuals or insurers would move to other states. Conversely, the overall-welfare case for according the federal government comprehensive authority over drug policy is hard to see. The costs of drugs are not imposed asymmetrically on out-of-staters, and states are not disabled from regulating or prohibiting drugs by the threat of exit.

Federalism: Scope of State Power

In the U.S. constitutional system, state legislation is subject to federal constitutional constraints. These constraints mainly concern individual rights – but not invariably. The so-called "dormant Commerce Clause" is a longstanding body of case law that elaborates a federalism constraint on state law (see Chemerinsky 2019). The worry underlying dormant Commerce Clause doctrine is that state legislatures might enact statutes that create costs for out-of-staters – costs which state legislatures are incentivized to discount, since their electorates are comprised of in-staters.

The core of Supreme Court dormant Commerce Clause doctrine is a non-discrimination rule: a law that discriminates against out-of-state economic actors is presumptively invalid, and will be upheld only if the state can establish a good reason for the discrimination. This non-discrimination rule is surely a sensible part of dormant Commerce Clause doctrine. However, the non-discrimination rule needs to be supplemented by some kind of scrutiny for facially neutral state laws. If in-state and out-of-state actors are differentially economically situated, a neutral state law might be net beneficial taking into consideration only in-state costs and benefits – and hence enacted by the state legislature – but net costly from a national point of view.

Indeed, *Pike v. Bruce Church*, 397 U.S. 137, 142 (1970), attentive to this concern, instructed courts to undertake a CBA with nationwide scope in adjudicating dormant Commerce Clause challenges: "Where the statute regulates even-handedly to effectuate a legitimate local public interest, and its effects on interstate commerce are only incidental, it will be upheld unless the burden imposed on such commerce is clearly excessive in relation to the putative local benefits." But the *Pike* CBA is now rarely used by the Court to strike down state laws. While *Pike* has not been overruled (see *South Dakota v. Wayfair*, 138 S.Ct. 2080 (2018)), it has effectively become a dead letter (Francis 2017).

V JUSTIFICATION?

What, if anything, justifies CBA's absence from U.S. constitutional doctrine? In addressing this question, I'll presuppose moderate welfarism. Recall that "moderate welfarism" denotes a wide family of ethical views: those that accord overall well-being a significant if not necessarily decisive role in determining the ethical status of choices. I find moderate welfarism to be very plausible and, I hope, so will many readers. It is not possible, within the brief compass of this chapter, to make the ethical case for moderate welfarism, and thus, I'll simply take it as given.

Some readers, to be sure, will reject moderate welfarism. From this perspective, the absence of CBA from constitutional doctrine is well justified. What is puzzling, rather, is why CBA should play an important role *anywhere* in the legal system, as it now does in U.S. administrative law. From the perspective of moderate welfarism, however, the puzzle runs in the other direction.

Consider a governmental actor who has selected a particular choice a, from a set of choices $\{a, b, ...\}$, including inaction. This actor could be a legislature, selecting among possible laws to enact; an administrative agency, selecting among possible regulations; or some other type of governmental actor.

Assume that the actor's choices are subject to judicial review. Consider two different possible types of doctrines that the reviewing court might employ: D+ and D*. D+ is aligned to overall well-being – in the sense that D+ characterizes a as legally permissible if a is at least as good in light of overall well-being as the alternative choices in the actor's choice set, and impermissible if a is significantly worse in light of overall well-being than some alternative(s). D* is not aligned to overall well-being in this sense.

From the perspective of moderate welfarism, it would be ethically better, pro tanto, for constitutional doctrine to take the form of D+ rather than D*. That is: it would be ethically better, in light of overall well-being, for constitutional doctrine to take the form of D+ rather than D*; and ethically appropriate, all things considered, unless there are non-consequentialist ethical factors (e.g., deontological constraints) in play that argue for D*.

I've described D+ and D* quite abstractly. But what, more concretely, are the characteristic features of a constitutional doctrine (D+) aligned to overall well-being? Well, it would seem, constitutional doctrine aligns to overall well-being by *incorporating* CBA. CBA is a methodology for operationalizing the overall-welfare criterion. It is a methodology whereby the analyst attends, consciously and carefully, to how the various possible choices being assessed compare in light of that criterion. So, it would seem, D+ is such that the reviewing court is instructed to assess the constitutional permissibility of the actor's choices by checking whether the actor has performed CBA and, if so, reviewing that analysis, or by undertaking its own CBA. Indeed, as we saw in Part II, administrative-law judicial review doctrines do incorporate CBA. And so, it would seem, should constitutional doctrine.

It might be objected that the distinctive function of *constitutional* doctrine is to effectuate non-consequentialist ethical factors. To make this objection more concrete, consider a moderate welfarism that includes deontological constraints. Constraints, of course, *override* ("trump") overall welfare; if the actor's choice a violates a constraint, then a is ethically impermissible even if a is the best choice in light of overall welfare. The moderate welfarist who endorses deontological constraints might try to explain the absence of CBA from constitutional law by arguing that (a) CBA can't be used to determine the content of deontological constraints, since the very point of constraints is to override overall welfare; and therefore (b) CBA doesn't figure in constitutional law, since the function of constitutional law is to effectuate constraints.

Indeed, *some* portions of U.S. constitutional doctrine might plausibly be seen as implementing deontological constraints. It is commonplace to refer to constitutional rights as trumps, to see them as constraining governmental choice notwithstanding considerations of overall welfare (Dworkin 1977). Yet much U.S. constitutional doctrine has no plausible nexus to deontological constraints. These doctrines neither implement plausible constraints, nor (in general) do they incorporate CBA. This is puzzling.

(1) *Rational basis review versus heightened scrutiny in rights doctrine*. As already mentioned, constitutional rights doctrine employs RBR as a default, and contains various triggers for heightened scrutiny. The nature of the trigger, and the nature of the more-than-RBR scrutiny, depends upon the right; often (but not always), heightened scrutiny consists in intermediate scrutiny or strict scrutiny.

It is quite contestable whether all of the various triggers for heightened scrutiny correspond to plausible deontological constraints. In any event, RBR certainly does not. The standing requirement that all legislation be rationally related to a legitimate governmental purpose *doesn't* ask the court to check whether the legislation subject to review infringes rights that trump overall welfare. But neither does RBR ask the court to undertake CBA; instead, as observed earlier, it is a means-end test. In short, for *any* moderate welfarist – whether she accepts or rejects deontological constraints – RBR is a puzzle.

(2) *Structural doctrines*. It's easy to see how deontological constraints might be reflected in doctrines protecting constitutional rights, but less clear how they would be reflected in structural doctrines. But let's grant that such a connection could obtain. That said, structural doctrines in U.S. constitutional law do not in fact implement plausible deontological constraints, nor (in general) do they reflect CBA. To illustrate: the Commerce Clause allows the federal government to regulate not only interstate activities, but also intrastate activities with a "substantial effect" on interstate commerce. Clearly, this test has nothing to do with deontological constraints. And yet Commerce Clause doctrine doesn't incorporate CBA. Thus, for *any* moderate welfarist – whether one who endorses some deontological constraints, or a welfare consequentialist who rejects deontological constraints – Commerce Clause doctrine is a puzzle.

In what follows, I consider possible justifications for the absence of CBA from U.S. constitutional doctrine even with respect to governmental choices that are "ethically regulated by overall well-being." That is to say, some governmental actor has selected a particular choice a, from a set of choices $\{a, b, ...\}$. Her choice from this set is not subject to a deontological constraint or other non-consequentialist ethical factor, and so the ethical status of *a* (relative to this choice set) is determined by overall well-being. For welfare consequentialists, *every* governmental choice is ethically regulated by overall well-being; for other moderate welfarists, at least some choices are.

What needs to be justified is a certain divergence between ethics and law, namely this: the governmental actor's choice is *ethically* regulated by overall well-being, and yet the *legal* doctrines guiding courts in reviewing this choice do not, in any way, incorporate a procedure for assessing choices in light of overall well-being (the procedure of CBA).

Text of the Constitution

One possible justification for CBA's absence from constitutional doctrine, even with respect to choices ethically regulated by overall well-being, points to the text of the Constitution. "Reviewing courts are *legally* obligated to follow the text of the Constitution, notwithstanding ethical considerations that may point in a different direction in the case at hand. Moreover, a judicial practice of following the text stabilizes the political system and thereby conduces to overall well-being in the long run."

However, the actual practice of the U.S. Supreme Court is only loosely textualist. Many extant doctrines have only an attenuated connection to the text. This is either because the relevant part of the text is quite open-ended, or because the Court has been willing to stretch the meaning of more specific text. This isn't to say that *all* of constitutional doctrine is loosely connected to the text, but that *much* is. (In these parts of constitutional law, what is doing the stabilizing work is not the text itself, but the corpus of Supreme Court case law.)

There are numerous non-CBA doctrines that the Court could swap for CBA without departing further from the text than it currently does. Here are some illustrative examples. Virtually all constitutional rights doctrines vis-à-vis the states are textually grounded in the open-ended language of the 14th Amendment's Due Process and Equal Protection Clauses; nothing in this language itself requires the tiers of scrutiny, or other non-CBA tests, rather than CBA, and indeed the word "due" (appropriate) in the Due Process Clause actually invites CBA. The First Amendment prohibits Congress from "abridging the freedom of speech." These words do not comprise a textual mandate for strict or intermediate scrutiny (the predominant form of First Amendment doctrine), rather than CBA, and indeed in the past, some justices argued for adjudicating First Amendment challenges via case-by-case balancing (Frantz 1962). The Fourth Amendment uses reasonableness language that seems to invite CBA. The text of the Constitution omits an equal protection clause governing the federal government, but nonetheless the Court has held that the federal government is subject to the very equal protection doctrines that bind state governments – doing so by pushing against the limits of the (already capacious) Fifth Amendment Due Process Clause to read it as having an implicit equal protection component.

As for structure: the Commerce Clause empowers Congress to "regulate Commerce ... among the several States" – which seems to confer regulatory power only with respect to interstate transactions, or perhaps also steps preceding or following interstate transactions – and yet the Court has stretched this language to permit the regulation of all intrastate economic activities that substantially affect interstate commerce. The text of the Commerce Clause hardly requires the "substantial effect" test as opposed to CBA. The dormant Commerce Clause lacks a textual basis entirely. Much doctrine concerning the internal structure of the federal government finds textual grounding in the open-ended terms "legislative," "executive," and "judicial."

Original Meaning

Originalists assert that the content of the Constitution is legally fixed by the criterion of original meaning. That is to say: the Court is legally obliged to craft its doctrine to accord with the original meaning of the relevant text, even if the text supports a different reading, and even if (in the Court's judgment) ethical considerations would argue for a doctrine that diverges from original meaning.

Whether the content of the Constitution is legally fixed by the criterion of original meaning is, to say the least, contestable. Suffice it to say that, on H. L. A. Hart's "rule of recognition" analysis of the content of law – all law is either part of the foundational rule of recognition generally accepted by judges, or derivable from the rule of recognition – a resort to original meaning is not legally mandated (Adler 2009). Some justices do appeal to original meaning as the master test, but others quite explicitly acknowledge their departures from that test. A striking example: The centrist justice Anthony Kennedy, in the same-sex marriage case, *Obergefell v Hodges*, 135 S.Ct. 2584 (2015), wrote:

> The identification and protection of fundamental rights is an enduring part of the judicial duty to interpret the Constitution. That responsibility, however, has not been reduced to any formula. Rather, it requires courts to exercise reasoned judgment in identifying interests of the person so fundamental that the State must accord them its respect.... That process is guided by many of the same considerations relevant to analysis of other constitutional provisions that set forth broad principles rather than specific requirements. History and tradition guide and discipline this inquiry but do not set its outer boundaries. That method respects our history and learns from it without allowing the past alone to rule the present. *Id.* at 2598 (internal quotations and citations omitted).

Indeed, many extant doctrines, in fact, lack an originalist warrant. This is true, for example, of doctrines protecting contraception, abortion,[8] and nonprocreative

---

[8] As mentioned earlier, constitutional protection for abortion was withdrawn by *Dobbs v. Jackson Women's Health* (2022). The case law protecting abortion, from *Roe v. Wade* (1973) up until *Dobbs*, had no originalist warrant.

sex, as well as same-sex marriage; of the recognition of gender discrimination (not merely race discrimination) as constitutionally suspect; of various components of race discrimination doctrine (e.g., the prohibition of segregated schools, and conversely the strong presumption against affirmative action); and of the broad scope of protected speech under the First Amendment. As Richard Fallon has observed, the entire tier-of-scrutiny structure, and the identification of various interests as "compelling" or "substantial," lacks originalist warrant (Fallon 2019, pp. 76–81).

In short: the moderate welfarist who (plausibly) denies that the content of the Constitution is legally fixed by the criterion of original meaning will see in originalism no obstacle to swapping CBA for current non-CBA doctrines (many of which in fact have no basis in original meaning).

Democratic Legitimacy

Might the absence of CBA from constitutional doctrine be defended on the grounds of democratic legitimacy? [See Ely (1980) for a classic presentation of constitutional theory animated by concerns for democratic legitimacy.] Note that moderate welfarists might deny that democratic legitimacy has intrinsic ethical weight (e.g., welfare consequentialists might insist that two laws with the same overall-welfare consequences are equally good, ethically, notwithstanding that one was enacted democratically while the second was not), and yet still accept that *legal* norms concerned with democratic legitimacy have a long-run ethical benefit (on the instrumental grounds that democratic institutions tend to be better for overall welfare).

Consider, then, two candidate roles for democratic legitimacy within U.S. constitutional law, denoted "DL-1" and "DL-2." DL-1: *A reviewing court should accord statutes or other democratically adopted legal texts a presumption of validity – a presumption that can only be overcome by sufficiently strong countervailing reasons.* It's plausible that DL-1 or something like it *is* part of U.S. constitutional law. Consider that RBR, the default level of judicial scrutiny of all statutes (state and federal), embodies a presumption of validity. A court is supposed to strike down the statute using RBR only if clearly indefensible as good public policy. The challenger must show that there is no plausible conception of legitimate public purpose and no reasonable view of the facts at hand which would support the statute.

CBA could be incorporated into constitutional doctrine consistently with DL-1. In particular, RBR could be swapped for a deferential, default test making reference to CBA. Such a test (for short, RB-CBA) could ask something like the following: Is the statute rationally related to overall well-being, or rationally related to legitimate considerations that the legislature might rationally take to override overall well-being? RB-CBA would allow the legislator to decide among accounts of well-being (hedonic vs. preference based vs. …); to select among conceptions of overall well-being (utilitarianism vs. prioritarianism vs. …); to select plausible non-consequentialist ethical factors; and to make factual judgments relevant to all of the above. Unlike RBR, RB-CBA is keyed to overall well-being – and so moderate welfarists should prefer RB-CBA to RBR. But, like RBR, RB-CBA accords significant deference to statutes, and so is consistent with DL-1.

Consider now DL-2, a second putative democratic-legitimacy norm. DL-2: *Unelected federal judges should not rely upon overall well-being or other mere "policy" considerations in crafting legal doctrine, except where such considerations have some antecedent democratic warrant (e.g., a statute that endorses CBA).* The idea behind DL-2 is that certain desiderata, such as overall well-being, are "policy" goals that are central to the legislative process but that judges should ignore. Note that DL-2 goes significantly beyond DL-1. It precludes CBA from entering constitutional doctrine even in the form of RB-CBA. It also precludes the court from relying upon CBA to invalidate decisions by any governmental actor, not merely legislatures.

I don't think DL-2 is actually embodied in U.S. legal practice. First, DL-2 is inconsistent with the fact that CBA is not entirely absent from constitutional doctrine. It does occasionally appear, as described above (most notably in the *Mathews* test within procedural due process doctrine). Second, and more significantly, DL-2 is inconsistent with the full scope of CBA's current role in administrative law doctrine – specifically, with the weight that courts give CBA in interpreting statutes. As described earlier (Part II), courts increasingly use what might be described as a pro-CBA presumption in the process of statutory interpretation. CBA is seen to be permitted unless there is clear evidence of congressional intent to the contrary, and sometimes required despite ambiguous language. *But this pro-CBA presumption used in reading statutes does not itself have a legislative warrant.* Like most other principles of statutory interpretation, it is court-made. Very few statutes explicitly require CBA, and Congress has never enacted a general presumption in favor of CBA.

First-order vs. Second-order CBA

The court's "first-order" doctrines, recall, are the rules that the Court uses, and instructs lower courts to use, in adjudicating challenges to state and federal lawmaking or other governmental action. It might be better, in light of overall well-being, for some first-order doctrines to abjure CBA. The application of CBA, to a given governmental choice, is hard to predict ex ante. This uncertainty might cause a pattern of behavior by governmental actors (or private individuals) that is worse, in light of overall well-being, as compared to behavior that would flow from certain first-order doctrines that are more determinate than CBA and, therefore, more predictable. Further, lower courts applying CBA to evaluate governmental action might make mistakes. The pattern of decisions by courts using CBA could be worse, in light of overall well-being, than if they were to use certain first-order doctrines that are more determinate and, therefore, easier to apply.

These sorts of considerations, familiar from the legal theory literature regarding rules versus standards, *could* provide persuasive moderate-welfarist grounds in favor of certain relatively determinate, non-CBA first-order doctrines, in some areas of constitutional law. But – of course – the argument at hand doesn't show that *any* relatively determinate non-CBA first-order doctrine is better for overall welfare than CBA. The Supreme Court – the body that promulgates first-order doctrines, in its majority opinions – would need to engage in second-order CBA. With a few exceptions,[9] there is little evidence of the Court doing that.

Judicial Expertise

Integrating information about how a given policy affects each of a variety of well-being dimensions (health, longevity, income, etc.), so as to arrive at an assessment of the policy with respect to overall well-being, is not straightforward. Quantitative CBA undertakes this integrative step in a rigorous, structured manner – via a well-being measure of some sort, be it money (money-metric CBA) or an interpersonally comparable well-being indicator (the SWF framework) – while qualitative CBA leaves the analyst to his or her intuitions. It's hard to see why unstructured intuition, in this instance, is epistemically more reliable than quantitative CBA. Just the opposite. Thus (we might plausibly conclude) quantitative CBA is the better tool. Its verdicts generally provide stronger evidence regarding how policies compare with respect to overall well-being, than do the verdicts of qualitative CBA.

Where does this leave constitutional doctrine? Federal courts deciding constitutional questions could, conceivably, undertake a de novo quantitative CBA. A trial court could do so via the various fact-finding processes available to such courts; for example, the parties to the case could hire CBA experts to testify or submit reports. An appellate court, although more restricted in its factfinding capacity, could do so via amicus briefing. Conceivably, an office of economic analysis could be created within the federal judiciary to assist the courts, just as the Supreme Court now uses a large library staff to marshal linguistic and historical evidence.

Admittedly, de novo quantitative CBA by the courts would be quite demanding of judicial resources. And one might worry that judges lack the expertise reliably to undertake CBA (notwithstanding the factfinding channels open to trial courts and even appellate courts).

Less ambitiously, courts can *review* quantitative CBA undertaken by other bodies (legislatures, administrative agencies). This now regularly occurs in the non-constitutional domain (see above, Part II), as part of arbitrary-and-capricious review

---

[9] See *Riley* v. *California*, 573 U.S. 373, 398 (2014), stating that the Court should use interest balancing to determine the doctrinal rules defining the categories of permissible warrantless searches, which rules will in turn guide police officers.

under the Administrative Procedure Act. Constitutional doctrine could be structured so as to incentivize non-judicial actors to engage in quantitative CBA – then to be reviewed by the courts. For example, the Supreme Court could incorporate CBA into some area of first-order doctrine and, concomitantly, instruct lower courts to apply the test more deferentially if the body whose action is under review had arrived at that action via a well-conducted, quantitative CBA.

A different route to integrating quantitative CBA into the workings of the federal courts is to have the Supreme Court bolster its own institutional capacity to perform this methodology, and then engage in second-order CBA so as to arrive at first-order doctrines which are applied (without CBA) by the lower courts.

One line of objection to incorporating CBA into constitutional doctrine runs as follows: (1) judges lack the capacity to undertake quantitative CBA; and (2) qualitative CBA is so intuitive and "mushy" as to provide little evidence regarding how policies compare with respect to overall well-being. Whether (2) is true depends on the non-CBA doctrine to which qualitative CBA is being compared. In any event, for the reasons discussed in the immediately preceding paragraphs, I believe that (1) is too downbeat about the prospects for incorporating quantitative CBA into constitutional law.

CONCLUSION

This chapter has examined the potential role of CBA in constitutional adjudication, using the United States as a case study. Notwithstanding the fact that CBA is a pervasive methodology in the academic literature on governmental policy, and notwithstanding its central place in U.S. administrative law, CBA is largely absent from constitutional adjudication. I've suggested that this absence is more problematic than it may, at first blush, seem. The reader's first reaction might well be: "*Of course* CBA is absent from constitutional doctrine, since constitutional rights trump the overall-welfare considerations reflected by CBA." Yet CBA plays virtually no role in *all* of constitutional doctrine, not merely fundamental rights doctrine. It's absent from structural doctrines, too; and the default RBR (rational basis review) standard that the Court uses to police legislation that doesn't infringe fundamental rights is not CBA. Nor, I argue, can CBA's absence be justified by appeal to the text (since the actual practice of the Supreme Court is only loosely textualist); or original meaning (since the actual practice of the Supreme Court is, on many questions, not originalist); or democratic legitimacy (since the Court could accommodate democratic legitimacy via a deferential version of CBA in reviewing statutes). The lack of judicial expertise in performing CBA *is* a significant consideration, but can be addressed in various ways – for example, by structuring doctrine so as to incentivize non-judicial actors to perform CBA (then to be reviewed by the courts), and by increasing the institutional capacity of courts to perform a de novo CBA where necessary.

ACKNOWLEDGMENTS

Many thanks to Joseph Blocher, Jamie Boyle, Michael Dorf, Richard Fallon, Brandon Garrett, Lisa Griffin, Ben Grunwald, Maggie Lemos, Paul Tucker, Ernie Young, and the editors for their comments.

RECOMMENDED READING

Adler, M. (2019). *Measuring Social Welfare: An Introduction*, New York: Oxford University Press.

Adler, M. & Posner, E. (2006). *New Foundations of Cost-Benefit Analysis*, Cambridge, MA: Harvard University Press.

Chemerinsky, E. (2019). *Constitutional Law: Principles and Policies*, 6th edn, New York: Wolters Kluwer.

Fallon, R. (2019). *The Nature of Constitutional Rights: The Invention and Logic of Strict Judicial Scrutiny*, Cambridge: Cambridge University Press.

Kagan, S. (1998). *Normative Ethics*, Boulder, Co: Westview Press.

Masur, J. & Posner, E. (2018). Cost-Benefit Analysis and the Judicial Role. *University of Chicago Law Review*, 85 (4), 935–986.

Sunstein, C. (2018). *The Cost-Benefit Revolution*, Cambridge, MA: MIT Press.

29

Revolution

Nimer Sultany

The people's power to resist tyranny, to overthrow unjust rulers, and establish their mode of government has a long pedigree in modern practice and political thought (Skinner 1978; Nabulsi 1999). Historians, political scientists, and political theorists often rightly assert that revolutions shaped the modern world (Foran, Lane & Zivkovic 2008; Halliday 1999). The transformative events of the Arab Spring in which mass mobilisations led to the overthrow of autocratic rulers in Tunisia, Libya, and Egypt (2011), Sudan and Algeria (2019), and to constitutional changes in several other states (Morocco, Jordan, Bahrain, and Oman) are the most recent illustration of the continued relevance and importance of revolution to legal and political thought and practice. These events further illustrate that revolutions unsettle long-standing institutional practices, captivate popular imagination, create hopes and fears, and set in motion a plethora of social and political struggles whose significance transcends the national boundaries of the particular states undergoing revolutionary transformations.

Attempts to define revolutions analytically often founder upon confronting historical plurality. The indeterminacy of definitions is reflected in changes in emphases of the study of revolution in historical sociology. These changes are often presented as "generational" with a recent announcement of the arrival of a fifth, but flawed, generation (Allinson 2019). Karl Korsch (2013) correctly argues that one cannot impose a general, abstract theory of revolution because of the historical specificity of each revolutionary practice. Revolution often denotes a sudden surge in popular mobilisation that leads to a rapid change in the political and social order. This mass movement displays a collective political agency committed to changing the extant order and it may or may not seize state power. It is often violent, although violence is not an essential characteristic. It characteristically advocates egalitarian and democratic ideals and includes both political and social elements.

The contestability of revolution and the absence of a universally accepted definition is unsurprising in light of normative and political disagreement about the desirability of revolutions and the change they seek to advance. Different philosophers and theorists offered competing definitions and contrasting assessments of the revolution's justifiability (Kouvelakis 2003; Flikschuh 2008; Zreik 2018). Yet revolution is more than merely a contested concept in the realm of ideas. It is an intervention in the world of events that aspires to draw a line between past and present, the old and the new. It is frequently argued that revolutions provide a "new beginning" (Arendt 1963), and "constitute a structural and ideological break from the previous regime" (Pincus 2009, p. 31). Yet the extent to which particular revolutions achieve rupture from the extant order and the desirability of specific ruptures are themselves subject to diverging assessments that may impact the applicability of "revolution" to the examined social and political changes.

Moreover, revolutions generate radically incompatible assessments because they inevitably create winners and losers due to the changes revolutionaries introduce to the social and political order (Dunn 2008). While winners and losers are bound to exist in any form of legal and political regulation, revolutions intensify political and social struggles, foreground existing fissures, magnify the existing order's inability to rectify injustices, mobilise the masses to demand radical change, and require the establishment of a new political-legal order to institute these changes.

This chapter argues that an adequate assessment of revolutions (and the role of law in revolutions) is often stymied by historical exclusions and theoretical myopia. Historical exclusions centralise certain experiences and present sanitized and one-sided narratives of the revolutionary experiences they centralise, especially with respect to violence, slavery, and colonialism. On the basis of such ideological uses of history, theoretical accounts overlook these social and political realities in order to legitimate particular revolutionary constitutions and to elevate them to the status of a paradigm or ideal type. This paradigm serves as the yardstick by which other experiences are assessed.

The main feature of this paradigm is that it postulates a distinction between political and social revolutions. It presents the American Revolution of 1776 as an exemplar for the political revolution that concerns itself with the establishment of government under law. In contrast, the French Revolution of 1789 is presented as an exemplar for the social revolution that also seeks to tackle social injustice. What follows from this distinction is an attribution of success and non-violence to the political revolution, and failure and violence to the social revolution making the US an exceptional case (Burke 1993; Arendt 1963; Palmer 2014; Wood 1993; Ackerman 2019). While a framing within a "Western Civilisation" (Palmer 2014; Wood 1993) is not always explicit, the paradigm generally ignores or dismisses major Global South experiences, many of which were social revolutions, such as the Haitian Revolution and the twentieth-century anti-colonial revolutions (Arendt 1963; Palmer 2014) or the Arab Spring (Ackerman 2019).

The problem is twofold: a comparative method that excludes or dismisses constitutional experiences outside the orbit of the Global North, and a theoretical apparatus that justifies this dismissal. This apparatus includes the dichotomies thus mentioned and presupposes an idealised yardstick of the liberal constitution as a form of higher law or normative contract that constrains politics. When employed in comparative methodology such dichotomies may "over-simplify complexity and almost invariably put the Western culture at the top of some implicit normative scale. Such self-confirming hierarchies threaten the comparatist's claim to non-ethnocentric, impartial research..." (Frankenberg 1985, p. 422). One should be careful then of the linear, monolithic narratives of "modern constitutionalism" and of generalisations about "the rise and fall of constitutions" (Frankenberg 2006, p. 447) or the rise and fall of revolutions (Takriti 2013).

In extreme cases, this narrative of failure of constitutionalism is deployed in explicitly orientalist (i.e., culturally essentialist) terms that depict Arab and Islamic constitutional history as a failure emanating from a cultural failure to join modernity (Kedourie 1992). In other writings, it is simply assumed that the normative role of constitutions is absent and that "constitutions without constitutionalism" is all there is to study in the Arab world (Brown 2001; for criticism see Sultany 2017a). In such cases, Maldonado (2013) notes, it is the failure of law that warrants attention and inclusion not its potential contribution to legal and constitutional theory.

The deficiency of this paradigm construction is not merely methodological, but also substantive and normative. It reduces the plurality of the revolutionary phenomena despite the conceptual contestability of the revolution, whether in respect to its applicability to particular realities or the emphasis on continuity with, or rupture from, the extant order. It ignores the revolution's dialectical nature by separating its assessment from the counter-revolution and thus exaggerates the role of violence in revolutions it disfavours, whereas it obscures the role of violence, slavery, and colonialism in the revolutions it favours. Finally, it presents a certain type of revolutionary constitutions (that are "political" not "social") as ones that legitimate the polity despite the contestability of the revolutions that generated them, and notwithstanding the incoherence and instability of these constitutions. Moreover, this paradigm elevates counter-majoritarian revolutionary constitutions to be a product of an exceptional act of founding that need not be repeated (or radically revised) despite the constitutional order's deficiencies, instability, and injustices.

In order to flesh out this argument, the discussion is divided into six sections. The first section discusses the common attributes of revolutionary experiences and the inadequacy of different frameworks to convey these experiences, such as transitional justice and the imposition of a success criterion. In order to further illustrate the problematic of the success criterion, the second section discusses prominent examples of both exclusions and selective inclusions in the comparative study of revolutions as well as the omission of the counter-revolution from the assessment of revolutionary success in social revolutions. The third section provides an intellectual history for the emergence of the paradigm that opposes the good, successful political revolution to the bad, failed, social ones. The fourth section highlights the paradigm's common exclusion or minimisation of violence, slavery, and colonialism from narratives of the political revolution. The fifth section highlights the intertwinement of social and political elements in all revolutions. Finally, the sixth section returns to the question of constituent power, the collective revolutionary agency, to highlight its contestations and examine its ability to legitimate the constitution.

I REVOLUTION, COLLECTIVE AGENCY, DEMOCRACY

Generally, revolution is distinguishable from other forms of protest and change because it is not a mere rebellion that rejects the extant order but stops short of reconstructing the political system. Unlike reform, revolution does not seek an internal change within the political order, because it seeks to restructure the political order itself rather than merely modify it (Nkrumah 1996; Luxemburg 2006). Unlike civil disobedience, revolution does not presuppose the regime's legitimacy and makes no appeal either to its underlying principles or unfulfilled ideals. Unlike a coup d'état, that often changes leaders without altering the body politic, revolution disrupts the continuity of state sovereignty and draws upon popular involvement (Takriti 2019a; Mayer 2000).

The element of popular involvement shows that revolutions are ill-captured by rule-based procedural definitions of revolutionary change. The most notable of these is Kelsen's (1946a) emphasis on the violation of procedural legitimacy as a hallmark of revolutionary change because it occurs outside prescribed constitutional rules. The focus in Kelsen's juristic-normative approach is on the loss of the legal order's efficacy and thus the occurrence of a change in the basic norm – the criterion for legal validity – by the establishment of a new effective order. In such a definition, the state is not understood as a political community. Instead it is reduced to a normative-legal relation that excludes social factors and neglects institutional continuities. Moreover, the distinction between revolution and coups collapses and no significance is assigned to the role of collective agency (Sultany 2017a).

Revolutions are captivating because they require mass mobilisation in order to challenge the systemic illegitimacy of the ruling regime and advocate a transformation of the polity. This popular mobilisation envisages a collective agency empowered to change the status quo. Counter-revolutionary literature conceptualises revolutions as historical events in which humans are swept away by the tide of history (Ozouf 1989). In this view, those who participate in revolutions are driven by passion rather than reason, are ruled by collective excitement rather than free will, and surrender their individuality to a formless rabble. Yet, revolutionaries celebrate human agency in making history and consider persons as conscious actors who seek to transform their conditions and control their destiny. Whereas counter-revolutionaries often lump revolutionary and fascist masses in a single "totalitarian" category, "revolutionary masses have nothing in common with the submissive, manipulated, disciplined, controlled, disempowered crowds of the fascist and Nazi rallies" (Traverso 2021, p. 12).

What underlies revolutions then is a particular attitude to history and reality. Revolutions "make possible the social reconstruction of reality, the reordering of things-as-they-are so they are no longer experienced as given but rather as willed, in accordance with convictions about how things ought to be" (Darnton 1989). The "givenness of things" (history, tradition, authority) is contrasted with the "conviction that the human condition is malleable, not fixed, and that ordinary people can make history instead of suffering it" (Darnton 1989).

In contrast to the common silencing and exclusion of majorities from actual rule, revolutionaries centralise the "forcible entry of the masses into the realm of rulership over their own destiny" (Trotsky 2017, p. xv). The emergence of "the people" as a political agent is a hallmark of revolutionary movements. This is particularly clear in the anti-colonial context. Amilcar Cabral (1966) argues, "the national liberation of a people is the regaining of the historical personality of that people, its return to history through the destruction of the imperialist domination to which it was subjected". In the Algerian context, Frantz Fanon (2018, p. 582) similarly argues that the:

> essence of any revolution of some depth ... is to bring movement to the masses, to enliven them by catalysing their energies, by setting them off on the conquest of their rights. Set in motion, they break with the structures that had kept them riveted to their immobility and passivity; they trigger the collapse of the system of oppression, reducing it to dust. Within this gigantic movement they become aware of themselves, of their strength and their creative capacity finds the means of its realization.

This requires accounting for both objective and subjective elements in conceptualising revolutions as an act of will in concert with others. In particular, popular mobilisation requires institutional organisation (Nabulsi & Takriti 2016). Rosemary Sayigh (2007) emphasises both in the Palestinian context the "organisational structure" and the "state of consciousness", because the revolution mobilises the masses and centralises them to enable them to break their chains. In addition to creating a quasi-state structure (a parliament and a government in exile), the Palestinian Revolution engendered a sense of collective empowerment by turning stateless refugees into political agents and militant fighters, by constructing a national consciousness amongst diasporic communities, and by developing an internationalist outlook and a network of solidarity (Nabulsi & Takriti 2016; Irfan 2020).

A revolution, then, is not merely a description of actual socio-political transformations that ensue from a historical event or a project of social engineering that a revolutionary regime embarks upon (Sewell 1996; Darnton 1989). It also denotes a consciousness that identifies a gap between human potentiality and human actuality and seeks to overcome this gap by changing the oppressive order that frustrates human potentiality (Calvert 1967). "Revolutionary consciousness", Gregory Calvert (1967, p. 16) maintains, "leads to the struggle for one's own freedom in unity with others who share the burden of oppression".

For this consciousness, liberation is a "never-ending process" that cannot be limited to the achievement of national independence (Said 1993, p. 274). Accordingly, anti-colonial revolutions draw connections between liberation from foreign subjugation and from domestic anti-egalitarian arrangements. Fanon writes (2018, p. 570):

> In Algeria, the war of national liberation is indistinguishable from a democratic revolution ... the expression 'Algerian revolution' expresses both a process of liberation from foreign yolk and the destruction of feudal relics from the middle ages, relics that must yield to democratic bases for a modern nation. The democratic revolution is preparing the advent of democracy.

This democratisation is not merely political-procedural but also socio-economic as it has to contend with the colonial legacy and democratise the economy upon independence: "The Algerian people wants to free itself from colonialism, but it does not conceive this liberation except in a revolutionary perspective entailing an end to feudalities and the destruction of all the economic structures of colonization" (Fanon 2018, p. 573).

This intertwinement of the social and political illustrates a substantive and contested feature of revolutions that stands in contrast to the virtual consensus over the centrality of a collective agency with a transformative agenda, often captured by the concept of "constituent power" – the people's political power to constitute their form of government. Yet the paradigmatic separation between political and economic changes – the focus on political democratisation and neglect of economic democratisation – fails to convey what is at stake in many revolutionary changes and glosses over the contestation over the meaning of democracy (and decolonisation) itself.

The problematic nature of this separation is evident in the utilisation of the prism of "civil society" or "transitions" or "transitional justice" to explain the cases of the collapse of communism in Europe and the fall of apartheid in South Africa. No matter how momentary or short-lived, revolutions engender a sense of empowerment and concerted collective action to realise a general interest. This unifying and empowering sense is distinct from the disunity of "civil society" that precedes the revolutionary event.

Likewise, "transitions" fail to convey the required rupture from the old regime in order to democratise and decolonise the polity. They reduce the required change into political proceduralism (Arato 2000a; Cornell 2014). For example, Drucilla Cornell (2014) points out that the "transitional justice" and "social contract" literature on South Africa is heavily focused on "democratic proceduralism" because it focuses on political emancipation while leaving the organisation of the economy at the mercy of neoliberal capitalist institutions. Accordingly, these approaches not only "foreclose revolutionary possibility" but also impede the emergence of "true decolonisation" (Cornell 2014, p. 7).

A transitional justice perspective is incapable of explaining the incompleteness of decolonisation in South Africa because of the need to problematise "civil society" itself.

In order to overcome the bifurcated mode of colonial control – under which "civil society was racialised, Native Authority was tribalised" – democratisation in Africa requires both "the deracialisation of civil power and the detribalisation of customary power" (Mamdani 1996, pp. 19, 25). The legacy of "decentralised despotism" by which colonial European powers ruled Africans require "dismantling" the colonially constructed customary power within civil society. Yet post-colonial constitutional orders "deracialise[d] the state but not civil society", and thus, left racial and economic privilege intact within civil society (1996, pp. 15–16, 20). Mahmood Mamdani concludes that the transition in the case of South Africa was one of "deracialisation without democratisation" because it left "intact the structures of indirect rule" (1996, p. 32).

Equally inadequate in conveying revolutionary change is "social movement theory" and its emphasis on "contentious politics". This approach depoliticises the revolutionary phenomena because it abstracts it from reality, emphasises the tactical over the substantive, and shies away from substantive value judgment (Takriti 2019b). Takriti correctly argues that "contention" lumps together a myriad of sociopolitical phenomena without sufficient attention to their particularities and normative connotations. Such an approach separates them from the material realities of human struggles that underlie them and declines to take a normative position in relation to power relations (Takriti 2019b).

An additional hindrance to an adequate comprehension of revolutions is the insistence on the imposition of a success criterion of capturing state power in defining revolutions or identifying them. While revolutions often aim at capturing political power in order to institute the required change that animated the revolution, that may not be achieved in all cases. This raises the question of whether "failed" collective mobilisations should be included in the revolutionary phenomena. For instance, Charles Tilly (1978 and 1995) requires – in addition to the presence of a "revolutionary situation" of a breakdown of sovereignty – a "revolutionary outcome" of a "displacement of power holders" and a "transfer of power". Likewise, M. N. Smith (2008, p. 408) requires a "profound and thoroughgoing substitution of one governing socio-political institution with another". Finally, Ackerman (2019, p. 3) focuses on "success stories – ones in which revolutionary outsiders have managed to oust establishment insiders from political authority".

Yet no success criterion should be stipulated as a definitional prerequisite for defining and identifying a revolution. First, revolutions are not mere events but a dialectical relation between an event and a process: an event that initiates a process, and a process that seeks to complete that which was initiated by the event (Kouvelakis 2003). Thus, a success criterion cannot be reduced to the outcome of the event itself (namely, the dethroning of the ruler). The problem with this criterion is that "it reduces entire processes to their end result" and "overlooks substantive elements" (Takriti 2013, p. 5).

Second, the reduction of success to capturing state power ignores other measures of success and the normative contestability of assessments of success. Once it is recognised that the revolution should not be reduced to a mere event, multiple criteria to determine success and failure in a revolutionary process would present themselves. This multiplicity requires a normative judgment regarding the achievement of success. Indeed, it is part and parcel of the revolutionary process that the participants argue about the ends of the revolution, whether they were achieved, and when should the revolution end. Limiting success to capturing state power may also preclude a discussion of the success in realising the revolution's goals and emancipatory potential after capturing power. Cornell's (2014) and Mamdani's (1996) discussion of South Africa, for instance, illustrates the complexity that narratives about a successful political revolution in South Africa obscure.

Third, "state-centrism" and the reduction of the revolution to a singular criterion undermine the richness of the revolutionary tradition because it excludes anti-colonial revolutions in the "Third World" (Takriti 2013, p. 6). Many of these revolutions failed to capture state power. Nevertheless, as the example of the Dhufar Revolution in Oman (1965–1973) illustrates, a liberation movement that occurred prior to the establishment of the state led to far-reaching social consequences (such as the abolition of slavery and changes in social structures) and political changes (such as formation of national identity, territorial consolidations, and the coexistence of multiple sovereignties during revolutionary mobilisation) (Takriti 2013).

It may be intuitive why political theorists and constitutional scholars would focus on "successful" revolutions because these establish constitutions that lend themselves to examination. Yet the existence of a constitution is an insufficient marker for the success of a revolution: "successful" revolutions do not necessarily produce constitutional documents (e.g., the Glorious Revolution), and some "failed" anti-colonial movements produced constitutional documents, such as Libya 1918, Syria 1919, and Morocco 1921 (Sultany 2017a). The fact that these documents were not formally backed by state enforcement does not explain the persistence of the "success" criterion. This is because it is also employed in cases where the revolutionaries capture power and establish an effective constitution, most notably the French and Russian revolutions. Despite their success in constitutional establishment and enforcement, these revolutions are still considered failed because the constitutions are considered temporary, ideological, or instrumental. This further shows the intertwinement of substantive judgment with formal criteria, in which success is associated with "political revolutions" and failure is associated with "social revolutions" given their aims and consequences.

The following section suggests that this focus on "success" is problematic. It either excludes Global South experiences entirely preventing a richer understanding of the plurality of the revolutionary phenomena (Arendt 1963), or alternatively, it selectively includes some of these experiences but flattens them to make them fit a ready-made narrative (Ackerman 2019). In both cases, however, the counter-revolution's contribution to the violence, failure, and instability of the revolution is often ignored.

II EXCLUSION, INCLUSION, DE-CONTEXTUALISATION

Many of the revolutions in the eighteenth and nineteenth centuries were directed against monarchies. Yet, the primary revolutionary form in the nineteenth and twentieth centuries were the anti-colonial revolutions in Latin America, Asia and Africa. The Haitian revolution (1791–1804) supplied an earlier example of this kind of revolution, when the slaves of Saint Domingo revolted against the French revolutionary regimes (James 2001). This transformative event was not merely a secessionist rebellion but a revolution demanding freedom and equality (Genovese 1992). Nevertheless, the revolution's exclusion from historiographical narratives of "the age of revolution" obscured its importance (Trouillot 1997).

Such exclusions – and the concomitant centrality of the American and the French revolutions – are consequential because of the historical experiences that are included for the purposes of theoretical exploration. Criticisms of Arendt's (1963) work, in this context, are instructive. Hobsbawm (1994, pp. 202, 203) highlights Arendt's exclusion of "everything outside the classical zone of western Europe and the north Atlantic", in particular China and Cuba, as well as her exclusion of revolutionary movements that preceded 1776. Bernal (2017, pp. 90–91) highlights Arendt's exclusion of the Haitian revolution. One can also add that Arendt's book was published in 1963 during the height of anti-colonial struggles, yet national liberation struggles, like in Algeria and Vietnam, are not discussed.

These historical exclusions pave the way for postulating the American and French experiences as paradigms for the revolutionary phenomena and as a yardstick by which other experiences are assessed. Global South revolutions against colonialism between World War II and the 1970s led to the independence of many countries such as Vietnam, Egypt, Iraq, Algeria, Mozambique, Angola, and Zimbabwe (1980). Confronted with the ruthless violence of colonial regimes, Global South revolutionary liberation movements often relied on armed struggle, guerrilla warfare, and popular mobilisation to achieve self-determination. Some liberation movements against settler colonial regimes like South Africa and Israel continued to later decades. In South Africa this led to the collapse of the apartheid regime in the early 1990s. The Palestinian Revolution has hitherto been less successful (Al-Hout 2006; Sayigh 2007).

Despite its claim to be inclusive, Bruce Ackerman's *Revolutionary Constitutions*, replicates similar blind spots. Published in 2019, during a decade in which the Arab Spring transformations dominated the news, the book fails to mention these revolutions or to include them in its theoretical modelling. Despite the focus on "success stories in which revolutionary outsiders have managed to oust establishment insiders from political authority" (Ackerman 2019, p. 3), Tunisia 2011 – matching the "success" criterion, at least until the presidential coup of 2021 – is ignored.

Ackerman's inclusion of some Global South countries in his discussion (Iran, India, South Africa, Burma) is marred by several difficulties. First is the theoretical framework.

Ackerman's modelling of constitutional legitimation contrasts the US/French-inspired revolutionary model with a British-inspired "reformist" and a Spanish/German-inspired "elite-construction" models. He presents revolution as a sequence of rebellion, construction, and long-term reform. This sequence moves from "high-energy" founding that delegitimises the existing order, to a stage of constitution making (or "constitutionalisation of revolutionary charisma"), and, finally, to a stage of "normalisation of revolutionary politics" after the departure of the founders (Ackerman 2019, pp. 8–9).

The problem with this modelling is that, as Waldron notes, it relies on a "capacious" understanding of revolution based on loosely connected events (Waldron 2019). In the context of post-colonial India, Thiruvengadam (2019, pp. 687–688) argues that Ackerman deploys "a very loose and abstract notion" of "revolution" that neither applies to Indian history nor recognises the contested nature of the revolutionary label in India. Moreover, Ackerman privileges a poorly defined "charismatic leadership" to the exclusion of other factors and explanations for constitutional legitimation (Arban et al. 2020).

Second is a selective, one-sided comparative inquiry that fits a pre-existing narrative and does not address the contested nature of the political and constitutional developments in each country. Ackerman selectively chooses facts that are "cherry-picked to confirm the argument" and provides no in-depth legal and constitutional discussions of the selected legal systems (Arban et al. 2020). The one-sidedness is clear in the case of the discussion of South Africa. If one ignores, as Ackerman does, critical discussions of South Africa's transition that foreground continuities (Cornell 2014; Mamdani 1996), it becomes unsurprising that he deems it a "success story". Similarly, Ackerman's discussion of the success of the "Zionist revolution" ignores critical scholarship that points out the anti-egalitarian and exclusive definition of "We the People" that excludes non-Jewish citizens who comprise one-fifth of the population (Masri 2017); that the lack of constitutional enactment after the moment of founding may have facilitated the denial of these Palestinian citizens' basic rights under a military government regime (1948–1966) and the massive confiscation of their lands (Kedar 2001); and that the subsequent rise of an activist supreme court did not significantly alter the "separate and unequal" status of this minority under a bill of rights that omits the right to equal protection of the laws (Sultany 2017b).

Finally, despite these inclusions Ackerman asserts that the US experience of founding is exceptional ("very special") even though it is "no longer unique" (2019, p. 361) because others followed in its footsteps. His comparative exercise advocates respect for foreign experiences not because of any assumption of novelty but because of a premise of similarity to the US model (Ackerman 2019, p. 362):

> Americans should treat the constitutional experience of nations like India or France, South Africa or Poland, with special respect. These countries are traveling down the very same Enlightenment pathway that the United States has been following since the Founding.

In addition to historical exclusion that ignores experiences and selective inclusion that flattens these experiences, there is a general tendency to de-contextualise revolutions in assessing their success. As a global phenomenon, however, revolution is rarely a process confined within national boundaries. On the one hand, revolutions may be world changing. Unlike rebellions, which are often "endemic and territorial", revolutions may be "epidemic and cosmic" producing the effect of – and fear from – contagion (Mayer 2000, p. 11). The French Revolution was "ecumenical" and the global reach of its radical message exceeded the American Revolution's (Hobsbawm 1996a, pp. 74–75; Arendt 1963, pp. 55–56). Europe's 1848 was "the first potentially global revolution" with its impact detected in Latin America (Hobsbawm 1977, p. 22). The October 1917 Russian Revolution was even "far more profound" and consequential than the French Revolution as it "produced by far the most formidable organized revolutionary movement in modern history" (Hobsbawm 1996b, p. 55). Anti-colonial liberation movements were "worldmaking" and not merely concerned with "nation building" because they connected between local struggles and wider imperial political and economic structures (Lee 2010; Getachew 2019). Many revolutionary movements in the twentieth century developed networks of solidarity, exchange, and training (Takriti 2013; Byrne 2016; Abou El-Fadl 2019). The 1979 Iranian Revolution was a "transnational revolution" both because it was embedded in global networks and because it generated far-reaching regional and international impact (Keshavarzian & Mirsepassi 2021). Finally, the Arab Spring evolved as a regional dynamics and inspired protesters in the Occupy Wall Street movement that swept through the United States.

In light of this global reach of revolutions, one needs to account for the recursive pattern of foreign and counter-revolutionary intervention. The nature of these interventions is often subject to scholarly debates, as in the case of the Mexican Revolution (1910–1919) (Foran 1996). These interventions influence the revolution's dynamics and character. Hobsbawm (1996a, p. 88) observes that the French Jacobins have to be contextualised within "a modern total war effort". Faced with a generalised condition of internal rebellion (60 out of 80 departments within the country), invasions by German and British armies, and financial bankruptcy, the Jacobin Republic succeeded in preserving the country's unity (Hobsbawm 1996a, p. 90). A similar danger of disintegration faced the Bolsheviks and the Russian Revolution of 1917: "Various counter-revolutionary ('White') armies and regimes rose against the Soviets, financed by the Allies, who sent British, French, American, Japanese, Polish, Serb, Greek and Rumanian troops on to Russian soil" (Hobsbawm 1996b, p. 63). Under such conditions, "It could have no strategy or perspective beyond choosing, day by day, between the decisions needed for immediate survival and the ones which risked immediate disaster" (Hobsbawm 1996b, p. 64).

The consequences of these foreign interventions is often detrimental to the prospects of revolutionary success, such as the counter-revolutionary role that Tsarist Russia played in 1848 to defeat the Spring of Nations and restore the monarchical order across Europe, and the role of the Gulf states – in particular, Saudi Arabia and the Emirates – in the Arab Spring (Davis 2011). In many cases, these counter-revolutionary interventions seek to maintain colonial and imperial domination, such as the British counter-insurgency operations to defeat the Dhufar revolution in Oman. Since 2011, Syria, Libya, and Yemen are three examples of foreign interventions diverting the course of the revolution into a prolonged civil war. The recursive pattern of counter-revolutionary mobilisation that is often supported by foreign interventions, and the disorder and carnage they lead to, are not a necessary attribute of the revolutionary movement itself nor do they necessarily follow from revolutionary goals and motivations. Therefore, a revolution should not be assessed on the sole basis of outcomes it did not necessarily lead to or fully anticipate. Nor is the anti-revolutionary argument – that supports counter-revolutionary interventions that create the chaos of which the revolution is subsequently accused – convincing either.

To conclude, the revolution and the counter-revolution are inseparable and need to be examined together (Mayer 2000). The problem with some scholarly accounts is that they are one-dimensional because they ignore the counter-revolution in their assessment of the revolution. This is particularly noticeable with respect to the treatment of the role of violence. Before turning to the role of violence, the following section provides a brief outline of the intellectual genesis of the dominant paradigm that frames and evaluates the role of violence. This is necessary in order to highlight the normative orientations that underlie particular assessments of revolutions and the longer lineage of scholarly traditions.

III GOOD REVOLUTION, BAD REVOLUTION

Philosophers have offered a variety of justifications for resistance, violent resistance, and revolutions (Finlay 2015; Delmas 2018). In the pursuit of such justifications, and when confronted with actual historical processes, some theorists have sought from the outset to differentiate between desirable and objectionable revolutions. A long-running strand in this context is the one expressed by Edmund Burke (1993) and Joseph de Maistre (1994) who set the tone for future negative assessments of the French Revolution as opposed to a more positive assessment of the Glorious Revolution and the American Revolution.

Conservative arguments against the French Revolution reject the idea of human-made rational order. "The very idea of the fabrication of a new government, is enough to fill us with disgust and horror", writes Burke (1993, p. 31). Tradition (Burke) or divinity (Maistre) determines humans' place in the world, not a rational construction of the social and political order. Burke and Maistre reject the idea of abstract and universal human rights and instead defend historical rights that are embedded in particular social structures (Burke 1993, p. 32). These pre-revolutionary, inherited privileges and vested interests are inscribed in an "ancient constitution" that the revolutionary constitution destroys. The destruction of the long-standing social and political order leads to divisiveness, disorder, and anarchy. Accordingly, compromise, moderation, and respect to authority are the preferred virtues (Burke 1993, pp. 34–36). In contrast, the Glorious Revolution is designated as a good revolution precisely because it affirmed the "ancient constitution": it maintained the monarchy and the line of succession, notwithstanding the change in the person of the monarch.

Yet, such a view overstates historical continuity by writing off historical rupture. The whig "ideology of customary law, regulated monarchy and immemorial Parliamentary right", that supports the Glorious Revolution, is based on a "myth of an Ancient Constitution" (Skinner 1965, pp. 151, 177). This myth asserts the continuity of ancient liberties, and the concomitant "continuity of English progress", despite the disruption caused by the Norman Conquest. Skinner (1965, p. 178) thus argues, "The 'whig' ideology ... amounted neither to genuine history nor to systematic political theory. It was more like political propaganda in historical dress."

On the other hand, Alexis de Tocqueville (2008) challenges the assumption of rupture at the basis of condemnations of the French Revolution and minimises its achievements and the broader sense of change and empowerment it brought. He argues that the Revolution was not as novel as often assumed, and that the ancient regime era had anticipated whatever change the Revolution brought about. Yet he too criticises the Revolution's "missionary zeal" and argues that it needs to be compared to religious revolutions.

In the Unites States, conservatives started already in the 1790s to blame the French Jacobins for "the popular disorder and degeneration of standards infecting America" and for the perversion of the American Revolution's "rational principles" (Wood 1993, p. 231). Gordon Wood credits these views for generating the long-standing "myth" that posits that the "American Revolution was sober and conservative while the French Revolution was chaotic and radical". Wood, however, maintains that "only if we measure radicalism by violence and bloodshed can the myth be sustained; by any other measure the American Revolution was radical" (1993, p. 231). This downplaying of the role of violence enables Wood to present the American Revolution as distinctive because it managed to be both radical and successful – in fact, "too successful" – whereas the French Revolution exemplifies a predictable failure (1993, p. 368).

The French Revolution, however, was not the only revolution to arouse American antagonism. Unwittingly, the "Black Jacobins" of the Haitian Revolution exposed the contradictions of the American Revolution and generated fears of contagion in the slave-holding US South. Revolutionaries like Thomas Jefferson feared that the rebellion might come back to haunt them, and the Federalists utilised the possibility of slave revolt to attack Jacobin and Republican ideas (Jordan 1968, pp. 381, 386, 387–388, 396). Southern states, Congress, and the Senate legislated a variety of measures in 1794–1795 and 1803 to bar the entry of freed blacks from the West Indies to the South (Jordan 1968, pp. 382–383). A "doctrine of revolution simply no longer served American interests and was, indeed, inimical to them" (Jordan 1968, p. 387).

The view that the American Revolution is exceptional and cannot be easily replicated, Michael Hunt (1987) maintains, is one of three key and interrelated ideological underpinnings of US foreign policy in its attitude toward political change abroad. In addition to a mission of national greatness as the agent of liberty and a racial worldview, the American Revolution emerges in this ideology as a "model of revolutionary moderation and wisdom" after erasing the traces of violence and radicalism that tainted it (Hunt 1987, p. 96). Crucially, a successful revolutionary transition requires adequate constitutional arrangements that protect human and property rights and for which the US Constitution serves as a model (Hunt 1987, pp. 96–97). From this perspective, a successful revolution is one that mimics the American Revolution's objectives and methods (Hunt 1987, p. 116). The travails of other peoples' revolutions "confirmed their racial or cultural inferiority and underlined their need for American tutelage" (Hunt 1987, p. 124).

Although subsequent generations of the conservative persuasion who followed Burke and Maistre resigned themselves to the idea of the modern constitution and universal suffrage (Gargarella 2010), later political theorists (such as Arendt 1963) and historians (such as François Furet 1981 and 2000) echoed the anti-Jacobin line of reasoning. These scholars now directed their negative assessment toward the Russian Bolsheviks and not only the French Jacobins whereas the American Revolution continued to serve as the exemplar for the good and successful revolution (Arendt 1963; Furet 1981 and 2000).

In contrast to Arendt's distinction between the American and French revolutions, her contemporary Palmer (2014, originally published in 1959) highlights the similarities between these revolutions in the face of those who deny or belittle the American Revolution's revolutionary character. He considers the American and the French revolutions as primary manifestations of a "single revolutionary movement" of "democratic revolutions" that lasted for forty years (1760–1800) in "Western Civilisation" (2014, p. 6). He thus presents "Western Civilisation" as a self-contained and coherent unit that is progressively evolving toward greater freedoms despite internal struggles and schisms. Palmer's temporal and geographical delineation of the "Western Civilisation" is arbitrarily determined, excluding in particular the Haitian Revolution against slavery (Armitage 2014, p. xx). Furthermore, "democracy" is thinly defined in opposition to aristocracy despite the anti-Federalist criticism of the US Constitution as "aristocratically designed" because it empowers an enlightened elite to rule in light of the founders' distrust in the capacities of the "selfish" many (Wood 1993, p. 255). The lack of universal suffrage (e.g., the disenfranchisement of women), the lack of a constitutional provision for the equal protection of the laws (till 1868), and the continuity of slavery further illustrate the thinness of "democracy". "As a violation of the ideology of equal rights", Winthrop Jordan writes, "slavery mocked the ideals upon which the new republic was founded" (Jordan 1968, p. 311).

Unlike Arendt, Palmer disassociates the French Revolution from the Russian Revolution, rejecting the latter's association with the Jacobins. Like her, however, he expresses a normative opposition to the twentieth-century socialist revolutions (2014, pp. 10–13). Thus, whether the good revolutions include or exclude France, they are equally opposed to divergences from the preferred US model. The existence of Jim Crow, at the time Arendt and Palmer wrote their books, failed to trouble the preference to this model.

Ackerman (2019) posits a similar opposition between what he calls constitutional and totalitarian revolutions, or "revolutions on a human scale" and "totalising revolutions". In the totalitarian variant, which seeks a radical "reconstruction of all aspects of social and political life" and leads to oppressive orders, he lumps together the French Reign of Terror, Lenin, Stalin, and Mao but also Hitler. On the other hand, constitutional revolutions "do not attempt a total makeover of society" but rather focus on a limited number of particular social or political concerns (2019, p. 28). In these revolutions the constitution "commits the new regime to a series of *revolutionary reforms*, not a totalizing transformation, of the old order" (2019, p. 29, emphasis in original). Moreover, transitional processes in constitutional revolutions are distinct from the totalitarian ones in which, according to Ackerman, "'real' revolutionaries fight the existing regime to the bitter end" (2019, p. 32). As previously discussed, such a statement ignores foreign interventions, counter-revolutionary mobilisations, and wars in the reality of the French and Russian revolutions. Without a substantive discussion, Ackerman presents "totalising" revolutions as if they were highly coherent, systemised, programmatic, and devoid of contingencies, internal inconsistencies, power struggles, and experimentation. His application of "totalising" seems internally inconsistent because he includes Iran – which is a "social revolution" (Foran 2005, pp. 74–87) – in "constitutional revolutions" and, at the same time, excludes socialist revolutions. Ultimately, Ackerman does not support or establish his binary distinction, and its concomitant generalisation, since he neither discusses nor quotes any "totalising" revolutionary texts nor refers to any historical literature and legal scholarship on the actual reality of these "totalising" revolutions (such as Mayer 2000). For instance, Eagleton argues (2011, p. 34), Marxism "is not intended to be a total philosophy. It does not give us accounts of beauty or the erotic, or of how the poet Yeats achieves the curious resonance of his verse. It has been mostly silent on questions of love, death and the meaning of life".

In fact, Ackerman's distinction turns out to be a version of the political versus social revolution. In the former, Ackerman argues, the revolutionaries focus on the "state" or the relatively autonomous political sphere (2019, pp. 29–30). Nevertheless, Ackerman seeks to distinguish himself from Arendt by claiming that constitutional revolutions can centralise social and economic justice and suggests the examples of India and South Africa (2019, p. 41). Despite this proclamation, Thiruvengadam (2019, p. 688) notes Ackerman's "neglect" of social and economic issues in his analysis of states like India and concludes that "the centrality of economic and developmental issues to the politics of the Global South is a distinguishing factor that Ackerman's analysis does not adequately acknowledge".

IV VIOLENCE, SLAVERY, COLONIALISM

This paradigm construction, then, oversimplifies realities and perpetuates myths, whether that of the British "ancient constitution" or US exceptionalism. Indeed, the more positive assessment of the Glorious Revolution and the American Revolution often relies on an idealised (that is to say, selective and sanitised) interpretation of these revolutions' actual reality and in particular the erasure of the role of violence.

Consider the case of the Glorious Revolution. In contrast to standard whig history, it was not "glorious". This is because it was neither non-violent nor a mere negotiated transition between elites devoid of popular involvement. Indeed, "the English endured a scale of violence against property and persons similar to that of the French Revolution" (Pincus 2009, p. 7). It was "violent, popular, and divisive" (Pincus 2009, p. 8). Edmund Burke's claims notwithstanding, the Glorious Revolution brought into existence a new political order rather than merely affirm the existing one (Pincus 2009, p. 3). Moreover, the whig view of the Glorious Revolution separates the revolution from what preceded it (the English civil war) and what followed it (the repression of the Jacobites and civil war in Scotland, and the continuation of the annihilation of the Irish from the sixteenth century onwards) (Losurdo 2020, pp. 42–44). Thus, historical accounts that contrast English stability with continental turmoil do not withstand scrutiny (Pincus 2009).

Similarly, Americans who were dismayed by the French Revolution and then by the 1848 revolutions abandoned earlier celebrations of "liberty achieved through violence" in the independence war and "developed a more organic image" of their own revolution that neglected the role of bloodshed in establishing the republic (Roberts 2009, p. 14). Consistent with this presentation, Arendt glorifies the American Revolution as evident in her assessment of the "superior wisdom" and "very high calibre" of the Founding Fathers (1963, pp. 94–95, 68). Her reason for preferring the American Revolution over the French Revolution lies in the absence of the social question and in the Americans' focus on the political aspects. By the social question Arendt does not mean the absence of poverty, but rather the absence of extreme forms of it (want and misery) (1963, pp. 60, 68). In her account, concern with "exploitation" generates "compassion" for the wretched of the earth and thus generates destructive "passions" (1963, p. 62). It is this absence of compassion and passions that enabled the American revolutionaries to focus on establishing a rational mode of government under law. In this model, constitution-making is perceived as "the foremost and noblest of all revolutionary deeds" and as the "end of the revolution" (Arendt 1963, pp. 158–159). In contrast, the French focus on the social question undermined the establishment of the political order and threw France into a "state of nature" exemplified by the Reign of Terror.

This analytical distinction between the social (bad) and political (good) revolution is based on selective historiography, an exclusionary scope of consideration, and ideological determinism. This distinction obscures the role of violence in the political revolution, magnifies its role in the social revolution, and then posits a necessary and essential link between the social revolution and violence. *Contra* Arendt, the violence and lawlessness unleashed and inflicted on parts of the population do not sharply distinguish between the American and the French revolutions.

The argument concerning the French "state of nature" seems devoid of consideration of the actual conditions that the French Revolution, and in particular the Jacobins, had to respond to. Moreover, it is infused with an ideological determinism that ignores ideological flexibility in revolutionary processes (Mayer 2000, pp. 9–10). Arendt's determinism is clear in her treatment of the Terror as a necessary, natural, and inescapable consequence of the Revolution's social character, thereby ignoring contingency (Parekh 1981, pp. 184–185).

Yet, not all of the Jacobins' objectionable actions follow inherently and deterministically from Jacobin ideas and values. Indeed, Higonnet (1998, p. 1) "rejects the idea that the essence of Jacobin politics culminated in the useless and immoral Terror of 1793–1794" and "holds that Jacobinism can still be a model for modern democrats". As Wahnich (2012, p. 100) points out, the "view of year II of the Republic as a period of terror and dread is essentially Thermidorian". The counter-revolutionaries, who defeated the Jacobins, laid the foundations for this narrative.

When compared to the actual effects of the American Revolution, it becomes unclear why scholars do not ascribe similar negative repercussions for the American Revolution. Defending the revolutionary character of the American Revolution, Palmer (2014, pp. 141–142) offers two "objective" numerical criteria that zero in on the violent and coercive treatment of the counter-revolutionaries, the loyalists. The American Revolution created an estimated 80,000 refugees because loyalists, who were on the losing side, had to flee the country (Wood 1993, p. 176). Compared to the French Revolution, the percentage of refugees created in North America was almost five times more (24 refugees in the thirteen colonies, and 5 in France, per thousand of population). The punitive actions against the loyalists included the curtailment of their rights, confiscation of their property, and the infliction of collective punitive measures. Compared to the French Revolution, and taking into account the difference in population size, the confiscation measures were analogous (Palmer 2014, p. 142; Losurdo 2020, p. 47). Whereas the French refugees returned to France, fuelling the counter-revolution, the American loyalists remained in Canada. Palmer thus opines that the loyalists' erasure from national consciousness enables a misleading view of a "consensus" devoid of conflict (2014, p. 142).

Despite the differences within the paradigm between those who ignore or marginalise the role of violence in the American Revolution (Arendt) and those who acknowledge aspects of it (Palmer), both sides conclude with an equally favourable judgment: "Palmer did not allow legacies of violence and inequality that scarred the Atlantic world, especially in the slave societies of the Americas, to cloud his progressivist narrative" (Armitage 2014, p. xx).

Slavery and colonialism are two additional major examples of distortion arising from an exclusionary scope of consideration and the minimisation of the role of violence. Arendt is aware of these two primary questions involving the American Revolution. Nevertheless, Arendt (1963, pp. 70–73) excludes slavery as both external to the social question and not peculiar to the American Revolution. Arendt then doubles down and claims that colonial lawlessness vis-à-vis the native nations was confined to the criminal actions of the few rather than an organised group effort (Arendt 1963, pp. 92–93). Similarly, Wood's (1993) omission of colonial violence against the natives allows him to celebrate the American Revolution's radicalism – in its resultant changes – while excluding violence from this radicalism. The Americans may be as radical as the French, but they are not as bloody and ruthless.

Once crucial historical facts are excluded from consideration, it becomes easier to idealise the Revolution and the "sound realism" of its founders: "there were no sufferings around them that could have aroused their passions, no overwhelmingly urgent needs that could have tempted them to submit to necessity, no pity to lead them astray from reason…" (Arendt 1963, p. 95).

In contrast to this idealisation, many scholars offered a more critical account of the founding that highlights omissions, exclusions, and violence. Some legal historians point out that the American Founders "had interests, prejudices, and moral blind spots" (Klarman 2016, p. 5). Following the general outlines of Charles Beard's argument (1913), these historians consider the American Revolution a "counter-revolution" or a "coup" and highlight the Founders' economic motivations (Klarman 2016, p. x):

> the Constitution was a conservative counterrevolution against what leading American statesmen regarded as the irresponsible economic measures [for tax and debt relief] enacted by a majority of state legislatures in the mid-1780s, which they diagnosed as a symptom of excessive democracy.

In addition to these anti-democratic economic motivations, Klarman argues, what ultimately emerged from the Convention's debates was a "proslavery" Constitution (2016, pp. 303–304; see also Finkelman 2014; Waldstreicher 2010; and Feldman 2021). Likewise, for Staughton (1967, pp. 180–183), the revolution was "betrayed" because the founders failed to act against slavery given their racial prejudice, strong commitment to private property, and "economic realism". He argues that the Revolution needs to be understood as part of an anti-colonial revolutionary sequence of a national independence war followed by another internal revolution (the Civil War), with the latter rectifying the incompleteness of the earlier: "America therefore did have a bourgeois revolution comparable to the French Revolution, but it was directed not against England but against slavery and took place not in 1776 but in 1861" (Staughton 1967, p. 14).

The maintenance of slavery in the US Constitution – and in most of the French revolutionary constitutions with respect to colonial dominions – stands in stark contrast with its abolition in the Haitian Revolution's constitutions (Kaisary 2015,

p. 400). The 1801 Haitian Constitution, it is argued, reveals "radically different conceptions of freedom" than the dominant ones in the Western liberal tradition of the time (Kaisary 2015, p. 394).

It thus seems that Arendt's exclusionary scope of consideration may be consequential to one's assessment of the revolution, including whether, and in what sense, and for whom it is revolutionary. A non-idealised understanding of revolutions should be dialectical because the revolution itself may be a counter-revolution on account of its exclusions and violence. Indeed, it may be simultaneously emancipatory and slave holding, anti-colonial and colonial. In this context, the colonial violence of the American Revolution is too fundamental to be ignored or dismissed as incidental. The Revolution can hardly be separated from the fate of the native nations in North America, some of whom fought with the British against the colonists (Calloway 1995, p. xv):

> The American Revolutionaries who fought for freedom from the British Empire in the East also fought to create an empire of their own in the West ... the Revolution elevated acquisition of Indian lands into a national policy ... The Revolution both created a new society and provided justification for excluding Indians from it.

The Revolution created "a new government and a new society increasingly committed to the notion that Indian country east of the Mississippi should not exist" (Calloway 1995, p. 24). The Declaration of Independence had made clear that one of the colonists' complaints against the British monarch is that he "endeavoured to bring on the inhabitants of our frontiers, the merciless Indian savages, whose known rule of warfare is an undistinguished destruction of all ages, sexes, and conditions" (quoted in Calloway 1995, p. 293). George Washington stipulated in 1779 that the war on the native nations should be punitive and merciless (Calloway 1995, p. 51; Ostler 2019, p. 72). Similarly, colonists' militias endeavoured to enforce the choice between expulsion and annihilation that Virginia's governor Thomas Jefferson offered to the natives (Calloway, p. 53; Ostler 2019, p. 64). The conclusion of a peace treaty with the British did not end the war against the natives. The colonists accelerated the appropriation of native lands, often through a "string of treaties" that capitalised on the reality of power relations that sanctioned the victors' justice (Calloway 1995, pp. 281–286; Banner 2007). The revolutionary leaders sought to "civilise" the natives by dispossessing them from their lands (Calloway 1995, p. 290). Given the massive dislocation, destruction of crops, demolition of villages, land grab, death, and hunger that befell the natives, it is hard to avoid the conclusion that the American Revolution was "one of the darkest periods in American Indian history" and that the "turmoil it generated in Indian country continued long after 1783" (Calloway 1995, pp. 290, 291). It would seem then that the American Revolution has produced its own "state of nature", as far as the native nations were concerned. Only by ignoring colonialism can one ascribe stability to the American Revolution and turmoil exclusively to the French Revolution.

In the same way French revolutionary constitutions had to contend with the question of territory, slavery, colonies, and Haitian revolution (Spieler 2009), the colonial war on the native nations influenced constitutional design. In contrast to orthodox accounts of the Philadelphia Convention, Ablavksy argues (2014, p. 1002), that the "debates over Indians played an important role in the Constitution's creation, drafting, and ratification, particularly in the push for a stronger federal state" and that the "conquest and dispossession of Native peoples were integral to the Constitution's ratification". Ostler (2019, p. 97) writes that "the Constitution's drafters and advocates saw the need to create an orderly and effective process for obtaining lands from Indians and recognized that meeting this objective might require war". Hamilton emphasised the benefit of a powerful central government in enabling the war against the natives, and "advocated for a standing army, a strong executive with powers of military command, and a Congress with powers of taxation" (Ostler 2019, p. 98). This Hamiltonian argument for a fiscal-militarist federal state was more successful than the Madisonian "paternalist" argument for centralization (that would restrain both states and native nations) (Ablavsky 2014, p. 1007). Federalists sought to secure the Constitution's ratification by winning over a state like Georgia that sought federal support for its war on the Creek Indians (Ablavsky 2014, pp. 1007–1008). This use of native nations "to justify the power of the new national state came with a cost", Ablavsky (2014, p. 1008) concludes, because:

> it elevated conquest of Indians to a constitutional principle. Although few Federalists were rabid Indian-haters of the sort common on the frontier, they had sold the Constitution by promising to use federal power against Indians.... Expansionist states and white settlers held the federal government to its bargain. The history of national violence against Indians that followed ratification fulfilled the Hamiltonian vision, as the dispossession and settlement of western lands became one of the central projects of the new federal state.

This state of affairs is normatively and theoretically consequential (Ablavksy 2014, p. 1008):

> both the Constitution's drafters and 'the people' worked to create a document committed in part to the violent expropriation of the western borderlands from Indians. This outcome was not a failure of the political process. It was, rather, the cost of the Constitution's embrace of democracy and union.

In light of this, it is surprising that Ackerman (2019) completely ignores the centrality of colonialism to the US Revolution. This selective approach to history and to comprehending revolution is also consequential for the deployment of the comparative constitutional method. In his account of the "Zionist revolution" in Palestine, Ackerman makes no reference to the native population or the fact that the Zionist settler colonial movement ethnically cleansed the vast majority of the population (see Morris 2004; Pappe 2006). Given his exclusive focus on charismatic leadership,

Ackerman lumps Iran and Israel in one category without distinguishing between an endogenous revolution producing a "new beginning" and a colonial takeover of another people's homeland (Ackerman 2019, pp. 49–50). It is thus surprising that Ackerman includes the "Zionist revolution" in the category of constitutional revolutions that "do not attempt a total makeover of society" when, in fact, it transformed Palestine's demography, territory, and property regime in 1948 and its aftermath (Kedar 2001).

These normative and theoretical implications extend beyond the recognition of the role of violence in a particular liberal revolution. It invites a candid reflection on the role of violence. It is not clear why it is easier for some scholars and politicians to justify the violence of war on foreign nations than to justify revolutions against unjust regimes (Mayer 2000, p. 5). Moreover, revolutionary violence does not necessarily introduce a novel element into social relations that did not exist prior to the revolution, as the horrific levels of violence in pre-revolutionary France illustrate (Darnton 1989). Finally, one also needs to account for the violence of modern states, especially in reaction to resistance movements. This violence may undermine the constitutional order's claim to be radically different from the lawlessness of the revolution. For instance, Marx (1990) highlights the role of the repressive state not only because of the forcible expropriation of the masses that the "social contract" disguises, but also in his reflections on the Paris Commune of 1871 (Marx 1978a, p. 646):

> The civilization and justice of bourgeois order comes out in its lurid light whenever the slaves and drudges of that order rise against their masters. Then this civilization and justice stand forth as undisguised savagery and lawless revenge…. A glorious civilization, indeed, the great problem of which is how to get rid of the heaps of corpses it made after the battle was over!

V SOCIAL REVOLUTION, POLITICAL REVOLUTION

Besides the attempt to ascribe violence exclusively to social revolutions, the very attempt to confine some revolutions to a political stage and exclude the social change that revolutions instigate, contributes to the myopia in understanding the revolutionary phenomenon. Arendt's condemnation of social revolutions and privileging of political revolutions faces two challenges: descriptively, it is difficult to find an example in which the social is absent from the revolutionary phenomenon; theoretically, the assessment of the extent to which a revolution is social is a contested normative question that invites a substantive judgment (Foran 2005, criticising Skocpol 1979). Historically, the primary examples for "political revolutions", such as the Glorious Revolution, were not merely political, as traditional accounts had suggested. Indeed, Lockean inspired labour-based notions of property "motivated many of the revolutionaries of 1688–89 to transform England from an agrarian to a manufacturing society, from a society bounded by limited raw materials to a society fuelled by the limitless possibilities of human creation" (Pincus 2009, p. 43). The US founders intended to protect private property and their establishment of a federal government facilitated conferring title (Ablavsky 2018), and in any event the 8-years long Revolutionary War produced a war economy that impacted socio-economic relations in a variety of ways (Wood 1993). On the other hand, Wahnich (2012, p. 86) questions the suggestion that the French revolutionary passion was a form of "politics of pity" that is focused on the "social question independent of politics". Instead, it was a "passion for declared, inviolable and sacred rights … for justice and equality" (Wahnich 2012, p. 90).

Thus, it is crucial to observe the intertwinement of social and political aspects in the reality of revolutions. "Every revolution", Marx (1978b, p. 132) writes, "dissolves the *old society* and to that extent it is *social*. Every revolution overthrows the *old power* and to that extent it is *political*". For Marx, the social and political should not be separated: a social change without capturing political power is illusory because it cannot be realised without overthrowing the old powers, and a political change without dissolving the old society is merely a competition between different classes over access to the state (Marx 1978b, pp. 131–132). In other words, instead of challenging relations of exploitation and social injustice by transforming economic structures and property relations to accomplish human flourishing, the power struggle would revolve around who manages this system of exploitation and who benefits from it. Thus, a revolution focused on capturing political power is focused on the state, whereas a social revolution "has a point of view of the whole" because it seeks to establish a humanised society that overcomes human alienation from the extant socio-political order (Marx 1978b, p. 131).

Consequently, Hegel's and Marx's criticisms of the French revolution as insufficiently social (Kouvelakis 2003) stand in stark contrast to Arendt's assessment. For Marx, partial interests motivate a political revolution, whereas a social revolution is motivated by the general interest. Whereas a political revolution, such as the French Revolution, "dissolves civil society into its elements", it does not revolutionise them (Marx 1978c, p. 46). Despite its social repercussions, a political revolution stops short of "human emancipation" because it creates a distinction between the "citizen", who is endowed with abstract rights such as equality, and "man", who remains embedded in stratified and unequal relations in civil society (Marx 1978c). In contrast to the relative autonomy of the state as a bureaucratic structure imposed on society, a social revolution democratises the state apparatus itself and brings it under social control (Marx 1978a, pp. 633–634).

The intertwinement of the social and political generates tensions in the revolutionary movement of which many revolutionaries are acutely aware. For instance, anti-colonial Arab revolutionaries like the leader of Egypt's 1952 revolution, Gamal Abdel Nasser, argued for the need to simultaneously achieve two revolutions: a "political revolution", in which the nation "recovers its right to self-government", and a "social revolution" that seeks to establish justice for all social classes. This task is challenging, he maintained, because the former requires national unity, whereas the latter entails disunity and social struggle (Abdel Nasser 1955, pp. 24–25).

In addition to the contestability of the political and social aspects, the intertwinement of these aspects requires caution against schematic understandings and formal distinctions. The social effect of revolutions is not simply a stage that follows the political stage. Revolutions bring a broader sense of political change and social transformation that is rarely detected in other forms of protest and change. When citizens seek to overthrow the political order that governs them they simultaneously seek to change themselves. This is because they are part of the regime that they seek to overthrow. On the one hand, the political regime's control over the state and its sustainability over time are enabled by citizens' patterns of behaviour and modes of socialisation – whether ones of cooperation, accommodation, acquiescence, indifference, or resistance (Schielke 2015). On the other hand, the "state" is intertwined with society because states do not simply provide security and regulate the economy. Their policies extend to all modes of social existence, such as subject formation, economic development, family planning, urban design, and welfare distribution, which seek to maintain stability, discipline, social cohesion, and a productive economy.

In light of this, revolutions are not easily confined to the political because revolutionary change often extends to ideas about the state, its role in society, and access to its apparatus. A revolution does not simply destabilise the "state" and its institutions but also the "social basis of the state" because it does not change only the networks of power and privilege that enable the regime but also the popular support that its hegemony maintains (Jessop 2016). The change in the social basis can be observed through different typical revolutionary measures that may include: dissolution of former ruling parties; lustration in processes of political representation and in the bureaucracy; constitutional reforms in electoral and representative systems; the entry of previously banned, or marginalised political movements (that represent different social classes than the ones that dominated the pre-revolutionary regime and benefited from its policies) into political competition and executive positions; and finally, the criminalisation of former regime officials, crony capitalists, and ruling families to tackle the endemic corruption of the old order and the confiscation of their property and restitution of their assets (Sultany 2017a).

The preceding discussion suggests that the distinction between social and political revolution can be conceptualised in two contradictory ways. Within the dominant paradigm this distinction seeks to contain revolutionary movements and aspirations to the establishment of "government under law", decries social revolutions that go beyond this goal, and (as the following section shows) further seeks through the model of "higher law" to limit these aspirations within a constitutional order that domesticates popular sovereignty. Its weakness lies in the forms of essentialism, ascriptions, and exclusions described thus far. This dominant view stands in contrast to the more critical perspective that recognises that human liberation is a work-in-progress because one form of exploitation or injustice may replace another.

VI REVOLUTION, LEGALITY, CONSTITUENT POWER

One reason for the persistence of injustice is the varying effect of revolutionary attempts to achieve rupture from the pre-revolutionary politico-legal order. The assessment of rupture is often premised on a distinction between legality (after founding) and legitimacy (of founding). This distinction is reflected in the dichotomy between the legitimating power of the people at the moment of founding (constituent power) and the legal constraints imposed on the people after the establishment of the new order (constituted power).

This question of the relation between revolution and legality should be distinguished from two separate inquiries. One involves the lawfulness of revolutions, that is, whether there is a legal right to revolution (Locke) or recognizing such a right leads to a contradiction in the constitutional order (Kant) (M. N. Smith 2008). The additional inquiry concerns the ethical attitude toward law during revolutionary struggle and prior to seizing power. For instance, Lukács (1968, p. 270) maintains "that the problem of legality and illegality is purely tactical in nature" that depends on the utility of the chosen course of action. Thus, the revolutionary masses "must be able to slough off both the cretinism of legality and the romanticism of illegality". Lukács writes (1968, p. 263):

> For by surrounding illegal means and methods of struggle with a certain aura, by conferring upon them a special, revolutionary 'authenticity', one endows the existing state with a certain legal validity, with a more than just empirical existence. For to rebel against the law *qua law*, to prefer certain actions *because* they are illegal, implies for anyone who so acts that the law has retained its binding validity.

Lukács' instrumental approach to legality seeks to de-fetishise the law and de-reify the state. He rejects the postulate of an inherent association of revolutionary activity with a consistent commitment to illegality. Revolutionary movements, then, are required to develop a nuanced position concerning the legal order. Yet, once the revolution succeeds in controlling the legal order, the primary question concerns the assessment of the relation of revolution to legality or the effect of a revolution on the legal system. This examination invites both sociological and theoretical inquiries.

Theoretically, different conceptions of law may impact our assessment of revolutionary rupture. Positivist jurists like Kelsen (1946a) focus on law as a system of rules and thus emphasise legal rupture between the old and the new legal orders given procedural violations that the revolution leads to. This approach proved influential as different constitutional courts utilised it to legitimate coups and new regimes by deducing the validity of legal systems from their efficacy (Mahmud 1994; Kumar 2016). In contrast, Dworkin's (1986) focus on principles can enable a semblance of continuity between pre-revolutionary and post-revolutionary legal systems despite the violation of the rules (Eekelaar 1973). Yet, a community's scheme of principles is abstract and contradictory (Waldron 2008; Raz 1992) and it is harder to identify a coherent scheme given the revolutionary attempt to delegitimise the previous regime. In light of this, there is no stable political valence and the scheme of principles may be utilised by counter-revolutionaries such as Burke (as in referring to the higher law of an "ancient constitution"). Thus, none of these approaches is able to proffer a systematic relationship between law and revolution because the law is incoherent and indeterminate (Kennedy 2008) and the revolution is a dialectical concept that includes its negation, the counter-revolution (Ritter 1984).

Sociologically, revolutionary rupture notwithstanding, the revolution inevitably absorbs a large part of the pre-existing legal system (Berman 1983; Schirazi 1997; Sultany 2017a). Moreover, it maintains institutional continuity – given the fact that the jurists who managed the old system maintain for the most part their position in the new system. These facts raise important questions concerning the legal effect on particular disputes during a revolutionary process. These jurists who mediate between competing claims are themselves implicated and impacted by the very social and political struggles they are regulating and resolving (Bourdieu 1987; Sultany 2017a). The rule of law they are asked to enforce is divided between past and future, actuality and potentiality, and different visions for the social order (Franklin 1970). Indeed, fundamental struggles over the meaning of the political community infuse the jurisprudential struggles over the meaning of the rule of law (Sultany 2017a).

Consequently, the existence of continuity in revolution and the existence of rupture (contradiction, incoherence, and gaps) in legality frustrate attempts to construct a clear-cut opposition in which revolution is associated with rupture and legality is associated with continuity. Thus, the revolution does not necessarily politicise the law or undermine its coherence because the law (whether pre-revolutionary or post-revolutionary) is already intertwined with politics and is already incoherent (Sultany 2017a).

Assessments of legality are conducted against the backdrop of the establishment of constitutional legitimacy. Yet, the fact that the revolution may be concurrently a counter-revolution; that the people simultaneously includes and excludes; that political and social aspects of revolutions intersect and conflict; that the revolution responds to violence but itself may be violent; and that the law before and after the revolution may be incoherent – require a more critical outlook on the legitimacy of founding than is often allowed.

Constitutional scholars and political theorists often associate the idea of revolution with the idea of the constitution as a higher law, fundamental law, or a "social contract" made by the people, in other words, the establishment of government under law (Arendt 1963; Loughlin 2010). In this sense, revolution is a legitimating concept for the political-legal order it gives birth to: the people give themselves the mode of government under which they live. It is by virtue of this popular act of political change, that brings forward a collective agency designated as "constituent power", that the newly established normative contract gets its authoritativeness and validity, or, in other words, its respect-worthiness and its binding force.

This social contract tradition is dramatised in the American Revolution and the French Revolution. These revolutions, and their associated declarations of rights, are often highlighted as crucial events for the birth, and subsequent ascendant hegemony, of liberal constitutionalism. It should be remembered, however, that similar assertions of natural rights and popular sovereignty have predated Rousseau's *Social Contract* and anticipated these two revolutions, as the Corsican Revolution and its associated constitution of 1755 illustrate (Carrington 1973). Furthermore, the subsequent European revolutions of the nineteenth century and their associated constitutions do not fit the narrative of a linear progression toward the consolidation of liberal constitutionalism (Mérieau 2019).

Revolution's legitimating power is often premised on the idea of constitutional vacuum (or rupture) at the moment of founding. Revolutionary rupture is manifested in the scholarly framing of revolutionary constitution-making as one of *ex nihilo* creation, in the sense that the people's constitution-making power unfolds unhindered by pre-existing constraints (Klein & Sajó 2012). Revolutionary constitution-making requires a change in the constitution-making power (or the identity of the sovereign), an abolition of the existing constitution, and the enactment of a new one (Arato 2000a; Schmitt 2008). In contrast, reformist constitution-making often takes the form of amendment in accordance with prescribed rules, reaffirms constitutional legitimacy, and seeks to stabilise the political regime in the face of demands for change (Sultany 2017a).

The assumption of a distinction between constituent power and constituted power fuels the debate and divides scholars into those who celebrate the unlimited power of the people (Sieyès 2003 [1789]; Negri 2009) and those who seek to domesticate it (Arendt 1963; Preuss 1994). Whereas Abbe Sieyès (2003 [1789]) celebrates the constituent assembly acting as a "surrogate" for the nation in its revolt, conservatives like Burke (1993, p. 45) and Carlyle (1902, pp. 248–262) are filled with horror and contempt at the prospect of such an act of democratic creation.

Yet, the theoretical distinction that generates the debate obscures historical realities. The assumption of rupture is often focused on formal abolition of written constitutions. It thus misses the judicial maintenance of constitutional continuity through unwritten norms and jurisprudential practice during revolutionary processes (as in Egypt after 2011). Constituent assemblies may face legal and practical constraints and may combine legislative and constituent functions (e.g., French Revolution; Algerian Revolution 1962; Tunisian Revolution after 2011). Thus, the problem may be less the absence of law as much as which kind of law, and less the "terrifying power" of the people in a "constitutional vacuum" as much as the blockage of democratic potentialities even in moments of perceived rupture (Sultany 2017a).

Likewise, Bernal (2017, p. 90) argues that the problem with dominant debates is that they represent founding as a theoretical problem rather than a political one and marginalise the people's constituent power in the process. The foundationalism that distorts the past is detrimental to the kinds of politics that can be pursued in the present. Constitutional theory, Bernal argues, needs to move beyond idealised binding origins and mythologised singular acts of founding. Instead, scholars should shift their gaze from a singularity to a plurality of founding, from theoretical to political dilemmas, and from settled to incomplete legitimacy that accounts for exclusions and under-representation. In the pursuit of such a democratisation, Bernal argues, the Haitian Revolution's model is a better guide than the American Revolution and theoretical models based on it (Bernal 2017, p. 77):

> Centered on a political conception of founding, it departs from an understanding of its problems as ones whose paradoxes cannot be foreclosed but instead remain open as problems that speak to real-world dilemmas of founding in which under-authorised actors seek to challenge existing institutions and establish new ones in a context wherein the authority and legitimacy of all ... are shaky and contestable.

Different strands highlight this contestability by insisting on the empirical reality of the people and its constituent power. The paradigm that privileges political revolutions, and excludes social revolutions, idealises constituent power. In contrast, Fanon and Nasser's anti-colonial invocation of a post-independence social revolution, and economic and racial analyses of the American Revolution are attempts to capture this sense of gap between the ideal and reality of constituent power. Likewise, Marx's distinction between the social and the political revolutions highlights the clash of interests and thus the limitations of the class-neutral conception of constituent power in the political revolution (Sultany 2021). Early republicans (like Machiavelli) provide a basis for criticising the conceptualisation of "the people" in modern constitutions "as a unitary entity of formally equal citizens, with class-blind representative forms that tend to shield from view the reality of elective oligarchy" (McCormick 2008). Whereas Sieyès considers the constituent assembly a proxy for the nation, a socialist like Marx warns against the fetishism of constitutionalism and analyses a French constituent assembly in the context of power struggles between differently situated parties (Marx 1978d, 1978e; Sultany 2021).

The insistence on the political nature of foundings is not merely a question of social democracy but also political democracy. This is illustrated in Trotsky's criticism of, and justification for, the consequent dissolution of the constituent assembly in the 1917 Russian Revolution. Trotsky (2017) criticises the elected constituent assembly as a delay tactic, a representation of the old order, and an expression of the reduction of the democratic revolution to formal democracy. Whereas Rosa Luxembourg agrees it was justified to dissolve the pre-revolutionary assembly because it represented the old order, she nevertheless argues that a new constituent assembly should have been established. One cannot generalise from the rejection of that particular assembly to "inadequacy of any popular representation whatsoever which might come from universal popular elections during the revolution"

(Luxemburg 2006, p. 208). For her, "the remedy [to the limits of democratic institutions] which Trotsky and Lenin have found, the elimination of democracy as such, is worse than the disease it is supposed to cure" (Luxemburg 2006, p. 210).

The questioning of "settled legitimacy", the representativeness of the people, the class-neutrality of constituent power, and the authoritativeness of the revolutionary founding are consequential. Scholars highlight political and theoretical attempts at the reduction of revolution to constitution (Negri 2009 on the US; Sultany 2017a on the Arab Spring). Indeed, historically, the very notion of constituent power was deployed to domesticate popular sovereignty (Rubinelli 2018).

Moreover, the argument for the openness of the constitutional order is crucial given the shrinking plurality of constitutional forms and the virtual closure of the ideological horizon in the age of neoliberal globalisation. This retreat is illustrated by the transition from the "social question" to a juridified and judicially enforced "social rights" (Gargarella 2010). The past of ideological battles over the constitution between conservatives, liberals, and radicals is sacrificed for a convergence over a limited institutional repertoire. The limited and limiting debates in constitutional theory over this repertoire convey an ideological function in which scholarly debates wish away contradictions at the basis of the political-legal order and quiet an enduring anxiety about its legitimacy (Kennedy 1979; Sultany 2012). Legitimacy, then, legitimates unjust political-legal orders (Sultany 2019).

Thus, some scholars question notions of constitutional legitimacy as misguided. Michelman (2000 and 2003b) argues that no constitution can serve as a contract for legitimacy because it is a *carte blanche* that awaits operationalization and thus its full implications – and hence its respect-worthiness – are unclear beforehand. Seidman (2013) rejects the authoritativeness of the US Constitution, claims that it should not be treated as a binding command, and calls for "constitutional disobedience". Such views provide a forceful challenge to the dominant paradigm.

CONCLUSION

Constitutional theory and the comparative study of constitutions need to recognise the richness of revolutionary traditions, the contradictions that revolutionary experiences generate, and the ultimate openness of the legal order to transformation. Idealising some revolutions and their constitutional experiences is a poor guide to the study of constitutions because it both masks the shortcomings of existing liberal constitutions and presents a non-realistic yardstick for the assessment of other constitutions. A comparison that idealises western revolutionary constitutions and discounts non-western ones is not fruitful either, because it presents no real assessment of either side of the comparison. What is required is not merely the inclusion of more experiences from the Global South than is often allowed on account of factual pluralism. Rather, there is a need to recognise these experiences as contributors to global theory, that is, as productive sites for theoretical elaboration. A unison of theory and practice in which a richer understanding of revolutionary experiences informs theoretical elaboration is preferable to the application of ready-made theory to newer and more cases. Such unison is likely to be more fruitful for a better understanding of current constitutional predicaments.

The legitimacy, stability, and durability of the constitutional order, even in liberal democratic states, are neither secure nor settled. Counter-majoritarian structures continue to deny the many the ability to rule, and wealth distributions privilege the few at the expense of the many. Capitalist political economy widens social inequalities, perpetuates poverty, and ruthlessly exploits nature for private profit. It thereby foments social unrest and endangers human survival. Social protests like Occupy Wall Street, Black Lives Matter, and Extinction Rebellion foreground the simmering tensions that lie beneath the liberal constitutional order in advanced capitalist states and its long-standing inability to realise social, racial, and climate justice. The rise of far-right populism across the globe in the past decade further exemplifies social malaise and showcases the fragility and manipulability of constitutional orders. Despite this fragility, injustice is resilient. Even where revolutions like in the Arab Spring succeed in toppling the constitutional order, the status quo reasserts itself.

Tensions and contradictions in the political-legal order are often overlooked in legal and constitutional discourses. Yet, the alienation that Hegel and Marx identify is all too apparent when public institutions and practices no longer command citizens' allegiance (Taylor 1979). Revolutions challenge rationalisations of objectionable practices and undermine the mediation of contradictions. As such, they often carry an emancipatory potential because they aspire to create the conditions that would enable human flourishing. This potential is not realised in all cases. As Hegel observed with respect to the French Revolution, revolutions often raise but leave unresolved the question of "the political realisation of freedom" and the required legal order for that realisation (Ritter 1984, pp. 47–50).

This unresolved nature of the question of freedom, democracy, and justice opens the door for further resistances and revolutions. Perhaps, then, Walter Benjamin (2003, p. 402) is correct to say: "Marx says that revolutions are the locomotive of world history. But perhaps it is quite otherwise. Perhaps revolutions are an attempt by the passengers on this train—namely, the human race—to activate the emergency brake".

RECOMMENDED READING

Arato, A. (2000a). *Civil Society, Constitution, and Legitimacy*, Lanham, MD: Rowman & Littlefield Publishers.

Bernal, A. M. (2017). *Beyond Origins: Rethinking Founding in a Time of Constitutional Democracy*, Oxford: Oxford University Press.

Calloway C. G. (1995). *The American Revolution in Indian Country: Crisis and Diversity in Native American Communities*, Cambridge: Cambridge University Press.

Fanon F. (2018). *Alienation and Freedom*. Edited by Jean Khalfa and Robert J. C. Young. London: Bloomsbury Publishing.
Hobsbawm E. (1996a). *The Age of Revolution, 1789–1848*, New York: Vintage Books.
James, C. L. R. (2001). *The Black Jacobins*, London: Penguin Books.
Kouvelakis, S. (2003). *Philosophy and Revolution: From Kant to Marx*, New York: Verso.
Losurdo, D. (2020). *War and Revolution: Rethinking the Twentieth Century*. Translated by Gregory Elliott. New York: Verso.
Luxemburg, R. (2006). *Reform or Revolution and Other Writings*, Mineola, NY: Dover Publications.
Nabulsi, K. (1999). *Traditions of War: Occupation, Resistance, and the Law*, Oxford: Oxford University Press.
Negri A. (2009). *Insurgencies: Constituent Power and the Modern State*. Translated by Maurizia Boscagli, 2nd edn, Minneapolis: University of Minnesota Press.
Sultany, N. (2017a). *Law and Revolution: Legitimacy and Constitutionalism After the Arab Spring*, Oxford: Oxford University Press.
Takriti A. R. (2013). *Monsoon Revolution: Republicans, Sultans, and Empires in Oman, 1965–1976*, Oxford: Oxford University Press.
Trotsky, L. (2017). *The History of the Russian Revolution*, London: Penguin Classics.

PART III

Institutions

PART III. A

The State

30

The State

Anna-Bettina Kaiser

I THE 'STATE' AS A TIME-SENSITIVE, NON-UNIVERSAL CONCEPT

Approaching the concept of the state is a challenging undertaking, for a variety of reasons. First, while a thin understanding of the 'state' was at least recognized in *classical* public international law based on state territory, its population and state authority (Crawford 2006, pp. 45 ff.),[1] the same is not true for the state as a concept of constitutional theory or constitutional law. Agreement on the concept of the state has never been reached. Instead, the concept is extremely time- and context-sensitive. Even though constitutional theory seeks to abstract from certain legal cultures, a constitutional theorist must not fall into the trap into which the traditional German 'General Theory of the State' ('Allgemeine Staatslehre') has so often fallen: namely, to assume that there is a universal concept of the state – that just happens to coincide with the one popularised in nineteenth century-Germany.

While there exists a pronounced continental European conceptual tradition of the state (Dyson 2009; Beaud 2013, p. 271), it is well known that neither England (Johnson 1978, p. 179) nor the US (Skowronek 1982, pp. 3 ff.) has a comparable tradition, although recent studies show that there is in fact ample evidence for the use of the concept of the state in these jurisdictions that has all too often been forgotten (for Britain: McLean 2012; for the US: Emerson 2019). Despite these recent, more nuanced analyses, it remains the case that alternative concepts such as 'government' or the 'Crown' have prevailed in Britain (Loughlin 1999; McLean 2012, p. 2 and chap. 7), whereas in the U.S., the term state is used only in limited contexts, such as the 'administrative state' (Sunstein and Vermeule 2020) or in relation to individual

---

[1] See Article 1 of the Convention on the Rights and Duties of States (Montevideo Convention), 26 December 1933, American Journal of International Law 28 (1934), Supplement, p. 75: "The State as a person of international law should possess the following qualifications: (a) a permanent population; (b) a defined territory; (c) government; and (d) capacity to enter into relations with the other states." Today, the concept of the state in public international law is highly controversial, too (Crawford 2006, pp. 96 ff.).

doctrinal concepts such as the 'state action doctrine' (Developments in the Law 2010; Minow 2017). Different terms such as 'Rechtsstaat', 'État de droit' and 'rule of law' only serve to underscore the discrepancies between the legal cultures (Heuschling 2002; Loughlin 2010, pp. 312 ff.; but see MacCormick 1984).

Meanwhile, a closer look reveals that even continental traditions themselves differ considerably. Even though the concept of the state played a central role in German public law (Dyson 2009; Möllers 2011b) and arguably still retains some meaning, its status seems uncertain. Thus, a consensus does not even exist in German constitutional law or theory – in spite of a centuries-long search for clarification. A strong statist tradition notwithstanding (Suleiman and Courty 1997), the same is all the more true for French constitutional law, where the concept had to be re-imported from German doctrine in the nineteenth century and has remained controversial ever since (Jouanjan 2004; Heuschling 2021; Jones 1993).

Second, 'state' is also a 'shared concept', in the sense that it is shared and analysed by several disciplines ranging from law, history, philosophy, and political science, to political economy and even theology. All of these disciplines have their own understandings. The sheer number of divergent perspectives will always leave us with highly different and blurred ideas of the state. Remarkably, at present political science seems to have the least problems with employing the concept of the state, applying it to (almost) all modern political systems (Levy, Leibfried, and Nullmeier 2015). This is true even for Anglo-American political science (Evans, Rueschemeyer, and Skopcol 1985).

Against this backdrop, this chapter will first ask why and how the concept of the state evolved in continental Europe and will examine why the term did not enter the legal terminology of England and later the US (sect. II). In a second step, it will introduce four influential concepts of the state from the constitutional theory of the nineteenth and twentieth centuries, as they have set the paths on which debate around the state still moves today (sect. III). Finally, the chapter will revisit the most famous critiques, to then answer the central question surrounding the 'state' in constitutional theory: what use does the concept retain today? (sect. IV).

II WHY THE CONCEPT OF THE MODERN STATE WAS INVENTED IN FRANCE AND DISMISSED IN ENGLAND

The geographical varieties in the use of the concept of the state identified above relate intimately to the divergent paths the development of the state has taken in the respective countries – or to be more precise: to the way in which conceptualizing the state from the early modern era onward has reacted to the political and institutional constellations in the respective countries. In order to explain how the concept and the historical development of state institutions connect, we have to look at the intermediate area between the history of institutions and the history of ideas. The contrast between the French and the English development shows this most clearly.

New concepts are typically the answer to new problems. This proves especially true in the case of the 'state'. The concept was invented in France to overcome the bloody confessional civil wars triggered by religious dissent after the reformation that had torn apart sixteenth- and seventeenth-century continental Europe (for the following, see Grimm 1986, pp. 89 ff.). Since the conflicting parties quarrelled over fundamental questions of truth, a compromise between them appeared entirely unlikely. A group of theorists around Jean Bodin, called 'les politiques', instead proposed the following solution: In order to restore peace, a third, 'neutral' party, the monarch, was to be endowed with the absolute power to subdue the conflicting parties. Thus, while it is true that Macchiavelli had already prominently introduced and popularised the word 'state' about 50 years earlier, the actual concept of the state was not modelled on the Italian city tyrants of the Renaissance, but on Bodin's doctrine of sovereignty and the overcoming of the feudal-estate conceptions of law (Schmitt 1958 [1941], p. 377 f.; the modern territorial states in fact soon replaced the Italian city-states in the European system of powers, Tilly 1990, chaps. 1 and 2). And indeed, it was Bodin's idea that was implemented by Henry IV of France in 1598. Thus, the absolutist state was born.

What was the key change from the previous era? Where the medieval order had been regarded as divinely given, this was no longer the case under the new circumstances. With this ontological change, the role of the monarch changed as well: Where his task had previously been to enforce and continue the existing divine order, it now became his responsibility to make laws by himself, and without invoking a divine mandate; it was he who set up the new order and was responsible for its content. The two realms, religion and public authority, thus became separated, and justice and positive law became distinguishable. This is why the genealogy of the modern state can also be told as a secularization narrative (Böckenförde 2020 [1967]). For the new, absolute power of the monarch Bodin coined the concept of sovereignty.[2] Sovereignty meant unifying all powers that had before been scattered between monarch and estates in one hand, (theoretically) unbound by the consent of others. 'L'état, c'est moi', is Louis XIV's famous comment. Accordingly, the jurisdiction of the courts, too, had to be limited to private litigation. The old Roman distinction between public and private law became decisive, although the French courts retained certain powers to control the monarch.

This conceptualization of the absolutist state rested on several institutional innovations which the monarch used to wrest political power from the estates and their medieval privileges (Tilly 1990; Ertman 1997). First and most obviously, the monarch needed a standing army to break free of the feudal system and its mutual obligations. Second and just as important, to exercise dominion over larger territories without remaining dependent on local traditional authorities, a professional administration had to be institutionalized. To staff these new administrations, lawyers were

---

[2] See David Dyzenhaus, Chapter 12, in this volume.

trained in Roman law at universities newly founded for this very purpose (Acemoglu and Robinson 2019; Gierke 1868–1913). Most crucial, however, was the question of how to finance these new structures. Indeed, the continental absolutist state was first and foremost a tax state to finance large standing armies (and later fleets) (Tilly 1990; Colley 2021). It started to become interested in economic growth to raise sufficient taxes.

In England, by contrast, the conflicts of the early modern era played out differently. The confessional conflicts of the seventeenth century did not end in absolutist Stuart rule, but in a strengthened parliament and in the relative independence of the common law courts. While the continental civil wars preceded absolutism, which appeared to be the only means of restoring peace, in England attempts at absolutism preceded civil war, which was waged to reject absolutism and which laid the foundations for the eventual establishment of parliamentary sovereignty (Grimm 1986, p. 94). Consequently, the centralised administrative, tax-raising state that had begun to take shape under Tudor rule and continued to develop in the eighteenth century in lockstep and in competition with its continental counterparts did so under the control not of the monarch, but of parliament, as 'King in Parliament' (Ertman 1997). It is ironic, then, that the abstract concept of the state, developed by Thomas Hobbes against the backdrop of the English Civil War, went on to play but a marginal role in British political thought (see Dyson 2009; but cf. Skinner 2009, p. 353 ff.). What is more, it is precisely this rejection of Hobbes' arguments that has been considered the central reason why the concept of the state itself came to be rejected in England (Johnson 1978, p. 179). By contrast, sentences like the following from the preface to the Leviathan (Hobbes 1991 [1651], p. 9) – 'For by art is created that great LEVIATHAN, called a COMMONWEALTH, or STATE (in Latin CIVITAS) which is but an artificial man; though of greater stature or strength than the natural, for whose protection and defence it was intended'; – resonated on the continent (Dyson 2009, p. 188) and were taken up early on in the German-Prussian tradition by Samuel von Pufendorf and Christian Thomasius.

These critical junctures proved path-dependent. While the continental, and particularly the German, tradition has remained highly interested in the abstract notion of the state (Ehmke 1962), the English approach was instead 'concerned with functions and powers rather than with how they all fit together to form a coherent pattern of authority.' Despite the presence of a highly effective administrative state, the *concept* of the state was hence 'dismissed as a piece of unnecessary mystification by a large number of Anglo-Saxon jurists and political philosophers' (Johnson 1978, pp. 182, 179). Factors that are seen as obstacles to the reception of the *concept* of the state are the common law system, the concept of parliamentary sovereignty, the Utilitarian tradition (which ironically in its reformist impetus required a modern state bureaucracy), and the different perceptions of the relationship between state and society. While, for instance, the traditional German understanding places the state above society (Ehmke 1962; Böckenförde 1976), in the British tradition the state has commonly been regarded as a *function* of 'civil society' (Johnson 1978, p. 182; McLean 2012, chap. 4), and has many times been relativized, perhaps most prominently in the thought of the English pluralists, such as John Figgis and Harold Laski (Runciman 1997). In more recent times, however, there have been authors from common law jurisdictions who have not just advocated taking up the concept of the state (Loughlin 2009, 2010, 2022; Skinner 1989, 2009), but have pointed to its existing traces in British legal thought that accompanied the development of a modern administrative and welfare state from the nineteenth century onward (McLean 2012). Both resistance to deregulation and privatization and the increased judicial control of the administrative state, which was triggered by the passage of the Human Rights Act in 1998, have been identified as factors that have made these earlier traces more explicit (McLean 2012, chaps. 8 and 9). Both issues already point to a potential answer to our underlying question of why a concept of the state might (still) be useful. This answer will be the subject of the next two sections.

III CENTRAL CONTROVERSIES IN THE CONTINENTAL INTELLECTUAL TRADITION ABOUT THE CONCEPT OF THE STATE IN THE NINETEENTH AND TWENTIETH CENTURY AND THEIR REPERCUSSIONS

Given the rich controversies about the concept of the state in the nineteenth and twentieth centuries, especially in continental Europe, it is impossible to reconstruct the debates in detail. I will instead emphasise four lines of thought that cover the spectrum on which debates around the state move and that each continue to resonate in the contemporary discourse. Perhaps unsurprisingly, given the historical and geographical variations in usage of the concept (see above I), these lines begin in the nineteenth-century German state theory (or react to it); more surprisingly, they end in recent revivals of state-related thought in international, including Anglo-American, debates.

Georg Wilhelm Friedrich Hegel: Sacralising the Concept of the State

On one side of the spectrum, we find Hegel's concept of the state. There is probably no thinker in the world who has done more to sacralise it. In his Philosophy of Right (*Philosophie des Rechts*) from 1821, the pinnacle of German idealism, he argues that the state is the 'divine will' (Hegel 1991, § 270, p. 292). He arrives at this view because he constructs a sequence of stages from the interest-led individual via the family on to bourgeois society and, finally, to the state where each stage grows in the degree to which it partakes in ethical life (*Sittlichkeit*). The state, then, at the peak, 'is the actuality of the ethical Idea' (Hegel 1991, § 257, p. 275). It is its task to unite the disunity of bourgeois society, not by force, but by reason. Unlike the liberals, Hegel does not want to liberate bourgeois society from the influence of the state, but conceives the state as independent from bourgeois society. He rejects individualistic natural law and contract theories. Accordingly, Hegel's concept barely provides for political participation. Instead, for him the 'unity' of the state requires an individual, the monarch, to represent it, with the executive serving him. It is commonly considered that this depiction of the monarch and the state bureaucracy tracked closely the political reality of Hegel's time, that is, late Prussian absolutism.

These positions notwithstanding, it is surprisingly difficult to classify Hegel as a thinker (not least because his writing is famously opaque). While many have drawn a line from Hegel to collectivist extremes and even proto-fascism (Popper 2011 [1945], pp. 217 ff.), the position the state takes in his theory is more complex – and in certain ways distinctly modern. It emerges from his analysis of bourgeois society and English liberal and economic thought, and his early criticism of the dysfunctionalities and (in modern parlance) externalities that a pure market society in his mind necessarily produces. Only a regulating and intervening state can, for Hegel, counterbalance these dysfunctionalities from the vantage point of the public and the common interest. It then comes as less of a surprise that Hegel not only thinks that precisely in a market society, liberal freedom can and must be limited by the state, but that he also believes that liberty can in fact only be fully achieved 'within' the state, that is, by means of the state and its interventions. For this reason, some recent interpreters see him as an early theoretician of welfare state elements (Siep 2017, p. 530).

Considering Hegel an early proponent of the regulatory state explains the remarkable success his thought had among the US-American Progressive thinkers towards the end of the nineteenth and the beginning of the twentieth century (Emerson 2019; for similar, albeit much weaker, developments in the United Kingdom McLean 2012, chap. 6). Faced with the spiralling inequality that the unfettered market forces produced during the American 'Gilded Age', the Progressives found in Hegel – once they had adapted his ideas to a democratic society – a theory of the state that did not simply see it as limiting human liberty, but as enabling liberty and indeed making it possible, through its regulations and interventions, for large parts of society (Emerson 2019, chap. 3). This ambivalence of the administrative state as either limiting private enterprise or correcting its externalities not just accompanied the construction of the American regulatory state from the 1870s onward (Skowronek 1982), it also remains present in the current debate surrounding not just the US administrative state.

Georg Jellinek: Searching for a Juristic Concept of the State

Nearly 80 years after Hegel's Philosophy of Right, it was Georg Jellinek, professor of law at Heidelberg, who conceptually developed and advanced the so-called General

Theory of the State (*Allgemeine Staatslehre*). What makes Jellinek interesting beyond the German context is that he was from the start taken up widely outside Germany – his *Staatslehre* was translated into French, Spanish, Italian, Czech, Russian, and Japanese – and his concept of the state eventually became foundational for classical modern public international law (Koskenniemi 2001, pp. 200, 203). Even today, his explanations are often the starting point for a definition of the state.

The General Theory of the State is a very peculiar German discipline that can only be understood against the background of how German public law scholarship had developed in the German Empire. At the time, the dominant methodological approach in Germany was a certain type of formalism (*staatsrechtlicher Positivismus*) that sought to 'cleanse' legal argument from its historical and political circumstances. Its best-known representatives were Carl Friedrich von Gerber and Paul Laband (Murkens 2013, pp. 12 ff.). While it is true that in their treatises on constitutional law the concept of the state played a significant role (that is why they were called treatises on 'state law' – *Staatsrecht*), it was the General Theory of the State that filled the gap that formalistic treatises on *Staatsrecht* had left. Only in the discipline of *Allgemeine Staatslehre* was the concept of the state analysed holistically – that is, not only as a legal term, but also from a historical and empirical perspective.

The discipline certainly peaked with Jellinek, who made great methodological progress in the analysis of the concept by applying his basic methodological, neo-Kantian convictions to it. Accordingly, he sought to distinguish between 'being' (empirical) and 'ought' (normative) in the concept of the state, even though he perceived both sides as phenomena of human consciousness. This method led him to his famous 'two-sided' theory of the state (*Zwei-Seiten-Lehre*). One side focused on the state as a legal concept, the other on the state as a social phenomenon. The advantage of this distinction was that, on the one hand, Jellinek was able to recognize the newly forming empirical social sciences (which his Heidelberg colleague Max Weber would very soon formalize), but at the same time acknowledge the autonomy of a distinctly legal approach (Stolleis 1992, p. 451).

As a social phenomenon, the state was for him 'the associational unity (*Verbandseinheit*) of a settled people equipped with original authority' (Jellinek 1914, p. 181, translation by author. – The inspiration for Weber is obvious). In the legal sense, by contrast, the state was primarily a corporate personality under public law (*Gebietskörperschaft*); the empirical 'association' thus becomes a legal personhood under the legal definition. This step of personifying the state is considered a German peculiarity, although it is already implied by Hobbes, and is still recognised today in German constitutional law. Both sides are connected: For a state to exist, it empirically needs state territory, people and ruling authority. Once it exists, however, the relations between the state and individuals can be understood as legal relations; precise rights and duties can be assigned to individuals.

Jellinek's theory was quickly received and widely discussed in French constitutional discourse. While it is true that France did not know the discipline 'General

Theory of the State' before – it was perceived as all-too-German – it was Raymond Carré de Malberg (1920–1922) who presented a first French General Theory of the State. Unlike his colleague Léon Duguit, who was the fiercest critic of German *Staatsrechtslehre* and who criticised its influence on the French concept of the state (Duguit 1913, p. 37), Carré de Malberg did not seek to eliminate the element of ruling authority ('puissance publique') as part of Jellinek's concept of the state and replace it by a rival French concept of the 'service publique'. In his view, ruling authority rightly formed a central component of the concept of the state. His accusation was rather that the Germans had 'abused the concept of ruling authority by turning it into an instrument of conquest, intended to give the German people a means of dominating and subjugating other peoples' (p. XIX, translation by author).

Even today, Jellinek's definition of the state is once again under discussion. Martin Loughlin (2009, pp. 5 ff.; 2022, pp. 51 ff.), for instance, takes it as a starting point when he argues strongly for the introduction of the concept of the state into British legal thought – and legal theory in general.

Carl Schmitt: Strengthening the Executive

Not long after the 3rd and last edition of Jellinek's General Theory of the State, it was Carl Schmitt who gave the concept of the state a central position in his theory. Unlike Jellinek, however, he was not interested in the genre of General Theory of the State, but centred his thinking on the state to a concrete constitution, that of the Weimar Republic. He defined the state (in Weimar times, deviating in other phases of his work) as the political unity of a people (Schmitt 1928, p. 3). For Schmitt, the concept of the state consequently presupposes that of the 'political' (Schmitt 1963 [1932], p. 20), where the political can be conceived as a conflictual state of nature. Thus, Schmitt's concept of the state – unlike Jellinek's two-sided theory of the state and even more contrary to Kelsen – no longer knows a legal side. Rather, he picks up an element of Jellinek's factual concept of the state, that is, the factual associational unity of the people, and expands it by including the element of the political (Möllers 2011b, p. 62). In the process, the concept of unity becomes central for Schmitt, though he did not use it uniformly. Since he is in any case unable to grasp the concept of unity in legal terms (Schmitt 1928, p. 8), he arrives at a substantial concept of unity that is ultimately oriented towards homogeneity.

The practical question that follows from Schmitt's construction is who can fulfil the unifying function within the state. Schmitt rules out both the legislature and the courts. While in his view the 'legislative state' remains a manifestation of the (German) constitutional monarchy of the nineteenth century, a 'jurisdictional state' (*Jurisdiktionsstaat*), where courts have the final say, would no longer even deserve to be called a state. For Schmitt, only the executive can provide the politically necessary function of creating unity. This translated into immediate political consequences under the Weimar Constitution: according to Schmitt, only the President of the Reich, as *pouvoir neutre*, was able to guarantee unity and legitimacy, against the 'societal' interests in parliament, against the political parties and not least against the social-democratic unions. Ultimately, it was he who proved to be sovereign in a state of exception.

This concept of an entirely unfettered executive has recently experienced an unlikely revival in US constitutional theory (Posner and Vermeule 2010; see also Sunstein and Vermeule 2020). Contrary to recent attacks on the US administrative state that consider its German heritage as potentially authoritarian and undemocratic (Hamburger 2014), the defenders of Schmitt's concept argue not just that the administrative state is a necessary actor in a modern society, but that it needs to be largely free from *legal* constraints to perform its various functions. The only check of any potency then remains the political process (Posner and Vermeule 2010, pp. 4–5). However, it is highly doubtful that the 'crisis of liberal legalism' in the control of executive action is anywhere near as extensive as this Schmitt revival argues.

Hans Kelsen: Demystifying the Concept of the State

Georg Jellinek's concept of state was also fiercely attacked by Hans Kelsen, who was at the same time one of Carl Schmitt's main intellectual opponents. For Kelsen as a legal positivist and founder of the Vienna School of Jurisprudence, Jellinek's two-sided theory was methodologically flawed (Kelsen 1928) and therefore unacceptable, for the following reason: In his mind, it was completely contradictory to assume, following Jellinek, that the state creates its legal order, but at the same time is itself bound by it (the so-called self-obligatory theory of the state, see Jellinek 1914, pp. 367 ff.). According to Kelsen, such a view, which hypostatizes a state behind the legal order, is purely ideological and aims at strengthening the state's authority. Kelsen's goal, by contrast, was to provide an account of the state 'free of ideology, and thus free of all metaphysics and mysticism' (Kelsen 1992 [1934], § 48, p. 99). With such an ideology-free analysis, Kelsen wanted to show that the state is a coercive social system and as such identical with the legal order (the so-called identity thesis, Kelsen 1992 [1934], § 48, p. 99). He explained this identity by pointing out that the fact that a human action is interpreted as state action is inconceivable without a legal order. It is the legal order that attributes human action to the state, making a state action out of a human action. To give an example: Only by way of the legal system does a person's wave become a police officer's order. Accordingly, contrary to the traditional doctrine, it is precisely not possible to speak of a state that precedes the legal order. And this is why Kelsen considered Jellinek's 'two-sided' theory of the state impossible to maintain, for as a system of norms, the state cannot be described sociologically (Somek 2006, p. 757).

It is immediately obvious that the continental theory of the state in the wake of Hegel was in need of such a methodological critique, of such an 'iconoclastic project' (Somek 2006, p. 754). However, it is hardly surprising that Kelsen found little success: the Anglosphere was sceptical about the concept of the state anyway.

And the continental tradition, in particular the German one, did not want to dispense with its concept of the state. This is all the more true since the legal positivism that Kelsen advocated was considered outdated in Germany after the Weimar Republic.

Remarkably, however, Kelsen's theory found a following in France. There, under the influence of Kelsen's student Charles Eisenmann, a Kelsenian tradition had been developing since the 1920s. It is in this context that the currently most sophisticated French theory of the state, presented by Michel Troper, should be understood. In his work 'Pour une théorie juridique de l'Etat' (1994), he first observes a crisis in the general theory of the state. Neither a link to its metaphysical tradition nor to radical legal-theoretical positivism is viable. The state is therefore in a theoretical void. Like Kelsen, Troper assumes that the state can only be understood in legal terms. However, he does not follow Kelsen's identity thesis. According to him, Kelsen contradicts himself when, on the one hand, he claims the identity of the legal order and the state, but, on the other, he himself must speak of the state within the legal order. Troper then calls for a renewed general theory of the state in the form of a meta-theory (Troper 1994, p. 22) that has been described as a neostructuralist programme aiming at a quasi-ethnological view of the respective legal systems (Schönberger 1999, p. 135).

IV IS THE STATE A USEFUL CONCEPT FOR A FORWARD-LOOKING CONSTITUTIONAL THEORY?

In order to be able to answer the central question whether, especially after Kelsen's insights and objections, the concept of the state can still be a meaningful concept for a forward-looking constitutional theory, we must first deal with two main objections: Is the concept of the state perhaps – as exciting as its intellectual history may be – a concept of the past that has long since become obsolete? And second: Should the concept of the state be replaced by other concepts, such as that of the constitution?

The Death of the State?

The death of the state has been announced by authors of very different directions, at different times, and for different reasons. Outside of legal discourse, Marx and Nietzsche were particularly influential in this respect. Marx famously proclaimed that under advanced communism the state would eventually wither away: the goal of the revolution, and the rule of the proletariat, should be to create a classless society that would make the state as an instrument of (bourgeois) control superfluous.

In the (German) legal discourse on the state, talk of the end of the state was introduced by Carl Schmitt of all people. As early as 1941, he declared the state to be a historical phenomenon of a certain epoch whose time had expired. From the institutional-historical development of the concept of the state (see above sect. II), he concludes that the modern state emerged under very specific historical conditions, that France then became the state par excellence, but that the concept remained restricted to continental Europe. The common assumption that the concept of the state was a general concept that applied to all peoples and times is misleading in his view. As he concluded: 'This elevation of the concept of the state to the general normal concept of the political form of organisation of all times and peoples will probably soon come to an end with the age of statehood itself' (Schmitt 1958 [1941], p. 376). In 1958, Schmitt supplemented his remarks with a short explanation: 'In the meantime, the hitherto closed unit [of the state] is opening up, from within through pluralisation, from without through integration' (Schmitt 1958, p. 385). This provided the central keywords for further debate.

Schmitt's student Ernst Forsthoff took up the thesis of the *internal* dissolution of the state prominently in his 1971 book, 'Der Staat der Industriegesellschaft' (The State of Industrial Society). What Forsthoff reacted to was the 'semisovereign state' (Katzenstein 1987) of the Federal Republic of Germany after 1949. It was one in which the federal government was bound up in a number of negotiating networks that severely limited its capacity for unilateral action: within the federal state, within the neocorporatist structures of the autonomous 'social partners', and within the party coalitions under proportional representation, the emergence of all of which Schmitt had analysed (and lamented) during the Weimar Republic. Similarly, there was an increasing number of voices that considered the state to be overburdened in many respects, especially if it had committed itself to be a welfare state, as the Federal Republic had done. When states increasingly involve private actors to pursue state purposes, this too was interpreted as a sign of a loss of state authority. These laments at times entered alliances with system-theoretic (Luhmann 1998) or neoliberal theories.

These and comparable swansongs of the state, however, also triggered a countermovement. The anthology 'Bringing the State back in' by the political scientists Evans, Rueschemeyer and Skocpol (1985), which reacted not to a corporatist environment, but to Robert Dahl's pluralist theory of democracy (Dahl 2006), proved to be particularly influential in reconceiving the state as an autonomous actor in problem-solving in modern societies. In Germany, too, a major discussion subsequently developed around the rediscovery of the state. Even the renaissance of a General Theory of the State was discussed not only in Germany (Schuppert 2003; Voßkuhle 2004), but also in France (Jouanjan 2004) and England (Loughlin 2009). What these interventions showed was that retaining the state as a concept to signify the independent problem-solving capacities of the (administrative) state as one actor in a modern society serves important descriptive and normative functions. This is in no way meant to deny the immense challenges that states face today (Poggi 1990, chap. 10). But, as the Covid crisis has shown, states have the capability of acting in an emergency and have also retained a certain superiority over the economic system, even in the United States.

But what about the dissolution of the state from *without*? Does the hyperglobalisation of the past thirty years render the (national) state a mute concept? The increasing international networks are typically interpreted not just as questioning state authority, but even as challenging the concept of state territory (Loughlin 2009, p. 17). What is more, global problems, such as the climate crisis, which transcend state borders, exceed an individual nation-state's capacity to solve them. Here, too, the question arises whether the state has had its day as an actor and ordering concept. Indeed, statehood has undoubtedly changed in times of globalisation. Its concept must therefore inevitably be adapted. To name the most prominent example, with regard to the relationship between the EU and its member states the term co-production of statehood is now used to illustrate shared statehood (Börzel 2013, p. 226). However, just as with the internal diffusion of statehood, it seems premature to abandon the concept of the state altogether in the case of external diffusion. At the extreme end, Brexit in particular shows that international linkages can also be reversed, even if Britain has had to pay a considerable price for this. But also with regard to global phenomena, such as environmental pollution, there are studies that come to the conclusion that it is quite unclear whether they weaken or strengthen the state, not least because their cooperation appears the most prominent means of addressing them (Mann 1997).

State and/or Constitution

But if we still accept that the institution and hence the concept of the state remain important, we need to address, in a second step, its relationship to the concept of the constitution. In recent times, the concepts are all too often used interchangeably; while 'state' is seen as the German, loaded term, 'constitution' appears as modern, fresh, and unburdened. In Germany, for example, the term 'Staatsrecht' was gradually replaced by 'constitutional law' (Verfassungsrecht) without any (major) change of content. In fact, the concept of the constitution has been so successful that it has long been applied to entities beyond the state, such as the EU (Weiler and Wind 2003). There is even talk of new forms of multi-level constitutionalism. Do these developments perhaps render the concept of the state expendable?

But this alternative between 'state' and 'constitution' seems to confuse two aspects. If the state retains its importance because at its core it is the instrument with which the public can collectively pursue its goals and solve its problems, both internally (most notably vis-à-vis the economy) and externally (collectively targeting climate change, for instance), this does not at the same time mean that we are allowed to play off this entity and its tasks against its constitutional constraints in the way that Schmitt and his followers have done. In fact, Kelsen can serve as an important reminder that, in systems with a written constitution, it is often the constitution itself that *creates* the state in its general outlines, as an organisation structured by law. This points, at the same time, to an important constructive role that the concept of the state plays in constitutional law: We need the concept of the state as an object of attribution so that no diffusion of responsibility occurs (Voßkuhle 2013, p. 383). In the same vein, Loughlin speaks of the state as a 'scheme of intelligibility' (Loughlin 2009, p. 8). Civil servants, for example, do not act in their own name, but for their state. It is obvious that such a concept of the state is – and can only be – a thoroughly legal one (Johnson 1978, p. 183).

The Place of the State in Constitutional Theory

To sum up: The state as a concept remains indispensable to constitutional theory, because it allows us to do several things. First, it permits us to analyse the precise relationship between state actors and society or the public and the private, empirically and normatively, by identifying the state as the vehicle for collective action in the name of public interest. This avenue brings constitutional theory into contact with political science and political economy that investigate from a comparative and normative perspective the relevant relationships between the state and, most importantly, the economy (Thelen 2014). It rests eventually on Hegel's insight that a modern liberal market society needs an autonomous decision-making centre to redress its externalities. Of course, such a concept must heed Kelsen's warning not to become metaphysical – not least because the charge of metaphysics has helped to bring into disfavour the state as a public, collective actor (Buchanan and Tullock 1990).

Second, the concept opens up both empirical avenues of investigation into the extent to which the state as an autonomous actor is insulated in its decision-making capacity from other actors, as well as the more fundamental normative question to what extent it should, or should not, be insulated in such a manner. Modern states are made up of complex decision-making structures and bound up in elaborate networks of democratic and judicial control. It is one of the most important tasks of constitutional theory to describe and to assess these structures and controls. We cannot fulfil this task without a concept of the state.

RECOMMENDED READING

Dyson, K. (2009). *The State Tradition in Western Europe. A Study of an Idea and Institution*, 2nd edn., Colchester: ECPR Press.

Emerson, B. (2019). *The Public's Law: Origins and Architecture of Progressive Democracy*, New York: Oxford University Press.

Grimm, D. (1986). The Modern State: Continental Traditions. In F.-X. Kaufmann, G. Majone, and V. Ostrom, eds., *Guidance, Control, and Evaluation in the Public Sector*. Berlin & New York: Walter de Gruyter, pp. 89–109.

Jellinek, G. (1914). *Allgemeine Staatslehre*, 3rd edn., Berlin: O. Häring.

Levy, J. D., Leibfried, S., & Nullmeier, F. (2015). Changing Perspectives on the State. In S. Leibfried, E. Huber and M. Lange et al., eds., *The Oxford Handbook of Transformations of the State*. Oxford: Oxford University Press, pp. 33–58.

Loughlin, M. (2022). *Against Constitutionalism*, Cambridge, MA: Harvard University Press.

McLean, J. (2012). *Searching for the State in British Legal Thought. Competing Conceptions of the Public Sphere*, Cambridge: Cambridge University Press.
Möllers, C. (2011b). *Staat als Argument,* 2nd edn, Tübingen: Mohr Siebeck.
Poggi, G. (1990). *The State. Its Nature, Development and Prospects*, Cambridge: Polity Press.
Skinner, Q. (2009). A Genealogy of the Modern State, *Proceedings of the British Academy*, 162, pp. 325–370.
Troper, M. (1994). *Pour une théorie juridique de l'Etat,* Paris: Presses Universitaires de France.

31

The Material Constitution

Marco Goldoni

The material constitution is an analytical instrument whose function is to provide a reconstruction of the constitutional order by integrating the analysis of the written or formal constitution with the formation of the social order. Its origin can be traced back to the doctrinal need of solving troubling puzzles about constitutional reality in European states: What counts as the constitution in a given jurisdiction? What is the identity of the constitutional order? When is the constitutional order undergoing a transformation?

Given its relatively unknown status in the Anglophone world, a working definition of the material constitution is a good starting point. The material constitution is *the political unity of a set of purposes or goals (fundamental norms) pursued by political subjects and institutions*. The material constitution is one term (the *explanans*) of an explanatory relation. The other pole (*the explanandum*) is the constitutional order. The analytical function of the material constitution is to grasp the relation between the organisation of the social order and the form of the constitution. It should be added that the material constitution does not necessarily stand against or behind the formal or (when available) written constitution, although this at times might happen. As such, the notion is not attached to a specific normative theory, and it can be understood from different methodological standpoints as long as the latter focus on the relation between fundamental social relations and the constitutional order. Furthermore, as an explanatory device, it can be applied to a multiplicity of constitutional experiences. In other words, it is not a notion limited to the explanation of liberal and democratic constitutional orders. For this reason, it is relevant for comparative constitutional studies as well.

Before exploring the history and the main aspects of the notion, it is necessary to introduce a distinction with another idea, the living constitution, in order to avoid potential misunderstandings. While there are some affinities, as both notions emphasise the importance of social organisation for constitution-making and interpretation, they are not the same. The living constitution's main concern revolves around the interpretation of the constitutional text (cf. D. Strauss 2010) and how to keep it updated – usually, through judicial means – when the social context has changed. Its main, but not exclusive, target is originalism. In short, the approach of the living constitution implies that 'law in action' ultimately should prevail over 'law in books'. While not irrelevant for the analysis of a specific material constitution, the notion of living constitution is more limited in scope and does not address the same set of questions addressed by an inquiry focussed on the material constitution.[1]

I MATERIALITY AND ITS CONCEPTIONS

As mentioned above, there are different theoretical entry points to the concept of the material constitution. The key difference is determined by the identification of the ordering principle of social relations. The common theme between these trends is that the material constitution emerges as the outcome of the organisation of fundamental social relations, but each tradition identifies those relations according to (at times profoundly) diverging criteria. Whether the principles or aims pertain to the dimension of economic organisation, national or religious identity, or around moral values and principles, the focus is always on how the constitutional order is strictly associated with the organisation of social relations (for an overview, see Grimm 2016, pp. 143–158).

Materialist Thought

In the history of political thought, the first conception of the material constitution was formulated within the materialist tradition. The key aspect of the Marxist version is the emphasis on the social structure. The author of *Das Kapital* did not write much about law and certainly not much about constitutional orders. Most of these observations have often been accused of being reductionist because they treat the constitutional order as the mere super-structure of the economic base. A classic example of this approach can be found in a famous passage from the *Critique of Political Economy*: 'The totality of [...] relations of production forms the economic structure of society, the real basis from which rises a legal and political superstructure, and to which correspond specific forms of social consciousness' (Marx 1996, pp. 159–160).

This view paved the way for the idea of the material constitution as the site where modes and relations of production are organised and articulated, while the formal law (and constitution) are simply overdetermined by this material basis. At least in this version, law seems to be a reflexion of an already instituted (pre-legal) system of production. The function of the legal system is to protect and consolidate those modes and relations. While there is debate in the Marxist field on whether Marx's

---

[1] It is not by chance that the notion of the living constitution is discussed in the US constitutional debate where it is necessary to interpret an old (and rarely amended) text. Bruce Ackerman (2007) uses this notion as well, but as it will become clearer below, his constitutional theory and his idea of constitutional regime can be better understood as a North American version of the material constitution.

oeuvre was consistently reductionist, the strongest reductionist formulation of the material constitution was put forward by the socialist thinker Ferdinand Lassalle in a couple of lectures given in 1862 on the concept of the constitution. As we shall see, Lassalle's conception contained an important intuition in contrast to the then hegemonic liberal conception of constitutionalism, but unfortunately developed the notion in a way that lacked any nuance. To the question 'what is the nature of the constitution?', Lassalle replied with the following definition: 'A constitution is the fundamental law proclaimed in a country which disciplines the organization of public rights in that nation' (Lassalle 1942). This is because, fundamentally, Lassalle thought that 'constitutional questions are not primordially legal questions, but a matter of relations of force' (ibid.). The latter implies that the material constitution is pure fact: a set of raw relations of domination whose power shapes the organisation of social relations. In the end, for Lassalle reference to the material constitution had an unmasking function: it showed to the public that the formal constitution was almost entirely irrelevant and merely served as a placebo for the dominated classes. According to the German thinker and politician, the reality of the constitutional order should be looked for at the material level of power relations and the formal constitution should be dismissed as a legitimising trick.

For the sake of accuracy, it should be noted that not all the materialist canon has fallen prey to the reductionist fallacy. In the twentieth century (see, for a reconstruction, Hunter 2021) a less reductionist version of the idea of the material constitution became prominent in Marxist scholarship. As noted by Bob Jessop (2019), Antonio Gramsci and Nicos Poulantzas have sketched conceptions of the material constitution that go beyond the distinction between base and superstructure. In a manner relevant to the contemporary theory of the material constitution, Gramsci explicitly mentions the distinction between governors and the governed and makes it an inherent aspect of the division of labour: 'one could say that that division is a consequence of the division of labour, a technical fact' (quoted in ibid., 127). Despite the fact that his political theory never mentions the idea of the material constitution, his lesson remains very important because by introducing the idea of hegemony it avoids the shortcomings of the reductionist version. Culture, education, and communication are deemed by Gramsci not simply as superstructural systems, but as equally important in governing and shaping a society both at the macro- and micro-level. With Gramsci, the materiality of the constitutional order is formed not only by labour, but also by the social and cultural imagination, which remains irreducible to sheer ideology.

Overall, the materialist contribution to the development of the material constitution can still offer two precious lessons: first, the organisation of the productive aspects of society (meaning: its political economy) is immanent to the development of the constitutional order (but it does not overdetermine it); second, the constitutional order should be addressed not just as ideology but as one of the historically-specific forms of struggle around principles of social organisation. Hence, the study of the material constitution should not be conducted simply as a critique of constitutional ideology.

Legal Institutionalism

The strand of thought that has produced the most refined and rich theories of the material constitution is legal institutionalism (for an introduction: La Torre 2010; Loughlin 2017). Common to all legal institutionalists are two features: first, the anti-positivist insight that modern constitutional orders develop around the distinction between the objective legal order (*ius*) and legislative/statutory law making (*lex*). Second, constitutional orders are supported by legal and political institutions whose function is to structure the connection between society and the state. It is impossible to give a full account of the rich institutionalist constellation and, therefore, only what could be deemed two of its most accomplished theorists will be discussed.

The first theorist is Carl Schmitt, particularly his constitutional theory (Schmitt 2008) and more specifically the 'concrete order' phase of his thinking (Loughlin 2015; Lindahl 2015). In formulating something akin to a material constitution, Schmitt was targeting the weaknesses of the Weimar constitution and its lack of a clear organising principle. But his guiding distinction between the constitution (*Verfassung*) and constitutional laws (*Verfassungsrechte*) captured something beyond the contingencies of the Weimar crisis. The first notion, which Schmitt also calls constitution in the absolute sense, is intertwined with the political unity of the social order and it operates as an active principle behind its development. Schmitt identifies six distinct but related aspects of the absolute constitution, but they are all 'expressing a (real or reflective) *whole*' (Schmitt 2008 [1928], p. 59). For Schmitt, the absolute character of the constitutional order is key and cannot be overestimated: it is only with the synthesis of concrete and normative senses of the constitution that authentic political unity can be achieved. The second notion, the constitution in the relative sense, is the aggregation of statute-like constitutional norms and other ordinary decisions whose legitimacy rests on the idea of the constitution in the first sense. This distinction allows Schmitt to criticise constitutional positivism as incapable of giving an account of the juridical dependency of the constitution in the relative sense from the constitution in the absolute sense. In fact, his main worry is how to achieve political unity and for this reason he postulates that the bearer of the constitution has to be a homogenous collective subject capable of taking existential decisions on its own political identity. At this point, Schmitt was still considering the social homogeneity of the collective as a given.[2] In the years following

---

[2] It should be reminded that this was a point of friction with Kelsen. Interestingly, the latter developed a conception of the material constitution as well. His starting point was that the material constitution would be a procedure, and in particular a distinctive lawmaking procedure, around which a society would find a temporary equilibrium (Vinx 2007, pp. 56–58).

his *Constitutional Theory*, Schmitt came to recognise the importance of moulding social homogeneity and investigated how institutions become the building block of the concrete order of each constitution (cf. Croce and Salvatore 2013, chaps. 3 and 4). Scared by the centrifugal forces of social pluralism, Schmitt thought that constitutional ordering ought to proceed by selecting the institutions compatible with the creation of social homogeneity. Nonetheless, the gist of his conception of the material constitution is already available at the end of the 1920s: the form of the political unity contains a constitutional core whose transformation (formal or informal) is equivalent to the dissolution of the unity itself in favour of a new constitutional regime (cf. Loughlin 2010, p. 215).

The second theorist is Costantino Mortati, who developed a systematic conception of the constitution in the material sense. Mortati wrote his most important book in 1940 (2025; cf. Rubinelli 2019a) after a long reflection on the governing function as a separate and autonomous State function and its relevance to Italian Fascism. Despite his aim being to show that the Fascist political regime had *de facto* changed the Italian constitutional order, his work transcends that context. The realist basis of his constitutional analysis avoided the essentialism of Schmitt's constitutional theory and any reference to entities such as the nation or the people. Instead of relying on the essentialism or the vagueness of these notions, Mortati identified the role of a bearer (a subject, or, in Gramsci's terms, a 'new prince') of the material constitution, whose political will left an imprint upon the organisation of the constitutional order and the pursuit of fundamental aims. Like Schmitt, Mortati recognises that the origins of the constitutional order are always political, and this fact reverberates in the history of the constitution itself. In the work of Mortati, this kind of subject, like in Gramsci, takes the form of the political party, an organised machine whose task is to mediate the entrance of the masses into state politics. Unlike Schmitt, Mortati thought that the principles of organisation of the political subject would carry with them normative force and radiate throughout constitutional creation. Only the political party could organise social relations in a way that is conducive to the pursuit of aims whose generality will reverberate across society.

Therefore, the key intuition developed by Mortati is that the organisation of social relations does already express in itself principles of organisation with a juridical nature (Mortati 2020, pp. 13–14). The main building block of this organisation are institutions, whose function is to maintain connected, but distinguished, social relations and constitutional development. According to Mortati, it is the process of differentiation that drives the organisation of social relations and produces the essential constitutional distinction between those who govern and those who are governed (cf. Loughlin 2003, p. 5).[3] The process of differentiation is not an act of sheer

---

[3] According to Mortati (2020, p. 123), this distinction is more fundamental than the Schmittian couple friend/enemy.

political will (although it is a fundamental political choice) because it is driven by principles or aims inherent to the process itself. For this reason, Mortati speaks of institutional facts, that is, facts that are inherently normative. It is in the notion of the institution that Mortati sees the bridge connecting social relations (and their cleavages) to the constitutional order. Furthermore, as it is for Schmitt, the identification of these institutional facts signals an unmodifiable constitutional core. Unlike Schmitt, however, Mortati does not pit the material versus the formal, but sees the material sense of the constitution as an integrative modality which, under normal conditions, include and explain the role of the formal constitution as well.

Legal institutionalism has provided other interesting versions of the material constitution but it is time to take stock. Two key points are still valuable for contemporary constitutional theory. First, unlike reductionist Marxism, legal institutionalism has put a juridical and political nexus at the core of the formation of the material constitution. In this way, it has also shown the juridical nature of the purposes or aims of each constitutional order. Any legal order has an orientation and strives to follow it. In other words, ordering is never an atelic activity, but it is always projected onto one or more objectives (Cover 1983, pp. 43–44). The second lesson is the introduction of institutions as the fundamental material component of the constitutional order. Institutions are supposed to act as the connecting devices between social relations and legal ordering. However, at least in the work of Schmitt and Mortati, they are rather the object of constitutionalisation than the subject of the constitution-making processes. Accordingly, state constitutions are still presented as a rather coherent and homogenous construction. The proliferation of societal sites in recent decades have made the latter claim much more questionable.

Societal Constitutionalism

Given the association with materialist and fascist doctrines, the institutionalist versions of the material constitution have not received much attention outside certain European states (mostly, France and Italy). Nonetheless, some of the issues addressed by the material conception of the constitution have not disappeared. In fact, in the second half of the twentieth century, one can detect traces of the notion in the work of important representatives of social theory. The question of materiality has taken up a new salience in different sociological schools (see Pottage 2012), from the structural inflection of the theory of fields to actor-network theory and systems theory. The latter is probably the stream of thought that has devoted most attention to constitutional orders and, in recent times, has developed fully fledged constitutional theories (see the impressive works by Thornhill 2011; Teubner 2012; Neves 2013). Three of their contributions are extremely relevant for the discussion of the material constitution as they all thematise the internal relation between societal ordering and constitutional formation. Teubner captures this relation in the most effective way when he makes reference to the idea of constitutionalisation as a complex self-description of society (Teubner 2012, p. 21).

The first important contribution from systems theory is the idea of the constitution as an evolutionary achievement which, according to Niklas Luhmann, is understood as the outcome of a structural coupling between the political and the legal system. This achievement has a double quality: it provides reserves of public power by bringing different systems to share structural elements but, at the same time, it preserves the autonomy of the social sub-systems and their functional differentiation. The second important contribution is Teubner's further expansion of Luhmann's intuition to the complexity of other social sub-systems. Teubner assumes that social sub-systems (not only the political system) can reflexively couple themselves with law and become constitutionalised. The state remains a fundamental institution, but ceases to be the exclusive site of the material constitution. In this way, Teubner has opened processes of the constitutionalisation of society to the autopoietic contribution of social fragments (1993). Yet, as he notes, 'constitutions outside the state need to satisfy the requirements of a "material" concept of constitution, according to which a constitution establishes a distinct legal authority which for its part structures a *societal* process (and not merely a political process, as is the case with nation-state constitutions)' (Teubner 2012, p. 74). Not all couplings successfully establish material constitutions, but only those that achieve a certain level of structural stability and reflexivity. The third important contribution is the belittling of the importance of political will in the formation of the material constitution. In this way, any residue of political opportunism is removed from constitutional theory. Societal constitutionalism does not exclude the existence of political will, but the latter has to be always mediated by the medium and the code of each social sub-system.

Yet, there are two important differences with the previous institutionalist versions that still apply and should be emphasised. First, systems are not organised around aims or purposes, but functions. The point of coupling sub-systems is indeed to allow them to perform their functions by employing law to supplement social reflexivity with secondary legal rules. In practice, structural couplings consolidate or stabilise social processes and avoid the risk that they become paralysed by their own paradoxes (Thornhill 2011, p. 18; Teubner 2012, p. 107). A crucial difference with previous versions of the material constitution is the recognition of growing social differentiation and the importance of preserving the operative autonomy of each sub-system. Once a society is assumed to be organised according to these coordinates, the institutionalist idea of the material constitution as a project (Kahn 2019) or as containing a spirit or principle, becomes secondary and marginal.

The second main difference is that institutions function as the recognition of the legal dimension of social relations. Yet, while institutionalists like Santi Romano and Mortati directly equate institutions with law, systems theorists hold that institutions are the product of the structural coupling between social sub-systems and the legal system. Under this description, law and politics maintain their full autonomy.

Allegedly, the innovative contribution of societal constitutionalism implies the recognition of the reflexive moment: social institutions in themselves do not contain any immanent principle or rule, and they become endowed with a material constitution only through a self-reflexivity engendered by structural couplings. This is where constitutionalisation does most of the work: it is supposed to stabilise the normative expectations of individuals and, at the same time, to open up constitutional orders to the inputs of social actors (e.g., movements).

II HOW TO MAKE ORDER

It is time to take stock of the previous overview and to summarise the main tenets of a contemporary conception of the material constitution. In doing so, some of the lessons previously highlighted will be synthesised in an attempt to show that the notion of the material constitution is still relevant for contemporary constitutional studies.

The primary question to be asked is: what should be identified as relevant ordering factors under conditions of modernity? In the following, four factors are taken as highly influential (but not exclusive) in moulding the material constitution: (1) formation of legal and political unity; (2) an effective governing activity; (3) political subjects that link social organisation and the governing activity by pursuing (4) a set of purposive norms (which can take, among others, the form of principles, aims or values). The starting point of this analysis is the recognition that the modern state remains the main form of political unity, but it is no longer the only relevant constitutional actor.

The reference to the state allows to identify in the creation of political unity a crucial factor of ordering. Political unity introduces spatial and temporal coordinates which enable the legal order to make sense of certain social interactions under its own terms. Of course, the construction of political unity within the constitutional order is a way to draw fault lines of inclusion and exclusion (Lindahl 2013). But part and parcel of the drawing of these lines is a moment of selection which defines what can be included or excluded in that order. This is not surprising: there is a typically modern attitude in the definition of political unity given that it takes place against the background of an increasingly complex social organisation driven by the principle of division of labour. In fact, the formation of political unity (and its determination as a concrete political unity) is inextricable from the organisation of labour as a productive and reproductive process of social and natural relations. But the relation between the organisation of productive activities and differentiation is not of a causal nature: the political moment still plays a key role in assembling and re-organising social relations. At the constitutional level, unity is the outcome of processes of differentiation and specification. Differentiation is a process which entails the distribution of roles and positions within productive social relations. In modern circumstances, differentiation is the first step towards the unfolding of the division of labour. Specification implies the ascription of roles and positions to certain social groups or elites. It goes without saying that specification is not a neutral process, but one that brings about social and, accordingly, legal hierarchies. Specification is propaedeutic to the individuation of the governing class. It should be noted immediately that these two processes (differentiation and specification) do not undermine the creation of political unity. To the contrary, under conditions of modern capitalism, they are part and parcel of the construction of unity. The latter is the end result of an assemblage of differentiation and specification. Ultimately, unity will be granted by fundamental norms; however, these norms cannot function as *a priori* conditions of knowledge. Fundamental norms will have to include or express the organising principles or values of differentiation and specification. Moreover, given that differentiation and specification are imbricated in the political economy of a concrete society, contradictions within the organisation of society might always play out and disrupt (or at least undermine) political unity in the longer term.

The processes of differentiation and specification bring us to the second ordering factor, *the art of governing*. Processes of differentiation and specification have to be steered, otherwise they cannot maintain political unity. This is an activity that is in charge of managing the organisation of powers and fundamental social relations. It is usually defined as governing and its analysis entails a move beyond a formalist understanding of a classic principle of constitutionalism. In modern times, the basic principle of constitutional organisation is the separation of powers (Möllers 2013). Constitutional doctrine understands it as the separation of functions (typically: legislative, executive, judicial) and their distribution to different organs. While the idea of different functions sheds light on the nature and the working of constitutional organs by describing their activities (e.g., adjudicating or executing), it remains insufficient for explaining the formation and development of the material constitution. The formal separation of powers can be observed from the perspective of the material constitution. Besides (or together with) functional differentiation, a *governing activity* that operates as an engine of unity for the different functions is necessary. There is political unity only as long as there is the capacity for unitary governing activities.[4] Yet, the construction of unity is not for the sake of unity, but for the purpose of setting up and consolidating a concrete constitutional order with its social organisation and its aims. Governing can mean several things, and historically its relation with the constitution has mutated. In the twentieth century, a continental constitutional tradition has tried to understand the art of governing as a fourth autonomous function (see Mortati 2001) to be placed 'above' the classic three functions. In this way, the governing function would not be confused with executive

---

[4] A critical point for political unity is represented by the other important constitutional principle of organisation of powers: federalism. Things become more complicated with the distinction between federation and confederation. While for the former term, it is relatively uncontroversial that the distribution of powers would still be compatible with a unitary form of government, it is less clear that the same can apply to confederations. See Stephen Tierney's contribution in this Handbook.

power and would steer all the other functions in order to ensure that, despite their difference in kind, they do not pull toward radically diverse directions. This is a key point. Functions might be distributed to different organs (the legislative function, for example, can be shared by the legislature and the executive, as is the case in most constitutional orders) but they always assume typical forms: the legislative function, for example, is characterised by lawmaking processes. But is it possible to typify the governing function? It looks like there is no typical form of the art of governing. For this reason, it is better to talk of a governing activity rather than function (see Loughlin 2003, p. 5). Governing is an activity that can be undertaken in many ways, and it is necessarily compatible with the forms of the standard three functions. For the same reason, there is no need to postulate that the governing activity is entrusted with one supreme organ (though, this has often been the case) or it is an exclusive state competence.[5] In fact, the art of governing has been increasingly the domain of the political system and, more specifically, of political parties. The awareness of the importance of political parties is far from being a novelty, and it cuts across different jurisdictions and constitutional schools: from the US (see Levinson and Pildes 2006) to the Commonwealth model (see Bellamy 2007, chap. 5). But in other realities as well, the political direction of the constitutional order is still determined by political parties.[6]

The mention of the role of political parties brings us to the third factor represented by the *subjects* undergirding and supporting the constitutional order. The creation and the maintenance of the material constitution requires a bearer (*Träeger*), that is, one or more social groups or political collective subjects whose political interests can shape the constitutional order and direct it along a specific trajectory. The bearer of a material constitution cannot be vague and underdetermined subjects such as the people or the nation. They also need to find expression in institutional form. As legal institutionalists have emphasised, the collective subjects or social groups are, in different degrees of complexity, and according to the context, already organised (and they carry within themselves the principles of their own organisation and the interests they want to pursue).[7] In order to be able to imprint their projects on the constitutional order, the dominant groups have to organise themselves and control certain structures of agency.

The connection between the art of governing and dominant political groups is realised by the fourth ordering factor. Governing activities can be understood only

---

[5] Another important distinction should be drawn with the principle of sovereignty. But as it should become clear, unlike governing, sovereignty is not an essential trait of the material constitution. The case of the EU represents a good example (see the following section).

[6] Though one could imagine other organisations or institutions being the main forces behind the art of governing.

[7] An insightful analysis of the work done by the representative claims of social groups (and their ordering force) is offered by Lindahl (2013, chap. 2). Lindhal's analysis is a healthy reminder of how even within social movements, structures and principles of organisation can unfold in a way that contains ordering principles.

as directed toward *fundamental political objectives*. The material constitution is formed around certain purposes which, on one hand, enable the consolidation of important political subjects, and on the other hand, operate as the point of convergence for different political groups. As is the case for the governing activity, fundamental political objectives do not have a typical or unique form or content. The substantive aims of a material constitution can be found expressed in various features of the formal constitution (e.g., in mission statements, as noted by King (2015), or as constitutional directive principles: Weis 2017), as well as in constitutional principles and values from time to time invoked by constitutional actors. Though it is often the case, it is not necessary that all the fundamental aims are written down. In modern constitutional orders, many things can become a fundamental aim, from the recognition of dignity as the fundamental constitutional value or the strict separation between church and state to price control or creation of a competitive market. But, of course, these aims have to be sufficiently broad and pervasive to entail either the preservation or the moulding of fundamental social relations. Accordingly, a change in one of the fundamental aims is tantamount to a constitutional transformation. This is the case because fundamental political aims carry with them juridical weight as well and they have to be factored in when legally interpreting the constitution.

III CONSTITUTIONAL ISSUES: IDENTITY, CHANGE, ORGANS AND SUPRANATIONAL CONSTITUTIONALISM

A fair question is whether it makes sense to speak of a material constitution under contemporary political and economic conditions. First of all, the notion has a distinctive Euro-centric flavour and it has been conceived without taking into account key constitutional phenomena like colonialism. Second, it is open to debate whether it can be used for the analysis of the constitutional order of increasingly complex societies. Without the possibility of an appeal to a fictitious social homogeneity, the key ordering role of leaders or political parties, one might legitimately question whether in the twenty-first century it is still relevant to speak of a material constitution rather than a number of plural non-constitutional fragments (see Krisch 2011), which stand in a relation of dialogue or conflict. The answer cannot be but a qualified one. For certain constitutional topics, the notion of the material constitution still carries an important epistemic value, in particular, for its capacity of explaining the constitutional dimension of political economies driven by a variety of forms of capitalism. Accordingly, the study of the material constitution is an exercise in constitutional understanding and not in normative design.

The area where the use of the notion is most valuable is that of constitutional change and identity. As for the latter, it is often the case that the material constitution can provide a guide to grasp constitutional reality when the form of the constitution is deceptive. In these cases, looking at the material constitution is the only way to grasp what is the 'real' constitutional order. A classic example is represented by the constitution of the Soviet Union. Even Kelsen (1948, p. 58) assumed that in order to identify the constitution of the Soviet Union, which formally contemplated democratic rights and freedoms, the public lawyer had to study not the written constitution, but the organisation of the Communist Party.

An analysis of constitutional change through the lenses of the concept of the material constitution can be truly rewarding. Constitutional change has troubled public lawyers since the inception of the discipline and in the last decades has been the source of a highly sophisticated debate (see Ackerman 1991; and, more recently, Roznai 2017; Albert 2019). The classic question revolves around the idea of inherent limits to constitutional change: is it legitimate to change a constitution through the channel provided by the procedure for constitutional amendments? And what is the difference between transformation and amendment? Looking at these important questions from the point of view of the material constitution may strengthen the accuracy of the analysis. In order to determine the nature and scale of constitutional change, the analysis ought to focus more on the material aspects than on the procedure followed for changing the constitutional order.

In this way, looking at the material constitution makes it possible to identify 'false negatives' and 'false positives'. A false positive can be avoided by not focussing simply on the formal constitution. For example, the re-organisation of the Swiss constitution in 1999, observed from the perspective of the material constitution, comes across not as an authentic constitutional change but as a simple rationalisation. The main principles and aims of the Swiss federation (and most of its political subjects) have not been changed by the codification of a new constitutional document (Biaggini 2011). Another example is provided by the 1992 Saudi Arabia's written constitution. This is not a sham constitution as it does not promise a fully fledged *constitutionalist* order. Rather, it mostly codifies the already existing order with the addition of a few marginal concessions (see Al-Fahad 2005, who speaks of 'ornamental constitutionalism').

On the other hand, false negatives can also be detected when a constitutional change has taken place without being formally registered in the written constitution. A classic (though clearly controversial) example is the New Deal (for a reconstruction sensitive to the re-organisation of the Welfare state, see Ackerman 1998), a sweeping package of reforms (extending from labour to social security), which was not approved through constitutional procedures of amendment. Yet, the scale and breadth of the social transformation of the labour market and the new type of social security introduced during the Roosevelt presidency, together with an impressive cycle of electoral hegemony, ushered in a new constitutional regime.[8] Another example is the emergence of the fascist regime in Italy. Formally, the 1848 constitution (*Statuto Albertino*) had never been abolished and there is no

---

[8] Ackerman makes a normative case for the legitimacy of this informal constitutional transformation: having won in a series of consecutive landslide victories the majority in Congress and the Presidency,

shortage of doctrinal opinion which has maintained that it was still valid during the fascist age (Palladin 2008, p. 35). But the core aspects of the constitutional order had been clearly transformed between 1922 and 1928: new labour-capital relation, the rise of a single-party political system, a new electoral law, the transformation of the Chamber of Deputies into a corporatist parliament, and the abolition of freedom of association. Despite the fact that the previous constitution had not been formally abolished, Gerhard Leibholz (2007, p. 115) observed that only some representative functions of the King had been maintained from the *Statuto Albertino*.

Another important dimension added by the study of the material constitution is the determination of what counts as a constitutional organ (as opposed to administrative agency) in a concrete legal order. This is important for democratic and liberal constitutional orders, as it helps in determining the standard of accountability of an institution. From the perspective of formalist constitutional analysis, the identification of an organ as constitutional has often appeared to be the outcome of circular reasoning. Usually, a constitutional organ has been identified as one of the essential components of the existence of the state and the determination of its form. The classic tripartite division of formal state functions is a representative example of that approach. However, for the definition of the form of the state, reference to its constitutional organs is usually made. In order to address the issue in a more satisfying way, it is better to look at the substantial connection between the fundamental aims of the constitutional order and the relevant organ. It is by looking at the degree of connection between the two that it becomes possible to define an organ as playing a constitutional function and, hence, being viewed as a constitutional power. In the last four decades, the transformation of some central banks into autonomous and independent institutions have made them organs whose capacity of constituting and regulating fundamental relations of credit and debit cannot easily be described in purely administrative terms (cf. Desan 2014).

Finally, another important question is whether it makes sense to speak of the material constitution of supranational organisations. As is known, it is doubtful that even the very idea of the constitution can be meaningfully applied to those legal orders. As already noted, the notion has always been conceived in a context that took for granted the state as the main unit of reference. For example, the unitary organisation of a spatial and temporal matrix has always been more easily associated with traditional forms of political power such as empires and states. For supranational and global legal entities, it is much more difficult to identify the bearers of the material constitution and their fundamental aims. The answer, indeed, varies from case to case.

> Roosevelt had sufficient political support based on a prolonged deliberative effort by the American public. Yet, the deliberative quality of the constitutional change does not undermine the fact that the two major changes (according to Ackerman himself) of constitutional regimes are associated to dramatic re-organisation of how production is organised. The abolition of slavery represents a swift constitutional change also because it makes possible the establishment of a different political economy.

An illustrative example is given by the European Union, whose constitutional nature, in the absence of a written constitution, is still controversial and debated. It is not clear, for example, which types of policies the EU constitutional order can accommodate, that is, whether it is open to any type of content (for a pluralist understanding, see Kaupa 2016). Yet, an analysis of the EU constitution through the lens of its material basis allows one to see that the EU has indeed a material constitution, although a relatively fragile one. It is a derivative constitutional order,[9] as its existence is not autonomous, but fully dependent on the member states. Nonetheless, as shown by Olivier Beaud (2009), its organisation instantiates a form of political unity, whose bearers are national governments, and whose fundamental aims are the realisation of the single market and the transformation of the member states through a shared set of economic and financial standards (Bickerton 2012). The main constitutional organs of this constitutional order are the European Council, the Council in its various formations (Puetter 2014) and the European Central Bank.

IV THE MATERIAL CONSTITUTION AND THE RULE OF RECOGNITION

As already mentioned, the reconstruction of the idea of materiality can be done in different ways and shape alternative views of the constitutional order. In fact, it is possible to conceive the material constitution both from a legal positivist and a non-positivist perspective. In particular, some clear affinities between the notion of the material constitution and the rule of recognition can be detected. It is possible, for example, to imagine the material constitution according to the influential conventionalist conception of the rule of recognition (Hart 1994, pp. 255–256; Marmor 2001, pp. 28–29). Philosophically,[10] conventions have been conceived as a way to solve coordination and strategic interaction issues (see the classic D. Lewis 1969). It has soon appeared that Hart's rule of recognition could be interpreted as a convention among officials for the identification of what counts as law in a given system. Hart himself, in the *Postscript* to the *Concept of Law*, admits that his practice theory of rules, while not applicable to moral rules, can explain which type of rule is the rule of recognition (Hart 1994, pp. 266–267). In this version, officials converge over a rule of recognition to solve their coordination problems. But in the following adaptations of the rule of recognition, the convention becomes constitutive of a social practice and also, at least partially, of its point and value (Marmor 2001, p. 19). One can see how this would translate into an explanation of what a material constitution is: the bearers of the constitutional orders are the officials or political institutional subjects who recognise a set of rules as the condition of existence of the

---

[9] For the distinction between original and derivative legal orders, see Romano 2017, 56.
[10] The conventions discussed in this section are quite not the same as those discussed in the British constitutional tradition, but this is a topic that is beyond the scope of this chapter.

constitutional system because of a convention which allows a convergence of the relevant actors around the same secondary rules. In short, the material constitution would be the equivalent of a set of constitutional rules of recognition. Once applied to the constitutional order, the great advantage of this conception is that it would not need to postulate consensus among officials over the content of substantial constitutional rules. Philosophically, legal conventionalism has always proved an appealing approach for those who wish to understand the reasons why agents decide to converge on certain secondary rules, even though their internal reasons for doing so might be quite different. This is the case because the validity of a conventionalist rule of recognition is based on content-independent reasons. As Andrei Marmor (2008, p. 10) has elegantly remarked, 'the reason for following a rule that is a convention depends on the fact that others follow it too' and not on its content. According to this account, the conventional rule respects two conditions: a condition of *dependency* and a condition of *arbitrariness*. The former postulates that one of the reasons for following a convention is that others do the same. The latter assumes that there is an element of arbitrariness in the choice of the convention. The conventional rule can be arbitrary (i.e., it could have been otherwise) even if it reflects moral or political convictions (Marmor 2001, p. 21). Ultimately, it is the rule-following behaviour that makes it a conventional rule and not its substantial content. This is a plausible way of making sense of contemporary (pluralist) constitutional orders and it explains the appeal of the conventionalist perspective. It cannot be denied, also, that this is a legitimate way of reconstructing the material constitution: eventually, the material constitution would be a compromise among political forces based on a convergence over a set of conventional rules whose adoption is largely independent from their content. For example, this would make a good explanation for a procedural constitutional order where alternative and agonistic political forces agree only over the procedure to settle their deep disagreements. But the approach suggested in this chapter is incompatible with such a conventionalist reading precisely because neither the condition of dependence nor arbitrariness can be met. If the art of governing, the kind of political subjects and the kind of aims pursed by them are defining elements of the material constitution, then the conditions of dependence and arbitrariness have to be excluded. Dependence should be excluded because the reason for identifying the relevant rules would be given by the purposes of the constitutional order. At the same time, arbitrariness cannot play a major role in a material constitution because often the determination of constitutional norms is driven by the selection of fundamental political aims. A conventionalist interpretation does not put enough emphasis on the political and material aspects of the constitutional order because it takes a social convention to be the organising principle of order. The coordination issue prevails over the content of the constitutional order. In this way, the juridical relevance of fundamental social and political facts is left outside of the realm of constitutional knowledge. Rather than a conventional rule of recognition, it is more accurate to speak of a material constitution in terms of a set of fundamental and purposive norms deeply intertwined with the social organisation of a political community. For the constitutional lawyer, the challenge lies in reconstructing the constitutional order in light of these fundamental norms.

RECOMMENDED READING

Ackerman, B. (1998). *We the People: Transformations*, Cambridge, MA: Harvard University Press.
Beaud, O. (1994). *La Puissance de l'État*, Paris: PUF.
Colón-Ríos, J. (2020). *Constituent Power and Law*, Oxford: Oxford University Press.
Goldoni, M., & M. Wilkinson (2018). The Material Constitution. *Modern Law Review*, 81 (4), 567–597.
Lassalle, F. (1942). On the Essence of Constitutions. *Marxist Archive*. Available from: www.marxists.org/history/etol/newspape/fi/vol03/no01/lassalle.htm.
Lindahl, H. (2013). *Fault Lines of Globalisation*, Oxford: Oxford University Press.
Loughlin, M. (2010). *Foundations of Public Law*, Oxford: Oxford University Press.
Mortati, C. (2025). *The Constitution in the Material Sense*, Abingdon: Routledge.
Neves, M. (2013). *Transconstitutionalism*, Hart: Oxford.
Poulantzas, N. (2000). *State, Power, Socialism*, London: Verso.
Romano, S. (2017). *The Legal Order*, Abingdon: Routledge.
Schmitt, C. (2008). *Constitutional Theory*, Durham, NC: Duke University Press.
Teubner, G. (2012). *Constitutional Fragments*, Oxford: Oxford University Press.
Thornhill, C. (2011). *A Sociology of Constitutions*, Cambridge: Cambridge University Press.

32

Federalism

Stephen Tierney

Federalism is a distinctive form of constitutional rule but one that has largely been neglected by both political and constitutional theory. Despite its widespread proliferation since the Second World War (Burgess 2012, p. 2; Elazar 1994, pp. xv, xvi–xvii), existing accounts of federalism tend to focus almost exclusively upon its institutional manifestation, describing different forms of federal government and analysing how these operate in practice. What is lacking is an account of the common conceptual underpinnings that unite these various institutional forms within the genus of one constitutional idea. In this chapter I argue that the core idea of federalism can only be arrived at by way of constitutional theory.

Constitutional theory explains both how and why law is used to manage political power. It has tended, however, to subsume federal constitutionalism within one, universal account of all modern democratic constitutions, assuming that unitary and federal constitutions perform the same functions. The key argument I put forward in this chapter is that different families of constitutionalism, while each does indeed serve the common function in the management of political power, perform this key public law task for specific purposes. Federalism, as one of these families, requires to be addressed as a discrete constitutional subject differing from unitary constitutionalism on this most fundamental register. A federal constitution manages and transforms political power for a discrete purpose that is fundamentally distinguishable from other constitutional forms; and this purpose manifests its discrete characteristics across the anatomy of constitutional law: foundations, subjects, authority, institutional design and dynamics of change. I contend that federalism must be addressed as a specific genus of constitutional government for the modern state which, in the act of constitutional union, gives foundational recognition and accommodation to the state's constituent territorial pluralism. The purpose of the federal constitution is to maintain the foundational relationship between pluralism and union through the creation and reconciliation of different orders of government. This marks a significant fork in the road between federal and unitary constitutionalism, not just in institutional terms but at the most fundamental level of constitutional identity and legitimacy.

A definition of federalism's purpose from the perspective of its legal-normative effect differs markedly from approaches which seek to identify the *political* purposes, which have lain behind particular decisions to promulgate a federal constitution, such as the building of a strong state, the consolidation of democracy across large territories, the division of governmental power in the name of liberty and the opportunity to experiment in policy development.[1] These political motivations have clearly been key factors in leading political actors to establish federal constitutions. However, there is a critical difference between the political motivations that tell us *why* a federal constitution is established and the act of federalising itself which concerns *what is done* in legal terms at that moment of promulgation. Making this distinction clear also demands that we address constitutional purposes in a categorically different way from political purposes. Constitutional purposes are tied to, and derive their meaning from, the nature of a constitutional founding and the fundamental ways in which political power is ordered in that moment: in the legal effects of that founding rather than in the political goals that the founders may have had. It is when we address federalism through the lens of constitutional foundations that we identify the particularity of constitutional purpose: the normative order which the constitution founds gives foundational constitutional recognition and accommodation both to territorial pluralism and to the relationship of union, which the act of constitutionalisation represents; in so doing it establishes a normative order designed specifically to manage this relationship as the fundamental totem of the polity's constitutional identity; the task of the constitution and the governmental fabric it creates is to manage the inherent tension between pluralism and union by way of legally-structured patterns of institutional and behavioural reconciliation. A diversity of political goals may have motivated this move but as constitutionalists we must focus our enquiry upon the legal consequences which it brings about.

The federal idea, therefore, represents a discrete tradition within modern constitutionalism. Collective territorial subjecthood is both the core feature of federalism and the key to understanding the legitimacy of normative authority within a federal constitutional order. This is in marked contrast to unitary constitutionalism, the underpinning legitimacy of which is understood exclusively through the lens of individualised subjecthood. In this chapter I discuss how federalism has generally been neglected by both political and constitutional theorists. I then make the argument that federalism, far from being an outlier in relation to modern state constitutionalism, is an entirely modern form of constitutional rule for the state, and therefore that it must be conceptually accommodated within modern constitutional theory in a similar way to unitary constitutionalism. The attempt, which we find within the literature, to side-line federalism as an alternative to the modern constitutional state stems from a tendency to elide

---

[1] For a classic statement of these traditional purposes see the opinion of O'Connor, J. in *Gregory v Ashcroft*, 501 U.S. 452 (1991).

the concepts of state and constitution themselves (Forsyth 1981, Beaud 2009). As I will argue below, this is conceptually misconceived. Nonetheless, the salience of territorial subjecthood to the founding of a federal constitution demands that federalism, while an order of rule for the modern state comparable to unitary constitutionalism, be addressed as an entirely distinct constitutional tradition. The normative fundamentality of constitutional foundations and the implications that flow from territorial as opposed to individualised constituent power act as discrete legitimising resources for federal constitutions. It is only in appreciating how at the moment of constitutional founding 'federal constituent power' launches and validates a new and distinctive genus of constitutional order that we can alight upon the real significance of federalism as a discrete idea of rule for the modern state.

I FEDERALISM AND THE THEORY DEFICIT

There is a vast literature on federalism that has scrutinised the political and constitutional structures of particular states (Aroney 2007; Morgan and Davies 2008; Gagnon 2009; and Umbach 2002); addressed the comparative dimension of federalism (Watts 1998; Burgess 2006 and 2012; Hueglin and Fenna 2006); analysed its institutional design (Filippov, Ordeshook, and Shvetsova 2004); offered assessments of the behavioural underpinnings of federal systems (Livingston 1956; Erk 2008); considered the implications of federalism for the functioning of political systems and state economies (Riker 1964); and addressed how federal relations play out in practice through party politics (Truman 1962), political culture (Cole et al. 2004) and political attitudes and identities (Friedrich 1968; Chhibber and Kollman 2004). Much of this work has served greatly to illuminate the practice of federalism and, in particular, the tensions and strains which attend it. But this literature has not in the end produced a clear conceptualisation of the legal-normative essence of federalism as a form of modern constitutional government. Indeed, conceptual confusion besets the constitutional idea of federalism.

Most of the analytical work that has been done on federalism has been conducted by political scientists. Their attention understandably tends to be directed to the practice of federal government rather than its conceptual substructure. Nonetheless, political scientists have brought important theoretical insights to the study of federalism, addressing for example its relationship to democracy (Stepan 1999; Forsyth 1981) and to the new turn in plurinational theory (Gagnon and Tully 2001; Keating 2001; Norman 2006). Others have taken strides in re-exploring the historical origins and traditions of federalism (Hueglin 1999; Hueglin and Fenna 2006), while further interventions attempt to take stock of the proliferation of federalism in a time of globalisation (Gamper 2005). But it is frequently noted nonetheless that more comprehensive theoretical interventions are lacking. Burgess argued in 2006 that as yet there was 'no fully fledged theory of federalism' (Burgess 2006, p. 1),[2] an observation also made by others,[3] some of whom contrast this gap with the plethora of theory concerning other systems of government. Wayne Norman, for example, observes: 'the role of the federal ideal in the standard histories of political thought has been *unjustifiably* neglected in our intellectual tradition' (Norman 2006, p. 82). He goes further in suggesting that federal scholarship has an active aversion to theory: 'federalist theorizing is almost entirely ignored by the mainstream tradition that has generally taken the frontiers of the nation-state as the frontiers of the discipline itself' (ibid.). Feeley and Rubin share this view: 'In light of its prominence as a governing arrangement and of the many and varied benefits advocates claim for it, one might expect there to be a vast and robust literature on federalism. Yet there is not. There is certainly no shortage of literature on federalism – in fact, there has been a deluge of it in recent decades – but virtually none of it presents a theory of the subject.' (Feeley and Rubin 2008, pp. 1–2; and see also Feeley 2012, p. 2).

When we turn to the canon of political theory, federalism has tended not to feature in theories of democracy (Weinstock 2001), and this omission has not been corrected in the past few decades, despite federalism becoming such a significant feature of constitutional practice. For example, federalism is rarely if ever discussed in the work of contemporary political philosophers as a factor which might impact upon their notions of justice, remaining 'understudied and poorly understood' (Levy 2007, p. 459). This is so even for scholars such as John Rawls (Rawls 1971, pp. 101, 357) or Jürgen Habermas (Habermas 1996) who came from, and spent their academic lives working within, federal constitutional systems. In discussing Rawls, Margaret Moore notes that his work tends to ignore the territorial dimension of government altogether: In 'A *Theory of Justice*' Rawls begins with the convenient simplifying assumption that the just society is closed: that it is a 'self-sufficient association of persons', thereby abstracting from the issue of the territory to which 'the just society' is entitled and the relationship of that territory to other territories.' (Moore 2015, p. 4). She goes on to observe: 'little attention was drawn to the fact that Rawls also assumed that justice operated within a *territorially* delimited political community (a state) and the territorial dimension of the state was not addressed in anything like adequate terms.' (Moore, 2015, p. 4). In a related way Norman observes that he and other political philosophers turning to address federal theory in the 1990s 'knew that our "mentors" – philosophers like Rawls, Nozick, and Dworkin – were silent on the mysteries of federalism. So too were almost all of their communitarian, feminist, and socialist critics during the 1970s and 1980s.... Standard texts in democratic theory generally avoided the topic, as did our field's principal journals,

---

[2] He continued: 'At best there is partial theory based upon rigorous conceptional analysis and the pursuit of terminological precision. At worst there is crass empiricism rooted in the failure to develop concepts and define the key terms.' (Burgess 2006, p. 1).

[3] In 2011 Scott argued: 'there is no theory of federalism' (Scott 2011, p. 1). Hueglin and Fenna agree: 'a general theory of federal state formation does not exist' (Hueglin and Fenna 2015, p. 98).

Ethics and *Philosophy and Public Affairs*.' (Norman 2006, p. 80) A helpful collection of those theoretical accounts of federalism that do appear within political philosophy is offered by Norman in a collection edited with Dimitri Karmis (Karmis and Norman 2005). However, the notable absence of 'greats' from this volume bears out Norman's observation.

It is perhaps not really a surprise that federalism has been so neglected given that it has tended to be either treated as a particular form of 'state' rather than constitution – an ungainly and distant relative of, rather than partner in, modern state constitutionalism (Forsyth 1981; Beaud 2009), or subsumed within one generic account of state constitutionalism and thereupon treated as just another way of dividing authority within any modern constitution, categorisable alongside separation of powers or checks and balances as an internal division of authority with no salient implications for the fundamental nature of the constitution's underpinning authority itself.[4] This is unsatisfactory. The crucial innovation that federalism introduces to politics is not as a distinct category of statehood but rather as a category of constitutionalism. We see this when we address statehood and constitutionalism in the context of sovereignty. Sovereignty has two dimensions – external and internal. The external or outward-facing perspective of sovereignty vis-à-vis other states and the international community is a singular concept that imbues the sovereign 'federal state' with a singular international personality of the same nature as that of the 'unitary state'. It, therefore, makes no sense from the perspective of constitutional theory to attempt to draw any meaningful distinction between federal 'states' and unitary 'states'. Federal constitutionalism is a distinct form of government but this does not imply a distinct form of statehood; the state is the default political construction of modernity, defined by its relationship to other states and in this way conceived in singular terms, for example, by international law's refusal to accept a state's internal constitutional arrangements, including federalism, as in any way qualifying the state's duty to perform its international obligations.[5] This is the characteristic of sovereignty shared by all modern federal systems emerging since Philadelphia.[6] In order to understand

---

[4] We see a combination of both approaches in Olivier Beaud's work. Beaud deploys two distinct categories in discussing federalism. First, there is 'federation', a *sui generis*, form of rule different from 'states'. Although Beaud attempts to differentiate 'federation' from the older term confederation, in fact, the two bear strong similarities: 'A Federation arises from the agreement between States that confederate to create a new political entity' (Beaud 2017, p. 35). Secondly, there are polities which he terms 'federal states' which are simply modern states like any other but with a federal constitution. The 'federal state' is not truly federal because in its internal constitutional form it rests upon a single source of sovereignty. A federation, by contrast, is built upon plural sources of sovereignty: the founding territories. For a further deployment of these two categories in an account of the European Union, see Larsen (2021).

[5] Vienna Convention on the Law of Treaties, Article 27.

[6] My concern is with the constitutional arrangements within states. I leave to one side efforts to conceptualise sovereignty within the multi-state European Union. See Bellamy (2019). Whatever legal form this body is deemed to have acquired it is founded upon international treaties that should not be conflated with the federal constitution of a state.

the federal idea as a distinctive concept of constitutional rule since 1789 we must view it squarely within the context of the modern state (K. Kelly 2017, pp. 174–175). It follows that the relative federal or unitary nature of a polity are features of *constitutionalism*, not of *statehood*.

Federalism shares with unitary constitutionalism the core generic purpose of modern constitutionalism: managing political power within a modern state. That said, it is not merely a form of authority division comparable to the division of institutional powers between executive and legislature, ultimately referable back to a monist source of constituent power resting in one undifferentiated 'people' in the way a unitary constitution is. A federal constitution's distinctiveness rests upon how, from the foundation of the constitution, it is characterised by an entirely distinct set of legitimacy-authority relations from those which underpin a unitary constitution; relations founded upon pluralised territorial subjecthood. Federalism's particularity emerges in how, as a form of modern government for the state, it offers a categorically different way of constitutionalising the state in the name of territorial rather than merely individual subjects. In the next part of the chapter, I take forward this argument, situating federalism squarely within modern constitutionalism.

II FEDERALISM AND MODERNITY

A number of scholars trace the origins of the federal idea to the pre-modern period, arguing that it is in fact an inter-temporal concept that both predates and potentially outlives the modern state (Elazar 1994; Hueglin 1999). It is my contention that while the notion of plural sites of government is certainly a feature of pre-modern Europe, and while there is some intuitive attractiveness in trying to draw links between this period and modern federalism, it is in general misconceived to equate pre-modern with modern constitutional concepts. Federalism as the constitutional form which we recognise today originated in the promulgation of the American constitution in 1789. Furthermore, whereas Locke conceived of federalism in reference to the external relations among independent entities (Locke 1988 [1689], 2.120), and while this remained an *idée fixe* among many of those contributing to the Philadelphia debates, what in the end emerged from these deliberations and from the Federalist Papers that did so much to articulate the nature of rule which they produced (Hamilton, Madison, and Jay 1961 [1787–88]), was the fashioning of a hybrid form of government that reached, as Tocqueville could see, towards a new idea – the notion that the modern state could accommodate multiple governments and that a constitution could be founded for that purpose. As Tocqueville observed, a new type of government did emerge at Philadelphia, even if its essence was not at that time fully unveiled: 'Human understanding more easily invents new things than new words ... a form of government has been found out which is neither exactly national nor federal; but no further progress has been made, and the new word which will one day designate this novel invention does not yet exist.' (Tocqueville 1835, pp.

237–238; Karmis 1998, pp. 67–72) The Philadelphia process was truly developmental as LaCroix also observes: 'a set of ideas about government that was later called "federalism" began to coalesce at the convention'. (LaCroix 2011, p. 2)

While it is mistaken to view the American constitution as itself synonymous with the constitutional idea of federalism, it is clearly the first instance of this essentially modern form of government for the modern state from which any attempt to define its underpinning constitutional conception must pay due attention.[7] A crucial step which marks out post-Philadelphian federalism from the more amorphous forms of segmented government described, for example, by Althusius (Althusius 1995 [1603]) in the pre-modern period is that, in constitutional terms, the seventeenth and eighteenth centuries witnessed the emergence of a category distinction between private and public orders of rule (van Caenegem 2012). Public authority took on a depersonalised form and adopted a clear line of hierarchy for each discrete polity, transforming the medieval idea of multiple and over-lapping sites of authority into a new concept that encapsulated ultimate, territorially bounded constitutional sovereignty for particular loci of rule. This process of husbanding political power was consolidated in the abstract idea of the state: a territorial locus within which the constitutionalisation of public rule could be embodied and nourished (Loughlin 2010). In short, the state became the sole source of political authority over a definable territory, replacing the intersectional orders of power and authority that characterised the pre-modern period in Europe. For Weber, the state also encapsulated the idea of one political community and the absolute and final source of political rule that emanated from it (Weber 1978). But Weber's vision of the state is in itself the theoretical culmination of the unitary essence of sovereignty theory in the tradition of Bodin (Bodin 1955 [1576]) and Hobbes (Hobbes 1991 [1651]). Federalism as a constitutional form within the state is in this context categorically different from amorphous orders of plural rule over the same space by cities, regions or the Holy Roman Empire. But it is its function as a form of constitutionalism for the state that marks out federalism as a modern idea of constitutional rule.

The founding of the American constitution was self-consciously aligned to the intellectual tradition of contemporary contract theory, drawing eclectically from a rich range of European philosophical resources (LaCroix 2011; Klarman 2016). It was at the same time a hard-headed attempt to construct a strong state for two

---

[7] 'The history of modern federal government ... begins with the adoption of the US Constitution in 1789 and the break with the historical practice of confederalism.' (Hueglin and Fenna 2015, p. 73). Clinton Rossiter also notes that: 'The Federalist converted federalism from an expedient into an article of faith, from an occasional accident of history into an enduring expression of the principles of constitutionalism' (Rossiter 1961, p. xii). The early connection between federalism and constitutionalism works in both directions: 'federalism has contributed significantly to the development of what we now think of as "a constitution"' (Hueglin and Fenna 2015, p. 275). It is partly on account of this elision that the specificity of federalism as a constitutional category has been lost within the broader innovation of modern republican government, which has tended to locate its source of legitimacy within a territorially-undifferentiated popular sovereignty.

main purposes: to remedy the centripetal defects of the Articles of Confederation under which the American states had been ruled since the revolutionary war, and to rival – and protect the new republic from – the increasingly powerful nation states of Europe. (Federalist No. 9 and 10 [in Hamilton, Madison, and Jay (1961)]). The dominant ideological turn which the American founders drew from European political thought was what we today would term liberal individualism. At the same time, the conception of the state evident in contemporary debates was one that built upon the monistic tradition of state sovereignty that had crystallised in early contract theory (Dienstag 1996). As such, the vision of the American polity that emerged was one that, in line with other projects of state-building at the time, eschewed the constitutional pluralism of the pre-modern period and its tendency towards faction and weakness, the pathology of which appeared to have been confirmed in the constitutional experiment from 1781 to 1789 (Federalist No. 9, 51 [in Hamilton, Madison, and Jay (1961)]). The simple mantra of one sovereign state for one conceptually unified and demotically undifferentiated people became the leitmotif of modern statehood, ultimately as much in the United States as elsewhere. But it is also in this act of constitution-making that the great tension at the heart of federal constitutionalism is made clear: a foundational commitment both to the central constitutional significance of the states and their individual governments on the one hand and to the union of these states in a common constitutional project on the other. The American constitution brought federalism into the fold of modern political statehood, constitutionalism and public law, and in doing so, transformed the federal idea from a more inchoate pre-modern conception of plural orders of rule. But it is also in this act that seemingly deep contradictions emerge: in the creation of a *singular* order of rule (the constitution) the legitimacy of which derives from, and the life of which is designed to accommodate, the existence of *plural* sources of territorial authority. The constitution was founded in the name of We the People of the United States, an ambiguous term, at once both monist ('the People') and pluralist (of the 'States') in expression. In order to understand this innovative turn in modern constitutionalism we must turn to constitutional theory.

III TOWARDS A CONSTITUTIONAL THEORY OF FEDERALISM

Constitutional theory has developed greatly as a discipline in recent decades (Loughlin 2005; Galligan 2008), and yet, as Amnon Lev puts it: 'The surge of interest in the foundations of public law has yet to extend to federalism.... As a result, we know very little about the intellectual foundations of the federation; what the values and ideas are that underpin this type of polity, inform its government and shape the normative expectations of the governed' (Lev 2019, p. 1). A significant problem for constitutional theorists is that where work in federal theory does exist it has tended to elide empirical analysis with normative prescription. This trend is not new – Alvin Jackson observes that the nineteenth- and early twentieth-century commentators on federalism 'were more concerned with earnest evangelism than with rigorous theology' (Jackson 2018, p. 30)[8] – but it is a feature of the late twentieth-century narratives. Michael Burgess noted that a pathological failing of federal scholarship was its tendency to deal 'simultaneously with fundamental moral questions as well as with amoral matter-of-fact issues' (Burgess 2006, p. 1). One prominent proponent of federalism was Ronald Watts whose very definition of federalism is overtly normative. In distinguishing federalism from 'federal political systems' and 'federations', he states: 'In this distinction, "federalism" is used basically not as a descriptive but a normative term and refers to the advocacy of multi-tiered government combining elements of shared-rule and regional self-rule' (Watts 2008, p. 8). Michael Burgess identified correctly that the respective approaches brought to the study of federalism by political theorists and politics scholars are in fact incommensurable: 'The moral basis to federalism derives from certain inherent virtues, such as respect, tolerance, dignity and mutual recognition, which lead to a particular form of human association, namely, the federal state or federation. The amoral foundation suggests that no such qualities inhere in federalism at all and that it is nothing more than a particular constitutional and/or political technique for achieving certain overarching goals such as territorial expansion or economic benefits and security.' (Burgess, 2006, p. 1).

While Watts' three-fold classification of federal forms and the pithy shared-rule/self-rule distinction (first drawn by Daniel Elazar – [see Elazar 1994]) may be insightful in explaining both different ways of thinking about federalism and why federalism has proven so attractive to human societies or political actors, they do not of themselves tell us *what federalism is* as a form of constitutional ordering of the modern state.[9] A stark example can be found in the fact that radical disagreement has even attended the very question of how many federal systems there are. Ronald Watts declaimed that there were merely 23 'federations' in the world (Watts 1998). This is seemingly in stark contrast with the late Michael Burgess, a passionate advocate of federalism, who argued in 2012 that, since 1945, approximately one-third of the states had adopted or were moving towards a federal constitutional system (Burgess 2012, p. 2). Daniel Elazar, an earlier pioneer in the revival of federal studies after the Second World War went further, asserting in the mid-1990s that of the world's 180 states, over half, with approximately 80 per cent of the world's population, were federal or had some kind of federal arrangement (Elazar 1994, pp. xv, xvi–xvii). It is extraordinary that leading scholars working in any field should arrive at such conspicuous disagreement as to the very scope of their discipline. However, on closer inspection, it transpires that very different meanings were being accorded by these scholars to the respective terms 'federal', 'federalism' and 'federation', the

---

[8] Feeley and Rubin (2008, pp. 5–6) also warn against the distorting effects of prescriptive accounts.
[9] As Feeley and Rubin put it: 'Despite the alleged tough-mindedness of political scientists ... and legal scholars, their treatment of the subject remains mired in sentimental attachment to the idea of federalism' (Feeley and Rubin 2008, p. 2).

last of these representing for Watts a sub-set of yet another category, 'federal political systems' (Watts 2008). On the one hand, the words 'federal' and 'federalism' were being used as general framework ideas, which resulted in an open-ended elision, through the term 'federal political system', of federalism with 'multi-level government' (Bache and Flinders 2004; Hooghe and Marks 2001). This contrasted with 'federal government' or 'federation'. Each of these two terms, in particular the latter, took on a very tight, institutionally focused definition, greatly reducing the number of 'real' federal constitutions in the eyes of commentators such as Watts. The upshot was, by the turn of the millennium, an increasingly inward-looking terminological debate around the very meaning of the words themselves, rather than a deeper engagement with the real meaning of federalism as a fundamentally distinctive constitutional idea, and hence of its adaptability to changing and more challenging circumstances (Choudhry and Hume 2011). As Burgess put, by the turn of the millennium, 'the definitional dogma of the past fifty years … [had] … outlived its usefulness.' (Burgess 2006, p. 2)

It is, in fact, not possible to define the federal idea merely through description of practice or through open-ended categories such as self-rule and shared rule. In order to understand the role of federalism as a *discrete legal category of constitutional rule* we must turn to constitutional theory. Unlike both political science which addresses political forces, behaviour, attitudes and institutions in a very broad purview, constitutional theory is concerned with a very specific area of social activity: the framing, founding, practice, and evolution of constitutions as legal orders of rule. It is concerned with transformation of political power into constitutional authority and with how the resulting legal-normative regime husbands and manages political forces through law.

Constitutional theory can also be contrasted with political philosophy. The latter locates the purpose of political rule in externally generated ideological values. Constitutional theory is also evaluative, but unlike political philosophy, constitutional theory is not an exercise in ideal theorising from first, abstract principles, and nor should it assume that constitutional practice is merely a vehicle for ideologically generated political and economic goals. Constitutionalism focuses upon the inherent purposes for which a constitution in general, and any particular constitution specifically, has been founded. The same approach should apply in seeking to determine the common purpose of particular families of constitutionalism, including federalism. In each of these cases these purposes should be drawn from the legal-normative ordering which the constitution brings into play.

That is not to say that constitutionalism is a merely descriptive exercise. Constitutional theory is an endeavour both to understand constitutionalism as the legal-normative conditioning of political practice and a benchmark with which to measure how such a legal order works against its own internal logic (Loughlin 2005). Evaluation is, therefore, an essential feature of constitutional theory as it attempts to synthesise the practice and theory of constitutional law. It is the integral relationship between these two dimensions that opens the door to evaluation, asking how well does the practice of constitutionalism meet its theoretical aims. This approach differs, however, from normative political philosophy in that this evaluative dimension is internally generated from the purposes of the constitution in question. A constitutional theorist asks what the legal purpose of a particular constitution is, and how this purpose is reflected in the constitution's institutional formation and practice. A 'good' constitution, therefore, is one that represents faithfully the purpose or purposes for which it was created. In this way constitutional practice, both in terms of how the constitution is initially framed and how its normative authority plays out, is central to the moral-normative evaluation that constitutional theory brings to bear. This evaluative dimension is essentially about function. What is the function that the constitution is intended to serve? Through the methodology of 'functional normativity' a constitutional theorist's key enquiry is essentially a quest to determine if a particular constitution does in fact serve that function and if so how effectively.

I have elsewhere applied this methodology of constitutional theory to the study of the constitutional accommodation of national pluralism (Tierney 2004) and in turn to constitutional referendums (Tierney 2012), but as a method of analysis it is also ideally placed to help unpack the federal idea. A search for the essence of federalism is complex because, unlike other political ideas such as 'democracy' or 'liberalism' which remain comparatively abstract and open to a vast array of different conceptual and institutional forms, the federal idea informs and is, in turn, further shaped by the practice of a specific form of government. Federalism is not just a political idea or ideological proposition, it is a particular category of constitutional practice. As a result, federalism must be located within the theory-practice nexus – and indeed praxis – which characterises constitutionalism itself. LaCroix captures neatly the essentially iterative engagement between theory and practice that shaped the emergence of the United States' federal constitution. 'The federal idea has origins because it was created; it is an intellectual artefact, not a transcendent or timeless idea that has always hovered around waiting to be applied to a particular project' (LaCroix 2011, p. 220).

The notion of functional normativity can help us circumvent the ultimately irresoluble debate as to whether federalism is at root an empirical or normative category by explaining the connection between the two in the very conceptualisation of modern constitutionalism. The key reason why federalism has never been adequately defined is due to the frequent zig-zagging between, on the one hand, empirical observations which do little to elucidate a wider conception of generic constitutional practice and, on the other, externally-generated normative assessments which also fail to focus upon the specificity of federalism within the arsenal of constitutional models. The key to resolving this bi-polar confusion is to address federalism as a specific approach to the management of political power, and in so doing articulate the particular constitutional purpose for which federal constitutions are specifically designed. This is more than an empirical exercise; it allows federal constitutions to be assessed and evaluated for their relative fidelity to this underpinning generic purpose.

Political scientists have certainly attempted to arrive at a synthesis between the idea of federalism and its institutionalisation. Michael Burgess was one commentator who struggled with the federal idea, trying to marry it in a coherent way to institutionalised 'federation' as a holistic encapsulation of federal practice. Where Burgess' account differs from an approach founded in constitutional theory, as indeed do those of so many politics scholars looking at federalism, is that he does not identify the specific discipline of constitutional theory as a way though the dichotomy between normative theory and empirical praxis. In the end Burgess falls back upon the binary he seeks to avoid, reaching for political theory as the only way to encapsulate the normative dimension of federalism: 'the federal principle is an organising principle and its fundamental purpose is essentially moral. Its *raison d'etre* is to furnish the basis for order and stability but in a framework that formally acknowledges, protects and promotes human dignity, difference and diversity. This is its moral content and purpose.' (Burgess 2006, p. 3)

This approach is at once both over-inclusive and insufficiently precise. In offering up values that are as open-ended as 'human dignity, difference and diversity', Burgess could be describing any democratic form of government: one struggles to imagine a democratic system that would not claim to protect and promote these values. The key question remains. What is it about the federal idea that distinguishes federalism from other democratic forms of government? In the end, the failure to answer this question lies not in Burgess' analysis; political theory simply cannot fill this gap. The search for the normative dimension of federalism cannot be an exercise in abstract political reasoning or a draw-down from a master-list of generalisable political values. Rather, it must be a functionalist approach that locates the inherent normative dimension of federalism in the constitutional functions it performs.

IV FEDERALISM AS A CONSTITUTIONAL IDEA

This leads us back to the generic purpose of federalism which I outlined in the introduction. I argued that to identify this we need to focus upon the significance of the federal foundational moment – a moment in which the federal constitution is born as a categorically different form of polity from that of a unitary constitution. The latter tends to be explained through an individualised conception of constituent power. The coming together of a group of people to form a constitution, lending legitimacy to it through consent. This may be fictional as a matter of political reality. The actual founding of particular constitutions is most often done by elite actors. But in this act the principle of representation is then applied as *ex post facto* justification for its foundational validity. The elites who in fact found the constitution do so in the name of 'the people', thereby supplying the legitimising link between the people and constitutional foundation. Although 'the people' may be a collective concept, the term has been taken to mean one group of (undifferentiated) individuals in whose name the constitution is founded and who then become the individual citizens of it. The foundation of a federal constitution challenges the universalisability of this account of the constituent act by positing a radically different, pluralised alternative. What marks the distinctiveness of the federal constitutional moment is the union of territories. Consequently, it is the salience of territorial subjecthood in the foundational constitutional moment that gives federalism its initial (and thereafter path-determining) orientation as a distinct model of constitutionalism.

In order to explain this significance, the first and most fundamental test for the constitutional theorist of federalism is to retrieve a specifically federal conception of constituent power: a conception that inheres in the nascent polity's constituent territories rather than simply in the individuals of whom these territories comprise. This is a dramatic step for constitutional theory: recognising that 'territorial constituent power' is the essential idea, and hence, source of legitimacy, that underpins a discrete 'federal constitutional moment'.[10] The initial drama rests not so much in what federal constituent power consists of, but in the very fact of its discrete existence as a rival to the purportedly universal account of modern constitutionalism. The key point of departure is, therefore, the very identity of the authors upon whom the notion of federal peoplehood and constituent power is built. The agents who come together to found the new constitution represent not one undifferentiated constituent body of individuals, but rather the constitution's 'constituent territories'.[11] By this formulation, federal constituent power can be explained as the foundational authority of the constituent territories of a nascent polity to form, together, the federal constitution for that polity.

This conceptual turn has implications for the meaning of the foundational act itself. The notion of territorial constituent power affects how we understand the nature and hence the legitimacy of the moment of constitutional creation. If the 'founding act' of constitution-making defines the political bond between 'the people' and its new system of government, the political bond that is created (and thereby constitutionalised) in a federal foundation cannot be – although it often is – cast in such conceptually unitary terms. Such a bond must be understood as uniting the founding territories – as a plurality – both to one another and to the governing system of constitutional authority created by these territories.[12]

---

[10] Indeed this idea continues to be resisted: 'States can move from a unitary structure towards a form of federal settlement without any formal constitutional change; there need not be any grand "constitutional moment"' (Barber 2018, p. 206).

[11] The name given to constituent territories varies from constitution to constitution: states, provinces, lander, cantons, autonomous communities and so on. See Watts (2008, p. 71). I use the term 'constituent territories' to identify the *foundational constitutional salience* of these constitutional subjects.

[12] As Madison, put it, 'Each State, in ratifying the Constitution, is considered as a sovereign body, independent of all others, and only to be bound by its own voluntary act…' James Madison, The Federalist No. 39 (in Hamilton, Madison, and Jay 1961). Madison's wider political purpose for the US constitution belied the implications of these words but they are notable as an early articulation of the implications and political potential of federal constituent power.

When we talk, therefore, of a federal people in constitutional terms, it must be with a notion of peoplehood very different from the monist account: a conception containing within it collective territorially-based pluralism, the nature and strength of which will vary from polity to polity. This has knock-on consequences for how we understand federal constituent power, not only at the founding moment but in the normative life of the polity. This in turn has further implications for the other building blocks of modern constitutionalism: subjecthood, authority, institutional design, and the dynamics of change.

Another dimension of the foundational moment must also be noted; its long-term implications for the ordering of the polity. Authorship endows legitimacy and hence authority upon the act of making a constitution, but legitimacy remains salient in two ways going forward: one concerns the ongoing authority of the constitution after the moment of creation, the second concerns the extent to which this authority is derived from the pre-constitutional setting from which it emerged. Foundational constituent power (*pouvoir constituent*) leads to constitutional form (*pouvoir constitué*) (Sieyès 2014 [1789]). The two remain connected symbiotically through a relationship of legitimacy between constitution and subjects. Hans Lindahl addresses this idea through the idea of reflexivity. The foundational moment gives validity to ongoing authority but at the same time the acceptance of the constitution's authority by its subjects today gives *ex post* validity to the foundational moment itself; and in this relationship we can, in fact, substantiate more clearly the nature of identity of both foundational and constitutional subjects (Lindahl 2008, p. 18). These metaphors apply also to the authority of a federal constitution. I have argued that federalism is a genus of constitutional government for the modern state which, in the act of constitutional union, gives foundational recognition and accommodation to the state's constituent territorial pluralism. The purpose of the federal constitution is both to reflect this foundational pluralism and to maintain the relationship between pluralism and union in the creation and reconciliation of different orders of government. In this way we see how authority within a federal constitution must be understood as an ongoing, symbiotic relationship between the foundational role of the constituent territories and the lived constitutional authority of these territories and their governments which the constitution creates in reflection of the salience of that foundational commitment. This is a commitment to plural governments but it is also a commitment to the central union government which they came together to form. The federal constitution becomes in this sense a third order of rule (Kelsen 1925, p. 198), which demarcates the respective authority of both levels of government; it provides the site for federal constitutional sovereignty to play out in the interaction of these different levels of rule, all in pursuit of the federal constitution's foundational purpose.

It is in this interconnection between foundational legal-normative legitimacy and ongoing authority, therefore, that we see the essence of federalism as a constitutional idea. It represents a fundamentally different foundational moment, with implications for the idea of constitutional subjecthood within the constitution; and it creates a legal-normative structure in which territories remain vital legal subjects, possessed of their own governments, and associating together in the central government of the polity. This reality in turn sets federalism upon its own normative path. The implications of this for constitutional theory have never been fully worked through. I submit that the entire anatomy of modern constitutionalism requires to be revisited across a range of registers, not just foundations, subjecthood and authority but also constitutional principles, institutional design, and the dynamics of change, all viewed through the distinct prism which federalism brings to modern constitutionalism, setting itself out as a categorically different form of ordering of legal authority from a unitary constitution. This is not a task that can be addressed in this chapter, but it is essential work if the full implications of the modern turn of federal constitutionalism is to be understood.

RECOMMENDED READING

Althusius, J. (1995 [1603]). *Politica Methodice Digesta, Atque Exemplis Sacris et Profanis Illustrata*. Edited and translated by Frederick S. Carney. Indianapolis: Liberty Fund.

Aroney, N. (2019). The Federal Condition. In Amnon Lev, ed., *The Federal Idea: Public Law between Governance and Political Life*. Oxford: Hart Publishing, pp. 29–51

Burgess, M. (2012). *In Search of the Federal Spirit: New Theoretical and Empirical Perspectives in Comparative Federalism*, Oxford: Oxford University Press.

Elazar, D., ed. (1994). *Federal Systems of the World: A Handbook of Federal, Confederal and Autonomy Arrangements*, 2nd edn, Harlow: Longmans.

Gagnon, A-G. & Tully, J., eds. (2001). *Multinational Democracies*, Cambridge: Cambridge University Press.

Hamilton, A., Madison, J, & Jay, J. (1961). *The Federalist Papers*. Edited by Clinton Rossiter. New York: New American Library.

Hueglin, T. O. & Fenna, A. (2015). *Comparative federalism: A Systematic Enquiry*, 2nd edn, Toronto: University of Toronto Press.

Karmis, D. & Norman W., eds (2005). *Theories of Federalism*, New York: Palgrave-Macmillan Publishing.

LaCroix, A. (2011). *The Ideological Origins of American Federalism*, Cambridge, MA: Harvard University Press.

Larsen, S. R. (2021). *The Constitutional Theory of the Federation and the European Union*, Oxford: Oxford University Press.

Lev, A., ed. (2019). *The Federal Idea: Public Law between Governance and Political Life*, Oxford: Hart Publishing, pp. 1–26

Palermo, F. & Kössler, K. (2017). *Comparative Federalism: Constitutional Arrangements and Case Law*, Oxford: Hart Publishing.

Tierney, S. (2004). *Constitutional Law and National Pluralism*, Oxford: Oxford University Press.

Watts, R. L. (2008). *Comparing Federal Systems*, 3rd edn, Kingston/Montreal: McGill-Queens University Press.

Wheare, K. C. (1946). *Federal Government*, Oxford: Oxford University Press.

33

Consociationalism

Joseph Lacey and Nenad Stojanović

All constitutions tell a story of the political community and a story of the regime (Nicolaïdis 2012, pp. 250–251). The story of the political community specifies who is included within the community, what political values and commitments citizens are expected to hold, as well as their rights, duties and perhaps some mention of historical legacy. The story of the regime outlines the institutional framework, the values upon which it is based and how it is expected to relate to the political community. This chapter will be concerned with societies where a central part of the story of the political community is that of deep diversity, while a central part of the story of the regime is the recognition and accommodation of this diversity by institutional means.

Deep diversity refers to a society divided by differences that are salient enough to consistently polarise groups over time in ways that make governing together difficult or, to quote John Stuart Mill (1977 [1861]), 'next to impossible'. Put differently, a political community is characterised by deep diversity when the differences between well-defined groups are strong enough to risk destabilising the political system. While societies with a particularly entrenched ideological cleavage on the traditional left-right scale have been identified as cases of 'extreme polarisation' (e.g., post-war Italy; Bogaards 2005, p. 504), the paradigmatic cases are forms of identity and belief systems that are less amenable to change and persuasion than those associated with political ideologies. Examples include countries segmented along racial, religious, ethnic, and/or linguistic lines (e.g., Belgium, Bosnia, Lebanon).

The varieties of instability that deeply diverse regimes threaten range from extreme difficulty in forming governments and making collective decisions to civil unrest and, at worst, civil war. A regime that seeks to address its problems of deep diversity in a *just* manner will typically give an important role to the value of equal recognition (Patten 2014). However exactly the meaning of equal recognition is defined (see De Schutter, this volume for various accounts), it will typically involve the affirmation that no group constituting the political community's deep diversity is superior to another, regardless of the nature of their identity or beliefs, or indeed their relative size as groups. Such recognition is generally institutionally expressed by ensuring some form of adequate political representation and safeguards to protect the fundamental interests of the core conflicting groups in the political community.

In some societies, a federal polity has been adopted as a (partial) solution to the problem of deep diversity. This involves the devolution of powers to territorially concentrated social groups with salient common identities in addition to a fair scheme of representation for these sub-federal units at the federal level (see Stephen Tierney, this volume for an account of federalism). Belgium (since 1994) and Canada (since 1867) are two powerful examples of the federal model.

Consociational regimes are different to, but not incompatible with, federal regimes. Their defining goal is social and political stability in a manner consistent with democratic values, while the unifying feature of the means to achieve that goal is the pursuit of measures that protect salient social groups (or segments) from blunt majority rule, especially in areas of particular concern for those groups. The problem of stability is central to consociational theory (Lijphart 1977, p. 1; McGarry and O'Leary 2009, pp. 47–69). Indeed, consociational theory's original progenitor, Arend Lijphart, has repeatedly underlined that the main goal of consociationalism is to show that it is possible to build and maintain peace and a 'stable' democracy in contexts of 'deeply divided societies' (Lijphart 1996, p. 258). As such, it stands in sharp contrast to theories that suggest that multi-ethnic countries are doomed to instability (e.g., Mill 1977 [1861]; Rabushka and Shepsle 1971). But can a consociational regime become sufficiently stable over time?

In this chapter, we claim that, despite its mission to secure social and political stability, consociations are themselves inherently unstable regime-types. We make our case in three steps before concluding with some reflections on an alternative to consociationalism, namely centripetalism.

In the next section, we define consociationalism and its ambiguous relationship with constitutional theory. Following this, we explore how the value of recognition is central to consociationalism and, as such, serves to structure the place of other democratic values within the consociational regime. The way in which recognition tends to be prioritised in consociations, we argue, results in democratic deficits that provide some of the resources to actors who would seek to challenge the regime from within. In the penultimate section, we build on this account, explaining that consociations are inherently unstable in the sense that they face the permanent risk of evolving into regimes dominated by the majority, or into a spiral of progressive disintegration. This brings us to the concluding section where, without making prescriptions, we outline the contours of the centripetal approach to the problem of political stability caused by deep diversity. The latter approach 'eschews consociational formulas and, instead, advocates institutions which encourage inter-communal moderation by promoting multi-ethnic parties, crosscutting electoral incentives and intergroup accommodation' (Reilly 2012, p. 260). In other words, the aim of centripetalists is 'to create incentives, principally electoral incentives, for moderates to compromise on conflicting group claims, to form interethnic coalitions, and to establish a regime of interethnic majority rule' (Horowitz 2014, p. 5). Even though there could (or should) be certain complementarities between the two approaches in the real world (see Bogaards 2019), it is important to note that, from a theoretical (ideal-type) viewpoint, centripetalism is not a sub-type of consociationalism but, rather, its main competitor in the contemporary literature on constitutional design for deeply divided societies.

I DEFINING CONSOCIATIONALISM

A consociational regime is typically defined in terms of four core features (Lijphart 1969, 1977, 1996). First, the main segments of the society should, via their representatives, share power in the executive. Second, these segments need self-rule, generally speaking but especially in certain policy areas that are especially salient. The segmental autonomy can be both territorial (most notably via federalism) and nonterritorial. Third, the principle of proportionality should guide decisions regarding the distribution of seats and resources. In particular, each segment should have (with regard to their population numbers) a proportionate share of seats in parliament and public administration. Consociationalists firmly believe that the former is to be achieved via an electoral system based on proportional representation. For the latter, the most straightforward tool is the adoption of formal or informal quotas. Finally, the fourth feature is minority veto. The idea here is that the first three features are necessary but still not sufficient to protect minorities, if the majority is determined to impose its will without taking into account the concerns of minorities. Typically, the veto right does not extend to all policy domains but regards only vital minority interests (e.g., the language rights of a linguistic minority).

While there have been some controversies on the exact definition of a consociational regime – for instance, critics have claimed that its key concepts have been defined with 'vagueness and elasticity' (Andeweg 2015, p. 693; see also Halpern 1986; Dixon 2012) – the general account we have provided has been standardly deployed since Lijphart first identified consociationalism as a distinctive way of organising a regime (Lijphart 1968). Furthermore, it should be underlined that the four core features of consociationalism represent an ideal-type institutional model with both descriptive and normative dimensions (Lijphart 1977, p. 1). Originally, the idea of consociationalism was formulated as a purely descriptive category, attempting to identify the logic of a peculiar institutional configuration in states like The Netherlands, Belgium, and Switzerland (Lijphart 1968, 1969). With time, however, the concept gradually took on normative weight. That is to say, its main features have been seen by many constitutional designers in deeply diverse societies as a legitimate way of addressing the problem of stability. As such, we have seen a spread of consociational regimes, or at least consociational practices, in some of the most diverse political systems and some of the most high-profile cases of political conflict over the last number of decades. Some of the most well-studied cases in recent times include Bosnia and Herzegovina, Belgium, Northern Ireland, Lebanon, and the European Union.

In many of these and other key cases in the consociational literature, the traditional four consociational features will be constitutionalised to some degree. Among other things, this means that they are recognised as forming an important part of the rules of the game that define the polity, while making them more difficult to change than ordinary legislation. Some regimes, however, do not necessarily go down the route of constitutionalisation, at least not on every dimension of consociationalism. In some instances, consociational 'practices' have emerged over time through civil compromises, while in other instances a regime struggling to maintain stability may experiment with elements of consociationalism initially, without necessarily committing to a grander constitutional project. A fitting example of the former is in the formation of the seven-person Swiss executive (the Federal Council), whose long-standing practice includes having one to three French-speakers and, occasionally, one Italian-speaker, in addition to German-speakers from the majority group. This is one significant way of giving recognition to all the main language groups in the country. Iraq (2005–2010) is a good example of a (unsuccessful) consociational experiment, where the constitution laid out a roadmap for the future adaptation of consociationalism, during which time the transitional power-sharing executive was constituted by representatives of the country's three largest ethnic groups (McGarry 2019, p. 1).

In recent years – as a response to certain critiques of the model, most notably those concerning practices deemed inimical to liberal democracy (e.g., ethnic quotas) – consociationalists have proposed the distinction between 'corporate' and 'liberal' consociations. In the corporate type, the groups entitled to power sharing, autonomy, proportional representation and veto are determined in advance. Rigid rules, entrenched in constitutions and other legal documents, regulate the distribution of seats and resources among the various segments. As an example, take the provision of the Belgian Constitution stipulating that Dutch and French speakers are entitled to the same number of ministerial positions in the federal executive.

In the liberal type, which today consociationalists prefer, informal rules and/or indirect mechanisms achieve the objectives of the four defining consociational features without necessarily fixing in advance the ratio between the groups (McCulloch 2014, p. 502; see Arendt 1963; McGarry and O'Leary 2009, p. 72). The central reason for this is a normative one. Essentially, wherever possible, it is widely agreed that consociations should stay as true as possible to familiar liberal democratic principles. The liberal model is viewed as being more attuned to the democratic ideas that political representation should be proportionate, in the sense of being as sensitive as possible to the weight of preferences and identities across the population. Rather than locking-in a fixed number of political representatives in perpetuity, for example, the liberal model allows for the electoral system to be sensitive to changing voting preferences and any related demographic shifts. For an example of this, we can return to the example of the Swiss Federal Council with a historical twist. Established in 1848, and elected by the Parliament by majoritarian rules, in its first decades, care was taken that two seats be given to the Catholics and the remaining seats to the Protestant majority. But as the religious divide became less salient, this informal quota gradually faded away and has no significance anymore. Hence, it has been argued that the absence of rigid and explicit quotas has helped to facilitate the disappearance of (rather than solidify) the Catholic-Protestant cleavage in Swiss society and politics (Stojanović 2020, p. 33). As we have seen, this informal religious quota has been outlasted by a linguistic one.

It is important to underline that the four features of a consociational regime are predominantly defined in terms of *outcomes* – that is, in relation to what we want to see in such a polity. Hence, consociationalists want to see an executive with representatives of all the main segments and a parliament where all groups are represented roughly in proportion to their demographic presence. They also want a degree of segmental autonomy and for minorities to have certain veto rights.

Now, despite the fact that consociationalism is defined by the observable outcomes, the literature has increasingly come to associate the idea of consociationalism with a particular set of *procedures*. The most prominent example is the choice of electoral system. Here, consociationslists clearly advocate the use of proportional representation and reject majoritarian electoral systems. The idea is that PR systems are better able to produce electoral outcomes that reflect the political diversity of the population, and thereby make coalition government more likely, as opposed to more majoritarian systems (e.g., first-past-the-post), which are more likely to produce overall electoral winners capable of governing without coalition partners. While there is a certain logic to this argument, this focus on procedures for a theory defined in terms of its outcomes can lead to dissonance. In particular, the consociational literature has largely neglected the fact that consociational outcomes can be and have been produced by a variety of procedural means. Continuing with the example of electoral system choice, the Swiss case illustrates how majoritarian (i.e., non-consociational) electoral rules can reliably produce outcomes that are in line with consociational theory.

Switzerland is one of Lijphart's original empirical cases of consociationalism (Lijphart 1969) and it remains an acclaimed example for consociationalist authors. O'Leary (2019, p. 569), for example, notes the first chamber of the Swiss federal parliament 'is elected by proportional representation' whereas the second 'represents the cantons'. The author omits to specify that the second chamber – one of the strongest second chambers in the world – is elected by *majoritarian* rules (with electoral competition taking place within each canton for two seats each, except for six cantons – formerly known as 'half-cantons' – that are entitled to one seat). He also omits to mention that, until 1919, even the first chamber used to be entirely elected by majoritarian rules. But most importantly, none of this was relevant for the desired outcome – that is, a more or less proportional representation of linguistic (and formerly also religious) groups in the Swiss parliament. In fact, linguistic groups have always been fairly represented in the second chamber as well as in the first chamber both before and after 1919 (Stojanović 2006). Group representation in the Swiss Parliament is entirely ensured by the geographical concentration of groups and the fact that electoral districts follow more or less the frontiers of these groups. Under such conditions, the choice between PR or a majoritarian system is next to irrelevant for ensuring group representation in Parliament.

To be sure, consociationalists are aware that the desired outcomes have been achieved also via non-consociational procedures – or, in Lijphart's words, that it is possible to have 'proportionality by non-PR methods' (Lijphart 1986) – but there is still an insistence on recommending the use of PR even in places where (e.g., Northern Ireland) the geographical concentration of groups together with a careful design of electoral districts would allow for the use of majoritarian rules without undermining proportionality within the assembly. More troubling for consociational theory, however, is when the desired outcome is achieved *thanks to* a method that is not prescribed or is even explicitly rejected by the theory. For example, consociationalists often praise the general practice that 'still accomplishes (informally) proportionality among German and non-German speakers [and] among Protestants and non-Protestants' in the Swiss Federal Council (O'Leary 2019, p. 569; see Lijphart 1977). Yet the rules governing the election of the Swiss executive by Parliament are not only majoritarian (to be elected, a member of the executive must gather the absolute majority of votes in the joint sessions of the two chambers of Parliament) but are actually quite close to the Alternative Vote system advocated by centripetalists and criticised by consociationalists (Stojanović 2016).

To sum up, consociationalism is a specific kind of regime, primarily associated with and defined by a particular set of outcomes such as executive power sharing and group autonomy. But consociational theory also purports to provide guidelines for the procedures that are supposed to bring about such outcomes, especially with regard to the choice of the electoral system. This can be misleading, though, as at least in some cases consociational outcomes are achieved via non-consociational procedures. With this brief overview of consociational regime we now proceed with a normative analysis of the values undergirding this regime type.

II THE VALUES OF CONSOCIATIONAL DEMOCRACY

As we have seen, consociationalism has developed from an empirical category into more than that: it is also a particular way of ordering values as a legitimate institutional response to the problem of stability in deeply diverse societies. To more fully understand consociationalism, therefore, we must be able to clarify what values it prioritises and how these values relate to one another.

The first thing to note is that consociationalism is better understood as an adverb than a noun. For consociations are always, or at least claim to be, consociational democracies. According to Mark E. Warren (2017), there are three problems internal to the idea of democracy that a society must resolve if it is to approach the democratic ideal. These problems are how to empower citizens in an inclusive manner; how to form collective agendas and wills; and how to make collective decisions. Furthermore, he identifies seven primary values or activities of self-government (as we shall call them) that are the essential tools required for political institutions and civil society to resolve these problems: voting, joining, resisting, representing, *recognising*, deliberating, and exiting. Warren believes that, in order to solve the three problems internal to democracy, it is necessary to ensure that all the activities of self-government are brought to bear on the organisation of political life and optimally employed across the regime and the political community. He resists the tendency to prioritise one value above others – such as the way in which deliberative democrats emphasise the value of deliberation (e.g., J. Cohen 1997) or aggregative democrats emphasise the value of voting (e.g., Downs 1957). Such an approach, according to Warren, will lead advocates to diminish or ignore entirely the potentially crucial role that other values can play in resolving the problems of self-government. And so, we find some deliberative democrats criticised for neglecting the importance of voting and others for neglecting the value of resisting (Mansbridge et al. 2012), while aggregative democrats have found themselves similarly criticised for failing to pay heed to the importance of values like deliberation and joining (e.g., B. Barber 1984).

Warren, however, does not develop his account to consider some of the problems that are *external* to the idea of democracy as self-government and which democracy may nevertheless be expected to resolve. One such problem is the problem of stability. And, as we have seen, this problem arises in a specific form in deeply divided societies. If a polity cannot take stability for granted, due to the conflictual identities characterising its political community, then we may expect some adjustment to how we might otherwise seek to mix democratic values across the regime and political community. In particular, it may be necessary to prioritise some values over others, leading to a diminishment in how other values find their expression in attempting to address the internal problems of democracy identified by Warren.

We posit that consociationalism, in its efforts to deal with the problem of stability in deeply diverse societies, amplifies the value of *recognition* dramatically. Though the way in which it does so will vary from context to context, this move will typically have some common consequences for other democratic values, potentially burdening consociational societies with specific kinds of democratic deficits as a result. As we shall argue, the peculiarly elitist manner in which consociations tend to emphasise the value of recognition leads to a narrow elevation of the values of representation and deliberation at the expense of the values of voting, joining, resisting, and exiting. As a result, consociations tend to find themselves hampered in their potential to reach high standards in solving the internal problems of democracy: of empowered inclusion; collective agenda and will formation; and collective decision-making.

From our definition of consociationalism above, it should be clear how recognition is the central structuring value. Grand coalitions and proportionality ensure that the voices of as many salient identities as possible are recognised and heard in collective decision-making. Meanwhile, segmental autonomy and vetoes ensure that the values and interests fundamental to the identities of these communities are recognised and protected. How then does this form of recognition impact upon the other activities of self-government identified by Warren?

Representing: The manner of representation in consociations risks being narrow in two primary ways. First, there is the narrowness of the constituency which representatives see themselves as representing. Under the normative ideal of partisanship, political representatives are expected to aim at the common good for all in their society, albeit from a committed ideological perspective (Muirhead 2006; White and Ypi 2016). In consociations, given the preference for PR electoral systems and segmental autonomy, political parties are more likely to be segmentally arranged such that they aim to represent one segment only, rather than building mutual relations with the whole of society. Second, in order to peacefully resolve conflict over potentially contentious issues, it is widely recognised in the consociational literature that political elites must be willing to depoliticise the most contentious issues dividing the segments as much as possible. Similarly, there must be a corresponding will among the segmented electorates to acquiesce in giving their representatives substantial leeway in reaching a negotiated compromise (Deschouwer 1994, p. 81; Andeweg 2019). As a result, at least on the depoliticised issues in question, the capacity for unelected representatives (such as civil society organisations and protest groups) to exert public pressure on the political system is substantially diminished. Representation, therefore, tends to take on an unusually narrow praxis in consociations, focused as it is upon the electoral arena at the expense of civil society.

Deliberating: The narrowness of representation that tends to affect consociations naturally impacts the nature of deliberations in such regimes. In the first instance, deliberation means being willing to engage in a process of reason-giving with others with the goal of reaching an accord that is mutually acceptable to all parties. It is a form of discourse entirely distinct from bargaining and negotiation. In these latter forms of discursive interaction, parties are not open to persuasion by the force of the better argument, but rather enter into discussions with a fixed position and the aim of achieving maximum concession from the other groups in order to advance that position (Mansbridge et al. 2010). In consociations, when representatives view themselves segmentally, they are equally likely to think of themselves as negotiators for their segment rather than deliberators for the wider good of the society. This phenomenon has the potential to enter a vicious and destabilising cycle commonly referred to as 'ethnic outbidding' (Zuber and Szöckick 2015).[1] According to G. Moore et al. (2014, p. 159):

---

[1] For examples in point see Belgium (Swenden 2015) and Bosnia (Jesse and Williams 2010, chap. 4); for partial counter-evidence, see the case of Northern Ireland (Mitchell, Evans and O'Leary 2009).

Ethnic outbidding occurs in the context of electoral politics when political parties compete for support within an ethnic group, having few incentives to cultivate support from other ethnicities. Each ethnic party seeks to demonstrate that it is more nationalistic than its competitors by raising its 'bid', protecting itself from claims by intra-group opponents that it is 'soft' on ethnic issues.... Once this auction-like scenario begins, the ethnic outbidding thesis predicts that the resulting extremist discourse will destabilise and ultimately prevent conflict regulation in divided societies.

Secondly, in consociations, civil society may also find itself at a deficit when it comes to deliberation. On the one hand, the division of society into segments means that citizens from different groups are less likely to encounter one another in deliberative contexts. This is particularly true when the segments are linguistically divided or constitute their own segmented mediatised public spheres (Lacey 2017).[2] On the other hand, due in large part to narrow representational focus on the electoral arena, and the depoliticisation of certain issues, we tend to find the ideal of mass deliberative politics at least partially abandoned in consociations (Dryzek 2009). In other words, the more citizens see politics or a particular set of issues as 'up to their elites', the less likely they are to become deliberatively engaged themselves. If deliberation is taking place, then it tends to be unusually concentrated at the elite level in consociations.

Joining: Naturally enough, if salient issues are depoliticised or at least left to elected officials to resolve, then citizens are less likely to perform one of the paradigmatic democratic functions of joining with one another to exert pressure on the political system. However, what may be even more problematic is that these are the lines along which citizens tend to become active. Depending on how entrenched and all-encompassing we find segmental division within the societies, to the extent that citizens do seek to self-organise politically or join political parties, they are likely to do so by joining with others who belong to their own segment only. This phenomenon has been observed most starkly in the Netherlands and Belgium, where a system of 'pillarisation' kept citizens from different segments isolated from one another as individuals were expected to organise politically (and indeed, socially and even economically) according to Christian, socialist, and liberal segments, overseen by the corresponding political parties (Lijphart 1969).

Resisting: The stability of any political system requires citizens at large to willingly obey the laws. However, democratic systems are typically expected to be able to endure some forms of resistance, like protest against or non-compliance with a particular policy. However, just as joining to exert influence on the political system may politicise an issue in destabilising ways, so will resisting the conclusions

---

[2] When concerted efforts have been made to bring citizens from distinct segments together under 'good deliberative conditions' – for example, through coordinated citizens assemblies – the capacity for citizens to deliberate together on contentious issues has been impressive. An example is the G1000 pilot in Belgium (Caluwaerts and Reuchamps 2018).

of negotiations by coalition government between social segments. The passivity required of the electorate for consociationalism to work, therefore, reduces the role of resisting in the political community, just as it reduces the role of joining.

Voting: As we have indicated, some form of PR is almost universally advocated as the electoral system appropriate to consociational democracies. As already noted, the major advantage of PR is that it ensures a wide representation of perspectives in parliament and makes coalition governments more likely and often also indispensable. While this may have its own advantages, especially to the extent that it requires rival parties to negotiate or even deliberate with one another, it has several disadvantages when it comes to voting. In particular, the more likely a coalition is, the less likely it is that the standard promissory model of representation applies (McCall Rosenbluth and Shapiro 2018). On this model, a party makes promises at election time and is then held to account for how well they have kept these promises. Electoral promises, however, become far less meaningful when coalition government is projected or guaranteed. In consociations, where grand coalitions rather than the bare minimum to form a majority are typical, the promissory model becomes especially weak. Consociations ensure that political representatives must be seen to be far more engaged in compromise and negotiation than in making and carrying out concrete electoral pledges. As such, we may expect consociations to be especially reliant upon what Jane Mansbridge (2003) has referred to as 'gyroscopic' (good-types) or 'descriptive representatives' (those that are 'like me' in some way). In the latter case, citizens select their representatives, not primarily on the basis of any promises that might be made, but rather by virtue of the fact that they share the same kind of social or cultural background. As a result, in such contexts the act of voting risks being dominated by 'ethnic voting' and in most extreme cases elections become mere ethnic headcounts.

Exiting: A general assumption of democratic systems is that citizens have meaningful choices in terms of self-government – if they don't like some policy or officeholder, they should have the option to change it. Voting for a different party in an election or to change the constitution in a referendum are just some ways of exiting previous political decisions. In one sense, consociations are remarkable for how they allow segments to have their own autonomy in entire policy areas, or at least for accommodative derogations from aspects of certain policies. These major exit options, as we have seen, are indispensable for the stability sought by consociational arrangements. However, there are important respects in which consociations may place strict limits on exit options. This is especially evident in the case of constitutionalising veto points. Once a veto is granted to a social segment as a matter of constitutional right, it thereby traps the other segments into the policy preferences of the former within the range of policies covered by the veto. Similarly, when the electoral system all but guarantees grand coalitions so that certain kinds of policy preferences are effectively locked-in, citizens' capacity to exert the electoral pressure for policy change that comes with standard electoral exit options are significantly reduced.

With this brief, and incomplete, overview of how values and the activities of self-government manifest themselves in a system designed to produce stability, we can more clearly see how consociations may have a more difficult time in resolving the three problems internal to democracy identified by Warren. Most significantly, through its emphasis on elite actors and its dependency on a relatively passive public, consociations are limited in their capacity to solve the problem of *empowered inclusion*. Through its narrow forms of institutional representation and deliberation, and its requirement that citizens forego some ordinary practices of joining and resisting, the participatory values undermining the ideal of self-government are somewhat relegated to the background. A consequence of this is that the second problem of self-government, concerning *the formation of collective agendas and wills*, is only partially resolved, namely, through the agenda and will-formation of the elite parts of segmented collectives.

A major achievement of consociations, when they are operating successfully, is their capacity to go some way towards resolving the third problem of democracy, which is *to reach collective decisions*, in particularly difficult circumstances. However, in contexts like consociations where there are veto players (whether formally specified or *de facto* through grand coalitions), the capacity to make collective decisions can be hampered (Warren 2017, p. 46). Deadlock, as consociationalists since Lijphart have recognised, is a perennial risk of institutionalising high consensus hurdles (Lijphart 1977, pp. 50–51). As a result of these veto points, citizens lack the capacity to contribute to collective decision-making by translating popular votes into clear outcomes, while they are limited in their ability to exit previous decisions and policy choices.

Pointing out these democratic deficits is by no means to undervalue the potential benefits of consociational arrangements. And it is not to say that all consociations will suffer from the same deficits in the same way. Indeed, as we have pointed out, some regimes are more consociational than others. It is, however, to acknowledge that there are democratic trade-offs associated with doing democracy consociationally. Most importantly, for our purposes in this chapter is the effect that such deficits may have on the stability of consociational regimes.

III THE INSTABILITY OF CONSOCIATIONAL DEMOCRACY

In attempting to explain the social conditions required for the stability of a just regime, defined as a fair system of cooperation over time, John Rawls (1993) introduced the idea of an overlapping consensus. Simply put, an overlapping consensus is achieved when, for their own reasons based on their worldviews, citizens endorse the core (constitutional) values and principles upon which political institutions are built and designed to deliver upon. It is this kind of consensus that Rawls believes gives stability to contemporary liberal democratic regimes, characterised as they are by a plurality of comprehensive doctrines and ways of life.

Rawls also underlines that stability in overlapping consensus is superior to a *modus vivendi*, that is, a mere balance of power among citizens who hold contending beliefs and perspectives on the world. 'After all, power often shifts, and when it does the social stability of a *modus vivendi* may be lost' (Wenar 2017). In Rawls' words, in a modus vivendi 'social unity is only apparent, as its stability is contingent upon circumstances remaining such as not to upset the fortunate convergence of interests' (Rawls 1993, p. 147).

In this section, we argue that a typical consociational regime is an ethnoi-cracy[3] closer to a *modus vivendi* than to a true overlapping consensus. Hence, its stability is fragile. Interestingly, what is called into question is not typically the liberal democratic norms that Rawls focused upon in explaining the conditions of a stable and just regime. It's perfectly feasible for all segments in a consociation to subscribe to the same liberal democratic norms. What is most likely to be the source of destabilising conflict are the (often constitutionalised) principles, institutions, and practices that give the regime its specific consociational flavour.

There are various ways in which particular actors within the segments may prevent the forging of a consociational overlapping consensus. As we shall now see, the common thread linking these actors is the claim that consociationalism is somehow at odds with the kind of liberal democratic principles that are often the sole focus of an overlapping consensus in the kind of non-consociational liberal democracies that Rawls had in mind.

One set of actors will typically arise from within the majority segment. They will highlight the democratic deficits of consociation (such as those outlined above) and try to capitalise on the democratic mantra 'one person, one vote' which amounts to an intuitively powerful demand for majoritarian electoral and decision-making rules, thus eschewing the philosophy of recognition behind such constitutional provisions that ensure power-sharing or special vetoes. When consociational compromises are loudly and continuously called into question by political actors in the majority segment and against the wishes of minority segments, consociationalism is under threat. When such calls are successful, leading to the (re)introduction of an unjust or oppressive majority-minority dichotomy, consociationalism fails.

A second set of actors will tend to push for an ever-stronger parity of segments (instead of citizens) in joint institutions and an ever-deeper segmental autonomy, especially via territorial federalism. These demands may come from a majority segment as an alternative strategy to making their own decisions, without reintroducing a majoritarian logic at the national level. Or these demands may come from the minority segment who do not believe that their interests are adequately protected through power-sharing at the national level. While federalism is compatible with

---

[3] Or, at best, it may be considered a demoi-cracy (in the sense of having multiple demoi), rather than a demos-cracy (in the sense of having a singular demos). See Stojanović (2020) for further discussion on this point.

consociationalism, we may expect that the more power is devolved to the segments, the less significant (and constraining) power-sharing at the federal level will be perceived. However, as exponents of 'the federal paradox' observe, federalisation tends not to sate demands for autonomy, but rather emboldens them to the limit of seeking complete secession (Erk and Anderson 2010). After all, as the logic goes, why would a segment continue to share any amount of power with another segment when they have already attained large amounts of autonomy, and full sovereignty no longer seems to be such a large step? When demands for secession are strong, consociationalism shows signs of faltering. When secession is achieved, consociationalism fails.

Summarily, rather than endorsing the non-majoritarian principles and the value of recognition upon which consociationalism is based, some groups may see it as a temporary compromise or *modus vivendi* to be eventually abandoned at an opportune moment. An illustrative example of this claim is a declaration made by Milorad Dodik, the leader of Bosnian Serbs: '[The Serbs' entity within Bosnia, called Republic Srpska or RS] will exist forever, Bosnia and Herzegovina as long as necessary'.[4] That declaration was made in the campaign for the 2010 elections. As we write these lines (October 2023), Mr. Dodik is still the leader of Bosnian Serbs. In February 2020, he addressed the Parliament of the Republic Srpska with the opening sentence (pronounced in English): 'Goodbye BiH [Bosnia and Herzegovina], welcome RSexit', thus unleashing the debate on a possible secession of the Serbs' entity from Bosnia.[5]

Belgium, another paradigmatic case of a consociational regime, provides a further illustration of the democratic impulse being exploited to challenge the consociational settlement (Lacey 2017, chap. 5). From 1970 to 2011, this consociation has seen six state reforms, with each one granting further autonomy to the Walloon and Flemish segments (including greater autonomy for the German-speaking community). This, however, has not put a stop to demands for the break-up of Belgium. The New Flemish Alliance, the largest party in the country (as of 2014 and 2019 federal elections), continues to draw attention to and exploit the democratic weaknesses of Belgium's consociational regime to build support for an independent Flanders.

Indeed, a cursory overview of the history of consociational regimes will reveal a large number of cases that have lapsed from consociational practice in favour of more or less majoritarian practices. Most significantly, two of Lijphart's original cases have been identified as consociations for periods of their history only: Netherlands (1917–1967) and Austria (1945–1966). Other 'experiments' with consociationalism have had a relatively short life-span. We have already seen this in the case of Iraq. Other examples include South Africa (1994–1999), Sudan (2005–2011), Fiji (1997–2006), and Kenya (2008–2013) (McGarry 2019).

---

[4] Source: European Forum (www.europeanforum.net/headlines/news_update_bosnia_and_herzegovina_18_24_september), accessed 6 March 2020.
[5] Source: www.youtube.com/watch?v=Hi9aiMd9ivM, accessed 11 October 2023.

This said, we should not exclude the possibility that a consociation could over time develop an overlapping consensus, instead of a mere *modus vivendi*. In fact, it is imaginable that citizens across segments support their constitutional settlement based on an overlapping consensus 'and will continue to do so even if their group gains or loses political power' (Wenar 2017). But how can this be achieved?

We believe that an important element in this debate is the question of *demos*. In our view, societies that used to be deeply divided but have gradually succeeded in construing an overarching political identity – that is, an 'effective and viable' demos (Miller 2018, p. 126) – have approximated an ideal of overlapping consensus. To put it differently, the common demos can be seen as the motivating force behind an overlapping consensus. As in the Rawlsian ideal, in such a regime, citizens are not required to abandon their various worldviews (stemming, for example, from their different languages and religions) in order to be part of the common demos. Abiding by basic laws of the demos 'is not a citizen's second-best option in the face of the power of others; it is each citizen's first-best option given her own beliefs' (Wenar 2017).

What does it mean in reality? It means that – given that citizens have a strong sense of belonging to the same political community or demos and not just to their social segment – it is more likely that citizens will accept majoritarian decision-making typical of liberal democracies. In other words, *if a consociation succeeds in developing a sufficiently strong common demos, then such a polity no longer needs to rely only on consociational institutions*: they can be abandoned altogether or combined with centripetal institutions based on a majoritarian logic (see Section IV). Examples in point are Austria, the Netherlands, and Switzerland. Each of these political systems have developed a strong common demos over time, such that they are no longer reliant upon consociational practices for their stability, even if certain vestigial consociational identifiers may remain (see Barry 1975).

On the surface, this might resemble one possible transformation of a consociational regime based on the *modus vivendi* approach (discussed above) that favours the majority segment. But that is not the case. In reality, the common demos *qua* overlapping consensus is superior precisely because it is *not* a *modus vivendi* based on the current balance of power and the 'us vs. them' logic. It is superior also because it is far more inclusive of a vast array of identities and worldviews that citizens have, whereas the typical consociation recognises and institutionalises only one dimension of people's identity (e.g., ethnicity or religion). The practical consequence of this is that in such a polity there is not 'the' majority vs. 'the' minorities. Of course, there are still majorities and minorities in a purely descriptive-statistical sense, but they are not closed and homogenous segments. Each is divided into various subgroups. Hence, cross-cutting cleavages reinforce the overlapping consensus associated with the common demos.

To sum up: consociations – especially those belonging to the 'corporate' type (McCulloch 2014) – are inherently unstable as long as they remain ethnoi-cracies based on a *modus vivendi* of clearly defined and homogenous segments, with a permanent risk to evolve either into regimes dominated by the majority or into a spiral of progressive disintegration. It is, however, possible that more 'liberal' consociational regimes provide stability for long enough that citizens begin to develop shared intentions or a common sense of purpose (O'Flynn 2017) and the corresponding sense of belonging together as a political community. Over time, as the polity matures and social and demographic shifts take place, identities once salient may recede or become entirely non-salient. In these cases, consociational practices may no longer be required: the need for robust forms of recognition subsides as the overarching demos becomes strong enough to handle a more majoritarian politics.

IV THE CENTRIPETAL ALTERNATIVE

In this regard, it is worth briefly mentioning another approach to the problem of stability in deeply divided societies, often referred to as centripetal democracy (Reilly 2012; Horowitz 2014; Lacey 2017). The overarching point of contrast between consociational and centripetal democracy is the emphasis they place on the value of recognition in their account. While centripetalists agree on the importance of providing diverse groups with institutional recognition, they aim to achieve that recognition through means that enable demos-formation across groups while softening the intensity of the segmental identities dividing the society in question. In other words, while consociationalism tends to recognise deep diversity by the way it institutionally entrenches segmental identities, centripetalism is more explicit in its attempt to incentivise the creation of a common identity among the segments, while not seeking to eliminate their distinctiveness.

Perhaps most intriguingly, centripetal democrats believe that the problem of stability in divided societies can be best achieved by adopting nuanced forms of majoritarianism. Among the centripetal tools that adherents of the approach advocate, depending on the specific society in question, are (a) certain types of majoritarian rather than PR systems (Reilly 2001, 2020; Horowitz 1991, 2004), (b) presidential instead of parliamentarian regimes with provisions ensuring nationwide and cross-ethnic support for the elected president (Horowitz 1985, pp. 635–638; Reilly 2012), and (c) forms of direct democracy (Stojanović 2011; Lacey 2017).

One of the main goals of such institutional proposals is to provide incentives for ethnically moderate parties and/or for multi-ethnic parties (Reilly 2001, p. 11) and, related to this point, to encourage cross-ethnic voting behaviour (Reilly 2020). Ethnically moderate parties are less likely to engage in ethnic outbidding. And, more promisingly, multi-ethnic parties will necessarily have a prior commitment to represent the whole rather than merely a part. A large part of the point of centripetal institutions is to make, via cross-ethnic voting, electoral victory and policy progress contingent on securing support from more than just one segment in society. In other words, political parties must be incentivised to run acceptable candidates with broadly appealing policies in constituencies across social segments. As Rabushka and Shepsle (1971) put it, centripetalists hold that:

> Candidates who can attract widespread support alone or as part of broad-based multi-ethnic parties or coalitions are seen as the best way of avoiding the tendency towards outbidding and extremism inherent in polarized electoral politics and ethnically exclusive party systems (quoted in Reilly 2000, p. 1).

Let us give just one example of how this might be achieved, by relying on the example of Indonesia, 'probably the best example of such a [strongly centripetal] system amongst contemporary democracies' (Reilly 2020, p. 5). While some elements of its democratic system are closer to the consociational model, many of them are clearly centripetal and in particular its presidential regime and the fact that direct presidential elections (introduced in 2004) require successful candidates to attain 'both a nationwide majority *and* at least 20% of the vote in over half of Indonesia's 34 provinces to avoid run-off election' (Reilly 2020, p. 7; see also Horowitz 2013, pp. 148–153).

Also, the procedure for the nomination of candidates requires collations of cross-national parties, and the parties themselves are legally obliged to have branches spread across most Indonesia's provinces (Horowitz 2013, pp. 178–179). Although it is not easy to establish direct causalities, Reilly observes that 'the more moderate presidential candidate has triumphed over sometimes much more extreme opponents in every election to date, greatly aiding the consolidation of Indonesian democracy' (Reilly 2020, p. 8). As for parties, Indonesia's party system has 'proved remarkably adept at encouraging cross-ethnic bargaining and in minimizing the role of ethnicity in politics' (Aspinall 2011, p. 311; quoted in Reilly 2020, p. 8).

To be sure, majoritarian institutions (electoral system, presidentialism, direct democracy) are not immune to abuse. For example, they can be misused by populists, either by facilitating their access to power or by augmenting the chances that populist proposals win the popular vote in referendums (e.g., the minaret ban in Switzerland). Hence, it is important that the risk of abuse be limited as much as possible by a system of check and balances and especially by entrenching fundamental rights in the constitution. But it is critical to remind the reader that our focus is on deeply divided societies. It is in such societies that, in our view, consociational solutions are also (and possibly even more) prone to abuse, because they are more likely to entrench group identities and promote radical (and, for that matter, populist too) ethno-nationalists.

This said, centripetalism should not be seen as a full-fledged alternative to consociationalism (see also Bogaards 2019). It is likely that building and sustaining democracy under conditions of deep societal diversity could benefit from both elements of equal recognition (emphasised by consociationalism) and institutional incentives for nationwide cross-communal parties, cross-ethnic voting and moderation (emphasised by centripetalism).

CONCLUSION

In this chapter we have discussed the problem of stability faced by deeply divided societies. We have critically assessed consociationalism, the most common institutional approach used to build and sustain democracy in such societies. Our analysis shows that the specific set of institutions put forward in the consociational democracy is highly problematic from the point of view of values that any democratic regime should convey and that it does not offer a fully satisfying response to the problem of democratic stability. We have concluded by discussing an alternative to consociationalism: centripetalism. Its normative underpinnings and institutional solutions are, in our view, more promising for tackling the problem of stability in deeply divided societies. At the very least, constitutional design should find ways to combine consociational insights based on the value of equal recognition with centripetal institutions that more explicitly aim to develop a common overarching political identity through democratic institutions.

RECOMMENDED READING

Bogaards, M. & Ludger, H. (2020). *Half a Century of Consociationalism – Cases and Comparisons. Special Issue of Swiss Political Science Review*, 25 (4): 341–574.

Brooks Kelly, B. (2019). *Power-Sharing and Consociational Theory*, London: Palgrave Macmillan.

Horowitz, D. L. (1991). *A Democratic South Africa? Constitutional Engineering in a Divided Society*, Berkeley: University of California Press.

Jakala, M., Kuzu, D., & Qvortrup, M., eds. (2018). *Consociationalism and Power-Sharing in Europe. Arend Lijphart's Theory of Political Accommodation*, London: Palgrave Macmillan.

Lacey, J. (2017). *Centripetal Democracy: Democratic Legitimacy and Political Identity in Belgium, Switzerland and the European Union*, Oxford: Oxford University Press.

Lijphart, A. (1977). *Democracy in Plural Societies*, New Haven: Yale University Press.

Lijphart, A. (2008). Introduction: Developments in power-sharing theory. In Arend Lijphart (ed.) *Thinking about Democracy: Power-Sharing and Majority Rule in Theory and Practice*. Abingdon: Routledge, 3–22.

Reilly, B. (2001). *Democracy in Divided Societies: Electoral Engineering for Conflict Management*, Cambridge: Cambridge University Press.

34

Corporatism

Steven Klein

Narrowly conceived, corporatism refers to the practice of state-supported, formalized bargaining between the organized representatives of labor and capital. Such corporatist institutions became a central feature of many twentieth-century capitalist societies. While corporatist bargaining arrangements have come under strain in an era of globalization and deregulation, they remain important political and economic institutions in many countries. Yet the labor-capital corporatism that took shape in the welfare state is just one moment in a larger constitutional and political debate about the ideal of corporatism. The concept of the corporate body, developed in late medieval political thought, was central to early modern theories of the constitutional state. The vision of a society organized into corporate bodies was revived in nineteenth-century Europe as a reaction to the supposedly disintegrating individualism of rights-based constitutional theories. In the twentieth century, these debates gave rise to rival democratic and authoritarian corporatisms, ideals that were realized, to varying degrees, as liberal constitutional states went into crisis.

Behind these debates about corporatism are more fundamental issues in constitutional theory. While in the twentieth-century corporatism became associated primarily with economic actors, a central question in corporatist theory was the broader constitutional status of non-state associations and organizations that often had their own political powers to govern their members and engage in quasi-legislative activity. Did such organizations exist at the pleasure of a sovereign state, or did they show that political authority was dispersed throughout society? In arguing for the independent legitimacy of such diverse corporate actors, proponents of corporatism were generally united in criticizing more liberal visions of constitutionalism for its abstraction and formalism. Many corporatist theorists thus advocated a sort of societal constitutionalism, where constitutional norms can be embodied in diverse institutions that are more proximate to individuals than the state – ranging from major professional and economic associations to a variety of civil society groups. The second major strain of corporatist thinking challenges the neglect of the role of organized power in rights-based constitutionalism. Corporatist institutions provide a formal role in the political process to organized societal interests, thereby recognizing the constitutional importance of forms of power beyond state coercion or equal voting rights. In this respect, corporatist institutions, with their focus on representing distinctive class perspectives, reintroduce into modern constitutions the elements of the mixed regime characteristic of ancient polities (McCormick 2011). Relatedly, corporatist institutions, and especially those focused on the economy, challenge the divide between public and private right, and in particular the image of private law that rests on the ideal of free contract. In place of the free labor contract, economic corporatist institutions construct "the economy as a polity," placing collective negotiations and problem-solving at the heart of economic institutions. Yet corporatist institutions varied widely in how inclusive these procedures were in practice, with many coming to privilege the interests of powerful insiders in a process scholars term labour market dualization. It remains an open question if corporatist institutions can overcome this dynamic and generate a genuinely inclusive and democratic process of societal constitutionalism.

The following discussion analyses corporatism both as a tradition in constitutional theory and as an empirical phenomenon that arose in the interwar and post-war periods. It argues that both can contribute to a theory of democratic constitutionalism that emphasizes the importance of organized collective power, and not just the problem of regulating state coercion or distributing formal voting rights. Section I provides an overview of corporatist ideas in European constitutional and political thought. In a stylized fashion, it emphasizes the contrast between integrative and pluralist understandings of corporatism, which came to inform rival conservative and socialist visions in the twentieth century. Section II examines the debate about post-war corporatist institutions and their role within liberal capitalist democracies. Sections III – V examine the broader theoretical and normative significance of corporatism for constitutional theory. Section III argues that corporatist theories contribute a notion of societal self-legislation via non-state organizations, while Section V focuses on corporatist theories' contribution to debates about social rights and economic constitutionalism. Section V analyses the relationship between corporatism and democracy. It contends that corporatism points to a conception of organized collective power and societal constitutionalism that challenges liberal proceduralists' vision of the democratic order.

I CORPORATISM IN THE HISTORY OF CONSTITUTIONAL THOUGHT

The concept of the corporation, which showed how a legal body could arise out of the plurality of individual members of a corporate entity, was an important inspiration for modern constitutional theories. Early modern theorists of the state looked to corporate ideas for a model of how a collective could constitute a self-governing unity out of the diversity of its members. As the centralized European state evolved, corporatist ideas then became a resource for two currents of political thought. The first sought to rescue the capacity for self-governance of organizations outside the state. According to such theories, these corporatist bodies had a reality beyond their legal recognition by the state and so were a source of political authority in their own right. Here, the central idea was the real, as opposed to juridical, personhood of non-state groups and associations. Such theories thus emphasized the corporatist challenge to the unitary model of the state associated with thinkers like Thomas Hobbes (Runciman 1997). The other strain of thought looked to corporatist institutions for more organic mechanisms of social integration than were provided for either by market-based modes of civil society or formal notions of political membership. Such theories proposed concepts of functional representation, whereby corporate bodies represented the social functions of their members, as opposed to the representation of interests provided by parliamentary models. This idea sought in the idea of corporatism a more genuine model of unity than was provided in juridical definitions of the state. These two currents of corporatism – one more pluralist, one more statist – form the backdrop for the twentieth-century debate over corporatism. While the idea of real group personalities would find its starkest expression in anarcho-syndicalism and functional representation in fascist theories of the state, many thinkers sought to combine elements of both and so to balance pluralism and statism in the theory of corporatism.

The term "corporation" comes from the Latin verb *corporare*, to embody. In the canonization of Roman law under Justinian, a corporation was a type of legal fiction that could embody a *universitas*, or entire collective of people, in a lasting entity that would outlive any individual. The Roman idea of the corporation became important to thirteenth- and fourteenth-century debates among European, and especially Italian, jurists that laid the foundation of modern constitutionalism (Canning 1980; Lee 2016). At the time, Europe was dotted with self-governing city-states and guilds which competed with hierarchical forms of feudal authority. For our purposes, the most interesting aspect of this debate was the effort to situate self-governing Italian city-states within the framework of authority derived from medieval interpretations of the Roman *lex regia*. According to the doctrine of *lex regia*, Augustus received a grant of authority from the Roman people that provided him absolute authority – a view that very much interested individuals such as the Holy Roman Emperor Frederick I. Against this view, the Italian jurist Bartolus and his student Baldus argued for the independent authority of the free people (*populus liber*) of Italian city-states – pointing to a more pluralist notion of political authority. To do so, Baldus drew on the Roman notion of a corporation. As a corporation, the *populus* was at once a unity and a plurality, a body made up of plural individuals but one that could act in a unitary way to issue laws. Even more radically, Baldus argued that corporate bodies had a self-constituting reality aside from the concessive grant that created their legal personality. He argued that "the members themselves – when 'rightly assembled' [*congregator bene*] – are perfectly capable of acting for the whole corporation" (Lee 2016, p. 75). Thus, the self-governed city-states did not need a singular representative to embody their corporate personhood. Rather, through their self-legislation they could form a unity out of the multitude of their members.

In the short term, these fourteenth-century corporatist arguments would generally recede in the face of defenders of the central state. Yet these arguments too were couched in the language of the corporation, with early modern theorists of state sovereignty such as Bodin, Grotius, and Hobbes all using categories drawn from the medieval theory of the corporation to explain the nature of sovereignty and the relationship between the sovereign and the government (Edelstein 2022; Lee 2016). The concept of the corporation was similarly influential in the constitutional thinking of the early American republic (Ciepley 2017). Speaking schematically, though, the period from the late medieval Italian jurists through to the nineteenth century was marked by attempts to consolidate the modern, centralized nation-state. The dominant motif of constitutional thought was the establishment of the territorial state through a system of individual rights that would counteract the pluralized authority advanced by theorists like Bartolus.

Yet this state-building project came to face deep challenges in the nineteenth century, challenges which would lead to a resurgence of corporatist thought. Especially in continental Europe, states faced lingering patterns of regionalism. More centrally, the system of private right that was meant to bind individuals qua individuals to the state faltered in the face of the class divisions produced by capitalism. Liberal constitutionalism was facilitated by the emergence of capitalism and the breakdown of the economic bases of feudal authority. But the political promise of the negative rights of liberal constitutionalism was increasingly undermined by the capitalist class system. For conservatives, this was a symptom of the disintegrative egoism embodied in the very notion of negative rights. For radicals, it demonstrated the need to extend democratic principles beyond the state and into the economy. In both cases, corporatist concepts proved crucial for articulating these concerns.[1]

This nineteenth-century revival of corporatist thought was a reaction to the upheaval caused by the French Revolution. Constitutional thinkers sought to combine principles drawn from the revolution with supposedly older corporatist traditions which would offset the destabilizing implications of revolutionary constitutionalism. Here we begin to see the second strain of corporatism, according to which corporate bodies provided an alternative mode of political representation and integration to electoral democracy. While pluralist thinkers tended to look to independent political bodies like city-states and guilds as their models, here the notion of medieval estates provided an ideal of functional representation. One of the clearest expressions of this hybrid is G. W. F. Hegel's constitutional proposals in *The Philosophy of Right* (Hegel 1991 [1821]). As Daniel Lee outlines, Hegel's proposals

---

[1] For an expansion of the line of argument in this paragraph, see Thornhill (2017).

were situated within a larger debate about constitutional reform in Prussia, one where conservatives came to advocate for a constitutional order centered around the *Stände* or feudal estates (Lee 2008). While Hegel partially sides with the French Revolution in advocating for a sphere of negative freedom in the domain of civil society, he also argues that the ideal of private right is self-undermining insofar as individuals' material dependence on the market tends to produce poverty and what Hegel calls "the rabble," as well as contingent moral concern through charity (Hegel 1991 [1821], §241, §244). The corporation, Hegel argues, overcomes this opposition between negative right and arbitrary moral concern. Hegel writes that in the corporation, "*the ethical returns* to civil society as an immanent principle" (Hegel 1991 [1821], §249). By this, Hegel means that the corporation combines both civil society's focus on meeting material needs through exchange – members of a corporation or guild still sell their labor on the market – with more substantive ethical principles, insofar as the corporation also guarantees their members a level of material well-being and social recognition. As a result, Hegel advocates for legislation through an assembly of estates (*Ständeversammlung*) rather than an elected parliament. Just as corporations can integrate individual freedom with an ethical principle of care for their members in civil society, so too in the state do corporations integrate democratic principles of electoral representation with more organic notions of representing the properly formed and organized interests of their members.

Hegel's defense of corporatism, as well as the larger debates about how to reconcile the principles of the French Revolution with Europe's old order, resonated throughout the nineteenth century. Much like Hegel, French thinkers such as the sociologist Emile Durkheim turned to the corporation to reconcile the individual and the community in the face of fears of social disintegration driven by industrialization and an emerging culture of individual rights. Durkheim thinks the separation between the political and economic spheres and the general distance of the state from daily life means that economic activity "is for the most part removed from the moderating action of any rules" (Durkheim 1997 [1893], p. xxxii). Durkheim looks to corporate bodies to establish "a professional morality and code of law within the various professions in the economy" and argues such corporations should become public institutions with the ability to regulate their members (Durkheim 1997 [1893], p. xxxvi). Corporately organized professional bodies could then become a "moral force capable of curbing individual egoism, nurturing among workers a more invigorated feeling of their common solidarity, and preventing the law of the of the strongest from being applied too brutally in industrial and commercial relationships" (Durkheim 1997 [1893], p. xxxix).

The late nineteenth century also saw the development of more pluralist corporatist theories. In France, the legal scholar Léon Duguit would build on Durkheim's vision of solidarity through corporate organizations to propose a more explicitly functionalist theory of representation. But the most influential account would emerge from Germany, where the legal theorist Otto von Gierke would provide a landmark historical account of the concept of the corporation in European law. Gierke was central to the recovery of medieval and early modern theories of the corporation, such as the work of Bartolus and Baldus.[2] Gierke argued that corporate bodies had a real personality independently of their legal grant of authority. He traced this idea back to medieval German notions of fellowship (*Genossenschaft*), which he argues was obscured by the absorption of Roman legal categories into European thought. This idea informed Gierke's critique of the German Draft Civil Code, which he felt was too based on the Roman divide between public and private law. Where the state recognizes private associations as corporations "private law wholly sheds its character of individual rights, and is transformed into social law" (Gierke 2019 [1889], p. 1108). These corporations have a "common sense and common life" that "serve the unending, manifold ideals and material purposes of human existence, in a way that cannot be achieved through independent action" (Gierke 2019 [1889], p. 1110). Gierke also saw corporatist ideas as a way of recognizing the class tensions within capitalist society without turning to the perceived statism of socialism. In his critique of the Civil Code, Gierke argued that "our private law must absorb a drop of socialist ointment" (Gierke 2019 [1889], p. 1113). Corporate institutions such as unions and guilds were one lubricant. Like Hegel and Durkheim, Gierke saw corporatist institutions as tempering capitalist economic institutions with principles of cooperation and mutual support. Yet he tended to emphasize, more so than Hegel, the pluralist nature of such associations.

Gierke's vision of corporatism in terms of a sphere of autonomous, self-governing entities that operate between the state and the market would prove influential. Yet Gierke himself was torn between his pluralist legal theory and his commitment to German state-building. His thought mirrored the already-noted tension within corporatist practice. Corporatist institutions were seen both as mechanisms for expressing a plurality of organized societal interests outside formal electoral representation *and* institutional mechanisms that could enhance the genuine unity of the state through a more organic notion of community. Subsequent debates about corporatism tended to polarize around this issue. In England, the pluralist school further developed Gierke's thought into a full-fledged critique of state sovereignty and defense of pluralism. Filtered through the translations and work of the English legal historian Frederic Maitland, Gierke influenced thinkers such as John Figgis, G. D. H. Cole, and Harold Laski (Hirst 1989; Laborde 2000; Runciman 1997). Figgis used the idea of real group personality to argue for religious pluralism and the need to keep church organizations autonomous from the state. From Gierke's notion of the real personality of non-state groups, Cole and Laski developed their socialist political theories. Cole built his comprehensive vision of guild socialism, where the

---

[2] These thinkers were important for Gierke's four volume history of the law of cooperatives *Das Deutsche Genossenschaftsrecht*, which was first (in part) translated by Frederic Maitland, as Gierke (1900).

economy would be reorganized around labor and consumer cooperatives, on the Gierkian idea that "the laws of other functional associations have the same binding character and social status as those of the State" (Cole 1920, p. 126, cited in Runciman 1997). Laski pushed further to a pluralist theory that rejected the notion of state sovereignty and called for the dispersion of political power throughout society. These thinkers drew inspiration from earlier models of self-governing guilds and municipalities and sought to adapt those ideas to the context of industrial capitalism and parliamentary democracy.

At the same time as the pluralist school was pushing corporatism away from the state, early fascist thinkers built on corporatist ideals of organic integration to construct their vision of the fascist state. In Germany, the influential legal theorist Rudolf Smend, reacting to the perceived chaos of the Weimar Republic, argued for integration into the state through corporate bodies that would ensure rights are matched to their obligations. He looked to Mussolini as a model and subsequently influenced Italian legal theories of the corporatist state (Caldwell 1997, chap. 5). A variety of thinkers in Italy, Spain, and Portugal built on the idea of organic unity and functional representation to argue that corporate organizations aligned with fascist parties provided a more authentic and immediate mode of political representation than liberal democracy.[3] These thinkers often drew together modern corporatist ideals with Catholic notions of subsidiarity, influencing the authoritarian and fascist movements in Catholic countries like Austria, Portugal, and Italy. But whether Catholic or not, these authoritarian versions of corporatism sought to subsume both the individual and the corporate bodies within the state. Such bodies did not have an autonomous, self-governing capacity but were rather mechanisms for ensuring that the unity of the state filtered into society. Thus, while pluralist theories blended into anarchism, the more integrative theories of corporatism lent themselves to fascist uses during the period of political crisis that followed World War I.

II THE CENTURY OF CORPORATISM?

While many theories of corporatism began from a plurality of self-regulating corporatist institutions – ranging from churches and universities to professional associations to volunteer groups – towards the end of the nineteenth century class conflict became the predominant axis of societal conflict, reconfiguring corporatist debates. The central question became whether corporatist forms of governance in the economy could help resolve increasingly politicized conflicts between labor and capital. This section provides an overview of the debates about the specifically economic form of corporatism that evolved alongside the welfare state.

---

[3] Sometimes this evinced fascinating cross-pollination: for example, the Spanish theorist of the corporatist state, Ramiro de Maeztu, had been a supporter of Cole's guild socialism before going to the right. For a more extended discussion of fascists theories of the corporatist state, see Pinto (2017).

During World War I, participant states developed various corporatist arrangements within the economy to pacify labor and maximize cooperation for military mobilization (Thornhill 2017). In the immediate post-war period, legal and political scholars used these institutional innovations as a basis for developing a theory of corporatism that focused on the politicization and even democratization of the economy. While important theorists developed these ideas in interwar Italy, the most prominent debate took place in Weimar Germany.[4] The Weimar Constitution, crafted by Gierke's student Hugo Preuß, included direct provisions for corporatist arrangements, albeit provisions that were never fully realized in practice. Designed to mollify advocates of the council democracy that arose during the German Revolution, Article 165 called for workers' councils within corporations as well as a national economic council, with the ability to draft laws, that would operate alongside parliamentary democracy. This produced an intensive debate among German public law scholars about the exact constitutional status of such corporatist self-regulation (Collin 2017). During this period, we see the increasing split between pluralist-democratic and centralist-authoritarian versions of corporatism. Social democratic thinkers like Hugo Sinzheimer, again largely influenced by Gierke, saw in corporatist institutions models for the autonomous emancipation and direct democratization of the economy alongside parliamentary democracy (Dukes 2014). At the same time, many Italian and German proto-fascist and fascist thinkers identified in corporatist institutions a mode of national social integration superior to parliamentary democracy, institutions that could embody national unity rather than the sectional interests of parties (Caldwell 1997; Pinto 2017). In either case, however, corporatism pointed to an organization, politicization, and constitutionalization of the formerly private sphere of economic activity – and so to a source of legal authority that rivalled parliamentary sovereignty.

Much like World War I, World War II fostered the creation of corporatist governance arrangements across belligerent states, arrangements that became central to the developed corporatism that was a key element of the post-war welfare state. Even as the most extreme forms of corporatism in fascist countries were dismantled after the war, all countries retained some degree of corporatist arrangements. And these arose alongside the post-war solidification of the notion of social rights and the institutional structures of the welfare state. Corporatism was a core component of a more general idea of coordinated capitalism or "embedded liberalism," where the market mechanism was replaced by a variety of political coordination mechanisms (Hall and Soskice 2001; Ruggie 1982; Shonfield 1965; Polanyi 2001 [1944]). They enabled the state to help coordinate wage policy and counter-cyclical state spending and existed alongside widespread acceptance that the state could play an active role in sectoral planning and strategic investment as part of a more general mixed economy. The normalization of corporatism now gave rise to an extensive debate

---

[4] For Italian debates, see Goldoni and Wilkinson (2018) and Rubinelli (2019a).

about how best to characterize such institutions as well as how to think about their macropolitical and macroeconomic effects. While earlier debates about corporatism involved philosophers and legal scholars, the study of these institutions proved foundational to the post-war comparative study of capitalist political economy.

Initially, scholars distinguished corporatist systems with reference to state-enforced monopolies on the representation of key economic interest groups (Schmitter 1974; Molina and Rhodes 2002). Corporatism was different from pluralism because the state recognized a single representative of the collective interests of labor or capital. And scholars pointed to the two-way intertwinement of the state and these collective actors; peak-level economic associations were deeply involved in the policy-making process, and the state played an active role in various aspects of collective bargaining in the economy. While corporatist arrangements varied between countries, for the purposes of scholarly debates the "ideal-type" became the system that evolved in Sweden, where peak-level employers' and workers' associations would negotiate sectoral wages and would coordinate macroeconomic policy with an elected pro-labor government. Another important model was Germany's system of codetermination, where workers would receive elected representation on the boards of major companies – a legacy of the Weimar constitution.

Yet as these corporatist systems evolved, they became important components of the general policy-making process in each country. While initially corporatism was seen as an alternative to other forms of pluralist interest-group politics, over time scholars of corporatism saw it as a particular mode of interest group activity, with higher degrees of concentration and formalized cooperation as part of what scholars called "policy concertation." Philippe Schmitter, for example, distinguished between state corporatism and societal corporatism, where the latter involves a more informal notion of spontaneously organized corporate interests, while in the former, the state directly constitutes the corporate institutions (Schmitter 1974). This broader definition captured the more diverse array of policy arenas in which corporatist actors were engaged. That is, corporatist institutions expanded beyond a strict focus on wage negotiations and macroeconomic policy and became, in the seminal formulation of Schmitter, "a particular ... institutional arrangement for linking the associationally organized interests of civil society with the decision structures of the state" (Schmitter 1974, p. 68). Corporatism, here, exists along a spectrum with pluralism, and many states have more corporate arrangements in some policy domains along with more pluralist arrangements in others.

Yet just as corporatism became a routinized facet of industrial democracies, such systems entered a crisis of both democratic legitimacy and macroeconomic effectiveness. First, "actually-existing" corporatism was far from the sort of economic democracy envisioned by thinkers like Sinzheimer. Both neo-Marxist and conservative critics highlighted the tendencies towards centralization, depoliticization, and unaccountability within these corporatist institutions. Jürgen Habermas observed how the functioning of the corporatist welfare state undermined the operation of critical public debate: "organizations strive for political compromises with the state and with one another, as much as possible to the exclusion of the public; in this process, however, they have to procure plebiscitary agreement from a mediatized public by means of a display of staged or manipulated publicity" (Habermas 1992 [1962], p. 232). New Left social movements were one reaction to this artificial publicity. Writing in 1974, Schmitter noted that corporatist arrangements are "being bombarded with demands for more direct forms of participation, undermining both the stability of established internal hierarchies of authority and their claims to democratic legitimacy" (Schmitter 1974, p. 127). Especially as German codetermination legislation limited the practice to the largest corporations and specific economic sectors, corporatist arrangements were increasingly seen as serving the interests of a core labor aristocracy operating in coordination with major corporations, groups divorced from broader societal currents and democratic movements.

These democratic challenges intersected with the economic crises of the 1970s to unravel the ideal-typical, peak-level corporatism. Changes in the structure of work, European integration, and increasing competitive pressures all undermined the viability of coordinated wage policy. Yet corporatism as a system of consultation and interest-group representation persisted through these transformations, even if in a more decentralized or informal manner. In some cases, corporatist institutions even re-emerged as a system of "policy concertation," with countries such as the Netherlands and Spain implementing peak-level "social pacts" to adapt to changing economic circumstances (Molina and Rhodes 2002, p. 309). Similarly, within the European Union there exists a complex system of consultation and negotiation with "social partners," which includes European-wide trade union and employer federations. This system of quasi-corporatist consultation is formalized by Article 152 of the *Treaty on the Functioning of the European Union* which states that the EU should "facilitate dialogue between the social partners, respecting their autonomy." While weakened, corporatist arrangements thus persist as an important element of constitutional democracies, existing as a system of formalized policy negotiation that operates alongside other forms of democratic representation such as elected parliaments.

III CORPORATISM AND SOCIETAL SELF-LEGISLATION

As we have seen, corporatism embodies a diverse historical tradition as well as an array of institutional manifestations. But within this broad field, some core constitutional concepts are distinctive to corporatist thought. What is corporatist constitutionalism? Here, I want to argue it has three pillars: (1) an ideal of society self-regulation and so of the autonomous law-making capacity of non-state actors;[5] (2) a distinctive vision of economic constitutionalism and economic democracy

---

[5] Albeit one that, in practice, always required extensive state involvement in and regulation of corporatist arrangements.

based around organized actors in the economy – one that incorporates but goes beyond social rights; and (3) a challenge to liberal proceduralism and a vision of democracy based on organized power. The first aspect situates corporatism relative to society, the second to the economy, while the third positions corporatist ideals relative to the state.

As we saw with Gierke, the development of corporatist ideas was closely tied to the concept of genuine group personhood. Corporatist theories point to the capacity of non-state actors for self-legislation and the production of legal norms. Corporatist constitutionalism challenges the exclusive legislative prerogative of the state, arguing instead that societal actors have autonomous quasi-legislative capacities. The debate about economic corporatism brought this out in the contexts of administrative and labor law. Rather than legislating things like working conditions or wages directly, the state delegates these competencies to corporate actors, albeit in close dialogue with the state and within general parameters. Yet for pluralist theories of corporatism the ideal of societal self-legislation extends to a variety of non-state groups and actors, such as religious organizations, universities, and professional associations. In this regard, corporatist theories are in the background for the late-twentieth-century revival of the concept of civil society, which emphasized the politics of "substitution," whereby civil society actors would take over functions otherwise carried out by the state (J. Cohen and A. Arato 1992; S. Klein and C.-S. Lee 2019). While such theories focused on the discursive and cultural benefits of an active civil society, corporatist theories point to the juridical dimension of civil society. For pluralists thinkers, civil society groups were genuine sources of obligation and authority that existed alongside the legal structure of the state. Thus, corporatism points to an ideal of societal self-legislation or self-regulation that exists alongside the formal law-making powers of the state. Corporatist arrangements often involve the delegation of official recognition of quasi-legislative powers to societal actors within a general framework.

One persistent question within the corporatist tradition is how autonomous this self-legislating capacity ought to be. Insofar as, for theoretical advocates of corporatism, corporatist arrangements are meant to correct for the supposedly disintegrative effects of private right doctrines, then advocates of corporatism viewed such institutions as mechanisms for improving integration into the state. From this perspective, corporatist arrangements are less about self-legislation than enhancing state legitimacy. More pluralist views of corporatism pointed to the ability of a variety of groups, ranging from religious organizations to medical and legal professional bodies to universities and so on, to produce their own quasi-legal standards governing their members based on their insider knowledge and expertise. Similarly, for those who see corporatist politics as a response to power imbalances within society that cannot be recognized within a private right framework – such as the tension between free labor contract and the power imbalance between labor and capital – corporatist arrangements are to be given greater leeway for self-direction. The role of the state is to help compensate for such power differences rather than integrate social groups through corporatist institutions.

IV CORPORATISM AND ECONOMIC CONSTITUTIONALISM

Alongside these pluralist theories of group self-legislation, corporatist thinkers also developed a vision of economic constitutionalism that complemented, even as it went beyond, notions of social rights central to the welfare state. Advocates of corporatism pointed to the failures of private right doctrines to respond to the inequalities generated by power imbalances within capitalist societies. The system of private right was predicated on the idea that workers could eventually move out of a dependent position and achieve independence as artisans or farmers. The development of industrial capitalism undermined this vision, giving rise to demands for various social rights that would compensate for market processes and protect workers against new social risks such as workplace injury or against sickness and old age. Today, such social rights are widely entrenched in constitutional structures or implicitly recognized as part of a political order (J. King 2018; K. Young 2012). They typically include rights to social security and in-kind provisions such as healthcare and housing, as well as rights to certain protections within the economic sphere, such as the right to form a union. Social rights thus tend to draw in public law principles like justice or the common good into the formerly private arena of contractual freedom.

Theorists of corporatism share the social rights critique of the capitalist economy. Many corporatist theories also reject the idea that the economy can be constituted through free contracts justified via the notion of private rights and autonomous choice. Because of the grand power disparities and the tendency of capitalist economies towards large-scale organizations and corporations, most workers simply accept the terms of contract offered. Moreover, the idea of private right fails to account for the new needs and risks associated with capitalist economies. Yet corporatist theories go beyond the rights-language of this aspect of the welfare state. For more liberal and left corporatist theories, social rights were only one component of a more ambitious democratization of the economy. They rejected the exclusive focus on top-down social rights secured by the state. Rather, the same set of concerns that gave rise to social rights – the new risks and inequalities generated by capitalism – also gave rise to a need to reorganize the economy on a more cooperative and democratic basis. Thus, corporatist theorists put more emphasis on responding to economic risks and power imbalances in the economy via the direct politicization and cooperative reorganization of economic institutions. In contrast, theories of social rights are indebted to T. H. Marshall's account of social rights as extending and complementing traditional economic rights (which Marshall includes within civil rights), ensuring people have the genuine basis on which to exercise their freedom of contract and so on (Marshall and Bottomore 1987). Yet this introduced tensions into the practice of corporatist politics. In some cases, such as the United

States, corporatist actors, such as trade unions, were often skeptical of centralized policies based on social rights such as public health care or collective wage setting, which they worried would encroach on the collective bargaining process. In other cases, such as Sweden, corporatist actors saw such central social welfare policies as enhancing their bargaining power and so ability to push for deeper democratization of the economy.

Corporatist theories thus often proposed an ideal of economic constitutionalism. For theorists of an economic constitution, like Sinzheimer, the economy was a domain of power relations that had to be regulated according to public law principles like equal voice, rather than a domain of private exchange or social risk. The economic constitution thus referred to what political principles would guide the organization of power within the economy. Rather than a dichotomy between public rights and private rights, democratic corporatism sought to draw suitably refined public law concepts into the legal regulation of economic relationships. Such theories thus view the organization of the economy as part of a constitutional order, rather than something that public law encases or regulates externally (Dukes 2014).

V CORPORATISM AND DEMOCRACY

Corporatism's relationship to democracy remains vexed. Within the corporatist tradition, theorists disagreed sharply about whether corporatist institutions are mechanisms for state integration or express a pluralist conception of political authority. And in both cases, there was not necessarily a strong connection to democracy. Indeed, pluralist theories of the real personhood of associations may require the defense of the right to organize such groups non-democratically and hierarchically. Similarly, as we saw, theories of functional representation often sought to substitute corporatist institutions for electoral mechanisms organized around principles of political equality. At the same time, for thinkers like Cole and Sinzheimer, corporatist ideas were to deepen and enhance democracy, especially within economic production. Yet even when that more democratic vision came into practice in the post-World War II era, critics contended that corporatist institutions became arenas for bargaining between entrenched, internally undemocratic insiders who struck deals at the expense of broader societal interests. Nonetheless, taken as an ideal and model, corporatist thought and institutions often support a distinctive vision of democracy. Taking up the more democratic variant of corporatism, this section considers how corporatist theories and institutions challenge the procedural formalism of many current approaches to constitutional democracy. Instead, corporatism is part of a more broadly understood political constitution, one which encompasses the organization of power in society, and not just the distribution of formal political rights. In this regard, corporatist theories echo pre-modern constitutionalism, according to which constitutions are both a formal-legal doctrine *and* the way in which polity is actually constituted through the organization of different political actors.

Procedural views of democracy, broadly speaking, begin from an ideal of resolving disagreements while respecting participants equal dignity or standing (Christiano 2008; Kolodny 2014; Viehoff 2014) The procedural ideal gets expressed in constitutional principles of universal suffrage and equally weighing individual votes, which are further complemented by political rights like free assembly. Those then translate into something like equal political influence through electoral procedures that give everyone equal weight in electing representatives, who along with political parties are meant to aggregate their constituents' preferences and values into a coherent policy program. Historically, this vision of democratic constitutionalism complemented the division between public law and private law. The same principle of equality that enshrined a sphere of equal rights in the private sphere grounded a standard of equal procedural rights in the public sphere.

On a more conceptual level, advocates of the procedural view argue that fair procedures equalize our power over each other. Such procedures thereby reconcile the existence of a coercive legal order with our basic autonomy and equality. Given conditions of deep disagreement, the existence of a coercive legal order would seem to entail that some individual or group exercises power over you in a way that conflicts with your deeply held beliefs. There is thus a deep puzzle regarding how to reconcile autonomy with the existence of a legal order. Proceduralist arguments then proceed in two steps: first, even with given conditions of disagreement, a legitimate legal order can provide the valuable good of coordination that prevents unilateral action to realize individual conceptions of justice. Yet the existence of such a legal order would then seem to violate our equality, insofar as it would entail that some individual or group (whoever makes the laws) exercises coercive power over us through the creation of the laws. By giving everyone the equal probability of being the decisive vote, however, a one-person, one-vote procedure can generate a legal order while positioning all participants as equals and so ensuring no individual or group exercises power over anyone.

Corporatist theories of democracy challenge the narrow conception of power with which proceduralist views operate (S. Klein 2021). Within liberal constitutional theories, the paradigmatic problem is regulating and controlling coercive state power. Within power debates, this variety of power is typically called "power-over" and refers to the ability to get an agent to do something they would otherwise not do. Yet as a variety of scholars have noted, this view of power is too narrow, identifying power with one subset of how it can operate (Abizadeh 2023). If we take power to mean the ability to realize one's goals in a social context, then the ability to overcome someone's resistance is only one aspect of power. Power also arises from the reliable ability to get others to cooperate in your endeavors. Corporatist institutions are one of the mechanisms that integrate cooperative forms of power into a constitutional order. For corporatist theories, political institutions do not just distribute coercive power over one another – the focus of the procedural views. They also influence and structure cooperative forms of power. Even as they are legally recognized, corporate bodies rely on the voluntary cooperation of their members to be effective. For example, within the economy, labor unions counteract the power of employers through the voluntary organization of their members and their willingness to cooperate to realize shared goals.

As a result, while electoral institutions provide a fixed distribution of power-over through their voting procedures, corporatist institutions, even where they are only relatively egalitarian themselves, can be an important mechanism in large-scale egalitarian feedback loops that produce the relatively equal distribution of both power-over as well as cooperative "power-with." From this perspective, political institutions are not just formal rules and procedures that distribute individual political rights but also mechanisms with regular effects on the organization and relative capacities of different societal actors. Thus, to understand the constitutional significance of corporatist institutions, we need to examine the feedback loops between the structure of the institutions and the broader balance of political power. In this regard, corporatist institutions also exist in a dynamic relationship with formal, electoral institutions. They can provide a check on the elitist tendencies of electoral institutions when they are cut adrift from non-state groups, like labor unions, by enabling forms of political organization and mobilization beyond electoral systems (Mair 2013). Indeed, scholars of comparative political economy have observed that the selection of different electoral institutions at key historical moments is in many respects endogenous to both the organizational structure of labor and capital as well as the perceived threat of a pro-labor government (Ahmed 2012). This is one reason, for instance, that we often observe a coincidence of corporatist economic governance arrangements in countries with more proportional electoral systems.

Corporatist institutions are thus part of the more informal, political constitution (Bellamy 2007) as opposed to the formal juridical constitution. In an influential discussion of corporatism, Gerhard Lehmbruch (1984) observes that corporatist arrangements were often hindered by formalization, something missed in the corporatist theories we examined earlier. Because the role of electoral institutions is "the aggregation of highly heterogeneous, individual acts of political choice," they need high degrees of formalization "to cope directly with the problems of maintaining stability, predictability, and responsiveness in representation." In contrast, "corporate representation presupposes a high degree of prior, inter-organizational aggregation: its stability and predictability rest upon the internal cohesion of relatively centralized association. And in the maintenance of such cohesion, a rigid formalization of procedures of inter-organizational coordination could prove to be counterproductive" (Lehmbruch 1984). Insofar as corporatist institutions rely on cooperative forms of power, such as the voluntary willingness of their members to participate in collective action like strikes, they require less formalization than institutions that rely on coercive power – and indeed the introduction of too much coercive power can introduce a logic of distrust that corrodes the functioning of the institutions. At the same time, the informal nature of representation to which Lehmbruch points can also conceal the operation of powerful insiders who dictate the terms of corporatist bargains. Such arrangements also tended to privilege already-organized and concentrated interests. While guild socialists like Cole thought that the corporate organization of production had to be balanced by the corporate organization of consumers through consumer co-operatives, corporatist arrangements were often seen as privileging the interests of labor and capital over that of consumers.

As we have already noted, thinkers such as Habermas and Schmitter drew attention to the internally undemocratic nature of much of actually existing corporatism. And this informality also makes corporatist institutions vulnerable to shifts in the underlying cooperative networks and so the larger economic context in which they operate, as we saw earlier. But here the contrast with formalized electoral institutions should not be overdrawn. Insofar as they also rely on various forms of informal cooperative power, especially political parties, they are also vulnerable to changes in their effective functioning if the underlying coalition structures of political parties shifts, even if formal rules do not markedly change – as has been evident in phenomena like the rise of anti-systemic parties, the weakening of traditional party systems, and the increasing use of extra-electoral mechanisms like referenda.

Lastly, corporatist arrangements make up a part of the "material constitution" (see Goldoni, Chapter 31, this volume) and indeed can be seen as embodying a modern form of the mixed regime. The material constitution refers to the "underlying material context, to the basic political and social conditions of possibility of constitutionalism and the dynamics of constitutional change" (Goldoni and Wilkinson 2018, p. 568). The material constitution points to how the organization of different societal actors, and especially economic actors and interests, generates the preconditions for the effective functioning of formal-juridical constitutional systems. Insofar as corporatist modes of representation operate alongside parliamentary systems, through organizational networks with electoral parties, they will partially condition the forms of representation and interest-aggregation that operate in other parts of the constitutional system. Moreover, corporatist institutions will form a point of connection between the constitutional system and the underlying material structure of capitalism. The changing fortunes of corporatism have affected other features of constitutional systems. The decline of labor parties with close ties to organized union associations has deeply altered the nature of democratic representation in many constitutional contexts, giving way to new forms of personality-driven parties, unstable multi-party alliances, or anti-systemic politics.

Here, again, it is worth recalling the dual connotations of the word constitution: both a formal-legal document and a general way that a political system is "constituted." For classical constitutional theories in ancient Greece and Rome, the constitution referred precisely to how political institutions expressed or related to material relations of wealth inequality and class orders. Modern public law constitutional ideals are founded on a notion of formal and juridical equality and equal treatment by the law, one that gets embodied in the principle of electoral representation based on equal voting rights. Yet the underlying material divisions to which classical notions of the mixed regime referred do not disappear, and indeed some scholars argue that the fiction of juridical equality becomes a cover for electoral aristocracy (Manin 1997; McCormick 2011). The concept of the material constitution reminds us of these connections between constitutional design and the underlying material structure of a society. Corporatist institutions are one institutional mechanism that reintroduces more materialist, mixed regime forms of constitutionalism into modern constitutional systems centered on formal equality. Corporatist institutions provide representation to groups on an explicitly materialist basis, incorporating workers as workers and so on, and explicitly embodying principles of representation and negotiation based on relative power. Yet we can also note how constrained such modes of corporate representation are as compared to other models of the mixed regime. They can only incorporate lower classes insofar as they are members of corporate organizations. As a result, they will often entrench the relative power of the most privileged segments of the working class. Given this partial recognition of the interests of workers, such institutions will then benefit from the relative secrecy of negotiations, enabling them to strike deals between representatives of labor and capital that may be politically unpalatable. These limitations of representation and transparency are part of what made such modes of corporatism vulnerable in changing economic conditions.

CONCLUSION

Modern corporatist institutions represent a key form of mediation between the constitutional system and both organized groups in society and the structure of capitalist economies. Even as their fate has waned since the 1970s, many constitutional systems continue to feature corporatist forms of interest representation and negotiation that operate alongside parliamentary and electoral democracy (Lijphart 2012). Such institutions challenge the public-private divide and introduce public law constitutional principles into the organization of the economy, emphasizing themes like equality of voice and inclusion as opposed to formal contractual freedom. And such principles go beyond, even as they encompass, the idea of social rights associated with the welfare state. Social rights compensate for the inequalities and risks generated by capitalist production, while corporatist institutions were attempts to politicize and partially democratize the actual governance of such production itself. Corporatist institutions also point to the capacity of organized societal actors to produce binding legal norms themselves, thus engaging in a form of cooperative self-regulation. Corporatist institutions thus often went beyond the opposition between formal rule of law and substantive social justice goals, providing societal actors latitude to reflexively determine their norms of mutual interaction even as the political system compensated for power imbalances.

Even as they only partially realize principles of inclusion and political equality, these corporatist institutions channel cooperative forms of power and can help mobilize democratic majorities against entrenched forms of power. The democratic possibilities of corporatism were recognized by many key corporatist theorists going back to early Italian city-states and finding fullest expression in the Weimar Republic. Such a democratic vision existed alongside more state-based, integrative theories of corporatism that saw in corporatist modes of representation an alternative to the supposedly atomizing and divisive nature of parliamentary politics. Most ambitiously, for thinkers like Sinzheimer and Cole corporatist ideals introduced a constitutional vision of equal political power into the organization of the modern economy. While corporatism as it took shape in the twentieth century fell short of this ideal, the ideal itself remains valuable in the face of our current conditions of concentrated economic power and hollowed out of formal democracy.

RECOMMENDED READING

Canning, J. P. (1980). The Corporation in the Political Thought of the Italian Jurists of the Thirteenth and Fourteenth Centuries. *History of Political Thought*, 1 (1), 9–32.
Cole, G. D. H. (2011 [1920]). *Guild Socialism Restated*. London: Routledge.
Durkheim, E. (1997 [1893]). *The Division of Labor in Society*. Translated by W. D. Hall. New York: The Free Press.
Durkheim, E. (2018). *Professional Ethics and Civic Morals*, London: Routledge.
Gierke, O. (1900). *The Political Theories of Middle Ages*. Translated by Frederic William Maitland. Cambridge: Cambridge University Press.
Gierke, O. (2019 [1889]). The Social Role of Private Law. (Translated by Ewan McGaughey). *German Law Journal* 19 (4), 1017–1116.
Habermas, J. (1992 [1962]). *The Structural Transformation of the Public Sphere: An Inquiry into a Category of Bourgeois Society*. Cambridge, MA.: MIT Press.
Hegel, G. W. F. (1991 [1821]). *Elements of the Philosophy of Right*. Edited by Allen W. Wood. Translated by H. B. Nisbet. Cambridge: Cambridge University Press.
Hirst, P. Q., ed. (1989). *The Pluralist Theory of the State: Selected Writings of G. D. H. Cole, J. N. Figgis, and H. J. Laski*, London and New York: Routledge.
Laborde, C. (2000). *Pluralist Thought and the State in Britain and France, 1900–25*, Basingstoke: Macmillan.
Mair, P. (2013). *Ruling the Void: The Hollowing of Western Democracy*, London: Verso.
Molina, O. & Rhodes, M. (2002). Corporatism: The Past, Present, and Future of a Concept. *Annual Review of Political Science*, 5 (1), 305–331.
Pinto, A. C., ed. (2017). *Corporatism and Fascism: The Corporatist Wave in Europe*, London: Routledge.
Runciman, D. (1997). *Pluralism and the Personality of the State*, Cambridge: Cambridge University Press.
Schmitter, P. (1974). Still the Century of Corporatism? *Review of Politics*, 36 (1), 85–131.

35

Guarantor (or the So-called "Fourth Branch") Institutions

Tarunabh Khaitan[*]

Guarantor institutions (such as electoral commissions and anti-corruption watchdogs, which supposedly comprise the so-called "fourth branch" of the state) are increasingly of interest to constitutional scholars (Tushnet 2021). In a given political context, a guarantor institution is a tailor-made constitutional institution, vested with material as well as expressive capacities, whose function is to provide a credible and enduring guarantee to a specific non-self-enforcing constitutional norm (or any aspect thereof). Broadly, the argumentative steps towards this conclusion are the following (Khaitan 2021b):

i. Constitutions, as risk-management tools for polities, generally seek to endure (self-consciously interim constitutions being an exception);
ii. In order for constitutions to endure, fundamental norms that constitutions commit to (hereinafter, *constitutional* norms) need credible and enduring "guarantees," understood in its colloquial (as opposed to private law) sense that a guaranteed outcome is one that is sufficiently likely to be obtained;
iii. Self-enforcing norms, that is, those norms that sufficiently powerful actors in a polity have an interest in effectuating, are automatically credible and likely to endure;
iv. The credibility and endurance of a non-self-enforcing constitutional norm, that is, fragile norms that powerful actors of the polity have self-interested reasons to want to frustrate, depend on the polity's cultural attitude towards that norm and the effectiveness of any institutional mechanism designed to enforce or realize it;

---

[*] Tarunabh Khaitan is the Professor (Chair) of Public Law at the London School of Economics and Political Science, and an Honorary Professorial Fellow at the Melbourne Law School. I am grateful to Anja Bossow, Bernie Andary, Samuel Keselman, Robert Lothman, and Jibran Khan for research assistance. I am also grateful to Jeff King, Richard Bellamy, Marcial Boo, Pablo de Greiff, Robert Hazell, Elliot Bulmer, Elizabeth Stephani, Vicky Jackson, David Wellstein, and participants of the "constitutional institutions" stream of the Prevention Project at the Centre for Human Rights and Global Justice (NYU) for helpful comments.

v. Even with respect to norms for which cultural restraints alone may not suffice, the traditional tripartite separation of power into the executive, legislative, and judicial branches may be enough to guarantee certain non-self-enforcing norms (arguably, a commitment to legality) (Waldron 2016d, chap. 3);
vi. For other non-self-enforcing norms, the three traditional branches – whether acting jointly or severally – are either unable (because they lack institutional capacity) or unwilling (because they are likely to have a conflict of interest) to provide a sufficient guarantee;
vii. To credibly guarantee the endurance of *such* non-self-enforcing (i.e., fragile) constitutional norms (such as the administration of free and fair elections), constitution-makers may sometimes have good reasons to create tailor-made, specific, *guarantor institutions* (such as electoral commissions) that sit outside the three traditional branches and are constitutionally entrenched (whether through legal or political means);
viii. In a given system, whether a regulator institution has a credibility-inspiring *guarantor* status depends on whether it enjoys a doubly constitutional character, that is, it must be a (legally or politically) *entrenched institution* seeking to credibly and enduringly make effective a (legally or politically) *entrenched norm*; if either of these entrenchments is missing, the institution is an ordinary or sub-constitutional regulator instead of a guarantor;
ix. Guarantor institutions tend to be vested with expressive capacity (i.e., the capacity to communicate) as well as material capacity (i.e., the capacity to undertake physical tasks) in order to discharge their functions, rendering their functional powers typically hybrid in nature;
x. Unlike integrity institutions, which typically only uphold the secondary duties of remedy or redress after a norm has been breached, guarantor institutions may be tasked with primary duties of norm enforcement as well as secondary duties of redressing breach; and
xi. Cultural factors aside, the effectiveness of guarantor institutions is a function of (a) its *expertise* and *capacity* to providing the said guarantee, (b) its *independence* from actors who are likely to have the ability and the willingness to frustrate the norm in question, and (c) its *accountability* to actors who are likely to have the ability and the willingness to secure the norm being guaranteed.

This chapter identifies and examines these three key factors that inform a guarantor institution's effectiveness in credibly serving its guaranteeing purpose over time (i.e., the factors identified in #xi. above). Admittedly, the polity's general cultural attitude to its constitutional norms is always a key variable in determining an institution's effectiveness. But cultural factors interact in complex forms with institutional design. While the best design can fail, and the worst may yet sail, design generally acts as a catalyst to broader political and cultural factors: good design can act as a positive catalyst and hasten desirable processes and outcomes, bad design is typically a negative catalyst. Furthermore, political culture itself is not static, and may change in response to design factors. Institutional design may not be the only thing that matters to outcomes, but it is not unimportant for that reason alone. Arguing that guarantor institutions are more trustee-like than agent-like in character, this chapter will defend the claim that the design of any guarantor institutions should seek to ensure that it has:

1. Sufficient expertise and capacity to perform its functions effectively;
2. Sufficient independence from political, economic, or social actors with an interest in frustrating the relevant norm it is meant to guarantee; and
3. Sufficient accountability to bodies with an interest in upholding the relevant norm.

I GUARANTORS AS TRUSTEES

Cultural and contingent factors aside, the effectiveness of guarantor institutions is a function of (a) its *expertise* and capacity to provide the said guarantee, (b) its *independence* from actors who are likely to have the ability and the willingness to frustrate the norm in question, and (c) its *accountability* to actors who are likely to have the ability and the willingness to secure the norm being guaranteed. This section explains why a guarantor needs to satisfy these requirements by way of a stylized rational-choice explanation.

In general, if transaction costs (such as information, temporal, decision, or enforcement costs) are higher when a principal does things directly, it is rational to delegate those tasks to agents with greater relative capacity than the principal, who will therefore incur lower costs (Majone 2001, p. 103). As such, agents are a means to enforce the *will* of their principal more efficiently than the principal could directly. On the other hand, it is rational to create a trust to manage a property for the benefit of the *interests* of the beneficiary if the trustee will do a better job at it than the settlor or the beneficiary acting directly. Unlike an agent, a trustee acts independently of both the settlor and the beneficiary, but always in the interests of the latter. For this arrangement to be rational, it must be the case that (for the duration of the trust) the trustee is likely to have greater relative *expertise* or *capacity* to perform its function of protecting the beneficiary's interest in the property than either the settlor or the beneficiary acting directly. This may be the case for a variety of reasons – the settlor may be unsure of her longevity or lack confidence in the beneficiary's ability in looking after his own interest.

Both the agent and the trustee have a *duty of loyalty* to the principal and to the beneficiary respectively. However, only the agent – with her duty to enforce the principal's will – is *under the control of* the principal (DeMott 2019, p. 25). The main danger with agency-type institutions is that they may fall short of carrying out the principal's will effectively or sufficiently. On the other hand, the trustee is, characteristically, *independent* of both the settlor and the beneficiary, and while duty bound to protect the beneficiary's interests in the entrusted property, she is under no duty to obey anyone's will. Because the trustee acts independently, rather than under anyone's control, judgments about her relative expertise (vis-a-vis to the settlor and the beneficiary) need to be made for longer time horizons (i.e., as long as the trust is expected to last). An unsure agent can always seek the principal's latest instructions; an unsure trustee usually must follow her best judgment. The trustee's continued comparative superiority to the settlor and the beneficiary is, therefore, essential if the creation of a trust is to be rational over time. Furthermore, trustees themselves can err or be captured. As a result, there may, sometimes, be a case for checking mechanisms to ensure that the trustee itself is acting as it is meant to act (e.g., by being legally accountable to the beneficiary for profits made from a breach of trust). The main reason to create agency-type institutions is to lower transaction costs, whereas the main reason to create trust-type institutions is to ensure that commitments made at T_0 are kept at T_1. Agencies protect *will*, trusts protect *interests*.

Constituted power cannot be entirely will-based; all constitutions must recognize and protect at least some interests. Even the most minimalistic, proceduralist, democratic constitution that only seeks to enforce the extant will of the people must – at least – assumes that it is in the interest of the people to have their contemporaneous will enforced. Taking the importance of the extant will of the people seriously *over time* therefore necessitates that even this minimally democratic constitution must seek to guarantee the *interest* in procedural democracy credibly and enduringly. Thus, no serious democratic constitution can rest on a will-based account alone: at the very least, securing the enforcement of the will of the future people is an interest that may, at some point, come into conflict with the will of the current people (or their agents). Because the will of the people can change, ensuring that the future will of the people, or the will of a future people, is also protected can only be expressed as their abiding *interest*. Most constitutions are not so minimalistic, and some make rather substantive commitments, either alongside or instead of democracy (Khaitan 2019). Many of these other long-term interests will need an effective guarantee against the powerful. If there are reasons to worry that constitutional actors may be tempted to frustrate these constitutional norms, it is rational for constitutions to design trustee-type institutions to make these commitments credible over time. It should be clear that guarantor institutions protect constitutionally-specified *interests*, and as such are better off reflecting the design of trustees than agents.

While illuminating, the application of the agency/trust models to explain constitutional institutions is not entirely straightforward. First, public law agents or trustees may not have clear (or any) conception of the relevant principal, settlor, entrusted property, beneficiary, or the agency/trust creating process. Second, in private law, agents and trustees are mutually exclusive binaries. In constitutional studies, since all constitutional actors (except, perhaps, "the people(s)") have fiduciary duties inasmuch as "they are quintessentially other-regarding and purposive" (Fox-Decent

2019, p. 913), it is better to imagine allocated *public* powers lying on a fiduciary spectrum, with *will-enforcing agents* closer to one end of this spectrum and *interest-protecting trustees* to the other (Lettanie 2019, p. 317). The closer an institution is to the agency end of this spectrum, the more likely it is to be tightly controlled by its principal; this is compatible with the claim that no public institution may purely be an agent. By contrast, the more independent an institution is, the more likely it is to be closer to the trusteeship end of this spectrum. Relatedly, operational constraints on more agentive bodies are likely to be procedural, to ensure that they mirror the will of their principal. On the other hand, bodies that are towards the trust end of the spectrum are likely to have their purposes (in terms of the interests they are meant to serve) defined more substantively. Despite their explanatory limitations, imagining agents and trustees as defining a spectrum of delegational possibilities, rather than binary categories, illuminates a key difference among public law institutions.

In the case of trustees that need to be vested with a considerable amount of power in order to do their job effectively, their considerable power can itself pose a risk for a polity. Therefore, a design that minimizes the risks they create is essential, because it might be better for a polity not to have a guarantor institution at all than to have one that is badly designed. In particular, guarantor institutions – as trustees – run the risk of:

- *Incompetence*, if they have insufficient expertise and capacities;
- *Capture*, if they are insufficiently independent of political parties, private interests, and other vested interests; and
- *Maladministration*, if they are insufficiently accountable to other legal and political institutions.

These three risks correspond to three features of the guarantor institution: their structural dimension concerns their expertise and capacity; their personnel dimension engages their independence; and their operational dimension invites attention to the need for accountability (see, for instance, Article 15 of the African Charter, on Democracy, which recognizes each of these design imperatives for guarantor institutions).

The key challenge in designing guarantor institutions is to give them enough power in all three dimensions they need to be effective, while ensuring that the risks of incompetence, capture, and maladministration are minimized. This can be particularly difficult, as some of these goals can be in tension with each other. For example, the need for independence from political parties to avoid partisan capture can cut against the need for democratic accountability to elected representatives to prevent maladministration. The design goal, therefore, is optimization, rather than maximization. Contextual and cultural factors will warrant careful consideration to determine the relative degree of challenge each of these risks poses, as well as the appropriate measures to mitigate them. In general, however, a few design features are likely to be relevant across the board in relation to each of these risks. The examples used in the discussions that follow are meant to illustrate the broader design principles, but they are too contextually specific to be useful as general recommendations.

II THE STRUCTURAL DIMENSION: AVOIDING INCOMPETENCE

The structural dimension of a guarantor institution concerns its structure, functions, processes, budgets, human resources, and (constitutional) status. To be competent, a guarantor must be structured effectively to ensure it has the necessary expertise and capacities to carry out its mandate. Expertise refers to possessing high levels of relevant domain knowledge, experience, and skill. Capacity is primarily a matter of an institution's *internal* composition and design – leadership and staffing quantities, personnel qualifications, internal organizational structure, decision-making process and procedures, and so on. Capacity, as distinct from expertise, is a function of the institutional powers, budget, personnel, and legal abilities with which the guarantor is vested. A guarantor may have the top experts in the field leading it, but it would still be incompetent if it is significantly understaffed, has a minuscule budget, or lacks the legal personality or powers necessary to perform its functions.

The nature of a particular guarantor's necessary expertise will depend on the nature of the norms it is tasked with guaranteeing. As constitutional actors, however, the leaders of guarantor institutions need to possess at least a minimal degree of constitutional understanding and experience working in public institutions. Such leaders are likely to have earned a reputation for sound judgment and institutional propriety – a reputation they are likely to be keen to preserve and augment. A degree of general expertise in the constitutional system and public life of the polity is a threshold requirement.

In addition, guarantors must also possess high-level specialist expertise in relation to their functions. Collins and Evans identify two high-level forms of expertise which allow their possessors to *do something* with expert knowledge, beyond merely possessing that knowledge: (i) *interactional expertise* is the high-level expertise that comes with mastering the language of a specialist domain which enables interaction with other experts, although without practical competence; (ii) *contributory expertise* is the possession of the high-level skill necessary to perform an activity competently (H. Collins & R. Evans 2007, pp. 13–14).

Depending on the nature of the norm being guaranteed, a guarantor may require contributory expertise (such as expertise in organizing election logistics for members of an electoral commission) or interactional expertise (e.g., an anti-monopoly and competition commission will need interactional expertise to understand business jargon, methods, and practices in order to determine what qualifies as anti-competitive practice) or (more likely) both. It may be useful to think of contributory expertise as *what* guarantors need to do, and interactional expertise in terms of *how* they should go about doing what they have to do – that is, in consultation with relevant actors, whether they be politicians, businesses, civil society, media, and so on. In fact, the importance of a high-level interactional expertise stems from the fact that guarantor institutions do not act in isolation, but are embedded in a complex constitutional context. They are closer to the political end of the law-politics spectrum than members of the higher judiciary, but closer to the law end of this spectrum than legislators and the political executive. It is a challenging position to occupy, making it essential that guarantor institutions are able to command the comity of other constitutional actors (including political parties in government and the opposition), and afford the same comity to them.

As constitutional actors engaged in constitutional politics, guarantors must also possess a modicum of interactional expertise in relation to politics. A constitutional guarantor ignores any likely political and constitutional implications of its actions at its own peril and could – sometimes – even imperil the constitution itself by acting ignorantly or recklessly. Guarantors must also be able to communicate decisions in ways that reduce the likelihood or intensity of backlash against their decisions. Furthermore, they often need to call upon the resources and expertise of other traditional branches to aid the performance of their own functions. As such, sufficient political *nous*, including the political wisdom to know when to intervene and when to refrain from acting, is likely to be essential for both a guarantor's effectiveness and its survival. Thus, guarantor institutions should typically not only have the relevant contributory expertise for their special function, but also interactional expertise to engage skillfully with other constitutional actors, including political parties, higher judiciary, other guarantor institutions, and civil society.

Effective leadership of a guarantor institution typically requires, either explicitly or implicitly, a general understanding of the constitutional system and interactional expertise with other constitutional actors. The most common explicit proxy for these types of expertise is a prior illustrious career in a relevant domain of public life. For example, the Indian Information Commissioners are to be "persons of eminence in public life with wide knowledge and experience in law, science and technology, social service, management, journalism, mass media or administration and governance" (Right to Information Act 2005, s 12(4)). Examples of provisions requiring specialist (interactional and contributory) expertise include the requirement on the German Information Commissioner to possess specific qualifications, experience, and skills in the field of data protection, alongside being qualified for judicial service or higher administrative service (Federal Data Protection Act 2017, s 11(1)).

The need for contributory expertise also explains, in part, why some guarantor institutions may function adequately with a single leader, while others need to be multi-member bodies: if the expertise needed for the effective discharge of its functions is unlikely to be found in a single individual, it makes sense to pool relevant types of expertise in a leadership committee. On the other hand, a single leader may suffice if the guarantor's mandate is narrow and requires only a single specialty. However, there may also be capture-related worries that may tilt the balance in favor of multi-member bodies more generally (*Seila Law LLC v Consumer Financial Protection Bureau*, 140 S. Ct. 2183 (2020) 15).

In order to understand the capacity-related needs of guarantor institutions, consider two examples of norms that a polity may wish to guarantee constitutionally: (a) reliable and up-to-date population data should be published periodically to inform public policy and electoral boundaries, and (b) actions of public servants should not be influenced by bribery. In order to guarantee these norms, a polity seeks to set up a census bureau and an anti-corruption agency, respectively. As a guarantor of norm (a), the census bureau will need to produce reliable and periodically updated census data through polity-wide surveys; with respect to norm (b), the anti-corruption agency will need to investigate suspected cases of bribery of public servants and charge them when there is sufficient evidence.

The two guarantors require very different types of personnel. A census bureau will likely need to employ a large number of surveyors who can go from door to door to collect population data or receive data digitally or by post (depending on the suitable method of data collection), and a sufficient number of statisticians, analysts, compilers, verifiers, and so on. The anti-corruption agency, on the other hand, will need a staff trained in investigative methods such as evidence gathering, witness interviewing, and criminal and evidentiary laws. The census bureau will need the legal ability and material capacity to collect and store citizens' private data; the anti-corruption agency may need the capacity and powers to interview suspects, collect evidence, make arrests, and so on. Both will need coercive and functional – rather than merely advisory – powers, as well as adequate budgets for paying the staff salaries, purchasing equipment, paying rents, and covering other operational expenses. Sometimes, guarantors may also need legislative (rulemaking) or judicial powers (with corresponding expressive capacities) depending on the duties they are required to perform. Retired judges from the higher judiciary are often tapped to serve with guarantors exercising judicial functions.

The need for expertise and capacity also shows why employing a single *generic* guarantor institution to protect all non-self-enforcing constitutional norms would not be effective – each norm requires a different type of expertise, and thus a different set of institutions. Creating a multiplicity of guarantor institutions may also entail the benefit of reducing capture risk, given that a single guarantor institution is more easily captured at a given point in time than several such institutions simultaneously (Tushnet 2021, p. 60).

Not all details relating to expertise and capacity in the structural dimension need to be constitutionalized, for effective guarantor institution design must strike a balance between entrenching key features and allowing some flexibility for adaptation to new circumstances. However, certain essential protections, such as adequate budgetary provisions or minimum staffing levels, may well require constitutionalization. Article 118 of the Nepali Constitution, for example, makes "the amount required as remunerations and facilities payable to the chiefs and officials of the Constitutional

Bodies" as well as "the administrative expenses of ... the Constitutional Bodies" chargeable directly to the federal consolidated fund without any need for prior legislative approval. It bears reiterating, however, that constitutionalization is a double-edged sword: just as poorly designed or captured guarantors are often worse than no guarantors at all, constitutionally protected poor design is worse than poor design that is more readily changeable. As always in debates on constitutional entrenchment, the polity's starting point matters.

III THE PERSONNEL DIMENSION: AVOIDING CAPTURE

The personnel dimension of guarantor institutions relates to the appointment, transfer, appraisal, removal, terms and conditions of employment, and post-employment prospects of their personnel, primarily directed to ensuring that they are independent of potentially hostile actors that have an interest in capturing them. In most democratic contexts, guarantor institutions will typically require independence from the ruling party/coalition and from any constitutional institutions it dominates. This is because of the simple reason that guarantor institutions seek to effectuate fragile non-self-enforcing norms, which – in democracies – tend to be fragile mainly because the ruling party will often have reasons to be hostile to them. An electoral commission captured by the ruling party and used to aid and legitimize any illegitimate power grab would be transformed from democracy's guarantor to its worst enemy. That said, the ruling party is not the only actor that can threaten the independence of a guarantor institution. Judicial councils tasked with ensuring judicial accountability and independence have unsurprisingly been shown to function less well, or even to be counter-productive, when constituted solely or largely by judges themselves (Bobek and Kosař 2014). Sometimes, a guarantor institution faces threat of capture from non-partisan actors other than politicians: a guarantor of truth and balance in news media reporting, for example, can be at risk of capture by profit-driven corporate media actors. The requirement of contributory expertise can also lead to appointment of industry insiders that can result in regulatory capture. In such cases, independence from these other (non-state) hostile actors should be part of guarantor institution design if the guarantor is to be effective in ensuring the guarantee it is meant to provide. In this section, we will consider two key modes that constitutions use to avoid capture: (i) by imposing *ex ante* and *ex post* disqualifications on groups of persons likely to have conflicts of interests, and (ii) by tweaking the partisan balance in committees that decide on appointments, removals, and transfers of members of guarantor institutions. Notably, these are only two of several tools used in practice.

Ex Ante and Ex Post Disqualifications

One key approach to mitigating the risk of partisan capture of guarantors is a bar on *ex ante* or *ex post* memberships or affiliations with organizations that could create a conflict of interest in guarantor institution personnel. Typically, this pertains to membership of political parties before and/or after belonging to a guarantor institution. Constitutions may also extend the ban to posts or offices that are acquired by running in partisan elections, or those contained within another uni-partisan body (like the political executive).

It is, for example, relatively common for partisan affiliations or the holding of a political office to be a disqualification for electoral commissioners, with this being the case in South Africa (Electoral Commission Act 1996, ss 9(2)(a)-(c), (f)) and the United Kingdom (House of Commons Disqualification Act 1975, sch 1(1)). Indeed, in the U.K., members of parliament (MPs) are barred from appointments to a number of institutions and offices that may possess guarantor status, including the Electoral Commission, the Equality and Human Rights Commissions, the National Audit Office, the Office of Communications, the Office for Budget Responsibility, the Auditor General, and the National Statistician (House of Commons Disqualification Act 1975, sch 1(1). See also, Article 240(6)(b) of the Nepali Constitution; Charter of the German Institute for Human Rights, para 10(a)).

The flipside of such *ex ante* disqualifications is that they reduce the pool of available talent, and designers will need to strike a balance – especially in smaller countries – between ensuring sufficient talent in the pool of candidates and reducing internal conflicts of interest. In some contexts, *ex ante* bans can remove from the talent pool the very skills and expertise that the job requires. One way of balancing these interests might be to impose a time-limited disqualification: for example, members of the Arizona Independent Redistricting Commission in the United States must not have held public office for three years preceding their appointment (Article IV(2)(1)(3) of the Constitution of Arizona). An example of time-limited *ex post* disqualification is the two-year bar that is imposed on the British Comptroller and Auditor General who after the end of her employment, cannot hold an appointed office by or on behalf of the Crown or provide any services to the Crown (Budget Responsibility and National Audit Act 2011, s 15(4)-(5)). It is worth noting that *ex post* disqualifications are likely to be effective only in contexts in which there is an effective term limit for the personnel of guarantor institutions. Non-renewable term limits also enable frequent changes in personnel, accruing the added benefit of reducing the risk of capture as well as the cost of capture to the institution if capture does occur, although at the cost of reducing the available talent pool.

An entirely different approach is adopted in contexts where design seeks to ensure the partisan neutrality of *the institution as a whole* by ensuring that affiliates of rival parties balance each other out as personnel of the institution (Tushnet 2019, p. 23; Tushnet 2021, p. 86). For example, under section 56 of the Constitution of Dominica, its Constituency Boundary Commission and its Electoral Commission have two members nominated by the Prime Minister and the Leader of the Opposition respectively, giving both institutions an overall balanced partisan character. Typically, this formula is used in politics where there are only two main political parties of approximately equal political strength. However, the possibility that these two parties will share an interest in perpetuating their duopoly through institutional means is a strong one (Issacharoff & Pildes 1998, p. 644), reducing the chances that this model can provide a credible and enduring guarantee to (extant or future) smaller opposition parties.

Partisan capture is far from the only risk that guarantor institutions face. Narrow private interests can also capture state institutions. That said, the risk of private capture of a guarantor is usually lower than that of ordinary regulators for institutions that either regulate other public institutions (anti-corruption agencies, for example, typically only regulate corruption in high state offices), or a wide variety of public and private actors rather than a single private industry (equality bodies, for example, regulate public institutions as well as private retailers, landlords, service providers, and so on). On the other hand, single-industry regulators – such as media regulators – are at a relatively high risk of private capture.

A potential risk of capture arising from private actors may be mitigated to a certain extent by imposing disqualifications for conflicted actors similar to partisan affiliations or memberships. For example, members of the American Citizens' Commission on Public Service and Compensation are not allowed to be registered lobbyists (2 U.S.C. 11 § 352(2) (2006)). Similarly, the Governor of the South African Reserve Bank cannot be affiliated in any capacity with financial institutions such as a banking institution, mutual building society, or building society (South African Reserve Bank Act 94 1990, s 4(4)). Insofar as industry insiders are frequently the people likely to have the necessary expertise to qualify as guarantors, the expertise requirement can sometimes increase the risk of industry capture – so, qualifications (and related expertise) requirements and disqualifications may have to be finely balanced, with stringent disclosure of conflicts rules (and other transparency requirements) on all applicants and appointees. Furthermore, just as a voice for opposition parties can guard against partisan capture – a role for civil society actors that have a proven record of seeking accountability from the industry in question can play the role in the personnel dimension to mitigate private capture risks. Similarly, the participation of the leaders of other guarantor institutions in appointment and removal bodies may ensure that personnel are properly vetted from the point of view of several constitutional norms.

Personnel Panels

Apart from disqualifications, constitutions also attempt to secure the independence of guarantors by carefully allocating the power to make personnel decisions (e.g., appointment, transfer, removal, post-retirement appointments/perks, conditions of service). In particular, they need to ensure that the personnel panel: (i) is likely to make decisions that enhance rather than decrease the expertise and independence of the guarantor and is itself unlikely to be captured, and (ii) can make time-bound decisions without the risk of irresolvable deadlocks. The South African Constitutional Court expressed these twin objectives (in a somewhat different, although still relevant, context):

'It would be inimical to the vital purpose of [the relevant constitutional provision] to accept that a motion …. may never [pass] except with the generosity and concurrence of the majority in that Committee. It is equally unacceptable that a minority within the Committee may render the motion stillborn when consensus is the decision-making norm' (*Mazibuko v Sisulu* 2013 (6) SA 249 (CC) 57).

Like so many design imperatives considered in this discussion, these two can pull in opposite directions. A panel in which the government and the opposition parties are required to reach a consensus in order to make appointments to guarantors is most likely to guarantee its independence from partisanship; this exact same process is also the most likely to lead to a deadlock, which – if it stalls key appointments – can effectively destroy the capacity of the guarantor to act. This is exactly what happened in Guyana, where provisions requiring cross-partisan consensus for the selection of the Chancellor and the Chief Justice resulted in a partisan deadlock and the posts remaining substantively unfilled for years (Campbell 2022).

It is still possible to optimize both objectives. At least in some recent democratic constitutions, the structure of these personnel panels is itself constitutionally entrenched. Assuming that the original design of the personnel panel enabled a good balance between these competing objectives, constitutional entrenchment makes it harder for the ruling party to sequentially capture the panel itself, and then – through it – other guarantors. On the other hand, if the original design is flawed, rigid forms of entrenchment can make it exceedingly difficult to improve upon the design flaws.

Let us begin with a closer look at the first objective. The first choice that constitutions face in relation to personnel panels is whether to create bespoke panels for each guarantor institution, or a single panel for all guarantors. Many older constitutions still vest appointment powers in the executive or the legislature (and, therefore, effectively with the party controlling at least one and potentially both political branches of the state, depending on the system of government – either way, cross-partisan consensus is not always necessary). Some of them, however, have created bespoke cross-partisan panels at least for some guarantors, usually through statutory means. Newer constitutions, on the other hand, frequently create single, high-level personnel panels to decide on all personnel-related matters for guarantor institutions (and frequently also for higher courts). This second option raises concerns regarding the form of cross-partisan makeup of the panel: should it be balanced between the government and the largest opposition party, or should it ensure a voice for minority parties? Finally, constitution-makers need to decide whether non-partisan members from the judiciary, other guarantor institutions, and civil society should be represented on the panel or otherwise included in the panel's decision-making process. The following examples illustrate a diverse number of ways in which different constitutions have sought to combine these possibilities.

1 Bespoke or General Personnel Panels

Jurisdictions like India and the United Kingdom have created bespoke personnel panels for some guarantor-type institutions. On the other hand, the Constitutional Council in the Nepali Constitution of 2015 is an example of a general personnel panel with constitutional status under Article 284. It is a six-member constitutional body comprising the offices of the Prime Minister, the Speaker, and the Deputy Speaker of the House of Representatives, the Chairperson of the National Assembly, the Leader of the Opposition, and the Chief Justice. Sri Lanka and Seychelles have also experimented with a general personnel panel for all constitutional guarantors (and senior judges).

2 Partisan Character

Uni-Partisanship: On the second question of the partisan make-up of the personnel panel, many older constitutions (such as India's) still allow the ruling executive to unilaterally make appointments to guarantor bodies, making them vulnerable to capture by the ruling party/coalition (although the Indian Supreme Court recently ordered that Election Commissioners shall be appointed by a panel with balanced partisan representation: *Anoop Baranwal v Union of India* MANU/SC/0190/2023. Parliament briskly replaced the balanced multi-partisanship ordered by the Court in the case with token multi-partisanship). More recent arrangements tend to involve opposition parties in personnel decisions in some manner. This can range from mandating consultations with the opposition to various forms of multi-partisan panels. The First Civil Service Commissioner in the U.K. cannot be appointed without consultation with the leaders of the two largest opposition parties in the House of Commons (based on vote share) as well as the First Ministers of Scotland and Wales (Constitutional Reform and Governance Act 2010, sch 1, para 2). Members of the Electoral Commission of the U.K. are appointed upon agreement of the Speaker of the House of Commons, but subject to consultation with the registered leader of each registered party (Political Parties, Elections and Referendums Act 2000, s 1(4), s 3(1)-(2)). The Elections and Boundary Commission of Belize has a chairperson and two members recommended by the Prime Minister after consultation with the Leader of the Opposition and another two recommended by the Prime Minister with the concurrence of the Leader of Opposition (Constitution of Belize s 88(2)).

Token Multi-Partisanship: The weakest forms of multi-partisan panels are those that include some opposition party members, but give the ruling party or coalition a decisive majority. Personnel of the Indian Lokpal (anti-corruption watchdog) are, for instance, appointed by a selection committee which includes the Prime Minister, the Speaker of the House, and the Leader of the Opposition, as well as the Chief Justice of India (Lokpal and Lokayuktas Act 2013, s 4(1)). Because the Speaker and the Prime Minister will almost always belong to the ruling party in its parliamentary system, the ruling party or coalition has twice the number of representatives as the opposition.

Proportional Multi-Partisanship: A somewhat stronger form of multi-partisanship in personnel panels is *proportional* multi-partisanship, in which the panel is composed of partisan members in proportion to the strength of the various parties in the relevant legislature. A committee of the National Assembly, proportionally composed of members of all parties represented in it, for example, plays a key role in the appointment of the members of the South African Election Commission (The Electoral Commission Act 1996, s 6(2)(c)-(d); s 6(3)-(4)). In another context, however, the South African Constitutional Court rejected proportional multi-partisanship by holding that that the inquiry into impeachable allegations against a President conducted by a legislative committee in which "parties are entitled to be represented in substantially the same proportion as the proportion in which they are represented in the Assembly" was unconstitutional (*Economic Freedom Fighters v Speaker of the National Assembly* 2018 (3) BCLR 259 (CC) 191–196). The Court was evidently concerned that the proportional multi-partisan system gave too much control of the process to the ruling party – a problem no doubt exacerbated by South Africa's dominant party system.

Balanced Multi-Partisanship: All of the preceding models give a decisive say in personnel matters to the ruling party/coalition. Under balanced multi-partisanship, on the other hand, the ruling party/coalition and the opposition party/parties get an exactly equal say. For example, the Constitutional Appointments Authority under section 140 of the Constitution of Seychelles (1993) has a balanced partisan makeup (albeit from only the two largest political parties). This Authority appoints the leadership of key guarantor institutions, and it alone can trigger a judicial inquiry into grounds for removal of the Attorney-General, the Auditor-General, the Ombudsman, or the members of the Electoral Commission (section 165(3)). Article 203 of the Thai Constitution of 2017 and Article 54 of the Belize Constitution also provide for balanced personnel panels. This model may be attractive in two-party political systems, as long as the problem of deadlock can be avoided.

The possibility of deadlock is the obvious problem in balanced multi-partisan panels. If either side holds out, it could result in no decision, thereby leaving key constitutional posts vacant. The Seychelles Constitution, therefore, has anti-deadlock provisions to incentivize time-bound appointments by automatically allocating the power of appointment to other constitutional actors if the relevant partisan players fail to act within a specified period.

Weighted Multi-Partisanship: In multi-party systems, balanced multi-partisanship may be unfair to parties other than the two largest parties. Given that some of these parties can nonetheless represent a sizeable proportion of the population, their exclusion from personnel panels can also be undemocratic and can facilitate a duopoly of the two largest parties. In such contexts, weighted multi-partisanship may be fairer than balanced multi-partisanship: weighted multi-partisanship overrepresents smaller/minority/opposition parties and underrepresents larger/majority/ruling parties in a manner that would ordinarily require a significant measure of cross-party support for decisions (Khaitan 2021a, p. 127). The concept resonates with Abebe's notion of "inclusive majoritarianism," which "rather than relying on the size of the legislative majority as a proxy to engender broad political consensus ... would pursue broad consensus more directly by ensuring that amendments have support beyond the ruling party or coalition" (Abebe 2020, p. 28). The idea behind weighted multi-partisanship is not just to give equal say to the government and opposition parties, but to also require partisan members on personnel panels to represent a relatively large portion of the electorate (rather than simply a majority thereof).

Article 256(6) of the Thai Constitution (2017) applies weighted multi-partisanship by requiring that certain constitutional decisions be approved by at least 20% of opposition party members, in addition to an overall legislative majority requirement. The idea can be adopted in relation to the partisan composition of personnel panels as well: for example, panels could include an equal number of members from each of the n largest political parties who together represent a specified super-majority of voters (depending on the context, this could range from 60% to 80%), subject to a minimum number of parties that must be included (again, depending on the context, this could be between three and seven or so of the largest parties).

Weighted multi-partisan panels are less susceptible to deadlocks compared to balanced multi-partisan panels, simply because several parties need to coordinate to exercise an effective veto. The likelihood of deadlocks can be reduced further by adopting decision-making rules that are unlikely to result in ties, such as single transferable vote (also known as ranked-choice voting), which can also ensure candidate moderation as a bonus by incentivizing the nomination of candidates who would appeal to multiple parties.

3 Non-Partisan Members

The final issue to be decided with respect to personnel panels is whether to include non-partisan members, and if so, which ones. Typically, non-partisan members tend to be judges and leaders of other guarantor bodies; in some contexts, civil society members are also included. In the Thai Constitution of 2017, members of the "Independent Organs" are selected by a committee that includes representatives of the judiciary and other guarantor institutions, alongside balanced multi-partisanship (Article 217). Those eligible for nominations to the Taiwanese Control Yuan (a personnel panel of sorts, mainly tasked with accountability-seeking functions) includes not only legislators, judges, and bureaucrats, but also professors, journalists, actors in cultural fields, and human rights activists.

Occasionally, the partisan and non-partisan parts of the panel are split into different stages in the process: members of the South African Election Commission, for example, are pre-selected by a panel composed of the President of the Constitutional

Court, a representative of the Human Rights Committee, and a representative of the Commission on Gender Equality and the Public Protector, who in turn propose them to a proportional multi-partisan panel of the National Assembly. One key risk of including civil society members is the special risk of the capture they entail, so the manner in which they are selected should itself be rigorously attuned to this risk.

Removal

Removal of leaders of guarantor institutions, who tend to have secured fixed terms, typically requires an established cause and a difficult, impeachment-type political or judicial process. A paradigmatic example is South Africa, where guarantor institutions such as the Electoral Commission, Auditor-General, Public Protector, and so on can only be removed by the President after a finding of misconduct, incapacity, or incompetence by a multi-partisan committee of the National Assembly and the subsequent adoption of a resolution by the Assembly to that end by a two-third majority (The Constitution of the Republic of South Africa, s 194(1)-(3)). By contrast, members of the U.K. Equality Commission can be dismissed by a minister, albeit for good cause, which allows the judiciary to police the propriety of the dismissal (see Equality Act 2010, sch 1, para 3(5)). The precise combination of removal mechanisms that is ideal will, needless to say, depend on contextual factors such as the robustness of political party competition and judicial enforcement of the rule of law.

Independence of Subordinate Staff

The discussion in this section has focused exclusively on the independence of the leadership of guarantor institutions. But these institutions also need subordinate officials in order to function properly. Constitutional framers may be wise to also pay attention to the independence of the bureaucratic staff of these guarantors. The Thai Constitution of 2017, for example, seeks to ensure the independence of the administrative staff of guarantor institutions by making them accountable directly to the institution concerned (rather than the political executive) (Article 220).

IV THE OPERATIONAL DIMENSION: AVOIDING MALADMINISTRATION

In the operational dimension, we need to take a closer look at the actions, omissions, procedures, and decisions of the guarantor institution. An expert, adequately resourced, independent guarantor still poses the risk of maladministration. Maladministration is a broad concept that includes unlawful acts, but also extends to bias, tardiness, mismanagement, overzealousness, under-regulation, overreach, selective regulation, inefficiency, and a range of related organizational shortcomings. Indeed, failures in any of the first two (structural or personnel) dimensions are also likely to result in maladministration. Maladministration of a constitutional norm is as risky as the norm in question is important for the given constitutional system. Assuming that constitutions are likely to go through the trouble of creating guarantor institutions primarily for relatively fundamental constitutional norms, maladministration of such norms is likely to be a serious risk.

Power without accountability is usually dangerous: in the context of one particular guarantor – anti-corruption agencies – this danger is particularly pronounced. Unconstrained investigatory powers can invite overzealousness, make the ACA a particular target for capture, or create a public perception that an unaccountable ACA is a threat beyond the scope of the corruption it aims to root out (see Heilbrunn 2004, p. 1). In many democracies, majority parties and special interests have weaponized anti-corruption drives to target opposition parties, making the accountability of ACAs an especially crucial design objective. Because ACAs are "deeply implicated in national politics," it is imperative for the ACAs to preserve their legitimacy by avoiding over-policing more marginal cases of corruption and focusing on core cases based on "sensitivity to the degree to which corruption impairs democracy" in a given context (Tushnet 2019, p. 454). Institutional design of ACAs thus "requires striking a balance between independence and accountability" with sensitivity to "the complicated interactions between" both necessary features (Tushnet 2019, pp. 447, 454). The point applies to other guarantors, too, with more or less urgency. In general, guarantor institutions need to be accountable in order to guard against maladministration.

Ensuring accountability of guarantors for acting illegally is relatively straightforward: judicial review is a common mechanism courts use to check the unlawful acts of other state actors. Subject to deference norms, there is little reason why guarantor institutions should be exempt. Furthermore, guarantor institutions may also be subject to the oversight of other guarantor institutions: for example, an anti-corruption agency may be empowered to investigate corruption allegations against electoral commissioners. However, there are limits to the ability of courts and other guarantors to hold guarantor institutions accountable legally (Bhat 2021), and so effectively guarding against maladministration also requires additional mechanisms for holding them accountable politically.

Political accountability of guarantor institutions for maladministration (especially when it falls short of illegality) is complex. To the extent that guarantors require some measure of political accountability, constitutions primarily make them answerable to elected politicians and to other guarantors. The trick is to facilitate that accountability, while ensuring the independence of guarantors from the ruling party/coalition. While light-touch reporting duties may be owed to the (uni-partisan) executive (see e.g., Article 294 of the Nepali Constitution), more exacting accountability powers are typically vested in the multi-partisan legislature or legislative committees (see, for example s 181 of the South African Constitution and Article 293 of the Nepali Constitution). As far as accountability to politicians goes, all the aforementioned design possibilities explored in relation to personnel panels remain available to accountability-seeking committees as well: their multi-partisanship can be token, proportional, balanced, or weighted. There may even be good reasons for the personnel panels, whether bespoke or general, to also double up as institutions that seek political accountability from guarantors.

Accountability to other guarantor institutions may also be desirable. Article 184 of the Constitution of Ghana (1992) makes its central bank accountable to the Auditor General, who then reports to Parliament. Normatively, Ghanaian-style accountability of guarantor institutions to politicians via other guarantors may well be a promising, and still under-explored, design possibility. Finally, some systems have explored accountability to civil society groups (Quah 2011, pp. 461–462; Heilbrunn 2004, p. 15).

Crafting political accountability mechanisms which are effective, without being overbearing, is an especially context-specific endeavor. The most that can be said at a general level is that they are an important safeguard for designing well-functioning guarantors, and the need for guarantor independence must be tempered with the need for guarantor accountability.

CONCLUSION

The three – relatively thin and *pro tanto* – design principles that I have argued for in this chapter demand that the design of any guarantor institutions should seek to ensure that it has:

  i. Sufficient expertise and capacity to perform its functions effectively;
 ii. Sufficient independence from political, economic, or social actors with an interest in frustrating the relevant norm it is meant to guarantee; and
iii. Sufficient accountability to bodies with an interest in upholding the relevant norm.

These principles are developed from real world examples of guarantor institutions (or institutions that have the potential to act as guarantors), although it is quite possible that no single extant guarantor satisfies all of them. These principles are conditionally normative: if a constitution wishes to effectively guarantee a specific non-self-enforcing norm, it should take these principles seriously when designing an institution to guarantee the relevant norm. They also suggest that political independence and political accountability of guarantor institutions need not trade off against each other: the group they need independence from overlaps with, but is not the same as, the group who they should owe accountability to. In a future work, I hope to explain *when* such guarantor institutions might together constitute a distinct – fourth – *branch* of the state.

RECOMMENDED READING

Ackerman, B. (2000). The New Separation of Powers. *Harvard Law Review*, 113 (3), 633–729.

Bhat, M. A. (2023). Between Trust and Democracy: The Election Commission of India and the Question of Constitutional Accountability. In S. Jhaveri, T. Khaitan and D. Samararatne, eds, *Constitutional Resilience Beyond Courts: Views from South Asia*. London: Bloomsbury Publishing.

Brown, A. J. (2014). The Integrity Branch: A 'System', An 'Industry', Or a Sensible Emerging Fourth Arm of Government? In M. Groves, ed., *Modern Administrative Law in Australia: Concepts and Context*. Cambridge, UK: Cambridge University Press, pp. 301–325.

Elliot, B. (2019). Independent Regulatory and Oversight (Fourth Branch) Institutions. *IDEA*. Available at: www.idea.int/publications/catalogue/independent-regulatory-and-oversight-fourth-branch-institutions (Accessed: 4 January 2022).

Federal Data Protection Act (2017). (Germany).

Fombad, C. M. (2018). The Diffusion of South African-Style Institutions? A Study in Comparative Constitutionalism. In R. Dixon and T. Roux, eds, *Constitutional Triumphs, Constitutional Disappointments*. Cambridge: Cambridge University Press, pp. 359–387.

Khaitan, T. (2021). Guarantor Institutions. *Asian Journal of Comparative Law*, 16 (S1), S40–S59.

Klug, H. (2019). Transformative Constitutions and the Role of Integrity Institutions in Tempering Power: The Case of Resistance to State Capture in Post-Apartheid South Africa. *Buffalo Law Review*, 67 (3), 701–742.

Lokpal and Lokayuktas Act (2013) (India).

Pal, M. (2023). The South Asian Fourth Branch. In S. Jhaveri, T. Khaitan and D. Samararatne, eds, *Constitutional Resilience Beyond Courts: Views from South Asia*. London: Bloomsbury Publishing.

Right to Information Act (2005). (India).

Samararatne, D. (2023). Sri Lanka's Guarantor Branch. In S. Jhaveri, T. Khaitan and D. Samararatne, eds, *Constitutional Resilience Beyond Courts: Views from South Asia*. London: Bloomsbury Publishing.

The Electoral Commission Act (1996) (South Africa).

Tushnet, M. (2021). *The New Fourth Branch: Institutions for Protecting Constitutional Democracy*, Cambridge: Cambridge University Press.

36

Central Banks

Jens van 't Klooster

Although their constitutional independence has varied historically, today most central banks are placed at arm's length from elected governments. Their independence, moreover, is often part of the written constitution, with at least 78 national constitutions referencing the status of their central bank (Constitute Project 2020). Under central bank independence, the power to issue public money is delegated to a committee of unelected officials within the central bank, often appointed on recommendation of the central bank. Positions come with long, fixed terms. Once appointed, only serious acts of misconduct can be the cause for dismissal. Central banks make their decisions in isolation from politicians. Their mandates, however, tend to provide central bankers with only the most generic guidance on what to do. What should legal and political theorists make of the institutional structures of central bank independence?

The most widely used democratic argument to justify central bank independence treats it as a case of bureaucratic delegation like any other. A prominent recent exponent of this view is former central banker Paul Tucker in his *Unelected Power* (2018). For him, delegation involves assigning to unelected officials a set of clearly defined instruments, which they are meant to use in pursuing clearly defined goals. Although accounts that treat central bank independence as a case of bureaucratic delegation usually do not deny that central bankers make some choices, major distributional choices are meant to be made in the act of delegation, rather than by the central bank itself. Setting monetary policy is treated as a technical issue, which concerns how to achieve goals in the most effective way, rather than setting those goals themselves. This approach thereby side-steps the many interesting questions that emerge once we acknowledge that central bankers do make important political choices.

This chapter provides an overview of the state of the art in constitutional theory with regard to the topic of central banks. It challenges accounts of central banking as involving limited discretion and distributional choices, as well as the narrow range of normative questions that such accounts raise. The chapter also provides a roadmap for a vast range of procedural and substantive issues raised by independent central banks, thereby highlighting just how much of the terrain remains unexplored.

The first part of the chapter studies the unique role of central banks within the broader "monetary constitution". Existing monetary constitutions involve both public and private money creation. Central banks do not usually provide credit to the real economy directly, which is typically the prerogative of private financial institutions. Central banks' most important tasks are to steer, regulate and supervise the issuance of private money. The structure of this monetary constitution is usually not written down in written constitutions narrowly understood. Rather, it receives effect from a range of legal texts, which include legislative instruments concerning banking, sovereign debt contracts and the central bank mandate.

The second part of the chapter turns to the politics of monetary policy and the way in which central bankers interpret their mandates. It is in this context that central bankers themselves routinely present their activities as an instance of bureaucratic delegation. For one, central bankers justify choices they make by suggesting that they are decided by their legal mandate. Central bankers also play down the far-reaching consequences of their choices and the policies that central bankers make are not meant to involve distributional choices. Where monetary policy impacts the economy, it is thought to be *neutral* in various senses of the term. I discuss these wide-spread ideas to show that central bankers make important choices and that monetary policy has a material impact on society that is anything but neutral.

The final part of the chapter turns to the question of what to make of central bank independence from a normative perspective. As I argue, some delegation of important decisions to unelected officials is almost unavoidable, often desirable and by itself not undemocratic. I then explain why we should nonetheless be reluctant to allow for extensive central bank discretion by highlighting six crucial issues that are currently not sufficiently understood: Their actual level of autonomy from governments, the effectiveness of accountability mechanisms, the effects of depoliticizing money on the broader political system, the effects of democratic insulation on the effectiveness of central banks, the specific practices of deliberation within central banks, and the scope for coordination with elected government.

I THE CENTRAL BANK AND THE MONETARY CONSTITUTION

The way in which the private and the public are interrelated in different historical capitalist societies has some strikingly invariant features (Braudel 1982; Ingham 2004; Arnon 2010; Desan 2014). Recently, this structure has been characterized as a hybrid public-private franchise system (Hockett & Omarova 2017) and as a money-credit constitution (Tucker 2018). I describe it as a monetary constitution, which is a hybrid of both public and private authority over money. I identify three key normative principles that characterize today's market liberal constitutions.

The Monetary Constitution

A helpful way of expressing the idea of a monetary constitution is as the total laws and constitutional conventions that govern: (i) how authority over the provision of money is distributed; (ii) which actions are permissible and which are compulsory for those who hold monetary authority; and (iii) how different actors are to exercise their authority (van 't Klooster 2018). This conception of the monetary constitution is wider than currently common uses of the term, where it refers to the central bank's mandate (Yeager 1962; Brennan & Buchanan 1980) or simply the conditions under which the central bank can issue public money. Milton Friedman, for example, talks of the need for "a monetary constitution, which takes the form of rules establishing and limiting the central bank as to the powers that it is given, its reserve requirements, and so on" (Friedman 1962, p. 255). This narrow conception ignores how a monetary constitution can also create a private sphere in which the state does not interfere with the issuance of money. Not all conceivable monetary constitutions involve both forms of authority. The authority over money could be entirely under public control. Socialist economies are examples but there are also proposals to prohibit private money creation within a broadly market-based economy (Jackson & Dyson, 2012; Kumhof & Benes, 2012; B. Weber 2018). Alternatively, as proposed by libertarian free bankers and some recent proponents of cryptocurrencies, the authority over money could be left entirely in private hands (Selgin 1988; Nakamoto 2008).

Existing monetary constitutions give effect to a hybrid system, which involves both public and private money creation (B. J. Moore 1988; Graziani 2003). Central banks issue cash and central bank deposits. A central bank deposit (also called reserve) is a balance on a central bank account, which is typically owned by a financial institution to settle large volume payments. Central banks issue money by either lending to commercial banks or by buying high-quality financial assets. These transactions, however, take place within financial markets far removed from most citizens. The central bank does not, save in exceptional circumstances, provide credit to the real economy. Citizens and non-financial firms currently do not receive cash directly from the central bank nor do they have central bank accounts (Barontini & Holden 2019). Instead, the volume of money circulating in the real economy is largely determined by banks, which issue new deposits through the act of granting loans to citizens and non-financial firms. Non-bank financial institutions (including hedge funds, insurance companies, and pension funds), meanwhile, engage in so-called shadow banking, where they seek to issue financial instruments with money-like characteristics, while simultaneously avoiding the strict regulatory framework applied to banks (Mehrling, 2010; Gabor & Vestergaard 2016; Murau 2017).

The Central Bank

Monetary constitutions are not written down in a document, nor are the key features of how authority over money is allocated a part of written constitutions narrowly understood. The key legal features that characterize today's market liberal monetary constitutions can be summarized in terms of three normative principles.

The first principle is that public money should be issued by a central bank rather than by the government. This serves to ensure that fiscal authorities do not pay for expenditures by issuing new money (A. Turner 2015; Ryan-Collins 2017). Instead, governments need to finance any expenditures in excess of tax revenues by issuing debt to the private sector, leaving the issuance of public money solely for the purposes of executing monetary policy decisions of the central bank. The creation of central banks is historically often motivated by the desire to place money creation at armlength from the Treasury. In some historical cases, such as the pre-twentieth century Bank of England, the issuer of public money is explicitly prohibited from lending to governments without parliamentary approval for each discreet line of credit (Bateman 2020). Some central bank laws explicitly prohibit operations whereby the central bank issues money to enable an expansion of government expenditure (so-called monetary financing). Even in the absence of an explicit rule, however, all hybrid monetary constitutions make a clear distinction between the monetary and the fiscal activities of the state.

Beyond being banned from paying for government expenditures, central banks are also expected to refrain from providing funds directly to individual citizens and non-financial firms. This is a second market liberal principle that informs the design of central bank mandates, which usually contain provisions that spell out eligible counterparties for central banks and the types of assets that they can trade in. Despite considerable historical variation (Braun & Downey 2020), central banks today tend to focus their activities on lending to banks and trading in government bonds, valuable metals, and other safe assets. Lending directly to citizens and firms, in contrast, is not usually an explicit part of the central bank toolbox. The past decade has made clear that existing central bank mandates provide legal options for central banks to influence the real economy, but central bankers remain very reluctant to do so (Johnson, Arel-Bundock, & Portniaguine 2019). By limiting central bank operation to the purchase of safe assets and lending to banks, the legislature codifies the hybridity of the monetary system. Where central banks are not actually constrained in their choice of instruments, the choice for a narrow toolbox can be understood as a constitutional convention. Lending to citizens and non-financial firms is often not strictly prohibited, but it is frowned upon and subject to moral condemnation.

The third market liberal principle that underpins hybrid monetary constitutions is that institutions that create widely used money forms are subject to a strict public regulatory framework (Admati & Hellwig 2014; Ricks 2016). Banks, in virtue of their ability to create money through lending, tend to be amongst the most tightly regulated private firms. At the same time, however, allowing for competition between banks is meant to incentivize an efficient allocation of credit. Competition is to incentivize them to offer high quality, or at least similar quality, products. Competition is also meant to cause profit rates for banks to gravitate around the general rate of profit in the economy. If a product or sector is particularly profitable, new competitors are meant to move into the market. The regulatory framework seeks to ensure that the owners that stand to benefit from profits also face any losses that result from the operations of the bank. Again, this objective is not typically an article in the written constitution, but rather part of the broader normative ideas which guide legislatures, central banks, and other public actors.

In giving effect to this third principle, central banks hold two key roles. First, many (but not all) central banks regulate and supervise financial institutions. The Financial Crisis of 2007 and 2008 has illustrated that financial institutions continually contest the actual legal and political constraints on private money creation (Pistor 2013; Murau 2017). Banks have an incentive to go to the limits of the regulatory framework, and sometimes beyond, which leads them to invent new financial products and other ways of skirting existing regulation. Central banks are often not only tasked with applying banking law but also devise the very regulatory standards that they apply. In the context of the Basel Committee for Banking Supervision central bankers set the main outlines of banking law (Brummer 2015). The second role that central banks have in relation to the private segment of the monetary system is that of designing and implementing monetary policy. Through monetary policy central banks seek to steer how much money banks create, which allows them to indirectly influence price levels. Monetary policy operations also serve financial market objectives such as that of serving as the lender of last resort of the banking system. Lending to banks is an important part of day-to-day central bank operations, which acquires existential importance to banks when customers withdraw deposits and money market funding runs out (BIS 2014). Today central bankers also hold various roles as market makers of last resort to stabilize asset prices and provide non-bank financial institutions with funding (Mehrling 2010).

II THE POLITICS OF MONETARY POLICY

The most interesting constitutional questions concerning central banks arise from their large discretion in exercising political power. To study the nature of the discretion available to central banks, I now turn to monetary policy, which is at the core of democratic justifications of central bank independence. I show that even within the confines of the hybrid monetary constitution, central bankers have considerable discretion, which routinely confronts them with important distributional choices.

Choices

To analyze the actual discretion available to independent central banks, I distinguish four interpretive steps that move from the central bank mandate to actual monetary policy operations (see Figure 36.1). In all four steps central bankers make important choices.

	Content	Constitutional authority
Mandate	General provision on goals and instrument	Legislature
Objectives	Empirical and quantitative operationalization of objectives and ordering their priority	Central bank and sometimes modest role for the executive
Monetary policy strategy	Operational targets and instruments	Multi-annual review within the central bank
Monetary policy setting	Setting the target value of the operational target	Central bank board or committee
Monetary policy Implementation	Trading to influence the operational target	Central bank board and market division within the central bank

FIGURE 36.1 Four steps in the interpretation of a central bank mandate

The first step in the interpretation of the mandate is to determine the objectives of monetary policy (Lastra 2015; Dikau & Volz 2021). The decision on the objectives operationalizes the aims of the central bank so that they can be measured empirically and quantitatively. This may involve various aims such as one or more specific inflation metrics, a growth number, unemployment statistic and/or exchange rate. Where a central bank has multiple targets of equal weight, it needs to decide how to settle conflicts. The objectives tend to be only spelled out in the mandate in general terms. The most austere mandates simply state that the central banks should pursue price stability without further qualification. The Bank of Japan Act, for example, states that monetary policy should be "aimed at achieving price stability, thereby contributing to the sound development of the national economy", with the qualification that "the basic stance of the government's economic policy shall be mutually compatible" (Bank of Japan Act of June 18, 1997, Article 2 and 5). Other central banks have an explicit mandate to support the economic policies of governments. Both the price stability objective and other objectives outlined in the mandate tend to be generic and only derive their meaning from interpretation. This vagueness is compounded when the mandate contains multiple aims. For example, the Federal Reserve is to "promote effectively the goals of maximum employment, stable prices, and moderate long-term interest rates" (US Federal Reserve Act, Section 2A), but the statute provides no guidance on how to deal with conflicts between these various objectives. The Federal Reserve has set its own target as that of "inflation at the rate of 2 percent, as measured by the annual change in the price index for personal consumption expenditures", whereas maximum employment is understood as a long-term equilibrium that changes over time and is debated at individual meetings (FOMC 2020). Although most central banks set their ultimate target themselves, some decide it together with the executive. The Reserve Bank of New Zealand makes this decision on the basis of a bilateral agreement with the government. Amongst the world's major central banks, the Bank of England alone receives an operationalization of its target from the Treasury.

The second step in the interpretation of the mandate is to determine a monetary policy strategy, which allows the central bank to achieve its objectives (Bindseil 2014). Monetary policy is geared towards influencing macroeconomic variables that are not under the direct control of the central bank. To pursue these objectives, the central bank needs to choose operational targets, which are targets that the central bank can directly control. Since the central bank's objectives tend to be in the real economy, the most direct operational targets have historically been the volume and sectoral distribution of private credit (Bezemer, Ryan-Collins, van Lerven, & Zhang 2018; Monnet 2018). The pre-2008 era saw broad convergence on short-term interest rates as the operational target of monetary policy, but since then central banks have broadened their interventions to influence long-term interest rates directly. Although exchange rate stability is often no longer a goal of the monetary policy, it remains an important consideration for achieving domestic price stability (Moschella 2015). Because monetary policy operations also have a crucial role in providing banks with short-term funding, the central bank must design its operational framework to look after these counterparties.

There is considerable variation in the extent to which central bank mandates address operational targets and instrument. Before the introduction of the Euro, the mandate of the German Bundesbank spelled out in meticulous detail what assets it was allowed to trade in. Today, the Federal Reserve is still only allowed to provide credit to individual and non-financial firms "in unusual and exigent circumstances" (Federal Reserve Act, article 13(3)). Other central banks, however, have a much more general power to trade in financial assets. The ECB, for example, is to pursue its objectives by "buying and selling outright (spot and forward) or under repurchase agreement and by lending or borrowing claims and marketable instruments, whether in euro or other currencies", as by trading in precious metals (ECB and ESCB status, Article 18). The mandate also permits the ECB to "conduct credit operations with credit institutions and other market participants, with lending being based on adequate collateral". But, crucially, what adequate means is not further specified. The ECB Governing Council can, by a two-third majority, decide on any "operational methods of monetary control as it sees fit" (ECB and ESCB status, Article 20). Periodic reviews of the monetary policy framework, such as those completed in 2020 by the Federal Reserve and in 2021 by the ECB, typically take place without a say for elected governments (ECB 2021; FOMC 2020).

The third step in the interpretation of the mandate is the actual setting of monetary policy (Bernanke, Laubach, Mishkin, & Posen 2001). This occurs in regular committee meetings. In setting monetary policy, the monetary policy committee chooses values for the operational targets with which to achieve its objectives. In setting monetary policy, central bankers tend to take its goals and the strategy as given and deliberate about the best way to act on it. This step is often emphasized in debates over central bank independence and it is here that the account of bureaucratic delegation fits best. Even at this stage, however, choices need to be made that go beyond establishing empirical facts and acting on them. Because the central bank has only incomplete knowledge of the state of the economy and the expected consequences of its policy interventions, the strategy rarely provides an unambiguous answer to what level the operational targets should have. Central bankers also have to decide on how to communicate their decisions (Braun 2015).

The fourth step of interpretation is the implementation of monetary policy, which concerns the operations that central bankers use to steer the operational target (Bindseil 2006, 2014). Operations, in this context, are typically financial market transactions in which the central bank either trades in specific financial assets or engages in direct lending and borrowing transactions. The central bank sets rules for its open market operations and standing facilities, the reserve requirements imposed on counterparties and indeed the rules that govern which institutions are eligible as counterparties. In the day-to-day trading context, the market division decides which assets to buy and what to accept as collateral.

Non-neutrality

Even if it is admitted that central banks make choices, we might still wonder whether they are not ultimately of a technical nature, finding the means to achieve a well-defined end. It is in this sense that central bankers often describe their operations as neutral.

Drawing on the theorem of the long-run neutrality of money, central bankers claim that monetary policy does little more than guiding the economy to an optimal state (Friedman 1968; Bernanke et al. 2001; Issing 2008). However, it is uncontroversial that monetary policy can have a pervasive impact on the economy in the short term. The initial effects of lower rates and other forms of monetary stimulus are to reduce unemployment and boost economic output. According to the theorem of the long run neutrality of money, nonetheless, the economy has a long-term equilibrium determined by supply-side factors. Should the central bank try to push the economy to operate above its long-term equilibrium the benefits will be transient. Employment and output growth result in higher prices which undo the effects of the initial stimulus. Even worse, workers and firms come to expect inflation over time so that they anticipate and thereby undo the short-term stimulus. Maintaining the same level of stimulus requires ever more inflation. Thus, as Friedman famously concluded, "there is always a temporary trade-off between inflation and unemployment; there is no permanent trade-off" (Friedman 1968, p. 11). The lesson that central bankers draw from the theorem of the long run neutrality of money is that monetary policy should only be used to push the economy towards its long-term equilibrium, but not beyond it. Establishing how far the economy is removed from the equilibrium is treated as a technical, not a political challenge.

As we have seen, however, neither the way in which the central banks define their targets nor the ways of pursuing them are determined by the mandate. Although it has always been clear that central bankers often cannot predict the impact of their policies (Blanchard & Katz 1997; Galbraith 1997), recent work has turned to consider the political aspects of those choices. There is now more appreciation of the pervasive uncertainty that surrounds real-time monetary policy making (Abolafia 2010; Best 2016), the politics of economic forecasting (Mudge & Vauchez 2018), the measurement of decisive economic variables (Mügge 2016; Heimberger & Kapeller 2017), and the trade-offs between financial and monetary stability (Tymoigne 2009; Gabor & Ban 2016; Tucker 2018, chap. 20). Central bankers also dramatically disagree on the most basic questions concerning the causes of inflation (Tarullo 2017; Rudd 2021). In short, rather than steering the economy to its long-term equilibrium, central bankers make their own choices in how they pursue price stability.

The pursuit of price stability has its own distributive impact. Most attention in recent years has gone to quantitative easing (QE) operations, which are thought to have disproportionately benefited wealthy households. To present just one startling statistic, the poorest 10% of the UK households saw their wealth increase an estimated GBP 3,000, while the wealthiest 10% made average gains of GBP 350,000 as a result of QE operations by the Bank of England (Bunn, Pugh, and Yeates 2018). QE operations also have distributive effects by shaping private sector investment. Arguably, the wealth effect has received a disproportionate amount of attention. In fact, it is just one of the many ways in which monetary policy affects economic distributions. Central banks seek to steer the business cycle by either boosting the economy or allowing it to go into recession. How the central bank does this and when it allows the economy to go into recession also has long-term effects on employment, wage growth and virtually every other economic indicator that affects the lives of people (Ball 1993; Galbraith 1997; Epstein & Yeldan 2009; Blanchard, Cerutti, & Summers 2015; Coibion, Gorodnichenko, Kueng, & Silvia 2017; Sokol & Pataccini 2021; Van Doorslaer & Vermeiren 2021).

There is also a second sense in which central bankers portray monetary policy as neutral, which concerns the impact of their operations on financial markets (van 't Klooster & Fontan 2020). In designing operations, central banks also pursue the dual objectives of protecting themselves against losses and market neutrality. Market neutrality of operations requires that beyond shaping markets to achieve the central bank's policy objectives, monetary policy should not benefit specific market participants, sectors, or asset classes. To this end, central bankers use various techniques of diversification and benchmarking or focus on government bonds and other public issuer assets.

In practice, however, the choice of instruments and the design of operations do have their own distributive consequences (Bindseil & Papadia 2009; CGFS 2015; Peer 2019). Central bank operations impact the availability of assets in financial markets directly, in the way that any market participant affects prices. Purchases of a certain asset class make it scarcer, while sales add to supply. Likewise, collateral eligibility also affects the demand for collateral of central bank counterparties. The mere announcement of a QE programme has immediate impact on market prices (Abidi & Miquel-Flores 2018). Because central banks seek to follow the market, their operations can also reproduce market failures. The European Central Bank's reliance on private credit ratings in evaluating sovereign bonds contributed to the European debt crisis (Orphanides 2017). Recognizing that capital markets unduly benefit carbon intensive industries (Matikainen, Campiglio, & Zenghelis 2017), central banks are currently in the process of finding ways to move beyond market neutrality (BoE 2021; ECB 2021).

Rather than having narrow roles and simple objectives, their key role in the hybrid monetary constitution leads central bankers to juggle a wide range of responsibilities. Central bankers create financial markets, both as regulators and through their monetary policy operations. Their choices benefit the common good, but also specific socio-economic groups and financial market constituencies (Braun 2020; Prins 2018). Hence, we should ask why the same standards of democratic accountability that apply to other areas of economic policy should not also apply to the monetary domain. This is the question that I now turn to.

III THE ETHICS OF CENTRAL BANK INDEPENDENCE

In the past decade, central bankers have, willingly or reluctantly, accepted new roles and proposed creative interpretations of their mandate to confront new challenges (Best, 2016; Dietsch, Claveau, & Fontan 2018; Goodhart & Lastra 2018; de Boer & van 't Klooster 2020). Although the legal text of the mandate in most cases remained essentially unchanged, central banks have experimented with a range of new instruments. Central banks also came to face new challenges far beyond that of maintaining price stability. Their financial stability objectives have expanded dramatically, moving from micro-prudential tasks targeted on individual institutions to macroprudential roles in stabilizing the financial system as a whole (Baker 2013; Thiemann, 2019). Climate change, meanwhile, creates new challenges, which central bankers have added to their remit by focusing on the financial risk that it creates and the way in which financial institutions deal with these (Bolton, Depres, Pereira da Silva, Samama, & Svartzman 2020; Smoleńska & van 't Klooster 2022). Despite all these new roles, it remains largely to their discretion how, if at all, central banks contribute to their government's environmental and climate-related objectives.

What should we make of the immense discretion that central bankers currently hold from a normative perspective? I first ask whether there is a democratic objection against the very fact of assigning a high level of discretion to unelected officials, which I argue is not the case. Instead, answering the question what to make of the institutions of central bank independence requires much closer empirical and normative scrutiny.

Is There a Democratic Case against Technocratic Discretion?

Bureaucratic delegation is widely recognized to be permissible in a democratic society (Richardson 2002; Christiano 2012). The only difficult normative question it raises is how exactly to demarcate the sort of choices that unelected officials are allowed to make from impermissible distributional choices. Accordingly, the account of central bank independence as bureaucratic delegation suggests a strict criterion for which roles in the public regulatory framework should be left to elected officials and which not. Unelected officials should not be setting their own goals but rather merely try to find ways to achieve goals assigned to them in the most efficient way (Tucker 2018; cf. Skinner 2021).

From this perspective, there is a simple answer to the question when major political choices can permissibly be delegated to unelected officials, namely: never. That answer, however, only serves to obscures the prevalence of technocratic discretion in advanced capitalist societies today. Rather than denying that central bankers as a matter of fact make political choices, we should question the conditions under which they should be allowed to make them.

Even for constitutional theorists committed to a strong conception of popular sovereignty there are good arguments against a blanket prohibition of technocratic discretion (van 't Klooster 2019, 2020; Jackson 2022). The first thing to note about democratic objections to central bank independence is their selectivity. Consider again the hybridity of existing monetary constitutions, wherein banks issue new money in the act of granting loans. Deciding who has access to finance, and under what conditions, can have life changing consequences and, hence, raises its own issues of justice (Meyer 2018b, 2018a; Hockett & James 2020). Credit provision is subject to pervasive biases along class, gender and race fault lines (Ongena & Popov 2016; Baradaran 2017; Quinn 2019). Banks routinely ban individuals from opening a banking account for spurious moral reasons. Who gets financed also shapes the lives of individuals indirectly by determining broader economic developments shaping what industries blossom and which disappear. Today, as we already saw, carbon-intensive industries continue to benefit from generous access to capital markets. The same democratic worries brought to bear against technocrats might be put forward against bankers. So, what, if anything, makes the power exercised by central bankers particularly problematic?

The permissibility of central bank independence only becomes an issue once there is a domain of public authority over money in the first place. In a largely private monetary constitution, there is very little for the public to decide hence the question of permissibility does not arise. But, surely that does not make such monetary system more democratic. Rather, we might very well wonder whether there are not pressing democratic reasons in favour of a pure public monetary constitution, which does away with private money creation altogether (B. Weber 2018).

Of course, we should ask how much discretion unelected officials should have. This is particularly true when they are insulated from more traditional structures of democratic accountability. Nonetheless, recognizing just how much needs to be decided in any given monetary jurisdiction, minimizing the discretion that is available to unelected officials will unduly constrain effective monetary governance. There are at least three kinds of reasons for giving final authority over important issues in the regulation of the hybrid monetary constitution to unelected officials (van 't Klooster 2020, p. 591).

First, technocratic discretion is almost unavoidable. In theory, the legislature could seek to spell out the correct way of dealing with all important choices, but this would quickly defeat the purpose of delegation. Over time, new choices unavoidably emerge and require new responses. The capacity of the legislature to reflect on monetary policy is limited, since it only one amongst an endless list of topics of concern. It is unavoidable that governments, therefore, leave some difficult political choices to unelected officials. By enshrining the independence of the central bank in constitutional structures, the legislature decides that it will focus its attention elsewhere. Central bank independence implies that the legislature has more time to scrutinize the annual budget.

The argument for unavoidability quickly turns into an argument for the desirability of central bank independence (Blinder 1999; Issing 2008; Tucker 2018). Governments might very well judge that it is better to leave some choices to unelected officials who have the time and expertise to decide how to deal with tricky political issues. A closely related problem is that of time-inconsistency (Kydland & Prescott 1977). Although governments may prefer low inflation in the long run, short-term electoral pressures may undermine that commitment. A central bank with a clear price stability mandate allows the government to make its commitment to financial markets credible. In this sense, assigning an area of policymaking to the final authority of an independent agency can itself be seen as a part of economic policy.

The third consideration, which I think should be decisive from the perspective of popular sovereignty, is that whether or not to delegate monetary policy should itself be a topic of democratic decision-making. How much discretion technocrats should have with regard to their instruments and goals is itself a political question. The account of central bank independence as bureaucratic delegation invokes a neat distinction between permissible bureaucratic and impermissible technocratic discretion. The vagueness of that distinction, however, is not accidental nor open to resolution through further conceptual clarification, but is rather itself a legitimate topic of political disagreement. Moreover, evaluating the permissibility of central bank discretion should take into account a range of tricky normative and empirical issues, turning it into a subject of pervasive and potentially irresolvable disagreement. Making such choices is exactly what legislatures are meant to do in the first place.

Central Bank Independence Today

Once we shake off the simple story of bureaucratic delegation it becomes clear that the normative evaluation of the central bank's constitutional role unavoidably requires weighing a range of substantive and procedural considerations. In earlier work, I proposed a normative framework for answering that question focusing on the way the central bank independence shapes deliberation and decision-making on monetary policy (van 't Klooster 2020). A justification for delegating monetary policy to an independent central bank should explain how it improves the quality of decision-making while involving acceptable losses of competences and policy instruments on the side of elected governments. Both sides of the equation, however, resist easy quantification. Most literature on the topic is authored by central bank researchers, who are reluctant to challenge independence (Blinder 1999; Dietsch et al. 2018, chap. 4). Despite some recent work by political scientists, lawyers and other social scientists, we are currently still far removed from having a clear answer to important questions. Consider six open issues that deserve more detailed study.

The first thing to ask about independent central banks is to what extent their choices really diverge from the policy preferences of citizens and their elected representatives. Traditionally, central bankers are thought to make better decisions because they are shielded from electoral pressures. In practice, however, popular opinion does matter to central banks. In fact, they tend to be acutely aware of their own tenuous legitimacy and this shapes their decision-making (Braun 2018; Ronkainen & Sorsa 2018; van 't Klooster & Fontan 2020). The rescue of banks in 2008 involved discretionary interventions on the side of central banks, but generally in coordination with the treasury and other government agencies (Calomiris & Khan 2015; Bateman 2020). The 2020 COVID-19 pandemic saw central bankers move beyond earlier taboos in lending on an unprecedented scale to governments and crisis-struck firms, but again they did so following a broad societal consensus.

If independent central banks indeed tend to follow the policy preferences of their domestic government, this would clearly alleviate the tension between popular sovereignty and central bank independence. A particularly clear illustration of how central banks follow national positions is visible in recent central bank concern for environmental issues. Climate change was virtually ignored before the 2015 Paris Agreement, whose Article 2.1c requires "making finance flows consistent with a pathway towards low greenhouse gas emissions and climate resilient development". From 2015 onwards, the Bank of England, the Banque de France and other, mostly European central banks became more vocal proponents of green priorities and founded the Network for Greening the Financial System (NGFS). Under the Donald Trump presidency, the US Federal Reserve did not join the NGFS and rarely addressed the issue of climate change in its public statements. The Fed announced it would become a member of the NGFS a few days after Joe Biden was elected. However, it is not clear that anything short of formal democratic authorization is sufficient to provide central banks with democratic legitimacy (Downey 2021, 2022).

Irrespective of how this first debate turns out, we should still worry about the informal nature of the existing arrangements of accountability. A long-standing worry with regard to central bank independence is that it disperses responsibility such that neither elected governments nor central banks are accountable for decisions (Friedman 1962). The creation of an independent central bank thus transforms the role of the executive, which gives up control over monetary policy. Parliaments no longer oversee monetary policy decisions as part of the legislature's role in the parliamentary control of executive taxation, borrowing and spending. The central bank board, whose member deliberate behind closed doors, sets monetary policy within the constraints imposed on it by the monetary constitution. As a consequence, central bankers can always blame governments and markets when things go awry. This problem is not new, but rather a perennial risk associated with central bank independence. As Milton Friedman already observed:

> In the past few years, I have read through the annual reports of the Federal Reserve System from 1913 to date, seriatim. One of the few amusing dividends from that ordeal was seeing the cyclical pattern that shows up in the potency that the authorities attribute to monetary policy. In years when things are going well, the reports emphasize that monetary policy is an exceedingly potent weapon and that the favorable course of events is largely a result of the skilful handling of this delicate instrument by the monetary authority. In years of depression, on the other hand, the reports emphasize that monetary policy is but one of many tools of economic policy, that its power is highly limited, and that it was only the skillful handling of such limited powers as were available that averted disaster. (1962, p. 233)

A similar dynamic of responsibility dispersal can be observed recently with regard to the distributive effects of monetary policy. Central bankers argue that they were forced to implement QE by the absence of fiscal policy. Within the mandate assigned to them by governments, QE was the only tool available to avert a recession (Haldane 2014). Although central banks moved beyond their existing toolkit to address the post-crisis recession, they sought to present their new policies as largely continuous with pre-crisis practices. Meanwhile, politicians routinely blame central banks for the adverse effects of accommodative monetary policy (or, more recently, inflation caused by political mismanagement of supply chains). The overall result is that no one accepts responsibility for general trajectory of the economy. Public scrutiny is also limited: Citizens have zoned out from monetary and financial politics, which they in any case have a very little ability to influence.

A third question concerns what the absence of public contestation does with the broader democratic system (Pinnow 2022). By ceding the power over money, politicians lose a tool to improve the lives of their constituents. Political scientists worry that the broader process of depoliticization, in particular with regard to economic policy, hollows out democratic politics, which in turn drives political disengagement and benefits the far right (Hay 2007; Mair 2013; Fawcett, Flinders, Hay, & Wood 2017). Money remains an arcane topic, however, whose impact on the lives of individuals is not a natural topic for public scrutiny even in the absence of independent central banks. This question is particularly tricky to study not just because of the complex social mechanisms involved but also because the absence of political systems with governmental control of monetary policy precludes comparative studies.

Since political insulation is supposed to improve the quality of central bank decision-making a third topic to consider is its potential benefits. Although central bankers are meant to be shielded from electorates by their independence, they can never afford to lose public support altogether. The Bundesbank carefully built its independent source of public support, which allowed it to use popular opinion to achieve its goals (Mee 2019). Few central banks have been able to replicate that feat (Lokdam 2020). In presenting their role as continuous with that of other government agencies, central bankers seek to foster a public perception of monetary policy as pursuing a clearly defined and broadly beneficial goal by means of a limited set of instruments. Even if that account is as we saw false, the efforts of central bankers to conform to it do shape their policies (van 't Klooster & Fontan 2020). Consider the choice to implement QE when the conventional tool of steering short-term interest rates became ineffective. QE was one of many tools available to central banks to supplement their pre-crisis practices. To what extent was the choice for QE and the way in which it was implemented motivated by the desire to maintain continuity with pre-crisis practices? The choice for QE, as we saw, did have its own distributive effects, which might have been different. The central bank's efforts to sustain legitimacy thus comes with its own social costs. Would it then simply be better to accept that central bankers make political choices and hope that they do the best they can? Or does the central bank's quest for legitimacy have its own beneficial consequences too? (C. Skinner 2021)

Democratic insulation not only shapes the central bank's policy space, but also gives a very specific shape to deliberation internal to the central bank. Central banking, in contrast to government-led policy, is meant to be a dispassionate affair subordinate to the common good. The importance of technical expertise, however, also means that central bankers often hail from a narrow range of career background in the financial sector or the government. In a comparative study of twenty central banks between 1950 and 2000, Adolph (2013, pp. 74, 75) shows that 95% of central bankers are men and 47% had spent their entire career in finance or government. Since low inflation is a crucial priority for the financial sector, whose assets tend to have a fixed nominal value, it is striking that those central bankers with a finance background prefer higher rates (and are hence willing to accept lower employment and growth). This suggests that central banks would take a broader range of interests into account if their board members were drawn from a broader range of societal backgrounds. A second way in which the existing institutions of central bank independence shape deliberation results is from the expertise available within central banks and the technical vocabulary in which choices are debated (Marcussen 2009; Abolafia 2010, 2012). The central bank's primary expertise concerns financial markets and business cycles, but many questions concerning the most desirable future path of economic development go beyond these topics. Consider once more whether central banks should take a more active role in stopping climate change. The climate transition will unavoidably result in certain industries flourishing and others disappearing. Employees will lose their jobs and consumers will have to adapt their lifestyles. Scholars of central banking should do more to explore how the specific expertise and career backgrounds of central bankers affects their ability to make these decisions.

To conclude: What should be done if we decide that central banks have in fact become too independent? Note that there is no strict contraction between formal independence and some degree of coordination with governments (de Boer & van 't Klooster 2020, 2021; Baer, Campiglio, & Deyris 2021; Monnet 2021). The mandate of the Bank of England explicitly invites the Treasury to weigh in on key strategic choices. More generally, where mandates contain a blanket provision in favour of supporting economic policy, governments could do more to weigh on the priorities that the central bank should support. One modality of coordination is to incorporate existing legislation into the design of monetary policy operations. For example, public taxonomies for green investment can be the basis for deciding which sectors of the economy monetary policy should support (van 't Klooster & van Tilburg 2020). In this way, coordination could improve the quality of decision-making. It could also improve the legitimacy of political choices made in the face of new challenges. A major question going forward will accordingly be how to structure effective coordination and whether, if at all, that would unduly limit the central bank's independence.

CONCLUSION

Legal and political theorists face many open questions when it comes to the institutional structures of central bank independence. Holding the most powerful levers of economic policy, they could achieve a wide range of objectives beyond price stability. Central banks could do a lot more to move the economy away from catastrophic environmental collapse, but should they? More generally, should central banks take the distributive effects of their policy into account when pursuing low inflation? Accounts of central bank independence as a case of bureaucratic delegation greatly simplify the moral questions raised by central banks. The most basic question to ask does not concern central banks per se, but rather the very shape of the monetary constitution. The democratic legitimacy of central banks can only become an issue after deciding where the private domain of money creation starts. The question of when delegation is permissible cannot be neatly separated from the question of how to govern the economy, so that the design of a central bank raises a wide range of procedural and substantive issues. This chapter has sought to bring the terrain that remains to be explored into focus. The past decades saw central bankers acquire an increasingly prominent role in economic policy. This makes a re-evaluation of the central bank's unique constitutional status highly pertinent. If it turns out that central bankers are not particularly well placed to deal with the major economic policy challenges of the twenty-first century, existing constitutional structures are no longer fit for the purpose and need to be revised.

RECOMMENDED READING

Adolph, C. (2013). *Bankers, Bureaucrats, and Central Bank Politics: The Myth of Neutrality*, New York: Cambridge University Press.
Baradaran, M. (2017). *The Color of Money: Black Banks and the Racial Wealth Gap*, Cambridge, MA: Harvard University Press.
Bateman, W. (2020). *Public Finance and Parliamentary Constitutionalism*, Cambridge: Cambridge University Press.
Bernanke, B., Laubach, T., Mishkin, F., & Posen, A. (2001). *Inflation targeting: Lessons from the international experience*, Princeton: Princeton University Press.
Braun, B., & Downey, L. (2020). *Against Amnesia: Re-Imagining Central Banking* (Discussion Note No. 2020/01). Zürich: Council on Economic Policies.
Bunn, P., Pugh, A, & Yeates, C. (2018). "The Distributional Impact of Monetary Policy Easing in the UK between 2008 and 2014." Staff Working Papers. Bank of England, March 27.
Coibion, O., Gorodnichenko, Y., Kueng, L., & Silvia, J. (2017). Innocent Bystanders? Monetary policy and inequality. *Journal of Monetary Economics*, 88, 70–89.
Conti-Brown, P. (2016). *The Power and Independence of the Federal Reserve*, Princeton: Princeton University Press.
Desan, C. (2014). *Making Money: Coin, Currency, and the Coming of Capitalism*, Oxford: Oxford University Press.
Dietsch, P., Claveau, F., & Fontan, C. (2018). *Do Central Banks Serve the People?* Cambridge: Polity.
Friedman, M. (1962). Should there be an independent monetary authority? In L. Yeager, ed., *In Search of a Monetary Constitution*. Cambridge, MA: Harvard University Press, pp. 219–243.
Hockett, R., & Omarova, S. (2017). The Finance Franchise. *Cornell Law Review*, 102 (5), 1143.
Mehrling, P. (2010). *The New Lombard Street: How the Fed Became the Dealer of Last Resort*, Princeton: Princeton University Press.
Monnet, E. (2021). *La Banque Providence: Démocratiser les banques centrales et la monnaie*, Paris: Seuil.
Pistor, K. (2013). A Legal Theory of Finance. *Journal of Comparative Economics*, 41 (2), 315–330.
Tucker, P. (2018). *Unelected Power: The Quest for Legitimacy in Central Banking and the Regulatory State*, Cambridge, MA: Harvard University Press.

PART III. B

The Executive

37

Presidentialism, Parliamentarism, and Their Hybrids

Steffen Ganghof

This chapter discusses the comparative constitutional theory of presidential government, parliamentary government and various hybrids. I refer to the relevant aspects of constitutions as forms of government or executive formats. These formats are generally defined by the *origin* and *survival* of the executive: how it gets into office and how it can be removed from office (Shugart and Carey 1992; Cheibub et al. 2014).

Normative theorists have taken surprisingly little interest in this basic aspect of constitutional design. This is reflected in two related ways. First, the comparative evaluation of executive formats has mainly been discussed in "instrumentalist" terms, broadly conceived. For example, when Martinez (2012, p. 558) summarizes the normative debate about executive formats, she is almost exclusively concerned with their causal effects, such as those famously hypothesized by Juan Linz (1990, 1994). With some exceptions to be discussed below, the idea that democratic institutions have intrinsic or non-instrumental value has not been systematically applied to forms of government. This predominance of instrumentalist reasoning contrasts sharply with debates about the design of electoral systems, legislative decision rules or systems of constitutional change and review (e.g., Bellamy 2007; Christiano 1996; Gaus 1996; Kolodny 2014; Schwartzberg 2013; Waldron 2006; Wilson 2019).

Second, the literature has focused almost exclusively on the three forms of government that dominate the real world of constitutional democracies: parliamentarism, presidentialism and semi-presidentialism. Many discussions proceed as if this trichotomy exhausted the choice set. There is very little work on the desirability of rarer executive formats, such as those in Switzerland or Australia, or formats that might yet have to be developed (but see Abizadeh 2021b; Ganghof 2021; Khaitan 2021a). The predominant focus on what path-dependent political processes – often driven by the self-interest of powerful actors – have produced may be justifiable in empirical research but is problematic in constitutional theory. The three dominant forms do not exhaust the logical space of possibilities, and it is not obvious that they represent the best way to realize or promote liberty and equality – or to defend liberal democracy against its enemies.

Going beyond the three dominant executive formats is also crucial for analytical reasons. When systematically comparing these formats, we need to distinguish two orthogonal dimensions: the *separation of powers* between the executive and the assembly, on the one hand, and *executive personalism*, the concentration of executive power in a single human being, on the other. The standard trichotomy fosters a conflation of these analytical dimensions. Only when we consider the full range of how democratic constitutions structure the relationship between the democratic principal and its representative agents, can we clearly distinguish the separation of powers from executive personalism.

This distinction is important because it may be that the "perils of presidentialism" (Linz 1990), to the extent that they exist, are to a great extent the perils of executive personalism. I suggest that constitutional designers may have good reasons to embrace the separation of powers, and hence to reject a pure parliamentary system, but they have even stronger reasons to reject presidentialism. The direct election of a fixed-term president is not – despite recurring claims to the contrary – inherently more democratic on proceduralist grounds, but it has important negative consequences, not least by attenuating some of the potential benefits of the separation of powers and accentuating its downsides. A promising but widely neglected strategy to achieve powers-separation without executive personalism is a "semi-parliamentary" system, which shifts the locus of powers-separation into the assembly (Ganghof 2018, 2021; Khaitan 2021a).

The next section clarifies this chapter's methodological approach. Section II then specifies the choice space by distinguishing six basic executive formats. Section III discusses proceduralist arguments for and against some of these. Section IV summarizes parts of the debate about the two pure types of presidential and parliamentary government. Section V then asks whether hybrids of the two pure types can achieve the best of both worlds. Section VI is a brief conclusion.

I METHODOLOGICAL APPROACH

Debates about the justification of democracy often distinguish between "proceduralist" and "instrumentalist" arguments, the former being concerned with the procedural fairness of decision-making, the latter with the quality of decision-making outcomes. When it comes to the evaluation of formal institutions, however, this distinction is insufficient, because there is a third object of evaluation located between formal procedures and substantive outcomes: democratic *processes*. It is possible to value democratic processes, in part, non-instrumentally yet formal procedures merely as instruments for achieving desirable processes and outcomes.[1] A number of democratic theorists defend this kind of position (e.g., Beitz 1989; Kolodny 2014; Wilson 2019). For example, one may deny that proportional electoral systems

---

[1] For further discussion, see Ganghof (2021, pp. 52–57).

are intrinsically valuable, but still favor them because they causally contribute to intrinsically desirable processes such as high turnout or government responsiveness to the preferences of the median voter. Much empirical research in political science is (implicitly) grounded in this kind of position.

In what follows, I first focus on narrowly "proceduralist" arguments, that is, those that see certain formal procedures as having non-instrumental value, if only conditionally (e.g., Christiano 1996, 2008). I then move on to the "instrumental" evaluation of executive formats, that is, based on their effects on desirable processes and outcomes. Note that, for the purposes of this chapter, I take no particular position on how to specify or weigh desirable processes and outcomes. I merely review the kinds of goals that the literature on executive formats has discussed. My main suggestion is that, based on a broad range of different design goals and priorities, the branch-based separation of powers is a double-edged sword, whereas executive personalism is more consistently perilous.

II SIX BASIC EXECUTIVE FORMATS

While much of the literature distinguishes only two or three basic forms of government, the logically implied possibility space encompasses at least six, four of which can be seen as hybrids of the two pure types (Figure 37.1). There is no consensus in the literature about whether all of them should be seen as hybrids or how they should be labelled. Here I follow the terminology used by Samuels and Shugart (2010, pp. 26–30) and amended by Ganghof (2021).

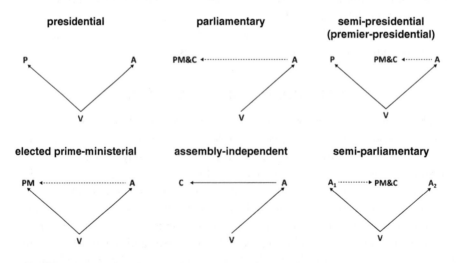

FIGURE 37.1 Six basic forms of government
Notes: Adapted from Ganghof (2021, chap. 2).
V = Voters, A = Assembly, P = President, PM = Prime Minister, C = Cabinet, → = Election, ⇢ = Dismissal

The upper row of Figure 37.1 shows the three most common executive formats. Under *parliamentary government*, the chief executive and cabinet are chosen by the assembly (fused origin) and can be dismissed by it for purely political reasons in a majoritarian procedure (fused survival). Under *presidential government*, chief executives are popularly elected and serve a fixed term in office (separate origin and survival). They can only be removed through special procedures such as impeachment. The most prevalent hybrid is *semi-presidential government* (Duverger 1980; Elgie 2011), which is now typically defined in terms of a directly elected, fixed-term president (separate origin and survival) and a prime minister and cabinet responsible to the assembly majority (fused origin and survival). The president may also have the constitutional right to dismiss the prime minister, however (not shown in Figure 37.1). In this case a distinct subtype of semi-presidentialism is established, which is labeled *president-parliamentary*. By contrast, in the *premier-presidential* subtype (shown in the figure) the prime minister and the cabinet are exclusively accountable to the assembly (Samuels and Shugart 2010, p. 30).

The lower row of Figure 37.1 shows the three rarer formats. Under *elected prime-ministerial government*, the chief executive is directly elected (separate origin) but still needs the continuous political confidence of an assembly majority to stay in office (fused survival). This system has been discussed in many countries and tried, unsuccessfully, in Israel from 1996 to 2001 (see Section V for further discussion). Versions of it also exist in Kiribati and at the subnational level in Italy (Edge et al. 2019; Fabbrini 2001). Under *assembly-independent government* in Switzerland, introduced in 1848, the assembly votes the cabinet into office (fused origin), but cannot dismiss it in a no-confidence vote (separate survival). Finally, *semi-parliamentary government* can be seen as the mirror image of semi-presidentialism (Ganghof 2018, 2021). It shifts the separation of powers into the assembly by allowing only one part of it to dismiss the prime minister and cabinet in a no-confidence vote (fused origin and survival), even though the assembly's other part has roughly equal democratic legitimacy and robust veto power (separate origin and survival).[2] Ganghof (2021) classifies the bicameral systems in Australia – at the federal and state levels – as well as Japan as semi-parliamentary (see also Taflaga 2018; Smith 2018). However, semi-parliamentarism may also be achieved within a single chamber by restricting the right to a no-confidence vote to a confidence *committee*. Note also that, since the semi-parliamentary separation of powers is assembly-based, one part of the assembly may be legitimized by sortition rather than elections (Abizadeh 2021b).

By comparing these six forms of government, we can analytically distinguish the separation of powers from what I call executive personalism. A separation of powers

---

[2] While many second chambers lack no-confidence power, they also lack the requisite democratic legitimacy. Conversely, some second chambers that are (almost) wholly directly elected, such as those in Italy or Romania, also possess no-confidence power. What makes semi-parliamentary bicameralism unique is the lack of this power *despite the requisite legitimacy*. The standard concepts of "symmetrical" or "strong" bicameralism (Lijphart 2012) cannot capture this uniqueness (Ganghof 2021, chap. 3).

between executive and assembly exists whenever the former is not fully fused with the latter – that is, whenever the chief executive and cabinet are not merely removable agents of the parliamentary majority. Executive personalism results when the chief executive is directly elected for a fixed term in office. The constitution personalizes executive power in this case because (1) elections vest power in a single person, rather a collective entity like a political party or an assembly, and (2) because this person cannot be removed from office by a representative assembly in a political and majoritarian procedure.

Given these definitions, each of the six formats in Figure 37.1 represents a particular combination of executive personalism and powers-separation:

- Presidentialism embraces both. Power is separated between the two branches by means of vesting executive power in a single human being.
- Parliamentarism rejects both. While parliamentary elections can be highly "personalized", prime ministers remain a removable agent of the parliamentary majority (as well as their own party).
- Semi-presidentialism embraces both to the extent that the president is – formally or informally – a politically powerful part of the executive.
- Prime-ministerial government embraces executive personalism in the direct election of chief executives, but limits it by making their survival in office dependent on assembly confidence;
- Assembly-independent government in Switzerland embraces executive personalism in the inability of the assembly to remove the government from office, but limits it by disallowing direct executive elections (and, in this specific case, also by dividing executive power between seven individuals who serve in the cabinet as equals);
- Semi-parliamentary government decouples executive personalism from powers-separation by making the origin of the prime minister and cabinet as well as their survival in office dependent on one part of the assembly but not the other.

Given space constraints, I largely neglect the important (potential or actual) variation in constitutional designs *within* each basic type (e.g., Albert 2009; Alemán and Tsebelis 2016; Cheibub et al. 2014; Cheibub and Rasch 2022; Colomer and Negretto 2005; Elgie 2011; Shugart and Carey 1992; Strøm et al. 2003). This within-type variation matters greatly, not only for empirical research but also with respect to the practical questions of constitutional reform. Here the focus is on understanding the basic options.

III PROCEDURALIST REASONS FOR AND AGAINST EXECUTIVE FORMATS

McGann (2006) makes an egalitarian case for pure parliamentary government. He argues that political equality (conditionally) requires pure proportional representation combined with simple majority rule in assembly decision-making. On this basis, parliamentary systems can be justified as a way to extend the resulting equality in legislative voting to the process of agenda-setting. The fairly constituted assembly majority selects and de-selects the government as the main agenda setter (McGann 2006, p. 85).

In sharp contrast, a range of authors have conjectured that presidential government is preferable on proceduralist grounds because chief executives are directly elected. Lijphart (1992, p. 13) suggests that direct presidential elections render presidentialism inherently "more democratic"; Arato (2000b, p. 321) claims that the critique of presidentialism "was rarely based on normative considerations for the simple reason that, under a democracy, direct elections are always preferable to indirect elections that can always deny office to the candidate the voters actually prefer;" Calabresi (2001, p. 67) even thinks this advantage of presidentialism may be "dispositive just by itself." While these claims focus on the selection of the chief executives, the underlying intuition can be extended to their deselection. That is, the *direct recall* of the chief executive by voters might be considered more democratically legitimate than their indirect removal through a no-confidence vote (Pérez-Liñán 2020).[3]

The contradictory arguments for parliamentarism and presidentialism reveal two general problems of proceduralist arguments about executive formats (Ganghof 2021, chap. 4). First, they tend to conflate distinct comparisons, which is most obvious in the above quote from Arato. Even if a presidential system with a directly elected president is preferable, on procedural grounds, to one with an indirectly elected president (e.g., election via an electoral college), it doesn't follow that a presidential system is also preferable to a parliamentary system.

Second, this does not follow because, in a representative democracy, political inequality has two dimensions (Dworkin 2000; Abizadeh 2021b). *Horizontal inequality* is the inequality between non-representatives, which is often thought to be reduced or prevented by using majority rule to make decisions and proportional representation to elect representatives (Christiano 1996; Waldron 1999a; McGann 2006). *Vertical inequality* is the inequality "intrinsic to representative democracy: between representatives empowered to decide legislation and policy and non-representatives who are not" (Abizadeh 2021b, p. 796). The two proceduralist arguments summarized above focus exclusively one dimension while neglecting the other. McGann's argument for parliamentarism is about reducing horizontal inequality, while the argument for direct presidential elections is about reducing vertical inequality. Once we consider both dimensions jointly, a purely proceduralist comparison is rendered inconclusive (Ganghof 2021, chap. 4).

---

[3] Pérez-Liñán's (2020) appears to rely mainly on a sociological notion of democratic legitimacy, which implies an instrumentalist version of this argument. The recent normative literature has generally neglected direct recall. This is true even for attempts to use the logic of principal-agent theory to reconcile the ideal of democratic equality with the obvious vertical inequality between voters and representatives (e.g., Kolodny 2014).

Another type of proceduralist argument aims at resolving the tension between horizontal and vertical equality by establishing a semi-parliamentary system with a randomly selected second chamber. The idea is that, since the extra power of office holding is inevitable and cannot be distributed equally, everyone ought to have "an equal chance or opportunity to hold office" (Abizadeh 2021b, p. 797). Citizens ought to be treated equally not qua selectors but qua *candidates for office*. Since there are also a number of instrumentalist concerns about sortition, though, Abizadeh proposes to mix elections and sortition within a semi-parliamentary constitution. The first chamber would be an elected confidence chamber, while the randomly selected second chamber would lack confidence power despite having equal – or, indeed, higher – democratic legitimacy and absolute veto power on ordinary legislation.

There are also proceduralist concerns about a semi-parliamentary constitution. Meinel (2021, p. 135) worries – in the context of a system with two *elected* parts of the assembly – that because only one of these parts can remove the government in a no-confidence vote and thus occupies a privileged position, a form of "symbolic" equality is undermined. He suggests that democratic representation ought to be "the representation by *equal* representatives," which in his view also implies equal power over the survival of the government. Ganghof (2021, pp. 63–65) rejects this view, arguing that what matters morally is the equal treatment, not of representatives, but of citizens.

IV THE PRESIDENTIALISM-VERSUS-PARLIAMENTARISM DEBATE AND BEYOND

Much of the contemporary instrumentalist debate about the two pure types of democracies has been framed by the arguments of Juan Linz (1990; see also Ackerman 2000, pp. 645–648). However, this debate has not systematically distinguished between the two aspects of presidential government: powers-separation and executive personalism. I argue that they must be separated analytically, as the respective discussions lead to very different conclusions. Powers-separation creates problems such as legislative deadlock but it also has important benefits. Executive personalism, in contrast, has mainly downsides. Moreover, it tends to accentuate the problems of powers-separation and attenuate its benefits.

The (Elusive) Advantages of Executive Personalism

Executive personalism is to a significant extent an overhang from monarchy (Colomer 2013; Nelson 2014; Scheuerman 2005; Prakash 2020, chap. 1). Historically, it has often been justified on the basis of some form of "antipartyism", that is, the idea that parties are, in one way or another, dangerously divisive (e.g., Muirhead and Rosenblum 2015, pp. 222–225; Samuels and Shugart 2010, pp. 39–40).

One justification that is at least continuous with pluralist and democratic ideals, espoused by Founding Fathers of the US Constitution such as James Wilson and Alexander Hamilton, sees executive personalism as a requirement of clear responsibility (Scheuerman 2005, p. 42). However, this view is not supported by the modern political science literature, which associates clarity of responsibility with the dominance of a single political *party* (Powell 2000, p. 52; Schwindt-Bayer and Tavits 2016, pp. 18, 20).

Other justifications are psychological. One suggestion – directly reflective of presidentialism's monarchical origins (Scheuerman 2005) – is that direct presidential elections lead to the selection of more charismatic leaders, which is considered instrumentally valuable (Calabresi 2001, p. 70). Another is that presidents are extraordinarily concerned with their legacies, which makes them "predisposed to seek coherent, durable policy solutions that will succeed in addressing the nation's key problems and enhancing social welfare" (Howell and Moe 2020, pp. 161–162). These arguments remain unconvincing, as they lack grounding in systematic psychological theory or empirical evidence and do not – upon closer examination – establish presidentialism's superiority over other forms of powers-separation (Ganghof 2021, p. 151).

Another important justification of executive personalism is an instrumentalist version of the argument from democratic legitimacy discussed above. Based on an sociological notion of democratic legitimacy, the idea is that the direct election and/or recall of presidents may increase public support for democracy – or, conversely, that parliamentary no-confidence votes "lack the legitimacy granted by direct popular participation" (Pérez-Liñán 2020, p. 201). While this may be a plausible hypothesis (but see Ganghof 2021, pp. 154–157), I am not aware of systematic empirical evidence to corroborate it (e.g., Tavits 2009; Welp and Whitehead 2020, p. 24).

The Perils of Executive Personalism

While the advantages of executive personalism are thus difficult to substantiate, Linz (1990) and other critics of presidentialism highlight its perils. Ackerman (2000, p. 663) even considers it "downright embarrassing for a constitution to ask free and equal citizens to place so much trust in the personal integrity and ideals of a single human being."

The empirical literature has corroborated many of these concerns. One important finding is that presidentialism facilitates the election of outsiders or newcomers (Carreras 2017; Samuels and Shugart 2010; see also Ginsburg and Huq 2018, pp. 180–181). Carreras (2014) shows that these outsiders also increase the likelihood of executive-legislative conflict – defined mainly but not exclusively as conflict over the approval of critical bills – as well as illegal attempts to dissolve the assembly.

Executive personalism also has important consequences for political parties. Samuels and Shugart (2010) show that parties in presidential and semi-presidential systems often become "presidentialized". Parties have strong incentives to give their leaders-as-executives considerable discretion in shaping their electoral and governing strategies and tend to lose their ability to hold these leaders to account. Executive personalism also tends to weaken party unity, especially within the party of the president. Carey (2007, p. 106) argues that popularly elected presidents have this effect because they can become powerful principals of individual legislators: "They present a potentially competing source of directives against those of party leaders within the legislature." All in all, parties are "unlikely, under most conditions, to act as voters' representational agents as they do in parliamentary systems" (Samuels and Shugart 2010, p. 247).

Chief executives may even be able to reverse the principal-agent relationship and dominate their parties rather than being responsible to them. This also means that they can often rely on "their" parties to undermine the separation of powers (Levinson and Pildes 2006). Even when parties are not strong enough principals to control "their" presidents, they may still be cohesive and polarized agents enough to shield them from effective checks and balances.

The negative causal effects of executive personalism are also indirect, resulting from the very constitutional measures to contain them. One example is impeachment and similar procedures, which – due to the absence of a no-confidence procedure – are needed as a constitutional safety net. Yet it seems to matter that these procedures are usually more cumbersome and time-consuming than no-confidence votes. Helmke (2017) argues that when presidents have weak partisan support in the assembly and can anticipate their removal, they are more likely to attack the legislature and the courts in a preemptive strike.

Another problematic constitutional safeguard is presidential term limits. They are widely embraced as a way to prevent too strong a concentration of powers in the hands of the president and reduce the likelihood of an authoritarian takeover. Yet they are also a major obstacle to one of the goals direct presidential elections are supposed to achieve: electoral accountability. Good last-term presidents cannot be re-elected, whereas bad ones cannot be sanctioned at the ballot box. Moreover, it has been argued, even by well-meaning and seemingly independent courts, that term limits violate democratic rights (Ginsburg and Elkins 2019). Some authors, therefore, propose to replace them with safeguards that only target *undue* electoral advantages of the incumbent (Cheibub and Medina 2019, p. 533; Mainwaring and Shugart 1997, p. 452). Yet there is much evidence to suggest that the lack of term limits endangers democracy (Baturo and Elgie 2019). Executive personalism thus creates a vexing trade-off "between the possibility of dictatorial takeover and a restriction of democratic choice" (Baturo 2014, p. 45). While this tradeoff might be mitigated, for example, by banning re-election only for consecutive terms (Dixon and Landau 2020), it cannot be avoided under presidentialism (see also Ginsburg and Huq 2018, pp. 181–182).

The Perils of Powers-Separation

Linz (1990) highlights two main problems of powers-separation. One is *dual legitimacy*: Since president and legislature are both directly elected, it may be unclear who is better legitimated to speak in the name of the people. The other is *rigidity in the face of deadlock*: The president and assembly may block each other's agenda, and since both serve fixed terms, there is no constitutional way to resolve an impasse. Linz also suggested that, partly as a result of these problems, presidential democracies are inherently less stable. In particular, the military may intervene as a way of resolving gridlock. The subsequent literature, however, has qualified Linz' worries – and this qualification is reinforced when we try to disentangle the effects of powers-separation from those of executive personalism.

The causal tendency of the separation of powers to lead to legislative deadlock, while important, should not be exaggerated. For one thing, the literature has shown that presidents – just like prime ministers – are often fairly successful in building executive and/or legislative coalitions (Cheibub et al. 2004; Cheibub 2007; Chaisty et al. 2018; Alemán and Tsebelis 2016). For another, when studies find that governments' legislative performance (i.e., the "success rates" of government bills) is lower under presidentialism as compared to parliamentarism, it is difficult to know how much of this effect is due to the separation of powers as such. It might partly be due to the added problems of executive personalism, such as the greater likelihood of outsider presidents noted above. Ganghof (2021, pp. 96–99) presents preliminary evidence to support this kind of interpretation. Legislative success rates under the semi-parliamentary – and hence non-personalized – separation of powers are comparable to those under pure parliamentarism, whereas success rates under presidentialism seem to be substantially lower.

Another reason why these differences exist in legislative success rates, is that executive personalism may make it harder to resolve the deadlock. Under the semi-parliamentary separation of powers, it can be resolved by a double dissolution of the two branches (chambers) (Ganghof 2021, chap. 7). A similar "double dissolution" and re-election of the executive and legislative branches has been proposed as a way to resolve legislative deadlock under presidentialism, too (Mainwaring and Shugart 1997, p. 453). Given executive personalism, however, such a mechanism runs the risk of increasing the "presidentialization" of political parties and weakening democratic checks and balances. The *muerte cruzada* ("mutual death") provision (Art. 148) in Ecuador's 2008 constitution seems to be a case in point. It allows presidents, once in the first three years of their term, to dissolve the assembly, force new legislative and presidential elections, and rule by decree on urgent economic matters in the interim. While the provision had been conceived as "quasi-parliamentary" and a way to "align the incentive structure of the Executive and the Legislative branches of government," Ecuador's president Rafael Correa "found a way to parlay his popularity into the threatened misapplication of the *muerte cruzada* provision with the aim to quell dissent" (Sanchez-Sibony 2018, p. 105).

The idea that presidentialism renders democracies unstable has also been qualified. On the one hand, Cheibub (2007) has shown that military coups in presidential democracies partly reflect the fact that these democracies were more likely to be preceded by a military regime. When this legacy of militarism is statistically controlled, the correlation between presidentialism and democratic breakdown disappears (see also Aydogan 2019). On the other hand, Maeda (2010, p. 1141) and Svolik (2015) argue that we need to distinguish military coups from authoritarian takeovers by democratically elected incumbents. Both find that presidentialism does increase the likelihood of the latter.

These findings, too, are consistent with the view that the danger for democracies is not the separation of powers as such but rather its combination with executive personalism. For one thing, systems of powers-separation that avoid executive personalism, such as those in Australia or Switzerland, do not seem to increase the likelihood of incumbent takeovers. For another, a *lack* of powers-separation can also facilitate incumbent takeovers, as democratic backsliding in parliamentary systems like Hungary exemplifies (Weyland 2020; Cheibub 2021; Ginsburg and Huq 2018, p. 108). After all, a traditional justification of the separation of powers is that it can be a defensive shield against the rise of tyranny (Hamilton, Madison, and Jay 2008).

The Promise of Powers-Separation

Linz's critics also highlight potential benefits of powers-separation that are the flip side of presidentialism's alleged perils.

Allowing voters to directly elect two separate agents not only creates "dual legitimacy" but also provides constitutional designers with a distinct way of balancing competing models or visions of democracy, such as those described by Lijphart (2012) and Powell (2000). Presidential systems can balance competing visions by varying the electoral design of the two separate branches (Shugart and Carey 1992, chap. 1). Assembly elections can be designed to represent voters proportionally in the process of coalition-building, while presidential elections are inherently majoritarian and thus allow voters to make a clear choice between competing government alternatives (Colomer and Negretto 2005; Cheibub 2007).

This balancing of democratic visions can lead to better outcomes. For example, Cheibub (2006) presents comparative evidence that, because voters are able to identify and punish those responsible for economic policies, presidential systems in which presidents are constitutionally able to dominate the budget process or to effectively veto legislation tend to have higher budget balances. Drawing on a similar line of reasoning, Ganghof (2021, p. 102) suggests that a well-designed semi-parliamentary separation of powers, with majoritarian elections in one chamber and proportional elections in the other, may help to achieve goals such as high turnout and low corruption.

The "rigidity" created by the lack of a no-confidence procedure has advantages, too: It liberates the assembly from the task of keeping the executive in office (Mainwaring and Shugart 1997, p. 463). As a result, specific legislative initiatives can be deliberated and decided on based on their merits rather than as matters of confidence in the leadership of the ruling party or coalition.

V HYBRIDS AS THE BEST OF BOTH WORLDS

If the perils of presidentialism – to the extent that they exist – are mainly due to executive personalism rather than the separation of powers, we gain a clear perspective on the relative attractiveness of the four hybrids in Figure 37.1. The most attractive ones might be those that reap some or all of the benefits of powers-separation while avoiding executive personalism. Based on this assumption, I proceed from the least to the most attractive hybrid.

Elected Prime Ministerial Government

This executive format failed in Israel because the intended benefits of powers-separation (separate origin) could not be reconciled with the simultaneous desire to contain executive personalism. Reformers wanted the benefits of giving voters two directly elected agents but were also afraid of vesting too much power in a single human being. Therefore, the version of the system that was eventually implemented required a parliamentary vote to install the government and allowed an absolute parliamentary majority to vote it out of office. Hence the independent electoral legitimacy of the prime minister made no difference to the cabinet's survival in office, and the bargaining power of small parties in a fragmented parliament remained unchanged (Ottolenghi 2001; Samuels and Shugart 2010, pp. 179–190).

Semi-Presidential Government

While semi-presidentialism has spread throughout the world, it is difficult to find principled justifications of the semi-presidential separation of powers. Robert Elgie (2011, pp. 14–15) found only two, both of which are questionable.

The first idea is that semi-presidentialism allows for power-sharing within the executive, especially in the context of a polarized society. This is unconvincing because – as discussed above – executive personalism makes presidents doubtful representatives of collective interests. If power-sharing is to be achieved within the executive, genuinely *collegial* government within the parliamentary or assembly-independent formats seems superior (Lijphart 2012; Linder and Mueller 2021).

The second idea is that semi-presidentialism provides a solution to the problem of deadlock under pure presidentialism. An oscillation of power between the president and the prime minister is thought to reinforce "the authority of whoever obtains a majority" (Sartori 1997, p. 125). This idea is derived from the French experience with the so-called *cohabitation* in the 1980s and 1990s, but it can hardly be generalized. Rather than leading to a convenient oscillation of power, semi-presidentialism can just as well lead to persistent intra-executive conflict (Åberg and Sedelius 2018, p. 15). France changed its constitution in 2000 to reestablish the president's dominance.

Of course, semi-presidentialism may also be justified explicitly in terms of the benefits of executive personalism. One prominent idea remains that only a single human being can create some desirable kind of political unity (Lacerda 2020, pp. 25–26). Yet the democratic credentials of this idea are doubtful, as is the empirical evidence for it.

Finally, semi-presidential systems create the danger that presidents become more dominant than under pure presidentialism. This is especially true if they have the right to dismiss the prime minister – as is the case under the "president-parliamentary" subtype – and/or to dissolve the assembly. Empirical studies associate these rights with democratic instability and authoritarian forms of presidentialism (e.g., Elgie 2011; Stykow 2019).

If semi-presidentialism is difficult to justify, why it has been so widely adopted? One reason is political self-interest. This form of government provides a constitutional compromise between those political forces that believe they can win the presidency and those that can at best hope to enter a coalition government (Elgie 2016, p. 60). Another explanation is the widespread belief – whether justifiable or not – that the direct election of the head of state is inherently more democratic. As Cheibub (2021, p. 5) puts it: "In an era in which 'democratic-ness' is probably the primary standard for evaluating institutions, it is natural that having direct elections for the head of state becomes the preeminent choice in constitution making."

Assembly-independent Government

The framers of the Swiss constitution deliberately contained executive personalism by avoiding direct executive elections. They wanted to prevent any "personal preeminence" and any "monarchical or dictatorial tendency" (Constitutional Reform Committee 1992[1848], p. 173). Still, since the assembly is liberated from keeping the government in office, Switzerland can realize one central benefit of powers-separation: the formation of legislative coalitions on an issue-by-issue basis.

Indeed, Switzerland is rather unique in that *no party*, regardless of whether or not it is included in the cabinet, is a true veto player; every party (that does not have a majority in one of the two chambers) can be excluded from the winning coalition.[4] This fact has been important for the evolution and resilience of the Swiss conventions of "consociational" democracy (Ganghof 2021, chap. 2). While Swiss cabinets have (with brief interruptions) included the same four parties since 1959, their common classification as "oversized" is misleading. In the case of disagreement, cabinet parties can be excluded; and legislative coalitions on individual bills can be, and frequently are, passed by minimal-winning coalitions. There is a great

---

[4] This is, of course, not to deny that the Swiss parliament's two chambers are *institutional* veto players.

deal of "hidden" majoritarianism in Switzerland, which implies – as per the median voter theorem – that the most powerful legislative actors are the parties in the political center (Linder and Mueller 2021, p. 192). The Swiss form of government may thus be particularly attractive for those normative theorists that understand the ideal of political equality as implying responsiveness to the position of the issue-by-issue median voter (Ward and Weale 2010).

Assembly-independent government in Switzerland is part of a demanding equilibrium, however, which involves not only powerful direct democratic procedures but also goes hand in hand with (1) the short-term irrelevance of elections for the composition of the government, (2) the inability of voters to decide between general political directions, and (3) very low levels of turnout. This helps to explain why this executive format has not been an export success.

Semi-Parliamentary Government

If the goal is to reap the benefits of powers-separation while avoiding the perils of executive personalism, semi-parliamentarism may be the most promising executive format. As suggested by Figure 37.1, it can achieve the benefits of the separation of powers, because voters directly elect two separate agents. At the same, executive personalism is avoided, as the prime minister and cabinet emerge from, and remain responsible to, one part of the assembly. This can either be a separate confidence chamber or a confidence committee within a single chamber.

Ganghof (2014, 2015) highlights the possibility that well-designed semi-parliamentarism might achieve an optimal compromise between presidentialism and parliamentarism as well as between different visions of democracy. Majoritarian elections to the confidence chamber can allow voters to clearly authorize a stable single-party cabinet, while this cabinet needs to seek issue-specific support in a separate, proportionally elected chamber of legislation, deliberation and control. Khaitan (2021a) develops the same optimization hypothesis with a more extensive theoretical focus on political parties. He suggests that well-designed semi-parliamentarism is indeed the optimal form of government. By contrast, Ganghof (2021) merely postulates semi-parliamentarism's superiority over presidentialism. Given the downsides of separation of powers-systems such as legislative deadlock, parliamentarism might still be superior, all things considered. Nevertheless, Ganghof (2021, chaps. 5–7) presents comparative evidence for twenty-nine democratic systems showing that the best-performing semi-parliamentary cases do balance conflicting democratic design goals in ways that are unavailable under pure parliamentary government.

Semi-parliamentarism also seems well-suited to reduce executive dominance and strengthen horizontal political accountability. This might not only make it an attractive response to the threat of democratic backsliding (Ganghof 2021, pp. 163–166) but is also relevant when considering political forms of accountability and checks as an alternative to strong forms of judicial review (Ackerman 2000; Waldron 2006, p. 1361; Watkins and Lemieux 2015). Gardbaum (2014, p. 636) suggests that the kind of political accountability achieved by Australia's form of bicameralism helps to explain why the country has resisted the constitutionalization and judicialization of rights. Semi-parliamentary government may thus be a complement to weaker forms of judicial review (Ganghof 2021, pp. 104–106).

One possible objection to this line of reasoning is that bicameralism is inherently supermajoritarian (e.g., Przeworski 2010, p. 142; McGann 2006, p. 184) and thus challenges the value of political equality just as much as strong judicial review. Yet Ganghof (2021, pp. 143–144) argues that well-designed semi-parliamentarism need not be supermajoritarian. For one thing, when a one-party cabinet with a first-chamber majority is centrally located in the ideological space and builds issue-specific minimal-winning coalitions in the second chamber, the first chamber is effectively "absorbed" by these coalitions (Tsebelis 2002). For another, when the second chamber's democratic legitimacy is at least equal to that of the first chamber, inter-branch deadlock could potentially be avoided by weakening the *first chamber*'s veto power. This would be analogous to presidential systems in which a presidential veto can be overridden by a simple or absolute assembly majority.

As is true for other forms of government, there is little consensus on the best design of semi-parliamentarism. Ganghof (2021, chap. 8) explores new designs that do not require fully fledged bicameralism and/or mimic the advantages of presidentialism by electing the chamber or committee of confidence in a single jurisdiction-wide district and making the separated, proportional part of the assembly the center of legislative decision-making. By contrast, Khaitan (2021a) prefers to stay closer to the Australian status quo of a first chamber that is elected in single-member districts and has superior democratic legitimacy, due to the second chamber having longer and staggered terms.

The preference for a legitimacy advantage of the confidence chamber can derive from the worry that when second chambers become as democratically legitimate as first chambers, they may usurp a confidence-supplying role (Khaitan 2021a, pp. 119–120). The latter did happen – to a certain extent and/or in specific times – in the Australian Commonwealth and Japan (Aroney et al. 2015, pp. 412–417; Thies and Yanai 2014, p. 70; Takayasu 2015, p. 161). In both cases, however, the reason was arguably not the second chambers' legitimacy but their direct or indirect veto power over the annual budget. The semi-parliamentary systems of the Australian states of New South Wales and Victoria, therefore, deny the second chamber any veto power over supply. Moreover, the transformation of a budget veto into de facto no-confidence power is not inevitable. In Australia, the 1974–1975 constitutional crisis has contributed to changing constitutional conventions in ways that constrain the misuse of the budget veto (Smith 2018, pp. 258–259; Stone 2008, p. 181). Moreover, whether such a veto must lead to the government's resignation depends on the details of constitutional design (Bach 2003, pp. 304–305).

CONCLUSION

Much work remains to be done in linking the constitutional design of democratic forms of government to the basic values of liberal democracy. To explore this linkage, we ought to avoid the conflation of two orthogonal design dimensions: (1) the *separation of powers* between two directly elected branches and (2) the *executive personalism* that results when one of these agents is a single human being that cannot be removed from office by any part of the assembly in a political and majoritarian procedure. I have suggested that the "perils of presidentialism" (Linz 1990), to the extent that they exist, are most of all the perils of executive personalism. The executive formats in Switzerland and especially in Australia show how the benefits of powers-separation can be reaped just as well or better when executive personalism is avoided. Whether these formats are superior to a parliamentary system, all things considered, remains an open question. Answering it will be easier when the benefits of powers-separation are clearly distinguished from the perils of executive personalism.

ACKNOWLEDGMENTS

For very helpful comments and suggestions, I would like to thank the editors of this volume as well as Tarunabh Khaitan and JD Mussel.

RECOMMENDED READING

Ackerman, B. (2000). The New Separation of Powers. *Harvard Law Review*, 113 (3), 633–729.
Cheibub, J. A. (2006). *Presidentialism, Parliamentarism, and Democracy*, New York: Cambridge University Press.
Constitutional Reform Committee (1992[1848]). Report on the 1848 Draft Constitution of Switzerland. In Arend Lijphart ed., *Parliamentary versus Presidential Government*. New York: Oxford University Press, pp. 173–174.
Elgie, R. (2011). *Semi-Presidentialism: Sub-Types and Democratic Performance*, Oxford: Oxford University Press.
Hamilton, A., Madison, J., & Jay, J. (2008 [1787/88]). *The Federalist Papers*. Edited by L. Goldman. Oxford: Oxford University Press.
Khaitan, T. (2021). Balancing Accountability and Effectiveness: A Case for Moderated Parliamentarism. *Canadian Journal of Comparative and Contemporary Law*, 7 (1) 81–155.
Lijphart, A., ed. (1992). *Parliamentary versus Presidential Government*, Oxford: Oxford University Press.
Linz, J., & Valenzuela, A., eds. (1994). *The Failure of Presidential Democracy: The Case of Latin America*, Baltimore: Johns Hopkins University Press.
Samuels, D., & Shugart, M. (2010). *Presidents, Parties, and Prime Ministers – How the Separation of Powers Affects Party Organization and Behavior*, Cambridge: Cambridge University Press.
Shugart, M., & Carey, J. (1992). *Presidents and Assemblies. Constitutional Design and Electoral Dynamics*, New York: Cambridge University Press.
Strøm, K., Müller, W., & Bergman, T., eds. (2003). *Delegation and Accountability in Parliamentary Democracies*, New York: Oxford University Press.
Tavits, M. (2009), *Presidents with Prime Ministers. Do Direct Elections Matter?* New York: Oxford University Press.

38

Prerogative

*Thomas Poole**

'That's your prerogative'. Used in an everyday setting, the word prerogative conveys a reluctant acceptance of someone's entitlement to do something as of right, without someone else's say-so or approval. That is also its essence when used to describe the general or inherent executive capacities of government. But when we try to say more about prerogative in this sense, things go rapidly downhill. One obstacle is that, while prerogative is important within certain systems of law and government, it is not a feature of others, or at least not obviously so. An inquiry into the general nature of prerogative has to contest with the fact that it is a far from universal concept. Another difficulty relates to its elusive qualities. Prerogative often seems to inhabit the margins around and gaps within constitutional order. Its content and scope – the powers, perquisites and immunities that might at any one time be summoned in its name, so far as these can indeed be ascertained – change substantially over time. As a result, the concept is often approached obliquely, with correspondingly disappointing results. Descriptive accounts get mired in the historical and local, adding thinly sketched functional material for ballast. Big-picture accounts tend to reach for the mystical. From Blackstone's 'mysteries of the Bona Dea' through Schmitt's 'miracle' to Loughlin's 'sublation', no other constitutional term provokes so much quasi-religious cliché (Loughlin 2010).

Much of this chapter chases prerogative down the rabbit hole. Taking its cue from Locke's remark that, at the beginning of political organisation, 'the government was almost all prerogative', it starts from the proposition that prerogative reflects a basic form of rulership. It represents, that is, a rudimentary expression of the command function (or imperium), a function bound up with de facto control over a territory and population. More precisely, I take the term 'prerogative' to signify what remains of that command function once institutions of law and government instantiate themselves around that basic core and in so doing transform it. The primary constitutional meaning of prerogative relates, then, to the capacities that

[*] London School of Economics & Political Science

remain once the command function is subsumed and reshaped by the stabilisation, institutionalisation and juridification of power that we associate with the constitutionalising process.

Constitutional theory often distills the complex character of the self-reflexive administrative capacity that emerges from these social operations down to an order of rules (and rules about rules). Framed in juristic terms, the relevant question becomes how best to express the idea of prerogative as residual command function within the order of rules that the constitution provides. Much of the literature on that question tends to share the same characteristic and ultimately the same fault. Most older texts, and some newer ones, rely on the claim that prerogative in the sense that I have described retains its original or authentic political quality. While paying due attention to their subtleties and nuances, I read these texts primarily with a view to identifying this shared characteristic, what animates it and where it can lead. I argue that in general the authors of these texts presuppose the existence of a 'sovereign prerogative', that is, an authority inherent to government that is distinct from, prior to, and in some sense superior to law. They suggest, in other words, that the 'original' command function stays more or less intact throughout the constitutionalisation process, capable when need arises of emerging from beneath the constitution's normative institutional crust.

I argue that the model of sovereign prerogative fails on two counts. Analytically, the claim that prerogative is an original power attempts to ascribe to the concept of something that it cannot possibly possess. Whatever the historical trajectory of a constitution, there is no such thing as a natural or original constitutional power (save possibly for the constituent power that may be said to undergird it). As a result, what is presented as a natural or quasi-natural power is in reality a disguised claim about how power ought to be allocated. Normatively, the claim that prerogative is outside and in some sense above the law introduces instability into our conception of constitutional order by postulating two distinct sources of authority. It also, in so doing, opens a path to bypassing or dismantling institutional structures designed to reinforce the idea of government subject to law, threatening the promise of free and equal citizenship that constitutional order seeks to elaborate.

It is for these reasons that modern constitutional orders have by and large abandoned sovereign prerogative in favour of the idea of 'constitutional prerogative'. That model begins by rethinking the residual nature of prerogative. One can hardly expect the rudimentary expression of the state's command function to emerge unscathed from successive waves of constitutionalisation. Even if we imagine the modern prerogative or its functional equivalent as specifying some of the same functions as its 'original' ancestor, these are now encoded within vastly different institutional and ideational structures. Their constitutional meaning is to be recalibrated accordingly. Prerogative power is now either authorised by a constitution or assumed to have been so. This means that, whatever the precise form of the constitution in which it appears, constitutional prerogative is understood to be general executive power that is derived, enumerated and limited, an arrangement which brings potentially conflicting sources of normative authority into conceptual alignment. (It might also be said to do the same for the constitution's past and present.) To the extent that sovereign prerogative was animated by the search for the Statesman capable of navigating the ship of state by means of the prudent exercise of superior intelligence, constitutional prerogative anticipates an order of statespersons, insisting on collective responsibility for the common good even on matters of statecraft.

Lest this sounds too neat a reconciliation, the chapter concludes with a sting in the tail. There are good reasons why we might want to reserve certain important functions to the central executive and to grant in respect of the exercise of some of these functions a wider degree of latitude. It follows that even if we empty the category of prerogative of any special significance, it is not clear that we have done much more than to shift the terrain on which executive power-grabs and other expressions of constitutional 'backsliding' may occur. Constitutionalising prerogative may foreclose more obvious routes to over-centralising power. (I do not altogether discount the counterintuitive proposition, which may be what Locke believed, that maintaining a distinct category of prerogative makes constitutional corruption, in fact, less likely.) But it is not clear that the same holds for less obvious routes. If that is indeed the case, constitutional interest shifts from first-order questions circling around the disruptive potential of prerogative to second-order matters relating to the exploitation of 'pseudo prerogatives' derived from open-textured grants of statutory or constitutional authority, or from obsequious judicial interpretation. It is one thing formally to curtail the prerogative; quite another to curb the 'prerogative disposition'.

I PRELIMINARY OBSERVATIONS

If prerogative has a certain ragbag quality to it, that may be because its content varies considerably across time and place. Some constitutional traditions, indeed, seem to find no obvious room for prerogative power. But it is still possible to think of prerogative as typically containing powers relating to foreign relations, war, national security, public order, emergencies, citizenship, border control, office-holding and pardon. We can provisionally classify these powers as relating to the somewhat indeterminate category 'matters of state', a somewhat indeterminate category but one that reflects the assumed origins of prerogative in the command functions of rudimentary political order. Likewise, the prerogative used also to play an important role in conquest and empire, now considerably less in relevant topics. Constitutions sometimes also contain prerogative powers to summon, prorogue and dissolve the legislature. Prerogative powers do not usually give exclusive jurisdiction to the executive over the fields to which they relate, nor do they necessarily give it a free hand. Constitutions often make provisions for power-sharing in the domains over which prerogative once held sway.

The most obvious feature of these powers concerns how they are exercised. They are executive powers which do not need authorising legislation or prior legislative approval to have lawful effect, powers under which government acts 'as of right' and so discretionary in a strong sense. The informality of prerogative powers relative to how governmental power normally operates through a framework of public laws provides a clue to their material essence. The powers that fall within this category tend to correspond to areas where the custodial responsibility of government is to the fore, its duty to protect the state. It is generally thought that distinct qualities are required for these governmental functions to operate effectively – 'decision, activity, secrecy, and dispatch' in the formulation of *Federalist* No.70 (riffing on Blackstone 1979, p. 242). The juridical structure in which prerogative powers operate tends to give expression to this apparent imperative. We need to be careful for several reasons, not least since these sources of power become increasingly entwined in modern governmental structures, an important factor later in my argument (Tilly 1990). But it may not be entirely improper to identify law and prerogative as two species of command emanating from two distinct sources of power. If law is the product of the state understood as normative institutional order or *potestas*, then prerogative, or directive authority, seems to be tied with the material (especially military) force of the state or *imperium*. (Blackstone 1979, p. 254).

II IN SEARCH OF THE STATESMAN

While our interest lies in the particular concatenation of powers and duties that characterises the modern constitution in at least one of its forms, I start with a general argument concerning law and discretionary power which animates this tradition of inquiry. The argument for prerogative – or, more generally, sovereign directive authority – is not a claim about the general capabilities of a system of government in its entirety, its accumulated and aggregated institutional capacities, but one concerning the capacity of a single institution to act apart from its general institutional normative environment. At its sharpest, the prerogative claim is that an individual site of intelligence, whether individual human or select group, that forms part of an institutional normative order but is also capable of independent action, should be able to determine a different course of action from that which would otherwise be determined by that order.

Plato's dialogue *Statesman* offers something like an Urtext for this claim, not just for its defence of directive power but also in the qualifications it makes to it. True statesmanship, Plato argues, is the practice of the art of ruling. Like a doctor whose treatment must fit the needs of individual patients, if rulers truly possess the art of government we must let them do the job according to what their superior skill determines. From the ruler's perspective, laws are like heuristics, to be dispensed with if that is what he considers for the best. Since general laws cannot prescribe with accuracy what is best and just for each member of the community at any one time, it follows that 'the best thing of all is not full authority for laws but rather full authority for a man who understands the art of kingship and has wisdom'. Like the weaver, the art of governing is to blend warp and weft, different personality types that otherwise might conflict, into harmonious unity. Understood as an activity of continuous creation, the true Statesman's power, conceived as an activity of continuous creation, is the closest realisation in our fallen state to natural conditions of divine ordering. As it partakes in the divine, it ought to be considered absolute. Within this constitution, for Plato the one true constitution (all others being more or less imperfect copies), 'what matters is that with or without persuasion, rich and poor, according to a written code or against it, the ruler does what is really beneficial', even if it involves compulsion (Plato 1992, 294a, 297a).

The Statesman as doctor; the Statesman as weaver. These images evoke the idea of ruling as a directive enterprise in which the leader, primary locus of intelligence and will, acts upon or disciplines the populace. Plato explores the idea that the governing relationship is like that between a shepherd and his flock earlier in the dialogue, only to reject the comparison. He elaborates a myth, more science fiction than speculative anthropology, which imagines how life was for our distant ancestors. That first epoch, the 'age of Kronos', coincided with a universe geared to happiness in which everything from the movement of the planets to the care of earthly life was managed by gods. Our ancestors, a simple species of humans who sprang like flora directly from the earth, were cared for by demi-gods. These proto-humans, in any case simpler beings, perceived those charged with their care as natural superiors, and the governing relationship that ensued, simple and unquestioning, could indeed be said to take the form of a pastorate.

But this epoch ended once the empyrean polarities were reversed, sending the solar system spinning in the opposite direction. The proto-humans were wiped out in the resulting cataclysm, replaced by our direct ancestors, who had previously lain dead in the earth but are now formed in the womb. Things in this, our own 'age of Zeus' are disordered, chaotic, and destined for ultimate destruction. Gods have withdrawn from the active management of human affairs, leaving us without natural superiors. But with chaos comes complexity. Our new imbrication within family structures into which we are born gives rise to memory and, with it, politics. Faced with a disorienting and deteriorating world, the best we can do to hold calamity at bay is to find leaders who possess the science of ruling. But such leaders as emerge are no longer like shepherds since they too are human, and so lack something that marks them out beyond peradventure marks rulers as special. Into the resulting legitimacy vacuum step various 'rivals of the king', doctors, priests, generals, sophists and so on, each claiming some special pastoral role. The ruler's task is now both more specific and more difficult. They must attempt to replicate, so far as possible under conditions of disenchantment, the natural order that existed under divine order, by seeking to join together contrasting lives into a unity of concord and fellowship.

But it is not just the more complicated situation rulers face in stabilising the legitimacy of their rule that complicates what might appear a highly directive form of government. Plato also adds an important qualification to the Statesman's plenary power. It is only the true statesman, one 'willing and able to rule with moral and intellectual insight and to render every man what is his due according to divine and human law with strict fairness' (Plato 1992, 301d), who has the right to claim absolute authority over those under their care. But Plato acknowledges that, even with the right sort of education and training, such a character is vanishingly rare – certainly, he sees no-one in his own time as exhibiting the right qualities. Plato accepts the consequences of this for constitutional design. The ideal constitution cannot function without a true Statesman. In fact such a constitution is positively dangerous absent the true Statesman since it gives godlike power to mediocre men, 'party leaders … supreme imitators and tricksters'. When the false Statesman attempts to copy the true Statesman it is tyranny (Plato 1992, 303c, 301c). Under non-ideal conditions, which in effect are the conditions we almost always inhabit, the right course of action is to ensure that laws are strictly adhered to and rulers prevented from claiming any extra-legal power.

III CONSTITUTING THE PRINCE

Plato's text indicates how the idea of superior discretionary authority is pervasive within political thought. It also outlines an important space in which discussion over prerogative takes place: the search for natural leaders in the absence of natural leadership. As an exercise in constitutional theory, though, our interest is more specifically geared toward understanding the concept of prerogative within the modern constitution. But to do that we must first go backwards in order to chart how a medieval category, with roots in Roman juristic thought, was later adapted to modern conditions of statecraft. Though not wishing to obscure the considerable variation thrown up during this process of development, I suggest that two main models of prerogative can be discerned. The *princely* model accords the executive authority a sovereign prerogative: a discretionary power, or reservoir of authority, assumed to correspond to an original command function, which is capable of operating at its own determination outside the law and if necessary against it. The *republican* model describes a constitutional form of prerogative in which general executive capacities are dispersed into enumerated, though still often quite general, separate discretionary functions. These prerogatives are taken to be vested by the constitution in an executive authority and subject to (often second-best) constitutional constraints. For much of the relevant period, it was the princely form that dominated, in various guises. Only recently has the republican model taken hold of the field.

If, as some suggest, Western philosophy is just a set of footnotes to Plato, it is tempting to say the same about juristic thought and Rome, though the lineage is often convoluted. The ideas that shape constitutional discourse, including the core notion of power generated by and subject to law, derive from a body of jurisprudence, itself sourced in Roman law, which medieval canon lawyers developed to explicate the juristic character of the papacy as an imperial structure (Blumenthal 1988). Prerogative became an important part of that story as the juristic framework began to be deployed in respect of the power of the secular prince. We might say that it offered in that context an especially acute 'hard case', the elaboration of which helped to redefine the character and characteristics of lordship, the defining topic of the age (Bisson 2009). Conceptualised as a special power that the prince possessed in contradistinction to non-sovereign lords, prerogative helped cement the difference between the two and was, as such, bound up with the consolidation of power around the Crown (Post 1964). But thinking juridically about public power also helped to foster a different way of conceptualising public power, one which we might call doctrinal on account of its tendency to recast princely power in terms of specific sovereign rights and capacities. This new way of thinking in turn prompted new questions about sovereign capacity, specifically whether the prince's field of action was circumscribed by the legal nature of his power. Answers varied considerably, but the juristic pack could certainly be shuffled to more constitutionalist ends. We see in this period the English jurist Bracton adamantly reject the notion that the prince's will could be superior to law, interpreting the maxim 'what pleases the Prince has the power of Law' to give a conciliar, almost impersonal or suprapersonal, account of kingly rule (Pennington 1993, p. 92).

The modern prerogative only comes into view with the rise of government as a more serious proposition from sixteenth century onward, a development we assess presently. The medieval debate interests us mostly in so far as it shaped much of the basic grammar, the ideas-stock and word-hoard, through which modern conceptions were rendered. Two distinctions played a particularly important role in that later process, the first relating to the space in which medieval administration took place, the second rather more conceptual in nature. The first distinction – between *gubernaculum* and *jurisdictio*, government and law – expressed the idea that while there might be limits on his legal powers, the king enjoyed largely uncontrolled discretion in respect of his administration. Prerogative, as the public authority of the ruler, lay within the sphere of his government (McIlwain 2008). The second distinction divided ordinary and absolute kingly power – *potestas absoluta et ordinata* (Pennington 1993). The former operated within the interstices of the laws, though it was not strictly bound by it; the latter described an anterior and superior capacity to act outside the laws – though jurists would continue to disagree about whether this equated to a capacity to act wilfully or arbitrarily for as long as monarchy remained an active proposition (Burgess 1993).

IV BIRTH OF GOVERNMENT

One might assume that the search for the statesman, elusive enough in Plato's day, became less viable as societies became more complex. In the long run that assumption may be said to have held good. But not so in the medium term. The cult of the Statesman reached something of an apogee in early-modern Europe, just when the apparatus of government assumed greater sophistication. Despite the impetus toward political concentration and constitutional formation after the Reformation, and the development of the idea of a sovereign entity housed within an abstract and impersonal state, far from freeing themselves from the figure of the prince, most states in the period embraced forms of 'absolutism'. The dominant tendency, that is, was to centralise and streamline authority around the executive, the King and his ministers, dismantling the consensual apparatus that had emerged in the Middle Ages and eliminating articulated constitutional checks on the royal prerogative (Thornhill 2011, pp. 112, 117). Why this was so is a difficult question. Most likely it was a response, in a period of quite staggering dislocation, to the sense of things falling apart. But perhaps the Machiavellian turn toward the politics of 'reason of state' also reflected how new currents of scientific reason impacted the sphere of politics. One can easily imagine in such an environment how recent conceptual and technological developments in government might well have produced a clearer sense of the state's own instrumentality, of how institutional power could be effectively harnessed in the furtherance of particular interests.

To connect these developments to prerogative, I examine two early-modern thinkers, Gabriel Naudé and John Locke, one now vastly more celebrated but both equally representative for our purposes. While their accounts are perhaps closer than one might expect, the differences between them are important since they reflect, I argue, the two dominant modern conceptions of prerogative in embryo form. Naudé's unqualified embrace of the new science of statecraft, sequestered within an invigorated and professionalised office of the executive, offers a blueprint for modern sovereign prerogative. A characteristic mix of old and new, Locke's account of prerogative keeps the basic medieval template but re-equips it to match the demands of dynamic modern statecraft. Locke anticipates a significant role for independent prudential action on the part of the executive, particularly in crisis management. But unlike Naudé he embeds prerogative (though not always neatly) within an evolving body of law law and custom. In what remains an idiosyncratic attempt to reconcile decisive government with a liberty-sustaining institutional ecosystem, we catch in Locke a glimpse of the constitutional prerogative. But only a glimpse. His retention of the notion of prerogative as an original (and in certain respects superior) power prevents the integration of princely power within the interstices of constitutional order.

V MASTER-STROKES OF STATE

Gabriel Naudé spent most of his career in service to a papal diplomat. His *Considérations politiques sur les coups d'état* (1639) advocated extraordinary and secret executive action, so-called 'master-strokes of State' (*coups d'état*), the 'Bold and extraordinary Actions, which Princes are contrain'd to execute when their

Affairs are difficult and almost to be despair'd of, contrary to the common Right, without observing any Order or Form of Justice, but hazarding particular Interest for the good of the Publick'. The book became the most famous manual of statecraft representative of the Machiavellian type in the seventeenth century. The identification of the executive as a superior source of both intelligence and agency generates the claim for that office constituting a superior sovereign agency beyond law. The power to command is presented as a true and authentic source of power, with law (in as much as it is discussed at all) seen as an artificial, and hence much less protean, source of power. There is no trace here of the equivocation and compromises of the medieval jurists. Naudé's clear and logical presentation drives the conclusion that prerogative must trump law whenever the executive sees fit:

> This law which is so common, and ought to be the principal Guide of all the Actions of Princes, *Salus Populi suprema Lex esto*, Let the Safety of the People be the Supreme Law, absolves them from abundance of the little Circumstances and Formalities to which Justice would oblige them, so they are Masters of the Laws to extend or mitigate, or confirm or abolish them, not as may seem good to themselves, but as Reason and the Publick Safety require[.]

Ignore for a moment the parallels between this passage and Locke's familiar definition of prerogative. There is another side to Naudé's text besides its more headline-grabbing elements that deserves attention. The last chapter of *Considérations politiques* concerns the desired characteristics of the Minister in effective charge of government policy. An idealised portrait of Richelieu, with whom Naudé associated, these passages emphasise softer and quieter attributes of statecraft. Secrecy is still pervasive, as in the discussion of master-strokes, but Naudé now suggests that the Minister's role is generally best accomplished not by confrontational gestures but the delicate application of almost imperceptible nudges. An almost otherworldly detachment on the Minister's part is called for: he 'should live in the World as if he were out of it, and beneath the Skies as if he were above them'. Successful government is based on information gathering, Naudé concludes, requiring a calculating coldness in applying the new science of politics to predict the future and contain risks of disorder.

Combining the layers in Naudé's text reveals a conception of the modern executive in which the blending of magisterial and ministerial capacities produces a dense concentration of reason and energy. While some aspects are specific to Naudé, the general picture is characteristic of its time and place. Plato's influence is still palpable, though largely subterranean, notably in the invocation of the godlike capacity to rain a 'Thunderbolt' on unsuspecting adversaries 'before the Noise of it is heard in the Skies', and in the superhuman omniscience demanded of the Minister. But now the stabilising intellect at the centre of the vortex of politics is invested with the properties of a machine or automaton, a theme destined to have a considerable future. In this way, the medieval juristic framework, crafted for the world of lordship and landholding, is adjusted to the new politics of statecraft. The notion of a space operating at least partially outside the sphere of ordinary law and justice is retained, and a sharper edge given to the idea of the executive as repository of legitimate violence.

But Naudé's text reveals another change. While medieval commentators emphasised stability as the chief attribute of rulership, early-modern thinkers began to see the executive as dynamic, decisive and calculating, liberating it from the bonds of convention in two rationalising moves. First, the disassociation of office from the person of the ruler. Though centralised more effectively around the figure of the king, effective public power was increasingly being held by Ministers, who retain office by virtue of their professional abilities. Government takes on classic attributes of bureaucracy: the functionary (Minister) accepts a specific duty of loyalty to the job and is at the service, not as before to a person (King), but of an objective and impersonal goal built into the organisation to which he is linked (State).

The second move works on the language of ordinary and absolute royal authority, realigning it to produce a dichotomy of prerogative and exception. Squarely aligning the power to command with new strategic imperatives, the move borrows heavily from the foreign policy field, itself recently reconfigured. Prerogative, in this new formulation, becomes the domestic analogue of diplomacy, its primary function being to coordinate inter-institutional dynamics through the application of prudence and persuasion. State power grows as the network of office holders increases, and the task of the executive, the nerve cell of this expanding operation, becomes more demanding and more important as a result. This understanding of prerogative as a category of directive communication, capable of ad hoc formulation as well as being expressed as rules, is exemplified in the quieter side of Naudé's exposition. But the portrayal is also consistent with the way prerogative would be discussed in Enlightenment thought. Blackstone, the most important eighteenth century legal analyst of prerogative, also highlighted prerogative's mediating capacity. (The same is true of Necker.) When 'balanced and bridled', Blackstone wrote, prerogative 'invigorates the whole machine and enables every part to answer the end of its construction'. Note the recurrence of the image of the machine. (Blackstone 1979, p. 233)

Blackstone's account deliberately excludes the exception (Blackstone 1979, p. 243). If the modern prerogative shadows diplomacy, the exception mirrors war and its potentially future-shaping logic. In recognising the capacity of decisive governmental action to effect potentially rupture-inducing moments, it reflects a distinctly modern understanding of the transformative possibilities of politics. The refashioning of prerogative helps inaugurate a new conceptual space, defined by the capacity consciously to make and remake constitutions, and which also become a feature Enlightenment thought. Take Rousseau as an example. His republicanism has no place for the kingly paraphernalia of Blackstone's *Commentaries*, including princely prerogatives. But his theory does advance a number of exceptional institutions: not only the dictator, who wields command authority in times of crisis, but also the enigmatic Legislator, who assumes a pre-eminent role in establishing a new constitution for the republic. Classical echoes are unmistakable. Yet the institution is nonetheless defiantly modern. Where the Statesman aims to knit together a pre-formed or natural political community, the Legislator must devise and inaugurate a new constitutional order by translating principles of political right into the conditions of that particular society. The Legislator's two main tasks thus resemble the two dimensions of Ministerial power in the *Considérations politiques*. To succeed in their respective roles, the Legislator and the Minister must possess singular political skills, combining the flamboyant, decisive and uncompromising on one hand, with the softer, more subtle and flexible on the other – both éclat and élan.

VI CONSTITUTIONALISING THE KING

Taking his cue from Naudé, whom we know Locke read, and the civil law writers on regal power and prerogative, Locke defined prerogative as a reserve power to command that operates outside and against the laws. 'This Power to act according to discretion, for the publick good, without the prescription of the Law, and sometimes even against it, is that which is called Prerogative' (Locke 1988, §160). Though there are certainly affinities between Naudé and Locke's work on prerogative, these should not be overemphasised. Naudé gives the impression of the executive as uncontrolled controller, rightful possessor of a monopoly of both political wisdom and violence, whereas in Locke's considerably subtler portrayal executive power is both weak and strong, subordinate and not subordinate. But perhaps the chief difference between the two is that Locke seeks to integrate a prudential account of executive power within a wider constitutionalist vision. Prerogative properly so called – that is executive discretionary power as opposed to arbitrary lordship – operates for Locke within an evolving band of law and custom which exerts non-trivial constraints on its exercise.

Locke generally refers to the active arm of government as the executive: the body, constitutionally subordinate to the legislative, that executes the laws. But he refers to the same institution when exercising prerogative power as 'the Prince' (or simply 'the King'). The choice indicates that Locke understands prerogative as a distinct mode of public power that implicates a different structure of authority from action under rules. The Prince, whether monarch or republican leadership, holds this special power in reserve for use at its discretion where the laws are not enough, either because the laws are silent or because what they prescribe is seen as obstructive to the public good. (The point works the other way: the Prince is identifiable as Prince because these powers are at its disposal.). But the terminological choice also shows how prerogative provided Locke with an entry point for exploring the situated or de facto nature of executive power and, beyond that, the progression from more or less arbitrary lordship to for the more structured and contained governmental discretion that characterises free association.

Taking first the idea of prerogative as a distinct source of authority, it might seem from Locke's illustrative examples that the power is restricted to public emergency situations. But that is not the case – nor can it be, on Locke's view. Prerogative emerges from the fact that the body in question exercises the functions of a supreme executive agent. It rests on a capacity to command the material resources of the state, or what Locke calls the 'force of Society', in situations where it is necessary to do so to secure the public good, which is a paramount obligation. Whereas the legal side of the office of government engages the executive capacity to implement the laws faithfully and justly, prerogative engages government's capacity as guardian or custodian of the political association. But since it does not source its authority in law, prerogative cannot itself make new laws, though it can generate rule-giving instruments – orders, measures, promulgations or edicts – that are authoritative to their addressees but do not carry the force of law.

More attention tends to be given to the social-contractual aspect of Locke's theory than its more evolutionary aspect. But the more developmental side of his thought, which features an account of how law and government gradually replace violence and arbitrary force, though always present, comes to prominence in the chapter of prerogative. I think there are two reasons for this. One is that Locke sees prerogative as a conventional power, de facto in nature whose effective parameters at any one time are largely determined by the conventions that have grown up around it. The second relates to the idea of trust, a central feature not just of prerogative but of all Locke's politics. What we are presented with on this front appears at first as an elemental, even back-to-basics, account of trust in the prerogative situation. The extra-legal status of prerogative, the way its exercise involves the Prince stepping outside of normal institutional power structures, sets the individual face to face with the Prince. That predicament, as Locke notes in a rather cryptic passage, resembles conditions encountered at a more rudimentary stage of political development:

> It is easy to conceive that in the infancy of governments, when commonwealths differed little from families in number of people, they differed from them too but little in number of laws: and the governors, being as the fathers of them, watching over them for their good, the government was almost all prerogative. A few established laws served the turn, and the discretion and care of the ruler supplied the rest.
> (Locke 1988, §162)

Some read this as a claim that we experience in prerogative a reversion from mature government (institutional normative order) to a more basic mode of rulership (interpersonal lordship) (e.g. D. Kelly 2017). But that reading is a poor fit with the rest of the chapter – let alone the rest of the *Second Treatise*. Locke says as much himself. He accepts that, since it can involve the Prince going out on a limb, prerogative may induce instability, but he is at pains to suggest that in practice this very rarely happens. This is not, as it can be read, the triumph of hope over experience. It is a reflection on the embedded nature of prerogative as we experience it. With the prerogative in its modern constitutional setting – that is, the context mapped by the *Second Treatise* – any 'reversion' to lordly discretion takes place within a conventional setting, one built up over time, that is normatively dense and populated by institutions. Even if those norms and institutions sometimes take a back seat, particularly in acute emergencies, their constitutional status is not disturbed by prerogative. Their presence conditions prerogative. This means that 'prerogative' in the sense used in the passage just quoted to describe rudimentary political forms is quite different from 'prerogative' in the modern sense of the term, understood as a category nested within a *habitus* of constitutional rule. Locke's prerogative (and ours) occupies a distinctive space within a settled deliberative ecosystem largely conditioned by law. Not only must its exercise reflect a good-faith attempt to stabilise the existing constitutional arrangements, as Locke stipulates, but also the effective power that can be claimed in its name is largely pre-determined by the conventions that enfold it.

This reading of Locke centres on the taming of prerogative, while recognising its continued prudential importance in modern statecraft. But it would be wrong to ignore the more unruly elements within his exposition, which can give the impression that Locke focuses on prerogative precisely to explore the never completely tameable nature of power (e.g., Dunn 1969). There is no question that Locke also sees prerogative, or prerogative-induced rupture, as an occasion for rebirth and reinvigoration, a position he interprets in political-theological terms, and that this perspective helps reinforce the idea that the executive's independent source of authority is more basic than the legal power of the state (Bates 2012). Calling prerogative an original power does much to sustain the claim for its supervening capacity over law. But it is at odds with the broader vision offered in the *Second Treatise* of government under law. There is an obvious tension between a civilising narrative which lauds the growth of law and government and the displacement of lordly discretion on the one hand, and an originality narrative which accepts, and sometimes celebrates, the special nature of de facto princely power as compared with institutional normative order on the other. As we shall see, later writers who adopted the same, broadly Lockean, strategy of squeezing and semi-taming prerogative also struggled with this tension.

VII LAW AND LEGISLATION

The writers considered so far wrote when legislation had yet to rise 'to the dignity of a general proposition'. Prerogative occupied more of the terrain on which governmental action took place (e.g., Hale 1976). Law's main task was to put a hedge around the space in which administration took place – directly through setting explicit statutory limits to what government was allowed to do, or indirectly through the allocation to legal subjects of rights and duties that could only be altered by legislation.

That model changed dramatically with the acceptance of legislation in the modern sense and the growth of the state's administrative capacities. Legislation answers the particular needs of modernity for government and self-government, facilitating the organisation of complex social interactions on the basis of a publicly accessible and presumptively coherent grand plan. The 'positivity' of legislation can be understood not just in the basic sense of the *source* of law as an expression of the will of the legislator, but also in a second sense, relating to its *function* – its capacity to place itself at the service of rational projects aimed at altering social reality (Baranger 2018). Authorisation for public action under general rules laid down by the legislator went over time from being an option, to normal practice, to a principle of government. This development, the practical adoption of the model of government authorised and limited by law, amounts to a process of constitutionalisation in the 'small c' sense. With the executive now working predominantly within the institutional structures of representative government, energy and reason, which previously might be seen as the preserve of the executive alone, become associated more closely with law and action under law.

If the widespread acceptance of legislation in its modern sense, grounded in the politics of interest, is the story of the nineteenth century, then a second development, the creation of a dense and complex bureaucracy that was the by-product of the age of reform, is more of a twentieth-century affair. To many, this new administrative state presented an instrument for realising social improvement. But others were unnerved by its machine-like quality, its unknowability and unpredictability, its apparent disdain for established patterns. Two juristic critiques emerged. The first targeted the way the administrative state seemed to dilute constitutional principles, including the rule of law and separation of powers (e.g., Dicey 2007). The second saw it as the triumph of technocracy over politics, and as such a lessening of what it means for a political community to be truly, authentically alive.

We associate the second critique with Carl Schmitt, for whom modern administration – or, rather, the absence of leadership he thought it entailed – was the death of politics and an assault on law properly understood (Schmitt 1991 [1919]). Schmitt is in some ways the natural inheritor of Naudé. Another in search of the Statesman, his work attempts to reconfigure princely prerogative to the radically unstable conditions of twentieth-century Europe. If Locke's tendency is to tame prerogative, Schmitt plans to unleash it. Prerogative represents for him an antidote to the political ills of the age, a means of escape from legal positivism, factional politics and the soulless logic of bureaucratic order into an authentic politics invested with a higher form of 'concrete' reason geared to preserving the political community as a substantive whole.

Schmitt's systematic realignment of the framework of prerogative and the exception gives him a route back to 'the political', to a politics that is substantive rather than procedural, decisive not deliberative, existential rather than concerned with muddling through. The centrepiece of this framework is to be found in Schmitt's characterisation of politics in terms of the friend/enemy distinction, which postulates that a group self-identifies as a political unit through its decision as to who counts as enemy. Schmitt identifies the designation of enemy with a preparedness to fight (Schmitt 1996 [1932]). It is the freighted quality of this designation, he suggests, which creates the peculiar density characteristic of political association. The political decision is the mechanism through which a multitude becomes a unity. Its essence inheres in a double movement: establishing an external boundary between 'us' and 'them' instigates an internal boundary between the law that binds 'us' and the condition of non-law that relates to, or concerning our relations with, 'them'.

Schmitt understood the dynamics that resulted from the enemy designation as a cascade, shaping the quality of the laws and decision-making within the shadow of those laws at the general level as well as the particular, and on a daily basis as well as in constitutional 'moments'. The political decision should be allowed to radiate, he argued, in as unmediated a way as possible throughout the constitutional order. Public law is ideally subject to and structured by the political, its content formed by iterative determinations on the enemy made most naturally in the constitution's outward-facing dimensions. The dominant theme of the treatise *Constitutional Theory* (1928) is precisely this prioritisation of the 'positive' concept of the constitution, 'the constitution of the complete decision over the type and form of the political unity', over the constitution in the negative or normative sense, referred to as the bourgeois Rechtsstaat. 'The political decision, *which essentially means the constitution*, cannot have a reciprocal effect on its subject and eliminate its political existence. *This political will remains alongside and above the constitution*' (Schmitt 2008 [1928], pp. 125–126).

Schmitt used the idea of 'the exception' to make sense of the internal ramifications of the political decision. The exception denotes a general category of constitutional theory and not merely a construct applied in emergency situations (though it is that too). It nonetheless remains opaque, since it is applicable to a range of phenomena, and is in certain respects misnamed, since Schmitt insists that the 'exception' should also be infused within the 'normal'. For the sake of clarity, I reserve the term 'exception' for a constitutional moment or similar event in which the constitutional order undergoes radical change, especially as a result of extra-constitutional action. I use the word 'prerogative' to describe the phenomenon Schmitt describes as operating at the everyday and particular level, that is, largely within the interstices (and around the margins) of the legal. My use of the term prerogative to describe one part of the operation of the political, though it is not an especially common term in his works, does have some textual support. Discussing the association between legal and theological concepts in *Political Theology*, Schmitt suggests that prerogative is 'analogous to the miracle in theology' (Schmitt 1985 [1922], p. 36). Just as the miracle transcends the laws of the natural world, so does prerogative exceed the bounds of the 'normal' legal system. Both share the structure of a capacity for extraordinary intervention invoked by a powerful figure.

On Schmitt's reading, the prerogative becomes the internal, intra-systemic analogue of the political ('exceptional') decision over who constitutes the enemy. Political decision and prerogative are *constitutive* of sovereignty: 'Sovereign is he who decides the exception.' (Schmitt 1985 [1922], p. 5) Note how the prerogative agent is here as elsewhere assumed by Schmitt as an individual man – the decisive leader, whose decisions express the will of the people, channeling his 'principally unlimited authority' (Schmitt 1985 [1922], p. 12) above or against the existing legal framework to the extent that he thinks necessary (Schmitt 2004 [1932], p. 69). Schmitt's theory foregrounds constitutional moments, situations of crisis, emergency or upheaval, but it does so in order to describe the constitutional normal. He sees these limit cases as showing us the way things really are. They uncover the pulsating life that we tend otherwise to stuff behind a juridical veneer. These elemental political moves animate the constitutional state through the radiating effect of prerogative. It is the means by which the exception becomes quotidian.

VIII THE PREROGATIVE STATE

Schmitt's argument for the supervening capacity of prerogative over law, based on the decisive character of the executive agent, is broadly familiar. So too are the oppositions that animate it: the authentic vs. the artificial, original vs. derived power, life vs. death (trapped in the machine). All are standard features of the general theory of princely prerogative. We have given space to Schmitt because of his bravura handling of those themes and because his work represents certainly, as specifically *constitutional* thought, a culmination of that theory. We also have a fairly good idea of what Schmitt's ideas looked like in practice. Though not the particular brand of (rightist authoritarian) concrete order he wanted, the Nazi regime, which Schmitt soon vociferously supported, contained many elements consistent with his theory. In his seminal work on the legal origins of the Nazi dictatorship, *The Dual State* (1941), Ernst Fraenkel identified Schmitt as the main theoretician of the National-Socialist state, turning to the term 'prerogative' to describe its basic juridical orientation. The system was a 'dual state', he argued, in the sense that 'the prerogative state', representing a special, floating, open-ended, politically-driven jurisdiction, hovered over 'the normative state' or institutional normative order.

Fraenkel's direct engagement with the Nazi legal system – though Jewish, as a great war veteran he was allowed to practice law until 1938, often representing dissidents (Morris 2020) – enabled him to distinguish the prerogative from the normative uses of law and to recognise the different ways *both* were made to serve the transition to dictatorship (Meierhenrich 2018). But the main driver of that process was unquestionably the semi-cannibalisation of the normal by the exception. Prerogative within the Nazi order took on the character of a general reservation – a supervening power that enabled 'the political', the content of which was the sole province of the regime, to float above the legal, intervening whenever so desired to divert, subvert or otherwise trump the operation of law: 'the presumption of jurisdiction rests with the Normative State. The jurisdiction over jurisdiction rests with the Prerogative State' (Fraenkel 2017 [1941], p. 57). The inversion of law and prerogative was consistent with what were in effect the martial law foundations of the Third Reich and in turn fed 'the cynical contempt for law which prevails among the power-intoxicated clique now dominating Germany' (Fraenkel 2017 [1941], p. 27). It is for *law* now to be tamed, and for prerogative to do the taming. In all its myriad forms – directions, commands, memos, suggestions, asides, even suppositions – prerogative is little more than a juridical veil for the wellspring of violence which fuels the regime.

IX THE REPUBLICAN PREROGATIVE

The year 1945 saw the end of the Nazi regime. It also marked the end of the primacy of prerogative in princely form, i.e. an original power to command with the capacity to supervene over law, a step which England had taken, despite what Locke might say, in 1689. The twentieth century had thrown up more than enough examples to skewer the fallacy of assuming that the proposition 'the true Statesman is one who breaks the laws' entails the conclusion that 'one who breaks the laws is a true Statesman'. Enough people now seemed to realise that there is no Statesman, at least of this sort, worth waiting for. Earlier, we encountered a wave of 'small c' constitutionalism, bound up with the rise of legislation, which instituted the principle that government should seek authority for its actions through enacted law. This principle, rolled back in many places under conditions of authoritarianism, re-emerged after the War as a tenet of liberal democracy. But this post-war consensus accommodated more substantive constitutional principles. The part of that development that interests us is how prerogative is closed around more tightly by law and a supporting culture of legality – the squeezing strategy we saw in Locke – but also and more deeply how the conceptual space occupied by prerogative is itself reconfigured so that its claim to act legitimately outside or above law are severely curtailed.

This development, which I call the constitutional prerogative, contains three central elements. While standard features of the post-war boom in constitution-making, parallel developments occurred in other forms of constitution. First, the rejection of the idea of prerogative as an original or authentic power of government. Like any other species of executive power, prerogative is now understood as a derived power authorised by a superior source, namely the constitution. It is as such subordinate to law, which represents the determination of the common good that is supreme within the constituted order. Second, the rejection of the idea of open-textured prerogative. The constitutional prerogative is enumerated: constitutions allocate to government particular prerogative functions (general executive powers) rather than acknowledge a pre-existing reservoir of discretionary prerogative authority. Third, the rejection of the idea of prerogative as inhabiting a space outside law and justice. The modern constitution makes sustained attempts to ensure control of prerogative powers consistent with their discretionary character. This may involve the specification of various 'second-best' design elements, such as ex-post legislative oversight and judicial review, that bring supervision of prerogative closer to the constitutional norm.

Though in many ways a distinctly modern phenomenon, the constitutional prerogative also has rather a long history. In *The Dual State*, Fraenkel continually juxtaposes the authoritarian regime he is describing with the English normative tradition, even describing the twentieth-century movement culminating in Fascism as 'a reaction against the heritage of the English revolutionary movements of the seventeenth century' (Fraenkel 2017 [1941], p. 48). The core of that tradition lay, he believed, in a hostility towards unconstrained prerogative allied to a scepticism of 'fancied emergencies'. The intuition seems to be that the constitutional subordination of prerogative, institutionally embodied in Parliament and the courts, is what really fuels the rule of law tradition, British constitutionalism's most important contribution to general constitutional theory. The same intuition animates Bagehot's well-known comment about the British constitution being a Republic that has insinuated itself beneath the folds of a Monarchy (Bagehot 2001).

If Fraenkel is right, there ought to be a seventeenth-century revolutionary root to these political sentiments. Though Locke fits broadly within this tradition, as we have seen, tensions remain in his work as a result of the retention of something resembling sovereign prerogative in an otherwise strongly constitutionalist account. We find a clearer statement of the thesis, which denies the prince any special original capacity and insists that the people hold all sovereign power some of which they may choose to vest in an executive agent, articulated by English revolutionary republicans (Poole 2015). Harrington's *The Commonwealth of Oceana* (1656), the most philosophically rewarding republican text, is an account of the founding of a republican constitution for England. Convinced that to secure political change you must change not just the system of government but the ideational framework in which it operates, Harrington insists that ultimate sovereignty within the constitution of Oceana always rests in the people: 'this free-born nation liveth not upon the dole or bounty of one man but, distributing her annual magistracies and honours with her own hand, is herself King People' (Harrington 1992 [1656], p. 98). This rhetorical crowning of the people has material implications. The term 'prerogative', previously associated with lords and kings, is now the property of the people. The people themselves are named the 'prerogative tribe', and wield the legislative power and the power of judicature. The executive or magistracy, a dedicated office of government, is placed firmly under the law, its officers publicly accountable for their actions.

This radical account of prerogative would have been inconceivable without various precursors – not just Machiavelli (of the *Dialogue*) whose influence loomed large over the English republicans but also the new political philosophy of Reformed Protestantism, notably Althusius's *Politica* (1603). The latter in particular, a theory of the self-governing polity established by citizens on the basis of consent expressed through binding covenants, contains an account of constitutionally derived and legally constrained magistracy at least as uncompromising as the one presented in *Oceana*. But one of the distinctive features of Harrington's inquiry relates to what we call, and he very nearly did, public reason. His theory manages to incorporate the politics of interest, then a cutting-edge category for understanding political action embracing prudential calculation, strategic thinking and reason of state. Harrington's objection is not to reason of state itself, which is a function of every state, but reason of state understood in terms of the private interest of particular rulers or ruling elites. To ensure against the latter, the existing political structure must be changed so that public reason prevails. The constitution should contain, then, various devices to guard against private-interest capture, including election, rotation, accountability and the agrarian law (a 'perpetual law' limiting wealth and property-holding).

X THE CONSTITUTIONAL PREROGATIVE

This may seem a little removed from the constitutional mainstream. But support for Fraenkel's position can also be found in A. V. Dicey, for whom prerogative and the rule of law were constant preoccupations. In terms of the narrative being advanced here, he is best understood as a liminal figure. In *The Law of the Constitution*, his chief work, prerogative is discussed in two ways. The first interpretation appears when writing directly on the subject. Dicey defines prerogative as 'the remaining portion of the Crown's original authority' and is as such 'the name for the residue of discretionary power left at any moment in the hands of the Crown, whether such power be in fact exercised by the King himself or by his Ministers' (Dicey 2013, p. 189). On this interpretation, prerogative is what the modern constitution retains from medieval kingship. Though the angle of inquiry is different, the substance of this position is not far removed from Locke. Both think of prerogative as subject to a long-term process of reduction, squeezed by tightening bands of law and sentiment. Both also assume that throughout this prerogative retains its character as a pre-existing, authentic and sovereign capacity – as 'the Crown's original authority' in Dicey's phrase. The same tension we found in Locke is to be found in (this version of) Dicey. On the one hand, we are told that the modern prerogative recognises a basic shift in the character of lordship. On the other, we are asked to assume the existence of an older and (in some sense) truer type of lordship that still animates prerogative in the present. The declining role of the monarch by Dicey's time makes the tension between those positions, if anything, more acute.

But Dicey offers a second interpretation of prerogative. In his extensive writings on martial law, a major topic of public interest, he accepted the orthodox characterisation of the situation as one involving the use of prerogative in situations of civil disorder or breakdown. Many contemporary writers understood martial law as an incident of a sovereign prerogative of war and peace, to which many would have given almost unlimited scope, especially in the imperial context. But this approach felt to Dicey too much like the French idea of the 'state of siege', in which constitutional guarantees are suspended, a position he regarded as anathema to British constitutionalism. He presented a very different conceptualisation of martial law, one which saw it as simply a manifestation of the general common law right and duty to suppress breaches of the peace. Though in practice that right might generally be invoked by government, that is just for the sake of convenience: in principle, the right is held by all legal subjects. There is no difference in law between the basic position of officials and ordinary citizens. Both are authorised to employ the force necessary to subdue breaches of the peace, and they are equally accountable in law if they use excessive or unnecessary force (Dicey 2013, pp. 352–366).

Dicey's analysis of martial law, striking in its egalitarian simplicity, mirrors his account of the rule of law (Dyzenhaus 2009b). It asks us not to abandon that idea, and the aspiration to restrain sovereign violence contained within it, even when threatened with serious disorder. The differences between his two treatments of prerogative should not be overstated. They both push in the same direction, an assertion of law and norm against force and exception. But the second interpretation is to be preferred, precisely because it does not assume the continuation in more or less pristine form of a type of power through which embryonic political order was formed. Whether constitutional order did in fact originate in that way does not matter. What matters is the way we think about the proper arrangement of power – who can claim what when – in the now and into the future.

This standpoint matters because it undercuts the assumption underlying the sovereign prerogative in the tradition from Naudé to Schmitt and which continues to exert a baleful influence on discussions involving prerogative to this day. For them, the core idea is that certain matters of state are best decided by a select individual or group, ideally possessing special characteristics. The republican response is that, however special, a select individual or group will tend to confuse the best interest of the state with its own best interest. Sovereign prerogative is private reason. It follows that the whole phenomenon of the Statesman is misconceived, even a little juvenile. The question of personality – whether a ruler is good, bad or ugly – is almost a side-issue. It is not about searching for the Statesman, but creating an order of statespersons. True politics, geared to the identification and realisation of the common good, demands procedural mechanisms that comprise conditions under which public reason can (or should) eventuate. It is a profoundly collective enterprise, a matter of democratic procedure (the common interest should be discussed by all) but also of democratic outcomes (the common interest). This approach must apply at least as much to important matters of state as to other matters of public interest. If there is a functional requirement for secrecy or small-group decision-making, then these can be put in place. But they must continue to operate within the interstices and under the control of the democratic institutions.

CONCLUDING REFLECTIONS

What I have said about constitutional prerogative might be open to the challenge that it addresses what is ultimately a substantive issue through a largely formal lens. That challenge can be partially deflected by observing that constitutional design is as much conceptual as institutional. Rearranging the way things are done influences how we perceive those things in the first place. It shapes expectations about what power ought to look like and how it ought to be used. But this cannot be a complete answer to the charge. As Marchamont Nedham, another Cromwell-era republican, was quick to realise, it is one thing to the kill a king, quite another to kill 'the king thing'. When it comes to political constitutions, that is to say, the relationship between institutional, conceptual and attitudinal structures is necessarily complex. Law and legality, save perhaps in a purely formal sense, is as much about culture – and habit – as institutions and processes. Especially where the unpurged relic of lordship continues to exert a hold over would-be subjects of aspirant lords, we can and do see the rise of a prerogative disposition among leaders even in cases where the constitution seems to shut off avenues for action under prerogative properly understood (Butler 2004, p. 56). This can take many forms but often includes action technically or ostensibly within the law but whose real effect is to stymie or circumvent its operation. Leaders who make these moves usually exhibit a careless or dismissive attitude to law and stress the primacy of decisive political leadership (Sajó 2021).

Prerogative operates at the hard end of constitutional politics, at the nexus where political violence, order, power and law meet. But it is not just this feature that makes it fascinating. It is also the way it makes us confront the past. I do not mean by this that with prerogative we encounter a long history of discretionary rulership that goes back beyond the age of kings, though this is true. It is more that this is a history that confronts us with its own historicity. The study of prerogative involves sifting through the various stories that have been told about it, stories which themselves have historical dimensions. Some would dismiss, or even celebrate, this as myth-making, something society does in order to make sense of itself politically. And there is no doubt an element to this. But we can also see it as applied conceptual history. One characteristic of that pursuit is to offer an account of how we got to this point by describing how things were at earlier points or at the outset. Though an exercise in rationalisation oriented to the present, it is also a method that incorporates historical data as part of the process of making sense of the concept being accounted for.

This process is not peculiar to prerogative. I think it goes to the heart of constitutional inquiry. Certainly, this is true if one studies constitutions first and foremost in terms of a process of ordering. Seen in long-term historical perspective, constitutions may be said to produce order of a certain character through the reassembling of base elements, most often fragments of order whether sourced in brute force, charisma, or the scratched surface of well-worn custom. Prerogative is a particularly interesting case of how, in repurposing the bric-à-brac of the past, constitutions also construct, even colonise, history. To the extent that prerogative is preserved in modern constitutions, it owes its continued existence to a process of recognition that is also a subordination and which generates an inclusion that is also partly exclusionary. Constitution implies reconstitution.

RECOMMENDED READING

Blackstone, W. (1979). *Commentaries on the Laws of England*, vol. I. Edited by S. Katz. Chicago: University of Chicago Press.
Butler, J. (2004). *Precarious Life: The Powers of Mourning and Violence*, London: Verso
Dicey, A. V. (2013). *The Law of the Constitution*. Edited by J. W. F. Allison. Oxford: Oxford University Press.
Fatovic, C. (2009). *Outside the Law: Emergency and Executive Power*, Baltimore: John Hopkins University Press.
Fraenkel, E. (2017). *The Dual State: A Contribution to the Theory of Dictatorship*, Oxford: Oxford University Press.
Locke, J. (1988). *Two Treatises of Government*. Edited by P. Laslett. Cambridge: Cambridge University Press.
Mansfield, H. (1989). *Taming the Prince: The Ambivalence of Modern Executive Power*, New York: Free Press; London: Macmillan.
Meinecke, F. (1957). *Machiavellism: The Doctrine of Raison d'État and Its Place in Modern History*. Translated by D. Scott. Introduction by W. Stark. London: Routledge.
Naudé, G. (2020). *Political Considerations upon Refin'd Politicks, and the Master-Strokes of State*. Translated by W. King. Edited by K. Watson. Independently published.
Plato (1992). *Statesman*. Translated by J. B. Skemp. Edited by M. Ostwald. Indianapolis and Cambridge: Hackett Publishing.
Poole, T. (2015). *Reason of State: Law, Prerogative and Empire*, Cambridge: Cambridge University Press.
Schmitt, C. (1985). *Political Theology: Four Chapters on the Concept of Sovereignty*. Translated by G Schwab. Cambridge, MA: MIT Press.

39

The Administrative State

Blake Emerson

The "administrative state" encompasses all those concrete arrangements of government in which constitutional theories are put to work. For instance, the republican-constitutional value of the rule of law is realized in the executive branch's implementation of legislation, judicial review of administrative acts, and bureaucratic structures that constrain the exercise of official discretion. But the administrative state does not merely fill up the details that constitutional theory outlines. Rather, administration consistently problematizes the constitution. It raises, configures, and provisionally resolves constitutional problems.

This chapter will examine the relationship between the administrative state and constitutional values and structures with reference to German and American legal and political theory. There are, of course, many other rich traditions of theorizing administration. But German and American thought are an important pair because the political histories of each are strikingly different yet linked together by common concerns and a shared intellectual history (Emerson 2019). This chapter recovers from these intertwined traditions three analytical approaches to the administrative state. The analytical framework draws inspiration from scholarship in public administration (Cook 2014), political science (Orren & Skowronek 2004), and comparative law (Rose-Ackerman 2017; Fisher 2007). The first analytical approach understands the administrative state to *implement* the constitution. The second understands the administrative state to *generate* new constitutional structures and values. The third understands the administrative state to *displace* the constitution with patterns and practices of rule that lie outside of the existing governance structure.

These frameworks foreground normative analysis of how the administrative state ought to relate to general democratic principles and the specific constitutional rules that institutionalize them. Here I contribute to a robust and growing literature on democracy and the administrative state, which treats welfare and regulatory agencies as potentially advancing rather than merely threatening popular self-government (Jackson 2022; Klein 2020; Ross 2018; Mashaw 2018; Rahman 2016; Rosanvallon 2011a; Richardson 2002). Scholars in this field vary in the degree to which they see administrative institutions as fitting squarely within existing democratic-constitutional arrangements or rather as creating new political configurations and commitments. I argue for a differentiated and developmental understanding of the relationship between democracy, constitution, and administration. The concrete administration of democratic values should allow constitutional rules to shift in light of social and historical context. The administrative state should not be strictly limited by, but rather should facilitate critical interrogation of, the constitution's current instantiation of democratic values. The administrative state can and should hold the constitution open for the introduction and proliferation of new institutional configurations and forms of public life.

I THE ADMINISTRATIVE STATE AND CONSTITUTIONALISM: THREE PARADIGMS

While the concept of the administrative state (*Verwaltungsstaat*) had been used occasionally in German scholarship since the nineteenth century (Cassese 2010), the term only came into wide circulation in the United States in the mid-twentieth century (F. M. Marx 1957; Waldo 1948). It referred to the state that had consolidated since the New Deal, in which a permanent bureaucratic officialdom played a central role in policymaking and implementation (Roberts 2020). This state was composed of civil servants, executive departments, and regulatory agencies, which stood in tension with extant political configurations and norms (Kornhauser 2015). Administrators were unelected officials who adjudicated disputes but were not part of the judiciary. They made rules with the force of law but were not part of the legislature. They enforced the law but were not strictly subject to presidential control. As the United States confronted fascism and totalitarianism abroad, the growth of bureaucratic government raised serious concerns about centralized, discretionary power at home (Ciepley 2006; Hayek 1944). Yet the administrative state confronted many analysts as a necessity of modern governance, deploying "expertness" to efficiently manage the economy and the complex constellation of interest groups within society (Landis 1938). Moreover, the administrative state did not arrive *ex nihilo*. It was created by the very constitutional branches – the legislature, and the executive, as well as the courts – which it sat uneasily alongside, between, and within.

The administrative state has once again become a subject of heated political and legal controversy in the United States today. Whereas the term in the US originally described a certain kind of state in which bureaucratic planning played a central role, today it usually refers to the administrative component of government, including in particular its regulatory agencies. Some conservative scholars condemn this administrative state as unconstitutional (Hamburger 2014; Lawson 1994). Chief Justice Roberts likewise expressed concern in *Free Enterprise Fund v. PCAOB* that the administrative state would "slip from the Executive's control, and thus from that of the people" (561 U.S. 477, 500 (2010)). Questions about the constitutional legitimacy of bureaucracy are hardly unheard of elsewhere, as in the long-standing discussion over the European Union's supposed "democratic deficit" (Murdoch, Connolly & Kassim 2018; Weiler, Haltern & Mayer 1995). Placing governmental power in the hands of the bureaucracy raises persistent worries about maintaining popular control and deliberative-democratic practices even in nations with longer histories of administrative governance. But the United States is perhaps unique in the intensity and constitutional tenor of disputes over the legality and legitimacy of national bureaucratic institutions. The investigations and impeachments of President Donald Trump pressed acutely on the conflict between presidential power and a "deep state" that constrains and even resists such political control (Skowronek, Dearborn & King 2021).

These anxieties and pathologies may be especially salient to the United States, but they aren't parochial. Rather, there are genuine, cosmopolitan problems of constitutional theory that the administrative state raises. These are best understood by taking a step back from the American context on its own and looking at a broader transatlantic discourse in which the administrative state emerged (Novak 2018; Stears 2002; Rodgers 1998; Kloppenberg 1986).

In the next sections, I disentangle three ways in which the administrative state has been understood to relate to constitutional structures and values in American and German thought: the administrative state as *instrumental* to the constitution, as *generative* of the constitution, and finally as *displacing* the constitution. These analytical frames inform normative arguments concerning the constitutional role of the administrative state, which variously treat the relations described as desirable, or as illegitimate, or even as downright dangerous. The discussion that follows touches on these evaluative perspectives in passing. Part III then outlines how these three models should together play a role within a developmental process of democratic constitutionalism.

The Administrative State Implements the Constitution

The administrative state is typically understood as an instrument or arm of constitutional government. That is to say, the body of officials, the organization of offices, and the procedural forms of administration implement already defined constitutional powers and values.

This instrumental understanding is most obvious in the alignment of the administrative state with the "executive power." The executive power is the power to put the law into effect, to enforce it against its addressees. To achieve consistent enforcement, the executive must be permanent or at least durable. John Locke accordingly described the executive as "*a Power always in being*, which should see to the *Execution* of the Laws that are made, and remain in force" (Locke 1988 [1689], §144). Without a permanent body to put the law into act, the law would be a norm without accompanying coercive power. As Alexander Hamilton observed in *Federalist* 70, "a government ill executed, whatever it may be in theory, must be in practice a bad government" (Hamilton 1961a [1788], p. 472).

Whether execution is "good" or "ill" on this model must first and foremost be judged by its fidelity to statutory law. Execution is a subordinate function, where a rule or a goal has already been set and the task of the executive is to make sure the rule is complied with or that the goal is pursued. The instrumental nature of administration makes efficiency paramount. An executive that carried out law in a way that was wasteful or ineffective with regards to the law's requirements and its ultimate ends would be deficient.

Locke and Hamilton's views predate the modern bureaucratic executive that took shape over the course of the nineteenth and twentieth centuries. But bureaucratic organization flows readily from the instrumental understanding. In the very first United States Congress of 1789, legislators established hierarchically organized, functionally differentiated departments of Treasury, Foreign Affairs, and War (Mashaw 2012). These ministries were not yet modern bureaucracies insofar as their officials were not salaried careerists; but in other respects the early American state mapped onto Max Weber's ideal type of bureaucracy (Parrillo 2014; Weber 1978). According to Weber, functional differentiation of government ministries enables specialization according to the competence of the officer and the jurisdictional grant. Hierarchical organization allows the heads of each ministry or department to control the conduct of subordinates so as to align the organization with publicly sanctioned purposes and interests. Bureaucratic organization institutionalizes "rational legal authority" by instituting "a continuous rule-bound conduct of official business" (Weber 1978, p. 218).

The instrumental understanding of the administrative state draws a sharp line between "politics and administration," the title of a pathbreaking work by one of the founders of American political science and public administration, Frank J. Goodnow (1900). "Politics," he argued, "has to do with policies or expressions of state will. Administration has to do with the execution of those policies" (ibid., p. 18). Administration encompassed the adjudication of concrete controversies between individuals and government as well as supervisory, scientific, technical, and accounting functions. Goodnow borrowed this distinction between the "will of the state" and the "deed of the state" from the German scholar Lorenz von Stein, who argued that "the deed must be subordinated to the will" so that the state's action was rational (Stein 1981 [1870], p. 14, author's trans.). For both Goodnow and Stein, administration was a matter of public action that corresponded to the general will that statutory law codified.

In order to ensure that the administrative act responds to the legislative will, both American and German theorists have relied on administrative hierarchy. The U.S. Constitution contemplates a hierarchical structure in which the President fulfills his duty to "take Care that the Laws be faithfully executed" by supervising the work of other executive and administrative officers (Metzger 2015). James Madison described a "chain of dependence" running from the elected president to appointed principal and inferior officers (Gales 1834, p. 499). Each subordinate officer is figuratively the instrument of their superior. In the context of the German federal republic, Ernst-Wolfgang Böckenförde (1987) spoke, in terms similar to Madison's, of a "chain of legitimation" running from the people to the legislature through to the hierarchical organization of the executive (ibid., p. 315, author's trans.). On this understanding, "the people" refers to the popular sovereign as a whole, which abstractly authorizes legislative and executive policymaking, rather than to any identifiable groups affected by administrative decision-making (Schmidt-Aßmann 1991).

There are, to be sure, important constitutional differences in how the implementation model operates. The American presidential system separates the president from the legislature and makes the former accountable to the people rather than to Congress. The German constitutional monarchies of the nineteenth century likewise bifurcated the executive from the legislature, placing the administrative staff subordinate to the crown, though of course the monarchs were not popularly elected. The Weimar Republic combined elements of presidential and parliamentary constitutions, whereas the contemporary Federal Republic is largely parliamentary. The instrumental conception of administration may be more or less apt for each of these arrangements. Under a parliamentary system, it appears to make good sense to treat the administration as an instrument of the law and of parliament, as the government is responsible to the parliament. Even if parliament and statutory law are not univocal, at the least the accountability of the government to the parliament aligns administration with the legislature. In constitutional monarchies and presidential systems, by contrast, the executive has its own source of legitimacy apart from legislation and its statutory enactment. It is, therefore, not entirely clear whether executive agencies in the United States are merely agents of the legislature or whether they may, also and separately, be instruments of the president's will (Pierce 1985; Kagan 2001). Some scholars accordingly propose that we consider the American administrative state as having two principals – the legislature and the president (Cox and Rodriguez 2020). Even in parliamentary systems where the executive is meant to be accountable to parliament, under the strains of modern government, the legislature may delegate to the executive such wide discretion that its policies in important domains are at best only formally authorized by law and weakly supervised by parliament (Lindseth 2004; Tompkins 2006). Rather than negotiating conflict between two principals, parliamentary regimes may undergo an inversion of the proper principal-agent relationship, with the executive tail wagging the legislative dog.

Once clear and specific lines of authorization break down, a purely instrumental account of administration loses its descriptive and normative purchase. If the legislative and executive officials are at odds, which is to prevail? What resources, if any, does the administrative state itself have to mediate conflicts between law and execution? Without some more substantive account of the administrative state – one that does not make it merely the arm of one constitutional power or another – we are left at an impasse.

The Administrative State Generates the Constitution

The limits of the instrumental model invite consideration of a less intuitive but arguably more deeply rooted conception of the administrative state. This conception treats the administrative state not as an efficient means for putting the laws and other preexisting constitutional powers into effect but rather as a source of constitutional value and constitutional change.

Constitution and administration arose historically in productive tension with one another. In France, for instance, de Tocqueville understood the intensive bureaucratic organization of *ancien régime* as helping to precipitate the French Revolution (Tocqueville 1856). Absolutist government undermined the intricate tapestry of feudal rights and began to erect in its place a direct and uniform connection between the central state authority and its subjects. Bodin's theory of absolutist monarchical sovereignty carved out a central place for official legality, as officials were authorized but constrained by the sovereign's legal command and could rely on those jurisdictional bounds to contest unlawful orders (McLean 2020; Lee 2013). Absolutism lay the legal and sociological foundation for demands for political equality. In Prussia, likewise, the quasi-constitutional General Code of 1794 was drafted under the enlightened absolutist regime of Frederick the Great. When Immanuel Kant (1996 [1784]) identified the Enlightenment with "the freedom to make public use of one's reason," he simultaneously recognized the state's claim to the obedience of its subjects – "argue as much as you please, but obey!" Enlightened absolutism enabled and subsidized the rise of private liberty even as it constrained it by hierarchical and authoritarian structures of the monarchical bureaucracy. Kant himself would go beyond the political conditions of his time in his normative account of the state. The state, in Kant's view, was necessary to establish and enforce objective rules delineating each person's sphere of equal freedom against every other's (Ripstein 2009). The ideal state would vest sovereign legislative authority in the united will of the people, whereas the "ruler" would command subjects to comply with law, and the judiciary would adjudicate disputed cases (Kant 2017 [1797], §45). And yet, Kant denied the people any right of revolution or resistance against an unlawful or unjust ruler, instead permitting only "reform" by the existing authorities (Ibid., §49). The monarchical executive, it seemed, was the appropriate instrument of gradualist constitutional reform.

Writing from within this contested project of Prussian constitutional reform, G. W. F. Hegel's *Philosophy of Right* (1821) continued to puzzle through the relationship between constitutional and administrative structure (Lübbe-Wolff 1981). Hegel outlined a constitutional order in which the administration would play a – perhaps the – central role. His normative understanding of law and political science embraced but fundamentally reformulated liberal and republican constitutional ideas. The Hegelian state respected and codified private rights of property, contract, and conscience, and emphasized the importance of the courts of law as forums to recognize and vindicate individual freedom. At the level of constitutional law (*Staatsrecht*), the state structure included a sovereign monarchical power symbolizing the unity of the state, a legislative power composed of representatives of the social estates, and a governmental or executive power (*Regierungsgewalt*).

Hegel's state was not merely a coercive power but rather the "actuality of concrete freedom" (Hegel 1991 [1821], §274). The right (*Recht*) of the state (*Staat*) was identical neither with the private rights of individuals in abstraction from their social context nor with positive law (*Gesetz*). Beyond both private interests and statutory law, the state defended the "public's right" to social relations and institutions in which each individual could recognize every other as free and equal members of the political community (ibid., §236). Given this understanding of law and of the state, the executive power necessarily involved more than merely carrying out the will of the legislature. Hegel described the professional civil service which staffed the government as the "universal estate," which had "the universal interests of society as its business" (ibid., §205). Drawing its members from the middle class, this professional bureaucracy would not play a narrow technical role but more broadly exercise practical reason to analyze and address social, economic, and moral conflicts (Shaw 1992).

The universal estate was constitutionally generative insofar as the meaning and requirements of freedom could not be determined by abstract philosophical reflection or by the general norms of statutory law on their own. The constitutional project of collective self-determination required the ongoing exercise of ethical judgment and steady application of public power by authorized officials. Hegel's *Staatsrecht* gave the bureaucracy a formative rather than purely instrumental role within the political structure of government and in its relation to civil society. Because the universal estate would share in the legislative power, it would not merely interpret and implement but also help to formulate basic statutory law.

This theory of the administrative state reflected the contemporaneous role of Prussian bureaucratic reform. The bourgeois social and economic forces that administrative intervention unleashed help to precipitate demands for liberal constitutional reforms in the revolutions of 1848–1849 (Koselleck 1989 [1967]). While the revolutions in the German states failed to topple monarchical authority, they left an enduring legacy of statist constitutionalism (Ross 2018; Clark 2012). The constitutional ideal of the *Rechtsstaat* – a state of law – was forged in the effort to constrain preexisting governmental powers according to statutory norms and judicial controls (Sordi 2017). The norms of *Rechtsstaatlichkeit* were not opposed to the use of state power but rather used it to preserve individual freedom, not only negatively, by guarding against arbitrary interference, but also positively, by providing for social welfare and regulation (von Mohl 1866; Stolleis 2001). The early formulation of the

Rechsstaat ideal thus understood the exercise of administrative police powers as part and parcel of the constitutional value of liberty.

The contrast between instrumental and generative conceptions of administration is evident in the ambiguous and contested relationship between *Regierung* (executive) and *Verwaltung* (administration) in German constitutional theory. The question whether the "political" nature of the former controls, is coterminous with, or is categorically distinct from the instrumental tasks of the latter has been open to constitutional and sociological dispute. Hans Kelsen (1925) understood *Regierung* as a relatively "free sphere of discretion" in which the highest administrative authorities would issue directives and regulations to subordinate administrative authorities (ibid., 245). But these discretionary acts were "legally constrained within a statutory sphere of authority" (id.). Government and administration were therefore not categorically distinct from the judiciary, insofar as each implemented pre-given statutory norms. Rudolf Smend, by contrast, understood *Regierung* as a "sphere of politics" in which the state "determined and implemented its essence," whereas administration involved ancillary, instrumental, and "technical" functions (Smend 1955 [1923], p. 79). Smend's understanding permits the executive leadership to exercise a generative constitutional role, above and beyond the requirements of law, to express and shape society according to an ethical conception of the political values that inhere in the constitutional state (Forsthoff 1961, p. 17). More recently, Christoph Möllers (2013) has rejected a purely instrumental conception of the executive, arguing instead that "the function of the executive is to mediate between democratic and individual self-determination" (ibid., p. 97). In that mediating role, where general statutory and political commitments are concretized, new understandings of how the demos is constituted out of its membership may emerge.

Constitutionally generative understandings of administration are not unique to German constitutional thought and history. It has also taken root in the American context. Consider, for instance, the famous claim of Franklin D. Roosevelt's President's Committee on Administrative Management that independent agencies in the U.S. constituted a "headless 'fourth branch' of government" (President's Committee on Administrative Management 1932, p. 32). As used by the President's Committee, the "fourth branch" label was an epithet. Independent agencies, which were not strictly subject to presidential control, were antithetical to the Committee's project of administrative centralization and presidential control. By contrast, for James Landis (1938), the foremost proponent of independent agencies during the New Deal, such agencies furthered, rather than undermined, republican constitutional values. In the face of swelling executive power in the hands of the president, Landis argued that independent administrative agencies would establish a new level of checks and balances and reduce the threat of arbitrary, unaccountable power.

Constitutionally generative understandings of administration faded away in the United States in the mid-twentieth century once administrative law secured a place for the permanent officialdom and a broad ideological consensus embraced the welfare state. Today, however, generative understandings of administration have reemerged as neoliberal political economy and politically conservative critics have put the legitimacy of economic and social regulation back into question. In response to these challenges, Brian Cook (2021) argues that the U.S. Constitution must be formally amended to establish a separate administrative branch uncorrupted by the influence of business interests and partisan politics. Cook has long explicitly endorsed a "constitutive" understanding of public administration, according to which the "the people, who are the ultimate sovereigns, and the institutions and officers of government in their representative and governing capacities, together constitute the regime" (Cook 2014, p. 17).

Jon D. Michaels (2017) argues, in a different vein, that the mid-century welfare state implemented an "administrative separation of powers" that replicated but reconfigured the separation of powers at the constitutional level. Michaels describes a division of functions and normative commitments amongst the political appointees who lead agencies and direct its policy, the civil servants who staff agencies and police legality, and the civil society groups who participate in the administrative process. This scheme does not merely replicate the separation of powers at the constitutional level but rather reconfigures it so that the state incorporates elements of the society it regulates. In this respect his approach is aligned with Hegel and von Stein's understanding of the relationship between the separate spheres of "state" and "civil society." For Hegel and Stein, the political unity of the state was set over against the antagonisms of civil society. Yet each understood the state to include, mediate, and ultimately harmonize discordant social interests. Michaels identifies a similar arrangement in the U.S. in the mid-twentieth century, where the state was separated from the market, yet the former incorporated social and political interests in different aspects of the administrative process. He sees the privatization of governmental functions and contracting out of services previously performed by tenured civil servants as corrupting this administrative separation powers.

The administrative state is not only generative of new political-structural arrangements but also of new individual rights. Scholars of "administrative constitutionalism" describe how agencies in the civil rights space have not only implemented pre-defined statutory and constitutional norms but positively shaped them. Sophia Lee (2010)'s pathbreaking research showed how agencies such as the Federal Communications Commission offered "creative," "selective," and "resistant" interpretations of the Equal Protection Clause. Other scholars have identified the administrative production of constitutional meaning with regard to sex discrimination (Eskridge & Ferejohn 2010), free speech (Kessler 2014), welfare rights (Tani 2014), involuntary servitude (Tani 2019), and fair housing (Emerson 2017a). Bertrall L. Ross II (2019) defends this practice of administrative constitutionalism as a form of "popular constitutionalism" on the basis of the special deliberative and institutional competencies of administrative agencies, which position them better than the courts to mediate democratic deliberation over individual rights.

Other scholars have extended the concept of administrative constitutionalism more broadly, beyond the explicit interpretation of constitutional rights. Rejecting claims that the administrative state was an unconstitutional outgrowth of the Progressive Era and the New Deal, Jerry Mashaw (2012) has unearthed a nineteenth-century "administrative constitution" that established both fundamental governance structures and means of protecting individual rights within executive-branch proceedings. Elizabeth Fisher (2007) describes administrative constitutionalism as a means by which the law constitutes and constrains the power of regulators, including by way of placing deliberative-procedural requirements on their decision making.

In all these instances public law scholars have understood administrative law as "concretized constitutional law," to borrow the famous phrase of the German jurist Fritz Werner (1959). Werner saw administration not merely as implementing the powers of the constitutional branches but as playing "the role of mediator," and working to "maintain a social equilibrium, so that the individual is not ground to dust by the ... struggles between associations" within a complex, industrialized, and interest-group based civil society (ibid., 532). Werner's concept of "concretization" captures the distinctive way in which administrative implementation can transform into constitutional generation. When administrative officials make constitutional norms materially and socially real through implementation, the constitutional norms are prone to shift in reaction to the factual circumstances, institutions, intersubjective relations they confront. At the contact point between state and civil society, administration mediates the evolution of constitutional norms over time.

This generative and constitutive understanding of the administrative state raises the specter of a third alternative analytic. If administration can alter constitutional structures and values, perhaps the administrative state can actually supplant, dislodge, or displace the constitution, either in whole or in part.

The Administrative State Displaces the Constitution

The instrumental and generative understandings of the administrative state's constitutional significance assume that there is indeed something that is constitutional about the administrative state. It is a source of constitutional values or an instrument through which constitutional purposes, powers, and values are put into effect. But there is another understanding of the administrative state that treats it as detached from and potentially antagonistic to the constitution. For some, this is a reason to indict the administrative state as inimical to constitutional principles. For others, the extra-constitutionality of the administrative state is its virtue. It enables us to escape strictures of the constitution or else simply avoid the high-altitude value disputes that often pervade constitutional law and politics.

The theory of constitutional displacement does not necessarily entail antagonism or hostility. It may simply be a way of differentiating the proper province of "administration" from that of "constitution." The American constitutional theorist W. W. Willoughby (1992 [1896], p. 199), for instance, argued that an administrative ordinance was of "equal validity" with legislative and constitutional norms – it simply operated within a different and more confined sphere. If administrative and constitutional law each stayed in their own lanes, the state and the constitution could persist alongside one another.

This understanding also permits scholars to argue for the durability of administrative state in the face of sweeping constitutional change. The preeminent German positivist scholar of administrative law, Otto Mayer, famously noted in the wake of the transition from the German Empire to the Weimar Republic that "constitutional law passes away, administrative law endures" (Mayer 1924). Mayer's famous dictum was probably inaccurate, and could only succeed by blinding the rational system of legal dogma he had developed to the massive developments of welfare and regulatory legislation that took place during and after World War I (Stolleis 2004; Badura 1967). Nonetheless, Mayer represents the inclination of scholars who wish to maintain the integrity of administrative law in the face of serious political and constitutional volatility – by insisting on a strict demarcation of the two spheres.

A more affirmative, reformist vision of constitutional displacement could be seen in Progressive Era and New Deal administrative law in the United States. By naming and articulating a separate branch of public law concerned especially with administration, reformers could keep constitutional constraints imposed by a hostile judiciary at bay. Instead of revising governance arrangement piecemeal, the Progressives sought to place state on a new footing altogether. The "new American state" would be governed by a combination of presidential leadership in legislation and delegation of authority to administrative experts (Skowronek 1982). This governance model aimed to dislodge the courts from their central role within the American constitutional order.

The New Deal put the Progressives' theory into practice. Across a decade of institutional conflict and accommodation, the courts came to defer to the policy judgments – and sometimes even the constitutional interpretations – not only of the legislature but also of administrative agencies (Tushnet 2011; Schiller 2007). This was not merely a story of judicial capitulation, however. Administrative lawyers responded to the constitutional rejection of welfare and regulatory legislation by honing the procedural regularity of administrative proceedings (Ernst 2014). They thus shifted the focus of legal analysis away from whether the statute in question delegated impermissibly broad power to the question of whether the agency had exercised that power in a manner that promoted fairness and reduced arbitrariness. Progressive scholars and judges then pushed judicial deference to agencies to include not only on questions of fact but also with regard to legal interpretations.

Such displacement did not in fact expunge constitutional concerns. The procedural repertoire of agencies remained redolent with tensions relating to due process and the separation of powers (Emerson 2017b). Nonetheless, Progressive administrative jurists created a set of a questions and a set of tools that delayed and marginalized explicit constitutional questions, which ordinary courts would be empowered to answer without deference to the political branches. Adrian Vermeule (2016) describes the result as a more-or-less permanent "abnegation" of the liberal-constitutional order. He argues that as the state has taken on tasks that call for complex and contested policy analysis rather than reasoned elaboration from principle, the administrative state has pushed the classical constitutional order aside. In a similar if less totalizing vein, Edward Rubin (2005) argues that the administrative state cannot be understood within the traditional system of constitutional branches. Rather, the modern state is constituted by policymaking networks that articulate public purposes not only through traditional electoral and legislative channels but also through interactions between civil society and administrative organizations. To be sure, neither Vermeule nor Rubin see the administrative state as violating specific constitutional rules. Rather, their point is that administration has rendered the political theory underlying the classical-liberal constitutional order descriptively and even normatively inapposite.

Carl Schmitt's diagnosis of the decline of parliamentary democracy in the Weimar Republic sounded in a similar register of constitutional displacement. He understood parliamentary "government by discussion" and the strict liberal separation between state and society to have broken down under the increasingly wide remit of the state's economic regulation. Whereas the Weimar Constitution had made a "decision for the bourgeois *Rechtsstaat*," (Schmitt 2008 [1928], p. 77) this decision proved untenable. In place of the old limited liberal state, the emergent institutional figure was a "total state characterized by an identity of state and society" (Vinx 2015, p. 132). In such a state, "the bureaucracy in the long run remains the superior partner and transforms the law of the parliamentary legislative state into the measures of the administrative state. The word *Rechtsstaat* should not be used here" (Schmitt 2004 [1932], p. 14).

Schmitt turned to the popularly elected *Reichspräsident* as a neutral power to preserve the constitution against the threat of destabilizing political forces – communism in particular. He shared with social-democratic thinkers such as Herman Heller and Franz Neumann a skepticism that legislative formalism on its own could suffice to preserve the legitimacy of the state in the face of overwhelming responsibilities of social and economic regulation (Dyzenhaus 1997; Scheuerman 1994). Heller and Neumann nonetheless remained committed to the principles of a "social *Rechtsstaat*," understanding social democracy as a means to live up to the unfulfilled emancipatory promise of the liberal *Rechtsstaat*. For them, the welfare state that grew during the Weimar Republic generated new social-constitutional configurations that furthered the egalitarian ideals that were implicit but hampered within classical-liberal constitutional forms. To Schmitt's mind, by contrast, the executive-administrative apparatus shoved the older constitutional order out the door. Understanding politics as defined by an essentially violent antagonism between friend and enemy, and relying on plebiscitary executive discretion for authority and legitimacy, Schmitt turned away from the *Rechtsstaat* and towards Nazi totalitarianism.

The Nazi regime transitioned in theory and practice from what Ernest Fraenkel (2017 [1941]) described as a "dual state" – in which administrative legality was preserved in limited spheres while lawless discretion pervaded others – to a "behemoth" altogether untethered from legal or substantive rationality (Meierhenrich 2018; Neumann 1944). Schmitt's student Ernst Forsthoff would go on to publish a National Socialist theory of the state, *The Total State,* that rejected the *Rechtsstaat* ideal wholesale. The Nazis' total state replaced separated powers and protections of individual rights with a regime "distinguished by the connection between the national socialist order and the bureaucratic administration" (Forsthoff 1935, p. 35). For Forsthoff in the Nazi years, the liberal-constitutional norms of limited government and negative liberty had been "discredited" and "overcome" (ibid., 45).

When Forsthoff rehabilitated himself as one of the foremost administrative law scholars of the Federal Republic, he nonetheless retained his view that the "social" aspects of the *Rechtsstaat* were outside of the scope of the constitution in the strict sense, even though the social character of the state was explicitly acknowledged in the Basic Law (Forsthoff 1954). Social administration remained as a non-liberal (or illiberal) displacement of liberal constitutional commitments, existing uneasily alongside the negative, exclusionary rights protected by the constitution itself.

This view was rejected by the Marxist constitutional law scholar Wolfgang Abendroth, who followed Heller in viewing the social state as intrinsic to the constitutional order (Abendroth 1968). Abendroth placed primary responsibility for implementing social democracy in the hands of the legislature, whereas Forsthoff's vision hewed more strongly to executive discretion. Neither Forsthoff's nor Abendroth's vision has carried the day. To guard against any future totalitarian displacement of liberal democracy, the German Constitutional Court has taken the lead to apply constitutional norms directly within the administrative sphere (Wahl 2006).

The specter of totalitarian displacement has played a profound role meanwhile in American administrative and constitutional law. Critics of the New Deal warned darkly of the threat of "Marxian" ideologies within the administrative state (American Bar Association 1938, p. 340). The President's Committee on Administrative Management's proposals for separation functions within administrative proceedings were motivated in part by the fear of fascism (Rosenblum 2022). The threat that the liberal constitutional order would be dislodged by some form of left or right totalitarianism not only challenged the overall growth of administrative power but reconfigured constitutional protections within administrative proceedings. The Administrative Procedure Act of 1946 and the accompanying organization of the executive branch have sought to channel administrative discretion with internal bureaucratic checks and judicial review.

Such constitution-preserving and constitution-generating developments within administrative law no longer mollify some conservative critics. They treat administrative law as a gross departure from, dislocation, and dismemberment of constitutional arrangements (Hamburger 2014, Lawson 1994). In particular, the delegation of rulemaking and adjudicatory power to administrative agencies has come under severe criticism and scrutiny. Without assessing the merits of these criticisms, the pathology they purport to diagnose is one of constitutional displacement. Critics understand social and economic regulation not as an instrument of constitutional government, nor as a source of constitutional meaning, but instead as inherently hostile to the constitution.

II THE ADMINISTRATIVE STATE AND THE DEMOCRATIC CONSTITUTION

The previous parts have developed three analytical frameworks for understanding how the administrative state and the constitution relate to one another. In this part, I show how this analytical framework sheds light on a normative problem: how to realize democratic principles in states that are both administrative and constitutional. Democratic principles provide lenses by which to assess how administration variously implements, generates, and displaces the constitution.

Democratic Principles and Democratic-Constitutional Rules

A democratic understanding of the constitution – one which is common to the United States, the Federal Republic, and many other modern states – treats free and equal people as the ultimate source of constitutional legitimacy. While there are certainly deep tensions and disagreements amongst different democratic theories, here I offer a general and inclusive account – one that most theorists of democracy could in part agree with. This account includes majoritarian, deliberative, and egalitarian principles. Democracy requires that each person have an equal right to contribute to collectively binding decisions, which means that at least some matters should be left to voting, either as to policies or as to representatives. Voting, on its own, however, may be insufficient to ensure that each person's interests and values are given due consideration. Many theorists agree that people must have the opportunity to deliberate with one another about shared concerns, to learn about problems at hand, and to convince one another as to appropriate courses of action (Cohen 1997; Benhabib 1996). Public deliberation within the public sphere and amongst civil society groups then guides and constraints the formal, legal decision-making structures of government (Habermas 1996). These procedural principles guard and help to implement a substantive concern with democratic equality. The conduct and structure of the state must manifest equal concern and respect for each of the communities' members (Shiffrin 2021; Christiano 2008; Dworkin 2000).

On some models, democracy is fundamentally committed to some degree of social egalitarianism (Anderson 1999; Kolodny 2014).

Democratic principles of this sort justify particular constitutional rules, relations, and structures. The majoritarian principle requires a right to vote and that voting determine significant matters of public policy. The people must enjoy regular opportunities to choose, judge, and replace officials or policies. The deliberative principle requires rights to free speech and association (Ely 1980) as well to adequately justified governmental decisions (Forst 2012). The egalitarian principle requires that law and policy guard against the subordination of some people to others, precluding, for example, invidious racial or gender discrimination, and providing basic social support that decrease the costs of exit from dominating institutions or relationships.

Each of these democratic principles is contestable. Some may reject one of the principles or insist on the inclusion of another. But the important point for my purposes is that democracy includes multiple commitments, the precise institutional entailments of which cannot be specified through conceptual analysis alone. This is for three related reasons. First, while democratic principles may be mutually supportive or constitutive, they are also prone to conflict with one another. People may vote for policies that undermine social equality or reduce the quality of public deliberation. Increasing requirements for deliberation or for reasoned decision-making may curtail the discretionary power of majorities, especially if unelected officials play a role in evaluating the quality of majoritarian decisions. Constitutionally binding requirements of social equality reduce the range of policies over which people may deliberate and vote. Given the internal tensions amongst democratic principles, a constitutional rule that advances one principle may detract from another. There is, therefore, likely to be significant scope for reasonable disagreement about the way in which these principles should be articulated and balanced in the rule-structure of the constitutional state.

Second, the factual landscape in which democratic principles operate changes over time and place. The institutional order that best fits the principles will depend on the social dynamics and history at issue. For example, in the wake of the American Civil War, there was good reason to condition the readmittance of the Confederate states to Congress on their approval of a constitutional amendment guaranteeing equal protection of the laws, even though that kind of heavily coerced decision-making would in other times be inconsistent with democratic principles. Likewise, some restrictions on free speech are arguably more justified in Germany in the wake of Nazi dictatorship than they are today in the United States. Majoritarian principles perhaps ought to have greater sway than deliberative principles where severe social inequality or sheer numbers prevents robust, rational deliberation over matters of policy. Even if we agree on democratic principles, and even if we agree on their relative weight as a general matter, the institutional configuration that best furthers them may vary depending on the risks and the opportunities of the social context and the historical moment.

Third, and perhaps most fundamentally, democracy itself disfavors rigid, authoritative, and permanent determination of the political structure that people inhabit (Dewey 1918). Democracy is ultimately concerned with recognizing the self-governing authority of free and equal persons. To claim that all of the fundamental requirements, procedures, and boundaries of democratic law and politics can be determined by philosophical inquiry prior to political experience is to deprive the people of such self-governing power. The people themselves must instead determine at least some of these matters for themselves, so long as they do not fail to give adequate leeway to majoritarian, deliberative, or egalitarian norms. The specific rules any democratic constitution imposes therefore must be understood as temporary and provisional institutionalizations of prior democratic principles that are each grounded in the equal freedom of the individuals who make up the people. Popular sovereignty requires that the constitution remain to some degree open in the present to refounding, reformulation, and contestation (Bernal 2017).

This perspective on democracy enables the administrative state to tarry with the constitution. If the constitution is only an imperfect and temporary approximation of democratic values in all their complexity, then it may be a virtue of the administrative state that it not only may generate but even, though only partially, displace the existing constitutional order. By creating a set of official practices that are related to but distinct from the constitutional order, the administrative state can serve as a proving ground for new forms of democratic law, politics, and life.

Administrative Development of the Democratic Constitution

With this understanding of the democratic constitution in view, we are in a position to assess how the administrative state ought to relate to it. This normative assessment will build on the analytical framework developed in Part II. I suggest that the open and provisional nature of the democratic constitution can be furthered by an administrative state that – in various institutional settings and at various times – alternately implements, displaces, and generates constitutional norms and institutions. None of the three modes in isolation is sufficient to give democratic principles their full leeway or *Spielraum*. The administrative state should enable constitutional rules to develop in light of the specific social and historical circumstances in which they are to be administered. This development should occur in a way that conditions the adoption of new democratic institutions on their mutual adjustment and dialogue with existing institutions. This developmental process would allow the people to alter the political order not only through heroic acts of constitution-making or formal amendment but also through the more mundane and practical arts of administration. I draw on my previous work (Emerson 2019) to provide an historical example of how administration can motivate democratic-constitutional change.

In the 1960s federal regulatory agencies such as the Equal Employment Opportunity Commission and the Department of Health Education and Welfare implemented the constitutional principal of *equality* by uprooting segregation in employment and education, respectively. The democratic significance of civil rights administration went beyond its commitment to equality, however. As creatures of statutory law, acting under some degree of supervision by the president, these agencies had *majoritarian* authorization and were subject to majoritarian constraints. Administrative agencies were also highly *deliberative*: they acted in dialogue with affected civil society groups, the other branches of the federal government, and state governments. The administration of civil rights law thus implemented democratic constitutional principles of equality, majoritarianism, and deliberation.

The first and most obvious target for these civil rights agencies were systems of legal segregation that denied people equal access to jobs or to schools on the explicit basis of their race. In the implementation of the principle of equality, agencies carried out legislative, executive, and judicial mandates using the enforcement mechanisms Congress gave them. EEOC processed discrimination complaints, attempted voluntary compliance, and collected racially disaggregated employment statistics. The Department of Health Education and Welfare threatened to withhold funding from segregated school districts.

As they implemented constitutional principles, however, these agencies *partially displaced* the existing constitutional structures. The courts were traditionally understood as the guardians of constitutional rights and expositors of constitutional norms. *Brown v. Board* (1954), which ruled public school segregation unconstitutional, set the paradigm for a judiciary that would defend the democratic principles embodied in the Constitution. On their own, however, judicial rulings did little to desegregate the South (Ackerman 2018). The civil rights movement thus pressed for legislative action that would not only enhance the judiciary's tools to combat Jim Crow but would also create administrative institutions to complement, amplify, and in some cases, challenge, the courts' interpretations. The Civil Rights Act of 1964 reconfigured the set of constitutional actors engaged in addressing the issue of civil rights. Not only the judiciary and the legislature but also administrative agencies would determine the meaning and implications of equality. In doing so, they would temporarily displace the central position held by some constitutional values, such as federalism, associational freedom, and private property, in favor of emergent values such as social equality and inclusion.

Constitutional displacement thus made space for moments of constitutional *generation*. Civil rights agencies confronted massive resistance from segregated institutions and were deluged with protests from the civil rights movement. Their encounter with the reality of segregation and the way minorities experienced it led them to extend and reformulate the equality norms that the Supreme Court had endorsed. EEOC officials concluded that discrimination existed not only when an employer exhibited explicit racial prejudice, but also where the employment practices more broadly created "a condition of pervasive exclusion" (Equal Employment Opportunity Commission 1970). EEOC thus developed interpretations of the Civil

Rights Act that prohibited apparently race neutral employment practices that had unequal effects on different racial groups without adequate business justification. Likewise, the Department of Health Education and Welfare, confronted with resistance by segregated southern school districts, imposed numerical quotas for integration. In this constitutionally "creative" and "resistant" process (Lee 2010), the institutionally specific tools of the administrative state – such as data analysis and the systematic, wholesale approach to social problems – offered a new understanding of constitutional values. Equality required not merely acting without regard to race but rather acting in a way that was conscious of and attempted to remedy past and present forms of racial exclusion and subordination.

After a period of openness and accommodation, the Supreme Court ultimately held this understanding at bay, denying it constitutional status and relegating it to a mere matter of statutory law. Thus, in *Washington v. Davis* (1976), the Court determined that the disparate impact theory of discrimination the EEOC had helped to develop only applied in statutory civil rights claims but not to constitutional equal protection claims. In this case, and others where it sidelined or relegated executive officials' constitutional interpretations, the Court short circuited an administrative process of constitutional development (Siegel 1997). Whether or not that course of development was justified is a matter for democratic debate. One might reasonably argue that an effects- and outcome-oriented understanding of equality advocated and implemented by administrative agencies was inconsistent with equal respect for each person regardless of their race. One might reasonably counter, as scholars of critical race theory have, that such formal equality, in fact, institutionalizes racism by prohibiting public actors from considering the racialized structures and practices in which individual identities and life-chances have been formed (Gotanda 1991; Crenshaw 1988). U.S. public law remains at an uneasy compromise today, with constitutional norms protecting a formal conception of equality and legislative and administrative law authorizing concern for equality of outcomes and conditions.

This historical example goes to show the complex but potentially fruitful normative relationship between the democratic constitution and the administrative state. Acting as an arm of constitutional institutions, the administrative state seeks to give effect to constitutional values. In doing so, however, it may compete with and displace other constitutional actors, specific constitutional rules, and even particular constitutional values. Administrative agencies may assume the role usually played by courts or legislatures or they may countermand the judgments of state and local officials. They may offer up new constitutional understandings for consideration by other political institutions and the people themselves.

It might be objected that administrative displacement of the constitution is, by definition, illegitimate. Complete displacement of a constitution generated by even compromised democratic means, or relied on by citizens for political participation, would certainly be not only unlawful but contrary to democratic norms. *Partial* displacement may be democratically legitimate, however. If the constitution contains or permits commitments that run contrary to fundamental democratic norms, such as exclusionary suffrage, inviolable property or contract rights, or racial or gender discrimination, democratic principles may require these rules to be transgressed and replaced. In these cases, administrative displacement may be an important component of a process of constitutional change that removes repugnant constitutional rules in the service of deeper democratic values. The administrative state is a particular useful and appealing avenue for such constitutional change because of its other, constitutionally instrumental and generative dimensions. To return to the example of civil rights, federal administrative action temporarily displaced the constitutional value of federalism by coercing state and local compliance with an effects-based understanding of equal protection. But this structural realignment of political relations and norms was authorized by legislative action, supervised by the presidency, and subject to judicial review. Administrative displacement of the constitution thus remained tethered to other recognized constitutional values and institutions, in a way that constrained and informed its innovations.

There is nonetheless moral danger in such moments. We leave behind the well-trodden safety of old constitutional paths and enter into uncharted terrain. While there is risk, so too is there opportunity. Partial constitutional displacement makes room for new understandings of constitutional value that had not been recognized by the traditional set of constitutional actors. Whether these new understandings are appropriate and valuable is a question for continuing democratic politics and theory. We, as scholars and as citizens, can regard the work of the administrative state and determine its constitutionality. We should not ask only whether the administrative state conforms to specific rules and structures of the existing constitutional order. Though that question is surely relevant, we should also ask whether administrative decisions and practices – even those that push the margins of current legal rules – have given greater effect to basic democratic principles than has the existing constitutional order.

CONCLUSION

This chapter has described three ways to conceptualize the administrative state's relation to the constitution. The administrative state may be understood to implement, generate, or displace constitutional values and structures. These three analytical frameworks foreground a normative understanding of how the administrative state may further democratic-constitutional principles. Any particular constitutional order is unlikely to institutionalize democratic principles of majoritarianism, deliberation, and equality in a completely and permanently adequate way. The constitution can evolve to better meet the democratic principles underlying it in and through administrative implementation, displacement, and generation of constitutional norms. Insofar as the administrative state is more closely tied than constitutional norms to social facts and values, it is able to adjust those norms in light of the social context in which they operate. Whether this adjustment is desirable and well-justified is a matter of public and scholarly debate. The important point, for the purpose of constitutional theory, is to recognize that the administrative state is one of the arenas in which constitution's meaning is carried out, contested, and constructed.

RECOMMENDED READING

Emerson, B. (2019). *The Public's Law: Origins and Architecture of Progressive Democracy*, New York: Oxford University Press.

Ernst, D. R. (2014). *Tocqueville's Nightmare: The Administrative State Emerges in America, 1914–1940*, New York: Oxford University Press.

Kagan, E. (2001). Presidential Administration. *Harvard Law Review*, 114(8), 2245–2385.

Lee, S. Z. (2010). Race, Sex, and Rulemaking: Administrative Constitutionalism and the Workplace, 1960 to the Present. *Virginia Law Review*, 96(4), 799–886.

Mashaw, J. L. (2012). *Creating the Administrative Constitution: The Lost One Hundred Years of American Administrative Law*, New Haven CT: Yale University Press, 2012.

Michaels, J. D. (2018). *Constitutional Coup: Privatization's Threat to the American Republic*, Cambridge, MA: Harvard University Press.

Rahman, K. S. (2016). *Democracy Against Domination*, New York: Oxford University Press.

Rose-Ackerman, S. (2021). *Democracy and Executive Power: Policymaking Accountability in the US, the UK, Germany, and France*, New Haven: Yale University Press.

Scheuerman, W. E. (1994). *Between the Norm and the Exception: The Frankfurt School and the Rule of Law*, Cambridge, MA: MIT Press.

Skowronek, S., Dearborn, J. A., & King, D. (2021). *Phantoms of a Beleaguered Republic: The Deep State and the Unitary Executive*, New York: Oxford University Press.

40

Executive Rulemaking

Susan Rose-Ackerman

Governments that hold power over time need bureaucratic organizations to work along with elected officials and their political appointees. Even bureaucracy's critics must come to terms with its necessity. The challenge is to establish a public law that enhances the democratic accountability of both bureaucrats and political appointees who have policymaking roles in the executive. Governments do not merely implement clearly articulated policies laid down by the legislature. As a practical matter, policymaking in the executive necessarily requires discretion and judgment. Political appointees work with civil servants to make policy under statutes that delegate authority either explicitly or through vague language requiring interpretation. Bureaucrats' technical expertise and programmatic experience are centrally important. However, giving discretion to career technocrats, full stop, is insufficient in a democracy that depends upon popular support. A skeptical public may be difficult to convince if complex policies rely on officials' claims to esoteric knowledge. Even if the executive's analysis is easily understandable, the general public will not necessarily agree with its policy prescriptions. Fairly managing the distribution of gains and loses is necessary for broad public acceptance.

Disparate policy views are normal in a democracy. Unanimous consent is not a realistic goal for most policy choices. Serious disagreements will typically persist. Consultation is necessary, but nothing would ever move forward if open-ended participatory processes must seek unanimous consent with no time limits. Majority rule in the legislature can produce legally enforceable norms legitimized by the democratic process. Once a statute delegates authority to a government ministry or agency, however, new legitimacy issues arise.[1] Democratic legitimacy requires that contesting policymaking frameworks be transparent to the public, not hidden

---

[1] I use the term "agency" in the American sense as a synonym for any public body, whether or not it is part of the cabinet structure of government. Thus, in the US, the term includes the Department of Commerce, whose head is a member of the cabinet; the Environmental Protection Agency, also in the core executive, but lacking cabinet status; the Food and Drug Administration, inside the Department of Health and Human Services; and the Federal Communications Commission, a regulatory commission with a multi-member board not under direct presidential control.

in esoteric language. Even for an agreed set of facts, there are alternative ways of aggregating costs and benefits to produce a policy recommendation. These options depend on competing views of the public good and on the proper role of the state in society.

Governments and regulatory agencies make policy through a range of instruments from soft-law guidelines and executive orders, on the one hand, to executive rules with the force of law, on the other. Legally enforceable rules have different labels in different countries. The United States calls them rules; in the UK they are labeled statutory instruments or delegated legislation; in Germany, the term is *Rechtsverordnungen*, and in France, they take the form of ordinances or decrees. This chapter concentrates on rules with the force of law and argues that a publicly accountable procedural framework can help legitimate these policy choices in the eyes of citizens. Based on the argument in my 2021 book *Democracy and Executive Power*, this chapter highlights the link between cross-country differences in rulemaking practices and underlying constitutional frameworks. It suggests how both bureaucratic expertise and public law can further democratic accountability in any system (Rose-Ackerman 2021). I critique governments' tendency to implement important policies through soft law or a string of adjudications instead of the issuance of general rules with the force of law.[2] My book discusses four established democracies, but the lessons learned from these comparisons can inform government-reform debates elsewhere, especially in emerging democracies and those in transition from an authoritarian past.

The tension between expertise and public acceptance is endemic to democratic government. Competent, technically trained bureaucrats are necessary but not sufficient. Individuals and organized groups should be able to present their relevant concerns and to articulate how the proposed alternatives will help or hurt them. They should not have the power to override statutory and political imperatives, but officials should be required to take account of outside input as they build on the statutory choices of the legislature to make their final policy decisions.

Although bureaucratic discretion is necessary and inevitable, one familiar conception of delegation to the executive, called the "transmission belt," fails to do justice to the realities of modern government. It supposes that the statutory text resolves all the key policy issues.[3] The bureaucracy carries out its mandate in a legalistic, adjudicatory fashion; policymaking only occurs during statutory drafting. Advocates of this model worry that public input will inject biased or partisan concerns into what should be an apolitical, professional policy decision. Worse yet, wealthy or well-organized interests may dominate the hearings and have too much influence

---

[2] A related problem is the delegation of rulemaking to private bodies that essentially make law in specialized areas. See Rose-Ackerman (2021, pp. 65–69), Strauss (2013–2014).

[3] Stewart (1975), pp. 1675–77, introduces the term and argues that it is unrealistic to expect it to apply in practice.

on the outcome.[4] Even if these concerns are valid, this restrictive model reflects an idealized vision of legislative activity and its ties to political-party platforms. It is blind to the reality of bureaucratic policymaking and ignores the weaknesses of the link between voting behavior and the democratic justification for regulatory policies. Instead, I begin from the proposition that voting and political parties are not the only proper routes for public sentiment to influence political/policy choices.

A citizen's support for a party or candidate running on a broad, diverse platform bears only a weak relationship to his or her views of particular executive decisions made months or years after the election. In my view, the ongoing policy problems facing incumbent governments need a stronger connection to the public than a paragraph in a composite platform issued during an election that may be several years in the past. Public input into executive rulemaking can invite participants to consider the broader merits of policy options, not only their own individual interests. Such considered evaluations of alternatives are a central link between citizens and officials in the administration and contribute to the democratic legitimacy of delegation.

Thus, administrative rulemaking procedures ought to require bureaucracies to reach beyond official circles and to consult broadly with the public. Consultation and public reason-giving contribute to the democratic legitimacy of discretionary regulatory actions. Government accountability extends beyond the individuals and property-owners who experience direct, personal effects from concrete decisions. Accountability also ought to extend to the justification of policy decisions with broad, diffuse effects on society, both positive and negative. The public-law literature emphasizes the protection of individual rights and the importance of preventing officials from acting outside the law – valid goals to be sure, but public consultation and reason-giving are no less important for the public accountability of executive policymaking. True, in a parliamentary system, ministers are accountable to the public through the cabinet's dependence on the parliamentary majority. Similarly, in a presidential system, the connection flows through the popular election of the chief executive. These are important routes for popular input and control, but I argue that they are insufficient.

There are four inter-related issues. First, why is executive-branch policymaking necessary? Shouldn't democratic legislatures resolve all the policy issues in the text of statutes? Second, even if delegation is a practical reality, how can it operate consistently with democratic principles? Third, how can the organization of the executive branch help to encourage public input and bureaucratic competence? Fourth, what role should courts play in enforcing the requirements of administrative law? I do not fully answer these questions in this short essay, but I illustrate their importance through my four case studies. The countries' disparate constitutional structures help to explain their divergent rulemaking practices, but I point

---

[4] See, for example, Lawson (1994).

to contemporary pressures that may be moving them all toward more accountable procedures.

I POLICYMAKING ACCOUNTABILITY AND THE RULE OF LAW

The "rule of law" stands for a number of different ideas (Davis & Trebilcock 2008). To some, the phrase implies nothing more than clear and market-friendly rules. Under that view, the courts should resolve legal challenges to government actions in ways that limit burden-shifting and interest-group capture while enhancing the efficacy of policymaking. To others, the talismanic phrase requires the protection of individual rights and legal redress for past wrongs.

My emphasis differs from both of these formulations by emphasizing the policymaking accountability of rulemaking procedures. The "rule of law" should constrain self-serving policy choices by politicians, bureaucrats, and private interest groups. However, it must do so without killing off valid exercises of discretion. Complex and fast-changing policy areas require the flexible application of professional expertise – not just when a statute is passed, but as ministers and their bureaucracies and political advisors confront new data and problems over time. One challenge for administrative law is to frame these on-going exercises of rulemaking discretion in ways that are compatible with democratic values. Judicial review should strengthen democracy, not restrict it through rigid, formalistic requirements. Courts should consider more than the substantive legality of rules. In my view, they should use their judicial authority to encourage agencies to comply with procedures for public consultation and public justification.

Three Types of Public Accountability

I argue for a notion of accountability that goes beyond mere fiscal rectitude to include policy implementation.[5] Consider three ideal-types: performance accountability, rights-based accountability, and policymaking accountability. Each has a valuable role, but I emphasize policymaking accountability.

Under *performance accountability*, political actors set the goals, and expert professionals carry them out in a competent and cost-effective way – using their specialized knowledge. It requires well-trained civil servants with high integrity.[6] In addition, administrative procedures should be transparent, so the public can check bureaucratic performance, and sanctions must discipline officials for illegal or incompetent actions (Magnetter 2003).

---

[5] "Accountability" is often difficult to translate. According to Carol Harlow (2002) some use the term only in the retrospective or fiscal accounting sense. She uses a broader meaning where "standard-setting is a vital element in the process of securing accountability" with "a prospective dimension". On the related terms in French see Ziller (2008). For a general discussion see Bovens, Goodin, and Schillemans (2014).

[6] On corruption in the civil service see Rose-Ackerman & Palifka (2016, chap. 2–5).

Performance accountability has always been a central concern of US public law, which regulates private industry to achieve objectives, such as the control of monopolies, protection of the environment, and the reduction of risk. This form of accountability is also important in France, Germany, and the UK, especially as they privatized state-owned enterprises and discovered a "new type of administration called regulation" that "consists of mostly sector-specific rules establishing markets and specific public obligations with regard to competition and certain social interests" (Schneider 2007). In Europe, with its state-owned utilities, the privatization of such firms led to the regulation of network industries – telecoms, energy, water, railroads – and also to regulation of public health, public transport, and financial services. Hence,

> ...regulatory law does not simply restrict economic freedoms in order to avert dangers for public or private interests. Instead, regulation organizes markets proactively, constructs new options for economic activities and directly or indirectly demands certain economic or social outputs. (Schneider 2007, p. 312).

This is a good statement of the aims of a system focused on performance accountability so long as one extends it to include environmental and social areas as well as regulations affecting the performance of particular sectors.

Rights-based accountability focuses on the protection of individuals against abuses of arbitrary power by public bodies. Even if an agency fulfills the requirements of performance accountability, it may nevertheless violate fundamental rights. Across the globe, public-law uses various formulations to express this point. In the US, the Bill of Rights plays a central role; across the Atlantic, judicial concepts of "natural justice" or *principes généraux du droit* fulfill an analogous function (Nicholas 1970). In Europe, the Convention on Human Rights (ECHR) of the Council of Europe and the European Union's Charter of Fundamental Rights affect the way rights are understood in Member States.

These modes of accountability are crucial, but they are not sufficient. Modern statutory regimes delegate vast areas of discretion to public and quasi-public agencies, and this can create a democracy deficit in the eyes of ordinary citizens. Election campaigns seldom emphasize technical regulatory matters, and elections are too infrequent and too rough-grained to link voter sentiment to the implementation of specific policies. Referenda are a poor substitute because of voter ignorance and apathy. Hence, additional steps must assure citizens that officials of the modern regulatory/welfare state are using their power in a way that is consistent with democratic values. Given the ubiquity of delegation, administrative law can be one way to promote the democratic character of policymaking. Hence, *policymaking accountability* goes beyond issues of competence, honesty, and the protection of rights. Statutes are frequently vague, unclear, and inconsistent, and they often leave difficult policy issues to the implementation stage (Rose-Ackerman 1995, 2021; Rothstein 2004). Whatever the risks and the countervailing political pressures, legislatures worldwide believe that the benefits of delegation outweigh the costs. In addition, sometimes, the executive makes policy on its own without any statutory framework, and these actions need democratic justification.

Policymaking accountability aims to inform citizens and interest groups that a policy choice is imminent and to give them an opportunity to express their opinions. At the same time, policymakers need to consult experts and to mediate conflicts between them in a transparent way. The views of the public and of the experts may diverge, and the regulatory authority should consider the evidence and the nature of public concerns before promulgating a rule. The authority should publish the final rule along with a justification that acknowledges the disputed nature of the choice. The final step in the process is independent judicial review that checks the policy decision for conformity with the underlying substantive statute and with procedural constraints designed to ensure public accountability.

Narrow and Broad Views of Public Law

In developing the concept of policymaking accountability, consider two stylized models of accountability that currently dominate the field of administrative law. The *narrow model* is dominant in some European legal circles. It focuses on administrative decisions in particular cases. The *broad model* incorporates this narrow concern but adds a role for administrative law in constraining and managing government rulemaking. I defend the broader view.

Under the narrow model, the review of administrative action concentrates on rights-based accountability, that is, on the protection of individual rights against state overreaching and on formal compliance with the law. The rights in question can be procedural, such as the right to be heard and to be judged by an impartial decision-maker, or they can be substantive and broad ranging, such as the right to "the free development of personality" affirmed in Art. 2 (1) of the German federal constitution (the *Grundgesetz*). In this model, the judiciary's basic task is to determine whether the bureaucracy's treatment of the individual is compatible with legally binding regulations, statutes, and the constitution.

The broad model, in contrast, takes policymaking accountability seriously. This approach is based on five building blocks: the inevitability of delegation, the need for technical expertise, the importance of political accountability both to elected officials and to voters, an openness to outside opinions, and recognition by the judiciary that administrative law can play a constructive role in promoting accountability.

Parliaments have limited time, expertise, and staff resources to confront the complexity and fluidity of real-world problems. At best, generalist legislators outline the policy that should guide the elaboration of technical and legal rules and guidelines, as well as the resolution of individual disputes. Realistically, that framework will leave many policy choices for the administration to resolve.

The narrow model contains a legitimacy gap that places much of the executive's work outside the realm of law. This could have one of two effects. Either executive rulemaking is political and, hence, not judicially reviewable or, conversely, a more aggressive judiciary could forbid such exercises of policymaking initiative and sharply limit their scope.

Of course, the legislature provides oversight of the bureaucracy through its power to determine budgets, review spending, hold hearings, establish commissions of inquiry, and the like. Members of opposition parties play an important role. However, just as the legislature does not have the time, expertise, or foresight to write detailed statutes in the first place, it lacks the ability to provide comprehensive oversight. Current political imperatives determine legislative priorities, and so the legislature is unlikely to monitor a wide range of government activities.

Policymaking accountability should not depend on the shifting attentions of the legislature. Furthermore, the presence of an honest and technically trained bureaucracy is insufficient. Writing rules with the force of law is a deeply political enterprise, but administrative law, nevertheless, should play a role in their promulgation. Political leaders inside the executive may not have strong incentives to be accountable to the public, even if they seek approval, at least pro forma, from the legislature. The broad view recognizes the legitimacy gap that this disconnect poses. It seeks ways to bring interest groups, stakeholders, civil society and business associations into the policy discussion, always understanding that no group can, on its own, claim to represent the public interest. Political accountability operating through an electoral connection has a superior claim to democratic legitimacy, but that claim is not sufficient to fill the legitimacy gap.

There is, of course, no magic formula for solving this problem. To move the discussion forward, four ideal types can help crystallize different options.

Models of Policymaking Accountability

The models differ in their organizational forms, appointment processes, and decision-making procedures. Call them: the chain-of-legitimacy model, the expertise model, the partisan-balance model, and the privatization model. Matching the options to substantive problems and finding ways to draw on the strength of each are major aspects of good rulemaking design.

Under the chain-of-legitimacy model (*Legitimationskette* in German), the democratic mandate flows from the voters to the political parties that they support to the legislature to the coalition that forms the government. Official policymaking by the cabinet is acceptable so long as it can be traced back to the will of the voters. The chain extends beyond legislative enactments to policy implementation by the cabinet and the bureaucracy (Böckenförde 1992, pp. 291–326). Agency heads may hold hearings or consult with an advisory body or a panel of experts, but the ultimate decision is in the government's hands. This view sees no role for rulemaking procedures that encourage public participation. It downplays the weaknesses of the link between voting behavior and the democratic imprimatur of particular regulatory policies. The route for redress is not the courts but the ballot box or a focused campaign to amend a statute or to replace those charged with implementing it. Taken to its extreme in presidential systems, the model empowers the elected head of state or government to issue decrees with the force of law in the absence of explicit delegation by statute (Carey & Shugart 1998). In the US, it supports the use of presidential executive orders, guidance documents, and memoranda that avoid the procedural requirements needed to promulgate a rule with the force of law (for a critique see Shane 2009).

This conception acknowledges that statutes can leave policy gaps for the executive to fill with secondary norms or regulations. Administrative discretion is consistent with democracy because policymakers in the executive are ultimately accountable to the voters along the chain of legitimacy.

Under the *expertise* model, a statute delegates authority to neutral, expert decision-makers. They may or may not need to accommodate or, at least, to consult with the public or politicians before making their final decisions. In extreme cases, the regulatory body does not depend on legislative appropriations to sustain its day-to-day operations. Central banks, for example, sometimes achieve this high degree of independence (Tucker 2018). This model applies to technical issues that are not politically contentious so that the legislature can safely delegate to specialists, and the courts defer to expert choices. However, in its pure form, it has limited reach. Many issues, although necessarily dependent on scientific competence, generate wide-ranging controversy. In such cases, expertise is not sufficient. Rather rulemaking procedures ought to include forms of public accountability, in which the government reaches beyond the scientific community to produce democratically acceptable policies.

When expert choices are subject to judicial review, judges routinely defer to agency expertise. Judicial review would then evaluate executive policies in light of technocratic criteria and remand decisions that appear to be in conflict (Rose-Ackerman 1992, pp. 33–42). This type of review could limit opportunities for the pathologies associated with "regulatory capture" that tilt so-called "expert" analyses in favor of the regulated industry (Stigler 1971; Carpenter & Moss 2014). Officials, then, would need to conduct an open and publicly justified process that permits oversight by civil society.

The US courts have struggled with their role in reviewing regulatory actions that draw on expertise. An iconic debate over so-called "hard look review" occurred in *Ethyl Corp v. EPA*, from the DC Circuit Court of Appeals.[7] In a concurring opinion, Judge David L. Bazelon argued that the courts should not "scrutinize the technical merits" of the decision but should, instead, review the process to be sure that it

---

[7] 29. 541 F. 2d 1 (D.C. Cir. 1976) (en banc), *cert. denied*, 426 U.S. 941 (1976).

"can be held up to the scrutiny of the scientific community and the public." Judge Harold Leventhal in a second concurrence countered that judges need to acquire the necessary technical knowledge to judge administrative actions. That debate continues, with some confusion over whether the court is checking to be sure the agency took a hard look at the alternatives or whether the judges themselves are taking a hard look at the agency's reasoning and the factual basis for a rule. Whatever the emphasis, the courts inevitably blend substance and process in assessing government actions.[8]

The *partisan-balance* model posits a multi-member board that makes decisions through a collegial process, operating by a majority or a supra-majority rule or by consensus. Paradoxically, explicit partisan balance aims to produce impartial decisions by forcing board members to compromise to fulfill their statutory mandates. It acknowledges the tension between political accountability and expertise. There are two variants: one based on institutional-constraints and a second, consisting of a group of establishment figures.

Under the institutional constraints version, politics enters at the appointment stage, but the design creates incentives for incumbents to operate as impartial professionals while in office. Sometimes, the appointment process seeks candidates who are broadly acceptable across the political spectrum. In the US, top agency appointees require the consent of two partisan bodies: the President and the Senate. In a parliamentary system, if approval requires a supermajority for confirmation, the government must often gain support from political opponents. Alternatively, different bodies may each select a portion of the agency's membership. In France, the National Assembly, the Senate, and the President independently choose officials to serve on multi-member commissions (Rose-Ackerman & Perroud 2014). Similarly, each house of the German parliament proposes sixteen members from each legislative chamber to serve on the Advisory Council for the Network Agency [§5(1) BEGTPG]. In this organizational type, members typically have diverse political priorities. Yet, they must transcend narrow partisanship to play a constructive role. Because appointments are meant to include a range of opinion, members have an incentive to make rules that will seem reasonable to broad sectors of the public. The danger, however, is partisans who fail to transcend their disagreements and condemn the agency to gridlock (M. Shapiro 2010).

In contrast, under the alternative version of the partisan-balance model, the appointees are establishment figures with reputations for practical wisdom and dedication to the public good. The danger is that they have little knowledge of the particular controversies under their mandate. Policy recommendations might be

---

[8] Discussion of hard-look review has focused on reasoned explanation and the public's access to information (Wagner [2010]); Stephenson (2006) (proposing that hard-look review can help reviewing courts overcome their comparative informational disadvantage or verify the substantive content of justifications provided by the government).

public-spirited but uninformed. To remedy that difficulty, the commission might have an expert staff and consult with representatives of the regulated industry and other stakeholders. This model bears a family resemblance to common-law adjudication. The notables on the commission hear arguments from experts and civil society groups, many of whom have narrow private interests in the outcome. As a practical matter, this process typically ends with a return to political accountability. The establishment figures make recommendation to the responsible minister who makes the final decision, sometimes after obtaining parliamentary approval.

Finally, under the *privatization* model, a statute turns over the regulatory task to a private or quasi-governmental institution that is largely independent of the legislature and the executive. These include professional self-regulation, industrial standard-setting, and corporatist self-government by a broader group of "stakeholders". Self-regulation is vulnerable to self-seeking behavior that raises entry barriers and entrenches monopoly profits (Stigler 1971). Often, these entities claim inherent or historical authority to regulate themselves. A statute merely confirms what they regard as their right – for example, medical or legal professional associations. An alternative variant, often labeled "corporatist", turns over a policy choice to a group of "stakeholders" under a statute that determines which groups can send members. A strong form of this model gives little role to the judiciary because of the body's position outside the political structure. "Administrative law" is then seen as a suspect category authorizing political meddling by judges. The courts resolve individual cases of maladministration and rights violation but stay clear of issues related to regulatory processes and the substance of policy.

Each of my four models has distinctive strengths and weaknesses. I have been treating them separately for analytic purposes, but in the real world, the variants overlap and interact. No combination represents a perfect solution. The challenge for the public administration is to balance political accountability to voters and elected politicians with technical competence. Rulemaking procedures should reflect the political values of the sitting government, incorporate state-of-the-art knowledge, and facilitate public input between elections. Comparative administrative law ought to play a central role in the construction of legitimate, responsive modern states. This requires cross-disciplinary dialogue and a search for common themes where the perspectives of political science, public administration, economics, history, and public law are in conversation. Public law should also help to contain excessive assertions of executive rulemaking power and monitor private or quasi-public entities that make their own rules to carry out public functions.

II RULEMAKING AND CONSTITUTIONAL STRUCTURES

Democratic systems differ in the incentives they provide to promote the political accountability of rulemaking. Comparative law traditionally draws a sharp distinction between presidential and parliamentary systems. However, the accountability practices adopted by different countries do not conform to a sharp presidential/parliamentary dichotomy. I illustrate this point by examining the rulemaking practices of the UK, Germany, France, and the US.[9]

I assign a different label to each democracy. The United Kingdom is a *common-law* parliamentary regime whereas Germany has a *written-constitution* parliamentary system. I distinguish between *strong* presidentialism in France, and *separation-of-powers* presidentialism in the United States. I highlight the differences between Britain and Germany and then argue that executive-branch accountability in France is closer to the practices in parliamentary Germany than to those in the UK with its common law regime. In contrast to all three European cases, the separation-of-powers in the United States creates political incentives that have produced the strongest laws requiring policymaking accountability in the executive.

Parliamentarianism: The United Kingdom and Germany

Begin with a stripped-down model that highlights the common features of the parliamentary systems in both Britain and Germany. In this simple model, voters choose between the competing candidates for prime minister selected by party leaders. The party or party coalition that gains majority support has sweeping lawmaking authority. However, a parliamentary vote of no confidence could lead to an abrupt end to the sitting government followed by a new election. In practice, both countries have built-in considerable stability. Germany requires that the sitting chancellor cannot leave office until the Federal President has approved a replacement selected by a majority of the Bundestag. Since 2011, the UK has had a Fixed Term Parliament Act (FTPA) that sets a five-year parliamentary term and limits the Prime Minister's ability to call a parliamentary election.[10]

Under these governmental structures, the governing coalition has no short-term reason to constrain its own discretion by empowering civil society or the courts.[11] This basic point also shapes the government's relationship to the bureaucracy. The governing coalition benefits from an apolitical civil service dominated by long-time professionals with the expertise required to implement the government's legislative

---

[9] The European Union presents yet another model of rulemaking in executive agencies. The promulgation of rules with the force of law is a relatively new phenomenon in the EU, where agencies traditionally served a primarily advisory function. See: C-70/12 United Kingdom v Parliament and Council, January 22, 2014, upholding the binding character of a rule promulgated by European Securities and Markets Authoring that referred to the agency's special expertise as a justification. The case did not deal with ESMA's procedures. On EU rulemaking see Rose-Ackerman, Egidy, and Fowkes (2015), pp. 216–260, and Mendes (2011).

[10] These constraints limit the sitting government's ability to time an election to gain an even larger legislative majority. In Germany, the vote is called a "constructive vote of no confidence" (*Grundgesetz*, Art. 67).

[11] I ignore special features of the German case discussed in Rose-Ackerman, Egidy & Fowkes 2015, and I omit the complications introduced by minority or coalition governments.

program. Within a parliamentary system, there is little long-term political gain from rigid restrictions on the promulgation and the repeal of rules. Here, the chain of legitimacy supporting the exercise of bureaucratic discretion is more than a metaphor. It is based on clear connections between voters, party platforms, and electoral victories.

These linkages, however, do not eliminate politics from administration. The victorious government may find that real-world complexities require unexpected revisions in its initial policy pronouncements – leading to exercises of rulemaking discretion that may generate controversy in civil society, especially if they appear to violate legislative mandates. Thus, in the UK political system, appointees in the prime minister's office work to coordinate policy across government departments (Tomkins 2006), and, in addition, ministers can appoint one or two "special advisors" to further their policy goals. The advisors are formally part of the civil service, but unlike the regular civil service, they need not be objective and impartial.[12]

This may lead the government to respond by turning to its specialist advisors and by invoking principles rooted in rights-based and performance accountability in its management of the civil service. It might impose internal controls on recruitment and promotion or establish procedures that permit individual citizens and firms to lodge complaints about their treatment. The government might also create specialized tribunals or administrative courts to check particular injustices.

Nevertheless, governing coalitions are unlikely to support laws that give citizens strong independent routes to demand policymaking accountability through appeals to the courts or other bodies. The cabinet may establish general oversight bodies, such as an audit office or an ombudsman staffed by experts. Their task is to assure that professional civil servants promote performance accountability. They will check the abuse of legal authority but are unlikely to further the democratic accountability of the governing coalition. The same is true of judicial review. At most, cabinet officers and top civil servants will support review of decisions made by low-level officials, especially when they involve the abuse of individual rights or indicate subpar bureaucratic performance. They are unlikely to seek limits on their own policymaking discretion.

These themes are visible in both Britain and Germany. Nevertheless, they play themselves out differently in the two systems – generating far more serious efforts at political accountability in *written-constitution* Germany than in its UK *common-law* analogue.

The British system provides a relatively pure example of the basic parliamentary model. Leaving the run-up to Brexit to one side, the government ordinarily

---

[12] The Constitutional Reform and Governance Act 2010, s. 7(4) states that civil servants must carry out their duties "(a) with integrity and honesty, and (b) with objectivity and impartiality." The Constitutional Reform and Governance Act 2010, s. 15 defines "special advisors." S. 7(5) states that they need only operate "with integrity and honesty." The Ministerial Code discusses special advisers in Sections 3.2–3.4. See Psygkas (2017), p. 194.

controls a majority of the House of Commons, and parliamentary sovereignty means that its statutes are not subject to judicial review except in the limited cases where the nation's courts declare a statute (without more) to be incompatible with the European Convention on Human Rights. The most important recent exceptions arose from challenges to government efforts to circumvent or limit parliamentary authority.[13] The lawsuits did not concern routes for public input into executive action over and above the role of parliament.

The government issues many regulations with the force of law – usually called Statutory Instruments (SIs).[14] Most require some review by the Commons; and unlike statutes, about one-quarter fall into a category that requires approval by both Houses. SIs can be subject to judicial review. However, parliamentary oversight of SIs is of relatively little significance; they are typically accepted without serious debate on the floor or in committee. According to Ruth Fox & Joel Blackwell (2014, p. 186), fewer than 0.01% were rejected between 1950 and 2014. The courts have sometimes intervened, but they tend to exercise restraint. Statutes impose procedural requirements on bureaucratic policymaking in specific areas, most notably the environment and for major infrastructure investments. Compliance with these procedures has engaged the courts in disputes over the adequacy of the administration's procedures.

The Supreme Court has invoked the principle of *ultra vires* to strike down SIs. However, parliamentary dominance is the root of these judgments, not a recognition of other routes to public accountability. Thus, Lord Neuberger wrote for a unanimous panel:

> Subordinate legislation will be held by a court to be invalid if it has an effect, or is made for a purpose, which is *ultra vires*, that is, outside the scope of the statutory power pursuant to which it was purportedly made. In declaring subordinate legislation to be invalid in such a case, the court is upholding the supremacy of Parliament over the Executive. R. *(on the application of The Public Law Project) v. Lord Chancellor* [2016], UKSC 39, ¶23.

Putting together the principle of ultra vires, scrutiny by the Parliament, the protection of rights, and statutory constraints on bureaucratic discretion, one can see a discernible shift toward greater policymaking accountability of the government. It remains to be seen, however, if this tendency will extend beyond the relations between the parliament and the government to include broader notions of accountability to citizens and organized civil society.

In Germany two institutional factors help to generate political accountability. The first is the prominent role of the Constitutional Court in the review of rights;

---

[13] R. *(on the application of Miller) (Appellant) v. The Prime Minister (Respondent); Cherry and Others (Respondents) v. Advocate General for Scotland* [2019], UKSC 41 [*Miller II*].

[14] Page (2001) links the issuance of SIs to the operation of the public administration and their important role in politics and policymaking.

the second, the status of the upper house. Neither one has had much effect to date on executive rulemaking procedures, but each could form the basis of such developments.

Most importantly, the written constitution reinforces the legitimacy of the German courts. Under the Basic Law, or *Grundgesetz*, the Constitutional Court plays a central role by requiring all government actors to respect fundamental principles of human dignity and democratic self-government. Just as in Britain, judicial scrutiny is constrained by the political dynamics of the parliamentary structure. The Basic Law authorizes parliament to delegate policymaking discretion to the government so long as the statute states the "content, purpose, and scope" of executive branch discretion (Art. 80(1) GG). The Grundgesetz does not regulate the process of issuing legally binding regulations that implement statutory objectives.

No government has tried to fill this vacuum in the modern republic. A statute setting out enforceable procedural requirements for public participation in rulemaking would limit the government's power to pursue its high-priority political initiatives. Instead, the government operates under a set of internal guidelines that are not judicially enforceable.[15]

The lack of statutory rule-making procedures, however, is not merely based on power politics. The chain of legitimacy that goes from voters through elected politicians to the government and professional bureaucracy is a living reality in national political life. Under this view, bureaucratic rulemaking should only be subject to political, not legal, constraints. Indeed, many German jurists go so far as to argue that the chain of legitimacy implies that independent efforts by the judiciary to assure bureaucratic accountability are unconstitutional. The Constitutional Court has never passed a definitive judgment on this issue. The administrative law code or *Verwaltungsverfahrensgesetz* (VwVfG) only authorizes judges to adjudicate grievances generated by particular agency decisions; it does not incorporate supervision of the broader processes leading to the issuance of rules and guidelines.

Over the past decade, these long-standing principles have been challenged by selective statutes requiring public consultations in some areas, mostly involving the impact of capital-intensive infrastructure projects on particular communities. These provisions have encouraged environmental activists to campaign for greater public consultation in bureaucratic decision-making, even where this is not required. In response, elected politicians have granted limited forms of civil society participation on an ad hoc basis.

Some academics have supported enhanced public consultation and participation in executive policy choices. In the 1990s, two prominent German professors of public law interpreted the Basic Law to require transparent and accountable

---

[15] §§ 62–68 Joint Rules of Procedure of the Federal Ministries (GGO). An English translation is at www.bmi.bund.de/SharedDocs/downloads/EN/themen/moderne-verwaltung/ggo_en.pdf?__blob=publicationFile&v=1.

procedures for setting the government's environmental and technical norms. Erhard Denninger (1990, pp. 178–180) argued that consultation ought to include environmental and public-interest groups, not just directly affected neighbors. Rudolf Steinberg (1994, pp. 94–98) made a similar argument, particularly for atomic power. More recently, Hermann Pünder (2014, 2015) argues that courts should not impose judicialized procedures on the administration. Rather, based on comparisons with America and Britain, he supports rulemaking procedures that enhance democratic legitimacy as well as providing legal protection for individual rights. He quotes a 1977 decision of the Federal Administrative Court dealing with the construction of the Hamburg metro. The court stated that "[t]he necessity for a dialogue between the administration and the citizen, corresponds to the constitutional appreciation of the position of the citizens within the state." (BVerfGE 45, 297, 335 (1977 [quoted in Pünder, 2014, p. 243])). The case dealt with a public construction project, not a rule, although the language could have broader application because the arguments for public participation are similar for executive regulations. The courts recognize the necessity of delegation for the effective functioning of modern government and understand that procedures can be a route to legitimate executive action, but they have not gone further to accept a role in policing the public accountability of rulemaking procedures. Nevertheless, some commentators recognize a distinction between doctrinal public law and a regulatory approach better adapted to modern realities (Eifert 2014). These developments could signal an appreciation of the fundamental significance of democratic values in the legitimation of executive branch policymaking. Overall, in spite of a parliamentary structure, German developments represent an emerging pattern of accountability that closely resembles developments in presidentialist France.

France: Strong Presidentialism

The French president is more powerful than a parliamentary chief executive. In the UK and Germany, legislative and constitutional constraints limit the chief executive's power to insist on a vote of confidence, but perhaps the most effective constraint is the risk of losing office if the vote fails, and voters head to the polls. Although the British prime minister and the German chancellor can call for a vote of confidence, under certain conditions, they will lose office if their opponents win. The French president does not take the same risk. He or she remains in office for the rest of the office's five-year term, whatever the outcome of the snap election (French Const. Art. 12, Bermann & Picard 2012). Given this fact, it is unlikely that the president's allies in the National Assembly will provoke a dissolution of the Assembly. American presidents are also weaker vis-á-vis Congress because they too lack the power to dissolve the Congress and call for an election.

The French constitution (Article, 9, 13) provides for a prime minister, appointed by the president and subject to approval by the National Assembly. If the president has a majority in that body, he or she will appoint a pliable ally. If the opposition parties do gain a majority in the Assembly, the president remains a powerful force because he or she chairs weekly Cabinet meetings, determines their agenda, and must formally sign all regulations approved by the Council of Ministers (Reitz 2006).

The president and the prime minister can propose statutes that delegate policymaking authority to the executive. Some issues have to be governed by statute, but in a range of policy areas, the government can issue ordinances and decrees (*ordonnances* and *décrets*) even if no statute exists. (Ordinances lapse unless approved by the legislature within a set period; decrees do not face that constraint although a subsequent statute may void a decree.) Presidents have no interest in passing statutes that impose procedural limits on executive rulemaking, and, in fact, no wide-ranging constraints appear in the statute books.

In practice, the most effective potential check on presidential power does not come from political opponents but from the bureaucracy itself. The elite corps in the Council of State or *Conseil d'État* (CE) predates the 1958 constitution of the Fifth Republic by at least a century. The CE has two roles. Not only is it at the apex of the administrative court system; it also plays a key role in reviewing the government's statutory and bureaucratic proposals before they are publicly advanced for consideration by parliament and the voters. This review takes place in secret and focuses on the extent to which proposals are compatible with the values and principles of the French system of public law. The CE consists of about 150 elite jurists most of whom dedicate their professional lives to public service, sometimes moving for a time into top positions inside the cabinet. Senior councilors resist governmental initiatives that they deem inconsistent with the basic values of French law. Moreover, the government risks subsequent enforcement difficulties if its proposed draft law or decree enters into force in spite of opposition from the CE. The constitutional structure, in short, combines strong presidential leadership with a significant check from an elite juristic institution.[16]

France's constitutional tribunal, the *Conseil Constitutionnel* (CC), has played a less significant role than its German counterpart. Until 2011, only parliamentarians or the president could raise constitutional challenges. Moreover, they could do so only before bills were enacted into law. Once the statute was on the books, regular courts refused to allow ordinary litigants to raise analogous objections. A constitutional amendment, however, now authorizes the CC to hear such challenges, based on referrals from France's two high courts. In contrast to Germany, this grant of authority challenges a centuries-old French tradition rejecting "government by judges." However, in *Association France Nature Environnement (AFNE)*, Conseil Constitutionnel, Décision n° 2011–183/184 QPC, 14 October 2011, the CC interpreted the constitution's Environmental Charter to permit such outside groups

---

[16] France & Vauchez (2017) raises doubts about the durability of that model as the private sector competes for elite officials.

to participate in a ministerial decision-making process. The decision only applies to environmental affairs. It remains unclear how aggressively the CC will exercise its new review powers and how well it will coordinate with other courts, but it has become an important actor within the French legal system.

Advocacy groups challenged French policy on climate change by bringing a joint action for failure to act (*un recours en carence fautive*) against the French government. They are basing their action on the same Charter for the Environment invoked in the *AFNE* case along with French statutes and international law. The groups notified the prime minister and other members of the government in late 2018 of their demands for government action. The French government rejected the groups' request, and the groups brought a case in the Administrative Court of Paris that issued a decision in February 2021 designed to force the government to act but without giving specific guidance. However, the litigation is ongoing.[17]

In 2015, France enacted its first Administrative Procedure Code that largely codifies the case law of the CE; it does not regulate rulemaking (Custos 2017). Despite this legislative affirmation of the status quo, other institutions have been more responsive to recent campaigns by those demanding greater public participation in bureaucratic initiatives, especially on environmental matters. The CE has experimented with different forms of public consultation. As already noted, the CC has used its new jurisdiction to expand participation rights in environmental matters.

United States: Separation-of-Powers Presidentialism

The American Constitution, Art. II, sect. 3, provides that the president shall "take Care that the Laws be faithfully executed," but it says nothing about the executive-branch institutions needed to fulfill this demand. The constitutional framework combines a separately elected president and legislature with the president's inability to dissolve Congress. Hence, the chief executive may face a Congress where a rival political party controls the House, the Senate, or both. Even if the president's party has a majority in both legislative branches, some of its members may oppose presidential initiatives that are unpopular in their home districts. As a consequence, Congressional leaders have a political interest in constraining executive branch discretion.

One option is to draft detailed substantive statutes. The president may accept restrictive language to gain Congressional consent to executive-branch initiatives. Such provisions will be more enduring than in Europe. In the US, if the presidency shifts to the opposing party, the new administrative will find it hard promptly to repeal or amend statutes, given the system's multiple veto points (Tsebelis 2002).

---

[17] *Notre Affaire à Tous v. France*, http://climatecasechart.com/non-us-case/notre-affaire-a-tous-and-others-v-france/. Updates of this and other cases in France and elsewhere are available at https://climatecasechart.com.

Even when delegation occurs, Congress has a strong incentive to keep it in check through oversight hearings, budgetary control, and commissions of inquiry.

However, direct oversight is insufficient. Given the broad-range of government regulatory activities, elected politicians have limited capacity to engage in intensive, ongoing oversight (McCubbins & Schwartz 1984).

Given that lacuna, the separation of powers generated political incentives for the legislature to act. Its most comprehensive response was the Administrative Procedure Act (APA), enacted in 1946, that aims to entrench public accountability for executive rulemaking. According to the APA §551(4), a rule is "an agency statement of general or particular applicability and future effect designed to implement, interpret, or prescribe law or policy or describing the organization, procedure, or practice requirements of an agency...." The key words here are "future effect." The "notice-and-comment" rulemaking procedures in §553 require general notice in the Federal Register of proposed rules, hearings open to all "interested persons," and publication of final rules along with "a concise general statement of their basis and purpose." The APA exempts certain rules and administrative actions, for example, "general statements of policy" and some policy areas, for example, military or foreign affairs, but its reach is broad. Even some agencies not required to follow notice and comment processes voluntarily follow them. The Act enlists the courts to enforce its requirements and to limit the electoral damage caused by policies hostile to the interests of legislators (Landes & Posner 1975). The APA §706(2)(D) states that a reviewing court shall set aside agency actions with substantive flaws, but it can also set aside actions if an agency does not follow the procedures required by law, including violations of the APA's own notice and comment procedures. Thus, the legislature recognizes the pragmatic value of delegation but uses the courts to constrain its exercise. This implies, of course, that the courts are both competent and have limited jurisdiction. In addition to ruling on the violation of constitutional rights and the abuse of power, judicial oversight can help to uphold democratic control, not to enact the judges' policy preferences. Difficulties can arise, however, when appeals to rights and the abuse of executive power have the effect of limiting the policymaking activities of the executive.

APA requirements for notice, hearings, and public reason-giving are broad and neutral. They do not favor particular political or economic interests. In practice, however, wealthy and well-organized interests are better represented at hearings and provide input both into proposed rules and in the post-comment period. In the end, however, the agency must docket all comments and provide a public, reasoned justification for its rules. If one assumes that organized economic interests seek to influence executive policymaking in all systems, in the U. S. much of that influence must be documented in the log of public comments. Nevertheless, critics argue that single-purpose agencies risk capture by the very industries they must regulate, or even that the legislature sought to create a regulatory structure that enshrined industry dominance (Posner 1974). Others make the same claim for groups supporting environmental and workplace regulation. If judicial review checks these tendencies, why would Congress build it into the structure of the law? One answer is that judicial review is a way for legislators to avoid making difficult policy choices. Because they face pressure from both special interests and ordinary voters, they write statutes that nominally favor interest groups but then set standards for judicial review that limit the damage. The legislators in David Mayhew's (1974) phrase "claim credit" for benefiting a powerful constituency while avoiding a severe impact on the general public. To some, this tendency argues for revival of the disused non-delegation doctrine that would limit the ability of Congress to include vague terms, such as "feasibility" in statutes.[18] The limits of policymaking delegation promise to be a contested issue going forward.

On the positive side of the ledger, empirical work suggests that extreme claims of regulatory capture are overstated and do not encompass the wide range of rulemaking experiences. Not surprisingly, business groups are very active, both in seeking to influence draft proposals and in submitting comments. Jason Webb Yackee and Susan Webb Yackee (2006) provide evidence of business influence but conclude that the process does allow open-ended participation and furthers the goal of "limiting the ability of federal agencies to regulate with impunity."[175] In other words, the process matters, and even if commercial bodies are central participants, it is preferable to put their input into the public rulemaking record. That way it can be countered by others, limiting the ability of insiders to influence policy choices out of the public eye. Of more immediate concern is the use of mechanical bots to flood agency websites with hundreds of thousands of comments.[19] The regulatory process is not meant to be a referendum on a draft rule, but agencies do need to develop effective ways to process such input without losing valuable observations.

CONCLUSIONS

Political economy helps to explain policymaking accountability under the rulemaking provisions of the US APA and its absence from my other cases. American separation-of-powers presidentialism produced political incentives for passage of the APA. The legislature, facing practical reasons to delegate policymaking to the executive, found ways to hold the executive to account. Going forward, however, critics see notice-and-comment rulemaking as pure window-dressing. They

---

[18] See Justice William Rehnquist's partial concurrence in *Industrial Union Dept., AFL-CIO v. American Petroleum Inst. (the Benzene Case)*, 448 U.S. 607, 671–688 (1980). Further effort at its revival failed in *Whitman v. American Trucking Ass'ns*, 531 U.S. 457 (2001) and *Gundy v. U.S.*, 139 S. Ct. 2116 (2019). In *Gundy* a strong dissent by Justice Neil Gorsuch may signal a willingness to revisit the issue in the future.

[19] Kevin Collier & Jeremy Singer-Vine, "Millions of Comments about the FCC's Net Neutrality Rules Were Fakes. Now the Feds Are Investigating," *BuzzFeed News*, December. 8, 2018, www.buzzfeed news.com/article/kevincollier/feds-investigation-net-neutrality-comments?mod=article_inline.

argue that it covers a deeply biased process that favors major economic actors. Others worry that it takes too much time and money and involves the courts in political/policy battles. At the same time, presidents, going back at least to Ronald Reagan, have attempted to take control of the administrative state, concentrating power in the White House. These centralizing moves limit the role of notice-and-comment rulemaking in cabinet departments and generate more executive control of so-called independent agencies. These developments may leave little space for diverse, outside voices. If critics of APA procedures succeed, they may find that the administration has become more closed and the president more powerful as presidents attempt to enhance their power over agency actions (Kagan 2001; Shane 2009; Strauss 2007). Nevertheless, there remains much to learn from America's successes and failures as democratic reformers everywhere try to design better forms of accountability for the twenty-first century.

At the same time, an opposing trend exists in the European cases that I study. The parliamentary systems of the UK and Germany as well as French-style presidentialism have no general statutory requirements for public input into executive rulemaking. Yet, the very lack of such laws is leading to organized pressure for more open and accountable policymaking processes. At present, these demands mostly involve the environment and large infrastructure projects, but the underlying concerns for democratic accountability raise fundamental issues with broad application to other areas of public life.

In Europe the expertise of the bureaucracy and its insulation from day-to-day politics were traditionally meant to preserve the public interest from the short-term partisan pressures of political actors. As faith in the civil service has eroded, the state faces demands for more openness and public participation, on the one hand, and more systematic, publicly justified reason-giving, on the other. Sometimes, expert social science conflicts with popular beliefs and interests. In all four countries, civil society organizations are pushing the courts and other oversight institutions to take more aggressive stands vis-á-vis unaccountable policymaking in public bureaucracies. Much of this activity, especially outside the US, focuses on the violation of individual rights. However, a deeper look at these developments suggests a broader concern with the democratic legitimacy of executive rulemaking.

Some polities have begun to respond to the pressures for more analysis and for expanded public participation, but public officials frequently resist them, and reforms have not coalesced around a consensus. Future developments are by no means clear, but the elements are in place to build upon recent reforms. There is plenty of room for innovative, cross-country learning as democracies struggle to produce well-reasoned policies that are responsive to popular concerns, not just to the interests of professional politicians or technocratic elites.

Some recognize the importance of this goal but argue that rulemaking hearings and dialogue are imperfect methods. They urge the greater use of public opinion polls and focus groups. They see open-ended public hearings as biased and unreliable measures of public opinion, and they claim that modern social science techniques would do a better job. Advocates for this position, however, too often understand "public opinion" in simplistic terms. In a representative democracy, bureaucratic policymakers should not merely seek a snapshot of public sentiment, especially because citizens' opinions often lack an informed confrontation with the problem at hand. Rather, the administration should create public fora to enable citizens to engage in meaningful discussion and debate.[20]

However, some contend that public hearings on proposed rules are an ineffective way to incorporate public sentiment into bureaucratic decisions. They argue that the public ought to be deeply involved in proposing options, debating the choices, and making the final decisions. The problem is figuring out how to accomplish such an ambitious goal. Positive examples exist at the local level in dense urban neighborhoods, small villages, and affinity groups. However, such intense public involvement is infeasible for policy issues affecting tens of millions of citizens. Think of national environmental regulations or the construction of a new high-speed rail line. Furthermore, seeking consensus is not a desirable goal if the distribution of power and wealth is unjust. Existing inequalities should not be baked into the menu of feasible options, especially if the poor lack the time and energy to reflect on their concrete interests in contested matters.

There is a final check on bureaucratic abuses of discretion: popular protest, with marches and rallies denouncing government initiatives. Even here, well-established forms of policy-making accountability matter. If they exist, it is more likely that the state will engage in constructive efforts to incorporate popular grievances into ongoing consultative processes or other efforts at popular inclusion. Of course, these measures may reduce, but won't eliminate, the risk of violent confrontations which may shake the very foundations of democratic legitimacy. In the final analysis, there is no substitute for responsible political leadership and thoughtful bureaucratic administration to sustain the credibility of modern activist government. Political accountability, as I have articulated it here, can play a valuable role in sustaining this project.

RECOMMENDED READING

Broeksteeg, H., Verhey, L., & Van den Driessche, I., eds. (2008). *Political Accountability in Europe: Which Way Forward?* Groningen: Europa Law Publishing.

Carpenter, D. & Moss, D. A. eds. (2014). *Preventing Regulatory Capture*, Cambridge: Cambridge University Press.

Eifert, M. (2014). Conceptualizing Administrative Law–Legal Protection Versus Regulatory Approach. In H. Pünder and C. Waldhoff, eds., *Debates in German Public Law*. Oxford: Hart, pp. 203–218.

---

[20] I canvass some of the options in Chapter 6 of *Democracy and Executive Power* (2021).

Harlow, C. (2002). Accountability in the European Union. In P. Alston and B. de Witte, eds., *Collected Courses of the Academy of European Law*. Oxford: Oxford University Press.

Kagan, E. (2001). Presidential Administration. *Harvard Law Review*, 114 (8), 2245–2319.

Mashaw, J. L. (2018). *Reasoned Administration and Democratic Legitimacy*, Cambridge: Cambridge University Press.

McCubbins, M. D., Noll, R. G., & Weingast, B. (1987). Administrative Procedures as Instruments of Political Control. *Journal of Law, Economics and Organization*, 3 (2), 243–277.

Nicholas, B. (1970). Loi, Règlement and Judicial Review in the Fifth Republic. *Public Law*, 1970, 251–276.

Reitz, J. C. (2006). Political Economy and Separation of Powers. *Transnational Law & Contemporary Problems*, 15 (2), 579–625.

Rose-Ackerman, S. (2021). *Democracy and Executive Power: Policymaking Accountability in the US, the UK, Germany, and France*, New Haven: Yale University Press.

Rose-Ackerman, S., Egidy, S. & Fowkes, J. (2015). *Due Process of Lawmaking: The United States, South Africa, Germany, and the European Union*, Cambridge: Cambridge University Press.

Rose-Ackerman, S., Lindseth, P., & Emerson, B., eds. (2017). *Comparative Administrative Law*. Cheltenham: Edward Elgar, pp. 284–301.

Rose-Ackerman, S. & Perroud, T. (2014). Policymaking and Public Law in France: Public Participation, Agency Independence, and Impact Assessment. *The Columbia Journal of European Law*, 19 (2), 225–312.

Ruffert, M., ed., (2007). *The Transformation of Administrative Law in Europe*, Munich: Sellier.

Shane, P. M. (2009). *Madison's Nightmare: How Executive Power Threatens American Democracy*, Chicago: University of Chicago Press.

Strauss, P. L. (2007). Overseer or "the Decider"? The President in Administrative Law. *George Washington Law Review*, 75 (4), 696–760.

PART III. C

The Democratic System

41

Constituent Assemblies

Joel Colón-Ríos

What are the elements uniting (or distinguishing) entities that in different jurisdictions and historical periods, have been officially called General Congresses, Constituent Parliaments, Constituent Congresses, National Constituent Assemblies, Constitutional Assemblies, Assemblies of Revision, Parallel Constituent Assembles, or Conventions, but at the same time are generically labelled (correctly or incorrectly) by political actors and academics as 'constituent assemblies'? In attempting to answer that question, the objective of this chapter is threefold. First, to describe the main features of the type of institution that can be accurately identified as a constituent assembly. This requires a conception that is broad enough to cover most constitution-making bodies that would be normally labelled as 'constituent assemblies', but specific enough as to discriminate against entities that lack certain features. I propose that, while constituent assemblies may be understood in terms of their form or function, it is the nature of their power what distinguishes them from other constitution-drafting mechanisms. My second objective is to enquire into the limits of the power of – a properly understood – constituent assembly. Third, and relatedly, to consider the effects that the attempt to constitutionally regulate such an entity has on its 'constituent' nature. In achieving these two last objectives, I will use the Colombian constitution-making (and amending) processes (and the associated jurisprudence) as a key example.

I FORM, FUNCTION, AND POWER

Constituent assemblies are, at the most general level, characterised by the fact that they engage in the activity of creating new constitutional content. However, they are not usually seen as engaging in the exercise of the amending power (that is, the power regulated by a constitution's ordinary rule of change), but the constituent one. Accordingly, they are not typically conceived as bound by any substantive restrictions derived from the constitutional text: explicit or implicit limits on constitutional reform, while reducing the scope of the ordinary amendment authority, do not apply to an entity engaged in the exercise of constituent power.[1] Moreover, once convened, constituent assemblies are usually free to adopt their own internal decision-making rules. In what follows, I will enquire more deeply into the nature of the type of entities that generally exhibit those features, by examining them from the perspective of their form, function, and power. As we will see later, some of these features may not be necessary elements of a constitution-making body correctly characterised as a constituent assembly.

From a *formal* perspective, the notion of a constituent assembly points toward a temporary constitution-making entity separate from the ordinary law-making authority. This entity would nonetheless be an *assembly*, although its members could be elected or appointed, and it could be convened in democratic or undemocratic contexts. It could be called by a military government, triggered by an extra-constitutional referendum or through a constitutionally regulated popular initiative process. It could also be given different functions: it could be tasked to adopt a new constitution or to alter an existing one. The nature of its power could also vary. It could be conceived as a sovereign entity with the authority to act as if it was the people, or as a drafting committee, whose decisions are not binding until ratified by the citizenry. From this formal perspective, a constituent assembly would thus be defined as an extra-parliamentary collegiate body producing constitutional law. The explanatory limits of this approach quickly come to light when confronted with actual constitutional practice: there have been many instances of ordinary legislatures temporarily acting, or doubling, as constitution-making entities and, when they do, they are usually identified by scholars and political actors as constituent assemblies or, sometimes, as constituent legislatures.

If one approaches constituent assemblies in terms of their *function*, this initial difficulty is avoided, for then what would make a constitution-making body a constituent assembly is having been temporarily tasked to engage in the creation of new constitutional content. Just as when understood from a formal perspective, a constituent assembly (functionally conceived) could be convened constitutionally or extra-constitutionally, and its power could be limited to that of proposing a draft constitution to the electorate (or to the legislature) or may include the authority to adopt it on behalf of the people. However, unlike in the formal approach, an ordinary legislature that at any point in time exercises any of those functions would also count as a constituent assembly. The functional approach nonetheless has some important limitations. While it may be able to accurately describe the nature of an ordinary legislature that has been given (or assumed) the task of creating a new constitution (or of altering an existing one in ways that go beyond the ordinary amendment process), it falls short of explaining the power of these types of entities. For example, some extra-parliamentary bodies convened for the creation of a new constitution have gone beyond that task and effectively assumed some of

---

[1] See for example, *Kesavananda Bharti Sripadagalvaru v. State of Kerala*, 1973 (SUP) SCR 0001 (India).

the ordinary functions of government in ways that sometimes also put into question their non-permanent nature.

To avoid that problem, one may say that under the functional approach, a constituent assembly must respect the specific functions it has been given (a legislative and constituent function in the case of an ordinary legislature tasked to engage in constitution-making; and a sole constituent function in the case of extra-parliamentary assemblies). This also means that it must dissolve (or, in the case of a legislature, that it would cease to act as a constitution-making body) after its constituent function is completed. At that point, however, the functional approach would tend to obscure the fact that the reason why some constituent assemblies go beyond the production of constitutional law and intervene in the exercise of the ordinary powers of government is a direct result of the way in which the relevant political actors understand the power these bodies are called to exercise. Put differently, constituent assemblies are usually seen as means for the exercise of an unlimited constitution-making authority that rests in the entire community, that is, as being called to exercise an uncontrollable (primary or original) constituent power on behalf of the people. Accordingly, a way of trying to circumvent the previously identified difficulty is to define constituent assemblies not in terms of their form or function, but in terms of the nature of their *power*.

Under this conception, a constituent assembly would be an entity called to exercise constituent power on a *mandate* directly attributable to the people. An ordinary legislature that has been vested with the task of adopting a new constitution would thus only be a true constituent assembly if its power can be understood as derived not from the constitution, but from the constituent subject itself. This would be the case of what Jon Elster (2006) has called 'mandated' constituent legislatures, which operate in situations where the electorate explicitly (i.e. *via* referendum) vests constitution-making jurisdiction to an otherwise ordinary legislature. These entities, under the power perspective, are correctly understood as constituent assemblies because their constitution-making jurisdiction can't be traced back to the existing constitution: it is based on a popular authorisation that has bypassed established constitutional rules.[2] In contrast, consider a constitution that authorises a legislature, or a joint-sitting of the legislative chambers, to engage in constitution-making activity. In this case, the legislature's constitution-making authority would be based on the constitution itself, and just as the ordinary legislative or executive functions, it would only be *indirectly* linked to a popular mandate. Those entities could thus be subject to whatever procedural or substantive limits are found in the constitution itself.

In that respect, under the 'power' perspective, a constitution-making body whose authority immediately derives from the constitution (i.e. one which is convened

---

[2] This is an example of Sieyès' (2003 [1789], p. 139) view that the same people could act as ordinary and extraordinary representatives. They could also be convened in a non-democratic way, such as the National Constituent and Legislative Assembly created by a Presidential decree in 1905 Colombia. See Legislative Decree no. 29 (Colombia) (1 February 1905). This type of assembly would present problems similar to self-created constituent legislatures, discussed below.

according to established constitutional provisions and in the absence of direct popular intervention) would not be understood as a true constituent assembly, but as an extraordinary mechanism[3] for the exercise of the amending power, that is, the type of power that is exercised under a constitution's amendment rule. 'Self-created' constituent legislatures (as Elster calls this third type of constituent legislature) present a special case. These are ordinary legislatures that assume, by themselves, a constituent function without having a popular mandate or constitutional authorisation to do so. These entities would also count as constituent assemblies from the 'power' perspective, even if they operate under a different, potentially not democratic, conception of constituent power. They would be, in a certain way, in a similar position to that of a sovereign parliament which decides (without a specific constitution-making mandate) to create a new constitution.[4] This would contrast with a situation where a parliamentary majority is elected on a programme that includes the creation of a new constitution. In such a case, the new parliament would arguably be in a position similar to a constituent assembly subject to a popular constitution-making mandate (even though, as noted below, the legal force of that constitution-making mandate would probably not be the same as if it was directed to a constituent assembly).

Although it does a better job of identifying what seem to be the key features of a constituent assembly, the *power* perspective also has important shortcomings. These are reflected in the following two questions: (1) Does the fact that a constituent assembly is not regulated by the existing constitution mean that it necessarily acts on a *free* or *sovereign* mandate, a mandate that allows it to act as if it was the constituent subject and produce *any* norms it wishes? and (2) Does a constitution-making entity, in order for its mandate to come directly from the constituent subject and not from the constitution itself, have to be convened extra-constitutionally, that is, in violation of the established rules of change? These questions go to the core of the nature of the power of a constituent assembly. The sections that follow will address them by examining in some detail the case of Colombia and some of its jurisprudence about constitutional change. I will argue that, even though constitutional theory and practice (in Colombia and in several other jurisdictions, most notably Venezuela) (Colón-Ríos 2020) has largely answered those questions in the affirmative, there are good reasons to support a different solution.

II CONSTITUENT ASSEMBLIES AND SOVEREIGNTY

Through his impressive work on constitution-making, Andrew Arato (2016, p. 117) has distinguished between constituent assemblies and constitutional conventions. For Arato, a key feature of the latter entities is their *double differentiation*: once

---

[3] See Pacheco (1845).
[4] This is why Alexis de Tocqueville's (1956, p. 74) once described the English Parliament as a constituent assembly in permanent session. See also Loughlin (2007).

a constitutional convention is in place, the ordinary legislature continues its usual work, while the convention cannot exercise ordinary governmental powers. Constituent assemblies, in contrast, are only *singly differentiated*: while they are in place the legislature cannot assume constituent functions, but the constituent assembly (which is here seen as a sovereign entity) is able to engage in the exercise of the ordinary powers of the state.[5] Arato's approach accurately describes different entities that have operated at various times and contexts, even if it does not sit easily with the terminology frequently used by political actors. There have been entities called 'conventions' that have acted as sovereign bodies[6], and entities called 'constituent assemblies' that possess the feature of double-differentiation[7]. Arato (2016, pp. 112, 115) himself describes the events in 1776 at Pennsylvania as involving "a sovereign constituent assembly ... under the name of a convention", and the constitution-making body initially convened in Venezuela in 1999 as an example of "the convention formula under the name constituent assembly".[8]

Arato's depiction of constituent assemblies nonetheless accurately reflects the ways in which they have been generally understood by Latin American courts: once convened, a constituent assembly is usually conceived as a sovereign body, an entity authorised to act *as if* it was the people. The influence of this conception is not surprising, since it appears to be based on a basic democratic principle: the people is sovereign and, accordingly, a popularly elected assembly convened to transform the constitutional order in fundamental ways cannot find itself constrained by positive law, it must be a sovereign entity. This is the conception exemplified in the decision of the Supreme Court of Justice of Colombia which examined the powers of the National Constituent Assembly of 1990. That conception, in my view, is based on a confusion between two concepts that should be kept separate: the concept of sovereignty and the concept of constituent power. As I have argued elsewhere, sovereignty, when referring to the power of a law (or constitution) making body, is the power of transforming any will into law (Colón-Ríos 2020). A sovereign entity would, in addition to creating novel constitutional forms, be able to transform into law a legislative, judicial, or executive will. Constituent power is by contrast an element of sovereignty but, as explained below, should be distinguished from sovereignty.

Consider, first, the relationship between a sovereign people and the general activity of law-making within a democratic constitutional order. In a democracy, the people

---

[5] Arato is of course not the only scholar to distinguish between constituent assemblies and conventions, even though not everyone understands the latter kind of entity as being double differentiated. For example, for Schmitt (2008 [1928], pp. 132–133), what differentiates assemblies and conventions is that the former are able to adopt a constitution without the need of popular ratification.

[6] This is the case of some state conventions in the United States. See Hoar (2004).

[7] See for example the 'Parallel Constituent Assembly' regulated by Article 314 of the current Constitution of Panama. The adjective 'Parallel' serves to emphasize its double differentiated character.

[8] As Arato explains, the Venezuelan "convention" ended up operating as a "sovereign constituent assembly".

is supposed to govern itself, even though it cannot come together and produce juridical acts. Rather, usually through a written constitution, the people – it is said – delegates to a legislative assembly the power to create laws, to the executive branch the power to execute them, and to the judiciary the power to adjudicate disputes about their application and meaning. Sometimes, the adoption of a new constitution or the alteration of the existing one becomes necessary. In those cases, the sovereign people may delegate the exercise of its power of constitutional change (its *constituent* power) to a special assembly, a *constituent* assembly. A key reason for proceeding in this way – that is, vesting on a special assembly (and not in the ordinary law-making body) the task of creating a new constitution – is related to the principle of the separation of powers: a (constituent) legislature would be acting as a judge in its own case and may be tempted to draft a constitutional text that augments its own powers. If a constituent assembly is understood as a sovereign entity, the separation of powers would also suffer a serious blow: all powers would be concentrated in it. But there is no reason for constituent assemblies to be necessarily seen in that way.

In the same way a legislature does not become a sovereign entity just by being called to exercise the legislative power, a constituent assembly, just as a result of having been called to exercise constituent authority, does not become a sovereign entity. In fact, despite been frequently described as 'sovereign' by lawyers and scholars, constituent assemblies are increasingly conceived as unable to *adopt* new constitutions: they are only able to draft a document that becomes constitutional law if popularly ratified. A constituent assembly is not the people; rather, it acts on its behalf. This view, if accepted, would have several consequences. First, unless authorised to do so, a constituent assembly would lack the power to adopt ordinary laws or of intervening with the constituted authorities. That is to say, the default position of a constituent assembly would be 'double differentiation'. Second, as in the power perspective discussed above, a constituent assembly would be acting on a mandate from the sovereign people. In contemporary constitutional practice, this mandate would normally emerge from a referendum question that asks the electorate a question like the following: 'Do you wish to convene a constituent assembly for the adoption of a new constitution?'

If the majoritarian answer to such a referendum question is 'yes', the people, acting through the electorate, would have instructed an assembly to draft a document that possesses the elements considered necessary within the society in question for something to count as a *constitution*. Naturally, the mandate to create a constitution, by itself,[9] does not include an authorisation to exercise the competences

---

[9] The case of Ecuador in 2007 is interesting in this respect, as the referendum question stated: "Do you approve that a Constituent Assembly with plenary powers is convened…". The reference to 'plenary powers' can be understood as including the authorisation to exercise a 'sovereign' authority (which would involve, for example, the authority to create ordinary laws), and that was how it was interpreted by the assembly. See for example, *Reglamento de Funcionamiento de la Asamblea Constituyente* (Ecuador) (12 December 2007).

vested on specific organs by the existing separation of powers regime.[10] Some referenda questions may involve a more specific mandate, a mandate to create a certain type of constitutional content and, in virtue of originating in the sovereign people, it could be understood as having the same binding qualities of a constitution (as suggested earlier this would not seem to be applicable to a sovereign parliament acting, or failing to act, on a mandate contained in the relevant party programme). In a non-revolutionary context (a context where the ordinary institutions of government continue to exist), a decision of a constituent assembly openly contrary to its mandate would thus appear to be open to judicial challenges: after all, (constitutional) courts' main task is to protect another popular mandate, the constitution.[11] As I will show below, the Supreme Court of Justice of Colombia rejected this approach and concluded that the National Constituent Assembly of 1990 was a sovereign entity, which was another way of saying that even if it was acting on a mandate, it could freely depart from it.

Convening the Colombian Constituent Assembly of 1990

The assembly that adopted the Colombian Constitution of 1991 was convened during a state of siege in place as a result of the climate of violence then present in the country. The first official act toward its convocation took place on 3 May 1990, when President Virgilio Barco decreed that in the presidential elections that would take place a few weeks later, electors would be asked the following question: "To strengthen participatory democracy, do you vote in favour of convening a Constitutional Assembly with representation of the social, political and regional forces of the nation, democratically and popularly established, to reform the Political Constitution of Colombia?"[12]. When the constitutionality of the decree was examined by the Supreme Court of Justice, the judges determined that the provisions regulating the state of siege not only authorised the executive to engage in repressive acts with the purpose of restoring order, but also to adopt "measures of political, economic, and social rehabilitation clearly directed at overcoming the crisis."[13] For the Court, consulting the electorate about the convocation of a 'Constitutional

---

[10] Perhaps the only exception would be cases in which those organs are preventing the constituent assembly from completing its task. In those scenarios, one could say that the mandate to adopt a constitution includes an implicit authorisation to act against any constituted authority that intentionally obstructs the adoption of a new constitutional text. See Jameson (1887).

[11] Even in the absence of a referendum, a constitution-making body could be seen as acting on a popular mandate. As Marx (1849) noted with respect to the Frankfurt National Assembly of 1848: "If the Assembly does not act in accordance with the mandate it has received, then this mandate lapses. The people then takes the stage itself and acts on its own authority".

[12] Decree no 927 (3 May 1990). Note that the referendum question did not refer to a 'Constituent' but a 'Constitutional' assembly, and to the "reform" of the constitution, not to its replacement (I will come back to this point below).

[13] Judgment no 59 (24 May 1990), Part V, para. 2.

Assembly' and counting the votes in favour and against it was an example of the latter kind of measure.

Shortly after this judgment, the recently elected president, Cesar Gaviria, issued another decree, where it was expressed that "the Nation, where sovereignty resides, has manifested through an electoral act its will to convene a Constitutional Assembly…".[14] A new election in which such an assembly would be formally convened and its members selected, was ordered. The explicit premise of President Gaviria's decree was the existence of a "popular mandate" in favour of constitutional reform.[15] Importantly, his decree included the following provisions, which sought to regulate the power of the future constitution-making body: "To strengthen participatory democracy … the following topics [the decree included a long list of topics],[16] after being approved by the people, will determine the scope of the assembly's competence and, accordingly, the content of the reform".[17] The decree also established that "the Assembly shall not consider matters not included in the list of topics approved by the people and, especially, shall not modify the terms in office of those officials elected this year, matters affecting commitments of the Colombian State resulting from international treaties, or the republican system of government".

Moreover, the decree stated that the assembly would not deliberate for more than 150 days and authorised it to dictate "transitional provisions when it considers it necessary, only to ensure the application of the reform", as well as to adopt its internal rules. Finally, the "text of Constitutional Reform" approved by the assembly would be sent to the Supreme Court of Justice, which would determine if it "complies with the list of topics approved by citizens".[18] The Court's review of the constitutionality of the decree began with an analysis of Article 2 of the Constitution of 1886, which stated: "Sovereignty resides essentially and exclusively in the nation, from where the public powers emanate…"[19] This meant, the Court expressed, that "the Colombian nation is the primary constituent power [*constituyente primario*], [and] can at any time give itself a constitution different to the one in place without being subject to the requirements established by it".[20] The actions of the primary (or original) constituent power, the Court added[21] (citing a previous judgment), "escape any limitation established by the juridical order" including, especially, the amendment rule of the existing constitution.[22]

---

[14] Decree no. 1926 (24 August 1990).
[15] Decree no 927 (n 43).
[16] The list included, for example, certain types of changes to the functions of the legislative chambers. Changes related to the democratization of the public Administration, the recognition of new Rights, the establishment of the referendum as part of the process of constitutional reform, and modifications to the 1886 constitution's emergency rule.
[17] Decree no. 1926 (n 45).
[18] ibid, Article 15.
[19] Judgment no 138 (9 October 1990), Part V, para. 5.
[20] ibid
[21] Judgment no 54 (9 June 1987).
[22] Judgment no 138 (n 50) Part V, para. 6.

Not surprisingly, the Court concluded: "whereas the competence of the National Constitutional Assembly that will be convened by the people as Primary Constituent Power in the elections that will take place on 9 December cannot be limited..., the Court will declare unconstitutional any limitations ... implying restrictions to the full exercise of its sovereignty".[23] This point of view, in a way, was already reflected in an aspect of the constitution-making process. That is to say, the National Constituent Assembly was not only authorised to draft a constitution but to adopt it: the new constitution would become valid without the need of popular ratification.[24] The result of the Court's decision was that, once convened, the assembly would be able to act as a sovereign entity, independently of the people that commissioned it. The limits contained in the previously mentioned decree (as well as the Court's jurisdiction to enforce those limits), were thus described as unconstitutional attempts to restrain the decision-making power of a sovereign constitution-making authority.[25] The attempt to present those limits as aiming towards the "strengthening of participatory democracy", a mandate that appeared in the referendum question itself, did not save them from invalidity.

However, while the specific topics listed in the decree were declared unconstitutional (and therefore removed from the juridical order), the mandate requiring "strengthening participatory democracy" survived the Court's review. That mandate, the Court determined, was part of the very reason why the constituent subject had decided to convene the assembly.[26] It was nonetheless a *non-justiciable* mandate: the assembly was free to determine what constitutional forms would strengthen participatory democracy and there would not be any institution with the power to review or invalidate its decisions as to the content of the new constitutional text. Moreover, the 150 days term (which was respected by the assembly) was also sustained (without discussion) by the Court. The judges, it seems, thought that being subject to a temporal limit was consistent with holding a sovereign constitution-making power, that is, one not bound to any legally enforceable substantive restrictions. Once convened, the assembly interfered in different ways with the legislative and judicial functions, that is, it acted as a sovereign entity. In fact, although the decree that authorised its convocation referred to the "reform" of the constitution, the assembly not only adopted an entirely new constitutional text, but placed itself over the established constituted powers.

This course of action was in a certain way anticipated in the assembly's first resolution. In that document, in which the assembly for the first time officially called itself

---

[23] ibid, Part V, para. 8.
[24] For an examination of the delegates' discussion about whether the draft constitution should be submitted to referendum, see Gil (2008, pp. 94–95).
[25] Judgment no 138 (n 50) Part V, para. 8.
[26] ibid, Part V, para 7.

"National Constituent Assembly" (abandoning the term "Constitutional Assembly", used in the referendum question and in the presidential decrees)[27], it was stated: "The acts sanctioned and promulgated by the National Constituent Assembly are not subject to any jurisdictional control."[28] The assembly later decided, for example, to "revoke the mandate" of the elected members of Congress and call for early elections.[29] Congress unsuccessfully objected to that course of action, issuing a resolution expressing that the assembly lacked the authority to intervene with the ordinary electoral cycle.[30] The assembly then determined that until new elections took place, "the current Congress and its commissions would enter into recess and would not be able to exercise any of their functions…"[31] During that period, Congress was replaced by a special commission that became known as the *Congresito*, comprised by 36 members elected by the assembly itself (some of them doubling as members of the National Constituent Assembly). The assembly also gave the President of the Republic the power to adopt laws subject to the *Congresito's* veto.

In this sense, during the transitional period, the assembly (acting through the *Congresito*) and the executive power, became a sovereign legislature. The assumption of an unlimited jurisdiction by the assembly (expressed once again in Transitional Article 59 of the new constitution) was challenged at the newly created Constitutional Court. It was argued, among other things, that what was convened in 1990 was a "constitutional assembly for the reform of the constitution, not a constituent assembly to abolish it".[32] Moreover, that the previously mentioned Transitional Article 59 was unconstitutional, because "the limits of the Assembly have been identified by the primary constituent power in the ballot that establishes its task of 'strengthening participatory democracy'", which mean that "the Assembly lacked the authority to dictate norms" contrary to democracy.[33] The Court rejected those arguments. Expressly referring to Carl Schmitt's definition of constituent power,[34] it described the assembly as acting on "a commission of the sovereign people".[35] But instead of using that conception to develop a clear separation between the (constituent) assembly and the popular sovereign, the Court determined that "the primary constituent power can be directly expressed through a plebiscite or a democratic National Constituent Assembly", and when that happens, an unlimited law-making authority emerges.[36]

---

[27] On the debate about the assembly's name, see Gil (2008, p. 123) and de la Calle (2004, p. 88)
[28] Constituent Act no 1 (9 May 1991), Artículo 2.
[29] See "Congreso: La Nuez del Revolcón", *El Tiempo*, 9 de junio 1991.
[30] ibid. See Gil (2008, 100–112).
[31] See Transitional Article 3, Constitution of 1991.
[32] Judgment C-544/92, Parte I, para 3.1
[33] ibid, Part I, para 4.3
[34] Ibid, Part II, para 10 (constituent power as "the political will, whose power or authority is capable of making the concrete, comprehensive decision over the type and form of its own political existence"). See Schmitt (2008, p. 125).
[35] Judgment C-544/92, Part II, para 10.
[36] ibid

III CONSTITUTIONS AND CONSTITUENT ASSEMBLIES

Perhaps to avoid a situation where a constitution-making body claims for itself sovereign authority, the constitution-making process which formally began in 2019 in Chile avoided, in the law and legal documents that regulated it, the terms '*constituent* power' and '*constituent* assembly'. The entity that drafted the (eventually rejected) new constitution (consistently with Arato's terminology) is instead called a 'constitutional convention'. Moreover, Article 135[37] of the current constitution (as amended in 2019 to regulate the constitution-making process), establishes: "The Convention, any of its members or a fraction of them, shall not vest in themselves the exercise of sovereignty, assuming other functions than those expressly recognised by this Constitution". The 2019 amendments also placed specific procedural and substantive requirements as to the content the new constitution could have. Article 133 maintains that decisions of the convention are to be made by a two-thirds majority of its members, and the previously mentioned Article 135 states: "The text of the New Constitution that is submitted to referendum will respect the republican character of the Chilean state, its democratic regime, judicial decisions that have become final and international treaties ratified by Chile…". However, Article 136 maintains that while "violations of the procedural rules applicable to the Convention" can be subject to a judicial challenge, decisions of the assembly as to the content of the new constitution (regardless of the substantive restrictions contained in Article 135) are final.

What is the nature of the power of a constitution-making body whose convocation, as in Chile, has been anticipated and regulated by the constitutional text? Once again, Colombian jurisprudence proves instructive. The Colombian Constitution of 1991 contains a mechanism for the convening of a future constituent assembly:

> **Article 374.** The Political Constitution may be reformed by Congress, by a Constituent Assembly, or by the people through a referendum…

> **Article 376.** By means of an Act approved by the members of both Houses, Congress may direct that the people in a popular election decides if it wants to convene a Constituent Assembly with the competence, term, and makeup that the same law shall determine. It shall be understood that the people has convened the Assembly if it is so approved by a majority [under a participation threshold of one-third of the registered electors]…. The ordinary powers of Congress to reform the constitution shall be suspended after the election so that the Assembly may fulfil its functions during the established term. The Assembly shall adopt its internal rules.

The reference to the "competence" of the constituent assembly in the first sentence of Article 376 seems to accept as valid what was determined inadmissible by the Supreme Court of Justice in 1990: the imposition of substantive restrictions on a constituent assembly. Nonetheless, at least at first sight, there is a fundamental

---

[37] Constitution of Chile (1980, as amended in 2019), Article 135.

difference between the entity convened in 1990 and a potential assembly called under Article 376: while the former can be understood as tasked with the exercise of the original constituent power, the second, being regulated by the constitution, is perhaps only a constituted authority, a special mechanism to exercise the amending power. Nevertheless, there are good reasons to think that the fact that the convocation of a constituent assembly is in some way regulated by law does not necessarily rule out the possibility of it being authorised to exercise the original constituent power.[38] In fact, the convening of the National Constituent Assembly of 1990 and the election of its members, as well as the totality of the constituent assemblies convened in Latin America since the nineteenth century, were *legally* called, either by a presidential decree, by a law, or by a constitutional provision (i.e., they all had their basis on some established, even if extra-constitutional, legal procedure).

The key question is thus what is the legal effect, if any, of substantive (or procedural) limits seeking to apply to an entity that enjoys a direct popular authorisation for the exercise of constituent power.[39] In Colombia, the Constitutional Court has not had the opportunity to fully consider that question (as no constituent assembly has been convened since 1990), but has issued some *obiter dicta* comments about it that are worth mentioning. For example, in 2003, and in the context of a discussion about the doctrine of unconstitutional constitutional amendments, the Court appeared to suggest that Article 376 provided an opening for the exercise of constituent power and, potentially, for the replacement of the Constitution of 1991:

> The power of constitutional reform, even if its exercise includes a referendum, is the work of neither the original constituent power nor of the sovereign people, but an expression of a juridical competence organised by the Constitution itself and, as a result, it is necessarily limited by the impossibility of replacing the Charter, as that would imply that the power of constitutional reform becomes the original constituent power.... That said, and without having to analyse this topic in detail in the context of this case, this Court considers that the Constitution of 1991 attempted to overcome ... the tension between popular sovereignty and constitutional supremacy through the creation of an opening to the original constituent power, providing a demanding [*agravado*] process of reform, that could eventually allow the juridically valid replacement of the existing Constitution. The establishment of a channel for the manifestation of the original constituent power is always imperfect, because constituent power, by its own nature, "rebels against its total integration in a system of norms and competences"[40], and in that sense does not admit a total institutionalisation.[41]

---

[38] On this point, see John Austin's (2000, p. 233) discussion about the periodic constitutional convention regulated by the Constitution of New York.
[39] Thanks to Vicente Benítez for his valuable comments and recommendations on this topic.
[40] The Court was here quoting from Burdeau (1969, p. 181).
[41] Judgment C-551/03, para. 40.

A problem with this approach is that it rests on a premise (i.e. the power of constitutional reform regulated by the constitution is a constituted power and, therefore, cannot be used to replace the constitution) that it is necessary to reject in order to accept the conclusion that the reform procedure established by the Constitution of 1991 provides an opening to the original constituent power that could result in its juridically valid replacement. It is thus not surprising that, a year later, the Court determined that the power of a constituent assembly convened under Article 376 is not unlimited. That provision itself, the Court maintained, "establishes that the law by which the people, through popular vote, decides to convene a constituent assembly, will determine the competence of the assembly, that is, the subject matter that the reform will address". Accordingly, "if the assembly goes beyond the scope of that competence, its acts would suffer from a vice susceptible of control by the Constitutional Court".[42] From this perspective, an assembly convened under a constitutional provision (in Colombia, Article 376) would be fundamentally different from an extra-constitutionally convened one, such as the National Constituent Assembly that adopted the Constitution of 1991. That is, the type of limit judicially enforceable against the former would lack any effect against the latter.

Moreover, according to the same judgement, even in the absence of legislation containing subject matter limitations, an assembly convened under Article 376 cannot replace the Constitution of 1991 with a new one: "...the reform power [exercised by an Article 376 assembly] cannot replace the Constitution from which its own competence derives".[43] But two years later, the Court appears to have modified again its view about this matter. In a 2005 decision, it expressed that the "only bearer of an unlimited constituent power is the sovereign people," who "can give a Constituent Assembly the competence of issuing a new Constitution, a possibility that is expressly permitted by Article 376".[44] And in a 2016 judgment, the Court qualified that statement by expressing that it is not possible to replace the constitution through a constituent assembly with a "limited competence", but that "a national constituent assembly expressly convened for that purpose, without other limits on its competence, can channel the exercise of constituent power" and result in the creation of a new constitutional order.[45] In short, an Article 376 assembly would have whatever specific constitution-making powers are directly attributable to a popular decision.

This more recent perspective, even if it is in tension with some of the previous expressions of the Court, is in my view the correct one: a constituent assembly convened under a constitutional provision can be tasked with the exercise of the original constituent power, but that does not mean that it becomes a sovereign entity. For that reason, it can be bound by subject matter restrictions. Those limits can

---

[42] Judgment C-970/04, para. 1.3.3. See also Judgment C-1200/03, para 2.
[43] ibid
[44] Judgment C-1040/05, para 7.10.2
[45] Judgment C-699/16, paras 35.1, 38. See also Judgment C-574/11, para 4.43.

require the assembly to only reform the constitution in certain ways (for example, to reform the functions of one of the legislative chambers) or to fundamentally change it but with respect to only one matter (for example, to replace a bicameral system with a unicameral one).[46] It could also be made subject to procedural restrictions as the ones applicable to the Chilean Constitutional Convention of 2021. From the 'power' perspective considered above, what would matter is that those limits can be directly attributed to the sovereign people (which would normally require popular ratification in a referendum). Now, there do not seem to be any reasons why the same principle would not apply to *any* constituent assembly, including an extra-constitutionally convened one. After all, what that would mean is that a constitution-making body, regardless of how it has been convened, is subject to democratic control; that the content of the resulting constitutional text would be, at least in some way, ultimately determined by a popular decision.

The Colombian Supreme Court of Justice seemed to have thought otherwise when it declared unconstitutional the provisions that vested it with the power to determine if the National Constituent Assembly of 1990 had respected a series of subject matter restrictions. This makes sense at first sight, because we would otherwise find ourselves before a situation in which a constituted power invalidates the acts of the constituent one. However, it is important to remember the following. A constituent assembly, even when extra-constitutionally convened, is not the bearer of the constituent power but a mechanism to exercise it. Accordingly, the possibility that its acts are invalidated by an institution that is regulated by law (e.g. by a court), should not be so quickly rejected. One potential problem is that in the context of a constituent assembly convened extra-constitutionally, the intervention of a court would not find its justification in the constitutional text. Nonetheless, one can imagine a situation where a constituent assembly convened extra-constitutionally attempts to clearly act beyond its mandate, such an action is subject to a judicial challenge, and a court, also acting extra-constitutionally (that is, with no basis in the constitution), decides to enforce the relevant mandate.[47] The success or failure of such an intervention will probably not depend on law, but on the balance of forces existing in the society in question.

CONCLUSION

This chapter examined the nature of constitution-making entities typically described as constituent assemblies. It considered them in terms of their form, function, and power, and argued that they are best understood as non-permanent constitution-making entities that act on a mandate directly attributable to the sovereign people

---

[46] See Judgment C-757/08.
[47] In this sense, the court would be exercising a sort of 'supra-constitutional' jurisdiction of the kind associated to judicial assessments of the effectivity of a revolution (Honoré 1967; Brookfield 2006).

(usually expressed through a referendum). It then explored, using the Colombian experience as an example, whether a constituent assembly can be subject to legally effective limits and whether the legal regulation of a constitution-making body necessarily rules out its status as a mechanism for the exercise of the original constituent power. A possible answer to those questions, the chapter argued, would be based on a distinction between a (sovereign) people and a (constituent) assembly. The fact that a constituent assembly acts on a mandate from the sovereign people does not necessarily make it a sovereign entity. There is no reason why a constituent assembly's (popular) mandate cannot include limits as to the constitutional content it is authorised to create and as to the specific procedures it should follow. The fact that these limits originate in a law or constitution is not a problem, as long as they are ultimately based on a popular decision.

RECOMMENDED READING

Arato, A. (2016). *Post Sovereign Constitution Making*, Oxford: Oxford University Press.
Arato, A. (2017). *Adventures of the Constituent Power*, Cambridge: Cambridge University Press.
Elster, J. (2006). Legislatures as Constituent Assemblies. In R. Bauman and T. Kahana, eds., *The Least Examined Branch: The Role of Legislatures in the Constitutional State*. Cambridge: Cambridge University Press, pp. 181–197.
Elster, J., Gargarella, R., Naresh, V., Rasch, B. E., eds. (2018). *Constituent Assemblies*, Cambridge: Cambridge University Press.
Ghai, Y. (2012). *The Role of Constituent Assemblies in Constitution Making*. International IDEA. https://constitutionnet.org/vl/item/role-constituent-assemblies-constitution-making-yash-ghai-international-idea-2012
Hoar, R. S. (2004). *Constitutional Conventions: Their Nature, Powers and Limitations*, Kessinger Publishing.
Jameson, J. A. (1887). *A Treatise on Constitutional Conventions: Their History, Powers, and Modes of Proceeding*, Chicago: Callaghan and Co.
Kruman, M. (1997). *Between Authority and Liberty: State Constitution Making in Revolutionary America*, Chapel Hill, N.C.: University of North Carolina Press.
Landau, D. & Lerner, H. (2019). *Comparative Constitution-Making*, Northampton: Edward Elgar.
Levinson, S. (2006). *Our Undemocratic Constitution*, Oxford: Oxford University Press.
Loughlin, M. (2007). Constituent Power Subverted: From English Constitutional Argument to British Constitutional Practice. In M. Loughlin and N. Walker, eds., *The Paradox of Constitutionalism*. Oxford: Oxford University Press, pp. 27–48.
Negretto, G., ed. (2020). *Redrafting Constitutions in Democratic Regimes*, Cambridge: Cambridge University Press.
Schmitt, C. (2008). *Constitutional Theory*, Durham: Duke University Press.
Sieyès, E. (2003). *Political Writings*, Indianapolis, Ind.: Hackett Publishing Company.
Tushnet, M. (2015). Peasants with Pitchforks, and Toilers with Twitter: Constitutional Revolutions and the Constituent Power. *International Journal of Constitutional Law*, 13 (3), 639–654.

42

Citizenship

Elizabeth F. Cohen and Cyril Ghosh

Democracies, nations, and states all require the drawing of myriad boundaries. One of the most fundamental of these boundaries is the political distinction between citizens and non-citizens. The process of distinguishing citizens from non-citizens commences with any nation-state's founding and continues as long as the country exists. In liberal democracies, rules governing the act of demarcating the citizenry are expressed in a body of texts that include constitutions, statutes, case law, and administrative law. Constitutions, whether written or unwritten, whether contained in a single text or scattered across multiple documents, either directly enumerate the rights and liberties of citizens or provide the overarching legal framework that governs their exercise. Constitutions also determine the juridical architecture within which legal redress may be sought when rights of citizens have been abrogated or infringed upon. Thus, to the extent that constitutional principles structure lawmaking, judicial opinions, and rulemaking, the contours of citizenship in liberal democracies may be said to be determined, in the last instance, by constitutions. Constitutions thus underwrite the right to have rights by furnishing a layer of protection from both public laws and private conduct that are violative of fundamental rights.

Despite the important function constitutions perform in governing citizenship most do not offer any clear definition of what citizenship means (Shaw 2020, pp. 37–39). In this way, they mirror uncertainty and dissensus about the definition of citizenship that exists in the scholarly literature as well as in citizenship practice. In the essay that follows, we do not attempt to settle these debates. Instead, we stipulate a few minimum conditions for calling a political status citizenship and provide an overview of the concept of citizenship and its relationship to constitutional theory. In so doing, we discuss the theories that ground the practice of citizenship, the norms that structure its administration, and the ways in which boundaries are established in order to delimit it. We also highlight boundary problems that are endemic in democratic citizenship even when it is well-defined by a body of constitutional jurisprudence and describe how these boundary problems create unavoidable complexity that we can observe in the lived political experiences of citizens around the world.

We begin the essay in Section I with a discussion of long-standing influential theories of citizenship. As is true of constitutional theory, more generally (D. Strauss 1999), an important chunk of disagreement about citizenship is generated by confusion about descriptive and prescriptive ways of thinking about citizenship. As we detail, citizenship invites us to tack between what we actually do and what we think we ought to do. But the two often lead us down radically different paths. In addition, here we synopsize some contemporary critiques and refinements of classic theories of citizenship. Citizenship's meaning and content are the subjects of our analysis in Sections II and III, respectively. Here, we continue our focus on the theme of contestation and demonstrate how citizenship is both understood and practiced in diverse ways. In Section IV, we address the question of who gets to be a citizen. In so doing, we look closely at the philosophical conundrum of infinite regress that is baked into the concept of citizenship from the outset. In Section V, we demonstrate how individuals frequently possess only a partial bundle of rights and liberties despite having the status of full citizenship. This phenomenon of semi-citizenship is both inevitable and ubiquitous. We conclude the essay with some remarks about how citizenship paradoxically signifies both equality and inequality of status.

One preliminary clarification to frame the discussion that follows: In contemporary discourse, the term citizenship is widely used to denote membership – generally passport-bearing or legal nationality – in a polity. Consequently, the word is often used overinclusively and might refer to subjects who live in countries ruled by monarchs, members of polities that have one-party or theocratic rule, as well as citizens in states that grant them the right to self-rule. In this essay, we favor an understanding of citizenship as bestowing formal legal membership in liberal democracies including irrevocable guarantees of meaningful opportunities for self-rule. We make this choice because we wish to distinguish citizenship from forms of subjecthood that do not confer rights to self-rule on an ongoing basis. People may be considered nationals of a state, but if they have no meaningful opportunity to participate in co-equal collective self-government, they are closer to having the status of subjects – members of a community who are subject to laws that they have little or no say in making – and not citizens.

I THEORIES OF CITIZENSHIP

Two normative schools of thought dominate the classical and modern canon of work about citizenship: civic republicanism and liberalism. In the classical literature, citizenship is closely associated with self-rule among equals and foregrounds the ideals of speech, deliberation, publicity, transparency, and collective decision-making, all intended to supplant what Aristotle (1996) calls rule by one or rule by the few. For Aristotle, citizenship is not an instrumental good. It is a good people pursue for its own sake. Aristotle also draws stark boundaries between citizens and non-citizens. The equality and independence of those capable of jointly self-governing distinguishes them from slaves, *metics*, women, and others who are not independent enough or otherwise qualified enough for the task of self-rule. Thus, citizens are an elite group of persons who are capable of thinking about the good life and excellence.

While Athenian citizenship is the touchstone for most people's idea of classical citizenship, J. G. A. Pocock's (1995) scholarship reminds us that Spartans practiced their own, highly regimented and militaristic, version of citizenship, where boys entered into military and political training at age 6, returning to the private sphere only after they were 30, and, in the interim, they rotated through agricultural, military, and political service. Roman citizenship, on the other hand, bifurcated the legal and the political, creating legal forms of status for conquered persons who did not qualify for political membership. These administrative categories thus enabled the Roman empire to maintain its dominion over a large, diverse population across vast territory. The challenges invariably associated with the scale and diversity of the empire were managed with the use of a highly bureaucratized polity that contained many layers and forms of membership.

Modern ideals of citizenship coalesced during the Enlightenment era, evolved throughout the sixteenth, seventeenth, and eighteenth centuries, and culminated in the American and French Revolutions. The philosophical foundations of modern constitutionalism date back to a tradition of Enlightenment political thought, principally the social contract theories associated with Hobbes, Locke, and Rousseau that justified rights claims as a function of membership in a political community of free and equal self-governing members. This Enlightenment ideal of self-government represented a dramatic departure from Aristotelian ideas of equality by expanding the conception to include all human beings. The American and French Revolutions codified these ideals into the American Declaration of Independence and the Declaration of the Rights of Man. The latter is one of the first modern documents to encode citizenship rights. The same is true of the US Constitution which places sovereignty squarely in the body politic.

During the course of the eighteenth, nineteenth, and twentieth centuries, contestation over the content of citizenship occurred within a circle of liberal theorists and between liberals, on the one hand, and critics of the liberal tradition, on the other. An iconic genealogy of modern citizenship is sociologist T. H. Marshall's 1949 lecture, "Citizenship and Social Class," in which he offers a developmental history of citizenship that describes civil rights as emerging in the eighteenth century, spurred both by social contractarian thought and the development of early capitalist forms that required private property and contract rights to flourish. Commitments to political rights, notably the right to vote and to be represented, followed in the next century. These are justified as a means to entrench and support civil rights via representation and franchise opportunities. Social rights come last, in the twentieth century, and in cases like the US, they develop unevenly.

Marshall's overarching argument that a set of complementary rights is central to citizenship dovetails with our stipulation that self-rule is central to citizenship.

But his view has been critiqued for omitting or undervaluing important rights that liberal, civic republican, and communitarian thinkers on citizenship believe are essential to a normatively robust conception of citizenship. Thus, many have called for adding economic citizenship and cultural citizenship to the list (Mann 1993; B. Turner 2001; Lara 2002a, 2002b). Others suggest that a separate right to work be considered fundamental to citizenship, although, to be sure, Marshall folded economic rights, including the right to work, into his definition of civil rights. And human rights scholars point out that rights-on-paper are not meaningful if, in practice, people are denied the opportunity to exercise those rights (Kingston 2019). This pushes contemporary theories of citizenship one notch past Hannah Arendt's oft-cited claim that citizenship is the "right to have rights."

Contemporary civic republicans have revived interest in their classical forebears, interrogating the thinness of accounts such as Marshall's. Civic republicans generally eschew individualism and embrace collectivism of the sort found in communitarian, neo-republican, and even neo-Aristotelian thought. While each of these three theoretical strains lands in a different place, they have in common a rejection of what they view as impoverished rights-centric understandings of citizenship (Nussbaum 1990).[1] Thus, Hannah Arendt revives classical concerns about who is capable of equality and notes that twentieth-century citizenship is degraded to the point of non-recognition by the dependence of political subjects on their citizenship to pursue their most basic self-interests (Arendt 1998). Some communitarian theorists of citizenship are dissatisfied with liberal notions of universal human rights because these rights are conceived at a level of abstraction that is so high that it makes them almost impossible to tie to "situated" human motivations (see, especially, Sandel 1996, pp. 3–25). Others, like Richard Bellamy, advocate a citizenship that is inextricably linked to democratic participation. For Bellamy, the "underlying rationale" of citizenship is "the establishment of a condition of civic equality" (Bellamy 2008, p. 12). Bellamy thinks citizenship ought to foreground solidarity and reciprocity (Bellamy 2008, p. 14).

Arguments about discursive models of citizenship, advanced most powerfully by critical theorists, draw in part from our active understandings of citizenship while incorporating some key tenets of liberal claims. Jürgen Habermas, for example, has proposed the view that the ideas of "communicative action" and "deliberative democracy" are central components of citizenship. In so doing, he has drawn attention to the role of mutual recognition in the public sphere (Habermas, quoted in Baynes 2000, p. 461). Others, such as Steven White, reject Habermasian foundationalism, which they believe ties Habermas to forms of consensualism that preclude more ideal versions of deliberation and engagement (S. K. White 2017). Some attempt to integrate liberal conceptions of autonomy with classic notions of virtue,

---

[1] Indeed, Martha Nussbaum's neo-Aristotelian leanings have taken her all the way to a version of cosmopolitanism not embraced by civic republicans.

and in so doing, propose the idea that citizenship is an "office" that one occupies, and that, among other things, this office demands loyalty (van Steenbergen, 1994, p. 46). Another critical theorist, Seyla Benhabib, advocates training our energies on "democratic iterations" that rely on "complex processes" of deliberation through which universalist rights claims and principles are contested and contextualized (Benhabib 2004, p. 179).

Highly normative accounts of citizenship are useful for working out an ideal theory of citizenship. But ideal theory has important limitations for understanding a concept like citizenship. Of particular importance is how these theories account for incomplete fulfillment of their normative standards. The most exclusively action- and virtue-oriented accounts detail the good embodied in, and arising from, specific actions but give readers less guidance about how to think systematically about inevitable citizenly shortcomings. One could take away from some virtue-centric accounts of citizenship that anyone who is lacking in a subset of key citizenly virtues or who fails to perform some of the signature acts of citizenship is not a citizen. We resist this conclusion because it contradicts what we know to be the case – that states do not decitizenize people for failing to exercise civic virtue or rights – and because it violates the spirit of our original stipulation that rights to self-rule be guaranteed to citizens in perpetuity.

Late twentieth-century scholarship on citizenship has interrogated the two dominant accounts of citizenship – liberal and civic republican – in ways that highlight and in some cases bridge gaps between norms and practices. Rogers Smith's account of US citizenship norms and their expression in law demonstrates how norms of citizenship in the US have always been characterized by "multiple traditions" (R. Smith 1997). These traditions accommodate a range of civic ideals, including but not limited to, civic republicanism, a "liberal consensus" approach (see, for example, Hartz 1955), and a tradition of "ascriptive hierarchies" that shore up exclusionary norms like those predicated on race, gender, and national origin. European citizenship too has been investigated as a racialized category from a number of perspectives, such as, migration and border enforcement (Andersson 2014), ethnic persecution and cleansing (Zahra 2016), and denationalization of undesirable ethnic minorities (P. Weil 2012).

Feminist writing on citizenship has moved to dismantle the long-dominant distinction both in liberal and in civic republican thought between the public and private spheres – while pointing out how the personal is indeed the political. The social contracts associated with liberal thought that are supposed to codify the consent of the governed have been critiqued as fundamentally sexist (and sexual) contracts (Pateman 2018). And the "gendered assumptions" regarding traditional family structures and gender roles that structure communitarian conceptions of citizenship have been demonstrated to be misguided (Lister 2003). Women's experiences of rights denials have been the source of further investigations of citizenship as scholars have advanced withering critiques of social and legal practices such as coverture laws, the marriage contract, the hyper-exploitation of female and feminized labor power, marital rape, wage inequality, and the systematic disenfranchisement of women.

Queer theoretic interrogations of citizenship (see, for example, Volpp 2017) complement these feminist critiques, as scholars have deconstructed dominant understandings of citizenship that foreground the experiences of a presumptively heteronormative subject and erase and/or inferiorize the sexually non-normative. The dovetailing of heteronormativity and late-capitalist neoliberal subjectivity has also provided fertile ground for scholarship in queer/sexual citizenship. Inquiries into the citizenship of children and the intellectually disabled have also generated a number of normative discussions, typically on the premise that the justifications for routinely denying members of these groups the right to vote, to own a gun, to live independently, and so on, have dubious foundations (Pincock 2018; also see Failer 2002).

Some theorists have pushed back against the idea of state-centric views of citizenship. In so doing, they have argued, both as a historical and as an empirical matter, that nation-states do not have the exclusive prerogative to bestow citizenship rights. These arguments may refer to both trans- or supranational institutions and subnational institutions. Drawing from international human rights norms and the concept of personhood, these scholars offer accounts of citizenship that range from the "postnational" to the cosmopolitan (Sassen 2002; W. Brown 2010; Soysal 2012; Tan 2017). For others, nation-states' claims to sovereignty in the domain of bestowing citizenship is in an ongoing process of being attenuated with the rise of dual- and multiple-citizenship, transnational migration, and globalization (see, for example, Bauböck 1994; Spiro 2016). Other scholars discuss multi-level citizenship and subnational citizenship, such as municipal or regional citizenship, quasi citizenship, confederated citizenship, the citizenship of indigenous populations in polyethnic states (Kymlicka 1995; Aleinikoff 2002), and supranational citizenship (in the EU) (see, for example, Maas 2017; Ramakrishnan and Colbern 2019).

Critics of a state-centric approach to citizenship have added normative and descriptive depth to our understanding of citizenship. However, there is reason to be skeptical that the state can be displaced as a final arbiter of the core rights and protections of citizenship precisely because when constitutional guarantees indemnifying individuals from conditions such as statelessness via denationalization are in fact enforced, they are enforced by states.[2] Human rights, such as those stipulated in the Universal Declaration of Human Rights, the International Covenant on Civil and Political Rights, and the International Covenant on Economic, Social and Cultural Rights, can be notoriously challenging to litigate outside the context of the state. In the absence of "universal jurisdiction" (K. Roth 2001; but see Kissinger

---

[2] See, for example, the US Supreme Court's interpretation of the Eighth Amendment here: "[Use] of denationalization as a punishment is barred by the Eighth Amendment," (*Trop v. Dulles* 356 U.S. 86, at 101 (1958); also see Waldron 2012c, p. 201). Between 1906 and the 1960s, denationalization was frequently practiced in the US (P. Weil 2012).

2001), the vast majority of disputes involving allegations of (human) rights violations are typically litigated within national and subnational jurisdictions under the penal laws of particular nation-states.

Finally, contemporary citizenship theory has adopted some non-anthropocentric approaches as, in the last few decades, a number of scholars have made the case for ecological or environmental citizenship that urge us to take seriously both the public and the private dimensions of citizenship obligations and invite a radical transformation of our relationships with the non-human world. In this view, reducing one's ecological footprint is a prime citizenship obligation and a normative commitment to sustainable development is an integral part of the wider concept of democratic citizenship (Jelin 2000; Dobson 2003, 2016; Revkin 2012). Complementing these ideas, some scholars engage themselves in the work of moral extensionism by extending the moral and ethical community to all sentient beings. In so doing, this scholarship advances the notion of animal citizenship (Singer 1990; Donaldson and Kymlicka 2011; Rowlands 2013).

II WHAT IS CITIZENSHIP?

Citizenship has been defined in various ways, including, as a status, standing, an institution, an instrument of political categorization, a set of actions related to virtue, civicness, a form of identification, a process, an affect, and more. Some of this disagreement is garden variety disagreement about how to define something that is simultaneously a part of our daily vernacular and a technical legal term. Disagreement about what the core elements of citizenship are (rights, virtues, blood lineage, actions, etc.) compound the concept's ambiguity. Other elements of confusion stem from citizenship's proximity to other concepts, such as, nationality, civicness, and membership, leading some to erroneously use it as a stand-in for other, usually subsidiary, concepts.

One of the most confounding sources of this confusion is disagreement about how citizenship is conferred or acquired. For example, classical civic virtue-based democratic theories of citizenship that predate the development of nation-state citizenship take it as axiomatic that citizens constitute their own citizenship through the cultivation of citizenly qualities and citizenly actions.[3] But plenty of evidence shows us that citizenliness and acts of citizenship are usually not, in and of themselves, constitutive of citizenship. Even in the ancient world one could not unilaterally declare oneself a citizen. This remains the case in contemporary polities. In the United States, courts have historically denied relief to all sorts of individuals who have claimed to

---

[3] For Aristotle, one such citizenly quality is proper interaction with strangers. These proper interactions involve treating others as [political] friends even in the absence of a deep emotional connection. One sign of this kind of civic virtue is the exercise of moderation, restraint, temperance, and not taking more than one's fair share. See Allen 2004, especially Chapter 9; also see Aristotle 1906, especially Book VIII.

possess eligibility for citizenship, such as black Americans,[4] Japanese people,[5] south Asian Indians,[6] and American Indians.[7] Only subsequent congressional statutes and constitutional amendments have overturned these verdicts. The Indian Citizenship (Amendment) Act of 2019 is another case in point. This amendment of the Indian Citizenship Act of 1955, passed by the Indian Parliament, grants amnesty and creates a pathway to citizenship for non-Muslim unauthorized migrants who have lived in India for certain specific durations and are citizens of a set of neighboring countries.[8] Under this law, no amount of citizenly behavior would allow analogously-situated Muslim migrants to become eligible for amnesty in India.

Equally, the Windrush Generation refers to thousands of people from former Caribbean commonwealth countries who came to the UK to work between 1948 and 1970 and remained in-country for many years, only to later be threatened with deportation and, in some cases, deported.[9] The individuals in question believed themselves to either have British citizenship or to be in possession of a status of citizenship that was indistinguishable from it.[10] But in 2010 the British Home Office destroyed their travel records and the government proceeded to inform them that they lacked adequate proof of their status to remain, to work, and to access basic rights like healthcare.

These episodes reveal that even the most legitimate claims to citizenship do not actually make someone a citizen when a state refuses to recognize those claims. If citizenship could be conjured by an individual or group's citizenly behavior, all kinds of boundary-enforcing laws would cease to be necessary. One could simply elect to gain representation, a passport, or specific goods simply via the performance of citizenly actions. But that is not how citizenship works in almost any circumstance. In other words, citizenship is never reducible to its performative components. On this view, citizenship is as citizenship does, not as we wish it would do. This is a solidly realist approach to citizenship, insofar as it places more weight on actual citizenship practices than on aspirational ideals.

This realist view of citizenship and its relationship to constitutional power renders citizenship as a structural relationship between individuals and the state. Citizenship in any given context is a particular legal status, circumscribed within a specific constitutional and juridical framework, and via which democratic states offer citizens both rights and liberties and the means for engaging in collective

---

[4] *Dred Scott v Sandford*, 60 U.S. 393 (1856).
[5] *Ozawa v United States*, 260 U.S. 178 (1922).
[6] *United States v Bhagat Singh Thind*, 261 U.S. 204 (1923).
[7] *Elk v Wilkins*, 112 U.S. 94 (1884).
[8] The Citizenship (Amendment) Act 2019.
[9] Windrush Compensation Scheme (Expenditure) Act 2020.
[10] The fact that the British Nationality Act 1948 stipulates that it is "An Act to make provision for British nationality and for citizenship of the United Kingdom and Colonies" does not help much to clarify matters.

self-rule. It is bestowed upon people via a set of formal legal procedures. But the way that guarantees of self-rule are institutionalized by constitutions can and will vary. For example, parliamentary and presidential democracies offer their citizens dramatically different means of representing themselves in the process of self-rule. Nor does self-rule mandate that sovereignty must reside in the people, as it does in the US. In the UK, for example, it resides in the Parliament. Despite these procedurally different experiences, full members of either type of state do have co-equal opportunities to engage in collective self-government. But, as we show in Section V below, all liberal democracies also fail to draw stark lines between members and non-members, rendering some of the people they as govern semi-citizens who have some but not all of the core rights set out by their constitutions, statutes, and case and administrative law. Citizenship's promise of egalitarian self-government cannot and does not extend to everyone governed by the law of the land.

III CITIZENSHIP'S CONTENT

We now turn to a discussion of citizenship as states administer it and citizens receive it. Here we take up the content of citizenship, furnishing an overview of the kinds of rights bestowed through, and the obligations and duties imposed on, citizenship. As indicated above, these rights and obligations are frequently to be found, not in any one document, but instead in a corpus of texts, including documents relating to a country's founding, its constitution, relevant statutes, and case law. In some cases, documents relating to supranational entities, such as the EU, may also determine how citizenship is experienced by individuals in any given country.

The rights most centrally associated with citizenship are: the irrevocable and unconditional right to (re)enter a country of one's citizenship, reside there, and move about without restrictions throughout the territory of that country (Carens 2013). Citizens also have access to consular services when traveling abroad. Permanent residents are in many places able to enjoy similar protections, but not with the same guarantees as citizens. Permanent residents can be deported and, in some countries, this happens frequently.[11] The right to vote in national elections is also frequently reserved for citizens. However, voting rights are extended to some categories of noncitizens in at least 45 countries at least in some elections (Ferris *et al.* 2019). The Maastricht Agreement allows citizens of various EU member countries to vote in local and regional elections of EU countries of which they are not citizens. Qualifying commonwealth citizens living in the UK can also vote in the British general elections.[12] In the US, from 1776 through the 1920s, as many as 40 states and

---

[11] In the US, annually, approximately 10% of all persons deported are Lawful Permanent Residents (American Immigration Council 2010).

[12] Electoral Commission, "Register to vote". Available from: https://web.archive.org/web/20210102043337/ https://www.electoralcommission.org.uk/i-am-a/voter/register-vote-and-update-your-details [Viewed 1 January 2021]

federal territories granted some noncitizens, particularly lawful permanent residents who declared their intent to become citizens, the right to vote in local, state, and in some cases even in federal, elections (Motomura 2006; Raskin 1993; Schuck 1998; Hayduk 2006).[13] While this practice virtually disappeared by the end of the twentieth century, at the present time, there is a resurgence of noncitizen voting rights, particularly in local elections such as those relating to school boards (Hayduk and Coll 2018; also see Hayduk 2006).

In some countries voting is not a right but instead a legal obligation that all citizens must fulfill. A number of countries in Central and South America have such compulsory voting laws, including Argentina, Brazil, Panama, Peru, and Chile. Australia (federal elections), Belgium, Greece, Turkey, and Singapore are other prominent countries with similar rules for voting. A number of these countries make exceptions for those who are elderly or for those who are illiterate and in some of these countries the rule is more strictly enforced than in others (E. F. Cohen and C. Ghosh 2019).

But compulsory voting is only one of a slate of obligations that states impose on their citizens. Another prominent citizenly obligation is jury service. In the US,[14] where jury trials are most widely used, and in Canada,[15] these obligations are restricted to citizens only. In the UK, jurors need to be registered voters in parliamentary and local elections but such individuals may be British, Irish, EU, and qualifying Commonwealth citizens.[16] In Australia, a federal law clearly states who may *not* serve on a jury and, as long as they abide by these restrictions, state laws can determine the composition of juries (Government of Australia 2016; also see Rubenstein 1995).[17]

As Richard Bellamy (2008) has pointed out, there is a long association of jury service to citizenship. Ancient Babylonia had jury trials where even commoners could serve on juries but the "linking of juries and popular democratic assemblies" did not appear until the Greek city-states (May 2019, p. 249). During the classical period, in Athens, participating in the assemblies (which was unpaid work) and jury service (which was paid work) were looked upon as two vital citizenly acts (Bellamy 2008).

---

[13] Peter Schuck points out that, in certain jurisdictions, even unauthorized migrants can vote in some elections. See Schuck (1998, p. 187).

[14] United States Courts, "Jury service" [online]. Available from: https://web.archive.org/web/20181227170823/http://www.uscourts.gov/services-forms/jury-service [Viewed 27 December 2018]. See also Spiro 2016.

[15] Ontario ministry of the attorney general, "General information about jury duty" [online]. Available from: https://web.archive.org/web/20181224042858/https://www.attorneygeneral.jus.gov.on.ca/english/courts/jury/general_jury_duty_info.php [Viewed 24 December 2018]

[16] Government of the United Kingdom, "Guide to jury summons" [online]. Available from: https://web.archive.org/web/20201128235733/https://assets.publishing.service.gov.uk/government/uploads/system/uploads/attachment_data/file/709844/jury-summons-guide-eng.pdf [Viewed 28 November 2020]

[17] For the Australian capital territory, "Each man and each woman whose name is on the Roll of electors for the Territory is, unless he or she is a disqualified person or is exempt from serving as a juror, liable to serve as a juror" (Government of Australia, 2016).

These days, however, Greek jurors, instead of serving independently on juries, usually serve on mixed courts together with judges, while jury trials have become common in many other countries of the world, particularly in cases involving serious crimes.

Most liberal democracies also impose the obligation to pay individual taxes on the personal incomes of their residents and citizens.[18] While residency, and not citizenship, is the predominant criterion that determines who ends up with this obligation, at least two countries, the US and Eritrea, mandate that their citizens need to pay taxes on their worldwide incomes no matter where they live (McKinnon 2012).[19] In some countries, such as Israel, Iran, and Turkey, citizens are obligated to perform some kind of military service.[20] In the US, eligible men are required by law to sign up for the Selective Service System, which supplies the federal government with a list of potential military draftees, should a need for conscription arise. In some federal and subnational jurisdictions,[21] laws mandate that all citizens must possess identity cards or some other form of documentation of their citizenship status.

Occasionally, duties that are not enforceable might also attach to citizenship. The Indian Constitution, for example, was amended in 1976[22] to add a set of moral obligations known as fundamental duties of citizens, which includes things like the duty "for a parent or guardian to provide opportunities for education of the child or ward between the age of six and fourteen" (Kurian 2016).

IV WHO GETS TO BE A CITIZEN?

The boundaries drawn by citizenship practices produce irregularity and liminality as well as neat and uncontested distinctions. In this section, we focus on the means by which states attempt to settle upon fixed determinants of citizenship, illustrating how both moments of establishment and ongoing practices in democratic states make irregularity inevitable.

Constituting a state democratically requires, antecedently, the act of constituting a decision-making people – a *demos* – who in turn decide how to constitute the polity.

---

[18] Countries that do not do so are usually reliant on alternative sources of revenue. Kuwait, the Cayman Islands, and Bahrain are some examples of countries that impose no personal income tax burden at all – on either their citizens or their residents (see E. F. Cohen and C. Ghosh 2019, chap. 4).

[19] However, US citizens might qualify for an exemption if their incomes are below a specified amount. This amount is adjusted for inflation every year. See Internal Revenue Service, "Foreign earned income exclusion". Available from: https://web.archive.org/web/20201127162731/https://www.irs.gov/individuals/international-taxpayers/foreign-earned-income-exclusion [Viewed 27 November 2020].

[20] All able-bodied men in Iran and Turkey, and both men and women in Israel, are mandated to perform mandatory military service. (Department of Justice 2020; Central Intelligence Agency 2020).

[21] See, for example, the German Personalausweisgesetz. Act on Identity Cards of 18 June 2009 (Federal Law Gazette I, p. 1346), amended by Article 4 of the Act of 22 December 2011 (Federal Law Gazette I, p. 2959).

[22] This list has since been amended.

But developing the rules that determine who gets to be a participant in this exercise involves identifying who is and who is not, or will or will not become, a legitimate member of the polity that is being instituted. Many democratic theorists believe this puts constitutions and citizenship rules in an infinite regress (Ochoa Espejo 2011; also see Goodin 2007, p. 43). Theoretically, the regress can continue infinitely,[23] never landing at a Rawlsian original position or a social-contractarian state of nature, all of which are of necessity thought-experimental fictions. But, in practice, the fact that democratic citizenries are established by undemocratically designating a set of initial decision-makers in no way consigns a state to an undemocratic future. We only refer to the regress because it tips us off to the fact that the drawing of distinctions between citizens and non-citizens is fraught and that some of the complications involved in boundary-drawing will entail prioritizing administrative, juridical, statutory, policy-making, constitutional, and other concerns over egalitarian norms.

Once established, democratic states apply norms, constitutions, law, and bureaucratic tools for arriving at and enforcing distinctions between citizens and non-citizens. A standard normative account of how democracies should draw boundaries that distinguish citizens from non-citizens is offered by Robert Dahl (1989). He describes two principles, the categorical and the contingent, that represent the two main ways a democracy can distinguish between citizens and non-citizens. The categorical principle stipulates that all people subject to the laws of the land ought to have a say in the making of those laws. The contingent principle states that only people who are qualified to exercise the rights of citizenship, but all such persons, ought to be full members of the *demos*.

In each case, it is easy to point to instances where the rule will fail to produce a neat boundary or where it will have other problematic consequences. The categorical principle is a version of political philosophy's "all affected" principle (Goodin 2007) and invites disputes about what it means to be affected by a country's laws and political decisions. Furthermore, many legitimately affected parties are not territorially present in the state that has affected them and in a multitude of other ways do not have the attributes of citizens. On the other side of the divide, imposing a contingent principle on citizenship opens up a plethora of opportunities for legitimating discrimination with standards that are facially neutral but in practice discriminate on a variety of bases. Making citizenship contingent upon exams, religious and cultural litmus tests, and other means of distinguishing qualifications for citizenship is fraught, often in ways that pass muster with ethnic democracies but violate too many core principles of liberalism to be used as boundary-setting mechanisms in liberal democracies. Dahl himself settles on a compromise in which he adopts a "modified categorical principle" that excludes from the *demos* children, persons deemed to be

---

[23] In this case, we are dealing with a regress that is "vicious." But, to be sure, regresses can also be "benign" in those cases where a proposition might entail another proposition, which might entail yet another proposition, and so on *ad infinitum* (see, for example, Cameron 2018).

cognitively unfit, and transient persons (Dahl 1989, p. 127). But any reader can see that any act of making decisions about who fits into these categories will inevitably trigger further debates about thresholds.

Additionally complicating matters is the fact that most liberal democracies do not confer citizenship in a way that comports with democratic norms but instead use versions of a principle of birthright citizenship, none of which is democratic. The two main principles of birthright citizenship are *jus soli* (citizenship by residency or birth in the territory) and *jus sanguinis* (citizenship by bloodline). Many countries rely on some combination of the two. These two principles govern not just who acquires what type of nationality when they are born, but also the range of choices open to adults who wish to change their status. Deciding how these norms will be balanced and prioritized also trigger a set of contestations.

Given the disparity between democratic norms and actual practices, it is no surprise that constitutions do not always determine even the roughest boundaries of the citizenry; nor do constitutions necessarily apply only to citizens. Some of the rights guaranteed by a constitution may accrue to noncitizens with equal force. Nor is it the case that the boundaries of any given demos likely will perfectly overlap with the boundaries of the territory and its population because people are mobile and cross territorial boundaries quite frequently. Some constitutions specify different statuses or sets of rights for people not living in-country, for people not living on mainland territory, for former colonial subjects, for people who are in-country but were not born with citizenship, for incarcerated persons, sexual minorities, children, religious minorities, and others. Anyone on the wrong side of these internal boundaries is rendered ineligible for some of the core rights of citizenship and must live with a partial- or semi-citizenship. Citizenship, thus, is experienced by many as a gradient category.

Most residents of liberal democratic states who do not have birthright citizenship in the place where they reside also need an opportunity to naturalize in order to achieve an approximation of the citizenship offered to natural-born citizens. Naturalization procedures, in turn, invite new threshold questions pertaining to variables such as time-in-residence, civic proficiency, money, and other barriers to obtaining full membership for those not born with citizenship. As scholars like Sara Wallace Goodman have shown, the barriers to naturalization vary widely from state to state, producing competition to enter places with generous policies during periods of mass forced migration, either for political, ecologic, or economic reasons (Goodman 2014; also see Kälin and Kochenov 2020).

There are two main organizing principles that shape access to citizenship for people born without *jus soli* or *jus sanguinis* grants of legal nationality. One prioritizes ties to a receiving country and the other the contributions that immigrants can make toward the receiving country's society and economy. The presence of family members or one's employment in a given country can represent one's ties to that country. At least since 1965, the US has given strong preference to family reunification and employment over things such as skills and contributions. Canada, on the other hand, is an example of a country that prioritizes an immigrant's potential to contribute to Canadian society and the Canadian economy, defined in terms of attributes the state prizes, such as advanced degrees, skills, work experience, and multilingualism. Australia,[24] New Zealand,[25] and the UK (Donald 2016), have also adopted versions of the points-based system that Canada has.

Most countries also require minimum time-in-residence within their territories before they allow immigrants to naturalize. These durations of time are supposed to serve as a proxy for, among other things, how much assimilation one has experienced and how many ties one might have developed in a receiving state. On the one hand, physical presence in the country, it is presumed, will lead to observable metrics of assimilation, such as the payment of income taxes, an immigrant becoming familiar with the language, history, culture, and politics of the country, them buying property, sending their children to school, them getting involved with the local community, and so on. On the other, these mandatory minimum lengths of stay are also supposed to represent abstract ideas like immigrants' loyalty toward, and acculturalization in, the society of the receiving state (E. F. Cohen 2015, 2018). The use of time here functions as a quantitative determinant of citizenship without taking the controversial step of putting citizenship up for sale to the highest bidder.

Nonetheless, a number of states have created visa regimes that prioritize fiscal and monetary contributions of a potential immigrant, or their highly specialized extraordinary talents, such as, say, in Olympic sports, or some forms of technical skills that are in short supply, over the more usual metrics of citizenship eligibility and readiness, such as family ties, employment, assimilation, or loyalty. Some of these visa regimes also circumvent the usual physical presence criterion (e.g., Austria).[26] Outright "cash-for-passport" programs and "talent for citizenship" exchanges are unusual and prompt ethical concerns about whether citizenship, which is conceived of as a means of self-government among equals, should be for sale (Shachar 2006, 2017; Shachar and Hirschl 2014).

V SEMI-CITIZENSHIP

In this section of this overview of citizenship, we turn to a discussion of the liminal category of people who do not have all the rights associated with full citizenship but

---

[24] Government of Australia, "Skilled independent visa (subclass 189) (points-tested) stream". Available from: https://web.archive.org/web/20180715224027/https://www.homeaffairs.gov.au/Trav/Visa-1/189- [Viewed 15 July 2018]

[25] Government of New Zealand, "About this visa: skilled migrant category resident visa". Available from: https://web.archive.org/web/20180715224216/https://www.immigration.govt.nz/new-zealand-visas/apply-for-a-visa/about-visa/skilled-migrant-category-resident-visa [Viewed 15 July 2018]

[26] Government of Austria, "Current residence abroad – granting of Austrian citizenship". Available from: https://web.archive.org/web/20180716001134/https://www.wien.gv.at/english/administration/civilstatus/citizenship/abroad.html [Viewed 16 July 2018]

who also do not get entirely excluded from citizenship. Their fate is the outcome of ambiguous, poorly enforced, or unattainable determinants. People who cannot, are not allowed to, or choose not to, meet the standards states set for full citizenship are usually neither fully included in nor fully excluded from the category: "citizen". They hold semi-citizenships; diverse statuses that are often difficult for individuals to navigate and sometimes also illegible to states. This liminal category of persons, those who are both haves as well as have-nots, experience citizenship as a gradient category – in the sense that it is possible for any given person to have more or less of it when compared to another person who is analogously-situated in a juridical sense.

Semi-citizenships are the outcome of conflicts over thresholds, such as, for example, how much time-in-residence is adequate to qualify someone as a citizen or whether someone who has seriously violated the laws is entitled to rights reserved for those who respect a society's social compact. Even in the most liberal democracies, until relatively recently sexual minorities could not expect all of their civil rights to be enforced, especially the right to conclude marriage contracts and adopt children. Sometimes these citizenship rights associated with citizenship might be withheld through statutory provisions; at other times, this might be the result of a constitutional stipulation. An example of the latter is the constitutional restriction of eligibility to run for the highest political office in the US, the presidency, to natural-born citizens.

Semi-citizenship may be held temporarily or permanently, and a person's citizenship may be augmented or impoverished over time. Children usually graduate into full citizenship, sexual minorities have been, frequently in the recent past, granted rights via judicial opinions and statutes, and in some places, such as the EU, via constitutional grants that themselves were the product of social movements. But in the UK and several other democratic states, the recent denaturalization of some naturalized citizens has prompted worries that our expectations about the permanence of citizenship are being undermined (Lenard 2016). On a much larger scale, recent changes to citizenship laws in India (referred to above) could potentially strip millions of Muslim residents of their right of domicile. Similarly, a proliferation of short-term visas and undocumented immigration in the post-WWII era has created entire classes of persons who live from renewal to renewal, building lives in places where they are able to access a few social and civil rights but never a full bundle of rights including political rights and rights of place and free movement.

Semi-citizenship statuses are generated by compromises among competing ways of thinking about who is entitled to be a citizen. The specific form they take – which parts of the citizenship bundle are included and excluded – varies from state to state but all democracies produce statuses that contradict constitutional commitments to equal status and standing for members. This essay opened with the non-controversial claim that democracies, nations, and states are constituted in part by boundaries such as those between citizens and non-citizens. However, scratching the surface of processes of boundary-drawing and -enforcement reveals that few are as stark and unambiguous in practice as most normative theory would suggest they ought to be.

CONCLUSION

It is paradoxical that citizenship was first theorized by Greek philosophers as a way to produce political equality and yet it has resulted in high-stakes forms of inequality. It was also first instantiated as a way of simplifying complex hierarchies of differentiated political statuses, but it has produced further differentiation in people's political statuses.

One might be tempted to think that better laws, more inclusive institutions, and fairer enforcement, would allow states to transcend what appears to be well-organized and entrenched hypocrisy. But none of the contestation we have described here is the product of simple bias. Nor do the conflicts have clear potential resolutions that have been ignored in favor of convenience or advantaging one's own in-group. Most of the disagreement we have described is inevitable and has no conclusive resolution. Contestations over foundings, authoritative definitions, content, and norms of citizenship can lead us in many quite distinct directions. The work of democratic communities is to continually interrogate their practices and assess whether they are realizing their normative commitments.

RECOMMENDED READING

Bauböck, R. (2006). *Migration and Citizenship: Legal Status Rights, and Political Participation*, Amsterdam: Amsterdam University Press.

Bellamy, R. (2008). *Citizenship: A Very Short Introduction*, Oxford: Oxford University Press.

Benhabib, S. (2004). *The Rights of Others: Aliens, Residents, and Citizens*, New York: Cambridge University Press.

Carens, J. (2013). *The Ethics of Immigration*, Oxford: Oxford University Press.

Carter, N. M. (2019). *American While Black: African Americans, Immigration, and the Limits of Citizenship*, New York: Oxford University Press.

Cohen, E. F. (2009). *Semi-Citizenship in Democratic Politics*, New York: Cambridge University Press.

Cohen, E. F. & Ghosh, C. (2019). *Citizenship (Key Concepts in Political Theory)*, Cambridge: Polity.

Cooper, F. (2018). *Citizenship, Inequality, and Difference: Historical Perspectives*, Princeton, NJ: Princeton University Press.

Donald, A. (2016). Immigration points-based systems compared. *The British Broadcasting Service* [online]. 1 June. [Viewed 19 August 2018]. Available from: https://web.archive.org/web/20180819133654/https://www.bbc.com/news/uk-politics-29594642.

Isin, E. F. & Turner, B. S., eds. (2002). *Handbook of Citizenship Studies*, London: Sage.

Joppke, C. (2010). *Citizenship and Immigration*, Malden, MA: Polity Press.

Kingston, L. N. (2019). *Fully Human: Personhood, Citizenship, and Rights*, New York: Oxford University Press.

Lister, R. (2003). *Citizenship: Feminist Perspectives*, 2nd edn, New York: NYU Press.

Lori, N. (2019). *Offshore Citizens: Permanent Temporary Status in the Gulf*, New York: Cambridge University Press.

Mamdani, M. (2018). *Citizen and Subject: Contemporary Africa and the Legacy of Late Colonialism*, Princeton, NJ: Princeton University Press.

Shachar, A. et al., eds. (2017). *The Oxford Handbook of Citizenship*, Oxford: Oxford University.

43

Elections

Daniel Weinstock

Elections are central to the institutional life of actually existing democracies. Though there are elections in states that one would hesitate to call truly democratic, there are at present no jurisdictions that count as democratic that do not ascribe a great deal of importance to the selection of representatives through elections. Elections are for us practically a criterion of what is to count as a democracy.

It is surprising, therefore, that there isn't more writing on normative issues surrounding elections. Democratic theory is a thriving area within political philosophy and constitutional theory, but writings in democratic theory do not often focus on elections. Some are pitched at a level of abstraction that would seem to make talk of democratic institutions such as elections irrelevant. Others focus on democratic alternatives to elections, on the basis of the claim that elections are not the best way to realize democratic principles, and that they should either be replaced by other kinds of democratic mechanisms, or at the very least that they should be made to coexist with such alternatives.

Given the centrality of elections to democracies as we know them, this is surprising. It also means that a great many questions of both theoretical and practical importance have been neglected. These questions include general ones, such as the question of *why* we should, in democracies, choose our democratic leaders through elections rather than in some other way. But it also includes questions to do with the institutionalization of elections. For example, the 2020 U.S. election has brought to the fore the question of what the specific mechanisms are through which the winners and losers in an election ought to be declared. It also elicited a host of practical questions of considerable normative interest, such as the question of whether, all things equal, all voters should vote on the same day, or whether "absentee," "mail-in," and early voting ought to be encouraged.[1] In fact, every aspect of the

---

[1] In the only contribution of which I am aware to the discussion of this latter question in political theory, Dennis Thompson, in arguing for same-day voting, claims that "when citizens go to the polls on the same day, visibly and publicly participating in the same way in a common experience of civic engagement, they demonstrate their willingness to contribute on equal terms to the democratic process." (Thompson 2002, p. 34).

organization of elections involves choices that raise important normative issues. We need to think about *why* democracies should choose their leaders via elections rather than in some other way, about *who* should get to make such decisions, about *how* elections are organized, both in the sense of how votes get grouped together in order to produce the membership of a legislature, and in the sense of how the mechanics of the electoral process are organized. This would include such questions as the organization and financing of electoral campaigns and the ways in which voters are registered. We also need to think about "when" questions: should elections be fairly easy to trigger, or should they occur according to a fixed schedule? And so on.

A separate though related set of questions has to do with the extent to which the rules that govern the electoral process ought to be seen as matter of constitutional law, and therefore, as relatively impervious to the cut and thrust of ordinary partisan politics and legislation. There are a number of ways in which such rules can be governed (or not) by constitutions. Most obviously, written constitutions typically contain democratic rights, and in particular, can guarantee the right to vote and to stand for office under certain qualifying conditions (for example conditions to do with age). In federal systems, they sometimes also specify constraints to do with the number of seats in legislatures that are to be granted to federal partners. It must be noted that the presence within written constitutions of clauses guaranteeing the right to vote does very little to specify what conditions the courts that are mandated to review legislation on the basis of these clauses will impose upon electoral arrangements in order to view the conditions laid down by these clauses as having been satisfied. This is true of all constitutionally entrenched rights. They can be interpreted in more or less demanding manners. The right to vote can be taken to be in place as long as some mechanism for meaningful electoral participation is in place, to be determined by democratically elected legislatures (Macfarlane 2016), or it can be interpreted as requiring the setting up of an electoral system that is substantively fair. For example, Yasmin Dawood has argued that courts should interpret the right to vote as a "structural" right that, one that encompasses such matters as the setting up and revision of electoral boundaries, and the regulation of campaign financing (Dawood 2012).

Electoral laws can moreover be taken by convention as elements of a polity's constitutional order. This is most obviously the case in countries such as the United Kingdom that have not had a written constitution. Its Representation of the People Act, as well as the more recent Political Parties, Elections and Referendums Act are usually seen as constitutional provisions.[2] (That certain statutes can by convention come to possess constitutional or quasi-constitutional status raises a deeper philosophical question to do with the identity conditions through which constitutional orders are individuated).

---

[2] Thanks to Richard Bellamy for having prompted me to consider this point, and for having provided me with relevant examples.

A third way in which constitutions and electoral rules intersect has to do with the relevance of constitutional provisions that do not directly speak to electoral matters to the constitutional permissibility of various rules that make up a polity's electoral system. For example, the landmark *Citizens United* case in the United States, which in essence removed all limits to private campaign contributions by conceptualizing monetary donations as protected speech, radically altered the campaign financing landscape in the US on the basis of an interpretation of the First Amendment to the US Constitution protecting free speech (McConnell 2013–2014). Michael Pal and Sujit Choudhry have in the Canadian context argued that unequal districting that tends to dilute the votes of ethno-cultural minorities violates not just voting rights guarantees contained in Section III of the Canadian *Charter of Rights and Freedoms*, but also Section XV, which has to do with equality rights (Pal and Choudhry 2014). The extension of the purview of constitutional provisions, especially provisions contained in Bills of Rights, is potentially limitless. It is hard to imagine an aspect of the manner in which states set up their voting practices that does not impinge upon some aspect of the rights protected in such Bills, especially when these rights are interpreted expansively. The question of the degree of deference that constitutional courts should manifest toward the electoral laws that result from legislation, and that of whether a bright line exists between aspects of electoral law and practice that should, as opposed to those that should not, invite constitutional scrutiny are of significant theoretical and practical import.

The aim of the present chapter is to contribute to bringing the political philosophy of elections from the periphery toward the center of the attention of political and constitutional theorists. Constraints of space prevent me from considering all of the issues that such a philosophy would need to consider. I will therefore focus on questions that have already started to receive some attention from philosophers and theorists. I will first consider the foundational question of *why* in a democracy we should elect our leaders rather than selecting them in some other way, taking care to distinguish the question of why we should choose *democracy* from that of why we should choose *elections* within a democracy. I will then consider the central question of how elections should determine winners and losers. How do we translate the huge number of votes that are cast in mass democracies into the choice of a comparatively small number of representatives? Third, I will consider democratic arguments against elections, and will consider a democratic mechanism with a significant historical pedigree within the theory and practice of democracy, that of selection of representatives by lot. Finally, I will briefly list some of the remaining questions that a more encompassing philosophy of elections would have to consider.

I WHY ELECTIONS?

Political philosophers have devoted a lot of attention to the question of how best to justify *democracy*. But the bulk of the philosophical literature on the justification of democracy has had to do not so much with arguing for the superiority of some set of democratic institutions over other such sets, but rather with arguing for democracy, usually understood in an institutionally unspecified way, as being preferable to other quite abstractly specified political theories. For example, many democratic theorists in the 1970s and 1980s were concerned with establishing some degree of equilibrium within the complex philosophical hybrid of "liberal democracy" between liberalism, which in the wake of the works of philosophers such as John Rawls and Ronald Dworkin, was felt to be on the ascendant, and democracy, which, it was felt, had become something of a theoretical afterthought. Liberalism, it was felt, sought to remove too many issues from the political agenda. Democratic theorists were concerned with reestablishing the prerogatives of collective self-rule and democratic deliberation.[3]

The justification of democracy has in the last couple of decades come to settle around a debate between two rival camps. Epistemic democrats believe that democracy is best justified because it is the form of government that gives rise to the best policies (Estlund 2008; Landemore 2013; Goodin and Spiekermann 2018). Others hold that democracy is best justified on the basis of the values that are constitutive of it. For some, it is the best way in which to instantiate the value of political equality (Christiano 2008). Others have seen it as flowing most naturally from the republican value of non-domination (Bellamy 2007, Pettit 2012, Shapiro 2016).

A justification of democracy is however not in and of itself a defense of *elections* as a way to select representatives. To equate democracy with electoral, representative democracy is to beg at least two important questions. First, it is to assume without argument that democracy is necessarily instantiated through a set of *representative* institutions. And second, it is to suppose that representatives should be chosen through elections. Both of these claims have been contested by some democratic theorists. Hélène Landemore has, for example, held that "because their democratic credentials are problematic, elections should not be raised to the level of a democratic principle" (Landemore 2020, p. 141). Thomas Christiano, though he is not as dismissive of elections as is Landemore, does not defend elections as such, but rather one specific kind of electoral system, namely, systems that incorporate what he refers to as "voluntary proportionality." He writes that "in my view, the *only* principle compatible with a principle of political equality in this context is a principle of voluntary proportionality between the number of citizens who support each of the different overall aims and the number of legislators committed to those aims in the legislature" (Christiano 1996, p. 220. My emphasis.). This suggests that for a theorist who is committed to egalitarian defenses of democracy as a theory of government, unless we are able to put in place a system of proportional representation, we are better off attempting to realize democracy through non-electoral means.

---

[3] See for example B. Barber (1984); Honig (1993); Gutmann and Thompson (1996).

What might a justification of elections, taken simply as such, involve? It requires showing that the fundamental elements of the institutional architecture of elections, rather than this or that particular instantiation of the general principles behind elections, have solid democratic credentials. It requires in other words showing that democracy is best instantiated through elections, whatever the specific way in which these elections are organized, as long as they are, recognizably, *elections*. I would submit that central to the institution of elections are the following three features.

1) Everybody gets to vote (the principle of *universal franchise*);
2) Everybody gets to run for office (the principle of *universal eligibility*); and
3) Whoever gets the most votes, wins (the principle of *plurality rule*).

Obviously, the first two of these principles are expressed in an overly simplistic way. First, it is simply not the case that everyone who has a presumptive case to possess the franchise should, all things considered, possess the franchise. Some people are excluded as a matter of principle. Children and most adolescents, permanent residents, felons and ex-felons, expatriate citizens – all of these categories and more are excluded from the vote in at least some electoral systems. Some people are moreover also excluded from eligibility for office. What's more, these two categories of exclusions do not overlap perfectly. While it is true that all those who are excluded from the franchise are also excluded from running for elected office, the reverse does not hold. For example, in some jurisdictions, some people who are allowed to vote are temporarily barred from running from office because of age restrictions.[4]

The debate between epistemic democrats and democratic theorists who argue for democracy on the basis of the values that it embodies is echoed at the level of justifications for elections, and in particular for the principle of majority rule. Key to the substantive case for the justification of elections is the idea that they are an effective way in which to embody the principle of equality in our decision-making procedures in a context in which disagreements persist after the vote. If democracy is about reaching consensus through, for example, extensive deliberation, and if consensus is furthermore viewed as a condition for equality, since in the absence of consensus some people's views will impact on the policy agenda less than others' will, then elections can be seen as, in effect, giving up. We have elections in large measure because we disagree, and we have to at some point arrive at decisions about how to exercise political authority even in the absence of agreement. Elections, in which each person's vote counts just the same as everyone else's, are a way of treating everyone as equals even as we acknowledge that some of our fellow citizens, perhaps substantial numbers of them, will be unhappy with the result of the process. This is the view that has been developed most forcefully by Jeremy Waldron (Waldron 1999a, pp. 109–110. See also Bellamy 2007, p. 226).

---

[4] For a systematic study of such exclusions, see Lopez-Guerra (2014).

A prominent strategy to construct an epistemic case for elections builds on recent work on Condorcet's Jury Theorem. That theorem, recall, states that citizens involved in a binary decision-making process only have to be slightly better than a coin-toss at determining the "correct" answer in order for decision-making procedures incorporating the independent judgments of a large number of such better-than-average judges to attain much higher rates of epistemic reliability. If we accept this result, *and* if we can see elections as Condorcetian decision-making schemes writ large, it follows that democracies have reasons to make use of elections to choose representatives (or, for that matter, to reach other decisions of collective import).[5]

Are these promising paths to the justification of elections as privileged democratic decision-making tools? They have both been subjected to criticism. To begin with the justification of elections as epistemic tools, it has been pointed out by many commentators that the simplifying assumptions made by Enlightenment thinkers such as Rousseau and Condorcet make it difficult to map them out onto real-world democratic practices. Rousseau, for example, thought that the principle of majority rule required that citizens' judgments be independent. The reasoning behind this condition is fairly clear: If we allow citizens to influence one another, then we throw a hostage to fortune, since the epistemic value of elections will in conditions in which the independence condition does not hold depend upon the epistemic worth of successful influencers. The question of how to assess voter competence when voters are presented with a choice between more than two alternatives also poses a challenge to the real-world applicability of such devices as the Condorcet Jury Theorem.[6]

The recent work of Jason Brennan (Brennan 2016) points to a more general problem with epistemic justifications of democracy in general, and of elections in particular. The problem is that the epistemic argument risks being self-undermining. If what we want is to select the decision-making procedure that reliably gives rise to the best results, then some form of epistocracy would seem to be preferable to decision-making processes that enfranchise everyone. Imagine it was possible to identify a tranche of, say, 10% of presumptive voters with the lowest competence for the ascertainment of the public good. Even if it turned out that including them in the pool of voters would give rise to *very good* results (imagine an epistemically very gifted society for example in which this tranche of potential voters is just slightly over the coin-toss threshold, whereas all other citizens are well beyond the threshold), eliminating them would give rise to epistemically *better* results. If epistemic bestness is what we are looking for, then it selects elections with a universal franchise only in

---

[5] The case for seeing Rousseau's defense of majority-rule as grounded in epistemic considerations of the kind that Condorcet had in mind has been argued in Grofman and Feld (1988). See also Barry (1965, pp. 222–223).

[6] For discussion of the independence condition in Rousseau's theory of the General Will, see Waldron (1989a). For discussion of the restriction of the Condorcetian argument to binary choices, see Estlund (1997) and List and Goodin (2001).

the case in which all citizens are equally cognitively well endowed. (Another epistemic road to democracy is David Estlund's, which involves making the claim that though democracy is justified in virtue of its epistemic virtues, reasonable persons can disagree about what the relevant epistemic standards are (Estlund 2008)).

To the extent that we judge this implication to be unacceptable, it is because we are tacitly allowing some non-epistemic standard to do normative work. Arguably, though one could imagine a benevolent epistocracy whose policymaking procedures were equally attuned to the well-being of all of its citizens, and that were therefore egalitarian in a welfarist sense, there is an important sense in which such a regime would not be treating all of its citizens *as* equals, to the extent that it denies them any say in the policymaking process, or in the selection of representatives. Some antecedent commitment to equality is quite clearly at work in justifying not just the principle of majority rule, but also that of universal franchise.

Are elections as the privileged mechanism for the choice of representatives a natural implication of the principle according to which citizens have equal worth? A commitment to egalitarianism would probably select elections as a way of representing the equal status of all citizens, but it would, for reasons that have been developed at great length by liberal theorists, include them within a broader range of institutions, some of which are designed to offset some of the foreseeable inegalitarian risks posed by electoral systems. To rehearse arguments that have been around at least since John Stuart Mill, the unfettered operation of electoral institutions risks giving rise to a number of problems that if unchecked speak against the egalitarian pedigree of elections and of the regimes that make use of them. First, in societies rifted along ethno-cultural, religious, or even class lines, the operation of the electoral process risks giving rise to "permanent minorities."[7] Whereas egalitarianism can tolerate democratic decision-making giving rise, in the absence of consensus, to winners and losers, it cannot countenance a system in which certain identifiable groups in virtue of their minority status are routinely defeated at the polls. Second, democracy requires in order to maintain its egalitarian *bona fides* that some mechanism be in place that filters out preferences that a majority may have about the satisfaction of other people's preferences, preferences the satisfaction of which may give rise to the violation of rights.[8] For example, it is possible that in certain contexts a majority might be led to voting for a party that proposes to limit the extent to which the members of a despised minority are capable of satisfying their religious preferences. A system that did not block this possible expression of majoritarian will could hardly be seen as treating its members equally. Some form of federalism or devolution of powers is a way of dealing with the first of these problems, insofar as it allows minorities to act like majorities at least with respect to certain policy domains. Judicial review of legislation on the basis of some form of Bill of Rights is

---

[7] For a thorough discussion of electoral design problems in divided societies, see Reilly (2001).
[8] See Dworkin (1978).

a standard way of dealing with the second, though, of course, not one that met with universal approval (Bellamy 2007, Waldron 1999a).

Thus, it would seem, to the extent that we are looking for something like a foundational answer to the question posed at the outset of this section, that our results are somewhat inconclusive. Elections do not seem to be specifically and uniquely called for by either of the principles that have in recent writing been thought to ground the justification of democracy. The epistemic defense only selects elections in limit cases in which they can be shown to be epistemically best. And egalitarian defenses provide a justification of elections at best as parts of a palette of institutions, some of which have as their primary function to offset some of the foreseeable inegalitarian effects of elections. Yet this is perhaps as it should be. That elections form part of a complex system of institutions and practices the interaction of which better allows for the realization of key political values than would any of the elements of this tapestry taken alone is likely as much of a justification of elections as we can hope for.

Ironically perhaps, the best justifications of elections may ultimately be those that have recently been put forward by self-professed sceptics about elections. For example, after having spent over 300 pages patiently debunking some of the claims upon which the epistemic case for democracy rests, namely, that ordinary citizens are tolerably competent at identifying their own interests and also at making conjectures as to the impact that their elected officials have upon the changes in states of affairs that impact their interests either adversely or positively, Achen and Bartels mount what they refer to as a "realist" case for elections. Among the virtues that they see elections as embodying is the fact that elections provide polities with "authoritative, widely accepted agreement about who shall rule" (Achen and Bartels 2016, p. 317). What's more, in their view, elections hold open the promise even to losers that they may very well be able to achieve power in subsequent elections, which means that they are more likely to accept the result of elections than to try to achieve power through some destabilizing, non-electoral route (ibid). The pacifying tendencies of electoral politics in turn in their view incentivize those in power to accept opposition parties. Adam Przeworski (2018), who is similarly skeptical of the more ambitious claims made by democratic theorists as to the ethical and philosophical grounding of democratic institutions such as elections, also emphasizes the pragmatic virtues of elections. They pacify society in his view among other things by providing potentially warring parties with a sense of the relative strength of their political opponents. Like Achen and Bartels, he argues that the prospect of alternation in power through elections minimizes the costs of losing any one election, and makes it more likely than not that transitions will occur peacefully.

II HOW SHOULD WE VOTE?

The basic idea is disarmingly simple. Some people propose their services to represent citizens in the making of public policy. They put forward their policy ideas, and whatever other personal credentials they deem relevant to the task of governing during a period of time running up to the day of the election. Voters consider the claims made by the candidates, and vote for the candidate they prefer. The votes are then counted, and the candidates who collects the most votes, win.

This characterization of elections is obviously a simplification. It corresponds at most to the manner in which heads of state are elected in presidential systems. But elections are not just about electing executives. Nor are they just about electing representatives, taken one by one. They are also about determining the composition of the legislature (Dummet 1997). They are about how to translate the votes of the entire polity into a finite set of representatives who will serve as its lawmakers.

Perhaps the most immediately intuitive manner in which to go about both selecting individual representatives and determining the composition of the legislature is to proceed additively. Divide the polity up into (usually, but not necessarily[9]) territorially concentrated units of roughly equivalent numbers of voters. Hold an election for a representative in each one of these constituencies on the simple, "Presidential" model briefly described above. Each constituency will return one representative. Each elected representative gets to go to the parliament. In modern democratic systems, the vast majority of those running for office will belong to political parties. The party with the largest number of elected members of Parliament usually gets to form the government. In rare cases, when no political party has managed to obtain the majority of seats in Parliament, parties that do not have the largest number of seats can form the government if they are better able than the party with the most seats to work with other parties so as to maintain the confidence of Parliament.

The system just described characterizes what are commonly referred to as "simple plurality" (SP) systems, sometimes also called "First Past the Post." It is characteristic of Westminster Parliamentary systems such as the United Kingdom's and Canada's. The feature most often associated with it is stability. SP systems tend to produce majority governments, which in virtue of their majority system are relatively immune from the danger of being defeated in the legislature before the end of their legally prescribed term. All that is needed in order to form a government is for some party to receive the most votes in a majority of the constituencies that make up the polity. That result can be achieved with far less than the majority of the votes even in the constituencies that the victorious party wins. Imagine a country made up of 100 constituencies in which three parties are serious contenders for seats. In a limit case, one can imagine a party winning 51 seats with as few as 35% of the vote, with the two other parties winning on the order of 30% each party. Imagine that, improbably, that same party receives no votes whatsoever in the 49 other constituencies. It would achieve a Parliamentary majority with somewhere on the order of 18% of the popular vote. SP systems are thus quite efficient in generating majorities out of pluralities of votes.

[9] The most systematic account we have of the notion of a constituency is in Rehfeld (2005).

A second feature of the SP system that is often seen as counting in its favor is that of *accountability*. When each voter can identify the single representative that she has voted into office, it is much easier than in other systems (which we shall be describing below) to assign responsibility when things go wrong (or, indeed, to bestow praise when things go right). Moreover, when governing parties enjoy majority status, there are fewer impediments to their implementing the platforms on the basis of which they were elected. In particular, they cannot justify themselves before their electorate for not having at least attempted to carry out their pledges on the basis of which they were elected by claiming that they were compelled to making compromises in order to keep an electoral coalition together (Weinstock 2015a, 2017).

Though accountability and stability count in favor of SP, it has considerable liabilities as well. It tends to leave very little place for minority voices. A political set of opinions that has some degree of support throughout the polity is within the context of such a system unlikely to get any representation at all. On some empirically plausible sets of circumstances, even a political party that has a relatively homogeneously spread out 20% share of the electorate is unlikely to receive any seats in Parliament at all. Thus, SP is disproportionate in two ways. It not only tends to inflate the Parliamentary representation of political parties that win the most votes, but it also tends to depress the influence of political parties that have substantial support, but not enough concentrated support to achieve seats in the legislature. Now, it is possible to overstate this concern. Indeed, under SP, the sets of political opinions that may only be favored by smaller segments of the electorate do not simply disappear. Rather, they tend to find their way into wings of the big-tent parties that the system tends to produce. Maurice Duverger famously stated that SP tends to produce two big parties, as it rewards size. Though Duverger's Law can be overstated – SP systems tend to be multi-party, either because of the regional electoral hold of some parties, because of the identification of parts of the electorate with more than two parties, or for a whole host of other possible reasons – it is nonetheless the case that bigger parties tend to be generated by this system. But rather than being tightly ideologically united, they tend to be pre-electoral alliances of political actors who under different electoral systems might perhaps be incentivized to try their electoral luck through different parties (McCall Rosenbluth and Shapiro 2018).

One of the ways in which to offset the problem of lack of proportionality that seems to be inherent in SP systems without losing the tie to constituency is by eliciting more information from voters on the ballot. Rather than asking them to simple pick a name, they could be asked to rank candidates, and in the case of ballots listing a first preference for a candidate without much popular support, to "transfer" at least part of the weight to that vote to the voter's second (or third, or…) choice. The mathematics involved in determining how to "discount" transferred votes, and what threshold to set to qualify a candidate for a seat in the legislature, can get quite complex, and there are highly technical disagreements among exponents of such systems about how to get it right. But the logic behind such systems is quite plain. It is within such systems usually not enough for a candidate simply to be preferred by a plurality. They will also have to do well in getting voters to list them as second or as third choices. By getting more information from voters than SP systems do, we are more likely better to represent the full range of voter preferences. A danger is that beyond a certain number, voters may not have reliable preferences between, say, their fourth and fifth ranked candidates. This risks introducing "noise" into the electoral system, noise that may in some mathematically possible cases have an actual impact on electoral results.

A concern with representativeness might also push one in a very different direction. Rather than breaking up a polity into electoral constituencies and having each one run its own election on something resembling the Presidential model, imagine the entire party being a single constituency. Everyone in the country votes in the same election. When the votes are counted up, each party receives seats in Parliament in proportion to their share of the overall vote. Each Party prepares a ranked list of candidates, and name members to the legislature by starting from the top of the list until the proportion is reached. In order to prevent "fringe" parties from exercising influence, a qualifying threshold is usually set as a condition of achieving any representation at all. These are systems of "closed list" proportional representation (PR), in which it is the party that determines the order in which candidates will enter Parliament. (PR systems can also exhibit greater or lesser degrees of "openness" depending on the degree to which voters get to at least partially determine that order).

PR has the advantage of allowing for the representation of a greater number of political ideas in the legislature. The system however has the tendency to produce fairly unstable governments, since the distribution of political opinion in an even just moderately diverse electorate means that a single party can rarely if ever elect a sufficient number of legislators to control the legislature. Coalition governments are therefore the norm, and their internal divisions make it the case that they tend to break down. What's more, they make accountability more difficult. The need to compromise and broker deals with coalition partners means that it is easier for elected representatives to renege on commitments to voters. And since pure PR systems violate what Michael Dummett has called the "constituency principle" – according to which "Parliament shall be composed exclusively of those elected to represent the constituencies" (Dummett 1997, p. 4) – such systems make it difficult for individual voters to be able hold identifiable representatives to account when they betray electoral trust.

One way of attempting to combine the best of both PR and SP systems while avoiding their drawbacks is in effect by combining them. Mixed-Member Electoral systems hand voters two votes. They treat one of their ballots the way they would in an SP system, and the other the way they would in a PR system. Representatives who win as constituency representatives are given seats in Parliament. And PR lists are then used in order to offset the disproportion that the SP-generated distribution of seats inevitably produces. Whether such MMP systems effectively allow for PR and SP's virtues to be expressed institutionally while limiting their drawbacks, or whether they just replicate these drawbacks while adding more besides, is a subject of very active academic debate (Shugart and Wattenberg 2001).

SP, PR, and MMP, despite their obvious differences, share one feature. The ballots cast by voters within each of these systems convey limited amounts of information. Voters are asked to indicate the party or candidate that they would prefer to see elected. Voters will sometimes indicate a preference through their ballots for candidates that they would not want to see elected, all things equal, but who they would prefer to another candidate who they "disprefer" the most. That voters can only express a fairly simple political preference through their vote has struck some theorists of elections as a flaw. It presents voters with a difficult dilemma – that of either using the limited expressive means available to them through the simple ballot to express an all things equal preference, or employing it "strategically" in order to lower the likelihood that a least preferred candidate might prevail. This flaw can be remedied, and the ensuing dilemma avoided, through the use of ranked ballots. Rather than indicating a single preference, voters are asked to rank some or all of the candidates on the ballot.

There are a number of ways in which votes can then be compiled. Single transferable vote systems tabulate winners by eliminating first-place choices that fail to achieve enough support, and "transferring" the votes of those who preferred eliminated candidates to their second (and third, and fourth) picks. Tabulation stops when seats are filled. STV systems differ along a number of dimensions. For example, some STV systems make use of a numerical quota that must be achieved by any successful candidate. Some systems only assign diminishing fractions of votes to voters' successive choices.

There have also been other proposals as to how to tabulate ranked ballots. For example, Borda counts give candidates points for each rival candidate ranked lower on ballots. Condorcet winners are determined by identifying the candidate that would beat all others in one-on-one electoral battles. The information needed in order to determine a "Condorcet winner" can be extracted from a ranked ballot by decomposing the information determined therein into head-to-head contests. There are in fact innumerable ways to use the information compiled through ranked ballots in order to determine winners. Implementing them and comparing their comparative virtues and liabilities can very quickly require the application of fairly advanced mathematics (Dummett 1984; Szpiro 2010).

Which of these electoral systems is "the best"? As posed, this question is unanswerable as there are just too many criteria that can be invoked in order to compare them. In comparing PR and SP systems, we've been able to determine some of them: stability, accountability, and representativity of the views held within the population. But as we get into the detail of different kinds of systems, especially of systems making use of ranked ballots, internal, technical criteria also emerge. For example, it is thought to be a virtue of an electoral system that it does not reward "strategic" voting, that is voting through which one seeks to contribute to the production of an electoral outcome by voting in a way that does not actually express one's political preferences. (The Gibbard-Satterthwaite theorem purports to show that no electoral system with more than two candidates is immune to strategic voting (Gibbard 1973)). Michael Dummett has pointed out that requiring of voters that they rank all candidates can produce "noise" that can actually have a substantive impact on the outcome of an election (Dummett 1997).

There are pragmatic considerations that must be taken into account as well. We may worry that, though ranked ballot systems simply require of voters that they rank candidates, the actual mechanisms for tabulating the information on their ballots may be so complex as to defy the understanding of many (or even most) voters. Perhaps a trade-off between the degree of precision that a system tries to achieve in faithfully mirroring the distribution of political preferences in a population, and the intelligibility of the procedures through which results are generated, is inevitable.

A point that in my view emerges quite clearly even from the foregoing pencil sketch of options of electoral systems is that in the same way as there is quite a conceptual distance to travel between arguments for democracy, and arguments for elections, similarly, there is a substantial gap between the arguments that we have canvassed in favor of elections, understood simply as decision-making procedures subject to the principles of majoritarianism, universal franchise and universal eligibility, and arguments for different electoral systems. All of the kinds of systems briefly canvassed here in some sense satisfy the majoritarian criterion, and they are all perfectly compatible with the rules of universal franchise and universal eligibility. Relevant normative questions only really come into view when we descend to a fairly detailed description of different possible systems.

Another observation worth making in the present context, one that may or may not be considered as introducing further criteria to the assessment of different electoral systems, is that different electoral systems create different sets of incentives for the creation of different kinds of political parties. There has in recent years been a greater appreciation on the part of political theorists of the important role that political parties perform in the political life of democratic societies (Goodin 2008; Rosenblum 2008; Bonotti 2017; McCall Rosenbluth and Shapiro 2018; J. White and L. Ypi 2016; Wolkenstein 2020; N. Barber 2018; Muirhead 2014). Political theorists have devoted quite a bit of attention to the various political functions that parties perform in a well-ordered liberal democracy. Parties, among other things, are seen as performing an important epistemic role for the electorate. By presenting voters with organized sets of policies underpinned by a small set of fundamental values, they organize political space for voters who may not normally pay much attention to policy matters, and allow them to make more informed choices than would otherwise have been the case. They also connect the electorate to the political process in the long periods between elections, thus preventing the kind of democratic demobilization that might occur were voters only to be connected to the political process at election time.

Of course, there are all kinds of political parties. Some are "big tent" parties that bring together people with quite different policy preferences, united only by a commitment to some very general political values ("liberty," "equality") and who end up compromising on party platforms to present to the electorate as a result of pre-electoral internal negotiations. Others are more narrowly focused on a very specific set of policy preferences, and in virtue of this fact are less amenable to internal negotiations and compromises. These different kinds of parties may in virtue of the quite different logics that animate them be more or less adept at performing the functions that "party theorists" have identified.

What is less often observed by the multiplicity of theorists who have begun to theorize about political parties is that the form that political parties take is a dependent rather than an independent variable (Weinstock 2019). Parties take shape as broader or narrower not just, and perhaps not even mainly, in virtue of endogenous preferences of party members, but rather because of the environment of political incentives in which the formation of political parties take shape. As we have already seen, SP tends to incentivize the creation of "big tent" parties capable of capturing large swathes of the electorate, whereas systems that present elements of proportional representation are more likely to generate ideologically more focused parties.

In another work, I've argued that the kinds of larger parties that tend to emerge from SP electoral systems are better positioned to fulfil some of the broader social and political functions that recent theorists of parties have ascribed to them than are parties that by their very nature are pitched in an ideologically narrower manner (Weinstock 2015a, 2017). I won't rehearse those arguments here, but merely point out that above and beyond the virtues that different electoral systems have simply *qua* electoral systems, they also create incentives for broader political action in general, and for the formation of different kinds of political parties in particular. Electoral systems help to create political cultures of very different kinds. This fact at least needs to be kept in view as we deliberate as to whether or not to engage in electoral reform.

III WHO SHOULD VOTE?

Myriad philosophical questions revolve around the matter of the extension of the democratic franchise, as well as around the related question of the moral modality associated with the franchise. Who should be granted the franchise, and should that franchise be thought of as a right, one that grantees are entitled to exercise of not as they see fit or as an obligation?

Let's briefly consider these questions, and the main lines of argument that they have elicited, in turn. First, as has already been mentioned, universal suffrage in a democratic state is never really *universal* suffrage. While some of the exclusions that have characterized liberal democracies in the past are now roundly rejected (for example, exclusions based on gender, on race, or on one's status as propertied or not), others are still subjects of live debate.

One such debate has to do with the requirement of residency. Should citizens who do not reside in the polity of which they are citizens enjoy the right to vote? If residency is to be considered a condition of the franchise, should those who move to another country of which they are not citizens lose the right to vote immediately upon switching residency, or should they be entitled to vote for a certain time after they have left their country of citizenship? And what about the case of dual, or even multiple citizens? (Weinstock 2010; Goodin and Tanasoca 2014) Should they be limited to only being able to vote in one of their countries of citizenship? If so, should they get to choose which of these countries the will vote in, or should they be limited to voting in the country that they reside in? Powerful moral intuitions seem to push us in different directions on this set of questions. On the one hand, some might argue that only those who are affected by a political decision should have a voice as to how that decision is made. Citizens who have not lived in a country of which they are citizens for years, and who may not have any intention of ever returning to that country would on this view not have a legitimate claim to voting in their country of citizenship because they will not be made to bear the consequences of their vote. (Those who hold this position owe an account of why citizenship is even a necessary condition for the franchise. If voting rights are conferred on the basis of the principle according to which one should only vote in elections that one is directly affected by, then permanent residency rather than citizenship would seem to be the operative principle).

On the other hand, there is a rival intuition according to which there should not be different categories of citizens, and that any citizen should in virtue of their citizenship have exactly the same rights as any other citizen. The right to vote is such a powerful marker of citizenship that were one to make distinctions among citizens, it should not be with respect to the crucially important marker of voting rights.

That this question is still very much in play can be ascertained by the fact that established liberal democracies are still changing their collective minds on the question of whether expatriate citizens should be allowed to vote. For example, expatriate citizens of the UK who had until very recently forfeited their right to vote after fifteen years of living abroad will now be able to vote in national elections.

Another criterion of exclusion has to do with age. Many countries have moved the voting age down over the course of the twentieth century. Canada, for example, lowered the voting age from 21 to 18 in 1970. Should it be lowered even more, say to 16? While some (including this author (Weinstock, 2020)) have (admittedly controversially) argued for the extension of the right to vote to children, there is no realistic prospect of this argument finding favor in any modern liberal democracy any time soon. However, the admission of adolescents, say, of 16 years of age, to the franchise is a question that has been on the agenda in a number of jurisdictions. Austria, for example, lowered its age requirement to 16 years in 2007, and many other countries have considered legislation that would also set the minimum voting age at that level.

As in the case of the residency requirement, the question of the right level at which to set the minimum voting age is underpinned by important philosophical questions. The question of political competency has been central to the debate over whether or not to lower the voting age. As studies increasingly tend to show that adult voters are quite uninformed about political matters, the justification for excluding adolescents on the basis of the fact that they too tend to be uninformed weakens. More fundamentally, the question of where to set the bar raises the question of what kind of competency we should expect from voters.

Whether or not to include non-resident and non-adult citizens to the franchise are at present the central questions to do with the *extension* of the franchise. Another set of questions has to do with the *modality* of the vote. Is there an obligation to vote for those who are members of the set of qualified voters, and if so, can that obligation be legally enforced? Conversely, is there an argument for the position that there is an obligation *not* to vote on the part of those who have not taken steps to obtain sufficient information relevant to their decision? Here again, powerful intuitions seem to push in different directions. Those who have argued for an obligation to vote have emphasized in different ways the obligation to do our part in sustaining a collective enterprise. Lisa Hill has argued, for example, that the legal obligation to vote helps us solve an assurance problem that voting would otherwise be beset by (Brennan and Hill 2014). Indeed, every vote only has an impact if it is part of a collective endeavor. But one can only be certain that this collective endeavor is actually being undertaken if one knows that others are being obligated to vote. on pain of legal sanction. Julia Maskikver has argued that by voting we satisfy a duty that can only be collectively borne to rid our fellow citizens of inadequate and unjust government. To those who argue that there are other ways in which citizens can contribute to the commonweal, Emilee Booth Chapman responds that such arguments are not sensitive to the centrality of voting among the various practices and institutions that make up the life of a complex modern democracy (Chapman 2019).

On the other hand, the claim that voting should be construed as a right that one is free to exercise or not rests on arguably equally powerful normative foundations. Most obviously, within the context of a broadly liberal democratic framework, making the vote into a legal obligation would seem to violate liberal strictures against undue perfectionism. Liberals should countenance the fact that some citizens are simply not interested enough in politics to take the time required to vote, and to inform themselves about the relevant issues, time that they might have devoted to pursuits that mean more to them. Moreover, in opposition to theorists such as Chapman, who have emphasized the centrality of voting to democracy, those who argue against an obligation to vote point out that there are multiple other ways in which citizens can contribute positively to the good of their communities (Freiman 2020).

More provocatively perhaps, some theorists have argued that there may, at least in the case of some citizens, be an obligation *not* to vote. According to this line of argument, voting is a paradigmatically other-regarding activity, one through which we impact not only our own interests, but those of others as well. When one does not know enough about the relevant issues to vote competently, then the risk is great that one will act harmfully in voting, and thus, that one should observe a moral (though perhaps not a legal) obligation not to vote (Brennan 2009).

Questions to do with the extension and with the modality of the electoral franchise are important and interesting in their own rights, but they also point us back to more fundamental questions to do with the value of the vote. In the next section, let's consider the views of theorists who believe that valuing democracy and valuing the vote are two very different things indeed, and that conflating the two has led theorists to overvaluing the vote as a democratic mechanism.

IV SHOULD WE VOTE?

We saw in Section I that the justification of elections is not as simple a matter as might have been thought. There is as we have seen a hiatus between the main justifications of democracy, and the justification of elections as a way of choosing political representatives. Moreover, the justifications that can be mounted for elections on the basis of the kinds of values that tend to be invoked in order to defend democracy present vulnerabilities. Equality-based justifications have to reckon with the inegalitarian consequences that elections untrammeled by other institutions can give rise to. And epistemic defenses risk being self-undermining, since democratic elections governed by the principle of universal suffrage and universal eligibility are unlikely to be epistemically best.

The lack of a robust justification of elections as uniquely privileged by democratic first principles has been exacerbated in recent years by the sense shared by pundits and by theorists of modern politics as well that we are currently undergoing something of a crisis of liberal democracy. In countries around the world, including in what had until now been thought to be the world's most robust democracies, such as the United States, there is the growing sense that the electorate has lost confidence in the institutions that had heretofore been thought to be central to the life of liberal democracy. Voters are increasingly heeding the call of populist politicians whose commitment to the core institutions of liberal democracy is at best tenuous. Many diagnoses have been proffered for the malaise of modern liberal democracies. For some, the root cause is economic. Globalization has made the workers of prosperous liberal democracies feel that their jobs and economic livelihoods are precarious, and that traditional political elites don't care. For others, the malaise is cultural. Patterns of migration have made many less privileged sectors of society feel like "strangers in their own land" (Hochschild 2016).

But some political philosophers have laid at least part of the blame at the feat of electoral systems and systems of political representation that have come to feel remote and unresponsive to many. Thus, Cristine Lafont has in a recent book claimed that "the generalized desire to 'take back control' is animating the current rise in populism," and that "it seems clear that reducing democratic deficits would require increasing the fair value of citizens' current rights and their opportunities to effectively shape the policies to which they are subject" (Lafont 2020 p. 2), something which in her view is incompatible with the institutional status quo obtaining in most democracies. Hélène Landemore begins her recent work with the observation that "everywhere, there is widespread backlash against established electoral elites, a backlash that can in turn empower authoritarian or populist rulers and ultimately threaten democracy's foundations," and argues further on in the book that elections "are by nature an ambiguously democratic selection mechanism, creating and thriving from inequalities between people" (Landemore 2020, pp. xiii, 42–43). David Van Reybrouck has argued that elections have now become an obstacle to democracy, rather than facilitating it. We have in his view become "election fundamentalists," and have forgotten that elections have only been seen for the last couple of hundred years as a privileged democratic mechanism, other democratic tools having had pride of place at other periods in the development of the democratic ideal and of democratic practice (Van Reybrouck 2014).[10]

Given the weak justificatory basis of elections, and given the suspicion voiced by some that elections as they are presently practiced in many liberal democracies may be part of the cause of the "crisis of democracy" that we are presently experiencing, it is not surprising that recent political theory has been replete with suggestions as to how elections might be complemented, or even replaced altogether, by other forms of decision-making and selection.

Alternatives to the election of representatives can be classed very roughly into two categories. Some object to the *representative* nature of representative democracy. On this view, the problem with modern democracy is that it has tended to take decision-making power out of the hands of people, and hand it over to electoral elites that have over time come to be increasingly disconnected from the electorate. Democracy should on this view accordingly make less use of representatives. Others object not so much to representation than to the way in which they are selected, namely, through elections. The former seek to reinvigorate other policymaking devices, such as mini-publics, Porto Alegre-style participatory budgeting, and citizens' initiatives that effectively bypass representation. The latter look to different ways in which to *select* representatives.

The dominant modality among those who argue for other ways in which to select representatives is that of lottery, or "sortition." The idea is to have representatives (or at least one chamber of representatives in bicameral legislatures) chosen by lot

---

[10] Part of the story told by Bernard Manin in his classic work *Principes du gouvernement représentatif* has to do with the historical "victory" of elections over other forms of selection of representative officials. (Manin 1995).

from the general population. Let me briefly consider the arguments for both of these proposed democratic selection and decision-making mechanisms, as well as some problems that they present.

The theorists who have defended the idea that at least some representatives should be selected by lot differ among themselves along a variety of dimensions. One of these dimensions has to do with the specific problems with elections that sortition is meant to fix. For Alex Guerrero (2014), the basic problem with an electoral system is that the mechanisms whereby elected representatives can be rendered effectively accountable are insufficient. This insufficiency is in his view the result of a number of complementary factors which create something of a "perfect storm" of factors that risk having legislatures captured by powerful elites. On the one hand, ordinary voters do not possess the knowledge required in order to hold elected representatives accountable, for example by voting them out of office if they have failed to fulfil their responsibilities adequately. But if elections are to be a mechanism of effective accountability, citizens must both understand the issues with respect to which they are evaluating the performance of representatives, and be sufficiently aware of what their representatives are doing with respect to these issues. If these two epistemic conditions are not satisfied by the electorate, then there are in effect no strings tying representatives to the interests and well-being of their constituents. As Guerrero puts it, "issue ignorance and conduct ignorance make monitoring difficult or impossible" (Guerrero 2014, p. 140) On the other hand, powerful elites are powerfully incentivized to control legislatures, especially given the magnitude of the stakes involved in the kind of legislation that can affect the interests of elites in all sorts of ways, and the lack of any other effective steering. As Guerrero puts it, "political power is more valuable to powerful interests the more that it is untethered from constituent interests and beliefs" (Guerrero 2014, p. 142). The selection of legislators by lottery removes much of the potential levers that such elites might otherwise possess in order to control the political behavior of elected legislators. And it compensates for the epistemic shortfalls of ordinary voters by putting citizens selected by lottery through a kind of policy bootcamp (Guerrero 2014, pp. 160–162).[11]

Given that one of the main concerns motivating Guerrero's lottocratic proposal has to do with the epistemic limitations of ordinary voters, it is unsurprising that the proposal seeks to limit the epistemic burden on lottocratically selected representatives. He imagines those persons selected by lot being seated not in normal legislatures tasked with drafting all manner of legislation, but in "single issue lottery-selected legislatures" (SILL). Among the reasons that he believes that SILLs should have singularity of focus is that the people who would be drawn into the legislative process would be "amateurs," and it might be expecting too much to expect them to be able to make competent decisions across the full range of policy domains (Guerrero 2014, p. 158).

---

[11] Another proposal that reduces the number of voters by lottery in order to increase each voter's epistemic level is by Lopez-Guerra (2011).

Guerrero is agnostic as to whether his "lottocratic alternative" should be considered as a full replacement for ordinary elected legislatures, or whether it should play some kind of a back-up role. It's fairly clear that as a full replacement for ordinary politics, the proposal is a nonstarter. The main concern is that it would exacerbate a problem that most modern theories of public administration have tried of late to escape, namely, the problem of legislative silos. Good policy-making does not strictly segregate policy domains. Rather, it sees them as part of a total package. This is so for a variety of reasons. First, formulating a platform and enacting a legislative agenda requires making trade-offs. Working with a limited fiscal pie, there is only so much that can be done, and investments in one domain always have to be evaluated in terms of the opportunity costs that they represent for other domains. Second, policy interventions do not always just affect a single domain. As we know, for example, from the literature on the social determinants of health, social policy in a wide range of domains has an impact on the health and well-being of populations. These crossover effects moreover have to be taken into account when policy is being formulated (as do crossover with respect to other policy indices, such as environmental impact and child welfare).[12] Third, a proposal such as Guerrero's, interpreted in "maximalist" fashion, would completely do away with political parties, and thus with the policy coherence that platforms developed on the basis of the underlying values that different political parties are committed to realizing. Guerrero is aware of the problem of coherence, but he views it as one of the many problems of "practical institutional design." I think that they go deeper than this. As the brief remarks above suggest, they go to the very heart of what policy and policymaking are. They are not about making policy proposals in entirely discrete areas, but rather about coming up with coherent policy ideas made in the light of the whole legislative platform of a governing party. If taking part in the legislative process in the more capacious sense I have just briefly sketched is beyond the ken of ordinary citizens chosen at random, then either the lottocratic alternative has to be abandoned, or its claims have to be quite radically scaled back.

A more modest, but nonetheless significant role for representatives selected by sortition has been proposed by Arash Abizadeh. For Abizadeh, the problem with electoral democracy that sortition would contribute to solving has to do with the inequality that is of necessity given rise to by electoral politics, which tends in his view to generate political elites, and it also has to do with the greater capacity that a randomly selected legislative assembly would have to consider legislation impartially, away from the cut and thrust of competitive elections, which tend to attract all kinds of powerful interests seeking to divert the course of the legislative process for their benefit. Abizadeh views sortition as fitting into a legislative scheme in which representatives chosen by lot would populate the "second" chamber in a bicameral system such as Canada's (Abizadeh 2019, 2021b; see also Gastil and Olin Wright

---

[12] I've developed these points at greater length in Weinstock (2015b) and (2015c).

2019). The division of labor that would be instantiated by a bicameral system in which the Senate is peopled by citizens selected by sortition would resemble the division of labor that presently obtains in many bicameral systems, where the Lower House is the only confidence chamber, and the Upper chamber is tasked with considering the legislation that has been sent to it by the elected chamber, and with proposing legislation with no budgetary implications. Electoral politics are still necessary in his view to maintain civil piece, and to provide an outlet for the political agency of ordinary citizens. The Upper chamber is the place where impartiality and equality obtain.

In performing a back-up role to the lower house in which most legislation originates, the idea of an upper chamber peopled by ordinary citizens has many attractions. Abizadeh stresses the fact that it would permit the realization of the virtues of political agency and of social peace that electoral politics give rise to, with the greater political egalitarianism and impartiality that a sortitioned second chamber would instantiate. While the bicameral system thus described has its attractions, it is clearly not an alternative to electoral politics, but rather a complement to such politics. The assumption that it makes is that, as it were, two imperfect systems of representation can improve the whole that they constitute when combined.

It would be a shame, however, if the adoption of a mixed bicameralism such as that proposed by Abizadeh occluded the institutional reforms that could very well improve the impartiality and egalitarianism of electoral politics. If citizen competence is a reason to distrust voters, then perhaps the solution is not to minimize their role, but rather to increase their competence through educational reforms. If money exerts too great an influence on the practice of elections, then laws limiting spending during election campaigns can be enacted. If we fear the creation of a political elite through elections that risks becoming disconnected from its constituents, then surely there are reforms that can be mitigated to prevent that happening to quite the degree that it presently does. Term limits can have the effect of making it more difficult to consider politics as a lifelong career. There are many small-scale institutional devices that could reform electoral politics from the inside by subtly changing the incentives that obtain within them that tend to give rise to the problems canvassed by defenders of the lottocratic alternative. It would be a shame if the pursuit of this alternative made us think that theorizing about such reforms had become superfluous.[13] It could be that the best justification of the lottocratic alternative is not the claim that it would allow us to fix otherwise unfixable problems with electoral politics, but rather, that it provides us with a much more attractive picture of *bicameralism* than those which are at present available either in theory or in practice.[14]

---

[13] Cf. Adrian Vermeule's "Institutional Design Writ Small" in Vermeule (2007).
[14] For an account of bicameralism's normative virtues, see Waldron (2012a).

I have focused this section on a prominent democratic alternative to elections. It is worth mentioning in passing that there is at present a considerable amount of theoretical work that is also being done on describing and defending alternatives to the natural concomitant of elections, namely *representation*. Direct democracy is back in vogue, and it is taking the form of the exploration of democratic devices such as grass-roots local democracy initiatives (Taylor, Nanz, and Beaubien Taylor 2020), legislative mini-publics (Landemore 2020), and of referenda initiated by citizens the results of which would be binding on legislators (Matsusaka 2020). Whether these alternatives to representation represent realizable, normatively defensible proposals will have to await another occasion.

CONCLUSION: A RESEARCH AGENDA

The foregoing pages have barely scratched the surface of the issues that would have to be considered in a full normative theory of elections. In closing, I'd like to make a plea for greater normative attention from philosophers and from constitutional scholars to what might be thought of as the micro-circuitry of elections. More attention has to be paid to the normative dimensions of the way in which elections are institutionalized, and in which what might at first glance seem to be normatively unimportant decisions are made. As the 2020 U.S. election shows, seemingly trivial practical questions of electoral organization raise sometimes deep normative questions, and can have momentous implications. We've already seen that the question of whether or not to encourage absentee and advance voting raise deep questions about what an election *is*. Is it a singular event, that requires quasi simultaneity in the casting of votes, or is it best thought of as a process, that can extend over days or weeks? Other questions abound. How should voters be registered to vote? Should their registration occur automatically, or should it require some kind of a positive manifestation of an intention? Are there any reasons to prefer particular *kinds* of ballots? The website of Elections Canada states that all ballots in Canadian elections are paper, and are counted by hand, because they are "user-friendly and cannot be hacked."[15] What counts as adequate invigilation of both the casting and the counting of votes? Some political theorists may view such questions of workaday institutional design as not deserving of normative scrutiny. They would be wrong.

As we have seen, the ethical and philosophical foundations of elections as a way of selecting our political leaders is surprisingly flimsy. The history of democracies could have taken a different turn, one in which elections were a marginal device relative to others. But history has not taken that turn, and for better or for worse, elections are considered by most of the world's population as a *sine qua non* of democracy. At the same time as we dream of possible alternatives to elections, ones

---

[15] www.elections.ca/content.aspx?section=vot&dir=bkg/safe&document=votSafe&lang=e Accessed on December 1, 2020.

that may tick more normative boxes than elections do, we should not neglect the task of thinking about ways of making elections as normatively attractive as they can be. Such a research agenda should consider both not only the theoretically rich and technically complex question of what electoral system is best relative to a range of relevant criteria, but also the humble but practically important question of how concretely to run a fair and free election.

RECOMMENDED READING

Achen, C. & Bartels, L. (2016). *Democracy for Realists. Why Elections do not Produce Responsive Government*, Princeton: Princeton University Press.

Brennan, J. & Hill, L. (2014). *Compulsory Voting*, Cambridge: Cambridge University Press.

Dummett, M. (1984). *Voting Systems*, Oxford: Oxford University Press.

Dummett, M. (1997). *Principles of Electoral Reform*, Oxford: Oxford University Press.

Gastil, J. & Olin Wright, E., eds. (2019). *Legislature by Lot*, London and New York: Verso.

Lafont, C. (2020). *Democracy without Shortcuts: A Participatory Conception of Deliberative Democracy*, Oxford: Oxford University Press.

Landemore, H. (2020). *Open Democracy. Reinventing Popular Rule for the Twenty-First Century*, Princeton: Princeton University Press.

Lopez-Guerra, C. (2014). *Democracy and Disenfranchisement*, Oxford: Oxford University Press.

Maskikver, J. (2020). *The Duty to Vote*, Oxford: Oxford University Press.

Matsusaka, J. (2020). *Let the People Rule. How Direct Democracy Can Meet the Populist Challenge*, Princeton: Princeton University Press.

McCall Rosenbluth, F. & Shapiro, S. (2018). *Responsible Parties. Saving Democracy from Itself*, New Haven: Yale University Press.

Przeworski, A. (2018). *Why Bother with Elections?* Cambridge, UK; Medford, MA: Polity Press.

Strangers in their Own Land. (2016). *Anger and Mourning on the American Right*, New York: The New Press.

Thompson, D. (2002). *Just Elections. Creating a Fair Electoral Process in the United States*, Chicago: University of Chicago Press.

44

Political Parties

Jonathan White and Lea Ypi

Political parties sit uneasily in constitutional thinking. While sometimes seen as essential agents of democratic life, in legal scholarship they have tended to be treated as groups whose power-seeking ambitions threaten to undermine the unity of the polity.[1] Parties, it is often said, divide citizens rather than encouraging them to deliberate, and polarise opinion instead of helping to institutionalise compromise. One function of a constitution, it is widely assumed, is to temper the divergence of political opinion. Already a current in ancient political thought, the assumption that an ideal constitution is one that enables different parts of the political community to mediate between potentially conflicting interests and principles has been prominent throughout modern democracy. Whether we focus on Aristotle's praise of the mixed constitution, Montesquieu's analysis of the separation of powers, or Madison's defence of checks and balances in the US constitution, underpinning all these accounts we find the idea that politics would run better – more efficiently, also more fairly – if strong opinions could be moderated or set to one side.

As we argue in the following, there are reasons to be sceptical of such an aversion to political division. It is not just that claims to be a moderate can be loaded and misleading, adopted by all who want to position themselves as responsible, unthreatening and uncontroversial. Even those who might deserve the label of moderate are the exponents, we suggest, of a dubious virtue. Existing political societies are far from just, even those widely viewed as democracies, and in an unjust order, moderation is a questionable outlook. Countering a polity's failings, and defending justice, is likely to depend on a more trenchant attitude. Political conflict deserves wider appreciation, and the key question becomes how it is organised – what demands are expressed, in the name of whom, and how they come to be embedded in structures. In societies like ours, still characterised by arbitrary uses of political, social and economic power, political parties remain central not only for connecting the different functions of government but also as champions of desirable legal change.

---

[1] For discussions of this ambiguity, see Bellamy (2007, chap. 6).

Parties have long been a cornerstone of modern democracy, and they remain critical to how conflict unfolds. Despite the fact that many constitutional orders have been configured with the goal of obstructing partisanship, parties of principle can be agents of productive adversarialism. Quite how they perform this role will depend on a number of features. There is a difference between how parties function in one-party systems, where a single party controls the constitution, sometimes with the help of smaller satellite parties, and multi-party systems where several parties compete with each other for control of legislative decisions and representation in the executive.[2] In the latter case, complications arise from the fact that parties are considered intermediary bodies between the private and public sphere. On the one hand, parties are spontaneous associations of individuals and, as such, belong to the realm of civil society, with a claim to as much freedom from interference as is necessary for civic participation to flourish (on the dual nature of parties between state and civil society, see Urbinati 2006). On the other hand, when the asymmetries that develop as a result of those spontaneous initiatives are left unregulated, for example when some parties are able to accumulate huge wealth and resources in campaign donations, this undermines the public role of parties in channelling the democratic will (Ewing et al. 2012).

When discussing the role that parties can play as agents of democratic change, it is important to be mindful of the background circumstances that enable or constrain that function. Our argument is that, in their ideal form, parties can be sites of participation, education and commitment even if in reality they often look like factions – a distinction to which we shall return. At their best, parties enable citizens to reflect on the background circumstances that shape the exercise of power, and to seek change that renders power democratically accountable. They are also ways in which the boundaries of political membership can be contested. Ultimately, they can be agents of transformation, reshaping the societies and institutional orders in which they emerge.

I CONSTITUTIONS AND CONFLICT: ON THE PROMISE AND PITFALLS OF MODERATION

Perhaps the most influential pioneer of the notion that political virtue lies in charting a position between extremes was Aristotle. In the *Nichomachean Ethics*, he defined virtue as 'a kind of moderation, inasmuch as it aims at the mean or moderate amount', pursuing a space 'between two vices, one on the side of excess, the other on the side of defect' (Aristotle 2000, Bk. 2). His appeal to the relative mean as the mark of wisdom and prudence, coupled with his defence in *Politics* of mixed government as the system that institutionalised these qualities, can be read as an

---

[2] For an instructive discussion of the differences, see N. Barber (2018), pp. 166–186. For excellent analysis of the intricacies of constitutional change in a one-party system, see Zhang (2012), chap. 4.

account of how the good political community aims to temper political conflict and achieve a form of equilibrium.

In a similar vein, David Hume lamented the negative effects of political conflict on shared institutions, distinguishing between divisions based on interest, principle and affection (Hume (1998 [1748]), p. 36). 'For my part', he argued, 'I shall always be more fond of promoting moderation than zeal' (Hume (1998 [1748]), p. 12). Yet Hume also recognised that the best way to temper political animosities was to design institutions so as to accommodate partisan instincts within a moderate system of checks and balances (see Landis 2018, pp. 219–230). His ideas both in the political essays and in the *History of England* provided the blueprint to which Madison later returned to defend an institutional model at the centre of which was the separation of powers as a way of countering political division. Madison's defence of a system that prioritised due process, the rule of law and legal checks and balances embodied a philosophical ideal of moderation animated by hostility to partisan politics (Spencer 2002, pp. 869–896).

If one adds such figures as Montesquieu, Burke, Constant and Berlin, one can reconstruct a body of constitutional and political thought that centres on the perils of extremism, adversarialism, division and zeal. This tradition of *moderation* combines the defence of a particular outlook on politics with a defence of the constitutional arrangements said to serve it. For its advocates, what defines moderation is the willingness to question oneself, to avoid Manichean simplifications and ideological rigidities, to engage in dialogue with adversaries, and to pursue a balance between competing ideas and interests. As one author who has traced the roots of this ideal puts it, 'moderation opposes absolute power, conflict, tension, polarization, violence, war and revolution. It can also be interpreted as an antonym of rigidity, stubbornness, dogmatism, utopianism, perfectionism, or moral absolutism' (Craiutu 2012, p. 14; cf. pp. 5, 20ff). Rather than a doctrine that can be systematised and written down, it is presented as a virtue displayed in practice, sensitive to particular circumstances. But moderation is not simply a sensibility: it also entails a body of commitments – by no means unique to it – based on preserving the rule of law, the separation of powers, political pluralism and toleration.

Moderation and hostility to partisanship, then, have tended to go hand in hand in the constitutional arrangements of many liberal democracies. But there are some immediate suspicions that a defence of moderation may raise. Is this a virtue that exists only in the eye of the beholder? Is one person's moderation likely to be another person's extremism? Clearly, it may sometimes just be a label by which to dignify a stance one agrees with. (Indeed, if one does not already have some sympathy with the stance, perhaps it will always have a touch of the extreme and the zealous about it.) The same views may look moderate or extreme depending on political circumstances, and on how one sketches the alternatives and the criterion of difference one applies. One may also wonder whether the virtue of moderation is not somehow dependent, even parasitic, on the existence of extremism and polarisation. As a reactive position, always responding to tendencies and events initiated by others, it seems conceptually incomplete. By definition, not everyone can be moderate on all things and at all times – it is a stance which cannot be universalised. Arguably though such problems attach to all forms of practical ethics, applied as they are to concrete situations based on the situated judgement of those involved. At first glance at least, there are good reasons to suppose that the moderate stance should be a pre-eminent one in political life.

That people will disagree on all manner of things forms part of the basic circumstances of politics. But, it may be said, if they cannot agree to put certain differences aside, there can be no life in common, no collective self-determination, indeed no basic social order. As Craiutu writes, 'to restore equilibrium in society, moderates tend to adopt some of the soundest attitudes and principles of all parties and facilitate agreements between them in order to calm passions and heal wounds. They seek to protect and foster the balance between diverse social and political forces and interests on which political pluralism, order, and freedom depend in modern society' (Craiutu 2017, p. 21). Some things in politics require consensus, or at least the suspension of conflict: procedures certainly, and perhaps also salient issues on which it is not possible to split the difference. Rawlsian public reason asks citizens to suppress comprehensive doctrines in the name of a more general political good.

The implication would seem to be that a polity's legal foundations need to be configured around agents of moderation so as to temper the dangers of political division. The judge on a constitutional court can be thought of as a quintessential figure of moderation – a person whose role is to avoid biases, dogmas and extremes of interpretation, and to reflect on the case and the facts at hand. It is no surprise that Rawls is often said to have a judicial conception of politics. Arguments for 'deliberative democracy' are another of the ways agents of moderation are championed in contemporary political thought. Common to the many different renditions of deliberative democracy is the idea that people of different viewpoints should interact in such a way as to avoid entrenched oppositions, being willing to revise their views in the light of the better argument, perhaps ultimately so as to arrive at a consensus (Gutmann and Thompson 2012).

In such perspectives, constitutional order is undermined by political divisions. Constitutions, it may be noted, tend to be founded as ways of ending civil wars and other deep disputes, and if they are to be something other than a self-serving imposition by the victorious they must moderate between extremes of outlook. They acquire legitimacy by entrenching in legal doctrine a newly found consensus, both in terms of acceptable procedures and values. Subsequently defending them, it may be said, then requires the same willingness to find positions of compromise. It depends on finding policies that all can put their names to, even as second-choice options. There would seem, accordingly, to be a good case for regarding moderation as the sensibility most in tune with preserving a democratic constitution and the life in common. Political divisions, adversarialism, still more 'extremism', would seem by contrast to be a destructive attitude – even an unpatriotic one, insofar as standing against one's compatriots can jeopardise the unity and security of a political community.

What reasons then might there be to be sceptical of this aversion to political conflict and the way it is conceptualised in certain strands of constitutional scholarship? First to observe is that the value of tempering conflict is at least conditional on the nature of the society to which it is applied. In a society that is fundamentally a just or nearly-just one, moderation may be an appropriate ideal – at least to the extent that all are committed to it. It may be a viable stance if the dangers to the constitution come from the margins. Perhaps this is the assumption most liberal democrats make about the constitutional order that commands their loyalty. But things look different if the status quo itself is corrupted and plausibly in need of far-reaching change. When political conflicts are due less to the psychological dispositions of the parties than to structural constraints of the societies in which they live, moderation is unlikely to offer the profound challenge required. It may, in fact, obstruct it. Observe that the tranquillity and depoliticisation of issues that moderates long for may very often be possible only when established powers and interests do not feel challenged or threatened. What is lamented as division is arguably the symptom of change being *resisted*, and its evaluation cannot be separated from an evaluation of the currents of change at stake. While not every context of sharp political division features a progressive force, every political context in which such a force appears is likely to be a divided one. Divisions emerge when the status quo is confronted by those pursuing a project of transformation.

Radical political change tends to depend on the actions of *groups*, and moderation is an outlook generally at odds with their political participation, indeed often intended to forestall it. Those who extol the virtue of moderation tend to cast it as something exercised by individuals. Political representatives, leaders, technical appointees, judges and individual citizens can exercise moderation, and can value others on the basis of their supposed moderation (e.g. by electing or appointing them). Institutions and legal structures too can be valued insofar as they encourage this disposition in individuals. But it is less clear that *collectives* engaged in political struggle can exercise or be prized for the virtue of moderation, since the moral universe of their members tends to be shaped in part by obligations to the collective, without which the latter would soon dissolve.

Constitutional arrangements designed to encourage moderation tend on the contrary to seek to *limit* the power of political groups or to pre-empt their formation. Structures of divided power, such as those established by the US constitution, have been explicitly conceived with this in mind, as the debates of the American Federalists about the ills of 'faction' bear testament to (Hamilton, Madison, and Jay 2008 [1787/88], No. 10). As a way of frustrating the actions of groups, moderation has a special relation to institutional complexity – the more complex the system, the harder for any parts of the political community to control it. Again, while this might be an attractive feature in a largely just society (albeit one with drawbacks, notably as regards popular participation), it is a clearly problematic one when a transformative politics is required. Programmes of change, and the agency needed to execute them, are likely to depend on the presence of organised collectives. Radical politics tends to be a politics of groups, valued for the ideas they stand for, whereas moderate politics tends to be a politics of individuals, valued for their personal qualities.

Just as consensual politics may be inadequate to the pursuit of radical progressive change, it may be inadequate even to the preservation of the good constitution. Its limits as a political stance are especially evident in circumstances when a polity's constitutional fundamentals are in jeopardy. Consider some of the things moderates may value: the rule of law, the separation of powers, political pluralism, the channelling of disagreement and toleration. A more adversarial stance than moderation may be required to maintain these when they are threatened by powerful forces, as the history of anti-fascist politics suggests. Likewise, while not all episodes of political conflict may feature desirable groupings, conflict itself should not be viewed as inherently bad – it is the context no less of positive transformations and defensive interventions. More than on moderation, building a constitution and maintaining it depends on groups willing to take an adversarial stand. Aristotle himself, for all his defence of moderation, observed that achieving a desirable equilibrium might depend on a willingness to overshoot: 'So much then is plain, that the middle character is in all cases to be praised, but that we ought to incline sometimes towards excess, sometimes towards deficiency; for in this way we shall most easily hit the mean and attain to right doing' (Aristotle 2000, Bk. 2). Certainly, it will not be enough to trim one's views to mediate between the currents of the moment: a more robust and principled stand is demanded, again something for which organisation, principled commitments and the motivation to promote them in association with others are important.

Defenders of moderation may concur, acknowledging that sometimes moderation needs to be abandoned, that it is 'not a virtue for all seasons' (Craiutu 2017, p. 3). They may say that there are extreme situations in which moderation ceases to be a virtue, or may say, with Aristotle, that 'it is not all actions nor all passions that admit of moderation' (Aristotle 2000, Bk. 2). But the question is whether such circumstances and actions are genuinely exceptional, or have been normalised in politics as we know it. Can the concerted effort to maintain constitutional processes and values really be no more than a temporary stance, adopted intermittently? In many liberal democracies, moderation's value has been historically undermined by the persistent presence of structures that entrench social divisions and trigger immoderate responses. When that is the case, the decision is not about whether to exercise moderation or not but how to ensure that political disagreements can be channelled in the right way.

Political participation is one of the areas where there seems to be a clear tension between an ethos of moderation and wider democratic norms. Moderation works best when politics is restricted to a minority with convergent ideas. 'Finding the middle or the mean in each case is a hard thing,' observed Aristotle, 'just as finding the middle or centre of a circle is a thing that is not within the power of everybody, but only of him who has the requisite knowledge' (Aristotle 2000, Bk. 2). Compromise is most easily achieved by those with the 'requisite knowledge' – when radical ideas are kept off the agenda, and when their sponsors are kept out of the process. The more people who participate, the more the boundaries of debate widen, and the more challenging the task of moderation becomes. Keeping public life oriented to pragmatic problem-solving is probably to restrict it to elites sharing similar views. Conversely, for those who value popular participation, a politics of groups engaged in adversarial exchange is likely to be more conducive. In 1950s America, fears of elite consensus and weak participation prompted the American Political Science Association to warn of the dangers of excessive moderation and agreement amongst political representatives. 'Alternatives between the parties,' they wrote, 'are defined so badly that it is often difficult to determine what the election has decided even in broadest terms' (APSA 1950, pp. 3–4). Unlike many of their counterparts in later decades, these scholars believed in a politics of strong, delineated programmes advanced by competing groups.

None of this is to exclude that groups may coalesce around undesirable views, and sometimes may entrench these views. Indeed, if this were not so, there would be little to be said for political conflict, since the political scene would lack objectionable figures to oppose. What can be said however is that political collectives mobilised around shared political commitments are the precondition of firmly held views that *are* of wider value.

Mobilised collectives adopting an adversarial stance are important both for the positive transformations they can lead in an imperfect polity, and for the defence of existing achievements in the good polity. They are of considerable instrumental value, that is. But they are also *intrinsically* desirable, at least to the extent that they are voluntary associations, and communities of principle rather than of unchosen identities or brute interests. Such collectives, whether single-issue movements or ideas-based parties as we shall come to, can be enriching for those who belong to them – ways in which the likeminded can learn from each other and strengthen their resolve and commitment. Civic education tends to be construed as a matter of factual knowledge about institutions and procedures, but it is also about building an understanding of the *logic* of politics – developing narratives and explanations that allow particular episodes to be connected to a larger scheme. Communities of principle are one of the key contexts in which such ideas are nurtured and disseminated, in the form of political narratives and ideologies. Such communities are places where solidarity and the habits of political involvement can develop, whether through participation in debates, protests or campaigns. They are ways to draw into politics those who would otherwise be disengaged, and whose interests and concerns would go ignored. The key question, we suggest, is what kinds of institution can allow collectives and conflicts of the *right kind* to take shape – ones that can be productive for the wider political community and indeed those beyond it. Here, we move to a discussion of *partisanship*.

II THE PLACE OF PARTISANSHIP

In recent years, political scientists, the media and politicians alike have tended to treat political parties as little more than vehicles for winning elections. In legal scholarship too, their function is often reduced to their role as agents that contribute to shaping legislative and executive power via electoral mechanisms. Their overriding goal, in these views, is to combine the preferences of citizens for the purpose of obtaining a share in government. What distinguishes parties from one another on this account is ultimately their skill in knowing which buttons to press to win votes – how to manufacture divisions in the electorate that they are best able to take advantage of. Attached to this perspective is a theory of motivation: party members, it is suggested, are in it largely for the spoils of office (see Muirhead and Rosenblum 2020 for critical discussion).

What the image of the party as the election-winning machine misses are the normative and transformative aspirations that partisans might proclaim, and that form the basis for a more discriminating understanding of what partisanship is (White & Ypi 2016). Historically, the members of parties have sought to distinguish themselves from other kinds of political formation that pursue merely sectional ends. The distinction between ideological and interest-based parties to which legal scholarship refers is one way of understanding this distinction. Philosophically, however, the contrast between parties and *factions* gets more directly to the core of how these different entities relate to public concerns. When parties started to position themselves in contrast to factions, they sought to distinguish themselves from entities committed to pursuing only the good of the part, and invoked political ideals intended to be applicable to a wider political constituency (White and Ypi 2016, esp. chap. 2). Though they might draw on particularist identities – ethnic, religious or class-related – partisans have always sought to incorporate them into a larger political project conceived as irreducible to these.

Ramsay MacDonald – co-founder and theoretician of the British Labour Party, and later its first Prime Minister – provides powerful illustration. 'Socialism', he wrote in his 1907 work of the same name, 'is no class movement. Socialism is a movement of opinion, not an organization of status. It is not the rule of the working-class; it is the organization of the community' (MacDonald, in Barker 1972, p. 162). His portrayal of the Labour Party in his 1919 piece on *Parliament and Revolution* expands on the same theme: 'it [the Party] believes in the class conflict as a descriptive fact, but it does not regard it as supplying a political method. It strives to transform through education, through raising the standards of mental and moral qualities, through the acceptance of programmes by reason of their justice, rationality and wisdom…. It walks with the map of Socialism in front of it and guides its steps by the compass of democracy' (MacDonald, in Barker 1972, p. 240).

This points to a more demanding idea of the party than the electoral machine. A party, one may argue, is an association that identifies itself in terms of a set of distinctly *political* ends, ranging from relatively specific policy goals to more abstract values and principles (White & Ypi 2016; cf. L. Herman 2017). Some may be specified in the party's founding text, while others will be dispersed across its election manifestoes and other significant policy statements. A party, moreover, aims to pursue these political ends across an extended period of time, connecting an historical tradition to an open-ended future horizon. The image of the party as an electoral machine misses the distinct temporality of partisanship: it is a long-term, cumulative activity. A party typically defines itself by goals that cannot be realised in the short term but that require constancy of political commitment across time – goals such as equality, justice and liberty. What is more, a party pursues such goals through the relatively slow mechanisms of political institutions – in contrast to more narrow and immediate forms of protest such as strikes and boycotts. The party is the organised expression of ongoing political allegiance: it is an association built up over time and projected into the future, centred on normative commitments intended to endure.

The party-faction distinction is crucial for understanding the difference between positive and negative forms of political division. Indeed, it is the neglect of this distinction, and with it the willingness to elide parties with self-interested groups, that supports calls for 'moderation' in party democracy. As collectives that appeal to sectional interests and identities, one may readily accept that *factions* promote forms of conflict that tend to be corrosive, or that at best are normatively insignificant. Think for instance of a farmers' lobby group. Standing for a particularist good, their representatives may feel little need to justify their actions in depth to anyone but those they claim to represent. Viewing their ends as materially given, they have little reason to devote serious effort to persuading others of the rightness of their cause. They need no comprehensive political narrative by which to widely communicate and justify their actions – simply a clear idea of whom they need to influence. Though they may seek to advance their ends through political institutions, they will generally view these merely as instrumentally useful rather than as a normatively valuable setting in which to enlist others to their side and acquire legitimacy for their struggles.

By contrast, collectives that plausibly see themselves as communities of principle, like parties properly understood, promote forms of conflict that are inevitably more open-ended. Communities of principle are consciously elastic groupings, unlike those based on pre-political interests and identities, since what define the circle of the like-minded are commitments that are generalisable and which others might be persuaded to share (cf. Rosenblum 2008, pp. 345 ff.; cf. Kelsen 2013 [1929]). Such conflicts of ideas are inherently dynamic, since their protagonists fight for constituencies that are politically rather than socially defined. Committed to pursuing their cause through public institutions, such groupings can be held electorally accountable for the claims they advance, and thus have reason to articulate them in accessible and generalisable ways. They are structurally disposed to seek some kind of *justification* for their actions. For the same reason, such collectives resist the territorialisation of conflict into spatially separated groups defined by socio-cultural criteria – groups that ultimately may seek to secede from each other.

It is important to underline that partisans are selective in the social conflicts they politicise – selective both in the sense that they draw and expand on conflicts which are in some form already present in society (hence they do not fabricate divisions from scratch), and in the sense that they prioritise some conflicts over others (in particular, those that can be rendered generalisable). For the same reason, a party then can never just go to 'the centre' in the way that anxious observers of partisanship might hope, because the centre is the evolving outcome of a process in which parties themselves are involved and which they must take responsibility for shaping. A party must decide how it wants to influence the process of centre-formation. It must select, from a range of resonant political messages, those that it wants to advance and those it must criticise. The 'median voter', if there is such a thing, is not what a party must chase but what it must help to define.

We have observed that political collectives can be sites of participation, education and commitment, and parties are arguably the pre-eminent example of this. While forms of spontaneous mobilisation and direct action can be significant here too, what parties offer is unique in several ways (White & Ypi 2010). Unlike social movements, they connect political mobilisation to the exercise of institutional power. Whether as governing parties of the executive, opposition parties of the legislature, or even as parties seeking admission to such institutions for the first time, they offer a focal-point for efforts to shape organised power. The kind of participation they offer is thus potentially more consequential, and more in tune with ideals of political equality and popular sovereignty, than that available to citizens acting individually or to movements confined to the streets. Built around an organisational structure, they can develop procedures of decision-making by which to enable ordinary members to shape political life (Wolkenstein 2019; Invernizzi Accetti and Wolkenstein 2017). And as associations expected to endure in time, they provide a context for lasting relations and ties of solidarity, unlike the temporary arrangements associated with social forms of protest. Political commitment involves the willingness to stick to a cause and to consistently oppose those who would thwart it: as continuing associations, parties are well suited to fostering it.

These are *democratic* arguments for partisanship and the conflicts it gives rise to, focused on the resources for active citizenship it makes available. Yet clearly, these resources are not always well actualised. If parties can be ways to harness the positive in political division, one of the constraints that partisans face has to do with the design of institutions, and whether they help to sustain partisanship or undermine it. Liberal electoral institutions are often configured precisely to *frustrate* a politics of firm commitments – one of the reasons many parties today are unpopular with the wider public. We have seen that, in the name of fostering moderation, constitutional designers have often aimed at institutional complexity and the division of power across multiple agents. They have sought ways to make it difficult for partisans to hold to their views, creating pressures for compromise at each step. In the contemporary world, one sees this expressed in the way certain forms of proportional-representation encourage the formation of governing alliances. 'Grand coalitions' – governments that include the two largest parties in an electoral system – have become a popular target of critique in a number of European countries in large part because of the way they interfere with the commitments by which parties define themselves. Being alliances that bring together those of varied political outlooks, typically of both left and right, they tend to depend on major compromises of principle (White 2018).

Not only may this alienate the supporters of the parties in question, but it may create public appetite precisely for the authoritarian politics it is meant to ward off, as citizens are drawn to charismatic figures who promise clarity of message and decisiveness. Sustaining meaningful partisanship requires the careful design of political institutions, weighing the merits of proportional representation, first-past-the-post systems, and mixed systems that combine elements of both (White 2021). And *intra*-party institutions are important too. Maintaining a party's programmatic profile depends on countering tendencies towards professionalisation and the usurpation of power by leaders. Mechanisms for the *recall* of party representatives are some of the more promising and currently underutilised ones (White & Ypi 2020b).

Notwithstanding the significance of institutions in fostering or frustrating parties of principle, it is important to conceive partisanship independently of any one constitutional settlement. Ultimately it is simply a method, a mode of politics, one that can be deployed to create new institutions and to reset political boundaries, not merely reproduce existing ones. Reshaping the demos, and challenging the exclusions involved in the existing exercise of power, is well within the scope of partisanship. Historically, it is through party-led interventions that previously detached social groups – economic, ethnic or religious – have been brought onto the legal and political stage. Once mass enfranchisement was achieved, it was the willingness of the masses to become politically involved, to engage in collective action and to vote which was at stake. In all such cases, the concept of 'the people' was to make its appearance in the context of partisan activity and was appealed to as a means to shape and articulate conflict, thereby cultivating the people as an active political force, not just as the passive bearers of rights.

As agents embedded in an institutional structure, albeit one always subject to critical scrutiny, partisans may contest the boundaries of participation most visibly by contesting the boundaries of a state's active citizenry. They may contest the make-up of those enfranchised and mobilised to participate politically, within a population already constituted: seeking to persuade non-voters to vote remains one of the principal examples. But because the commitments partisans espouse are intended to be broad in their social appeal, there is no necessary link between their constituency of support and an existing political territory. Historically, this is illustrated by moves to expand enfranchisement beyond national and ethnic boundaries, as in the case of the French revolutionaries' attempt to extend the category of citizens to all those who shared the ideals of the Revolution (Merker 2009). Partisanship extending across state borders, guided by a common supranational ideological orientation, has also been witnessed in more recent history, sometimes resulting in the founding of institutions that tend towards a fundamentally reconstituted people – the European Union being one example. The partisan process of defining the people thus takes place on a continuum extending from the reshaping of who participates in existing institutions to the revision of constitutional arrangements themselves.

III CONTEMPORARY PARTIES AND THE FEAR OF POLARISATION

While acknowledging the historical worth of parties and partisanship, some doubt whether its contemporary forms can be anything like as constructive. Parties in western democracy today, it is often said, have long given up confronting each other on the important political questions. The large majority have converged on broadly the same socio-economic model, leading them to operate as 'cartels' (Katz & Mair 2009; cf. Ignazi 2017). The divisions they present are often not socio-economic but 'cultural' ones – intractable to be sure, and the source of much passion, but arguably not the ones on which progressive campaigns depend. An exercise in substitution, it is said, sees partisans ramp up the significance of so-called 'values issues' (abortion, gender rights) and boundary issues (migration, intercultural relations), precisely to compensate for their timidity before socio-economic power. Are we not dealing with a political form that has long decayed – or to put it differently, do we not live in a world of *factions* rather than parties?

Politics reflects the societies in which it unfolds, and there can be no doubt that wider socio-economic conditions have taken their toll, both on the programmes to which partisans commit themselves and the demographic make-up of those who choose to join them. But parties retain untapped resources for renewing their identity as associations of principle. Ongoing experiments with intra-party deliberation, the recall of representatives, and the networking of parties with wider social movements are some of the most significant, and the basis for future iterations of the party form (Wolkenstein 2019; White & Ypi 2020a). What is alarming today though is how easily parties tend to be denounced as the agents of discord, irrespective of what is at stake in their disagreements.

One form such doubts take in contemporary political analysis is the critique of 'polarisation'. In countries around the world, deep divisions of an irreconcilable kind are said to threaten social cohesion and the capacities of law-making institutions. A US think-tank declares that 'political polarization – the vast and growing gap between liberals and conservatives, Republicans and Democrats – is a defining feature of American politics today'.[3] Reflecting on the challenges facing democracies around the world, the *Financial Times* observes that 'as societies grow more polarised, democratic agreement has never been so much in demand. Yet only in historic crises have institutions been harder pressed to do their job.'[4] While the concept of polarisation has been most prominent in the two-party system of the United States, it has been applied more widely too across a variety of types of electoral system.

A recent overview of studies of polarisation by two distinguished political scientists (Fiorina and Abrams 2008) highlights some key features of the concept as follows. Central, first, is the presence of a division of outlook on salient matters, amongst representatives, ordinary citizens, or both. On issues from taxation to foreign policy, climate change to migration, polarisation describes the co-presence of differing views, in a more or less antagonistic relation. It suggests different opinions held with some intensity, and blended in some measure with different understandings of the facts. Although disagreement may hinge on just a small number of issues, talk of polarisation tends to escalate when it is felt that divisions of opinion *cluster* – that is, when views on one matter pair with those on another, amounting to a broader clash of political vision. Polarisation suggests a clash between two main bodies of opinion. Moreover, Fiorina and Abrams explain, 'an implicit assumption most of us make is that the two modes of the distribution lie at the extremes, not near the center' (Fiorina and Abrams 2008, p. 566).

Polarisation tends to be weighed negatively on various grounds. It may be suspected that strong divergences of view entail mutual antipathy, that the 'extremes' are ill-disposed to tolerate one another, leading to poor-quality public debate and institutional dysfunction. The inability of the US Congress to pass laws in the face of animosity between Republicans and Democrats is commonly cited as an example of a legislature paralysed by deep disagreement; the rise of an authoritarian executive is often presented as the logical consequence. Equally, polarisation may be viewed negatively on intrinsic grounds, as the expression of divisions felt to be aberrant, unnecessary, perhaps even manufactured. It may suggest the community's deviation from a normal condition of harmony. Talk of polarisation tends to be accompanied by denunciations of 'tribalism' amongst those identified with extreme positions.[5] In particular, there is often an undercurrent of scepticism towards *partisanship*, insofar as party discipline and party attachment is thought to increase polarisation (and is sometimes taken as the measure of it). 'Elite polarisation' (amongst

---

[3] www.pewresearch.org/topics/political-polarization/.
[4] *Financial Times* (11th August 2019): www.ft.com/content/6bc199c8-b836-11e9-96bd-8e884d3ea203
[5] For example, http://nymag.com/intelligencer/2017/09/can-democracy-survive-tribalism.html?abcid=intel-test-4-16&abv=1

party representatives) is often said to drive 'mass polarisation', suggesting that these divisions are in some way an artefact of partisanship (Muirhead 2006).[6]

Notwithstanding the familiarity of such concerns, the concept of polarisation is problematic. Some of the reasons are empirical. The spatial metaphor it relies on – the notion that parties, for instance, can be 'far apart' or 'close' – is potentially misleading, however intuitive it may be.[7] Proximity in space may suggest proximity to consensus, yet the sociology and psychology of disagreement suggests otherwise: the 'narcissism of small difference' often steps in. Then there are such problematic notions as 'the centre', an artefact of the spatial metaphor, by reference to which degrees of polarisation are calibrated. As Hans Daalder notes (Daalder 1984), a Left-Right spectrum invites the superimposition of a normal-distribution curve at its centre, implying – sometimes spuriously – that views located away from the centre will be held only by a small minority. Note also, again as a function of this schema, that observations of 'polarisation' tend to imply that both parties to disagreement are moving symmetrically away from each other. Obscured is the possibility that all are moving in one direction to different degrees, or that one party is remaining constant while others reinvent themselves. Diagnoses of polarisation can be oblivious to the entire political spectrum moving 'to the right', suggesting instead that agency and responsibility is to be equally apportioned.

But one needs to be cautious with the concept of polarisation also because there is an implicit *normative* theory here, based on a reassertion of the ideal of moderation. Diagnoses of polarisation suggest that what is wrong with contemporary parties is the fact that they may sharply disagree. Responsible parties, it is implied, appeal to centrist voters, and seek agreement with their opponents where possible – they are 'bi-partisan', in the American phrase. The good polity is the consensual one, and divisions are dangerous because they threaten the common good. Such narratives tend not to scrutinise too hard the substance of politics at 'the centre': for those who speak of the ills of polarisation, the desirability of the centre tends to be assumed. Talk of polarisation generally says little about the *content* of disagreement or the reasons triggering it: it implies that one form is analogous to another, and discounts

---

[6] Polarisation can describe both a static state – the polarised society – and a process, one tending towards *increasing* extremism. Technological trends are often invoked as evidence of the latter – the 'bubbles' and 'cascades' produced by social-media networks, insulating people from counter-views and, with the help algorithmic feedback effects, entrenching their perspectives ever further (Sunstein 2007). The public sphere thereby comes to be compromised by a multitude of micro-spheres that rarely overlap. Polarisation provokes anxiety partly for the very reason that it is felt to have this dynamic quality – its contours are becoming more pronounced.

[7] Note how such concepts presuppose the view of an observer, somewhat detached from the conflict itself. The spatial imagery makes sense *from a distance*, from a position exterior to both 'poles'. The observer of polarisation adopts the aerial view, looking down on events from above, or they locate themselves on the same plain but away from the main clusters of opinion. Rarely will those identifying with one viewpoint in a contest have reason to use notions like polarisation or 'the extremes': these are concepts for those keen to avoid taking sides.

the possibility that sometimes one of the 'poles' may deserve trenchant opposition while the other requires relentless defence. It also neglects the fact that sometimes the status quo must be challenged rather than defended.

The critique of polarisation misdiagnoses the shortcomings of parties today, for it is not political conflict itself which is the problem. What matters is how it comes to be articulated, under what circumstances, and in the name of what and who. As those who retain a pre-eminent position in the politics of the state, yet also still networked with the wider society, parties enjoy an enduring capacity to shape the substance of political division. Whether conflict takes a destructive or constructive course depends ultimately on how partisans choose to exercise this capacity, and more generally on whether those of a principled outlook can displace the opportunists amongst the ranks of today's parties.

CONCLUSION

Anxieties about the dangers of political division are widespread. On one level these are an expression of how politics has come to be studied today – in the detached perspective of the scientist, looking down on conflict from above, keen to avoid taking sides. On another level, and more profoundly, concerns about the dangers of political division are testament to the appeal of a normative ideal of politics centred on the avoidance of extremes – a politics of moderation. The critique of political division is premised on the defence of a legal system which expects representatives to compete for the support of the median voter.

As we have argued, moderation makes for an ambivalent ideal. It may be a viable one if the point of departure is a largely just order. It is much less so if one takes seriously the possibility of an unjust status quo and the need to pursue far-reaching change. Moderation offers few resources for political transformation, and even modest changes are likely to provoke a defensive response from established powers, giving rise to the circumstances of polarisation so widely decried. Even those who consider the status quo acceptable will acknowledge that often it must be defended against immoderate opponents. Whether in contexts of transformation or constitutional consolidation, something more than moderation is required – an outlook of firm principle and commitment, pursued in a clash with adversaries.

Contemporary parties are often criticised as agents of division. In commonly expressed concerns about rising 'polarisation', the ideal of moderation is invoked once more. But what contemporary politics needs is not less polarisation but polarisation of the right kind, channelled by stronger institutions of partisanship. Present-day parties are beset by difficulties, but that is no reason to wish parties away. Partisans are structurally disposed to denominating conflict in terms of political ideas rather than social identities and interests, and to locating it within a cross-temporal frame. As organisations, parties can be sites of education, participation and political commitment, alongside ties of solidarity. To be sure, political commitment can sometimes be put to bad purposes – the single-mindedness of the partisan can be a negative quality, depending on how it is exercised and the ends to which it is put. But it seems an indispensable resource by which to carve a more just and legitimate order. Rather than try to neuter parties in the name of moderation, better to join them and seek to re-shape them. Finding ways to reinvigorate parties by removing the asymmetries of power that affect public life is one of the central challenges for democracy today.

RECOMMENDED READING

Biezen, I. & Saward, M. (2008). Democratic Theorists and Party Scholars: Why They Don't Talk to Each Other, and Why They Should. *Perspectives on Politics*, 6 (1), 21–35.
Bonotti, M. (2017). *Partisanship and Political Liberalism in Diverse Societies*, Oxford: Oxford University Press.
Herman, L. (2017). Democratic Partisanship: From Theoretical Ideal to Empirical Standard. *American Political Science Review*, 111 (4), 738–754.
Invernizzi Accetti, C. & Wolkenstein, F. (2017). The crisis of party democracy, cognitive mobilization and the case for making parties more deliberative. *American Political Science Review*, 111 (1), 97–109.
Kelsen, H. (2013). *The Essence and Value of Democracy*. Edited by N. Urbinati and C. Invernizzi-Accetti. Lanham, MD: Rowman & Littlefield.
Mair, P. (2013). *Ruling the Void*, London: Verso.
Muirhead, R. (2006). A Defence of Party Spirit. *Perspectives on Politics*, 4 (4), 713–727.
Muirhead, R. (2014). *The Promise of Party in a Polarized Age*, Cambridge, MA: Harvard University Press.
Muirhead, R. & Rosenblum, N. (2020). The Political Theory of Parties and Partisanship: Catching Up. *Annual Review of Political Science*, 23 (1), 95–110.
Rosenblum, N. (2008). *On the Side of the Angels: An Appreciation of Parties and Partisanship*, Princeton: Princeton University Press.
Schattschneider, E. E. (1942). *Party Government*, New York: Holt, Rinehart & Winston.
White, J. & Ypi, L. (2016). *The Meaning of Partisanship*, Oxford: Oxford University Press.
Wolkenstein, F. (2019). *Rethinking Party Reform*, Oxford: Oxford University Press.

45

Legislatures

Richard Ekins[*]

The legislature is a central constitutional institution. It exercises legislative power and is the preeminent lawmaking body in any well-ordered polity. Its relationship with government and with the people makes deliberation within the legislature, and the contest for control of the legislature, the focus of democratic politics (Ekins 2012, p. 9). This chapter explores the nature of the legislature and its relationship to constitutional government, focusing in particular on the importance of legislative agency and the dynamics that frame its exercise. Like a prince, the legislature is a single agent, responsible for and capable of making reasoned lawmaking choices; unlike the prince, the legislature is made up of many persons, which complicates legislative deliberation and action.

The chapter begins by reflecting on the objects of legislative action, arguing that authorising a legislative assembly to legislate changes who legislates but not what it is to legislate. The object of legislative deliberation and action should be the common good and securing this end requires agency. The assembly faces many challenges in exercising agency, which it is structured to overcome, partly by way of its relationship to government, a relationship that goes well beyond acts of legislation. The relationship between legislature and government shapes the character of a constitutional order and bears on the relationship between legislature and the people. The legislature's duty is to represent the people, which makes self-government possible. The legislature should deliberate and act for the people and be accountable to the people, with legislative deliberation taking its place in a wider public conversation. The legislature's capacity for agency informs how legislative acts should be understood to change the law. This capacity, and the legislature's relationship to government and the people, also helps explain the moral importance of legislative freedom and informs how one should evaluate limits on that freedom.

[*] Professor of Law and Constitutional Government, University of Oxford. I am grateful to Grégoire Webber, Sir Stephen Laws, Jeff King and Richard Bellamy for helpful comments on an earlier draft; the usual disclaimer applies.

I FROM PRINCE TO PARLIAMENT

There are good reasons for the legislature's central place in constitutional order. The way to understand the institution's distinctive character and capacity is to follow these reasons, to ask why one should establish (or maintain) a legislature, serve as a legislator, understand legislative acts to change what the subject of law has duty to do, etc. (Ekins 2019a, pp. 142–143) The reasons form a subset of the wider truth that there are some goods that cannot safely be secured or promoted without law (Finnis 2011, p. 1). Part of the virtue of law as a form of social order is that law may be made and changed (amended or repealed) by deliberate action, rather than happenstance (Ekins 2012, pp. 118–119; Hart 1994, pp. 95–96). Part of what forms laws into a system is that they are able to be made or changed by deliberate action – not as a side-effect of adjudication but openly and directly when some person or body concludes that there are good reasons for legal change. In other words, if a political community is to enjoy the rule of law, if it is to secure its common good, then some person or body must exercise the authority to change the law by free choice.

Who is to exercise this authority? The first principle of constitutional order is that those with capacity to coordinate others should exercise authority (Finnis 2011, p. 246). This entails a duty to govern (Green 2007). In many times and places, it has been reasonable for a single person to rule (Ekins 2013, p. 172 and Ekins 2019a, p. 153). The ruler's duty is in part to deliberate about how and when to make and to change the law. The moral need for law, and for law with the distinctive capacity of legislation to secure the rule of law, calls for legislative authority. In making law by promulgating his choice about what should be done, the prince exercises legislative power. The advantage of noting that, and in thinking about how, the prince legislates is that one isolates the moral need that legislation aims to meet and clarifies what it is to legislate. The prince is able to legislate because (like other persons) he is an agent and is able to consider the reasons for making or changing the law and to respond to those reasons with intelligent choice which he conveys to his subjects by promulgating his lawmaking choice, ideally in canonical form. The unity of the prince qua natural person brackets the difficult questions that arise about the rational capacities of a multi-member legislative assembly. Postponing those questions helps one avoid overlooking the reasons why legislation is required and the way in which a single agent would meet them.

Like a prince, the legislative assembly should exercise agency to choose how to change the law. That is, authorising an assembly to legislate changes who legislates not what it is to legislate. This understanding of legislative action is denied by Dworkin and Waldron who, despite sharp differences on some points, largely share a theory about legislative action. For Dworkin, the point of the legislature, the rationale that grounds attending to its activities, is political fairness. The output of the legislative process is not a choice made by a rational agent, but a political event that should be taken into account, by Hercules J and others, at least in relation to questions of policy (Dworkin 1986, chap. 9; see further Ekins 2011, pp. 452–454). Questions of principle are reserved to courts alone because the legislative process (democratic politics) cannot engage them. Legislators respond to voter preferences, Dworkin argues, not to arguments of principle (Dworkin 1985, pp. 344–345; see further Ekins 2012, pp. 77–83). This resonates with public choice analyses of legislative behaviour, in which legislators are assumed to be self-interested, to be the plaything of lobbyists and to be dominated by electoral incentives (Tollison 1988; see further Ekins 2012, pp. 83–85). It is a misleading and unappealing account of legislative behaviour, which does not do justice to the breadth and depth of legislative reasoning across time and place. The separation of powers for which Dworkin argues should be rejected out of hand by any reasonable legislator, who will see his or her (and the assembly's) duty to be to reason about principles, rights and justice.

Waldron departs from Dworkin in arguing that legislation is a principled source of law, which courts should not have authority to question or quash (Waldron 1999a, Waldron 1999b). But he follows Dworkin in denying that the legislature is an agent able to reason and choose. Indeed, he argues that legal philosophy goes astray in taking for granted a model of lawmaking by a prince, neglecting the distinctive features of legislative assemblies which make the analogy inapposite (Waldron 1999a, pp. 28–43). Better, he says, to think about legislation by analogy to custom, as the people's law rather than the prince's law (Waldron 2000, pp. 517–521). This is in some ways an attractive picture. However, the problem with custom is precisely that it is haphazard and unclear; legislation addresses these shortcomings and makes truly positive law possible (Ekins 2012, pp. 121–123; Gardner 2012). The advantage of custom, as Waldron outlines it, is that it is grounded on the people's own practices and is not an imposition from above. Not all impositions from above (or outside) are unjust, I would say, but it is true that in making provision for legislation to be enacted there are good reasons to involve the people, such that legislation is adopted as if it were chosen by the people rather than foisted upon them (Ekins 2013, pp. 180–182). And indeed, the history of legislative power is in many places a history of a prince extending to his people a right to participate in the making of the law that shall govern them.

The English kings and queens summoned parliaments who might represent the realm and thus agree to taxes and changes in the law. The great jurist and statesman Sir John Fortescue argued that the king's limited authority to rule alone meant that English kingship was political rather than regal (Fortescue 1997, pp. 83–87).[1] Political kingship was a form of mixed government, inviting the representatives of different estates in the realm to participate in rule, giving counsel and advice and deciding whether or not to assent to legislative changes or new taxes. Initiative remained with the king and parliaments were an instrument of royal authority, not in the sense that the king could do as he pleased, but rather that the King-in-Parliament enjoyed unrivalled authority, able to bind the political community

---

[1] On political and regal kingship, see further Finnis 1998.

jointly in momentous courses of action. While the king might be compelled to summon parliament, this was also a recognised means to augment royal authority by inviting representatives from across the realm to join the king in high decision (Loughlin 2013, pp. 45–48). In turn, this enabled representatives to demand that kings limit themselves to the agreed terms, which made statute ever more authoritative and invited rivalry between king and parliamentarians for relative power *within* the King-in-Parliament, which all agreed spoke authoritatively for all. The history of the English, and then British, Parliament is a history of unified royal authority being separated, with legislative power exercised not by the king alone but by the King-in-Parliament, in which the king held initiative but could not act without assent of the Houses of Parliament. Over time, the king's effective role waned, with parliamentarians themselves legislating. This is a history of change in who it is that legislates.

The rise of parliaments is in some ways clearly driven by proto-democratic principle. Rule by the king alone would be unjust, for it would deny others a share in government and would expose the realm to the risks of regal kingship, in which a bad king may be a tyrant (Ekins 2012, pp. 155–158 and Ekins 2013, pp. 174–175). But is the turn from prince to parliament best understood to be the working out of democratic principle? Schmitt reasoned not, arguing that while the expansion of parliamentary power vis-à-vis the monarch was supported on democratic grounds, it was at the same time, and in the end more fully, the working out of a liberal theory of government (Schmitt 1985 [1926]). The organising principle of parliamentary rule, Schmitt maintained, was government by discussion, rather than the democratic principle of popular unity that one finds in the work of Rousseau and others, thinkers who were decidedly cautious about deliberation (Tuck 2019). There is something to this analysis insofar as parliaments, while representing the realm in one sense, might also be committed to excluding the (ordinary) people from their own rule. In other words, requiring participation in government to be mediated through representative form may be a technique to discipline and to limit that participation. However, this pathology should not obscure the more important truth that in its central case the legislative assembly is an institution that anchors self-government – with legislative deliberation and action the focus of democratic politics and the dynamics of parliamentary government the means by which a free people rules itself.

I shall take up later the question of how and why the legislature represents the people. My point for present purposes is that in relation to legislating, parliaments worked with and then replaced princes. The prince's duty to respond to the reasons for changing the law was a duty long shared with parliamentarians and now a duty exercised by the legislative assembly itself. The question, to which I now turn, is how a multi-member assembly is able to reason and choose.

II THE PROBLEM OF LEGISLATIVE AGENCY

Whoever exercises legislative authority, whether prince or assembly, must respond to reasons for changing the law by choosing how the law is to change. The difficulty which an assembly is likely to encounter in reasoning and choosing may be termed the problem of legislative agency. As Waldron notes, the legislative assembly is a large group, with members drawn from a wide range of backgrounds, who disagree sharply about what is to be done (Waldron 1999a, pp. 24–25). He relies on these features to argue that the legislature is not capable of acting like a prince and does not form and act on intentions, but instead exercises authority indirectly. Others argue to similar effect that legislative agency is impossible, taking the assembly to be a site of competition and bargaining rather than to be capable of coherent choice (Shepsle 1992; see further Ekins 2012, pp. 40–46). This view is articulated by political scientists who are sceptical about the coherence of legislative behaviour, stressing the arbitrariness of legislative outcomes. It is echoed also by public choice theory's (unrealistic) conception of legislators as automata (Ekins 2012, pp. 83–84 and Mackie 2004).

In legal theory, the argument has largely focused on the question of legislative intent. Dworkin takes for granted that because the modern legislature is a group rather than a person it cannot have mental states and thus does not form and act on intentions (Dworkin 1986, chap. 9). What is termed legislative intent must instead be constructed (invented) by the interpreter, who is then forced to answer a series of unanswerable questions about who counts as a legislator, what mental states count, and how to combine them. The pretence, Dworkin says, should be abandoned and the legislative process seen as a machine for aggregating preferences. Waldron adopts Dworkin's critique but aims to explain the legislative process as a means to exercise authority without intentions, as a kind of voting machine that may generate principled outcomes justified by reference to utilitarianism, Condorcet's theorem or the wisdom of the multitude (Waldron 1999a, pp. 129–142). Likewise, Raz and Gardner argue that the legislature is only able to form the minimal intention to enact (adopt) the conventional meaning of the statutory text (Raz 2009, Gardner 2012).

These theories wrongly assume that groups cannot form and act on intentions or constitute agents. They also fail to explain how legislative authority is intelligible, viz. how the legislature is capable of changing the law for good reasons, and thus why one should authorise an assembly to legislate. They cannot explain how the reasonable legislator understands his or her joint action. For that legislator, from whose perspective one sees the central case of the legislature, the institution is not a machine or a process but an agent with responsibility for changing the law, a responsibility which requires the making of reasoned, coherent lawmaking choices. It is possible for the legislature to make such choices, to form and act on lawmaking intentions, because the legislature is a purposive group with a shared end, which takes pains to structure itself to make the exercise of agency possible (Ekins 2012, chap. 8). The standing intention of all legislators makes majority voting count, such that a vote on third reading for a legislative proposal means that the legislature, singular, makes this choice.[2] Proposals are introduced, developed and adopted on the

---

[2] I set aside the complications of a second chamber and royal assent (or presidential veto).

footing that they are proposals fit to be chosen by a single rational agent, setting out a reasoned, coherent scheme for legal change. This understanding, and the prospects for reasoned coherence, is safeguarded by internal legislative hierarchy, with some legislators authorised to frame the agenda and exercise unequal control.

While legislative structure differs by time and place, nowhere does a legislative state of nature prevail (Cox 2006), for without hierarchy legislative action is near impossible. This hierarchy, which does not vitiate the formal voting equality of each legislator, may consist in legislative office-holders, such as Speaker or committee chairs, and/or recognition of political party affiliation and leadership. Like Burke, I take each legislator to be responsible for acting for the common good of the whole political community, which he or she represents, rather than the good of some narrow part thereof. I do not mean that the object of legislative action is uncontested. On the contrary, legislating takes place in the 'circumstances of politics' (Waldron 1999a, p. 102), where there is much disagreement about what is to be done. But in a well-ordered assembly, the disagreement is about the common good of all.

The responsibility of legislators is consistent with party membership, with the party adopting a common approach to questions of legislative controversy and coordinating many legislators to act jointly. Schmitt argued that the Burkean model was increasingly outdated, with party and corporate interests predominating over independent judgment in representing the polity (Schmitt 1985 [1926], pp. 49–50). Others have since argued similarly that deliberation within the legislature is irrelevant, with decisions made elsewhere (Hardin 2000). Party political discipline may well be drawn too tightly, with legislators unable freely to reason and act. However, overly strict party discipline is not somehow entailed by legislative structure. It is instead a pathology, which is constantly open to question and challenge within the legislature and beyond, and is likely to prove unstable, precisely because the Burkean model continues to hold a rational appeal. My point is not that each legislator is or should be a law unto himself or herself, but rather that legislators are well-placed to contribute to the common good by reasoning with their fellows, including especially those in the same political party, and thus representing the realm and acting for its good (Burke 1949 [1774]). Party discipline helps support the assembly's capacity to exercise legislative agency.

The wider constitutional structure will frame how the assembly makes provision for agency. In the Washington model, the President has a share in legislative power (Weinberg 2018), which is no surprise insofar as the presidency is effectively an elective, political (rather than regal) monarchy. Within the assembly, no person or body exercises executive power, and thus, there will not be a structural incentive to form a coherent, unified group which might provide leadership across the board. Instead, agenda power is widely distributed amongst party leaders and committee chairs – and across both chambers – and Congress may act relatively more like a meeting of rival ambassadors than like a Parliament deliberating jointly about a single, shared common good (cf. Burke 1949 [1774]). There are high barriers to action, with legislation only enacted if each of a series of veto-players can be overcome. Thus, new legislation is less likely to be enacted, old legislation is less likely to be amended, and legislative agency is on the whole harder to exercise. This is a structure that is designed to enable policy to be developed in multiple sites, including both chambers of Congress and the Presidency. It is also a structure designed to complicate the exercise of legislative power in order to minimise the risk of abuse. The result has been the partial atrophy of Congress because of the difficulties of discharging this role and also because of a shift to different methods of policy making (Posner and Vermeule 2010), with Congress aiming to shape policy by way of its control of the budget and appointment of executive agencies.

In the Westminster parliamentary system, the government's initiative is vital, for it makes coherence possible. The government consists in senior parliamentarians in whom a majority of others, especially in the lower house, have confidence.[3] The government is largely responsible for framing the legislative agenda, with discussion standardly centring on a proposal moved and managed by those with responsibility for its coherence. It does not follow that the parliamentary discussion is irrelevant, as if the votes were already assured. On the contrary, close study of Westminster legislative practice confirms that the legislative process results in changes in legislative proposals, with government making amendments and/or anticipating amendments (Russell and Gover 2017). The government's unequal control over the framing of amendments is important to help ensure that the legislative proposals that are finally chosen are fit for choice by a single agent. While other legislators may move bills, or table amendments, they are unlikely to advance to enactment without government support, or at least acquiescence, and governments often adopt and adapt such bills, or accept responsibility for framing amendments, precisely in order to ensure coherence.

Many legislative assemblies are bicameral, which requires coordination between two chambers before legislation may be enacted. In one way, this poses a further challenge to legislative agency, but the challenge is readily surmountable, especially if one chamber has the whip hand, as the lower house often has in a parliamentary system. If both chambers independently develop proposals on the same subject, which then require reconciliation, there is a risk of incoherence; if one chamber develops proposals moved by another the risk is relatively muted. Much turns on whether the executive (government) has an active presence within the bicameral assembly, shepherding legislative proposals and taking responsibility for their coherence even if not able to guarantee that they will be adopted if one or other chamber takes exception. Scholars have long recognised the practical importance of leadership within the legislature. But some wrongly take the government's participation in the legislative process somehow to compromise its integrity, as if legislation would ideally be developed freely by legislators without executive interference. It is with just such an argument in mind that Waldron has decried New

---

[3] This is a simplified formulation of the confidence principle; I state it more fully in Section III below.

Zealand's legislative practice, contrasting it with its American equivalent (Waldron 2005). While Waldron has cause to lament the thinness of some deliberation within New Zealand's Parliament, he is wrong to aim to exclude government. Forming and supporting a government is a key way in which parliamentarians make it possible for them jointly to exercise legislative agency, as well as to exercise influence over government more generally (Ilbert 1901, pp. 213–219).

III WORKING WITH GOVERNMENT

Legislating is a means of governing. However, the legislature does not itself govern. It is not well-placed to direct the great offices of state or to form and maintain a coherent policy across the full range of subjects that require government attention. The brief English experiment with government by legislature, in the wake of the execution of Charles I, did not end well. But the legislature has a vital role to play in making government possible, partly by assenting to the levying of taxes and the enactment of primary (and some secondary) legislation. This role grounds the legislature's capacity to exercise influence over taxation, legislation and policy at large, but also makes it imperative that legislature and government work together. The relationship between legislature and government is at the heart of the constitution. The legislature has a share in governing but its primary role is to hold the government to account, considering and challenging its initiatives. The mode of sharing, and the way the role is discharged, varies sharply from Washington to Westminster.

In the parliamentary system, Parliament forms an electoral chamber for government, not in the sense that it literally elects a government, but rather that political support in the Houses of Parliament, especially the lower House, is necessary if one is to govern. The constitutional entitlement to form (and then to remain) the government requires such support. The King appoints as Prime Minister whichever parliamentarian seems best placed to form a government that will command the confidence of the House of Commons (Cabinet Manual, chap. 2; Craig, Ekins and Laws 2019). The Prime Minister advises His Majesty to appoint other ministers who jointly form a government. Ministers exercise executive powers, and frame the legislative agenda, and are answerable to the Houses of Parliament and especially to the House of Commons for their conduct. The government is entitled to govern, including to frame the legislative agenda, unless the House of Commons withdraws its confidence in the government, at which point another government should be formed or an election held.[4] While the government consists in senior parliamentarians (legislators), the Cabinet is not a committee of the House of Commons (cf. Bagehot 2001 [1867], chap. I). It may be undone by withdrawal of confidence, which,

---

[4] Ekins and Laws 2019a and 2019b; the government remains in office (and continues to govern) until the election returns a new political configuration, which may support it in office or result in a change in government, but the purdah convention limits its freedom during this period to initiate major policy changes.

as I say, may lead to an alternative government being formed, in which the House reposes confidence, or to an election that returns a new political configuration.

The government must account to Parliament, and may be undone by Parliament, which is what makes it responsible. Is the government then the servant of the Houses of Parliament? No. The government provides leadership within the Houses of Parliament and does not act on the directions of the Houses, save insofar as they take the form of Acts of Parliament, which are almost never enacted against the policy of the government in power when the legislation was enacted. The government cannot neglect Parliament and any government that treats Parliament with contempt, or high-handedly, is courting trouble. The government cannot take votes in Parliament for granted, even if it may expect to win. Instead, it has to maintain its relationship with the backbench, build and cultivate support, and anticipate objections, all in the awareness of the risk that the opposition may exploit opportunities (Ekins 2012, pp. 171–172). The government leads within Parliament, but this is not executive dominance or legislative weakness. In a parliamentary system, the government should enjoy legislative support, as well as legislative challenge. The government's power to set the legislative agenda is valuable precisely because good government requires the coordinated exercise of executive and legislative power.[5] It does not follow that the legislature and the executive (government) simply collapse into one another.[6] The capacity of governments to act with legislative support is vital to democratic participation, with legislative scrutiny and opposition (challenge) vital in turn to responsible, contested government.

While the government is not elected as such, the general election that forms the House of Commons is a contest for the right (opportunity) to form the next government. Electoral success paves the way to the formation of a government because of relative capacity to command legislative confidence. Nested within the House of Commons, armed to challenge and question the government at every point, is His Majesty's Opposition, which aims to present itself as the government in waiting.[7] The government's political challenge is to maintain its legislative coalition and resist the opposition's attempts to fracture that coalition and to appeal to the country at large. The government is strong but dependent, with its location within Parliament and the challenge it receives from the opposition, within the Houses and before the country, helping to enable political accountability.

In the presidential system, by contrast, the executive has its own entitlement to rule apart from the balance of political forces within the legislature. Here too, both institutions must work together if government is to be possible, but a conflict

---

[5] I do not mean to say that *only* a parliamentary system can deliver good government, although I do think there are some major problems with presidential systems. My point is that good government requires coordination of executive and legislative power, for which a constitution must make some provision, for example by empowering the government to frame the legislative agenda.

[6] For a subtle discussion of the risk of conflation, see O'Donovan 2007, pp. 195–196.

[7] Webber, this volume, and Webber 2017.

(impasse) is relatively more likely. For it is not obvious whether the legislature or the executive will be held responsible if or when the relationship breaks down and the system makes provision for the executive and legislature to have rival agendas. On the contrary, the parliamentary system is unstable unless and until a working relationship between government and parliament can be struck, which then must be maintained. In the Washington system, major government programmes will often involve congressional support for presidential initiatives. However, the standing difficulty of securing legislative support for presidential initiative, or of arranging for executive policy to be in harmony with the views of a majority in Congress, makes coherent government simply harder to secure. Congress and the President are rival sources of policy-making initiative, even if in practice the executive has come to be the main source, by reason of its greater capacity to form and maintain a coherent agenda and the weight of public expectation that it will do so (Posner and Vermeule 2010). The presidential veto is a means by which the President may prevent congressional action that threatens coherent government, which is to say the implementation of his agenda. The political difficulty of ensuring legislature and executive work together encourages greater use of emergency powers, or executive lawmaking powers, or even outright constitutional breach (Linz 1994). In the United States, it often culminates in legislative gridlock, making Congress relatively less central to government.

Impeachment aside, neither Congress nor President can dislodge the other. But in the traditional Westminster model, the government and the House of Commons are both able to bring an early end to their working arrangement, if the Prime Minister advises dissolution, which triggers an election, or if the Commons withdraws confidence. Thus, Washington and Westminster make rather different provision for the coordination of executive and legislative power, with the former animated much more than the latter by the imperative of making new government action costly.

IV REPRESENTING THE PEOPLE

In the central case, the legislative assembly is a representative institution. Its members are drawn from (elected by) and answerable to citizens and it acts on behalf of the political community, especially in acts of legislating, but also, in the parliamentary system, in forming and challenging the government. While the prince may act for the good of all, his claim to represent the people is different in kind from the assembly's, because he is not chosen by those for whose good he acts and he is not answerable to them (Ekins 2012, pp. 148–152, pp. 157–161). And even if the prince was elected, one person alone cannot represent the community well. There are many good reasons to authorise an assembly rather than a prince to legislate, but its connection to the people has particular force. In making provision for who is to exercise legislative power, an assembly's capacity to enable the people to share in their own government, to make self-government possible, is significant.

The legislature's representative capacity is sometimes questioned in arguments for judicial review of legislation (Ekins 2013, pp. 165–169). Eisgruber (2001) argues that the legislature is not *impartial*, for it does not act for the good of all but only for the interests of the majority. (The court, by contrast, is assumed to be impartial and to act for the good of all and thus to be more truly representative than the legislature.) Hence, the legislature is conflated with the majority and legislative decisions are derided as majoritarian, which is taken to entail either that the legislature is the instrument of majority tyranny or that it would be unless constitutional rights are upheld *against* the legislature by the courts (Dworkin 1996c). The political process is widely assumed inevitably to exclude politically marginal groups, such that, again, the legislative assembly is the quintessential majoritarian institution and a standing danger to minority rights.

This line of argument misconceives how the legislative assembly relates to the electoral majority and how and why an electoral majority is entitled to rule. For Lincoln, '[a] majority held in restraint by constitutional checks and limitations, and always changing easily with deliberate changes of popular opinions and sentiments, is the only true sovereign of a free people' (Lincoln 1861). I consider how constitutional limitations might be squared with legislative freedom in the final part of this chapter. The legislature acts on majority vote, and requires political support in the country to act. The outcome of a general election, in which each citizen has an equal vote, settles which persons have authority to legislate and, in a parliamentary system, to govern. This is a fair means to allocate authority. The technique of majority voting, which is the salient alternative to unanimity, does not entail that the legislature – or the electorate – acts for the good only of some (Webber et al. 2018). Rather, in deciding what measures should be adopted for the common good, a majority vote in the legislature settles the question. In the circumstances of politics, barring a total failure of solidarity, this is a fair means to decide what should be done. It reposes authority to an institution that takes seriously the political equality of citizens, which in turn helps ground the authority of the institution, for its decisions are likely to enjoy wider political support and to be accepted as fairly made.

The promise of the legislative assembly is to reproduce the community in a form fit to reason, where the community thus personified will choose how the law should change. The assumption that the legislature simply acts for the good of a voting majority is ungrounded, neglecting not only the moral psychology of voters and legislators but also the fractured nature of political majorities. When legislative authority is exercised unjustly, for private rather than common good, as it of course sometimes is, this is an abuse rather than the outworking of the institution's true character. The assembly, or at least the main part thereof, should be elected, because this extends political agency to voters, who may respond to reasons in voting for or against a candidate for election. Elected representatives predictably form a political elite, but one that is dependent on (and answerable to) the masses, much as government is dependent on parliament. The assembly's deliberation and action are nested within a wider public conversation, with the number of legislators and the breadth and depth of their connections to voters and other groups providing much needed information. Legislative deliberation is the sharp end of this public conversation (Ekins 2019b). Deliberation often happens outside plenary session or committee hearings, but the necessity of ministers providing an account to the Houses and the ongoing provision for debate focuses attention (Ilbert 1901, pp. 230–234).

Legislators provide leadership and form a governing elite. But they are accountable to, and in important ways subject to, voters and other citizens. The legislature's function is not to execute some antecedent will of the people (Ekins 2012, p. 94; Ekins 2013, p. 175). If anything, the legislature forms up and articulates a will of the people, in its deliberation and choice, on this or that question (Ekins 2019a, p. 156). However, the legislature's lawmaking choices, while authoritative, are also fully contestable. Indeed, one important virtue of legislation is that it remains open to successive legislatures freely to amend or repeal. The legislature forms the will of the people by deliberating about and deciding what is to be done, in a way that makes provision for lively political contest in and between elections.

Representation has its risks. Legislators may come to disdain the people, which might manifest in adoption of an unduly narrow franchise or simply an unwillingness fully to engage or answer to voters (Ekins 2020). In this way, legislators might form not an accountable, contingent elite but a semi-detached, stable caste. This in turn may fuel popular disdain for legislators and legislature, leading to disillusionment with democratic politics and openness to its demise or subversion. The legislature's representative character might also risk the legislature coming to understand itself to rival the people, with representation forming a (liberal, oligarchic) curb on popular excess. While the legislature should not think that its duty is to carry out instructions issued by the people, part of its rationale is to make politics possible, to make wider public conversation matter, such that the exercise of legislative power is carried out by an agent that is the community personified. It is thus vital that the legislature remain the site of robust party political competition and that legislators strive to maintain fellow feeling with, and sympathy for, voters. A failure on the part of legislators to understand the common good, to prefer the interests of a class apart, is a real risk. It is, however, much less of a risk than with a prince, or mandarins, judges, generals, or technocrats, all of whom lack a standing, reciprocal connection to those for whose good they should act.

It is a mistake to conceive of the legislative assembly as a second-best alternative to direct democracy. Rather, it is an improvement on rule by a prince, where one shares responsibility for the exercise of legislative power amongst many hands, consistently with political equality. The persons and parties who form the legislature, and who contest elections to serve in the legislature, may be held to account by the electorate for its decisions. It is sometimes, but not often, reasonable for the legislature to make provision for direct popular decision on some question such as, for example, whether to enter or exit the EU or whether to reform the electoral system (Webber et al. 2018). But this choice is a limited one, for which the legislature must make provision and which it must implement, not in reopening the question, but in making further choices consequent on it. This is a dangerous technique because it can encourage an absence of – or rather the avoidance of – responsibility. In general, it is better to be ruled by an assembly (and government) than by all. For, while we are all entitled to share in our government, governing by way of a representative assembly makes responsible government possible.

V LAWMAKING AND STATUTORY INTERPRETATION

The legislature's authority is exercised in acts of legislation. Constitutional lawmaking aside, the Acts of Parliament or Congress or equivalent are the highest form of lawmaking in a democratic constitutional order. (Or at least they are the highest form of deliberate, openly acknowledged lawmaking; constitutional interpretation may be higher still, but it works a change in the law by stealth.) How one should understand legislative acts is an important constitutional question. The general answer, I say, is that they should be understood precisely to be *acts* of the legislature (Ekins 2012, pp. 246–247). That is, the legislature exercises its authority by forming and acting on intentions about how the law is to change, intentions which are choices about what law should be adopted. Legislating is an exercise of rational agency and the assembly's lawmaking choices are conveyed in some intended meaning. In other words, the legislature's capacity frames how subjects of the law rationally respond.

Contrast the arguments of Raz, Manning and Waldron that the legislature can only intend the conventional meaning of the statutory language it enacts. Manning would add that the stability of this conventional meaning is the currency of legislative bargains (Manning 2005, 2006). This analysis is premised on a misconceived theory of how language uses works and how legislators work together. In fact, language users routinely intend more or less than the conventional meaning of the semantic content they utter and legislators understand legislative proposals to convey meanings that are not reducible to the semantic content of the statutory text and which do articulate a reasoned plan of action. Pace Dworkin, for whom legislation is a political event that the court takes into account, there is good reason to conclude that the legislature forms and acts on lawmaking intentions.

Aquinas understood law to be an ordinance for the common good, formed in the mind of the ruler and then adopted by the ruled as if it were their own Finnis (1998, pp. 255–256). The law the legislature makes is the reasoned scheme that it chooses to adopt and promulgates in acts of legislation. The duty of the subject of law is to infer the legislature's intended meaning and thus to adopt as his or her own the plan of action the legislature has authoritatively chosen. In adjudicating disputes, the judge is in the same position as other subjects of the law. In inferring the legislative intent, subjects of the law – including judges – reasonably take for granted that the legislature acts for common good (Ekins 2012, p. 245). One reads legislation aiming to infer the intelligent and intelligible scheme the legislators chose, a scheme inferred from the semantic content of the text uttered in the context of enactment. Constitutional principles form part of that context, common to legislator (drafter) and judge (Laws 2020). But the judge (or citizen) should not be entitled to displace legislative intent by reference to constitutional principle.

Interpretation goes astray if it takes legislation to be antithetical to rights or principle. Reasoning about the common good is to reason about justice, rights, and principles. One should read legislation on the premise that it articulates the legislature's reasoned conclusion about how justice is to be done in some context or how rights and other principles are to be specified, whether as the main objects of legislative action or as side-constraints on some other object (Webber et al. 2018). Any theory of statutory interpretation that assumes that legislation standardly infringes rights is dubious, with the theory encouraging courts to misconceive and then to subvert statute. That said, the subject of the law should avoid letting slip a focus on the legislative intent in enacting the particular statute, a loss of focus which some techniques of statutory interpretation may wrongly encourage.

The way in which legislative acts are understood, and the importance of reasoned agency in their exercise, informs how one should think about statutory interpretation. It is relevant to constitutional adjudication too, in which courts decide whether legislation passes constitutional muster. Proportionality analysis often goes wrong in taking for granted a parody of legislation, which fails adequately to address the complexity of legislative reasoning (Yowell 2018; Ekins 2014; Webber et al. 2018).

VI LEGISLATIVE FREEDOM AND ITS LIMITS

In a well-ordered political community, the legislature has freedom to legislate, which is to say that the assembly is free to consider the reasons for legal change and to decide when or whether to enact legislation. The legislature may responsibly tolerate custom or case law, standing ready to intervene if or when need be. It is free to take as much time to deliberate and choose as it sees fit. And its deliberation and lawmaking choice is in important ways creative and open (Ekins 2012). The extent of legislative freedom in this or that jurisdiction turns on constitutional limits. However such limits are drawn, only some uses of its freedom will in fact be reasonable or justified. The merits of the exercise of legislative freedom will often be hotly disputed within and beyond the assembly. And controversy is often likely to continue after enactment, with legislation routinely amended or repealed.

A few legislatures still enjoy plenary legislative authority, most notably the Westminster Parliament. This authority is consistent with constitutional government. Indeed, it has long been taken to be a central part of the British constitutional order, making the political dynamics and conventional restraints within Parliament and the country decisive, and making continuing room for radical political and legal change if and when politics permits (Ekins 2019b). This openness is thought to help chasten extremism, and to encourage a self-tempering equilibrium – radical change will only endure if one's successors do not undo it (Tuck 2019). This analysis takes for granted, of course, that the change in question is such as to permit peaceful succession in time. But then the more fundamental premise is that a political community's main security against tyranny is politico-cultural rather than legal (Goldsworthy 1999, 2010). This has not been a foolish wager in the British experience, for Parliament's freedom has been framed and limited by political competition, by internal structure and by constitutional convention.

Plenary legislative authority does not mean arbitrary fiat. The object of legislative deliberation and choice remains the common good, and legislation is fully open to criticism, or in extremis to resistance, on the grounds that it fails to do justice. The point is that responsibility for determining whether existing law, or proposed legislation, is or is not just remains with the assembly. In exercising this responsibility, the political dynamics of parliamentary democracy, the restraints of culture and convention, will all help frame what is done.

Some constitution makers, and/or the people, have reasonably imposed limits on the legislature, limiting legislative authority to minimise the risk of abuse or to settle in advance some point (Ekins 2013, pp. 173–174). In particular, the constitution may often aim to establish a stable structure in which multiple institutions – federal and state, presidential and congressional – can take up their places, a structure that the legislature is disabled from recasting. This choice is often a reasonable exercise of self-government, but it does risk the atrophy or abdication of continuing self-government insofar as the strictures are drawn too tightly and unduly limit the capacity of legislatures, state and federal, to form a means by which the people may decide how they should be governed.

Legislative freedom is the centrepiece of the Westminster constitution (Ekins 2017a and 2019b). It is important, even if more limited, in many other constitutional schemes. However, for some scholars, the whole point of constitutional order is to restrain legislative freedom, which is understood to be the main threat to minority rights and constitutional government. Weinrib (2016) argues that the problem with legislatures is that without the restraint of constitutional adjudication they are simply unaccountable, because individuals cannot bring before an independent tribunal their objection to legislative decisions that violate their dignity or their right to just governance. Dworkin (1996c) takes the legislative process to incarnate majoritarian, statistical democracy, in which respect for rights warrants the external discipline of judicial review. Schauer (2006) too sees the virtue of judicial review to be its externality from the legislative process. The alternative, Harel and Kahana (2010) argue, is that the legislature is judge in its own cause, whereas in truth each individual is entitled to demand that legislation that interferes with his or her rights be justified in court.

The mistake here is to overlook the way in which the legislature, while forming a single agent capable of reason and choice, is constituted by a multitude of persons who are rivals for electoral support and who challenge one another, in a context where today's choice may be contested and reversed tomorrow (Webber et al. 2018). The legislative choice is the upshot of a fair process for collective decision. In inviting courts to review the merits of the choice, and to quash legislation on the grounds that it appears to the judges in question to be unjust or disproportionate, one unfairly unravels that fair process for collective decision-making. And one transfers from legislators to judges the responsibility for deciding what the law should be, in a context where judges are obviously and by design not accountable to citizens for how they exercise this responsibility.

It is no answer to say that rights are different and warrant special protection over and against ordinary legislating. Rights are the subject of legislative deliberation and choice and standardly require legislative specification (Webber et al. 2018; Ekins and Webber 2018). The common framing of legislation as hostile, or antithetical, to rights is misconceived. While courts may reasonably uphold clear, specific constitutional commitments posited in advance, modern rights adjudication more often invites and requires them to determine whether some legislative act strikes a fair balance between the public good and individual interests. This approach risks misconstruing the complexity of legislative reasoning and at best simply invites judges to decide for themselves whether the legislators have acted reasonably. This is a form of constitutional order that fails to do justice to the moral need for legislation and to the capacities of the legislative process to provide for reasoned lawmaking consistent with popular participation in self-government. Apart from enforcement of clearly specified constitutional rights, the main route of challenge to legislation should always be within the legislature itself or by way of the wider political and electoral dynamics that frame the assembly's action.

The legislature's accountability to the people is fundamental to self-government. Political accountability should be cultivated, not abandoned. The assumption that the legislature is uniquely vulnerable to capture by populism or to domination by the executive is unsound (Webber and Yowell 2020). Legislative freedom makes democratic politics matter, which is the best answer to the populist concern that the people are unjustly excluded from their own government. The constitutional and (especially) supra-national limitations that are often pressed by those who fear legislative freedom are in fact likely to provoke a populist insurrection. The legislature is an institution framed to take up responsibility for reasonable lawmaking, working with government but holding it to account, and being accountable in turn to the people. Ensuring that the legislature remains free to act, and supporting its capacity to exercise that freedom well, is a matter of the highest public importance.

CONCLUSION

The way to explain the legislature is to reflect on the need for legislation – for legislating – and thus on the shape of an institution that is well-placed to legislate. The legislative assembly takes the place of the prince, reasoning about what should be done and choosing what to make law. The exercise of legislative authority requires the legislature to exercise agency, forming and acting on intentions about how the law is to change. Legislative agency consists in the joint action of the many legislators, who share a concern for the common good but disagree about how best to secure it. Legislators deliberate about how to act, with party political discipline helping to support their coordinated action over time. Political competition takes its place within, and in relation to, an institution that in the end acts as a single agent, making reasoned choices about how the law is to change. The legislature's relationship to government is a central constitutional dynamic. The constitution should make provision for coordination between executive and legislative power if good government is to be possible. Whether nested within the assembly or not, the government should provide leadership in legislating, initiating proposals for action. The government is exposed to challenge by (other) legislators, including for its exercise (or failure) of leadership. The form of the legislature makes it possible for the people to have a share in public deliberation and decision, much more than would be the case if they only elected a single office holder. The reasons for the legislature thus explain its structure and agency, with the many legislators forming themselves into an institution that is at the heart of democratic politics and which is capable of taking up the responsibility for legislating, which is to respond to reasons with intelligent choice.

RECOMMENDED READING

Bauman, R. & Kahana, T. eds. (2006). *The Least Examined Branch: The Role of Legislatures in the Constitutional State*, Cambridge: Cambridge University Press.
Ekins, R. (2012). *The Nature of Legislative Intent*, Oxford: Oxford University Press.
Feldman, D., ed. (2013). *Law in Politics, Politics in Law*, Oxford: Hart Publishing.
Goldsworthy, J. (2010). *Parliamentary Sovereignty: Contemporary Debates*, Cambridge: Cambridge University Press.
Ilbert, C. (1901). *Legislative Methods and Forms*, Oxford: Clarendon Press.
Mill, J. S. (1865). *Considerations on Representative Government*, London: Longman.
Norton, P. ed. (1990). *Legislatures*, Oxford: Oxford University Press.
Nourse, V. (2016). *Misreading Law, Misreading Democracy*, Cambridge, MA: Harvard University Press.
Waldron, J. (1999a). *Law and Disagreement*, Oxford: Oxford University Press.
Webber, G., Yowell, P, & Ekins, R. et al. (2018). *Legislated Rights: Securing Human Rights through Legislation*, Cambridge: Cambridge University Press.

Wintgens, L. ed (2005). *The Theory and Practice of Legislation: Essays in Legisprudence*, Aldershot: Ashgate.

Yowell, P. (2018). *Constitutional Rights and Constitutional Design: Moral and Empirical Reasoning in Judicial Review*, Oxford: Hart Publishing.

46

Referendums

Silvia Suteu

The constitutional theory literature on referendums has expanded in recent years, in part as acknowledgement of the need for rigorous theorising following high profile instances of their use. This literature covers a wide spectrum of investigations, spanning topics as disparate as whether and how referendums can be understood and designed as deliberative democratic instruments (Tierney 2012); referendums' complex relationship to representative democracy (Daly 2015; Trueblood 2020; Thompson 2022); the role of courts in shaping referendum campaigns and interpreting their results (Choudhry and Howse 2000); the sequencing of interconnectedness between referendums and micro-deliberative tools such as citizens' assemblies (Suteu and Tierney 2018); and the rationales one might have for using referendums as tools for conflict settlement (Qvortrup 2014; Levy *et al.* 2021; Bernal 2022).

This wide-ranging scholarship includes both referendum enthusiasts and sceptics, offering a diverse assessment of the legitimacy, usefulness, and dangers of referendums. The positive case for the referendum in constitutional practice tends to start from taking seriously its democratic potential. It gives a consequential voice to the people, including often to previously disenchanted voters mobilised by the salience of the question and the directness of the vote at referendum. As such, it can help reinvigorate democratic politics. Additionally, the referendum campaign can perform an educational role, especially when enough time and resources are dedicated to providing voters with information and spaces for them to deliberate and form considered opinions on their choices. In instances where the referendum vote concerns a highly divisive issue such as secession or membership/integration in supranational structures, the direct appeal to the people can garner the popular support needed to proceed. There is also an anti-establishment role that referendums can play, especially when their results are binding, such as prodding elites to act on issues hitherto not on the political agenda, checking elite self-dealing, and breaking inter-institutional deadlock.

Sceptics, conversely, believe these benefits overstated or elusive. Instead, they point to the high risk of elite control of the referendum process, to the poor quality of information usually relied on during referendum votes, and to the potentially highly divisive nature of referendums. Some referendum features, in turn, can cut both ways. For example, their very bluntness and finality is decried by their detractors while praised by those who believe referendums to be useful, under certain circumstances, precisely for their ability to cut through political impasses. In addition, as I will discuss below, most constitutional theorists favourably disposed to the use of referendums view it as complement to rather than replacement for mechanisms of representative constitutional democracy.

In the time since referendums have captured the constitutional theorist's attention, the questions she has had to grapple with have augmented and deepened. While it is true that the ultimate concern remains whether and how to make recourse to the people by way of a direct vote cast at referendum – ultimately, how to ensure this is a legitimate democratic exercise and not one co-opted or abused – important changes in the political and societal landscape mean that new problems must additionally be addressed. Among these are the rise of social media as well as the distorting and potentially pernicious effects of echo chambers, conspiracy theories, and disinformation rife online. Another consequential development has been the rise of various democratic innovations that interact in interesting and potentially productive ways with referendums, especially deliberative mini-publics. These have been proposed by some as tools to complement and even fix some of the shortcomings of referendums, as part of what has been called a deliberative turn in constitutionalism (Levy *et al.* 2018).

In what follows, I propose to look at three long-standing issues of concern to the constitutional theorists of referendums, but attempt to do so through an updated lens. That is, I will look at debates and critiques of referendums as a democratic instrument in light of recent developments in referendum theory and practice that have potentially challenged received wisdom. These issues are: the ambiguous place of referendums within democratic theory, including its relationship to direct, representative, and deliberative democracy; the complex interplay between referendums as majoritarian tools and minority rights; and the novel opportunities and distinct challenges to informed voter consent in the digital era, not least disinformation and fake news.

The chapter shows that, for all its faults, the referendum as a tool of democratic collective decision-making remains central to constitutional theorists' imaginary, whether they identify as political constitutionalists, deliberative constitutionalists or otherwise. The objections raised against referendums depend very much on the wider constitutional architecture, the limits and safeguards present, the institutional actors who can sanction abuse, and the overall place of public participation within the wider constitutional culture. In addition, any such objections must be tailored to the referendum itself, as opposed to voting in general – as we will see, a distinction which is sometimes lost among the instrument's detractors. Finally, the chapter discusses the possibility that one of the biggest ills of referendums, their vulnerability to manipulation through disinformation, may be a symptom of the more widespread breakdown of democratic institutions plaguing constitutional democracies the world over. I end the chapter with the argument that constitutional theory should move beyond analysing referendums within the old democratic paradigm and to start thinking creatively about how they can be insulated from the sustained, large-scale, and insidious attacks they have been subjected to.

As will become evident, my approach to referendums is reflective of my overall views on the methodology of constitutional theory, that is, it is highly comparatively informed and contextualised (Suteu 2022a). I wish to resist generalisations and extrapolations from individual case studies that risk sanding over the distinctive place of referendums within different constitutional systems. This is not necessarily distinct from other constitutional theoretical evaluations of the referendum instrument (see, e.g., Moeckli 2011 arguing for the need to take stock of referendums within their specific constitutional context). It is, instead, a reaffirmation of the necessity of comparative insight that spans beyond the dominant examples in the field and that ensures the theoretical discussion of referendums remains embedded in a given constitutional system. That is a fine balance to strike between deep contextualism and responsible comparatism, but one well worth pursuing in the hitherto often nation-focused study of referendums.

I REFERENDUMS' AMBIGUOUS RELATIONSHIP TO DEMOCRACY

It may seem an odd place to begin a contribution on referendums, but determining their relationship to democracy is not straightforward. The purported settled view would be to regard referendums as the quintessential mechanism of direct democracy. With variations as to referendum type (consultative or mandatory, bottom-up or initiated by the government or legislature), this view nevertheless holds that by giving the people a direct vote, referendums are indeed an instrument of democratic self-government (for a discussion ultimately endorsing bottom-up and binding referendums, see Cheneval and El-Wakil 2018). Insofar as the vote is not only direct but also equal, rejecting referendums has been equated to rejecting democracy (Bogdanor 1981, p. 93). Its collective nature makes it an act of democratic sovereignty that must therefore be viewed as authoritative (Galligan 2001, p. 109). Such views categorise the referendum as an alternative both to traditional channels of lawmaking, the hallmarks of representative democracy, and to citizen-led micro-forums that have increasingly been promoted by deliberative democrats. As we will see, however, constitutional theorists remain divided about the democratic nature of referendums.

To some constitutional theorists, a well-designed and well-run referendum on a question of constitutional importance acts as the closest tool we have to approximate a sovereign act of the people (Tierney 2012). Rather than decry the majoritarianism inherent in the referendum vote, these theorists welcome its capacity to crystallise the voice to the demos (or demoi, where plural), to act collectively, and to complement rather than supplant the institutions of representative democracy. Tierney, for example, cautions against mistaking practical objections about the running of referendums for principled ones and argues instead that, with careful planning and in the right political conditions, a referendum can be not only democratically legitimate, but also deliberative. Design choices about the timing of the referendum, the question asked, the campaign rules, and the implementation of the result will, according to Tierney, buttress or undermine the democratic credentials of any given referendum. Importantly, his is a defence of the constitutional referendum as a sovereign act that nevertheless is bound by the limits of constitutionalism, insofar as "the people" is too large and diverse a body to manifest itself without the intervention of representational forces; thus, even in a constitutional democracy mandating the use of referendums, 'popular sovereignty and representation can never be separated from one another.' (Tierney 2012, p. 136)

An example of squaring this circle is offered by King in his case for a written constitution for the UK, as part of which he proposes an amendment formula that would include, first, careful deliberation and legislation by Parliament, followed by a ratificatory referendum that engenders a national conversation and ownership over the proposed bill (King 2019b, pp. 32–33). Additionally, one could argue that processes of negotiating secessionist claims offer the best illustration of Tierney's defence of the referendum tool insofar as they by definition bring into focus a fractioned demos and involve a constitutive vote on the future of the polity. Scotland's road to the 2014 independence referendum may be a positive example here, though its replicability outside of its distinctive political and constitutional conditions is dubious, including within Scotland itself (Suteu 2022b).

Conversely, Catalonia's fraught attempts to move forward the cause of independence is a good illustration of how, within a more rigid constitutional system with a constitutional court willing to intervene forcefully, the referendum (or threat of one) cannot on its own shift the political winds towards a negotiated solution (Bossacoma Busquets 2020). Since 2009 when changes to the region's autonomy status first sparked controversy, Catalonia has been at the centre of multiple and often contested decisions by the Spanish Constitutional Tribunal, different electoral configurations at both national and regional levels, and a European Union reluctant to make room for sub-national sovereignty claims. Within that complex context, the infamous 2017 referendum on independence only exacerbated the competing visions of nationhood within the Spanish constitutional system, rather than help reconcile them (Cetra *et al.* 2018).

To these examples of the positive role that referendums can play in processes of constitution-making and constitutional change, we can add others, informed by practice in systems where it is an embedded and recurring constitutional tool of decision-making. I have argued elsewhere, for example, drawing on the Romanian example, that the referendum plays a unique role as deadlock-breaking mechanism during periods of divided government in semi-presidential systems (Suteu 2019). In such scenarios, serious institutional conflict is accompanied by the competing authority claims of the directly elected legislature *and* president, with the people voting during a referendum performing the role of arbiter. An example would be presidential impeachment by parliament requiring confirmation via a popular vote. The dangers of politicisation and elite control remain, of course, and Charles de Gaulle's use of the referendum to amend the French Constitution in 1958 is but one famous illustration (Tierney 2012, pp. 132–137). In the case of post-impeachment referendums, too, the danger is that the vote is more likely to support a popular president regardless of any transgression that might have led to impeachment in the first place. Nevertheless, by going to the ballot, the institutional conflict is resolved by the same democratic authority source behind both the head of state and parliament. More broadly, we should recognise the distinctive constitutional role referendums can play depending on whether they are embedded in a presidential, semi-presidential, or parliamentary system.

Not everyone agrees with the more positive case for referendums illustrated above. Daly, for example, shares Tierney's civic republican starting commitments but disputes his reading of referendums as sovereign or constituent acts (Daly 2015). Instead, Daly argues, referendums perform the function of a check on government power and have the virtue of being able to foster a wider culture of civic participation. His is a call to appreciate the modest but important role that referendums afford the people and an attempt to walk the tightrope between seeking to actualise self-government and believe in an unmediated form of democracy. Rather than as a bottom up exercise of popular sovereignty, the referendum for Daly is part of a mixed constitution in which it does not compete with the legislature but instead performs the function of an additional check on parliament helping to mitigate legislative self-dealing. Daly's view is thus one that ascribes to the referendum a narrower role within the constitutional order. This 'domestication' of the referendum arguably reduces its radical potential to the point of disabling it entirely. The broader argument that referendum use is legitimate when integrated within a mixed system combining direct and representative elements, meanwhile, is one that most constitutional theorists today would agree with.

Trueblood has similarly argued that understanding referendums as a form of unmediated democracy, typically also then invoked as the basis for their normative justification, is erroneous and misleading (Trueblood 2020). She has argued that a referendum vote is no less mediated than regular elections insofar as the triggering of a referendum vote, the question on the ballot, the personalisation of the campaign, and the aggregation and interpretation of the result all centre the representatives. Instead, Trueblood has argued, referendums are best viewed and defended as a distinctive mechanism to give specific (as opposed to general, as in elections) direction to these representatives (Trueblood 2020, p. 447). Thus, the referendum is better understood as a check on the representative process rather than an instrument to supplant it, even temporarily. The latter, in Trueblood's view, led to the misguided reading of the Brexit referendum vote as an instruction to representatives that needed to be given effect to despite the failings of the process preceding it (Trueblood 2022). Political constitutionalists like Bellamy, who have otherwise been less critical of the Brexit vote and have defended it as reasonably democratic, would nevertheless agree that its consequences and implementation were not predetermined (Bellamy 2023). This line of critique, moreover, appears very much influenced by the particulars of the UK constitution, wherein the referendum sits uneasily with the principle of parliamentary sovereignty and is regulated by ad hoc legislation which sometimes, as in the case of Brexit, incompletely sets out its operation. To the comparatist, many of these concerns are not so much problems of principle but of institutional design and, therefore, easily resolved. Clearer rules on referendum initiative and items to be subjected to a referendum vote, stipulating the legislative steps following a referendum vote, tighter referendum campaign rules and mechanisms for accountability – these are all design elements on which there exists ample comparative material and which would seem to alleviate many of Trueblood's concerns.

In my view, a more significant error often seeping into these debates is pitting the referendum at its worst against representative democracy at its best (the nirvana fallacy). For example, when arguing that referendums are more prone to elite capture or that representative institutions tend to be more deliberative in their decision-making, the evidence must be evaluated in a specific institutional and temporal context. For instance, we must account for the breakdown of representative institutions themselves as democratic mediators and deliberative agents, as well as for their own propensity to be captured by elite interests. As explained in the next section, when condemning referendums as more likely to disadvantage minorities than the representative democratic process, the claim should not be assessed in the abstract but as against representative institutions' own track record in this area. For example, condemning Hungary's 2016 immigration and 2022 anti-LGBTQ referendums in isolation would completely miss the consistent dismantling of democratic and rule-of-law safeguards of the Orban government and its capture of representative institutions and most media since 2010. When it comes to fragile democracies, moreover, the independence, institutional capacity, and commitment to democracy of state institutions may make a single-issue, one-off event such as a referendum vote less, not more, susceptible to manipulation. We know from comparative practice, in fact, that authoritarian leaders do not necessarily reject representation and that they are far more ambivalent towards referendums than might be thought (Pinelli 2011, Halmai 2019). In contexts where they have captured representative institutions and where popular votes may bring unpredictable results, this ambivalence makes sense.

A second cautionary note is against missing the referendum's specific democratic potential. One example is the referendum as a tool for overcoming political stalemate, such as on the regulation of highly charged topics such as abortion or same-sex marriage, and for evading political self-dealing, such as on electoral reform. For all their faults, referendums can and do occasionally throw up surprises for the political class, however intent it may be on controlling them. Dictators losing but accepting the outcome of referendums in Uruguay and Chile in the 1980s and Zimbabwe in 2000 are older but stark examples (Altman 2010, p. 108). There may well be a case to be made that, regardless of their faults, referendums are necessary in situations where politicians are otherwise judges in their own cause. These are said to be instances where 'representative government with referendums is in this respect superior to representative government without them' (Thompson 2022, p. 209).

The focus then turns from how to design referendums as 'pure' exercises of direct democracy to how to integrate them within representative democracy in any given context (see also Bellamy 2023). Deliberative democrats have similarly, rightly, moved away from evaluating the referendum as a deliberative tool on its own and are asking instead how it can be integrated into a deliberative system (Parkinson 2020). This allows it to play a role in large-scale, deliberative democracies even while not itself being expected to produce deliberation as such. The referendum then shifts from deliberative pariah to a useful mechanism not so much insofar as it aggregates preferences or settles issues (two purported virtues of referendums), but insofar as it helps clarify issues, promotes a national conversation, educates the public, and brings to light what it is thinking (LeDuc 2015, Chambers 2018b). Such approaches offer a way out of a zero-sum thinking about the relationship of referendums and democracy and allow the constitutional theorist in particular to focus on the institutional and principled preconditions for the referendum to play a beneficial role in a constitutional democracy.

II REFERENDUMS AND MINORITY RIGHTS

Long-standing assessments of direct democracy have criticised its propensity to trample minority rights (Bell 1978; Gunn 1981; Gamble 1997). Whether it be popular initiatives such as California's Proposition 8 or referendums such as Switzerland's on banning minarets, the unmediated majoritarianism of these mechanisms has been viewed as facilitating the expression and often the enforcement of the basest of anti-minority impulses in society (Eskridge 2010; Moeckli 2011). Without the safeguards of representative institutions, it is argued, direct democracy cannot escape perpetuating the tyranny of the majority over various types of minorities (Lewis 2012). Indeed, these examples confirm that such participatory instruments have been used successfully for reactionary goals. Moreover, precisely because they purportedly give voice to the hitherto silent majority, there is a symbolic claim accompanying such anti-minority initiatives and referendums: whatever the so-called 'political correctness' of elites in the legislature or judiciary may dictate, the majority will strike back.

The relationship between referendums and minority rights was never as black and white as this, however. When reflecting on instances of recourse to the people via referendum, their vote has not always resulted in the diminution of rights of minorities. This raises more interesting questions of when and under what conditions are referendums conducive to positive outcomes for minorities. How much are they the exception that proves the rule? Are they flukes or outcomes that can be predicted or designed in some way? While some studies may have reassessed how minorities fare in direct democracy and posited a more complex relationship, with minorities often themselves able and willing to use mechanisms such as popular initiatives and referendums to protect their vital interests (Hajnal *et al.* 2002), generalising or replicating this finding remains contested (Haider-Markel *et al.* 2007). Moreover, as Simone Chambers has argued, if we find that minority enhancing referendums are a very small set of referendums, this finding may well necessitate a broad rejection of most forms of referendums (Chambers 2018b).

Much rides on the type of democratic and constitutional concerns raised by different participants in this debate. Political scientists are better placed to answer questions of causality, but they have struggled with a small and skewed sample: On the one hand, referendums on minority rights remain relatively rare; on the other hand, the accurate comparison would be between minority rights infringement via referendums versus via the ordinary lawmaking process, and that is often difficult to track (Matsusaka 2020, p. 203). Even when identifying a series of referendums with negative outcomes for minorities in a given national context, looking at the number of failed citizens' initiatives that might have raised that number even higher forces a re-evaluation. This could be said about Switzerland, for example, whose infamous referendums on banning minarets and forcibly expelling foreign criminals conceal the greater number of discriminatory popular initiatives that never made it to a vote (Fatin-Rouge Stefanini 2017, p. 378).

Constitutionalists, by comparison, understand the referendum tool as interconnected with the other elements of the constitutional system and view its effects as often difficult to single out. They tend to be more preoccupied with the legal safeguards instituted within the system to ensure that referendums on minority rights are either prevented altogether or else their potentially dangerous effects mitigated. Among these safeguards are retaining the power to initiate a referendum in the hands of the political branches; taking certain topics off the table entirely for popular votes; mandating high courts to exercise *ex ante* powers of review over the referendum question/bill; and *ex post* judicial review of the referendum result to ensure its conformity with the constitution and/or international legal obligations such as international human rights norms or norms of *jus cogens* (Moeckli 2018; Bernal 2022). To both the political scientist and the constitutionalist, therefore, the question of whether minorities fare poorly in referendums is difficult to answer in the abstract and without regard to very particular local conditions.

Two recent examples help illustrate the interplay between institutional design, constitutional system and culture, and the outcomes of referendums on minority rights. One is the successful 2015 referendum in Ireland on the recognition of same-sex marriage. The second is the unsuccessful referendum on amending the constitutional definition of the family in Romania. Success in this instance refers simply to whether the votes met the local requirements for the referendums to have been considered valid and their outcomes implemented.

The Irish example in particular has been touted as proof of the potentially progressive deployment of the referendum tool in advancing the case of minorities, in this instance sexual minorities. The final vote saw 62% of Irish voters approve the legal recognition of same-sex marriage. The fact that the referendum was preceded by a constitutional convention composed of half politicians and half regular citizens deliberating on the question also seemed to reinforce deliberative democrats' optimism that micro-deliberation can shift entrenched attitudes and promote inclusivity and consensus-building (Suiter and Reidy 2020).

Unknowns remain, however, about the impact the preceding constitutional convention had on voters' attitudes during the referendum campaign and about whether the winds of societal change meant the referendum outcome would have been the same regardless of the preceding micro-deliberative exercise. Moreover, the intensely personal nature of the referendum campaign appears to have been consequential, even while it extracted a high price from the very members of the minority group whose rights were being subjected to a popular vote (Tobin 2016). This in turn raises the important but underexplored question of whether, regardless of the final outcome of the vote, having minority rights subjected to a popular vote in itself causes harm.

Equally unclear remains whether the Irish example is easily replicable elsewhere, that is, whether the local conditions prevailing there around the time of the same-sex marriage referendum are so distinctive as to caution against generalisation. The country is small and homogenous enough to allow for deliberation during the referendum campaign to an extent difficult to attain in bigger and more polarised societies (Suteu 2015). Moreover, the relative frequency with which constitutional referendums are held – given that they are mandatory as part of the procedure for constitutional amendment – has been said to have engendered a 'healthy amendment culture' (Doyle and Walsh 2020, Doyle 2021). This refers, first, to the general acceptance of putting the issue to a popular vote, which helps focus public debate on the substantive question asked rather than on the decision to go to referendum in the first place. Second, it also refers to a certain consensual, cooperative and responsible political culture, institutional cooperation among constitutional actors, and general acceptance of the finality of the vote even in the face of continued normative resistance to it.

Nevertheless, in the same-sex marriage referendum as later in the 2018 abortion one, the Irish public proved to be more progressive than the legal status quo had been reflecting and voted to advance rather than curtail rights. To note these positive examples is by no means tantamount to recommending referendums as the preferred method of legislating for minority rights. However, while these Irish examples may not be easily replicated, they show that under the right conditions the referendum can act as a tool that not only does not stifle but brings about swifter legal progress.

Moving now to a second, very different example, I wish to discuss Romania's 2018 referendum on the constitutional definition of the family. The question asked of the voters was whether the reference to 'spouses' in the constitutional provision on equality within the family should be replaced with 'man and woman'. The move was an anticipatory strike seeking to pre-emptively entrench a heteronormative, religious understanding of marriage and the family precluding any (but at the time, non-existent) campaigns to legally recognise same-sex marriage within the country. The referendum was the result of a citizens' initiative that had met the procedural requirements of gathering over 500,000 signatures spread geographically across the country's counties. It had also passed all safeguards mandated by the Romanian Constitution: double certification by the Constitutional Court, including as not contravening the constitutional eternity clause banning the suppression of rights, and easily met the two-thirds majority requirement in both chambers of Parliament. Neither the Court, through cursory reasoning in its certification of the amendment bill, nor Parliament, through meagre and rushed debate, can be said to have performed a noteworthy deliberative function. The referendum is a mandatory final step in the constitutional amendment process, meant to provide the popular seal of approval to this lengthy, multi-actor process. There is a turnout quorum of 30% to be met for the referendum result to be validated.

The 2018 referendum vote followed a period of intense societal debate on an issue that had not been on the political agenda previously but on which Romanian society had repeatedly scored among the most conservative in Europe. The campaign mobilised a variety of institutional and civil society actors, sometimes in surprising configurations that eschewed traditional left-right or even party loyalties (Norocel and Baluta 2021). Calls for boycotting the vote soon came from an array of societal actors, not just LGBTQ alliances. Some argued it would have excluded single-parent and other non-traditional family arrangements. Others resented the immersion of religion into lawmaking, fearing it would open the floodgates to more church influence in the future. Others still perceived the referendum as timed to distract from the corruption charges levied against the then-leader of the ruling party. Many also failed to see the salience or urgency of the issue, which had not been on the public agenda prior to the initiative (Gherghina *et al.* 2019). The boycott was thus a broad church, arranged informally through social media, and brought together those who opposed the vote on substantive grounds (but knew that they would likely be in the minority at the ballot box) and those who viewed it as an attempt at political distraction. While earlier indicators had suggested a high turnout, the turnout quorum was not met after only a fifth of voters turned up. The government's attempts to avoid this – including by controversially extending the vote over two days – were unsuccessful. In spite of the Yes vote garnering 93.4% of the ballots cast, the referendum failed.

The Romanian example illustrates just how interwoven a referendum is with a country's broader constitutional architecture. Even where it is a mandatory element in the amendment process and where the initiation, certification, and implementation procedures are nominally robust, as here, there is no guarantee that minority rights are safe. The Romanian example also shows that it is not always the institutional safeguards we might expect (typically the legislature and/or constitutional court) that step in to prevent the erosion of rights via a popular vote. In this instance, the referendum turnout threshold was exploited to block the attempted constitutional change at the last minute. The boycott of the vote was a strategic choice of a multitude of actors not necessarily acting in concert or motivated by the same reasons. Nevertheless, the institutional feature of the turnout threshold allowed for informal societal mobilisation to block the constitutional amendment where the representative institutions and mechanisms had failed to do so.

The Romanian experience is of course not generalisable, not even in its regional context. For example, in 2015, Slovenia voted against a bill that would have legalised same-sex marriage, meeting a 20% turnout threshold. Nevertheless, the country recognised same-sex civil partnerships in 2003 and in 2022 legalised same-sex marriage after the Slovenian Constitutional Court ruled its ban unconstitutional. In contrast, despite the failed 2018 referendum, Romania continues to offer no legal recognition of same-sex unions. A further comparison may be drawn to Hungary, which has an even higher turnout threshold of 50% required to validate referendum outcomes. This was in turn what allowed its infamous 2016 anti-migrant and 2022 anti-LGBTQ in education referendums to fail despite overwhelming support for the government position among votes cast. The Hungarian examples are that much more noteworthy as they occurred in the context of state capture of political institutions and of the media and an impotent political opposition; despite these conditions, enough people in Hungary mobilised strategically against voting so as to ensure the voting threshold was not met.

The argument, then, is not that the failed referendum somehow ushered in a progressive shift in Romanian society or among its lawmakers. What I wished to showcase, instead, is how immersing ourselves in the constitutional features of a given system reveals the relationship between referendums and minority rights to be even more complex than often accounted for in the literature. While the issue originated in a citizens' initiative, had it been left to the Romanian representative institutions alone, they were poised to endorse the constitutional redefinition of the family without much concern for its discriminatory nature. This is true not just of the Constitutional Court and Parliament, but also of all but one of the major political parties. Instead, it was the informal public sphere that allowed alliance-building and mobilisation against the initiative and led to its ultimate demise.

III REFERENDUMS AND INFORMED VOTING

One of the main bones of contention between defenders of referendums and their detractors has to do with the capacity of the voters to make an informed decision. Regardless of where the decision to initiate the referendum originates or how its outcome is to be enforced, a question arises as to whether the vote cast reflects not only an accurate aggregation of individual views, but also a certain degree of reflection following reasoned, informed societal debate. Relevant here are familiar concerns about voter interest and expertise. In addition, the danger of elite control and manipulation arises insofar as the information presented to the public may be incomplete, misleading, or simply overly technical for answering the question put to a referendum. The Brexit vote has often been given as a negative example. It was not just the lack of knowledge on European Union membership that was thought to have made putting it to a referendum vote a serious gamble, but also the knock-on policy implications of the vote: the fact that, while purporting to be a single-issue vote, the decision in effect carried far-reaching policy implications of which voters remained ignorant (Bellamy 2023, p. 9).

In addition, there is a fear that populist leaders are especially adept at drumming up emotive voting via referendums and relying on them to entrench their political power and to promote illiberal policies. The fear is that the complexity of the issues, such as large packages of constitutional amendments, and the unpopularity of the targets, such as immigration or minorities, make voters especially prone to disinformation. Examples here include Turkey's 2017 constitutional reform referendum (seen as sealing President Erdogan's attempt to institutionalise his grip on power) and Hungary's 2016 anti-migrant and 2022 anti-LGBTQ referendums (viewed as attempts by Prime Minister Orban to stir anti-minority sentiment and redirect attention from his administration's failings). Viewed as a populist event, the Brexit vote itself could be added here as an example of falsehoods (e.g. on the threat of unregulated immigration or spending redirected to the healthcare system) being deployed strategically to mislead voters.

It is important to distinguish concerns about voter information and expertise in general and those specific to referendums. Indeed, many of the objections raised against referendum voting are no less relevant to election voting. In both instances, it has been argued that, while based on imperfect information, the popular vote is defensible on democratic grounds. Thus, we know that voters use voting cues and heuristics to determine how to cast their ballot (Hobolt 2009, p. 35). Voters may defer to trust proxies such as their representatives, political parties and other elites; they may cast a general ballot on the basis of a single issue of importance to them (e.g. immigration, abortion, gun control, climate change etc.); and they often rely on 'information shortcuts', meaning 'small pieces of information that signal the consequences of a vote without conveying much of the underlying content' (Matsukata 2020, p. 172). Several studies have in fact found that voters can indeed make informed decisions at referendum and that they can distinguish between propaganda or 'spin' and quality information, or at least that they are no more vulnerable to these than they are during the regular electoral process (Hobolt 2009, Bernhard 2012). Thus, even while a voter may not be fully versed on the complexities of European policy, they may nevertheless make a reasonably well-informed decision on the question of deepening European integration or, indeed, exiting the European Union.

The case remains, however, that the referendum campaign is a very particular type of electoral event and that the quality of the information provided to voters matters. For whereas periodic elections require voters to choose representatives that are then tasked with deciding policy and adopting legislation over time, the referendum puts the voter into the shoes of one-off decision-maker. Renwick *et al.* have proposed four axes along which to assess information quality if it is to lead to a 'fully democratic referendum': accuracy, balance, accessibility, and relevance (Renwick *et al.* 2020). They posit that all four can be cultivated via controlling campaign finance, confronting misinformation, creating and disseminating quality information, and promoting quality discussion. Moreover, while they find these cannot be fully designed to conform to democratic expectations, they are reasonably optimistic that sufficient strategies can be implemented to ensure defensible outcomes. The picture emerging from their study of the ideal referendum information campaign is one in which institutional actors act in good faith to distribute truthful, balanced, readily findable, intelligible, engaging, and relevant information to voters, from sources they can trust, and with the possibility of an electoral commission stepping in to sanction deviations before they skew the vote. I raise two observations in response.

On the one hand, Renwick *et al.* suggest interlinking deliberative mini-publics with large-scale referendums as a means to plug information shortcomings in the latter (Renwick *et al.* 2020, pp. 532–533; see also Chambers 2018b). The reasoning appears at first hand appealing: if voters are more likely to trust a mini-public such as a citizens' assembly than their political representatives, and if the information provided by the former can be trusted as accurate and balanced, then the democratic process is enhanced when referendums are preceded by such micro-deliberative exercises. Ireland's experience with a constitutional convention and a citizens' assembly preceding referendum votes on same-sex marriage and abortion, respectively, has cast an outsize shadow over this debate. Optimists believe that the Irish mini-publics have led to greater understanding of referendum issues by extending the time allocated to discussion, producing rigorous and informed materials, and delivering decisions made by ordinary citizens who benefit from more societal trust (Suiter and Reidy 2020). The empirical evidence on the replicability of these findings is incomplete, however. Furthermore, sceptics have suggested the case for the impact of mini-publics in the Irish referendums has been overstated (Carolan 2015, 2020).

Beyond the empirical question, it bears remembering that the principles informing mini-publics and referendums differ significantly and the democratic legitimacy they inculcate does as well. The former are focused on small-scale reasoned debate among carefully selected citizens, given the time and space to learn, exchange views, and possibly change their minds; the latter are large-scale processes where deliberation may or may not occur but certainly during which views are formed and exchanged in a less structured and controlled manner (Suteu and Tierney 2018). Because of these different dynamics, and because of the vulnerability to disinformation in referendums discussed below, we must remain cautious about assuming mini-publics can plug the information gaps and shortcomings inherent in a referendum campaign.

On the other hand, much of the literature in both political science and constitutional theory elaborating conditions for an informed referendum vote tends to operate within rather traditional boundaries. It assumes a public sphere within which traditional institutions such as the government and traditional media are the main information actors. It also assumes that what individuals require in making an informed decision is knowledge that is deemed sufficient and vetted for accuracy and impartiality or balance. However, the realities of the rise of disinformation and the distinct dynamics of online political engagement continue to pose challenges for both the scholar and the lawmaker (Baume *et al.* 2021). These raise problems that are qualitatively different from the traditional information shortcomings. The prospect arises that a referendum vote in the digital era of disinformation is even further from representing voters' informed, reasoned preference than we thought. In short, that the democratic legitimacy of voting may itself be illusory in the face of disinformation forces too large to mitigate.

Defining disinformation matters. We are talking about more than misleading or indeed false information. Instead, disinformation can be defined as 'intentional falsehoods or distortions, often spread as news, to advance political goals such as discrediting opponents, disrupting policy debates, influencing voters, inflaming existing social conflicts, or creating a general backdrop of confusion and informational paralysis' (Bennett and Livingstone 2021, p. 3). Another definition similarly highlights its intentionality, as well as its reliance on opinion disguised as fact, on moving beyond the true/false dichotomy, and on 'misinformation by inundation', that is, flooding the public with so much irrelevant information as to obscure truth altogether (Nadakavukaren Schefer 2021). What makes disinformation so pernicious is that it is intentionally crafted and disseminated to maximise political damage. It is carefully curated for the mediums through which it circulates, especially online platforms, where echo chambers and confirmation bias reign supreme and where individuals search for emotive content to confirm and entrench pre-existing positions. Disinformation is especially difficult to fight and prepare against because it also relies on the relational features of the internet: people are not isolated information processors, but rely on their social networks and both produce and distribute large volumes of disruptive content (Bennett and Livingston, p. 6). The problem is one of sheer volume and unwieldiness of distribution, so much so that 'the propagation of misleading content is not a bug, it is a feature' (Bennett and Livingston, p. 7).

The Brexit vote has been amply shown to have fallen victim to such disinformation (Renwick *et al.* 2020, Hansson and Kroeger 2021). As the UK Parliament's Digital, Culture, Media and Sport Committee Report noted in this regard, we have always experienced propaganda and political bias in voting campaigns. However, this has now taken on new forms and 'been hugely magnified by information technology and the ubiquity of social media,' to the point that 'the very fabric of our democracy is threatened' (House of Commons Digital, Culture, Media and Sport Committee 2019, p. 5). The scale and speed at which the Internet functions, its propensity to create echo chambers, reinforce biases, reduce the common ground and plurality of voices, polarise views, and spread hatred and fake news together pose an unprecedented threat to democracy as a whole. This has been compounded by the fact that most people now rely on online sources for information and the sophisticated individual targeting made possible by the big data ecosystem.

Bennett and Livingston propose an additional argument in this context, one which should especially worry the constitutional theorist. They argue that at the heart of this 'disinformation disorder' is a crisis of legitimacy of authoritative institutions:

> In a well-functioning public sphere, institutions anchor public debate in a mix of competing political goals and values, authoritative evidence claims, and norms and processes for communicating and resolving disagreements. Yet those norms of reasoned debate between competing viewpoints have given way to wilful distortion and reckless prevarication that disrupt the basic functioning of democratic public spheres. For every fact that seems key to discussing important issues such as immigration or climate change, opponents are ready with alternative facts that distort perceptions of problems and solutions. Institutional arenas designed to articulate and resolve political differences through reasoned debate based on evidence are disrupted and fail to provide the gatekeeping roles that once kept politics bounded by a more or less shared set of institutional norms and processes. (Bennett and Livingston 2021, p. 4)

In other words, we risk focusing on the symptoms rather than the cause of the problem. To these authors, the latter has to do with the gatekeepers of information in the democratic public sphere – the judiciary, scientists, the media, political parties, an apolitical civil service – having lost their legitimacy and their ability to mediate and vet contested political claims to the public. The enormity of the diagnosis is striking: we are talking about the erosion of the entire liberal democratic edifice. Without 'repairing the basic functioning of democratic institutions', we may well be doomed (Bennett and Livingston 2021, p. 34).

The reason for emphasising the enormity of the challenge is to ring the alarm for constitutional theorists, indeed, constitutionalists more generally. We cannot do analogue constitutional theory in a digital world. With regard to referendums specifically, to previous concerns about their overly aggregative, majoritarian features we must add the danger that they are especially vulnerable to disinformation and fake news. The single-issue nature of the referendum, its very bluntness as a yes/no vote, and the potentially highly charged nature of referendum campaigns make it a uniquely vulnerable instrument in the age of disinformation.

This is not merely an attempt at awareness-raising, however. The conceptual work constitutional theorists do may itself be under more stress than might be immediately apparent. For example, the familiar contours of the debate surrounding the 'will of the people', and whether the referendum is a good mechanism to approximate it, change when opinion-formation itself falls prey to sophisticated online targeting. Another example refers to the rationale for protecting speech and what constitutes protected expression given the rise of anonymous, not easily attributable, and sometimes non-human digital communication that floods electoral events especially. American scholars, for instance, must grapple with how the rise of fake news, disinformation, deep fakes, and other ills of the digital world has challenged the First Amendment doctrine of free speech and admit that existing constitutional categories may no longer be fit for purpose (Sunstein 2020, Napoli 2018). In light of the far-reaching electoral impact such tools have already had, theirs is by no means a purely theoretical endeavour.

Additionally, the safeguards constitutional design has come up with thus far to curtail the excesses and limit the prospects of capture of referendums need updating and rethinking. As we saw during the Brexit vote and since, accountability mechanisms currently in place appear ill-suited for stopping disinformation in real time: the court process is lengthy and occurs after the fact; electoral management bodies often lack the capacity and competence to intervene effectively; and representative institutions may find it too politically costly to attempt to push back against a highly emotive public vote, even in the face of its distortion. The UK Parliamentary Committee report on disinformation rightly noted that legal tools exist and should be used better, including privacy laws, data protection legislation, antitrust and competition law, and electoral law (House of Commons Digital, Culture, Media and Sport Committee 2019, p. 6). It also rightly pointed to the need for comparative learning on legislative tools to address disinformation (House of Commons Digital, Culture, Media and Sport Committee 2019, pp. 12–13). However, much more work is needed on how best to regulate disinformation given the risks to political rights especially. Whatever certainties we thought we had about the regulation of the public sphere and the careful balancing of rights and limitations must be revisited and reconstructed in a digital world rife with disinformation.

The work will not begin at zero, however. Legislatures across the world have reacted to these challenges, trying to protect the integrity of the voting process. Examples of new legislation seeking to defend voting against disinformation include Germany's 2017 Network Enforcement Act, Canada's 2018 Elections Modernization Act, and France's 2018 Law against the Manipulation of

Information, among others. They reflect different immediate aims of the legislator – e.g. the German law requires the removal of fake news from big online platforms under threat of penalty, targeting 'big fish' platforms of more than two million users; the French law has been interpreted by the Conseil Constitutionnel to apply to 'manifestly false' information, thereby restricting its scope of application; whereas the Canadian law sought to expand spending rules to online advertising and limit foreign involvement to prevent undue influence in the national electoral process (see discussions in Baume *et al.* 2021 and Pal 2020). They also reflect national understandings of the constitutional protection of speech. This explains, for instance, the German law requiring removal of online hate speech. All have been subject to criticism on free speech grounds, as well as on efficacy grounds. They have also been criticised for continuing to operate with outdated or unworkable notions, such as speedier removal of misinformation than existing monitoring institutions could reasonably achieve or a tenuous distinction between false and truthful information. To these we can add objections to legislation purporting to tackle fake news that is in fact a veil for censorship and the pursuit of political opponents, as have been levied against Singapore's 2019 Protection from Online Falsehoods and Manipulation Act.

While imperfect, however, such legislative steps demonstrate the acute need for clear and innovative thinking in tackling the disinformation age. Undoubtedly, the task is monumental, not least as it is embedded in broader debates about the transformation of the fourth estate in the digital era, treating social media platforms as broadcasters, ascribing liability for content, and stemming the ever-growing intrusion of 'surveillance capitalism' into our lives (Pal 2020).

CONCLUSIONS

Referendums remain uniquely appealing in constitutional theory and practice for their ability to crystallise public opinion and concentrate collective decision-making on a single issue. The same features that some view as the referendum's defects – its majoritarianism, directness, bluntness etc. – are what makes them appealing to others. Indeed, one implicit observation running through this chapter has been that it is impossible to assess the democratic credentials of referendums in the abstract. They must be evaluated in their respective constitutional setting, with due regard to how they interact with other institutions in the system. The pieces of this puzzle are many and include the numerous possible institutional avenues for triggering a referendum, the actors involved in the referendum's design, campaign and implementation, safeguards and accountability mechanisms, as well as other participatory tools such as mini-publics with which referendums may be interlinked.

A separate point worth noting is that the either/or logic often applied to the study of referendums' relationship to democracy is not the most productive. For the longest time, the referendum was presumed to be the quintessential instrument of direct democracy and as such considered a poor fit with the representative democratic system. More recently, with the deliberative turn in democracy, the referendum again became the archetypal villain, insofar as it was taken to encapsulate the ills of unmediated, purely aggregative, majoritarian voting. I have sought to show, however, that such readings tend unfairly to pit the worst of the referendum against the best of representative or deliberative mechanisms, respectively. Moreover, such zero-sum thinking is unhelpful: many constitutional systems around the world are mixed democracies, neither purely representative, direct, or deliberative. Indeed, some of the most promising avenues of research on the institutional design of referendums revolve around their integration with other democratic tools that can mitigate referendum deficiencies. Examples include integrating ratificatory referendums as part of law- and constitution-making processes and mandating deliberative mini-publics as agenda-setting tools preceding national referendums.

Finally, it bears remembering that the digital age is also an age of disinformation, fake news, and distortion of information, opinion-formation, and voting. The threat is not unique to referendums but manifests itself distinctively in the context of referendum campaigns. These are vulnerable in specific ways to disinformation, be it because of their focus on single issues that are often highly salient, their direct appeal to the voting public, the gaps in their regulatory framework, etc. Ultimately, disinformation distorts the vote to such an extent that it raises serious questions about the democratic legitimacy of the overall decision. Disinformation's power is premised on the breakdown of democratic institutions and erosion of trust in them. The task for the constitutional theorist thus becomes to think through ways to rebuild that trust, reinvigorate the democratic process, and safeguard against future breakdowns. The referendum itself may be revisited and reimagined as part of this task.

RECOMMENDED READING

Albert, R. & Stacey, R. eds. (2022). *The Limits and Legitimacy of Referendums*, Oxford: Oxford University Press.

Baume, S., Boillet, V., & Martenet, V., eds. (2021). *Misinformation in Referenda*, London: Routledge.

Bellamy, R. (2023). Political Constitutionalism and Referendums: The Case of Brexit. *Social & Legal Studies*. 32 (6), 973–995.

Bernhard, L. (2012). *Campaign Strategy in Direct Democracy*, Basingstoke: Palgrave Macmillan.

Carolan, E. (2020). Constitutional Change Outside the Courts: Citizen Deliberation and Constitutional Narrative(s) in Ireland's Abortion Referendum. *Federal Law Review*, 48 (4), 497–510.

Cetra, D., Casanas-Adam, E., & Tarrega, M. (2018). The 2017 Catalan Independence Referendum: A Symposium. *Scottish Affairs*, 27 (1), 126–143.

Hobolt, S. B. (2009). *Europe in Question: Referendums on European Integration*, Oxford: Oxford University Press.

King, J. (2019). The Democratic Case for a Written Constitution. *Current Legal Problems*, 72 (1), 1–36.

LeDuc, L. (2015). Referendums and Deliberative Democracy. *Electoral Studies*, 38, 139–148.

Matsusaka, J. (2020). *Let the People Rule: How Direct Democracy Can Meet the Populist Challenge*, Princeton: Princeton University Press.

Moeckli, D. (2011). Of Minarets and Foreign Criminals: Swiss Direct Democracy and Human Rights. *Human Rights Law Review*, 11 (4), 774–794.

Morel, L. & Qvortrup, M., eds. (2017). *The Routledge Handbook to Referendums and Direct Democracy*, London: Routledge.

Parkinson, J. (2020). The Roles of Referendums in Deliberative Systems. *Representation: Journal of Representative Democracy*, 56 (4), 485–500.

Suteu, S. & Tierney, S. (2018). Squaring the Circle? Bringing Deliberation and Participation Together in Processes of Constitution-Making. In R. Levy et al., eds., *The Cambridge Handbook of Deliberative Constitutionalism*. Cambridge: Cambridge University Press, pp. 282–294.

Swiss Political Science Review (2018) Debate: Do Referendums Enhance or Threaten Democracy? *Swiss Political Science Review*, 24 (3), 291–358.

Tierney, S. (2012). *Constitutional Referendums: The Theory and Practice of Republican Deliberation*, Oxford: Oxford University Press.

47

Citizens' Juries/Minipublics

Cristina Lafont

Constitutionalists typically defend political and legal mechanisms or institutions that (a) provide due process which treats those involved with equal concern and respect, not least by upholding their rights to liberty; and (b) support some publicly defensible notion of the common good, including notions of well-being. Most contemporary constitutionalists think that democracy plays a crucial role in achieving these goals, but they worry that, in practice, democracy often falls perilously short of its full potential. Democracies often fail to be sufficiently representative of all options and interests, minority voices tend not to be adequately heard, citizens can often be swayed by prejudice and ill-informed opinion and, more generally, political decisions are commonly made too quickly without surveying the relevant interests and information in an impartial manner. For a variety of reasons, minipublics are increasingly seen as institutions that could help mitigate such problems and improve democracy in ways that would also further its commitment to constitutionalism. In fact, many scholars and practitioners defend minipublics as being the most apt institutions for directly considering constitutional questions or even for making a constitution itself. This chapter assesses these claims.

Deliberative minipublics – such as citizens' juries, citizens' assemblies, consensus conferences, and Deliberative polls – offer innovative ways for citizens to engage in political deliberation and governance.[1] These institutional innovations provide a space for high quality face-to-face deliberation where randomly selected participants who would otherwise not interact receive balanced information on an issue, are exposed to a variety of relevant social perspectives, and have the opportunity to weigh the reasons and arguments "for and against" specific policies during facilitated group discussions before reaching a considered judgment. Beyond these basic features, different types of minipublics vary in terms of the selection and number

---

[1] For a detailed analysis of the key similarities and differences between these types of minipublics see G. Smith and M. Setälä (2019, pp. 3–5). For more information on citizens' juries see Crosby and Nethercut (2005); on citizens' assemblies see Fournier et al. (2011), and Warren and Pearse (2008); on planning cells see Dienel and Renn (1995); on consensus conferences see Joss (1998); and on Deliberative Polls see Fishkin (2018).

of participants (from 10 to 200), the amount of time spent together (a few days or a series of weekends), and the expected output: after the deliberative experience participants are asked to either issue a recommendation or, as is the case in Deliberative polls, to provide their post-deliberative opinions on the policies in question so that they can be compared to their pre-deliberative opinions. This information can be made available to policy makers, voters, or the general public.

In recent decades, minipublics have proliferated around the world.[2] They have been used to address a wide variety of topics ranging from constitutional and electoral reform to the adoption of a common currency, new technologies, health care reform, the protection of minorities, environmental policies, and so on. Although their political role is still relatively marginal, minipublics have become the focus of interest and study for an ever-growing number of political theorists and practitioners. The empirical evidence from decades of analysis explains the growing interest in these institutions. Because of their careful design, minipublics enable a form of political deliberation among ordinary citizens that is quite unique in terms of both its epistemic quality and its democratic representativeness. Indeed, on both counts the high-quality deliberation that takes place within minipublics stands in stark contrast to the political discourse that predominates in other political institutions and in the public sphere of actual democratic societies. The design features responsible for the most relevant differences can be briefly summarized as follows:

1. The techniques of stratified random sampling help to ensure *inclusion* and *diversity* (especially the inclusion of marginalized social groups in terms of both *presence* and *voice*). This gives minipublics a higher level of representativeness than other political institutions where the presence and voice of powerful social groups tends to predominate. This is particularly the case regarding political deliberation in the public sphere.
2. The random selection of participants from the common citizenry prevents co-option by politicians or capture by organized interest groups. It helps to ensure the political *independence* and *impartiality* of participants and increases the chances that their deliberations are oriented toward the public interest. By randomly generating a heterogeneous group of strangers with no shared social

---

[2] Minipublics have been developed in several waves over the past decades. In the 1970s Ned Crosby developed citizens' juries in the US and simultaneously Peter Dienel developed planning cells in Germany. In the 1980s consensus conferences were pioneered in Denmark and James Fishkin developed Deliberative Polls in the US. In the 2000s citizens' assemblies were launched in British Colombia (2004), Ontario (2006) and the Netherlands (2006) to discuss proposals for electoral reform. They offered a model for subsequent assemblies that have been established with broader mandates such as the recent Irish Citizens' Assembly (2016–18) that issued reports on several topics, some of them constitutional in nature. A more recent development would be institutions that include both randomly selected citizens and other political actors. The best-known examples are the Convention on the Constitution in Ireland (2013–14) and the G1000 in the Netherlands. Due to their "mixed" composition, these institutions fall outside the standard meaning of the term "minipublics."

bonds, who would not otherwise interact, it is possible to avoid negative group dynamics such as polarization and groupthink.
3. The provision of information helps secure balanced briefing materials as well as the inclusion of all relevant social perspectives. The presence of trained moderators facilitates mutual deliberation, helps weigh the pros and cons of different proposals, and prevents collective deliberation from being hijacked. This enables participants to reach considered judgments on the political issues at hand.

Recent, extensive empirical analysis largely confirms the high epistemic and democratic quality of deliberation within minipublics.[3] The evidence shows a clear positive impact on the level of information, satisfaction with the process, and an enhanced interest in civic engagement among participants. This is not to say that all findings are positive. Some design features of minipublics raise concerns which are the object of heated debates (e.g., regarding the degree of self-selection involved, the optimal length and outputs, etc.). What is not contested, however, is that minipublics enable a form of inclusive deliberation that far surpasses the epistemic and democratic quality of political discourse that pervades other political institutions – be it within the legislature, judiciary or civil society organizations. Indeed, the empirical evidence clearly indicates that when citizens are given the time, resources and support to become informed and deliberate about policy issues, they can engage with complex policy issues and reach considered judgments. Given these impressive findings, many scholars and practitioners enthusiastically recommend the proliferation of minipublics as a key institutional tool for overcoming current democratic deficits. For many of them, minipublics have become their exclusive focus and the paradigm for realizing deliberative democracy. Yet, the proper political role of minipublics remains contested. Minipublics could be formally institutionalized in a variety of ways and for a variety of purposes. Proposals abound and are continuously added to the discussion. However, given their novelty, it is far from clear that all potential uses of minipublics would equally promote the democratic aims that are of concern to constitutionalists. Some uses could actually increase rather than decrease current democratic deficits. Let's see why.

I PROPOSALS FOR POLITICAL USES OF MINIPUBLICS

There are many ways that minipublics could be embedded in the political process. Minipublics could be *endowed with special* powers and functions within the overall political system, they could *supplement* some existing institutions by sharing their powers and functions, or they could *replace* institutions by simply taking over their powers and functions. Regardless of which specific option one favors, it is clear that

---

[3] See e.g., Gerber et al. (2018); Fishkin (2018); Esterling et al. (2021).

in order to make an impact, minipublics would need to have some form of *effective power* to influence the political process. Indeed, democratic theorists and practitioners who are involved with minipublics often complain about their relative lack of impact. So far, the record shows that the recommendations of minipublics often fail to be taken up by the relevant political actors (government officials, administrators or voters) and that they are ultimately not implemented. This is not to say that an increase of minipublics' power to influence the political process would be without problems. Any significant increase in minipublics' political power is likely to generate "powerful incentives for interest groups and partisan elites to try to manipulate deliberative forums" (Neblo 2015, p. 181). However, this is a general worry that arises for any institution with some significant level of political power. If minipublics became politically influential this problem would arise regardless of the specific way in which they were embedded in the political process. Needless to say, the more political power that is conferred upon minipublics the more acute this problem is likely to become (see Landa and Pevnik 2021).

Proposals for institutionalizing minipublics can be situated on a spectrum. On the weakest side of the spectrum, minipublics can be convened for the purposes of mere consultation about policy issues that have already been determined and without conferring any agenda-setting capacity or decision-making authority upon them. This minimal political role reflects most current practice where, at most, minipublics have the power of influencing political actors such as legislatures or administrative agencies through non-mandatory, one-off processes in which they are convened to discuss some preselected policy issues. Since minipublics are not permanent institutions and most citizens are unfamiliar with them they can easily be ignored. With very few exceptions, their political impact so far has been fairly marginal. By contrast, on the other side of the spectrum we find proposals that envision much more ambitious political roles for minipublics. These proposals would confer various powers and authorities upon minipublics such as the power of legislative review (e.g., by establishing assemblies of randomly selected citizens which would complement or partially replace existing legislative assemblies of elected representatives), the power of constitutional review (e.g., by replacing or complementing Constitutional Courts with constitutional juries), or the power of constitutional amendment (e.g., by replacing or complementing constitutional assemblies of elected representatives with minipublics).[4]

Recent debates on the proper political role of minipublics have focused on the question of whether it would be democratically legitimate to confer decision-making authority upon minipublics by following proposals that lie on the strongest side of

---

[4] For some examples, see the contributions to "Legislature by Lot: Transformative Designs for Deliberative Governance," special issue, *Politics & Society* 46, no. 3 (2018): 299–451, esp. Gastil and Wright, "Legislature by Lot"; also Ghosh (2010) and (2018); Guerrero (2014); Landemore (2020); Leib (2004); O'Leary (2006); Spector (2009); Van Reybrouck (2016); Zurn (2011).

the spectrum. This issue is contested. Many deliberative democrats would hesitate to go as far as to hand over actual political power (e.g., of legislation or constitutional interpretation) to minipublics. However, it is important to note that legitimacy concerns arise not only with respect to proposals that would empower minipublics to make binding political decisions. Proposals that favor institutionalizing minipublics merely for the purposes of public consultation, which are much more popular among deliberative democrats, can also give rise to legitimacy concerns. Indeed, within debates on whether and how the political uses of minipublics can be democratically legitimate the central question is not simply about *how much power* their participants ought to exercise but rather, above all, *the capacity* in which they are supposed to exercise that power. The risk is that, in contrast to other political actors, minipublics' participants can easily be taken as proxies for the citizenry as a whole.

Minipublics are special in comparison to other political institutions in that they are composed of ordinary citizens who are supposed to exclusively act in that capacity, that is, as members of the citizenry itself. The minipublics' composition is supposed to reflect or descriptively represent the composition of the citizenry as a whole but, at the same time, their members have neither been selected by the citizenry nor are they required to act as political representatives of the individuals or groups that they represent in a descriptive sense. There is no sense in which female participants are supposed to defend the views of women or Californians the views of other Californians. They are and remain members of the citizenry who, as such, represent only themselves. They participate as individual citizens with total freedom to express whichever views and opinions they happen to have and to change them in whichever way they see fit. But, for that very same reason, they are in no way accountable to citizens who are outside of the minipublic. This is problematic in light of potential differences of opinion between participants and non-participants. The purpose of having a process of public consultation is for officials to be able to find out the opinion and will of the citizenry regarding certain policy decisions. But if minipublics' participants and non-participating citizens disagree about the decisions at hand, then who is supposed to speak in the name of the citizenry? Whose views ought to count as the views of "the public" that officials are supposed to consult? John Parkinson illustrates the problem with a real example of a citizens' jury convened to consider hospital restructuring in Leicester, England. In that case, decision-makers were confronted with the results of a citizens' jury's deliberation recommending one course of action, and a petition of 150,000 signatories demanding another (Parkinson, 2006, p. 33). The citizenry neither elected the minipublics' participants nor had any way of holding them accountable. As such, the normative basis upon which officials should take the judgments of the minipublics' participants to have more recommending force than the judgments of the citizenry is unclear. It is true that, according to deliberative democrats, only post-deliberative, considered judgments, and not just raw preferences and opinions, provide the legitimate basis for justifying political decisions to all those who are bound by them.

However, unless and until the minipublics' considered judgments *become* the considered judgments of the actual people who will be bound by the decisions in question they can't accrue any legitimacy under that criterion. Justifying political decisions only to members of the random sample won't do.

If one focuses on this issue it is possible to see that there are two fundamentally different ways of thinking about the purpose of institutionalizing minipublics but only one of them would serve genuinely democratic aims.

II TWO PATHS FORWARD: EMPOWERING MINIPUBLICS OR USING MINIPUBLICS TO EMPOWER THE CITIZENRY?

Proposals that institutionalize minipublics are often justified as a way of reaching democratic aims. Institutionalized minipublics are seen as vehicles for empowering the citizenry in various ways: from increasing the venues of political participation available to citizens to improving the responsiveness of the political process to citizens' needs, interests, and policy objectives, to enhancing citizens' democratic control of political institutions, and so forth. Involving the citizenry in the political process is essential to ensure that citizens can identify with the laws and policies to which they are subject so that they can come to endorse them as their own, as the democratic ideal of self-government requires. Providing citizens with genuine opportunities to influence political decisions is supposed to serve the democratic aim of preventing a *disconnect* or misalignment between citizens' interests, reasons, and ideas and the actual laws and policies that they must obey. From this perspective, the appropriate standard for evaluating proposals for democratic improvement is whether they will prevent or minimize such a disconnect or whether they may risk increasing it.

However, if we examine proposals for institutionalizing minipublics with this standard in mind, it becomes clear that not all of them would have the democratizing effects that their defenders often suggest. Clearly, any proposals that confer decision-making authority directly upon minipublics while also expecting the citizenry to blindly defer to its recommendations would, over the long-term, generate a disconnect between the interests and ideas of the citizenry and the laws and policies that they must obey. As can be seen from many examples of actual minipublics, those who participate often drastically change their views on the issues at hand as a consequence of having access to proper information and high-quality deliberation. However, since the rest of the citizenry has not had a similar opportunity, it seems reasonable to expect that over time the cumulative effect of making political decisions that are based on the judgments of minipublics' instead of the actual judgments of the citizenry would be that the latter would cease to identify with the laws and policies to which they are subject and won't be able to endorse them as their own. Note that this difficulty is not avoided by proposals that limit the role of minipublics to public consultation. From a democratic point of view, these proposals face a dilemma. If, after the consultation process, the actors with decision-making authority (e.g., politicians, administrators, and voters) are expected to follow their own judgment, instead of the minipublics' recommendations, then organizing minipublics would seem to lack impact and purpose, that is, consulting them will be at best redundant (when there is agreement) and at worst useless (when there is disagreement). By contrast, if these actors are expected to blindly follow the recommendations of the minipublics, instead of following their own judgments, then an alienating disconnect between the citizenry's own views and the political decisions to which they are subject will eventually result. The long-term effect of making political decisions based on the considered judgments of minipublics' participants *instead of the actual judgments of the citizenry* is that the latter would have difficulty seeing themselves as participants in a democratic project of self-government. Institutionalizing minipublics in the hope that they would do the thinking and deciding for the rest of the citizenry would not be a way of increasing the democratic control of the latter over the political process. The problem with this way of thinking about the potential uses of minipublics is that it focuses on increasing the involvement and influence of *a few randomly selected citizens* in the political process, while non-participants – the citizenry as a whole – are simply ignored. However, if minipublics are to have any democratizing effect, then the focus needs to be on ways that we can use minipublics to improve the involvement and influence of *the citizenry as a whole* in the political process.

To do so, minipublics would need to serve two important democratic functions: first, they could help *improve* the quality of public deliberation such that the citizenry can also reach a considered opinion on the important political decisions they are bound to obey and, second, they could help make the political system more *responsive* to considered public opinion on the political decisions at hand.[5] The democratic potential of using minipublics for political purposes stands or falls with the possibility of scaling up the impact of minipublics' deliberation to deliberation in the wider public sphere.[6]

Minipublics' Potential Contribution to the Generation of Considered Public Opinion

At this particular historical juncture, there are plenty of reasons to be worried about the increasing deterioration of political deliberation in the public sphere. In addition to long-standing threats such as the excessive influence of money in political discourse, the potential for manipulation by powerful social groups and the exclusion of marginalized voices from public discourse, recent technological innovations such as social media and big data collection are generating new types of threats – and

---

[5] In what follows I draw on Chapter 5 of Lafont (2020).
[6] See Niemeyer (2014).

doing so at a faster rate than society can cope with. The business model behind social media has led to the creation of "filter bubbles" that preselect the information going to consumers according to their preferences. As a consequence, they almost never receive information, news, or opinions that they do not already agree with. As we are currently witnessing, these features of social media not only increase group isolation and polarization but also facilitate the spread of fake news and the microtargeted manipulation of voters. If we add to these threatening developments the decline of traditional news outlets that operate under norms of impartiality, accuracy, accountability, and so on, it is no longer clear how or even whether citizens will be able to keep sufficiently politically informed so as to sustain a meaningful shared debate with their fellow citizens, even on the most fundamental political problems that they face. At this historical moment, the danger that a shared sense of community among the citizenry simply vanishes seems alarmingly real.[7]

In that context, it is not surprising that deliberative democrats who are familiar with the workings of minipublics are enthusiastic about the quality of political deliberation that they enable participants to engage in. Indeed, the deliberative conditions available to minipublics' participants are the exact opposite of those that prevail in most social venues that are currently available to citizens in all relevant dimensions (e.g., inclusion, diversity, access to reliable and balanced information, independence, impartiality, orientation toward the public interest). Thus, it does not seem far-fetched to imagine that as more and more citizens become familiar with the workings of minipublics they would become as enthusiastic about them as deliberative democrats already are, and for the same reasons. Indeed, if deliberative minipublics were institutionalized for a variety of purposes and their uses spread to the local, regional, national, and even the transnational levels, then they could become an extremely valuable resource to the citizenry precisely at a time when reliable sources of inclusive, well-informed, impartial political deliberation are becoming harder and harder to come by. Now, this way of looking at the democratic potential of minipublics involves an important change in perspective. Instead of thinking of microdeliberation within minipublics as an *alternative* to macrodeliberation in the public sphere we should think of it as a *resource* for macrodeliberation. How could minipublics help improve the quality of deliberation in the public sphere?

To begin with, minipublics could serve some important functions that are not all that different from those that traditional media outlets have fulfilled. As with the latter, their contribution to the citizenry would not be that they do the thinking or make the decisions for them. Rather, their contribution would simply be to make the most relevant arguments for and against the political decisions available to them. Minipublics could do so by filtering out irrelevant or patently manipulative considerations while highlighting the key information, potential trade-offs, and long-term consequences of the available alternatives as evaluated from the various

[7] I analyze this issue at length in Lafont (2023).

political perspectives that resonate with the citizenry of a political community at a given time. Minipublics are particularly well suited to serve this function. Precisely because their participants are a mirror of the people as a whole, the reasons and considerations that lead them to form their considered judgments are likely to be those that resonate with the rest of the citizenry (Fishkin 2018, p. 72). Moreover, by highlighting the considerations that are most relevant in reaching a considered judgment on the political issue at hand, minipublics would not only function to reduce the costs of acquiring that type of information but they could also serve an emancipatory function as well. As Simon Niemeyer explains it, minipublics can provide citizens with the necessary resources to sort out the "wheat from the chaff," that is, the information behind claims made in sincerity and good faith as opposed to the misinformation conveyed by distorted claims that are strategically deployed to subvert (rather than inform), and which are therefore unsustainable in the face of deliberative scrutiny. By testing the available arguments and providing their considered judgments to their fellow citizens, minipublics could play a constructive role in building proper public discourses.

I cannot provide an exhaustive account of all the possible ways in which minipublics could help generate considered public opinion on important political issues if their use were generalized and citizens became familiar with their functioning. The point of mentioning some of these important functions is only to counteract the widespread assumption that minipublics could only help improve political deliberation by having their participants do the thinking for the rest of the citizenry. Here, it is important to keep in mind that minipublics' participants are as diverse as the citizenry itself and are therefore as likely to disagree in their considered opinions on contested political issues as the rest of the citizenry is. For this reason, non-participants should not be expected, let alone required, to blindly follow the recommendations of the minipublics' majority. However, this does not make minipublics' recommendations useless. To the contrary, they can provide crucial information to the citizenry. In contrast to regular polls citizens can trust that, within minipublics such as deliberative polls, the reasoning given by both the majority and the minority of participants reflects the considered judgments of each and that it does not reflect misinformation or manipulation by powerful interest groups. Knowing the interests, values, and lines of reasoning that actually resonate with our fellow citizens for contentious political issues is essential even (or, perhaps, especially) in cases where we disagree with them. For knowing the actual sources of contention and disagreement on specific political issues (as opposed to the many manipulative claims and pseudo-arguments that circulate in the public sphere but cannot withstand deliberative scrutiny) would enable us to figure out the kind of information, evidence, arguments, or counterarguments that we would need to provide in order to move the public debate on these political issues forward. Thus, by sorting out the "wheat from the chaff" minipublics would provide extremely valuable information to both sides of ongoing political debates without having to do the thinking for them.

Now, in order to assess the full democratic potential of institutionalizing minipublics we need to pay attention to their potential contributions not only to ongoing political debates in the public sphere, but also to political decision-making. In the latter context, however, the difference between the opinion of the majority and the minority becomes essential. In democratic societies, for any political issue that can be legitimately decided by majority rule the decisional majority's opinion determines the policies to which all citizens are subject. Since majority opinion and actual policies are supposed to be aligned, in political struggles that shape what counts as majority opinion, the stakes could not be higher. It is in the context of this struggle that the information provided by minipublics acquires additional political significance. The alignment or misalignment between majority opinion, public policies, and minipublics' recommendations offers an interesting way of organizing the potential political uses of the latter so that their benefits or drawbacks can be better assessed. Following this idea (and for simplicity's sake), I distinguish the following four general categories under which the many potential uses of minipublics can be subsumed: empowered, contestatory, vigilant, and anticipatory uses of minipublics. My brief analysis, however, does not aim to cover the innumerable applications of minipublics currently under discussion within the vast empirical literature on applied deliberative democracy or to answer empirical questions about institutional design for each of these types of minipublics. I analyze some possible political uses of minipublics in order to identify the specific democratic values that could be served in each case, while offering a few examples of how the relevant political actors could best engage them in each case. This analysis also shows how minipublics could not only help generate considered public opinion but, even more importantly, how they could help empower the citizenry to make the political system more responsive to considered public opinion. The analysis does not assume that citizens would need to know all the details about the workings of different types of minipublics, but it does assume that citizens would have become sufficiently familiar with their key features (e.g., inclusion, diversity, access to reliable and balanced information, independence, impartiality, and orientation towards the public interest).

Empowered Uses of Minipublics

As mentioned above, proposals in favor of empowering minipublics to make binding political decisions on legislation, constitutional interpretation, or constitutional amendment abound. Critics of such proposals argue that empowering minipublics to do the thinking and deciding for the citizenry would increase rather than decrease democratic deficits. It would make it harder and harder for non-participating citizens to identify with the political decisions to which they are subject and come to endorse them as their own. However, if minipublics have no decisional power at all, then they can hardly be expected to make an impact. In this context is important to keep in mind that what matters from the point of view of democratic legitimacy is not so much whether or not minipublics are empowered to make some political decisions but, above all, *the specific way in which they are embedded in the political process.*

From a democratic perspective, it makes all the difference in the world whether minipublics are designed as ways to *empower* the citizenry or as ways to *bypass* the citizenry and connect directly (and exclusively) with the political system. Any institution that serves a function will exercise some decisional power. If the institution in question is designed to serve participatory aims then the fact that it itself exercises some decisional power is not a problem *per se*. With this idea in mind, let's focus on some uses of minipublics that could serve genuinely participatory aims.

Contestatory Uses of Minipublics

One reason to embed minipublics in the political process is the expectation that the majority opinion reached by the minipublic after deliberation will *differ* from the majority opinion of the population on the political issue at hand. Discussions of this type of mismatch tend to focus on the difference in the deliberative *quality* of the outcome. However, in my view, the fact that the difference concerns the *majority opinion* has even greater significance. To the extent that the political decisions in question are supposed to be made by majority rule, showing that considered majority opinion differs from current majority opinion gives minorities a powerful tool to challenge consolidated majorities *in their own terrain*, so to speak. It is one thing for a minority to simply claim that they are right and that the majority is wrong. It is quite another to provide some independent evidence indicating that the majority of a representative sample of the population came to endorse their view after having been properly informed. The fact that the minority view became a majority view under these circumstances can be a powerful political tool. In the context of a political struggle on the contested political issue in question, the independent evidence provided by minipublics could help minorities challenge consolidated majorities and hold them to account.

As mentioned above, a distinctive and valuable feature of minipublics is the better ability to secure effective inclusion of marginalized voices and social perspectives. In virtue of achieving higher statistical representativeness minipublics are able to offer a mirror of the people that is unmatched by any other available mirror that allows the citizenry to see itself. The mirrors offered by other institutions in the political system (from the judiciary to the legislature, the media, the public sphere, etc.) tend to be highly exclusionary and therefore reflect back a quite distorted image of 'the people.' Even in democratic societies it is hard to ensure effective inclusion in public political debate or even voting, given the factual disenfranchisement of marginalized groups and the difficulties of providing a proper hearing to their interests and views. Even if new venues for citizen participation are created, self-selection, which tends to favor the wealthy and educated, can worsen rather than improve the underrepresentation of the powerless and marginalized. Thus, even democratic political systems lack venues for finding out what would happen if the general public or the powerful groups that define the majority culture could actually listen to the needs, views, and arguments of minorities and marginalized groups.

Assuming the general public is aware of the unique features of the venue that minipublics provide, minipublics could be used by organized social groups in their political struggles to contest the views of consolidated majorities on specific political issues. The more the minipublics' opinions differ from actual majority opinion the more this should signal to the public the need to examine the available information and the relevant perspectives so as to scrutinize their soundness and their potential need for revision. This could lead to more nuanced positions on polarizing issues or it could prompt a general reconsideration of popular but unjust views held by consolidated majorities. However, this is not to suggest that the public should take the evidence provided by the minipublics' opinions as decisive or authoritative. The function of minipublics should not be to shut down political debate but, to the contrary, reignite and facilitate the *ongoing* public debate on contested political issues. Minipublics can enrich those wider debates by enhancing the voices of silenced or marginalized groups and perspectives in the public sphere. Precisely because the recommendations of the minipublic *differ* from actual public opinion, the distinction signals the need to *transform* public opinion accordingly. This means that political actors must address the minipublics' recommendations to *both officials and the public* with the aim of shaping ongoing political debate in the public sphere.

Minipublics could be inserted in the political process not only for the purposes of political but also legal contestation. Out of the many possibilities here I shall simply mention two. Civil society groups could include the recommendations of minipublics when filing *amicus curia briefs* to the Supreme Court as independent evidence for challenging the assumption that raw public opinion actually reflects views "deeply rooted in the country's history and traditions." The evidence in question should not be taken as authoritatively settling the issue. Still, the special features of minipublics (their independence, impartiality, representativeness, etc.) confer on their recommendations a status of independent evidence that no other evidence that parties may provide from like-minded sources (groups, organizations, etc.) can match. If minipublics are working as intended, outside parties can do nothing to influence the outcome.

Stronger forms of institutionalization in the context of constitutional review could also be beneficial. For example, it could become standard practice that in cases involving suspect classifications of groups with a history of discrimination, which trigger a higher level of scrutiny, some type of minipublic is routinely convened to provide the Supreme Court with additional information on what considered majority opinion of the country on the policy issues in question at a given time may be. Again, there is no need to claim that this information should be authoritative about the right way to interpret constitutional rights. The considered opinion of the majority may still be unduly hostile toward protecting the rights of unpopular minorities. But the information may nonetheless be valuable as an indication of how far the considered judgment of the majority is moving in a particular direction. Precisely because minipublics would not have decisional status, the political contestation that is likely to surround the interpretation of their opinions by different political groups would not be detrimental, especially if it manages to spark a broader debate in the public sphere as well – which important Supreme Court cases tend to do. The level of empowerment that minipublics have in this context could be increased. For example, the Supreme Court could be required to take up their recommendations in the legal reasoning justifying its decisions and to offer an explicit, reasoned justification whenever it rules against them. I mention this intermediate possibility not as a proposal I necessarily endorse, but simply as an illustration of the fact that political empowerment comes in degrees. As such, for any possible use of minipublics the level of empowerment can range from the weakest option of conferring a merely non-binding and advisory role upon them to the strongest possible option of conferring the binding power to make final decisions – decisions unchecked by the citizenry or by any other political institution. Opposing the strongest form of empowerment because it bypasses the citizenry does not necessarily entail endorsing the weakest form as the only legitimate option.

Vigilant Uses of Minipublics

The analysis of contestatory uses of minipublics was based on cases where the minipublics' recommendations *differ* from the actual majority opinion on some political issue. The driving idea was that the more minipublics' recommendations differ from actual public opinion the more this should signal to the public the need to *scrutinize public opinion*, that is, to reexamine the available information and reconsider the soundness of the views and arguments supported by the majority culture on the issue in question. But perhaps even more significant are cases when the minipublic's recommendations coincide with the majority opinion but *differ* from existing policy. This mismatch should signal to the public the need to *scrutinize the political system*. The more minipublics' recommendations are aligned with public opinion but differ from the actually enacted policies the more it signals to the public that the political system is not properly responsive to their views, interests, and policy objectives. The evidence provided by minipublics could draw additional support from the general public to social and political groups mobilized against whichever forces are impeding the proper flow of influence between the process of opinion and will formation in which citizens participate and the enacted policies. By enhancing the responsiveness of the political system to the interests, views and policy objectives of the citizenry, such critical or vigilant uses of minipublics would serve the important political function of enhancing *democratic control*. Whereas the contestatory uses would strengthen *political equality* in the *horizontal* dimension (i.e., between socially powerful citizens and less powerful or marginalized citizens), the vigilant uses of minipublics would strengthen *political equality* in the *vertical* dimension (i.e., between ordinary citizens and political officials).

Minipublics could also be employed to enhance the agenda-setting power of ordinary citizens by giving them more effective influence in the selection of policy objectives to which the political system must respond. Citizens could be regularly polled to rank important political issues that need to be tackled but which have not yet been addressed and minipublics could then be convened to make recommendations concerning top-ranked issues. This process would provide public visibility to the issues in question. This would be particularly helpful concerning political issues that elected officials may see as intractable or not worth confronting. Because officials have little incentive to tackle such issues they are therefore likely to remain forever unresolved – even if the overwhelming majority of citizens agree on what the right political solution would be. Think of the policy proposals for enforcing background checks on gun sales in the US, which are supported by 85% of the population, but cannot make it through the legislature.

Situations of political gridlock or the capture of political institutions by powerful interest groups provide one of the key motivations behind proposals to confer decisional status on minipublics, so that they can achieve what the legislature (perhaps even the judiciary) is demonstrably unable to do with respect to some political issues. As Leib argues in the context of his proposal to create a popular branch of government modeled on minipublics, empowered minipublics could make an essential contribution in situations when citizens are frustrated by the legislature's unwillingness to take action or when legislatures find themselves unable to reach a reasonable compromise. Minipublics without decisional status would seem to make no contribution at all. If the citizenry already overwhelmingly endorses some political solution already, organizing a minipublic is likely only to reinforce the opinion the citizenry already holds, and thus would seem to fulfill no function.

However, the fact that the minipublic offers a *considered* majority opinion can be extremely powerful for the citizenry. It can effectively counteract arguments to the effect that the majority's support for some popular policy is due to the citizenry's lack of information or familiarity with the complexity of the problems involved; or that it is due to irresponsible wishful thinking that fails to take the potential consequences, legal constraints, or any other relevant dimensions into account that only experts (but not ordinary citizens) can supposedly fully grasp. Popularity for self-defeating policy objectives is not unheard of, as when citizens favor both expanding public services and lowering taxes at the same time. When this is the case, following the political will of the majority could be extremely harmful. In such public political debates, the contribution of a minipublic could be invaluable. It would force the political system to provide the needed information so that participants in the minipublic could engage in an independent examination of the soundness of the arguments in question. Whatever the minipublics' conclusions may be, the public availability of these arguments would be a great improvement over the status quo. Indeed, for ordinary citizens it would be a win-win situation. If the arguments were right, they would have independent evidence that might lead them to change their political opinions accordingly instead of having to blindly trust the bare assertions of potentially self-interested parties. If the arguments were wrong, this would strengthen the ability of ordinary citizens to pressure the relevant political actors into action by removing their demonstrably unsupported excuses for inaction.

Anticipatory Uses of Minipublics

So far, I have considered two different forms of misalignment between majority opinion, public policies, and minipublics' opinions. But, from a democratic perspective, another form of misalignment can be even more worrisome. These are situations when the public has no opinion at all about the political issues at hand. This type of *disconnect* does not have to be problematic. For low stakes issues that are technical in nature or serve merely an administrative purpose, there may be no need at all for citizens to even form an opinion on the policies in question. But it is worrisome when the public does not know anything about policies or legal developments that can negatively impact their well-being or their fundamental rights.

Such public ignorance can have various roots. The policies in question may concern technological innovations with *unpredictable consequences* so the public does not know what may be at stake. Think of new gene editing technologies such as clustered regularly interspaced short palindromic repeats (CRISPR), which may permanently alter the human genome. Or the public may not know because the political decisions in question are *migrating beyond national borders*. International trade agreements are a paradigmatic example. Although they can have a tremendous impact on the domestic economy of a country and its ability to protect the fundamental rights of its citizens, they are negotiated beyond national borders, often by the executive branch of government, without strong oversight by the legislature, under the unilateral influence of powerful lobbies, and surrounded by secrecy. In the absence of public political debate and proper media coverage most citizens do not even know that they should know about the political issues in question, given what is at stake. Disguised as remote foreign relations matters, transnational agreements are not perceived by the citizenry as having domestic policy implications that may have severely harmful consequences but which will be much harder to reverse, given the number of countries involved. Transnational negotiations lack the *visibility* in the domestic public sphere needed to generate a political debate in which citizens could either endorse or reject such policies.

Under current conditions of globalization, embedding minipublics in transnational political processes could have, in my opinion, the highest democratizing impact. From a participatory perspective, the function of minipublics would not be to directly *shape* the policies in question but to instead enhance the *visibility* of what is at stake so as to enable public debate among citizens. Their primary role would not be to recommend some policies over others, but rather to acquire sufficient information so as to be able to *identify*, among the various policies under consideration, those whose potential impact on citizens' well-being, fundamental rights, and interests are so high that the public needs to know about them in order to collectively determine in public debate which priorities, interests and values should guide the political decisions in question. By *anticipating* what citizens would think if they knew more about what is at stake in political decisions that, for a variety of reasons, fall under the radar of the public sphere, and by providing public *visibility* to those decisions where the stakes are so high that the citizenry should not remain ignorant, minipublics would fulfill the crucial political function of enhancing democratic control. Instead of becoming another shortcut for bypassing the citizenry, minipublics could be deployed against many of the existing shortcuts in order to force the political system to take the long road of properly involving the citizenry.

CONSTITUTIONAL MINIPUBLICS?

As already mentioned, proposals for embedding minipublics in the political process are not limited to ordinary policy decisions but are also often extended to processes of constitutional review and constitutional amendment.[8] Although there is an increasing number of proposals under discussion, so far very few minipublics have addressed constitutional questions. Prominent examples are the Citizens' Assemblies for electoral reform organized in British Columbia in 2008 and in Ontario in 2016, the Irish Constitutional Convention organized in 2013, and the Icelandic Constitutional Assembly in 2011. In terms of formal institutionalization, Mongolia offers a pioneering example. In 2017, it became the first country to pass a law requiring the use of deliberative polls in advance of all constitutional amendments. Although constitutional deliberation has distinctive features that need to be considered when evaluating the pros and cons of potential uses of minipublics for constitutional purposes, in the constitutional context the question of whether such uses would enhance or undermine democratic aims is as fundamental, if not more, than it is with regard to ordinary policy decisions.

Proposals for embedding minipublics in processes of constitutional review or constitutional amendment are typically defended on democratic grounds. The suggestion is that letting ordinary citizens participate in such processes is a net democratic gain, especially if one compares it with the alternative of conferring the power to make such fundamental political decisions upon other political actors such as

---

[8] See e.g. Spector (2009); Ghosh (2010); Zurn (2011). For an interesting discussion of pros and cons of constitutional minipublics, see Elstub and Pomatto (2018).

judges, lawyers, and political elites. However, framing the issue in this way is quite misleading. For unless embedding minipublics in the constitutional process helps to ensure that the citizenry as a whole can identify with the constitution to which they are subject and endorse it as their own, then the democratic quality of the process would not actually improve. Making constitutional decisions on the basis of the considered judgments of the few – be it Supreme Court judges, minipublics' participants, or political elites – instead of the actual judgments of the citizenry would not enhance the democratic quality of those decisions. In order to serve genuinely democratic aims, proposals for using minipublics within processes of constitutional review and/or amendment need to identify institutional ways of securing a strong feedback loop between deliberation within constitutional minipublics and deliberation in the wider public sphere throughout the process. As with any other political uses of minipublics, only if the desirable qualities of minipublic deliberation can positively impact and improve the quality of deliberative process of opinion and will-formation in which the citizenry participates would the institutionalization of minipublics contribute to enhance the democratic legitimacy of constitution-making processes. This is one of the most important challenges facing the design and implementation of minipublics for political uses.

RECOMMENDED READING

Crosby, N. & Nethercut, D. (2005). Citizen Juries: Creating a Trustworthy Voice of the People. In J. Gastil, and P. Levine, eds., *The Deliberative Democracy Handbook*. San Francisco: Jossey-Bass, pp. 111–119.

Dienel, P. C. & Ortwin R. (1995). Planning Cells: A Gate to "Fractal Mediation." In O. Renn, T. Webler, and P. Wiedeman, eds. *Fairness and Competence in Citizen Participation: Evaluating Models for Environmental Discourse*. Dordrecht: Kluwer Academic, pp. 117–140.

Elstub, S. & Escobar, O., eds., (2019). *Handbook of Democratic Innovation and Governance*, Cheltenham: Edward Elgar.

Fishkin, J. (2019). *Democracy when the People are Thinking*, Oxford: Oxford University Press.

Fournier, P., van der Kolk, H., & Carty, R. K. (2011). *When Citizens Decide: Lessons from Citizen Assemblies on Electoral Reform*, Oxford: Oxford University Press.

Gastil, J. & Wright, E. O. (2018). Legislature by Lot: Envisioning Sortition within a Bicameral System. *Politics & Society*, 46 (3), 303–330.

Ghosh, E. (2010). Deliberative Democracy and the Countermajoritarian Difficulty: Considering Constitutional Juries. *Oxford Journal of Legal Studies* 30 (2), 327–359.

Goodin, R. E. & Dryzek, J. S. (2006). Deliberative Impacts: The Macro-Political Uptake of Mini-Publics. *Politics & Society*, 34 (2), 219–244.

Grönlund, K., Bächtiger, A. & Setälä, M., eds. (2014). *Deliberative Mini-publics: Practices and Prospects*, Colchester: ECPR Press.

Lafont, C. (2020). *Democracy without Shortcuts. A Participatory Conception of Deliberative Democracy*, Oxford: Oxford University Press.

Landemore, H. (2013). *Democratic Reason: Politics, Collective Intelligence, and the Rule of the Many*, Princeton, NJ: Princeton University Press.

Leib, E. J. (2004). *Deliberative Democracy in America: A Proposal for a Popular Branch of Government*, University Park: Pennsylvania State University Press.

MacKenzie, M. K. & Warren, M. E. (2012). Two Trust-Based Uses of Minipublics in Democratic Systems. In J. Parkinson, and J. Mansbridge, eds., *Deliberative Systems: Deliberative Democracy at the Large Scale*. New York: Cambridge University Press, pp. 95–124.

Niemeyer, S. (2014). Scaling Up Deliberation to Mass Publics: Harnessing Mini-Publics in a Deliberative System. In K. Grönlund, A. Bächtiger, and M. Setälä, eds., *Deliberative Mini-Publics: Involving Citizens in the Democratic Process*. Colchester: ECPR Press, pp. 177–201.

Smith, G. & Setälä, M. (2019). Mini-Publics and Deliberative Democracy. In A. Bächtiger, J. S. Dryzek, J. Mansbridge, and M. Warren, eds., *The Oxford Handbook of Deliberative Democracy*. Oxford: Oxford University Press, pp. 300–314.

Spector, H. (2009). The Right to a Constitutional Jury. *Legisprudence*, 3 (1), 111–123.

Zurn, C. (2011). Judicial Review, Constitutional Juries and Civic Constitutional Fora: Rights, Democracy and Law. *Theoria*, 58 (2), 63–94.

PART III D

The Legal System

48

Constitutional Courts and Supreme Courts

Christine Landfried[*]

Constitutional and supreme courts having the power to declare parliamentary laws and acts of public authority unconstitutional, can be found all over the world. Out of 193 states, 164 have constitutional adjudication, including 76 states with specialized constitutional courts (v. Bogdandy, Huber, Grabenwarter 2020, p. 2). These impressive figures should not obscure the fact that the rule of law is increasingly in danger in fragile democracies (Issacharoff 2015). While in the second half of the twentieth century more and more authoritarian countries were transformed into democracies based on constitutions and constitutional review, the situation has changed since the beginning of the twenty-first century. Populist political parties are gaining influence in democracies and, once populists win majorities in parliaments, constitutional review gets under attack. In Poland it took fifteen months from October 2015 until December 2016 to destroy the independence of the constitutional court (Garlicki 2019, pp. 145 et seq.). These developments remind us not "to take the rule of law for granted" (Baer 2018, p. 336).

In such a situation, it does make sense to analyze the pros and cons of constitutional review. Two practices have been developed: the diffuse review by the judiciary with supreme courts as the final appellate body in common law countries, often called the American model, and the concentrated review by constitutional courts outside the ordinary judiciary in civil law countries, often called the European model. The tendency toward a convergence of diffuse and concentrated constitutional review "should not obfuscate differences that have so far persisted rather unabridged" (Lübbe-Wolff 2020b, p. 162). In this chapter the contending institutional frameworks will be compared. It remains to be seen, whether this comparison allows us to judge which practice performs any better in fulfilling the function of constitutional review. But what is the role of constitutional review in a democracy?

It is my hypothesis that constitutional review can be a potential for democratic governance, provided that there is a difference between judicial and political decision-making (Landfried 2019, pp. 3 et seq.). Once, judicial independence allows for a way

---

[*] I am deeply grateful to Gertrude Lübbe-Wolff for generously giving advice and sharing her knowledge of judicial deliberation.

of reflecting about social problems that differs from the mode of politics, constitutional adjudication increases the rationality of democratic governance and can be characterized as legitimate and effective. This understanding of successful constitutional review makes two normative claims. On the one hand, we have to pay attention to the political system in which constitutional and supreme courts operate in order to adequately analyze constitutional review (Lafont 2020, p. 225). In relation to this overall context, these courts should complement and not replace political discourses (Habermas 1996, p. 266). On the other hand, constitutional and supreme courts should contribute to social integration by establishing a mechanism to correct procedural and substantive injustices, thereby enriching the discourse about a "justifiable" (Forst, this volume, p. 131) political order with a legal perspective. Also, conflicts which "are kept out of politics" through "social forces and institutional practices" (Lukes 2005, p. 28) could come up on the agenda of apex courts before they are destructive to social cohesion.

This normative approach neither means to underestimate the dangers of constitutional review for democratic governance nor to overlook those decisions of apex courts that prevented corrections of procedural and substantial injustices. Rather, the normative concept informs us about the qualities of courts and politics necessary to enable legitimate and effective constitutional review. The crucial quality is according to my hypothesis a specific mode of judicial reasoning enabled by judges who combine the independence from politics with attentiveness to social grievances (Fiss 1979, p. 16), by democratic appointment procedures for constitutional judges, and finally by citizens and politicians who are committed to democracy as well as to constitutionalism. To test my hypothesis, it becomes essential to explore, whether the institutional frameworks of constitutional and supreme courts actually facilitate or impede the realization of these preconditions of constitutional review.

I will develop my argument as follows. First, I will discuss the idea of constitutional review, the concepts for realizing this idea, and the preconditions of legitimate and effective constitutional review. Second, the focus will be on the institutional frameworks of constitutional and supreme courts. The appointment rules for constitutional judges, the procedures of abstract and concrete review, and the modes of judicial decision-making are described. And third, the gradual convergence and the persistent differences between constitutional and supreme courts will be examined. In concluding, the comparative merits and problems of concentrated versus diffuse review are evaluated, and a specific division of labor between judges and legislators is suggested that promises legitimate and effective constitutional review enhancing the overall reflexive capacity of democratic governance.

I THE IDEA OF CONSTITUTIONAL REVIEW BY COURTS

Relation between Constitutionalism and Democracy

Constitutional review means that either all courts of a legal system with a supreme court as the final appellate body or a specialized constitutional court can declare laws and acts of government unconstitutional. At first glance, this appears very much against democratic governance. How can it be that judges having only indirect legitimacy are entitled to decide that acts of democratically elected parliaments and governments are null and void? To understand the rationale of constitutional review, it is important to have a look at the relation between constitutionalism and democracy. Constitutions in the modern sense originated in the revolutions of America and France at the end of the eighteenth century. These revolutions were about fundamental changes of politics building up a new political order in which "We the people" is the only legitimate source of all public authority. In a constitution free and equal citizens agree upon the principles and rules of government. In order to effectively structure democratic processes and to limit political power, a constitution must have priority over parliamentary laws (Grimm 2020a, p. 346).

The supremacy of the constitution is a consequence of the very meaning of a constitution as the fundamental law structuring politics and binding the representatives of the people. But the idea to entrust courts with the power to decide about the constitutionality of laws does not necessarily follow from having a constitution. Constitutional review is just one mechanism, though an often used one, to make sure that laws are in accordance with the fundamental law. In Finland, to give an example, a parliamentary commission and not a court decides ex-ante about the constitutionality of legislative acts, and this decision is binding for parliament, even though it is not expressly required by the constitution (Tuori 2020, p. 199).

Both aspects, the supremacy of the constitution over parliamentary acts and the question which institution would be best suited for constitutional review, have already been discussed before the ratification of the American Constitution by Alexander Hamilton. In the Federalist Papers no. 78, he wrote: "No legislative act (…) contrary to the Constitution, can be valid." And he was convinced that courts should have the power of review. "The complete independence of the courts of justice is peculiarly essential in a limited Constitution. By a limited Constitution, I understand one which contains certain specified exceptions to the legislative authority; (…) Limitations of this kind can be preserved in practice no other way than through the medium of courts of justice, whose duty it must be to declare all acts contrary to the manifest tenor of the Constitution void. Without this, all the reservations of particular rights or privileges would amount to nothing" (Hamilton, Madison, and Jay 2008 [1787–1788], no. 78).

In Hamilton's opinion it would not be rational to assume that the legislature should be the judge of its own powers. Otherwise, the representatives of the people were superior to the people themselves, and elected representatives could not only do what "their powers do not authorize, but what they forbid" (Federalist, no. 78). However, the problem is that the constitution often allows different interpretations of what is not authorized and what is forbidden. What concepts have been developed to realize the idea of constitutional review by courts and to achieve that judges are not "superior to the people themselves" but support the people as the constituent power?

The Origins of Diffuse and Concentrated Constitutional Review

The *concept of diffuse constitutional review by courts* has been invented in the United States of America. With "diffuse review" we describe a concept in which all courts when deciding about concrete "cases or controversies" have the power to declare a law or a public act unconstitutional. The supreme court is in such a system part of the ordinary judiciary and functions as the final appellate body for deciding about concrete litigation including constitutional questions. The publication of concurring and dissenting opinions is a common practice following the "seriatim" mode in the common law tradition in which each judge is giving an opinion. The individual judge plays an eminent role also in public.

In the American Constitution nothing is said about constitutional review by courts. Rather, the concept was introduced by the decision of the Supreme Court in *Hylton v. United States* in 1796.[1] In this case a federal tax law was judged to be constitutional. Alexander Hamilton as Minister of Finance gave a speech before the Supreme Court in support of the government lasting for about three hours![2] The new mechanism of constitutional review was confirmed in *Marbury v. Madison* in 1803.[3] Chief Justice John Marshall empowered with this decision each judge and each court to declare that "a legislative act contrary to the constitution is not law." Would it be otherwise, "then written constitutions are absurd attempts, on the part of the people, to limit a power, in its own nature illimitable."[4]

The concept of diffuse or generalist constitutional review has been especially influential in common law countries. Examples are Australia, Canada, and India. Most Anglophone African countries with common law traditions have adopted the concept of decentralized review as well (Fombad 2017, p. 28). However, there are exceptions from the equation of diffuse review with common law traditions. We find diffuse judicial review in a number of civil law countries as, for example, in Norway and Japan (Saunders 2017, p. 36). Vice versa, there are common law countries in which we would expect diffuse, but actually do find specialized constitutional review as, for example, in South Africa.

The *concept of concentrated constitutional review* is built upon a specialized constitutional court outside the ordinary judiciary being the only court entrusted with constitutional review. The architect of specialized review by constitutional courts has been legal scholar Hans Kelsen. Being the author of the Austrian Constitution of October 1920, he combined legal theory and legal praxis in the most fruitful way. He integrated his idea of a specialized constitutional court into the Austrian Constitution. As recent research is showing, Kelsen advocated in his first drafts

---

[1] *Hylton v. United States*, 3 U.S. (3 Dall), 171 (1796).
[2] Supreme Court Justice James Iridell in a letter to his wife of 26 February, 1796.
[3] *Marbury v. Madison*, 5 U.S. (1 Cranch), 137 (1803).
[4] Ibid., p. 177.

constitutional review of state laws, not of federal laws. However, when this proposal caused a lot of protest by politicians of the states, the constitutional court was entrusted with the power to decide about the constitutionality of federal as well as of state laws (Grimm 2020b, p. 14).

The core of Kelsen's theoretical argument is the hierarchy of the legal system, in which each public act that claims legal validity and compliance must be authorized by a higher-ranking norm and be limited by this norm (Grimm 2020b, p. 15). Each legal act has a creative and a norm-implementing element. For the legislature the higher norm is the constitution (Kelsen 1929, pp. 30 et seq.). This is why parliament, when drafting laws, must comply with the rules laid down in the constitution. The question is how to guarantee the necessary compliance of the legislator with the norms of the constitution. Kelsen proposed that not parliament itself, but an independent, specialized constitutional court would be the best candidate for controlling the constitutionality of laws. According to him, one can draw clear lines between the political realm of parliament being the "positive legislator" with a lot of freedom for creatively shaping policies on the one hand, and the legal realm of the constitutional court being the "negative legislator" with a restricted scope of action limited by the constitution on the other hand (Kelsen 1929, p. 56).

The concept of a specialized constitutional court was implemented after the Second World War in Germany, Italy, and Spain. The experience of fascism had shown that democratically elected majorities can act against the principles of democratic constitutionalism and, in the end destroy democracy, fundamental rights, and the respect for human dignity. Also, post-communist states like Poland and Hungary established constitutional courts. These specialized constitutional courts are equipped with far-reaching competences as, for example, the competence of abstract as well as concrete review of legislation. In Germany and Spain citizens have the right to file a constitutional complaint after judicial remedies are exhausted.

The reality of the specialized concept of constitutional review in Europe demonstrates that the theoretically assumed dichotomy between constitutional courts being "negative" legislators contrary to parliaments being "positive" legislators, does not work. Especially the importance of fundamental rights in modern constitutions has led to topics of constitutional adjudication which enlarge the creative element of judicial interpretation. Constitutional judges, when deciding about the constitutionality of laws, are inevitably becoming "positive" legislators. Therefore, the question arises, on what conditions is constitutional review compatible with democratic governance, and might even enhance social integration.

The Preconditions for Legitimate and Effective Constitutional Review

Constitutional and supreme courts are neither purely legal nor purely political institutions. The object of these courts is political, and their decisions have political effects. But the process of judicial decision-making should be different from politics and follow legal criteria (Grimm 2019b, p. 309). According to my hypothesis, the mode of judicial decision-making is the litmus test to find out whether these courts practice constitutional review in a democratically adequate way or transgress their competencies. The central condition for legitimate constitutional review by courts is a way of judicial decision-making that is different from political decision-making. The rationale of apex courts is to decide on the basis of legal reasoning and of interpretive rules comprising a creative element but nevertheless legally constructed (Grimm 2019b, p. 314), while the rationale of politics is to campaign, to win majorities, and to engage for a political agenda. To solve problems in a democracy we need complex structures of decision-making facilitating the cooperation of actors with different social and professional experiences, skills, and priorities. Constitutional and supreme courts raise the level of complexity required for democratic governance. They do not substitute (Habermas 1996, p. 266), but complement political discourses with a different perspective.

The ability of apex courts to maintain a specific mode of judicial decision-making, in turn, depends upon a variety of conditions that constitute the relationship between such courts and the more general system of democratic governance. Judicial independence is an important condition for a deliberative approach (Lübbe-Wolff 2020b, p. 178) and constitutes the capacity of apex courts to correct procedural and substantive injustices. This independence has not only to do with the behavior of judges, but also with the vitality of the democratic system.[5] The commitment of citizens and politicians to democracy, fundamental rights, and the supremacy of the constitution is therefore crucial for the success of review by apex courts. This commitment requires politicians to decide about contested policies in the democratic process instead of always waiting for the courts to solve the problems. "Parliament, the executive, and courts are ... part of a joint enterprise for the betterment of society" (King 2012, p. 139). The political context also plays a role when it comes to the appointment of the judges. Democratic and transparent procedures for the appointment of judges have an impact on judicial reasoning. These procedures can, for example, promote or prevent a politically divided court thereby influencing the openness for arguments. And finally, a specific judicial mode of deciding does not mean that judges should not care for the problems or expectations of society. The authority of a judge to review public acts is based on his or her ability to be detached from politics, yet attentive to social grievances (Figure 48.1).

The assumption of a distinction between political and judicial decision-making has been and continues to be criticized by legal scholars and political scientists alike. Such critics argue that the quality of judicial reasoning would not be superior to political reasoning, on the contrary. In judicial reasoning the "real issues at stake" about rights "get pushed to the margins" (Waldron 2006, p. 1383). Constitutional

---

[5] M. Shapiro (2019, p. 35), when defining "building blocks" of constitutional review, describes "democracy as the grand building block of review though the two are at odds."

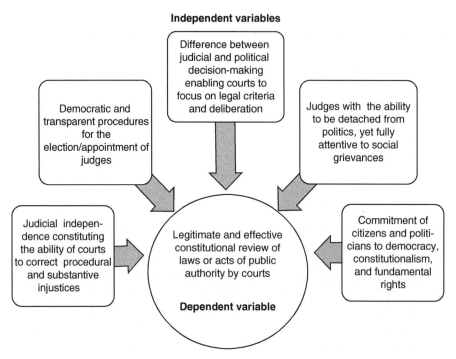

FIGURE 48.1 The preconditions for legitimate and effective constitutional review by courts
For a graph describing the specific preconditions of constitutional review in the European legal space see Landfried 2023, p. 597

review of a parliamentary decision "that has been taken according to the due democratic procedures could only be legitimate," if legal procedures were "fairer and more attentive" to principles like equal participation and representation (Bellamy 2007, p. 244).

Yet, my argument is not that judicial decision-making must be better than political decision-making. Rather, it should be different. This difference, well-grounded in different tasks of legislation and constitutional review, could enhance the overall "discursive level of public debates" (Habermas 1996, p. 304) by looking at a social or political problem from a legal perspective. The legitimacy and effectiveness of constitutional review is grounded in the capacity of apex courts to open up such an additional space for the reflection about procedural and substantive justice as well as in the capacity to correct with its binding decisions constitutionally "unjustifiable forms and outcomes of public, political justification" (Forst, this volume, p. 131). Constitutional judges must be politically independent and at the same time sensitive to political problems. "The right of the Judge to speak, and the obligation of others to listen, depends (…) on his ability to be distant and detached from the immediate contestants and from the body politic, yet fully attentive to grievances, and responsive in terms that transcend preferences and that are sufficient to support a judgment deemed 'constitutional'" (Fiss 1979, p. 16). Of course, the question arises: Is the real world of constitutional review of legislation by courts governed by such an approach?

II THE INSTITUTIONAL FRAMEWORKS OF CONSTITUTIONAL AND SUPREME COURTS

The Appointment Rules for Constitutional Judges

The important role of parliaments and governments in the processes of recruitment and appointment of judges has to do with the political role of constitutional and supreme courts. The intention is to provide the judges of apex courts with indirect democratic legitimacy. One can say – with all due caution – that the legislature in various combinations with the executive is the dominant actor of electing constitutional judges in countries with concentrated review, while the executive in various combinations with the legislature or independent commissions is particularly influential in appointing constitutional judges in countries with diffuse review.

To give some examples: In countries with concentrated review the spectrum ranges from Germany and Portugal, where the parliamentary chambers elect the constitutional judges, to Austria and France, where judges are partly elected by the legislature and partly by the executive, to Italy and Spain, where parliament, government, and the judiciary share the authority of recruiting the judges. The appointment rules in countries with diffuse review vary from Australia, where the executive alone appoints the judges, to the United States of America prescribing the nomination by the President and approval by the Senate, to the United Kingdom with an independent Judicial Appointments Commission mainly consisting of lawyers. Especially the election or approbation of judges for specialized constitutional courts increasingly requires a supermajority. Such supermajority requirements "are on the rise throughout the world" (Lübbe-Wolff 2020b, p. 167), and have the function to get judges who are accepted across political party lines.

A comparison between the electoral rules for the judges of the German Federal Constitutional Court and the appointment rules for the judges of the United States Supreme Court can illustrate some advantages and disadvantages of the different models. The German Federal Constitutional Court is composed of two senates with eight judges each. Half of the sixteen judges are elected by the Bundestag, and half of the judges by the Bundesrat for a non-renewable term of twelve years. A candidate needs a two thirds majority to get elected by one of the parliamentary chambers. There is an informal quota arrangement that the major political parties in parliament have the right to nominate a certain number of candidates.

A political influence on the election of constitutional judges is legitimate as long as the influence of political parties is embedded into a transparent selection and election process. And here, the deficit of the electoral rules in Germany becomes obvious. The selection and election process of constitutional judges in Germany is not at all transparent for the general public. A reform in 2015 did not change this situation. Let us take the election of half of the judges by the Bundestag. A few members of the parliamentary groups of those political parties that are entitled to nominate a certain proportion of judges negotiate who could be selected as a candidate. Afterwards, a small committee of the Bundestag agrees in confidential proceedings on a candidate and proposes him or her to the plenary. The plenary of the Bundestag finally elects this candidate without any debate. Such a procedure misses the transparency and publicity required for a democratic procedure. Therefore, it would make sense to have public hearings in the electoral committees of the two parliamentary chambers and give the public the chance to learn about the future constitutional judges.

Admittedly, the experience of some of the public hearings for supreme court judges in the American Senate is not encouraging. Yet, such hearings enable the public to express informed criticism. An example is the appointment of Judge Brett Kavanaugh in 2018. After the hearing, 2400 legal scholars wrote a letter to the Members of the Senate arguing that the aggressive and biased behavior of the candidate disqualified him from being a judge of the Supreme Court. According to their opinion, the candidate demonstrated that he is not committed to judicious inquiry: "Instead of trying to sort out with reason and care the allegations that were raised, Judge Kavanaugh responded in an intemperate, inflammatory and partial manner."[6]

While in Germany the introduction of public hearings for candidates in committees of the parliamentary chambers is discussed, in the United States the introduction of a supermajority rule of sixty Members of the Senate for the approval of candidates has been proposed in order to counteract a growing polarization of the Supreme Court (Resnik 2005, p. 638). This polarization is expressed by the many 5 to 4 decisions in which two factions are in opposition to each other, a conservative one with judges nominated by a President from the Republicans and a liberal one with judges nominated by a President from the Democrats. During the last decade from 2010 until 2019 there have been 61 opinions out of a total number of 727 full opinions that were decided by a majority of the five conservative judges against the four liberal judges.[7] These decisions often had a great impact on American politics as, for example, the decision of *Citizens United* v. Federal *Election Commission*[8] that invalidated a legislative reform intended to reduce the influence of big money on elections. With this decision the Supreme Court changed the landscape of campaign finance in favor of an even more unfair distribution of the opportunities for political participation than it was already the case.

---

[6] New York Times, 3 October 2018.
[7] Supreme Court Statistics. In: 125 Harvard Law Review 362–134 Harvard Law Review 610.
[8] 558 U.S. 310 (2010).

The formation of political factions in the Supreme Court interferes with the function of constitutional review "to counteract rather than fuel political polarization" (Lübbe-Wolff 2016, p. 51). Therefore, it would make sense to require a supermajority for the approbation of candidates by the Senate. Such a rule "could create incentives for the President to put forth individuals about whom a broad consensus of approval exists" (Resnik 2005, p. 638).

The examples of Germany and the United States demonstrate that countries with concentrated and countries with diffuse constitutional review can learn from each other. This also applies to the length of time for which the judges are in office. The rules range from a non-renewable period of time, often between 9 and 12 years, in countries with concentrated review to life tenure or a mandatory retirement age, usually practiced in countries with diffuse review. The disadvantages of life tenure are twofold. On the one hand, constitutional judges must take into regard social change and be attentive to new understandings of what is constitutionally justifiable. A court with rare and accidental renewals is not well prepared for this task. On the other hand, life-tenure in combination with a split court has an impact on judicial decision-making. If a politically aligned majority can assume to be the majority for a long time, the chance to be open for the arguments of the other side gets shrunk (Lübbe-Wolff 2020a, p. 11). This is why it would make sense to abolish life tenure for judges of the US Supreme Court (Resnik 2005, p. 638).

The Procedures of Abstract and Concrete Review

In countries with concentrated review constitutional court judges alone are exercising constitutional review, and they only decide constitutional questions. The ordinary judiciary has its own appellate supreme courts, which sometimes causes tensions between these supreme courts and constitutional courts about the competence of statutory interpretation (Garlicki 2007, p. 66).

The procedures for constitutional review by specialized constitutional courts are the abstract and concrete review, and the individual constitutional complaint. Not all constitutional courts have at their disposal all three procedures. The abstract review, as the name implies, gives constitutional courts the authority to decide about the constitutionality of statutes without reference to any specific case of private law or public law litigation. Usually, abstract review of legislation can be initiated by members of parliaments and governments. In Germany, for example, the abstract review procedure may be set off by the federal government, by a state government, or by a quarter of the Members of the Bundestag. In Italy, the federal and regional governments, and in France the President, the Presidents of the Assembly and of the Senate as well as sixty Members of the Assembly and sixty Senators are entitled to use the procedure.

A constitutional court, empowered to declare statutes unconstitutional, necessarily has an impact on policy-making, though not in all policy areas to the same degree (Landfried 1994, p. 114). In addition to the existing procedures, constitutional courts have developed new forms of sanctions to escape the simple choice of declaring a law constitutional or unconstitutional. One of these forms, often used in Austria, France, and Germany, is the "authoritative interpretation" (Stone Sweet and Shapiro 2002, p. 365), a declaration that a particular interpretation of a statute is the only constitutional one. Such declarations often entail precise prescriptions for the implementation of a statute and, in the end, result in policy-making by constitutional courts. Thus, the intention of constitutional courts to practice more judicial restraint by this new form of sanction is turned into the opposite.

In countries with common law tradition all judges of all courts have the authority to declare a law unconstitutional and to suspend its application in the concrete case. The supreme court is the final court of appeal, and the selection of cases is guided by the general legal importance of an issue. This can be illustrated by the rule structuring the selection of cases at the UK Supreme Court.[9] The case must raise "an arguable point of law of general public importance which ought to be considered by the Supreme Court at that time, bearing in mind that the matter will already have been subject of judicial decision…" (Reed 2020, p. 26).[10] The UK Supreme Court is defining which legal problem is of interest for the general public right now. Once a case has been selected, the "importance of adversarial elements" (Lübbe-Wolff 2020b, p. 164) comes into play and continues to be a specific feature of constitutional review in common law systems. Now the focus is on solving the questions of the concrete case. As a result, the procedures of concrete and abstract review are getting closer to one another.

But aren't the procedures the same anyway? For the US Supreme Court it is argued that the techniques of concrete review are "indeed virtually identical" (Stone Sweet and Shapiro 2002, p. 365) to those of abstract review in European countries. "No matter how formally concrete their review, US courts are fully aware that their major constitutional decisions are not simply 'doing justice' in particular, concrete past circumstances, but announcing general policy norms applicable to many different and not fully predictable circumstances in the future" (Stone Sweet and Shapiro 2002, p. 372). In this interpretation the concrete case appears to be "simply a vehicle" (Stone Sweet and Shapiro 2002, p. 37) for the Supreme Court to solve an abstract public policy problem. It is not taken into account that the common law tradition of hearing concrete cases affects judicial decision-making. "A mixed docket both informs those who sit on a high court about workings of law in a range of situations and insulates a court from being understood only through its high profile

---

[9] In the United Kingdom with its tradition of parliamentary sovereignty courts cannot annul or suspend an Act of Parliament. On a few occasions, Parliament has decided to give the courts the power to question legislation. The courts are, for example, authorized to declare laws incompatible with the ECHR. Also, they can challenge a law made by the Government under powers delegated by Parliament.

[10] A third of the applications, about 75 cases, are accepted each year. Cp. Reed 2020, p. 26.

constitutional work" (Resnik 2005, p. 645). Such an impact is easily overlooked if we interpret the concrete and abstract review as being more or less the same. Therefore, we should maintain the distinction in order to explore where exactly the procedures overlap, and how we can explain processes of convergence.

Another persistent difference between constitutional and supreme courts with regard to procedures is the way in which review of legislation is activated. Concrete review in common law countries is activated by applications for appeal to any of the higher courts, while in civil law countries the access to abstract review is usually limited to politicians. Once constitutional review is activated – how do constitutional and supreme courts proceed?

The Processes of Judicial Decision-Making

Filtering mechanisms, the publication of separate opinions, and the majority requirements for judicial decisions are influencing constitutional review (Lübbe-Wolff 2020b, pp. 163 et seq.). Here again, we observe processes of gradual convergence of constitutional and supreme courts as well as persistent differences.

Filtering mechanisms can change the character of an apex court with constitutional review power. An example is the transformation of the US Supreme Court by the Judiciary Act of 1925. Before this act, virtually everyone had the right to appeal to the US Supreme Court "as of right." Since 1925 citizens can petition the court to grant a "writ of certiorari" bringing the case from the lower to the Supreme Court for review. The Court can turn down these petitions without giving any reasons. The denial of review is entirely discretionary. It is up to the Court to select its docket and define which cases are important. "The Act transformed the Court from a tribunal of last resort into the manager of the system of federal law, responsible for supervising the development and legitimacy of national law."[11] Thus, the US Supreme Court has changed into the direction of a constitutional court.

Another process of approximation between constitutional and supreme courts relates to the publication of concurring and dissenting opinions. More and more supreme courts nowadays are favoring "judgments of the court." Even in the United Kingdom, where the Law Lords used to deliver all their own "speeches," the current practice "is generally to favor a single majority judgment, so that the reasoning of the majority is expressed in a unitary way" (Reed 2020, p. 32). In 2015–2016, the UK Supreme Court agreed in 63% of the cases upon a single judgment (Reed 2020, p. 32).

While supreme courts are increasingly pursuing unanimous judgments,[12] more and more constitutional courts of countries in the civil law tradition have introduced the

---

[11] Post, R. C. (2023). The Taft Court: Making Law for a Divided Nation, 1921–1930. Volume X of the *Oliver Wendell Holmes Devise History of the Supreme Court of the United States*, Cambridge: Cambridge University Press, p. 603.

[12] Ibid., pp. 604–605. The US Supreme Court deviates from this trend. Only 34% of the full opinions from 2005–2017 were unanimous.

publication of dissenting opinions. There are of course exceptions from this gradual approximation. The Italian and the Austrian constitutional courts, for example, do not allow for dissenting opinions. Dissenting opinions can enhance the deliberative quality of judicial decision-making. When one or more members of the court do not agree with the majority, the potential dissenters will try to persuade the majority and vice versa. The arguments of the majority become more precise when challenged by counterarguments of judges who have the choice of writing a dissenting opinion. When in the end the disagreement is so profound that one or more judges publish a dissenting opinion, the different interpretations of the constitution are made transparent to the public.

An important difference between constitutional and supreme courts continues to exist with regard to the majority requirements for decisions. "In common law jurisdictions, to this day, a majority of votes is required only for the dispositive part ('outcome') of a decision, not for the reasons (…) In the civil law tradition, the rules (…) are often not quite clear, but at least with respect to reasons concerning the law, the dominant view is that all of them need majority support" (Lübbe-Wolff 2020b, p. 162). This is why supreme courts in the common law tradition can opt for decisions in which the majority of judges supporting the result is split with respect to the reasons. On the one hand, such an approach of "multiple reasoning" informs the public about the difference of arguments between judges. "Multiple reasoning" is especially adequate in developing areas of law indicating "a number of possible paths for future development" (Reed 2020, p. 33). On the other hand, there is less of a commitment toward finding compromises for a single judgment giving clear guidance for the legal system.

In contrast, the rule of constitutional courts to find a majority for both, outcome and reasons, produces "a habit of intense efforts to convince and converge" (Lübbe-Wolff 2020b, p. 166). This approach promotes a deliberative approach of decision-making and an orientation toward the building of compromises. Yet, a high degree of compromise-orientation combined with the culture to avert the publication of a dissent, can reduce the transparency for the public. A recent example is the judgment of the Second Senate of the German Federal Constitutional Court on the European Central Bank's public sector purchase program.[13] The decision was taken by a majority of 7 to 1. Of course, the public would have liked to know the arguments of the judge who voted against the majority. All we know is the numerical distribution of votes.

III THE GRADUAL CONVERGENCE AND THE PERSISTENT DIFFERENCES

In the analyzed areas of appointment rules, review procedures, and modes of judicial decision-making we observe processes of gradual convergence and at the same time persistent differences between constitutional and supreme courts.

---

[13] German Federal Constitutional Court, Judgment of the Second Senate of 5 May 2020, 2 BvR 859/15 et al.

Differences exist with regard to the appointment of judges. Constitutional court judges, being outside the ordinary judiciary, are appointed by elected representatives for a statutorily fixed time, often for nine to twelve years. There are many variations from the election by parliamentary chambers to combinations with some judges elected by parliament and some named by the executive and the judiciary. An advantage for the function of constitutional review in a democracy is the relatively short and non-renewable tenure supporting judicial independence and the attentiveness of judges to social change. The role of politicians in the appointment process adds to the indirect democratic legitimacy of the judges. But at the same time the political bargaining process about candidates reduces the transparency for the public, and hence democratic legitimacy.

Supreme court judges, being part of the ordinary judiciary, are usually appointed by the head of state on advice of elected governmental institutions or independent commissions for life time or up to a certain retirement age. It is an advantage of recruitment systems with judicial appointment committees that judges can be selected without taking into account their political orientation. However, for supreme court judges who are deciding about political topics with political consequences, such a recruitment pattern comes at the expense of the electoral link to democratically representative institutions. Life tenure can additionally reduce the openness of judges for social and political developments.

A process of *partial convergence* between constitutional and supreme courts is typical for the procedures of abstract and concrete review. Supreme courts that have discretion to pick their cases (docket control) increasingly focus on constitutional questions. But this trend should not be overestimated. Even the US Supreme Court that has developed in the direction of a specialized constitutional court, deals with "constitutional" review in the strict sense in a limited number of cases (Zurn 2007, p. 283). In roughly a third (34.2%) of the 727 full opinions of the US Supreme Court from 2010 until 2019 the principal issue was constitutional.[14] Also, a growing number of cases concerning constitutional matters does not mean that the concrete cases are just "vehicles" for developing constitutional law. Concrete review is not totally transformed into abstract review of legislation. The overall experience of supreme court judges in a broad range of legal fields influences their approach to constitutional matters.

Gradual convergence and persistent differences characterize judicial decision-making. An approximation can be observed with regard to separate opinions. Many constitutional courts changed their approach from exclusively publishing "opinions of the court" and introduced the option of separate opinions. Vice versa, supreme courts that traditionally emphasized the individual opinion of each judge are now encouraging "opinions of the court." An ongoing difference between constitutional and supreme courts is the role of

---

[14] Supreme Court Statistics. In: 125 Harvard Law Review 362–134 Harvard Law Review 610. It has to be emphasized that the categorization of cases as primarily "constitutional" is difficult. Cp. note in 132 Harvard Law Review 447, p. 459: "Cases invoking a mixture of statutory interpretation and constitutional adjudication are particularly difficult to classify."

hearings in judicial decision-making. For supreme courts these hearings are of utmost importance. These hearings are open to the public and generally well attended. Robert Reed (2020, p. 33), President of the UK Supreme Court, describes these hearings as "the most important stage in collective decision-making (…), where interventions by members of the court can be persuasive." Finally, a remaining difference between constitutional and supreme courts with consequences for judicial deliberation has to do with the majority requirements for decisions (Lübbe-Wolff 2020b, p. 162). A majority of votes for the result and the reasoning is required for decisions of constitutional courts, encouraging compromises, while a majority of votes only for the result is required for decisions of supreme courts facilitating multiple reasoning.

Types of constitutional review by courts[15]

	Civil law tradition	Common law tradition
Type of apex court with constitutional review power	Constitutional Courts	Supreme Courts
Concept of constitutional review	Concentrated, specialized; Constitutional courts alone have the power of declaring a statute unconstitutional and therefore null and void.	Diffuse, generalist; All courts have constitutional review power with the supreme court being the final appellate body.
Appointment of judges	Appointments by parliamentary chambers or by combinations of legislature, executive and judiciary; Supermajority requirements for the election by parliaments; Tenure often between 9–12 years, usually non-renewable	Appointments by the executive on advice or approval of parliamentary chambers; Increasingly, appointments are mediated by independent commissions; Life tenure or retirement at a certain age
Procedures	Abstract and concrete review Constitutional complaint	Predominantly concrete review
Processes of judicial decision-making	Originally, per curiam (pronouncing a single "opinion of the court"); In more and more countries separate opinions are allowed; Great variety of the extent of deliberative decision-making; Usually, the majority of votes is required for the outcome and the reasons of a decision	Originally, seriatim (each judge pronouncing his or her opinion); Trend to "judgments of the court" with separate opinions; Great variety of the extent of deliberative decision-making; Generally, the majority of votes is only required for the outcome of a decision.

[15] The great diversity of the institutional frameworks of constitutional review with many mixed forms between the concepts is of course not covered by such ideal types, cp. M. Weber (1964, p. 738).

CONCLUSION

Apex courts with constitutional review power have to ensure that democratically elected majorities do not misuse their power but are acting in accordance with the sovereignty of the people expressed in the constitution. They offer a mechanism to correct procedures and political outcomes that are not well-reasoned and constitutionally unjustifiable. It is their function to contribute to the integration of a society by developing constitutional law in distance to politics but sensitive to political and social problems.

The establishment of constitutional courts in Europe after the second World War has been a success. These specialized courts outside the ordinary judiciary have contributed to the social anchoring of the constitution. People feel that fundamental rights are not just written on paper. This is why the trust of citizens in constitutional courts is in comparison to other public institutions very high. However, the appreciation of the constitution and of constitutional courts require a basically functioning democracy. The populist attacks on constitutional courts in Hungary and Poland are a serious setback for concentrated constitutional review, demonstrating that courts have limited resources to resist such attacks. "In the final effect, courts and judges may not survive a collision with the political branches." This assessment of the situation in Poland by Lech Garlicki (2019, p. 162), a former Justice of the Polish Constitutional Court, is an alarm signal.

We have to keep in mind such politically induced dangers for judicial independence when evaluating the merits and problems of constitutional courts. Many properties of specialized constitutional courts have passed the reality test. The appointment procedures by elected representatives in various combinations provide constitutional judges with indirect democratic legitimacy without diluting their independence. Supermajority requirements for the election of judges prevent the building of political blocs within courts. Appointments of judges for a limited time are enabling courts to be attentive to social change. And finally, as far as we can tell from the decisions of constitutional courts and learn from the descriptions of former constitutional judges, judicial reasoning differs from political reasoning. A comparative study of the jurisdiction of apex courts arrives at the conclusion that "judicial argument" is the "core of judges' activity" (Robertson 2010, p. 21). Of course, the possibility that constitutional judges cover up their political preferences with legal arguments cannot be ruled out. Deficits in the clarity of arguments and methodological shortcomings usually are the first signs of such a transgression of judicial power. But empirical research does not prove that such an attitude is the norm.

In spite of the many advantages, concentrated review by constitutional courts is in my opinion not superior to diffuse review by supreme courts.[16] The concepts are shaped for different legal cultures and have been established in different historical

---

[16] Cp. for the opposite opinion Zurn 2007, pp. 274 et seq.

situations. Constitutional court judges with the monopoly of issuing binding interpretations of the constitution can concentrate on constitutional topics. Supreme court judges being the final arbitrators of appeal decide constitutional questions in the context of concrete cases of private law and public law litigation. This basic difference does not prevent mutual learning processes. Constitutional courts could profit from more transparent appointment procedures for judges, while the status-quo strengthening effect of life tenure for supreme court judges is worth considering, just to mention two examples.

The decision of the people as the constituent power to entrust courts with such a challenging task as being a corrective mechanism for failures of justice (Forst, this volume, p. 131), does not come without problems. Critics argue that the global trend toward constitutional review is an attempt of political and economic elites "to defend established interests" and "to insulate policy-making from the vagaries of democratic politics" (Hirschl 2015, p. 107). There is evidence for such a bias in several decisions of campaign finance (Landfried 1994, p. 119) or social rights adjudication (J. King 2012, pp. 186 et seq.). Yet, constitutional review cannot altogether be characterized as being in the interest of the political and economic elites.

Rather, the problem of both, constitutional and supreme courts, lies in a gradual process of a judicialization of politics (Landfried 1994, p. 118). More and more political questions are decided by courts, thereby reducing political alternatives. Judges and politicians contribute to this process. Judges, when transgressing their competencies, and politicians, when focusing in their legislative work too much on judicial arguments, diminish the difference between judicial and political decision-making. The very existence of a constitutional or a supreme court changes the political discourse, because there is an anticipatory effect of possible future judgments of the courts on policy-making. The argument that a planned statute could be declared unconstitutional has an effect on politics. Members of Parliament try to formulate their drafts as near as possible not only to previous, but also to predicted decisions of apex courts.

The more the constitutional or supreme court is appealed to, the more close-meshed the constitutional interpretations become. Of course, there is nothing wrong with politicians taking seriously the constitutional dimensions of their decisions. But first of all, politicians must be committed to solve problems on the basis of political discourses. The constitution, not the constitutional court should be guiding democratic politics. Otherwise, the political process becomes overloaded with legal arguments, and the difference between political and judicial reflection is shrinking.

This is why legitimate constitutional review based on the difference between judicial and political decision-making requires a division of labor between apex courts and politics (Landfried 2019, p. 7). How could such a division of labor be organized, if it is to strengthen democratic governance? John Hart Ely has interpreted constitutional and supreme courts as referees "policing the process of representation" (1982, p. 73). The referee "is to intervene only when one team is gaining unfair advantage, not because the 'wrong' team has scored" (p. 103). Likewise apex courts have to ensure that each and every person of a society can participate in the political process on an equal basis (p. 73). Yet, according to this approach, it is not the task of constitutional and supreme courts to impose values.

This distinction between political processes and political values is convincing but not sufficient. The task of constitutional judges goes beyond the interpretation of procedures and their substantive dimension (J. King 2012, p. 180). As modern constitutions do not only regulate the procedures of governance, but also constitute a normative order, judges interpreting this text cannot avoid to assess values. Therefore, I am proposing a more flexible interpretation of the division of labor between apex courts and politics. When it comes to the evaluation of procedural justice (processes), apex courts have broad competence and power shifts in favor of constitutional review. When it comes to the evaluation of substantive justice (outcomes), the competence of constitutional and supreme courts is more restricted, and the authority shifts in favor of democratic politics. Such a division of labor enables constitutional and supreme courts to correct violations of the constitution without transgressing judicial competencies.

The architectural maxim "form follows function" can be applied to constitutional review. The *form of judicial decision-making follows the integrative function* of constitutional review by opening up a new arena for reflecting and deciding with legal methods about the constitutionality of legislation. The institutional framework of apex courts – the form – must be adequate for legitimate constitutional review based on judicial deliberation. As has been demonstrated, concentrated as well as diffuse review have specific institutional deficits, such as an insufficient transparency of the appointment process or life tenure giving single judges too much power and reducing the capacity of a court to keep pace with social developments. Constitutional and supreme courts could learn from each other in order to strengthen their potential for a deliberative approach of constitutional review for the benefit of democratic governance. This is all the more important, as the architectural maxim also applies the other way around.[17] *The integrative function of constitutional review follows form*, and profits from a mode of judicial decision-making that enables judges to be distant from politics and at the same time attentive to social and political grievances.

RECOMMENDED READING

Bellamy, R. (2007). *Political Constitutionalism. A Republican Defense of the Constitutionality of Democracy*, Cambridge, UK: Cambridge University Press.

Ely, J. H. (1982). *Democracy and Distrust. A Theory of Judicial Review*, Cambridge, MA and London: Harvard University Press, 4th printing.

---

[17] Morrison, T., Weiler, J.H.H. (2009). Introduction to the Art Collection of 22, Washington Square North, New York, p. 4.

Fiss, O. M. (1979). Forms of Justice. *Harvard Law Review*, 93 (1), 1–58.
Fombad, C. M. (2017). An Overview of Contemporary Models of Constitutional Review in Africa. In C. M. Fombad, ed., *Constitutional Adjudication in Africa*, Oxford: Oxford University Press, pp. 17–48.
Garlicki, L. (2007). Constitutional courts versus supreme courts, *International Journal of Constitutional Law*, 5 (1), 44–68.
Grimm, D. (2009). Constitutions, Constitutional Courts and Constitutional Interpretation at the Interface of Law and Politics. In B. Iancu, ed., *The Law/Politics Distinction in Contemporary Public Law Adjudication*, Utrecht: Eleven International Publishing, pp. 21–34.
Häcker, B. & W. Ernst, eds. (2020). *Collective Judging in Comparative Perspective*, Cambridge: Intersentia.
Issacharoff, S. (2015). *Fragile Democracies. Contested Power in the Era of Constitutional Courts*, Cambridge, UK: Cambridge University Press.
Landfried, C., ed. (2019). *Judicial Power. How Constitutional Courts Affect Political Transformations*, Cambridge, UK: Cambridge University Press.
Lübbe-Wolff, G. (2016). Cultures of Deliberation in Constitutional Courts. In P. Maraniello, ed., *Justicia Constitucional*, Vol. 1, Resistencia – Chaco: ConTexto Libreria, pp. 37–52.
Lübbe-Wolff, G. (2022). *Beratungskulturen. Wie Verfassungsgerichte arbeiten, und wovon es abhängt, ob sie integrieren oder polarisieren*, Berlin: Konrad-Adenauer-Stiftung.
Morrison, T., Weiler, J. H. H. (2009). Introduction to the Art Collection of 22, Washington Square North, New York.
Saunders, C. (2017). Constitutional Review in Asia: A Comparative Perspective. In A. H. Y. Chen, A. Harding, eds., *Constitutional Courts in Asia: A Comparative Perspective*, Cambridge, UK: Cambridge University Press, pp. 32–59.
Stone Sweet, A. & Shapiro, M. (2002). Abstract and Concrete Review in the United States. In M. Shapiro, A. Stone Sweet, eds., *On Law, Politics, and Judicialization*. Oxford: Oxford University Press, pp. 347–375.

49

Judicial Independence

David Kosař and Samuel Spáč

Judicial independence appears on most laundry lists of principles of the rule of law (Crawford 2003; Rawls 1971, p. 239; Raz 1979a, pp. 216–217; Waldron 2011b). Although the wording varies, all major international human rights treaties stipulate the right to a fair trial by an independent tribunal. Judicial independence is also advanced by the United Nations and explicitly mentioned in most national constitutions.

Despite being nearly universally recognised as a virtue, judicial independence has been challenged in almost all parts of the world, from Latin America, where politicians such as Venezuelan President Hugo Chávez (Taylor 2014) both expanded the size of the Supreme Court and dismissed and prosecuted judges (Castagnola 2018), to the European Union, where Hungary (Uitz 2015) and Poland (Sadurski 2019) have recently witnessed similar attacks on the judiciary. These attacks have often been legitimised as attempts to 'restore' rather than undermine judicial independence on the grounds that any judgment critical of the government reflects an unwarranted political bias and disrespects the will of the people. Indeed, some commentators consider judicial independence to be so open to differing interpretations (Tiede 2006, p. 130) as to be a useless concept, that should be unpacked into its smaller components to be studied meaningfully (Kornhauser 2002).

We are less cynical about the idea. According to our theory, judicial independence exists where powerful actors are unable or unwilling to inappropriately interfere with the workings of the judiciary. By the 'workings of the judiciary' we mean both judicial decision-making and judicial governance. By 'powerful actors' we mean any actors that hold formal or informal powers to exercise pressure on the judiciary. Such actors include not only politicians, oligarchs, organised crime, and interest groups, but also judges in such environments where they are considerably involved in the judicial governance and have a reasonable chance of systematically skewing how the courts operate. The reasons why powerful actors may be *unable* to interfere with the workings of the judiciary are manifold – they may have neither formal powers nor informal means to do so, or they have them, but judicial resistance coupled with the pressure from the media, the people, supranational bodies, or foreign states eventually block their efforts. Powerful actors are *unwilling* to interfere with the workings of the judiciary primarily for two reasons (Popova 2012) – due to political culture (belief in the rule of law) or for strategic reasons (cost-benefit analysis). Traditionally, *inappropriate* interferences (sometimes referred to as *undue influence*) are primarily those that are not done to correct a lack of 'good behaviour' of judges. However, due to the complexity of judicial governance (Šipulová et al. 2023), such interferences may include actions that are not necessarily connected to the 'good behaviour' of judges, such as packing a judicial council, abusive case assignment, reducing mandatory retirement age or judicial salaries, establishing new courts, or offering golden parachutes for judges. What is inappropriate is contextual and country specific. For instance, lustration and vetting of judges, which would be considered inappropriate in consolidated democracies, are acceptable measures in countries that transition to democracy.

Courts are thus independent when powerful actors do not consistently impose their preferences in disputes in which they have a stake, either by capturing the courts through formal changes of laws governing the judiciary, through rigging these laws in their favour, or by skewing judicial decision-making. We thus distinguish between three levels of judicial independence: *de jure* institutional independence, *de facto* institutional independence, and decisional independence. The first two concern judicial governance (often referred to as structural independence) broadly understood (Šipulová et al. 2024), whereas the third focuses on actual judicial decision-making (sometimes referred to as behavioural independence). We argue that each level should be analysed independently, and the connections between them carefully explained and elaborated, because it is perfectly plausible that different actors interfere with the workings of the judiciary at each level. The executive may push the court packing plan through the parliament (*de jure* independence level), a court president may rig case assignment and ensure that a case is allocated to a judge favourable to governmental views (*de facto* independence level), but mafia may bribe this judge to decide this particular case differently (*decisional* independence level). This implies that judicial independence is a relational concept, which means that we always need to specify the potential source of dependence. While independence from politicians is at the heart of normative importance of independent courts to the rule of law, judges can be dependent on other actors ranging from organised crime to court presidents.

Importantly, judicial independence is not an end in itself, but a means to an end (Burbank & Friedman 2002), which is to provide fair and impartial justice and effective judicial protection. Nevertheless, judicial independence is not sufficient for fair and impartial decision-making. Independent judges can still decide with impetuousness and whimsicalness (Kramer, this volume, chap. 10). The judiciary may be uncritical about current government, business thinking or the police even without undue pressure for reasons of conformism (van Dijk 2024; Brinks 2008) or judicial apoliticism (Hillbink 2007). It may also become partisan (Kramer, this volume, chap. 10) and predisposed to find in favour of one of the parties, regardless of or despite the law and the facts, again without external pressure. Judges thus can be biased for other reasons than the lack of independence. Nor is judicial independence able, in itself, to ensure effective judicial protection. If courts have narrow powers, they cannot protect citizens' rights effectively even if they are independent (Toharia 1975; Brinks 2005, p. 597). Similarly, if litigation is prohibitively expensive, judicial proceedings extremely delayed or judgments not implemented, independent courts do not provide effective judicial protection. Finally, judicial independence cannot guarantee that courts are responsive to the society. Again, judicial independence is a prerequisite to responsive judicial review, but it is not a sufficient condition (Dixon 2023). A promising way to make judges more responsive to society is to focus less on the insulation of the judiciary and more on providing a plural and inclusive system of judicial appointments and accountability (Brinks & Blass 2017).

This chapter proceeds as follows. Part I conceptualises judicial independence and identifies two major approaches to it – institutional and output-oriented. Part II proposes a unified theory of judicial independence. Part III concludes.

I DEFINING JUDICIAL INDEPENDENCE

Any conceptualisation of judicial independence can be located on a continuum from understanding the concept at the level of individual judges' decision-making to understanding it at the institutional level, as the separation of the judiciary from the executive and legislative branches of power. A varied vocabulary has been used to describe the different perspectives resulting from these two levels. Some distinguish between independence as certain ends and independence as the means to realise those ends (Burbank & Friedman 2002); some distinguish between independence understood as values and as mechanisms (Shetreet 2011), others label the former 'impartiality' (Malleson 2002; Geyh 2013) and the latter 'structural insulation' (Popova 2012); some differentiate between individual and collective independence, hence differentiating between independence understood in institutional terms and independence understood as a characteristic of an individual judge (Russell 2001); some write about independence as a separation from the executive branch on the one hand, and independence as an amount of discretion judges enjoy, on the other (Tiede 2006); other authors draw a distinction between institutional, decisional and behavioural independence – the first referring to independence at the level of the judiciary as a whole, the other two at the level of individual judges (Popova 2012, pp. 14–19). In the language of this Handbook, one end of the continuum understands judicial independence as an institutional quality, the other treats it as a modality.

This distinction does not necessarily help us to understand what judicial independence actually is. It shows that independence in the literature means various things, yet does not clarify how we can use independence analytically. To make independence a more tangible concept, it is necessary to emphasise that it is a relational concept. As Russell writes, judicial independence 'is first and foremost a concept about connections – or, more precisely, the absence of certain connections – between the judiciary and other components of political system.' (Russell 2001, p. 2) An important implication of this claim is that it defines independence as the result of a relationship between the judicial system and the rest of the political system. However, he does not clarify what falls under the 'political system'. Indeed, he claims that 'general theory cannot decisively settle whether or not pressure on judges generated from within the justice system ... constitute a violation of judicial independence, any more than it can determine whether the media pressure ... is altogether incompatible with judicial independence.' (Russell 2001, p. 4)

In a similar fashion, Ferejohn (1999, p. 375) defines independence as a 'consequence of self-restraint by powerful actors.' However, two questions regarding this conceptualisation need to be addressed: who are the 'powerful actors'? And why would they restrain themselves from influencing courts? Popova provides an answer to the latter. While her analysis focuses only on politicians as powerful actors, she distinguishes between the *capacity* and *willingness* of these actors to influence the judiciary (Popova 2012, pp. 20–23). Capacity refers to the channels these actors can use to pressure courts – both formal and informal. Willingness refers to a conscious choice made by these actors (Landes & Posner 1975; Hanssen 2004). Popova (2012) provides two answers to why politicians may refrain from utilising their capacity to threaten independence. First, it can be the result of a strategic calculation that the costs outweigh the benefits (a strategic rationale). Second, politicians may have a strong belief in the ideal of the rule of law that prevents them from applying any pressure on courts (an ideational rationale).

However, leaving independence to the will of 'powerful actors' alone treats judges – or the judiciary in general – as the mere objects of powerful actors' capriciousness. But judges are not necessarily passive (Matthes 2022). Judicial independence also depends on the *capacity* and *willingness* of judicial actors and their allies to resist undue pressure (Šipulová 2021). This capacity depends on factors such as the size of their salaries, cohesiveness, embeddedness in transnational judicial networks, and ability to seek support at supranational courts. Judicial actors may be more empowered to exercise resistance in instances when the judiciary feels supported by the media (Trochev & Ellett 2014), the Bar and the civil society (Shafqat 2018), the public (Clark 2011), or by supranational courts (Bonelli & Claes 2018). The willingness of judges and of their allies to resist may be somewhat similar to that of politicians. Their strategic calculation would depend on whether the possible risks were sufficiently small for judges to disregard the desires of powerful actors (Helmke 2002). Likewise, the stronger their belief in the rule of law the greater the judicial willingness is likely to be to resist even when the risks are high. Judicial independence thus depends on the interplay between the powerful actors' capacity and willingness to influence courts and the capacity and willingness of judicial actors and their allies to resist such actions. The described relationship can be expressed in a formula presented in Figure 49.1.

FIGURE 49.1 Judicial independence formula

That said, we also need to acknowledge that judges themselves can endanger judicial independence and other constitutional values. In other words, when judges are equipped with substantial powers to exert influence over the judiciary, they pose as much of a threat as any other powerful actor. The underlying assumption of various international soft-law standards – that judges, unlike politicians, do not have interests of their own which could endanger the independence of the judiciary – proved wrong (Bobek & Kosař 2014; Parau 2018; Šipulová et al. 2023). Numerous examples in the academic literature contradict this assumption and make clear that judicial independence can be threatened also by actors inside the judiciary (Sillen 2019).

For instance, in Poland, new judges installed by Jaroslaw Kaczyński to the Constitutional Tribunal and the Supreme Court became enablers of democratic decay (Sadurski 2019). In Slovakia, judiciary representatives used their substantial powers to compromise judicial independence through rigging the process for selecting judges so as to choose their relatives and loyal candidates (Spáč 2022) and abusing accountability mechanisms, such as promotion, remuneration, and the disciplining of judges (Kosař 2016). The Ukrainian judicial leadership nurtured informal channels for influencing judges which allowed for the politicisation of justice (Popova 2012). In Latin America, judicial self-governance was misused to 'foster sectoral privileges of judicial personnel or to allow unchallenged, arbitrary interpretations of law' (O'Donnell 2004, p. 35). In Mexico, the Supreme Court controlled the staffing of all courts through informal means that led to patronage and corruption within the judiciary (Pozas-Loyo & Rios-Figueroa 2018).

In all these cases, the judiciary may be independent from external interference but internal interferences by the judges themselves could compromise judicial governance as well as judicial decision-making. Judicial leadership in fully autonomous judiciaries may still engage in nepotism, act as a transmission belt for politicians, or take bribes. External independence simply does not necessarily translate into internal independence of judges nor to independent judicial decision-making. As a result, we argue that when analysing judicial independence, it does not matter from whom the undue interferences stem, what matters are their consequences and severity.

Institutional Approaches to the Definition of Judicial Independence

Institutional approaches focus on the degree of separation of the judiciary from the other branches of power. They perceive judicial independence as a feature of institutional design. Scholars commonly use this perspective (Fiss 1993; Larkins 1996; Finkel 2008; Hanssen 2004; Garoupa & Ginsburg 2009), as do policy-makers and democracy promoters. This institutional emphasis is unsurprising. For political scientists, institutions provide the locus for politicians' attempts to foster – or hamper – independence. Hence, it is logical to analyse independence at this level, even though it is impossible to secure the absolute separation of the judiciary from other branches of power. Legal scholars and policy-makers have also preferred particular institutional solutions such as judicial councils, in particular, in the democratisation context in Latin America and post-communist Europe. They have believed that new institutions would change the prevailing judicial culture and strengthen judicial independence (Blankenburg 1995; Hammergren 2002).

Even Russell, who proposes that independence can be threatened at both the collective and the individual levels, claims that it makes more sense to focus on the institutional framework when analysing judicial independence. Although the capacity and willingness of judges to act impartially cannot be guaranteed by their insulation from other branches of power, without it their independence in the exercise of their power cannot be ensured (Russell 2001). Similarly, Fiss (1993) also favours an institutional approach to independence, labelling it 'political insularity', to ensure that judges are protected from political interferences in order to allow for the possibility of their being impartial. Larkins, too, writes about the insulation of the judiciary from the government, although he does so with regard to specific cases in which the government is directly involved as a party in the litigation. Admittedly, it is not always straightforward to assess in which cases the government is or is not interested – and hence whether it has a preference over the how the dispute is decided. Either way, what Larkins claims is that 'it is important that judges not be subject to control by the regime, and that they be shielded from any threats, interference, or manipulation which may either force them to unjustly favour the state or subject themselves to punishment for not doing so' (Larkins 1996, p. 608).

Shetreet (2011, p. 3) also admits that the 'modern conception of judicial independence is not confined to the independence of an individual judge and his or her personal and substantive independence. It must include the collective independence of the judiciary as an institution'. The institutional approach is similarly central to Rios-Figueroa's definition when he perceives judicial independence as a 'relation between actor A that delegates authority to an actor B, where the latter is more or less independent of the former depending on how many controls A retains over B' (Rios-Figueroa 2006). This definition not only holds that independence is a structural feature, but recognises that independence is not reducible to a binary variable but is a continuum, where B can be independent from A to varying degrees.

However, there are some authors who dispute the usefulness of the institutional approach to the definition of judicial independence. The main reasons for such critiques come from a rule of law standpoint, as there is no institutional set-up that would directly secure what independence should aim to secure – namely, that judges are equipped to remain impartial even when the cases before them involve actors who can play some role in deciding about their careers. According to Kornhauser, the institutional approach cannot ensure the delivery of such values as economic growth or democracy, and therefore, any endeavour aimed at fulfilling the institutional prerequisites of independence should be abandoned (Kornhauser 2002).

Nevertheless, the findings by Voigt, Gutmann and Feld (2015) provide evidence in favour of the focus on institutions. They show that it is not de jure independence – institutional design – but de facto independence – how formal powers are used – that offers a significant predictor of economic growth. On the one hand, this finding undermines the notion that creating structurally insulated institutions is sufficient to ensure an adequate performance by the judiciary. On the other hand, though, it demonstrates that protection from political interference in the appointment and dismissal of judges, their jobs and financial security, all are important factors for properly undertaking judicial duties.

Output-Oriented Approaches to the Definition of Judicial Independence

The approach to defining judicial independence as a feature of the output of the judicial system is much rarer in the literature. However, the logic behind it is more straightforward. If we care about independence to ensure fair and impartial decision-making, then all judicial decisions – the output of all cases – should be based solely on the law and facts relevant to cases. Clark (2011, p. 5) thus understands independence as the ability of courts 'to make decisions that are unaffected by political pressure from outside of the judiciary'; Melton and Ginsburg similarly argue that independence means the 'ability and willingness of courts to decide cases in the light of the law without undue regard to the views of other government actors.' (Melton & Ginsburg 2014, p. 190) Other scholars broaden the definition by stating that judges should be independent from all litigating parties – there should not be any connection, feeling of gratitude, threats, bribery or, in some instances, cultural ties as they could cause a judge to identify with one party more than the other (Fiss 1993, p. 58; Larkins 1996, p. 608). These criteria for independent judicial decision-making can be related to the qualities of disinterestedness and open-mindedness Kramer associates with impartiality as an aspect of the rule of law (Kramer, this volume, chap. 10).

Here, we need to add two caveats. The first clarifies Larkins' position, as his definition seems too broad. He stresses the political dimension of judicial independence by emphasising that independent judges 'are not manipulated for political gain' (Larkins 1996, p. 611). The second concedes that judges who 'have no interest in the issues of the case' is an unrealistic objective. If only such judges were considered independent, they would have to be chosen from people absolutely excluded from society with no personal life experiences, or only be allowed to decide cases that they can under no circumstance relate to – if such are even imaginable. Other authors consider independence as the ability to pursue justice as they understand it, free from undue pressures (Karlan 2007); Aydin posits that 'a judge is independent when she can take decisions based on her preferences and interpretation of law' (Aydın 2013, p. 108). The problem with this definition, however, is that it might allow for whimsicalness on the part of a judge, and as such be in conflict with impartiality as open-mindedness, which implies a certain conscientiousness (Kramer, this volume, chap. 10).

Despite the seeming clarity of this approach, most definitions of this kind lack analytical precision. For instance, Herron and Randazzo expect independent judges not to be influenced 'by exogenous factors during the adjudication process' (Herron & Randazzo 2003, p. 423), yet for the purpose of analysis use as a measure of independence an index (Ishiyama Smithey & Ishiyama 2002) centred on the structural aspects of the concept. Popova (2012) and Clark (2011) do better. Their measures of independence focus on how frequently, and to what extent, the judiciary delivers decisions that are contrary to the preferences of certain actors who can either formally or informally exert pressure on the judiciary. Tiede (2006, p. 131) agrees that independent judges need to be independent at the institutional level. She adds the condition of impartiality only after there is a certain level of insulation, as she argues that judicial independence 'can and should be defined as the judiciary's independence from the executive, as measured by the amount of discretion that individual judges exercise in particular policy areas.' Russell also admits that there are two different approaches to independence, one understood as the autonomy of judges from other parts of the political system, the other as a type of behaviour or set of attitudes observable in judges' behaviour (Russell 2001).

All in all, while it is quite common to define judicial independence as a feature of the output of the system, scholars only rarely study large-N samples of judicial decisions empirically and instead focus on normative analyses of isolated decisions. If there is no consensus regarding the connection between the institutional (structural guarantees) and output-oriented (whether each judicial decision reflects an independent process) approaches, there is no evidence undermining the idea that the two are related (Varol, et al. 2017). Nevertheless, although it may be widely accepted that judges should 'do justice' in accordance with the law and their interpretation of it, free from any undue influence, it needs to be emphasised that this 'independence' should not be unconstrained (Burbank & Friedman 2002, p. 9). As we have noted, such freedom would only be justified if it meant judges used it to 'do justice' impartially and fairly rather than in a partisan or whimsical way.

II A UNIFIED THEORY OF JUDICIAL INDEPENDENCE: A PROPOSAL

In this chapter we propose an understanding of judicial independence which connects approaches focusing on institutional factors with those focused on outcomes. In order to do so, we introduce three levels on which we can study and analyse judicial independence. These levels are institutional *de jure* independence, institutional *de facto* independence and decisional independence that can be observed either at a systemic level or at the level of individual judges. We propose that these three levels should be analysed independently, with an assumed link between them. This assumption goes as follows: institutional *de jure* independence (what the law says regarding judicial governance) should translate into institutional *de facto* independence (how the legal rules concerning judicial governance are applied in practice), both of which should result in *decisional* independence (how judges actually decide). These three levels can be roughly summarised also as legal independence, legal independence 'as applied', and decisional independence, but it must be born in mind that in our conceptualization the former two deal exclusively with judicial governance (structural guarantees), whereas the third focuses on judicial decision-making (whether each decision reflects an independent process).

The purpose behind our proposal to analyse these three levels independently is that the link between them is only assumed. At each level, judicial independence is a consequence of the interplay between the capacity and willingness of powerful actors to exercise undue influence on courts and the capacity and willingness of judicial actors and their allies to resist such actions. To put it differently, at each of the three levels, the capacity and willingness to exercise undue influence, on the one hand, and the capacity and willingness to resist, on the other, interact anew. Hence, judicial independence on the subsequent level either increases, decreases or stays the same compared to the level which preceded it. In the following sections, we set out the questions regarding independence raised by each level, analyse what is meant by independence at each level, identify the relevant 'powerful actors,' and list possible factors that may enhance or threaten judicial independence.

Institutional De Jure Independence

Institutional *de jure* independence is concerned with how the law allocates formal powers to administer the judiciary. It thus focuses on what the law says regarding judicial governance. The rationale for such independence lies at the heart of the separation of powers. As James Madison put it, 'The accumulation of all powers, legislative, executive, and judiciary, in the same hands, whether of one, a few, or many, and whether hereditary, self-appointed, or elective, may justly be pronounced the very definition of tyranny' (Hamilton, Madison, and Jay 2003 [1787–1788], Federalist No. 47, p. 234). The questions that may be raised at this level include the following: How is the judiciary structurally insulated from other branches of power by law? What does the constitution say about appointment, promotion and dismissal of judges? Who holds the powers to administer the judiciary (such as case allocation) according to statutory law? Who sets the rules concerning judicial procedure, the salaries of judges and other matters of judicial governance broadly understood? (Šipulová et al. 2023).

The capacity to alter judicial institutions belongs almost exclusively to political branches that can 'create, modify, and destroy judicial structures as well as ... establish and alter the system of appointing, removing, and remunerating judges,' (Russell 2001, p. 13), among other competences. Political branches can increase as well as decrease the amount of independence at this level. Yet, as a considerable literature shows, such increases in institutional *de jure* independence can often be explained as instances of strategic action – to protect short-term political interests (Ramseyer 1994; Stephenson 2003; Hanssen 2004), ensure that the judiciary will not be used against politicians who have been voted out of office, (Ginsburg 2003; Finkel 2008), or motivated and driven by judges (Kosař 2016).

What does institutional *de jure* independence consist in? There have been several attempts at measuring who holds the formal powers related to the governance of the judiciary. These contributions focus on what the legal rules say on how judges are selected, appointed, promoted, disciplined, dismissed, and demoted (Ishiyama Smithey & Ishiyama 2002; Voigt, et al. 2015), who plays a dominant role in the system of judicial governance (Garoupa & Ginsburg 2009), and various less prominent aspects such as the control of administrative and financial resources, or the education of judges (Šipulová, et al. 2023). De jure institutional independence is an important first step in understanding judicial independence, but it is an unhelpful construct especially in emerging democracies, such as Latin America (Brinks 2005) and post-communist countries (Popova 2012; Kosař 2016), because it tells us little about whether powerful actors actually interfere in selection, promotion and disciplining judges or other aspects of judicial governance. That is why we need to study *de facto* institutional independence.

Institutional De Facto Independence

At the level of institutional *de facto* independence, the focus is placed on how legal rules concerning judicial governance (law on paper) are applied in practice (law as applied). Depending on the degree of congruence, 'law as applied' may converge to or diverge from 'law on paper' and it can do so in both directions. For instance, if the law says that disciplinary motions against judges can be initiated by several actors, for example, the Ministry of Justice, the President, the Chief Justice, and court presidents, it does mean that all of these actors will actually do so. Disciplinary motions can be weaponised by the Minister of Justice, such as in Poland (Gajda-Roszczynialska & Markiewicz 2020), or abused by the Chief Justice who wants to settle the score with his critics within the judiciary, such as in Slovakia (Kosař 2016). Similarly, if the law stipulates life terms for judges, it does not mean that judges actually can serve them. Judges can be forced to 'voluntarily' resign, such as in Argentina and other Latin American countries (Castagnola 2018). On the other hand, a flawed formal design that allows the executive to exercise undue influence on the workings of the judiciary 'on paper' can be remedied by constitutional conventions (Stephenson 2021) and informal norms (Pozas Loyo & Rios Figueroa 2022).

We should care about the de facto institutional independence for two main reasons. First, powerful actors can consistently utilise their powers to select or promote judges who will decide cases in their favour, so no other pressure will be necessary to secure desired outcomes (Silverstein 2008). Second, they can use their powers to demonstrate their capacity to motivate judges to either carry out or abstain from certain actions. Generally, it can be very well anticipated that if powerful actors utilise their powers at this level in a way that either substantively changes the composition of the judiciary in favour of attitudes that would be more aligned with theirs, or would be visible to judges and recognised by them, they may force judges to behave in a desired way. A tentative definition of independence at this level, therefore, could be that the judiciary is independent when decisions regarding its composition and other issues of judicial governance are not made in a manner that would reflect the partisan preferences of any powerful actor.

The capacity to influence the judiciary at this level partly depends on the answer to the question asked at the previous level: who holds the formal powers? Most commonly, these powers belong either to the political branches, the judiciary itself, occasionally to some expert bodies, or to the people. However, the formal division of powers according to law often does not tell us whether the holders of these powers have capacity to use these powers effectively. Certain institutions can be weak, lack information or personnel, or may not have the necessary legitimacy. This information asymmetry and power vacuum can be exploited by other actors and various informal norms. De facto capacity can thus vary a lot from de jure capacity.

Whether powerful actors are willing to interfere in the workings of the judiciary is a matter of strategic choice based on the estimated costs and benefits of such actions. Costs are mainly dependent on two factors – public confidence and the perceived legitimacy of such actions. As to public confidence (Urbániková & Šipulová 2018), what matters is the relative degree of confidence in the judiciary compared to other political actors. If the judiciary is perceived as untrustworthy while politicians enjoy great public confidence, then the costs of politicians using their formal powers for their own benefit will be low. If the situation is reversed, the costs of such actions will be much higher. The legitimacy argument relates to how these tasks have traditionally been performed, and whether these mechanisms are perceived as legitimate. Even though justices in federal courts in the United States are selected and appointed by politicians, and even though they are selected on the basis of their ideological proximity to the selector, the process was not perceived as a serious risk to independence (Ferejohn 1999).

The benefits of using formal powers to change the composition of the judiciary increase when powerful actors perceive the need to exercise control over the judiciary in order to secure desired outcomes or to ensure the desired atmosphere within the judiciary. For instance, politicians – particularly autocrats and wannabe autocrats – may rely on courts if electoral competition becomes more intense, as courts may provide an important bulwark in protecting their hold on power (Epperly 2019). Contrarily, the benefits decrease if actors are strongly supportive of the rule-of- law ideal and democratic institutions – including the separation of powers, or, for instance, when they do not want to endanger economic growth by scaring off investment (Voigt, et al. 2015). As the internal workings of judicial systems are not a particularly salient topic among the public, the judiciary's and judges' ability to resist these pressures is rather limited. It depends on the ability of the judiciary to attract the attention of the public and hence increase the political costs of such actions.

As institutional *de facto* independence is closely related to *de jure* independence, the dimensions that can be studied largely overlap. Powerful actors can mainly exercise pressure in matters of court personnel through administrative powers or via financial channels. Scholars often emphasise the first of these dimensions – hence decisions about personnel, especially judges themselves. Among indicators of *de facto* independence Voigt, Gutman and Feld include average term length, the difference between term length in law and reality, instances of the removal of judges before the end of their terms, or the stability of salaries (Voigt, et al. 2015). They also look at the stability of a number of judges and changes in the legal framework related to apex courts – hence the stability of the institutional setting and the level of enforcement of judicial decisions. Additionally, Kosař analyses who initiates disciplinary motions against judges and for what, as 'what really matters is not what the law says about mechanisms of judicial accountability (*de jure* judicial accountability), but how mechanisms of judicial accountability operate in practice (*de facto* judicial accountability).' (Kosař 2016, p. 149) Even court-packing, understood as an intentional irregular change in the composition of the existing court, both quantitative and qualitative, may occur through the use of *de facto* powers (Kosař & Šipulová 2023).

There are several contributing factors that may decrease independence at this level. They can be divided into two broad categories – rewards and sanctions. Rewards, such as promotion, career advancement or remuneration, can be applied selectively or abusively to create an incentive structure that may motivate judges to act in a strategic way. This is particularly true for judiciaries with the civil-service model of judicial careers which, to some extent, function as bureaucracies (Spáč 2018). As Russell (2001, p. 17) writes, 'If those who control career advancement within the judiciary are perceived to reward or punish a particular ideological orientation in judicial decision-making, judicial independence can be seriously compromised', which suggests that the decision-making of an ambitious judge can become a matter of conformity. Powerful actors can also provide financial motivation to judges through salary bonuses and other material perks.

Sanctions that may threaten independence likewise take many forms. They include not only accountability perversions – most prominently selective accountability recognisable through the unfair application of rules to specific judges or groups of judges (Kosař 2016, pp. 68–72), but also such tools as arbitrary dismissal of judges, weaponizing disciplinary proceedings against critics within the judiciary, arbitrary transfers of judges to other courts, and informal tools such as reassigning judges to smaller offices, supplying them with worse equipment and the like. The exertion of influence through the material conditions in which judges' work can be observed at the level of both individual judges and courts. What both share is the unfair application of rules that allow one to distinguish between winners and losers with regard to a certain formal power. Finally, powerful actors may provide rewards for judges to retire or threaten them (or their family members) with sanctions if they reject doing so. As a result, these judges leave offices prematurely and these vacant offices can be subsequently filled by judges who are more in sync with their preferences (Castagnola 2018).

Decisional Independence

Unlike the previous two levels, decisional independence focuses directly on judicial decision-making. Decisional independence can be analysed at the systemic level,[1] and also at the level of individual judges or cases. The former is concerned with a certain predictability in adjudication about specific actors or group of actors, while the latter looks at individual instances where independence can be compromised.

At the systemic level, scholars usually focus on the relationship between judicial power and political powers, operationalised either as the degree of opposition to politicians (Herron & Randazzo 2003; Clark 2011) or as consistency with the desired outcomes of a specific group of actors (Popova 2012). From the rule of law perspective, we believe this is the more important level for the assessment of judicial independence. At the individual level, independence is at stake at all times. Judiciaries consist of hundreds, or thousands of individuals and it can be safely assumed that at least some are always susceptible to succumbing to pressure.

At the level of the individual judge, the concern lies with the ability of judges to decide cases impartially and fairly according to their assessment of the law and the facts of the case. Here, it is necessary to distinguish between independence at the level of a case, on the one hand, and at the level of the rules or laws they apply, on the other (Popova 2012). We argue that judicial independence relates to the former and the pressure – through both formal and informal channels – to decide cases in a particular fashion. The latter refers to a situation where the laws are designed so as to unfairly favour certain actors, such as in the apartheid-era South Africa (Dyzenhaus 1998a). This situation concerns not judicial independence, but rather the fairness of legislation.

---

[1] Indeed, this dichotomy is an over-simplification – the level of judicial independence can differ between courts or types of cases. For instance, if all levels of the judiciary except for the Supreme Court decide independently, yet powerful actors can obtain desired result when they appeal to the highest court, the independence of the judiciary as a whole is compromised.

To be able to decide impartially and fairly judges need to be, first and foremost, free from fear that there will be any repercussions from their decision-making, beyond the regular and legal ways in which judges can be reprimanded. Karlan writes, 'If judges were imprisoned or physically attacked for their decisions ... they would lack the minimal safe space within which to perform a judicial role.' (Karlan 2007, p. 1043). Judges who need to worry about their safety, or about the safety of people in any way affiliated with them, are certainly very vulnerable to outside pressures. Within this category fall attacks or threats of violence coming from individuals, organised criminal groups, but theoretically from the state apparatus as well. Another unambiguously illegal way to pressure judges is corruption, and specifically bribery or the misuse of public office for a private gain. According to Rios-Figueroa, corruption is most likely in a setting where the judiciary is either too dependent on other branches of power, or it is totally independent – in terms of institutional *de jure* independence – and lacks effective accountability mechanisms (Rios-Figueroa 2006). Research in post-communist Europe showed that tolerance of corruption is associated with institutional trust, particularly trust towards self-governing bodies and judicial associations (Beers 2012).

Another tool of direct influence over judicial decision-making is the so-called 'telephone justice'. This originally referred to the use of informal mechanisms to pressure judges by politicians in Russia but could also be found in other post-communist judiciaries (Ledeneva 2008; Popova 2012) as well as in Latin America (Brinks 2005, p. 599), and need not be connected only to political actors. It consists of oral commands that are not necessarily to be perceived as a sign of corruption, and relates to the existence of informal rules that in certain cases enjoyed supremacy over formalised law, disobedience to which could put judges' careers at risk as their jobs depended on political patrons. Additionally, such patterns of behaviour may still be present in post-communist judiciaries if a sufficient change of personnel has not taken place. As Ledeneva states, 'Although it is ridiculous to suggest that every court case in Russia is decided according to directives from above or on the basis of alternative incentives, it is perfectly possible to imagine that a way to influence a particular case can be found if necessary.' (Ledeneva 2008, p. 347) Despite the fact that 'telephone justice' may have been tolerated in the past, in democratic regimes or regimes declaring themselves to be democratic it is surely not acceptable, and if it persists it must be considered an external threat to the independence of an individual judge.

From these external pressures on judicial decision-making we must distinguish the situation when a judge, courts or the judiciary as a whole imposes its values through a consistent preference for specific actors in disputes; for instance, in the criminalisation of the African-American minority in the United States (Russell-Brown 2009). As Karlan (2007, p. 1051) states, 'Judges should strive to overcome their irrational and unconscious prejudices against certain sorts of cases or litigants'. Some authors refer to this trait as 'independence as a state of mind' (van Dijk 2024). However, according to us, succumbing to prejudices is a failure of impartiality (in the sense of being open-minded, courageous and willing to argue on the basis of legal principles), not independence, which in our understanding is always relational.

Identifying powerful actors at the level of decisional independence is a complicated task. First, it is extremely difficult to uncover corruption and commands via 'telephone justice' or 'informal talks', because the relevant actors want to keep these influences hidden. Second, decisional independence can be threatened without any pressure being exercised on individual judges, because it can be done also at the previous two levels. Popova (2012) operationalises independence as a state where no actor can consistently secure a preferable outcome. Independence so defined can be undermined if powerful actors interfered with the workings of the judiciary informally at the *de facto* level – mainly through mechanisms of selection, promotion, and removal of judges; or when some actor or group of actors can utilise informal channels to pressure judges in specific types of cases.

We can thus say, recalling the Anna Karenina principle,[2] that while independent judiciaries are roughly all alike, every dependent judiciary is dependent in its own way: through being captured, rigged or skewed. Captured or rigged judiciaries are dependent, because their independence is compromised through formal or informal pressures in judicial governance, which then also translates into their judicial decision-making. Skewed judiciaries are not independent, because powerful actors interfere directly with their judicial decision-making.

The judiciary is 'captured' when powerful actors, holding formal powers to modify judicial governance, use them so as to lead the judiciary consistently to deliver favourable outcomes. A 'rigged' judiciary works correctly on paper, but somewhere between the institutional framework and the judicial decision-making certain actors can replace, modify or side-step de jure structural guarantees and distort judicial governance in their favour. A rigged judiciary, therefore, relates to both the utilisation of informal channels and to a large-scale ability to pressure a variety of courts and judges, which again results in judicial decisions unfairly favouring the powerful actors. Finally, a 'skewed' judiciary is one in which powerful actors exercise undue pressure on judges deciding on specific cases they have a stake to find in favour of one of the parties, regardless of or despite the legal merits. This may happen through various mechanisms ranging from telephone justice to 'informal talks' and bribes.

On the individual level of judicial independence, virtually anybody who has an informal channel to hand can pressurise a judge. The willingness of powerful actors to influence judges is, as always, dependent on a cost-benefit analysis related to a specific case. Factors favouring a willingness to influence are the ease of access to judicial actors, knowledge about the level of corruption in the country, and the

---

[2] As Tolstoy writes in the novel Anna Karenina: "Happy families are all alike, each unhappy family is unhappy in its own way."

ability to bribe a judge, or the perception of possible criminal repercussions in the event of attempted bribery. The benefits of any exercise of pressure on judges lie in the eyes of the beholder in combination with trust for the judicial system, a court or a judge, or the general attitude towards concepts such as fairness or justice.

The capacity and willingness of judicial actors to resist undue influence on judicial decision-making is very much related to individual judges' integrity and readiness to misuse their power and fulfil some actors' ambitions (Šipulová 2021). Their capacity depends on their physical and financial security, supportive judicial networks and existence of mechanisms on how to hold the interfering actor accountable. Their willingness to resist is certainly dependent on the tools utilised by powerful actors. When a factor of fear comes into the picture and judges feel threatened, their willingness to resist undue influence dramatically decreases. The willingness to resist bribes is also determined by peer pressure, existence of free media that are willing to expose improper interferences into judicial decision-making, a judge's perception of her role in society, trust in the institution, a general attitude towards democratic institutions, acceptance of corruption in the society and the idea of fairness in the judicial process. Standard deterrents against judicial corruption such as security of tenure and adequate remuneration are necessary, but often not sufficient, and must be accompanied by well-functioning accountability mechanisms and in venal societies also by vetting mechanisms and special anti-corruption units.

CONCLUSION

In this chapter we have presented a theory of judicial independence that may be useful for the analysis of judicial systems, as well as for policy-makers involved in the design of judicial institutions. We define judicial independence as a state when powerful actors are unable or unwilling to inappropriately interfere with the workings of the judiciary. Judicial independence is a relational concept and always results from the interplay between the capacity and willingness of powerful actors to inappropriately interfere with the workings of the judiciary, and the capacity and willingness of judicial actors and their allies to withstand such actions. We distinguish three levels of judicial independence: *de jure* institutional independence, *de facto* institutional independence, and decisional independence. We propose that, for analytical clarity, each level should be analysed independently, and the connections between them be explained and elaborated very carefully, because at each of these three levels independence is not necessarily affected by the configuration of the other levels.

Based on this analysis, we identify several possible outcomes. Courts are independent when powerful actors do not consistently impose their preferences in disputes in which they have a stake, either by capturing the courts through formal changes of laws governing the judiciary, through rigging these laws in their favour, or by skewing judicial decision-making. By contrast, a dependent judiciary is the one that is captured, rigged or skewed.

RECOMMENDED READING

Brinks, D. M., & Blass, A. (2017). Rethinking Judicial Empowerment: The New Foundations of Constitutional Justice. *International Journal of Constitutional Law*, 15 (2), 296–331.

Burbank, S. B. (2007). Judicial Independence, Judicial Accountability and Interbranch Relations. *The Georgetown Law Journal*, 95 (4), pp. 909–927.

Castagnola, A. (2018). *Manipulating Courts in New Democracies: Forcing Judges off the Bench in Argentina*, New York: Routledge.

Ferejohn, J. (1999). Independent Judges, Dependent Judiciary: Explaining Judicial Independence. *Southern California Law Review*, 72 (2–3), pp. 353–384.

Garoupa, N. & Ginsburg, T. (2009). Guarding the Guardians: Judicial Councils and Judicial Independence. *American Journal of Comparative Law*, 57 (1), pp. 103–134.

Karlan, P. S. (2007). Judicial Independences. *Georgetown Law Journal*, 95 (4), pp. 1041–1059.

Kosař, D., & Šipulová, K. (2023). Comparative Court-Packing. *International Journal of Constitutional Law*, 21 (1), 80–126.

Popova, M. (2012). What is Judicial Independence? In *Politicized Justice in Emerging Democracies: A study of Courts in Russia and Ukraine*. New York: Cambridge University Press, pp. 14–25.

Russell, P. H. (2001). Toward a General Theory of Judicial Independence. In P. H. Russell and D. M. O. O'Brien, eds., *Judicial Independence in the Age of Democracy: Critical Perspectives from around the World*. Charlottesville: University Press of Virginia, pp. 1–24.

Tiede, L. B. (2006). Judicial Independence: Often Cited, Rarely Understood. *Journal of Contemporary Legal Issues*, 15 (1), pp. 129–161.

Voigt, S., Gutmann, J., & Feld, L. P. (2015). Economic growth and judicial independence, a dozen years on: Cross-country evidence using and updated set of indicators. *European Journal of Political Economy*, 38 (C), pp. 197–211.

50

Bills of Rights

Richard Bellamy

Ever since the French Declaration of the Rights of Man and the Citizen of 1789, Bills of Rights have been regarded as the core of constitutionalism. Moreover, such bills have typically been seen as the preserve of an independent judiciary. As Article 16 of the Declaration affirmed, 'A society where rights are not secured or the separation of powers established has no constitution at all'. Bills of Rights so conceived have often been portrayed as constraints upon – and even in opposition to – democracy. As Ronald Dworkin put it in an essay on 'Constitutionalism and Democracy', constitutionalism consists of 'a system that establishes legal rights that the dominant legislature does not have the power to override or compromise' (Dworkin 1995, p. 2). However, as scholars critical of this stance point out (Bellamy 2007, chap. 1; Webber et al. 2018, p. 2), individual rights have standardly been secured through legislative action, and Bills of Rights in a number of countries are legislative instruments that the legislature has a central, and in some jurisdictions final, role in upholding and interpreting (Gardbaum 2013; Hiebert and Kelly 2015). Meanwhile, even those who conceive of Bills of Rights in terms of a justified constraint on certain democratic processes and particular decisions or actions of democratically authorised politicians and officials, have increasingly come to concede the need for such an arrangement to have some form of democratic legitimacy. They propose that this legitimacy may be achieved either through the rationale for such Bills of Rights mirroring the arguments for democracy in respecting the autonomy and equality of individuals (Dworkin 1996b, pp. 15–19; Habermas 1996, chap. 3.1), or via the actual enactment of such Bills of Rights through some form of democratic process (Ackerman 1991), such as a constitutional referendum. Yet, if democratic legitimacy is a requirement for such Bills, then, as other scholars note, rights may be more appropriately defined and established through the normal legislative process of a democratically elected legislature (Waldron 1999a, Part 3; Bellamy 2007, chap. 1 and 4)

This chapter focuses not on the possible *content* of a Bill of Rights, such as whether it should contain social and economic rights or only civil and political rights, but on the *form* any such Bill needs to take to be legitimate in a manner congruent with the moral norms of equal concern and respect underlying both constitutionalism and democracy. It explores four conceptions of Bills of Rights and the different ways they relate to democratic theory and practice. I start with the view of a Bill of Rights as distinct from normal legislation and that is ultimately the responsibility of the courts to defend. I distinguish between substantive and procedural accounts, in which the first focuses on upholding the rights necessary to ensure the outputs of democratic decisions reflect democratic norms whereas the second seeks to uphold the rights required for a due democratic process. I then turn to legislated rights and the possibility of Parliamentary Bills of Rights. Finally, I examine the role of democratic constitutional politics as a means for justifying and legitimising a Bill of Rights, be it upheld by a legislature or a supreme court.

I DWORKIN AND THE SUBSTANTIVE CASE FOR BILLS OF RIGHTS

Ronald Dworkin defended the role of a Bill of Rights and rights-based judicial review as part of a general approach to law as 'a matter of principle', based on a 'moral reading' of the Constitution. An American who held senior academic positions in Britain as well as the United States, he saw the USA's constitutional arrangements and the role the Supreme Court had come to play within them as 'providing the most important contribution our [United States] history has given to political theory' (Dworkin 1996b, p. 6), one from which the UK along with the rest of the world had much to learn. Yet, he also contended that this contribution was poorly understood even by US constitutional lawyers and legal theorists, not least in their concern that rights-based judicial review might be undemocratic through raising a 'counter-majoritarian' difficulty (Dworkin 1996b, pp. 6–7). By contrast, Dworkin wished to defend the view that such an arrangement was compatible with, and even required by, democratic norms (Dworkin 1996b, pp. 17, 20).

Dworkin's case involves three related arguments. First, he contrasts a constitutional and rights-based with a statistical and majoritarian conception of democracy. He considers that the former possesses the intrinsic democratic quality of treating all citizens as equals to a fuller degree than the latter (Dworkin 1996b, pp. 21–26). Second, he argues that it also has superior instrumental qualities in ensuring governmental and legislative decisions treat those who are subject to them with equal concern and respect (Dworkin 1996b, pp. 26–29). Finally, he contends that judges are not acting either as 'a bevy of Platonic Guardians' or on their own discretion and ideological opinions when making their judgments (Dworkin 1985, p. 27; 1996b, p. 22). Rather, their decisions are constrained by the abstract moral principles of the constitution, on the one hand, and the need to interpret them in a manner that reflects the integrity of judicial decision-making – and with it the political morality of the community, on the other (Dworkin 1985, pp. 28–31; 1996b, pp. 12–15).

With regard to the first argument, Dworkin considers a constitutional conception of democracy as securing each citizen's equal status as a 'moral member' of the political community by guaranteeing they have 'a *part* in any collective decision, a *stake* in it, and *independence* from it' (Dworkin 1996b, p. 24, emphasis in the original). He regards these three elements as being intrinsic to the very idea of democracy – part of its inner rationale – and requiring constitutional protection. The first two might be thought to be inherent to a democratic process involving equal votes for all citizens and decision by majority rule. However, Dworkin raises the traditional liberal objection that such processes may give rise to collective decisions that ignore the interests and opinions of particular minorities and individuals. They may have played no part in making that decision if the majority could simply ignore their votes, and have no stake in it if it simply marginalised their interests.

In at least some writings (e.g., Dworkin 1977, pp. 234–235; 276), Dworkin appeared to countenance such majoritarian decisions as legitimate in what he called 'policy' areas, where he considered the justified public goal was to achieve the greatest satisfaction of the greatest number of what he called an individual's 'personal' preferences for what gave them satisfaction in their own lives. However, he regarded such decisions as potentially illegitimate on matters of principle, that involved the rights of individuals to be treated as equals. The importance he gave to the third element of 'independence' comes into play here. Dworkin considered majoritarianism inappropriate for such decisions, since it risked a majority of individuals being able to impose on a minority their 'external' preferences for how other people should live their lives that involved a discriminatory prejudice against certain cultural or ethnic groups. In these cases, the state should remain neutral and give as much scope as possible to the rights of all individuals to act according to their own moral values (Dworkin 1977, pp. 235–238; 276–278).

For decisions of a principled kind, entailing upholding the rights of individuals to an equal part and stake in a collective decision and especially their equal ability to remain independent from it, he considered courts likely to prove a more appropriate venue than the legislature (Dworkin 1996b, pp. 30–31). Whereas democratic politicians might often have electoral incentives to pander to majoritarian prejudices that involved side-lining minority rights, judges had a professional training and obligation to reason in ways that respected them. Consequently, though he granted he had not provided thereby a 'positive argument in *favour* of judicial review' of legislation on the basis of an entrenched bill of rights (Dworkin 1996b, p. 33), he did consider he had shown such a system was not in conflict with democracy (Dworkin 1985, pp. 23–28; 1996b, pp. 33–34).

As we shall see below, those favouring a legislative conception of Bills of Rights contend the legislature is also a 'forum of principle', in which democratic representation gives all concerned a part in debating moral questions and acknowledges their stake in any collective decision (Waldron 1999a, pp. 289–291; (2003) pp. 388–394). These critics contend legislatures do not so much ignore rights as seek to weigh them – both against each other and alongside other moral values – in an attempt to balance competing evaluations of the relative importance and understandings of individual and public interests. True, such balancing is likely to involve 'external' preferences about how society should be most justly organised. But these preferences need not be just those of bigoted reactionaries protecting their privileges but may also be those of progressive liberals seeking equality for all (Bellamy 1999, pp. 174–179).

Although Dworkin conceded that legislators also had a duty to make constitutional judgments and adopt the 'moral reading', he never explored the institutional structures that might make this possible. Moreover, he believed that given 'the most straightforward interpretation of American constitutional practice shows that our judges have final interpretive authority, and that they largely understand the Bill of Rights as a constitution of principle ... we have no reason ... to strain for one that seems more congenial to a majoritarian philosophy' (Dworkin 1996b, p. 35). And if that history is America's greatest contribution to political theory, as he claims, by extension it offers a model that Dworkin and others have thought even countries with a different tradition – such as the UK – had good reasons to adopt (Dworkin 1985, pp. 31–32; Dworkin 1990; Dworkin 1996a).

Perhaps. This might be true if judges really did make decisions in the principled way Dworkin advocates they should. However, the evidence points to their being influenced by similar ideological commitments to those Dworkin considers mar legislative decisions. As a result, the claim that the Court is upholding the underlying democratic values of the Constitution in overruling the legislature becomes problematic. At best, it is offering an alternative reading of those values to the legislature, but then why should we prefer the Court's interpretation to the legislature's? Surely, in such a situation a democratic process is far more likely to possess the intrinsic democratic qualities Dworkin associates with constitutional democracy than a judicial process, which effectively involves judges acting as trustees for citizens. Pace Dworkin, treating the Constitution as the purview of the Court impairs the sense of responsibility politicians and citizens should feel to consider its meaning and implications for the policies they adopt. In other words, his proposal creates the very problem he claims it resolves. True, Dworkin countered that Supreme Court judgments can spark such a general popular debate (Dworkin 1996b, pp. 30–31), but to the extent that is so it is a discussion to which all but the justices are mere bystanders (Waldron 1999a, pp. 290–291).

Dworkin's defence of the intrinsic democratic qualities of rights-based judicial review proves questionable, therefore, and so casts doubt on his second argument, the instrumental claim that a judicially protected Bill of Rights improves the likelihood that legislative outputs and executive actions will uphold the moral equality of citizens (Dworkin 1985, pp. 27–28). Dworkin suggests that Courts are more likely than legislatures to protect the rights of Black citizens or of a woman's right to abortion because of the risk of majority tyranny inherent to the democratic process. This is an empirical claim, and a dubious one. While judgments such as *Brown vs Board of Education* and *Roe vs Wade* might appear to provide *prima facie* support for

Dworkin's argument, the evidence proves more complex. In both cases the Court can be regarded as having followed what was at that time majority federal opinion (Sunstein 1993d, p. 147). In fact, Courts generally respond to broader social pressures, with the US Supreme Court following sustained national opinion (Dahl 1957). Of course, it can be argued that as such they can overcome localism – evident in *Brown* in particular – and short termism, both of which can have a distorting effect, while still tracking popular preferences over the long term and, therefore, possessing democratic legitimacy. That still weakens the degree to which these judgments can be characterised as overcoming the majoritarianism of democracy. In fact, the effectiveness of these judgments depended on their being aligned with a federal majority capable of mobilising legislative action to provide the resources necessary for them to be implemented. For example, a decade after *Brown* only 1.2% of black children in the South attended desegregated schools – the main change only came with the civil rights movement and the passage by Congress of the Civil Rights Act and the Voting Rights Act in 1964 and 1965 (Tushnet 1999, pp. 147–150). At the same time, the fact that a Court rather than a legislature prompted the change has arguably weakened the democratic legitimacy such measures might otherwise have possessed and had the effect of politicising the Court and encouraging those opposed to these policies to seek to capture it. As Billings Learned Hand (1958, p. 71) predicted at the time, the more the Supreme Court has come to be conceived as what he called a 'third legislature', alongside the House of Representatives and the Senate, the more their known or expected political convictions have become an important determinant in their appointment. As a result, the judgments of Supreme Court Justices now reliably reflect the political views expressed at their confirmation hearings (Segal and Cover 1989). Given the Court settles disagreements over its rulings by a simple majority vote, the Court currently embodies precisely the dilemma Dworkin associated with the legislature: namely, that a socially conservative majority of six, thanks to President Trump's three appointees, can not only consistently override the three more liberal appointments of Presidents Clinton and Obama, possibly weakening or even overturning earlier rulings of the Court, as they have done with regard to *Roe* in *Dobbs v. Jackson Women's Health Organization*, but also undermine acts of democratic legislative majorities such as Obamacare, including – in *Shelby County v. Holder* – rolling back safeguards against racial discrimination provided by the Voting Rights Act.

Meanwhile, the Court has long used arguments that parallel the emphasis Dworkin gives to 'independence' to strike down legislation that allegedly favours the public welfare over individual rights. This line of reasoning underpinned the judgments of the so-called *Lochner* era, when the Supreme Court struck down some 150 pieces of Labour legislation, including regulations limiting child labour, on grounds that they offended freedom of contract (Waldron 1999a, p. 288). Similar reasoning with regard to the exercise of free speech underpinned *Buckley v Valeo* and *Citizens United v. FEC*. One of the many oddities of Dworkin's contrast between principled decision making, entailing respect for individual rights, and policy decisions, concerned with the general welfare, is that individual rights assume a public infrastructure to be exercised on a fair and equitable basis. Dworkin's 'independence' argument seems to be inspired by the Court's argumentation in *Roe*, that links abortion to 'privacy' and the right of women to make a choice on the basis of their personal preferences rather than having a religiously motivated 'external' preference imposed on them. Yet, as Mary Anne Glendon has noted (1991, p. 65), separating the right to an abortion from public funding and social support for abortions in many jurisdictions in the US leaves pregnant women 'largely isolated in their privacy'.

In fact, there is no clear empirical correlation between the protection of minority rights and the existence of strong form rights-based judicial review grounded in an entrenched Bill of Rights. If one looks at standard indices for the protection of civil and political liberties, such as the Freedom House Reports, then a majority of the highest performing countries, many ranked far higher than the United States, do not have strong form judicial review: these include the four Scandinavian countries, which have a very weak form of review; the Netherlands and Australia, that do not permit judicial review of statutes in rights cases; the UK and New Zealand, that have declaratory powers but leave the law in force; and the Canadian constitution that permits parliament a legislative override (King 2019b, p. 13 and n. 30). Majoritarian democracy has more than a contingent link to human rights protection because in sharing power equally, at least in formal terms, it favours the promotion of public policies that promote the equal rights of voters (Christiano 2011). By contrast, as the traditional utilitarian criticism of natural rights contended, there is a danger that appeals to rights that are unrelated to, and even deployed against, the public welfare, serve merely to protect the unwarranted privileges of privileged minorities. That danger risks being exacerbated by the narrower and less accessible forum of a Court – not least if that Court has been captured by the privileged minority.

It might be countered that many of these problems stem from the politicisation of courts and the appointment process, and might be alleviated if the latter was more independent from political influence. This leads us to Dworkin's third argument and the qualities he considered a judge should possess. As we saw, Dworkin denied his ideal judge would be a Platonic Guardian, as his former mentor, Judge Learned Hand, had feared might be the case. Hand (1958, p. 73) had confessed he would find rule by such Platonic ideal judges 'most irksome' even if he knew how to choose them, which he 'assuredly' did not. As he remarked, 'I would miss the stimulus of living in a society where I have, at least theoretically, some part in the direction of human affairs.' As we shall see, at least one school of thought holds the proper role of rights-based judicial review is to secure every citizen plays such a part in the democratic process. However, Dworkin down plays that view. His prime concern is to ensure everyone has an equal stake in decisions even if they may not have had a part in making them. Nevertheless, he denies this is a matter of a judge deciding as per a Platonic Guardian what policies might best achieve that result. Rather, they look for answers proposed by the principles enshrined in constitutional law and 'anchored in history, practice and integrity'. But as he conceded, 'we must not exaggerate the drag of that anchor. Very different, even contrary, conceptions of constitutional principle – of what treating men and women as equals really means, for example – will often fit language, precedent, and practice well enough to pass these tests' (Dworkin 1996b, p. 11).

Yet, if 'personal moral conviction' ultimately proves more important than the 'craft of a judge' in deciding contentious issues of constitutional principle, then the case for assigning them to a judicial rather than a political process becomes ever more tenuous. That seems particularly the case given that Dworkin acknowledged that many constitutional judgments required judges to address 'intractable, controversial, and profound questions of political morality that philosophers, statesmen, and citizens have debated for many centuries.' Yet, if so why should people and their representatives simply have to 'accept the deliverances of a majority of the justices, whose insight into these great issues is not spectacularly special' (Dworkin 1996, p. 74). Why should we regard a simple judicial majority as having greater weight than a legislative majority among a far greater number of representatives elected by, and accountable to, millions of citizens? (Waldron 2016a, pp. 197, 237–239).

Dworkin's account fails to convince. However, a case may still exist for two accounts of rights based judicial review that he rejects yet seem more closely aligned with democracy than his. The first, explored in the next section, stresses that its role is to improve the functioning of the democratic process. The second, different versions of which occupy the subsequent two sections, contends courts act on a mandate provided by the democratic process itself. It is to these two alternatives that we now turn.

II ELY AND THE PROCEDURAL CASE FOR BILLS OF RIGHTS

The democratic objection to Dworkin's substantive view of the Bill of Rights has been that the identification, weighing and elaboration of the fundamental values of a political community is the prerogative of citizens themselves, albeit indirectly through their elected representatives. However, that response arguably begs the question as to whether the process through which these values are debated and enacted into law is itself one in which all with a stake in the decision play an equal part, and whether the goods represented by these values are equally available to all. A number of theorists sympathetic to the democratic critique of the substantive account, seek to address this objection by adopting a procedural account of a Bill of Rights as providing the basis for judicial review aimed at upholding due process and non-discrimination in the formulation and application of the rights established by law.

This position shares with Dworkin the tradition of treating the 14th Amendment to the US Constitution, one of the three Reconstruction Amendments following the

Civil War, as encapsulating and securing all the other rights amendments through its citizenship, privileges and immunities, and – most particularly – the due process and equal protection clauses. However, on J. H. Ely's influential reading of these clauses, they should be viewed as securing what he calls 'participational' rather than substantive goals (Ely 1980, pp. 74–75). As he put it, 'they ask us to focus not on whether this or that substantive value is unusually important or fundamental, but rather on whether the opportunity to participate either in the political processes by which values are appropriately identified and accommodated, or in the accommodation these processes have reached, has been unduly constricted' (Ely 1980, p. 77).

As Ely noted, it is fairly uncontroversial that the judiciary is both competent and suited to make such 'participational' assessments of criminal and administrative procedure. His account simply broadened this competence to include issues of voter qualification and apportionment as a proper concern of the courts, alongside a wider concern with ensuring equal access to public goods and services. He held this procedural approach was a better characterisation than Dworkin's substantive approach of the series of progressive judgments on desegregation (notably *Brown* in 1954) and reapportionment (such as *Baker v Carr* in 1962) of the US Supreme Court under Chief Justice Earl Warren from 1953–1969, on which both drew for inspiration. True, issues such as the drawing of electoral districts are clearly 'political questions' – and had been judged non-justiciable for that reason in *Colegrove v. Green*, a US Supreme Court decision of 1946. Yet, they are also issues on which it might be thought politicians ought not to be judges in their own cause, given the incentives to gerrymander and in other ways to skew the electoral process to their own advantage.

Though Ely's approach has proved popular with many scholars who are otherwise critical of rights-based constitutional judicial review (e.g. Dahl 1989, pp. 191, 359 n.9), critics of his views have objected that these issues cannot be determined without reference to substantive values not only with regard to process but also to outcomes. The choice and interpretation of these values will be every bit as controversial as the moral reading of the Constitution advocated by Dworkin, involving very similar judgments concerning matters of principle (Waldron 1999a, pp. 295–296; Bellamy 2007, pp. 110–114). For example, consider such questions as whether equality in voting is satisfied simply by all citizens possessing one vote, or requires that every constituency has roughly the same number of voters, so that each vote has more or less the same weight in the aggregation process? And what about the weighting of the federated units in a federal system – should this reflect population size or be the same for all, to ensure each unit gets treated equally? Should there be special representation rights or even self-government rights for certain minority groups to ensure their voice and presence gets adequate representation? And how should votes be aggregated so as best to ensure equality – is a plurality system sufficient or should some form of proportional system be adopted, and if so what kind? All these questions involve taking a stance on what equality entails in a given context, and when and how it is appropriate to treat people the same and when relevant differences make it apposite to treat them differently. At the same time, whatever view is taken will have consequences for the functioning and outcomes of the political system. For example, a more proportional system is likely to encourage a multi-party over a two-party system, and produce coalition governments. This may give certain small parties considerable bargaining power on issues they particularly care about. How far this scenario will be regarded as justifiable, though, will depend on context and evaluations of the policy positions and character of the groups involved with regard to certain substantive values.

Inspired by Justice Stone's argument in Footnote 4 of *United States vs Caroline Products Co* of 1938 regarding 'discrete and isolated minorities', Ely tries to get around such substantive value judgments by suggesting that enhancing participation is justified when it overcomes intentional discrimination by a dominant majority ('we') against a dominated minority ('they'). Ely had in mind the ways white politicians in southern states had made black voters a consistent and marginalised minority. His concern was with the politics of presence rather than the politics of ideas or interests per se (Phillips 1995). He observed how the vote of minorities could be systematically diluted even when constituencies met the formal requirement of being equally populous by being so designed as to consistently deny representation to particular groups (Williams 1998, pp. 90–94). The difficulty lies in whether such forms of unjustified discrimination can be identified without making controversial substantive judgments as to which groups might be deserving of representation qua group. Discrimination against certain groups or views may be justified. Even in the case of a 'consistent' and 'intense' minority it will be relevant to ask what they feel intensely about and whether their consistently minority and marginalised status might not be justified. After all, this minority might hold eccentric or obnoxious views and as such be a 'they' that 'we' could ignore justifiably.

This possibility has at least figured in German Federal Constitutional Court deliberations on the constitutionality of the 5% threshold required of parties seeking representation in either the national or European parliaments. In these cases, the Court took account of the need for a degree of governmental stability, that might be difficult at the national level with an overly fragmented party system. However, wary of making 'political' decisions by reference to fundamental values, their decisions have tended to rest on simple numeric uniformity as a metric for ensuring the equality of votes and voters (Miles 2020, chap. 6). Yet, as Ely had appreciated, that can be something of a blunt instrument, consistent with more sophisticated gerrymandering techniques, as partisan districting in the United States vividly indicates (Williams 1998, pp. 102–109).

None of the above denies that issues of political process are matters of constitutional concern. On the contrary, Ely deserves credit for drawing attention to the constitutional role played by representative institutions and the political process more generally in ensuring citizens have both an equal part and stake in legislative decisions. As he notes, the US Constitution is mainly concerned with process and institutional design rather preserving certain substantive values (p. 92), and he approvingly quotes Madison's contention in *Federalist* 51 that the aim of these arrangements was to 'render an unjust combination of a majority of the whole very improbable' (p. 80). However, Madison omitted to acknowledge, or more surprisingly Ely to remark, that they were also so designed in order to protect the grave injustice of slavery by giving disproportionate weight to those states – by the time of the Civil War a minority – where slave ownership was most prevalent.[1] As I remarked above, empowering minorities against majority rule need not favour equality or justice. On the contrary, it can entrench or be productive of inequality and injustice.

Even the best institutional designs can have perverse effects in different contexts and may over time need reform. However, we have seen that in adjudicating on the participational equity of different reforms, the Court cannot avoid reference to fundamental values, as Ely desired. Moreover, while its independence may render a Court more likely to be impartial in deciding such issues than the legislature, Ely shared Madison's worry that 'a power independent of society' offered 'at best' but 'a precarious security' in this regard. After all, 'it may as well espouse the unjust views of the major, as the rightful interests of the minor party, and may possibly be turned against both parties' (quoted in Ely 1980, p. 80). Indeed, as disturbing, one should add, it may well espouse the 'unjust views of the minor against the rightful interests of the major party'. For example, the US Supreme Court does not have a great record in this regard. In *Buckley*, *First National Bank of Boston v. Bellotti*, and *Citizens United*, it interpreted the First Amendment right to free speech to declare unconstitutional majority campaign finance legislation designed to curb the disproportionate electoral influence of corporations and others with deep pockets. It is the possibility of the tyranny of the minority, and the way rights-based judicial review may support the privileges of the powerful, that partly motivates those who propose an alternative model of legislative bills of rights.

III WALDRON, TUSHNET, BELLAMY AND THE CASE FOR LEGISLATIVE BILLS OF RIGHTS

If the United States and to an extent Germany have formed the backdrop to many of the most influential discussions of constitutional Bills of Rights backed by strong form judicial review, the United Kingdom and Commonwealth countries more generally have – along with the Nordic states – served as exemplars of an alternative model of legislative Bills of Rights, in which the legislature and parliamentary committees play a determining role in rights protection alongside the courts (Gardbaum

---

[1] The most notorious measure was the 'three fifths compromise' incorporated into Article 1 Section 2 Clause 3, that counted three-fifths of each state's slave population toward that state's total population for the purpose of apportioning the House of Representatives and direct taxes. It was repealed by Section II of the 14th Amendment of 1868.

2013; Follesdal and Wind 2009). Scholars adopting this position argue that rights are more legitimately and appropriately specified through legislation by democratically elected politicians rather than through constitutional rights-based judicial review (Waldron 2006; Bellamy 2012). However, they regard politicians – both legislators and the executive, as well as administrators – as being subject to the rule of law, and hence as being subject to review by the courts regarding the degree they have acted with legal authorisation. The key difference lies in a Bill of Rights either having the status of an ordinary statute, as in the UK, or able to be repealed by simple majoritarian means, as in Canada or Victoria in Australia. As with the UK Human Rights Act, therefore, a Bill of Rights need not be an entrenched part of the constitution such as the German Basic Law or the US Bill of Rights. It may be a law that the legislature gives itself to abide by and under which it may be held accountable by the courts. Even so, that accountability need not be of a 'strong' kind, whereby a court can have the authority not to apply or even to strike down legislation it considers fails to comply with the requisite legal standards. Such arrangements usually involve 'weak' forms that allow courts to scrutinise laws for conformity with a Bill of Rights yet not to moderate or decline to apply it, although they may trigger its reconsideration by the legislature (Tushnet 2006). The issue to be addressed here, therefore, is whether such an arrangement satisfies the democratic objections to Bills of Rights, while addressing the concerns of advocates of substantive and procedural rights-based judicial review to ensure that key individual rights have protection against government or legislative action or inaction.

The case for a democratic Bill of Rights starts from the contention that the basis of, balance between, and policy implications of rights are often matters of reasonable disagreement. As a result, rights cannot be placed outside politics – for these disagreements over the interpretation of rights reflect to a large degree the normal range of political differences (Bellamy 2007, chap. 1; Waldron 2006). None of these scholars doubts that important interests are represented by rights. They may even agree on which rights should figure in any Bill of Rights – after all, there is widespread agreement on the main international rights conventions. However, agreement on rights in the abstract leaves broad scope for disagreements as to how they should be evaluated in concrete cases, and these disagreements arise from divergent moral and political judgments rather than being purely legal disputes of a technical nature. These scholars contend that it is the very importance of rights to all individuals within a political community, along with the reasonable moral and political disagreements they may hold about them, that justifies their being handled politically rather than juridically within a democracy.

The reasoning here reflects the standard and more general instrumental and intrinsic arguments for democracy, while paralleling certain liberal egalitarian accounts of rights, such as Dworkin's. The instrumental argument for democracy holds that the most legitimate and effective way of ensuring all individuals' rights are given equal consideration in the making of collective decisions is to give them an equal influence and control over the making of those decisions. This argument assumes that the collective decisions of any given political community are likely to have an equal impact on the interests of the individuals who comprise it, giving each of them an equal stake in the political process. If we accept that no individual's well-being is more important than that of any other, and – following J. S. Mill – view each individual as the best guardian of his or her own interests, then democracy will offer the most justified form of decision-making. For, 'if individuals interests are equally at stake in a political process, those individuals as a matter of fairness, have a right to play an equal part in that process to ensure their interests are taken equally into account' (Jones 1994, p. 180). As we noted above, rights protect particularly important individual interests. Moreover, securing these interests requires a public infrastructure and services, such as a legal system and police service, capable of providing the public goods on which the supply of even negative rights depend. As a result, rights involve collective decision making concerning the priorities of the political community. If the system of rights is to be equal for all, then equal participation in the political process that determines its scope and shape becomes in essence the 'right of rights' (Waldron 1999a, p. 232). The intrinsic argument for democracy comes in here, and mirrors the liberal egalitarian understanding of rights as entailed by the moral requirement to treat individuals with equal concern and respect. For the right to participate on equal terms in the co-determination of rights encapsulates the principled demand that one be considered and treated as an equal that lies behind this version of the very idea of rights (Bellamy 2007, chap. 4).

This democratic argument concurs with the view that the sort of rights enumerated in a Bill of Rights reflect special interests, but considers this specialness as being most suitably recognised in the way they are handled by politicians rather than in their being taken out of the hands of politicians and placed in those of the courts, and ultimately some supreme or constitutional Court. However, can the proponents of this position meet the concerns raised by the advocates for substantive and procedural rights-based judicial review rehearsed above? One potential dilemma lies in the way both these other views consider rights as having especial force to defend the interests of minorities and to constrain the discretion available to those who possess political power more generally by insisting they uphold the rights of those subject to their coercive authority. By contrast, the democratic account appears to place rights under the protection of the power holders possessing the support of the majority. To assuage this concern, democratic rights theorists argue both that democratic majoritarianism possesses greater constitutional qualities than these critics acknowledge, and that there are democratic mechanisms, some of which involve weak forms of judicial review, that can protect minority interests better than strong forms of judicial review.

As we saw, Dworkin considers majoritarianism a 'statistical' view of democracy, suitable for gauging which policies might best promote the general welfare but not for addressing matters of principle. By contrast, the democratic account sees majoritarianism as exemplifying equal concern and respect precisely because of its statistical qualities – one person, one vote means each citizen counts equally, while the process is neutral between their views and weighs them impartially (Waldron 1999a, pp. 113–116). At the same time, majoritarian voting can be combined with principled deliberation. As with majority voting on multi-member constitutional courts, so too in elections and in the legislature a majority vote is the end of the process rather than its entirety. Prior to that, political mechanisms of various kinds can – and in most democratic systems to varying degrees do – serve to motivate a principled debate that engages with differing perspectives on the rights and other moral considerations involved in any policy decision (Bellamy 2007, chap. 6). In line with the argument of Madison in Federalist 52, reported above, these mechanisms tend to force majorities to engage with minorities. Indeed, in complex, pluralist societies majorities rarely form a homogenous and coherent group but need to be constructed from among different minorities – a feature often reflected in the need for coalition building in multiparty systems. Consequently, party competition in election campaigns, and the need for politicians to fish for votes among a variety of constituencies, incentivises them to frame even partisan views as programmes benefitting the population as a whole and that take account of certain minority interests. Meanwhile, within the legislature the interaction between government and opposition can serve a similar purpose; as can the presence of a second chamber with scrutiny powers, such as the House of Lords (Waldron 2016c, chap. 4 and 5). These mechanisms institutionalise different kinds of checks and balances that serve the constitutional purpose of controlling the exercise of political power so as to encourage treating those subject to it with equal concern and respect.

These political mechanisms for dividing and sharing power can serve a similar role in regard to rights protection to the separation of judicial from executive and legislative power. For example, Learned Hand proposed the suspensive veto power of the House of Lords as a political alternative to judicial review (Hand 1958, p. 68). Meanwhile, a legislative Bill of Rights can lead to an explicit engagement of the legislature with rights principles. Under the UK Human Rights Act, for example, there is pre-legislative scrutiny for compliance with the Act by the Joint Committee on Human Rights of the Lords and Commons, with Ministers obliged to give a declaration of compatibility when presenting the legislation for approval. Although Section 4 of the Act allows for weak review, whereby courts may challenge that compatibility when considering individual cases, the law remains in force and the decision on whether to revise or disapply rests with the legislature – though by and large it does amend the legislation in response to the court's ruling (J. King 2015). As a result, a Bill of Rights can enhance democratic deliberation of rights without ceding democratic control of the process (Bellamy 2011).

Some scholars have argued that when linked to even weak form review, pre-legislative rights-based scrutiny leads politicians to operate under the shadow of a potentially adverse judicial decision, reinforcing the tendency for legislatures governing with courts to govern as courts would do (Hiebert 2006; Kavanagh 2009). However, part of the democratic case is that the constraints of legal reasoning that justifiably operate when deciding individual cases are less appropriate for the purposes of framing general legislation. As Dworkin argued, judicial decision-making is bound by precedent and the text. However, contrary to his claims, these constraints, weak though they may be in practice, can distort due consideration of the principles at stake since they become arguments not about the principles themselves but about the meaning of a certain formulation of those principles found in the Bill itself and the ways they have been interpreted in the past. An advantage claimed for the legislature is that they may address the moral issues raised by a policy directly, including those not stated in any Bill of Rights, without such legal distortions (Waldron 1999a, pp. 289–291). Research on pre-legislative review suggests it retains certain of these qualities, and may additionally offer a steer to courts as to how legislation should be interpreted as well as anticipating, and being bound by, how a court might interpret it, or at least promote a dialogue between the legislature and the courts (Hiebert 2005). At the same time, though, weak review offers the possibility for a legislature to think again should a particular case draw attention to an unanticipated consequence of a general measure, highlighting how legislation may impact in harmful ways on certain individuals in particular circumstances (Bellamy 2012).

Of course, the adequacy of these political processes will depend in part on how far they promote equal concern and respect for the interests of those subject to the legislation. Many of the most contentious rights issues relate to the interests of those who have no representation at all, such as immigrants and refugees, or who form discreet and isolated minorities or belong to historically discriminated groups, who have difficulty getting their interests placed on the electoral or legislative agenda (J. King 2015). Courts are often seen as providing a more accessible and responsive forum for such groups than the legislature. Yet, changes achieved in ways that appear to circumvent democratic politics risk lacking legitimacy, while the legal forum also proves more accessible to some groups than others and may favour in some circumstances certain privileged minorities resistant to legislative change. Although the aim of achieving rights equally for all may be a general one, the political and legal mechanisms most appropriate to achieving it are likely to be particular to the prevailing political complexion and cleavages of each political community at a given time. Mechanisms that may have seemed justifiable at one period, such as short-term mandates in the US House of Representatives or the equal representation of states in the US Senate, can become less so in the light of experience or in changed circumstances (A. King 1997). A dilemma thereby arises as to whether change can be left to the normal political process or not. One suggestion, to which we now turn, is that democratic constitutional change and legitimation can be best achieved outside the normal political process, through referendums for example. Of course, an issue also arises as to how and by whom the rules of such constitutional politics are to be set, thereby prompting the prospect of an infinite regress. It is to how these issues might be confronted that we now turn.

IV ACKERMAN, KING, AND THE CASE FOR THE DEMOCRATIC ENACTMENT OF BILLS OF RIGHTS

As we have noted, a persistent criticism of judicial review based on an entrenched Bill of Rights consists of the charge that it lacks democratic legitimacy. Moreover, we have also seen the counter claim that this mechanism offers a means to uphold democratic values remains open to this criticism on the grounds that it sidelines and constrains actual democratic processes and their attendant virtues. A legislative Bill of Rights offers one response to this critique, yet has been criticised in its turn for making rights vulnerable to self-serving interpretations or even abrogation by any party able to secure a majority and willing to bolster its power through unscrupulous methods, be it by pandering to populist prejudice or manipulating electoral rules. A response to both sets of criticisms involves what has been termed a dualist conception of democracy, whereby constitutional politics is distinguished from normal politics.

Dualist democracy as advocated by Bruce Ackerman (1991) contrasts the democratic process surrounding certain exceptional constitutional moments from the normal day-to-day operation of the democratic system between such moments. The former frames the latter, providing a democratic basis for how a Bill of Rights might come to be agreed and subsequently be interpreted via the courts. On his account, the need for a super majority to effect any major constitutional amendment or shift in the way the constitution is understood means that such changes will only arise at times of national crisis, such as the aftermath of the Civil War or the Great Depression. As a result of this mix of exceptional circumstances and the need to overcome high practical hurdles, constitutional politics proves to be broader and more deliberative and principled and less narrowly partisan, self-interested and policy orientated than normal politics. Each successive moment gives rise to a new constitutional regime, in which the Supreme Court is empowered to uphold a given understanding of the constitution (Ackerman 2014, pp. 2–5).

Ackerman identifies three such constitutional regimes in the USA: the Founding, Reconstruction, and the period of the New Deal-Civil Rights. He contends that in each of these periods a national crisis – the weaknesses of the Articles of Federation, Civil War, and the Great Depression, and the civil rights movement – precipitated the need for a major constitutional innovation. These crises galvanised significant popular support for change and ultimately led to either the supermajority required for ratification of the constitution and amendments by both Congress and the states, or allowed a party committed to these changes to win both the Presidency and Congress and ultimately appoint judges favourable to the change on the Supreme Court. Ackerman regards the de jure super majoritarian requirements for formal constitutional amendments and ratification under Article 5 of the US constitution, and the de facto super majoritarian constraints imposed by the separation of powers and the life terms of Supreme Court justices to altering the balance of the Court, both ensure that the prevailing interpretation of the constitution has been endorsed by We the People (Ackerman 2014, pp. 4–8).

Ackerman considers dualist democracy as providing rights-based judicial review with democratic legitimacy and allows for the judicial interpretation of rights to be progressively updated on the basis of popular consent. Yet, his account proves flawed. For a start, it omits the slave supporting constitutional order of the 1840s and 1850s culminating in the *Dred Scott* ruling; the economic liberal constitutional order associated with Lochner spanning from 1897 to 1937, the Reagan conservative era from the 1980s to 2000 and the prospect of an emerging reactionary Trump era (what follows draws on Tushnet 2020, Parts 1 and 2). All these periods represent constitutional orders marked by the minoritarian capture of the political and legal system as a result of the very counter-majoritarian divisions and separations of power Ackerman admires for their alleged super majoritarian consequences. Typically, they have involved a denial of procedural rights through forms of partisan voter suppression, such as Jim Crow, and gerrymandering of electoral districts, allowing capture of the state legislatures and House of Representatives. These measures have reinforced the minoritarianism of the Senate, where minority rule is inbuilt through the equal representation of states and amplified by the impact of the filibuster; and of the Electoral College, where the winner-takes-all rule employed by most states for the allocation of their seats has a similar effect. Meanwhile, capture of the Presidency and Congress by such means has allowed the packing of the Supreme Court with partisan appointees who not only often fail to challenge the biased application of procedural rights but also have added to them through judgments such as *Buckley v. Valeo* and *Citizens United v. Federal Election Commission* that have enhanced rather than constrained the influence of money in elections. As a consequence, substantive rights from working rights legislation to abortion rights, gun control and healthcare, have been likewise interpreted in ways that systematically operate against the views and interests of national majorities. Far from reflecting a more deliberative and consensual form of constitutional politics, these constitutional orders have provided mechanisms for the constitutionalisation of normal politics to entrench minority partisan positions. True, popular mobilisation was often needed to do so, yet this has tended to be populist rather than democratic in character. Sadly, the phenomenon of constitutionally reinforced democratic backsliding exists beyond the United States, as the examples of Hungary and Poland illustrate.

These criticisms of Ackerman's scheme do not deny the importance of the New Deal/Great Society constitutional order of the 1930s–1960s. Nor do they dispute his emphasis on the primacy of politics. However, they do underscore the possibility and dangers of pursuing normal politics through constitutional means, and note that conservatives have proven all too adept at deploying such tactics: the last time the Supreme Court had a chief justice nominated by a Democratic President was 1953, while the Court last had a majority of justices nominated by Democratic Presidents in 1969.

It might be more reasonable to expect a departure from normal politics to something more akin to what Ackerman expects from constitutional politics during formalised constitutive moments, such as the drafting and ratification of a constitution. Of course, if the involvement of the people is restricted to ratifying a document drawn up in camera by an elite, one may doubt how far such a constitution can be considered the expression of 'We the People' – especially if this exercise took place several generations ago, so that at best the dead bind the living. Ackerman's scheme is designed to overcome these dilemmas (Waldron 1999a, chap. 12). However, as Jeff King (2019a) has suggested, a more direct route might be to have a drafting convention that involves actual popular input, and to hold it every generation. Certainly, that promises an improvement in democratic legitimacy. Yet, it lacks the advantages of being able to adapt a constitutional order piecemeal, through an ongoing process of trial and error in the way a legislative Bill of Rights allows. As in Ireland, it could be possible to harness the amendment of such a Bill to popular input from citizens' assemblies and endorsement by a popular referendum, but still retain parliamentary control over the process (Daly 2015). Whether such an arrangement manages to capitalise on the best rather than the worst of all the schemes rehearsed here, though, is likely to depend on context.

CONCLUSION

Bills of Rights have come to be seen as almost synonymous with constitutions and constitutionalism. Yet they can take a number of forms and be related to democratic politics in a variety of different ways. Those sceptical as to the advantages of an entrenched and codified Bill of Rights, defended by a strong form of judicial review, are rarely sceptical as to the importance of rights as defences of important human interests, not least the capacity for autonomous action. Rather, they consider the democratic formulation and enactment of such rights as intrinsic to their exercise and the best instrumental defence of their being made accessible on an equal basis to all. Such a conception proves consistent with a legislative Bill of Rights combined with weak form judicial review, which may even include a direct role for its popular amendment and endorsement (Bellamy 2012). As with most constitutional devices, the effectiveness and legitimacy of any Bill of Rights will tend to rest on its continued acceptance by both the general public and those authorised with its interpretation and implementation. Those advocating a democratic Bill of Rights in the aforementioned sense do so in part because they consider it as conducive to ensuring its on-going popular endorsement.

RECOMMENDED READING

Bellamy, R. (2011). Political Constitutionalism and the Human Rights Act. *International Journal of Constitutional Law*, 9 (1), 86–111

Bellamy, R. (2012). Rights as Democracy, *Critical Review of International Social and Political Philosophy*, 15 (4), 449–471.

Dworkin, R. (1996a). Does Britain Need a Bill of Rights? In *Freedom's Law: The Moral Reading of the American Constitution*. Oxford: Oxford University Press, pp. 352–372.

Dworkin, R. (1996b). Introduction: The Moral Reading and the Majoritarian Premise. In *Freedom's Law: The Moral Reading of the American Constitution*. Oxford: Oxford University Press, pp. 1–38.

Ely, J. H. (1980). *Democracy and Distrust: A Theory of Judicial Review*, Cambridge, MA.: Harvard University Press.

Fabre, C. (2000). A Philosophical Argument for a Bill of Rights. *British Journal of Political Science*, 30 (1), 77–98.

Habermas, J. (1995). On the Internal Relation between the Rule of Law and Democracy. *European Journal of Philosophy*, 3 (1), 12–21

Hand, L. (1958). *The Bill of Rights*, Cambridge, MA.: Harvard University Press.

Hiebert, J. L. (2006). Parliamentary Bills of Rights: An Alternative Model? *Modern Law Review*, 69 (1), 7–28.

Tushnet, M. (1980). Darkness on the Edge of Town: The Contribution of John Hart Ely to Constitutional Theory, *Yale Law Journal*, 89 (6), 1037–1062.

Waldron, J. (1999). *Law and Disagreement*, Oxford: Oxford University Press, ch. 10.

51

Administrative Law

Farrah Ahmed

Why would a handbook of constitutional theory include a chapter on administrative law? For some, the inclusion of this chapter is natural, as there is no difference between administrative and constitutional law. In jurisdictions with codified Constitutions, we might call the rules that are traditionally or generally found in codified Constitutions 'constitutional' and other public law rules 'administrative'. But this labelling convention does not point to any important difference between the two bodies of law. Other scholars think of administrative law as constitutional law as it applies to certain officials, administrators: "administrative law is best understood as a project in which judges and other legal officials seek to work out the constitutional principles that discipline the decisions taken by those who act on behalf of the state" (Dyzenhaus 2016, p. 30). On either view, "[t]he twofold division of public law (into constitutional and administrative law) is of no great significance" and the relationship between these two bodies of law is of no great significance either (Cane 1996, p. 1).

This chapter develops and defends an opposing view: the relationship between administrative law and constitutional law is significant. The chapter develops the idea that these bodies of law regulate institutions in a delegator-delegate relationship. This idea, the chapter argues, helps us make sense of the nature and content of administrative law, as well as how it relates to constitutional law.

This chapter makes the argument in the context of common law judicial review of administrative action, with examples from England and Wales. However, the argument is likely to resonate in other jurisdictions as well, as the idea that administrators are delegates is commonplace. One economic theory of administrative law of "all the advanced capitalist democracies" proposes that "administrative law ... is designed for one purpose: to reduce to an optimal level the agency costs that arise when public officials are appointed as agents to carry out tasks for the benefit of their principals, where the principals are, in various contexts, the people, the legislatures, or the ministry" (Bishop 1990, p. 489). In the US, where administrative law diverges from common law doctrine, the "transmission belt theory" of "the agency as a mere transmission belt for implementing legislative directives in particular cases" fits with the idea that administrators are delegates (Stewart 1975, p. 1675; Criddle 2006, p. 121). In India, a key ground of review is excessive delegation, that is, 'essential legislative functions' cannot be delegated by the legislature to the executive (Massey 2012).

Against a scholarly literature which treats the precise relationship between administrative and constitutional law as insignificant, the first part of the chapter explores and fine-tunes the best available account of the relationship: namely, that offered by John Gardner. Gardner argues (roughly) that administrative law regulates institutions whose powers are delegated and constitutional law regulates those that delegate. The chapter then defends this view from criticism by elaborating on the nature of delegation in public law. Next, the chapter shows how this understanding of the relationship between administrative law and constitutional law ('the delegation theory') illuminates the nature of administrative law, makes sense of the scope and content of common law administrative law and yields important theoretical insights about the nature of public law.

I ADMINISTRATIVE LAW AND CONSTITUTIONAL LAW

In the course of an essay on the possibility of a written constitution, John Gardner writes:

> [T]he distinction between questions of constitutional law and questions of ordinary public law (also known as administrative law) lies in the type of institutions that these respective parts of the law regulate. Administrative law regulates institutions whose powers are delegated ['administrators']. Constitutional law regulates those that do the delegating, i.e. institutions whose powers are not delegated but are, as it is sometimes put, inherent or original ['constitutional institutions'].
> (Gardner 2011, p. 170)

Gardner later clarifies that the pedigree of the institution does not determine the category to which it belongs. Institutions are 'constitutional' when significant practical (but not necessarily legal) impediments stand in the way of their powers being revoked.

For instance, on one understanding of the US Constitution, the powers of the US Congress, President and Supreme Court might be revoked by a reconstituted Constitutional Convention (like the 1787 Philadelphia Convention); but this far-fetched possibility does not change the constitutional status of Congress, the President or the Supreme Court. In the UK, even if Parliament and the High Court began life with delegated powers from the Crown, they are constitutional institutions today because the delegation is now practically irrevocable. Thus, in the UK, constitutional institutions include Parliament, the Crown and the High Court; administrative institutions include local councils, tax inspectors and tribunals.

With this clarification, on Gardner's account:

1. constitutional institutions are state institutions whose powers are either inherent or practically irrevocable by the delegating institutions,
2. administrators are delegates of constitutional institutions which can revoke the delegated powers, and
3. constitutional law regulates constitutional institutions while administrative law regulates administrators.

I would tweak this slightly in response to recent work reminding us of the significance of rules of tort in regulating official action (Varuhas 2018). Tort law applies to a range of actors; but it does not regulate administrators *qua* administrators. The tweaked distinction is now: constitutional law regulates constitutional institutions *qua* constitutional institutions; administrative law regulates administrators *qua* administrators.

This understanding of the significance of delegation in the relationship between administrative and constitutional institutions is supported by a wealth of common law sources. In *GCHQ*, Lord Fraser explicitly bases judicial review of statutory and prerogative powers on their delegation from Parliament and the Crown respectively.[1] In *ex parte Lain*, Parker LJ[2] endorses the view that the decision of the Criminal Injuries Compensation Board was subject to administrative law because it is 'a servant of the Crown charged by the Crown, by executive instruction, with the duty of distributing the bounty of the Crown'.[3] Diplock LJ described the Board members as 'agents of the Crown'.[4]

Many judges and scholars[5] have characterised non-state bodies exercising de facto state powers as delegates of Parliament or the Crown to explain why they are subject to administrative law and held to the duties of (other) administrators (Donnelly 2007; McLean 2012, p. 260). In *Aga Khan*, Lord Hoffmann suggested that whether 'the Club might de facto be a surrogate organ of the government'[6] was relevant to amenability on the grounds that 'governmental power may be exercised de facto as well as de jure'.[7] Judgments in *Datafin* characterise the Takeover Panel as akin to a delegate in a delegation relationship created by implicit, rather than express, understandings to explain its amenability to review. Lloyd LJ characterised the set-up as 'an implied devolution of power'[8] and Nicholls LJ as 'indistinguishable in its

---

[1] *Council of Civil Service Unions v Minister for the Civil Service* [1985] AC 374, 399.
[2] In comments that have been cited with approval, e.g. *R v The Disciplinary Committee of the Jockey Club Jockey Club, ex p Aga Khan* [1993] 1 WLR 909 (per Sir Thomas Bingham MR).
[3] *R v Criminal Injuries Compensation Board, ex p Lain* [1967] 2 QB 864, 882 (Lord Parker CJ).
[4] Ibid. 888 (Lord Diplock); see also *Council of Civil Service Unions v Minister for the Civil Service* [1985] AC 374, 409.
[5] McLean argues that contracting out arrangements were based on a theory of the firm which treated "the Minister as the principal and the chief executive as her contractual agent".
[6] *R v Disciplinary Committee of the Jockey Club, ex p Aga Khan* [1993] 1 WLR 909, 932.
[7] *R v Disciplinary Committee of the Jockey Club, ex p Aga Khan* [1993] 1 WLR 909, 931.
[8] Ibid. 849.

effect from a delegation by the council of the Stock Exchange to the Panel ... of its public law task'.[9] Sir John Donaldson MR was influenced by the 'willingness of the Secretary of State ... to use the Panel as the centrepiece of his regulation of that market'.[10]

Later cases also implicitly and explicitly characterise non-state bodies subject to administrative law as delegates of Parliament or the Crown. In *Servite*, Moses J[11] found that Servite was *not* amenable to judicial review because it 'was not acting as agent of Wandsworth (Council)' which 'had no power to delegate its obligations'.[12] Burton J of the High Court in *Leonard Cheshire* followed *Servite* in using 'true delegation' as part of the test of amenability.[13] The Court of Appeal in *Hampshire County Council v Beer* also used language strongly suggestive of implicit delegation as the test of amenability: the body in question had 'stepped into the shoes' of the Council[14] and was 'taking the place of central government or local authorities'.[15]

There is therefore support for the delegation theory, particularly the idea that administrators are delegates of constitutional institutions, and that administrative law regulates these delegate administrators. But many are still sceptical that anything of significance hangs on the relationship between constitutional and administrative law, in part because despite Gardner's account, "the dividing line between constitutional and administrative law [is] hard to locate and somewhat artificial" (Elliot & Thomas 2014, p. 4). But (to my knowledge) there has been only one principled defence of this scepticism which grapples with Gardner's proposed distinction of the two bodies of law. David Dyzenhaus mounts a challenge to Gardner's view; addressing this challenge indicates how the delegation theory needs to be developed.

Dyzenhaus explains Kelsen's view that "the parliament in any legal order creates law at a very high level but still at a level below the constitution. So the parliament, like an administrative body, exercises authority delegated by the level above..." (Dyzenhaus & Thorburn 2016, p. 21). This poses a challenge for Gardner's distinction because that distinction is based on the difference between (administrative) 'institutions whose powers are delegated' and constitutional institutions 'that do the delegating' (Gardner 2011). The distinction, Dyzenhaus suggests, is undermined if

---

[9] *R v Panel on Take-overs and Mergers, ex p Datafin plc* [1987] QB 815, 852.
[10] Ibid. 838, 835.
[11] In a judgment Lord Mance called "illuminating and persuasive": *YL v Birmingham City Council* [2008] AC 95, 139–140.
[12] *R v Servite Houses ex p Goldsmith* [2001] LGR 55, 69.
[13] *R (Heather) v Leonard Cheshire Foundation* [2001] EWHC Admin 429. While the Court of Appeal offered different reasons for its decision, its focus was on the Human Rights Act 1998, so these comments on amenability to judicial review from the High Court (examined with "obvious care and skill" *R (Heather) v Leonard Cheshire Foundation* [2002] 2 All ER 936, 939) remain valuable.
[14] *Hampshire County Council v Beer (Graham) (t/a Hammer Trout Farm)* [2004] 1 WLR 233, 248. For similar language in agency law, see *Imageview Management Ltd v Kelvin Jack* [2009] EWCA Civ 63 (per Jacob LJ).
[15] Ibid.

it turns out that the powers of constitutional institutions are also delegated, albeit by the constitution.

To put it in Dyzenhaus' terms, it looks as though both constitutional and administrative law involve ensuring that state institutions abide by their "formal authorization rules" (Dyzenhaus & Thorburn 2016, p. 16). He concludes that on this view: "Constitutional law is then the ultra vires principle of administrative law writ large, the principle that a body that wields delegated power cannot go beyond the terms of its mandate" (Dyzenhaus & Thorburn, 2016, p. 21).

Dyzenhaus' important objection points to the need for greater attention to the nature of delegation in public law. His objection, like many discussions of delegation, equates delegation to 'authorisation by a rule'. Dyzenhaus is supported in this equation by the terms of the debate between ultra vires and common law theorists, particularly ultra vires theorists' identification of the duties of Parliamentary delegates with the terms of the empowering statute (Dyzenhaus & Thorburn 2016, p. 30).

However, the next section will argue, contra Dyzenhaus, that there is more to delegation than authorisation to do something. It will sketch an account of delegation which allows us to see why the relationship between administrative and constitutional law is significant and which makes sense of the scope and content of common law administrative law.

II ADMINISTRATORS AS DELEGATES

In what sense are administrators delegates? If we are looking for answers, two places are particularly promising. First, judges and commentators explicitly and implicitly explain the common law grounds of review of administrative action by reference to the idea that administrators are delegates (Ahmed 2021). Indeed, this idea is directly expressed in some grounds of judicial review, for example, *delegatus non potest delegare* (a delegate cannot delegate a power further). Second, private law regulates delegates through the law of agency, which has developed ideas about the identity and duties of agents. The private law understanding of delegation may well shed light on the nature of delegation in public law, given the well-established continuities between the two (Oliver 1999). In my previous work, I offered an account of public law delegation that draws on these resources (Ahmed 2021). On this account, the idea of delegation contrasts with the idea of 'formal authorisation by a rule' in at least three ways.

First, not all delegates are delegates by virtue of 'formal authorisation rules'. Some relationships of delegation develop over time from implicit, rather than express, understandings between the delegator and delegate. The ordinary understanding of delegation often involves explicit agreement between the delegator and delegate (e.g. when I ask my friend to bid on my behalf at an auction and she agrees). However, the ordinary understanding of agency or delegation also admits of cases of delegation that develop over time from implicit, rather than express, understandings between the delegator and the delegate. The law of agency recognises such agency relationships if agent and principal 'have agreed to what amounts in law to such a relationship even if they do not recognise it themselves' (Bennett 2013, p. 4; Criddle, Miller, & Sitkoff 2019, p. 26). Moreover, even though the paradigm case of delegation involves a delegate who consciously agrees to act as a delegate, the ordinary understanding of delegation also admits "unwitting agents" as instances (even if non-paradigm instances) of agents (see e.g. numerous descriptions of Donald Trump as an "unwitting agent" of Russia: Morrell 2016; Porter 2019).

In public law, the clearest cases of delegation in the absence of formal authorization rules involve judicial review of non-state non-statutory bodies exercising *de facto powers*. In *Datafin*, and other cases discussed earlier, bodies exercising de facto powers were characterised and treated as delegates of Parliament or the Crown, even though neither Parliament nor the Crown laid down 'formal authorization rules' granting them powers.

Secondly, not all delegates exercise the *powers* of their delegator by invoking a rule that authorises them to do so. It is a mark of a delegate that they have the ability to exercise (at least some of) the legal powers of their delegators (Leow 2019, pp. 107–113). ('Legal power' refers to the ability to change a person's legal position by performing an act with the intention to change their legal position, for example, powers to contract, marry or decide legal disputes (Perry 2015, pp. 660–664)). But delegates may be able to exercise the legal powers of their delegators in different ways.

In the most straightforward case, the delegator may legally *devolve* their powers to the delegate, as government officials regularly do to other government officials or bodies, so that the delegate has the ability to exercise the delegator's powers. But alternatively and importantly, the delegate's acts may also consistently *trigger* an exercise of the delegator's powers because the delegator has a legal or non-legal rule (e.g. a policy or social rule) (Perry & Ahmed 2014) of exercising these powers in response to the delegate's act.[16] For example, if a doctor is found guilty of misconduct by a professional body, government officials may have a policy of legally barring them from practice on the back of the professional body's findings. This second, indirect way in which delegates can exercise their delegator's powers shows why delegation cannot be reduced to 'authorization by a rule'.

We can see examples of delegates indirectly exercising delegator's powers by triggering their exercise in important public law cases. In *Datafin*, there was 'the unspoken assumption' that the Takeover Panel could trigger the exercise of statutory powers;[17] bodies with statutory powers treated breach of the Takeover

---

[16] This rule must be particular to the delegate; if the delegator would have exercised the power in response to that action regardless of who had performed it, this does not indicate a relationship of delegation.

[17] *R v Panel on Take-overs and Mergers, ex p Datafin PLC* [1987] QB 815, 826, 834 (Donaldson MR).

Code administered by the Panel as *ipso facto* constituting misconduct under their own rules.[18] Sir John Donaldson in *Datafin* acknowledged this when he said that the Panel's determination 'is merely *one step in a process* which may have the result of *altering ... legal rights or liability*' (i.e. they can indirectly exercise a legal power).[19]

In a similar case, *R v Advertising Standards Authority ex p The Insurance Service plc*,[20] the Advertising Standards Authority was a company whose objects included the promotion and enforcement of advertising standards. Government regulations charged the Director General of Fair Trading to consider certain complaints about advertising. But the regulations authorised the Director General to demand that the complainant demonstrate that 'established means of dealing with such complaints' had been invoked.[21] The upshot was that the Director General would use his powers under the regulations if and only if a complaint to the Authority had not 'produced a satisfactory result',[22] that is, had not been complied with. Thus, failure to follow the Advertising Standards Authority's decision would lead to the Director General of Fair Trading using her or his powers under regulations. Here again, the Authority was a delegate who could exercise the delegator's powers *not* because it was authorised to do so by a rule, because it possessed the ability to trigger an exercise of the powers of its delegator.

Thirdly, there is more to delegation than 'authorisation by a rule' because delegates have duties beyond strictly following the terms of such authorisation. This is because a delegate holds an office, that is, 'a position, devoted to a characteristic kind of action ... whose grounding in [particular] purposes gives rise to particular duties and privileges that derive from the position' (Sabl 2002, p. 1; Roughan 2018, p. 210).

I have argued elsewhere that administrative law reflects the moral duties that administrators possess as delegates of Parliament. These moral duties should be understood by reflection on the three aspects of delegation relevant to administrative law:

a. mandate delegation, which involves the delegate performing certain extremely well-defined actions and exercising very little discretion;
b. effectuate delegation, which involves delegates effectuating – or giving concrete form to –the general or abstract purposes of the delegator and;
c. expressive delegation, which involves delegates expressing the delegator's values or state of mind.

---

[18] Ibid. 834–835.
[19] *R v Panel on Take-overs and Mergers, ex p Datafin PLC* [1987] QB 815, 837 quoting from *R v Criminal Injuries Compensation Board, ex p Lain* [1967] 2 QB 864.
[20] [1990] 2 Admin LR 77, 77–93.
[21] Ibid. 80–81.
[22] Ibid. 81.

Judicial review of administrative action under the common law is available on specified grounds: that an administrative action was *ultra vires*, based on irrelevant considerations, made without hearing affected parties, etc. But common law courts have never offered an account of why judicial review is available on these specified grounds. I have argued elsewhere that reflecting on these three aspects of delegation in public law helps us to appreciate moral duties that administrators have qua delegates of constitutional institutions (Ahmed 2021); these moral duties closely track the grounds of review in common law administrative law.

Private law recognises that delegates have duties qua delegates by holding agents not just to their contractual duties, but to fiduciary duties which arise by virtue of their position as agents. Private law duties on agents to exercise powers for the purpose for which they were conferred, to exercise discretion 'in a manner that is not capricious, arbitrary or so outrageous in defiance of reason that it can be properly categorised as perverse' and not to delegate power further (without the principal's permission) (Bennett 2013, pp. 88–89; Munday 2016, p. 196). These private law duties have a parallel in familiar common law grounds of review of administrative action (Munday 2016, p. 196). It is a strength of the delegation theory that it makes sense of such similarities of the duties of delegates across public and private law. For if delegates have moral duties qua delegates, we would expect that these duties are found across the public-private divide, even if the precise content of these duties depends on the particular delegator and terms of delegation.

III EXPLAINING ADMINISTRATIVE LAW WITH DELEGATION

Return now to Dyzenhaus' objection to Gardner's proposed distinction between administrative and constitutional law based on administrators' character as delegates. Dyzenhaus points out that administrators – those subject to administrative law – are not the only delegates relevant to public law theory; constitutional institutions are also delegates. This objection hits the mark if we equate delegation to authorisation by a rule. But if we accept the argument made in the previous section that that there is more to delegation than such authorisation, where does that leave Dyzenhaus' objection?

It could be argued that, even on the understanding of delegation offered here, constitutional institutions might be thought of as delegates of (say) constituent assemblies or conventions (like those which created the US or Indian constitutions), or even 'the People', just as administrative institutions are delegates of constitutional institutions. Perhaps Indian Parliament, for example, is the delegate of the 1946–1950 Indian Constituent Assembly, even though the latter has ceased to exist. If we accept this, then Gardner's proposed distinction between constitutional and administrative law and institutions does not point to a difference in their fundamental character. Rather, constitutional and administrative institutions are consecutive links in a chain of delegation.

Much more would need to be said in support of this version of Dyzenhaus' objection. The idea of constituent power that animates it is controversial (Loughlin, this volume) and does not find support in Dyzenhaus' own thinking (Dyzenhaus 2012a). Moreover, administrative and constitutional institutions, on Gardner's view developed here, are linked by a *working relationship* of delegation through which they govern. The paradigm case of delegation in ordinary usage, and in public and private law, presupposes that the delegator currently exists; it might be contrasted with devolution which suggests a transfer of power or authority. While we may admit of the possibility of a delegate of a deceased person, or an obsolete assembly, this is a marginal case of delegation which contrasts with the paradigm case of a living (usually functioning) delegator. Indeed, one could argue that there is a fundamental difference in character between administrators who are delegates of *existing* institutions, with which they share a working relationship, and constitutional institutions which (we accept for argument's sake) are delegates (in some sense) of obsolete institutions.

In any case, if we were to accept this version of Dyzenhaus' objection, the upshot would be that Gardner's account overstates the difference between constitutional and administrative law. But even if Gardner overstates this difference, his key insight for the purpose of this chapter is that the *relationship* between these two bodies of law is significant, and worthy of attention.

Dyzenhaus' objection forced us to interrogate how we understand delegation. The previous section sought to show – through a response to Dyzenhaus' characterization of delegation – that, properly understood, delegation helps us understand and make sense of administrative law. Thinking about administrators as delegates of constitutional institutions offers a way to make sense of the grounds of judicial review of administrative action, taken together, as the grounds reflect the duties of delegates (in public and private law). Thinking about administrators in this way also helps resolve another puzzle: the scope of administrative law, particularly its availability against non-state actors. The account of delegation offered above anticipates that some non-state bodies will qualify as delegates of state bodies, and will have the ability to indirectly exercise their delegator's state powers. Thinking of administrators as delegates of constitutional institutions thus has the capacity to make sense of the scope of administrative law as well. This way of thinking about administrative law, and its relationship with constitutional law, is therefore very significant.

To underscore this significance, the rest of this section critically reviews other theories of administrative law to demonstrate the advantages of the delegation theory. Our understanding of administrative law is enriched by important work identifying 'public law values', constructing empirically-grounded accounts of administrative law practice, offering accounts of the idea of public law and modelling administrative law (Craig & Rawlings 2003, pp. 14–17; Harlow & Rawlings 2009, pp. 46–47; McLean 2012, p. 266; Bell, Elliot, Murray et al. 2016, pp. 23–244; Nason 2016; Loughlin 2010; Loughlin 2003; Rawlings 2008; Harlow & Rawlings 2009, pp. 1–48).

The focus in what follows is on interpretive theories of administrative law, as they aim to illuminate, make intelligible and make sense of administrative law, as does the delegation theory.

First, Trevor Allan's theory – justifying judicial review by reference to individual rights and interests – is the most influential of these (Allan 1994, p. 223). Allan argues that we can understand "the purposes and operation" of judicial review in terms of justice, fairness and equality, understood in a particular way. Justice requires that when public authorities seek to curtail rights, they should be bound to act within the limits of their legal powers, and that public authorities should give effect to statutory rights (ibid.). Fairness – understood by Allan as 'the fulfilment of popular will' – supports judicial review to compel a public authority to perform its statutory duty 'imposed in the public interest'. Equality and the rule of law require that 'administrative action should discriminate between citizens [only] for proper reasons, sufficiently related to legitimate governmental purposes, as those may be gleaned from the statute'; they also require that the government acts within its jurisdiction so that 'no one shall suffer disadvantage at the hands of government except in the proper exercise of lawful authority' (ibid., p. 173). There is much more to say about Allan's theory – spread over several books and papers – than any single chapter could say. There is also much that could be said by way of criticism and response. The main criticism of Allan's theory relates to the most vital indicator for the success of an interpretive theory – *fit*.

Allan urges us to understand public law "primarily as protecting individual rights" (ibid., p. 214). This understanding sits uneasily with the common conception of duties under judicial review as "owed to the public at large rather than to individuals" (McLean 2012, p. 205). This understanding is also significantly out of step with legal doctrine. As Jason Varuhas argues, "it remains difficult to imagine how significant and traditional doctrines of review such as improper purpose, delegation, relevant considerations, bias, review for factual error, and 'bog-standard' *vires* review, which forms the central plank of many review challenges ... could be recalibrated around a right-centred approach" (Varuhas 2013, p. 379; McLean 2012, p. 235). The possibility of intra-governmental disputes, particularly, the availability of judicial review *to* government actors, sits uneasily with a rights-focussed theory of judicial review (Poole 2005, p. 161). Allan's theory does not fit with standing rules which allow public-spirited individuals and groups to bring cases even when their individual rights are not affected, a point appreciated by judges (Varuhas 2013, pp. 381–382, 410–411). The right-centred approach is also at odds with the remedies available under judicial review, in particular the limited availability of damages under the common law (Varuhas 2013, pp. 383–384). Allan's 'rose-tinted' account of judicial review – where judges exercise 'independent', even 'personal' moral judgement – has also been criticised; as one critic rhetorically asks, "is the author's public law one which students of immigrations law, or race relations or social security, would recognise" (Allan 1994, p. 199; Munro 1994, pp. 456–458)? Overall, as Thomas Poole concludes, Allan's theory contrasts with the 'traditional British understanding of the practice' where 'the primary function of judicial review is to enforce the commands of Parliament as expressed for the most part, in enacted statutes' (Poole 2003).

A second category of theory of judicial review features the rule of law. The ideal of the rule of law has grown to require not just Fullerian principles relating to certainty, stability and consistency, but natural justice, access to courts, fundamental human rights, socio-economic rights, legal literacy and even more (Craig 2005; Barber 2004). Even those who appeal to the rule of law admit that it is a protean, imprecise and contested concept and that the "precise content of the rule of law is notoriously controversial" (Elliott 2001, p. 100; Tomkins 2010, p. 7).

Compare this with an interpretive theory of contract law viewing 'contract as promise', which has the potential to achieve the ends of an interpretive theory because thinking about contracts in relation to promises may plausibly reveal the intelligibility, coherence and significance of the features of contract law. This is because promises are common social phenomena, whose basic features and normative force are well-understood. In contrast, it would be very difficult to craft an illuminating and coherent explanation of judicial review based on the unwieldy ideal of the rule of law.

Perhaps unsurprisingly then, theorists often appeal to the rule of law, not in interpretive theories of judicial review, but in evaluations of legal arrangements or in arguments about the legal and constitutional basis for judicial review. For instance, some of Allan's work seeks to evaluate legal and political arrangements against the ideal of the rule of law (Allan 2003, p. 125). And, according to Mark Elliot's influential version of the ultra vires doctrine, Parliament has a "general intention that the discretionary power which it confers should be limited in accordance with the requirements of the rule of law" (Elliott 2001, p. 110); courts give effect to this intention of Parliament by elaborating what the rule of law requires of administrators exercising their discretion (ibid., pp. 90–110). This view is attractive especially since judges appeal to the rule of law in judicial review decisions.

Despite its significance in his account of the legal and constitutional basis of judicial review, Elliott argues that the rule of law is at best "able to furnish the courts with a principled *starting point* in their determination of precisely how governmental power should be controlled. It cannot ... dictate the precise conclusions at which the courts should arrive", that is, "the exact content of the controls which apply to discretionary powers" (ibid., p. 105). It is unsurprising then that there has been no systematic account of how (a coherent defined understanding of) the rule of law explains specific grounds of review (ibid., p. 99). Elliott is clear that his focus is not on the grounds of judicial review. His "focus ... is on how the law of judicial review is accommodated, at a structural level, by the unwritten constitutional order of the United Kingdom, rather than on the substantive content of the grounds of review deployed by the courts" (ibid., p. 12) or the "specific principles of judicial review" (ibid., p. 106). We might follow Elliott in thinking about the rule of law "when it is applied to a particular legal system" as "simply a convenient label which described the fundamental values on which that system is based", those values being "broadly rooted in the normative heritage which the rule of law ethos represents" (ibid., p. 104). Again, this explains the attractiveness of the rule of law as the legal and constitutional basis for judicial review, but not as the basis for an interpretative account of administrative law. By contrast, the idea of delegation is able to ground such an account, where the rule of law cannot.

In a third category of interpretive theories of judicial review is Adam Perry's 'Plan B' theory. Perry argues that 'judicial review is a planned activity to supervise the planning of officials, in case they fail to do so adequately themselves. The grounds of review are the same grounds on which officials would, ideally, review their own decisions' (Perry 2017, p. 22). While 'Plan B' is an attractive account of judicial review, which fits the doctrine well, the delegation theory presents advantages. 'Plan B' understandably takes judicial review of an official's exercise of statutory powers as a typical case, but it does not explain at all judicial review of de facto powers, a significant feature of judicial review. 'Plan B' also does not explain judges' claim to *transparency*. The law understands itself as providing moral reasons for action and as being transparent, that is, judges' purported reasons for decisions are taken to be their true reasons for decisions (Smith, 2004, pp. 3–37). A theory which makes sense of administrative law must respond to this feature.

Of course, no one would expect judges – especially given the pressures of deciding particular cases before them – to articulate an account of judicial review with the sophistication of Perry's, drawing carefully as it does on philosophical thinking about plans and the nature of law. But the core idea behind Plan B is 'simple' (Perry, 2017, pp. 1, 2, 7). Generations of common law judges have had opportunities to reflect (and comment) on the foundations of judicial review in the course of deciding cases. Perry's account does not offer us evidence that they relied on (even in a rudimentary form) something approximating the Plan B theory; and it does not offer us an explanation of why they would not or could not have done so. In comparison, the delegation theory explains judicial review of de facto powers, and does offer an explanation of judges' claim to transparency. This account shows that judges have explicitly and implicitly appealed to the idea that administrators are delegates over a range of judicial review cases.

In the fourth and final category of interpretive theory of judicial review are fiduciary theories of judicial review, particularly influential in Canadian public law. According to fiduciary theories of government, 'public officials enjoy a position of power and owe obligations comparable to those of agents, trustees and other fiduciaries' (Criddle et al. 2018b, p. 1). Fiduciary theories argue that the state, government or administrators – by analogy or definition – are fiduciaries of those subject to them, and that administrative law duties parallel the duties that private law attaches to fiduciary relationships (Sossin 2003; Criddle 2006; Fox-Decent 2011). In the English context, Dawn Oliver's work has uncovered the striking parallels between fiduciary law relating to trustees and administrative law (Oliver 1999, p. 309). She shows that trustees, like administrators, must not delegate powers without authority, act capriciously or outside the scope of their power, act unfairly between beneficiaries, and take irrelevant considerations into account, use their powers to effectuate the purpose (of e.g. the trust) or breach legitimate expectations without a hearing (Oliver 1999, p. 309). A judge may also interfere if trustees had "taken into account irrelevant, improper or irrational factors, or their decision was one that no reasonable body of trustees properly directing themselves could have reached".[23] The parallels are so striking that some have gone so far as to suggest that the legal basis of judicial review is in fact equitable (Turner 2016, pp. 326–366), though there are reasons to doubt this conclusion. Timothy Endicott for instance notes "(1) how deeply different the role of a fiduciary is, from the role of administrative agencies in general, and (2) how different the role of judges is in enforcing trustees' fiduciary duties, from their role in reviewing the lawfulness of administrative decision making" (Turner 2016, pp. 367–379).

Fiduciary theories accurately capture some important features of judicial review, and aspects of these theories – particularly the analogy between administrative law and fiduciary law – have inspired the delegation theory offered here. But fiduciary theories have been criticised for lack of fit with doctrine in Canada and England, with critics throwing doubt on the appropriateness of the analogy between administrative law and private law fiduciary relationships (ibid.; Criddle et al. 2018a, p. 35). These problems are unsurprising because many fiduciary theories are meant as responses to the problem of political authority, rather than interpretative accounts of particular areas of law (Criddle et al. 2018a, pp. 21–48).

The delegation theory has strong resonance with such fiduciary theories, but it differs significantly, if subtly. These differences allow the delegation theory to evade much of the criticism directed at fiduciary theories. Unlike fiduciary theories, the delegation theory is highly attentive to doctrine. Further, criticisms of fiduciary theories aimed at the parallels that they draw between officials and *trustee-type* fiduciaries do not implicate parallels that the delegation theory draws between administrators and *delegates or agents* (Gold & Miller 2014, p. 397; Criddle et al. 2018a, pp. 306–330). Finally, the delegation theory is unaffected by controversies over 'whether and, if so, how conventional fiduciary duties can be extended from bilateral relationships to public administration for diverse constituencies' (Criddle et al. 2018a, pp. 7, 306–330). Unlike fiduciary theories which centre on the relationship between the state or state officials (as fiduciaries) and 'the people' as beneficiaries, the delegation theory centres on the relationship between Parliament and the Crown (as principals) and administrators (as agents) (Criddle et al. 2018a, p. 51). The delegation theory thus evades many objections raised against the indeterminacy, imprecision and challenges associated with the diverse beneficiaries at the heart

---

[23] *Edge v. The Pensions Ombudsman* [1998] 3 W.L.R. 466; ibid.

of fiduciary theories (Criddle et al. 2018b, pp. 6–7; Leib, Ponet, and Serota 2014, p. 397).

The delegation theory, as a way of thinking of administrative law and its relationship with constitutional law, thus has attractions even over its sophisticated competitors.

CONCLUSION

The relationship between constitutional and administrative law is usually seen as a non-problem, as the conventional wisdom is that there is no distinction between them, or that nothing of significance hangs on their relationship. The sense that there is nothing significant about the constitutional-administrative law relationship is reinforced by the blurring of the boundary between them in many jurisdictions that are prominent 'exporters' of public law. In the US, important scholarship questions the boundary between these areas of law in order to better respond to the core constitutional concerns of administrative law (Metzger 2010). In South Africa, complex connections between administrative law and constitutional text and principle make untangling their relationship challenging (Hoexter 2017; O'Regan 2017). In India, the expansive interpretation of 'Fundamental Rights' has obscured the distinctive nature of administrative law norms (Ahmed and Jhaveri 2021).

Inattention to the relationship between the two bodies of law is not a problem if the relationship really is insignificant. This chapter suggests that, at least in jurisdictions sharing common law grounds of review, the relationship *is* significant. Bearing down on the nature of the relationship – one of delegation – contributes to significant theoretical debates. Thinking of administrators as delegates helps make sense of the grounds of review and the scope of administrative law and has had advantages over other interpretive theories of the subject.

Taking the idea of administrators as delegates seriously, this chapter suggests, also has the potential to contribute to debates on the legal or constitutional basis of judicial review. These debates implicate large and difficult issues: the nature of parliamentary sovereignty; the nature of a common law constitution; the existence of an 'undistributed middle' and the correct approach to statutory interpretation. While the delegation theory does not aim to address these issues and uncover the legal or constitutional basis of judicial review, it contributes to these discussions. The ultra vires doctrine shares an insight with the delegation theory: that administrators stand in a relationship of delegation to Parliament (Elliott 2001, p. 194). In providing a detailed account of the nature of this delegation, the delegation theory enriches the ultra vires doctrine. Equally though, on the other side, common law theorists receive comfort and aid from the delegation theory's recognition that administrators' status as delegates (as opposed to legislative intent alone) may ground administrators' duties. It is a short step from this recognition to acceptance that the common law holds administrators to these duties, as it does with other moral duties. Moreover, by drawing attention to the parallels between agency law and administrative law, the delegation theory also lends plausibility to 'mixed' accounts of the legal basis of judicial review, according to which some grounds of review derive from statute (analogous to an agent's contractual obligations) and some from the common law (analogous to an agent's fiduciary obligations) (Adams 2018, p. 31). The delegation theory draws attention to an important way in which the mixed accounts reflect the coherence of legal control of delegates across the public-private law divide. Thus, the delegation theory could contribute to each side of the debate about the constitutional basis for judicial review of administrative action, and enrich the overall debate.

RECOMMENDED READING

Allan, T. (1994). *Law, Liberty and Justice: The Legal Foundations of British Constitutionalism*, Oxford: Oxford University Press.
Cane, P. (1996). *Administrative Law*, Oxford University Press.
Dyzenhaus, D. (2000). Form and Substance in the Rule of Law: A Democratic Justification for Judicial Review? In C. Forsyth, ed., *Judicial Review and the Constitution*. Oxford: Hart.
Elliott, M. (2001). *The Constitutional Foundations of Judicial Review*, Oxford: Hart.
Elliott, M., & Varuhas, J. (2017). *Administrative Law: Text and Materials*, 5th edn, Oxford: Oxford University Press.
Forsyth, C. (2000). *Judicial Review and the Constitution*, Oxford: Hart.
Harlow, C., & Rawlings, R. (2009). *Law and Administration*, 3rd edn, Cambridge: Cambridge University Press.
Loughlin, M. (2010). *Foundations of Public Law*, Oxford: Oxford University Press.
McLean, J. (2012). *Searching for the State in British Legal Thought*, Cambridge: Cambridge University Press.
Oliver, D. (1999). *Common Values and the Public-Private Divide*, Cambridge: Cambridge University Press.
Rawlings, R. (2008). Modelling Judicial Review. *Current Legal Problems*, 61(1), 95–123.
Sunkin, M., & Payne, S. (1999). *The Nature of the Crown: A Legal and Political Analysis*, Oxford: Clarendon Press.

52

Horizontal Effect

Oliver Gerstenberg

It is wise, I think, to limit the basic liberties to those that are truly essential.... The reason for this limit ... is the special status of these liberties. Whenever we enlarge the list of basic liberties, we risk weakening the protection of the most essential ones and recreating within the scheme of liberties the indeterminate and unguided balancing problems we had hoped to avoid by a suitably circumscribed notion of priority.

J. Rawls, Political Liberalism (1993), p. 296.

INTRODUCTION: THE DUALITY OF ROLES OF FUNDAMENTAL RIGHTS

It is common ground that a bill or charter of constitutional rights regulates the relationship between an individual and the state. Fundamental rights create negative obligations for the state – duties not to interfere with life, liberty, conscience, speech, privacy etc. To what extent, if at all, though, do fundamental rights also have a bearing on relations between individuals? Can they also obligate the state to actively promote liberty in society? Are they focused merely on state abuse but silent on social inequality – or can they, in addition to their role as negative basic liberties, be mobilized by marginalized and despised groups in society as politically and legally transformative vehicles for social justice?

Undeniably, conflicts where claims of fundamental rights are plausibly asserted on either side of a lawsuit have become an enduring, increasingly common phenomenon. Wherever you look, examples of this development abound: your right to free speech may clash with my personality rights; my "right to conduct a business" may collide with your fundamental right to equal treatment and non-discrimination; more generally, constitutionally sensitive conflicts routinely arise, for example, between capital and labor; between financial service providers and vulnerable consumers; between vulnerable groups themselves, and so on.

Under the doctrine of "indirect horizontal effect" – which is hugely influential across jurisdictions worldwide (Tushnet 2008b, p. 196; Gardbaum 2011,

p. 396) – fundamental rights do not create direct obligations between private individuals. Parties to a dispute cannot simply invoke fundamental rights against one another ("direct horizontal effect"). Instead, the percolation of constitutional value is mediated by ordinary law. Fundamental rights merely influence and shape the way in which the regular courts must go about their business of construing and developing private-law norms. The regular courts charged with *developing* the ground-rules of property, contract, tort and the like are required to do so in the light of the underlying principles and value-orderings of the constitution. Constitutional courts, in turn, will monitor and *review* the regular courts in that process in order to ascertain whether those courts, in their interpretations of private-law norms, have sufficiently given effect to those values.

However, the "constitutionalization" of private law through the indirect horizontal effect of fundamental rights has not always been seen as an unmixed blessing. At first sight, of course, you might unambiguously welcome this trend because it promises an "ever closer" alignment of the market-making ground-rules of private law with the democratically-endorsed dignitarian and social values of the constitution. The normative promise, in other words, is of safeguarding the unity of the legal order and, ultimately, of ensuring the primacy of politics over markets. Yet the duality of roles of fundamental rights – as negative liberties and as "positive" rights and "constitutional value-decisions" that percolate into private law – has given rise to at least two persistent interconnected concerns.

The first concern is that the expansion of substantive constitutional norms beyond the negative basic liberties and their penetration into private law eliminates the domain of private law and private autonomy that is an essential characteristic of liberal societies. Down the slippery slope of constitutionalization might eventually lie a point where private law – which, of course, itself lays autonomous claim to providing a fair equilibrium between competing interests – simply becomes redundant, as sceptics fear. If private-law solutions are being subjected to incessant constitutional-legal second-guessing, value-based adjustment and transformative constitutional-judicial tinkering, then people simply no longer have the security and independence that the status of market-citizenship properly requires. Citizens have to guess about what the law is and are unable to plan their affairs. Private law discourse here expresses, if you will, a deep-seated conservative impulse – a constant protest against colonialization through constitutional-legal intervention and disruption.

The second – and in surprising ways similar and overlapping – concern about constitutionalization, however, is raised by progressive- or democratic-minded critics. An expansive doctrine of indirect horizontal effect, those critics allege, transfers substantial regulatory authority from democratic legislatures to constitutional courts. The problem, as those critics argue, is that citizens in modern, morally divided societies often divide – deeply, sharply, sincerely, and often reasonably – over contentious matters of social justice and questions of fair balance. Given those facts of social disagreement, the role of a legitimacy-conferring democratic constitution lies in providing a shared framework for politics going forward, not in entrenching a comprehensive judicial blueprint for all political decisions (Grimm 2019a, p. 30; Michelman 2019, p. 64f). A constitution – apart from its regulatory role – must also offer democratically responsible citizens a shared *justificational framework* (Michelman 2019, p. 64 f.) for critique, justification and ongoing reform through processes of public deliberation. However, any top-down imposition of constitutional-legal judgments through some *judicial fiat* about what is good or right may compromise that justificational role. Where matters of grave moral moment arise but where agreement does not yet exist between and among reasonable citizens, such imposition may violate the duty of civility of respect toward people with whom one often reasonably disagrees. Indirect horizontal effect may in this way become a path toward foreclosure of democratic deliberation and, indeed, a path toward a weakening of social protections against economic liberties. An even stronger (version of this) concern says that constitutionalization is paradoxical because it dramatically raises the ideological stakes in given conflicts, making them mutually irreconcilable and undermining the possibility of meaningful dialogic engagement in an advanced democracy (Kennedy 2014, pp. 188 ff).

This chapter argues that neither of these two concerns – about private autonomy and about democratic sovereignty – necessarily arises in connection with the doctrine of indirect horizontal effect. In its first step (mentioned below, Section I), this chapter explores both these mutually corresponding concerns about the doctrine's consequences. In the second step (Section II), however, I argue that an expansive doctrine of indirect horizontal effect need not have the consequence of shifting substantive regulatory authority from legislatures and ordinary courts to constitutional courts. The reason is that the act of *reviewing* – by the constitutional court – typically entails explicit recognition of a margin of discretion on the part of the reviewee charged with *developing* the law: the regular courts and legislatures. When operating within that margin, those courts and legislatures enjoy an important leeway in developing nonconstitutional law in ways that are constitutionally tenable. I argue that we should think of open-textured fundamental rights as deliberative rights to be mobilized in order to touch-off a process of reconsideration of routine private-law solutions in situations of myopia and normative shortfall as regards the position of the vulnerable in society. In parsing selected examples from the case law, I suggest that there exists an empirical link between a legal order's commitment to dignitarian-social values, on the one hand, and the expansion of the doctrine of indirect horizontal effect, on the other.

I THE CRITIQUE OF CONSTITUTIONALIZATION

The "indirect horizontal effect" of fundamental rights and the autonomy of private law (the first concern)

Private Law as the True Constitution

About a century ago, Max Weber famously addressed the problem of incorporating social values into law. However, he framed the problem as a tragic, unresolvable one – as a clash between "legal formalism," on the one hand, and "[n]ew demands for a 'social law' to be based upon such emotionally coloured ethical postulates as 'justice' or 'human dignity,' and directed against the very dominance of a mere business morality," on the other, which have arisen with the "modern class problem" (Weber 1978, p. 886). According to Weber, concepts such as "economic duress, or the attempt to treat as immoral, and thus as invalid, a contract because of a gross disproportion between promise and consideration" are based on norms which "from the legal standpoint" are "entirely amorphous and … are neither juristic nor conventional nor traditional in character but ethical" – and which claim as their legitimation only "substantive justice rather than formal legality." The threat to formal legality, as Weber added, was compounded by the "status ideologies of the lawyers themselves" and by the "demand for 'judicial creativeness' at least where the statute is silent." For "[b]eing confined to the interpretation of statutes and contracts, like a slot machine into one which one just drops the facts (and the fees) in order to have it spew out the decision (plus opinion), appears to the modern lawyer as beneath his dignity."

By contrast, the tradition of ordoliberalism no longer saw a tragic conflict. It associated the rule of law with limited government and the function of providing a secure framework for the spontaneous order of free markets. This conception prioritizes economic liberties and emphasizes the importance of rules fixed in advance that allow private actors to foresee with certainty how public authority will use its coercive power in given circumstances. The ground rules of private law – property and freedom of contract – are often thought to meet this requirement *par excellence* and to epitomize the pure form of law. For example, Hayek described private law as a self-policing form of governance without coercion. Coercion occurs, he argued, whenever there is "such control of environment or circumstances of a person by another that, in order to avoid greater evil, he is forced to act not according to a coherent plan of his but to serve the ends of another" (Hayek 1960, p. 133). Coercion, however, can be eliminated, if a person is governed entirely by general rules which are applied impersonally and equally to all. Where general rules of this kind are in place, a person can command only in ways, and for reasons, that are set by laws that the person did not herself choose and cannot change. Accordingly, private law is not an "anomaly bound to disappear" (Hayek 1976, p. 47); instead, "public law passes but private law persists" (Hayek 1973, p. 135). Private law in this way becomes a shorthand for a conception of the rule of law focused entirely on the importance of legal predictability and private autonomy as stand-alone values.

The Doctrine of "Indirect Horizontal Effect" and Private Autonomy

As Mark Tushnet in his various writings on "indirect horizontal effect" has observed, the GFCC's 1958 *Lüth* decision[1] is usually described as the origin of the idea that substantive constitutional norms should shape the way ordinary courts develop private law norms (Tushnet 2008b, p. 219; Tushnet 2005b, p. 177). In reaction to the horrors of Nazi Germany, the German Basic Law (BL) is strongly premised on the principle of human dignity. As the GFCC ruled in *Lüth* and daughter cases, while fundamental rights are subjective rights of freedom of the individual against interference by public power, it is also the case that the German Basic Law "has set up an objective value system," which is "centred around the human personality … and its dignity … as the basic constitutional decision for all spheres of law." This value-system "accordingly also manifestly influences the civil law: no provision of civil law may be in contradiction with it; each one must be interpreted in its spirit." The regular courts at all times are required to bring the ground-rules of private law "into harmony with [the Basic Law's] system of values" and to develop these rules accordingly. Correspondingly, the GFFC does not act as a "super-revisionary court" ["Superrevisionsinstanz"]. Instead, the role of the GFCC – as guardian of the Basic Law and in its role as a "specialist," not "generalist" court (Michelman 2011, p. 289; on the latter distinction: Kelsen 1942) – is limited to checking "whether the challenged decisions of ordinary courts sufficiently give effect to the Basic Law's fundamental rights and reflect the required balancing of conflicting rights with a tenable outcome."[2] Broadly speaking, the general clauses which can be found in in statutory private law provisions – open-textured concepts such as "good faith," "good morals," "unethical behavior," and "fairness" – cater for such an incorporation and serve as preferred entry-ways for constitutional value-orderings into private law. As the GFFC has put it more recently, in the context of indirect horizontal effect fundamental rights "do not generally create direct obligations between private actors." Instead, it is incumbent on the regular courts "to give effect to fundamental rights in the interpretation of ordinary law."[3] Even as the dispute at all times remains a private-law dispute, the constitutional court's role lies in *overseeing* and *reviewing* the decisions by the regular courts, but never in *displacing* the ordinary courts' role of construing and developing the background rules of property, contract,

---

[1] Lüth, BVerfGE 7, 198 (1958), translated in D. Kommers, The Constitutional Jurisprudence of the Federal Republic of Germany 363 (1997).

[2] Recht auf Vergessen II (Right to be forgotten). Order of the First Senate, 6 November 2019 – 1 BvR 276/17.

[3] Stadium ban, – 1 BvR 3080/09 – Order of the First Senate, 11 April 2018.

or tort law. In particular, fundamental rights influence "the balancing of the freedoms of equally entitled rights holders," meaning that "[t]he freedom afforded one right holder must be reconciled with the freedom afforded another."[4] To this end, the regular courts must strike the required balance according to the "principle of practical concordance ... which requires that the fundamental rights of all persons concerned be given effect to the broadest possible extent" with an eye to the "circumstances of the individual case." The "decisive factors" in striking that contextual balance include "the inevitable consequences resulting from certain situations, the disparity between opposing parties, the importance attached to certain services in society, or the social position of power held by one of the parties."[5]

In this way, the doctrine of indirect horizontal effect aims to uphold a separation between constitutional law and the background rules of private law, while also opening the latter to the transformative influences of the former. This distinction between "developing" and "reviewing" is – as Tushnet (2005b, p. 178) has pointed out – the center-piece of this doctrine (see also Michelman 2011, pp. 289, 293).

In interrelated ways, the European Court of Human Rights (ECtHR) has opted for a two-pronged approach, dividing states' obligations into two categories: negative and positive obligations. Art. 1 ECHR requires the Contracting Parties to "secure to everyone within their jurisdiction the rights and freedoms defined in ... [the] Convention." The ECHR's Protocol 13 (Preamble) refers to the "inherent dignity of all human beings." Accordingly, virtually all of the ECHR's standard-setting provisions have this dual aspect, actively requiring the national authorities, including the courts, to take the necessary measures to safeguard a right, even in private-law relations. In similar ways, Art. 51 (1) and (2) of the Charter of Fundamental Rights of the EU (CFREU) oblige Member States to promote the application of the CFREU in accordance with their respective powers. The Preamble to the CFREU, too, confirms that the EU is founded on "indivisible, universal values," including human dignity. As a consequence, in ways resonating with the doctrine of indirect horizontal effect, national courts, in a formally private-law dispute between private parties, must take into account the value-orderings of the CFREU.

However, the doctrine of indirect horizontal effect immediately raises the concern that the intended separation between constitutional law and ordinary private law, in actual practical effect, collapses. As constitutional value-orderings penetrate the entire legal order and begin to monopolize the interpretation of ordinary law, the possibility arises that the reviewing constitutional courts might begin to arrogate to themselves the monopoly of the ordinary courts to apply and develop ordinary law in great detail. Constitutional courts could end up determining quite precisely what the background rules of private law are (Tushnet 2005b, p. 178 f.; H. Collins 2014, pp. 27 ff.; Gerstenberg 2004, pp. 766 ff.), with the consequence of the administration

---

[4] Ibid.
[5] Ibid.

of justice more or less eventually coming under the complete control of the constitutional court. As Lech Garlicki (2007, p. 49) has authoritatively summarized the problem, "no genuine separation between constitutional jurisdiction and ordinary jurisdiction is possible in the modern *Rechtsstaat*" as a matter of institutional fact.

This, however, raises the possibility of constitutional courts transforming themselves into quite aggressive – even autocratically self-programming, as regards the substantive scope and outreach of constitutional law – agents and pacemakers of social and economic transformation. Many private lawyers object that indirect horizontal effect and the dual aspect of fundamental rights as "negative" and "positive" rights together, and working in tandem, will fatefully lead to a colonialization of private law by constitutional law that will not only seriously disturb the coherence of the private-law system, but ultimately also pose a threat to its libertarian ideals of private autonomy. A constitution that also protects "positive" rights, critics argue, can no longer be a bulwark of negative basic liberties (Epstein 2014, pp. 77–80).

Consider this standard concern as it has been articulated in the specifically German post-*Lüth* context by E.-W. Böckenförde – who was a pre-eminent German constitutional scholar and a former judge at the GFFC (1993–1996). Böckenförde began by pointing out that the quarrel over whether third-party effect is direct or merely indirect turns out to be "a secondary, if not marginal problem" (Böckenförde 2017a, p. 243) when fundamental rights are regarded also as constitutional principles that influence statutory interpretation. Instead, he argued that the real problem – amounting to a "growth crisis in the development of fundamental rights" –, lay elsewhere: expanding fundamental rights beyond the core defensive negative liberties gives them an indeterminate range. Yet Böckenförde at the same time insisted that securing freedom also includes the social conditions for realizing freedom and also – against the grain of a then German school of thought – that this must have a *constitutional* bearing. For what good are freedom of contract and the freedom to engage in gainful work, he asked, if you are forced to accept whatever conditions just in order to survive (p. 377 f.)? However, given the indeterminate range of rights as objective principles, proportionality-analysis – unmoored from the directives of ordinary law – "is not constrained by pre-existing standards" (p. 254). As a consequence, the proliferation of proportionality-analysis eventually opens up constitutional law to "the inflow of the value-related subjective views of judges [and] law teachers ... and ... to the sanctioning of the conceptions of values that actually—or seemingly—prevail within society" (pp. 227 and 232) – inflows that might or might no longer be consistent with the rule of law. That would entail a fateful shift from the "parliamentary-legislative" to a "constitutional-jurisdictional state."

Consider now Mark Tushnet's (2017b) illuminating critique of E.-W. Böckenförde's influential argument. Böckenförde's specific version of this standard concern, as Tushnet insightfully observes, rests on "an essentialist understanding of the courts as institutions" (2017b, p. 480f) an understanding which is based on the – Weberian, as one might add – proposition that the "background private-law rules of property and contract form an integrated set with its own 'rational' integrity that cannot be 'rationally' disrupted by value-based constitutional-legal interventions" (p. 481). Yet notice that Tushnet's pertinent observation does not remove the problem altogether. For, even if we drop those essentialist assumptions, we still may have independent reasons for remaining, as Tushnet (2017a, p. 303) says of himself, "deeply sceptical of claims that legal doctrine – of whatever sort, categorical rules, proportionality, case-specific balancing, categorical balancing, and more – has virtues like transparency, relative objectivity, and the like (and so of claims that any specific doctrinal formulation optimizes several of those virtues)." Tushnet's formulation turns our attention to the second – the progressive or democratic-minded – critique of an over-expansion of the regulatory role of constitutional law.

The Progressive or Democratic-Minded Critique (The Second Concern)

1 Social Constitutionalism, the Problem of the Mutual Accommodation of Competing Values ("Practical Concordance"), and the Duty of Civility (Frank Michelman)

Contemporary political-liberal thought has been alive to the problem of incorporating values of social justice into constitutional law.

The basic problem is this: in a modern, morally pluralistic society, where citizens deeply divide over questions of justice, a constitution is supposed to serve as a shared "public platform of justification" (Michelman 2019, p. 64) which enables citizens to shift conversation from endlessly contestable questions of whether an impugned state measure is truly just to the different – more readily answerable question, as is hoped – of whether the measure is *legitimate* under a good-enough constitution.

However, as Frank Michelman explains our predicament, in modern liberal societies legitimacy-endangering moral and interpretive disagreement "cannot be expected to stop at the water's edge … [but], inevitably, will extend even to setting the bounds of the central ranges of the … constitution's named essential guarantees" (p. 66) themselves. When it comes to fair balance and the mutual adjustments between contextually competing rights, judges (but also the public at large) – in their assignments of priority to specific rights, liberties, and opportunities – will hold different and mutually incompatible (though reasonable) conceptions of justice which can guide the balancing-process. Judges and citizens – as Michelman says (following Rawls) – are faced with "an indefinitely numerous 'family' of underlying liberal conceptions of justice," each vying for our support and recommending different (reasonable) balances case-by-case. Pervasive moral dissensus occurs not only "at the level of constitutional-legal application," but reaches into "the level of a constitution's underlying conception of justice" (p. 67) itself, casting doubt onto each and every proposed "unified, coherent scheme" of rights that is supposed to provide guidance and orientation to judges in the process of balancing. As Michelman drives home this point: "[t]he hitch comes with the need ... to supply an underlying normative conception by which to guide reciprocal adjustments of the ranges of liberties listed in a constitution ... to maintain them in a unified, coherent scheme. ... The troubling question is whether any guiding criterion [for fair balance] that you and I ... might propose will not be subject to reasonable intra-liberal disagreement in conditions of pluralism" (p. 65).

Accordingly, the terms of a legitimation-worthy constitution must be neither "too thick," nor "too thin." Where "matters of grave moral moment" arise, and where "agreement does not yet exist throughout the population of reasonable citizens," its terms must never lead to "permanent foreclosure of questions over which reasonable citizens divide" ("too thick"), but leave those questions for "future continuing examination in the democratic venues of political life" (p. 65). Yet, those terms must nevertheless still also be robust enough (not "too thin") to "carry a core of common meanings ... sufficient to render both mutually coherent and widely persuasive the claims of citizens to each other of the worthiness of any conforming regime for continued support" and to achieve social solidarity and cooperation. For "a procedural pact with core terms unsettled is no pact at all" (p. 73). A legitimacy-conferring constitution, accordingly, must "cater for sufficiency at all times, but never at any time an excess, of publicly settled meanings for the constitutional essentials" (p. 65).

As Michelman stresses, "sufficiency at all times" is not just a prudential requirement – reflecting considerations of expedience and compromise – but a moral one (2018, p. 95 f.). For political-liberal thought posits a fundamental duty of civility: an obligation of respect toward disagreeing fellow-citizens as our moral peers and codeliberators who equally share the constitution. There is a moral dilemma for citizens, caught between their sincerely-held convictions of substantive justice, on the one hand, and their commitment to respect toward codeliberators with whom they disagree, on the other. For a constitution to be able to serve as a public standard, test, or platform of justification in a divided society (its "proceduralizing" or "justificational" function), there are "limits on what [it] can say and in how much concrete detail," even if the boundaries will, of course, vary and shift from time to time (2018, p. 85). On the one hand, we want constitutional law to be perpetually open to modifications, extensions etc., as times and conditions change and understandings evolve. On the other hand, under conditions of interpretive pluralism a gap must persist between your and my considered convictions of the true requirements of human rights and our observance of moral obligations of civility that obtain between fellow citizens in a democratic polity.

Rawls himself – on whose work Michelman draws – envisaged a society based on reciprocity – with institutions that affirm the good of all citizens. The underlying "criterion of reciprocity" expresses the "intrinsic normative and moral ideal" of a political conception of justice: democratic citizens "are prepared to offer one another fair terms of social cooperation ... and ... they agree to act on those terms ... as free and equal, and not as dominated or manipulated, or under the pressure of an inferior political or social position" (Rawls 1996, p. xliv). Rawls also was adamant that in contractual transactions, "the tendency is rather for background justice to be eroded even when individuals act fairly: the overall result is away from and not toward background justice." As he explained, "[t]he fact that everyone with reason believes that they are acting fairly and scrupulously honoring the norms governing agreements is not sufficient to preserve background justice" (p. 267). However, what follows from Michelman's "troubling question" is that under conditions of deep moral dissensus just any justice-seeking constitutionalization of private law – whether driven by "reciprocity," "non-domination," or any similar such *substantive* criterion – may leave us trapped in the Goldilocks-dilemma as we seek to incorporate values of justice into constitutional law.

2 Duncan Kennedy's "Hermeneutics of Suspicion"

For a long time, a related message of deep conflict and indeterminacy has emerged from within realist and critical legal scholarship. According to Kennedy (2020), constitutionalization is a "paradigm shift" in a "genealogy" of forms of "legal consciousness," which he defines as "the body of ideas through which lawyers experience legal issues" (1980, p. 5).

Within "classical legal thought" ["CLT"], as Duncan Kennedy terms it, the courts defined their task as policing the conceptual boundaries that defined spheres of both state power and of private citizens. These spheres did not overlap: the delegated power of each legal actor – of the state, on the one hand, and of the private citizens, on the other – remained "absolute within but void outside its sphere" (1980, pp. 5 and 7). Hence, "a defining characteristic" of CLT "was the assimilation of a great deal of law to a single subsystem dominated by the concept of a power absolute within its sphere" (1980, p. 21). Given that understanding, courts viewed themselves as applying boundary-defining techniques that rendered their analysis "an objective, quasi-scientific one" (1980, p. 7). The crucial point here is that this conception of the judicial role and technique did not (or only very marginally) involve the balancing of competing public and private interests.

By contrast, *constitutionalization* involves the practice of "reviewing a recurring ideologically-sensitive practice by application of a test derived directly from the constitution" (2020, p. 111). And this entails an ever "greater supervision of public actors of all kinds (and some private ones as well) by the highest constitutional court in the system" (2020, p. 112). Yet the problem lies in the absence of a "test derived directly from the constitution" that actually "transcend[s] politics" (2020, p. 120). For, inevitably, any constitutional test, especially in horizontal conflicts, relies on proportionality-analysis: "[judicial] balancing … seems the only workable solution, even if it is a solution of last resort" (2011, p. 213).

Judicial balancing, however, "is particularly vulnerable to the charge of easy manipulability for covert ideological purposes" (2020, p. 110) and to "ideological corruption" (2014, pp. 118 ff). Any Herculean judicial effort to "legitimately exercise moral judgment" in the search for the right answer based on the constitution will simply backfire by setting in motion an all-pervasive "hermeneutics of suspicion" on all sides towards just any claim of "legal necessity" (2014, p. 132). Constitutionalization inevitably raises the ideological stakes. Any presumptively neutral balancing-procedure will be weaponized by diverse "ideological intelligentsias" (2014, p. 132). In their respective pursuit of "rival contradictory coherentist theories" – all "players [in the game of litigation] understand that the rules of the game are stakes of the game, and strategise upon that basis" (2020, p. 107). Constitutionalization increases the power of judges "to determine the winners of ideological conflicts" (2019, p. 34) and eventually destroys the "key legitimation claim [in contemporary capitalism] that conflict occurs within a framework that is stable, neutral between persons, and democratically legitimate." At the end of the road, it enables "liberals and conservatives ... [to] gamble on preserving their constitutional triumphs of the past against the threat that mobilized right- or left-wing popular majorities would pose if they had unrestricted legislative power" (2014, p. 136). Hence, a constitutionalized private law, far from being neutral or above politics, is "just another terrain of ideologically motivated struggle."

Notice, however, that Duncan Kennedy also says that he "agree[s] with the presupposition ... that legal reasoning is not so completely indeterminate that the only possible explanation of any and all legal outcomes is ideological, or at least extra-juristic" (2014, p. 130). When legal interpreters are "arguing to a potentially persuadable audience and against real or hypothetical opponents" in search for "a right answer" (2014, p. 127) the fact that they will "experience some answers as errors means that the range of interpretive possibilities is limited." Legal interpreters devote time and resources "to stabilizing and destabilizing rival answers," and this kind of "work in the legal medium" involves "framing and reframing the argument," precisely "in the hope that we will end up able to affirm the necessity of an answer." As Kennedy insists, "[t]he correct legal argument is not a 'fact of nature', nor yet a subjective will o' the wisp, but something phenomenally real but defeasible by a new argument that will be, precisely, more effective" (2014, p. 130). The challenge, then, is to understand how this constructive conception of "work in the legal medium" can be vindicated.

Interim Conclusion: Over-Constitutionalization?

Those sharing private law's "conservative impulse" resist constitutionalization out of an anxiety about the integrity of private-law solutions and about keeping private autonomy sacrosanct. Surprisingly, however, democratic-minded critics, too, express anxiety about constitutionalization, out of a mixture of two overlapping motives. First, an anxiety that constitutionalization might undermine social solidarity by raising the stakes and by creating a discourse-undermining spirit of non-negotiable confrontation which, in a morally deeply divided society, might leave codeliberators without just any shared common justificational framework. The constitution might itself be drawn into the interminable partisan divisions of divided societies. The regulatory function of a constitution and its justificational function may come apart, as Michelman has put it. Second, out of a concern that the syndrome of constitutionalization and judicialization might betray the progressive-liberal cause. Absent an overlapping consensus on a shared common constitutional-justificational framework, courts might read the right in question adversely to the outcomes you hoped to promote, inadvertently turning constitutionalization into a path to a weakening of social protections against economic liberties ("process over substance"), in ways incurable by progressive legislation, thereby entrenching a "constitutional asymmetry" between law and politics (Scharpf 2010; Grimm 2019a), as an (un)intended consequence. Both these anxieties form part of the over-constitutionalization critique.

If we nevertheless want to hold on to the idea that fundamental rights can transformatively shape – rather than arrest – the development of private-law norms in response to concerns about economic bias, then how do we get out of this impasse? For sure, debates over reasonable balances of relevant public values in the public sphere may eventually "make their own contribution toward consolidations of evolving public views of the central cores" of the constitutional essentials, as Michelman says. After all, despite the force of the realist critique we *also* experience constitutional interpretation as a collaborative search for a right answer, as Kennedy insists. An answer – as I will suggest below – lies in a retreat from an unnecessarily judicially-supremacist conception of judicial review. Courts – even where review must be strong-form – exert an important forum-creative and agenda-setting role in the context of balancing. Rather than create a spirit of non-negotiable confrontation, indirect horizontal effect may constructively *enhance democratic deliberation* in ways often underappreciated by conservative and progressive critics alike. It is this idea of an experimentalist constitutional learning process that we need to develop, as I will argue.

II HOW CONSTITUTIONALIZATION SUCCEEDS: TOWARD A DEMOCRATIC-EXPERIMENTALIST REFORMULATION OF THE DOCTRINE OF "INDIRECT HORIZONTAL EFFECT"

The sustainability of the distinction between "developing the law" and "reviewing" and democratic experimentalism

I think Mark Tushnet is correct in insisting on the crucial importance of the distinction between the act of "reviewing" and acts of "developing the law." The "act of reviewing," as Tushnet points out, "entails acknowledging that the body being reviewed (here, the ordinary courts) have some discretion in specifying the law they are charged with developing" (Tushnet 2005b, p. 179). Constitutional courts will "act with respect to background rules [of private law] just as they should act with respect to legislation" by determining whether "some judicially developed legal rule" is consistent with "some ... reasonable specification of the abstract [constitutional] norm's meaning in the enactments' context" (Tushnet 2008b, p. 224) and in this way constitutionally tenable.

Notice that the underlying crucial distinction between "reviewing" and "developing the law" renders it unlikely that an expansive doctrine of indirect horizontal effect has the consequence, feared by its critics, of shifting substantial authority from legislatures and regular courts to constitutional courts. First, for reasons of simple practicality: intervening only sporadically and exceptionally, constitutional courts may even be the "weaker participants" (Garlicki 2007, p. 67 f.) in a partnership with ordinary courts on whose ongoing cooperation and domain-specific contextual expertise they strongly depend. As ordinary courts give effect to fundamental rights in the interpretation of ordinary law, constitutional courts may, in fact, recede into the background.

The second reason has to do with interpretive uncertainty. Substantive constitutional norms are typically stated at a relatively abstract level, in highly open-textured language. However, those abstract value-statements – such as equality, free speech, and privacy – do not generate uncontroversial answers to particular issues. Rights do create a shared common framework, but this framework does not necessarily lead to agreement at the point of application. In other words, there is always a gap – an interpretive gap – between general and abstract constitutional norms and their contextualizing applications.

This interpretive gap can, however, at least be narrowed *in time* through process and procedure. The reviewing constitutional court will typically afford the ordinary courts and legislatures with an experimental leeway for the case-specific development of ground-rules of private law that are – as regards their underlying conception of fair balance – constitutionally tenable. Open-textured fundamental-rights norms, in turn, may serve as seismographs and portals for changing values in societies that are changing. The role of the reviewing constitutional court, however, is here far less dictatorial than both conservative and progressive-minded critics fear. Where interpretive uncertainty prevails, the constitutional court can at least require attention to relevant reasons; invite litigants and stakeholders to explain their mutually antagonistic constitutional-interpretive views; and indicate where the justificational burden on either side must lie. In that process, the constitutional court can indicate which groups or classes of individuals in society are particular vulnerable, and for what specific kind of reasons. The reviewing constitutional court can touch-off and monitor a process of meaningful *dialogic* engagement between various stakeholders in the ongoing clarification of the applied meaning of a right. In sundry domains – think of consumer law, employment law, commercial law, or family law (and many others) – the reviewing constitutional court can be *judicially assertive* in indicating where the socially-protective threshold must lie below which the development of ordinary law by the regular courts and legislatures must never fall. It thereby lends voice, participation, public respectability and visibility to the vulnerable in the society and their reasons. The constitutional court can, in turn, become more judicially tolerant where best practice at the decentralized level of the regular courts or at the legislative level consolidates. In this multilevel constitutional-interpretive process, the relationship between constitutional courts, legislatures, and ordinary courts (and also courts-beyond-the-state) is far less supremacist, in either direction, than critics assume. It far more resembles what has been called a deliberative polyarchy (Sabel and Simon 2017; Gerstenberg 2018) by inviting a jurisprudence of mutual monitoring and peer-review, as the next section will suggest.

Transformations: Constitutional Private Law

Consider some few – but exemplary – constitutionally supplied framework criteria for the development of what you may think of as a *constitutional private law* in the context of Europe's multilevel system of law.

First, recall the *Bürgschaftsfall*: the eponymous 1993 ruling of the GFCC (BVerfGE 89, 214) on bank guarantees by family members, which confirms the distinction between acts of "reviewing" and acts of "developing" ordinary private law. The case concerned a series of claimants, including spouses and children, of a party which had mortgaged the family home, in order to secure a business loan from a bank. The banks had required that, in return for the loans, the spouses or children – who were without any (prospect of) significant income or wealth – would have to guarantee those debts, because "it's only for the files." But there would be no loan without their signature. The validity of these contracts was challenged. The Federal Court of Justice for civil matters ("FCJ") – Germany's highest "ordinary court" – refused to control the content of such contracts, essentially arguing that freedom of contract, properly understood, must also include the freedom to engage in risky undertakings, without the state's tutelage, as a matter of private autonomy. After all, such guarantees lay in the interest of borrowers themselves who would otherwise never be able to secure a bank loan at all and would have a valuable incentive not to maladminister their businesses. The underlying regulatory and constitutional question – should banks really be allowed to *colonize* intra-family feelings of loyalty, love, and solidarity in that way, under the guise of freedom of contract – did not figure in the FCJ's reasoning. Even where the banks dutifully informed the spouse or children of the exorbitant risks incurred, providing *information* did nothing to relieve family members of their *moral dilemma* as *consenting* spouses or children to which the (cartelized) practice of the banks systematically exposed them.

The FCC roundly rejected the position taken by the FCJ. The GFCC insisted that, as a general matter, the private-law framework of freedom of contract must always be in alignment with the constitutional imperatives of the Basic Law itself. The GFCC argued that not only the banks but, indeed, both parties to the contract were entitled to the fundamental constitutional guarantee of private autonomy enshrined in Art. 2(1) of the Basic Law. Relying additionally on the Basic Law's principle of the social state in Articles 20(1) and 28(1), the GFCC deployed the concept of *structural* imbalance to declare the contract void: "in cases ... where one party to a contract may be recognized as being structurally weaker, and if the consequences for the weaker contracting party are significantly imbalanced, the civil law order must react and make correction possible [and] may not content itself with the conclusion that: 'contract is contract'." The – welcome and subsequently widely accepted – outcome in these cases notwithstanding, it remained a fair and obvious question whether the GFCC's conceptual framing of the issue as one of *private autonomy* adequately described the above regulatory problem (Teubner 2000, p. 388 ff.). Regardless of where you stand on this, however, the important point is this: The GFCC – in ways that resonate with Tushnet's analysis – combined strong-form review of the ordinary courts' jurisprudence – invalidating such contracts – with a leeway for the development of ordinary-law remedies by those courts and the legislature. The FCC stated an unequivocal and principled constitutional baseline, but left institutional development that met that threshold to other actors.

Second, again as regards the relationship between banks and vulnerable consumers, recall the CJEU's 2013 landmark case C-415/11 *Mohammed Aziz*.[6] The case is of interest for two reasons. First, because Aziz provides an opportunity to test the widespread assumption that the CJEU is marred by a persistent and deep structural bias in favor of economic integration to the detriment of the non-economic constitutional values (critically of this view: Pochet 2019; affirmingly: Scharpf 2010; Bellamy 2019). Second, because *Aziz* offers a vivid illustration of the devastating impact of the economic and financial crisis in Europe on vulnerable individuals, in particular in strongly exposed countries like Spain. Many consumers had mortgaged their family homes to secure unaffordable loans and subsequently lost their homes due to a malign combination of over-indebtedness, lopsided contract terms, and ancillary national procedural law regimes that clearly prioritized the interests of the banks in fast, "simplified" enforcement over the interests of vulnerable consumers. Mr. Aziz, a Moroccan worker on a small income in Spain and without savings, had used his family home as a security for a mortgage loan but lost his job. The mortgage loan contract concluded between him and the Spanish bank contained several unfair terms – for example, an acceleration clause, allowing the bank, in the event of consumer default with just one of monthly installments, to *automatically* recall the totality of the loan and to make a unilateral quantification of the amount owed. In addition, in case of arrears, the bank was entitled – under domestic Spanish law – to initiate simplified enforcement procedures, which precluded any consideration of the fairness of the underlying standard contract terms. When Mr Aziz fell behind

---

[6] C-415/11 *Mohammed Aziz v. Caixa d'Estalvis de Catalunya, Tarragona i Manresa (Catalunyacaixa)*, Judgment of 14 March 2013. ECLI:EU:C:2013:164.

with his monthly payments, the bank invoked this process, and, as a result, Mr. Aziz was evicted from his home. The home was sold, by auction, at only half its value.

In *Aziz* and subsequent rulings, the CJEU transformed Art. 7 CFEU – respect for private and family life and home – into an anti-eviction principle: "The loss of a family home is not only such as to seriously undermine consumer rights ..., but it also places the family of the consumer concerned in a particularly vulnerable position" (C-34/13 *Monika Kušionov v SMART Capital a.s.*). The CJEU in this way required the ordinary domestic courts to read the general clause in Art. 3 of the Council Directive 93/13/EEC on unfair terms in consumer contracts – which referred to terms that are "unfair" and contrary to "good faith" – in the light of the principle enshrined in Art. 7 CFEU, extending proportionality analysis into private law. In addition, the CJEU required a legislative change of wayward Spanish procedural law so as to prevent the definite and always irreversible loss of the family home in such constellations. The CJEU thus raised the level of social protection beyond the level initially envisaged by domestic law and lent voice and credibility to people in Mohammed Aziz's position.

For sure, in *Alemo-Herron*,[7] the CJEU held that the transfer-of-undertakings Directive 2001/23 – read in the light of freedom of contract flowing from Art. 16 CFREU – meant that "an undertaking must be able to assert its interests effectively in a contractual process to which it is party and to negotiate the aspects determining changes in the working conditions of its employees with a view to its future economic activity." However, in *AGET Iraklis*,[8] the CJEU's Grand Chamber, arguably in response to *Lochner*-style concerns voiced in the literature, ruled that freedom of contract may "be subject to a broad range of interventions on the part of public authorities that may limit the exercise of economic activity in the public interest," because the "European Union is ... based ... on a highly competitive *social* market economy." Hence, Greece's anti-redundancy measures – once properly redrafted – survived the legal challenge and did not violate the economic freedom of establishment. In subsequent rulings – such as *Bauer* and *Broßonn*,[9] *Max Planck*,[10] *Cresco*,[11] and several others – the CJEU's Grand Chamber held that the "right to paid leave" under Art. 31(2) CFREU expresses "a particularly important principle of European Union social law" which also

---

[7] C-426/11 *Mark Alemo-Herron and Others v Parkwood Leisure Ltd.* Judgment of 18 July 2013. ECLI:EU:C:2013:521.

[8] C-201/15 *Anonymi Geniki Etairia Tsimenton Iraklis (AGET Iraklis) v Ypourgos Ergasias, Koinonikis Asfalisis kai Koinonikis Allilengyis.* Judgment [CC] of 21 December 2016. ECLI:EU:C:2016:972.

[9] C-569/16 and C-570/16 *Stadt Wuppertal v Maria Elisabeth Bauer and Volker Willmeroth v Martina Broßonn.* Judgment [GC] of 6 November 2018. ECLI:EU:C:2018:871.

[10] C-684/16 *Max-Planck-Gesellschaft zur Förderung der Wissenschaften eV v Tetsuji Shimizu.* Judgment [GC] of 6 November 2018. ECLI:EU:C:2018:874.

[11] C-193/17 *Cresco Investigation GmbH v Markus Achatzi.* Judgment [GC] of 22 January 2019. ECLI:EU:C:2019:43.

governs private employment relationships. And in *Egenberger*,[12] contradicting the jurisprudence of the GFFC, the CJEU's Grand Chamber held that the meaning of "genuine, legitimate and justified occupational requirement" (in Article 4(2) of Directive 2000/78) could not be determined by a *faith-based organization (church) unilaterally* but must be established in the light of the principle of equal treatment in Art. 21 CFREU through proportionality analysis. In all these rulings the CJEU instigated legal and political reform, ratcheting up standards of protection for the vulnerable beyond the levels envisaged by national law (for further analysis, cf. Gerstenberg 2021).

Third, also the European Court of Human Rights (ECtHR) plays a significant role in the constitutionalization of private employment law. In the 2017 case *Bărbulescu v. Romania*,[13] a private employer's internal regulations strictly prohibited the use of social media on the firm's IT equipment during working time except on the firm's business. Any breach of this code of conduct – which had been signed by the applicant as well – would be sanctioned by dismissal. Subsequently, the employer confronted the applicant with a transcript of the messages which the applicant, in breach of the code, had exchanged with his brother and his fiancée during a period when he had been monitored, including messages of a personal and intimate nature. Before the Romanian courts, the applicant, claiming unfair dismissal, unsuccessfully argued that Romanian courts had failed to strike a fair balance in giving priority to the employer's interest in the smooth running of his company over the applicant's personality rights. The ECtHR's Grand Chamber ruled that the Romanian courts had approached the issue in a wrong attitude by failing to understand the importance of Art. 8 ECHR (right to protection of privacy relating also to personal correspondence) in the sphere of private-law employment relations. Although "the essential object of Art 8 [ECHR] is to protect individuals against arbitrary interference by public authorities, it may also impose on the State certain positive obligations to ensure effective respect for the rights protected in Art. 8 [ECHR]."[14] *Any* restrictions on an individual's professional life may fall within Article 8 if they have repercussions on the manner in which an individual constructs his or her social identity in relationships with others and the outside world. The Grand Chamber required Romania to set up, as part of its labor law code, a "legislative framework" governing communication of a non-professional nature in the workplace. Romania retained a wide margin of appreciation in establishing it. However, "adequate and sufficient safeguards against abuse ... [and] proportionality and procedural guarantees against arbitrariness are essential."[15] While

---

[12] C-414/16 *Vera Egenberger v Evangelisches Werk für Diakonie und Entwicklung e.V.* Judgment [GC] of 17 April 2018. ECLI:EU: C:2018: 257.
[13] *Bărbulescu v. Romania* (Appl. No. 61496/08). Judgment [GC] of 5 September 2017.
[14] *Ibid.*, Rec. 108.
[15] *Ibid.*, 120.

the parties to an employment contract remained free to regulate a significant part of the content of their relations, an "employer's instructions cannot reduce private social life in the workplace to zero."[16] Contrary terms in an employer's code of conduct were unenforceable unless there were "specific reasons" – expressing a necessary business purpose – "justifying ... the monitoring measures" by way of proportionality analysis.[17]

Many other illustrations could be added to illustrate the point: The need for indirect horizontal effect will be most strongly felt in constellations where a justice-deficit at the level of private law becomes so troubling as to tarnish the legitimacy-conferring constitutional-legal order itself. By not expanding the outreach of fundamental rights into private-law relations, courts in those circumstances would simply become complicit in the *underprotection* of constitutional essentials and in *interpersonal exploitation* (King 2024). Yet the horizontal expansion of fundamental rights doesn't eliminate private autonomy. Given the increased *statutorification* of constitutional norms, these fears about private autonomy are in truth directed against the modern regulatory state itself and less against indirect horizontal effect and proportionality analysis (similarly, Tushnet 2005, p. 180). Moreover, an expansive doctrine of indirect horizontal effect doesn't mean that – as regards the politically salient issues of the day – political sovereignty inevitably passes from legislatures and ordinary courts to constitutional courts. The regular courts and legislatures retain (and are actively being provided with) an important experimental leeway within a constitutional framework to address the balancing problem in an attitude of constitutional principle. Constitutionalization doesn't necessarily "depoliticize" socially salient issues: for constitutional meaning – having emerged from deliberation – always remains under discussion and can change if further deliberation recognizes meanings that hitherto have not been recognized or favored or even been explicitly discarded. As the above examples illustrate, constitutional framework criteria – such as "structural disadvantage," "significant imbalance," "non-discrimination," "freedom to conduct a business," "right against unfair dismissal," and "right to a paid holiday" – are themselves evolving concepts. They are subject to iterative correction, revision, and updating over the sequence of cases in the light of stakeholder deliberation in the wider public. Constitutional courts play a key role in keeping deliberation open to the voices of the marginalized or vulnerable. Indeed, the case law invites us to think of these constitutional criteria as unfinished *democratic* projects which are owned, ultimately, by the democratic citizens themselves as codeliberators. We might simply say: constitutionalism evolves, over the spread of cases, "project-by-project" – in ways that are more experimental, judicially-collaborative, and inclusive; more critically responsive to changing societies; and perhaps in anticipation of *future* consensus.

[16] *Ibid.*, 80.
[17] *Ibid.*, 140.

CONCLUSION

The doctrine of indirect horizontal effect need not have the negative consequences some of its critics suggest, of over-constitutionalization and judicialization to the detriment of either private autonomy or democratic sovereignty. There is no apostasy from deliberative democracy in the doctrine of indirect horizontal effect when read along the lines set out. The distinction between reviewing and developing the law ensures a certain degree of autonomy for private-law relations. Yet, at the same time, the distinction opens up new pathways of legislative and jurisprudential reform – sometimes in response to mounting pressure from a vigilant public sphere talking back to courts. Indeed, an expansive doctrine of indirect horizontal effect of fundamental rights can be seen as a means of reigniting democratic deliberation – a process of constitutional reasoning about the applied meaning of underlying dignitarian-social constitutional value-orderings and fair balance – and, *mutatis mutandis*, of extending those commitments of the constitution into the future.

RECOMMENDED READING

Alexy, R. (2010). *A Theory of Constitutional Rights*, Oxford: Oxford University Press (esp. pp. 349–364).

Böckenförde, E.-W. (2017). Fundamental Rights as Constitutional Principles. In *Constitutional and Political Theory. Selected Writings*. Oxford: Oxford University Press, pp. 235–265.

Collins, H. (2014). On the (In)compatibility of Human Rights Discourse and Private Law. In H. Micklitz, ed., *Constitutionalization of European Private Law*. Oxford: Oxford University Press, pp. 26–60.

Gardbaum, S. (2011). The Structure and Scope of Constitutional Rights. In T. Ginsburg and R. Dixon, eds., *Comparative Constitutional Law*. Cheltenham: Edward Elgar, pp. 387–405.

Gerstenberg, O. (2004). What Constitutions Can Do (but Courts Sometimes Don't): Property, Speech, and The Influence of Constitutional Norms on Private Law. *Canadian Journal of Law and Jurisprudence*, 17 (1), 61–81.

Grimm, D. (2016). *Constitutionalism. Past, Present, and Future*, Oxford: Oxford University Press (esp. Chapter IV).

Grimm, D. (2017). *Verfassung und Privatrecht im 19. Jahrhundert. Die Formationsphase*, Tübingen: Mohr Siebeck.

Kennedy, D. (2011). A Transnational Genealogy of Proportionality in Private Law. In R. Brownsword, H.-W. Micklitz, L. Niglia, and S. Weatherill, eds., *The Foundations of European Private Law*. London: Hart Publishing, pp. 185–220.

Kennedy, D. (2019). A Political Economy of Contemporary Legality, forthcoming. In Poul Fritz Kjaer, ed., *The Law of Political Economy: Transformations of the Function of Law*. Cambridge University Press. At https://papers.ssrn.com/sol3/papers.cfm?abstract_id=3334107.

King. J. (2024). The Rule of Law. In R. Bellamy and J. King, eds., *The Cambridge Handbook of Constitutional Theory*. Cambridge: Cambridge University Press, pp. 297–315.

Michelman, F. (2011). The Interplay of Constitutional and Ordinary Jurisdiction. In T. Ginsburg, and R. Dixon, eds., *Comparative Constitutional Law*. Cheltenham: Edward Elgar, pp. 278–297.

Rawls, J. (1996). *Political Liberalism*, Columbia University Press.

Tushnet, M. (2005). The Relationship between Judicial Review of Legislation and the Interpretation of Non-Constitutional Law, with Reference to Third Party Effect. In A. Sajó and R. Uitz, eds., *The constitution in private law relations. Expanding constitutionalism*. Utrecht: Eleven Int'l Publ., pp. 167–182.

van der Walt, J. (2014). *The Horizontal Effect Revolution and the Question of Sovereignty*, Berlin, Boston: De Gruyter.

PART III E

The Global System

53

Global and National Constitutionalism

Carmen E. Pavel

Partly due to misunderstandings about how and whether it works, international law remains a neglected step-sister in legal philosophy and constitutional theory. While failures of international treaties to shape state behavior are well known, it remains true that many of the thousands bilateral and multilateral treaties signed by states are effective and change the relationships states have to each other and to their own citizens. Indeed, as Louis Henkin observed a few decades ago, "almost all nations observe almost all principles of international law and almost all of their obligations almost all of the time" (Henkin 1979, p. 47). States have managed, against significant odds, to create cooperative arrangements across a wide range of issues in international politics, from the division of territorial sea and ocean resources to air transport, telecommunication, trade, territorial rights, decolonization, human rights, and the protection of the environment (Dunoff, Ratner, and Wippman 2015; Alter 2014; Brownlie 2003; Dixon and McCorquodale 2003). Despite these successes, states continue to have difficulties making commitments to each other to respect rights and solve collective action problems. They fail to agree on solutions to well-recognized problems such as climate change, and when they do agree on solutions, such agreements can be unstable and easy to unravel. Can we shore up the commitments states have made to each other so far and pave the way for better, more stable cooperative agreements in the future?

I want to explore a constitutional treaty as a commitment device among states. Briefly stated, the case for a global constitution is that it could make the relations among states and between states and their citizens more just, by defining and entrenching the basic principles of political interaction across borders, by creating mechanisms for cooperation on matters essential for the survival of individuals and groups, by limiting the use of arbitrary political power, both of other states and of international institutions, and by articulating and protecting a range of rights for individuals and states.

Constitutional language is developed and differentiated in international law scholarship. It builds on two other distinctive literatures: the constitutionalization of the European Union, and constitutionalism within the state. Some international legal scholars refer to global constitutionalism as an ethos or a disposition, or better yet a heuristic to describe the various features of international law, which give it unity, stability, and coherence. This language can be traced back to some of the most influential mid-twentieth century scholars of international law such as Hans Kelsen (Kelsen 1952; Fitzmaurice 1957; Kleinlein and Peters 2018). Klabbersm, Peters, and Ulfstein describe the evolution of international law as one long process of constitutionalization (Klabbers, Peters, and Ulfstein 2009; Jakubowski and Wierczyńska 2016). Erika De Wet and Aoife O'Donoghue claim that the constitutional character of international law can be traced to its core value system, which grew and became shared through processes of international law formation among states (De Wet 2006; O'Donoghue 2014). Another sense in which the language of constitutionalization is used in international law is to describe the organization of various legal regimes such as the World Trade Organization (WTO) as constitutional or constitutionalized (McGinnis and Movsesian 2000; Peters 2016). Finally, some argue that apart from the constitutions of particular legal regimes, international law possesses a constitution which outlines its fundamental principles in the UN Charter (Fassbender 1998, 2009; Macdonald 2000; Sloan 1989).

These descriptive-cum-constructivist strands of thought draw an equivalence between processes of legalization and institutionalization on the one hand, and constitutions and constitutionalization on the other. In their common narrative, constitutionalism is thus an explanatory project of understanding and interpreting the various features of international law, and thus reconstructing it in a language familiar from domestic constitutional law. While such an approach may yield attractive insights, my account of constitutionalism differs significantly. I will focus instead on a more foundational, normatively demanding conception of constitutionalism, one which presupposes a written agreement which articulates and defends the primacy of robust, hierarchically superior rules and principles to guide basic state interaction, fundamental rights for individuals and groups, and mechanisms of judicial review and direct effect (Krisch 2012, pp. 39–40; Dunoff and Trachtman 2009b, pp. 4–5). Given this normative focus, for the purposes of assessing whether international law possesses a constitution, the common narrative may be distracting. The existing literature on international law constitutionalism refers to acts such as the Uruguay Round or the UN Charter as constitutions for specific areas of international law or international law as a whole break (Dunoff 2009, pp. 178–205; Pavel 2021a, pp. 140–174). The language of constitutionalism confers legitimacy on areas of law that are not constitutional in the traditional normative sense and thus are devoid of the basic features which make constitutionalism morally desirable. Such treaties do not create legal hierarchies (except partially), do not articulate fundamental rights for individuals or groups, fail to establish direct effect of treaty rules in national legislation, and do not commit to judicial review of national legislation or of the acts of international organizations.

However, there is a supranational legal arrangement which is considered to have many of these features: the European Union (Isiksel 2016; Kumm 2005; Eeckhout 2013; Schütze 2009). In a series of rulings (e.g. Costa v ENEL in 1964), the Court of Justice of the European Union (CJEU) declared the supremacy of the EU law over member states. The CJEU also offers a supranational judicial review system which checks the conformity of national laws with EU law. Finally, EU law is said to have direct effect and to nullify national legislation which comes into conflict with it. Some scholars argue against describing the EU as a constitutional legal system (Lindseth 2010; J. H. H. Weiler 2003; N. Barber 2019; Bellamy 2019). They point to the instances in which states such as Germany, Italy, and Spain have pushed back against the assertion of supremacy, direct effect, and constitutional review by the CJEU to describe the interrelationship between member states and EU law as one of pluralism and constitutional tolerance rather than hierarchy and subordination. Whether one group or another proposes the most correct understanding of legal authority and constitutionalism within the EU is less important for my inquiry. What is more relevant is the possibility of constitutional rules and constitutional authority beyond and above the state, which the EU demonstrates plainly, even if in incomplete form. Similar to this new model at the EU level, the most important inspiration for constitutionalism in the international law remains the traditional model of domestic constitutionalism, on which I will build in the remaining of the chapter.

What I offer here is not a morally neutral way of understanding the role of constitutions and constitutionalism. Constitutions structure political and legal systems in distinctively principled, value-driven directions. Their moral purposes are fundamental to the content and design of constitutional rules. Therefore, I will be focusing on normatively rich, morally demanding forms of constitutionalism as a model for global constitutionalism. Such a model does not baptize any political system including totalitarian, autocratic ones with the legitimating label of constitutional systems. Instead I offer an account of constitutionalism which can serve as a framework for desirable constitution – making and constitutional change.

This chapter captures what is morally significant about the practice of constitutional law and explains the continuity of thinking in terms of constitutional rules at both the domestic and international level. I will argue that despite the obvious challenges of the scale and nature of the commitment problem in international politics, and the character of the collective agents involved, we can apply constitutional thinking on a global scale to deal with some of the most pressing problems the world is confronted with today. I will describe constitutionalism as a solution to the paradox of commitment faced by states and show why their inability to resolve it is a source of global public bads. I will then explain the ways in which constitutions act as commitment devices on a national scale. The next step involves showing what role a global constitution can play in international law. Finally, I will outline some of the institutional design choices which can accompany constitution-making at the global level.

1 COMMITMENT PROBLEMS AMONG STATES

The fates of individuals living in different states are deeply intertwined nowadays. Tourists and migrant workers, communicable diseases, pollution, commerce, scientific research, ideas, weapons, drugs, and news cross borders at levels and speeds unprecedented in human history. In some ways, states' ability to solve problems arising from their ever-denser interactions have been nothing short of impressive. Over the last two centuries, states have developed sophisticated bilateral and multilateral treaties, customary norms, and legal institutions such as courts which establish rules of behavior, help monitor compliance, and solve disputes. According to Phillipa Webb, over fifty courts, tribunals, and quasi-judicial bodies now operate in international law (Webb 2013). These courts have issued thousands of binding rulings, 91% of them since 1990 (Alter 2014, p. 4). Their decisions have helped states settle long-festering disputes, divide contested territory, and avoid the costs of uncertainty and conflict (Simmons 2002; Follesdal 2020).

The Montreal Protocol for the Protection of the Ozone Layer is among the more successful treaties to date. It enjoys universal membership from all states and close to 100% compliance. It has persuaded states to phase out over one hundred chemicals damaging the ozone layer (Gillis 2018). Other examples of successful multilateral treaties include the United Nations Convention on the Law of the Sea (UNCLOS – 1982), which regulates, among other things, control over coastal waters, the allocation of fishing rights, pollution, criminal jurisdiction, seabed mining, marine scientific research, and passage through straits for shipping and military vessels; the Convention on International Civil Aviation (1944), which coordinates access to international air routes; and a broad range of trade agreements governed by the World Trade Organization.

Yet, these successes are overshadowed by serious commitment problems in international politics. First, states continue to cause harm to their immediate neighbors and to other states due to unresolved governance issues in regional or global commons. Egypt and other countries in the Nile river basin are still fighting over an equitable way to divide its water resources (The Associated Press 2020). Aggressive fishing methods in the open seas destroy marine habitats, and conflicts over territories such as those in the South China Sea continue to challenge peaceful coexistence among neighboring states (Sample 2010; Phillips, Holmes, and Bowcott 2016). Second, recurring massive human rights abuses in states like North Korea, China, Myanmar, Syria, Yemen, South Sudan, and Ethiopia call for more effective modes of international accountability to reduce the states' ability to harm their own citizens and the citizens of other states (Macfarquhar and Shadid 2012; Paddock 2020; Pavel 2015).

Third, states often understand the imperatives of international cooperation which formalizes rules of behavior and constraints or redirects state action, but are reluctant to reduce their own discretion to act free from interference. States create treaties and rules but fail to endow them with mechanisms for interpreting the rules, settling disputes, and enforcing them. Or when they create those mechanisms, they are reluctant to give them the authority necessary to be effective, thus leaving them too weak to serve the roles they were designed for. This is what Andrew Guzman called the 'Frankenstein problem' of international law. States create formal agreements and institutions at the international level with a life of their own which are able to restrain and impose costs for non-compliance (Guzman 2013). States understand this risk to their sovereign autonomy and seek to guard against it. They do so by creating weak, inefficient institutions that lack the proper authority to constrain states and impose sanctions. The Frankenstein problem is the problem of commitment on a global scale.

Fourth, certain feature of international law and domestic constitutional rules make this problem worse. Unlike the domestic legal order, where individuals are bound by rules with or without their consent, state consent is the cornerstone of international law. Most treaties do not apply to states without their consent and Article 34 of the Vienna Convention on the Law of Treaties states clearly that 'A treaty does not create either obligations or rights for a third State without its consent'. Further, Article 35 requires *written express consent* from a third-party state to accept legal obligations under a treaty. There are a number of exceptions to this rule, such as the obligations arising from the UN Charter. In addition, there are other sources of international law which apply to states without their consent, such as customary rules and jus cogens.[1] Nonetheless, the result of the oversized role the state consent plays in international law is that states can choose not to consent to treaties which are essential for solving collective action problems, they can consent to a treaty but not to the authority of institutional mechanism, which interprets and applies the rules through the practice of reservations, and they can withdraw consent from a treaty they have joined due to say, a change in government. State consent significantly weakens the commitments states make to the rules of international law, by making those commitments subject to the political whims of its leaders and the winds of political change (Guzman 2011; Pavel 2021b).

Fifth, national constitutional systems play a big role in whether states' commitment to international law is secure (Pavel 2021a). Many constitutions are understood implicitly or explicitly to establish the supremacy of domestic constitutional rules within each national legal system. They do so by creating legal hierarchies and giving domestic institutions the last word in determining the validity of international law on a state's territory and for its citizens. This means that when national and international laws come into conflict, national institutions can interpret international rules and determine their weight in the municipal context. The implication of domestic constitutional supremacy is that

---

[1] Even for customary rules there is an exception according to which when states explicitly and repeatedly dissent from a rule, the rule does not apply to them as a persistent objector (Green 2016).

international legal rules often have the power which domestic institutions say they do, and the various judgments domestic institutions make can diverge and even be at odds with each other and with those of international courts and tribunals. Despite the fact that the VCLT says explicitly in Article 27 that states cannot use domestic legal provisions as a justification for breaching their international legal obligations, in practice the enforcement of this rule is weak and states tend to proceed as if they can ignore it.

Finally, a lack of commitment results from perceived deficiencies of the international legal system itself. Understandably, some states regard the inequalities in states' legal obligations and the weakness of enforcement and the paucity of authoritative dispute resolution mechanism as shortcomings of legitimacy and fairness in international law itself, and refuse to commit to rules which create differential treatment. For example, the jurisdiction of the International Criminal Court (ICC) concerning genocide, crimes against humanity, war crimes, and crimes of aggression applies to states with their consent, with the exception of referrals from the Security Council. However, the Security Council is unlikely to refer its permanent members with veto powers in cases in which they are suspected of committing these crimes, creating the legitimate worry that powerful states can shield themselves and their allies from accountability. It is not surprising then that the ICC is perceived as biased and that some states have begun to withdraw from the Rome treaty which created it (Christiano 2020; Gutierrez 2019).

These inequalities speak to deficiencies in the rule-of-law features of international law. Few international legal rules apply equally and impartially to all states; access to dispute resolution mechanisms is the exception rather than the norm, and protections against the arbitrary exercise of power by international institutions is very limited. This is most clear in the case of the Security Council, which controversially took on legislative functions (Talmon 2005), and for which there is no opportunity for institutional review (judicial or otherwise). The Kadi case before the CJEU shows that there can be some pushback, but it is severely limited.[2] These deficiencies spark fears that states or their citizens will be unfairly targeted, that they will not have access to remedies in cases where other states violate their obligations, and that the costs of dispute resolution is extremely high. This legitimacy deficit underlies accusations of hypocrisy targeted at big powers who can get away with less compliance than smaller, less economically advanced states, and at the international institutions which do little to prevent this from happening.

---

[2] *Kadi and Al Barakaat International Foundation v Council and Commission* Court of Justice of the European Union, 2008. In this case a Saudi national with assets in Sweden, Yassin Abdullah Kadi, and a non-profit foundation for Somali refugees called Al Barakaat, argued before the CJEU that the Council of European Union decision which gave effect to a Security Council Resolution to freeze the assets of those suspected of aiding terrorism violated their rights of right to property and the right to effective judicial review. The court ruled for the defendants in a 2008 decision.

All of these features highlight the paradox of commitment which obtains among states in international politics. States would benefit from more effective rules which reduce conflict, enable cooperation and coordination, and resolve collective action problems, but they are reluctant to restrict their own freedom in the name of those rules and the institutions tasked with interpreting and enforcing them. The difficulty to keep commitments made is not just a feature of states, but of human rationality itself. Social relations are marred by profound problems of commitment. Respecting other people's rights, keeping promises, contributing to public goods are commitments whose successful realization takes willingness to bear costs, restrain one's actions, and develop a long-term view of one's and other people's interests. Commitments are hard because they involve limitations on one's freedom to act for the sake of one's future capacity to act. The paradox of commitment, namely the difficulty of restraining freedom in order to enhance it, is a well-understood problem in political science (Ferejohn and Sager 2002; Elster 2000; North 1993; North and Weingast 1989; Holmes 1995; Isiksel 2016). James Buchanan called it the 'paradox of being governed:' 'men want freedom from constraints, while at the same time they recognize the necessity of order' (Buchanan 2000, p. xv). The ability of individuals to make binding commitments expands their opportunity set. By becoming reliable, trustworthy, restrained in their treatment of others, individuals can form rewarding personal relationship, exchange, cooperate, solve collective action problems, and create stable, mutually beneficial institutions.

Effective solutions to commitment problems are many and depend on a range of background conditions for their realization. I will focus on one solution that is less explored in the case of international law, namely a constitutional agreement which encourages states to pre-commit to certain basic principles of international cooperation, institutions, and decision-making procedures, and to courts with compulsory jurisdiction and power of judicial review. But before I make the case for a constitutional agreement for international law, I will summarize the case for constitutions as pre-commitment devices in national legal systems.

II NATIONAL CONSTITUTIONS AS PRE-COMMITMENT DEVICES

What are constitutions for? The standard answer says that constitutions organize, empower, and constrain government power (Holmes 1995; Sunstein 2001; Elster and Slagstad 1988; McIlwain 2008). They create and articulate the power of specific political and legal institutions. They also oppose absolutism by dispersing power among political branches, protecting rights, enabling political accountability, limiting the executive, and strengthening due process and the rule of law. On this account, constitutions are uniquely fit to organize the political institutions of modern, large, complex societies. When we speak of morally desirable constitutions, we speak of developed, institutionally differentiated domestic legal systems, characterized by legal hierarchies, entrenched rules structuring political interactions, and the primacy of law over politics.

Constitutions are sometimes seen as effective precommitments to ensure that people bind themselves to rules which ensure respect for rights, the rule of law, and procedures for solving disagreements. Ferejohn and Sager argue that:

> 'By enshrining various aspects of procedure or substance in a written document that announces itself as the supreme source of law, and by making that document difficult to change, a people can achieve a future better than any they could otherwise attain. The usual examples center on using a constitution to commit to protecting private property, to accord political and legal recognition to unpopular minorities, and more generally to respect and further the rule of law and democracy.' (Ferejohn and Sager 2002, p. 1929)

Constitutions distill agreements on second order rules, namely, the fundamental principles and constraints which will guide the design of first order rules, and on the scope and limits of the authority of institutions tasked with creating implementing these rules. By making these agreements on higher order rules and principles hierarchically superior to ordinary legislation, difficult to change, and enforceable in courts, citizens create legal and political orders which enable them to achieve a better future. Constitutions ensure against the political risk of despotic governments, against devaluing the basic principles of freedom and equality, and against temptations to exempt political officials and governments from accountability for their actions.

The popular metaphor for understanding constitutions as pre-commitment devices is that of Ulysses tying himself to the mast. He does this to resist the Sirens' song, which he knew would make him act irrationally and possibly lead to his crew's demise. Similarly, constitutions place constraints on groups' future capacity to act, and these constraints end up increasing trust and expanding the capacity of individuals to pursue their goals (Elster 1984). Constitutional rules need not be intended as precommitment devices, and indeed often they are not seen this way by their original signatories (Elster 2000, pp. 88–90).[3] Rules can have other motivations, such as enabling effective decision-making, or designing the working of electoral politics. Yet over the long run, the language of the constitution sets limits on the acceptable form such politics can take and inhibits government agencies from operating outside of the bounds of the law (Ferejohn and Sager 2002, p. 1930).[4] A government bound to protect minority rights or to respect an independent judiciary can be entrusted to

---

[3] In his second book on precommitments, Ulysses Unbound (Elster 2000), Elster pulls back from the claim that constitutions are precommitment devices.

[4] Ferejohn and Sager contend that 'here, burnt bridges-as where parties to a cease-fire are assured against attack by the incapacity of their enemy to reach them may be the more apt metaphor. On this account, it is a weakened rather than a strengthened federal government that made the relative indelibility of our constitutional provisions appealing to the generation that drafted and ratified the Constitution.' (2002, p. 1930)

have more power and do more than one that is not so bound. Constitutional rules both incapacitate and empower, and these two functions are related.

Moreover, it is rational for constitutional assemblies to adopt these pre-commitments and for citizens to ratify them as a mechanism for generating a well-ordered society. As Ferejohn and Sager put it, 'It is sensible to make a commitment precisely in those circumstances in which it is reasonable to think that, absent the commitment, one may be tempted to deviate from one's chosen course of action' (Ferejohn and Sager 2002, p. 1936). Under normal circumstances, without constitutional restraints, individuals and groups can be expected to deviate from behavior and choices which are morally desirable, such as protecting minority rights or defending the rule of law.

There are a number of explanations for deviations from desirable behavior: ethnic and racial discrimination, low tolerance for unpopular minorities, time-inconsistent preferences, weakness of will, new technological circumstances, and high discount rates for the future. These are problems which both individuals and groups face. But groups have additional challenges. Foremost among them is that groups must deal with conflict and disagreement over the most fundamental principles of social cooperation (Sunstein 2001, pp. 49–50; Waldron 1999a, pp. 147–188). People disagree on how to interpret fundamental values like liberty, equality, and rights, how much power political institutions such as the executive and the courts should have, and what rules should govern decision-making. One path to forging agreement is to rely on constitutional rules to create consensus on higher order principles. Constitutions are necessary even when people disagree radically, as they do in international politics, and *precisely because they disagree*, as a system of deliberation and debate which structures the various parties' confrontations and compromises with one another. Once basic agreement is reached, constitutions make it more stable.

Constitutional rules act as *external* commitment devices which reinforce *internal* commitments which constitution-makers already possess or come to accept in light of the political compromises they negotiate. These rules are instrumental to the realization of, and can develop concomitantly with internal commitments (Ferejohn and Sager 2002, pp. 1947–1948). For example, a commitment to democratic politics can be institutionalized in various ways through constitutional rules, and once such rules are accepted, they become part of the normative expectations people have with respect to political dynamics. To think of constitutional rules as external commitment devices is to realize that they depend, to an important extent for their success, on the widespread acceptance and the strength of constitutional rules as internal commitments. Constitutional rules that are not backed by a culture that supports them and that lacks institutions which interpret, apply, and enforce them are mere words on paper. This is why mechanisms such as judicial review are important for the effective and consistent implementation of constitutional rules.

Typical constitutional commitments are not like unchangeable physical constraints. They do not *guarantee* that commitments will be honored. Acting contrary to commitments is still possible. But they can *increase the likelihood* that the agent will follow through with their commitments. This is why it is prudent for persons and groups/collective agents to 'restructure (their) circumstance so as to make it more likely that (they) will honor (their) commitment' (Ferejohn and Sager 2002, p. 1937). Constitutions reaffirm the commitments publicly and raise the costs of not following through with them.

III AGAINST CONSTITUTIONS AS COMMITMENT DEVICES

The idea of a constitution as a commitment device, or at least of some of the features that come with it, do not enjoy universal support. In fact, prominent scholars see judicial review as an illegitimate restriction on popular will (Waldron 1999a; Tushnet 1999; Bellamy 2007; Seidman 2013). For example, despite being a committed defender of constitutionalism, Waldron rejects both a bill of rights and judicial review as anti-democratic. He argues that 'respect for individual rights is not compatible with a purely predatory image of legislative majorities' (Waldron 1999a, p. 258). If the basis of these constitutional mechanisms is that majorities can be wrong or unjust, we are selling democracy short. Representatives in parliament, as rights bearers, will not be indifferent to the fact that their decisions may infringe on rights. The corrections of errors in judgment will be made through democratic action and legislative deliberation. Unless they are allowed to do so, restraining the legislators' capacity via judicial review amounts to a denial of self-government (Waldron 1999a, p. 264). The specification of rights is complex, difficult and subject to disagreement, and we have no reason to prefer the specification a group arrive at a point in time t_1, when a constitution is written, to t_2, when a democratic majority prefers to specify them differently (Waldron 1999a, pp. 266–275).

Richard Bellamy puts the point even more emphatically. Bellamy objects not only to judicial review, but to the idea of a written constitution as such. Written, unchangeable constitutions ossify particular legislative, procedural, and moral commitments, whereas the democratic will is constantly learning and evolving, expressing itself in ways that faithfully reflects the political agendas of current majorities (Bellamy 2007, pp. 90–140). His main objection to judicial review, for example, is that courts take away the most basic constitutional right, namely that of deciding how to handle ongoing issues loyal to existing democratic preferences. To entrust the power to judges is to set up a system of arbitrary rule and ultimately domination. Like Waldron, who maintains that giving power to unelected judges to settle difficult questions about what rights individuals should have is tantamount to a form of aristocracy, Bellamy also believes that judicial review undermines political equality (Bellamy 2007, pp. 164, 257; Waldron 1999a, p. 264).

Although Waldron, Bellamy, and others raise difficult questions about how to best instantiate the democratic will, I am not persuaded by these criticisms. First, there should always be a means to evaluate if the government is using its power in legitimate ways and consistent with existing law. Legal rules do not ensure their faithful application and legislative assemblies cannot perform the function of checking the actions of the public officials, including their own, for consistency with the law. The administrative and executive machinery of the state are not self-monitoring either and they should not be entrusted to be. Judicial review is not applied to legislative majorities exclusively, but also to the police, bureaucracies, and other non-elected public servants. Once laws are promulgated, we need to make sure these other bodies respect and interpret them in ways that are not unduly burdensome on citizens. Courts enforce basic rules of political engagement and appropriate boundaries for various governmental roles.

Second, I think the dangers of majorities trampling on minorities' rights continues to be downplayed by defenders of political constitutionalism. Constitutionally entrenched rights of political participation and to various freedoms can ensure both adequate voice as well as safeguards for unpopular minorities. Finally, judicial review is the most important avenue given to individuals to call the government to account (Walen 2009, pp. 341–344). For individuals to have legal standing to ask the government to give an account of its actions is fundamental in itself and secures other significant political values, such as equality, liberty, rule of law, and lack of arbitrary interference.

An appeals or review court is no more dominating than any other public institution whose officials are unelected, as long as they have a well-defined and justified function within a legal and political system. There will always be differences in political status between judges and citizens just as there will be differences between elected officials and citizens in a large democracy with complex roles and responsibilities (Walen 2009, pp. 344–345). I do not have the space to develop these insights and they have been made elsewhere at length. And although the context of international law is different, the same general considerations apply, not just to individuals and groups but also to states and international organizations bound by a global constitution. But let me begin to build the case for a global constitutionalism next.

The main question is whether constitutionalism appropriate for the structuring relations among states. Talk of constitutionalism in international law may seem premature and naive. Especially during a period of retrenchment from international cooperation, and inward-looking domestic policies driven by a health pandemic and populist politics, placing faith in a rule-governed interaction among states could strike one as unreasonably optimistic. Whether it is optimistic depends on us being able to predict how states will react to a growing list of cross-border challenges such as climate change, the ever-present possibility of violent conflict, large scale violations of the rights of individuals, trade wars, refugees, poverty, and disease. Predictions of this sort are difficult, and they are not my aim here. Rather I want to investigate whether *in principle*, constitutionalism provides a plausible solution to a problem states face in their interactions with each other and their citizens: the problem of commitment.

IV CONSTITUTIONALIZING INTERNATIONAL LAW

International law is nowadays a complex network of rules, organizations, discourses, and practices which regulate state behavior and the behavior of nonstate actors. Moreover, international law already contains rules and principles with quasi-constitutional status. Among them are the principles of state equality and noninterference, restrictions on the use of force, jus cogens norms such as prohibitions against torture and genocide, and the secondary rules for the validity of treaties codified in the Vienna Conventions on the Law of Treaties (1969). The UN Charter also states in Article 2 paragraph 6 that the United Nations shall ensure that nonmembers act in accordance with its principles in order to ensure international peace. Certain rules of international criminal law similarly operate on a nonconsensual basis, such as the referral mechanism of the Security Council to the ICC. Thus, international law already contains rules which restrict the consensual character of treaty-based law, in recognition of the fact that no legal system can operate on a purely voluntary basis. Article 103 of the Charter codifies a limited quasi-constitutional hierarchy in asserting the supremacy of Charter rules over contrary international law.

But, as I explain elsewhere (Pavel 2021a, pp. 160–170), the status of all these quasi-constitutional rules is contested, they are ambiguously defined in international treaties, when they are defined at all, and the mechanisms for their interpretation and application are weak or non-existent.[5] Take the principle of noninterference, codified in Article 2 of the UN charter, paragraphs 4 and 7. Paragraph 4 says that 'All Members shall refrain in their international relations from the threat or use of force against the territorial integrity or political independence of any state, or in any other manner inconsistent with the Purposes of the United Nations', while paragraph 7 adds that 'Nothing contained in the present Charter shall authorize the United Nations to intervene in matters which are essentially within the domestic jurisdiction of any state or shall require the Members to submit such matters to settlement under the present Charter'. Yet the Charter does not clarify what matters are 'essentially within the domestic jurisdiction of any state', leading to uncertainty about a number of international legal provisions which would seem to require some form of interference for enforcement, such as the prohibition against genocide. These tensions between fundamental principles of international law such as noninterference and prohibition against genocide have led some scholars to argue that humanitarian intervention is both legal and illegal at the same time (Hurd 2011; Frank 2005).

What this shows is that fundamental international legal principles could be more precisely and coherently articulated through a constitutional agreement which strengthens states' resolve to uphold them as the building block of an international

---

[5] For example, there is no agreed list of jus cogens norms (see, for example, The Fourth report of the *Special Rapporteur*, Mr. Dire Tladi (71st session of the ILC (2019)) https://legal.un.org/ilc/guide/1_14.shtml accessed May 23, 2021).

legal order and enables more effective mechanisms for their interpretation, balancing, and application. If we take seriously that at their most basic, constitutions are 'convenient ways of laying out the formal contours of the mechanisms for exercising public power' (Tushnet 2018a, pp. 10–11; Waldron 2016d, p. 26), a constitution for international law would establish the basic rules as well as provide for means of resolving conflicts among them.

Still, some might worry that the disagreements about the basic rules of international justice at the international level is too great for any compromise of broad principles and procedures to be possible. And it is true that disagreement on values and principles is magnified by the sheer size as well as the diversity of legal and political practices at the international level. This makes constitutionalism more, not less, necessary, because it can serve as an essential mechanism for finding compromise on radically different understandings of political and legal principles. Without erasing disagreements, constitutions make them more tractable, by encouraging compromises on higher order rules (Hardin 1999). As Waldron puts it, a constitution can:

> make politics possible among a people who disagree, often quite radically, about values, principles, rights, justice, and the common good. Even in the midst of their disagreements they need rules that can define a politics – a system of decisions and systems of debate and deliberation that can house the various parties and factions in their confrontations with one another. (Waldron 2014b, p. 1169; 2016d, pp. 23–26)

It is unlikely that Waldron himself would transfer this insight to international law (Waldron 2011a). Nonetheless, I find it illuminating for thinking about how to tackle disagreement at the global level. The main role of the constitution is to enable peaceful and fair terms of political interaction for people who disagree, and an international constitution can be regarded as a mechanism to facilitate agreement on the most basic principles of interaction at the global level. Still, constitutions do more than resolve disagreements. They ensure that the weak are not at the mercy of the strong, and this is the most salient challenge characterizing relations among states, as the conflicts in the politics of international trade demonstrate (Barton et al. 2008; Steinberg 2002). For instance, smaller, less developed states are less likely to retaliate against the violation of trade rules by more economically powerful states, and less likely to initiate proceedings at the Dispute Settlement Body of the WTO when this happens (Shaffer 2009). As the Federalist put it, constitutional law frames regular political interaction so that it does not depend on 'accident and force' (Waldron 2014b, p. 1168; Hamilton, Federalist no. 1). International politics is particularly prone to accident and force, to the rule of the strong over the weak, and to the vagaries of economic might and military power.

As an external commitment device, a constitutional agreement would build on states' internal commitments for a peaceful international order, and facilitate compromises on higher order rules of coexistence, cooperation, and the resolution of collective action problems. Constitutionalism at the global level depends on and cannot exist without an important degree of internal commitment from states. As part of that commitment, we can expect states to insist, and rightly so, on the robust protection of sovereign autonomy. A commitment to state autonomy does not introduce a new, foreign norm to the international legal system, but rather constitutionalizes an already well-entrenched and widely observed rule (Roth 2011; Ratner 2015). Many fundamental international law documents to date include important provisions to protect states against interference from other states, and one would assume, international organizations and rules. The UN Charter, VCLT, even the more recent Responsibility to Protect doctrine (R2P) assumes it as a fundamental principle of international law, only liable to be trumped in the most severe cases of violations by states of the rights of their citizens. A global constitution would include, like most state-based constitutions, a range of other substantive rules for framing international legal and political interaction, procedures for making decisions which affect all states, and institutions entrusted with guaranteeing and stabilizing constitutional rules.

To sum up, the main reasons for global constitution-making are:

- To make peaceful interaction and cooperation possible among peoples who disagree, often quite radically, about values, principles, rights, and justice.
- To frame and define the interactions of states by constitutional rules, rather than power, prejudice, and military force.
- To use the rights of states, individuals, and groups as fundamental building blocks of an international order.
- To realize the rule of law in international law, including equality before law, access to courts, and due process.

Many questions remain unanswered about global constitutionalism, including how to persuade states that commitment problems in international law make this solution worth considering, what are the fair procedures by which various countries can be consulted and their views aggregated into a set of rules which serves the interests of states and their citizens rightly understood, what is the range of morally acceptable compromises on substantive rules and decision procedures, and what can be done to reduce the likelihood of constitution-making processes misfiring and coopting some of the more pathological dynamics of international politics. I do not have the space to answer all these questions here, but note that those are issues as much for an international constitution as they are for a domestic one, and we have a range of possible ways to address them borrowing from domestic constitutional practice. The aim of this chapter has been rather to offer some preliminary reasons to persuade states to consider constitutionalism as a solution to commitment problems in international law. I will conclude with a few brief observations on compliance challenges and institutional design options for an international constitution.

CONCLUSION: INSTITUTIONALIZING A GLOBAL CONSTITUTION

Framed in this way, the case for a global constitution is not very different from a case one could make for constitutionalism within the political community of a state. Constitutionalism manages political conflict and makes the conciliation of disagreements possible. It does so by creating rules which define the political process, a system of deliberation and decision which frames and limits the ways in which conflict is allowed to shape outcomes and requires that political action is governed by law. Constitutions entrench norms of liberty and equality for legal subjects, typically in the language of rights, empower and differentiate between different sources of legal and political power, and disperse and separate the power of the various institutions involved in the making, interpretation, and application of the law, by enabling them to check each other's power. They further create mechanisms and procedures for solving coordination and cooperation problems. Instituting constitutional rule means that any exercise of legal power outside of constitutional limits is power without right. Without constitutional rules, international politics falls prey to power politics, vulnerable states are swept up by the brute force and inertia of the big military and economic powers, rule of law protections for states and individuals are weak, human security is at risk, and the threat of violence remains ubiquitous as the primary means of structuring the interaction among states.

Once a constitution is established as a set of external commitment devices to shore up states' internal commitments, compliance could be achieved via its coordinating function. A constitution sets up a regular process for making decisions and it 'conserves political energy' since the processes and mechanisms for decisions, and their side-constraints, do not have to be worked anew every time. Constitutions enable long-term planning by entrenching some compromises that enable parties to set aside their disagreements (Tushnet 2018a, p. 37). Indeed, as Hardin explains, in the domestic context, coordination among a sufficient part of the population on constitutional rules is sufficient for virtually all the rest of the people to go along with it:

> Coordinating a substantial part of a populace on some institution, practice, or norm is commonly sufficient to make it the interest of virtually all to go along with that institution, practice, or norm. When enough of us drive to the right, the rest of us will have an interest in driving to the right also, no matter what preferences we might have in the abstract' (Hardin 1999, p. 14).

Coordination at the global level through a constitutional agreement might work the same way, even if it starts with only some states endorsing it. If a constitutional solution is regarded as a stable, mutually beneficial agreement, which confers benefits on complying states, a mimetic process of norm diffusion can encourage other states to join or those who have already expressed support for it. Constitutions depend for their effectiveness as commitment devices on the internal commitments of legal subjects, or a substantial number of legal subjects. They rely, in other words, on the voluntary acceptance of the rules by the most powerful players. No constitutional system works where the subjects and institutions with the most power (the executive, the army) do not voluntarily accept its constraints, because there is usually no one above them to ensure conformity to the law. The same will be true of a constitution of international law: major political powers as well as international institutions will have to commit to its rules and allow them to establish the framework for their interaction long term. This is why beliefs about the legitimacy of constitutional rules are so important: they lay the groundwork for internal commitments and pro-constitutional social norms, which ultimately elicit compliance with external constraints. The more legal subjects believe in the legitimacy of the constitutional project, the more widespread compliance with it becomes.

Constitutional rules are neither self-explanatory nor self-enforcing. In addition to substantive rules and decision procedures for making law and policy, constitutional systems need interpretive and enforcing institutions. A constitutional court that settles disputes about constitutional rules, ensures that international law and state law is made in conformity with them, and serves as a court of last resort of other international courts is an important external commitment device. Constitutional review has become a widespread principle of constitutional design. Although Tushnet himself rejects constitutional review, he notes that 'essentially all modern constitutions reject parliamentary supremacy in favor of some form of constitutional review' (Tushnet 2018a, p. 41), with important exceptions in New Zealand, the United Kingdom, and Israel. He continues '*that* constitutional review has triumphed is uncontroversial; *why* it has triumphed requires some explanation. The best scholarly accounts focus on a variety of so-called "insurance" models of constitutional review.' In a quantitative analysis of 204 countries for the period 1781–2011 Tom Ginsburg and Mila Versteeg provide new evidence for this theory. Compared to alternative accounts, they find the most support for the idea that constitutional review is a form of political insurance adopted by constitution-makers to protect specific legal settlements in the face of political uncertainty (T. Ginsburg and M. Versteeg 2014, pp. 588–589). This is consistent with the idea of a constitution as a device to secure commitment over time.

That a constitutional text includes constitutional review does not make it automatically effective. Its effectiveness depends on a number of factors, but important among them is the legitimation beliefs that powerful agents (that in the case of international law are states) hold in relation to it and their willingness to comply with its decisions. Illustrative is the case of the constitutional court in Russia in the 1990s, where a series of controversial decisions involving presidential power led to the court being suspended for several years (Sharlet 1993). For international courts, there are other, less abrupt or visible ways to disable their operation, such as when states refuse to submit themselves to their authority, fail to comply with their decisions, defund them, and undermine the nomination/election of judges. This is why the designing of the courts and of the rules which govern them are an essential part of a constitutional agreement to support it.

An international constitution will have to strike a delicate balance between the commitments states have already demonstrated by their participation in international law, and encouraging them to take on new rule-of-law commitments and institutionalize them in the right way. Any constitutional process works this way. Whether that is possible for the divisive arena of international politics remains to be seen. As a way to advance the conversation on what is possible, I have made the case that constitutionalism is worth investigating as a way to address commitment problems states face in their dealing with each other and their citizens. Wherever a significant body of law regulates the interactions of the members of a community or the interactions among communities (whether organized as a state or not), constitutions are appropriate as authoritative mechanisms to regulate the use of power (both private and public), realize common principles, protect rights, and institute the rule of law.

RECOMMENDED READING

Bellamy, R. (2007). *Political Constitutionalism: A Republican Defence of the Constitutionality of Democracy*, Cambridge: Cambridge University Press.

Ferejohn, J. & Sager, L. (2002). Commitment and Constitutionalism. *Texas Law Review*, 81 (7), 1929–1963.

Ginsburg, T. & Versteeg, M. (2014). Why Do Countries Adopt Constitutional Review? *The Journal of Law, Economics, and Organization*, 30 (3), 587–622.

Guzman, A. (2013). International Organizations and the Frankenstein Problem. *European Journal of International Law*, 24 (4), 999–1025.

Isiksel, T. (2016). *Europe's Functional Constitution: A Theory of Constitutionalism Beyond the State*, Oxford: Oxford University Press.

Kleinlein, T. & Peters, A. (2018). International Constitutional Law. In *Oxford Bibliographies*. Available from: www.oxfordbibliographies.com/view/document/obo-9780199796953/obo-9780199796953-0039.xml.

Krisch, N. (2012). *Beyond Constitutionalism: The Pluralist Structure of Postnational Law*, Oxford: Oxford University Press.

Kumm, M. (2005). The Jurisprudence of Constitutional Conflict: Constitutional Supremacy in Europe before and after the Constitutional Treaty. *European Law Journal*, 11 (3), 262–307.

Pavel, C. (2021). *Law Beyond the State: Dynamic Coordination, State Consent, and Binding International Law*, New York: Oxford University Press.

Pavel, C. (2021). The Rule of Law and the Limits of Anarchy. *Legal Theory*, 27 (1), 70–95.

Ratner, S. (2015). *The Thin Justice of International Law: A Moral Reckoning of the Law of Nations*, Oxford: Oxford University Press.

Waldron, J. (1999a). *Law and Disagreement*, Oxford: Oxford University Press.

Walen, A. (2009). Judicial Review in Review: A Four-Part Defense of Legal Constitutionalism. A Review Essay on Political Constitutionalism. *International Journal of Constitutional Law*, 7 (2), 329–354.

54

Regional Integration

Turkuler Isiksel[*]

I THE EU AS A REGIONAL INTEGRATION ORGANIZATION

Competing conceptions of constitutionalism abound, but most presuppose a particular form of political ordering, namely the sovereign state. What do we gain, and what do we lose, when we try to adapt constitutionalism to organizations that neither possess the attribute of sovereignty nor aspire to it, and whose task is instead to promote cooperation between states? Because constitutionalism serves both as a normative ideal and also as an institutional arrangement, this question could be addressed at different levels of analysis. Likewise, the theory and practice of postnational constitutionalism runs on parallel tracks: while scholars disagree about the desirability of constitutionalizing international organizations, it has been argued that organizations like the EC/EU (Stein 1981), the WTO (de Búrca & Scott 2001; Cass 2005), NAFTA (Afilalo 2001), and the UN (Fassbender 1998) have already appropriated certain recognizable features of constitutional rule.

This chapter focuses on the promises and drawbacks of adapting constitutionalism to a specific type of international organization, namely that designed to promote regional integration. Following Mattli (1991, p. 41), I define regional integration as a process by which states that share a distinctive geopolitical space transfer decision-making authority over select areas of policy to a set of jointly established institutions that promote long-term cooperation. Most regional integration schemes fall in the economic domain and, more specifically, promote market integration. To that end, they establish customs unions and eliminate obstacles to the circulation of goods and services (and, occasionally, of capital and labor). Some regional organizations also address externalities of market integration, such as by promoting labor or environmental standards. Not all regional integration schemes have an economic focus: some promote security and/or military objectives, sometimes in tandem with economic cooperation (Katzenstein 2005). Finally, regional human rights bodies, which are typically semi-autonomous organs of broader regional governance institutions, form a distinctive but high-profile category of their own. Unlike organizations tasked with generating

---

[*] This essay draws on and expands arguments presented in Isiksel 2016.

collective goods such as security or free trade (where one member's failure to fulfil its obligations can diminish returns for all partners), their role is to ensure member state compliance with fundamental rights and foster accountability for violations.

Of course, not all regional integration projects succeed. The empirical conditions under which they do remain hotly contested (Börzel and Risse 2019). Even when states stand to benefit from cooperation and desire the same ends, sovereignty generates a paradox: in the absence of a global enforcer, states cannot guarantee to one another that they will not succumb to short-term incentives to renege on their commitments (Shepsle 1991, p. 246). In order to overcome the paradox of commitment and unlock the benefits of cooperation, therefore, they must find ways of mutually and credibly limiting their prerogatives. Scholars of early modern absolutism have shown that in the domestic realm, constitutional mechanisms have helped sovereigns overcome the paradox of commitment (North and Weingast 1989; Root 1989; North 1993; Holmes 1995). Likewise, in the international context, regional organizations can facilitate commitment by providing coordination, decision-making, compliance monitoring, and dispute settlement mechanisms (Mattli 1991, p. 54). Depending on their institutional structure, some regional and multilateral organizations command what looks like domestic constitutional functions and powers, such as the authority to make and unmake binding norms, exercise judicial review, impose sanctions, and adjudicate individual rights claims.

This chapter argues that while such mechanisms can enhance cooperation by locking in states' commitments, the fact that most regional organizations are created to pursue specific policy ends creates a significant divergence between constitutional mechanisms on the one hand, and the political principles that those mechanisms have been prized for advancing, on the other. The chapter advances this argument primarily with reference to the EU. Of course, treating the EU as an exemplar of regional integration is methodologically and normatively problematic (Alvarez 2003, pp. 429–431; Sbragia 2008; Lombaerde et al. 2010). Regional institutions across the globe are abundant and richly varied. Assuming that the EU is simply more advanced along a developmental path that all integration schemes are destined to tread perpetuates a troubling Eurocentric civilizational narrative that hampers our ability to understand other political experiments on their own terms (McCarthy 2009). Furthermore, in the words of Alberta Sbragia, "the EU is so deeply institutionalized that its internal political and inter-institutional dynamics are unique within the world of regional integration" (Sbragia 2008, p. 35). Few other regional organizations have the authority to make binding decisions in such a broad range of issue areas, let alone without requiring unanimous member state consent. Furthermore, the EU has pursued a uniquely legalized tack towards integration (Abbott et al. 2000; Stone Sweet 2004), resulting in constitutional structures that resemble domestic federal arrangements far more than they do other regional integration projects.

While the distinctiveness of the EU's historical and political trajectory precludes us from generalizing its experience to other international organizations, some aspects of that experience may well be more broadly applicable. Rather than providing a comprehensive and authoritative institutional frame for civic association, as modern states do, regional organizations – the EU included – typically pursue a more focused set of policy goals. This feature not only distinguishes regional integration organizations from sovereign states; it also makes them a distinctive framework for the practice of constitutional rule. This chapter focuses on the consequences of instrumentalizing constitutional mechanisms in the multilateral pursuit of substantive policy objectives. Specifically, it evaluates the implications of using constitutional mechanisms to facilitate the goal of regional market integration.

In the next section, I will address the methodological and definitional challenges raised by adapting constitutionalism to governance frameworks beyond the state. Then, Section III will outline the institutional features that motivate the claim that the EU is constitutionalized, and entertain objections to that claim. In Section IV, I will argue that although the EU does not satisfy the expectations of a democratic conception of constitutionalism, it nevertheless has important lessons for constitutional theory. Insofar as regional integration in Europe is structured around a substantive policy objective, namely economic and monetary union, the EU's constitutional system amplifies a rationale that is germane to any constitutional system, but has sometimes been overlooked by constitutional theorists. I call this *the rationale of effective government* and contend that it is a type of legitimacy claim in its own right. In liberal democracies, constitutionalism is expected not only to enable participatory self-government and safeguard individual freedom, but also to facilitate the effective exercise of public power. These three distinct rationales are not incompatible, but they are often in tension with one another. Because the EU has been designed to help states govern more effectively, its legal system, while deficient from a democratic point of view, is continuous with this third rationale of constitutional rule.

In Section V, I will address the counter-argument that there is an irresolvable conflict between constitutionalism and democracy, which implies that the EU is not at all distinctive in this respect. I will argue that the extent to which constitutionalism and democracy are compatible depends in large part on constitutional design. Using a matrix developed by Versteeg and Zackin (2016), Section VI will argue that the EU's constitutional order is particularly undemocratic because it is <u>both</u> highly specific <u>and</u> deeply entrenched. Finally, Section VII will situate this argument within the context of a wider literature on the uses of constitutionalism in non-democratic contexts. The EU case reminds us that constitutional mechanisms are modular and can be designed to advance many different ends, including facilitating regional integration. We cannot assume, however, that their effects will be emancipatory by default.

II COMPETING APPROACHES TO CONSTITUTIONALISM BEYOND THE STATE

The first modern constitutions emerged alongside projects of nation- and state-building. Whether in the US, France, Haiti, or Latin America, they helped to frame a new, modern type of political community that cohered not only around a set of emancipatory principles, but also around claims to exclusive sovereignty, shared identity, and territorial control. It may, therefore, seem incongruous to transplant the idea of constitutionalism to multilateral organizations that are made up of sovereign states, and which do not themselves claim exclusive authority in the name of a cohesive political community. Beyond this, however, postnational constitutionalism poses an even more profound problem. Given that any genealogical, normative, or institutional account we might give of constitutionalism is bound up with the political form of the sovereign, territorial state, theorizing constitutionalism beyond the state cannot be a simple matter of applying a particular definition of that concept to new institutions (Walker 2002). Even if we grant that supranational variants of constitutionalism will look different from domestic ones, we are faced with the vexing question of how we can describe the former as a recognizable instance of constitutionalism at all (Walker 2003).

For over two decades, scholars have debated whether postnational institutions (like regional integration organizations) can or should be considered in constitutional terms, and whether redesigning such entities along constitutional lines would be desirable. It is worth noting two competing approaches to this puzzle. According to what I will call the *orthodox approach*, constitutionalism is not identical with having a constitution; nor is constitutionalism a mere arrangement of political institutions. Rather, it is the instantiation of a particular theory of political legitimacy. Eighteenth-century American revolutionaries, Sartori argues, "re-conceived" constitutionalism as a counterpoint to absolutism, using it to refer to "*the* distinctive political order which would protect their liberties" (Sartori 1962, p. 860). Consequently, Sartori asserts, the term *constitution* "means—a frame of political society, *organized through and by the law*, for the purpose of restraining arbitrary power" (p. 860). Although many polities have constitutions, few are so organized. If we detach constitutionalism from this original function of protecting individual liberty from governmental action, as Potemkin constitutions do, "the distinction between constitution and constitutional government really becomes meaningless" (p. 861).

Sartori's point is not the banal one that constitutionalism is a normative concept. He does not simply think that constitutionalism correlates with "legitimate government"; rather, constitutionalism embodies a *particular theory of political legitimacy* whose priority —for Sartori— is realizing individual freedom through limited government. Thus, whereas a constitution that prioritizes the principle of popular sovereignty (for instance, by rejecting entrenchment and subjecting all decision-making to majority rule) may be deemed legitimate under a democratic conception, for Sartori it would merely be an instance of *nominal* constitutionalism because it would not sufficiently constrain the exercise of political power (Sartori 1962, p. 861). Sartori's claim is not simply that constitutions are legitimate to the extent that they ensure limited government, but also that constitutions which fail to do so are not deserving of the name.

While Sartori exemplifies an orthodox approach to constitutionalism insofar as he identifies the latter with certain principles of legitimacy, an alternative approach understands constitutionalism in more descriptive terms. On this view, constitutionalism refers to a particular way of structuring public authority. For instance, according to Dunoff and Trachtman (2009a, pp. 10–14), international norms have a constitutional character to the extent that they perform three related functions: "enabling the formation of international law"; "constraining the formation of international law"; and "filling gaps in domestic constitutional law that arise as a result of globalization." Like domestic constitutional systems, postnational legal systems can fulfil these functions by means of allocating authority along vertical and horizontal institutional axes, ordering norms along a hierarchical structure (typically, though not universally, with entrenched norms at the top), ensuring compliance through judicial review, and empowering individuals to challenge certain norm violations. These constitutional functions can be analyzed in normative terms, of course, but they are not defined by the fulfilment of any particular principle like limited government or democratic self-rule.

In the next section, I will use the approach recommended by Dunoff and Trachtman to argue that the EU makes extensive use of conventional constitutional mechanisms. In fact, once we take stock of the distinctive means by which constitutional systems structure the exercise of legal and political authority – including, but not limited to such mechanisms as judicial review, individual rights, hierarchical structure, entrenchment, separation of powers – it is virtually impossible to find a single combination of them that would *include* archetypal constitutional systems such as the US or Germany or India *and exclude* the European Union. More importantly, in shifting the discussion toward constitutional mechanisms and functions, we can better appreciate the different ends that those mechanisms promote, the values and objectives they prioritize, and the practices they foster. This is the claim that I will advance in the next section.

III CONSTITUTIONAL ELEMENTS OF THE EUROPEAN UNION

Notwithstanding the theoretical aporias of constitutionalism beyond the state, the European Union (EU) has acquired many of the recognizable characteristics of a constitutional system (Stein 1981; Weiler 1981 and 1991). Although the EU, like any other regional organization, remains anchored in a series of international agreements, its judiciary has used its interpretive leeway to create a highly distinctive, supranational legal order that is held up by three mainstays that have been largely acknowledged by member states over successive treaty amendments. (Stone Sweet 2004). First, as the Court of Justice proclaimed in a series of landmark rulings beginning with *Costa* v. *ENEL* in 1964,[1] European Community (EC) law takes precedence over the laws of member states in the event of a conflict. The categorical terms in which the Court of Justice frames the supremacy doctrine have been questioned

---

[1] Case 6/64, Flaminio Costa v. E.N.E.L. [1964] ECR 585

by national courts, who periodically contest the interpretive authority that flows to the Court of Justice of the EU (CJEU) as a result of it. Nonetheless, European integration has created a complex new hierarchy of norms, weaving supranational rules directly into national legal systems (Weiler 1981; Alter 2001; Stone Sweet 2004).

Second, a comprehensive system of judicial review integrates member state courts into an EU-wide legal order by tasking them with applying supranational norms (Burley & Mattli 1993; Dehousse 1998; Edward 2003; Stone Sweet 2004; Schmidt & Kelemen 2013). Under the preliminary reference procedure (Art 267 TFEU), national courts are empowered (and courts of last instance are required) to refer questions about the application of EU law to supranational judiciary. In turn, the CJEU has directed these courts to disregard *any* domestic norm that comes into conflict with EU law, effectively giving ordinary national courts powers of judicial review normally reserved for constitutional courts and thereby restructuring the domestic constitutional systems of member states in areas touched by EU law (Stein 1981; Maduro 2005b). Moreover, because it is their own courts rather than a distant supranational body ordering member states to fulfill their supranational obligations, EU law has enjoyed remarkably diligent application domestically, at least relative to much of public international law.

The EU's third constitutional mainstay is the doctrine of direct effect, which gives individuals rights originating exclusively in EU law. In 1963, the Court of Justice ruled that individuals could invoke certain provisions of the Treaty of Rome in front of national courts to challenge national norms. In the ensuing decades, the Court gradually expanded the remit of direct effect by finding more and more Treaty provisions and secondary legislation as capable of giving rise to individual rights. The most litigated among them remain those known under European law as "fundamental freedoms," namely, the freedoms of movement of persons, services, goods, and capital. To the extent that the EU legal order regards individuals as its legal subjects, gives them rights against member states, and triggers judicial review of national law, it transcends the conventional paradigm of international law and mirrors domestic constitutional orders (Pescatore 1983). Importantly, however, these protections relate primarily to cross-border economic activity rather than a comprehensive array of fundamental human interests as would be the case with a traditional constitutional system.

In 1986, the European Court of Justice went so far as to christen, in *Les Verts v. European Parliament*,[2] the Treaty of Rome the "constitutional charter" of the European Community.[3] To explain this choice of terminology, it declared that

---

[2] Case 294/83 Partie Ecologiste 'Les Verts' v. European Parliament [1986], ECR 1339.
[3] In fact, as early as 1956, Advocate-General Lagrange argued that even though the Paris Treaty establishing the European Coal and Steel Community was an international agreement, "it is nevertheless, from a material point of view, the charter of the Community, since the rules of law which derive from it constitute *the internal law of that community.*" He added that the model of the ECSC was "more closely related to a federal rather than to an international organization." (Opinion of Advocate General Lagrange in Case 8/55 *Fédération Charbonnière de Belgique v High Authority* [1954–6] ECR 245, 12 June 1956, Section VI) (emphasis original).

"The European Economic Community is a community based on the rule of law, inasmuch as neither its Member States nor its institutions can avoid a review of the question of whether the measures adopted by them are in conformity with the basic constitutional charter, the Treaty."[4] Implicit in this statement is a conception of constitutionalism as the (judicially enforced) rule of law, where no exercise of public power is exempt from constitutional scrutiny by the judiciary. Coining a formulation that it has since invoked many times, the Court held that "the EC Treaty [establishes] *a complete system of legal remedies* and procedures designed to enable the Court of Justice to review the legality of acts of the institutions."[5] According to the Court, the supranational legal order qualifies as *constitutional* because it subjects all legislative and executive acts to the authority of higher order norms as laid down by the treaties.

To be sure, this narrative underplays the twin claims, never relinquished and periodically brandished by national courts, that member state constitutions underwrite the validity of EU law and, therefore, that member state constitutional courts retain the prerogative to police the bounds of the EU's authority (at least insofar as it claims validity within their legal systems) (Slaughter, Stone Sweet, and Weiler 1998; Kumm 1999; Craig and de Búrca 2015, ch.9). However, the normative basis of EU law can no longer be construed, without significant loss of descriptive power, as the mere emanation of the will of member state principals. Even the episodic confrontations that materialize between the EU's judiciary and those of member states underline the extent to which they have come to form a "composite system of constitutional adjudication" (von Bogdandy and Schill 2011, 1419; Maduro 2003). The point is not only that the EU has many legal features we associate with constitutional rule, but also that it has effected profound constitutional transformations *within* member states.[6] In fact, the metaphor of supranational, national, and subnational "levels" of decision-making is no longer helpful, since neither EU norms nor institutions hover above states as a distinct source of authority. Instead, they are deeply imbricated with domestic (including sub-national) norms and institutions (Hooghe and Marks 2001). The EU is more accurately understood as a composite polity that both supervenes on and is embedded within member states. If the EU cannot be treated as a self-contained polity or legal system, neither, arguably, can its member states, marking their collective constitutional transformation.

There are two major objections to describing the EU, a regional organization, as a constitutional system in its own right. According to the first, the EU lacks the attribute of sovereignty and, as such, its authority can only be derivative. It is a

---

[4] Case 294/83 Partie Ecologiste 'Les Verts' v. European Parliament [1986], ECR 1339, para.23.
[5] Ibid.
[6] See Case 106/77, *Amministrazione delle Finanze dello Stato v. Simmenthal SpA* [1978] ECR 629; Joined cases C-46/93 and 48/93, *Brasserie du Pêcheur SA v Bundesrepublik Deutschland and The Queen v Secretary of State for Transport* [1996] ECR I-1029. See also Maduro 2005a, pp. 339–340.

constituted, not constitutive, legal system (Lindseth 2010, p. 53). According to the second, the EU's legitimacy has never been based fully, or even primarily, on the principle democratic self-rule. In a world where the sovereign state's legitimacy is largely predicated on enabling popular self-rule (J. Cohen 2012), the two objections often go together: the EU cannot be understood in constitutional terms because it rests on a series of international agreements rather than on a popular act of self-founding. The decisions to establish and empower supranational institutions were not made by a pan-European constitutional assembly nor in the name of a *pouvoir constituant*; rather, they were made by the representatives of sovereign states with the understanding that they entailed a limited grant of authority. Insofar as they exercise power delegated to them by states, EU institutions lack the "legitimacy resources" that member state institutions, like regional and national parliaments, command (Lindseth 2010, p. 11).

This objection neatly illustrates the central problem of the post-national constitutionalism debate, namely that it tends to reflect underlying conceptual disagreements about the very meaning of constitutionalism. According to Dieter Grimm, a leading scholar of comparative constitutionalism, "every principle of legitimacy other than democracy would undermine the function of the constitution," which he understands as "to establish legitimate rule and to regulate its exercise by the rulers comprehensively" (Grimm 2010, p. 10). "[I]t is inherent in a constitution in the full sense of the term," Grimm writes, "that it goes back to an act taken by or at least attributed to the people" (Grimm 2004, p. 75). Because Grimm builds the democratic criterion into the very definition of constitutionalism, a regime cannot count as constitutional *and* fail to be (democratically) legitimate. Equally importantly, his formulation of the concept is inapplicable to non-sovereign forms of political community, however democratic they may be. Exploring the genealogy of constitutional regimes, Grimm writes that they presuppose "an object being capable of being [comprehensively] regulated" (Grimm 2010, p. 11): "a concentration of all prerogatives on a certain territory in one hand" (Grimm 2010, p. 11). The necessary interrelation Grimm sets up between sovereignty, democracy, and constitutionalism implies that developments which detract *either* from the sovereign authority *or* democratic prerogatives of constitutional states also undermine constitutionalism *as such*, and are moreover incapable of being remedied through "compensatory constitutionalism" at the supranational level (Peters 2006). As for the EU, while Grimm concedes that its treaties "fulfill the functions of a constitution," it "differs from a constitution because it does not have its source in an autonomous act of a European constituent power" (Grimm 2017, p. 89).

Grimm's argument exemplifies what I termed the *orthodox approach* in Section II insofar as it associates constitutionalism with a particular theory of legitimacy (in this case, one founded on popular sovereignty). On this view, as long as institutional features such as supremacy, direct effect, and judicial review cannot be traced to the will of a sovereign *demos*, we cannot dignify the EU with the constitutional title. In the remainder of this essay, I will argue that this critique is partially right: Grimm's observation that the EU fails to fulfill the democratic aspirations associated with constitutionalism *à l'ancienne* is unobjectionable. However, as I will argue in the next section, the orthodox approach cannot capture what is distinctive about the EU's constitutional system in the first place. Even if we think that democratic constitutionalism is the most (or perhaps the only) desirable kind of constitutionalism, we should be prepared to admit that it is neither the only conceptually coherent idea of constitutionalism available, nor the only type we find when we look at existing constitutional systems. If we insist on a narrow understanding of the phenomenon, moreover, we miss an opportunity to develop a more comprehensive understanding and critique of constitutionalism as an existing practice. The empirical universe of political regimes that make use of constitutional mechanisms is now far wider than liberal democracies. It is essential to understand just what constitutional mechanisms do in such contexts, particularly if we care about preserving an emancipatory vision of constitutionalism. Furthermore, examining the promises and limitations of constitutionalism in the context of a regional integration organization gives us an opportunity to shed new light on some of the familiar problems of constitutional theory, such as the tension between entrenchment and democratic self-rule, or the role of constitutions in promoting or hampering effective government. I now turn to these problems.

IV FUNCTIONAL CONSTITUTIONALISM IN THE EU

Critics of the EU often contend that decisions made at the EU level are too far attenuated from majoritarian control by citizens. The democratic deficit thesis has been debated so extensively for so long that there is little need to revisit it. Its upshot is that despite the ever-expanding powers of the European Parliament and its persistent attempts to involve national parliaments in its policy-making processes, the EU does not approximate any model of democracy, whether representative, deliberative, or direct. Although critics are right to decry the dearth of citizen control over EU decision-making, they often miss what is distinctive about the EU as a political system; namely that its legitimacy has never been based on the ideal of democratic self-rule. Rather, the EU's legitimacy claims are best understood in functionalist terms: the point of delegating certain policy functions to a regional organization is not to give the people more power, but to render policy-making (in certain domains at least) more effective than it would be at the nation-state level. This is not to say that such a claim is well-founded as an empirical matter, much less to affirm it normatively. Rather, my point is that the EU, like many other regional organizations, exists primarily to enhance the "problem-solving" capacity of its member-states by allowing them to cooperate (Scharpf 1999, p. 2; Majone 2005, p. 38).[7]

---

[7] This is often referred to, following Fritz Scharpf's (1999) formulation, as "output legitimacy." However, whereas Scharpf understands output legitimacy as a form of *democratic* legitimacy, I contend that effective government is a criterion of legitimacy independent of and external to democracy itself, not least because it is also available to autocratic regimes.

As I have argued in greater detail elsewhere (Isiksel 2016, pp. 51–56), the EU's constitutional features should be understood in light of this functionalist rationale. As stated in the introduction, one of the main obstacles to international cooperation among states that otherwise seek the same objectives is the problem of credible commitment. In the absence of an overarching authority to enforce mutual promises, states are ensnared by the paradox of commitment: their untrammeled authority narrows their opportunity set, while reducing their discretion can help them achieve benefits that would otherwise elude them (Shepsle 1991, p. 246; Ferejohn and Sager 2003). The range of domestic measures that are required to build and sustain a single market illustrate this problem well. The lifting of protectionist measures, the elimination of state subsidies, and the adoption of shared environmental, consumer, or labor protection standards are costly to implement domestically. The EU's experience suggests that regional organizations can turn to constitutional mechanisms to alleviate some of these problems. Entrusting decision-making, monitoring, and enforcement authority to supranational bodies like the EU Commission, the Court of Justice, and the European Central Bank narrows member states' discretion and allows the latter to reap the benefits of long-term cooperation.

However, solving the paradox of commitment comes at a hefty democratic price. Policies locked in at the EU level cannot easily be challenged through the usual democratic channels. Even the broadest, most well-mobilized democratic coalitions at the domestic level struggle to overturn them, because the institutions that enshrine those policies have been deliberately insulated against contestation. The only (legal) ways to successfully revise major EU norms are to do so through the Council, through litigation before the Court of Justice, or through treaty revision (which usually requires a unanimous decision by 27-member states *and* successful domestic ratification).

Of the many public goods that regional organizations are established to pursue, the EU prioritizes one in particular: generating material affluence through market integration. Because market integration implicates almost all other policy domains, member states have gradually expanded the scope of cooperation at the EU level, simultaneously reducing the room for maneuver that domestic legislatures and elected governments have. After all, for domestic democratic institutions to unilaterally reject policies established at the EU level would be tantamount to that member state's reneging on its commitments. In other words, the trade-off between democratic legitimacy and policy effectiveness is endemic to the EU's design and, by implication, so is the democratic deficit. Insofar as the EU's constitutional mechanisms are configured to administer substantive policy goals, they amount to a form of constitutional rule I have termed *functional constitutionalism* (Isiksel 2016). According to traditional models of constitutional rule such as those reviewed above, the authority of constitutional norms is justified with reference to their role in facilitating democratic self-rule or protecting individual freedom (or some combination of the two). By contrast, in a system of functional constitutionalism, the authority of constitutional norms rests on an appeal to effective governance which, in the EU's case, is measured by the benefits (real or perceived) of economic integration.

It is in part because the rationale of making government effective is integral to *any* constitutional system that the EU is recognizable as one. Although the legitimacy of *any* political system (constitutional or not) rests at least in part on how well it can meet the basic needs of citizens and administer the basic tasks of government, some of the hallmark experiments in constitutional rule, not least that of the US, were justified with reference to the imperative of empowering political institutions to deliver public goods such as public security and defense, economic growth, and financial stability (Isiksel 2016, pp. 40–49). Notwithstanding the ubiquity of this logic, however, constitutional theorists have often framed the challenge of constitutional legitimacy as a dichotomous one: that is, as one of balancing individual freedom with popular sovereignty. By contrast, I contend that the puzzle of constitutional legitimacy entails a trilemma, whereby the aspiration of democratic self-rule must be reconciled not only with respect for individual liberty and the rule of law, but also with the demands of effective government. To be sure, different constitutional regimes strike this balance differently. I refer to the EU's system as functional constitutionalism because it prioritizes the goal of a well-administered economic union over (among other things) democratic self-rule.

V IS CONSTITUTIONALISM NECESSARILY NON-DEMOCRATIC?

Of course, the EU's constitutional system would hardly be exceptional if *all* constitutionalism is fundamentally at odds with democratic self-rule. After all, constitutionalism – at least in its conventional sense as the subjection of public power to a legally established framework of higher norms – presents a famous democratic problem (Bickel 1986; Waldron 1999a). Although constitutional norms are not universally or uniformly difficult to change (Versteeg and Zackin 2016), constitutionalism is often associated with the entrenchment of certain fundamental political norms (Rubenfeld 1998, p. 1105). That is, constitutions are often understood to insulate the basic parameters of the political system from alteration through the ordinary legislative process. As such, they can frustrate the ability of democratic publics to exert their will, revisit past decisions, and refashion the law to their circumstances (Waldron 1999a; Schwartzberg 2007). If laws are legitimate to the extent that they are author(iz)ed by those whom they govern, then any attempt to bridle majority will, including through entrenched constitutional rules, is potentially heteronomous. Whenever popular will frequently chafes against constitutional rules, therefore, the latter are democratically suspect and in need of a legitimizing rationale.

According to some constitutional theorists, democracy itself provides such a rationale (Ely 1980; Michelman 1988; Ackerman 1991; Habermas 1996; Bellamy 2007). Such accounts justify the procedural and/or substantive constraints that constitutional norms impose on ordinary politics in terms of their role in facilitating the exercise of collective self-rule. The key democratic functions of constitutional norms include determining the conditions of equal political participation for citizens, establishing and empowering representative institutions, and setting out the parameters for legal (including constitutional) change.

However, the compatibility of constitutionalism with democracy hinges partly on all higher order norms being subject to revision in response to the democratic will of citizens (Levinson 2008). The defining feature of contemporary politics is that "we disagree about the substantive outcomes that a society committed to the democratic ideals of equality of concern and respect should achieve" (Bellamy 2007, p. 4). We need democratic politics precisely because fundamental values are not timeless, and constitutional rules must not fall out of step with what a particular political community at a particular time considers these values to be (Schwartzberg 2007). Accordingly, the possibility of constitutional amendment in response to popular mobilization is necessary (though not sufficient) to ensure that the ground rules of political life are inclusive, current, and corrigible. Entrenched norms can reify existing asymmetries of power, prolong injustice, and thwart attempts at widening the circle of democratic inclusion. Sooner or later, we can expect a rigid constitution to become an "imperial yoke" that hegemonizes rather than emancipates (Tully 1995, p. 5). Furthermore, empirical studies suggest that constitutional rigidity may be destabilizing, as it may make extra-constitutional paths to political change seem more attractive (Elkins et al. 2009, pp. 140–141).

Unfortunately, however, the prospect of constitutional entrenchment creates an incentive for political actors to use constitutional amendment/reform to ensure "hegemonic preservation" (Hirschl 2004). When ruling elites feel threatened by an impending shift in public support toward their rivals, they may try to reinforce their substantive policy preferences by constitutionalizing them. Accordingly, while public choice theorists insist that constitutionalism hinges "on a categorical distinction ... between outcomes generated within defined rules and the rules themselves" (Brennan and Buchanan 1985, p. 20), strategic uses of constitutional entrenchment have led many democratic theorists to question the viability of such a distinction. According to critics, constitutional arrangements reflect elite interests and expedient bargains just as often as they enshrine principled commitments and open-ended procedures (Beard 1913; Schwartzberg 2007). There are two possible ways to address this realist critique. The first is to double down on the distinction between the rules of the political process and its outcomes. It is precisely because entrenchment risks perpetuating existing patterns of domination that constitutional norms should be framed, as far as possible, in ways that neither dictate nor prejudice future policy choices. Although no set of constitutional rules can be completely neutral with regard to the policy outcomes they sanction or generate, the realist critique – somewhat counter-intuitively – would seem to reinforce the distinction between the political process and its outcome(s) as a normative ideal.

The second way to meet the realist critique is to reject entrenchment and endorse relatively mutable constitutions (for instance, those that can be amended through the regular legislative process). While the constitution's role in circumscribing the arena of permissible political contestation implies that it should be resistant to abrupt alteration and partisan manipulation (Elster 2000, p. 100), the fact that constitutional norms can be unjust, oppressive, or just plain ill-conceived implies that they should also be corrigible (Schwartzberg 2007, p. 25). However, as Versteeg and Zackin (2016) observe, mutable constitutions also tend to be specific; that is, they tend to contain detailed, substantive policy prescriptions. In other words, they blur the conventional distinction between the rules of the political process and its outcomes. Constitutional specificity raises some of the same democratic concerns as the rigidity of constitutional norms: detailed constitutions may impose greater constraints on the ordinary political process, potentially limiting democratically elected policy-makers' ability to respond to citizens' demands. In response, Versteeg and Zackin contend that mutable constitutions can "promote tighter control of the citizenry over the policy-making process" relative to the sparse but entrenched model, provided that drafting and amendment processes are inclusive (Versteeg and Zackin 2016, p. 671).

As an empirical matter, Versteeg and Zackin contend, rigid constitutions tend to be sparse, and specific constitutions tend to be mutable (pp. 658, 660). In view of the foregoing discussion, this empirical relationship can also be framed as a normative principle: constitutional norms should either be relatively amenable to modification through democratic mobilization, or open-ended enough to accommodate democratically-sanctioned policy shifts. In other words, a constitution can only discharge its democracy-enabling function provided that it can strike a hydraulic balance between rigidity and specificity.[8] If it is onerous to change, then it should define the scope of political decision-making as broadly as possible, doing little more than establish the parameters of an inclusive, dynamic system of democratic self-rule. Conversely, a constitution that mandates detailed, substantive policy outcomes should be relatively easy to amend through the ordinary democratic process, because the desirability of those outcomes is likely to be contested and to change over time.[9] Of course, constitutions that are easy to amend may not be as reassuring from a democratic point of view, since they leave the basic parameters of democratic rule vulnerable to short-sighted political manipulation. However, a constitution that advances a partial and detailed policy agenda is less vulnerable to democratic objection if it can easily be amended following an electoral alternation of power.

VI SUPRANATIONAL ENTRENCHMENT: ANTI-DEMOCRATIC AND ANTI-CONSTITUTIONAL

Versteeg and Zackin's finding that constitutions are either sparse and rigid, or specific and mutable is something of an empirical puzzle. If entrenchment and specificity

---

[8] The metaphor of constitutional hydraulics is inspired by Gerken 2007.
[9] Dixon and Landau (2018) advocate "tiered constitutional design" as a way of calibrating this relationship. On this model, different sorts of constitutional provisions are subject to different amendment rules, harnessing the respective advantages of flexibility and rigidity in ensuring the stability and democratic quality of a constitutional system.

represent alternate solutions to "some of the agency problems associated with constitutional design" (p. 661), then framers who are worried about constitutional compliance may be motivated to adopt both (a belt-and-suspenders approach). More cynically, elites who want to preserve their own political preferences may fill the constitution with *both* entrenched *and* detailed prescriptions when they have the opportunity. Perhaps due to the difficulty of credible commitment by sovereign states, the EU's legal system embodies a perfect example of this combination. EU norms are detailed and specific in the way of ordinary statute on the one hand, and change-resistant in the way of entrenched constitutional norms, on the other. The treaties that establish the EU do not simply set out the parameters of the supranational policy-making process; they also mandate detailed and demanding policy outcomes. Although we would expect this sort of constitutional document to be mutable, moreover, EU norms are unusually rigid. Major treaty change requires unanimous approval and ratification by all member states. Even the simplified revision procedures introduced by the 2009 Treaty of Lisbon require a unanimous Council vote *and* approval by the European Parliament. In short, judged by the hydraulic standard of democratic constitutionalism I proposed earlier, the EU's constitutional order is all out of whack. In Grimm's influential formulation, it is "over-constitutionalized" (Grimm 2017, p. 99).

The problem goes well beyond the treaties. As I observed earlier, the Court of Justice asserts that *all* EU law (that is, secondary legislation as well as treaty norms) have the status of higher norms vis-à-vis domestic legal norms and are binding on domestic institutions. It holds that supranational norms prevail even when they conflict with hallowed provisions of a member state's constitution, which gives them the *de facto* status of higher law within member state legal orders (although this is stridently contested by national courts). Thus, it is not simply EU treaties that are constitutionalized vis-à-vis member state law, but the entire body of the *acquis*. Furthermore, although EU regulations and directives govern relatively prosaic matters, revising them ultimately requires securing either a qualified majority or unanimity among all member states representatives in the Council as well as Parliamentary input and/or approval. A member state that wishes to challenge the domestic application of EU rules (or their interpretation by the CJEU) must pursue arduous legislative or treaty amendment routes.

This combination of attributes (namely, the entrenched and voluminous nature of supranational norms) generates an unusually heavy burden of legitimation for the EU to shoulder. As I argued earlier, the entrenchment of constitutional norms in the domestic context is often justified with reference to the fact that these norms *enable* the exercise of democratic self-rule. By contrast, the EU's legal system has been configured to *constrain* shifting domestic majorities from overturning the long-term commitments of their respective member states. As such, the EU can hardly avail itself of the standard democratic justification for constitutional rule. Furthermore, as the EU's competences have grown, the domains of policy that remain open to democratic contestation and revision have shrunk. The direct applicability of many EU-level decisions short-circuits the power of national parliaments to contest, revise, and adapt supranational legislation. Legislative instruments that require transposition into domestic statute allow national parliaments limited room for adjustment in light of their constituencies' preferences, on pain of infringement actions. Even in purely domestic matters, national legislatures are constrained by the duty of sincere cooperation enumerated in Treaty of European Union Art 4(3), which enjoins member states from jeopardizing the EU's objectives in *any* area of domestic policy (Craig and de Búrca 2015, p. 226).

Thwarting mobilized publics from effecting policy change through electoral means is a risky proposition in any political context. In the supranational realm, however, the risk takes on existential dimensions. First, the absence of a clear distinction between the binding force of constitutional and ordinary EU norms as they apply *within* member states makes supranational law excessively brittle, because *any* derogation – no matter how well-rooted in principle or democratic assent – constitutes non-compliance and can be viewed as a threat to integration. Second, given the categorical application of the doctrine of supremacy and the detailed requirements of the *acquis*, it is virtually impossible to ensure even constitutional discipline across all member states. Third, the entrenchment of EU norms thwarts democratic hopes of effectuating major policy changes through the ballot box. This is particularly troubling in the economic domain, where policy choices have strong ramifications for distributive justice and public goods provision. In the early decades of integration, the constitutionalizing dynamics set into motion by the Court of Justice not only promoted market *integration*, but also created a substantive preference in favor of market *liberalization* (Scharpf 1999, pp. 44–52). In particular, the market freedoms that the Court of Justice derived from the Treaty of Rome and christened "fundamental freedoms" have served to elevate the *telos* of unhindered market activity above other political values (Höpner and Schmidt 2020, p. 183). Although the EU has since stepped into the regulatory domain in earnest, the strict rules it enforces in the areas of fiscal and monetary policy, including those relating to borrowing, deficits, revenue, and redistribution, effectively place momentous matters of social justice beyond the reach of majoritarian politics (Streeck 2015).

Finally, the *de facto* entrenchment of ordinary rules prevents the EU from reacting to crises nimbly, forcing EU institutions and member states to work around the EU's own procedures in emergency situations. The financial and sovereign debt crisis of 2009 showed that in the face of capital flight, mounting debts, and a credit crunch, member states, the Commission, and the European Central Bank were willing to resort to workarounds whose conformity with the EU's treaty law was highly suspect (Craig 2014, p. 25). For its part, the Court of Justice subordinated its judicial review role to the imperative of saving the monetary union, relaxing the constitutional limits on the EU's operations to facilitate the supranational crisis response.[10] It is hardly surprising that faced with an emergency, political actors sacrificed adherence to rigid rules to the exigencies of the moment. In short, the sovereign debt crisis revealed a paradox: over-constitutionalization can ultimately undercut constitutionalism itself. The fact that the EU has had to circumvent its own constitutional strictures in order to save the economic and monetary union suggests that it may be too hidebound even for its own ends.

VII THE EU'S PROMISES AND LIMITATIONS AS A CONSTITUTIONAL REGIME

The idea of constitutionalism that emerged from the eighteenth-century revolutions represents an effort to tame sovereign power and, as such, remains a partial success. While liberal democracies have succeeded in conditioning the domestic exercise of public power in light of principles of individual and collective freedom, however, they leave the external exercise of sovereign power relatively unchecked. Traditional constitutional authority is "coextensive with the state"; meaning that "[t]he constitutional order ends at the borders of a state" (Dobner 2012, p. 143). As Kant noted, however, the internal and external aspects of the constitutional project are not easily separable in practice, since the lawlessness of the international realm perpetually threatens to disrupt the orderly world of domestic constitutionalism (Kant 2007 [1784], p. 8:28). Stable liberal regimes are beset not only by their ideological rivals but also by security dilemmas endemic to a disordered international realm. As Altiero Spinelli and Ernesto Rossi observed in their wartime plea for European unity, "the absolute sovereignty of national states" creates an inescapable "desire to dominate, since each one feels threatened by the strength of the others" (Spinelli and Rossi 1941). The project of replicating constitutional mechanisms at the level of international organizations, including regional ones, may be seen not only as an extension of domestic constitutionalism but its *conditio sine qua non* (Kumm 2009, p. 271).

Seen through this lens, the EU's principal achievement is the establishment of an extensive, complex, and demanding system of norms and procedures to govern cooperation, competition, and contention among member states. In the epigrammatic words of the European Court of Justice, the EU represents "a new legal order of international law for the benefit of which the states have limited their sovereign rights, albeit within limited fields, and the subjects of which comprise not only the member states but also their nationals."[11] Like a domestic constitutional system, then, the EU brings states under a "fundamental law, or a fundamental set of principles, and a correlative institutional arrangement, which would restrict arbitrary

---

[10] See Case C-370/12 *Thomas Pringle v the Government of Ireland, Ireland, and the Attorney General* [2012] ECLI:EU:C:2012:756.

[11] Case 26/62 Van Gend en Loos v Nederlandse Administratie der Belastingen [1963] ECR 1

power" (Sartori 1962, p. 855). In addition to transforming the external aspect of sovereignty, EU law shapes member states' obligations toward their own citizens and toward non-citizens within their jurisdiction, at least in policy areas that fall within its zone of competence as defined by the treaties.

And yet, the same standard that highlights the EU's unique achievements also reveals its limitations. Judged by its own promise to extend the constitutional ideal beyond the confines of the sovereign state, the EU has struggled to realize the normative principles with which constitutional rule has been associated since the popular revolutions of the eighteenth century. These shortcomings are not immediately evident on paper. After all, despite having started out with the limited mandate of sectoral and market integration, subsequent rounds of treaty revisions have complemented the brisk texts of the original treaties with lofty political commitments. For instance, Article 2 of the Treaty on European Union proclaims that "the Union is founded on the values of respect for human dignity, freedom, democracy, equality, the rule of law and respect for human rights, including the rights of persons belonging to minorities." It asserts that "these values are common to the Member States in a society in which pluralism, non-discrimination, tolerance, justice, solidarity and equality between women and men prevail." Furthermore, the EU's primary law now includes a state-of-the-art catalogue of fundamental rights guarantees. Overall, European integration has undeniably gained an extensive political dimension in addition to its economic priorities.

At the same time, the EU has yet to fashion effective and usable institutional mechanisms for monitoring and enforcing the foundational norms of constitutional democracy. Accordingly, the values boldly proclaimed in Article 2 are at best a troubling reminder of the disjunction between the EU's aspirations and its practical configuration. The EU's most formidable institutional prerogatives are still market-oriented, while the political values inscribed into the treaties have not been accompanied by a systemic realignment of the EU's competences or governance framework. In fact, far from having transcended its original focus on market integration, the EU has subordinated ever-wider swaths of public policy to the *telos* of the market.

To sum up, although the EU has been criticized for *over*-constitutionalization, it also suffers from *under*-constitutionalization. On the one hand, by constitutionalizing the market integration project, it entrenches policy choices that need not – and in fact should not – be entrenched, including those that affect social welfare provision, wealth redistribution, collective bargaining rights, or employment policies, effectively removing them from democratic contestation. On the other hand, it is under-equipped (and less than enthusiastic) when it comes to enforcing the principles that define constitutionalism as an emancipatory project. What is troubling from a democratic point of view is not the fact that EU law removes certain prerogatives from the scope of national decision-making or even that its norms are arduous to alter, but that the substantive scope of these constraints have little to do with constitutionalism's defining commitment, namely securing the wider conditions of individual freedom and democratic self-rule.

The analysis I have presented in this chapter dovetails with a growing – but relatively recent – strand of scholarship among constitutional theorists and scholars of comparative constitutionalism that centers on the practice of constitutionalism in non-democratic contexts (Somek 2003; T. Ginsburg and T. Moustafa 2008; Ginsburg and Simpser 2013; Isiksel 2013; Tushnet 2015; Scheppele 2018; D. Landau 2018). Just a decade or two ago, associating constitutionalism with any regime type other than liberal democracy would have seemed a *non-sequitur*. As authoritarian and hybrid regimes have reconfigured constitutional mechanisms to pursue ends other than democratic self-rule, however, constitutional theory has moved away from treating the eighteenth century republican model(s) as authoritative. The kind of value pluralism that Isaiah Berlin saw as endemic to the ethical realm is also at work in the world of constitutional practice (Berlin 1991). Existing constitutional regimes pursue a range of different political ends, ranging from democracy to authoritarianism, social democracy to free markets, and liberal neutrality to religious homogeneity. Constitutional rule – and its various features including legal entrenchment, individual rights, and judicial review – are versatile in terms of the normative priorities they can support. This is not to say that all existing constitutional systems are equally legitimate from a normative point of view. It is rather to observe that our knowledge of constitutionalism is incomplete if we fail to understand the role that it plays in non-democratic contexts, and to issue a troubling reminder, if such was needed, that the bond between constitutionalism and liberal democracy is contingent and fragile.

RECOMMENDED READING

Alter, K. (2001). *Establishing the Supremacy of European Law*, Oxford: Oxford University Press.

Bellamy, R. & Castiglione, D. (2018). *From Maastricht to Brexit: Democracy, Constitutionalism and Citizenship in the EU*, London: ECPR Press.

Bickerton, C. (2012). *European Integration: From Nation-States to Member States*, Cambridge: Cambridge University Press.

Börzel, T. A. & Risse, T. (2019). Grand Theories of Integration and the Challenges of Comparative Regionalism. *Journal of European Public Policy*, 26 (8) pp. 1231–1252.

Börzel, T. A. & Risse, T. (2021). Grand Theories of Integration and the Challenges of Comparative Regionalism. *Journal of European Public Policy*, 26 (8) pp. 1231–1252.

de Burca, G. & Weiler, J. H. H., eds. (2012). *The Worlds of European Constitutionalism*, Cambridge: Cambridge University Press.

Dunoff, J. & Trachtman, J., eds. (2009). *Ruling the World? Constitutionalism, International Law, and Global Governance*, Cambridge: Cambridge University Press.

Eleftheriadis, P. (2020). *A Union of Peoples. Europe as a Community of Principle*, Oxford: Oxford University Press.

Ferejohn, J. & Sager, L. Commitment and Constitutionalism. *Texas Law Review*, vol. 81, pp. 1929–1963.

Grimm, D. (2017). *The Constitution of European Democracy*, Oxford: Oxford University Press.
Isiksel, T. (2016). *Europe's Functional Constitution. A Theory of Constitutionalism beyond the State*, Oxford: Oxford University Press.
Katzenstein, P. J. (2005). *A World of Regions: Asia and Europe in the American Imperium* (Ithaca: Cornell University Press).
Larsen, S. (2021). *The Constitutional Theory of the Federation and the European Union*, Oxford: Oxford University Press.
Lindseth, P. (2010). *Power and Legitimacy: Reconciling Europe and the Nation-State*, Oxford: Oxford University Press.
Maduro, M. P. (2005). The importance of being called a constitution: Constitutional authority and the authority of constitutionalism. *International Journal of Constitutional Law*, 3 (3), pp. 332–356.
Stone Sweet, A. (2004). *The Judicial Construction of Europe*, Oxford: Oxford University Press.
Versteeg, M. & Zackin, E. (2016). Constitutions Unentrenched: Toward an Alternative Theory of Constitutional Design. *American Political Science Review*, 110 (4), pp. 657–674.
Walker, N. (2008). Taking constitutionalism beyond the state. *Political Studies*, 56 (3), pp. 519–543.
Weiler, J. (1999). *The Constitution of Europe. Do the New Clothes Have an Emperor?* Cambridge: Cambridge University Press.
White, J. (2019). *Politics of Last Resort: Governing by Emergency in the European Union*, Oxford: Oxford University Press.

55

International Organisations

Anne Peters

The world is today populated by around 5000 international organisations.[1] The exact number is not known, not least because it is not entirely clear which entities fall under that heading. Typical international organisations are inter-state in form and possess international legal personality (Golia & Peters 2022).[2] This chapter mainly deals with those.

"Constitutional theory" (as a reflection about the meaning, functions, and design of constitutions) can be analytic (identifying and explaining its elements) or normative (in the sense of presenting the "best" model of constitution for a given polity). In the law of international organisations, both dimensions are underdeveloped. This chapter seeks to address the dual gap by, first, identifying in an analytic exercise three waves of hidden constitutional models of international organisations, and second, proposing that the third wave should be developed into a model that fits our time.

I KEY CONCEPTS AND OVERVIEW OF THE ARGUMENT

The premise of the chapter is that it makes sense to speak of constitutions and constitutional law in the context of international organisations in the first place, and even if only as "a bit of a legal fiction" (Kochi 2020, p. 214).[3] I will argue that the founding documents of international organisations can be usefully "re-characterised" as constitutions (Gathii 2001). This view seems justified by political practice. Notably the

---

[1] Union of International Associations, Yearbook of International Organizations 2020–2021: Guide to Global Civil Society Networks Vol. 3 (Union of international Organizations, Brussels: 2020), p. XXXV.

[2] Art. 2(a) of the 2011 ILC Articles on the Responsibility of International Organizations (ARIO) (UN GA Res. 66/100 of 9 December 2011, (2011) *Yearbook International Law Commission* vol. II, Part Two, 39–104). The concept of international organisation includes atypical entities which enjoy some quantum of autonomy and pursue a global public interest.

[3] This premise has been denied by parts of scholarship and legal practice, which have been either indifferent or have found the constitutional paradigm for international organisations to be descriptively false (analytically worthless or legally "impossible") or normatively undesirable.

early founding instruments of many such organisations were officially designated as "constitution"[4] or "Charter".[5] The question what this means (if anything) needs to be reflected by constitutional theory.

The term "constitution" is ambiguous, loaded, and contested. This chapter espouses a broad concept of constitution that is in line with the normal usage of the word. Not only constitutions which embody the principles of constitutionalism are the proper object of constitutional theory. Also legal documents that establish and organise a given polity (following whatever normative principles) are constitutions in a less ambitious sense. Applied to international organisations, we can say that both types of constitutions contain provisions about the mission or mandate of the organisation, about the organs/bodies and their competences, and also regulate the relationship between the organisation and those who are legally subjected to it. Both types of constitutions function as a legal basis for the organisation (they "constitute" it) which at the same time determines the scope of its activity, and they give some sense of purpose and guidance. But my view is that constitutions imbued with constitutionalism ("with a capital C"), that enshrine the constitutionalist "trinity": rule of law, human rights, and democracy (Kumm, Lang & Wiener 2014, p. 3) are preferable and should be a normative aspiration, also for international organisations.

This chapter traces, throughout the evolution of the law of international organisations, two waves of theories which have espoused the two conceptions of constitution just mentioned: The first wave revolved around the small c-constitution in the more neutral sense (Section II). The second wave postulated constitutions "with a capital C" that embody constitutionalism (Section III). In the current constellation of a global shift of power and ideology, a third model for constitutions of international organisations, more responsive to the global social question and to the demands of the global south, is emerging (Section IV). I ultimately argue (in the concluding section) that this third model deserves to be pulled out into the light and should be fleshed out further. It should, on the one hand, not fall back on the small-c constitution and, on the other hand, take on board new principles, notably social transnational solidarity and contestatory democracy. This intellectual contribution can provide a basis for responses to the current pushbacks against international organisations.

II FIRST WAVE CONSTITUTIONAL FRAMING

The first wave of constitutional thought about international organisations was not inspired by liberal constitutionalism in the "trinitarian" sense, espousing rule of law, democracy, and human rights (Peters 2016). However, it qualified the organisations' founding documents as constitutions and attached a legal significance to this

---

[4] See e.g. the ILO (1922), UNESCO (1945), WHO (1946), and FAO (1946).
[5] UN (1945).

quality. The approach was more a constitutional imagery or a mere portrayal of the founding document rather than a full-fledged theory.

Constituting and Enabling International Organisations

The first generation's qualification of the organisations' founding document as a constitution gave rise to the extreme view that the document was *no international treaty at all* (Rosenne 1966). The later, more moderate doctrine framed the founding instruments as Janus-faced documents, for example, as "constitutional treaties" or "treaty-constitutions". The ICJ described these documents' hybridity as follows: "From a formal standpoint, the constituent instruments of international organizations are multilateral treaties (…). But the constituent instruments of international organizations are also treaties of a particular type."[6] The aborted "Treaty Establishing a Constitution for Europe" of 2004 captured the hybridity in its official name.[7]

Despite the lack of normative ambition in the sense of liberal constitutionalism, the term "constitution" evoked (as a minimum) the 'constitutive' (i.e. positively constructive) function of a constitution. More specifically, the c-word had a number of interrelated and overlapping legal implications. The first implication was the existence of legal patterns in the institutional set-up of actors which were in fact hugely diverse. The doyen of the discipline, Henry Schermers, called this "unity within diversity" (Schermers and Blokker 2018).

The second consequence was that the founding act constituted a "living" (i.e., dynamic) entity.[8] Put differently, the c-word undergirded the framing of an international organisation as an institution, understood as an identifiable and distinct set of legal structures and processes. For example, Judge Alvarez, in an ICJ advisory opinion on the UN, stressed "that an *institution*, once established, *acquires a life of its own*, independent of the elements which have given birth to it, and it must develop, not in accordance with the views of those who created it, but in accordance with the requirements of international life".[9] The "life of its own" then has numerous technical consequences for the procedures and limits of revisions of the founding document (Peters 2013).

---

[6] ICJ, *Legality of the Use by a State of Nuclear Weapons in Armed Conflict*, Advisory Opinion, ICJ Reports 1996, 66, para. 19.
[7] Treaty of 29 October 2004, OJ 2004 C 310/1. It was rejected by the populations of France and the Netherlands and never entered into force.
[8] See Milan Bartos in the ILC: "And practice showed that international organizations were *living entities* with an *influence of their own*" (718th meeting, Wednesday, 10 July 1963, at 9 h 30 a.m., Relations between States and intergovernmental organizations (A/CN.4/161), Yearbook of the International Law Commission 1963, vol 1, 300 ff, 305–306, para. 69 (emphasis added)).
[9] ICJ, Conditions of Admission of a State to Membership in the United Nations, Advisory Opinion of 28 May 1948, ICJ Reports 57, Individual Opinion by M. Alvarez, pp. 67 et seq., p. 68 (emphasis added).

The third consequence of the constitutional quality of the founding document was that the secondary law produced by the organisation became a special body of law, possibly outside public international law (Zacklin 1968 (2005), p. 199). It, fourthly and relatedly, gave rise to a new legal order. These effects were called "institutional" or "constitutional" effects of the organisations' foundation and work (Simon 1981, p. 474). Fifth, the constitution led to the "autonomy" (Sørensen 1983) of the organisation and/or of its legal order – autonomous both from the members and from ordinary public international law (Cahier 1998, p. 387). With regard to the EU (then still called the European Economic Community (EEC)), the ECJ spoke of a *"new legal order* of international law" in *Van Gend & Loos* (1963).[10] In *Costa v. ENEL* (1964), the ECJ stated: "By contrast with ordinary international treaties, the EEC Treaty has created *its own legal system*".[11]

The organisations' legal order is "new" (or "autonomous"), because its basis is no longer the treaty but the "original" public authority of that entity. Hans Peter Ipsen famously spelled this out for the European Community: "A line of continuity between founding treaty on the one side, and the constitution of the Community and legal order of the Community on the other side, does not exist" (Ipsen 1972, p. 195 (my translation)). Although the EU is a particularly strong ("supranational") organisation whose law enjoys supremacy and frequently a direct effect in the member states, I maintain that these features do not set aside the EU categorically from all other international organisations.

These mentioned legal implications are relevant for all organisations, and had as a motive or consequence to explain and justify their empowerment and even expansion. A famous illustration for the unleashing potential of the constitutional framing is the former World Bank President Ibrahim Shihata's analysis of the Bank's founding document as a constitution (Shihata 2000). Shihata's key concern here was flexibility and adaptability to changing circumstances. He advocated for a dynamic interpretation of the Bank's Articles of Agreement in the style of a living instrument, while avoiding an illegitimate over-reach. Along a similar line, a senior legal counsellor of the WTO praised the "[i]nnovative analytical approaches" which bolster the organisations' "successes in moving beyond the legal and policy frameworks originally imposed on them" (Marceau 2011, p. 13).

Concomitantly, the founding states were seen to suffer a transformation: from contractors to members of the new institution. The states thus cease to be the "masters of the treaty."[12] Rather, they are subdued to the organisations which are enabled by their "constitution" to keep the members in check. This has been most visible for the WTO Agreement, which – conceived as a constitution – functions as a

---

[10] ECJ, case C-26/62, *Van Gend & Loos v. Administratie der Belastingen*, 05.02.1963, ECR 1963, 1, 12.
[11] ECJ, case C-6/64, *Costa v. ENEL*, 15.07.1964, ECR 1964, 587, 593.
[12] But see for a defence of the EU member states as the masters of the treaties: German Constitutional Court, *Lisbon Treaty*, judgment of 30 June 2006, 2/BvE 2/08, para. 334.

constrainer of protectionist measures adopted by members whose parliaments and executives are excessively lobbied by rent-seeking societal groups. By virtue of its claimed constitution-based powers, incarnated in the judicialised dispute settlement system whose bodies engage in balancing (which is seen to be a constitutional type of reasoning), the WTO is able to rectify what is often depicted as distortions of the democratic processes by rent-seeking groups in the members' trade policies (Cottier 2000; Cass 2005; Dunoff 2006; Petersmann 2007).

In this vein, the International Criminal Court (an untypical international organisation which is in functional terms a court) has also been described as performing "quasi-constitutional functions as a last resort in states in which the rule of law is not well-functioning" by restraining powerful state actors (political and military leaders) from committing the worst kinds of abuses (Elderkin 2015, p. 240). The imagery of the organisations' "constitution" bears a family resemblance with the political-science-driven theory of functionalism for international organisations (Albi & Bardutzky 2019, p. 24). Both approaches mainly seek to make the organisations work. And this is exactly their problem, too.

Critiques

Probably the organisations' founders did not have any political ambitions when they called the basic documents "Constitution" or "Charter." Nevertheless, the constitutional framing was then used – as we have seen – by some actors to justifying a dynamic interpretation of the organisations' basic document. The loading of the term was thus complicit to what has been blamed as "mission creep." The dark side of the constitutional language's empowering effects came to light once the activity of international organisations was stepped up and began to be felt in earnest both by states and by affected individuals. It then became obvious that the talk of constitution was prone to furnish a veneer of legitimacy to organisational overreach. The critique emerged that the "use of the constitutional metaphor – and the legal hermeneutic it implied – present perhaps an extreme demonstration of how little the constituent instruments of international organizations have acted as any kind of constraint upon their expansion" (Sinclair 2017, p. 280). The need for "constraint" then motivated a revision of the constitutional theory of international organisations.

III SECOND WAVE CONSTITUTIONAL THEORY

The change of the geopolitical situation marked by the fall of the Berlin wall in 1989 and the accompanying victory of market-economy and capitalist economic policy beliefs, as symbolised by the Washington consensus of 1990 (Williamson 1990) gave rise to a new dynamism in the practice of international organisations. This activity boost then triggered a turn in the theory, shifting the focus of attention from *constituting* to *containing* international organisations. With this move, the constitutional theory of international organisations transformed itself into constitutionalism whose traditional objective has been the constraint of governmental power (von Humboldt 1792 [1851]).

The Need for Containment and Accountability

The historic constellation of 1989/1990 boosted international organisations in an unprecedented degree. The WTO was founded in 1994, the ICC was established in 1998 (and took up work in 2003). The World Bank and International Monetary Fund stepped up their conditionality policies. The system of investor-state arbitration hosted by the World Bank exploded in activity after 1996. The ILO adopted its declaration on core labour standards in 1998, the Human Rights Council was established in 2006, and so on.

The UN Security Council was "unblocked" in 1990, as the P5 stopped vetoing each other's draft resolutions. The Council began to authorise economic sanctions, first the comprehensive boycott imposed on Iraq (which lasted from 1991–2003), then "smart" sanctions against individual terror suspects and politically exposed persons. The detrimental repercussions for the well-being of targeted and otherwise affected persons, in the case of Iraq the entire population, soon became visible. The same is true for the entire gamut of robust measures undertaken or authorised by the UN, such as the territorial administration of entire countries (e.g., by UNMIK and Eulex in Kosovo) and peace missions with broad mandates ranging from repatriation of refugees to election monitoring. The Security Council also engaged in quasi law-making with resolutions on financing terrorism (Res. 1373 (2001)), on weapons of mass destruction (Res. 1540 (2004)), on "Foreign Fighters" (Res. 2178 (2014)), and more. It established criminal tribunals (the ICTY and ICTR). Finally, between 1990 and 2011 (until the alleged overstepping of the mandate for the protection of civilians in Libya marked a turning point), the Security Council recurringly authorised military interventions under Chapter VII.

All these activities have deployed tangible effects for the lives of those who are subjected to them and additionally regularly produce negative externalities. The resulting harm may be wanted or unwanted, foreseeable or unforeseeable, it may be due to design or due to operational mistakes. Once such harms materialised, it is unsurprising that the weak "legitimacy" of international organisations was raised as a problem and that "accountability" became the new buzzword (Coicaud & Heiskanen 2001).

The second wave of constitutional theory was an attempt to close the accountability gap. It sought to apply the "trinity" of constitutionalism (rule of law, human rights, and democracy) to international organisations. In its Rule of Law Declaration of 2012, the UN General Assembly affirmed that "human rights, the rule of law and democracy are interlinked and mutually reinforcing and that they belong to the universal and indivisible core values and principles of the United Nations," and – importantly – that these values also apply at "the international level."[13] In line with the mentioned political and economic developments of the 1990s and early millennium, the revised constitutional theory of international organisations was "liberal" in a political and an economic sense; it breathed the spirit of both Wilhelm von Humboldt and the Washington consensus.

Containment through Rule of Law and Institutional Balance

Officials of international organisations, notably the UN, claim that international organisations are themselves under the international rule of law.[14] In practice however, this commitment is barely honoured. It is not even entirely clear which laws bind the organisations. The ICJ has stated that international organisations are international legal persons which are, generally speaking, 'bound by any obligations incumbent upon [them] under general rules of international law.'[15] But this dictum leaves open *which* obligations are 'incumbent' on the organisations (Daugirdas 2016). Also, the legal consequences of organisational actions violating international law are spelt out only in a non-binding text, the 2011 ILC Articles on the Responsibility of International Organizations.[16]

A possible "constrainer" could be a separation of powers which was in eighteenth-century constitutionalism seen as the most important device for safeguarding liberty.[17] In order to make this benchmark commensurate to international organisations, whose organs and bodies clearly do not mirror the legislative, executive, and judicial branches in states, the guideline could be reformulated as a quest for an "institutional balance," to use the term as coined by the ECJ.[18] The idea is transferrable to other international organisations (Cullen 2020). The "vertical" separation of powers between the organisations and the member states is no functional equivalent and does not obviate any need for additional "horizontal" checks and balances,

---

[13] United Nations, General Assembly, Declaration of the High-level Meeting of the General Assembly on the Rule of Law at the National and International Levels (Res. UN Doc. A/67/PV.3, adopted on 30 November 2012, para. 5).

[14] See, e.g., United Nations, Secretary General. The Rule of Law and Transitional Justice in Conflict and Post-conflict Societies. Reports: UN Doc. S/2004/616, submitted on 23 August 2004, para. 6: The rule of law is "at the very heart of the UN's mission". ICTY, case No IT-94-1-AR72, *Prosecutor v. Duško Tadić, Decision on the Defence Motion for Interlocutory Appeal on Jurisdiction*, Appeals Chamber of 2 October 1995, paras. 26–28 for the UN Security Council.

[15] ICJ, *Interpretation of the Agreement of 25 March 1951 between the WHO and Egypt*, Advisory Opinion of 20 December 1980, ICJ Rep. 1980, 72, para. 37.

[16] Note 2.

[17] French Declaration of the Rights of Man and Citizen (*Déclaration des droits de l'homme et du citoyen*), 26 August 1789, Art. 16: "A society in which the observance of the law is not assured, nor the separation of powers defined, has no constitution at all."

[18] ECJ, case 70/88, *European Parliament v. Council*, 22 May 1990, ECR 1990, I-02041 [*Tschernobyl*], paras. 23 and 31; ECJ (GC), case C-284/16, *Slowakische Republik v. Achmea BV*, of 6 March 2018, para. 32.

because the purpose and practice of these member states' checks do not primarily protect the liberty of those affected by organisational action. Systematic attention paid to "horizontal" checks and balances inside international organisations, and respect for and re-enforcement of a separation of functions in international organisations through interpretation, practice, and procedural rules might contribute to containing organisations where necessary. This could help to distinguish sweeping "ultra vires"-allegations from legitimate concerns.

Human Rights and Remedies

The next limb of the constitutionalist trinity are human rights. Human rights are affected by the intensified activity of various organisations. Organisational actions, ranging from economic sanctions over project financing, debt restructuring, and investment promotion, up to intellectual property protection, have triggered the quest for human rights protection against international organisations. This quest has been honoured to some extent. Despite the reluctance of the organisations themselves, especially the international financial institutions,[19] an overall factual trend towards improved human rights protection against international organisations is discernible (Heupel & Zürn 2017). The doctrinal questions such as the source of obligations, their scope (in the absence of a clear concept of "jurisdiction" of organisations), the rights' contents in the respect–protect–fulfil framework, and the legal possibilities for the lawful curtailment of human rights by the organisations are under intense juridic scrutiny and debate. However, the lack of access to remedies for human rights violations committed by or in complicity with international organisations remains a serious problem. International courts before which individuals could institute judicial proceedings against international organisations or their organs do not exist.[20] In several organisations, much weaker complaint mechanisms, short of judicial remedies, have been offered to natural persons or groups. Examples are the World Bank inspection panel (since 1993), the United Nations Mission in Kosovo (UNMIK) Human Rights Advisory Panel (HRAP) (since 2007), the European Union Rule of Law Mission in Kosovo (EULEX) Human Rights Review Panel (HRRP) (since 2010); or the ombudsperson for the Security Council's 1267/1989/2253 Al Qaeda (later "ISL/Al'Daesh") sanction regime. However, all these

---

[19] Then General Counsel to the IMF squarely denied the bindingness of social human rights for the IMF: François Gianviti, "Economic, Social and Cultural Human Rights and the International Monetary Fund" (undated working paper), para. 56 at p. 43; the working paper is referred to in CESCR, *Report on the 25th, 26th and 27th Session 2001* of 2 June 2002 (UN Doc. E/C.12/2001/17), p. 145. See for the World Bank: Environmental and Social Framework Setting, Environmental and Social Standards for Investment Project Financing of 4 August 2016: "A vision for sustainable development", p. 5, para. 3.

[20] Even in the EU, which forms the sole exception, the CJEU has only a limited jurisdiction for proceedings brought by individuals against legal acts issued by EU institutions themselves under fairly narrow conditions (see Art. 263(4) TFEU).

mechanisms remain isolated, are only moderately effective, and certainly do not amount to a *de facto* judicial review. The situation is better for employees of these organisations. Internal complaint mechanisms in the form of administrative tribunals have been improved in the past decade.[21] Second wave liberal constitutional theory has contributed to the understanding that human rights can and must be applied to international organisations. It has made clear that human rights have become "part of a script for legitimate IOs" (Heupel & Zürn 2017, p. 314). The approach has moreover offered the tools for nuancing the intensity and scope of the human rights obligations. The constitutionalist mindset has finally thrust a spotlight on the paucity of remedies against international organisations.

Democracy: Deliberation, Participation, and Transparency

The third limb of the constitutionalist trinity is democracy. Democracy as a normative ideal means that all those potentially substantively affected by a political decision ("quod omnes tangit...") should have an equal say in it. Starting from that premise, third wave liberal constitutional theory has established the democratic principle as a relevant benchmark for the activity of international organisations (Wheatley 2010; Goodin 2016, Teubner 2018). The debate has shown that the idea of democratic procedures in international organisations does not face principled and absolute obstacles (such as the absence of a unified global demos). However, the democratisation of the activity of international organisations must cope with eminently practical problems, notably with the sheer size and diversity of the democratic constituency, and the two-level governance structure of organisations and their member states.

On the basis of the "all substantially affected" (or more narrowly: "all subjected") idea, not all activities of all international organisations need to be fully democratised. The proper degree of democratisation depends on how intensely the actions of a given organisation affects people on the ground. This in turn hinges on the substance, scope, and on the bindingness (de jure or de facto) of their legal acts (Krajewski 2019, para. 12). Along this line, the quest for more democratic decision-making has been rightfully addressed most of all at the Security Council's sanctions (trade embargoes, travel bans, asset freezes) and at various measures by the World Bank, IMF, and the WTO which have intense financial and economic repercussions on countries and their populations.

I have proposed a "dual" or two track-model of democracy for global governance which combines a range of improvements in member states' democratic procedures regarding the international organisations (first track) with direct citizens'

---

[21] The IMF established an Administrative Tribunal in 1994; an EU Civil Service Tribunal was established in 2005; the United Nations Administrative Tribunal was transformed into a two-tiered system with a United Nations Appeals Tribunal in 2009.

engagement on the international level, and in the workings of the organisations themselves (second track). The first track requires the involvement of the national parliaments in the decision-making of the international bodies and the empowerment of the organisations' own parliamentary assemblies which are composed of members of national parliaments, too. The second track consists in more 'directly' democratic, or at least proto-democratic or *'ersatz'*, mechanisms, such as the participation of civil society organisations and the transparency of meetings and documentation of the organisations (Peters 2009).

Empirically speaking, the above-mentioned *ersatz* features have become increasingly prominent. Thereby, the international organisations' decision-making rules "move closer to democratic models" (Grigorescu 2015, p. 277). International organisations have become more participatory and transparent, notably since 1990 as a turning point (Zweifel 2006; Tallberg et al. 2013). Increasing involvement of civil society organisations, new accreditation schemes, and new rules of procedure in organisations and conferences (mainly during the reform era of 1990–2005)[22] have consolidated a "participatory status" of CSOs, which gives them a voice but not a vote.[23] Recent reforms include the "Civil Society Mechanism" in the Committee on Food Security (CFS) in FAO (since 2010, in response to the world food price crisis)[24] and the democratisation of UNITAID, a "global health agency," hosted by the WHO. Examples for an increase of transparency are the 2015 process of selection of the UN Secretary-General, "guided by the principles of transparency and inclusiveness"[25] and the access to information policies of many organisations.[26]

However, both transparency and participation are less developed in the more powerful organisations (in the field of finance and security), and also less developed

[22] See, e.g., WTO, Guidelines for arrangements on relations with Non-Governmental Organizations, WT/L/162, Decision of 18 July 1996; World Bank, Consultation with civil society organizations, general guidelines for world bank staff (2000); WHO, Policy for relations with non-governmental organizations, Report by the Director-General, 14 April 2003, A56/46; Permanent Council of the Organization of American States (OAS), Review of the Rules of Procedure for Civil Society Participation with the OAS, 31 March 2004, CP/CISC-106/04; African Union (AU), Statute of the Economic, Social and Cultural Council of the African Union (ECOSOC), approved by the Assembly, Decision on ECOSOC of 8–9 July 2004, Assembly/AU/Dec.48(III) Rev.1.

[23] Council of Europe, *Participatory Status for International Non-governmental Organisations with the Council of Europe*, Res. (2003) 8, 19 November 2003, adopted by the Committee of Ministers at the 86st meeting of the Ministers' Deputies.

[24] Doc. CFS: 2010/9, Proposal for an International Food Security and Nutrition Civil Society Mechanism for Relations with CFS, September 2010, acknowledged by the final report of the 36th session of the Committee on the World Food Security of 11–14 and 16 October 2010, para. 32. www.fao.org/3/k9551e/k9551e.pdf.

[25] GA Res 69/321 "Revitalization of the work of the General Assembly", 11 September 2015, paras. 35–35; Joint letter of the Presidents of the General Assembly and the Security Council to all Member States to invite candidates, 15 December 2015.

[26] See for access to documents, e.g., the World Bank Policy on Access to Information, 1 July 2010; Regulation (EC) No 1049/2001 of the European Parliament and of the Council of 30 May 2001 Regarding Public Access to Documents, OJ 2001 No. L145/43, 31 May 2001.

for the most consequential phases of activity, notably decision-making (as opposed to the phase of monitoring) (Tallberg et al. 2013, p. 260). Moreover, the options for participation are often shallow. Civil society actors seem to recognise their ineffectiveness and do not necessarily use them well. Another problem is that business actors tend to have, in fact, more entry points for participation than civil society organisations. Finally, the overall intensity of transparency and participation of civil society organisations (hearings, deliberations, access to documents) in the work of international organisations is still low, compared to states.

The low intensity of these practices and the selectiveness of actors has led sceptics to doubt whether such practices can be properly called "democratic" at all. My view is that deliberations and voice are approximations to the election and recall of governors, and might be called "proto-democratic" even if not democratic in a full sense.

Critiques of Second Wave Constitutional Theory

The second wave of constitutional theory has introduced the principles of rule of law, human rights, and democracy to the sphere of international organisations and has sought to apply them, albeit with due modification. This theory has laid open that the trinitarian principles have so far not been sufficiently implemented in the everyday functioning of international organisations. Therefore, the second wave constitutional demands have by no means been satisfied.

The next question is whether the second wave's demands remain relevant in the current global constellation or whether the liberal constitutionalist benchmark and guideline is wrong in the first place. The critique is that far from contributing to more global justice, liberal constitutionalism, as applied to international organisations and promoted by them, has cemented and deepened global injustice (Gill & Cutler 2014; von Bernstorff 2019; Kochi 2020). It is this radical challenge that the third wave of constitutional theory needs to address.

IV THIRD WAVE CONSTITUTIONAL THEORY

The fundamental critique directed against second wave constitutional theory is related to changes in the real world that are economic, ecologic, psychological, and political. The fallouts of ruthless economic globalisation are ecologic disaster, impoverishment, and emotional and intellectual disorientation of large groups of people. On top, democratic procedures are being eroded by globalisation, by the dismantling of democracy inside superficially democratised states, and by the rise of undemocratic states. Four specific issues need to be addressed by a third wave of constitutional theory. First, it needs to revisit liberalism's focus on the "unencumbered self" (Michael Sandel), the concomitant rise of human rights in international law in general and in the law of international organisations more specifically. Second, it needs to address the challenge of an allegedly pernicious legalism. This requires more work on the development of the democratic side of the constitutional theory, involving the establishment of global forums for political opposition and procedures that would allow to regularly reverse the organisations' power-holders.

Third, it needs to address the neo-liberal tilt of constitutional theory, its lopside towards the so-called "first generation" rights, which served as a justification for a strong protection of property and investment unaccompanied by social cushioning. Fourth, it needs to address the colonial legacy. These four concerns will be discussed one by one.

Individualism: Rights and Responsibilities

A growing strand of international legal scholarship is highly critical towards international law's imbuement with human rights. This critique needs to be addressed by the constitutional theory of international organisations. The reproaches are that the "righting", or "rightsification" of international law – as manifest in the application of human rights to international organisations – reflects possessive individualism, overstates human rationality (epitomised in the image of homo economicus as the rational benefit-maximiser), and falls too short for tackling inequities in the world order.

Against this critique, I submit that the focus on individuals as the ultimate normative point of reference should not be given up in the law of international organisations. The expansion of the scope of the legal analysis to individuals, as opposed to focusing exclusively on the relationship between the organisation and its members, is a lasting achievement of both waves of constitutional theory. Already the initial constitutional imagery took individuals in its purview. This has been explicitly stated only for the EU: in the leading case *Van Gend & Loos*, the ECJ held that the "subjects" of the Community legal order "comprise not only member states but also their nationals".[27] The direct legal relationship between the organisation and natural persons is often considered to be a hallmark of the EU. I submit that, beyond the EU, individual human beings are the stakeholders (besides the member states) of all international organisations because their well-being is the true justification of both the organisational activity and ultimately of their states, too. This fact needs to be recognised in law (Peters 2011; Klabbers 2015; Besson 2021).

Along this line, second wave liberal constitutionalism has placed the individual squarely on the centre-stage. It has rejected the view that individuals are entirely and properly "mediated" (i.e. completely represented) by their home states in international organisations (Peters 2009). The principal normative reason for looking

---

[27] ECJ, case 26/62, *Van Gend & Loos*, ECR 1963, 3 under II.B. The Court repeated that statement with a view to fending off the protocol on accession of the EU to the ECHR (ECJ, Opinion 2/13 of the Court (Full Court) of 18 December 2014 – *Accession to the ECHR*, para. 157).

beyond the member states is the fact that the military, economic, financial, and legal effects of organisational behaviour are relevant for the satisfaction of needs, for the realisation of interests, and the enjoyment of rights of human beings. The organisations thus shape the latters' normative situation, often independent from their citizenship in a member state.

Therefore, a direct legal and political relationship between the organisations and individual human beings needs to be worked out more. Such mechanisms should take into due account the individual's embeddedness in a social community, the relational nature of individual rights, and the bounded rationality of humans. It should also insist on political and legal responsibilities of individuals that must accompany the exercise of rights. Such a redirection is needed not the least for accommodating a range of cultural, political, and legal traditions (often non-western) which cherish the values of community and duties. But this nuancing does not imply that the law of international organisations should remain exclusively focused on the relationship between the organisation and the member states. Because of the normative deficits of mediation, the reference point of the individual human being should not be given up in the course of revision. The individual should remain in the centre of the constitutional theory of international organisations.

Democracy: Politicisation and Contestation

Current political concerns and concomitant action underscore rather than question the exacerbated relevance of a further democratisation of international organisations. Democratic backsliding in numerous states risks to weaken the organisation's internal quasi-democratic procedures (T. Ginsburg 2020). It has already been shown that new organisations sponsored and shaped by China (the AIIB and the NDB) are less participatory and transparent than the older western-dominated organisations (Heldt & Schmidtke 2019). Facing this trend, the normative commitment should be to at least uphold the degrees of transparency and participation reached in international organisations.

Another tendency is to exit from international organisations. For example, Brexit was directed against the fact that EU membership curtails British popular sovereignty. The official documents justifying the British withdrawal do not condemn any specific failure or illegitimacy of the EU but merely point to "national self-determination" and to the "democratic decision" in the UK[28] and express the people's desire to "take back control of their money, their borders, their laws, and their waters and to leave the European Union".[29] However, under conditions of global interdependence, national control (which is ostensibly more democratic) is

---

[28] UK withdrawal letter (required by Art. 50 TEU) signed on 29 March 2017 by Prime Minister Theresa May.
[29] Prime Minister Boris Johnson, Statement on the Withdrawal Agreement of 24 December 2020.

often undercut. After Brexit, the British parliament may take more decisions but these will become less relevant for the British people because important decisions affecting their lives are taken elsewhere. This fact reduces the output dimension of democracy (Rodrik 2011). In the end, the exit from an international organisation only superficially satisfies the quest for democracy, but it cannot bring about broad and deep democratisation without a parallel democratisation of the work of international organisations themselves.

Non-western states have often voiced the quest for "more democratic" international organisations, meaning the inclusion of all states in the decision-making of international organisations (Boysen 2019, p. 496). In that terminology, "democracy" is the antidote to an inter-*state* oligarchy and decidedly not a call for direct citizens' participation in the working of international organisations. The agenda of full inclusion and state equality should for reasons of analytical clarity not be pursued under the heading of democracy, because it does not call for majority voting among states, and because the representation of individuals by their states is egregiously skewed to the detriment of inhabitants of big states. I will discuss this point in the context of the colonial legacy.

A new strand of democratic thinking that can be roughly associated with the third wave of constitutional theory deserves more attention. The key claim of the new theories is that even improved participation, transparency, and voice will not guarantee any alternativity and reversibility of governance on the global level. The new quest is, therefore, that international organisations should much more actively give a platform to the radical opposition and should institutionalise ongoing contestation and conflict (Ley 2015; Volk 2012, pp. 571–573).

An overlapping line of research diagnoses and applauds an ongoing "politicisation" in the work of international organisations, as processes through which certain issues become objects of public contention and debate. Because politicisation introduces new demands for resources, justice, or recognition, the process is inevitably contestatory.

These new conceptions are valuable, but in my view do not obviate the need to upstep participation and transparency which are indispensable pre-conditions for a deeper democratisation of international organisations.

To conclude, the revision of the democratic theory and a reflection about more democratic practices inside international organisations need to go on. Schemes of participation and transparency (online citizens' assemblies, notice-and-comment procedures on international treaty projects), ideally accompanied by more contestatory devices (such as alternative summits), are necessary pre-conditions for collective self-government on a global level, because information and deliberation about the organisational politics are the first step towards critique and (a still theoretical) recall of the power-holders. In combination with an upstepped involvement of national parliaments (e.g., through early warning mechanisms, liaison committees, parliamentary delegates in bodies of the organisations), these schemes are for the time being second-best surrogates for currently unfeasible fully democratised decision-making in international organisations.

Human Welfare as a Task for International Organisations

Another ongoing revision of global constitutional thought (both on the macro-level and as applied to international organisations) is the espousal of a welfare dimension. International organisations need to work more than ever towards improving the material living conditions of humans and mitigate poverty and inequality of wealth and income. This revision has become necessary for coping with the "groundswell of discontent" with globalisation, as the then-managing director of the International Monetary Fund, Christine Lagarde, put it (Lagarde 2016).

In a 2005 study, the World Bank has acknowledged that "the distributive effects of trade liberalization are diverse, and not always pro-poor". The Bank also found that "the preservation and expansion of the world trade system hinges on its ability to strike a better balance between the interests of industrialized and developing nations", because "the world trade system is still biased against the poor".[30]

More attention to the social limb of global governance would thus notably demand reforms of the WTO, whose regime has neglected the distributive effects of trade liberalisation and has arguably deepened problems of food insecurity and scarcity of pharmaceuticals in the global south (Joseph 2011; Lang 2011). The more social policies and social rights are missing or are dismantled in the domestic sphere, "the more trade policy needs to assume these protective functions" (Cottier 2013, p. 53). Under the heading of a "Geneva Consensus", then Director-General of the WTO, Pascal Lamy, stated in 2006 that "we have not yet completed the economic decolonization". He urged the negotiating WTO-members "to continue the rebalancing of our rules on favour of developing countries".[31]

The current paralysis of the WTO (the stalemate of the institutional reform debate and the sidelining of the organisation by bilateral and regional trade agreements) is largely owed to the unwillingness or inability of the members to agree on the welfarist demands formulated mainly by the states of the global south.[32] My view is that the identification of a public purpose, the analytical attention to the social consequences of the WTO-rules, and the acknowledgment of responsibility for the negative externalities would be facilitated on the basis of a constitutional vision of the WTO.

---

[30] World Bank, Economic Growth in the 1990s: Learning from a Decade of Reform (World Bank: Washington DC 2005), 19.

[31] Speech of the Director-General of the WTO, Pascal Lamy: "It's time for a new 'Geneva Consensus' on making trade work for development" (in Emile Noel Lecture New York University Law School, New York, 30 October 2006), <www.wto.org/english/news_e/sppl_e/sppl45_e.htm>, accessed 21 April 2021.

[32] See, e.g., China's Proposal on WTO Reform, Communication from China, 13 May 2019 (WT/GC/W/773), point 2.2. ("Rectifying the Inequity in Rules on Agriculture").

Renewed attempts for strengthening the social dimension of the constitutions of international organisations need to overcome the normative deficiencies of the historic blueprints (such as the post Second World War embedded liberalism (Ruggie 1998, pp. 89–90) and the 1970s New International Economic Order (NIEO)[33]). They must also respond to the current global realities of ecological disaster, global supply chains, and a much-increased global mobility of persons who vote with their feet against states that do not offer them life chances. The most important normative supplement are human rights. The historical NIEO was human-rights-free and state-focused. In contrast, a "new" NIEO would need to marry both agendas: it would have to be an NIEO plus human rights. It would recognise not only a moral but also legal cross-border social responsibility for individuals. Such a legal cross-border responsibility for the welfare of individuals is already visible in international law, in the international anti-poverty regime, in the new standard procedures such as social human rights due diligence and social impact assessments, and notably in the rise of social rights (Peters 2018). Most of these trends are relevant for international organisations. For example, international social rights have been so far mainly operationalised in political and economic conflicts involving international organisations.

A constitutional label for the welfare work of international organisations could be "solidarity" (Wellens 2010), a principle that is firmly rooted in the constitutional vocabulary of nation states. Especially the COVID-19 pandemic has motivated international organisations such as the UN and the WHO to appeal to "solidarity".[34] This new talk (some might say "cheap talk") on global solidarity can build on a pre-existing textual basis which has however not given firm contours to the concept.[35] But despite this vagueness, solidarity has been identified as an "emerging structural principle of international law" (Wolfrum 2006).

The uptake of the welfare dimension in the most important international organisations is necessary for salvaging global constitutionalism as a macro-paradigm from its neo-liberal entrapment. At the same time, it would accommodate the preferences of the populations of the global south and non-western world and thus fits in the current post-colonial constellation.

A Post-colonial Sensibility

The constitutional theory of international organisations (just as the macro-paradigm of global constitutionalism) must acquire a post-colonial sensibility (Havercroft

---

[33] See for a re-appraisal of the NIEO the contributions in the special issue of *Humanity* of spring 2015 (pp. 1–237) under the guest editorship of Samuel Moyn.

[34] UN GA Res. 74/270 (2 April 2020); GA Res. 74/274 (20 April 2020); WHO, WHA, "COVID-19 response", Second plenary meeting, A73/VR/2 (Doc. 73.1. of 19 May 2020).

[35] See for the latest document in the relevant process of the Human Rights Council: Draft declaration on the right to international solidarity and Report of the Independent Expert on human rights and international solidarity (UN Doc. A/HRC/35/35 of 25 April 2017).

et al. 2020). This sensibility has been awakened by TWAIL scholars, and it accommodates the economic and political clout of the post-colonial states. The rise of China, which insists on its position as "the largest developing country in the world",[36] is not only a power shifter but also a discourse-shifter giving the global south a greater leverage.

With all due caution against instrumental and cynical employment of the postcolonial vocabulary by the rising and potentially neo-colonial actors, the shift of perspective is a welcome development which merits reinforcement. Global constitutionalism needs to concretely address the colonial legacy and its repercussions in the working of international organisations. This legacy consists in organisational designs, processes, and outcomes that reflect the political and economic interests and normative preferences of the rich states of the north more than those of the poorer and less industrialised states of the south. The fundamental asymmetries of political and economic power are not sufficiently accommodated by the formal principle of state equality in the diverse bodies, and of course also shine up in those important organisations and organs which formalise unequal legal positions such as the international financial institutions and the UN Security Council (Viola 2020).

A key demand of the third wave constitutional theory is, therefore, the *inclusion* of the so-far underprivileged member states and civil society organisations of the south. As mentioned, this demand has constantly been voiced by the states of the south under the heading of "democracy".[37] For example, the 1994 Agenda for Peace states that "Democracy within the family of nations … is a principle that means affording to all States, large and small, the fullest opportunity to consult and to participate."[38] Along that line, the UNGA has been regularly adopting resolutions on the "promotion of a democratic and equitable international order" which convey this inter-state meaning of democracy, and regularly against the votes of the member states of the global north. These resolutions ask for reforms of the international organisations in the direction of a "full and equal participation" of states of the global south in the decision-making mechanisms.[39]

The insistence for the inclusion of all states in the work of international organisations in the sense of dismantling state oligarchies is justified. The discernible trend in that direction is laudable. An example is the transformation of the prior Governing Council of the UN Environment Programme, which was a club of only

---

[36] "China's International Development Cooperation in the New Era" – The State Council Information Office of the People's Republic of China (Third White Paper on China's foreign aid), 10 January 2021, n.p.

[37] See, e.g., Joint Statement by the Foreign Ministers of China and Russia on Certain Aspects of Global Governance in Modern Conditions of 23 March 2021: "In this context, we call on the international community to (…) build up cooperation (…) to contribute to the establishment of a fairer, more democratic and rational multipolar world order."

[38] UN Secretary General, *Agenda for Development* (UN Doc. A/478/935 of 6 May 1994), para. 134.

[39] See last UN GA Res. 75/178 of 28 December 2020, preamble (p. 3) and para. 6(g) (adopted with 55 no-votes basically of the European states and the US).

58 member states, into an UN Environmental Assembly with universal state membership in 2010.⁴⁰

Importantly, such inclusion cannot be fully realised through formal legal equality but additionally needs some forms of positive action that create material preconditions enabling the underprivileged member states to exercise their membership rights, and possibly additional compensatory preference schemes. The slogan of a "democratic *and equitable* legal order" alludes to this aspect by replacing the term "equal" with "equitable". In a nutshell, such positive action schemes already exist (such as the principle of common but differentiated responsibility in the climate regime, the WTO Enabling Clauses, and the principle of *"inégalité compensatrice"* in the law of development cooperation). These would need to be stepped up further and expanded. Otherwise, the hearings and deliberations conducted under the headings of transparency and participation remain largely empty rituals (Boysen 2021, p. 315).

The theoretical framework undergirding this revision is, besides post-colonialism, an "antagonist" and "radical" constitutionalism (Kochi 2020, p. 195) a "constitutionalism of dissent" (Volk 2012, p. 571). These conceptual variants of constitutionalism build on political philosophies of republicanism and a more "political constitutionalism" (Bellamy 2007), coupled with contestatory theory (Wiener 2018).

These intellectual strands share the basic idea that constitutionalism should no longer be primarily about containment (as in classic liberal constitutionalism) but more about the facilitation of political action ("politicisation"). The main function of these types of constitutionalism is to channel and institutionalise the possibility of permanent political controversy. From that perspective, all processes and institutions must be designed so as to encourage dissent, and should actively grant space to opposing voices (not only to the moderate civil society organisations prone to co-optation in the business of global governance). By foregrounding contestation and conflict, the political character of decision-making in global governance is uncovered (Volk 2012, p. 567).

The mentioned conceptions were mainly developed for accommodating the violent anti-globalisation protests. They can be applied to respond to the alienation and frustration of both state and non-state actors of the global south. At the same time, developing international organisations into an *"additional* institutional framework, which enables, allows, and encourages dissent and contestation" (Volk 2012, p. 573) might help to mitigate the rise of authoritarianism on the level of the nation states.

CONCLUSIONS

Our globalised condition will continue to undermine the problem-solving regulatory capacities of national governments and parliaments. Withdrawals from

---

⁴⁰ UN GA Res. of 27 July 2012 (Doc. A/RES/66/288 of 11 September 2012), para. 88 lit. (h).

international organisations will probably not only reverse welfare gains but will also fail to deliver democratic and rights-abiding outcomes. Therefore, international organisations are here to stay. But they are facing huge challenges in words and deeds, manifest in withdrawals, cut-backs of funding, and sidelining.

Confronted with ideational and material challenges, and in the midst of a changing world order, an updated constitutional theory of international organisations is warranted (Lake, Martin & Risse 2021). In the face of multilateral saturation and potential overreach, the purely "constitutive" first wave-constitutional theory that disregarded the containment of international organisations has become untenable. But also the second wave, liberal constitutionalism, has turned out to be flawed. This chapter has argued that the emerging third wave of constitutional theory of international organisations should be fleshed out more. That third wave can build on "islands of the constitutional" (Teubner 2012, p. 52) in international organisations but it should not "return to the business of global constitutionalism as usual, whatever this is assumed to have been" in the early millennium (Saunders 2019, p. 25).

Rather, the renewed constitutional theory should rebalance lopsided political-human rightism, while retaining rights (including *social* rights) as an indispensable building block. It should upscale quasi-democratic decision-making procedures (which have so far only been prepared by transparency and participation schemes), and politicise them with the help of contestatory processes. It should rectify the north–south imbalance, that is inter alia rooted in the colonial heritage. And it must tackle the global social (and ecological) questions upfront.

We cannot expect any theory to "resolve" the problems that international organisations are facing, because intellectual paradigms are no mathematical model or rigid recipe but can offer only a reservoir of legal ideas for re-interpretation and reform. Also, a constitutional (as any legal) analysis cannot in itself prevent or bridge the gap between the constitutional principles on paper and the lacking, possibly slackening implementation in the changing ideational world climate. A recast constitutional theory of international organisations can only deploy the power of ideas – not more but also not less.

RECOMMENDED READING

Bernstorff, J. von (2019). The Decay of the International Rule of Law Project (1990–2015). In H. Krieger, G. Nolte, & A. Zimmermann, eds., *The International Rule of Law – Rise or Decline?* Oxford: Oxford University Press, pp. 33–55.

Boysen, S. (2021). *Die postkoloniale Konstellation*, Tübingen: Mohr Siebeck.

Cottier, T. (2000). Limits to International Trade: The Constitutional Challenge. In The American Society of International Law (ed.), International Law in Ferment: A New Vision for Theory and Practice, Proceedings of the 94th Annual Meeting (5–8 April), pp. 220–224.

Daugirdas, K. (2016). How and Why International Law Binds International Organizations. *Harvard Journal of International Law*, 57 (2), 325–381.

Humboldt, W. von (1851). *Ideen zu einem Versuch, die Grenzen der Wirksamkeit des Staates zu bestimmen*, written in 1792, Breslau: Trewendt.

Joseph, S. (2011). *Blame it on the WTO?: A Human Rights Critique*, Oxford: Oxford University Press.

Kochi, T. (2020). *Global Justice and Social Conflict: The Foundations of Liberal Order and International Law*, Abingdon, Oxon: Routledge.

Krajewski, M. (2019). International Organizations or Institutions, Democratic Legitimacy. In A. Peters, & R. Wolfrum, eds., *Max Planck Encyclopedia of Public International Law*. Oxford: Oxford University Press.

Lagarde, C. (2016). Making Globalisation Work for All, Sylvia Ostry Lecture, Toronto (13 September).

Ley, I. (2015). Opposition in International Law: Alternativity and Revisibility as Elements of a Legitimacy Concept for Public International Law. *Leiden Journal of International Law*, 28 (3), 717–742.

Peters, A. (2009). Dual Democracy. In J. Klabbers, A. Peters, & G. Ulfstein, *The Constitutionalization of International Law*. Oxford: Oxford University Press, pp. 263–341.

Peters, A. (2016). International Organizations and International Law. In J. Katz Cogan, I. Hurd, & I. Johnstone, eds., *The Oxford Handbook of International Organizations*. Oxford: Oxford University Press, pp. 33–59.

Peters, A. (2018). Global Constitutionalism: The Social Dimension. In T. Suami, A. Peters, D. Vanoverbeke, & M. Kumm, eds., *Global Constitutionalism from European and East Asian Perspectives*. Cambridge: Cambridge University Press, pp. 277–350.

Saunders, C. (2019). Global Constitutionalism – Myth and Reality. In J. N. E. Varuhas, & S. Wilson Stark, eds., *The Frontiers of Public Law*, Oxford: Hart, pp. 19–40.

Sinclair, G. F. (2017). *To Reform the World: International Organizations and the Making of Modern States*, Oxford: Oxford University Press.

Tallberg, J., Sommerer, T., Squatrito, T., & Jönsson, C. (2013). *The Opening up of International Organizations: Transnational Access in Global Governance*, Cambridge: Cambridge University Press.

Volk, C. (2012). Why Global Constitutionalism Does not Live up to its Promises. *Goettingen Journal of International Law*, 4 (2), 551–574.

Zacklin, R. (1968). *The Amendment of the Constitutive Instruments of the United Nations and Specialised Agencies*, Brill (reprint 2005).

PART IV

Challenges for Constitutional Democracy

56

Inequality

Roberto Gargarella[*]

Modern constitutions are, above all, a pact among equals: they represent a contract that aims to include everyone, on an equal footing. So, two of the main, foundational documents of constitutionalism, namely the U.S. Declaration of Independence and the French *Déclaration des droits de l'homme et du citoyen* of 1789, adopted as one of their central missions the affirmation of a principle of equality. The US document stated it as "self-evident" that "all men" were "created equal." Meanwhile, Article 1 of the French Declaration of Rights claimed: "Men are born and remain free and equal in rights." These declarations represented a significant departure from the then widespread assumption according to which human beings were unequal by nature. The American and French Revolutions thus symbolized the coming of a new moral paradigm, defined by the ideas of natural rights and equality among all human beings. From then on, most of the enacted constitutions included explicit references, of different kind and intensity, to the principle of equality.

The problem is that, from its very origins, the ideals of constitutionalism encountered enormous difficulties that prevented them from becoming a reality. Almost every area covered by the equality principle – whether we refer to the rights of racial, sexual or ethnic minorities, or to the workers' rights – was transformed into a space for legal and political dispute. In what follows, we shall explore a few of those "disputed territories" and pay attention to the continuous, unfinished battle between the constitutional ideal of equality and a political practice systematically oriented to defy it. We shall examine that dispute through the lens of the Constitution, focusing on its two main parts: its Declaration of Rights, and its Separation of Powers.

I CONSTITUTIONAL EQUALITY: INITIAL LIMITS

The principle of constitutional equality was usually qualified, from its very origins, in ways that authorized the unequal treatment of some. Very early, in his famous 1774 speech to the electors of Bristol, Edmund Burke proclaimed that "government

---

[*] I want to thank Vanina Domizzi for her wonderful research assistance. Project financed/Co-financed by the European Union (ERC, Project 101096176 — ICDD). The views and opinions expressed are solely those of the author and do not necessarily reflect those of the European Union or the European Research Council. Neither the European Union nor the granting authority can be held responsible for them.

and legislation are matters of reason and judgment, and not of inclination," assuming that "the majority" were in fact guided by mere "opinions," rather than "reason." In the US, John Adams, one of the main political figures behind the U.S. Constitution, affirmed the principle that men were "free and equal" but suggested, immediately thereafter, that "the Creator" had established physical and intellectual inequalities among people, from which it was possible to derive and justify additional inequalities.[1] Simón Bolívar, one of Latin America's main independence leaders, seemed to have shared Adams' approach on the matter. He affirmed the idea that "all men are born with equal rights," but immediately qualified that claim by stating that "it does not follow that all men are born equally gifted to attain every rank" (Bolívar 1951, vol. 1, p. 182).

In order to circumvent the demands of the equality principle, other influential public figures of the time tried a different route. Notably, James Madison, the most significant voice among the Americans' "founding fathers," advanced a distinction between "persons," and "citizens," which would allow the "framers" to preserve the inferior status of slaves untouched. Madison made this point evident at the core of his most famous writing, namely *Federalist Paper* n. 10. When he had to define the concept of "factions" – a concept around which the entire Constitution was erected – Madison stated: "By a faction, I understand a number of citizens, whether amounting to a majority or a minority of the whole, who are united and actuated by some common impulse of passion, or of interest, adversed to the rights of other citizens, or to the permanent and aggregate interests of the community." Madison used the word "citizens" – in the *Federalist Papers* or at the Federal Convention – when he wanted to make clear that he was not taking into consideration the interests of slaves. The result of this was that the issue of slavery remained fundamentally foreign to the scope of the Constitution of 1787.

The point is that the main commitment of constitutionalism – namely, the commitment to the "equality of all" – was seriously undermined in practice, from its very origins.[2] One of the most serious implications of this initial and subtle movement

---

[1] "By the law of nature," Adams asserted, "man differs by nature from man, almost as much as man from beast.... A physical inequality, an intellectual inequality, of the most serious kind, is established unchangeably by the Author of nature; and society has a right to establish any other inequalities it may judges necessary for its good" (quoted in Rossiter 1982, p. 112).

[2] By recognizing that modern constitutions were "forced" to speak the language of equality (one could argue that those documents would have found impossible to gain legitimacy without speaking that language), I do not mean to affirm that the structure of modern constitutions was aimed at advancing the democratic ideal. By contrast, I tend to assume that, in many occasions, those constitutions came to "improperly" limit, rather than enhance or favor, democratic self-government. I understand that there is a good argument suggesting reading most constitutional limitations upon self-government (i.e., a list of fundamental rights) as "enabling" devices. Examples like that of Ulysses and the sirens came to show, for instance, that what in principle appeared as a severe limitation and loss of freedom – tying one's hands to the mast; writing freedom of expression in the constitution – could be an excellent way of expanding or ensuring future freedom (Elster 1984, Holmes 1995). The idea is that there are limits that can make us a free, in the same way that there are "enabling" constitutive rules.

toward the preservation of an unequal status quo was the establishment of distinctions between people, in terms of their political rights. Political rights were thus subjected to repeated and diverse restrictions: literacy and economic requirements; limitations to the political participation of women, slaves, and domestic servants; and also restrictions related to age, income, property, capacity, religion, nationality, and ethnic origin (Ternavasio 2002; Sábato 2010; Sábato y Lettieri 2003).

II FORMAL EQUALITY AND "STATUS QUO NEUTRALITY"

The idea of "formal equality", which has played a crucial role since the origins of modern constitutionalism, has usually being understood as implying that all individuals must be subject to the same rules and standards. It advocates for a "neutral" State, which denies the possibility of making unjustified distinctions between individual and groups.

Following a commitment to formal equality (and, consequently, trying to leave behind the old legislation through which the State subjected some people to an inferior status), the first Venezuelan Constitution of 1811 not only proclaimed legal equality between all races, but also abolished the most prominent, existing legal privileges of the Church and the Army – the special *"fueros"* that both corporations enjoyed. In Argentina, the so-called *Assembly of the year xiii* (1813), also promoted numerous reforms to secure basic freedoms and formal equality. These reforms included a law of "free birth"; the abolition of the *mitas* and *yanaconazgos* (institutions through which Native Americans were forced to work on behalf of state, church or private citizens); and the suppression of all titles of nobility. All these initiatives represented crucial, but also limited steps, in the direction of obtaining more equal societies. Clearly, groups that were previously relegated to a second-class status did not become equal just because the State ceased to make and enforce unjustified legal distinctions between groups. This is why, for instance, Argentina's 1853 Constitution had to insist – 40 years after the solemn declarations presented by the

---

However, it is still difficult to see some clauses of the constitution, – that is, strong protections to private property; consecration of a free market as the only economic alternative – as more than strict limits upon democracy: these should be seen as purely democracy-disabling rules. In fact, as the same Jon Elster put it, a few years after he had presented the now famous Ulysses example, "in politics, people never try to bind themselves, only to bind others" (Elster 2000, p. ix). References about the undemocratic features of constitutions can also be found, for instance, in Robert Dahl or Sanford Levinson. See, for instance, Robert Dahl's book *How democratic is the American Constitution*, where he tries to respond the question about "how well does our constitutional system meet *democratic* standards of the present day?" He wonders: "if our constitution is in some important ways defective by democratic standards, should we change it, and how?" (Dahl 2003, 3–4). Seemingly, Sanford Levinson, writing about the US Constitution, stated: "the Constitution is both insufficiently democratic, in a country that professes to believe in democracy, *and* significantly dysfunctional, in terms of the quality of government that we receive.[it] is a human creation open to criticism and even to rejection" (Levinson 2008, p. 9).

Assembly of the year xiii – that "in the Argentine Nation there are no slaves" (Article 15 of the Constitution) and that the Nation did not "allow prerogatives of blood or birth" (Article 16). The fact is that the initial efforts in the direction of formal equality had proved to be not only ineffective, but also consistent with the preservation of profound inequalities and social distinctions.

In the United States, formal equality among the races began to slowly gain force after the Civil War, particularly through the enactment of the Civil Rights Act of 1866 (which guaranteed the right to equal protection by law, although it was vetoed by President Andrew Johnson), and then through the Fourteenth Amendment (which came to replace the fragile Civil Rights Act). Those political decisions were directed at repairing a situation of active State violation of the rights of Black Americans who, after the abolition of slavery (through the 1865 Thirteenth Amendment), still suffered discrimination. The legal discrimination that continued to affect the black community derived both from politics, that is, from local legislatures that adopted "Black Codes" following the war (Black Codes that restricted their rights to hold property and enforce contracts, for example); and from the Judiciary (i.e., through infamous decisions such as *Dred Scott v. Sandford* 60 U.S. 393, 1857). With or without the help of the law, the situation of discrimination toward the African-American community seemed to remain intact, and constitutionalism appeared unable to react to that situation.

Using the concept of "status quo neutrality" constitutional scholar Cass Sunstein described how the US Court – particularly since its decision in *Lochner v. New York*, 198 U.S. 45 (1905), over decades, took legally created inequalities as "natural and prepolitical." "Ownership rights are not treated as legally created at all" – he claims – "they appear to be part of nature" (Sunstein 1993d, p. 68). Sunstein illustrates his view with cases such as *Plessy v. Ferguson*, 163 U.S. 537 (1896), where the U.S. Supreme Court upheld the constitutionality of racial segregation laws for public facilities as long as the segregated facilities were equal in quality – what came to be known as the "separate but equal" doctrine; *Lochner v. New York*, 198 U.S. 45 (1905), which was a famous labor law case in which the US Supreme Court held that limits to working time violated the Fourteenth Amendment; and *Muller v. Oregon*, 208 U.S. 412 (1908), where the US Court did not recognize sex-based discrimination in a state's decision through which women were provided by state mandate lesser work-hours than allotted to men. Sunstein found "extraordinary similarities" among the three cases, and particularly between *Plessy* and *Muller*, where the Court "saw the sphere of sex and race difference as natural and pre-political, when in fact that sphere is in important respects a creation of law" (Sunstein 1993d, p. 64).

III MINORITY GROUPS AND THE QUEST OF SUBSTANTIVE INEQUALITY

In previous paragraphs, we recognized that the modern constitutional commitment to "formal equality" did not imply the disappearance of serious and long-standing social inequalities. For instance, that the African-American community continued to suffer discrimination even after the abolition of slavery in the same way that indigenous groups in Latin America continued to live in extreme marginality after the abolition of forced labor. These circumstances help us understand why the principle of "substantive equality" began to gain more importance, as a supplement or as a substitute for the old principle of "formal equality." According to the principle of substantive equality, the ideal of equality is not satisfied when some individuals or groups live as a "second-class" for morally irrelevant distinctions made and enforced by the law.[3]

In the United States, the path from formal equality to a more substantive version of it can be summarized in the Supreme Court's transit from *Plessy* (1896) to *Brown* (1954). In *Plessy*, a case that we already mentioned, the Court had affirmed the infamous doctrine of "separate but equal." Although in this decision it abandoned the harsh discriminatory approach that it had assumed in *Dred Scott*, the Court still refused to adopt a fully color-blind approach to the law. As Justice Harlan maintained in his dissent: "arbitrary separation" represented "a badge of servitude wholly inconsistent with the civil freedom and the equality before the law established by the Constitution."

After *Plessy*, the US Court began to build a different approach to the ideal of "equal justice under law." In fact, the US Court paved the way to *Brown* through cases such as *Sweatt v. Painter* and *McLaurin v. Oklahoma State Regents*, both from 1950, where the main tribunal argued for "substantial equality in … educational opportunities." The fundamental change in the Court's approach appeared, however, in *Brown v. Board of Education of Topeka*, 347 U.S. 483 (1954), with Justice Earl Warren acting as the Chief Justice. Through its decision, the Tribunal finally put a full stop to the prevailing doctrine of "separate but equal" and recognized that school segregation violated the Equal Protection Clause. For the Court, to separate children in grade and high schools from others of similar age and qualifications "solely because of their race generates a feeling of inferiority as to their status in the community that may affect their hearts and minds in a way unlikely to ever be undone."

After *Brown*, the judicial dispute in racial matters became extended to other areas of the law – from Criminal Law to malapportionment and racial gerrymandering. One area where those judicial disputes became particularly intense was the one

---

[3] Thinking in terms of what we are calling substantive justice, philosopher John Rawls maintained that the circumstances within which we are born and develop – say, our race and ethnicity, the social class to which we belong, the cultural environment, etc. – are not just or unjust per se, but rather the product of a "natural lottery." The idea was that the basic institutions of an egalitarian society had to be organized in ways that discounted the burden of those circumstances (Rawls 1971). For Sandra Fredman, substantive equality requires to redress disadvantage; address stigma, stereotyping, prejudice, and violence; enhance voice and participation; and accommodate difference and achieve structural change (Fredman 2016).

related to affirmative action. The US Supreme Court has been debating the issue for decades now. For instance, in *Regents of the University of California v. Bakke*, a case from 1978, the Supreme Court ruled that colleges could not use racial quotas because they violated the Equal Protection Clause – race could be instead used as one factor for admission. At the beginning of the century, in *Grutter v. Bollinger*, 539 U.S. 306 (2003), it held that a student admissions process that favored "underrepresented minority groups" did not violate the Fourteenth Amendment's Equal Protection Clause so long as it took into account other factors evaluated on an individual basis for every applicant. However, in *Gratz v. Bollinger*, an undergraduate policy in which a point system gave specific "weight" to minority applicants was overturned six to three.[4]

IV THE DISPUTE OVER SOCIAL RIGHTS

Since the beginning of the twentieth century, constitutions began to include social rights in their texts, as a way of recognizing the situation of disadvantage in which a growing part of the population – namely the working class – lived. The first constitution to incorporate social rights was the 1917 Mexican Constitution. The Mexican Constitution decisively changed the history of world constitutionalism. Since its adoption, and little by little, most countries in the Latin American region began to change their basic constitutional structure. In fact, and following Mexico's early example, most countries began to include long lists of social rights in their constitutions: Brazil modified its Constitution in 1937; Bolivia in 1938; Cuba in 1940; Uruguay in 1942; Ecuador and Guatemala in 1945; and Argentina and Costa Rica in 1949. This was the way in which Latin American Constitutions expressed the main social change that had taken place in the region during the first half of the twentieth century, namely the incorporation of the working class as a decisive political and economic actor.

In Europe, some of the most interesting social aspects of the influential Weimar 1919 Constitution seemed to be directly based on Russian 1918 Constitution. Similarly, the Spanish Republican Constitution of 1931 was inspired by the constitutional examples of Mexico, Russia, and Weimar. Presently, almost all the European constitutions include social rights in their texts, even though some of them still "subscribe to the widely held view that those rights are subordinate to civil and political rights," and most of them "do not ground social rights on the claim that they are part and parcel of political citizenship" (Fabre 2005, pp. 20, 23).

Despite these important constitutional efforts in the direction of social justice, the fact is that, all around the world, and during decades, courts showed resistance

---

[4] Ronald Dworkin, one of the main advocates of legal egalitarianism, maintained during years that affirmative action programs, if properly tailored, did not violate, but rather honor, the Equal Protection Clause of the Constitution (Dworkin 2000, pp. 409–410; Dworkin 1998).

toward the enforcement of social rights. In order to justify their restrictive approach on the subject, courts resorted to numerous strategies, which allowed them to establish a sharp distinction between liberal rights (freedom of speech; freedom of association; the right to vote; etc.), and social and economic rights. Judges said that liberal and social rights were very different in nature; that social rights were more expensive than liberal rights; that social rights were "positive" rights, which – unlike "negative" rights – required the presence of an "active state," and not its mere "abstinence"; that social rights were "collective" rights that affected numerous people – and so deserved a significantly different treatment. For those reasons, they concluded courts could not "activate" or enforce those rights without violating the principle of the *separation of powers*, or without assuming tasks that they were not *democratically* authorized to perform. They claimed it was the duty of the political branches to "activate" or give actual life to those rights: only they were democratically authorized to define how to use the national budget and, in addition, only they had the technical and practical capacities to define and implement a common social policy. As a consequence, and over many decades, social and economic rights became judicially non-enforceable rights.

By the end of the twentieth century, however, the status of social rights began to change. That change was the product of various causes, from the "internationalization of law," to the coming of serious changes at the level of doctrine. Critical debates around these issues had emerged, since the late 1970s, in different countries, from the United States to Germany and Italy (Alexy 2002; Brinks 2020; Fabre 2000; Ferrajoli 1999; Forbath 2001; J. King 2012; Langford 2009; Michelman 1979; Tushnet 2008b; Young 2012). Through these renewed discussions, the fragility of the arguments that were traditionally offered against the enforcement of social rights became manifest. For one, legal doctrinaires began to accept, as a common ground, that "all rights were costly," as Stephen Holmes and Cass Sunstein famously argued (Holmes and Sunstein 1999). In Latin America, Víctor Abramovich and Christian Courtis popularized a similar line of argumentation: "The distinction [between positive and negative rights]," they maintained, "is notoriously weak. All rights, whether civil, political, economic or cultural, imply costs, and prescribe both negative and positive obligations" (Abramovich and Courtis 2009, pp. 975–976; Abramovich and Courtis 2002; for a different view, see J. King 2012, pp. 7–8).

This doctrinal evolution accompanied a slow change in the orientation of the courts. The well-known *Grootboom* case,[5] which was decided in South Africa in 2001, probably represents the best example in this respect.[6] In its historic decision, the South African Court ruled against the Government by maintaining that since

---

[5] *Republic of South Africa v. Grootboom*, Case n. CCT 11/00.
[6] In the also famous *Treatment Action Campaign* case, in South Africa, the Constitutional Court would go some steps further, and command the state to prescribe the required HIV medicines at stake (Nevirapine) "without delay," and to take "reasonable measures" to facilitate its use.

the state's program on housing made no provision for the relief of the appellants, the government's policy could not be considered reasonable.[7] *Grootboom* exercised an enormous impact within the legal community, particularly among those who had largely assumed a, contrary, negative approach to those matters (Sunstein 1993a).[8] Many other Western courts joined this "social rights-revolution" and began to assume a more "active" role concerning the enforcement of social rights.[9]

In Latin America, this significant and gradual movement toward the judicial enforcement of social rights became particularly prominent. This was so for diverse reasons, including the very robust constitutions that emerged in the entire region during the twentieth century; the fact that most countries had ratified international treaties on the subject (in particular, the International Covenant on Economic, Social, and Cultural Rights); and also the pressing demands of vast disadvantaged sectors. Particularly, the Colombian Constitutional Court built a robust jurisprudence in the area, using and developing renewed legal tools (like the *tutela*) that helped the court in the enforcement of social rights (Parra 2016; Cepeda 2004).[10] However, the case of Colombia – like other similar ones – raises a disturbing question, related to the co-existence between a progressive social rights jurisprudence, and very deep social inequalities, of all kinds.[11]

In the meantime, international courts continue to appear timid and undecided in the matter. More than 70 years after economic and social rights (ESR) were recognized as Human Rights within the American continent (which took place through the adoption

---

[7] See also the interesting decision *State of Punjab vs. Mohinder Singh Chawla*, AIR 1997 SC 1225, where the Indian Court interpreted the right to health as integral to the right to life, and thus worthy of the "most imperative constitutional (protection)."

[8] Examining the *Grootboom* decision, Cass Sunstein changed his initial view on the matter of the judicial enforcement of social rights. He claimed: "The Court's approach suggests [] for the first time, the possibility of providing that protection in a way that is respectful of democratic prerogatives and the simple fact of limited budgets" (Sunstein 2001, p. 14).

[9] One remarkable exception in this respect was the US court. However, during the 60s, the Court moved "toward ruling that the Constitution requires government to provide a decent minimum for all." This development took place through cases like *Harper v. Virginia State Board of Elections*; *Griffin v. Illinois*; *Douglas v. California*; and *Shapiro v. Thompson* (for opposing views on the matter, see Michelman 1969, Bork 1979). In spite of all these efforts, the fundamental change that was taking place in the Court's orientation, particularly in the area of social rights, reached an abrupt end with the election of Richard Nixon as the President of the country, and the appointment of four new (and conservative) justices in the Court. Even though the new majority "did not dramatically shift the Court to the right," the area of social and economic rights was "the one crucial exception" (Sunstein 2006, p. 154). By 1975, "the whole idea of minimum welfare guarantees had become implausible" (ibid., p. 153).

[10] In Germany, for example, the Federal Constitutional Court took an important step forward when it interpreted the principle of the Social Welfare State covered by Article 20(1) of the German basic law in conjunction with the right to human dignity established by Article 1(1), to find the first explicit social right in the German Constitution, namely the right to a minimum guarantee of existence.

[11] "The jarring contrast between the evident discrimination and disadvantage present in Colombian society, with the progressive of case law evident in the courts, must prompt questions of effectiveness" (Delaney 2008, p. 55).

of the American Declaration of the Rights and Duties of Man in 1948), "the legal satisfaction of ESR is still a controversial topic, as the regional Human Rights Tribunal – the Inter-American Court of Human Rights – seems to find multiple difficulties when requested to issue binding decisions concerning the guarantee of the mentioned Human Rights" (González-Salzberg 2011, p. 120).[12] The situation seems still more worrisome in the European context, where "as the European Court of Justice has reminded us, social rights are still conceived as 'exceptions' to market freedoms, and are only admitted if they manage to pass a severe proportionality test" (Pisarello 2007, p. 133).

V GENDER INEQUALITY

So far, we have seen how, since the beginning of the twentieth century, constitutionalism began to address the growing demands of the working class and some of those brought by racial minorities who had long suffered severe discrimination. However, after so many decades, constitutionalism seemed to still pay insufficient attention to the interests of other ample and crucial sectors of society, including those of women and indigenous groups – two groups who have continued being "the disadvantaged among the disadvantaged." Let me refer, first, to the issue of women's rights, and then focus on the topic of aboriginal rights.

In almost all of cases, women began to enjoy full political rights only by the first half of the twentieth century (with the exception of New Zealand, where women obtained the right to vote in parliamentary elections in 1893). This occurred, first in some Nordic countries (Finland in 1906, Norway in 1913, Denmark and Iceland in 1915), and then – very slowly – in the rest of the world: in the Netherlands in 1917, in Austria, Canada, Czechoslovakia, Poland and Sweden in 1918, in Germany and Luxembourg in 1919, and in the United States in 1920. In Great Britain, women gained full political rights only after the 1928 Equal Franchise Act, which equalized the franchise to all persons over the age of 21 on equal terms, while in Greece women had to wait until 1952, in Switzerland until 1971 and in Portugal until 1976 (for a general discussion on the topic, see Williams 2000).

As usual, this growing political equality between men and women did not deny that women continued living in situations of serious disadvantage with regard to men. Very commonly, women suffered serious forms of discrimination, which the law enforced or did not help to eliminate – from genital mutilation to the denial of medical services that only they needed.

---

[12] For instance, while in the case "Five Pensioners" the Tribunal declared that economic, social and cultural rights have both an individual and a collective dimension, "it stated that its progressive development should be measured concerning the entire population and not a limited group of individuals," which raised a number of criticisms. Later on, in "Discharged and Retired Employees of the Comptroller" the Tribunal "declared that the States are under the positive obligation of adopting measures in order to guarantee the satisfaction of ESR, but this obligation was considered to be subject to the economic and financial resources of the States" (ibid., p. 132).

Courts began to take women's rights more seriously only in the late twentieth century. For instance, the US Court began to change its approach on gender issues by the second half of the twentieth century, and after having affirmed, over years, that the Fourteenth Amendment did not prevent sex discrimination. In *Reed v. Reed*, 404 U.S. 71 (1971), the Court also extended the Equal Protection Clause to safeguard women from sex discrimination, in situations where there was no rational basis for the discrimination. Later on, in *Craig v. Boren*, 429 U.S. 190 (1976), it determined for the first time that statutory or administrative sex classifications were subject to intermediate scrutiny under the Fourteenth Amendment's Equal Protection Clause.[13]

In the area of reproductive and abortion rights, women's fundamental interests have been grievously postponed. In fact, reproductive rights became part of the list of human rights only in 1968, after the United Nation's International Conference on Human Rights. At that time, the non-binding Proclamation of Teheran proclaimed that "parents have a basic human right to determine freely and responsibly the number and the spacing of their children," thus becoming the first international document to refer to reproductive rights. The idea of reproductive rights was then recovered in the Cairo Program of Action, in 1994; and then by the Beijing Declaration, in 1995.

Despite these recent legal efforts made by International Human Rights Law, millions of women still suffer from discrimination and mistreatment in the area, and particularly in what regards their abortion rights (Yamin and Gloppen 2011). According to a recent report by the Center for Reproductive Rights, "while a majority of women live in countries where they can exercise their right to abortion, 41 percent of women live under restrictive laws. The inability to access safe and legal abortion care impacts 700 million women of reproductive age. For the World Health Organization, 23,000 women die of unsafe abortion each year and tens of thousands more experience significant health complications. Legal restrictions on abortion do not result in fewer abortions, instead they compel women to risk their lives and health by seeking out unsafe abortion care."[14]

---

[13] The situation seems still more worrisome in what regards the rights of sexual minorities, and despite some recent important Supreme Court decisions. For instance, in *Romer v. Evans* (1996), the Court deemed unconstitutional a Colorado amendment that came to deny homosexuals "minority status, quota preferences, protected status or (a) claim of discrimination"; and in *Lawrence v. Texas*, 539 U.S. 558 (2003), the Court overruled its previous decision in *Bowers v. Hardwick* (1986), and ruled that American laws prohibiting private homosexual activity between consenting adults were unconstitutional. More recently, in *Obergefell v. Hodges*, 576 U.S. (2015), in a 5–4 decision, the Court ruled that the fundamental right to marry is guaranteed to same-sex couples by both the Due Process Clause and the Equal Protection Clause of the Fourteenth Amendment to the United States Constitution. The Court also stated that all fifty states had to perform and recognize the marriages of same-sex couples on the same terms and conditions as the marriages of opposite-sex couples, with all the accompanying rights and responsibilities.

[14] Center for Reproductive Rights, https://reproductiverights.org/worldabortionlaws, accessed 28th December, 2019.

VI INDIGENOUS RIGHTS AND ITS LIMITS

One of the areas where legal changes toward greater equality appears to be more limited concerns indigenous rights. In Latin America, a region that includes a vast indigenous population, the first significant legal changes on the matter appeared only by the end of the twentieth century. In Nicaragua, it emerged an initial initiative in this respect after the conflict that confronted the Sandinista government with the indigenous group of the Miskitos, in 1987. Following this example, by the end of the twentieth century, numerous Latin American constitutions incorporated references to aboriginal communal rights, including the right of indigenous peoples to the property of the land that they had traditionally inhabited (Constitutions of Argentina, Bolivia, Ecuador, Nicaragua, Panama, Paraguay, Peru); and the right of use and enjoyment of natural resources (Bolivia, Brazil, Mexico, Nicaragua).

The gradual emergence of a right to "prior consultation" (the right to "free previous and informed consultation" *FPIC*), represents one of the most interesting novelties in the area. This new "right" derives from the International Labor Organization, and its Convention 169 about Indigenous and Tribal Peoples. According to Article 6.1 of the Convention, governments shall "consult the peoples concerned, through appropriate procedures and in particular through their representative institutions, whenever consideration is being given to legislative or administrative measures which may affect them directly." The FPIC achieved a special significance in recent years, given a social context characterized by the growing demands of indigenous groups, and the predominance of economic policies increasingly characterized by predatory economic initiatives.[15]

Unfortunately, local authorities have frequently defied the force of this right to previous prior consultation. In numerous countries, legislatures ignored or undermined the requirements so far established by the ILO Convention. In some occasions, national authorities considered their obligations satisfied, after simply informing indigenous communities about the economic initiatives they were about to adopt. In other cases, they continued with the implementation of their development plans even though those plans were rejected in the consultation processes (Rodríguez-Garavito and Arenas 2005). In Mexico, the Yaqui tribe had its prior consultation rights confirmed, time and again, by the Court, with almost no practical effect (Sieder 2016). In Ecuador, a crucial Mining Law was approved with no prior consultation. These legal difficulties were added to many

---

[15] This explosive combination has generated social tensions that frequently resulted in violent confrontations. We may remember, for instance, the protests that were triggered in Ecuador, after President Correa approved, in 2011, a mining law that favored the interests of transnational groups; or the massive protests that emerged in Bolivia, by the same time, after the government decided to construct a transnational road through the protected Indigenous Territory of Isiboro Secure National Park (TIPNIS). More tragically, there was also the massacre of "Bagua", in Peru 2009, which occurred as a consequence of the indigenous protests against oil exploitation in the Amazon.

other practical problems, which in the end deprived the right to prior consultation of its force and meaning – these practical problems included, typically, insufficient funds; lack of information; and lack of transparency (Rodríguez-Garavito and Arenas 2005).

In the context of these political difficulties, judicial authorities did not always come to the rescue of the FPIC, even in countries such as Ecuador or Bolivia, where Constitutions favorable both to indigenous rights and the protection of natural resources were enacted.[16] In Bolivia, for example the Constitutional Court advanced a restrictive reading of the FPIC on different occasions. For instance, in decisions SS. CC. 2.003/2010-R and 0300/2012, the Court limited the cases in which prior consultation was required, and also affirmed – against the explicit letter of the Convention – that the consultation could proceed after (and not necessarily before) the enactment of the law. Similarly, in Ecuador, political and judicial authorities tended to join forces to legalize the exploitation of natural resources, without attention to the limits imposed by the Constitution, the "sumac kawsay" (the surprising "right of nature" incorporated into the Constitution), and the ILO Convention.[17]

VII INEQUALITY THROUGH THE ORGANIZATION OF POWERS

While Constitutions tend to speak the language of equality and adhere to different forms of it through their Declarations of Rights, they simultaneously tend to reinforce inequality through the way they organize the Structure of Powers. In a silent form, but almost invariably, they consecrate a significant difference of power between "the few" and "the many", the rich and the poor, those who occupy public positions and the citizenry at large. In this way, social and economic inequalities have become imprinted into the Constitution through its Organization of Powers. We can find manifestations of this phenomenon in almost every aspect of the organization of powers.

Perhaps the most visible expression of these inequalities is the one related to the executive branch, particularly but not only in presidential systems like the US. Notably, in any democratic system, the concentration of decision-making powers in

---

[16] Those Constitutions, it must be noted, even made explicit reference to the "sumac kawsay" or principle of the "Good Living" –a concept revived from the ancestral Quechua knowledge, which came to incorporate in the Constitution a different interpretation of the "cosmos," related to communal, rather than capitalistic values.

[17] By contrast, the intervention of the Inter-American Human Rights Court in these matters has frequently been positive. The Inter American Court had the chance to intervene in those affairs in a number of times. For instance, the Court established that consultation processes constituted a "general principle of International Law" (*Saramaka v. Surinam*, sentence of the 12th August 2008). Also, the Inter American Court had the chance to define its view on the matter further, in the case *Sarayaku v. Ecuador* (2012).

"one single man" should be considered the most obvious challenge to the ideal of an egalitarian distribution of political authority.[18]

In Latin America, and since the early nineteenth century, numerous constitutions adopted the strongest forms of presidentialism, which philosopher Carlos Nino defined as "hyper-presidentialism" (Nino 1997). The polemic choice of hyper-presidentialism was usually presented as necessary for ensuring order and political stability. The model of a strong executive was adopted in most Bolivian constitutions, from the one written by Simón Bolívar, in 1826, to those of 1831, 1834, 1843, and 1851. In Colombia, the failed projects of 1826, 1828, and 1830, were all inspired by Bolívar's presidentialist ideas. So too with the enormously influential Constitution of 1886, which also represented an important example of an hyper-presidentialist and centralized Constitution. In Peru, the Constitutions of 1826 and 1839, which allowed the delegation of "all the necessary powers" to the president in case of crisis; and also the Constitution of 1860, represented significant efforts to strengthen the authority of the Executive. In Chile, the Constitution of 1833, which established an executive power invested with political, legislative and military powers, became the most stable Latin American Constitution of the nineteenth century.

In Europe, the idea of the executive as a decisive "national arbiter" has also played an important role. The roots of this view may be found in Benjamin Constant's notion of the "moderating power," that is to say a "neutral power," in charge of balancing and limiting the excesses of the other branches (Constant 1997, p. 327). Constant's proposal was adopted in Portugal, 1822; and also in the 1848 "Statuto albertino" of the Kingdom of Sardinia, on which the 1861 Italian Constitution came to be based. The idea of the executive as the "arbiter" or "moderating power" also came to play an important role in French contemporary constitutionalism. It appeared, for example, in Charles de Gaulle's famous speech before the municipal council of Bayeux (June 16th, 1946).[19]

---

[18] This challenge to equality should be deemed even more serious when that unequal distribution of powers is justified through arguments based on the distrust of the citizens' democratic capacities -as it was the rule, for instance, in the US context. For instance, in numerous writings and speeches, Alexander Hamilton made clear not only that the President would receive exceptional powers, but he also explained the reasons that justified that polemic institutional choice. Particularly in *Federalist Papers* n. 71 and 76, he justified the concentration of powers in the hands of the President in relation to the (democratic) *distrust* that many of the "Framers" had toward the political capacities of the people at large ("a single well-directed man with a single understanding cannot be distracted by that diversity of views, feelings and interests, which frequently distract and warp the resolutions of a collective body").

[19] In the referred speech, de Gaulle referred to the work of "an elite which spontaneously sprung from the depths of the nation" with "feeling of moral superiority" and "contempt for agitation, pretenses or discussions." From that standpoint, he suggested that "new democratic institutions compensate by themselves the effects of our perpetual political turmoil," and affirmed the importance of creating a "national arbiter" that "above political contingencies" can show "the road to continuity in the midst of debates."

Now, among the inequalities that are established by constitutions through the organization of powers, none has been more theorized and debated than those that relate to the judicial branch. The tensions that exist between judicial review, equality, and democracy seemed clear from the very initial discussions on the subject – thus, in the initial criticisms of anti-federalist *Brutus*, and in Alexander Hamilton's remarkable response to them in *Federalist Papers* n. 78; or in Justice Marshall's famous opinion in *Marbury v. Madison* (5 U.S. 137 1803). In the mid-twentieth century, Alexander Bickel presented this problem with singular force in his influential book *The Least Dangerous Branch*. There, Bickel referred to the challenge that judicial review posed to democracy: when courts declare a law invalid – he claimed – what in fact happens is that they thwart "the will of the representatives of the actual people of the here and now," thus exercising control "not in behalf of the prevailing majority, but against it" (Bickel 1962, p. 17).

Recently, legal scholars have begun to recognize and question the challenge that judicial review poses to the constitutional value of equality. Jeremy Waldron has forcefully advocated this view in the past decades. He has demonstrated that, in a society of equals (in a society where people are equal in their moral dignity), where people reasonably disagree over fundamental public issues (this is what he called "the fact of disagreement"), it is something of an "insult" that the opinion of a few judges should prevail (as the "final word") over the opinion of all the rest (Waldron 1993b, 1999a, 2014a).

VIII CONCENTRATION OF POWERS VS. EXPANSION OF RIGHTS

The previous considerations suggest something important concerning the limits of the constitutional reforms that were carried out in the last century. Those reforms have been concentrated on the declaration of rights (i.e., though the inclusion of new participatory, social, economic, and cultural rights), leaving the traditional structures of the organization of powers basically unchanged. In that way, contemporary Constitutions have been "modernized," but only in one of its main parts, namely the one that establishes the Bill of Rights. In that way, these new Constitutions tended to become split into two parts: "21st century-style" Declarations of Rights (rich, social, democratic), and "18th century-style" organizations of powers. One of those parts appeared in that way deeply committed to the principle of equality, while the other appeared oriented at making political inequalities stable.

Now, one could claim that legal reformers did what they could, the best they could. One could also say that we should at least celebrate the improvement we got when our constitutions adopted robust lists of social and economic rights. However, the problem is that the non-reformed parts of the Constitution do not remain "silent" or "indifferent" in relation to those areas that are reformed. On the one hand, the two main sections of the Constitution are inter-related: what we do or not do in one part of the Constitution has usually an impact on the rest of the Constitution. Typically, the incorporation of more fundamental rights into the Constitution means the creation of more powerful judiciaries (given the privileged role they play in the enforcement of rights). On the other hand, the "engine room" of the Constitution, this is to say the section related to the organization of powers, includes most of the mechanisms required to "give life" to constitutional rights (Gargarella 2010, 2013). One consequence of this is that the most powerful branch of power – usually, in our time, the Executive Power – begins to work against the implementation of those rights that threaten to affect its dominance or hegemony (i.e., participatory rights): strong presidents tend to resist all kinds of delegation of powers.

In addition, the problem of the dissociation between the declaration of rights and the organic part of the Constitution needs to be understood in a *dynamic rather than in a static way*. The inequalities that are incorporated into the Constitution, through the concentration of powers, tend to expand and reproduce over time, and affect the functioning of the rest of the Constitution. For instance, in strongly presidential systems, the executive tends to use the powers and means under its control (including coercive and economic means) in order to enlarge his or her own capacities. Rosalind Dixon has explored this issue, and for instance demonstrated how many contemporary executives used "rights as bribes" (Dixon 2018). She illustrates her point through the "path-breaking environmental and indigenous rights protections in Ecuador in 2008, and the adoption of social rights, and especially equal voting rights, for Indo-Fijians under the 2013 Fijian Constitution." For her, rights are sometimes "used by democratic political leaders to increase support from national social movements, or foreign governments and NGOs, for the formal expansion of their own power or prerogatives, in ways that often undermine norms of democratic competition or accountability, or by authoritarian leaders to gain support for the adoption of a new constitution that legitimizes their ongoing hold on power" (Dixon 2018, p. 4).

Powerful executives tend to work for the increasing expansion of their own powers, usually at the expense of the rest of the structure of "checks and balances." This phenomenon generates the gradual deterioration of the entire institutional system. Tom Ginsburg and Aziz Huq call this phenomenon one of "democratic erosion," which they define as "the risk of slow, but ultimately substantial unraveling along the margins of rule-of-law, democratic, and liberal rights" (Ginsburg and Huq 2018, p. 39). "Democratic erosion" implies a "process of incremental but ultimately still substantial, decay in the three basic predicates of democracy – competitive elections, liberal rights to speech and association and the rule of law, across different institutions, against a baseline of some ongoing level of democracy" (ibid., pp. 43–44).[20] In line with what was said above, the authors also recognize that "the most formidable motor of erosion [of the entire institutional system] would be the presidency, which over time has acquired a plethora of institutional, political, and rhetorical powers above and beyond the meager list set out in Article II of the US Constitution" (Ginsburg and Huq 2018, p. 141). In fact, with the coming to power of authoritarian leaders, in the United States, Hungary, Poland, Turkey, etc., numerous authors began to call attention to the risk of "democratic backsliding" (Ginsburg and Huq 2018; Levitsky and Ziblatt 2018; Sunstein 2018a; Przeworski 2019). Usually, the first victim of "democratic backsliding" and the gradual erosion of the system of "checks and balances" is the judiciary, which – as experience has shown – after being captured by those in power, becomes a crucial instrument for the consolidation of the new regime.

IX DIALOGIC CONSTITUTIONALISM AND EQUALITY

Let me conclude this analysis on a more positive and optimistic note. The fact is that the strong tendency that contemporary constitutional systems show toward the concentration of powers and the gradual debasement of democracy, contrasts with other initiatives, favorable to more inclusive and deliberative forms of democracy. These alternative tendencies can be found in judicial and political alternatives that usually follow demands coming from civil society. These new experiences teach us something extremely important: namely, that *the meaning of the Constitution can be discussed and defined in an egalitarian way, and through the participation of "all the affected," situated on an equal footing.* In other words, constitutional interpretation may be properly exercised by civil society.

The fact is that, since the beginning of the new century, we have seen the emergence of participatory experiences that suggest the presence of a new way of thinking and developing constitutionalism. These practices include the use of public hearings; more inclusive decision-making processes; participatory judicial remedies; and so on. Alternatives of these kinds have made clear that the decision about fundamental public issues need not (and should not) be reserved to experts or elites: fundamental political decisions can (and should) be the result of an open, collective conversation. Let me briefly explore these alternatives both at the judicial and political level.

The judiciary: Judges have been contributing to this "dialogic" type of constitutionalism in different ways: sometimes through decisions aimed at "correcting" the political decision-making process and making it more "inclusive" or more

---

[20] "Years ago" – the authors claimed – the emergency powers and military coups were important to "fast democratic breakdowns," which usually yielded to "a clearly authoritarian form of government." In contrast, the "slow erosion" of democracy would constitute the more common phenomenon of our time – a phenomenon that usually ends up with "some kind of competitive authoritarian structure" (Ginsburg and Huq 2018, p. 39).

"deliberative"; sometimes by opening its own decision-making process to the participation of other previously unheard voices, etc. Many of these developments suggest that judges can make a decisive contribution to the cause of an egalitarian democracy where "all those potentially affected" participate on an equal footing in the discussion about fundamental public issues. For instance, the remarkable series of public hearings called by Argentina's Supreme Court in 2004 in *Matanza-Riachuelo River Basin* represent an early and interesting example of this possibility. *Doctors for Life*, a case that was decided by the South African Constitutional Court, constitutes another interesting instance of this new development. In that ruling, judges reflected upon the constitutional obligation of legislators to facilitate public involvement in its legislative processes and ensured that the decision-making process did not unjustly excluded the voices of disadvantaged groups.[21]

On another occasion, *Olivia Road*, the South African Court tried another thought-provoking route of dialogic intervention, through what came to be called a process of "meaningful engagement."[22] In a crucial passage of its decision, the Court stated:

The City of Johannesburg and the applicants are required to engage with each other meaningfully and as soon as it is possible for them to do so, in an effort to resolve the differences and difficulties aired in this application in the light of the values of the Constitution, the constitutional and statutory duties of the municipality and the rights and duties of the citizens concerned. (Chenwi 2015, p. 185; Liebenberg 2012, p. 14; Liebenberg 2015)[23]

Courts can also make an important contribution to public dialogue through the means and remedies they choose in order to implement their decisions. For instance, in the famous T 760/8 decision by the Colombian Constitutional Court, the Colombian Tribunal decided to intervene in the restructuring of the National Health System. Through its ruling, the Court required the reorganization of the existing plans through transparent and participatory mechanisms; and demanded the reconstructive process to be supervised by public audiences (Yamin and Parra 2009).

Politics: More interesting still are the political experiences of inclusive deliberation and citizens' assemblies that have emerged all around the world in recent years. One could consider, in that respect, the 1998 Australian Assembly that, notably, was composed of professional politicians and regular citizens; the participatory assemblies of British Columbia 2005 and Ontario 2006, which organized citizens' conventions (whose members were selected by lot) aimed at discussing

---

[21] *Doctors for Life International v. The Speaker of the National Assembly and Others*, CCT 12/05, 17, August 2006.

[22] *Occupiers of 51 Olivia Road, Berea Township and 197 Main Street Johannesburg v. City of Johannesburg and others*, 2008 (3) SA 208 CC.

[23] However, as I have tried to show in a previous work, alternatives of the kind also constitute a "territory of dispute." See, for instance, the jurisprudence of the South African Court in cases such as *Joe Slovo* (Gargarella 2019; Liebenberg 2012).

and proposing new electoral systems; the deliberative experience developed in the Dutch Citizen Forum in 2006; the "crowdsourcing" Constitutional Convention of Iceland (2009–2013); the deliberative assemblies of Ireland in 2012 and 2016 (that were also composed of members elected through lottery), which ended with two successful referendums, one on gay marriage and the other on abortion. These citizens' assemblies arguably provide the main institutional hope of our time. Their promising functioning suggest that our political systems can work in a better way, and also teach us that the interpretation of our main constitutional values can be – in spite of everything – the result of an actual conversation among equals.

RECOMMENDED READING

Christiano, T. (2010). *The Constitution of Equality: Democratic Authority and Its Limits*, Oxford: Oxford University Press.
Cohen, G. (2008). *Rescuing Justice and Equality*, Cambridge: Harvard University Press.
Dahl, R. (2003). *How democratic is the American Constitution?* Conn.: Yale University Press.
Dixon, R. (2018). Constitutional Rights as Bribes. *Connecticut Law Review*, 50 (3), pp. 769–818.
Dworkin, R. (2000). *Sovereign Virtue: The Theory and Practice of Equality*, Cambridge: Harvard University Press.
Elster, J. & Slagstad, R. (1988). *Constitutionalism and Democracy*, Cambridge: Cambridge University Press.
Fabre, C. (2000). *Social rights under the Constitution. Government and the Decent life*, Oxford University Press, Oxford.
Fiss, O. (2003). *The Law as it Could Be*, New York: New York University Press.
Gargarella, R. (2010). *The Legal Foundations of Inequality*, Cambridge: Cambridge University Press.
Gargarella, R., Domingo, P., Roux, T., eds. (2016). *Courts and Social Transformation in New Democracies*, London: Routledge.
Ginsburg, T., Huq, A. (2018). *How to save a Constitutional Democracy*, Chicago: University of Chicago Press.
Graber M., Levinson, S., Tushnet M., eds. (2018). *Constitutional democracy in crisis?*, Oxford: Oxford University Press.
Landau, D. (2013). Abusive Constitutionalism. *UC Davis Law Review*, 47 (1), pp. 189–260.
Langford, M. (2009). *Social Rights Jurisprudence: Emerging Trends in International and Comparative Law*, Cambridge: Cambridge University Press.
Levitsky, S., Ziblatt, D. (2018). *How Democracies Die*, New York: Crown.
Loveman, B. (1993). *The Constitution of Tyranny*, Pittsburgh University Press.
Michelman, F. (1979). Welfare Rights in a Constitutional Democracy. *Washington University Law Quarterly*, 1979 (3), 659–693.
Przeworski, A. (2019). *Crises of Democracy*, Cambridge: Cambridge University Press.
Tushnet, M. (2008). *Weak Courts, Strong Rights*, Princeton: Princeton University Press.
Young, K., ed. (2019). *The Future of Economic and Social Rights*, Cambridge: Cambridge University Press.

57

Populism

Paul Blokker

Populism in relation to constitutionalism is a widely discussed, and in distinctive ways, a critical topic. In the literature on the phenomenon, there is a prevalence to identify populism as antithetical to constitutional democracy (see, e.g., Halmai 2018; Mudde 2013; Müller 2016, 2018; Scheppele 2018)[1] and as eroding the idea and fundamentals of constitutionalism. However, as this chapter will show, much depends on the definitions offered of populism and constitutionalism, and the analytical commitment to study both as historical phenomena with important contextual differences. As I will argue in this chapter, constitutionalism as such is a contested phenomenon, and populism frequently takes up different forms of critique on the predominant legal understanding of constitutionalism. Furthermore, populism is a phenomenon that manifests itself in different ways, displaying diverse guises depending on distinctive ideological position (left- or right-wing), but equally showing variety in terms of positioning regarding characteristic issues, such as sovereignty, the definition of the political community, or relations to constituent power.

In this chapter, I will first give an overview of the recent debate on populism and constitutionalism. The discussion will end indicating promising recent scholarship, which is critical of the general, pejorative "anti-populist" view of populism as the antithesis of constitutionalism. Hence, such scholarly work attempts to develop a more comparative, theoretically fine-grained, and contextually sensitive treatment of manifestations of "populist constitutionalism," elaborating comparative, empirical analysis as an indispensable dimension for an in-depth understanding of the populist phenomenon. Second, I will argue that in order to understand the populist reaction to contemporary liberal-constitutional democracy, constitutionalism as an ideal and practice needs to be put in a historical-comparative perspective. The latter highlights postwar "legal constitutionalism" as a contested political project, and acknowledges alternative historical understandings of constitutionalism. The liberal-legal form constitutionalism that emerged after 1945 is as such contested,

---

[1] For a rich comparative approach, which however stresses the idea that populism is a threat to liberal democracy, see Landau (2018).

and some of the populist critiques can be shown to portray affinity with various alternative understandings of constitutionalism. Third, populism itself needs to be understood as a multifaceted phenomenon, and the suggestion is that the relation of populism with constitutionalism can be explored on at least four dimensions: inclusion – exclusion; past-orientation – future-orientation; reformism – constituent power; and national – transnational outlook. In the fourth part, I will explore these dimensions in what could be identified as the two main forms of populism – left- and right-wing populism – and will provide various examples of "really existing" populist constitutionalism.

I THE DEBATE ON POPULISM AND CONSTITUTIONALISM

The Anti-populist Thesis

In much of the recent literature, populism is understood as a political manifestation that erodes or negates – or at the very minimum threatens – constitutional democracy. As Jan-Werner Müller has put it, "populism is inherently hostile to the mechanisms, and ultimately, the values commonly associated with constitutionalism: Constraints on the will of the majority, checks and balances, protections for minorities, and even fundamental rights" (Müller 2016, p. 68; Urbinati 2014).

Populists are seen as impatient with procedures and institutions, and as loath to intermediary bodies, as they prefer unmediated relations between the populist ruler and the people. Populists prefer direct "natural" or "pure" forms of politics, in contrast to indirect and artificial ones (Urbinati 1998, p. 111). In Wojciech Sadurski's words, "[p]opulist regimes are impatient with freedom of speech for minorities," "they dislike slow, patient deliberation in parliaments, preferring a 'winner takes it all,' plebiscitary model of politics, under which the leader (usually a charismatic leader) obtains a carte blanche for the period of his or her parliamentary or presidential term" (Sadurski 2020, p. 8). Sadurski further refers to the "antipathy of modern populists to the separation and dispersion of powers that is seen as a constraint upon the political will of a homogeneous community" (Sadurski 2020, p. 9). In sum, "populisms have this common denominator: they abhor pluralism, minority rights, and constitutional constraints upon simple majority rule" (Sadurski 2020, p. 9).

This means, according to many observers, that constitutionalism is in stark contrast to populism. In the view of Gabor Halmai, "[t]hose who perceive democracy as liberal by definition also claim that populism is inherently hostile to values associated with constitutionalism: checks and balances, constraints on the will of the majority, fundamental rights, and protections for minorities" (Halmai 2018, pp. 328–329). In Halmai's opinion, the term "populist constitutionalism" – as those of "illiberal" or "authoritarian constitutionalism" – is an oxymoron, in that constitutionalism consists in "legally limited power of the government" and populist, just as alleged illiberal or authoritarian versions fail to live up to the "requirements of constitutionalism" (Halmai 2018, p. 329).

In Sajó and Uitz's book on legal constitutionalism, one can equally find a rather strong distinction between the idea and practice of constitutionalism, on one hand, and populism, on the other. Sajó and Uitz argue that "[c]onstitutionalism stands for minorities (at least in the minimum sense that they have the right or legal possibility to be part of the majority, or become the majority)," whereas the populist approach stands for the "unity of the people and those who are 'outside' (the others or 'them') do not count" (Sajó and Uitz 2017, p. 9). In their discussion, Sajo and Uitz relate populism to a range of contemporary challenges to constitutionalism – which includes not only right-wing, nationalist political forces – but also a whole range of radical challenges to the legal-constitutional idea, which are similar in their display of an "intellectual political dislike of constitutionalism." In Sajo and Uitz's account, this means that "whenever [such sceptical forces] were able to shape constitutions, constitutional practices, and constitutional law, this was detrimental to fundamental principles of constitutionalism" (Sajó and Uitz 2017, p. 9).

In a contribution by Chris Thornhill, the objection to "legal globalism" by populist governments is stressed, and populist politics is depicted as a politics in which "people are invited to imagine themselves as constantly engaged in the exercise of *constituent power*, and the government is perceived as legitimate if the popular will acts as a live political force in the state, assuming higher authority than constituted institutions and institutional actors that usually mediate popular interests in legitimate form" (Thornhill 2020, p. 3). As Thornhill further argues, "[t]his conception of popular agency means that, under populist rule, formal legal and organizational structures for facilitating political representation lose purchase and elections acquire strongly plebiscitary dimensions." Thornhill's approach to populism coincides with the arguments above in that his view identifies a deep tension between the populist invocation of unlimited political (majoritarian) power, on the one hand, and constitutional structures, embedded in global norms and liberal legalism, on the other. His view is original, and quite radical, in contrast, in that he deeply questions normative understandings of popular sovereignty and constituent power. In Thornhill's not implausible reading, effective democratic societies only emerged in the post-1945 context, and the effectiveness of their democratic rule-making, in his understanding, derived importantly from societies' integration into international systems of legal norms, and those involving human rights in particular. Thornhill understands the main threat to constitutionalism as stemming from the strong emphasis on populism on national sovereignty and the rejection of international norms and institutions.

The accounts above, which tend to understand the relation between populism and constitutionalism as an antithesis, ultimately build on a rather distinctive understanding of constitutionalism, that is, the post-Second World War paradigm of constitutionalism or "legal constitutionalism" (Sajó and Uitz 2017, p. 9; Gyorfi 2016).

This understanding regards constitutionalism in particular as an anti-totalitarian project, which aims at safeguarding representative, liberal democracy from radical threats from both left- and right-wing forces. The concerns of such "anti-populist" positions are equally legitimate and real in current times, in which many established constitutional democracies face strong pressures (US, UK), while more recently established democracies, such as Hungary and Poland, are now turning against the anti-totalitarian project and are constructing alternative, self-identified "illiberal democratic" systems.

The anti-populist account, however, suffers from three major problems. First of all, it tends to regard legal forms of constitutionalism as the only historically available manifestation of constitutionalism, which is a highly debatable claim. Second, it tends to conflate populism with (radical) right-wing, conservative populism, while ignoring major differences between populist parties, between populist political projects, and distinctive societal contexts. Third, the anti-populists tend to endorse a normative understanding of legal constitutionalism, which is little inclined to engage with and analyze the potential problems and tensions such a model contains.

Despite the urgency of the very real threat against liberal–constitutional democracy in contemporary times, it is equally urgent to detect and reveal specific in-built tensions in the postwar legal-constitutional project. Such insights might shed light on the thrust and mobilizing force of the current wave of populist "counter–constitutionalism" and – rather than making us re-propose an unlikely return to the status quo ex ante – may help us to think in more fruitful and innovative ways about constitutional democracy. As Mark Tushnet has recently argued,

> treating efforts to transform the courts as a strong point – "assaults on judicial independence" – against populism is a defense of the failed status quo, not a politically neutral defense of a central component of every good constitution. (In its best form, the argument against institutional transformation is something like this: the costs of transformation, such as a reduction in judicial independence, are so great that the failed status quo is preferable. I think it not unreasonable for populists to disagree, given their – again, often accurate – understanding of the costs of persisting with the status quo) (Tushnet 2018c, p. 644).

Hence, Tushnet proposes, together with Bojan Bugaric, that populism is to be understood as a pluralist phenomenon, which shares a "family resemblance, but the family is an extended one whose dispersal around the world has produced members who could have little to say to each other at a family reunion" (Bugaric and Tushnet 2021, p. 2348). Bugaric and Tushnet's approach indicates the need for a comparative, pluralist approach, which allows for different manifestations of both populism and constitutionalism, and which acknowledges potential conflict between populism and constitutionalism, but such conflict is not understood as a general conflict, and while in some cases populism clearly violates constitutional norms, in other cases it does not (Bugaric and Tushnet 2021).

II CONSTITUTIONALISM: ONE OR MANY?

I suggest that it is crucial – as also suggested by Bugaric and Tushnet – to approach the populism-constitutionalism nexus from a historical perspective. A crucial starting point for understanding current manifestations of populism and constituent politics is the post-1945 emergence of a distinctive constitutional imagination. The postwar paradigm of constitutionalism is grounded in a distinctive constitutional imaginary, strongly emphasizing aspects of stability and order, and granting judicial institutions important review powers. This postwar paradigm, identified here as having crystallized into the institutional blueprint of "legal constitutionalism," is what deeply informs the global constitutional landscape as well as the constitutional visions of many constitutional scholars. It is also this particular conception and project of constitutionalism from which the current academic interest in populism departs.

The emergence of a universal, legal-constitutional model of society is related to a tendency toward judicialization in modern societies, which includes a "profound shift of power away from legislatures and toward courts and other legal institutions around the world" (Ferejohn 2002, p. 41). Judicialization further refers to a growing importance of legal norms in social interaction – not least in the form of human rights – shifting political demands and claims away from representative and participatory democratic institutions to the legal arena. In the last few decades, the legal-constitutional paradigm has gained dominance in the global constitutional landscape, but is clearly not without contestation (Thornhill 2020). A number of competing constitutional narratives have become visible, and in some cases, are explicitly formulated against some of the key tenets of legal constitutionalism. Three of such competing narratives may be seen as particularly relevant: political constitutionalism; communitarian constitutionalism; and democratic constitutionalism (cf. Koch 2020).

Until fairly recently, the legal constitutional model appeared to be predominantly challenged by political and constitutional theorists endorsing an alternative model: political constitutionalism (Bellamy 2007; Tomkins 2005) (evidently, the political-constitutional perspective is strongly related to actual societal contexts, not least that of the UK). A key point of contention regards the role of apex courts, and more particularly, the role of judicial review of, most prominently, legislative acts. As Mac Amhlaigh states, the

> Most popular front of contestation between political and legal constitutionalism has been with regard to the question of whether courts or legislatures should have ultimate decision-making authority on the identification, interpretation, and application of the fundamental values, usually expressed as fundamental rights, of a particular legal order or constitutional settlement (Mac Amhlaigh 2016, p. 175).

The political-constitutionalist conception challenges the (hegemonic) legal-constitutional idea by taking a rather different view of the role and substance of the constitution, and its relation to democratic politics. Political constitutionalism reevaluates the role of judicial institutions in constitutionalism and reasserts the importance of parliamentary institutions.

A second alternative take on constitutionalism is grounded in communitarian views of constitutional democracy. The communitarian view is equally aimed against legal constitutionalism, and puts value in the historical and cultural bases of constitutional orders; a crucial dimension is the idea of constitutional identity. The communitarian constitutional view prioritizes local moral understandings over alleged universally valid norms. Communitarian constitutionalism may turn into an illiberal form of constitutionalism, prioritizing community interests to individual interests, and actively promoting a collectivist vision of communal life. In the communitarian view, courts are playing a "secondary rather than counterbalancing role" in that constitutionalism is understood as a community-preserving project (Thio 2012, p. 133).

A third alternative to legal constitutionalism is that formulated in different manifestations of what could be called "democratic constitutionalism," in which critical, radical-democratic, bottom-up, and agonistic dimensions of democratic politics are at the forefront. Legal constitutionalism is criticized as deficient in terms of its democratic nature. For instance, in Joel Colon-Rios' version of "weak constitutionalism," democratic constitutionalism "rests on the idea that ordinary citizens should be allowed, to the extent to which it is practically possible, to propose, deliberate, and decide on important constitutional transformations through the most participatory methods possible." (Colon-Rios 2011, p. 23). Democratic constitutionalism consists of a critical, normative suggestion of how to radically rebalance legal constitutionalism in favor of a democratic-participatory dimension in constitutionalism, in a critique of elitism and technocratic politics.

In sum, the postwar project of legal constitutionalism is confronted with, and challenged by, competing constitutional visions and narratives, which criticize its depoliticizing tendencies, its individualist and abstract, universalist nature, its lack of acknowledgement of conflicting views, and dearth of possibilities for civic engagement. Contemporary manifestations of populist critique tend to show affinity with, and perhaps even borrow from, different and competing constitutional narratives in their critical attitude toward legal constitutionalism.

III VARIETIES OF POPULISM

The relation between populism and constitutionalism appears hence not simply as a purely antithetical one (Bugaric and Tushnet 2021). Manifestations of populism (as we will see below, right- and left-wing versions differ importantly) relate to different constitutional narratives, and criticize the hegemony of legal constitutionalism on various grounds. As I have discussed above, in part the variety of populist critique is due to the various available positions on, imaginations, and political projects of, constitutionalism, to some of which populists show a fairly close affinity (such as to that of communitarian visions of the community in the case of right-wing, conservative forms of populism). But populism itself equally needs to be approached as an internally variegated phenomenon. This variety of manifestations of populism is, however, frequently overlooked in scholarly debates on populism and constitutionalism, where the antithetical/anti-populist, and in many ways, simplifying, interpretation appears dominant. This means that populism is frequently equated with illiberal, ethno-national, and tendentially authoritarian ideas and practices. However, as inter alia Rob Howse has aptly remarked, much of the anti-populist critique stems from a relatively narrow view of liberal, representative democracy and a rather thick view of what constitutionalism entails, which anti-populist observers intend to defend in a rather uncritical fashion (Howse 2018).

As, however, the prominent scholar of ideology Michael Freeden has argued, the equation of "populism with democratic illiberalism requires further elaboration," not least because both liberalism and populism come in many forms and shapes. Freeden in a way "normalizes" populism in that he considers it "a slippery concept to define, attracting a range of cultural and geopolitical connotations that overlap only with difficulty," a condition which can, however, be seen as pertaining to "other ideological variants" too (Freeden 2016, pp. 1–2).

The relation between populism and constitutionalism is hence better analyzed by means of comparative analysis, which takes into account various intrinsic dimensions of the populist phenomenon. Comparative analysis requires analytical dimensions that allow one to capture the defining characteristics as well as forms of diversity in manifestations of populism. Defining dimensions regard core, overlapping characteristics of populism. Here, I suggest such core dimensions of populism include: a friend-enemy logic in populist political mobilization; a critical attitude toward liberal democracy, which, according to populists, is inadequate in promoting popular sovereignty; and a frequently crucial role for constituent power in populist projects (in other words, a critical approach to existing legal norms and rules). These very same defining characteristics relate equally to significant differences between forms of populism. In terms of such differences, I have elsewhere proposed (Blokker 2019b) the following dimensions: an inclusionary versus exclusionary forms of populism (the friend-enemy distinction is differently defined by populists); an orientation toward the past or the future (popular sovereignty has to be recuperated from a past ideal situation or rather conquered in the name of some real utopian vision); a reformist or radical orientation (invoking constituent power or not); and, finally, definitions of the political community in national or more cosmopolitan terms (cf. Blokker 2019a; Koch 2020).

Inclusion versus Exclusion

Populism is frequently displayed as a politically exclusionary force. Populism tends to understand society as divided between the pure people and its enemies. Populists attempt to mobilize the people as a unitary, collective actor against designated enemies. The exclusionary tendency of the construction of the people – and the related process of othering – appears to point to a necessary closure of a political community toward those that are defined as external. But this is not necessarily the case. Admittedly, key dimensions of populism are its anti-elitist and antiestablishment positions, also coming through in critical approaches to judicial institutions, and populists' claim to promote the cause of the underrepresented and marginalized parts of society. But the mobilization of the latter groups and the promotion of their interests does not necessarily lead to an exclusionary approach. Populism in some cases promotes the conquest of existing institutions by popular forces. In this, they attempt to sweep away the political hegemony of the enemies, replace it by the rule of the popular forces, while attempting to reduce any further political and public participation or influence of these enemies. But other forms of populism, while equally making strong claims against elites, promote political and material inclusion of previously excluded groups in – reformed – existing institutions, endorsing pluralism, and redistributive justice. As Kate Nash argues in her discussion of populist forces criticizing legal constitutionalism in Europe (Nash 2016), distinctive left-wing populist forces such as Podemos use patriotic language identifying the people, but the people is not defined in a closed manner, and is understood as including non-national, marginalized groups such as migrants.

An exclusionary or inclusionary thrust in populist political forces has potentially great implications for the constitutional projects such forces pursue. While comparative work regarding populism and constitutionalism in Latin America and Europe is relatively scarce,[2] preliminary investigations indicate that highly important differences exist in terms of inclusionary, participatory and bottom-up, democratizing dimensions of (distinctive phases of) constitutional reform in Latin America if compared to the outright majoritarian, nationalist, and conservative projects in (East-Central) Europe (Kaltwsser 2013).

Past versus Future

A second diversifying dimension to populism is that relating to conservatism and utopianism, or backward-looking and forward-looking projects of populism. Populist movements ought to be understood as reactionary, in the specific sense of reacting to a specific political order or a distinctive status quo. In other words, a hegemony of some sorts is criticized in the name of popular sovereignty. This brings back into the discussion an insight that was frequently made in the early 2000s: that populism is intrinsic to liberal democracy. The populist reaction is hence against the liberal-democratic status quo and decries its detrimental effects on popular sovereignty

---

[2] For analyses of Latin America, see, among others, Nolte and Schilling-Vacaflor (2012); Díaz de Valdés and Verdugo (2019).

and the interests of the ordinary people. The critical dimension is clearly a negative dimension, arguing against the current political and institutional constellation. This critical approach toward liberal-democracy – while at the same time claiming to remain within the democratic endeavor is – what distinguishes populism across the board.[3]

It is on the positive (constructive) dimension that populist projects start to differ importantly. The invocation of popular sovereignty is importantly about the claim to retrieve a lost promise – that is, of the rule of the people. And hence, populists seek to retrieve something that according to them existed in the past, or that has been part of a societal project but was then corrupted. A crucial distinction is subsequently between two types of populism. The first is one that perceives the liberal-democratic project as ultimately deeply flawed and hence in need of being replaced by a radically different understanding of democracy – that is, emphasizing collective, cultural, and historical dimensions against liberal democracy's individualism, deeply skeptical of the ontological presuppositions of the liberal-individual idea. The second is one that accepts some of the fundamentals of liberal-democratic society – the individual, related human rights, popular self-government – but perceives the current liberal-democratic as greatly distorted in realizing such ideals.

Reformist versus Constituent Politics[4]

The constructive dimension of populism can further be diversified in reformist forms versus constituent forms of populist politics. In much of the debate on populism, the latter dimension fails to be discussed. As recently stressed by Andrew Arato (2020) as well as by Kolja Möller, *constituent power* has a crucial role in various populist projects: studies on populism tend to overlook that the "invocation of 'the people' is not only a matter of bolstering mere political discourse, but of constitutional politics addressing the higher-ranking dimension of the legal and political community, the distribution of powers, and the overall design of rule-making and application" (Möller 2018, p. 17). As Möller further claims, "[p]opulism does not only refer to certain policy issues, but invokes 'the people' as constituent power on which the political community relies." (Möller 2018, pp. 17–18; Corrias 2016). The reformism–constituent politics dimension is clearly not unrelated to the different stages or manifestations of the "life trajectory" of populist movements, ranging in their development from spontaneous, bottom-up protest movements, to professionalized parties, to government coalition partners, and to actual governing parties (Arato 2020).

---

[3] Whether the populist claim to represent the marginalized and the victims of (neo-) liberal elites corresponds to actual social support among such groups is a matter I cannot address here. The fact of the matter is that populism in power often leads to the centralization of power and a clear manifestation of hierarchy, in obvious contrast to the democratic promise of populism as such.

[4] Bugaric and Tushnet indicate a similar distinction in terms of "mere policy" versus "rights" domains (Bugaric and Tushnet 2021).

Not surprisingly, it is in particular in the latter context, of government responsibility, that constituent claims are being made, and frequently put into practice. Radical constituent politics includes the adoption of an entirely new constitution (as in the case of Hungary or the "neo-Bolivarian" experiences of Latin America, such as that of Venezuela), but can also take a disguised or "pseudo-constituent" form, in terms of the increased violation and hollowing out of the existing constitutional order (Poland since 2015 is a case in point). A key claim of such populist manifestations of constituent power is that the existing or preceding order profoundly lacks in legitimacy and protects the interests of elites. In contrast, reformist populist forces may place demands on the constitutional order (as in the case of Marine Le Pen in the 2017 presidential campaign, the constitutional amendments proposed by the Italian Five Star Movement[5], or the suggestion by Geert Wilders in the Netherlands to change the first article of the Dutch Constitution), but without promoting a comprehensive change or revision of the constitutional order.

National and Transnational Populism

A final dimension regards the dimension of political community. The larger part of the literature tends to equate the populist quest for the people as one of a necessarily national character. This is not least because of the taken-for-granted linkage between popular sovereignty and liberal democracy. Conceptually and historically there appears much to be going for such a form of methodological nationalism, as the people has predominantly been imagined to be forming a national political community.

An important part of the political manifestations of populism can, admittedly, be grouped under the notion of national populism. But it also needs to be recognized that an equation of populism with the national political community may reduce our capacity to understand the phenomenon. As amongst others, Rogers Brubaker has pointed out, the people comes in different guises – plebs, demos, nation, or ethnos (Brubaker 2017, p. 359). What emerges from these observations is that the people can be constructed in very different ways, and its specific relations to elites and outsiders depends on the specific populist project one looks at. National populism may develop an international dimension in terms of the coordination between national populist movement for a common purpose – as has occurred with regard to the elections of the European Parliament – in the lead-up to which populist forces mobilized in order to attempt to conquer the EU institutions. A different,

---

[5] The Five Star Movement is understood here as – at least originally – endorsing important left-wing ideas, such as the democratization of existing institutions through direct-democratic and participatory instruments, and ecological and sustainable development objectives, even if the Movement itself often claims to be beyond left and right, and in the recent past formed a coalition with the radical rightwing *Lega* (currently, it is part of a coalition government with the center-left Partitio Democratico).

transnational form transcends international collaboration in that it constructs the people in truly transnational terms: as a post-national, marginalized subject, mobilized against exploitative and hegemonic transnational elites.

IV LEFTWING VERSUS RIGHTWING POPULISM

Manifestations of populism vary. The argument presented here is basically in agreement with the recent statements by Bojan Bugaric and Mark Tushnet, who hold that the general view that populism is inherently incompatible with constitutionalism is problematic, and claim that while "some variants of populism are incompatible with modern liberal constitutionalism," this is not always the case and depends very much on the distinctive interpretations of populism as well as of constitutionalism at stake (Bugaric and Tushnet 2021). In their view, in a manner similar to my argument above, "there are many populisms and at least a few constitutionalisms" (Bugaric and Tushnet 2021, p. 2346). One significant distinction that has been made relatively frequently is between the right-wing and left-wing populisms. In an attempt to define these two versions of populist political projects, and their relations with constitutionalism, I will draw on the categories discussed above, and provide various examples. The intention is not to reduce either version to "bad" or "good" versions of populism, as might sometimes seem to be implied in discussions of distinctive positions (Mouffe 2018; Furedi 2017; Baudet 2013). Rather, the argument intends to show that on both sides of the political spectrum important tensions may emerge (which to significant extents may be attributed to the problematic notion of the "people" as such) (Arato 2016, chap. 6; Rosanvallon 2011b).

Both right- and left-wing versions of populism tend to show important affinities with existing ideological positions. Some authors, such as Mudde and Kaltwasser (2013) and recently Arato and Cohen (2021), understand this affinity in terms of so-called "host ideologies," given the fact that in their view populism is at most a "thin ideology," which needs thicker content to mobilize people. In the case of right-wing populism, this frequently means affinities with conservatism (cf. Blokker 2020), nationalism, and fascism (Finchelstein 2019). What is particularly strong in right-wing populism is a set of traditional views on society, the nation, and the family. In left-wing populism, there is a close affinity with social-democratic ideas (cf. Frega 2020). The question indeed emerges whether left-wing populism can be considered a continuation of socialdemocracy or not. On the one hand, left-wing populism "contains without doubt a basis of overlap with the social-democratic project," but at the same time it represents a reaction to social-democracy, criticizing the latter's corruption due to technocratic, elitist and neoliberal tendencies (Frega 2020, pp. 243–247). The question of continuity is further complicated by the fact that there are varieties of left-wing populism, some of which contain clear references to national sovereignty and even "patriotic" forms of exclusion (for instance, against migrant workers), and which seek some kind of return to the original social-democratic project. Other manifestations, however, take a much more pluralist and even cosmopolitan stance (cf. Blokker 2019b). In many ways, leftwing populism should be understood as a reaction to the failure of social-democracy to live up to its core ideals of equality and emancipation.

While it will not be possible to give a definite answer to the question of continuity here, one important dimension that distinguishes more radical forms of left-wing populism from social-democracy is in the critique of the liberal-constitutional, rule of law state, and in attempts at activation of forms of constituent power in the name of the people. Roberto Frega identifies social-democracy's "nucleus of principles" as including adherence to human rights as well as a liberal-constitutionalist conception of democratic legitimacy (Frega 2020, p. 243). In fact, one distinctive feature of populism is the collapse of ordinary and constitutional politics (Arato 2019), which may (at least in theory) pave the way for more democratic forms of constitutionalism, but in practice is prone to lead to authoritarian tendencies. This is particularly clear in the development of forms of populist regimes, where the combination of leaderism, centralization, and "abusive constitutionalism" has pushed left-wing populism toward plebiscitarian democracy and authoritarianism (various examples in Latin America, in particular Venezuela, are relevant here, see De La Torre and Burbano de Lara 2020).

A significant difference between (forms of) left- and right-wing populisms emerges from the dimension of inclusion-exclusion, and the related understanding of the people. As noted by Mark Tushnet, an important difference between left- and right-wing versions of populism regards the populist attitude toward equality (Tushnet 2018c; cf. Frega 2020). Left-wing populists tend not to deny a liberal, universalistic understanding of equality, but rather criticize national as well as global elites for promoting restrictive understandings of equality which prevent extensive reform on the basis of social-democratic ideas of social redistribution. The rights-based critique of left-wing populism criticizes the defense of the core of "classical liberal rights" and promotes the restriction of such classical rights (e.g. property rights) in the name of programs of redistributive justice (Tushnet 2018c, p. 645). The core struggle is hence against powerful and wealthy elites, revealing a close affinity with a social-democratic program of socio-economic redistribution. For instance, in Bernie Sanders' "political revolution," he argued that "today in America we not only have massive wealth and income inequality, but a power structure which protects that inequality. The handful of super-wealthy campaign contributors have enormous influence over the political process, while their lobbyists determine much of what goes on in congress." Instead, he claimed, "it's time we had democratic socialism for working families, not just Wall Street billionaires and large corporations" (cited in: Macaulay 2018, pp. 185–188). Sanders' political program explicitly identified the need to use constitutional means to change the status quo:

Returning to a government of, by, and for the people – not the billionaires and giant corporations – will not be easy. We need not some, but all of the measures highlighted here. As president, I will be able to accomplish some of these on my own. But others will require agreement of Congress or, in the case of a constitutional amendment, two-thirds of the Congress and three-quarters of the states. We aren't going to get there just by electing a president who believes in and is committed to restoring our democracy. We're going to get there by building a movement – a movement with enough power not only to elect a president but to insist that all of our elected representatives return power to the people, a movement that not only identifies the deep corruption of our politics but rejects cynicism and instead insists on solutions, action and accountability.[6]

In more radical manifestations of left-wing populism in Latin America, the constituent dimension took an illiberal slant and moved away from a project respecting liberal rights and constitutionalism. Constitution-making processes in Venezuela and Ecuador, for instance, sought to include the excluded, but ultimately marginalized oppositional forces. New constitutions codified "social, economic, cultural and multicultural rights, but also centralized and concentrated political power, particularly favouring charismatic presidents and weakening horizontal forms of accountability" (De La Torre and Burbano de Lara 2020, p. 1459).

In right-wing populism, the core focus is on a national "in-group" against a range of enemies (including elites on the top, but equally migrants at the bottom). This close affinity of right-wing populism to nationalist perceptions of the political community is frequently noticed. This relation is often expressed – even if not exclusively so – in terms of a past-oriented approach regarding national (constitutional) traditions, the constitutional protection of national identity and history, and the usage of constitutional instruments to deconstruct the existing political-constitutional order or those that were in place until recently. This is evident in a number of instances of East-Central European conservative populism, such as the attention Hungarian populists and right-wing forces for the alleged "historical constitution" of Hungary (Scheppele 2000; Hörcher 2017) or in the Polish idea of a "Fourth Republic." The idea of a Fourth Republic, raised in contrast to the current Third Republic of Poland, is "supposed to be the product of a moral revolution entailing a rebirth of religious and patriotic values, an uncompromising decommunization, and the strengthening of collective memory" (Brier 2009, p. 64). Already in 2005, the Polish conservative populist PiS party proposed a new constitution, to replace the 1997 one, which "clearly defines moral values and national traditions forming the axiological foundation of the Basic Law."[7] In right-wing versions of populism, then, the "inherent equality of all human beings" tends to be denied, and, in contrast, the political majority tends to be equated with a homogenous, ethno-nationalist

---

[6] Bernie Sanders, *On the issues*, 2016, on file with the author.
[7] Prawa i Sprawiedliwosci, *Konstytucja rzeczypospolitej Polskiej*, 2005, on file with the author.

people, which is to be prioritized in political action and constitutional norms. This entails that the liberal, universalist understanding of human rights is replaced by a strictly domestically understood view of rights, pertaining to, and emerging from, a distinctive political community.[8] In this regard, populist governments rhetorically act against foreign or domestic actors that either represent foreign interests or promote the rights of groups that such populists consider not part of the in-group (as, for instance, is frequently the case in their attitude toward human-rights NGOs).

From the above, it appears that the distinction of future-oriented versus past-oriented outlooks of populist parties is relatively easily superimposed onto a left-wing right-wing distinction. This is however not the case. Admittedly, in different ways, left-wing populist parties tend to be future-oriented, in the sense of seeking significant alternatives to the existing political-juridical order, for instance, by promoting ideas of participatory and deliberative democracy (as in the case of the Spanish Podemos, the Italian Five Star Movement, or the Greek Syriza party), or by actively promoting further supranational integration as an alternative to nation-states (as in the case of the Democracy in Europe Movement, DiEM25, Blokker 2019b). At the same time, however, left-wing populism includes important past-oriented dimensions, not least in terms of a return to experiences of the domestic welfare state or the retrieval of lost national sovereignty, in a form of "re-spatializing power" (García Agustín 2020, p. 34). Bernie Sanders, for instance, in his 2016 presidential campaign used the narrative of Franklin Delano Roosevelt and the New Deal as a story of "America lost" and to be rediscovered (Macaulay 2018, p. 183). Another case in point is the, in various ways original, Italian left-wing association *Patria e Costituzione* ("Fatherland and Constitution"), recently established by the left-wing politician Stefano Fassina, the main aim of which is to "retrieve the dignity of labour and popular sovereignty." For *Patria e Costituzione*, the return to national sovereignty is the only way to fight neoliberal globalism, and to contrast the "class warfare from above unleashed by the political and financial elites of the United States and Europe" (Damiani 2020, p. 54):

> The "United States of Europe" or the so-called "democratization of the European Union" are a conservative mirage of a neo-liberal order founded on the devaluation of work and on the hollowing out of constitutional democracy. The only way to restore social and political value to work is the revitalization of popular and national sovereignty: this means focusing on implementation of the principles of the Constitution of 1948, whose spirit of solidarity and socialist orientation is essential for rebuilding both the economic and social functions of the democratic state and a renovated form of mixed economy. This is the road to relaunching industry,

---

[8] In some cases, such as PiS in Poland, right-wing conservatism is combined with social and redistributive policies in favor of the Polish population. In other manifestations, in particular Fidesz in Hungary, authoritarian neoliberal policies are ardently pursued, in an attempt to build a "workfare state" (cf. Stubbs and Lendvai-Bainton 2020, p. 555).

generating full employment, governing the market and restoring to the citizens, through the parties, the power to impact the general direction of the country. What we need, therefore, is an authentic *constitutional patriotism*.[9]

The emphasis in left-wing populism of this kind is to retrieve economic sovereignty and enhance socio-economic equality, which is different from the ethno-nationalist-culturalist projects found on the right end of the political spectrum (as painstakingly explained in *Patria e Costituzione's* manifesto). At the same time, it is difficult to deny that an emphasis on "constitutional sovereignty," as in the case of *Patria e Costituzione*, and a rejection of supranational integration have close affinity with right-wing populism, which tends to strongly emphasize political, national sovereignty and explicitly deny the legitimacy of supranational juridical institutions (as, e.g., stated in the electoral program of the Italian *Lega* in 2018, which prioritizes the powers of the Italian Constitutional Court, as articulated in the 2017 electoral program of the German *Alternative fuer Deutschland*, or as emphasized in the statements of the Dutch *Platform voor de Democratie*). AfD stated in its 2017 program:

> The Constitution may not be changed, and no significant international treaty be entered into, without the direct approval of the German people. Vice versa, the people themselves should have the right to initiate changes to the Constitution. In particular, the relinquishing of national sovereignty to the EU and other institutions would be scotched without prior approval by the German people (AfD 2017, p. 8).

In terms of constitutional change, left- and right-wing populisms equally display a variety of forms of engagement. The example of *Patria e Costituzione* above is one of a "left-left" defense of the existing national-constitutional order, rather than change, but other left-wing forces in Italy do promote forms of democratic innovation through constitutional amendment, such as in the proposal of the Five Star Movement for the introduction of new direct-democratic and participatory instruments in the Italian Constitution. Equally in other cases of leftwing populism, such as that of the Greek Syriza, endorsements of constitutional reform have been made. The left-wing populist party Syriza, led by Alexis Tsipras (allied with the rightwing, populist party Independent Greeks, *ΑΝΕΛ*), started up a reform process in 2016, in which it inter alia sought to strengthen majoritarian and presidential institutions as well as of the instrument of referendums (Grigoriadis 2018, pp. 48–49). But the most elaborate examples can be found in the "neo-Bolivarian" constitution-making projects in Latin America, in particular in Venezuela, Colombia, and Ecuador. According to Bolivia's populist leader, Evo Morales, "all sectors [of the population] want a Constituent Assembly committed to refoundation, and not simply constitutional reform" (cited in: King 2013, p. 366). As Phoebe King has argued, in all three

---

[9] Patria e Costituzione, "Il Manifesto per la Sovranità Costituzionale," 2019. Available at: www.patriaecostituzione.it/manifesto-per-la-sovranita-costituzionale/; emphasis in original.

Latin American cases, the new constitutions were highly aspirational in their intent to lead to a "better future," and promoted a radical social-democratic agenda both in terms of popular participation and in terms of popular inclusion through the extension of social equality (King 2013, p. 367). The neo-Bolivarian constitutional projects were intended to radically change the existing order into the direction of "true democracy." In the European context, the most evident left-wing populist invocation of constituent power is that made by the transnational movement DiEM25' established by Yanis Varoufakis, the former Greek minister of finance in the Syriza government of 2015. It puts a strong emphasis on popular sovereignty and citizen participation. In DiEM25's manuscript "European Constituent Assembly," put forward in April 2018, it states that it will "show the corrupt elites that there is a European demos, and put democracy at the center of the European project." The mission is indeed to "take power back from the elites." DiEM25 employs a strategy of constituent power in its call for a constituent assembly, in which it claims that "Europe must abandon the already defunct phase of treaties towards a constitutional momentum: A common approach with a pan-European perspective is necessary." The project, which DiEM25 pursues with other left-oriented social movements and forces throughout Europe, is to draw up a new Constitution for Europe: "A constitutional text would serve as a fundament that defines a new sovereign political entity, a new legitimate community of equals, a framework from which law and rights stem. The Constitution, elaborated by the peoples of Europe, would become the source of legitimacy and sovereignty. It will be the beginning of a new age: [T]he age of 'We, the People of Europe!'" (DiEM25, A Manifesto for Democratising Europe;[10] Panayotu 2017, p. 5).

The dimension of reformist or constituent power is equally relevant for right-wing populism. As mentioned above, Geert Wilders of the Dutch Partij voor de Vrijheid (the Freedom Party) argued in 2005 in favor of the amendment of Article 1 of the Dutch Constitution, which refers to freedom of expression and non-discrimination, so that it would refer to the "dominant culture" of the Netherlands, the Judeo-Christian tradition and humanism. Marine Le Pen elaborated a more extensive set of constitutional reforms in a separate document, entitled "La Révision Constitutionnelle Que Je Propose Aux Français Par Référendum," during the presidential campaign of 2017, which contained the following opening lines:

> The institutions of our country, organized by the Constitution of October 4, 1958, have been distorted by successive constitutional reforms. In addition, their operation has been deeply disturbed by the ongoing federal and anti-democratic development of the European Union. Today, our institutions no longer guarantee the fundamental principles for which they were built: sovereignty of the people is regularly trampled on, Democracy is weakened and our rulers no longer defend

---

[10] DiEM25 (2016). "A Manifesto for Democratising Europe," available at: https://diem25.org/manifesto-long/.

the national interest. The institutional reforms that I propose to you will require for the larger part constitutional amendment. ... My intention is not to upset the organization or the political order in France, but to return to the original spirit of our Constitution, by strengthening its democratic character considerably. All the reforms presented in this document have the same objective: to give back to our country the institutional instruments to defend its sovereignty, its identity, its prosperity and true Democracy.[11]

Le Pen's project is clearly more comprehensive, and has affinity with more radical, constituent projects, such as in the case of Hungary. Not only was the post-1989 Hungarian Constitution replaced by the new Fundamental Law in 2011, but constituent power has continued to be exercised in terms of a series of comprehensive amendments, so far seven in total. In the Hungarian case, the populist government that has continuously been in power since 2010 has arguably managed to install a veritable populist regime.

A final significant dimension to populism is related to populist understandings of a relevant political community, mostly between views that prioritize the national (or regional) community and those that entertain some form of transnational or cosmopolitan outlook. Generally, populism is equated with nationalist views and definitions of the people, but it has become clear that there are significant examples of transnational populism, in which views of the political community tend to transcend the national dimension (Moffitt 2017, pp. 409–410; De Cleen et al. 2020; Blokker 2019b). The dimension of relevant political community seems to portray a relatively clear-cut distinction between left- and right-wing versions: whereas on the right, it is difficult to identify any cosmopolitan position, on the left one finds both more nationalist and more internationalist, and even cosmopolitan-oriented approaches of populism. The latter tend to frame friend-enemy distinctions in terms of socio-economic class terms, criticizing global capitalist elites for exploiting local working classes, while indicating – in the cosmopolitan version – transnational solutions to neoliberal capitalist arrangements (cf. Tushnet 2018c, p. 648; García Agustín 2020).

The different identifications of political communities by left- and right-wing populists has important implications for constitutional views. Left-wing, cosmopolitan populists approach what they understand as the problem of global, neoliberal capitalism from a perspective of the necessity of a transnational alternative (as in the case of the aforementioned transnational movement DiEM25, or in some ways also in the Latin American, "neo-Bolivarian" revolutions and calls for a "Fifth International"), which includes calls for constitutionalization beyond the nation-state. Right-wing populists certainly engage in international interaction and networking, but the latter tends to be confined to forms of a "Populist International," which so far, at least in

---

[11] Marine Le Pen, "La Révision Constitutionnelle Que Je Propose Aux Français Par Référendum," 2017, on file with the author.

the context of Europe, has not led to extensive forms of mobilization around constitutional ideas.[12]

CONCLUDING REMARKS

I have argued in the chapter that the relation between constitutionalism and populism cannot be reduced to a purely antithetical one. A more complex relation between constitutionalism and populism is due to the pluralist dimensions to both: constitutionalism consists of a historical project, and as such is, and has been, contested by contender positions on the role of constitutions and the understanding of constitutionalism as a form of governance. Populist forces tend to be critical of the postwar hegemony of legal constitutionalism, and articulate forms of critique that resonate in some ways with contending views of constitutionalism, such as political, communitarian, or democratic positions. Varieties of populism are further the result of different populist positions on core dimensions of populism, which I have suggested to include: inclusionary versus exclusionary forms of populism; an orientation toward the past or toward the future; a reformist or radical orientation; and, finally, definitions of the political community in national or more cosmopolitan terms. As becomes clear from a number of examples in the last part of the chapter, which discusses left- and right-wing manifestations of populism, significant differences exist with regard to populist attitudes toward constitutional law, constitutionalism, and rights, differences which cannot be reduced to either a left- or a right-wing stance. The best way forward in analyses of the relation between constitutionalism and populism is that suggested by Bugaric and Tushnet, that is, an empirical-comparative approach, which "must be highly sensitive to context" (Bugaric and Tushnet 2021).

RECOMMENDED READING

Alterio, A. M. (2019). Reactive vs structural approach: A public law response to populism. *Global Constitutionalism*, 8 (2), 270–296.
Arato, A. (2019). Populism, Constitutional Courts, and Civil Society. In C. Landfried, ed., *Judicial power: how constitutional courts affect political transformations*. Cambridge: Cambridge University Press, pp. 318–341.
Blokker, P. (2018). Populist constitutionalism. In C. de la Torre, ed., *Routledge handbook of global populism*, London/New York: Routledge.

---

[12] It has to be admitted, though, that some right-wing intellectuals do make suggestions into such a direction, as in the calls for "Europe of the Peoples," and, more importantly, a "Charter of the Rights of the Peoples of Europe" (Becchi 2019, pp. 16, 18–9). As expressed in Art. 1 of this proposed Charter, the intent is clearly "international" and not "cosmopolitan": "Art. 1 The European peoples recognize each other reciprocally as free and equal. The European peoples are the holders of their own rights, and as such autonomous and independent in relation to those [rights] attributed by international law to the states in which they live and to the individuals who make up these states" (p. 31).

Blokker, P. (2019a). Populism as a constitutional project. *International Journal of Constitutional Law*, 17 (2), 536–553.

Bugaric, B. & Tushnet, M. (2021). Populism and constitutionalism: an essay on definitions and their implications, *Cardozo Law Review*, 42 (6), pp. 2345–2393.

Corrias, L. (2016). Populism in a Constitutional Key: Constituent Power, Popular Sovereignty and Constitutional Identity. *European Constitutional Law Review*, 12 (6), 6–26.

Kaltwasser, C. R. (2013). Populism vs. Constitutionalism? Comparative Perspectives on Contemporary Western Europe, Latin America, and the United States. The Foundation for Law, Justice and Society Policy Brief.

Landau, D. (2018). Populist Constitutions. *University of Chicago Law Review*, 85 (2), 521–543.

Müller, J.-W. (2018). Populism and Constitutionalism. In C. R. Kaltwasser et al., eds., *The Oxford Handbook of Populism*. Oxford: Oxford University Press, 590–606.

Nash, K. (2016). Politicising Human Rights in Europe: Challenges to Legal Constitutionalism From the Left and the Right. *International Journal of Human Rights*, 20 (8), 1295–1308.

Oklopcic, Z. (2019). Imagined ideologies: Populist figures, liberalist projections, and the horizons of constitutionalism. *German Law Journal*, 20 (2), 201–224.

Scheppele, K. L. (2019). The opportunism of populists and the defense of constitutional liberalism. *German Law Journal*, 20 (3), 314–331.

Thio, L.-A. (2012). Constitutionalism in Illiberal Polities. In M. Rosenfeld & A. Sajó, eds., *The Oxford Handbook of Comparative Constitutional Law*. Oxford: Oxford University Press, pp. 133–152.

Thornhill, C. (2020). Constitutionalism and populism: national political integration and global legal integration. *International Theory*, 12 (1), 1–32.

Walker, N. (2019). Populism and constitutional tension. *International Journal of Constitutional Law*, 17 (2), 515–535.

58

Climate Change

Jocelyn Stacey[*]

Climate change, it is often said, is the greatest challenge of our time. It is difficult to adequately capture the full scale of biophysical and social impacts unfolding in our climate disrupted world. No humans have ever lived on a planet as hot as ours now is (IPCC 2018, p. 4). Climate breakdown has dramatically visible impacts in the forms of hurricanes, floods, and fires that are more intense and more frequent than in the past. Some impacts are similarly tragic but quieter: the heat waves that exact a growing death toll, the bleached coral reefs, the creeping sea-level rise that threatens coastal cities and ecosystems. Some of its impacts are slower moving and profound: altering the planet's food systems, and hastening the sixth mass extinction. While the worst of these impacts may still be preventable through collective human action, they threaten in some manner every living creature on the planet. The deep injustice of climate change, however, is that those who have contributed least to the problem stand to suffer the most. Children and future generations, Indigenous Peoples, non-human species, those living in poverty around the world (whose contribution to greenhouse gas emissions is dwarfed by the carbon footprints of wealthy individuals and nations) are all disproportionately harmed by climate change.

The definitive statement of our knowledge of climate change has long been the reporting by the Intergovernmental Panel on Climate Change (IPCC). Since 1990 the IPCC has reported the scientific consensus that climate change is occurring, it is human-caused, and it will have significant impacts on the planet (IPCC 1990). In the fall of 2018, the IPCC issued a special report on *Global Warming of 1.5°C*, which detailed the anticipated catastrophic impacts of exceeding 1.5°C (IPCC 2018, p. 8). Despite international commitments "[h]olding the increase in global average temperature to well below 2°C above pre-industrial levels and pursuing efforts to limit the temperature increase to 1.5°C" (*Paris Agreement*, Article 2(1)(a)), current estimates have the planet on track for 3.5–4°C of warming by the end of the century

---

[*] Many thanks to Natasha Affolder and Hoi Kong for their helpful feedback on an early draft of this chapter. Thanks very much to the editors for their detailed feedback and to Imalka Nilmalgoda, Allard Law JD 2021 for her excellent research assistance. All errors remain my own.

(UNEP 2019a). Under this projected trajectory, impacts are likely to be truly catastrophic due to the likely transgression of global tipping points and cascading climate impacts (Lenton et al. 2019).

The scale of the climate crisis makes it difficult to know where to begin. It is an all-encompassing, boundary-shattering global phenomenon with existential implications. Writing about one's personal capacity to process the profundity of climate change, novelist James Bradley, observes, "we manage not to think about it, or when we do only briefly or glancingly. …. This inability to discuss the question is the expression of a larger erasure, a desire not to engage with the conflagration that is already engulfing our world" (Bradley 2019).

This chapter represents an attempt to face up to the challenge of climate change from the perspective of constitutional theory. It takes seriously the discourse of "climate emergency" and it argues that emergency is a theoretically defensible framing of the problem. It argues that the emergency framing directs us to a theory of constitutionalism that is up to the task. This is an ambitious goal for a short chapter, but a necessary and productive one. As we will see, engagements between constitutional theory and climate change have thus far been targeted and disparate. By drawing out the strengths and gaps in these existing literatures, we can situate these debates in an overarching theoretical framework and spark new scholarly conversations about the role of constitutional theory in a climate disrupted world.

This chapter begins by introducing existing scholarly conversations that squarely address the relationship between constitutionalism and climate change in three areas: rule of law, rights, and federalism. It then turns to its main argument: the climate emergency is a theoretically defensible and productive understanding of our planetary reality and a constitutional theory based on the requirement of public justification answers the challenge of how the climate emergency can be governed by law.

I RULE OF LAW, RIGHTS, FEDERALISM, AND CLIMATE CHANGE

As climate change engulfs our world, it leaves little untouched, including constitutions and constitutional theory. States worldwide have begun to incorporate climate change into constitutional text and legal literature has followed these developments (May and Daly 2019). However, climate change is virtually absent from existing debates that are self-described as constitutional theory. Conversely, the literatures that do engage questions of constitutional theory in relation to climate change do not tend to identify as such.

This part turns to pockets of existing scholarship to identify key debates about how states are constitutionally constrained in how they address climate change. It does so for two purposes. First, it shows that while there are notable direct engagements between climate change and constitutional theory, these have been targeted and disparate. While not exactly "brief and glancing" in the words of Bradley above, these engagements are limited in how they have addressed the challenges that climate change poses for constitutional theory. However, these debates do reveal important insights and gaps that can inform broader constitutional theorizing. Thus, the second purpose of this section is to extract those core insights and gaps to harness for future theorizing.

This is necessarily a partial sketch of the universe of scholarship that addresses the plurality of intersections between climate change and constitutional theory. As Affolder writes about climate law, "[w]hen the relevant literatures are this vast and the legal developments so fast-moving, any commentary is partial, possibly outdated, and ignorant of important new developments and literatures" (2019, p. 5). Moreover, the all-encompassing nature of climate change means that law and scholarship labelled as climate change "may not even be where the action is or needs to be." (Affolder 2021, p. 10 citing to Rolfe 2010; Setzer & Vanhala 2019). When writing about climate change "we are challenged to see what we have and to imagine what we want" (Editors *Climate Law* 2010, p. 1). I am mindful of these limits and am transparent about the scope of this part.

This chapter takes constitutional theory to mean the elaboration of basic assumptions about constitutional order as well as arguments "to justify a set of prescriptions about how certain controversial constitutional issues should be decided" (D. Strauss 1999, p. 582). Undoubtedly, each chapter in this text has important implications for climate change whether in relation to its causes or potential responses. Here, however, I address three constitutional concepts: the rule of law, rights, and federalism. In this part, I focus on five bodies of literature that most directly address matters of constitutional theory. Three literatures – rule of law for nature, environmental constitutionalism, and law in the Anthropocene – speak principally to the rule of law. Climate law literature closely follows climate rights litigation. Climate governance literature addresses federalism. Within these literatures, the experiences of Anglo-American and common law jurisdictions receive significant attention and international human rights law plays an influential role. These literatures are methodologically diverse and each places a different emphasis on critique, reform, and description.

Rule of Law

The rule of law is "an essentially contested concept" about which there are enduring debates (Waldron 2002). At the core of this concept, however, is the commitment to a system of laws which apply equally to all, including those who exercise public power. Its concerns are preventing and responding to the exercise of arbitrary public power.

The strength of the literatures that engage with the rule of law from the perspective of climate change is the fundamental nature of the critique that they present to conventional western conceptions of the rule of law. Within these literatures, climate change is understood, not as the narrow policy problem of reducing greenhouse gas emissions, but rather as part of a set of intertwined social and ecological failures. This set of intertwined challenges is captured squarely by those who write on law in the Anthropocene, the Anthropocene being the description of our present geological epoch in which human activity is the dominant force of global change (Crutzen 2006). These scholars argue that the Anthropocene "is more than simply a new term to describe global environmental decline.... Instead, the Anthropocene foregrounds the reality of the deeply connected human-nature relationship." (Stephens 2019, p. 123). Taken as such, the Anthropocene presents fundamental challenges for law and regulation (Jaria-Manzano & Borràs 2019). Law can no longer presume that nature is either an object that can be set aside for protection nor a resource for endless exploitation (Natarajan and Khoday 2014). Climate change impresses upon us the reality of the ecological truism that everything is connected.

These literatures critique the failure of both the theory and practice of the rule of law. From the perspective of these literatures, conventional definitions of the rule of law exemplify the problem of the human-nature divide and are "structurally complicit" in climate change (Grear 2014; see also Kotzé 2016; Humphreys 2014). They point out that the ultimate constraints on the exercise of public power are ecological limits, which are absent from conventional western notions of the rule of law (Jaria-Manzano & Borràs 2019; Cullinan 2011). And they highlight the inherent arbitrariness of public decision-making that does not reflect ecological reality. These literatures elaborate ideals of climate justice, which respond to the reality that the effects of this arbitrary decision-making are disproportionately borne by marginalized communities and future generations. Some scholars also argue that the state's legal obligations extend to the natural world, which has its own inherent value that ought to be recognized through legal subjectivity.

The responses offered by these critics reflect the boundary-shattering phenomenon of climate change. They argue for radically-inclusive notions of the rule of law: inclusive of nature as legal subject and rights-bearer (Voigt 2013), inclusive of future generations of humans (Lewis 2018), and inclusive of new substantive content of the rule of law drawn from ecological principles (Cullinan 2011; Filguiera & Mason 2011; Burdon 2011), and applied at the global scale in the form of global constitutionalism (Kotzé 2016). For instance, many scholars argue that the rule of law ought to incorporate the principle of ecological sustainability. Sourced from science, Indigenous knowledge, and commitments expressed in domestic and international laws, the principle of ecological sustainability seeks to ensure that the planet retains its life-sustaining capacity (Collins and Sossin 2019; Bosselman 2013). As a legal principle, ecological sustainability counsels self-restraint, humility, and cooperation (Bosselman 2013; Jaria-Manzano 2019). On this view, understanding ecological sustainability as an inherent feature of the rule of law is one step toward rectifying the division between human and nature that many scholars view as the underlying problematic in the Anthropocene.

Importantly, these literatures do not reject the rule of law as fundamental constitutional concept. They seek a recommitment to it in practice (UNEP 2019b, Kotzé 2018, Robinson 2014, Kotzé 2012) and, as described above, they seek a more expansive commitment to formal equality that constrains the exercise of (unsustainable) public power. Speaking about the challenge for international environmental law in the Anthropocene, Stephens writes that "a central conundrum will be how to maintain [an] ethical and principled core that serves principles of ecological integrity, fairness and justice, and not to embrace a 'survivalist' ethic which discards fundamental values in service to wholly instrumentalist and utilitarian objectives" (2019, p. 137). Thus, these critical literatures do not advocate for abandoning the rule of law project, but rather reimagining and reinvigorating it in response to compounding ecological and climate crises.

The strength of these literatures is echoed in the introspection undertaken by scholars who identify the need to take a hard look at the failures of environmental and international law (e.g., Stephens 2019; Natarajan and Khoday 2014). The limitation of these literatures is that they exist as separated pockets of critique in the fields of environmental and international environmental law. To achieve the aims of fundamental reorientation envisioned by these scholars, their insights need to be in conversation with scholarship that spans the entire legal spectrum (Mitchell 2018). As we will see in Part 2, the climate emergency, understood *as emergency*, can help bridge these scholarly conversations.

Rights

Climate law scholarship canvasses the potential for constitutional rights and rights-based litigation to shape responses to climate. Tracking the "rights-turn" and ascendency of climate rights litigation, this literature addresses the potential for rights recognition and enforcement as a response to climate change (Setzer & Vanhala 2019; Peel & Osofosky 2018).[1] The strength of this literature is its success in making the impacts of climate change visible and concrete within a familiar legal frame (Jodoin et al. 2020). Scholars expertly advocate for the extension of doctrinal concepts and adaptation of institutional roles to the challenge of climate change. However, the limit of this literature, as we will see, is its focus on high-profile cases and the tendency to lump together all rights-based climate litigation as a transnational phenomenon.

The 2006 Inuit Circumpolar Conference (ICC) petition to the Inter-American Commission on Human Rights is credited with catalyzing the 'rights turn' in climate

---

[1] The focus of much climate rights literature is the potential for rights protection for vulnerable groups; however, critical and TWAIL perspectives on the limits of rights are crucial as well: See, e.g., Natarajan 2015.

litigation (Lewis 2018; Peel & Osofsky 2018). Speaking powerfully about the petition, Sheila Watt-Cloutier stated:

> "Climate change is not about bureaucrats scurrying around. It is about families, parents, children, and the lives we lead in our communities in the broader environment. We have to regain this perspective if climate change is to be stopped. Inuit understand these connections because we remain a people of the land, ice, and snow." (Osofsky 2007)

The ICC framed its claim as violations of the rights to life, health, physical integrity, use and enjoy traditional lands, and personal property (Inuit Circumpolar Conference 2005). The petition was a powerful early example of the human rights dimensions of climate change.

Though the Commission declined to adjudicate the claim, the ICC petition garnered significant academic attention. Since then, climate rights literature has focused on elucidating the relationship between human rights, environmental rights, and climatic harms (Humphreys 2010; Knox 2009), and identifying the myriad ways in which climate change amplifies ongoing rights violations around the world: for example, violations of rights to life, health, equality, property, water, and food security (Sinden 2019; Lewis 2018).

More specifically, climate law scholarship tracks the proliferation of climate litigation worldwide (Setzer & Vanhala 2019)[2] and seeks to make sense of its impact on climate governance (Jodoin et al. 2020; Peel & Osofsky 2018; Peel & Osofsky 2015; Lin 2012; Boyd 2011), public perception (Nosek 2018; Weaver & Kysar 2017), and the communities seeking judicial relief (May & Daly 2019). Take for instance, the high-profile and complex *Juliana* litigation in the United States, a lawsuit filed by 21 youth plaintiffs who allege that the federal government's ongoing actions to promote the fossil fuel industry violates the public trust doctrine and the youth plaintiffs' federally protected constitutional rights to life, liberty, property, and equal protection (Our Children's Trust). The lawsuit generated the remarkable finding by the Oregon District Court "that the right to a climate system capable of sustaining human life is fundamental to a free and ordered society."[3] In relation to this type of climate litigation, scholars have sought to identify and dispel potential doctrinal barriers, for example, justiciability and causation (Heinzerling 2019; Peel & Osofsky 2018; Blum & Wood 2017; Kysar & Weaver 2017) and have explored the potential and limits of the judicial role in this sphere (Burgers 2020; Barritt & Sediti 2019). Scholars note that some of the most promising climate rights litigation is emerging from the Global South where climate vulnerability is already acutely felt and judicial remedies are more creative (Peel and Lin 2019; Barritt & Sediti 2019).

---

[2] The Sabin Centre for Climate Change Law at Columbia Law School maintains a database: http://climatecasechart.com.
[3] *Juliana v United States*, 217 F. Suppl. 3d 1224, 1250 (D. Or. 2016).

Climate law scholarship has taken on the difficult task of making sense of the vast and rapidly expanding practice of climate litigation. These cases are situated in different legal traditions, engage every scale of legal system (from subnational to international), and mix-and-match private and public law causes of action. Scholarship that addresses this eclectic mix often misses detailed attention to the specifics of constitutional interpretation, though good examples certainly exist (e.g., Chalifour 2015). At the same time, this scholarship focuses on the highly visible spaces of climate law and, in particular, a small number of high-profile cases that are viewed as filled with positive potential for climate action (Affolder 2021 Setzer & Vanhala 2019; Bouwer 2018). Showcasing these prominent examples may come at the expense of elucidating the ways in which constitutional text, doctrine, and norms perpetuate the climate crisis by, for instance, protecting corporate disinformation campaigns (Nosek 2018; Weinstein 2018) or criminalizing Indigenous land and water defenders (Spiegel 2021).

Federalism

Climate governance literature addresses intergovernmental dynamics of climate law and policy in federal jurisdictions. As we see below, the strength of this body of literature is its attention to detailed analysis that captures the nuance, complexity, and movement of climate law and policy within states. The limitation of this literature, however, is the narrow frame which it places on climate law, focusing predominantly on "end-of-the-pipe" measures such as emissions standards and carbon pricing. While this literature is attentive to federalism's underlying tension between unity and diversity, its narrow frame misses deeper questions about sovereignty and state stability.

Much climate governance literature works from the background assumption, emerging from studies of the US, Canada, and Australia, that the federal government is in the best position to effectuate environmental and climate policy (Rabe 2011; Thomson & Arroyo 2011). On this view, federalism is presumed to act as a barrier to needed climate action. The arguments for this are familiar to environmental scholars: sub-national pollution standard-setting is said to be more vulnerable to industry and union pressure, and there exists a credible threat of industry and commerce exiting the subnational jurisdiction for another with weaker environmental regulation (Wood et al. 2010; Stewart 1977; cf Schreurs 2008). Empirical research lends some support to these arguments that subnational jurisdictions act as barriers to effective climate mitigation (Steurer et al. 2020; Harrison 2013).

Real-world dynamics between national and sub-national units are more complex. Climate governance scholars have sought to capture this complexity through a number of descriptors: compensatory, diagonal, iterative, contested, and cooperative federalism (Derthick 2010; Osofosky 2011; Carlson 2008; Rabe 2011; Kaswan 2008; Thomson and Arroyo 2011). All agree that, whatever its form, effective climate mitigation requires action by all levels of government and cooperation within federations (e.g., Brown 2012; Derthick 2010; Kaswan 2008). This scholarship tracks the climate mitigation initiatives of subnational jurisdictions, their influence on federal policy, and is always mindful of the need to guard against federal overreach.

The limited scope of this body of work is that it focuses on design without investigating prior questions of sovereignty or the continued existence of the federation (Choudry and Hume 2011). This lack of deeper theoretical inquiry perhaps explains the absence of Indigenous jurisdiction from federalism literature, despite the profound impacts of climate change on Indigenous Peoples (Whyte 2017) and the ongoing exercise of Indigenous authority over lands, waters, and communities. Yet, in settler federations, the impact of climate change on Indigenous Peoples tends to be construed as a rights issue rather than an issue of governance or jurisdiction.

Existing climate law scholarship has engaged with constitutional theory in targeted ways. In this part we have seen where this literature has excelled in critique, reform, and description of legal responses to climate change. We have also seen that the targeted nature of these pockets of scholarship leave gaps unexplored. We now turn to the question of how constitutional theory might engage more systematically with the profound challenge of climate change.

II THE CLIMATE EMERGENCY AND CONSTITUTIONAL THEORY

This part argues that the discourse of "climate emergency" offers a useful entry point for framing the role of constitutional theory in relation to climate change. It first makes the case that climate change constitutes an emergency. It then defends a theory of constitutionalism premised on the requirement of public justification that can be sustained even during an emergency and thus is an appropriate theory of constitutionalism for a climate-disrupted world. While this theory has been articulated and defended more fully elsewhere (Stacey 2018; Dyzenhaus 2006a), this part shows how a theory of public justification incorporates the strengths of the existing literatures discussed above while also charting new pathways for addressing the gaps and limitations.

The Climate Emergency

Emergencies are generally understood to be sudden, extreme events that threaten the state and which demand immediate, coordinated, and effective state action in response. Within legal and political theory, emergencies are conceptualized as instances which seem to demand departure from ordinary rule-of-law requirements in order to effect exceptional emergency powers. For instance, John Locke understood prerogative power as the reserve of discretionary power that could be drawn upon in times of urgent and unforeseen emergency (Locke 1764, §§159–161).

Rossiter, and others, identify the Roman constitutional dictatorship as a model of emergency power that provides for flexible emergency measures while remaining subject to some separate and minimal legal constraints (Rossiter 2002; Gross and Aolain 2006).[4] At the furthest extreme, Carl Schmitt, the controversial Nazi legal theorist, argued that the exception (the emergency) could not be governed by law (Schmitt 1985), an argument that has been seriously mooted since the 9/11 terrorist attacks (Posner and Vermeule 2010; Agamben 2005).

Emergencies place constitutionalism under strain. In theory, the Schmittian claim that "sovereign is he who decides on the exception" reveals the political – not legal – nature of the constitution (Schmitt 1985 [1922]; Dyzenhaus 2006a). In practice, Schmitt's claim finds some traction in the historical record which provides countless instances of the executive's use of exceptional measures which undermine human rights (through, e.g., indefinite detention, torture, forcible removal from lands) and which go largely unchecked by legislative or judicial branches. Within constitutional theory, wartime represents the paradigmatic case of the use of emergency powers to depart from – or circumvent – constitutional constraints, but the use of emergency powers to respond to insurrection, economic crisis, or natural disasters are all commonplace (Loevy 2016, Scheppele 2005). The normalcy of emergency has led many scholars to observe that the "contemporary danger [is not] a space beyond law, but the expansion of legally authorized zones of discretionary executive power." (Zuckerman 2006). The response, as we see below, is to resist the hollowing out of such legal authorization to a thin veneer of formalism and rather to insist that rule by law implies rule of law in a substantive sense (Dyzenhaus 2006a).

The phrase "climate emergency" emerged as a way of making sense of the increasingly worrying projections by the IPCC and others which indicate that emissions are on track for widespread catastrophe (IPCC 2018). In 2020, relying on a suite of climate vital signs that extends beyond emissions (e.g., growing livestock populations, tree cover loss), over 11,000 scientists concluded "clearly and unequivocally that planet Earth is facing a climate emergency" (Ripple et al. 2020).

Commentators use the framing of the climate emergency to draw on the history of wartime efforts that mobilized swiftly and dramatically transformed the economy (Seth Klein 2020; Stiglitz 2019). Now comparisons between the climate emergency and the COVID-19 pandemic seem more apt (Seth Klein 2020). These commentators argue for a powerful state, one that acts efficiently and perhaps exceptionally to radically decarbonize society to protect those most vulnerable to climate harms. These calls are reflected, in some sense, in the thousands of jurisdictions worldwide which have issued declarations of climate emergency with commitments to net-zero emissions (Climate Emergency Declaration). In this narrative, the disruptive and

---

[4] Emergency powers also feature prominently in Latin American constitutional law scholarship, which also points to the limits of Anglo-American and European scholarship: Gonzalez-Jacome (2011).

energizing nature of the emergency serves to mobilize progressive action to slow climate breakdown and mitigate its worst effects.

The climate emergency is an uncomfortable fit with the concept of emergency as portrayed in constitutional theory (Stacey 2022). Climate change is not sudden in the way an earthquake, for example, is sudden. The greenhouse effect that drives climate change has been known since at least 1896 and national governments have been aware of the need to curb anthropogenic emissions since at least the 1970s. Human and ecological communities have been experiencing impacts associated with climate change for decades, with calls for systemic action going largely unheeded. It is possible, for example, for small island states to plan in accordance with law their migration in anticipation of inundation from rising sea levels. Moreover, emergencies are typically considered temporary disruptions in which emergency powers play a role in preserving the possibility of a return to normal. In contrast, climate change demands, not temporary measures, but rather a transformative response away from carbon-intensive systems of production and ways of life.

Despite these potential objections, it is worth taking seriously this framing of climate emergency from the perspective of constitutional theory. Climate change is a "legally disruptive" phenomenon (Fisher et al. 2017) and, with appropriate nuance, we can see how the climate emergency can both disrupt and illuminate constitutional theory.

Understood as an emergency, climate change is not simply the technological or political challenge of rapid decarbonization. Rather it "is part of a family of interlocking problems ... all planetary in scope and all speaking to the fact of an overall ecological overshoot on the part of humanity" (Chakrabarty 2016, p. 380). Climate change is perhaps the most notorious member of this family in how it calls our attention to humanity's inextricable dependence on the complex, dynamic, living relationships that make up our planet. These relationships – the webbing of human and non-human life connected through the systems that sustain us all – form complex systems (Holling and Gunderson 2002). The dynamics of complex systems are difficult to reliably predict. Relationships are non-linear, timeframes are long, and the probability of extreme events is surprisingly high and cannot be discounted in advance (Underdal 2010). It is not only that our understanding of environmental and climate issues is constantly evolving, but also that the issues themselves are evolving too. Moreover, the most extreme events are irreversible and existential: e.g., catastrophic floods and wildfires, destruction of ecosystems and traditional ways of life, and species extinction. Complexity is irreducible and our vulnerability to catastrophic environmental harm is omnipresent (Jasanoff 2003). The constitutional concept that responds to this combination of existential and epistemic challenges is the emergency.

More specifically, climate breakdown contains the possibility of extreme and existential threats that constitute emergencies in the conventional sense. Each instance of severe wildfire, deadly heat wave, record-shattering hurricane or flood, consistent with projections in a climate-disrupted world, will require resort to urgent, emergency measures in order to protect individuals and communities. The use of these emergency powers brings all the risks of executive aggrandizement and restrictions on civil liberties that attract the concern of constitutional theorists.

While many of these climate impacts are foreseeable in a general sense, the specific and local manifestation of climate impacts is and will remain uncertain in light of the changing nature of the problem (Mehta et al. 2019; IPCC 2014, p. 9). As the planet crosses ecological thresholds and tipping points, cascading disasters will require new responses that account for unforeseen intersecting hazards.[5] We know now to expect from climate change, to some extent, the unexpected. This is consistent with our understanding of complex systems. It means that lawmakers face the ever-present possibility of catastrophic climate harm and the inability to reliably know in advance which specific decisions will precipitate this harm.

Climate change also disrupts how law confronts questions of time, requiring consideration of "deep pasts and deep futures" (Chakrabarty 2016, p. 380). The climate emergency engages the same enduring "anxiety about change versus continuity" that dominates theoretical debates about emergencies (Loevy 2016, p. 281). Climate change is not a "toggle switch" that is triggered on or off through a declaration of a state of emergency (Scheppele 2005, p. 838). It is rather an emergency that exposes all the complexity and dynamism contained in the real-world operation of emergency powers (Loevy 2016).

Framing climate change as an emergency is thus defensible at a theoretical level. Moreover, understanding climate change as an emergency, in theoretical terms, means that it is more than the accumulation of individual declarations of emergency that respond to the most acute climate impacts. Climate emergency presents an entry point for conceptualizing the constitutional relationship between humans and our environment. As an encompassing theoretical concept, it requires a theory of constitutionalism that is equally comprehensive. Because we are faced with the ever-present possibility of climate disaster, with both existential and unpredictable features, we need a theory of constitutionalism that holds even (and perhaps especially) in the extreme case.

The climate emergency is attractive to those seeking transformative change in the state, whether oriented toward climate justice or eco-fascism (Mann and Wainwright 2018). But the argument here is not an invitation or a license for the exercise of arbitrary power. It is rather a challenge for constitutional theory to explain how, when faced with unprecedented climate and ecological breakdown, the state can nonetheless operate with legal and democratic authority. We will now see that the theory of public justification responds to this challenge. Moreover, the theory of public justification embraces the strengths of existing literature on climate change and constitutional theory, while also responding to its limitations.

---

[5] If this seems extreme, consider that in 2020 the United States, Cambodia, and Vietnam all experienced catastrophic wildfires or floods at the same time as the COVID-19 pandemic.

Responding to the Climate Emergency

David Dyzenhaus articulates a constitutional theory of public justification and defends this theory against Schmitt's challenge to show that, even in the face of exception, the state can still be governed by law (Dyzenhaus 2006a). Dyzenhaus's theory of constitutionalism requires the exercise of public authority to be publicly justified on the basis of deep-seated constitutional principles (e.g., fairness and reasonableness). On this view, all institutions of the state participate in the "rule-of-law project" working to hold each other to account to ensure decisions are publicly justified (Dyzenhaus 2006a). For instance, where courts have historically failed to demand robust justification of the executive in emergencies, he argues creative institutional design in the administrative state may address this failure.

Dyzenhaus argues that the rule *of* law must follow rule *by* law. He observes that public officials are subject to the "compulsion of legality"; that is, they are compelled to claim to act with legal authorization (rule by law) in order to be perceived as acting with legitimacy (Dyzenhaus 2012b). Dyzenhaus continues:

> "the compulsion of legality can set in motion two very different cycles of legality. In one virtuous cycle, the institutions of legal order cooperate in devising controls on public actors that ensure that their decisions comply with the principle of legality, understood as a substantive conception of the rule of law [public justification]. In the other cycle, the content of legality is understood in an ever more formal or vacuous manner, resulting in the mere appearance or even the pretence of legality. Here, the compulsion of legality results in the subversion of constitutionalism." (Dyzenhaus 2012b, p. 452)

The theory of public justification posits that the emergency is a normal and predictable part of the constitutional order, one in which claims of legal authority will be made, contested, defended, rejected, or revised. The executive can implement novel emergency measures to respond to an unforeseen situation, but in so doing must participate in the everyday rule-of-law project with the same requirement of public justification as in non-emergency times.

This theory of public justification focuses on the ultimate end of the rule of law: protecting and facilitating the responsible agency of those subject to law. I understand responsible agency as the recognition of one's capacity for purposive action and one's responsibility to respect others as such (Stacey 2018; Rundle 2012). Core constitutional principles such as fairness and reasonableness mean that decision-makers must always have within their contemplation the agency of those affected by the exercise of public authority. The responsible agency of legal subjects is further realized through mechanisms for contestation and demanding adequate public justification (Rundle 2012).

These principles are constitutional because they are constitutive of legal authority. On this view, the rule of law is not a system of commands, but rather an ongoing commitment to a reciprocal relationship between lawmaker and legal subject that is realized through public justification (Dyzenhaus, 1998b; Fuller 1969). Unlike any specific text (which could be suspended or amended in an emergency), compliance with these principles is non-derogable because they flow "from the constitutional nature of the democratic state with its inherent commitment to the rule of law." (Dyzenhaus 2012b, p. 455) To derogate from the requirement to publicly justify the exercise of public authority on the basis of core commitments is to cede the claim to act with legal authority (Dyzenhaus 2006a).

The problem, Dyzenhaus argues, with other theories of emergency powers is that they rest on a dualism that abandons the legal and moral resources needed to recover legality from the exception (Dyzenhaus 2006a). When emergency powers are conceived of as sitting outside constitutional order, legal order hinges on political decision about when legal order will be suspended and restored. Alternatively, accommodative theories of emergencies posit that emergency powers can be compliant with the rule of law through prior legislative or constitutional authorization of emergency. But this creates a substantive/procedural legal dualism in which "the rule of law is reduced to a regime of delegations of authority in which the constraints are purely formal" (Dyzenhaus 2012b, p. 444).

I have argued in depth elsewhere that Schmitt's challenge and Dyzenhaus's public justification response can explain what the rule of law requires of environmental decisions (Stacey 2018). It helps illuminate how and why environmental law is often perceived as somehow exceptional or extra-legal. Philippopoulous-Mihalopoulos explains, "[t]he inability of environmental law to deliver such certainty as adequately as other legal branches do, seems to target precisely the ability of environmental law to become or even to be law" (Philippopoulous-Mihalopoulos 2011, p. 22). Understanding environmental issues as an emergency reflects, for instance, judicial practice which frequently subjects environmental decisions to a hollow, procedural cycle of legality (Stacey 2018).

In contrast, the requirement of public justification posits rule-of-law imperatives that are constitutive of legal authority at all times. This requirement meaningfully protects and promotes the responsible agency of legal subjects through the realization of fair and rational decision-making. Because the specific contours of those minimum features of publicly-justified decisions are responsive to the particular context in which public authority is being exercised, the theory responds to the dynamic and multifaceted character of our destabilizing climate. The declaration of a wildfire emergency, the expropriation of waterfront property for flood plain restoration, the approval of major fossil fuel infrastructure, to have legal authority, all must be publicly justified in accordance with core constitutional principles.

This theory of the rule of law is one in which all public actors act as partners in the rule-of-law project. This means that there are no pockets of public authority that are confined to the political or the technical or scientific such that they are exempt from the rule-of-law requirement of public justification. Decisions that implicate climate change – whether through perpetuating it, or addressing it – are part of this interpretative rule-of-law framework. Where conventional forums for public justification (i.e. tribunals and courts) fall short, the rule of law demands institutional creativity to sustain the rule-of-law project (Stacey 2018; Dyzenhaus 2006a). Indeed, the creative potential latent in the theory of public justification is in many ways consistent with current grassroots climate activism, which is successfully advocating for creative institutional design in the form of citizens assemblies and climate justice committees.

The public justification theory of the rule of law takes seriously the complex, dynamic, and existential characteristics that constitute the climate emergency. It posits rule-of-law requirements which can be met in all instances, through context-sensitive interpretations of core constitutional principles and also through creative institutional design that require decision-makers to publicly justify their decisions to those affected. It makes democratic requirements of publicity, participation and reason-giving internal to the rule of law. It explains that the exercise of discretionary public power in the time of climate crisis is not outside the rule of law (due to its political or biophysical nature), and that public decisions must adhere to minimum requirements of fairness and rationality to have both democratic and legal authority.

Rule of Law

The rule of law response outlined above seizes on the strengths of the existing literature introduced in Part I, while also responding to its weaknesses. Like these existing literatures, the public justification response to the climate emergency operates at the level of fundamental theory. It is not limited to a specific environmental law or policy reform. Rather it is oriented toward systemic change in how the rule of law is realized in practice, which transcends any one area of law.

The comparative advantage of the theory of public justification over other literatures, however, is that it draws strength from established theories of constitutionalism and deliberative democracy. Public justification provides a framework for transformation, but unlike existing literatures, it relates to existing constitutional architecture and provides a mechanism for constitutional change through public deliberation.

Because it is a theory of democratic legality, public justification means that the contours of core constitutional principles are not fixed. Rather they are responsive to particular decision-making contexts and the need to recognize and facilitate the responsible agency of those subject to the law. Elsewhere I have argued that the precautionary principle and sustainability are necessary for realizing the requirement of public justification in environmental decision-making (Stacey 2018). This is because these principles address how decisions can be fair and reasonable even in the face of uncertain and potentially far-reaching environmental consequences. Public justification can thus provide an interpretive framework for situating the ecological principles identified by existing literatures as necessary for responding to ongoing environmental crisis. Through the requirement of public justification, ecological principles can be made internal to the rule of law.

Finally, the theory of public justification provides an interpretive framework which makes space for a more expansive understanding of legal subjectivity. Public justification presupposes the responsible agency of the legal subject. This is a relational conception of the legal subject (Rundle 2012), which better reflects how individuals are always embedded in social and ecological communities. Moreover, responsible agency can be extended to future generations and non-humans. In this vein constitutional theory can learn from Indigenous legal orders (Clifford 2019, Watts 2013), deliberative democracy (e.g., Eckersley 2004), and other literatures (e.g., Honig 2017, Latour 1993), which recognize the agency of nonhuman others and explore the roles for their agency in public decision-making.

Rights

The climate emergency is a jarring proposition for rights theorists. Emergencies can be, and often are, used to suspend constitutional rights protection. It is entirely foreseeable that the notion of "climate emergency" will be harnessed to perpetuate human rights abuses. Past emergencies make painfully clear the devastating consequences of rights infringements made in the name of bringing a crisis to an end. Moreover, understanding climate as emergency seems to undercut the notable successes of rights-based climate challenges and the growing momentum building from these successes. As Brown puts it, "certainly rights *appear* as that which we cannot not want" (2002, p. 421).

Recall though, that the climate emergency directs us to the theory of public justification as the appropriate rule-of-law response. The climate emergency thus helps to bring the literature on climate rights litigation into conversation with broader theorizing about constitutional rights and to provide an interpretive framework for rights definition, rights conflicts, and remedies for rights violations. I highlight two important avenues for future theorizing on constitutional rights and climate change.

The first avenue for future theorizing is understanding climate rights litigation not solely in terms of claims brought by vulnerable individuals and communities, but rather by engaging with climate rights litigation in all its forms. Climate rights litigation needs an interpretive framework that also accounts for instances in which rights are used to try to block progressive climate action and instances which engage intersecting vulnerabilities (e.g., renewable energy infrastructure or climate adaptation measures in or near marginalized communities).

A constitutional theory of public justification can supply such an interpretive framework. On this view, constitutional rights fit into a theory of public justification; not the other way around (Bellamy 2015, Pettit 1997). Placing rights in this context shifts the focus to the interconnected nature of rights and away from worries of when and how they can receive absolute protection in a finite world. Understanding rights as part of a theory of public justification allows rights theorists to draw on the work of deliberative democrats, who detail the theory and practice of permissible reason-giving (Stacey 2018, Kong 2015). As one example, Levy and Orr posit deliberative alternatives to "crude proportionality methods" that they argue have greater potential to address and accommodate multiple constitutional interests (2017, p. 13). Accommodative reasoning methods, sensitive to the tensions between constitutional rights and values, and to the particular constitutional context, contain much potential for deepening the engagement between rights theories and their implications for a climate-disrupted world.

The second avenue is how a theory of public justification contributes to understanding appropriate remedies for rights violations. While recalling that in emergencies courts are not always well-suited to assess whether adequate justification has been provided, they nonetheless remain crucial actors in the rule-of-law project (Mureinik 1992, Dyzenhaus 2006a). As others have elaborated, judges can play a democracy-enhancing role through remedial creativity (e.g., Fredman 2008). For instance, in one prominent climate rights case, *Leghari v Pakistan*, it was not the court that directly supervised and ensured compliance with national climate goals; rather the High Court of Lahore constituted a Climate Change Commission for this purpose and then supervised the work of the Commission.[6] Courts can thus help promote Dyzenhaus's virtuous cycle of substantive legality – public justification – through remedial creativity rather than resorting to a procedural conception of the rule-of-law or endorsing a form of extra-legal measures (see also, Hailbronner 2017).

Placing climate-rights litigation in the context of public justification helps highlight their success, without supposing "simplicity" or "imaginary cut-and-driedness" of constitutional rights challenges (Mureinik 1992, p. 469). These challenges are successful because they are an important realization of the responsible agency of the children, youth and other vulnerable individuals who have contested state action and they have begun to compel justification from public decision-makers where other mechanisms for securing such justification have failed. At the same time, the theory of public justification helps to shift the focus toward important theoretical challenges for justifying and remedying infringements in light of the complex and existential nature of climate change.

Federalism

As we saw in Part I, climate governance literature details design choices and intergovernmental dynamics in federations. The legally disruptive nature of the climate emergency, however, requires constitutional theory to confront deeper assumptions

---

[6] *Ashgar Leghari v. Federation of Pakistan*, Case No. 25501/2015 (Lahore High Court, Order of 4 Sept. 2015). Note that the Court held that fundamental rights to life, dignity, access to information and property were violated. The Pakistan Constitution does not, at present, contain explicit environmental rights protections.

of sovereignty and stability. We will now see that theory of public justification provides a framework for engaging with these deeper questions.

The climate emergency brings questions of sovereignty to the foreground. Choudry and Hume observe that classical federalism assumes the federal political unit is a nation which inhabits a territory and exercises self-government (2011). Similarly, Tierney suggests the issue of sovereignty is one that "constitutional theory has only scratched the surface of" in the context of federalism (2018, p. 64). Understanding climate change as an emergency provokes the deeper inquiry that Tierney suggests is needed. The climate emergency reveals profound questions of divided sovereignties within federations, as climate harms threaten the territory of some subnational units while climate mitigation threatens resource extraction and, in some cases, the political identity of others.

The theory of public justification, which responds to the climate emergency, provides a framework for these inquiries. The theory of public justification refocuses on the intrinsic rationale for federalism; that is, protection of the autonomy of both individuals and subnational communities. As noted above, I understand autonomy as responsible agency. Therefore, to the extent that political national and subnational communities adhere to a federal state, they must act as responsible agents. This means that they are responsible for offering justifications for the exercises of their authority which have climatic impacts on other responsible agents in the federation. At the same time, as responsible agents, they are owed such justification when the law acts on them.

While the exercise of authority under a federation's division of powers must be justified on the basis of any specific constitutional text, that text must be understood against the backdrop of responsible agency. Any recognition of responsible agency must at least entail the claim to continued existence as a responsible agent in the federation. Decisions that deny the right to continued responsible agency cannot be justified as fair and reasonable. As evidence mounts of the profound, long-term and, in some instances, existential impacts of climate change, the boundaries of acceptable justification must account for the foundational threat any exercises of power pose to sustaining the responsible agency of their partners. Thus, laws or policies of a partner in a federation, which are premised on explicit or implicit climate change denial, risk running afoul of the constitutional commitments to fairness and rationality realized through public justification.

Moreover, the climate emergency intensifies the need for recognition of Indigenous sovereignty in federations, as the authorization of extractive resource industries and impacts of climate change continue to erode the practice of Indigenous laws, governance and traditional ways of life. In some instances, theories of federalism may be appropriate for reconstituting the relationship between settler institutions and Indigenous Peoples (Hamilton and Nichols 2019). The theory of justification can again provide a framework for pursuing this inquiry, so long as the responsible agency of Indigenous Peoples entails a respect for pre-existing and ongoing legal orders as sources of authority (Napoleon and Friedland 2014). Development of shared constitutional principles for justifying the exercise of authority may also mean looking to international theories of legal authority to understand how settler-Indigenous relations can proceed on a nation-to-nation basis (e.g., Brunnée and Toope 2013).

Finally, the climate emergency also brings to the fore issues of stability. While federalism literature tends to assume stability and ignore the question of whether a state should continue to exist (Choudry and Hume 2011), the climate emergency is, if anything, unstable. Large-scale migration and shifting political communities have long been a predicted consequence of climate disruption which will generate tension and conflict over resources and political identity. In addition, nation states are literally disappearing due to a changing climate. The constitutive question of whether a nation should continue to exist (and if so, how) is *the* pressing question for small island states as well as nations whose populations will be dramatically affected by landscapes rendered uninhabitable due to climate change. As countries prepare to pick up and move (e.g., Kiribati) questions of existence and design will be intertwined in ways that will expand the conventional boundaries of federalism theory. The theory of justification can explain how such constitutive decisions can nonetheless be made with legal authority.

The climate emergency reveals deep challenges and opportunities for theorizing federalism. Climate change threatens settled assumptions of sovereignty and stability, even in classical federal states. Changing climatic conditions will suggest that federalism theory must expand outward from classical federalism to post-conflict settings, post-colonial theory and transnational federalism. As constitutional theory expands in these ways, the theory of justification has the potential to frame future debates about the responses of federations to the climate emergency and all the political, social and biophysical tensions that it entails.

CONCLUSION

Climate change necessitates a particular understanding of legal authority that is capable of governing during an emergency. Unlike a conventional emergency, the climate emergency is all-encompassing, enduring and revealing of humanity's inescapable connection to our environment. This chapter has argued that developing a constitutional theory of public justification can explain how the state can operate with democratic and legal authority in our climate disrupted world.

This chapter has addressed the rule of law, rights and federalism as three examples of the challenges that climate change poses for constitutional theory. It has outlined some strengths and limitations of existing bodies of literature that address climate change across these three constitutional concepts. And it has sought to show that a theory of constitutionalism, which takes seriously the climate emergency, can build on these strengths and respond to these limits.

There are many varied meanings and motivations behind the use of "climate emergency." Here I have argued that it is worth taking this concept seriously from the perspective of constitutional theory. The climate emergency is a product of our epistemic and existential relationship to the environment. It is disruptive in every way. The constitutional concept that best responds to this set of immanent characteristics of climate change is the emergency. Facing up to the climate emergency has important implications for constitutional theory. It is not an abandonment of constitutionalism; rather it reveals deep challenges for constitutional theory which must be engaged. I have argued that these challenges can be addressed through a theory of public justification, grounded in the commitment to core constitutional principles which respect and enhance the responsible agency of those subject to the law.

The climate emergency is unlike conventional emergencies in that it is not a temporary and exceptional event from which we return to the status quo ante. It is rather an emergency that demands societal transformation. There is no reason to think that constitutional theory is exempt from this transformational imperative.

RECOMMENDED READING

Affolder, N. (2021). Transnational Climate Law. In Peer Z., ed., *Oxford Handbook of Transnational Law*, Oxford: Oxford University Press, pp. 247–268.

Dyzenhaus, D. (2006a). *The Constitution of Law: Legality in a Time of Emergency*, Cambridge: Cambridge University Press.

Humphreys, S. ed. (2010). *Human Rights and Climate Change*, Cambridge: Cambridge University Press.

IPCC (2018). Summary for Policymakers. In: Masson-Delmotte, V., P. Zhai, H.-O. Pörtner et al, eds., *Global Warming of 1.5°C. An IPCC Special Report on the impacts of global warming of 1.5°C above pre-industrial levels and related global greenhouse gas emission pathways, in the context of strengthening the global response to the threat of climate change, sustainable development, and efforts to eradicate poverty*. Available from: www.ipcc.ch/site/assets/uploads/sites/2/2019/05/SR15_SPM_version_report_LR.pdf

Jaria-Manzano, J. I. & Borras, S. eds. (2019). *Research Handbook on Global Climate Constitutionalism*, Cheltenham, UK: Edward Edgar Publishing.

Kotzé, L., ed. (2017). *Environmental Law and Governance for the Anthropocene*, Oxford: Hart Publishing.

Levy, R., et al, eds. (2018). *The Cambridge Handbook on Deliberative Constitutionalism*, Cambridge: Cambridge University Press.

Loevy, K. (2016). *Emergencies in Public Law: The Legal Politics of Containment*, Cambridge: Cambridge University Press.

Setzer J. & Vanhala, L. (2019). Climate change litigation: A review of research on courts and litigants in climate governance. *Wiley Interdisciplinary Reviews: Climate Change*, 10 (3), e580.

Stacey, J. (2018). *The Constitution of the Environmental Emergency*, Oxford: Hart Publishing.

Watt-Cloutier, S. (2016). *The Right to Be Cold*, Toronto, Ontario: Penguin Canada.

59

Migration

Sarah Song

International migration involves exit (emigration) and entry (immigration). Public debate in liberal democratic countries has focused mostly on immigration, with the issue often framed in binary terms. On one side are those who regard borders as unjust and inefficient. Most migrants want little more than to make better lives for themselves. What moral or political theory could justify preventing people from moving where they want to go? Global egalitarians and libertarians join with immigrants' rights advocates in arguing for generally open borders. On the other side of the debate are those who think states have a virtually unlimited right to restrict immigration. Cultural nationalists view immigration as posing a challenge to the national identity they value. Some social democrats and economic nationalists favor immigration restrictions for a different reason: protecting domestic workers from the competitive pressures said to be generated by immigration.

The topic of migration raises a number of challenging questions for constitutional democracies about the legitimacy of state power, the basic rights of individuals, and the substance and boundaries of citizenship. If people wish to migrate across borders, why shouldn't they be able to? States exercise power over borders, but what, if anything, justifies this power? Is it morally permissible for constitutional democracies to prevent their citizens from exiting the country and exclude prospective migrants from entering? If they are justified in excluding some and accepting others, how should they decide whom to admit?

This chapter examines how contemporary political theorists and philosophers have answered these questions with the aim of providing an overview of the main contributions to the ongoing normative debate on migration. It begins with a discussion of the "conventional view" that says states have the right to control migration and then turns to discuss arguments for "open borders." The third section examines critique of open borders. The fourth section considers more recent arguments for the conventional view and makes the case for a particular position.

I THE CONVENTIONAL VIEW

Many people take for granted that states have the right to control migration. After all, states exercise power over borders, regardless of whether there is any compelling justification for it. Until recently, political theorists and philosophers had mostly been silent on the topic of migration and other issues that spill across borders. To take one prominent example, John Rawls developed his theory of justice for a democratic society "conceived for the time being as a closed system isolated from other societies" (1971, p. 8). Rawls is not alone. Many theorists writing about justice, equality, rights, and democracy mostly take for granted that their theories apply within the context of the nation-state, to those who are already members.

One notable exception is Michael Walzer. He was one of the first scholars to explicitly examine the issue of political membership in debates about distributive justice. Political membership is "conceivably the most important" social good because it has historically determined access to other fundamental goods (1983, p. 29). It can only be distributed by taking people in. For Walzer, it is obvious who should decide how to distribute the good of membership: "we who are already members do the choosing" (p. 32). To elaborate the nature of political community and whether it has the right to control migration and membership, Walzer compares political communities with three more local associations: neighborhoods, clubs, and families.

The first analogy is with *neighborhoods*, which he defines as a random association of people living in close proximity. Because neighborhoods have no formal admissions policies, people are able to move into and out of neighborhoods for reasons of their own, subject only to the constraints of the market. Should countries be like neighborhoods, permitting people to move to whatever country they want? Walzer argues they should not. Political communities have an obligation to provide for the security, welfare, and culture of their members. If they are not able to select among would-be members, "it is likely that neighborhoods will become little states," leading to "a thousand petty fortresses" (p. 39). In a world of open borders, neighborhoods might maintain some "cohesive culture" for a generation or two on a voluntary basis but over time the cohesion would disappear. Walzer suggests the state's right to control immigration rests on the goal of preserving distinctive cultures:

> The distinctiveness of cultures and groups depends upon closure and, without it, cannot be conceived as a stable feature of human life. If this distinctiveness is a value, as most people ... seem to believe, then closure must be permitted somewhere. At some level of political organization, something like the sovereign state must take shape and claim the authority to make its own admissions policy, to control and sometimes restrain the flow of immigrants (p. 39).

This cultural imperative grounds Walzer's case for the state's right to control immigration but he adds a qualification: the right to restrict entry does not entail a right to restrict exit. Controlling immigration is necessary to defend "the liberty and welfare, the politics and culture of a group of people committed to one another and to their common life," but controlling emigration involves coercing people who no longer wish to be members (p. 39). Except in times of national emergency when everyone has a duty to work for the country's survival, citizens must be free to exit their country. The right of exit is one constraint on the state's right to control migration. This moral asymmetry between immigration and emigration suggests a second analogy.

Countries are like *clubs* in having admissions committees. Clubs have the right to control who can become a member, but they cannot prevent members from leaving. We might regard the U.S. Congress as the admissions committee charged with determining categories for admission and exclusion and setting numerical limits. To say that states, like clubs, have a right to control immigration is not to say anything goes. In debating particular admissions standards and the kind of community they want to create, Walzer says members can appeal to the "shared understandings" of members. He does not specify what sorts of constraints there should be on admissions standards; his point is that the distribution of membership in a society is "a matter of political decision" (p. 40). The club analogy, however, misses an important feature of the moral life of contemporary political communities.

This leads to a third analogy with *families*. Unlike members of a club, members of a political community often believe they are morally bound to open the doors of their country to particular individuals, those recognized as "national or ethnic 'relatives.'" In this regard, states are like families, "for it is a feature of families that their members are morally connected to people they have not chosen, who live outside the household" (p. 41). The implications of this "kinship principle" for immigration policy include giving priority to the relatives of citizens and taking in co-ethnics who are persecuted by other states. As Walzer puts it, "Greeks driven from Turkey and Turks from Greece, after the wars and revolutions of the early twentieth century, had to be taken in by the states that bore their collective names. What else are such states for?" (p. 42).

Taking stock of these analogies, Walzer emphasizes what is unique to political communities: they are *territorial states* that possess jurisdiction over a particular territory. Unlike neighborhoods, clubs, and families, states have the right to control the physical location and movement of members and nonmembers in the territory. Yet, like clubs, they have the general right to set its own admissions policy, and like families, they have an obligation to take in those recognized as part of the "national family." As he puts it,

> Admission and exclusion are at the core of communal independence. They suggest the deepest meaning of self-determination. Without them, there could not be *communities of character*, historically stable, ongoing associations of men and women with some special commitment to one another and some special sense of their common life (p. 62).

For Walzer, the agent of collective self-determination, the "we" who controls admission into the territory and into political membership, is a culturally distinctive community.

Walzer suggests one more constraint on the right of states to control migration. They are bound by the principle of mutual aid: positive assistance must be provided to foreigners outside the territory if it is "urgently needed" and the risks or costs of giving it are relatively low for the other party. Wealthy countries can usually fulfill this duty by sending foreign aid and development assistance to poorer countries. However, in the case of "persecuted and stateless" people, the duty of mutual aid can only be met by taking them in (pp. 33, 45). In light of this qualification, we can say the "conventional view" advanced by Walzer is not a case for "closed borders." Rather, while liberal democratic states have a general right to control immigration in accordance with its national priorities, it must open its doors to refugees, family of current citizens, and forcibly displaced co-ethnics.

II OPEN BORDERS

Many scholars reject the conventional view in favor of open borders. They begin from the basic liberal premise of the moral equality of all human beings and interpret liberal principles as requiring a policy of open borders. Joseph Carens, the leading proponent of open borders, has argued,

> Citizenship in Western liberal democracies is the modern equivalent of feudal privilege – an inherited status that greatly enhances one's life chances. Like feudal birthright privilege, restrictive citizenship is hard to justify when one thinks about it closely (1987, p. 252).

Carens's analogy with feudalism is meant to highlight the unfairness implicit in being born a citizen of a wealthy country. Like being born into a wealthy family, citizenship acquired in virtue of birth in the territory of, or to parents who are citizens of, wealthy liberal democratic states is like winning the lottery. It is, to borrow a phrase from Rawls, "so arbitrary from a moral point of view" but so strongly determines our prospects in life (1971, p. 72).

In his early work, Carens builds his case for open borders by drawing on utilitarianism, libertarianism, and liberal egalitarianism. These theories start with the premise of the equal moral worth of all human beings. If we take this premise seriously, we have no basis for distinguishing between citizens and foreigners who seek to become citizens, whether the moral standard is maximizing utility, respecting the right to liberty, or ensuring equal basic liberties and some measure of material equality. Carens devotes greatest attention to applying Rawls's theory to the issue of immigration. He revises Rawls' device of the original position such that parties adopt a global standpoint and select principles of justice that apply to everyone in the world, not just fellow citizens. From this hypothetical global standpoint, not only would parties not know what their social class background or life plans were, they would also not know which country they would be citizens of. As a result, they would choose to add freedom of international movement to the list of basic liberties that all individuals are entitled to. This right of free movement grounds a *pro tanto* duty on the part of liberal democratic states to open their borders.

More recently, a number of additional arguments for open borders have been advanced. They fall into two main categories. The first appeals to equality of opportunity. The basic claim is that respecting the moral equality of all human beings requires a commitment to global equality of opportunity. Carens has argued that the principle of equal opportunity requires that "access to social positions should be determined by an individual's actual talents and capacities, not limited on the basis of arbitrary native characteristics (such as class, race, or sex)" (1992, p. 26). Citizenship is another arbitrary characteristic, so it follows that citizenship status is not an appropriate basis upon which to distribute access to rights and opportunities. By restricting immigration, states deny equal opportunity to those who are entitled to it. In this regard, immigration restrictions constitute an unjust form of discrimination akin to discrimination on the basis of class, race, and sex. As Darrel Moellendorf argues, everyone in the world should have the same opportunity sets: "if equality of opportunity were realized, a child growing up in rural Mozambique would be statistically as likely as the child of a senior executive at a Swiss bank to reach the position of the latter's parent" (2002, p. 49). Other theorists regard global equality of opportunity as an important element of global justice (Caney 2001 and Shachar 2009). The implication is that global equality of opportunity requires open borders.

A second set of arguments for open borders rests on the value of freedom. One argument says freedom of movement is a fundamental human right in itself. People have an interest in immigration that is fundamental to their well-being, and this interest is said to be of sufficient weight to ground a duty on others to respect the right to immigrate. Kieran Oberman argues we have a general interest in having access to "the full range of existing life options," which includes both "attachments" (options we have already chosen) and "possibilities" (options we haven't chosen but may wish to pursue in the future) (2016, pp. 35, 40). To access the full range of life options, people must have the right to immigrate to countries of their choosing.

A second freedom-based argument for open borders proceeds by way of analogy. It says freedom of international movement is a logical extension of rights we already take to be fundamental: the right of domestic free movement and the right to exit a country. Carens has pressed the consistency claim between *domestic* and *international* freedom of movement:

> Every reason why one might want to move within a state may also be a reason for moving between states. One might want a job; one might fall in love with someone from another country; one might belong to a religion that has few adherents in one's native state and many in another; one might wish to pursue cultural opportunities that are only available in another land (2016, p. 239).

Carens concludes that liberals should regard freedom of international movement as a basic human right, which grounds a duty on the part of states to open their borders.

Another consistency argument is made with regard to *exit* and *entry*. The right to exit one's country is widely recognized as a human right. The Universal Declaration of Human Rights (1948) includes "the right to leave any country" in its list of human rights. Philip Cole (2000) has argued that the right to exit a country entails the right to enter another. There must be a "symmetry" between exit and entry: "one cannot consistently assert that there is a fundamental human right to emigration but no such right to immigration." Cole argues that the liberal asymmetry position (defended by Walzer as discussed above) is "not merely ethically, but also conceptually, incoherent" (pp. 52–53).

A third freedom-based argument for open borders has been made by libertarians. We can find this argument periodically in the opinion pages of the Wall Street Journal (1984): "Our greatest heresy is that we believe in people as the great resource of our land … so long as we keep our economy free, more people means more growth, the more the merrier." The empirical assumption here is that complete or even partial elimination of migration barriers would bring vast economic gains, especially for migrants and the firms who employ them. The economist Michael Clemens (2011) provides a provocative metaphor: policies restricting migration are tantamount to leaving "trillion-dollar bills on the sidewalk." In a world without border restrictions, people would move from low-wage to high-wage regions out of a desire to improve their economic well-being and huge economic gains would result. Clemens suggests we could see overall gains of 20–60 percent of global GDP.

The libertarian argument rests on freedom of contract and exchange. Libertarians regard the state as a voluntary association among consenting property owners. As Hillel Steiner (1992) has argued, "If I am willing to lease, sell, or give away space to other persons and am under no contractual obligation to refrain from doing so, the state has no authority to establish whether they are insiders or outsiders before permitting me to do so." Steiner argues libertarians should strongly oppose legislated restrictions on international migration since such restrictions are taken as defending neither contractual agreements nor property rights. The role of the libertarian state is limited to enforcing "individuals' moral rights which consist exclusively of property and contractual rights." Thus, "migration restrictions aimed at protecting the *value* of property rights—let alone broader cultural values are entirely beyond its rightful authority" (pp. 91–93). So long as migrants do not violate the security and property rights of others, the libertarian state should not prevent their migration.

Proponents of open borders acknowledge some qualifications to their case for open borders. For example, Carens says if migrants pose a threat to national security, states are justified in excluding them. Another potential qualification arises if "too many immigrants came within a short period," which might lead to a breakdown in public order in the receiving country and leave everyone worse off in terms of liberty and welfare (2013, p. 276). However, Carens is quick to add that the national security qualification is contingent and self-limiting: it only justifies the exclusion of specific migrants who can be shown to pose an actual threat. He also doubts that states would ever reach a circumstance in which the public order qualification would kick in. These weak qualifications do little to constrain the claim that borders should generally be open and people should generally be free to move if they wish.

III CRITIQUE OF OPEN BORDERS

Arguments for open borders have been challenged in a variety of ways. I focus on three. The first objection, advanced by Michael Blake (2005), contests the claim that immigration restrictions violate moral equality. Blake agrees with Carens that citizenship, like race and sex, is morally arbitrary, but he maintains that it is morally relevant because it demarcates the boundaries of state coercion. Because state coercion invades a person's autonomy, liberal states owe some form of justification to those it subjects to coercion. Because foreigners are not subject to state coercion in the same way citizens are, what liberal states owe to foreigners is different from what they owe to citizens. According to Blake, what the liberal state owes to citizens is political equality and the rights associated with political membership, including the right of political participation and the right of domestic freedom of movement. By contrast, liberal states have duties of humanitarian assistance and perhaps other global obligations, but they do not have a duty to grant admission to foreigners who wish to immigrate.

Blake's argument assumes that the scope of state coercion falls within the territorial borders of the state. Arash Abizadeh (2008) has challenged this assumption, arguing that virtually all foreigners are subject to the coercion of the world's most powerful states. Any state that takes democratic legitimacy seriously must justify border controls to everyone subject to them. Justification must take the form of equally enfranchising all those subject to coercion in a cosmopolitan scheme of democratic institutions. Abizadeh's argument rests on two assumptions: that the justification of coercion must take the form of equal enfranchisement of all those subject to coercion (not just citizens) and that a state's immigration policy coerces everyone in the world.[1]

A second objection rejects the claim that freedom of international movement is a human right. To be sure, people must be able to move freely in physical space in order to fulfill their basic interests, but how extensive must the scope of free movement be? David Miller (2016) has argued that our interest in freedom of international movement does not rise to the level of a human right. Human beings have a range of generic interests they are entitled to pursue, but in deciding on the specific form these interests should take, they must take account of what is feasible. For example, practicing a religion means "finding a faith one can believe in, but also finding a community of believers – a church, mosque, and so forth – that one can actually join given practical constraints on time, money, and distance." Contra

---

[1] For critique of both premises, see Miller 2016.

Oberman, Miller argues a person's human rights are fulfilled when they live in a country that provides an "adequate range" of life options, options that are "sufficient" for a "decent human life" (pp. 51–52). In cases where the state cannot or will not provide its citizens with an adequate range of options, as in the case of refugees, international migration may be required, but the obligation to admit in such cases arises from a remedial responsibility to address injustice, not a human right to immigrate. In many cases, respecting people's freedom to move about within their country is sufficient to protect their basic interests.

A third objection focuses on the libertarian case for open borders. Neo-Lockeans like Steiner conceive of the political community as akin to a voluntary association of homeowners or business associates, but the cottage "community" that Steiner analogizes to the state operates *within* the jurisdiction of the state. Similarly, when an American employer signs a labor contract with a foreign worker, their agreement presupposes the broader context of the political community, including the system of laws that recognizes and enforces their contract and provides the public roads by which the worker travels to his employer (Song 2017). When a foreign worker sets foot on an American employer's property, he enters not only a parcel of private property but also the territorial space of the political community. The libertarian approach fails to distinguish between private property rights of individuals and firms and the territorial rights of states.

IV COLLECTIVE SELF-DETERMINATION, THE TERRITORIAL STATE, AND IMMIGRATION CONTROL

While some theorists have advanced new lines of argument for open borders, others have developed novel arguments for the conventional view. I critically examine three accounts, all of which appeal to the value of collective self-determination but ultimately rest on other values: national identity, property rights, and freedom of association. I identify some shortcomings of these accounts to set the stage for an alternative view.

Miller offers a liberal nationalist account, which develops the cultural argument advanced by Walzer in explicitly nationalist terms. According to Miller, the right of states to control immigration is grounded in the right of *nations* to be self-determining. Citizens are not merely co-participants in a scheme of social cooperation or subject to the same coercive legal regime; "they also relate to one another as fellow nationals, people who share a broadly similar set of cultural values and a sense of belonging to a particular place" (2016, p. 26). Members of the nation have an interest in the character and preservation of their national culture. Immigration generates racial and ethnic diversity, which affects the pace of change of the national culture. In earlier work, Miller says, "immigration need not pose problems, provided only that the immigrants come to share in a common national identity, to which they may contribute their own distinctive ingredients" (1995, p. 26). However, "immigration might pose a problem" in certain circumstances: "where the rate of immigration is so high that there is no time for a process of mutual adjustment to occur; consider recent immigration to California, where a large number of immigrants have arrived in a relatively short space of time. In such cases the education system and other such mechanisms of integration may be stretched beyond their capacity" (128). In more recent work, Miller points to studies suggesting the racial and ethnic diversity generated by immigration may reduce social and political trust, which in turn may reduce public support for social welfare programs and the deliberative institutions of democracy (2016, p. 64). Nationalists conclude that if immigration does have this kind of impact, receiving states are justified in restricting immigration for the sake of protecting their national culture.

Miller's nationalist argument rests on empirical claims that may not be accurate. If high levels of immigration do not have negative impacts on social trust, social welfare provision, or democratic participation, then it is not clear what reasons are left for excluding migrants. It may be the goal of preserving a distinctive national identity. One troubling aspect of the nationalist view is that by grounding immigration control in the imperative of preserving national identity, it may open the door to racial and ethnic exclusions. Miller explicitly rejects racial exclusions: "To be told that they [immigrants] belong to the wrong race or sex (or have the wrong color) is insulting, given that these features do not connect to anything of real significance to the society they want to join" (2014, p. 204). Yet, visions of national identity have always been contested, and race and ethnicity have historically played a central role in shaping what it means to be American, British, French, and so on. Consider the Chinese Exclusion Act, the national origins quota system, and the many other U.S. immigration and citizenship policies shaped by racial, ethnic, and other ascriptive ideologies (Ngai 2004; R. Smith 1997). Racial and xenophobic sentiments are not relics of the past; they are evident today in the rise of far-right parties in Europe and the "white nationalists" who helped usher Donald Trump into the White House. Liberal nationalists have sought to eliminate racial and xenophobic elements from their visions of national culture, emphasizing linguistic and cultural elements consistent with liberalism. Yet, the challenge for any nationalist view remains what to do when a nation's commitment to racial and ethnic visions of national identity overtakes its commitment to liberal principles.

A second novel defense of the state's right to control immigration draws on Lockean property theory. Locke himself began with the theological premise that God gave the earth to humankind in common and argued that individuals come to hold private property rights in particular parcels of land in virtue of mixing their labor with and adding value to that land (1980 [1689]). Contemporary Lockeans have set aside the theological premise and developed the labor theory of value. As A. John Simmons puts it, "those who innocently work to discover, make, or usefully employ some unowned good ought to be allowed to keep it (if in so doing they harm no others).... [I]t would be wrong for others to take it away" (1992, p. 223). Ryan

Pevnick adopts this Lockean intuition to justify the state's right to control immigration. In virtue of the labor they have contributed, citizens have property rights in their "collective accomplishments" (2011, p. 33). Like owners of a family farm, citizens are "joint owners" of state institutions:

> Like the family farm, the construction of state institutions is a historical project that extends across generations and into which individuals are born. Just as the value of a farm very largely comes from the improvements made on it, so too the value of membership in a state is very largely a result of the labor and investment of the community (p. 38).

The right of joint ownership includes the right to determine the future course of their institutions and the right to decide who can join the group (p. 44). Pevnick suggests some qualifications on the legitimate claims of joint-owners: they cannot exclude outsiders who are in desperate need and children of "disliked minorities" who are born in the territory but have not yet contributed to the public institutions (pp. 12, 66).

Pevnick's account suffers the same problem as Steiner's libertarian theory discussed above, although Steiner draws on Locke to argue for open borders. Both conflate property rights and territorial rights of which the right to control immigration is a part (Song 2017). As the owner of my home, I can use and benefit from it and exclude people from entering, but my ownership claim does not entail the right to determine who can make the rules governing my home and all the homes of my fellow citizens. The latter is a fundamentally jurisdictional right that belongs to states. In addition, although Pevnick acknowledges states are not voluntary associations and emphasizes instead the role of labor in conferring ownership rights upon citizens, consent plays an unacknowledged role in conferring ownership rights. As he puts it, "In the case of illegal immigrants, by entering the country illicitly such individuals took their place in their community without the consent of the citizenry." He acknowledges that unauthorized migrants make contributions through working and paying taxes, but he contends that citizens have no obligation "to pass ownership of their institutions to illegal immigrants" because the migrants have "put themselves in this situation without the consent of the citizenry" (2011, pp. 164–165). Migrants' labor is insufficient to ground a claim to joint ownership; the consent of citizens is necessary. But we can apply this same consent standard to the citizens whom Pevnick regards as joint-owners of public institutions: very few citizens have become part of the collective of joint-owners by way of consent.

A third novel argument for the conventional view, advanced by Christopher Heath Wellman, is based on freedom of association. Wellman takes Walzer's club analogy to its logical conclusion. He starts with the premise that freedom of association is "an integral component of self-determination" (2011, pp. 39–40). Freedom of association includes both the right to include and the right to exclude potential associates. Wellman quotes Stuart White on this point: "When a group of people gets together to form an association of some kind (e.g., a religious association, a trade union, a sports club), they will frequently wish to exclude some people from joining their association. What makes it *their* association, serving their purposes, is that they can exercise this 'right to exclude'" (1997, pp. 360–361). Wellman extends the value of freedom of association beyond small-scale associations to the state itself, arguing by way of analogy:

> Just as an individual may permissibly choose whom (if anyone) to marry, and a golf club may choose whom (if anyone) to admit as new members, a group of fellow citizens is entitled to determine whom (if anyone) to admit into their country (2011, p. 37).

Wellman acknowledges this presumptive right can be overridden by competing considerations, but he concludes,

> even if egalitarians are right that those of us in wealthy societies have stringent duties of global distributive justice, and even if libertarians are correct that individuals have rights both to freedom of movement and to control their private property, legitimate states are entitled to reject all potential immigrants, even those desperately seeking asylum from incompetent or corrupt political regimes that are either unable or unwilling to protect their citizens' basic moral rights. (2008, p. 109)

Among existing defenses of the conventional view, Wellman's comes closest to a position of "closed borders."

The club analogy upon which Wellman's argument rests does not hold up. States are not voluntary associations; we do not freely enter them. The non-voluntariness of political membership raises the stakes of membership (Song 2017). Exclusion from a particular state can be hugely consequential in a way that exclusion from golf clubs typically is not. If one golf club refuses to admit me, I can join another or form my own. If a state refuses to admit me, I can't form my own nor easily join another. If no golf club will admit me, the consequences are nowhere near as dire as the consequences of being a stateless person. In light of these differences, the burden falls on proponents to elaborate why freedom of association remains so fundamental for states. Wellman says control over rules of admission and membership are significant because new members will subsequently have a say in determining the future course of the association. In other words, freedom of association flows from the right of collective self-determination, but Wellman does not develop the connection. Rather than relying on problematic analogies, we need to examine the idea of collective self-determination and its connection to immigration control.

If there is any compelling argument for the state's right to control immigration, I believe it rests on the right of collective self-determination (Song 2018). The three accounts examined above appeal to collective self-determination to justify a state's right to control immigration, but they go awry in ignoring what is distinctive about political community as a form of association. Collective self-determination is the moral claim of a collective to rule itself. It is recognized as a fundamental right in UN charters and covenants. Article 1 of the International Covenant on Civil and Political Rights states, "All peoples have the right of self-determination. By virtue of that right they freely determine their political status and freely pursue their economic, social and cultural development." Collective self-determination has an internal and external dimension. The internal dimension is the idea of popular sovereignty: the people are the ultimate source of political authority and they must authorize the binding collective decisions that the government makes in their name. The external dimension finds expression in international law: a group of people has a right to significant independent control over their collective life without the interference of those outside the collective.

If we examine the role of collective self-determination in domestic and international discourse, we can see its distinctive value. Colonized peoples have appealed to the idea of self-determination in mobilizing against colonial governments. Even proponents of humanitarian intervention in cases of genocide and other mass atrocities argue that occupiers have an obligation to restore the occupied country to independence after the emergency has passed and a decent political order has been established. The claim of self-determination by colonized and occupied peoples is a claim about who has authority to rule. The claim of self-determination says the legitimacy of political rule depends on authorization by the people governed by those institutions. To be legitimate, political institutions must reflect the will of the people. The people must be authors of those institutions in some meaningful way.

A people can be self-determining through a range of institutional arrangements, democratic and nondemocratic. A people has the right to establish democratic institutions but this does not mean that they must do so. Collective self-determination is less demanding than democracy (J. Cohen 2006). Democracy requires *equal* rights of participation in collective decision-making by all those subject to those decisions. By contrast, collective self-determination requires that binding collective decisions result from and are accountable to a political process that represents the diverse interests of those who are subject to the decisions. Collective self-determination requires at least the following kinds of institutional mechanisms. First, there must be protections for basic rights and liberties, including the right to bodily integrity, subsistence, and freedom of speech and association. Second, there must be institutional mechanisms of accountability, including the right to dissent from and appeal collective decisions. Third, government must provide public rationales for its decisions in terms of a conception of the common good of the society. Collective self-determination grounds the right of democratic and nondemocratic states to control immigration.

Any attempt to justify the state's right to control immigration based on collective self-determination must meet several challenges (Fine 2013). First, it must provide a coherent account of the collective who is to be self-determining. Second, it must connect the self-determining collective to a particular territory. Third, it must explain why the state's interest in controlling immigration outweighs the claims of prospective migrants to be admitted to the territory such that it can be said to have a general right to control immigration. Can these challenges be met?

First, we should regard the collective not as a nation, joint-owners of state institutions, or members of a voluntary association but as "a people" engaged in the shared political project of collective self-governance. What are peoples and how are they constituted? The idea is invoked in democratic theory and practice to refer to the agent in whose name political power is exercised. We can identify prominent invocations of peoplehood in foundational political documents around the world. The U.S. Constitution opens with the words "We the People of the United States." The French Declaration of the Rights of Man and Citizen begins: "The representatives of the French people."

Peoplehood is considered synonymous with the more familiar idea of the nation, but we should distinguish them. The idea of peoplehood is more capacious. To be a member of a nation, one must share the national identity. Conceptions of nationhood may include a component of willingness on the part of members of the nation, a "daily plebiscite," to use Ernest Renan's phrase (2018), but for nationalists, sharing the cultural attributes associated with national identity is essential for membership in the nation. By contrast, what is essential about peoplehood is participation in shared institutions that aim at collective self-governance. Political cooperation, not cultural identity, is what defines peoplehood. Many nations count as peoples, but the category of peoples is broader and includes groups whose members do not necessarily share a cultural identity.

How are peoples individuated or distinguished from one another if not in virtue of shared cultural markers? The most prominent alternative to the nationalist view is what we might call the statist view, which says the state creates a people by exercising its coercive power over individuals in the territory. On the statist view, the state is prior to and necessary for the creation of a people. By contrast, on the peoplehood view, "a people" comes into being in virtue of participating together in ways that express an aspiration to be authors, not merely subjects, of the rules governing collective life. A people can come about through participating in already established state institutions, and in this regard, a people is not actually prior to the state. But it is the fact of acting together in ways that aspire to self-rule, not the mere fact of subjection to state coercion, which makes a group of individuals "a people." One implication is that a group of people who have not achieved statehood but who participate in ways that strive for collective self-determination may be considered a people.

The second challenge is to explain the connection between the self-determining collective and its right over a particular territory. The state is unique from other types of associations in being a fundamentally territorial entity. The state requires control over a particular territory in order to function as a state. But why is the state entitled to control access to the *particular* territory it claims for itself? We need to show that the people who are represented by the state have the right to occupy the territory in question. A state's claim of territorial rights over a particular territory depends on a prior entitlement to the area it governs. It is not the state but the occupants of the territory who hold these prior entitlements: only if the individuals residing in a particular place have a rightful claim of occupancy does the state, which represents those individuals, have legitimate jurisdiction over it. This right of occupancy is a pre-institutional claim of those who not unjustly inhabit a place to reside there permanently, to make use of the area for valued practices, and to be immune from expropriation or removal (Stilz 2013). What grounds the right of occupancy is the importance of stable residence for the pursuit of our life projects. As Hobbes argued, a person entering the social contract retains some rights, including "to his own body (for example) the right of defending, whereof he could not transfer; to the use of fire, water, free air, and place to live in, and to all things necessary for life" (1999). The implication is that the state's territorial rights derive ultimately from an individual's right to place. People have a right to occupy a particular place because stable residency in a particular place is necessary for personal well-being.

The most straightforward case of legitimate occupancy involves a group of people who settle on uninhabited land and reside on it continuously. This scenario is reflected in the familiar narrative of the U.S. being a "nation of immigrants." But if we look at history, we find not only voluntary migration but also colonialism, conquest, slavery, theft of land, and the mingling of peoples over time. This complicated history generates more questions than answers about who is entitled to establish jurisdiction in any particular geographic area. For example, much territory that is today regarded as U.S. territory was annexed against the will of its original inhabitants who were either forcibly expelled or incorporated into the territory. What are the implications for the occupancy claims of those residing on the U.S. territory today and for the territorial rights claims of the U.S. government?

These are hard and important questions that I cannot pursue here, but briefly I do not think the legitimate occupancy condition necessarily unravels the case for the territorial rights of states. Where the agents and victims of the unjust appropriation are still alive and easily identifiable, the agent that was causally responsible for the injustice bears a responsibility to remedy the injustice. What about cases where the perpetrators and victims of the injustice are long gone? White settlers and government officials who expropriated Native American land are causally and morally responsible for the harms caused to Native Americans, but given that none of the original parties who perpetrated the injustices are still alive, who bears responsibility for remedying the effects of the injustice suffered by Native American descendants?

One approach rests on establishing causal connections between perpetrators and victims, but it runs into the practical difficulties of making such connections in the case of injustices perpetrated long ago. We must also consider current occupants of the land, many of whom arrived after the injustices were perpetrated and have built their lives on the land. In response, some have argued that historical injustices should be regarded as having been "superseded" and the focus instead should be on securing the rights and well-being of current members of the political community (Waldron 1992). By contrast, others argue that democratic political communities must acknowledge and respond to past injustices to foster inclusion of those disadvantaged by past injustices. The responsibility to remedy the enduring effects of past injustices is a political responsibility that falls on all current members of the political community (I. M. Young 2011). Remedies might take symbolic and material forms, including apologies, return of stolen property, monetary compensation, and legal and constitutional provisions recognizing the self-government rights and land use rights of indigenous communities. The exact form that remedy should take will depend on a number of factors, including what those harmed by the past injustice want and the impact of granting the remedy on the state's obligations toward all members of the political community. There are no easy answers, but I believe the difficult questions raised by the legitimate occupancy condition can be addressed through taking historical injustice seriously.

A third challenge is to explain why the state's interest in controlling immigration outweighs the claims of prospective migrants to be admitted such that there is a general right to control immigration. There are clearly circumstances in which states are morally required to admit prospective migrants as in the case of refugees fleeing violence and persecution. Such cases constitute "obligatory admissions," cases where the decision to admit prospective migrants is required by justice (Carens 2013). In cases where states have played a causal role in turning people into refugees, they bear a remedial responsibility to take refugees in to repair the harm they have caused (Souter 2014). Another source of the duty to assist refugees is more universal in scope, the humanitarian concern that grounds the principle of mutual aid. What distinguishes refugees and other "necessitous migrants" from other migrants is their pressing need for protection against serious harm (Song 2018). It is akin to a duty of rescue in emergencies: when someone faces the threat of death or serious harm, we have a duty to rescue them if we can do so without causing serious injury to ourselves. Refugees are in need of rescue from persecution by their home states or the failure of their home states to protect them from violence by third parties.

What about cases in which prospective migrants are not at risk of serious harm? Various defenders of the conventional view argue that states have a *prima facie* right to restrict the entry of such migrants. The decision to admit prospective migrants is not morally required; rather, it constitutes what we might call "discretionary admissions" (Blake 2002). There are at least two fundamental interests that underlie the political community's right to control immigration. One is the interest of individuals in being free from unwanted obligations. Membership in a political community is a source of special rights and obligations, and meeting the membership-based obligations imposes burdens on all members to do their part. As Blake has argued,

> The would-be immigrant who wants to cross into a given jurisdiction acts to impose a set of obligations upon that jurisdiction's current residents. That obligation limits the freedom of those residents by placing them understanding obligations to act in particular ways in defense of that migrant's rights. In response to this, legitimate

states may refuse to allow immigrants to come in, because the residents of those states have the right to refuse to become obligated to those would-be immigrants (2013, pp. 119–120).

There is another fundamental interest not captured by Blake's account, one that is irreducibly collective. It is the interest in collective self-determination. Collective self-determination enables, through its exercise, a distinctive kind of freedom, what Rousseau calls "moral liberty" and what we can call political freedom: "obedience to the law one has prescribed for oneself" (1987, pp. 150–151). Collective self-determination is a form of political freedom that is only possible through membership in a collective. So, if a demagogue were to seize power without the support of the people he seeks to rule, he would not take something away from the individuals *qua* individuals; instead, he takes something from the group as a whole, the right to collective self-determination. If prospective migrants enter without authorization, they sidestep the political process by which members of the political community can define who the collective self is and determine its future course. A state's qualified right to regulate immigration flows from the right of a people to govern themselves (Song 2018).

The collective self-determination argument for the state's right to control immigration offers a middle ground in a highly polarized debate about migration. In contrast to restrictive nationalists who argue for "closed borders," we can acknowledge universal obligations to assist the world's persecuted and poor. In contrast to proponents of "open borders," we can recognize the moral significance of political membership: it grounds the particular rights and obligations of citizenship, which are more extensive than the rights and obligations we have in virtue of our humanity. When it comes to migration, morality requires states to take in refugees and other necessitous migrants, but it does not demand open borders or uncontrolled freedom of movement. What is required is a policy of what I call "controlled borders and open doors," which gives priority to those fleeing persecution and violence as well as those with family ties to current members (Song 2018). It also recognizes that insofar as immigration negatively impacts the wages and working conditions of workers already here, including recently arrived migrant workers, liberal democratic states may be justified in restricting immigration.

CONCLUSION

The issue of migration will continue to pose challenges to constitutional democracies because it implicates fundamental questions about the legitimacy of state power, the bases and scope of individual rights, and the substance and boundaries of citizenship. As a result, it is important to grapple with one's views about these basic questions in pursuing debates about what kind of immigration policies to pursue.

RECOMMENDED READING

Abizadeh, A. (2008). Democratic Theory and Border Coercion: No Right to Unilaterally Control Your Own Borders. *Political Theory*, 36 (1), 37–65.
Blake, M. (2013). Immigration, Jurisdiction, and Exclusion. *Philosophy & Public Affairs*, 41 (2), 103–130.
Brock, G. & Wellman, C. H. (2011). *Debating the Ethics of Immigration: Is There a Right to Exclude?* Oxford: Oxford University Press.
Carens, J. (1987). Aliens and Citizens: The Case for Open Borders. *Review of Politics*, 49 (2), 251–273.
Carens, J. (2013). *The Ethics of Immigration*, Oxford: Oxford University Press.
Fine, S. (2013). The Ethics of Immigration: Self-Determination and the Right to Exclude. *Philosophy Compass*, 8 (3), 254–268.
Miller, D. (2016). *Strangers in Our Midst: The Political Philosophy of Immigration*, Cambridge, MA: Harvard University Press.
Oberman, K. (2016). Immigration as a Human Right. In Sarah Fine and Lea Ypi, eds., *Migration in Political Theory: The Ethics of Movement and Membership*. Oxford: Oxford University Press, pp. 32–56.
Pevnick, R. (2011). *Immigration and the Constraints of Justice: Between Open Borders and Absolute Sovereignty*, Cambridge: Cambridge University Press.
Shachar, A. (2009). *The Birthright Lottery: Citizenship and Global Inequality*, Cambridge, MA: Harvard University Press.
Song, S. (2017). Why Does the State Have the Right to Control Immigration? In: J. Knight, ed., *NOMOS LVII: Migration, Emigration, and Immigration*. New York: New York University Press, pp. 3–50.
Song, S. (2018). *Immigration and the Limits of Democracy*, Oxford: Oxford University Press.
Souter, J. (2014). Towards a Theory of Asylum as Reparation for Past Injustice. *Political Studies*, 62 (2), 326–342.
Walzer, M. (1983). *Spheres of Justice: A Defense of Pluralism and Equality*, New York: Basic Books.
Wellman, C. H. (2008). Immigration and Freedom of Association. *Ethics*, 119(1), 109–141.

60

Constitutional Hardball

Mark Tushnet[*]

A family of paradoxes or tensions hovers around the concept of liberal constitutionalism. The paradox of toleration arises because liberals must (it is said) tolerate and allow the dissemination of the views of the intolerant, whose programs if implemented would eliminate liberal constitutionalism. Militant democracy, a prominent candidate to overcome the paradox through institutional design, is according to Jan-Werner Müller (2012), prima facie illiberal. At a higher conceptual level Ernst-Wolfgang Böckenförde (2020 [1967]) contends that "the liberal, secularized state draws its life from presuppositions it cannot itself guarantee." And, at the very highest, John Gardner (2011) asks, "Can There be a Written Constitution?"[1]

The practices described as constitutional hardball seemingly are part of this family. Constitutional hardball consists of practices that are consistent with the formal requirements of constitutional democracy but that destabilize and potentially transform it. After defining the term and examining how political actors defend specific examples of constitutional hardball, this Chapter examines why political actors engage in hardball, focusing first on their short-term political motivations and then turning to the function of constitutional hardball within reasonably well-functioning constitutional democracies. The Chapter ends with a discussion of what might be done to convert constitutional hardball into ordinary political maneuvering, concluding that such efforts are unlikely to succeed and might be inappropriate (though not illiberal) efforts to halt more or less ordinary transformations in political practices.

A preliminary note on the argument's scope is appropriate. The concept of constitutional hardball emerged from a consideration of constitutional developments in the late twentieth-century United States, and that nation's political history will provide most of the examples offered in this Chapter. I believe there is good reason to think, though, that the concept has some purchase in aiding thinking about other

---

[*] William Nelson Cromwell Professor of Law emeritus, Harvard Law School. I thank Vicki Jackson, David Pozen, Neil Siegel, L. Michael Seidman, and Oren Tamir for helpful comments.
[1] For what it's worth, Gardner's answer is Yes.

constitutional systems, especially, I will argue, in connection with significant transformations within a democratic constitutional order.

I CONSTITUTIONAL HARDBALL DEFINED

Norms, or more accurately their breach or violation, are at the foundation of the practice of constitutional hardball. Constitutional hardball occurs when politicians disregard norms limiting what they have the sheer power to do (within constitutional limits).[2] Or, as one formulation put it, "it consists of political claims and practices – legislative and executive initiatives – that are without much question within the bounds of existing constitutional doctrine and practice but that are nonetheless in some tension with existing pre-constitutional understandings," the latter of which are defined as "the 'go without saying' assumptions that underpin working systems of constitutional government" (Tushnet 2004, p. 523).

Several additional definitional matters deserve attention. The norms breached in constitutional hardball lie at one point in a continuum that extends from "mere" usages – common practices followed perhaps unreflectively and out of habit, relatively easily displaced – to conventions, regular practices followed by nearly everyone out of a sense of obligation deriving from political morality. For present purposes little turns on specifying whether constitutional hardball rests on breaches of norms, usages, or conventions, because what matters is that some important political actors – typically leaders of political parties – no longer believe themselves to be constrained by the barriers to breach.

These leaders see partisan advantage flowing from breaching, and they conclude that the advantage outweighs whatever benefits their parties get from conforming to the usages, norms, or conventions. These calculations typically depend upon an evaluation of the system's operation over a sustained period, and perhaps we should distinguish between isolated norm-breaches, occasioned by a single dramatic problem, for example, and a sustained series of breaches, treating only the latter as constitutional hardball itself.

Their partisan adversaries will describe constitutional hardball as conforming to the letter but not the spirit of the constitution. They describe the outcome of constitutional hardball as "backsliding." In contrast, hardball's practitioners will respond that truly implementing the constitution requires departures from outdated practices not formally required by the constitution. "Court-packing" and similar practices associated with staffing constitutional courts can sometimes support constitutional regression, as in Hungary, but sometimes can be sought to remove obstacles to implementing a normatively attractive constitutional vision, as with Franklin

---

[2] What those limits are is of course contestable, and the more important the stakes are in disregarding norms, the more pressure there will be to develop creative constitutional arguments to support the proposition that the norms are in fact constitutionally embedded and perhaps even judicially enforceable.

Delano Roosevelt's court-packing plan of 1937.[3] This suggests that we should not associate constitutional hardball as inevitably "anti-constitutional" or the like: Its normative character depends upon the normative value of its practitioners' political program.

Political parties run on platforms or manifestos. When they take office their ability to implement their programs is limited, first, by the constitution's provisions both substantive and procedural, and second, by politics. A party might not be able to implement one of its programs despite its electoral victory for many reasons. The program might be unconstitutional – or, more precisely, party leaders might fear that it would be found unconstitutional, in which case they will have expended political capital to no good end, or they might fear that the constitutional arguments will gain purchase among the electorate, which will punish the party at the next election.

Even if there are no substantial constitutional arguments against implementing the program party leaders might decide not to pursue it. The party might have won because its platform overall was more popular than the loser's, but some component of its platform might be unpopular. The party might have the votes to implement the program but its leaders forgo doing so because they worry about the electoral consequences in the next election.

Similarly with procedures. Constitutions provide some guidelines to procedures for enacting statutes: revenue laws must be introduced in the lower house, the opposition must be given seats on significant parliamentary committees, and the like. In general though constitutions leave many procedures open to legislative choice. On many matters a governing majority has the formal power to push through its proposals without regard to constitutionally prescribed procedures. Here too, politics can constrain politicians. As with substantive policies they may fear electoral consequences if they are seen by the public to "overreach" procedurally, for example, by failing to give the opposition a fair chance to articulate its objections even though the majority is certain to prevail. In addition, considerations of constitutional morality may come into play: Some political actors may believe that conforming to existing norms is simply the right thing to do – sometimes even at the cost of being able to achieve their policy goals (less so, probably, if the cost is loss of office).

Often they may worry, though, that as the saying goes, turnabout is fair play: If they simply override the minority now, they might find that when they lose office they will become the victims of the same maneuvers. This concern can generate reasonably stable norms about how politicians should behave with respect to each other. Steven Levitsky and Daniel Ziblatt have described two important norms: "mutual tolerance," meaning that politicians should treat each other as opponents

---

[3] Kosař and Šipulová (2023) offer a useful definition of court-packing that nonetheless implicitly builds in a normative element, as the article's title suggests.

who disagree about what's good for the nation and not enemies who must wipe the other one out if the nation is to survive, and "forbearance," meaning that politicians should refrain from exercising the full power they actually have (Levitsky & Ziblatt 2018).

Other norms are more concrete. For a while in the United States, for example, there was a norm that major legislation should not be pushed through on a purely partisan basis: The majority party should get at least some significant number of members of the minority to sign on to such legislation. And often there is a norm that the opposition should be allowed to introduce amendments to government legislation even when the amendments are doomed to defeat. In some constitutional systems the norm is that important policy changes should be exposed to public comment and debate, including legislative debate, before substantial steps are taken to enact them. In some systems the prime minister's obligation to submit her or his resignation is regulated by norms identifying, for example, what kind of defeat in parliament counts as a vote of no confidence. And some norms are even more precise: The U.S. Senate's rules require unanimous consent to move forward with debate and votes if its committees are in session; insisting on complying with that rule would paralyze the Senate because the occasions for invoking it are so common; the norm, therefore, is that a Senator will not refuse unanimous consent except in truly extraordinary cases.

The idea that constitutional systems contain conventions is closely related to the idea of norms associated with constitutional hardball. Conventions differ from the norms of interest here in several ways. Typically, we describe constitutional conventions as defining the contours of constitutionally permissible actions in systems with unwritten constitutions.[4] The norms associated with constitutional hardball describe practices that are clearly or at least arguably consistent with a nation's written constitution. And typically conventions operate on a high level of political practice whereas norms operate closer to the ground of daily legislative politics. The distinction is captured in the observation that for a practice to be a convention it must be of constitutional significance whereas norms can regulate "ordinary" or subconstitutional practices.

Many scholars believe that constitutional hardball is a problem because norm breaches are almost by definition destabilizing. That belief is supported by the observation that politicians charged with breaching a norm typically deny that they are doing so: they argue that there is no norm in the premises, or that the norm actually does not prohibit what they are doing. Yet, though constitutional stability

---

[4] So, for example, in a student coursebook Hilaire Barnett writes that a convention is a "a non-legal rule which imposes an obligation on those bound by convention, breach or violation of which will give rise to legitimate criticism; and that criticism will generally take the form of an accusation of '*unconstitutional conduct.*'" Barnett (2002, p. 31) (emphasis added).

is a value, it is not an ultimate one. Constitutional orders change, and sometimes they should change. Constitutional hardball may be a method of inducing desirable constitutional change – and is almost always a signal of some disorder in the existing constitutional system.

II DEFENDING SPECIFIC PRACTICES OF CONSTITUTIONAL HARDBALL

Identifying specific "plays" of constitutional hardball itself poses important analytic questions. One fundamental question is to distinguish between forbearance according to a norm and forbearance because of concern about ordinary electoral consequences. The latter results from ordinary political calculations unaffected by normative concerns. The former results from political calculations as well but of a different sort.[5] As already noted, norms arise because they are to the mutual advantage of the majority and minority, on the assumption that political parties will sometimes be in the majority, sometimes in the minority. They result from calculations not about the electoral consequences of breaching this norm now but from a second-order calculation about the consequences of disregarding the norm, both in connection with the particular norm if the majority becomes the minority and in connection with the overall system of norms of reciprocity.

The possibility that forbearance arises from first-order calculation complicates analysis. Consider one of the most well-known asserted norms, that against a U.S. president running for a third term (before the U.S. Constitution was amended to include a two-term limit). Several presidents after George Washington who were in their second term considered running for a third. Each decided against it. Close examination of their decisions suggests, though, that each decision was primarily a first-order one: the prospects of victory were not great enough to warrant the effort. And, to the extent that those calculations were affected by worrying that voters would object to a third term, we cannot tell whether the feared objections rested upon a principle or norm or, instead, upon a concern about the policy unwisdom of a third term.

First-order calculations thus can generate observed behavioral regularities that are associated with norms but that do not actually involve behavior according to norms. A politician who deviates from the regular course can assert that there is simply no norm in the premises to be breached. The politician's action is ordinary politics, not constitutional hardball.

---

[5] My discussion focuses on norms and political calculations rather than on norms as expressions of principled ("above politics") considerations. I believe that the latter view of norms generates some of the unease about constitutional hardball, but that it does not provide much analytic purchase on questions about when constitutional hardball occurs or about its significance for a constitutional order.

Another form of the argument that some action is not truly hardball acknowledges the existence of some norm generally associated with the behavior but characterizes (or re-characterizes) the norm so that it does not apply in the circumstances. Real-world political events always occur in complex factual settings, and we can typically pick out factual circumstances that (a) give a decent normative explanation of why the regularities resulted from adhering to a norm (rather than first-order calculations) and (b) do not include some features of the current situation that are also normatively relevant. The argument then is that the norm is inapplicable to the situation at hand.

An extended example will be helpful here. In February 2016, an election year, U.S. Supreme Court Justice Antonin Scalia died. A month later President Barack Obama nominated Merrick Garland to fill the seat. Senate Majority Leader Mitch McConnell, a Republican, announced that the Senate would not hold hearings on the nomination before the November elections. Faced with the argument that the Senate had some sort of duty to give Garland a hearing, McConnell asserted that in modern times the Senate had not confirmed a nomination made during a presidential election year – a factual claim that was accurate if one defined the claim's terms carefully – and that leaving the seat vacant until the election was consistent with the principle that the electorate's views about who should make the nomination, soon to be determined, should govern. Then, when Justice Ruth Bader Ginsburg died in September 2020, also an election year, Senator McConnell processed the nomination of her successor expeditiously. Some of his defenders offered a fig-leaf justification: In 2016, Obama was ineligible for reelection and voters could not use Garland's nomination as a factor in their decisions about who to vote for, whereas in 2020 President Donald Trump was on the ballot and voters could build the nomination into their decisions.[6]

When Democrats criticized Senator McConnell's actions as inconsistent with settled norms, Republicans responded not only by defining the norm in a way that made their actions consistent with it but also by asserting that they were actually following precedents established by Democrats. The primary precedent they invoked was that of Robert Bork's Supreme Court nomination in 1987. As Republicans describe the events Democrats had characterized Bork's views in a grossly unfair manner and subjected him to personal attacks, thereby breaching norms of civility and forbearance that had previously characterized the nomination process. Democrats responded in turn that Bork had at least received a hearing, at which the public was exposed to his views and concluded (as Democrats saw things) that his views were indeed extreme and unacceptable, and a vote on the nomination was defeated on the merits.

---

[6] The justification was a fig-leaf because Senator McConnell was actually relying upon a different feature of constitutional hardball, the argument that no norm governs the Senate's decisions about how to process Supreme Court nominations, meaning that the question is one of simple constitutional and political power.

The matter of interest here is the form of these arguments, not their accuracy or strength. Arguments about whether a norm has been breached take forms familiar from common-law reasoning. The factual circumstances of prior actions (analogous to prior cases) are described in ways that identify a principle applicable or irrelevant to the matter at hand. The descriptions are defended by referring to some general principles associated in the context of constitutional hardball with democratic norms.

The similarity between common-law reasoning and arguments about specific practices said to be examples of constitutional hardball should not be surprising. Neither setting offers a canonical text to be interpreted, only prior actions. And, importantly, in neither setting is it permissible to say that sheer will (in the common law) or power (in constitutional hardball) is sufficient to justify the action to be taken. Principle extracted from prior practices and generalized is to govern.

For all these reasons the assertion that a politician is playing constitutional hardball is typically a partisan claim: the target of the criticism denies that anything special is occurring. Either there is no norm barring the politician's action, or, the constitution provides the ground for the ultimate objection to the very idea of constitutional hardball. The nation's political norms, it can be said, are exhausted by the textual constitution. Some constitutional provisions set out the terms of some forms of mutual toleration and forbearance, of course, but beyond that the constitution countenances whatever political moves are made based on first-order calculations. Here, there is no idea of constitutional hardball independent of unconstitutionality – or, put another way, the idea of constitutional hardball does no work that the constitution itself does not do.

The difficulties just canvassed are similar to those encountered when analysts attempt to identify non-textually based political conventions: behavioral regularity yes, convention no; convention yes but of narrow scope; no convention beyond the text. Sometimes, though, politicians acknowledge that they are breaching a norm that they had previously regarded as valuable. Norm-breaches can occur when the second-order calculation comes out against complying with the norm. That can happen for several reasons. Adhering to the norm might prevent the party from implementing a truly important part of its program – and the party might suffer electorally from that failure. The party breaching the norm might conclude that truly exceptional circumstances exist, which justify introducing a bit of instability into the overall system (and perhaps hoping that the pre-breach equilibrium can be restored relatively quickly after the emergency passes). This might explain Franklin Delano Roosevelt's decision to run for a third presidential term in 1940 when the expansion of the then-current European war was clearly on the horizon – which might be described as establishing that the "no third term" norm had built into it an "exceptional circumstances" exception that simply happened not to have been satisfied in prior cases. Or, for norms regulating the minority party's behavior, the minority might fear that adhering to the norms – or to the entire system of norms in place – will prevent the minority from becoming the majority. Here, there is no "mutual" advantage to be had by adhering to the norm.[7]

III WHY CONSTITUTIONAL HARDBALL OCCURS: A "REGIME-CENTERED" ANALYSIS

Politicians decide to play constitutional hardball when, from their point of view, the stakes are quite high – especially, the survival of the nation's political system in the face of serious external or internal threats, or the prospect that their party will be bulldozed out of existence – and existing norms block the adoption of policies suitable to deal with the threats. They must somehow distinguish these situations from ones in which the stakes are so to speak ordinary: losing a governing majority or remaining in the minority for the foreseeable future. Politicians have incentives to exaggerate the threats the nation faces if their party fails electorally, yet in ordinary times even the exaggerated claims do not generate constitutional hardball. What then might be the conditions that tip politicians over the threshold?

Here, a perspective drawn from U.S. political science, specifically the subfield known as American political development (APD) may be useful, though application of a "developmental" perspective to other nations' constitutional histories is quite limited as yet. The core of APD is the argument that U.S. constitutional and political history has seen a succession of political "regimes" or orders. Each order has a set of core institutions central to its functioning, ideas that animate its policies, and modes of political mobilization to generate sustained electoral success for supporters of the institutions and proponents of the ideas.[8] And, central to the argument, the institutions, ideas, and modes of political action characteristic of one order differ from those of its predecessor and successor.

Development is of course a process that takes place in time. A crude version has it that constitutional orders are initiated, function well for a while, then decay, to be replaced by another. A more refined version notes that a new constitutional order begins to form in the interstices of the order in place, as politicians see signs that the existing order is in decline and search out and generate new

---

[7] A version of this problem occurs in "asymmetrical" hardball, where one party beaches norms and the other continues to adhere to them. See Fishkin and Pozen (2018). Mutuality of advantage disappears, yet the party that is now disadvantaged persists in adhering to the norm. For additional discussion, see Section IV below.

[8] For relevant studies, see Skowronek (1982); Skowronek (1997); Orren and Skowronek (2004). For application of a developmental approach to political orders outside the United States, see Streeck and Thelen (2005); Pierson (2011); Bermeo (2003) (dealing with constitutional breakdowns but not expressly deploying the concept of constitutional hardball). In the U.S. context it is important that during each constitutional order both major political parties buy into the order's institutions and ideas. That might be true elsewhere but, again, developmental-focused studies of the constitutional features of other nations are limited. For a somewhat wooden application of Skowronek's analysis of the US president-led system of political development to Australia's prime-ministerial system, see Laing and McCaffrie (2013).

ideas and institutions that they hope will characterize a new constitutional order. As they attempt to win enough elections to put a new order in place they might – indeed probably will – engage in innovative forms of political action. These can include rejection of the norms of political behavior associated with the order they are challenging: in short, they start playing constitutional hardball. Another way of putting this point: Only time reveals whether politicians were playing (problematic) constitutional hardball or were gradually building a new constitutional order.

This analysis suggests that we should observe constitutional hardball whenever politicians see the possibility of a regime transition on the horizon: sometimes in a two-party system with well-organized and ideologically opposed parties after a period in which one party has dominated and might have worn out its welcome, sometimes in a system of multi-party coalition governments when one party seems poised to win a majority.[9]

For expository purposes consider a quite simplified account of constitutional orders that focuses solely on the distinctive way in which political parties are organized and compete. Party systems come in numerous forms: competition between two or a small number of relatively stable parties, yielding a succession of governments (of the right or the left, for convenience); multiparty systems with some parties being coalitions ("workers and farmers," for example), others being organized around coherent ideological platforms (Green parties at least at their outset), yet others being the vehicles for one or a handful of ambitious politicians ("personalistic" parties); and of course many variants.

The norms governing political action will vary depending upon the form party competition takes in a constitutional order. The United States between the 1930s and the early 2000s provides an example. The Democratic and Republican parties during that period consisted of complex coalitions of groups identified by both interests and ideologies: Southern conservatives animated by a racist domestic ideology and a modestly isolationist foreign policy but whose poorer constituents benefited from social welfare programs joined in the Democratic party with Northern urban liberals who favored civil rights, the social welfare state, and an interventionist foreign policy; western "rugged individualists" and wealthy investors and businesspeople joined in the Republican party to oppose dramatic expansions of the social welfare state, with the westerners far more isolationist than the wealthy elites and the latter generally supportive of civil rights as to which the westerners were either indifferent or opposed. Today the German Christian Democratic and Social Democratic parties have a similar "internal coalition" structure.

---

[9] cf. Laing and McCaffrie (2013), p. 83 (contrasting for their purposes nations "with histories of strong executive leadership and two major parties" and those "with histories of multi-party coalition governments that combine progressive and conservative forces within a single executive.").

Where two relatively stable parties that are coalitions compete, as in these cases, each will be concerned about the possibility that some within the coalition will migrate to the other. The possibility of these shifts in the parties' internal coalition generates an understanding that the parties might well rotate in office as components of the internal coalitions circulate between the parties. That understanding generates the norm of forbearance: "We will refrain from doing everything we can while we're in office because we understand that someday soon we will be out of office and don't want our opponents to do to us what we might have done to them." More formally politicians in these circumstances see themselves as playing a set of repeated Prisoners' Dilemmas games with no obvious termination point and quickly learn that cooperation is better than defection.

Parties can change their internal structure, though. Historically, the German parties were ideologically organized but became internal coalitions. In the United States the late 1990s and early 2000s saw the Republican party first, the Democratic party later and less strongly, shift from internal coalitions to ideologically organized. The reasons for these changes are complex, sometimes associated with external forces (globalization and an associated neoliberal ideology being the prime candidate for the German change, for example), sometimes simply with ambitious politicians' observation that a promising path to victory appears to have opened as a constitutional order decays (probably the best explanation for the change in the United States).

We can characterize party competition between ideologically organized parties in at least two ways. Depending upon the ideologies, the competition may seem to have high stakes from the outset: In Weimar Germany the competition between Socialists, Communists, and Nazis was high stakes, and generated strongly confrontational forms of political action including actions within the parliament that paralyzed it and actions "on the street" organized around politics. Alternatively, politicians may come to believe that the Prisoners' Dilemmas games are going to end relatively soon and (rationally) decide that defection is a better strategy than cooperation. Constitutional hardball results.

This developmental account provides a political explanation for constitutional hardball.[10] It may also go some way to explaining "asymmetrical" constitutional hardball in the United States and perhaps elsewhere. Politicians may disagree about the imminence of a constitutional order's replacement. Those who see it coming

---

[10] India provides an important additional example. There a long period of one-party dominance was replaced by a few decades of coalition government and now by a return to one-party dominance. The developmental perspective suggests that we should be able to observe constitutional hardball as the shifts in party structure were imminent. And indeed at the first transition there was a truly dramatic form of constitutional hardball, the declaration of a state of emergency that repressively shut down ordinary politics for several years.

soon will play hardball to give themselves the upper hand when the new order actually materializes. Those who believe that the old order is here to stay for a while will adhere to existing norms and hope that those who agree with them will find constitutional hardball so distasteful as to disqualify the other side from office. Or, perhaps more important, the rate of change within parties may differ. Here too the U.S. example is instructive: Both major parties have become more ideologically coherent than they were in the late twentieth century, but the Democratic party continues to have a significant "coalitional" dimension – insiders routinely observe that policy and personnel decisions have to satisfy "the groups" – that is much weaker and perhaps even absent in the Republican party. The more ideologically coherent party will find it easier to play hardball than the coalitional one.

The foregoing is an extremely simplified account of what are in reality quite complicated political stories, and, once again, the developmental perspective has not been brought to bear extensively on constitutional orders outside the United States.

The bottom-line point, though, is clear: Constitutional hardball is a signal of proposed or impending constitutional change, and the change might be for the better rather than for the worse. This suggests an additional point: Constitutional hardball matters when it is systematic rather than isolated – when a political party disregards a large number of norms in close succession, rather than one or two over a several-year period. Further, constitutional hardball is quite costly when it fails – that is, when the change in constitutional orders that its players propose does not eventuate. A failed insurrection accomplishes nothing; a successful one might put a better order in place.

Here too a contrast with constitutional conventions is useful. Such conventions change, of course, but the arguments associated with changes in conventions differ from those associated with constitutional hardball. Consider the alteration in the convention that a minister is responsible for misconduct that occurs in his or her ministry and must resign when misconduct is revealed. Initially, the principle of ministerial responsibility was a form of vicarious liability, the obligation to resign arising whenever any misconduct was revealed. The convention changed to one in which a minister had to resign when the misconduct was substantial and now may be one in which resignation is required only when the misconduct was of such a magnitude that the minister knew or should have known that it was occurring – a form of personal rather than vicarious liability. The reason for the change is obvious: the expansion of government ministries to the point where misconduct is almost inevitable at lower bureaucratic levels.

The argument for changing a convention is that the conditions identifying the occasions for invoking the convention have changed. That is a standard form of common-law reasoning. Yet, it is not an argument regularly made in connection with constitutional hardball. The reason is that constitutional hardball occurs before regime change happens rather than afterwards.

IV HOW CAN CONSTITUTIONAL HARDBALL BE FOUGHT (AND SHOULD IT BE)?

Levitsky and Ziblatt describe the norms that constitutional hardball places under pressure as "guardrails" against democratic destabilization. How can those guardrails be maintained?

1. *Public institutions.* We might look to public institutions to do so. A model exists in the theory and practice of militant democracy. According to that theory "anti-constitutional" parties can be barred from the ballot, individual candidates disqualified from running, and party members removed from the public services (including police agencies). Analogously a parliamentary committee on good conduct could (in theory) discipline legislators for breaching civility norms, an electoral monitoring body could publicize and perhaps even sanction candidates who demonize their opponents.

The practice of militant democracy shows that such a strategy is unlikely to succeed. As already noted, militant democracy is prima facie illiberal, making it vulnerable to a "tu quoque" criticism by its targets. The scope of militant democracy and analogous practices has to be rather narrow because of its illiberal character – more precisely, the tension between it and principles of free expression. The practice has a political feature as well: The range within which it can be effectively deployed against destabilizing parties is itself narrow. Barring from the ballot a party that has no chance of winning is pointless (and costly in free expression terms). Barring a party that has substantial support already has proven to be quite difficult, precisely because the party's existing electoral strength is a resource it can use to fight its disqualification.[11] And, because practices of constitutional hardball are by definition lawful, explaining why they result in sanctions will be quite difficult: How could it be permissible for a parliamentary majority to impose sanctions on a minority that insisted upon strict compliance with unanimous consent rules?

Put in the context of constitutional hardball, these observations can be summarized as observing that attempts by public institutions to implement remedies for constitutional hardball will themselves be subject to constitutional hardball.

2. *Self-help, or anti-hardball.* Consider a case of asymmetrical hardball. The party playing hardball less often is at a disadvantage. Can it do anything about that on its own? Suppose its opponent is playing hardball because it believes that the stakes are quite high, that (in the United States) the Democratic Party seeks to bring socialism to the nation or that the Republican Party wants to dismantle the administrative state.

---

[11] Militant democracy measures directed at specific individuals, even party leaders, might be more likely to succeed, for example when targeted leaders face opposition within their own political party. And, if the targeted leaders were the strongest proponents of hardball, their removal might shift their party into a more evolutionary path of constitutional change. (I thank Oren Tamir for this observation.)

The target of hardball might try to demonstrate that the stakes are not so high as to justify hardball.[12] It can forgo promoting programs that its opponents can characterize as aggressive or overreaching, lowering the actual stakes. Instead of large-scale regulatory efforts, Democrats can promote marginal changes or nudges; instead of deregulating across-the-board, Republicans can identify areas where regulations can be pruned without sacrificing public safety or health. Similar programmatic adjustments might lower the stakes in other systems under pressure.

The "lower the stakes" strategy faces two difficulties. Some members of the party that has been the target of hardball (the party's "hardliners") will want the party to pursue the programs that the other party regards as raising the stakes too high. Lowering the stakes means abandoning the programs that the hardliners believe are central to the party's mission. The difficulty here is internal to the party, and not all party leaders will be skilled enough to keep the hardliners on board with a "lower the stakes" strategy.

The other difficulty is external to the party. The strategy can succeed only if the opposing party comes to believe that the stakes have indeed been lowered. At a minimum, the party seeking to lower the stakes has no control over how the opposing party will characterize the proposed programs: Some that seem modest to the proponents can be characterized as massive, or as the camel's nose under the tent, by their opponents, and such characterizations may be especially likely once a game of hardball has already begun.

Lowering the stakes is not directed at hardball practices themselves but at one possible cause of hardball. "Anti-hardball" is a related but somewhat different strategy.[13] Anti-hardball tactics focus on specific forms of hardball: the "confirmation wars" in the United States, for example. They occur because each judicial nomination is itself a high-stakes matter. Anti-hardball would make each one a low-stakes one, for example by ensuring that one nomination will occur every two years. As David Pozen, the originator of the idea, notes, attempts to implement such a change will themselves be subject to hardball tactics. The same is probably true of every other specific hardball tactic that we might try to modify: If a Senate majority refuses to hold a hearing for a judicial nominee, instituting a rule requiring hearings will be the target of hardball tactics (not in connection with nominations, of course, but in connection with the process by which the Senate makes its rules).

Self-help might relieve some of the pressure on constitutional guardrails, but seems unlikely to be a generally useful strategy.

3. *An informal game-theoretic analysis (herein of escalating tit-for-tat strategies).* As mentioned above, the best strategy for people engaged in repeated Prisoners'

---

[12] Some libertarian theorists argue that a well-designed constitution confines public authority to low-stakes matters. Whatever its merits as a normative theory, acting on such an interpretation of any existing constitution, for example by nominating only judges who agreed with that interpretation would be a hardball play.

[13] For the term, see Pozen (2019).

Dilemma games with no specified endpoint is a forgiving tit-for-tat one: Cooperate as long as the other side cooperates, punish a defection in one round with your own defection in the next, but return to cooperation as soon as the other side does. Where the participants know all this, and especially when they can explain their strategies to each other, they seem to converge on using the forgiving tit-for-tat strategy – which means that no one ever defects, to everyone's benefit.

We might think that adopting such a strategy in connection with constitutional hardball might produce similarly attractive outcomes. A defection here is a breach of one of the norms of interest. Faced with such a breach, the other side would respond with an equivalent breach of the same or some other norm, indicating clearly that it was doing so as a response to the prior breach. The hope is that (perhaps after a few rounds of play) the parties will agree to adhere to the norms that they have breached once or twice – maintain the guardrails, in short.

This might be true even if the tit-for-tat strategy resulted in some degree of escalation. The usual example in the United States, with parallels elsewhere, again involves the courts. Some Democrats favored "Court-packing" – adding some additional members to the Supreme Court to offset the hardball installations after the deaths of Justices Scalia and Ginsburg. A common objection was that if Democrats did that, Republicans would do the same the next time they had the chance: If Democrats added four seats in 2022, Republicans given the chance to do so in 2025 or 2029, would add six – to the point that the Court would eventually have 57 justices.[14] Proponents of a tit-for-tat strategy could respond that at some point everyone would realize that the escalation had gotten out of hand – that the nation was no longer benefiting from the Court's interventions simply because it was too large. Sanity would be restored, the Court's size reduced, and the parties would have learned the lesson that they should not play hardball with respect to staffing the Supreme Court. The broken guardrail would have been repaired.[15]

Here too one can see several difficulties. One is obvious: Even if the "restore sanity" scenario comes to pass, interim costs will have been incurred, and they might be substantial. A second is more subtle and arises from the forms of argument associated with constitutional hardball. The tit-for-tat strategy requires that participants agree that one of them has shifted from cooperating to defecting. As we saw in connection with the Garland episode, one characteristic argument about norm-violations

---

[14] For readers unfamiliar with U.S. advertising, the number was adopted in tribute to a famous advertisement for a ketchup that came in 57 varieties.

[15] Escalating tit-for-tat can sometimes draw new actors into the dispute. In some constitutional systems, for example Australia and the United Kingdom (but not the United States), there has been a norm against targeting the judiciary – and in particular specific judges – for the political nature of their decisions, and a norm against extra-curial comments more or less directly addressing political matters. A hardball-practicing politician in such systems might criticize specific judges for their decisions, and the judges, previously disengaged from politics, might respond. If these cross-institutional effects persist, we might fairly describe what has occurred as the kind of sustained hardball that has constitutional significance.

is, "You did it first." In the present setting: One participant announces that it has a forgiving tit-for-tat strategy and is now defecting only because the other participant breached the norm in the prior round. The other participant responds, "Wait a minute. True, we did defect, but only because we were following a forgiving tit-for-tat strategy ourselves, in response to *your* prior breach. According to your own stated principle, this time around you should return to cooperating, and the fact that you haven't tells us that you are not committed to the norm at all."

A deeper difficulty awaits. The tit-for-tat strategy arises when two people play repeated Prisoners' Dilemma games with no termination point. Politics is not that. The players are aggregates, not individuals: to adapt a classic article's title, parties are a they not an it (Shepsle 1992). Party members come and go, abandoning politics for other pursuits, dying off, and the like. New members might not be committed to the strategies their predecessors chose. Perhaps more important, they cannot be chastised for "defecting" in a new round of the Prisoners' Dilemma game because they were not there when the prior round was played. The forgiving tit-for-tat strategy cannot get off the ground under these circumstances.

Constitutional hardball might be associated with only some structures of party politics. Sometimes parties are "strong," in the sense that their leaders can impose discipline on members to adhere to a single "line" – in the present context, a strategy – over a significant period of time. The game-theoretic argument might explain why we do not observe constitutional hardball when major political parties are strong. Yet if the strong parties are also ideologically coherent they might regularly see the political stakes as high enough to justify hardball tactics. As argued earlier, parties that are internal coalitions might be weak – unable to impose discipline – but for that very reason norms of forbearance might arise.

As discussed earlier, though, parties themselves change. Strong ones can become weak, weak ones strong; internal coalitional parties can become ideologically coherent ones, and the reverse. Political scientists using the developmental approach to understand U.S. constitutional development have sketched some of the circumstances occasioning these and related changes: policy failures as the constitutional order's characteristic policies are over-extended to domains where they do not work well (or fail to be extended to domains where they should be extended and would work well); policy innovations modeled on the order's distinctive ideas that turn out to be mistakes; and more. Stable strategies are quite unlikely to emerge when such changes occur. Or, put another way, constitutional hardball becomes more likely as a constitutional order decays.

The foregoing argument against the game-theoretic analysis can be captured in a simple point: Politics might indeed be a repeated Prisoners' Dilemma game with no termination point, but the rounds will end for individual players, who know that they will not be in office indefinitely, and party leaders might believe that the next round might be the last one. Seeking to maintain the guardrails by appealing to a politician's or a party's long-term interests can succeed but only under specific conditions.

4. *Civil society (or institutions other than those of government itself).* Public institutions that seek to repair guardrails weakened by hardball tactics will face the same tactics when they attempt to do so. Might non-public institutions? Classically, those institutions were the market, the family, and religion; today we would include nongovernmental organizations (NGOs) and would refer more broadly to civil society. People engaging in market transactions can come to appreciate the value of forbearance and toleration as they negotiate with trading partners; almost all religions have some version of the Golden Rule ("do unto others as you would have done unto you"); family members learn that they should not pursue their own personal self-interest single-mindedly but should take others' interests into account; many important NGOs pursue the public's interest rather than merely sectoral ones. Constitutional hardball is inconsistent with the principles expressed in actions within these civil society institutions. As constitutional hardball emerges perhaps the institutions of civil society can help repair the guardrails.

A number of difficulties attend the use of these institutions to fight constitutional hardball. (a) In general, their effects on values work themselves out over rather extended periods of time, perhaps too long to be effective when constitutional hardball actually comes to be played.

(b) Related, perhaps the role of civil society institutions in promoting anti-hardball political values is a side-effect of their core roles, and necessarily so.[16] A sermon criticizing some politician's actions as inconsistent with the Golden Rule might be substantially less effective in reinforcing norms of forbearance than one showing that all major religions have their own versions of the Golden Rule that apply to everyone's activities, not politicians' alone.

(c) Perhaps civil society no longer has much ability to inculcate the politically relevant norms needed to repair guardrails. Modern commercial transactions involve few of the face-to-face negotiations that generate trust; fewer and fewer people may have deep religious convictions; so many family structures have arisen that we cannot count on "the family" as such to be an institution that generates the "right" kind of politically relevant values.

(d) In any event civil society itself can become a focus of constitutional hardball. The conventional phrase for this phenomenon is "the culture wars," in which politicians are soldiers. One front in the culture wars involves legal regulation of civil society because its institutions are inevitably structured by law. Religious institutions may be induced to forgo taking political positions by tax laws, or might be given privileged status vis-à-vis aspects of government regulation, or might become the vehicles for the governing majority. Civil society institutions might have some

---

[16] For the idea of "states that are essentially by-products" that cannot be intentionally aimed at, see Elster (1983, Part II).

constitutional protections, but the contours of their constitutional protection are often ill-defined, giving opportunities for political actors to seek to define the permissible range of such institutions' actions with reference to the existing or emerging constitutional order's values.

Culture wars too are associated with constitutional orders. Such orders have distinctive motivating ideas, and among those ideas will be ones affecting civil society. Consider for example what will count as effective education for civic responsibility. A constitutional order will define the legal contours of permissible action by civil society organizations with reference to the dominant ideology about civic education. And as politicians see the possibility that a new constitutional order will come into being they will formulate ideas about civic education appropriate to that constitutional order, which might differ from the parallel ideas in the existing order. That might lead them to play constitutional hardball about the legal contours defining civil society.

The mechanisms sketched above might each do a bit to combat constitutional hardball, and in the aggregate they might be able to reduce it to a minor phenomenon. They might be able to repair the guardrails. Should we treat this as unequivocally good?

The developmental perspective suggest that guardrails break down as a constitutional order decays. We might wonder whether it is socially valuable to do something to let such an order stumble on for a few more years before its inevitable demise. Perhaps repairing the guardrails would preserve the order indefinitely. That is good only if the order itself, even in its decayed form, is better than the one that would replace it. Earlier, we noted that claims about constitutional hardball were inevitably partisan, meaning that each one's value could be evaluated only by directly bringing political criteria to bear. Now we have seen that the claim that constitutional hardball is a problem worth worrying about is partisan in the same sense.

CONCLUSION

Constitutional hardball poses a challenge to constitutional democracies in place. Whether it poses a challenge to constitutional democracy as such is a different question. Constitutional democracies change, sometimes for the bad ("constitutional retrogression" or back-sliding), sometimes for the good ("transformative constitutionalism"). The developmental perspective sketched here suggests that constitutional hardball emerges when a substantial shift in a nation's constitutional order is in prospect. That shift might be bad or good, and the mere fact that we see hardball being played does not tell us which it will be. And, even worse, it might be that the side playing hardball more effectively might want to degrade democracy and yet, when things settle down, their opponents might prevail and improve the constitutional order.

A Burkean who believes that change is in itself bad, or someone who is simply risk averse, might be nervous about constitutional hardball. There may be little they can do about it, though, if it arises when a constitutional order has decayed but has not yet been replaced.

RECOMMENDED READING

Balkin, J. (2020). *The Cycles of Constitutional Time*, Oxford: Oxford University Press.
Chafetz, J. & Pozen, P. (2018). How Constitutional Norms Break Down. *UCLA Law Review*, 65 (4), 1430–1459.
Fishkin, J. & Pozen, D. E. (2018). Asymmetrical Constitutional Hardball. *Columbia Law Review*, 118 (3), 915–982
Ginsburg, T. & Huq, A. (2018). *How to Save a Constitutional Democracy*, Chicago: University of Chicago Press.
Levitsky, S. & Ziblatt, D. (2018). *How Democracies Die*, New York: Crown Publishers.
Pozen, D. E. (2019). Hardball and/as Anti-Hardball. *New York University Journal of Legislation & Public Policy*, 21 (4), 949–955.
Tushnet, M. (2004). Constitutional Hardball. *John Marshall Law Review*, 37 (2), 523–553.

Bibliography

Abbott, K. W., Keohane, R. O., Moravcsik, A., Slaughter, A.-M., & Snidal, D. (2000). The Concept of Legalization. *International Organization*, 54 (3), 401–419.
Abbott, K. W., Levi-Faur, D., & Snidal, D. (2017). Theorizing Regulatory Intermediaries: The RIT Model. *The Annals of the American Academy of Political and Social Science*, 670 (1), 14–35.
Abdel-Nasser, G. (1955). *The Philosophy of the Revolution*, Cairo: Mondiale Press.
Abebe, A. (2020). The Vulnerability of Constitutional Pacts: Inclusive Majoritarianism as Protection Against Democratic Backsliding. In A. Abebe et al., eds., *Annual Review of Constitution-Building 2019*. Stockholm: International IDEA, pp. 21–33.
Abendroth, W. (1968). Zum Begriff des demokratischen und sozialen Rechtsstaates im Grundgesetz der Bundesrepublik Deutschland. In E. Forsthoff, ed., *Rechtsstaatlichkeit und Sozialstaatlichkeit*. Darmstadt: Wissenschaftliche Buchgesellschaft, pp. 114–144.
Åberg, J., & Sedelius, T. (2018). A Structured Review of Semi-Presidential Studies: Debates, Results and Missing Pieces. *British Journal of Political Science*, 50 (3), 1111–1136.
Abidi, N., & Miquel-Flores, I. (2018). *Who Benefits from the Corporate QE? A Regression Discontinuity Design Approach*. ECB Working Paper No. 2145. Frankfurt-am-Main: European Central Bank.
Abizadeh, A. (2008). Democratic Theory and Border Coercion: No Right to Unilaterally Control Your Own Borders. *Political Theory*, 36 (1), 37–65.
Abizadeh, A. (2019). In Defense of Imperfection: An Election-Sortition Compromise. In J. Gastil, & E. O. Wright eds., *Legislatures by Lot. Transformative Design for Deliberative Governance*. London and New York: Verso, pp. 249–255.
Abizadeh, A. (2021a). Counter-Majoritarian Democracy: Persistent Minorities, Federalism, and the Power of Numbers. *American Political Science Review*, 115 (3), 742–756.
Abizadeh, A. (2021b). Representation, Bicameralism, Political Equality, and Sortition: Reconstituting the Second Chamber as a Randomly Selected Assembly. *Perspectives on Politics*, 19 (3), 791–806.
Abizadeh, A. (2023). The Grammar of Social Power: Power-to, Power-with, Power-despite, and Power-over. *Political Studies*, 71 (1), 3–19.
Ablavsky, G. (2014). The Savage Constitution. *Duke Law Journal*, 63 (5), 999–1089.
Ablavsky, G. (2018). The Rise of Federal Title. *California Law Review*, 106 (3), 631–695.
Abolafia, M. Y. (2010). Narrative Construction as Sensemaking: How a Central Bank Thinks. *Organization Studies*, 31 (3), 349–367.
Abolafia, M. Y. (2012). Central Banking and the Triumph of Technical Rationality. In K. Knorr-Cetina, & A. Preda, eds., *The Oxford Handbook of the Sociology of Finance*. Oxford: Oxford University Press, pp. 94–112.

Abou El-Fadl, R. (2019). Building Egypt's Afro-Asian Hub: Infrastructures of Solidarity and the 1957 Cairo Conference. *Journal of World History*, 30 (1–2), 157–192.
Abramovich, V., & Courtis, C. (2002). *Los derechos sociales como derechos exigibles*, Madrid: Trotta.
Abramovich, V., & Courtis, C. (2009). Apuntes sobre la exigibilidad judicial de los derechos sociales. In R. Gargarella, ed., *Teoría y crítica del derecho constitucional*. Buenos Aires: Abeledo Perrot, pp. 1–12.
Acemoglu, D., & Robinson, J. (2009). *Economic Origins of Dictatorship and Democracy*, Cambridge: Cambridge University Press.
Acemoglu, D., & Robinson, J. A. (2019). *The Narrow Corridor: How Nations Struggle for Liberty*, New York: Penguin Books.
Achen, C., & Bartels, L. (2016). *Democracy for Realists: Why Elections Do Not Produce Responsive Government*, Princeton: Princeton University Press.
Ackerman, B. (1991). *We the People: Foundations*, Cambridge, MA: Harvard University Press.
Ackerman, B. (1998). *We the People: Transformations*, Cambridge, MA: Harvard University Press.
Ackerman, B. (2000). The New Separation of Powers. *Harvard Law Review*, 113 (3), 633–729.
Ackerman, B. (2004). The Emergency Constitution. *Yale Law Journal*, 113 (5), 1029–1091.
Ackerman, B. (2006). *Before the Next Attack: Preserving Civil Liberties in an Age of Terrorism*, New Haven: Yale University Press.
Ackerman, B. (2007). The Living Constitution. *Harvard Law Review*, 120 (7), 1737–1812.
Ackerman, B. (2011). Lost Inside the Beltway: A Reply to Professor Morrison. *Harvard Law Review Forum*, 124 (13), 13–41.
Ackerman, B. (2014). *We the People: The Civil Rights Revolution*, Cambridge, MA: Harvard University Press.
Ackerman, B. (2018). *We The People Volume 3: The Civil Rights Revolution*, Cambridge, MA: Harvard University Press.
Ackerman, B. (2019). *Revolutionary Constitutions: Charismatic Leadership and the Rule of Law*, Cambridge, MA: Belknap Press.
Acton, L. (1862). Nationality. *Home and Foreign Review* 1 (July 1862), 1–25.
Adams, T. (2018). Ultra Vires Revisited. *Public Law*, 2018 (1), 31–43.
Adler, M. (2009). Social Facts, Constitutional Interpretation and the Rule of Recognition. In M. Adler, & K. E. Himma, eds., *The Rule of Recognition and the U.S. Constitution*. New York: Oxford University Press, pp. 193–233.
Adler, M. (2012). *Well-Being and Fair Distribution: Beyond Cost-Benefit Analysis*, New York: Oxford University Press.
Adler, M. (2016). Benefit-Cost Analysis and Distributional Weights. *Review of Environmental Economics and Policy*, 10 (2), 264–285.
Adler, M. (2019). *Measuring Social Welfare: An Introduction*, New York: Oxford University Press.
Adler, M., & Posner, E. (2006). *New Foundations of Cost-Benefit Analysis*, Cambridge, MA: Harvard University Press.
Admati, A., & Hellwig, M. (2014). *The Bankers' New Clothes: What's Wrong with Banking and What to Do about It*, Princeton: Princeton University Press.
Adolph, C. (2013). *Bankers, Bureaucrats, and Central Bank Politics: The Myth of Neutrality*, New York: Cambridge University Press.
AfD. (2017). *Manifesto for Germany. The Political Programme of the Alternative for Germany*.
Affolder, N. (2021). Transnational Climate Law. In P. Zumbansen, ed., *Oxford Handbook of Transnational Law*. Oxford: Oxford University Press, pp. 247–268.

Afilalo, A (2001). Constitutionalization Through the Back Door: A European Perspective on NAFTA's Investment Chapter. *NYU Journal of International Law and Politics*, 34 (1), 1–55.
Afonso Da Silva, V. (2013). Deciding without Deliberating. *International Journal of Constitutional Law*, 11 (3), 557–584.
Agamben, G. (1998). *Homo Sacre: Sovereign Power and Bare Life*. Trans. by D. Heller-Roazen. Redwood City: Stanford University Press.
Agamben, G. (2005). *State of Exception*. Translated by Kevin Attell. Chicago and London: University of Chicago Press.
Agamben, G. (2014). What Is a Destituent Power? *Environment and Planning D: Society and Space*, 32 (1), 65–74.
Agirdag, O. (2014). The Long-Term Effects of Bilingualism on Children of Immigration: Student Bilingualism and Future Earnings. *International Journal of Bilingual Education and Bilingualism*, 17 (4), 449–464.
Agrama, H. A. (2012). *Questioning Secularism: Islam, Sovereignty, and the Rule of Law in Modern Egypt*, Chicago: Chicago University Press.
Ahmed, A. (2012). *Democracy and the Politics of Electoral System Choice: Engineering Electoral Dominance*, Cambridge: Cambridge University Press.
Ahmed, F. (2021). The Delegation Theory of Judicial Review. *Modern Law Review*, 84 (4), 772–810.
Ahmed, F., & Jhaveri, S. (2021). Deconstitutionalising and Localising Administrative Law in India. In S. Jhaveri, & M. Ramsden, eds., *Judicial Review of Administrative Action across the Common Law World: Origins and Adaptations*. Cambridge: Cambridge University Press, pp. 273–288.
Ahmed, F, & Perry, A. (2014). The Quasi-Entrenchment of Constitutional Statutes. *Cambridge Law Journal*, 73 (3), 514–535.
Ahmed, F., & Perry, A. (2018). Standing and Civic Virtue. *Law Quarterly Review*, 134 (April), pp. 239–256.
Albert, R. (2009). The Fusion of Presidentialism and Parliamentarism. *The American Journal of Comparative Law*, 57 (3), 531–578.
Albert, R. (2010). Constitutional Handcuffs. *Arizona State Law Review*, 42 (3), 664–716.
Albert, R. (2013). The Expressive Function of Constitutional Amendment Rules. *McGill Law Journal*, 59 (2), 225–282.
Albert, R. (2014a). The Importance of Constitutional Amendment by Constitutional Desuetude. *American Journal of Comparative Law*, 62 (3), 641–686.
Albert, R. (2014b). The Structure of Constitutional Amendment Rules. *Wake Forest Law Review*, 49 (4), 913–976.
Albert, R. (2015). Amending Constitutional Amendment Rules. *International Journal of Constitutional Law*, 13 (3), 655–685.
Albert, R. (2019). *Constitutional Amendments*, Oxford: Oxford University Press.
Albi, A., & Bardutzky, S. (2019). Revisiting the Role and Future of National Constitutions in European and Global Governance: Introduction to the Research Project. In A. Albi, & S. Bardutzky, eds., *National Constitutions in European and Global Governance: Democracy, Rights, the Rule of Law*. The Hague: T.M.C. Asser Press, pp. 3–37.
Aleinikoff, A. (1987). Constitutional Law in the Age of Balancing. *Yale Law Journal*, 96 (5), 943–1005.
Aleinikoff, A. (2002). *Semblances of Sovereignty: The Constitution, the State, and American Citizenship*, Cambridge, MA: Harvard University Press.
Alemán, E., & Tsebelis, G., eds. (2016). *Legislative Institutions and Lawmaking in Latin America*, Oxford: Oxford University Press.

Alexander, L. (2009). Constitutionalism. In Christiano, T., & Christman, J., eds., *Contemporary Debates in Political Philosophy*. Oxford: Wiley-Blackwell, pp. 283–300.
Alexy, R. (2002). *A Theory of Constitutional Rights*, Oxford: Oxford University Press.
Alexy, R. (2005). Balancing, Constitutional Review, and Representation. *International Journal of Constitutional Law*, 3 (4), 572–581.
Al-Fahad, A. (2005). Ornamental Constitutionalism: The Saudi Basic Law of Governance. *The Yale Journal of International Law*, 30 (2), 375–396.
Al-Hout, S. (2006). *My Life in the PLO: The Inside Story of the Palestinian Struggle*, New York: Pluto Press.
Allan, T. R. S. (1994). *Law, Liberty and Justice: The Legal Foundations of British Constitutionalism*, Oxford: Oxford University Press.
Allan, T. R. S. (2003). *Constitutional Justice: A Liberal Theory of the Rule of Law*, Oxford: Oxford University Press.
Allan, T. R. S. (2013). *The Sovereignty of Law: Freedom, Constitution and Common Law*, Oxford: Oxford University Press.
Allen, D. S., (2004). *Talking to Strangers: Anxieties of Citizenship since Brown v. Board of Education*, Chicago: University of Chicago Press.
Allinson J. (2019). A Fifth Generation of Revolution Theory? *Journal of Historical Sociology*, 32 (1), 142–151.
Alter, K. (2001). *Establishing the Supremacy of European Law*, Oxford: Oxford University Press.
Alter, K. (2014). *The New Terrain of International Law: Courts, Politics, Rights*, Princeton: Princeton University Press.
Alterio, A. M. (2019). Reactive vs Structural Approach: A Public Law Response to Populism. *Global Constitutionalism*, 8 (2), 270–296.
Althusius, J. (1995 [1603]). *Politica Methodice Digesta, Atque Exemplis Sacris et Profanis Illustrata*. Edited and translated by Frederick S. Carney. Indianapolis: Liberty Fund.
Altman, D. (2010). *Direct Democracy Worldwide*, Cambridge: Cambridge University Press.
Alvarez, J. (2003). The New Dispute Settlers: Half-Truths and Consequences. *Texas International Law Journal*, 38 (3), 405–444.
Amar, A. R. (1999). Intratextualism. *Havard Law Review*, 112 (4), 747–827.
Amar, A. R. (2012). *America's Unwritten Constitution: The Precedents and Principles We Live By*, New York: Basic Books.
American Bar Association, Special Committee on Administrative Law. (1938). *Annual Reports of the American Bar Association* 63, 331–368.
American Immigration Council. (2010). The Ones They Leave Behind: Deportation of Lawful Permanent Residents Harm U.S. Citizen Children. Available from: https://web.archive.org/web/20201028021851/ www.americanimmigrationcouncil.org/research/ones-they-leave-behind-deportation-lawful-permanent-residents-harm-us-citizen-children [Viewed 4 January 2020].
American National Election Studies. (2020). Available from: https://electionstudies.org/data-center/.
Amery, L. S., (1964). *Thoughts on the Constitution*, Oxford: Oxford University Press.
Andenæs, J. (2003). *Statsforfatningen i Norge*, Oslo: Universitetsforlaget.
Anderson, E. (1999). What Is the Point of Equality? *Ethics*, 109 (2), 287–337.
Anderson, E. (2010). *The Imperative of Integration*, Princeton: Princeton University Press.
Anderson, E. (2017). *Private Government: How Employers Rule Our Lives (and Why we Don't Talk about It)*, Princeton: Princeton University Press.
Andersson, R. (2014). *Illegality, Inc.: Clandestine Migration and the Business of Bordering Europe*, Berkeley: University of California Press.

Andeweg, R. B. (2015). Consociationalism. In J. D. Wright, ed., *International Encyclopedia of the Social and Behavioral Sciences*, 2nd edn, vol. IV. Oxford: Elsevier, pp. 692–694.

Andeweg, R. B. (2019). Consociationalism in the Low Countries: Comparing the Dutch and Belgian Experience. *Swiss Political Science Review*, 25 (4), 408–425.

Ankersmit, F. R. (2002). *Political Representation*, Stanford: Stanford University Press.

Anonymous. (1855). Parliamentary Opposition. *The Edinburgh Review*, 101, 1–22.

Anscombe, G. E. M. (1981). Rules, Rights, and Promises. In *Ethics, Religion, and Politics: Collected Philosophical Papers*. Vol III. Oxford: Blackwell.

APSA. (1950). Summary of Conclusions and Proposals. *American Political Science Review*, 44 (3), Part 2, Supplement, 1–14.

Arato, A. (2000a). *Civil Society, Constitution, and Legitimacy*, Lanham: Rowman & Littlefield Publishers.

Arato, A. (2000b). The New Democracies and American Constitutional Design. *Constellations*, 7 (3), 316–340.

Arato, A. (2016). *Post Sovereign Constitution Making: Legitimacy and Learning*, Oxford: Oxford University Press.

Arato, A. (2017). *The Adventures of the Constituent Power: Beyond Revolutions?* Cambridge: Cambridge University Press.

Arato, A. (2019). Populism, Constitutional Courts, and Civil Society. In C. Landfried, ed., *Judicial Power: How Constitutional Courts Affect Political Transformations*. Cambridge: Cambridge University Press, pp. 318–341.

Arato, A. (2020). How We Got Here? Transition Failures, Their Causes and the Populist Interest in the Constitution. *Philosophy & Social Criticism*, 45 (9–10), 1106–1115.

Arato, A., & Cohen, J. (2021). *Populism and Civil Society: The Challenge to Constitutional Democracy*, Oxford: Oxford University Press.

Arban, E., Bottini, E., & Samararatne, D. (2020). Bruce Ackerman, Revolutionary Constitutions: Charismatic Leadership and the Rule of Law, Belknap Press: Harvard University Press, 2019. *Modern Law Review*, 83 (5), 1108–1112.

Arendt, H. (1963). *On Revolution*, New York: Viking Press.

Arendt, H. (1970). Reflections on civil disobedience. *The New Yorker*. 12 September. pp. 70–105.

Arendt, H. (1973). *The Origins of Totalitarianism*, new edn, New York: Harcourt.

Arendt, H., (1998). *The Human Condition*, Chicago: University of Chicago Press.

Aristotle (1906). *The Nichomachean Ethics of Aristotle*. Translated by F. H. Peters, 10th edn, London: Kegan Paul, Trench, Trübner & Co.

Aristotle (1975). *Nicomachean Ethics*. Translated by H. Rackman. Cambridge, MA: Harvard University Press.

Aristotle (1996). *The Politics: In The Politics and The Constitution of Athens*. Edited by S. Everson. Cambridge: Cambridge University Press.

Aristotle (2000). *Nicomachean Ethics*. Edited and translated by Roger Crisp. Cambridge: Cambridge University Press.

Aristotle (2009). *Nicomachean Ethics*. Translated by David Ross. Edited by Lesley Brown. Oxford: Oxford University Press.

Armitage, D. (2014). Foreword. In R. R. Palmer, (ed.),(2014). *The Age of the Democratic Revolution: A Political History of Europe and America, 1760–1800*, Princeton: Princeton University Press, pp. xv–xxii.

Arneson, R. J. (2004). Luck Egalitarianism Interpreted and Defended. *Philosophical Topics*, 32 (1/2), 1–20.

Arnon, A. (2010). *Monetary Theory and Policy from Hume and Smith to Wicksell: Money, Credit, and the Economy*, Cambridge: Cambridge University Press.

Aroney, N. (2007). *The Constitution of a Federal Commonwealth: The Making and Meaning of the Australian Constitution*, Cambridge: Cambridge University Press.

Aroney, N. (2015). Law and Convention. In B. Galligan, & S. Brenton, eds., *Constitutional Conventions in Westminster Systems*. Cambridge: Cambridge University Press, pp. 24–50.

Aroney, N., et al. (2015). *The Constitution of the Commonwealth of Australia: History, Principle and Interpretation*, Port Melbourne: Cambridge University Press.

Aroney, N. (2019). The Federal Condition. In A. Lev, ed., *The Federal Idea: Public Law between Governance and Political Life*. Oxford: Hart Publishing, pp. 29–51.

Asad, T. (2012). Thinking about Religious Belief and Politics. In R. Orsi, ed., *Cambridge Companion to Religious Studies*. New York: Cambridge University Press, pp. 36–57.

Aspinall, E. (2011). Democratization and Ethnic Politics in Indonesia: Nine Theses. *Journal of East Asian Studies*, 11 (2), 289–319.

Aulard, A. (1882). *Les orateurs de la Révolution Française*, Paris: Hachette.

Austin, J. (1861). *Lectures on Jurisprudence, or The Philosophy of Positive Law*, 2nd edn, volume I, London: John Murray.

Austin, J. (1885). *Lectures on Jurisprudence, or The Philosophy of Positive Law*, 5th edn, London: John Murray.

Austin, J. (2000). *The Province of Jurisprudence Determined*, Amherst: Prometheus Books.

Austin, L., & Klimchuk, D., eds. (2014). *The Rule of Law and Private Law*, Oxford: Oxford University Press.

Australian Election Commission. (© 2018). Compulsory voting. Available from: https://web.archive.org/web/20180715211955/ www.aec.gov.au/Voting/Compulsory_Voting.htm [Viewed 15 July 2018].

Avineri S. (1971). *The Social & Political Thought of Karl Marx*, Cambridge: Cambridge University Press.

Avril, P. (1997). *Les conventions de la constitution*, Paris: Presses Universitaires de France.

Aydın, A. (2013). Judicial Independence across Democratic Regimes: Understanding the Varying Impact of Political Competition. *Law & Society Review*, 47 (1), 105–134.

Aydogan, A. (2019). Constitutional Foundations of Military Coups. *Political Science Quarterly*, 134 (1), 85–116.

Ayres, I., & Braithwaite, J. (1992). *Responsive Regulation: Transcending the Deregulation Debate*, New York: Oxford University Press.

Azoulai, L., & Rasnača, Z. (2016). The Court of Justice of the European Union as a Self-Made Statesmen. In D. Patterson, & A. Södersten, eds., *A Companion to European Union Law and International Law*. Hoboken: John Wiley & Sons, pp. 166–178.

Bach, S. (2003). *Platypus and parliament: The Australian Senate in Theory and Practice*, Canberra: Department of the Senate.

Bache, I., & Flinders, M. (2004). *Multi-level Governance*, Oxford: Oxford University Press.

Bache, I., Bartle, I., & Flinders, M. (2016). Multi-level Governance. In C. Ansell, & J. Torfing, eds., *Handbook on Theories of Governance*. Northampton: Edward Elgar Publishing, pp. 486–498.

Bader, R. M. (2018). Moralized Conceptions of Liberty. In D. Schmidtz, & C. Pavel, eds., *The Oxford Handbook of Freedom*. Oxford: Oxford University Press, pp. 59–75.

Badura, P. (1967). *Das Verwaltungsrecht des liberalen Rechtsstaates*, Goettingen: Verlag Otto Schwartz.

Baer, S. (2018). The Rule of – and Not by Any – Law. On Constitutionalism. *Current Legal Problems*, 71 (1), 335–368.

Baer, M., Campiglio, E., & Deyris, J. (2021). It Takes Two to Dance: Institutional Dynamics and Climate-Related Financial Policies. *Ecological Economics*, 190, 107210.

Bagehot, W. (2001 [1867]). *The English Constitution*, Oxford: Oxford University Press.
Bailly, J.-S. (1804). *Mémoires*, Paris: Levrault.
Baker, A. (2013). The New Political Economy of the Macroprudential Ideational Shift. *New Political Economy*, 18 (1), 112–139.
Baker, E. C. (2007). *Media Concentration and Democracy: Why Ownership Matters*, Cambridge: Cambridge University Press.
Baldwin R., & Black, J. (2010). Really Responsive Risk Based Regulation. *Law and Policy*, 32 (2), 181–213.
Baldwin, R., Cave, M., & Lodge, M. (2010). *Oxford Handbook of Regulation*, Oxford: Oxford University Press.
Baldwin, R., Cave, M., & Lodge, M. (2012). *Understanding Regulation: Theory, Strategy, and Practice*, Oxford: Oxford University Press.
Balkin, J. (2011). *Constitutional Redemption: Political Faith in an Unjust World*, Cambridge, MA: Harvard University Press.
Ball, L. (1993). *What Determines the Sacrifice Ratio?* Working Paper No. 4306. National Bureau of Economic Research.
Banai, A. (2013). Language Recognition and Fair Terms of Inclusion: Minority Languages in the European Union. In S. G. de Latour, & P. Balint, eds., *Liberal Multiculturalism and the Fair Terms of Integration*. Basingstoke: Palgrave Macmillan, pp. 194–210.
Banfield, A. (2015). Canada. In B. Galligan, & S. Brenton, eds., *Constitutional Conventions in Westminster Systems*. Cambridge: Cambridge University Press, pp. 189–203.
Banner, S. (2007). *How the Indians Lost Their Land: Law and Power on the Frontier*, Cambridge, MA: Harvard University Press.
Baradaran, M. (2017). *The Color of Money: Black Banks and the Racial Wealth Gap*, Harvard University Press.
Barak, A. (2012). *Proportionality*, Cambridge: Cambridge University Press.
Barak, A. (2015). *Human Dignity: The Constitutional Value and the Constitutional Right*, Cambridge: Cambridge University Press.
Baranger, D. (2018). *Penser La Loi: Essai sur le législateur des temps modernes*, Paris: Gallimard.
Barber, B. (1984). *Strong Democracy. Participatory Politics for a New Age*, Berkeley: University of California Press.
Barber, N. (2004). Must Legalistic Conceptions of the Rule of Law Have a Social Dimension? *Ratio Juris*, 17 (4), 474–488.
Barber, N. (2010). *The Constitutional State*, Oxford: Oxford University Press.
Barber, N. (2016). Why Entrench? *International Journal of Constitutional Law*, 14 (2), 325–350.
Barber, N. (2018). *The Principles of Constitutionalism*, Oxford: Oxford University Press.
Barber, N. (2019). The Two Europes. In M. Cahill, R. Ekins, & N. W. Barber, eds., *The Rise and Fall of the European Constitution*. Oxford: Hart Publishing, pp. 89–104.
Barère, B. (2002 [1794]). Rapport du comité de salut public sur les idiomes. In M. de Certeau, D. Julia, & J. Revel, eds., *Une politique de la langue. La Révolution française et les patois: l'enquête de Grégoire*. Paris: Gallimard, pp. 323–331.
Barker, B. (1972). *Ramsay MacDonald's Political Writings*, London: Allen Lane.
Barnett, H. (2002). *Constitutional and Administrative Law*, 4th edn, London: Cavendish Publishing.
Barnett, R. (2003). Constitutional Legitimacy. *Columbia Law Review*, 103 (1), 111–148.
Barnett, R. (2004). *Restoring the Lost Constitution: The Presumption of Liberty*, Princeton: Princeton University Press.
Barontini, C., & Holden, H. (2019). *Proceeding with Caution: A Survey on Central Bank Digital Currency*, Basel: Bank for International Settlements.

Barradas de Freitas, R. (2016). Three Questions for Moderate Sceptics. *Analisi e Diritto*, 305–319.
Barritt, E., & Sediti, B. (2019). The Symbolic Value of *Leghari v Federation of Pakistan*: Climate Change Adjudication in the Global South. *King's Law Journal*, 20 (2), 203–210.
Barroso, L. R. (2012). Here, There, and Everywhere: Human Dignity in Contemporary Law and in the Transnational Discourse. *Boston College International and Comparative Law Review*, 35 (2), 331–393.
Barry, B. (1965). *Political Argument*, London: Routledge and Kegan Paul.
Barry, B. (1975). Political Accommodation and Consociational Democracy. *British Journal of Political Science*, 5 (4), 477–505.
Barry, B. (2001). *Culture and Equality*, Cambridge: Polity.
Barry, N., & Miragliotta, N. (2015). Australia. In B. Galligan, & S. Brenton, eds., *Constitutional Conventions in Westminster Systems*. Cambridge: Cambridge University Press, pp. 204–216.
Bartels, L. (2008). *Unequal Democracy*, Princeton: Princeton University Press.
Barton, J., Goldstein, J., Josling, T., & Steinberg, R. (2008). *The Evolution of the Trade Regime: Politics, Law, and Economics of the GATT and the WTO*, Princeton: Princeton University Press.
Bateman, W. (2020). *Public Finance and Parliamentary Constitutionalism*, Cambridge: Cambridge University Press.
Bates, D. W. (2012). *States of War: Enlightenment Origins of the Political*, New York: Columbia University Press.
Baturo, A. (2014). *Democracy, Dictatorship, and Term Limits*, Ann Arbor: University of Michigan Press.
Baturo, A., & Elgie, R., eds. (2019). *The Politics of Presidential Term Limits*, Oxford: Oxford University Press.
Baubök, R. (1994). *Transnational Citizenship: Membership and Rights in International Migration*, Brookfield: Edward Elgar.
Baudet, T. (2013). *Oikofobie*, Amsterdam: Prometheus.
Baume, S., Boillet, V., & Martenet, V., eds. (2021). *Misinformation in Referenda*, London: Routledge.
Baynes, K. (2000). Rights as Critique and the Critique of Rights: Karl Marx, Wendy Brown, and the Social Function of Rights. *Political Theory*, 28 (4), 451–468.
BBC News. (2019). Citizenship Amendment Bill: India's New "anti-Muslim" Law Explained. 11 December. Available from: https://web.archive.org/web/20201129115229/ www.bbc.com/news/world-asia-india-50670393 [Viewed 29 November 2020]
BBC News. (2020). Windrush Generation: Who Are They and Why Are They Facing Problems? 31 July. Available from: https://web.archive.org/web/20200825024907/ www.bbc.com/news/uk-43782241 [Viewed 25 August 2020].
Beard, C. (1913). *An Economic Interpretation of the Origins of the Constitution of the United States*, New York: Macmillan.
Beaud, O. (1999). *Le Sang contaminé. Essai critique sur la criminalisation de la responsabilité des gouvernants*, Paris: Presses Universitaires de France.
Beaud, O. (2005). De quelques particularités de la justice constitutionnelle dans un système federal. In C. Grewe, O. Jouanjan, E. Maulin, & P. Wachsmann, eds., *La notion de la "justice constitutionnelle"*. Paris: Dalloz, pp. 49–72.
Beaud, O. (2009). *Théorie de la Federation*, Paris: Presses Universitaires de France.
Beaud, O. (2013). Conceptions of the State. In M. Rosenfeld, & A. Sajó, eds., *Oxford Handbook of Comparative Constitutional Law*. Oxford: Oxford University Press, pp. 269–282.
Beaud, O. (2017). The Founding Constitution Reflections on the Constitution of a Federation and Its Peculiarity. *Jus Politicum; Revue de Droit Politique*, 17, 33–63.

Becchi, P. (2019). *Manifesto sovranista. Per la liberazione dei popoli europei*, Rome: Giubilei Regnani.
Becher, M., & Stegmuller, D. (2021). Reducing Unequal Representation: Labor Unions and Equal Representation: The Impact of Labor Unions on Legislative Responsiveness in the U. S. Congress. *Perspectives on Politics*, 19 (1), 92–109.
Beck, U. (1992). *The Risk Society*, London: Sage Publications.
Bedau, H. (1968). On Civil Disobedience. *Journal of Philosophy*, 58 (21), 653–665.
Beers, D. J. (2012). Judicial Self-Governance and the Rule of Law: Evidence from Romania and the Czech Republic. *Problems of Post-Communism*, 59 (5), 50–67.
Beetham, D. (1991). *The Legitimation of Power*, London: Macmillan.
Beetham, D. (2013). *The Legitimation of Power*, 2nd edn, London: Palgrave Macmillan.
Beitz, C. (1989). *Political Equality*, Princeton: Princeton University Press.
Beitz, C. (2009). *The Idea of Human Rights*, Oxford: Oxford University Press.
Beitz, C. (2013). Human Dignity in the Theory of Human Rights: Nothing but a Phrase? *Philosophy and Public Affairs*, 41 (3), 259–290.
Bell, D. (1978). The Referendum: Democracy's Barrier to Racial Equality. *Washington Law Review*, 54 (1), 1–29.
Bell, J., Elliott, M., Murray, P., & Varuhas, J., eds. (2016). *Public Law Adjudication in the Common Law World: Process and Substance*, Oxford: Hart.
Bellamy, R. (1999). *Liberalism and Pluralism: Towards a Politics of Compromise*, London: Routledge.
Bellamy, R. ed. (2005). *The Rule of Law and the Separation of Powers*, London: Routledge.
Bellamy, R. (2007). *Political Constitutionalism: A Republican Defence of the Constitutionality of Democracy*, Cambridge: Cambridge University Press.
Bellamy, R. (2008). *Citizenship: A Very Short Introduction*, Oxford: Oxford University Press.
Bellamy, R. (2011). Political Constitutionalism and the Human Rights Act. *International Journal of Constitutional Law*, 9 (1), 86–111.
Bellamy, R. (2012). Rights as Democracy. *Critical Review of International Social and Political Philosophy*, 15 (4), 449–471.
Bellamy, R. (2014a). *Croce, Gramsci, Bobbio and the Italian Political Tradition*, Colchester: ECPR Press/Rowman and Littlefield.
Bellamy, R. (2014b). The Democratic Legitimacy of International Human Rights Conventions: Political Constitutionalism and the European Convention on Human Rights. *European Journal of International Law*, 25 (4), 1019–1042.
Bellamy, R. (2015). Rights, Democracy and Republicanism. In A. Nierderberger, ed., *Republican Democracy*, Edinburgh: Edinburgh Press, pp. 253–275.
Bellamy, R. (2016). Turtles All the Way Down? Is the Political Constitutionalist Appeal to Disagreement Self-Defeating? A Reply to Cormac Mac Amhlaigh. *International Journal of Constitutional Law*, 14 (1), 204–216.
Bellamy, R. (2019). *A Republican Europe of States. Cosmopolitanism, Intergovernmentalism, and Democracy in the EU*, Cambridge: Cambridge University Press.
Bellamy, R. (2023). Political Constitutionalism and Referendums: The Case of Brexit. *Social & Legal Studies*, 32 (6), 973–995.
Benhabib, S. (1996). Toward a Deliberative Model of Democratic Legitimacy. In S. Benhabib, ed., *Democracy and Difference: Contesting the Boundaries of the Political*. Princeton, NJ: Princeton University Press, pp. 67–94.
Benhabib, S. (2004). *The Rights of Others: Aliens, Residents, and Citizens*, New York: Cambridge University Press.
Benjamin, W. (2003). *Selected Writings*. Volume 4, 1938–1940, Cambridge, MA: Harvard University Press.

Bennett, H. (2013). *Principles of the Law of Agency*, Oxford: Hart.
Bennett, W. L., & Steven Livingston, eds. (2021). *The Disinformation Age: Politics, Technology, and Disruptive Communication in the United States*. Cambridge: Cambridge University Press.
Bentham, J. (1834). *Traités de Legislation*. Translated as C. K. Ogden ed., The Theory of Legislation. London: Kegan Paul.
Bentham, J. (1843a). Anarchical Fallacies. In J. Bowring, ed., *The Works of Jeremy Bentham*, vol. II. Edinburgh: William Tait, pp. 489–534.
Bentham, J. (1843b). *Plan of Parliamentary Reform. Vol. III of Works*. Edited by W. Stark. London: George Allen and Unwin.
Bentham, J. (1977). A Fragment on Government. In *A Comment on the Commentaries and A Fragment on Government*. Edited by J. H. Burns, & H. L. A. Hart. London: The Athlone Press.
Bentham, J. (1990). *Securities against Misrule and other Constitutional Writings for Tripoli and Greece*, Oxford: Oxford University Press.
Bentham, J. (1999). *Political Tactics*, Oxford: Oxford University Press.
Benton, L. (2006). Constitutions and Empires. *Law and Social Inquiry*, 31 (1), 177–198.
Benvenisti, E. (1999). Margin of Appreciation, Consensus and Universal Standards. *NYU Journal*, 31 (3), 843–854.
Bergallo, P. (2013). El género en el constitucionalismo latinoamericano contemporáneo. Draft on file with the author.
Berlin, I. (1969). *Four Essays on Liberty*, Oxford: Oxford University Press.
Berlin, I. (1991). *The Crooked Timber of Humanity*, New York: Alfred A. Knopf.
Berlin, I. (2013). The Pursuit of the Ideal. In *The Crooked Timber of Humanity*. Princeton: Princeton University Press, pp. 1–20.
Berman, H. J. (1983). *Law and Revolution: The Formation of the Western Legal Tradition*, Cambridge: Harvard University Press.
Bermann, G. A., & Picard, E., eds. (2012). *An Introduction to French Law, Alpjem aam dem*, Rijn: Wolters Kluwer.
Bermeo, N. (2003). *Ordinary People in Extraordinary Times: The Citizenry and the Breakdown of Democracy*, Princeton: Princeton University Press.
Bernal, A. M. (2017). *Beyond Origins: Rethinking Foundings in a Time of Constitutional Democracy*, New York: Oxford University Press.
Bernal, C. (2022). Plebiscites and Peace: Comparative Lessons from the 2016 Colombian Plebiscite for Peace. In R. Albert, & R. Stacey, eds., *The Limits and Legitimacy of Referendums*. Oxford: Oxford University Press, pp. 241–263.
Bernanke, B., Laubach, T., Mishkin, F., & Posen, A. (2001). *Inflation Targeting: Lessons from the International Experience*, Princeton: Princeton University Press.
Bernhard, L. (2012). *Campaign Strategy in Direct Democracy*. Basingstoke: Palgrave Macmillan.
Bernstorff, J. v. (2019). The Decay of the International Rule of Law Project (1990–2015). In H. Krieger, G. Nolte, & A. Zimmermann, eds., *The International Rule of Law – Rise or Decline?* Oxford: Oxford University Press, pp. 33–55.
Besson, S. (2021). *Reconstruire l'ordre institutionnel international*, Paris: Fayard, Collège de France.
Best, J. (2016). Rethinking Central Bank Accountability in Uncertain Times. *Ethics & International Affairs*, 30 (2), 215–232.
Bezemer, D., Ryan-Collins, J., van Lerven, F., & Zhang, L. (2018). *Credit where it's due: A historical, theoretical and empirical review of credit guidance policies in the 20th century*. UCL Institute for Innovation and Public Purpose Working Paper Series No. 2018–11. Retrieved from www.ucl.ac.uk/bartlett/public-purpose/publications/2018/nov/credit-where-its-due.
Bhargava, R. ed., (1998). *Secularism and Its Critics*, Oxford: Oxford University Press.

Bhat, M. A. (2021). Governing Democracy Outside the Law: India's Election Commission and the Challenge of Accountability. *Asian Journal of Comparative Law*, 16 (S1), S85–S104.

Bhat, M. A. (2022). Between Trust and Democracy: The Election Commission of India and the Question of Constitutional Accountability. In S. Jhaveri, T. Khaitan, & D. Samararatne, eds., *Constitutional Resilience beyond Courts: Views from South Asia*. London, UK: Bloomsbury Publishing.

Bhatia, G. (2018). The Sole Route to an Independent Judiciary? The Primacy of Judges in Appointment. In A. Sengupta, & R. Sharma, eds., *Appointment of Judges to the Supreme Court of India: Transparency, Accountability, and Independence*. Oxford: Oxford University Press, pp. 135–145.

Biaggini, G., 2011. Switzerland. In Oliver, D., & Fusaro, C., eds., *How Constitutions Change: A Comparative Study*. Oxford: Hart Publishing, pp. 303–328.

Bickel, A. (1962). *The Least Dangerous Branch: The Supreme Court at the Bar of Politics*, New Haven: Yale University Press.

Bickel, A. (1986). *The Least Dangerous Branch: The Supreme Court at the Bar of Politics*, 2nd edn, New Haven: Yale University Press.

Bickerton, C. (2012). *European Integration*, Oxford: Oxford University Press.

Bilancia, F. (2001). Brevi note su costituzione materiale, legalitá ed Unione Europea. In A. Catelani, & S. Labriola, eds., *La costituzione materiale*. Milan: Giuffrè, pp. 143–156.

Bilodeau, A., Turgeon, L., White, S., & Henderson. A, (2015). *Seeing the Same Canada? Visible Minorities' Views of the Federation*, IRPP Study No.56.

Bindseil, U. (2014). *Monetary Policy Operations and the Financial System*, New York: Oxford University Press.

Bindseil, U., & Papadia, F. (2009). Risk Management and Market Impact of Central Bank Credit Operations. In U. Bindseil, F. Gonzalez, & E. Tabakis, eds., *Risk Management for Central Banks and Other Public Investors*. Cambridge: Cambridge University Press, pp. 271–302.

Bingham, T. (2010). *The Rule of Law*, London: Penguin.

BIS. (2014). *Re-thinking the Lender of Last Resort*, Basel: Bank for International Settlements.

Bishop, W. (1990). A Theory of Administrative Law. *Journal of Legal Studies*, 19 (2), 489–530.

Bisson, T. (2009). *The Crisis of the Twelfth Century: Power, Lordship, and the Origins of European Government*, Princeton: Princeton University Press.

Black, C. (1997). *A New Birth of Freedom, Human Rights, Named and Unnamed*, New Haven: Yale University Press.

Black, J. (2001). Decentring Regulation: Understanding the Role of Regulation and Self-Regulation in a "Post-Regulatory" World. *Current Legal Problems*, 54 (1), 103–146.

Black, J. (2002). Regulatory Conversations. *Journal of Law and Society*, 29 (1), 163–196.

Black, J. (2003). Enrolling Actors in Regulatory Systems: Examples from UK Financial Services Regulation. *Public Law*, 63–91.

Black, J. (2008). Constructing and Contesting Legitimacy and Accountability in Polycentric Regulatory Regimes. *Regulation and Governance*, 2 (2), 137–164.

Black, J. (2013a). Reconceiving Financial Markets – From the Economic to the Social. *Journal of Corporate Law Studies*, 13 (2), 401–442.

Black, J. (2013b). Calling Regulators to Account: Challenges, Capacities and Prospects. In N. Bamforth, & P. Leyland, eds., *Accountability in the Contemporary Constitution*. Oxford: Oxford University Press, pp. 354–388.

Blackstone, W. (1979 [1765–1769]). *Commentaries on the Laws of England*, vol. I. Chicago: University of Chicago Press.

Blake, M. (2002). Discretionary Immigration. *Philosophical Topics*, 30 (2), 273–289.

Blake, M. (2005). Immigration. In R. G. Frey, & C. Heath Wellman, eds., *A Companion to Applied Ethics*. Malden, MA: Blackwell, pp. 224–237.

Blake, M. (2013). Immigration, Jurisdiction, and Exclusion. *Philosophy & Public Affairs*, 41 (2), 103–130.

Blanchard, O. (2018). Should We Reject the Natural Rate Hypothesis? *The Journal of Economic Perspectives*, 32 (1), 97–120.

Blanchard, O., & Katz, L. F. (1997). What We Know and Do Not Know About the Natural Rate of Unemployment. *The Journal of Economic Perspectives*, 11 (1), 51–72.

Blanchard, O., Cerutti, E., & Summers, L. (2015). *Inflation and Activity – Two Explorations and their Monetary Policy Implications*. Working Paper No. 21726. National Bureau of Economic Research.

Blankenburg, E. (1995). The Purge of Lawyers after the Breakdown of the East German Communist Regime. *Law & Social Inquiry*, 20 (1), 223–243.

Blick, A. (2012). The Cabinet Manual and the Codification of Conventions. *Parliamentary Affairs*, 67 (1), 191–208.

Blick, A. (2015). Constitutional Reform. In B. Galligan, & S. Brenton, eds., Constitutional Conventions in Westminster Systems. Cambridge: Cambridge University Press, pp. 249–260.

Blinder, A. (1999). *Central Banking in Theory and Practice*, Cambridge, MA: MIT Press.

Blokker, P. (2018). Populist Constitutionalism. In C. de la Torre, ed., *Routledge Handbook of Global Populism*. London, New York: Routledge.

Blokker, P. (2019a). Populism as a Constitutional Project. *International Journal of Constitutional Law*, 17 (2), 536–553.

Blokker, P. (2019b). Varieties of Populist Constitutionalism: The Transnational Dimension. *German Law Journal*, 20 (3), 332–350.

Blokker, P. (2020). Populist Understandings of the Law: A Conservative Backlash? *Participation and Conflict*, 13 (3), 1411–1416.

Blondel, J. (1997). Political Opposition in the Contemporary World. *Government and Opposition*, 32 (4), 462–486.

Blum, M. C., & Wood, M. C. (2017). "No Ordinary Lawsuit": Climate Change, Due Process, and the Public Trust Doctrine. *American University Law Review*, 67 (1), 1–88.

Blumenthal, U.-R. (1988). *The Investiture Controversy: Church and Monarchy from the Ninth to the Twelfth Century*, Philadelphia: Pennsylvania University Press.

Bobek, M., & Kosař, D. (2014). Global Solutions, Local Damages: A Critical Study in Judicial Councils in Central and Eastern Europe. *German Law Journal*, 15 (7), 171–206.

Böckenförde, E.-W. (1976). Die Bedeutung der Unterscheidung von Staat und Gesellschaft im demokratischen Sozialstaat der Gegenwart. In E.-W. Böckenförde, ed., *Staat, Gesellschaft, Freiheit*, Frankfurt-am-Main: Suhrkamp, pp. 185–220.

Böckenförde, E.-W. (1987). Demokratie als Verfassungsprinzip. In *Staat, Verfassung, Demokratie*. Frankfurt-am-Main: Suhrkamp, pp. 289–378.

Böckenförde, E.-W. (1991). *State, Society, and Liberty: Studies in Political Theory and Constitutional Law*. Translated by J. Underwood. Oxford: Berg Publishers.

Böckenförde, E.-W. (1992). *Staat, Verfassung, Demokratie*, Frankfurt-am-Main: Suhrkamp.

Böckenförde, E.-W. (2017a). *Constitutional and Political Theory: Selected Writings*. Edited by M. Kunkler, & T. Stein. Oxford: Oxford University Press.

Böckenförde, E.-W. (2017b). The Constituent Power of the People: A Liminal Concept of Constitutional Law. In M. Kunkler, & T. Stein, eds., *Constitutional and Political Theory: Selected Writings*. Oxford: Oxford University Press, pp. 168–185.

Böckenförde, E.-W. (2020 [1967]). The Rise of the Modern State as a Process of Secularization. In M. Künkler, & T. Stein, eds., *Religion, Law, and Democracy: Selected Writings*. Oxford: Oxford University Press, pp. 152–167.

Bodin, J. (1955 [1576]). *Six Books of the Commonwealth*. Abridged and translated by M. J. Tooley. Oxford: Blackwell.
Bodin, J. (1962 [1576]). *The Six Bookes of a Commonweale*. Translated by R. Knolles. Edited by K. D. McRae. Cambridge, MA: Harvard University Press.
Bodin, J. (1992 [1576]). *On Sovereignty*. Edited and translated by J. Franklin. Cambridge: Cambridge University Press.
BoE. (2021). *Options for greening the Bank of England's Corporate Bond Purchase Scheme* [Discussion Paper]. London: Bank of England.
Bogaards, M. (2005). The Italian First Republic: "Degenerated Consociationalism" in a Polarised Party System. *West European Politics*, 28 (3), 503–520.
Bogaards, M. (2019). Consociationalism and Centripetalism: Friends or Foes? *Swiss Political Science Review*, 25 (4), 519–537.
Bogdandy, A. v., & Schill, S. (2011). Overcoming Absolute Primacy: Respect for National Identity under the Lisbon Treaty. *Common Market Law Review*, 48 (5), 1417–1453.
Bogdandy, A. v., P. M. Huber, & C. Grabenwarter (2020). Constitutional Adjudication in the European Legal Space. In Bogdandy, A. v., P. M. Huber, & C. Grabenwarter, eds., *Constitutional Adjudication: Institutions, vol. III of The Max Planck Handbooks in European Public Law*. Oxford: Oxford University Press, pp. 1–17.
Bogdanor, V. (1981). *The People and the Party System*, Cambridge: Cambridge University Press.
Bogg, A., & Estlund, C. (2018). The Right to Strike and Contestatory Citizenship. In H. Collins, G. Lester, & V. Mantouvalou, eds., *Philosophical Foundations of Labour Law*. Oxford: Oxford University Press, pp. 229–251.
Bolívar, S. (1951). *Selected Writings of Bolívar*. Compiled by V. Lecuna. Edited by H. Bierck. Translated by L. Bertrand. New York: The Colonial Press.
Bolton, P., Depres, M., Pereira da Silva, L. A., Samama, F., & Svartzman, R. (2020). *The Green Swan: Central Banking and Financial Stability in the Age of Climate change*, Basel: Bank for International Settlements.
Bonelli, M., & Claes, M. (2018). Judicial Serendipity: How Portuguese Judges Came to the Rescue of the Polish Judiciary (ECJ 27 February 2018, Case C-64/16, Associação Sindical dos Juízes Portugueses). *European Constitutional Law Review*, 14 (3), pp. 622–643.
Bonotti, M. (2017). *Partisanship and Political Liberalism in Diverse Societies*, Oxford: Oxford University Press.
Borio, C. (2011). Central Banking Post-crisis: What Compass for Uncharted Water? *Bank of International Settlements*.
Bork, R. (1971). Neutral Principles and Some First Amendment Problems. *Indiana Law Journal*, 47 (1), 1–35.
Bork, R. (1979). The Impossibility of Finding Welfare Rights in the Constitution. *Washington University Law Quarterly*, 1979 (3), 695–702.
Börzel, T. (2013). EU-Staatlichkeit – ein Oxymoron?, Der Staat, Beiheft 21, pp. 221–235.
Bossacoma Busquets, P. (2020). *Morality and Legality of Secession: A Theory of National Self-Determination*, London: Routledge.
Bosselmann, K. (2013). Grounding the Rule of Law. In C. Voigt, ed., *Rule of Law for Nature*. Cambridge: Cambridge University Press, pp. 75–93.
Bourdieu P. (1987). The Force of Law: Toward a Sociology of the Juridical Field. *Hastings Law Journal*, 38 (5), 805–853.
Bourdieu, P. (2014). *On the State: Lectures at the Collège de France 1989–1992*, Cambridge: Polity.
Bouwer, K. (2018). The Unsexy Future of Climate Change Litigation. *Journal of Environmental Law*, 30 (3), 483–506.

Bovens, M. (2012). Analysing and Assessing Public Accountability: A Conceptual Framework. *European Law Journal*, 13 (4), 447–468.
Bovens, M., Goodin, R., & Schillemans, T., eds. (2014). *The Oxford Handbook of Public Accountability*, Oxford: Oxford University Press.
Bowles, S. (2016). *The Moral Economy: Why Good Incentives Are No Substitute for Good Citizens*, New Haven: Yale University Press.
Boyd, D. R. (2011). *The Environmental Rights Revolution*, Vancouver: UBC Press.
Boysen, S. (2019). Remants of a Constitutional Moment: The Right to Democracy in International Law. In A. von Arnauld, K. von der Decken, & M. Susi, eds., *The Cambridge Handbook of New Human Rights*. Cambridge: Cambridge University Press, pp. 465–480.
Boysen, S. (2021). *Die postkoloniale Konstellation*, Tübingen: Mohr Siebeck.
Bradley, J. (2019). Unearthed. *Meanjin*. Available from: https://meanjin.com.au/essays/unearthed/.
Braudel, F. (1982). *The Wheels of Commerce. Vol. II of Civilization and Capitalism, 15th-18th Century*. Berkeley: University of California Press.
Braun, B. (2015). Governing the Future: The European Central Bank's Expectation Management during the Great Moderation. *Economy and Society*, 44 (3), 367–391.
Braun, B. (2018). Central Bank Planning? Unconventional Monetary Policy and the Price of Bending the Yield Curve. In J. Beckert, & R. Bronk, eds., *Uncertain Futures: Imaginaries, Narratives, and Calculation in the Economy*. Oxford: Oxford University Press, pp. 194–218.
Braun, B. (2020). Central Banking and the Infrastructural Power of Finance: The Case of ECB Support for Repo and Securitization Markets. *Socio-Economic Review*, 18 (2), 395–418.
Braun, B., & Downey, L. (2020). *Against Amnesia: Re-Imagining Central Banking*. Discussion Note No. 2020/01. Council on Economic Policies.
Brazier, R. (1999). *Constitutional Practice: The Foundations of British Government*, 3rd edn, Oxford: Oxford University Press.
Bredin, J.-D. (1988). *Sieyès: La clé de la revolution française*, Paris: Editions de Fallois.
Brennan, G., & Buchanan, J. M. (1980). *The Power to Tax: Analytical Foundations of a Fiscal Constitution*, Cambridge: Cambridge University Press.
Brennan, G., & Buchanan, J. (1985). *The Reason of Rules*, Cambridge: Cambridge University Press.
Brennan, J. (2009). Polluting the Polls: When Citizens Should Not Vote. *Australasian Journal of Philosophy*, 87 (4), 535–549.
Brennan, J. (2016). *Against Democracy*, Princeton: Princeton University Press.
Brennan, J., & Hill, L. (2014). *Compulsory Voting: For and Against*, Cambridge: Cambridge University Press.
Brest, P. (1980). The Misconceived Quest for the Original Understanding. *Boston University Law Review*, 60 (2), 204–238.
Brier, R. (2009). The Roots of the "Fourth Republic" Solidarity's Cultural Legacy to Polish Politics. *East European Politics and Societies*, 23 (1), 63–85.
Brilmayer, L (1989). Consent, Contract, and Territory. *Minnesota Law Review*, 74 (1), 1–35.
Brinks, D. (2005). Judicial Reform and Independence in Brazil and Argentina: The Beginning of a New Millennium? *Texas International Law Journal*, 40 (3), 595–622.
Brinks, D. (2008). *The Judicial Response to Police Killings in Latin America: Inequality and the Rule of Law*, Cambridge: Cambridge University Press.
Brinks, D. (2020). Social Rights Constitutionalism in Latin America. In C. Hubner, & R. Gargarella, eds., *The Latin American Handbook of Constitutional Law*. Oxford: Oxford University Press, pp. 744–757.

Brito Vieira, M., & Runciman, D. (2008). *Representation*, London: Polity Press.
Brookfield, F. M. (2006). *Waitangi and Indigenous Rights: Revolution, Law and Legitimation*, Auckland: Auckland University Press.
Brown, A. J. (2017). *A Theory of Legitimate Expectations for Public Administration*, Oxford: Oxford University Press.
Brown, A. J. (2014). The Integrity Branch: A "System", An "Industry", Or a Sensible Emerging Fourth Arm of Government? In M. Groves, eds., *Modern Administrative Law in Australia: Concepts and Context*. Cambridge, UK: Cambridge University Press, pp. 301–325.
Brown, D. M. (2012). Comparative Climate Change Policy and Federalism: An Overview. *Review of Policy Research*, 29 (3), 323–333.
Brown, M. B. (2009). *Science in Democracy: Expertise, Institutions, and Representation*. Cambridge, MA: MIT Press.
Brown, N. J. (2001). *Constitutions in a Nonconstitutional World: Arab Basic Laws and the Prospects for Accountable Government*, New York: SUNY Press.
Brown v. Louisiana, 383 U.S. 131 (1966).
Brown, W. (2002). Suffering the Paradoxes of Rights. In W. Brown, & J. Halley, eds., *Left Legalism/Left Critique*, Durham: Duke University Press, pp. 420–434.
Brown, W. (2010). *Walled States, Waning Sovereignty*, New York: Zone Books.
Brownlee, K. (2012). *Conscience and Conviction: The Case for Civil Disobedience*, Oxford: Oxford University Press.
Brownlee, K. (2020). *Being Sure of Each Other: An Essay on Social Rights and Freedoms*, Oxford: Oxford University Press.
Brownlie, I. (2003). *Principles of Public International Law*, 6th edn, New York: Oxford University Press.
Brubaker, R. (2017). Why Populism? *Theory and Society*, 46 (5), 357–385.
Brudnick, I. A., (2018). *Congressional Salaries and Allowances: In Brief*. Congressional Research Service Report RL30064. Washington: Library of Congress. Available from: www.senate.gov/CRSpubs/9c14ec69-c4e4-4bd8-8953-f73daa1640e4.pdf.
Brummer, C. (2015). *Soft Law and the Global Financial System*, Cambridge: Cambridge University Press.
Brundage, J. A. (2008). *The Medieval Origins of the Legal Profession: Canonists, Civilians, and Courts*, Chicago: University of Chicago Press.
Brunnée, J., & Toope, S. J. (2013). *Legitimacy and Legality in International Law: An Interactional Account*, Cambridge: Cambridge University Press.
Bryce, J. (1888). *The American Commonwealth*, London: Macmillan and Company.
Bryce, J. (1995 [1915]). *The American Commonwealth*, Indiana: Liberty Fund.
Bryde, B.-O. (1982). *Verfassungsentwicklung: Stabilität und Dynamik im Verfassungsrecht der Bundesrepublik Deutschland*, Baden-Baden: Nomos.
Buchanan, A. (1988). *Ethics, Efficiency, and the Market*. Totowa: Rowman and Littlefield.
Buchanan, A. (2003). *Justice, Legitimacy and Self-Determination*, Oxford: Oxford University Press.
Buchanan, James M. 2000. *The Reason of Rules*. 10 edition. Indianapolis, IN: Liberty Fund.
Buchanan, A. (2013). *The Heart of Human Rights*, Oxford: Oxford University Press.
Buchanan, J. M. (1995–1996). Federalism and Individual Sovereignty. *Cato Journal* 15 (2–3), 259–268.
Buchanan, J. M. (2000). *The Limits of Liberty: Between Anarchy and Leviathan. Vol. VII of The Collected Works of James M. Buchanan*, Indianapolis: Liberty Fund.
Buchanan, J. M., & Tullock, G. (1990). *The Calculus of Consent. Logical Foundations of Constitutional Democracy*, Indianapolis: Liberty Fund.
Bugaric, B., & Tushnet, M. (2021). Populism and Constitutionalism: An Essay on Definitions and Their Implications, *Cardozo Law Review*, 42 (6), 2345–2393.

Buiter, W. (2014). Central Banks: Powerful, Political and Unaccountable? *Journal of the British Academy*, 2, 269–303.
Bungham, T. (2007). The Rule of Law. *Cambridge Law Journal*, 66 (1), 67–85.
Bunn, P., Pugh, A. & Yeates, C. (2018). The Distributional Impact of Monetary Policy Easing in the UK between 2008 and 2014. Staff Working Papers. Bank of England, March 27.
Burbank, S. B., & Friedman, B. (2002). Reconsidering Judicial Independence. In S. B. Burbank, & Friedman, B., eds. *Judicial Independence at the Crossroads: An Interdisciplinary Approach*. Thousand Oaks: Sage Publications, pp. 9–42.
Burdeau, G. (1969). *Le statut du pouvoir dans l'État. Vol. IV of Traité de Science Politique*. Paris: LDGJ.
Burdon, P. (2011). The Great Jurisprudence. In P. Burdon, ed., *Exploring Wild Law: The Philosophy of Earth Jurisprudence*, Kent Town, SA: Wakefield Press, pp. 59–75.
Burgers, L. (2020). Should Judges Make Climate Law? *Transnational Environmental Law*, 9 (1), 55–75.
Burgess, G. (1993). *The Politics of the Ancient Constitution: An Introduction to English Political Thought, 1603–1642*, University Park: Pennsylvania State University Press.
Burgess, M. (2006). *Comparative Federalism: Theory and Practice*, London: Routledge.
Burgess, M. (2012). *In Search of the Federal Spirit: New Theoretical and Empirical Perspectives in Comparative Federalism*, Oxford: Oxford University Press.
Burgess, M., & Gagnon, A-G., eds. (2010). *Federal Democracies*, London: Routledge.
Burke, E. (1949 [1774]). Speech to the Electors of Bristol. In R. Hoffmann, & P. Levack, eds., *Burke's Politics, Selected Writings and Speeches*. New York: AA Knopf, p. 115.
Burke, E. (1993). *Reflections on the Revolution in France*. Edited by L. G. Mitchell. Oxford: Oxford University Press.
Burley, A.-M., & Mattli, W. (1993). Europe before the Court. *International Organization*, 47 (1), 41–76.
Buscaglia, E., & Dakolias, M. (1999). *An Analysis of the Causes of Corruption in the Judiciary*, Washington: World Bank.
Butler, J. (2004). *Precarious Life: The Powers of Mourning and Violence*, London: Verso.
Butterfield, H. (1951). *The Whig Interpretation of History*, London: G. Bell and Sons Ltd.
Byrd, S. B., & Hruschka, J. (2010). *Kant's Doctrine of Right: A Commentary*, Cambridge: Cambridge University Press.
Byrne, J. (2016). *Mecca of Revolution: Algeria, Decolonization, and Third World Order*, Oxford: Oxford University Press.
Cabral, A. (1966). The Weapon of Theory. Available from: www.marxists.org/subject/africa/cabral/1966/weapon-theory.htm.
Cagé, J. (2018). *Le Prix de la Démocratie*, Paris: Fayard.
Cagé, J. (2020). *The Price of Democracy: How money Shapes Politics and What to Do About It*, Cambridge, MA: Harvard University Press.
Cahier, P. (1998). L'ordre juridique interne des organisations internationals. In R.-J. Dupuy, ed., *A Handbook on International Organizations*, Leiden: Martinus Nijhoff, pp. 377–397.
Cairns, A. (2000). *Citizens Plus. Aboriginal Peoples and the Canadian State*, Vancouver/Toronto: UBC Press.
Calabresi, S. (2001). The Virtues of Presidential Government: Why Professor Ackerman Is Wrong to Prefer the German to the US Constitution. *Constitutional Commentary*, 18 (1), 51–104.
Calabresi, S. and Lawson, G. (2007), "The unitary executive, jurisdiction stripping and the Hamdan opinions", *Columbia Law Review* 107, 1002–1048.
Caldwell, P. (1997). *Popular Sovereignty and the Crisis of German Constitutional Law: The Theory and Practice of Weimar Constitutionalism*, Durham: Duke University Press.

Callon, M., & Muniesa, F. (2005a). Economic Markets as Calculative Collective Devices. *Organization Studies*, 26 (8), 1229.

Callon, M., & Muniesa, F. (2005b). Peripheral Vision: Economic Markets as Calculative Collective Devices. *Organization studies*, 26 (8), 1229–1250.

Calloway, C. G. (1995). *The American Revolution in Indian Country: Crisis and Diversity in Native American Communities*, Cambridge: Cambridge University Press.

Calomiris, C. W., & Khan, U. (2015). An Assessment of TARP Assistance to Financial Institutions. *Journal of Economic Perspectives*, 29 (2), 53–80.

Caluwaerts, D., & Reuchamps, M. (2018). *The Legitimacy of Citizen-led Deliberative Democracy: The G1000 in Belgium*, Abingdon: Routledge.

Calvert, G. (1967). In White America: Liberal Conscience vs. Radical Consciousness. In C. Davidson, ed., *Revolutionary Youth & the New Working Class: The Praxis Papers, the Port Authority Statement, the RYM Documents and Other Lost Writings of SDS*. Pittsburgh: Changemaker Publications 2011. pp. 11–20.

Cameron, R. (2018). Infinite Regress Arguments. *The Stanford Encyclopedia of Philosophy*. Available from: https://plato.stanford.edu/entries/infinite-regress/.

Caminker, E. H. (2003). Thayerian Deference to Congress and Supreme Court Supermajority Rule: Lessons from the Past. *Indiana Law Journal*, 78 (1), 73–122.

Campbell, K. (2022). Formula for Appointing Chancellor, CJ "makes no sense"; Constitutional Reform Could Fix Deadlock – Nandlall. *Newsroom*. April 6. Available from: https://newsroom.gy/2022/04/06/formula-for-appointing-chancellor-cj-makes-no-sense-constitutional-reform-could-fix-deadlock-nandlall/.

Canada. (1970a). *Proclamation declaring that apprehended insurrection exists and has existed as and from the 15th October, 1970* (16 October 1970). SOR/70-443. Ottawa: Queen's Printer for Canada.

Canada. (1970b). *Public Order Regulations*, P.C. 1970–1808, 16 October 1970, SOR/70-444. Ottawa: Queen's Printer for Canada.

Cane, P. (1996). *Administrative Law*, Oxford: Oxford University Press.

Cane, P. (2003). Theories and Values in Public Law. In P. Craig, & R. Rawlings, eds., *Law and Administration in Europe: Essays in Honour of Carol Harlow*. Oxford: Oxford University Press, pp. 14–17.

Caney, S. (2001). Cosmopolitan Justice and Equalizing Opportunities. *Metaphilosophy*, 32 (1–2), 113–134.

Caney, S. (2014). Justice and the Basic Right to Justification. In R. Forst, ed., *Justice, Democracy and Justification. Rainer Forst in Dialogue*. London: Bloomsbury, pp. 147–166.

Canning, J. P. (1098). The Corporation in the Political Thought of the Italian Jurists of the Thirteenth and Fourteenth Centuries. *History of Political Thought*, 1 (1), 9–32.

Canovan, M. (2001). Sleeping Dogs, Prowling Cats and Soaring Doves: Three Paradoxes in the Political Theory of Nationhood. *Political Studies*, 49 (2), 203–215.

Canovan, M. (2005). *The People*, Cambridge: Polity Press.

Carens, J. (1987). Aliens and Citizens: The Case for Open Borders. *Review of Politics*, 49 (2), 251–273.

Carens, J. (1992). Migration and Morality: A Liberal Egalitarian Perspective. In B. Barry, & R. E. Goodin, eds, *Free Movement: Ethical Issues in the Transnational Migration of People and of Money*. University Park: University of Pennsylvania Press, pp. 25–47.

Carens, J. (2000). *Culture, Citizenship and Community. A Contextual Exploration of Justice as Evenhandedness*, Oxford: Oxford University Press.

Carens, J. (2013). *The Ethics of Immigration*, Oxford: Oxford University Press.

Carey, J. M. (2007). Competing Principals, Political Institutions, and Party Unity in Legislative Voting. *American Journal of Political Science*, 51 (1), 92–107.

Carey, J. M., & Shugart, M. S., eds. (1998). *Executive Decree Authority*, Cambridge UK: Cambridge University Press.
Carlson, A. (2008). Iterative Federalism and Climate Change. *Journal of Scholarly Perspectives*, 4 (1), 3–13.
Carlyle, T. (1845). *Oliver Cromwell's Letters and Speeches: With Elucidations*, vol. I, New York: Wiley & Putnam.
Carlyle, T. (1902). *The Bastille. Vol. I of The French Revolution: A History*, London: Chiswick Press.
Carney, G. (1989). An Overview of Manner and Form in Australia. *Queensland University of Technology Law Journal*, 5, 69–96.
Carolan, E. (2015). Ireland's Constitutional Convention: Behind the Hype about Citizen-led Constitutional Change. *International Journal of Constitutional Law*, 13 (3), 733–748.
Carolan, E. (2020). Constitutional Change Outside the Courts: Citizen Deliberation and Constitutional Narrative(s) in Ireland's Abortion Referendum. *Federal Law Review*, 48 (4), 497–510.
Carpenter, D., & Moss, D. A., eds. (2014). *Preventing Regulatory Capture*, Cambridge: Cambridge University Press.
Carré de Malberg, R. (2004 [1920–1922]). *Contribution à la théorie générale de l'État spécialement d'après les données fournies par le Droit constitutionnel français*, Paris: Dalloz.
Carreras, M. (2014). Outsiders and Executive-Legislative Conflict in Latin America. *Latin American Politics and Society*, 56 (3), 70–92.
Carreras, M. (2017). Institutions, Governmental Performance and the Rise of Political Newcomers. *European Journal of Political Research*, 56 (2), 364–380.
Carrington, D. (1973). The Corsican Constitution of Pasquale Paoli (1755–1769). *The English Historical Review*, 88 (348), 481–503.
Carter, I. (1999). *A Measure of Freedom*, Oxford: Oxford University Press.
Carter, I. (2011). Respect and the Basis of Equality. *Ethics*, 121 (3), 679–710.
Casaleggio, G., & Grillo, B. (2011). *Siamo in guerra. Per una nuova politica*, Milan: Chiarelettere.
Cass, D. (2005). *The Constitutionalization of the World Trade Organization*, Oxford: Oxford University Press.
Cassese, S. (2010). Die Entfaltung des Verwaltungsstaates in Europa. In von Bogdandy, Cassese, S., & Huber, P., eds., *Handbuch Ius Publicum Europaeum, Bd. III, Verwaltungsrecht in Europa: Grundlagen*. Heidelberg: C.F. Müller, §41.
Cassese, S. (2015). *Dentro la Corte. Diario di un giudice costituzionale*, Bologna: Il Mulino.
Casson, D. (2008). Emergency Judgment: Carl Schmitt, John Locke, and the Paradox of Prerogative. *Politics & Policy*, 36 (6), 944–971.
Castagnola, A. (2018). *Manipulating Courts in New Democracies: Forcing Judges off the Bench in Argentina*, New York: Routledge.
Cavanaugh, W. T. (2009). *Myth of Religious Violence: Secular Ideology and the Roots of Modern Conflict*, New York: Oxford University Press.
Cecot, C., & Viscusi, W. K. (2015). Judicial Review of Agency Benefit-Cost Analysis. *George Mason Law Review*, 22 (3), 575–617.
Celikates, R. (2016). Democratizing Civil Disobedience. *Philosophy and Social Criticism*, 42 (10), 982–994.
Central Intelligence Agency. (2020). The World Factbook: Military Service Age and Obligation. Available from: https://web.archive.org/web/20180716003832/ www.cia.gov/library/publications/the-world-factbook/fields/2024.html [Viewed 16 July 2018].
Cepeda, M. (2004). Judicial Activism in a Violent Context: The Origin, Role, and Impact of the Colombian Constitutional Court. *Washington University Global Studies Law Review*, 3, 529–700.

Cepeda Espinosa, M. J., & Landau, D. (2017). *Colombian Constitutional Law*, Oxford: Oxford University Press.
Cetra, D., Casanas-Adam, E., & Tarrega, M. (2018). The 2017 Catalan Independence Referendum: A Symposium. *Scottish Affairs*, 27 (1), 126–143.
CGFS. (2015). *Central bank operating frameworks and collateral markets*. Committee on Payments and Market Infrastructures Papers No. 53. Basel: Bank for International Settlements.
Chaisty, P., Cheeseman, N., & Power, T. (2018). *Coalitional Presidentialism in Comparative Perspective: Minority Presidents in Multiparty Systems*, Oxford: Oxford University Press.
Chakrabarty, D. (2016). Humanities in the Anthropocene: The Crisis of an Enduring Kantian Fable. *New Literary History*, 47 (2–3), 377–397.
Chalifour, N. J. (2015). Environmental Justice and the Charter: Do Environmental Injustices Infringe Sections 7 and 15 of the Charter? *Journal of Environmental Law and Practice*, 28 (1), 89–124.
Chambers, S. (2018a). Kickstarting the Bootstrapping: Jürgen Habermas, Deliberative Constitutionalization and the Limits of Proceduralism. In R. Levy, H. Kong, G. Orr, & J. King, eds., *The Cambridge Handbook of Deliberative Constitutionalism*. Cambridge: Cambridge University Press, pp. 256–268.
Chambers, S. (2018b). Making Referendums Safe for Democracy: A Call for More and Better Deliberation. *Swiss Political Science Review*, 24 (3), 305–311.
Chambers, S. (2019a). Democracy and Constitutional Reform: Deliberative Versus Populist Constitutionalism. *Philosophy and Social Criticism*, 45 (9–10), 1116–1131.
Chapman, E. B. (2019b). The Distinctive Value of Elections and the Case for Compulsory Voting. *American Political Science Review*, 63 (1), 101–112.
Cheesman, N. (2014). Law and Order as Asymmetrical Opposite to the Rule of Law. *Hague Journal on the Rule of Law*, 6 (1), 96–114.
Cheibub, J. (2006). Presidentialism, Electoral Identifiability, and Budget Balances in Democratic Systems. *American Political Science Review*, 100 (3), 353–368.
Cheibub, J. (2007). *Presidentialism, Parliamentarism, and Democracy*, New York: Cambridge University Press.
Cheibub, J. (2021). Intrinsic Backsliders? Presidentialism and Democratic Backsliding. *Democracy and Autocracy* (American Political Science Association, published by the Weiser Center for Emerging Democracies (WCED), University of Michigan), 19 (1), 4–8.
Cheibub, J., & Medina, A. (2019). The Politics of Presidential Term Limits in Latin America: From Re-democratization to Today. In A. Baturo, & R. Elgie, eds., *The Politics of Presidential Term Limits*. Oxford: Oxford University Press, pp. 517–534.
Cheibub, J. A., & Rasch, B. E. (2022). Constitutional Parliamentarism in Europe, 1800–2019. *West European Politics*, 45 (3), 470–501.
Cheibub, J., Elkins, Z., & Ginsburg, T. (2014). Beyond Presidentialism and Parliamentarism. *British Journal of Political Science*, 44 (3), 515–544.
Cheibub, J., Przeworski, A., & Saiegh, S. (2004). Government Coalitions and Legislative Success under Presidentialism and Parliamentarism. *British Journal of Political Science*, 34 (4), 565–587.
Chemerinsky, E. (2019). *Constitutional Law: Principles and Policies*, 6th edn, New York: Wolters Kluwer.
Cheneval, F., & el-Wakil, A. (2018). The Institutional Design of Referendums: Bottom-Up and Binding. *Swiss Political Science Review*, 24 (3), 294–304.
Chenwi, L. (2015). Democratizing the Socio-Economic Rights Enforcement Process. In H. Alviar García, K. Klare, & L. Williams, eds., *Social and Economic Rights in Theory and Practice*. London: Routledge, pp. 178–197.

Chiassoni, P. (2019). *Interpretation Without Truth*, New York: Springer.
Chhibber, P., & Kollman, K. (2004). *The Formation of National Party Systems: Federalism and Party Competition in Canada, Great Britain, India and the United States*, Princeton: Princeton University Press.
Choudhry, S., & Howse, R. (2000). Constitutional Theory and the Quebec Secession Reference. *Canadian Journal of Law & Jurisprudence*, 13 (2), 143–169.
Choudhry, S., & Hume, N. (2011). Federalism, Secession & Devolution: From Classical to Post-Conflict Federalism. In Ginsburg, T., & Dixon, R., eds., *Comparative Constitutional Law*. Cheltenham, UK: Edward Elgar, pp. 356–383.
Christiano, T. (1996). *The Rule of the Many: Fundamental Issues in Democratic Theory*, Boulder: Westview Press.
Christiano, T. (2008). *The Constitution of Equality: Democratic Authority and Its Limits*, Oxford: Oxford University Press.
Christiano, T. (2011). An Instrumental Argument for a Human Right to Democracy. *Philosophy and Public Affairs*, 39 (2), 142–176.
Christiano, T. (2012). Rational Deliberation among Experts and Citizens. In J. Mansbridge, & J. Parkinson, eds., *Deliberative Systems: Deliberative Democracy at the Large Scale*. Cambridge: Cambridge University Press, pp. 27–51.
Christiano, T. (2020). The Arbitrary Circumscription of the Jurisdiction of the International Criminal Court. *Critical Review of International Social and Political Philosophy*, 23 (3), 352–370.
Christiano, T., & Braynen, W. (2008). Inequality, Injustice and Leveling Down. *Ratio*, 21 (4), 392–420.
Christin, O. (1997). *La paix de religion*, Paris: Seuil.
Cicero, M. T. (2017 [52 BC]). *On The Commonwealth and On The Laws*. Translated by J. E. Zetzel. 2nd edn, Cambridge: Cambridge University Press.
Ciepley, D. (2006). *Liberalism in the Shadow of Totalitarianism*, Cambridge, MA: Harvard University Press.
Ciepley, D. (2017). Is the U.S. Government a Corporation? The Corporate Origins of Modern Constitutionalism. *American Political Science Review*, 111 (2), 418–435.
Çıdam, C. (2017). Radical Democracy Without Risks? Habermas on Constitutional Patriotism and Civil Disobedience. *New German Critique*, 44 (2), 105–132.
Clark, C. (2012). After 1848: The European Revolution in Government. *Transactions of the Royal Historical Society*, 22, 171–197.
Clark, T. S. (2011). *The Limits of Judicial Independence*, New York: Cambridge University Press.
Clarke, M. V. (1964). *Medieval Representation and Consent: A Study of Early Parliaments in England and Ireland, with Special Reference to the Modus Tenendi Parliamentum*, New York: Russell & Russell.
Clifford, R. (2019). Saanich Law and the Trans Mountain Pipeline Expansion. Centre for International Governance Innovation. Available from: www.cigionline.org/articles/saanich-law-and-trans-mountain-pipeline-expansion.
Clemens, M. (2011). Economics and Emigration: Trillion-Dollar Bills on the Sidewalk? *Journal of Economic Perspectives*, 25 (3), 83–106.
Cobbe, J. (2019). Administrative Law and the Machines of Government: Judicial Review of Automated Public-Sector Decision-Making. *Legal Studies*, 39 (4), 636–655.
Coglianese, C., & Lazer, D. (2003). Management-based Regulation: Prescribing Private Management to Achieve Public Goals. *Law & Society Review*, 37 (4), 691–730.
Cohen, C. (1966). Civil Disobedience and the Law. *Rutgers Law Review*, 21 (1), 1–17.
Cohen, C. (1971). *Civil Disobedience: Conscience, Tactics, and the Law*, New York: Columbia University Press.

Cohen, E. F. (2015). The Political Economy of Immigrant Time: Rights, Citizenship and Temporariness in the Post-1965 Era. *Polity*, 47 (3), 337–351.
Cohen, E. F. (2018). *The Political Value of Time: Citizenship, Duration and Democratic Justice*, New York: Cambridge University Press.
Cohen, E. F., & Ghosh, C. (2019). *Citizenship (Key Concepts in Political Theory)*. Cambridge, UK: Polity.
Cohen, G. A. (2008). *Rescuing Justice and Equality*, Cambridge, MA: Harvard University Press.
Cohen, G. A. (2011a). Equality of What? On Welfare, Goods and Capabilities. In G. A. Cohen, ed., *On the Currency of Egalitarian Justice, and Other Essays in Political Philosophy*. Edited by M. Otsuka. Princeton: Princeton University Press, pp. 44–60.
Cohen, G. A. (2011b). *On the Currency of Egalitarian Justice, and Other Essays in Political Philosophy*, Princeton: Princeton University Press.
Cohen, J. (1996). Procedure and Substance in Deliberative Democracy. In S. Benhabib ed., *Democracy and Difference: Changing Boundaries of the Political*. Princeton: Princeton University Press, pp. 407–437.
Cohen, J. (1997). Deliberation and Democratic Legitimacy. In J. Bohman, & W. Rehg, eds., *Deliberative Democracy: Essays on Reason and Politics*. Cambridge, MA: MIT Press, pp. 67–92.
Cohen, J. (2006). Is There a Human Right to Democracy? In C. Sypnowich, ed., *The Egalitarian Conscience: Essays in Honour of G. A. Cohen*. Oxford: Oxford University Press, pp. 227–250.
Cohen, J. (2009). *Philosophy, Politics, Democracy: Selected Essays*, Cambridge, MA: Harvard University Press, pp. 154–180.
Cohen, J. (2012). *Globalization and Sovereignty. Rethinking Legality, Legitimacy, and Constitutionalism*, Cambridge: Cambridge University Press.
Cohen, J., & Arato, A. (1992). *Civil Society and Political Theory*, Cambridge, MA: MIT Press.
Cohen, J., & Sabel, C. (1997). Directly Deliberative Polyarchy. *European Law Journal*, 3 (4), 313–342.
Cohen, S. (2011). *Folk Devils and Moral Panics*, London: Routledge.
Coibion, O., Gorodnichenko, Y., Kueng, L., & Silvia, J. (2017). Innocent Bystanders? Monetary Policy and Inequality. *Journal of Monetary Economics*, 88, 70–89.
Coicaud, J.-M., & Heiskanen, V., eds. (2001). *The Legitimacy of International Organizations*. Tokyo: United Nations University Press.
Cole, G. D. H. (1920). *Social Theory*, London: Methuen & Co.
Cole, D. (2003). *Enemy Aliens: Double Standards and Constitutional Freedoms in the War on Terrorism*, New York: New Press.
Cole, D. (2004). The Priority of Morality: The Emergency Constitution's Blind Spot. *Yale Law Journal*, 113, 1753–1800.
Cole J. (1999). *Colonialism & Revolution in the Middle East: Social and Cultural Origins of Egypt's 'Urabi Movement*, Cairo: The American University in Cairo Press.
Cole, P. (2000). *Philosophies of Exclusion: Liberal Political Theory and Immigration*, Edinburgh: Edinburgh University Press.
Cole, R., Kincaid, J., & Rodriguez, A. (2004). Public Opinion on Federalism and Federal Political Culture in Canada, Mexico, and the United States. *Publius*, 34 (3), 201–221.
Colley, L. (2021). *The Gun, the Ship, and the Pen: Warfare, Constitutions, and the Making of the Modern World*, London: Profile.
Collin, P. (2017). The Legitimation of Self-Regulation and Co-Regulation in Corporatist Concepts of Legal Scholars in the Weimar Republic. *Politics and Governance*, 5 (1), 15–25.

Collings, J. (2015). *Democracy's Guardian: A History of the German Federal Constitutional Court 1951–2001*, Oxford: Oxford University Press.
Collins, H. (2014). On the (In)compatibility of Human Rights Discourse and Private Law. In H. Micklitz, ed., *Constitutionalization of European Private Law*, Oxford University Press, pp. 26–60.
Collins, H., & Evans, R. (2007). *Rethinking Expertise*, Chicago: University of Chicago Press.
Collins, L., & Sossin, L. (2019). In Search of an Ecological Approach to Constitutional Principles and Environmental Discretion in Canada. *University of British Columbia Law Review*, 52 (1), 293–343.
Collins, P. H. (2008). *Black Feminist Thought: Knowledge, Consciousness, and the Politics of Empowerment*, 1st edn, New York: Routledge.
Colomer, J. (2013). Elected Kings with the Name of Presidents. On the Origins of Presidentialism in the United States and Latin America. *Revista Lationamericana de Politica Comparada*, 7 (1), 79–97.
Colomer, J., & Negretto, G. (2005). Can Presidentialism Work Like Parliamentarism? *Government and Opposition*, 40 (1), 60–89.
Colón-Ríos, J. (2011). The Three Waves of the Constitutionalism-Democracy Debate in The United States: And an Invitation to Return to the First. Victoria University of Wellington Legal Research Papers VUWLRP.
Colón-Ríos, J. (2020). *Constituent Power and the Law*, Oxford: Oxford University Press.
Comella, V. F. (2013). *The Constitution of Spain: A Contextual Analysis*, Oxford: Hart Publishing.
Commission on the BP Deepwater Horizon Oil Spill and Offshore Drilling. (2011). *Deep Water. The Gulf Oil Disaster and the Future of Offshore Drilling*. Washington, DC: Government Publishing Office.
Conly, S. (2013). *Against Autonomy*, Cambridge: Cambridge University Press.
Constant, B. (1997). *Ecrits politiques*, Paris: Gallimard.
Constitute Project. (2020). Constitute The World's Constitutions to Read, Search, and Compare. Available from Constituteproject.org website: www.constituteproject.org/ (Accessed: 9 September 2020).
Constitutional Reform Committee. (1992[1848]). Report on the 1848 Draft Constitution of Switzerland. In A. Lijphart, ed., *Parliamentary versus Presidential Government*. New York: Oxford University Press, pp. 173–174.
Cook, B. J. (2014). *Bureaucracy and Self-government: Reconsidering the Role of Public Administration in American Politics*, Baltimore: JHU Press.
Cook, B. J. (2021). *The Fourth Branch: Reconstructing the Administrative State for the Commercial Republic*, Lawrence, KS: Kansas University Press.
Cooray, L. J. M. (1979). *Conventions. The Australian Constitution and the Future*, Sydney: Legal Books.
Cordelli, C. (2021). *The Privatized State*, Princeton: Princeton University Press.
Cornell, D. (2014). *Law and Revolution in South Africa: uBuntu, Dignity, and the Struggle for Constitutional Transformation*, New York: Fordham University Press.
Cornell, N. (2015). Wrongs, Rights, and Third Parties. *Philosophy and Public Affairs*, 43 (2), 109–143.
Corrias, L. (2016). Populism in a Constitutional Key: Constituent Power, Popular Sovereignty and Constitutional Identity. *European Constitutional Law Review*, 12 (6), 6–26.
Cottier, T. (2000). Limits to International Trade: The Constitutional Challenge. *Proceedings of the Annual Meeting (American Society of International Law)*, 94, 220–224.
Cottier, T. (2013). Poverty, Redistribution, and International Trade Regulation. In K. Schefer, ed., *Poverty and the International Economic Legal System*. Cambridge: Cambridge University Press, pp. 48–65.

Cover, R. (1983). Nomos and Narrative. *Harvard Law Review*, 97 (1), 4–68.
Cox, G. (2006). The Organization of Democratic Legislatures. In B. Weingast, & D. Wittman, eds., *The Oxford Handbook of Political Economy*. Oxford: Oxford University Press, pp. 141–161.
Cox, A. B., & Rodridguez, C. (2020). *The President and Immigration Law*, New York: Oxford University Press.
Craig, P. (1997). Formal and Substantive Conceptions of the Rule of Law. *Public Law*, 467–487.
Craig, P. (2014). Economic Governance and the Euro Crisis: Constitutional Architecture and Constitutional Implications. In M. Adams, F. Fabbrini, & P. Larouche, eds, *The Constitutionalization of European Budgetary Constraints*. Oxford: Hart Publishing, pp. 19–40.
Craig, P. (2005 [2017]). Formal and Substantive Conceptions of the Rule of Law: An Analytical Framework. In R. Bellamy, ed., *The Rule of Law and the Separation of Powers*. London: Routledge, pp. 95–115.
Craig, P., & de Búrca (2015). *EU Law. Text, Cases, and Materials*, 6th edn, Oxford: Oxford University Press.
Craig, P., & Rawlings R., eds. (2003). *Law and Administration in Europe: Essays in Honour of Carol Harlow*, Oxford: Oxford University Press.
Craig, R., Ekins, R., & S. Laws (2019). *Lost in Transition: The Conservative Leadership Contest and the Confidence of the Commons*, London: Policy Exchange.
Craiutu, A. (2012). *A Virtue for Courageous Minds: Moderation in French Political Thought. 1748–1830*, Princeton: Princeton University Press.
Craiutu, A. (2017). *Faces of Moderation: The Art of Balance in an Age of Extremes*, Philadelphia: University of Pennsylvania Press.
Crawford, C. C. (1915). The Suspension of the Habeas Corpus Act and the Revolution of 1689. *The English Historical Review*, 30 (120), 613–630.
Crawford, J. (2003). International Law and the Rule of Law. *Adelaide Law Review*, 24 (1), 3–12.
Crawford, J. (2006). *The Creation of States in International Law*, 2nd edn, Oxford: Oxford University Press.
Crenshaw, K. (1988). Race, Reform, and Retrenchment: Transformation and Legitimation in Anti-discrimination Law. *Harvard Law Review*, 107 (7), 1331–1387.
Crenshaw, K. (1994). Demarginalizing the Intersection of Race and Sex: A Black Feminist Critique of Antidiscrimination Doctrine, Feminist Theory and Antiracist Politics. In A. Jaggar, ed., *Living With Contradictions: Controversies in Feminist Social Ethics*. Boulder: Westview Press, pp. 29–52.
Cretney, S. (1998). *Law, Law Reform and the Family*, Oxford: Oxford University Press.
Criddle, E. (2006). Fiduciary Foundations of Administrative Law. *UCLA Law Review*, 54 (1), 117–183.
Criddle, E., Fox-Decent, E., Gold, A., Hui Kim, S., & Miller, P., eds. (2018a). *Fiduciary Government*, Cambridge: Cambridge University Press.
Criddle, E., Fox-Decent, E., Gold, A., Hui Kim, S., & Miller, P. (2018b). Fiduciary Government: Provenance, Promise, and Pitfalls. In Criddle et al., eds., *Fiduciary Government*. Cambridge: Cambridge University Press, pp. 1–18.
Criddle, E., Miller, P., Sitkoff, R., eds. (2019). *The Oxford Handbook of Fiduciary Law*, Oxford: Oxford University Press.
Croce, M., & Goldoni, M. (2020). *The Legacy of Pluralism*, Stanford: Stanford University Press.
Croce, M., & Salvatore, A. (2013). *The Legal Theory of Carl Schmitt*, Abingdon: Routledge.

Crosby, N., & Nethercut, D. (2005). Citizen Juries: Creating a Trustworthy Voice of the People. In Gastil, J., & Levine, P., eds., *The Deliberative Democracy Handbook*. San Francisco: Jossey-Bass, pp. 111–119.

Cruft, R. (2019). *Human Rights, Ownership, and the Individual*, Oxford: Oxford University Press.

Crutzen P. J. (2006). The "Anthropocene". In Ehlers E., & Krafft T., eds., *Earth System Science in the Anthropocene*. Berlin, Heidelberg: Springer, pp. 13–18.

Cullen, M. (2020). Separation of Powers in the United Nations System? Institutional Structure and the Rule of Law. *International Organizations Law Review*, 17 (3), 492–530.

Cullinan, C. (2011). *Wild Law: A Manifesto for Earth Justice*, 2nd edn, Devon, UK: Green Books.

Culver, K., & Giudice, M. (2010). *Legality's Borders*, Oxford: Oxford University Press.

Custos, D. (2017). The 2015 French Code of Administrative Procedure; an Assessment. In S. Rose-Ackerman, P. Lindseth, & B. Emerson, eds., *Comparative Administrative Law*. Cheltenham, UK: Edward Elgar, pp. 284–301.

Daalder, H. (1984). In Search of the Center of European Party Systems. *American Political Science Review*, 78 (1), 92–109.

Dahl, R. A. (1957). Decision-Making in a Democracy: The Supreme Court as a National Policy Maker. *Journal of Public Law*, 6 (2), 279–295.

Dahl, R. A. (1989). *Democracy and Its Critics*, New Haven: Yale University Press.

Dahl, R. A. (1998). *On Democracy*, New Haven: Yale University Press.

Dahl, R. A. (2006). *A Preface to Democratic Theory*, 3rd edn, Chicago: Chicago University Press.

Daly, E. (2015). A Republican Defence of the Constitutional Referendum, *Legal Studies*, 35 (1), 30–54.

Daly, P. (2016). Administrative Law: A Values-Based Approach. In J. Bell, M. Elliott, P. Murray, & J. Varuhas, eds., *Public Law Adjudication in the Common Law World: Process and Substance*. Oxford: Hart Publishing, pp. 23–44.

Damiani, M. (2020). *Populist Radical Left Parties in Western Europe: Equality and Sovereignty*, London, New York: Routledge.

Dana, J., Cain, D., & Dawes, R. (2006). What You Don't Know Can't Hurt Me. *Organizational Behavior and Human Decision Processes*, 100, 193–201.

D'Angelo, J., & Ranalli, B. (2019). The Dark of Sunlight. *Foreign Affairs*, 98 (3), pp. 155–168.

Darag, A. (2016). Politics or piety? Why the Muslim Brotherhood engages in social service provision. Brookings Rethinking Islam Series. Available from: www.brookings.edu/wp-content/uploads/2016/07/Amr-Darrag-FINAL-3-1.pdf.

Darnton R. (1989). What Was Revolutionary about the French Revolution? *New York Review of Books*. 19 January 1989.

Darwall, S. (2006). *The Second Person Standpoint: Morality, Respect and Accountability*, Cambridge, MA: Harvard University Press.

Darwall, S. (2012). Bipolar Obligation. In R. Shafer-Landau, ed., *Oxford Studies in Metaethics*, vol. VII. Oxford: Oxford University Press, pp. 333–358.

Daugirdas, K. (2016). How and Why International Law Binds International Organizations. *Harvard Journal of International Law*, 57 (2), 325–381.

Davidson, S. (1992). *The Inter-American Court of Human Rights*, Dartmouth: Aldershot.

Davis, K. C. (1969). *Discretionary Justice: A Preliminary Inquiry*, Baton Rouge: Louisiana State University Press.

Davis, K. E., & Trebilcock, M. J. (2008). The Relationship between Law and Development: Optimists Versus Skeptics. *American Journal of Comparative Law*, 56 (4), 895–946.

Davis, M. (2011). Spring Confronts Winter. *New Left Review*, 72, 5–15.

Dawood, Y. (2006). Democracy, Power, and the Supreme Court: Campaign Finance Reform in Comparative Context. *International Journal of Constitutional Law*, 4 (2), 269–293.

Dawood, Y. (2012). Electoral Fairness and the Law of Democracy: A Structural Rights Approach to Judicial Review. *University of Toronto Law Journal*, 62 (4), 499–561.

de Boer, N., & van 't Klooster, J. (2020). The ECB, the Courts and the Issue of Democratic Legitimacy after Weiss. *Common Market Law Review*, 57 (6), 1689–1724.

de Boer, N., & van 't Klooster, J. (2021). *The ECB's Neglected Secondary Mandate: An Interinstitutional Solution*, Brussels: Positive Money Europe.

de Búrca, G., & Scott, J. (2001). *The EU and WTO: Legal and Constitutional Issues*, Oxford: Hart Publishing.

De Cleen, B., Moffitt, B., Panayotu, P., & Stavrakakis, Y. (2020). The Potentials and Difficulties of Transnational Populism: The Case of the Democracy in Europe Movement 2025 (DiEM25). *Political Studies*, 68 (1), 146–166.

Dehousse, R. (1998). *The European Court of Justice: The Politics of Judicial Integration*, New York: St. Martin's Press.

de Jouvenel, B. (1966). The Means of Contestation. *Government and Opposition*, 1 (2), 155–174.

Delaney, P. (2008). Legislating for Equality in Colombia: Constitutional Jurisprudence, *Tutelas*, and Social Reform. *The Equal Rights Review*, 1, 50–59.

de la Calle, H. (2004). *Contra todas las Apuestas: Historia Íntima de la Constituyente de 1991*, Bogotá: Editorial Planeta.

de la Torre, C., & Burbano de Lara, F. (2020). Populism, Constitution Making, and the Rule of Law in Latin America. *Partecipazione e conflitto*, 13 (3), 1453–1468.

D'Elia-Kueper, J., & Segal, J. (2017). Ideology and Partisanship. In L. Epstein, & S. Lindquist, eds., *The Oxford Handbook of U.S. Judicial Behavior*. Oxford: Oxford University Press, pp. 304–319.

Della Mirandola, G. P. (1996). *Oration on the Dignity of Man*. Translated by A. Robert Caponigri. Washington, DC: Gateway Editions.

Della Porta, D., Peterson, A., & Reiter, H., eds., (2006). *The Policing of Transnational Protest*, Aldershot: Ashgate.

Delmas, C. (2018). *A Duty to Resist: When Disobedience Should Be Uncivil*, New York: Oxford University Press.

Delmas, C. (2019). Civil Disobedience, Punishment, and Injustice. In K. Ferzan, & L. Alexander, eds., *The Palgrave Handbook of Applied Ethics and the Criminal Law*. Switzerland: Palgrave Macmillan, pp. 167–188.

Delmas, C. (2020). Uncivil Disobedience in Hong Kong. *Boston Review*. 13 January. Available from: http://bostonreview.net/global-justice/candice-delmas-uncivil-disobedience-hong-kong.

de Maistre, J. (1884). Etude sur la Souveraineté. In *Archives de la Révolution Française*.

De Maistre, J. (1994). *Considerations on France*. Translated and edited by R. Lebrun. Cambridge: Cambridge University Press.

DeMott, D. (2019). Fiduciary Principles in Agency Law. In E. Criddle, P. Miller, & R. Sitkoff, eds., *The Oxford Handbook of Fiduciary Law*. Oxford: Oxford University Press, pp. 23–40.

Denninger, E. (1990). *Verfassungsrechtliche Anforderungen an die Normsetzung im Umwelt- und Technikrecht*, Baden-Baden: Nomos.

Department of Justice, Government of the United States. (2020). Country Policy and Information Note. Iran: Miltary Service. Available from: https://web.archive.org/web/20201128232832/www.justice.gov/eoir/page/file/1274581/download. [Viewed 28 November 2020].

Derthick, M. (2010). Compensatory Federalism. In B. Rabe, ed., *Greenhouse Governance: Addressing Climate Change in America*. Washington, DC: Brookings Institution Press, pp. 58–72.

Desan, C. (2014). *Making Money: Coin, Currency, and the Coming of Capitalism*, Oxford University Press.
Deschouwer, K. (1994). The Decline of Consociationalism and the Reluctant Modernization of Belgian Mass Parties. In R. S. Katz, & P. Mair, eds., *How Parties Organize: Change and Adaptation in Party Organizations in Western Democracies*. London: Sage, pp. 80–108.
De Schutter, H. (2011). Federalism as fairness, The Journal of Political Philosophy 19(2), 167–189.
De Schutter, H. (2014), Testing for Linguistic Injustice: territoriality and pluralism. Nationalities Papers. 42:6, 1034–1052. De Schutter, H. (2017) Two principles of equal language recognition. Critical Review of International Social and Political Philosophy, 20:1, 75–87.
De Schutter, H. (2016). The Liberal Linguistic Turn: Kymlicka's Freedom Account Revisited. *Dve Domovini – Two Homelands* (44), 51–65.
De Schutter, H. (2022). Linguistic Justice for Immigrants. *Nations and Nationalism*, 28 (2), 418–434.
De Schutter, H. (2023). Taming Dignity for Multiculturalism. *Critical Review of International Social and Political Philosophy*, 26 (1), 22–38.
de Tocqueville, A. (1856). *The Old Regime and the Revolution*. John Bonner, trans. New York: Harper & Brothers.
Developments in the Law. (2010). State Action and the Public/Private Distinction, *Harvard Law Review*, 123 (5), 1248–1314.
De Wet, E. (2006). The International Constitutional Order. *International & Comparative Law Quarterly*, 55 (1), 51–76.
Dewey, J. (1918). Philosophy and Democracy. In *John Dewey, The Middle Works, 1899–1924* vol. XI. Edited by J. A. Boydston. Carbondale: Southern Illinois University Press, pp. 41–53.
De Wilde, M. (2010). Locke and the State of Exception: Towards a Modern Understanding of Emergency Government. *European Constitutional Law Review*, 6 (2), 249–267.
De Wilde, M. (2012). The Dictator's Trust: Regulating and Constraining Emergency Powers in the Roman Republic. *History of Political Thought*, 33 (4), 555–577.
Díaz de Valdés, J. M., & Verdugo, S. (2019). The ALBA Constitutional Project and Political Representation. *International Journal of Constitutional Law*, 17 (2), 479–488.
Dicey, A. V. (1915). *Introduction to the Study of the Law of the Constitution*, 8th edn, London: Macmillan and Co.
Dicey, A. V. (1982 [1915]) *Introduction to the Study of the Law of the Constitution*, 8th edn, Indianapolis: Liberty Classics.
Dicey, A. V. (2007). *Lectures on the Relationship between Law and Public Opinion in England during the Nineteenth Century*, Indianapolis: Liberty Fund.
Dicey, A. V. (2013). *The Law of the Constitution*. Edited by J. W. F. Allison. Oxford: Oxford University Press.
Dicke, K. (2002). The Founding Function of Human Dignity in the Universal Declaration of Human Rights. In D. Kretzmer, & E. Klein, eds., *The Concept of Dignity in Human Rights Discourse*. The Hague: Kluwer Law International, pp. 111–120.
Dienel, P. C. (1999). Planning Cells: The German Experience. In U. Khan, ed., *Participation Beyond the Ballot Box*. London: UCL Press, pp. 81–93.
Dienstag, J. F. (1996). Between History and Nature: Social Contract Theory in Locke and the Founders. *Journal of Politics*, 58 (4), 985–1009.
Dietsch, P., Claveau, F., & Fontan, C. (2018). *Do Central Banks Serve the People?* Cambridge: Polity.
Dikau, S., & Volz, U. (2021). Central Bank Mandates, Sustainability Objectives and the Promotion of Green Finance. *Ecological Economics*, 184, 107022.

Dinan, J. (2006). *The American State Constitutional Tradition*, Kansas: University of Kansas Press.
Disch, L. (2015). The Constructivist Turn in Democratic Representation: A Normative Dead-End? *Constellations*, 22 (4), 487–499.
Dixon, M., & McCorquodale, R. (2003). *Cases and Materials on International Law*, 4th edn, New York: Oxford University Press.
Dixon, P. (2012). The Politics of Conflict: A Constructivist Critique of Consociational and Civil Society Theories. *Nations and Nationalism* 18 (1), 98–121.
Dixon, R. (2018). Constitutional Rights as Bribes. *Connecticut Law Review*, 50 (3), 767–818.
Dixon, R. (2023). *Responsive Judicial Review: Democracy and Dysfunction in the Modern Age*, Oxford: Oxford University Press.
Dixon, R., & Landau, D. (2018). Tiered Constitutional Design. *The George Washington Law Review*, 86 (2), 438–512.
Dixon, R., & Landau, D. (2020). Constitutional End Games: Making Presidential Term Limits Stick. *Hastings Law Journal*, 71 (2), 359–418.
Dixon, R., & Tushnet, M. (2021). Constitutional Democracy and Electoral Commissions: A Reflection from Asia. *Asian Journal of Comparative Law*, Online First.
Dobner, P. (2012). More Law, Less Democracy? Democracy and Transnational Constitutionalism. In P. Dobner, & M. Loughlin, eds., *The Twilight of Constitutionalism*. Oxford: Oxford University Press.
Dobson, A. (2003). *Citizenship and the Environment*, Oxford, UK: Oxford University Press.
Dobson, A. (2016). *Environmental Politics: A Very Short Introduction*, Oxford, UK: Oxford University Press.
Dodd, V., Gayle, D., & Murray, J. (2019). Police Seek Tougher Powers against Extinction Rebellion. *The Guardian*. 19 October. Available from: www.theguardian.com/environment/2019/oct/19/police-seek-tougher-powers-against-extinction-rebellion (Accessed: 1 November 2019).
Donald, A. (2016). Immigration Points-based Systems Compared. *BBC*. 1 June. Available from: https://web.archive.org/web/20180819133654/ www.bbc.com/news/uk-politics-29594642 [Viewed 19 August 2018].
Donaldson S., & Kymlicka, W. (2011). *Zoopolis: A Political Theory of Animal Rights*, Oxford, UK: Oxford University Press.
Donnelly, C. (2007). *Delegation of Governmental Power to Private Parties: A Comparative Perspective*, Oxford: Oxford University Press.
Donohue, L. (2008). *The Cost of Counterterrorism*, Cambridge: Cambridge University Press.
Dorf, M. (2008). The Morality of Prophylactic Legislation. *Current Legal Problems*, 61 (1), 23–47.
Dougherty, V. M. (1994). Absurdity and the Limits of Literalism: Defining the Absurd Result Principle in Statutory Interpretation. *American University Law Review*, 44 (1), 127–166.
Dowdle, M. (2006). *Public Accountability: Designs, Dilemmas and Experiences*, Cambridge: Cambridge University Press.
Downey, L. (2021). Delegation in Democracy: A Temporal Analysis. *Journal of Political Philosophy*, 29 (3), pp. 305–329.
Downey, L. (2022). Governing Money Democratically: Rechartering the Federal Reserve. In D. Allen, et al., ed., *Governing Money Democratically: Rechartering the Federal Reserve*. Chicago: Chicago University Press, pp. 340–366.
Downs, A. (1957). *An Economic Theory of Democracy*, New York: Harper.
Doyle, O. (2021). Order from Chaos: Typologies and Models of Constitutional Change. In X. Contiades, & A. Fotiadou, eds., *Routledge Handbook of Comparative Constitutional Change*. London: Routledge, pp. 45–60.

Doyle, O., & Walsh, R. (2020). Deliberation in Constitutional Amendment: Reappraising Ireland's Deliberative Mini-Publics. *European Constitutional Law Review*, 16 (3), 440–465.
Driskill v. Parrish (1845). 7 F. Cas. 1100 (C. C. D. Ohio) (No. 4,089).
Dryzek, J. S. (2009). Democratization as Deliberative Capacity Building. *Comparative Political Studies*, 42 (11), 1379–1402.
Duchacek, I. (1970). *Comparative Federalism: The Territorial Dimension of Politics*, New York: Holt, Rinehart and Winston.
Duchacek, I. (1986). *Territorial Dimension of Politics: Within, among, and across Nations*, Boulder: Westview.
Duguit, L. (1913). *Les transformations du droit public*, Paris: Colin.
Dukes, R. (2014). *The Labour Constitution: The Enduring Idea of Labour Law*, Oxford: Oxford University Press.
Dummett, M. (1984). *Voting Procedures*, Oxford: Oxford University Press.
Dummett, M. (1997). *Principles of Electoral Reform*, Oxford: Oxford University Press.
Duncan, G. (2015). New Zealand. In B. Galligan, & S. Brenton, eds., *Constitutional Conventions in Westminster Systems*. Cambridge: Cambridge University Press, pp. 217–232.
Dunn, J. (1969). *The Political Thought of John Locke*, Cambridge: Cambridge University Press.
Dunn, J. (1999). Situating Democratic Political Accountability. In A. Przeworski, S. C. Stokes, & B. Manin, eds. *Democracy, Accountability, and Representation*. Cambridge: Cambridge University Press, pp. 329–344.
Dunn, J. (2008). Understanding Revolution. In J. Foran, D. Lane, & A. Zivkovic, eds., *Revolution in the Making of the Modern World: Social Identities, Globalization and Modernity*. London: Routledge, pp. 17–26.
Dunoff, J. (2006). Constitutional Conceits: The WTO's "Constitution" and the Discipline of International Law. *European Journal of International Law*, 17 (3), 647–675.
Dunoff, J. (2009). The Politics of International Constitutions: The Curious Case of the World Trade Organization. In J. Dunoff, & J. Trachtman, eds., *Ruling the World?: Constitutionalism, International Law, and Global Governance*. Cambridge: Cambridge University Press, pp. 178–205.
Dunoff, J., & Trachtmann, J. (2009a). A Functional Approach to International Constitutionalization. In J. Dunoff, & J. Trachtman, eds., *Ruling the World? Constitutionalism, International Law, and Global Governance*. Cambridge: Cambridge University Press, pp. 3–35.
Dunoff, J., & Trachtman, J., eds. (2009b). *Ruling the World? Constitutionalism, International Law, and Global Governance*, Cambridge: Cambridge University Press.
Dunoff, J., Ratner, S., & Wippman, D. (2015). *International Law: Norms, Actors, Process: A Problem-Oriented Approach*, New York: Wolters Kluwer.
Durkheim, E. (1997 [1893]). *The Division of Labor in Society*. Translated by W. D. Hall. New York: The Free Press.
Duverger, M. (1980). A New Political System Model: Semi-Presidential Government. *European Journal of Political Research*, 8 (2), 165–187.
Duxbury, N. (1999). *Random Justice*, Oxford: Oxford University Press.
Dworkin, G. (1988). *The Theory and Practice of Autonomy*, Cambridge: Cambridge University Press.
Dworkin, R. (1977). *Taking Rights Seriously*, Cambridge, MA: Harvard University Press.
Dworkin, R. (1978 [1977]) *Taking Rights Seriously*, 5th edn, Cambridge, MA: Harvard University Press.
Dworkin, R., (1981). The Forum of Principle. *New York University Law Review*, 56 (2–3), 469–511.
Dworkin, R. (1985). *A Matter of Principle*, Cambridge, MA: Harvard University Press.

Dworkin, R. (1986). *Law's Empire*, Cambridge, MA: Harvard University Press.
Dworkin, R. (1990). *A Bill of Rights for Britain*, London: Chatto & Windus.
Dworkin, R. (1994). *Life's Dominion: An Argument about Abortion, Euthanasia and Individual Freedom*, New York: Vintage Press.
Dworkin, R. (1995). Constitutionalism and Democracy. *European Journal of Philosophy*, 3 (1), 2–11.
Dworkin, R. (1996a). Does Britain Need a Bill of Rights? In *Freedom's Law: The Moral Reading of the American Constitution*. Oxford: Oxford University Press, pp. 352–372.
Dworkin, R. (1996b). Introduction: The Moral Reading and the Majoritarian Premise. In *Freedom's Law: The Moral Reading of the American Constitution*. Oxford: Oxford University Press, pp. 1–38.
Dworkin, R. (1996c). *Freedom's Law: The Moral Reading of the American Constitution*, Cambridge, MA: Harvard University Press.
Dworkin, R. (1998). Affirming Affirmative Action. *The New York Review of Books*. 22 October.
Dworkin, R. (2000). *Sovereign Virtue: The Theory and Practice of Equality*, Cambridge, MA: Harvard University Press.
Dworkin, R. (2006). *Justice in Robes*, Cambridge, MA: Harvard University Press.
Dworkin, R. (2011). *Justice for Hedgehogs*, Cambridge, MA: Harvard University Press.
Dworkin, R. (2013). *Religion without God*, Cambridge, MA: Harvard University Press.
Dyevre, A. (2015). Technocracy and Distrust: Revisiting the Rationale for Constitutional Review. *International Journal of Constitutional Law*, 13 (1), 30–60.
Dyson, K. (2009). *The State Tradition in Western Europe. A Study of an Idea and Institution*, 2nd edn, Colchester: ECPR Press.
Dyzenhaus, D. (1997). *Legality and Legitimacy: Carl Schmitt, Hans Kelsen, and Hermann Heller in Weimar*, Oxford: Clarendon Press.
Dyzenhaus, D. (1998a). *Judging the Judges, Judging Ourselves: Truth, Reconciliation and the Apartheid Legal Order*, Oxford: Hart Publishing.
Dyzenhaus, D. (1998b). Law as Justification: Etienne Mureinik's Conception of Legal Culture. *South African Journal on Human Rights*, 14 (1), 11–37.
Dyzenhaus, D. (2005). The State of Emergency in Legal Theory. In V. V. Ramraj, M. Hor, & K. Roach, eds., *Global Anti-Terrorism Law and Policy*. Cambridge, UK: Cambridge University Press, pp. 65–89.
Dyzenhaus, D. (2006a). *The Constitution of Law: Legality in a Time of Emergency*, Cambridge: Cambridge University Press.
Dyzenhaus, D. (2006b). Schmitt V. Dicey: Are States of Emergency Inside or Outside the Legal Order? *Cardozo Law Review*, 27 (5), 2005–2040.
Dyzenhaus, D. (2007a). Deference, Security and Human Rights. In B. Goold, & L. Lazarus, eds., *Security and Human Rights*. Oxford: Hart Publishing, pp. 125–156.
Dyzenhaus, D. (2007b). The Politics of the Question of Constituent Power. In M. Loughlin, & N. Walker, eds., *The Paradox of Constitutionalism: Constituent Power and Constitutional Form*. Oxford: Oxford University Press, pp. 129–145.
Dyzenhaus, D. (2008). The Compulsion of Legality. In V. V. Ramraj ed., *Emergencies and the Limits of Legality*, Cambridge: Cambridge University Press, pp. 33–59.
Dyzenhaus, D. (2009a). Review Article: How Hobbes Met the "Hobbes Challenge". *Modern Law Review*, 72 (3), pp. 488–506.
Dyzenhaus, D. (2009b). The Puzzle of Martial Law. *University of Toronto Law Journal*, 59 (1), 1–64.
Dyzenhaus, D. (2010). *Hard Cases in Wicked Legal Systems*, Oxford: Oxford University Press.
Dyzenhaus, D. (2012a). Constitutionalism in an Old Key: Legality and Constituent Power. *Global Constitutionalism*, 1 (2), 229–260.

Dyzenhaus, D. (2012b). States of Emergency. In M. Rosenfeld, & A. Sájo, eds., *Oxford Handbook of Comparative Constitutional Law*. Oxford: Oxford University Press, pp. 442–460.
Dyzenhaus, D. (2014). Proportionality and Deference in a Culture of Justification. In G. Huscroft, B. Miller, & G. Webber, eds., *Proportionality and the Rule of Law*. Cambridge: Cambridge University Press, pp. 234–258.
Dyzenhaus, D. (2016). The Idea of a Constitution: A Plea for *Staatsrechtslehre*. In Dyzenhaus D., & Thorburn, M., eds., *Philosophical Foundations of Constitutional Law*. Oxford: Oxford University Press, pp. 9–32.
Dyzenhaus, D. (2019). Introduction: The Politics of Sovereignty. In H. Heller, ed., *Sovereignty: A Contribution to the Theory of Public and International Law*. Oxford: Oxford University Press, pp. 1–59.
Dyzenhaus, D. (2020). The Janus-Faced Constitution. In J. Bomhoff, D. Dyzenhaus, & T. Poole, eds., *The Double-Facing Constitution*. Cambridge: Cambridge University Press, pp. 17–53.
Dyzenhaus, D., & Thorburn, M., eds. (2016). *Philosophical Foundations of Constitutional Law*, Oxford: Oxford University Press.
Dzur, A. W. (2012). *Punishment, Participatory Democracy, and the Jury*. Oxford: Oxford University Press.
Dzur, A. W. (2013). Twelve Absent Men: Rebuilding the American Jury. *The Boston Review*, 38 (4), 30–35.
Eagleton, T. (2011). *Why Marx Was Right*, New Haven: Yale University Press.
Eatwell, R., & Goodwin, M. (2018). *National Populism: The Revolt against Liberal Democracy*, London: Penguin.
Eberle, C., & Cuneo, T., (2015). Religion and Political Theory. In E. Zalta, ed., *Stanford Encyclopedia of Philosophy* (Winter 2017 Edition). Available from: https://plato.stanford.edu/archives/win2017/entries/religion-politics/
Eberlein, B., Abbott, K. W., Black, J., Meidinger, E., & Wood, S. (2014). Transnational Business Governance Interactions: Conceptualization and Framework for Analysis. *Regulation & Governance*, 8 (1), 1–21.
Ebrahim, H. (1999). *The Soul of a Nation: Constitution-making in South Africa*, Oxford: Oxford University Press.
ECB. (2021). The ECB's Monetary Policy Strategy Statement. 8 July. Available from: www.ecb.europa.eu/home/search/review/html/ecb.strategyreview_monpol_strategy_statement.en.html (last Accessed: 18 July 2021).
Eckersley, R. (2004). *The Green State: Rethinking Democracy and Sovereignty*, Cambridge, MA: MIT Press.
Edelstein, D. (2022). Rousseau, Bodin, and the Medieval Corporatist Origins of Popular Sovereignty. *Political Theory*, 50 (1), 142–168.
Edge, P., Corrin, J., & Than, C. (2019). The Appointment and Removal of the Head of Government of the Kiribati Republic. *A Report for Daphne Caine MHK, October 2019*. Oxford Brookes University.
Editors Climate Law. (2010). Editorial. *Climate Law*, 1 (1), 1–2.
Edward, D. (2003). National Court – the Powerhouse of Community Law. *Cambridge Yearbook of European Legal Studies*, 5 (1), 1–13.
Eeckhout, P. (2013). Human Rights and the Autonomy of EU Law: Pluralism or Integration? *Current Legal Problems*, 66 (1), 169–202.
Eekelaar, J. M. (1973). Principles of Revolutionary Legality. In A. W. B. Simpson, ed., *Oxford Essays in Jurisprudence*. Oxford: Clarendon Press, pp. 22–43.

Ehmke, H. (1962). "Staat" und "Gesellschaft" als verfassungstheoretisches Problem. In K. Hesse, S. Reicke, & U. Scheuner, eds., *Staatsverfassung und Kirchenordnung. Festgabe für Rudolf Smend zum 80. Geburtstag*, Tübingen: Mohr Siebeck, pp. 23–49.

Eifert, M. (2014). Conceptualizing Administrative Law – Legal Protection Versus Regulatory Approach. In H. Punder, & C. Waldhoff, eds., *Debates in German Public Law*. Oxford: Hart, pp. 203–218.

Eisgruber, C. (2001). *Constitutional Self-Government*, Cambridge: Harvard University Press.

Eisgruber, C., & Sager, L. (2007). *Religious Freedom and the Constitution*, Cambridge, MA: Harvard University Press.

Ekins, R. (2011). Legislative Intent in *Law's Empire*. *Ratio Juris*, 24 (4), 435–460.

Ekins, R. (2012). *The Nature of Legislative Intent*, Oxford: Oxford University Press.

Ekins, R. (2013). How to Be a Free People. *American Journal of Jurisprudence*, 58 (2), 163–182.

Ekins, R. (2014). Legislating Proportionately. In G. Huscroft, B. Miller, & G. Webber, eds., *Proportionality and the Rule of Law: Rights, Justification, Reasoning*. Cambridge: Cambridge University Press, pp. 343–369.

Ekins, R. (2017a). Legislative Freedom in the United Kingdom. *Law Quarterly Review*, 132, 582–605.

Ekins, R. (2017b). Objects of Interpretation. *Constitutional Commentary*, 32 (1), 1–25.

Ekins, R. (2019a). Intentions and Reflections: *The Nature of Legislative Intent* Revisited. *American Journal of Jurisprudence*, 64 (1), 139–162.

Ekins, R. (2019b). Constitutional Conversations in Britain (in Europe). In G. Sigalet, G. Webber, & R. Dixon, eds., *Constitutional Dialogue: Rights, Democracy, Institutions*. Cambridge: Cambridge University Press, pp. 436–465.

Ekins, R. (2019c). Models of (and Myths About) Rights Protection. In L. Crawford, P. Emerton, & D. Smith, eds., *Law Under a Democratic Constitution: Essays in Honour of Jeffrey Goldsworthy*. Oxford: Hart Publishing, pp. 224–247.

Ekins, R. (2020). The Dynamics and Objects of Democratic Agency. Comment on Tuck 2019. Available from: www.kcl.ac.uk/c-ppl/assets/inaugural-lecture-series/r-ekins-revised-comment-on-richard-tuck-ytl-annual-lecture.pdf.

Ekins, R., & Laws, S. (2019a). *Securing Electoral Accountability*, London: Policy Exchange.

Ekins, R., & Laws, S. (2019b). *Endangering Constitutional Government: The Risks of the House of Commons Taking Control*, London: Policy Exchange.

Ekins, R., & Webber, G. (2018). Legislated Rights in the Anglo-American Tradition. *Faulkner Law Review*, 10 (1), 129–169.

Elazar, D., ed. (1994). *Federal Systems of the World: A Handbook of Federal, Confederal and Autonomy Arrangements*, 2nd edn, Harlow: Longmans.

Elderkin, R. (2015). The Impact of International Criminal Law and the ICC on National Constitutional Arrangements. *Global Constitutionalism*, 4 (2), 227–253.

Electoral Commission. Register to vote. Available from: https://web.archive.org/web/20210102043337/https://www.electoralcommission.org.uk/i-am-a/voter/register-vote-and-update-your-details [Viewed 1 January 2021].

Elgie, R. (2011). *Semi-Presidentialism: Sub-Types and Democratic Performance*, Oxford: Oxford University Press.

Elgie, R. (2016). Varieties of Presidentialism & of Leadership Outcomes, *Daedalus*, 145 (3), 57–68.

Elias, N. (2000). *The Civilizing Process*, Oxford: Blackwell.

Elkink, J. A., Farrell, D. M., Reidy, T., & Suiter, J. (2016). Understanding the 2015 Marriage Referendum in Ireland: Context, Campaign, and Conservative Ireland. *Irish Political Studies*, 32 (3), 361–381.

Elkink, J. A., Farrell, D. M., Marien, S. Reidy, T., & Suiter, J. (2019). The Death of Conservative Ireland? The 2018 Abortion Referendum. UCD Geary Institute for Public Policy Discussion Paper Series. Available at www.ucd.ie/geary/static/publications/workingpapers/gearywp201911.pdf.

Elkins, Z, Ginsburg, T, & Melton, J. (2009). *The Endurance of National Constitutions*, Cambridge: Cambridge University Press.

Elkjaer, A. M., & Iverson, T. (2020). The Political Representation of Economic Interests: Subversion of Democracy or Middle-Class Supremacy? *World Politics*, 72 (2), 254–290.

Elliot, B. (2019). Independent Regulatory and Oversight (Fourth Branch) Institutions. *IDEA*. Available from: www.idea.int/publications/catalogue/independent-regulatory-and-oversight-fourth-branch-institutions (Accessed: 4 January 2022).

Elliott, M. (2001). *The Constitutional Foundations of Judicial Review*, Oxford: Hart.

Elliott, M., & Thomas, R. (2014). *Public Law*, Oxford: Oxford University Press.

Elliott, M., Varuhas, J., & Stark, S., eds. (2018). *The Unity of Public Law? Doctrinal, Theoretical and Comparative Perspectives*, Oxford: Hart Publishing.

Elster, J. (1983). *Sour Grapes*, Cambridge: Cambridge University Press.

Elster, J. (1984). *Ulysses and the Sirens: Studies in Rationality and Irrationality*, rev. edn, Cambridge: Cambridge University Press.

Elster, J. (2000). *Ulysses Unbound*, Cambridge: Cambridge University Press.

Elster, J. (2006). Legislatures as Constituent Assemblies. In R. W. Bauman, & T. Kahana, eds., *The Least Examined Branch: The Role of Legislatures in the Constitutional State*. Cambridge: Cambridge University Press, pp. 181–197.

Elster, J. (2007). Unwritten Constitutional Norms. Working Paper. Columbia University.

Elster, J. (2013). *Securities Against Misrule: Juries, Assemblies, Elections*, Cambridge: Cambridge University Press.

Elster, J. (2016). Icelandic Constitution-Making in Comparative Perspective. In V. Ingimundarson, P. Urfalino, & I. Erlingsdóttirr, eds., *Iceland's Financial Crisis*. London: Routledge, pp. 187–202.

Elster, J. (2017). Constitutions and Constitution-Making. 10 September 2017. Available from: www.hr.fudan.edu.cn/_upload/article/64/c3/6a6475fd465ba83bf340746409e9/32b0f60b-8a82-48af-9e16-1a6f80fd6111.pdf (Accessed: 28 February 2020).

Elster, J. (2018). The Political Psychology of Constitution Making. In J. Elster, R. Gargarella, V. Naresh, & B. E. Rasch, eds., *Constitutent Assemblies*. Cambridge: Cambridge University Press, pp. 207–246.

Elster, J., & Slagstad, R., eds. (1988). *Constitutionalism and Democracy*, Cambridge: Cambridge University Press.

Elstub, S., & Escobar, O., eds., (2019). *Handbook of Democratic Innovation and Governance*, Cheltenham: Edward Elgar.

Elstub, S., & McLaverty, P. (2014). Introduction. In S. Elstub, & P. McLaverty, eds., *Deliberative Democracy: Issues and Cases*. Edinburgh: Edinburgh University Press.

Elstub, S., & Pomatto, G. (2018). Minipublics and Deliberative Constitutionalism. In R. Levy et al. eds., *The Cambridge Handbook of Deliberative Constitutionalism*. Cambridge: Cambridge University Press, pp. 295–310.

Ely, J. H. (1980). *Democracy and Distrust: A Theory of Judicial Review*, Cambridge, MA: Harvard University Press.

Emerson, B. (2017a). Affirmatively Furthering Equal Protection: Constitutional Meaning in the Administration of Fair Housing. *Buffalo Law Review*, 65 (1), 163–235.

Emerson, B. (2017b). The Administration of Constitutional Conflict: Structural Transformations in American Public Law, 1877–1946. *Quaderni Fiorentini*, 46, 385–415.

Emerson, B. (2019). *The Public's Law: Origins and Architecture of Progressive Democracy*, New York: Oxford University Press.
Emerson, B. (2021). The Departmental Structure of Executive Power: Subordinate Checks from Madison to Mueller. *Yale Journal on Regulation*, 38 (1), 90–174.
Emerson, T. I. (1963). Toward a General Theory of the First Amendment. *Yale Law Journal*, 72 (5), 877–956.
Emmert, F. (2008). Rule of Law in Central and Eastern Europe. *Fordham International Law Journal*, 32 (2), 551–586.
Endicott, T. (2012). Legal Interpretation. In A. Marmor, ed., *The Routledge Companion to Philosophy of Law*. New York: Routledge, pp. 109–122.
Endicott, T. (2014). Proportionality and Incommensurability. In G. Huscroft, B. Miller, & G. Webber, eds., *Proportionality and the Rule of Law*. Cambridge: Cambridge University Press, pp. 311–342.
Endicott, T. (2016). Equity and Administrative Behaviour: A Commentary. In P. Turner, ed., *Equity and Administration*. Cambridge: Cambridge University Press, pp. 367–379.
Endicott, T. (2018). The Public Trust. In Criddle et al. pp. 306–330.
Engel, R., & Swartz, K. (2014). Race, Crime, and Policing. In S. Bucerius, & M. Tonry, eds., *The Oxford Handbook of Ethnicity, Crime, and Immigration*. Oxford: Oxford University Press, pp. 135–165.
Engst, B. et al. (2017). Zum Einfluss der Parteinähe auf das Abstimmungsverhalten der Bundesverfassungsrichter – eine quantitative Untersuchung. *JuristenZeitung*, 72 (11), 816–826.
Epperly, B. (2019). *The Political Foundations of Judicial Independence in Dictatorship and Democracy*, Oxford: Oxford University Press.
Epstein, B. (2015). *The Ant-Trap: Rebuilding the Foundations of the Social Sciences*, Oxford: Oxford University Press.
Epstein, G. A., & Yeldan, A. E. (2009). *Beyond Inflation Targeting: Assessing the Impacts and Policy Alternatives*, Cheltenham: Edward Elgar Publishing.
Epstein, R. (2014). *The Classical Liberal Constitution: The Uncertain Quest for Limited Government*, Cambridge, MA: Harvard University Press.
Equal Employment Opportunity Commission. (1970). "They Have the Power, We Have the People": The Status of Equal Employment Opportunity in Houston, Texas, 1970. Washington, DC: EEOC.
Erdos, D. (2010). *Delegating Rights Protection: The Rise of Bills of Rights in the Westminster World*, Oxford: Oxford University Press.
Erikson, R. (2015). Income Inequality and Policy Responsiveness. *Annual Review of Political Science*, 18 (1), 11–29.
Erk, J. (2008). *Explaining Federalism: State, Society and Congruence in Austria, Belgium, Canada, Germany and Switzerland*, London: Routledge.
Erk, J., & Anderson, L. M. (2010). *The Paradox of Federalism: Does Self-Rule Accommodate or Exacerbate Ethnic Divisions?* London and New York: Routledge.
Ertman, T. (1997). *Birth of the Leviathan. Building States and Regimes in Medieval and Early Modern Europe*, Cambridge: Cambridge University Press.
Ernst, D. R. (2014). *Tocqueville's Nightmare: The Administrative State Emerges in America, 1914–1940*, Oxford: Oxford University Press.
Eskridge, W. (2010). The California Proposition 8 Case: What Is a Constitution For? *California Law Review* 98 (4), 1235–1252.
Eskridge, W., Jr. & Ferejohn, J. A. (2010). *A Republic of Statutes: The New American Constitution*, New Haven: Yale University Press.

Esping-Andersen, G. (1990). *The Three Worlds of Welfare Capitalism*, Princeton: Princeton University Press.
Esterling, K. M., Fung, A., & Lee, T. (2021). When Deliberation Produces Persuasion Rather than Polarization: Measuring and Modeling Small Group Dynamics in a Field Experiment. *British Journal of Political Science*, 51 (2), 666–684.
Estlund, D. (1997). Beyond Fairness and Deliberation: The Epistemic Dimension of Democratic Authority. In J. Bohman, & W. Rehg, eds., *Deliberative Democracy*. Cambridge, MA: MIT Press.
Estlund, D. (2008). *Democratic Authority: A Philosophical Framework*, Princeton: Princeton University Press.
Eule, J. N. (1987). Temporal Limits on the Legislative Mandate: Entrenchment and Retroactivity. *Law and Social Enquiry*, 12 (2–3), 381–459.
Evans, P. B., Rueschemeyer, D., & Skocpol, T. (1985). *Bringing the State back in*, Cambridge: Cambridge University Press.
Ewing, K. D, Rowbottom, J., & Tham, Joo-Cheong (2012). *The Funding of Political Parties: Where Now?* London: Routledge.
Fabbrini, S. (2001). Features and Implications of Semi-Parliamentarism: The Direct Election of Italian Mayors. *South European Society and Politics*, 6 (2), 47–70.
Fabre, C. (2000). *Social Rights under the Constitution. Government and the Decent Life*, Oxford: Oxford University Press.
Fabre, C. (2005). Social Rights in European Constitutions. In G. de Búrca, & B. de Witte, eds., *Social Rights in Europe*. Oxford: Oxford University Press, pp. 15–28.
Fabre, C. (2006). *Whose Body Is It Anyway?* Oxford: Oxford University Press.
Failer, J. L. (2002). *Who Qualifies for Rights?: Homelessness, Mental Illness, and Civil Commitment*, Ithaca: Cornell University Press.
Fairclough, A. (1987). *To Redeem the Soul of America: The Southern Christian Leadership Conference and Martin Luther King, Jr.*, Athens: University of Georgia Press.
Fallon Jr, R. H. (1997). "The Rule of Law" as a Concept in Constitutional Discourse. *Columbia Law Review*, 97 (1), 1–56.
Fallon, Jr., R. (2019). *The Nature of Constitutional Rights: The Invention and Logic of Strict Judicial Scrutiny*. Cambridge: Cambridge University Press.
Fanon, F. (2018). *Alienation and Freedom*. Edited by J. Khalfa & Robert J. C. Young. London: Bloomsbury Publishing.
Farrand, M., ed. (1937). *The Records of the Federal Convention of 1787*, New Haven, CT: Yale University Press.
Farrell, D., Suiter, J., & Harris, C. (2019). "Systematizing" Constitutional Deliberation: The 2016–2018 Citizens' Assembly in Ireland. *Irish Political Studies*, 34 (1), 113–123.
Fassbender, B. (1998). The United Nations Charter as Constitution of the International Community. *Columbia Journal of Transnational Law*, 36 (3), 529–619.
Fassbender, B. (2009). Rediscovering the Forgotten Constitution: Notes on the Place of the UN Charter in the International Legal Order. In J. Dunoff, & J. Trachtman, eds., *Ruling the World?: Constitutionalism, International Law, and Global Governance*. Cambridge: Cambridge University Press, pp. 133–147.
Fatin-Rouge Stefanini, M. (2017). Referendums, Minorities and Individual Freedoms. In L. Morel, & M. Qvortrup, eds., *The Routledge Handbook of Referendums and Direct Democracy*. London: Routledge, pp. 371–387.
Fatovic, C. (2004). Constitutionalism and Presidential Prerogative: Jeffersonian and Hamiltonian Perspectives. *American Journal of Political Science*, 48 (3), 429–444.
Fatovic, C. (2009). *Outside the Law: Emergency and Executive Power*, Baltimore: John Hopkins University Press.

Fatovic, C., & Kleinerman, B. A., eds. (2013). *Extra-Legal Power and Legitimacy: Perspectives on Prerogative*, Oxford: Oxford University Press.

Fawcett, P., Flinders, M., Hay, C., & Wood, M. (2017). Anti-Politics, Depoliticization, and Governance. In *Anti-Politics, Depoliticization, and Governance*. Oxford: Oxford University Press, pp. 3–25.

Federalist Papers. (1787). Edited by I. Kramnick. London: Penguin, Harmondsworth.

Feeley, M. (2012). The Political Theory of Federalism. *Flinders Journal of History and Politics*, 28, 1–15.

Feeley, M., & Rubin, E. (2008). *Federalism: Political Identity and Tragic Compromise*, Ann Arbor: University of Michigan Press.

Fehr, E., & Fischbacher, U. (2006). The Economics of Strong Reciprocity. In H. Gintis, S. Bowles, R. Boyd, & E. Fehr, eds., *Moral Sentiments and Material Interests: The Foundations of Cooperation in Economic Life*. Cambridge, MA: MIT Press, pp. 151–192.

Feinberg, J. (1970). The Nature and Value of Rights. *The Journal of Value Inquiry*, 4 (4), 243–257.

Feinberg, J. (1986). *Harm to Self. Volume III of The Moral Limits of the Criminal Law*, Oxford: Oxford University Press.

Feinberg, J. (1988). *Harmless Wrongdoing. Volume IV of The Moral Limits of the Criminal Law*, Oxford: Oxford University Press.

Feldman, L. (2008). Judging Necessity: Democracy and Extralegalism. *Political Theory*, 36 (4), 550–577.

Feldman, N. (2021). *The Broken Constitution: Lincoln, Slavery, and the Refounding of America*, New York: Farrar, Straus and Giroux.

Fenton, W. N. (1998). *The Great Law of the Longhouse: A Political History of the Iroquois Confederacy*, Norman: University of Oklahoma Press.

Ferejohn, J. (1999). Independent Judges, Dependent Judiciary: Explaining Judicial Independence. *Southern California Law Review*, 72 (2–3), 353–384.

Ferejohn, J. (2002). Judicializing Politics, Politicizing Law. *Law and Contemporary Problems*, 65 (3), 41–68.

Ferejohn, J. (2008). The Citizen's Assembly Model. In Warren, M., & Pearse, H. eds., *Designing Deliberative Democracy: The British Columbia Citizens' Assembly*. Cambridge: Cambridge University Press, pp. 192–213.

Ferejohn, J., & Pasquino P. (2002). Constitutional Courts as Deliberative Institutions. Towards an Institutional Theory of Constitutional Justice. In S. Wojciech, ed., *Constitutional Justice, East and West*. The Hague: Kluwer Law International, pp. 21–36.

Ferejohn, J., & Pasquino, P. (2004). The Law of the Exception: A Typology of Emergency Powers. *International Journal of Constitutional Law*, 2 (2), 210–239.

Ferejohn, J., & Sager, L. (2002). Commitment and Constitutionalism. *Texas Law Review*, 81 (7), 1929–1964.

Ferrajoli, L. (1999). *Derechos y garantías. La ley del más débil*, Madrid: Trotta.

Ferrajoli, L. (2011). *Principia Iuris: Teoría del Derecho y de la Democracia*. Vol I. Madrid: Trotta.

Ferris, D. et al. (2019). Noncitizen Voting Rights in the Global Era: A Literature Review and Analysis. *Journal of International Migration and Integration*, 21 (3), 949–971.

Filgueira, B., & Mason, I. (2011). Is There Any Evidence of Earth Jurisprudence in Existing Law. In P. Burdon, ed., *Exploring Wild Law: The Philosophy of Earth Jurisprudence*, Kent Town, SA: Wakefield Press, pp. 192–203.

Filippov, M., Ordeshook, P. C., & Shvetsova, O. (2004). *Designing Federalism: A Theory of Self-Sustainable Federal Institutions*, Cambridge: Cambridge University Press.

Finchelstein, F. (2019). *From Fascism to Populism in History*, Berkely: University of California Press.

Fine, S. (2013). The Ethics of Immigration: Self-Determination and the Right to Exclude. *Philosophy Compass*, 8 (3), 254–268.
Finer, S. E. (1999). *Empires, Monarchies, and the Modern State. Volume III of The History of Government*, Oxford: Oxford University Press.
Finkel, J. S. (2008). *Judicial Reform as Political Insurance: Argentina, Peru, and Mexico in the 1990s*, Notre Dame: University of Notre Dame Press.
Finkelman, P. (2014). *Slavery and the Founders: Race and Liberty in the Age of Jefferson.* 3rd edn, London: Routledge.
Finlay, C. (2015). *Terrorism and the Right to Resist: A Theory of Just Revolutionary War*, Cambridge: Cambridge University Press.
Finnis, J. (1998). *Aquinas: Moral, Political and Legal Theory*, Oxford: Oxford University Press.
Finnis, J. (2011 [1980]). *Natural Law and Natural Rights*, 2nd edn, Oxford: Oxford University Press.
Fioravanti, M. (2007). Siéyès et le jury constitutionnaire: perspectives historico-juridiques, *Annales historiques de la Révolution française*, 349, 87–103.
Fiorina, M., & Abrams, S. (2008). Political Polarization in the American Public. *Annual Review of Political Science*, 11, 563–588.
Fish, S. (2000). Mission Impossible. Settling the Just Bounds Between Church and State. In S. M. Feldman, ed., *Law & Religion. A Critical Anthology*. New York: New York University Press, pp. 383–410.
Fisher, E. C. (2007). *Risk Regulation and Administrative Constitutionalism*, London: Bloomsbury Publishing.
Fisher, E. et al. (2017). The Legally Disruptive Nature of Climate Change. *Modern Law Review*, 80 (2), 172–201.
Fishkin, J. S. (2018). *Democracy When the People Are Thinking. Revitalizing our Politics through Public Deliberation*, Oxford: Oxford University Press.
Fishkin, J. S., & Pozen, D. E. (2018). Asymmetrical Constitutional Hardball. *Columbia Law Review*, 118 (3), 915–982.
Fiss, O. (1979). Forms of Justice. *Harvard Law Review*, 93 (1), 1–58.
Fiss, O. (1993). The Limits of Judicial Independence. *The University of Miami Inter-American Law Review*, 25 (1), 57–76.
Fitzmaurice, G. (1957). The General Principles of International Law Considered from the Standpoint of the Rule of Law. *Recueil des cours – Académie de Droit International*, 92, 1–227.
Flavin, P. (2016). Labor Union Strength and Equality of Political Representation. *British Journal of Political Science*, 48 (4), 1075–1091.
Fleming, J. ed. (2011). *Getting to the Rule of Law: NOMOS L*, New York: New York University Press.
Flikschuh K. (2008). Reason, Right and Revolution: Kant and Locke. *Philosophy & Public Affairs*, 36 (4), 375–404.
Follesdal, A. (2020). Survey Article: The Legitimacy of International Courts. *Journal of Political Philosophy* 28 (4), 476–499.
Follesdal, A., & Wind, M. (2009). Introduction: Nordic Reluctance Towards Judicial Review Under Siege, *Nordic Journal of Human Rights*, 27 (2), 131–142.
Fombad, C. M. (2017). An Overview of Contemporary Models of Constitutional Review in Africa. In C. M. Fombad, ed., *Constitutional Adjudication in Africa*. Oxford: Oxford University Press, pp. 17–48.
FOMC. (2020). *Statement on Longer-Run Goals and Monetary Policy Strategy*, Washington, DC: Federal Open Market Committee.

Foner, E. (2019). *The Second Founding: How the Civil War and Reconstruction Remade the Constitution*, New York: W.W. Norton & Company.
Fontana, D., (2009). Government in Opposition. *Yale Law Journal*, 119 (3), 548–623.
Foran, J. (1996). Reinventing the Mexican Revolution: The Competing paradigms of Alan Knight and John Mason Hart. *Latin American Perspectives*, 23 (4), 115–131.
Foran, J. (2005). *Taking Power: On the Origins of Third World Revolutions*, Cambridge: Cambridge University Press.
Foran, J., Lane, D., & Zivkovic, A., eds. (2008). *Revolution in the Making of the Modern World: Social Identities, Globalization and Modernity*. Abdingdon Oxon: Routledge.
Forbath, W. (2001). Constitutional Welfare Rights: A History, Critique and Reconstruction. *Fordham Law Review*, 69 (5), 1821–1892.
Forst, R. (2002). *Contexts of Justice. Political Philosophy Beyond Liberalism and Communitarianism*, Berkeley: University of California Press.
Forst, R. (2012). *The Right to Justification: Elements of a Constructivist Theory of Justice*. Jeffrey Flynn (trans.). New York: Columbia University Press.
Forst, R. (2014). *Justification and Critique. Towards a Critical Theory of Politics*, Cambridge, UK: Polity Press.
Forst, R. (2016). The Justification of Basic Rights. *Netherlands Journal of Legal Philosophy*, 45 (3), 7–28.
Forst, R. (2017a). *Normativity and Power. Analyzing Social Orders of Justification*, Oxford: Oxford University Press.
Forst, R. (2017b). Political Liberalism: A Kantian View. *Ethics*, 128 (1), pp. 123–144.
Forst, R. (2017c). Toleration. In E. Zalta, ed., *Stanford Encyclopedia of Philosophy* (Fall 2017 Edition). Available from: https://plato.stanford.edu/archives/fall2017/entries/toleration/.
Forst, R. (2019). The Justification of Progress and the Progress of Justification. In A. Allen, & E. Mendieta, eds., *Justification and Emancipation. The Critical Theory of Rainer Forst*. University Park: The Pennsylvania State University Press, pp. 17–37.
Forst, R. (2020a). The Point of Justice: On the Paradigmatic Incompatibility of Rawlsian "Justice as Fairness" and Luck Egalitarianism. In J. Mandle, S. Roberts-Cady, & J.Rawls, eds., *Debating the Major Questions*. Oxford: Oxford University Press, pp. 148–160.
Forst, R (2020b). The Constitution of Justification. Replies and Comments. In E. Herlin-Karnell, & M. Klatt, eds., *Constitutionalism Justified. Rainer Forst in Discourse*. Oxford: Oxford University Press, pp. 295–346.
Forsthoff, E. (1935). *Der totale Staat*, 2nd edn, Hamburg: Hanseatische Verlaganstalt.
Forsthoff, E. (1954). Begriff und Wesen des sozialen Rechtsstaates. *Veröffentlichungen der Vereinigung der deutschen Staatsrechtslehrer*, 12, 9–36.
Forsthoff, E. (1961). *Lehrbuch des Verwaltungsrechts*, vol. I, 8th edn, Munich, Berlin: C.H. Beck'sche.
Forsthoff, E. (1971). *Der Staat der Industriegesellschaft. Dargestellt am Beispiel der Bundesrepublik Deutschland*, München: C. H. Beck.
Forsyth, M. (1981). *Union of States: The Theory and Practice of Confederations*, Leicester: Leicester University Press.
Fortas, A. (1968). *Concerning Dissent and Civil Disobedience*, New York: The American Library.
Fortescue, J. (1997). *On the Laws and Governance of England*. Edited by S. Lockwood. Cambridge: Cambridge University Press.

Foucault, M. (2007). *Security, Territory, Population: Lectures at the Collège de France 1977–1978*. Edited by M. Senellart. London: Palgrave Macmillan.
Fournier, P., et al. (2011). *When Citizens Decide: Lessons from Citizen Assemblies on Electoral Reform*, Oxford: Oxford University Press.
Fox, R., & Blackwell, J. (2014). *The Devil in the Detail: Parliament and Delegated Legislation*, London: Hansard Society.
Fox-Decent, E. (2008). Is the Rule of Law Really Indifferent to Human Rights? *Law and Philosophy*, 27 (6), 533–581.
Fox-Decent, E. (2011). *Sovereignty's Promise: The State as Fiduciary*, Oxford: Oxford University Press.
Fox-Decent, E. (2019). New Frontiers in Public Fiduciary Law. In E. Criddle, P. Miller, & R. Sitkoff, eds., *The Oxford Handbook of Fiduciary Law*. Oxford: Oxford University Press, pp. 910–924.
Fraenkel, E. (2017 [1941]). *The Dual State: A Contribution to the Theory of Dictatorship*, Oxford: Oxford University Press.
France, P., & Vauchez, A. (2017). *Sphère Publique, Intérêts Privés: Enquête sur un Grand Brouillage*. Paris: Presses de Sciences Po, 2017. [Available in English as Vauchez, A., and France, P. (2021). *The Neoliberal Republic: Corporate Lawyers, Statecraft, and the Making of Public-Private France*, Ithaca: Cornell University Press.]
Francis, D. (2017). The Decline of the Dormant Commerce Clause. *Denver Law Review* 94 (2), 255–319.
Frank, T. (2005). Legality and Legitimacy in Humanitarian Intervention. In T. Nardin, & M. Williams, eds., *Humanitarian Intervention: NOMOS XLVII*. New York: New York University Press, pp. 143–157.
Frankenberg, G. (1985). Critical Comparisons: Re-Thinking Comparative Law. *Harvard International Law Journal*, 26 (2), 411.
Frankenberg, G. (2006). Comparing Constitutions: Ideas, Ideals, and Ideology – Toward a Layered Narrative. *International Journal of Constitutional Law*, 4 (3), 439.
Frankfurt, H. (1997). Equality and Respect. *Social Research*, 64 (1), 3–15.
Franklin, J. H. (1978). *John Locke and the Theory of Sovereignty: Mixed Monarchy and the Right of Resistance in the Political Thought of the English Revolution*, Cambridge: Cambridge University Press.
Franklin, M. (1970). Legal Method in the Philosophies of Hegel and Savigny. *Tulsa Law Review*, 44 (4), 766–797.
Frantz, L. (1962). The First Amendment in the Balance. *Yale Law Journal*, 71 (8), 1424–1450.
Fraser, N., & Honneth, A. (2003). *Redistribution or Recognition? A Political-Philosophical Exchange*, London: Verso.
Fredman, S. (2008). *Human Rights Transformed: Positive Rights and Positive Duties*, Oxford: Oxford University Press.
Fredman, S. (2016). Substantive Equality Revisited. *International Journal of Constitutional Law*, 14 (3) 712–738.
Freeden, M. (2016). After the Brexit Referendum: Revisiting Populism as an Ideology. *Journal of Political Ideologies*, 22 (1), 1–11.
Freeman, A. (1990). Antidiscrimination Law: The View from 1989. In D. Kairys, ed., *The Politics of Law: A Progressive Critique*. New York: Pantheon Books, pp. 121–150.
Freeman, S. (2000). Deliberative Democracy: A Sympathetic Comment. *Philosophy and Public Affairs*, 29 (4), 371–418.
Frega, R. (2020). Il populismo di sinistra come altro della socialdemocrazia. In A. Masala, & L. Viviani, *L'età dei populismi*, Rome: Carocci, 227–254.

Freiman, C. (2020). *Why It's OK to Ignore Politics*, London: Routledge.
Fricker, M. (2007). *Epistemic Injustice: Power and the Ethics of Knowing*, Oxford, Oxford University Press.
Friedman, M. (1962). Should there be an Independent Monetary Authority? In L. Yeager, ed., *In Search of a Monetary Constitution*. Cambridge, MA: Harvard University Press, pp. 219–243.
Friedman, M. (1968). The Role of Monetary Policy. *American Economic Review*, 58 (1), 1–17.
Friedmann, D. (2016). *The Purse and the Sword: The Trials of Israel's Legal Revolution*, Oxford: Oxford University Press.
Friedrich, C. J. (1963). *Man and His Government: An Empirical Theory of Politics*, New York: McGraw Book Company.
Friedrich, C. J. (1968). *Trends of Federalism in Theory and Practice*, London: Frederick A. Praeger Publishers.
Fujiwara, D., & Dolan, P. (2016). Happiness-Based Policy Analysis. In M. Adler, & M. Fleurbaey, eds., *The Oxford Handbook of Well-Being and Public Policy*. New York: Oxford University Press, pp. 286–317.
Fuller, L. L. (1969). *The Morality of Law*, rev. edn, New Haven: Yale University Press.
Fung, A. (2004). *Empowered Participation: Reinventing Urban Democracy*, Princeton: Princeton University Press.
Fung, A. (2007). Minipublics: Deliberative Designs and Their Consequences. In S. W. Rosenberg, ed., *Deliberation, Participation, and Democracy: Can the People Govern?* New York: Palgrave Macmillan, pp. 159–183.
Fung, A., & Wright, E. O. (2003). *Deepening Democracy: Institutional Innovation in Empowered Participatory Governance*, London: Verso Books.
Furedi, F. (2017). *Populism and the European Culture Wars: The Conflict of Values between Hungary and the EU*, London, New York: Routledge.
Furet F. (1981). *Interpreting the French Revolution*. Translated by E. Forster. Cambridge: Cambridge University Press.
Furet F. (2000). *The Passing of an Illusion: The Idea of Communism in the Twentieth Century*. 2nd edn, Chicago: University of Chicago Press.
Gabor, D., & Ban, C. (2016). Banking on Bonds: The New Links Between States and Markets. *JCMS: Journal of Common Market Studies*, 54 (3), 617–635.
Gabor, D., & Vestergaard, J. (2016). Towards a Theory of Shadow Money. INET Working Paper. Institute for New Economic Thinking.
Gadamer, H., (2004). *Truth and Method*. Translated by J. Weinsheimer and D. G. Marshall. London, New York: Continuum.
Gagnon, A.-G., ed. (2009). *Contemporary Canadian Federalism*, Toronto: University of Toronto Press.
Gagnon, A-G, & Tully, J., eds. (2001). *Multinational Democracies*, Cambridge: Cambridge University Press.
Gaita, R. (2001). *A Common Humanity*, London: Routledge.
Gajda-Roszczynialska, K., & Markiewicz, K. (2020). Disciplinary Proceedings as an Instrument for Breaking the Rule of Law in Poland. *Hague Journal on the Rule of Law*, 12 (3), 451–483.
Galbraith, J. K. (1997). Time to Ditch the NAIRU. *The Journal of Economic Perspectives*, 11 (1), 93–108.
Gales, J., ed. (1834). *The Debates and Proceedings of the Congress of the United States*, vol. I. Washington, DC: Gales and Seaton.
Gallie, W. B. (1956). Essentially Contested Concepts. *Proceedings of the Aristotelian Society*, 56, 167–198.

Galligan, B. (2001). Amending Constitutions through the Referendum Device. In M. Mendelsohn, & A. Parkin, eds., *Referendum Democracy: Citizens, Elites, and Deliberation in Referendum Campaigns*. Basingstoke: Palgrave, pp. 109–124.

Galligan, B., & Brenton, S., eds. (2015). *Constitutional Conventions in Westminster Systems: Controversies, Changes, and Challenges*, Cambridge: Cambridge University Press.

Galligan, D. J. (2008). Constitutional Paradox or the Potential of Constitutional Theory. *Oxford Journal of Legal Studies*, 28 (2), 343–367.

Gamble, B. (1997). Putting Civil Rights to a Popular Vote. *American Journal of Political Science*, 41 (1), 245–269.

Gamper, A. (2005). A "Global Theory of Federalism": The Nature and Challenges of a Federal State. *German Law Journal*, 6 (10), 1297–1318.

Gandhi, M. (2005). *Gandhi: Selected Writings*. Edited by R. Duncan. Mineola: Dover Publications.

Gandhi, M. (1923). *Young India 1919–1922*, New York: B. W. Huebsch, Inc.

Ganghof, S. (2014). Bicameralism as a form of Government (or: Why Australia and Japan Do Not Have a Parliamentary System). *Parliamentary Affairs*, 67 (3), 647–663.

Ganghof, S. (2015). Is the "Constitution of Equality" Parliamentary, Presidential or Hybrid? *Political Studies*, 63 (4), 814–829.

Ganghof, S. (2018). A New Political System Model: Semi-parliamentary Government. *European Journal of Political Research*, 57 (2), 261–281.

Ganghof, S. (2021). *Beyond Presidentialism and Parliamentarism: Democratic Design and the Separation of Powers*, Oxford: Oxford University Press.

Gans, C. (2016). *A Political Theory for the Jewish People*, Oxford: Oxford University Press.

García Agustín, Ó. (2020). *Left-Wing Populism: The Politics of the People*, Bingley, UK: Emerald Group Publishing.

Garcia, L., Grande, I., & R. Cussó (2017). La Question Moreno face à l'essor du séparatisme en catalogne. L'identité duale est-elle nationale? *Pôle Sud*, 47 (2), 119–132.

Gardbaum, S. (2010). A Democratic Defense of Constitutional Balancing. *Law and Ethics of Human Rights*, 4 (1), 78–106.

Gardbaum, S. (2011). The Structure and Scope of Constitutional Rights. In T. Ginsburg, & R. Dixon, eds., *Comparative Constitutional Law*. Cheltenham: Edward Elgar, pp. 278–297.

Gardbaum, S. (2013). *The New Commonwealth Model of Constitutionalism: Theory and Practice*, Cambridge: Cambridge University Press.

Gardbaum, S. (2014). Separation of Powers and the Growth of Judicial Review in Established Democracies (or Why has the Model of Legislative Supremacy Mostly been Withdrawn from Sale?). *The American Journal of Comparative Law*, 62 (3), 613–640.

Gardiner, S. R., (1906). *The Constitutional Documents of the Puritan Revolution, 1625–1660*, 3rd edn, Oxford: Oxford University Press.

Gardner, J. (2011). Can There be a Written Constitution? In L. Green, & B. Leiter, eds., *Oxford Studies in Philosophy of Law*. Oxford: Oxford University Press, pp. 162–194.

Gardner, J. (2012). *Some Types of Law*. In J. Gardner, *Law as a Leap of Faith: Essays on Law in General*, Oxford: Oxford University Press, pp. 54–88.

Gardner, J. (2018). *From Personal Life to Private Law*, Oxford: Oxford University Press.

Gargarella, R. (2003). The Majoritarian Reading of the Rule of Law. In J. M. Maravall, & A. Przeworski, eds., *Democracy and the Rule of Law*. Cambridge: Cambridge University Press, pp. 147–167.

Gargarella, R. (2010). *The Legal Foundations of Inequality*, Cambridge: Cambridge University Press.

Gargarella, R. (2013). *Latin American Constitutionalism, 1810–2010: The Engine Room of the Constitution*, Oxford: Oxford University Press.
Gargarella, R. (2019). Why Do We Care about Dialogue. In K. Young, ed., *The Future of Social and Economic Rights*. Cambridge: Cambridge University Press, pp. 212–232.
Garlicki, L. (2007). Constitutional Courts Versus Supreme Courts. *International Journal of Constitutional Law*, 5 (1), 44–68.
Garlicki, L. (2019). Constitutional Court and Politics. The Polish Crisis. In C. Landfried, ed., *Judicial Power. How Constitutional Courts Affect Political Transformations*. Cambridge: Cambridge University Press, pp. 141–162.
Garnsey, P. (2007). *Thinking about Property: From Antiquity to the Age of Revolution*, Cambridge: Cambridge University Press.
Garoupa, N., & Ginsburg, T. (2009). Guarding the Gardians: Judicial Councils and Judicial Indpendence. *The American Journal of Comparative Law*, 57 (1), 103–134.
Gastil, J., & Wright, E. O. (2018). Legislature by Lot: Envisioning Sortition within a Bicameral System. *Politics & Society*, 46 (3), 303–330.
Gastil, J., & Wright, E. O. (2019). Legislature by Lot, Envisioning Sortition Within A Bicameral System. In Gastil, & Wright, eds., *Legislature by Lot. Transformative Designs for Deliberative Governance*. London, New York: Verso, pp. 3–38.
Gathii, J. T. (2001). Re-Characterizing the Social in the Constitutionalization of the WTO: A Preliminary Analysis. *Widener Law Symposium Journal*, 7 (1), 137–174.
Gauchet, M. (1995). *La révolution des pouvoirs: La souveraineté, le peuple, et la représentation, 1789–1799*, Paris: Gallimard.
Gaus, G. (1996). *Justificatory Liberalism: An Essay on Epistemology and Political Theory*, New York: Oxford University Press.
Gaus, G., & Vallier, K. (2009). The Roles of Religious Conviction in a Publicly Justified Polity: The Implications of Convergence, Asymmetry and Political Institutions. *Philosophy and Social Criticism*, 35 (1–2), 51–76.
Gee, G., & Webber, G. (2010). What Is a Political Constitution? *Oxford Journal of Legal Studies*, 30 (2), 273–299.
Gerbaudo, P. (2019). *The Digital Party: Political Organization and Online Democracy*, London: Pluto Press.
Gerber, M., et al. (2018). Deliberative Abilities and Deliberative Influence in a Transnational Deliberative Poll (EuroPolis). *British Journal of Political Science*, 48 (4), 1093–1118.
Gerhardt, M. (2000). *The Federal Appointments Process*, Durham: Duke University Press.
Gerhardt, M. (2019). *The Federal Impeachment Process: A Constitutional and Historical Analysis*, 3rd edn, Chicago: Chicago University Press.
Gerken, H. (2007). The Hydraulics of Constitutional Reform: A Skeptical Response to Our Democratic Constitution. *Drake Law Review*, 55, 925–943.
Gerrards, J., & Senden, H., (2009). The Structure of Fundamental Rights and the European Court of Human Rights. *International Journal of Constitutional Law*, 7 (4), 619–653.
Gerstenberg, O. (2004). What Constitutions Can Do (but Courts Sometimes Don't): Property, Speech, and The Influence of Constitutional Norms on Private Law. *Canadian Journal of Law & Jurisprudence*, 17 (1), 61–81.
Gerstenberg, O. (2018). *Euroconstitutionalism and Its Discontents*, Oxford: Oxford University Press.
Gerstenberg, O. (2021). Fundamental Rights and Democratic Sovereignty in the EU: The Role of the Charter of Fundamental Rights of the EU (CFREU) in Regulating the European Social Market Economy. *Yearbook of European Law*, 39 (1), 199–227.
Genn, H. (2009). *Judging Civil Justice*, Cambridge: Cambridge University Press.

Genovese, E. D. (1992). *From Rebellion to Revolution: Afro-American Slave Revolts in the Making of the Modern World*, Baton Rogue: Louisiana State University Press.
Getachew, A. (2019). *Worldmaking After Empire: The Rise and Fall of Self-Determination*, Princeton: Princeton University Press.
Geuss, R. (2008). *Philosophy and Real Politics*, Princeton: Princeton University Press.
Geyh, C. G. (2013). The Dimensions of Judicial Impartiality. *Florida Law Review*, 65 (2), 493–551.
Gherghina, S., Racu, A., Giugal, A., Gavris, A., Silagadze, N., & Johnston, R. (2019). Non-voting in the 2018 Romanian Referendum: The Importance of Initiators, Campaigning and Issue Saliency. *Political Science* 71 (3), 193–213.
Ghosh, E. (2010). Deliberative Democracy and the Countermajoritarian Difficulty: Considering Constitutional Juries. *Oxford Journal of Legal Studies* 30 (2), 327–359.
Ghosh, E. (2018). Deliberative Constitutionalism: An Empirical Dimension. In Levy, R., Kong, H., Orr, G., & King, J., eds., *The Cambridge Handbook of Deliberative Constitutionalism*. Cambridge: Cambridge University Press, pp. 220–232.
Gibbard, A. (1973). Manipulation of Voting Schemes: A General Result. *Econometrica*, 41 (4), 587–601.
Gibson, J. L., & G. A. Caldeira (2009). Confirmation Politics and the Legitimacy of the U.S. Supreme Court: Institutional Loyalty, Positivity Bias, and the Alito Nomination. *American Journal of Political Science*, 53 (1), 139–155.
Gierke, O. (1868–1913). *Das deutsche Genossenschaftsrecht*, 4 vols., Berlin: Weidmannsche Buchhandlung.
Gierke, O. (1900). *The Political Theories of Middle Ages*. Translated by F. W. Maitland. Cambridge: Cambridge University Press.
Gierke, O. (1958). *Political Theories of the Middle Age*. Translated by F. W. Maitland. Cambridge: Cambridge University Press.
Gierke, O. (2019 [1889]). The Social Role of Private Law. Translated by E. McGaughey. *German Law Review*, 19 (4), 1017–1116.
Gil, R. Z. (2008). *De la Expectativa al Desconcierto: El Proceso Constituyente de 1991 Visto por sus Protagonistas*, Cali: Pontificia Universidad Javeriana.
Gilad, S. (2014). Beyond Endogeneity: How Firms and Regulators Co-construct the Meaning of Regulation. *Law & Policy*, 36 (2), 134–164.
Gilardi, F. (2009). *Delegation in the Regulatory State: Independent Regulatory Agencies in Western Europe*, Cheltenham: Edward Elgar Publishing.
Gilardi, F., Jordana, J., & Levi-Faur, D. (2006). Regulation in the Age of Globalization: The Diffusion of Regulatory Agencies across Europe and Latin America. In Hodge, G., ed., *Privatisation and Market Development: Global Movements in Public Policy Ideas*. Edward Elgar Publishing, pp. 127–147.
Gilens, M. (2010). *Affluence and Influence*, Princeton: Princeton University Press.
Gilbert, M. (2018). *Rights and Demands*, Oxford: Oxford University Press.
Gill, S., & Claire Cutler, A., eds. (2014). *New Constitutionalism and World Order*. Cambridge: Cambridge University Press.
Gilley, B. (2006). The Meaning and Measure of State Legitimacy: Results for 72 Countries. *European Journal of Political Research*, 45 (3), 499–525.
Gillis, J. (2018). The Montreal Protocol, a Little Treaty That Could. The New York Times, October 19, sec. Science. Available from: www.nytimes.com/2013/12/10/science/the-montreal-protocol-a-little-treaty-that-could.html.
Ginsburg, D., & Menashi, S. (2010). Nondelegation and the Unitary Executive. *University of Pennsylvania Journal of Constitutional Law*, 12 (2), pp. 251–276.
Ginsburg, T. (2003). *Judicial Review in New Democracies: Constitutional Courts in Asian Cases*, Cambridge: Cambridge University Press.

Ginsburg, T. (2020). Authoritarian International Law? *The American Journal of International Law*, 114 (2), 221–260.
Ginsburg, T., & Elkins, Z. (2019). One Size Does Not Fit All: The Provision and Interpretation of Presidential Term Limits. In A. Baturo, & R. Elgie, eds., *The Politics of Presidential Term Limits*. Oxford: Oxford University Press, pp. 37–51.
Ginsburg, T., & Huq, A. (2016). *Assessing Constitutional Performance*, Cambridge: Cambridge University Press.
Ginsburg, T., & Huq, A. (2018). *How to Save a Constitutional Democracy*, Chicago: University of Chicago Press.
Ginsburg, T., & Moustafa, T., eds. (2008). *Rule by Law: The Politics of Courts in Authoritarian Regimes*, New York: Cambridge University Press.
Ginsburg, T., & Simpser, A., eds. (2013). *Constitutions in Authoritarian Regimes*, New York: Cambridge University Press.
Ginsburg, T., & Versteeg, M. (2014). Why Do Countries Adopt Constitutional Review? *The Journal of Law, Economics, and Organization*, 30 (3), 587–622.
Glendon, M. A. (1991). *Rights Talk: The Impoverishment of Political Discourse*, New York: Free Press.
Godwin, A., & Schmulow, A. (2021). *Cambridge Handbook of Twin Peaks Financial Regulation*, Cambridge: Cambridge University Press.
Goitein, E., (2020). Opinion: The Power Trump Can Wield Like a Dictator. *New York Times*. 12 February [viewed 12 June 2020]. Available from: www.nytimes.com/2020/02/12/opinion/trump-emergency-act.html.
Gold, A., & Miller, P., eds. (2014). *Philosophical Foundations of Fiduciary Law*, Oxford: Oxford University Press.
Goldoni, M. (2012). At the Origins of Constitutional Review: Sieyès' Constitutional Jury and the Taming of Constituent Power. *Oxford Journal of Legal Studies*, 32 (2), 211–234.
Goldoni, M., & Wilkinson, M. (2018). The Material Constitution. *Modern Law Review*, 81 (4), 567–597.
Goldsworthy, J. (1999). *The Sovereignty of Parliament: History and Philosophy*, Oxford: Clarendon Press.
Goldsworthy, J. (2010). *Parliamentary Sovereignty*, Cambridge: Cambridge University Press.
Golia, A., & Peters, A. (2022). The Concept of International Organization. In J. Klabbers, ed., *The Cambridge Companion to International Organizations Law*. Cambridge: Cambridge University Press, pp. 25–49.
Gomez, M. A. (2018). *African Dominion: A New History of Empire in Early and Medieval West Africa*, Princeton: Princeton University Press.
Gonzalez-Jacome, J. (2011). Emergency Powers and the Feeling of Backwardness in Latin American State Formation. *American University International Law Review*, 26 (4), 1073–1106.
González-Salzberg, D. (2011). Economic and Social Rights within the Inter-American Court. *International Law: Revista Colombiana de Derecho Internacional*, 9 (18), 117–154.
Goodhart, C., & Lastra, R. (2018). Populism and Central Bank Independence. *Open Economies Review*, 29 (1), 49–68.
Goodin, R. (1988). *Reasons for Welfare*, Oxford: Oxford University Press.
Goodin, R. (2007). Enfranchising All Affected Interests, and Its Alternatives. *Philosophy and Public Affairs*, 35 (1), 40–68.
Goodin, R. (2008). The Place of Parties. In *Innovating Democracy. Democratic Theory and Practice After the Deliberative Turn*, Oxford: Oxford University Press, pp. 204–223.
Goodin, R. (2016). Enfranchising All Subjected, Worldwide. *International Theory*, 8 (3), 365–389.

Goodin, R., & Dryzek, J. S. (2006). Deliberative Impacts: The Macro-Political Uptake of Mini-Publics. *Politics & Society*, 34 (2), 219–244.
Goodin, R., & Jackson, F. (2007). Freedom from Fear. *Philosophy and Public Affairs*, 35 (3), 249–265.
Goodin, R., & Spiekermann, K. (2018). *An Epistemic Theory of Democracy*, Oxford: Oxford University Press.
Goodin, R., & Tanasoca, A. (2014). Double Voting. *Australasian Journal of Philosophy*, 92 (4), 743–758.
Goodman, M. (2005–6). Human Dignity in Supreme Court Constitutional Jurisprudence. *Nebraska Law Review*, 84 (3), 740–794.
Goodman, S. W. (2014). *Immigration and Membership Politics in Western Europe*, New York: Cambridge University Press.
Goodnow, F. J. (1900). *Politics and Administration: A Study in Government*, London: Macmillan.
Gordon, S. (1999). *Controlling the State: Constitutionalism from Ancient Athens to Today*, Cambridge: Harvard University Press.
Gotanda, N. (1991). A Critique of "Our Constitution Is Color Blind." *Stanford Law Review*, 44 (1), 1–68.
Gould, C. (2004). *Globalising Democracy and Human Rights*, Cambridge: Cambridge University Press.
Gould, C. (2014). *Interactive Democracy: The Social Roots of Global Justice*, Cambridge: Cambridge University Press.
Government of Australia. (2016). Juries, no. 47 of 1967. Available from: https://web.archive.org/web/20160309085701/ www.legislation.act.gov.au/a/1967-47/19680101-44861/pdf/1967-47.pdf [Viewed 9 March 2016].
Government of New Zealand. About this visa: skilled migrant category resident visa. Available from: https://web.archive.org/web/20180715224216/https://www.immigration.govt.nz/new-zealand-visas/apply-for-a-visa/about-visa/skilled-migrant-category-resident-visa [Viewed 15 July 2018].
Graber, M. (2010). *Dred Scott and the Problem of Constitutional Evil*, Cambridge: Cambridge University Press.
Gramsci, A. (1989). *The Modern Prince and Other Writings*. Translated by Louis Marks. New York: International Publisher Company.
Gravelle, S. (1988). The Latin-Vernacular Question and Humanist Theory of Language and Culture. *Journal of the History of Ideas*, 49 (3), 367–386.
Gray, G., & Silbey, S. (2014). Governing Inside the Organization: Interpreting Regulation and Compliance. *American Journal of Sociology*, 120 (1), 96–145.
Graziani, A. (2003). *The Monetary Theory of Production*, Cambridge: Cambridge University Press.
Grear, A. (2014). Towards "Climate Justice?": A Critical Reflection on Legal Subjectivity and Climate Injustice: Warning Signals, Patterned Hierarchies, Directions for Future Law and Policy. *Journal of Human Rights and the Environment*, 5, 103–133.
Green, J. (2016). *The Persistent Objector Rule in International Law*, Oxford: Oxford University Press.
Green, L. (2007). The Duty to Govern. *Legal Theory*, 13 (3–4), 165–185.
Greene, J. (2011). The Supreme Court as a Constitutional Court. *Harvard Law Review*, 124 (1), 124–153.
Greenwald, G. (2011). Obama Libya War Powers Debate: Obama's Lawyers Are Worse than Bush's. *Huffpost*. 19 June [viewed 12 June 2020]. Available from: www.huffpost.com/entry/obama-libya-lawyers-war-powers_n_879951

Greenwood, R., Oliver, C., Lawrence, T. B., & Meyer, R. E., eds. (2017). *The Sage Handbook of Organizational institutionalism*, Los Angeles, London: Sage.
Gregg, P. (1984). *King Charles I*, Berkeley: University of California Press.
Grégoire, H. (2002 [1794]). Rapport sur la nécessité et les moyens d'anéantir les patois et d'universaliser l'usage de la langue française. In M. de Certeau, D. Julia, & J. Revel, eds., *Une politique de la langue. La Révolution française et les patois: l'enquête de Grégoire*. Paris: Gallimard, pp. 331–351.
Griffin, J. (2008). *On Human Rights*, Oxford: Oxford University Press.
Griffith, J. A. G. (1979). The Political Constitution. *Modern Law Review*, 42 (1), pp. 1–21.
Grigorescu, A. (2015). *Democratic Intergovernmental Organizations? Normative Pressures and Decision-Making Rules*, Cambridge: Cambridge University Press.
Grigoriadis, I. N. (2018). *Democratic Transition and the Rise of Populist Majoritarianism: Constitutional Reform in Greece and Turkey*, Cham, Switzerland: Palgrave Macmillan.
Grimm, D. (1986). The Modern State: Continental Traditions. In F.-X. Kaufmann, G. Majone, & V. Ostrom, eds., *Guidance, Control, and Evaluation in the Public Sector*. Berlin & New York: Walter de Gruyter, pp. 89–109.
Grimm, D. (2004). Treaty or Constitution? The Legal Basis of the European Union after Maastricht. In E. O. Eriksen, J. E. Fossum, & A. J. Menendez, eds., *Developing a Constitution for Europe*. New York: Routledge, pp. 7–89.
Grimm, D. (2010). The Achievement of Constitutionalism and Its Prospects in a Changed World. In P. Dobner, & M. Loughlin, eds, *The Twilight of Constitutionalism?* Oxford: Oxford University Press, pp. 3–22.
Grimm, D. (2016). *Constitutionalism: Past, Present and Future*, Oxford: Oxford University Press.
Grimm, D. (2017). *The Constitution of European Democracy*, Oxford: Oxford University Press.
Grimm, D. (2019a). Constitutionalisation without Constitution: A Democracy Problem. In N. W. Barber, M. Cahill, & R. Ekins, eds., *The Rise and Fall of the European Constitution*. Oxford: Hart Publishing, pp. 23–40.
Grimm, D. (2019b). What Exactly Is Political about Constitutional Adjudication? In C. Landfried, ed., *Judicial Power. How Constitutional Courts Affect Political Transformations*. Cambridge: Cambridge University Press, pp. 307–317.
Grimm, D. (2020a). Neue Radikalkritik an der Verfassungsgerichtsbarkeit. *Der Staat*, 59 (3), 321–353.
Grimm, D. (2020b). *Recht oder Politik? Die Kelsen-Schmitt-Kontroverse zur Verfassungsgerichtsbarkeit und die heutige Lage*, Berlin: Duncker & Humblot.
Griswold, E. (1968). Dissent – 1968 Style [The George Abel Dreyfous Lecture on Civil Liberties, given at the Tulane University School of Law, New Orleans, La.]. *United States of America Congressional Record – Proceedings and Debates of the 90th Congress, Second Session*. 114 (8), 9407–10822.
Grodzins, M. (1996). *The American System*. Edited by D. J. Elazar. Chicago: Rand McNally & Company.
Grofman, B., & Feld, S. (1988). Rousseau's General Will: A Condorcetian Perspective. *American Political Science Review*, 82 (2), 567–576.
Grönlund, K., Bächtiger, A., & Setälä, M., eds. (2014). *Deliberative Mini-publics: Practices and Prospects*, Colchester: ECPR Press.
Gross, O. (2003). Chaos and Rules: Should Responses to Violent Crises Always be Constitutional? *Yale Law Journal*, 112 (5), 1011–1134.
Gross, O. (2004). Prohibition on Torture. In S. Levinson, ed., *Torture: A Collection*. Oxford: Oxford University Press.

Gross, O. (2008). Extralegality and the Ethic of Political Responsibility. In V. V. Ramraj, ed., *Emergencies and the Limits of Legality*. Cambridge: Cambridge University Press, pp. 60–93.
Gross, O., & Ni Aolain, F. (2006). *Law in Times of Crisis: Emergency Powers in Theory and Practice*, Cambridge: Cambridge University Press.
Grotius, H. (1901). *Rights of War and Peace*, New York: M. Walter Dunne.
Guastini, R. (2019). An Analytical Foundation of Rule Scepticism. In D. Duarte, P. M. Lopes, & J. S. Sampaio, eds., *Legal Interpretation and Scientific Knowledge*. New York: Springer, pp. 13–27.
Guerrero, A. (2014). Against Elections: The Lottocratic Alternative. *Philosophy and Public Affairs*, 42 (2), 135–178.
Guinier, L. (1994). *The Tyranny of the Majority*, New York: The Free Press.
Gunn, P. (1981). Initiatives and Referendums: Direct Democracy and Minority Interests. *Urban Law Annual Review*, 22, 135–159.
Gunningham, N. (2010). Enforcement and Compliance Strategies. In Baldwin, R., Cave, M., & Lodge, M., eds., *Oxford Handbook on Regulation*. Oxford: Oxford University Press, pp. 120–145.
Gunningham, N., & Sinclair, D. (2009). Organizational Trust and the Limits of Management-based Regulation. *Law & Society Review*, 43 (4), 865–900.
Guntermann, E. (2020). Does Economic Inequality Undermine Political Equality? Testing Two Common Assumptions. *Electoral Studies*, 69, 102–202.
Gushee, D. (2013). A Christian Theological Account of Human Worth. In C. McCrudden, ed., *Understanding Human Dignity*. London: The British Academy, pp. 275–288.
Gutierrez, J. (2019). Philippines Officially Leaves the International Criminal Court. *The New York Times*, March 17, sec. World. Available from: www.nytimes.com/2019/03/17/world/asia/philippines-international-criminal-court.html.
Gutmann, A. (2000). Religion and state in the United States: A Defense of Two-Way Protection. In N. Rosenblum, ed., *Obligations of Citizenship and the Demands of Faith*. Princeton: Princeton University Press, pp. 127–164.
Gutmann, A. (2003). *Identity in Democracy*, Princeton: Princeton University Press.
Gutmann, A., & Thompson, D. (1996). *Democracy and Disagreement*, Cambridge, MA: Harvard University Press.
Gutmann, A., & Thompson, D. (2004). *Why Deliberative Democracy*, Princeton: Princeton University Press.
Gutmann, A., & Thompson, D. (2012). *The Spirit of Compromise: Why Governing Demands It and Campaigning Undermines It*, Princeton: Princeton University Press.
Guzman, A. (2011). Against Consent. *Virginia Journal of International Law*, 52 (4), 747–790.
Guzman, A. (2013). International Organizations and the Frankenstein Problem. *European Journal of International Law*, 24 (4), 999–1025.
Gyorfi, T. (2016). *Against the New Constitutionalism*, Cheltenham, UK: Edward Elgar Publishing.
Habermas, J. (1975). *Legitimation Crisis*, Boston: Beacon Press.
Habermas, J. (1979). *Communication and the Evolution of Society*, London: Heinemann Educational.
Habermas, J. (1984). *The Theory of Communicative Action. Volume 1: Reason and the Rationalization of Society*, Boston: Beacon Pres.
Habermas, J. (1985). Civil Disobedience: Litmus Test for the Democratic Constitutional State. Translated by J. Torpey. *Berkeley Journal of Sociology* 30, 95–116.
Habermas, J. (1996). *Between Facts and Norms: Contributions to a Discourse Theory of Law and Democracy*, W. Rehg, trans. Cambridge, MA: MIT Press.
Habermas, J. (1990). Discourse Ethics: Notes on a Program of Philosophical Justification. In *Moral Consciousness and Communicative Action*. Cambridge, MA: MIT Press, pp. 43–115.

Habermas, J. (1992 [1962]). *The Structural Transformation of the Public Sphere: An Inquiry into a Category of Bourgeois Society*, Cambridge, MA: MIT Press.
Habermas, J. (1995). Reconciliation Through the Public Use of Reason: Remarks on John Rawls's Political Liberalism. *The Journal of Philosophy*, 92 (3), 109–131.
Habermas, J. (1996). *Between Facts and Norms: Contributions to a Discourse Theory of Law and Democracy*. Translated by W. Rehg. Cambridge, MA: MIT Press.
Habermas, J. (2001). Constitutional Democracy: A Paradoxical Union of Contradictory Principles? *Political Theory*, 29 (6), 766–781.
Habermas, J. (2008). *Between Naturalism and Religion*. Translated by Ciaran Cronin, Cambridge: MIT Press.
Habermas, J. (2010). The Concept of Human Dignity and the Realistic Utopia of Human Rights. *Metaphilosophy*, 41 (4), 464–480.
Habermas, J. (2012). *The Crisis of the European Union: A Response*, Cambridge: Polity.
Hackett, E., & Haslanger, S., eds. (2006). *Theorizing Feminisms: A Reader*, Oxford: Oxford University Press.
Haider-Markel, D., Querze, A., & Lindaman, K. (2007). Lose, Win, or Draw? A Reexamination of Direct Democracy and Minority Rights. *Political Research Quarterly*, 60 (2), 304–314.
Hailbronner, M. (2017). Transformative Constitutionalism: Not Only in the Global South. *The American Journal of Comparative Law*, 65 (3), 527–565.
Hajnal, Z., Gerber, E., & Louch, H. (2002). Minorities and Direct Legislation: Evidence from California Ballot Proposition Elections. *The Journal of Politics*, 64 (1), 154–177.
Haldane, A. (2014, May). *Unfair Shares*. Presented at the Bristol Festival of Ideas event, Bristol.
Hale, M. (1976). *The Prerogatives of the King*. Edited by D. E. C. Yale. London: Selden Society.
Hall, P., & Soskice, D. (2001). *Varieties of Capitalism: The Institutional Foundations of Comparative Advantage*, Oxford: Oxford University Press.
Halliday, F. (1999). *Revolution and World Politics: The Rise and Fall of the Sixth Great Power*, London: Palgrave.
Halliday, S. (2004). *Judicial Review and Compliance with Administrative Law*, Oxford: Hart Publishing.
Halmai, G. (2018). Is There Such Thing as "Populist Constitutionalism"? The Case of Hungary. *Fudan Journal of the Humanities and Social Sciences*, 11 (3), 323–339.
Halmai, G. (2019). Populism, Authoritarianism and Constitutionalism. *German Law Journal* 20 (3), 296–313.
Halpern, S. M. (1986). The Disorderly Universe of Consociational Democracy. *West European Politics*, 9 (2), 181–197.
Hamburger, P. (2014). *Is Administrative Law Unlawful?* Chicago: University of Chicago Press.
Hamilton, A. (1961a [1788]). The Federalist No. 70. In J. Madison, A. Hamilton, J. Jay, & J. E. Cooke, eds., *The Federalist*. Middletown: Wesleyan University Press, pp. 471–480.
Hamilton, A. (1961b [1787]). The Necessity of a Government as Energetic as the One Proposed to the Preservation of the Union. In A. Hamilton, J. Madison, & J. Jay, eds., *The Federalist Papers*. Edited by C. Rossiter. New York: New American Library, pp. 153–156.
Hamilton, A., Madison, J., & Jay, J. (1961 [1787–88]). *The Federalist Papers*. Edited by C. Rossiter. New York: New American Library.
Hamilton, A., Madison, J., & Jay, J. (2003 [1787–88]). *The Federalist; With Letters of Brutus*. Edited by T. Ball. Cambridge: Cambridge University Press.
Hamilton, A., Madison, J., & J. Jay (2008 [1787–88]). *The Federalist Papers*. Edited by L. Goldman. Oxford: Oxford University Press.

Hamilton, D., & Darity, W. 2010. Can "baby Bonds" Eliminate the Racial Wealth Gap in Putative Post-Racial America? *Review of Black Political Economy*, 37 (3–4), 207–216.

Hamilton, R., & Nichols, J. (2019). The Tin Ear of the Court: Ktunaxa Nation and the Foundation of the Duty to Consult. *Alberta Law Review*, 56 (3), 729–760.

Hammergren, L. (2002). Do Judicial Councils Further Judicial Reform? Lessons from Latin America. Carnegie Endowment Rule of Law Series' Working Paper No. 28.

Hampshire, S. (2000). *Justice Is Conflict*, Princeton: Princeton University Press.

Hand, L. (1958). *The Bill of Rights*, Cambridge, MA: Harvard University Press.

Hanretty, C., & Koop, C. (2011). Measuring the Formal Independence of Regulatory Agencies. *Journal of European Public Policy*, 19 (2), 198–216.

Hanssen, A. F. (2004). Is There a Politically Optimal Level of Judicial Independence? *The American Economic Review*, 94 (3), pp. 712–729.

Hansson, S., & Kroeger, S. (2021). How a Lack of Truthfulness Can Undermine Democratic Representation: The Case of Post-referendum Brexit Discourses. *British Jurnal of Politics and International Relations*, 23 (4), 609–262.

Hardin, R. (1999). *Liberalism, Constitutionalism, and Democracy*, Oxford: Oxford University Press.

Hardin, R. (2000). Democratic Epistemology and Accountability. *Social Philosophy and Policy*, 17 (1), 110–126.

Hardin, R. (2013). Why a Constitution? In D. Galligan, & Versteeg, eds., *Social and Political Foundations of Constitutions*. Cambridge: Cambridge University Press, pp. 51–72.

Harel, A. & Kahana, T. (2010). The Easy Core Case for Judicial Review. *Journal of Legal Analysis*, 2, 227–256.

Harlow, C. (2002). Accountability in the European Union. In P. Alston, & B. de Witte, eds., *Collected Courses of the Academy of European Law*. Oxford: Oxford University Press.

Harlow, C. (2006). Global Administrative Law: The Quest for Principles and Values. *European Journal of International Law*, 17 (1), 187–214.

Harlow, C., & Rawlings, R. (2009). *Law and Administration*, 3rd edn, Cambridge: Cambridge University Press.

Harrington, J. (1992 [1656]). *The Commonwealth of Oceana*. Edited by J. G. A. Pocock. Cambridge: Cambridge University Press.

Harris, D. (2003). *Profiles in Injustice: Why Racial Profiling Cannot Work*, New York: New Press.

Harrison, K. (2013). Federalism and Climate Policy Innovation: A Critical Reassessment. *Canadian Public Policy*, 34 (Suppl. 2), S95–S108.

Hart, H. L. A. (1955). Are There Any Natural Rights? *Philosophical Review*, 64 (2), 175–191.

Hart, H. L. A. (1973). Rawls on Liberty and Its Priority. *University of Chicago Law Review*, 40 (3), 534–555.

Hart, H. L. A. (1982). Bentham on Legal Rights. In *Essays on Bentham*. Oxford: Oxford University Press.

Hart, H. L. A. (1994 [1961]). *The Concept of Law*, 2nd edn, Oxford: Clarendon Press.

Hart, J. (2003). *The Rule of Law 1603–1660: Crown, Courts, and Judges*, London: Routledge.

Hartz, L. (1955). *The Liberal Tradition in America: An Interpretation of American Political Thought since the Revolution*, New York: Harcourt, Brace & World.

Haslanger, S. (2012). *Resisting Reality: Social Construction and Social Critique*, Oxford: Oxford University Press.

Havercroft, J., Eisler, J., Shaw, J., Wiener, A., & Napoleon, V. (2020). Decolonising Global Constitutionalism. *Global Constitutionalism*, 9 (1), 1–6.

Hay, C. (2007). *Why We Hate Politics*, Cambridge: Polity Press.
Hayduk, R. (2006). *Democracy For All: Restoring Immigrant Voting Rights in the United States*, New York: Routledge.
Hayduk, R., & Coll, K. (2018). Urban Citizenship: Campaigns to Restore Immigrant Voting Rights in the US. *New Political Science*, 40 (2), 336–352.
Hayek, F. A. (1944). *The Road to Serfdom*, Chicago: Chicago University Press.
Hayek, F. A. (1960). *The Constitution of Liberty*, Chicago: Chicago University Press.
Hayek, F. A. (1973). *Rules and Order. Vol. I of Law, Legislation, and Liberty*, Chicago: Chicago University Press.
Hayek, F. A. (1976). *The Mirage of Social Justice. Vol. II of Law, Legislation, and Liberty*, Chicago: Chicago University Press.
Hazell, R. (2015). The United Kingdom. In B. Galligan, & S. Brenton, eds., *Constitutional Conventions in Westminster Systems*. Cambridge: Cambridge University Press, pp. 173–188.
Heard, A. (1989). Recognizing the Variety Among Constitutional Conventions. *Canadian Journal of Political Science*, 22 (1), 63–82.
Heard, A. (1991). *Canadian Constitutional Conventions*, Oxford: Oxford University Press.
Heath, J. (2020). *The Machinery of Government*, Oxford: Oxford University Press.
Heidelberg Institute for International Conflict Research. (2021). *Conflict Barometer 2020*, Heidelberg: HIIK.
Heimberger, P., & Kapeller, J. (2017). The Performativity of Potential Output: Pro-cyclicality and Path Dependency in Coordinating European Fiscal Policies. *Review of International Political Economy*, 24 (5), 904–928.
Heinzerling, L. (2019). A Meditation on Juliana v. United States. SSRN. Available from: https://papers.ssrn.com/sol3/papers.cfm?abstract_id=3395471
Hegel, G. W. F. (1967 [1821]). *Philosophy of Right*. Edited and translated by T. M. Knox. London: Oxford University Press.
Hegel, G. W. F. (1991 [1821]). *Elements of the Philosophy of Right*. Edited by A. Wood. Translated by H. B. Nisbett. Cambridge, UK: Cambridge University Press.
Heilbrunn, J. (2004). *Anti-Corruption Commissions Panacea or Real Medicine to Fight Corruption?* Washington, DC: World Bank Institute.
Heldt, E., & Schmidtke, H. (2019). Global Democracy in Decline? How Rising Authoritarianism Limits Democratic Control over International Institutions. *Global Governance*, 25 (2), 231–254.
Heller, H. (1987 [1930]). Rechtsstaat or Dictatorship? *Economy and Society*, 16 (1), 127–142.
Heller, H. (1996 [1934]). The Nature and Structure of the State. *Cardozo Law Review*, 18 (3), 1139–1216.
Heller, H. (2019 [1927]). *Sovereignty: A Contribution to the Theory of Public and International Law*, Oxford: Oxford University Press.
Helmke, G. (2002). The Logic of Strategic Defection: Court-Executive Relations in Argentina under Dictatorship and Democracy. *American Political Science Review*, 69 (2), 291–303.
Helmke, G. (2017). *Institutions on the Edge: The Origins and Consequences of Inter-Branch Crises in Latin America*, Cambridge: Cambridge University Press.
Helms, L. (2004). Five Ways of Institutionalizing Political Opposition: Lessons from Advanced Democracies. *Government and Opposition*, 39 (1), 22–54.
Henkin, L. (1979). *How Nations Behave: Law and Foreign Policy*, 2nd edn, New York: Columbia University Press.
Hennette-Vauchez, S. (2011). A Human *Dignitas*: Remnants of the Ancient Legal Concept in Contemporary Dignity Jurisprudence. *International Journal of Constitutional Law*, 9 (1), 32–57.

Herman, L. (2017). Democratic Partisanship: From Theoretical Ideal to Empirical Standard. *American Political Science Review*, 111 (4), 783–754.
Herman, E. S., & Chomsky, N. (1988). *Manufacturing Consent: The Political Economy of the Mass Media*, New York: Pantheon Books.
Herron, E. S., & Randazzo, K. A. (2003). The Relationship Between Indpendence and Judicial Review in Post-Communist Courts. *The Journal of Politics*, 65 (2), 422–438.
Heuschling, L. (2002). *État de droit, Rechtsstaat, Rule of Law*, Paris: Dalloz.
Heuschling, L. (2021). État de droit: The Gallicization of the Rechtsstaat. In J. Meierhenrich, & M. Loughlin, eds., *The Cambridge Companion to the Rule of Law*. Cambridge: Cambridge University Press, pp. 68–85.
Heupel, M., & Zürn, M. (2017). *Protecting the Individual from International Authority: Human Rights in International Organizations*, Cambridge: Cambridge University Press.
Hickey, T. (2019). The Republican Core of the Case for Judicial Review. *International Journal of Constitutional Law*, 17 (1), 288–316.
Higonnet P. (1998). *Goodness Beyond Virtue: Jacobins During the French Revolution*, Cambridge, MA: Harvard University Press.
Hiebert, J. L. (2005). Interpreting a Bill of Rights: The Importance of Legislative Rights Review. *British Journal of Political Science*, 35 (2), 235–255.
Hiebert, J. L. (2006). Parliamentary Bills of Rights: An Alternative Model? *Modern Law Review*, 69 (1), 7–28.
Hiebert, J. L., & Kelly, J. B. (2015). *Parliamentary Bills of Rights: The Experiences of New Zealand and the United Kingdom*, Cambridge: Cambridge University Press.
Hillbink, L. (2007). *Judges beyond Politics in Democracy and Dictatorship: Lessons from Chile*, Cambridge: Cambridge University Press.
Hirschl, R. (2004). *Towards Juristocracy: The Origins and Consequences of the New Constitutionalism*, Cambridge, MA: Harvard University Press.
Hirschl, R. (2010). *Constitutional Theocracy*, Cambridge, MA: Harvard University Press.
Hirschl, R. (2015). The Origins of the New Constitutionalism: Lessons from the "Old" Constitutionalism. In S. Gill, & A. C. Butler, eds., *New Constitutionalism and World Order*, Cambridge: Cambridge University Press, pp. 95–107.
Hirst, P. (1989). *The Pluralist Theory of the State: Selected Writings of G. D. H. Cole, J. Figgis, and H. J. Laski*, London and New York: Routledge.
Hirst, P. (1990). *Representative Democracy and Its Limits*, Cambridge: Polity Press.
Hoar, R. S. (2004). *Constitutional Conventions: Their Nature, Powers and Limitations*, Whitefish: Kessinger Publishing.
Hobbes, T. (1991 [1651]). *Leviathan*. Edited by R. Tuck. Cambridge: Cambridge University Press.
Hobbes, T. (1994). *Leviathan*. Edited by E. Curley. Indianapolis: Hackett.
Hobbes, T. (1988). Leviathan, ed. Richard Tuck, Cambridge: Cambridge University Press.
Hobbes, T. (1999). *The Elements of Law, Natural and Politic*. Edited by J. C. A. Gaskin. Oxford: Oxford University Press.
Hobolt, S. B. (2009). *Europe in Question: Referendums on European Integration*, Oxford: Oxford University Press.
Hobsbawm, E. (1977). *The Age of Capital 1848–1875*, London: Abacus.
Hobsbawm, E. (1994 [1973]) *Revolutionaries: Contemporary Essays*, London: Phoenix.
Hobsbawm, E. (1996a [1962]). *The Age of Revolution, 1789–1848*, New York: Vintage Books.
Hobsbawm, E. (1996b). *The Age of Extremes: A History of the World, 1914–1991*, New York: Vintage Books.
Hochschild, A. R. (2016) *Strangers in their Own Land. Anger and Mourning on the American Right*, New York: The New Press.

Hockett, R., & James, A. (2020). *Money from Nothing: Or, why we should stop worrying about debt and learn to love the Federal Reserve*, New York: Melville House.
Hockett, R., & Omarova, S. (2017). The Finance Franchise. *Cornell Law Review*, 102 (5), 1143.
Hockin, T. A. (1971). The Roles of the Loyal Opposition in Britain's House of Commons: Three Historical Paradigms. *Parliamentary Affairs*, 25 (1), 50–68.
Hoexter, C. (2017). South African Administrative Law at a Crossroads: The PAJA and the Principle of Legality. Admin Law Blog, 28 April 2017. Available from: adminlawblog.org/2017/04/28
Hohfeld, W. N. (1964 [1919]). *Fundamental Legal Conceptions as Applied in Judicial Reasoning and Other Legal Essays*, New Haven: Yale University Press.
Holling, C. S., & Gunderson, L. H., eds. (2002). *Panarchy: Understanding Transformations in Human and Natural Systems*, Washington, DC: Island Press.
Holmes, O. W. (1913/1920). Law and the Court. In O. W. Holmes, ed., *Collected Legal Papers*. New York: Harcourt, Brace, and Co.
Holmes, S. (1993). Gag Rules or the Politics of Omission. In J. Elster, & R., Slagstad, eds., *Constitutionalism and Democracy*. Cambridge: Cambridge University Press.
Holmes, S. (1995). *Passions and Constraint: On the Theory of Liberal Democracy*, Chicago: University of Chicago Press.
Holmes, S. (2012). Constitutions and Constitutionalism. In M. Rosenfeld, & A. Sajo, eds., *The Oxford Handbook of Comparative Constitutional Law*. Oxford: Oxford University Press.
Holmes, S., & Sunstein, C. (1999). *The Cost of Rights*, New York: W.W. Norton & Company.
Hong, L., & Page, S. (2004). Groups of Diverse Problem Solvers Can Outperform Groups of High-Ability Problem Solvers. *Proceedings of the National Academy of Sciences of the United States*, 101 (46), 16385–16389.
Honig, B. (1993). *Political Theory and the Displacement of Politics*, Ithaca: Cornell University Press.
Honig, B. (2009). *Emergency Politics*, Princeton: Princeton University Press.
Honig, B. (2017). *Public Things: Democracy in Disrepair*, New York City: Fordham University Press.
Honneth, A. (1995). *The Struggle for Recognition: The Moral Grammar of Social Conflicts*, Cambridge: Polity Press.
Honoré, A. M. (1967). Reflections on Revolutions. *Irish Jurist*, 2 (2), 268–278.
Honoré, T. (1994). The Basic Norm of a Society. In S. L. Paulson, & B. Litchewski Paulson, eds., *Normativity and Norms: Critical Perspectives on Kelsenian Themes*. Oxford: Oxford University Press, pp. 89–112.
Hood, C. (1983). *The Tools of Government*, London: Macmillan.
Hood, C., Rothstein, H., & Baldwin, R. (2001). *Government of Risk*, Oxford: Oxford University Press.
Hooghe, L., & Marks, G. (2001). *Multi-level Governance and European Integration*, London: Rowman and Littlefield.
hooks, bel. (2000). *Feminist Theory: From Margin to Center*, London: Pluto Press.
Höpner, M., & Schmidt, S. (2020). Can We Make the European Fundamental Freedoms Less Constraining? A Literature Review. *Cambridge Yearbook of European Legal Studies*, 22, 182–204.
Hörcher, F. (2017). Is the Historical Constitution of Hungary Still a Living Tradition? A Proposal for Reinterpretation. In A. Górnisiewicz, & B. Szlachta, eds., *The Concept of Constitution in the History of Political Thought*. Warsaw, Berlin: De Gruyter, pp. 89–112.
Horowitz, D. L. (1985). *Ethnic Groups in Conflict*, Berkeley: University of California Press.

Horowitz, D. L. (1991). *A Democratic South Africa? Constitutional Engineering in a Divided Society*, Berkeley: University of California.
Horowitz, D. L. (2004). The Alternative Vote and Interethnic Moderation: A Reply to Fraenkel and Grofman. *Public Choice*, 121 (3/4), 507–516.
Horowitz, D. L. (2013). *Constitutional Change and Democracy in Indonesia*, New York: Cambridge University Press.
Horowitz, D. L. (2014). Ethnic Power-Sharing: Three Big Problems. *Journal of Democracy*, 25 (2), 5–20.
Horwill, H. (1908). The Problem of the House of Lords. *Political Science Quarterly* 23 (1), 95–111.
Horwill, H. (1925). *The Usages of the American Constitution*, Glasgow: The University Press.
House of Commons Digital, Culture, Media and Sport Committee. (2019). *Disinformation and "Fake News": Final Report*, Eighth Report of Session 2017–19, HC 1791, 18 February 2019.
Howard, J. (2019). Dangerous Speech. *Philosophy & Public Affairs*, 47 (2) 208–254.
Howell, W., & Moe, T. (2020). *Presidents, Populism, and the Crisis of Democracy*, Chicago: University of Chicago Press.
Howse, R. (2018). Populism and its enemies. Draft paper, on file with the author.
Hueglin, T. O. (1999). *Early Modern Concepts for a Late Modern World: Althusius on Community and Federalism*, Waterloo: WLU Press.
Hueglin, T. O., & Fenna, A. (2006). *Comparative Federalism: A Systematic Enquiry*, Peterborough, Ontario: Broadview Press.
Hueglin, T. O., & Fenna, A. (2015). *Comparative Federalism: A Systematic Enquiry*, 2nd edn, Toronto: University of Toronto Press.
Humboldt, W. v. (1920 [1792]). *Ideen zu einem Versuch, die Grenzen der Wirksamkeit des Staates zu bestimmen*, Leipzig: Meiner Verlag. [translated as W. v. Humboldt (1854) *The Sphere and Duties of Government*. Translated by Joseph Coulthard. London: John Chapman].
Hume, D. (1978 [1739–40]). *A Treatise of Human Nature*. Edited by L. A. Selby-Bigge & P. H. Nidditch. Oxford: Clarendon.
Hume, D. (1983). *A History of England*, vol. 6. Indiana: Liberty Fund.
Hume, D. (1985 [1742]). On the Independence of Parliament. In E. F. Miller, ed., *Essays: Moral, Political, Literary*. Indianapolis: Liberty Fund.
Hume, D. (1998 [1748]). Of Parties in General. In K. Haakonssen, ed., *Political Essays*. Cambridge: Cambridge University Press.
Humphreys, S. ed. (2010). *Human Rights and Climate Change*, Cambridge: Cambridge University Press.
Humphreys, S. (2014). Climate Justice: The Claim of the Past. *Journal of Human Rights and the Environment*, 5, 134–148.
Hunt, M. H. (1987). *Ideology and U.S. Foreign Policy*, New Haven: Yale University Press.
Hunter, R. (2021). Marx's Critique and the Constitution of the Capitalist State. In P. O'Connell, & U. Otzsu, eds., *Research Handbook on Law and Marxism*. Chetelham: Edward Elgar, pp. 190–208.
Huq, A. (2019). *A Tactical Separation of Powers?*, University of Chicago, Public Law Working Paper No. 709. Available from: https://papers.ssrn.com/sol3/papers.cfm?abstract_id=3369820
Hurd, I. (2011). Is Humanitarian Intervention Legal? The Rule of Law in an Incoherent World. *Ethics & International Affairs*, 25 (3), 293–313.
Hurka, T. (2005). Proportionality in the Morality of War. *Philosophy and Public Affairs*, 33 (1), 34–66.

Hussain, N. (2003). *The Jurisprudence of Emergency: Colonialism and The Rule of Law*, Ann Arbor: University of Michigan Press.
Hutchins, E. (1995). *Cognition in the Wild*, Cambridge, MA: MIT Press.
Hylland, A. (2007). Opening the archives (in Norwegian). Working Paper. University of Oslo.
Ignazi, P. (2017). *Party and Democracy: The Uneven Road to Party Legitimacy*, Oxford: Oxford University Press.
Ihara, C. K. (2004). Are Individual Rights Necessary? A Confucian Perspective. In K.-L. Shun, & D. B. Wong, eds., *Confucian Ethics: A Comparative Study of Self, Autonomy, and Community*. Cambridge: Cambridge University Press, pp. 11–30.
Ilbert, C. (1901). *Legislative Methods and Forms*, Oxford: Clarendon Press.
Ingham, G. K. (2004). *The Nature of Money*, Cambridge and Malden, MA: Polity.
Ingham, S. (2019). *Rule by Multiple Majorities: A New Theory of Popular Control*, Cambridge: Cambridge University Press.
Inuit Circumpolar Conference. (2005). Petition to the Inter American Commission on Human Rights Seeking Relief from Violations Resulting from Global Warming Caused by Acts and Omissions of the United States.
Invernizzi Accetti, C., & Wolkenstein, F. (2017). The Crisis of Party Democracy, Cognitive Mobilization and the Case for Making Parties More Deliberative. *American Political Science Review*, 111 (1), 97–109.
Ionescu, G., & de Madariaga, I. (1972). *Opposition: Past and Present of a Political Institution*, Harmondsworth: Pelican Books.
IPCC. (1990). Policymaker Summary of Working Group I (Scientific Assessment of Climate Change). In *Climate Change: The 1990 and 1992 IPCC Assessments*. Available from: www.ipcc.ch/site/assets/uploads/2018/05/ipcc_90_92_assessments_far_wg_I_spm.pdf
IPCC. (2014). Summary for policymakers. In Field, C. B. et al., eds., *Climate Change 2014: Impacts, Adaptation, and Vulnerability. Part A: Global and Sectoral Aspects. Contribution of Working Group II to the Fifth Assessment Report of the Intergovernmental Panel on Climate Change*. Cambridge, UK, and New York, NY: Cambridge University Press.
IPCC. (2018). Summary for Policymakers. In: Masson-Delmotte, et al., eds., *Global Warming of 1.5°C. An IPCC Special Report on the impacts of global warming of 1.5°C above pre-industrial levels and related global greenhouse gas emission pathways, in the context of strengthening the global response to the threat of climate change, sustainable development, and efforts to eradicate poverty*. Available from: www.ipcc.ch/site/assets/uploads/sites/2/2019/05/SR15_SPM_version_report_LR.pdf
Ipsen, H. P. (1972). *Europäisches Gemeinschaftsrecht*, Tübingen: J. C. B. Mohr (Paul Siebeck).
Irfan, A. (2020). An Unusual Revolution: The Palestinian *Thawra* in Lebanon, c 1969–1982. Durham Middle East Papers.
Isaac, R., Mathieu, D., & Zajac, E. (1991). Institutional Framing and Perceptions of Fairness. *Journal of Constitutional Political Economy*, 2 (3), 329–370.
Ishay, M. (2004). *The History of Human Rights: From Ancient Times to the Globalization Era*, University of California Press.
Ishiyama, J. (2012). Explaining Ethnic Bloc Voting in Africa. *Democratization*, 19 (4), 761–788.
Ishiyama Smithey, S., & Ishiyama, J. (2002). Judicial Activism in Post-Communist Politics. *Law & Society Review*, 36 (4), 719–472.
Isiksel, T. (2013). Between Text and Context: Turkey's Tradition of Authoritarian Constitutionalism. *International Journal of Constitutional Law*, 11 (3), 702–726.
Isiksel, T. (2016). *Europe's Functional Constitution: A Theory of Constitutionalism Beyond the State*, Oxford: Oxford University Press.

Issacharoff, S. (2015). *Fragile Democracies. Contested Power in the Era of Constitutional Courts*, Cambridge: Cambridge University Press.
Issacharoff, S., & Pildes, R. H. (1998). Politics as Market: Partisan Lockups of the Democratic Process. *Stanford Law Review*, 50 (3), 643–717.
Issacharoff, S., & Pildes, R. H. (2004). Between Civil Libertarianism and Executive Unilateralism: An Institutional Process Approach to Rights During Wartime. In M. Tushnet, ed., *The Constitution in Wartime: Beyond Alarmism and Complacency*. Durham: Duke University Press, pp. 161–197.
Issing, O. (2008). *The Birth of the Euro*, Cambridge, New York: Cambridge University Press.
Jackson, A. (2018). The Failure of British and Irish Federalism, circa 1800–1950. In R. Schütze, & S. Tierney, eds., *The United Kingdom and the Federal Idea*. Oxford: Hart, pp. 29–47.
Jackson, A., & Dyson, B. (2012). *Modernising Money: Why Our Monetary System Is Broken and How it Can be Fixed*, London: Positive Money.
Jackson, K. (2022). All the Sovereign's Agents: The Constitutional Credentials of Administration. *William & Mary Bill of Rights Journal*, 30 (3), 777–824.
Jackson, P. (2003). Warlords as Alternative Forms of Governance. *Small Wars and Insurgencies*, 14 (2), 131–150.
Jackson, V. (2012). Comparative Constitutional Law: Methodologies. In M. Rosenfeld, & A. Sajó, eds., *The Oxford Handbook of Comparative Constitutional Law*. Oxford: Oxford University Press, pp. 54–74.
Jacobson, G. (2010). *Constitutional Identity*, Cambridge, MA: Harvard University Press.
Jaconelli, J. (1999). The Nature of Constitutional Convention. *Legal Studies*, 19 (1), 24–46.
Jaconelli, J. (2005). Do Constitutional Conventions Bind. *Cambridge Law Journal*, 64 (1), 149–176.
Jakubowski, A., & Wierczyńska, K., eds., (2016). *Fragmentation vs the Constitutionalisation of International Law: A Practical Inquiry*, London: Routledge.
James, C. L. R. (2001). *The Black Jacobins*, London: Penguin Books.
Jameson, J. A. (1887). *A Treatise on Constitutional Conventions*, 4th edn, Chicago: Callaghan and Co.
Jansen, R., & Aelen, M. (2015). Biases in Supervision: What are they and how can we deal with them? DNB Occasional Studies 1306. Netherlands: De Nederlansche Bank.
Jaria-Manzano, J. I. (2019). Law in the Anthropocene. In J. Jaria-Manzano, & S. Borras, eds., *Research Handbook on Global Climate Constitutionalism*. Cheltenham, UK: Edward Edgar Publishing, pp. 31–49.
Jaria-Manzano, J. I., & Borràs, S. (2019). Introduction to the Research Handbook on Global Climate Constitutionalism. In J. Jaria-Manzano, & S. Borras, eds., *Research Handbook on Global Climate Constitutionalism*, Cheltenham, UK: Edward Edgar Publishing, pp. 1–16.
Jasanoff, S. (2003). Technologies of Humility: Citizen Participation in Governing Science. *Minerva*, 41 (3), 223–244.
Jasanoff, S. (2017). Science and Democracy. In U. Felt et al., eds., *The Handbook of Science and Technology Studies*. Cambridge, MA: MIT Press, pp. 259–288.
Jasanoff, S., Markle, G. E., Peterson, J. C., & Pinch, T., eds. (2001). *Handbook of Science and Technology Studies*, London: Sage Publications.
Jefferson, T. (1905 [1810]). Letter from Thomas Jefferson to John B. Colvin, 20 September 1810. In P. L. Ford, ed., *The Works of Thomas Jefferson*. vol. XI. New York, NY: GP Putnam's Sons. Article 2, Section 3, Document 8.
Jelin, E. (2000). Towards a Global Environmental Citizenship. *Citizenship Studies*, 4 (1), 47–63.

Jellinek, G. (1905). *Allgemeine Staatslehre*, 2nd edn, Berlin: O. Häring Verlag.
Jellinek, G. (1914). *Allgemeine Staatslehre*, 3rd edn, Berlin: O. Häring Verlag.
Jennings, I. W. (1959). *Cabinet Government*, 3rd edn, Cambridge: Cambridge University Press.
Jennings, I. W. (1961). *The British Constitution*, Cambridge: Cambridge University Press.
Jennings, I. W. (1963). *The Law and the Constitution*, London: University of London Press.
Jennings, I. W. (1969). *Parliament*, 2nd edn, Cambridge: Cambridge University Press.
Jesse, N. G., & Williams, K. P. (2010). *Ethnic Conflict: A Systemic Approach to Cases of Conflict*, Washington, DC: CQ Press.
Jessop, B. (2016). *The State: Past, Present, Future*, Cambridge, UK: Polity.
Jessop, B. (2019). Critical Theory of the State. In E. Christodoulidis, R. Dukes, & M. Goldoni, eds., *Research Handbook on Critical Legal Theory*. Cheltenham: Edward Elgar, pp. 114–134.
Jestaedt, M. et al (2020). *The Federal Constitutional Court – The Court without Limits*, Oxford: Oxford University Press.
Jhaveri, S., & Ramsden, M., eds. (2021). *Judicial Review of Administrative Action: Origins and Adaptations across the Common Law World*, Cambridge: Cambridge University Press.
Jodoin, S. et al. (2020). Realizing the Right to be Cold? Framing Processes and Outcomes Associated with the Inuit Petition on Human Rights and Global Warming. *Law and Society Review*, 54 (1), 168–200.
John Paul II. (1995). Encyclical Letter "Evangelium Vitae." Vatican. Available from: http://w2.vatican.va/content/john-paul-ii/en/encyclicals/documents/hf_jp-ii_enc_25031995_evangelium-vitae.html
Johnson, N. (1978). Law as the Articulation of the State in Western Germany: A German Tradition Seen from a British Perspective. *West European Politics*, 1 (2), 177–192.
Johnson, J., Arel-Bundock, V., & Portniaguine, V. (2019). Adding Rooms onto a House We Love: Central Banking after the Global Financial Crisis. *Public Administration*, 97 (3), 546–560.
Jones, H. S. (1993). *The French State in Question. Public Law and Political Argument in the Third Republic*, Cambridge: Cambridge University Press.
Jones, N. (2017). Let immigrants reunite with their parents: NZ people's party. *New Zealand Herald*. 7 July. Available from: https://web.archive.org/web/20181009012654/www.nzherald.co.nz/nz/news/article.cfm?c_id=1&objectid=11886934 [Viewed 9 October 2018]
Jones, P. (1994). *Rights*, Basingstoke: Macmillan.
Jordan, W. (1968). *White Over Black: American Attitudes toward the Negro, 1550–1812*, Chapel Hill: University of North Carolina Press.
Jordana, J., & Levi-Faur, D., eds. (2004). *The Politics of Regulation: Institutions and Regulatory Reforms for the Age of Governance*, Cheltenham: Edward Elgar Publishing.
Joseph, S. (2011). *Blame it on the WTO?: A Human Rights Critique*, Oxford: Oxford University Press.
Joss, S. (1998). Danish Consensus Conferences as a Model of Participatory Technology Assessment. *Science and Public Policy*, 25 (1), 2–22.
Jouanjan, O. (2004). Braucht das Verfassungsrecht eine Staatslehre? – Eine französische Perspektive. *Europäische Grundrechtezeitschrift*, 31 (13), 362–370.
Jouanna, A. (1998). Les temps de guerre de religion en France, 1559–1598. In A. Jouanna et al., eds., *Histoire et dictionnaire des guerres de religion*. Paris: Laffont, pp. 6–445.
Jubb, R. (2019). Disaggregating Authority: What's Wrong with Rawlsian Civil Disobedience. *Political Studies*, 67 (4), 955–971.
Juoin, C. (2019). *La constitution matérielle de l'Europe*, Paris: Pedone.

Kadi and Al Barakaat International Foundation v Council and Commission. 2008. Court of Justice of the European Union.
Kagan, E. (1992). The Changing Faces of First Amendment Neutrality: R.A.V. v St Paul, Rust v Sullivan, and the Problem of Content-Based Underinclusion. *Supreme Court Review*, 1992, pp. 29–77.
Kagan, E. (1996). Private Speech, Public Purpose: The Role of Governmental Motive in First Amendment Doctrine. *University of Chicago Law Review*, 63 (2), 413–517.
Kagan, E. (2001). Presidential Administration. *Harvard Law Review*, 114 (8), 2245–2385.
Kagan, S. (1998). *Normative Ethics*, Boulder: Westview Press.
Kahn, P. (2003). Comparative Constitutionalism in a New Key. *Michigan Law Review*, 101 (8), 2677–2705.
Kahn, P. (2004). *Putting Liberalism in Its Place*, Princeton: Princeton University Press.
Kahn, P. (2011). *Political Theology*, New York: Columbia University Press.
Kahn, P. (2019). *The Origins of Order*, New Haven: Yale University Press.
Kahneman, D. (2011). *Thinking Fast and Slow*, Farrar, Straus and Giroux.
Kahneman, D., Slovic, S. P., Slovic, P., & Tversky, A., eds. (1982). *Judgment under Uncertainty: Heuristics and Biases*, Cambridge: Cambridge University Press.
Kahneman, D., & Tversky, A., eds. (2000). *Choices, Values, and Frames*, Cambridge: Cambridge University Press.
Kairys, D., ed. (1990). *The Politics of Law: A Progressive Critique*, New York: Pantheon Books.
Kaisary, P. (2015). Hercules, the Hydra, and the 1801 Constitution of Toussaint Louverture. *Atlantic Studies*, 12 (4), 393–411.
Kaltenbrunner, A., & Painceira, J. P. (2017). The Impossible Trinity: Inflation Targeting, Exchange Rate Management and Open Capital Accounts in Emerging Economies. *Development and Change*, 48 (3), 452–480.
Kaltwasser, C. R. (2013). Populism vs. Constitutionalism? Comparative Perspectives on Contemporary Western Europe, Latin America, and the United States. The Foundation for Law, Justice and Society Policy Brief.
Kamm, F. (2013). *Ethics for Enemies*, Oxford: Oxford University Press.
Kammen, M. (2006). *A Machine That Would Go of Itself: The Constitution in American Culture*, London: Routledge.
Kälin, C., & Kochenov, D., (2020). The nationality index. *The Nationality Index*. Available from: www.nationalityindex.com/. [Viewed 29 November 2020.]
Kant, I. (1991). *Kant: Political Writings*, 2nd edn. Edited by H. S. Reiss. Translated by H. B. Nisbett. Cambridge: Cambridge University Press.
Kant, I. (1996 [1784]). An Answer to the Question: "What Is Enlightenment?" In I. Kant, ed., *Practical Philosophy*, Edited and translated by M. J. Gregor. Cambridge, UK: Cambridge University Press, pp. 11–22.
Kant, I. (2007 [1784]). Idea for a Universal History with a Cosmopolitan Aim. In G. Zöller & B. Louden eds., *The Cambridge Edition of the Works of Immanuel Kant: Anthropology, History, and Education*. Translated by A. Wood. Cambridge: Cambridge University Press.
Kant, I. (2012 [1785]). *Groundwork of the Metaphysics of Morals*. Edited and translated by Mary Gregor, Jens Timmerman. Cambridge: Cambridge University Press.
Kant, I. (2017 [1797]). *The Metaphysics of Morals*. Edited by L. Dennis, translated by Mary Gregor. Cambridge: Cambridge University Press.
Kantorowicz, J., & Garoupa, N. (2016). An Empirical Analysis of Constitutional Review Voting in the Polish Constitutional Tribunal, 2003–2014, *Constitutional Political Economy*, 27 (1), 66–92.
Kaplow, L. (2019a). On the Design of Legal Rules: Balancing versus Structured Decision Procedures. *Harvard Law Review*, 132 (3), 992–1065.

Kaplow, L. (2019b). Balancing versus Structured Decision Procedures: Antitrust, Title VII Disparate Impact, and Constitutional Law Strict Scrutiny. *University of Pennsylvania Law Review*, 167 (6), 1375–1462.

Karlan, P. (2007). Judicial Independences. *The Georgetown Law Journal*, 95 (4), 1041–1059.

Karlan, P., & Cole, D. 2020. "Ruth Bader Ginsburg, 1933–2020." New York Review of Books, October. Available from: www.nybooks.com/articles/2020/10/22/ruth-bader-ginsburg/.

Karmis, D. (1998). Fédéralisme et relations intercommunautaires chez Tocqueville: entre prudence et négation des possible. *Politique et Sociétés*, 17 (3), 59–91.

Karmis, D., & Norman W., eds. (2005). *Theories of Federalism*, New York: Palgrave-Macmillan Publishing.

Kaswan, A. (2008). A Cooperative Federalism Proposal for Climate Change Legislation: The Value of State Autonomy in a Federal System. *Denver University Law Review*, 8 (4), 791–839.

Kateb, G. (1992). "Remarks on the Procedures of Constitutional Democracy," In *The Inner Ocean: Individualism and Democratic Culture*, Ithaca: Cornell University Press.

Kateb, G. (2014). *Human Dignity*, Cambridge, MA: Harvard University Press.

Katz, R., & Mair, P. (2009). The Cartel Party Thesis: A Restatement. *Perspectives on Politics*, 7 (4), 753–766.

Katzenstein, P. J. (1987). *Policy and Politics in West Germany. The Growth of a Semisovereign State*, Philadelphia: Temple University Press.

Kaupa, C. (2016). *The Pluralist Character of the European Economic Constitution*, Oxford: Hart Publishing.

Kavanagh, A. (2002). Original Intention, Enacted Text and Constitutional Interpretation. *American Journal of Jurisprudence*, 47 (1), 255–298.

Kavanagh, A. (2009). *Constitutional Review Under the UK Human Rights Act*, Cambridge: Cambridge University Press.

Keane, J. (2009). *The Life and Death of Democracy*, London: Simon & Schuster.

Keating, M. (2001). *Plurinational Democracy: Stateless Nations in a Post-sovereignty Era*, Oxford: Oxford University Press.

Kedar, S. (2001). The Legal Transformation of Ethnic Geography: Israeli Law and the Palestinian Landholder 1948–1967. *New York University Journal of International Law & Politics*, 33, 923–1000.

Kedourie, E. (1992). *Politics in the Middle East*, Oxford: Oxford University Press.

Keller, S. (2004). Welfare and the Achievement of Goals. *Philosophical Studies*, 121 (1), 27–41.

Keller, S. (2009). Welfare as Success. *Noûs*, 43 (4), 656–683.

Kelly, D. (2017). From King's Prerogative to Constitutional Dictatorship as Reason of State. In B. Kapossy, I. Nakhimovsky, & R. Whatmore, eds., *Commerce and Peace in the Enlightenment*. Cambridge: Cambridge University Press, pp. 300–336.

Kelly, K. (2017). Woodrow Wilson and the Challenge of Federalism in World War One. In A. Lev, ed., *The Federal Idea: Public Law Between Governance and Political Life*. Oxford: Hart, pp. 167–188.

Kelly, R. (2020). Short Money. House of Commons Research Briefing Paper SN01663. [online] London: House of Commons Library.

Kelsen, H. (1925). *Allgemeine Staatslehre*, Berlin: Verlag Julius Springer.

Kelsen, H. (1928). *Der soziologische und der juristische Staatsbegriff. Kritische Untersuchung des Verhältnisses von Staat und Recht*, 2nd edn, Tübingen: J.C.B. Mohr.

Kelsen, H. (1929). Wesen und Entwicklung der Staatsgerichtsbarkeit. In *Veröffentlichungen der Vereinigung der Deutschen Staatsrechtslehrer*, 5, 30–88.

Kelsen, H. (1932). Wer soll der Hater der Verfassung sein? [Who Should be the Guardian of the Constitution?], *Die Justiz*, 6 (11/12), 576–628.

Kelsen, H. (1942). Judicial Review of Legislation: A Comparative Study of the Austrian and American Constitution. *Journal of Politics*, 4 (2), 183–200.

Kelsen, H. (1946a). *General Theory of Law and State*. Translated by Anders Wedberg. Cambridge, MA: Harvard University Press.

Kelsen, H. (1946b). Natural Law Doctrine and Legal Positivism. In H. Kelsen, *General Theory of Law and State*. Translated by Anders Wedberg. Cambridge, MA: Harvard University Press, pp. 389–446.

Kelsen, H. (1948). *The Political Theory of Bolshevism*, Los Angeles: University of California Press.

Kelsen, H. (1952). *Principles of International Law*, New York: Rinehart & Company, Inc. republished by New Jersey: The Lawbook Exchange, Ltd. in 2003.

Kelsen, H. (1967 [1960]). *Pure Theory of Law*, 2nd edn, Berkeley: University of California Press.

Kelsen, H. (1981). *Das Problem der Souveränität und die Theorie des Völkerrechts*, 2nd edn, Aalen: Scientia Verlag.

Kelsen, H. (1992 [1934]). *Introduction to the Problems of Legal Theory*, Oxford: Clarendon Press.

Kelsen, H. (2013 [1929]). *The Essence and Value of Democracy*. Edited by N. Urbinati & C. Invernizzi-Accetti. Lanham: Rowman & Littlefield.

Kelsen, H. (2015). Who Ought to be the Guardian of the Constitution. In L. Vinx, ed., *The Guardian of the Constitution: Hans Kelsen and Carl Schmitt on the Limits of Constitutional Law*. Cambridge: Cambridge University Press, pp. 174–221.

Kennedy, D. (1979). The Structure of Blackstone's Commentaries. *Buffalo Law Review*, 28 (2), 205–382.

Kennedy, D. (1980). Towards an Historical Understanding of Legal Consciousness: The Case of Classical Legal Thought in America, 1850–1940. *Research in Law and Sociology*, 3, 3–24.

Kennedy, D. (1997). *A Critique of Adjudication: Fin de Siècle*, Cambridge, MA: Harvard University Press.

Kennedy, D. (2008). A Left Phenomenological Critique of the Alternative to Hart/Kelsen Theory of Legal Interpretation. In his *Legal Reasoning: Collected Essays*. Aurora: The Davies Group Publishers.

Kennedy, D. (2011). A Transnational Genealogy of Proportionality in Private Law. In R. Brownsword, H. Micklitz, L. Niglia, & S. Weatherill, eds., *The Foundations of European Private Law*. London: Hart Publishing, pp. 185–220.

Kennedy, D. (2014). The Hermeneutic of Suspicion in Contemporary American Legal Thought. *Law Critique*, 25 (2), 91–139.

Kennedy, D. (2020). A Political Economy of Contemporary Legality. In P. F. Kjaer, ed., *The Law of Political Economy: Transformations of the Function of Law*. Cambridge: Cambridge University Press, pp. 89–124.

Keshavarzian, A., & Mirsepassi A., eds. (2021). *Global 1979: Geographies and Histories of the Iranian Revolution*, Cambridge: Cambridge University Press.

Kessler, J. K. (2014). The Administrative Origins of Modern Civil Liberties Law, *Columbia Law Review*, 114 (5), 1083–1167.

Khaitan, T. (2019). Constitutional Directives. *Modern Law Review*, 82 (4), 603–632.

Khaitan, T. (2021a). Balancing Accountability and Effectiveness: A Case for Moderated Parliamentarism. *Canadian Journal of Comparative and Contemporary Law*, 7 (1), 81–155.

Khaitan, T. (2021b). Guarantor Institutions. *Asian Journal of Comparative Law*, 16 (S1), S40–S59.

Kim, S. E., & Margalit, Y. (2017). Informed Preferences? The Impact of Unions on Workers' Policy Views. *American Journal of Political Science*, 61 (3), 728–743.

Kincaid, J., & Cole, R. (2004). Public Opinion on Federalism in Canada, Mexico and the USA in 2003. *Publius*, 33 (3), 145–162.

King, A. (1997). *Running Scared: Why America's Politicians Campaign Too Much and Govern Too Little*, New York: Martin Kessler Books.

King, A. (2009). *The British Constitution*, Oxford: Oxford University Press.

King, D. (1995). *Actively Seeking Work? The Politics of Unemployment and Welfare Policy in the United States and Great Britain*, Chicago: University of Chicago Press.

King, D. (1997). *Separate and Unequal: Black Americans and the US Federal Government*, Oxford: Oxford University Press.

King, J. (2008). Institutional Approaches to Judicial Restraint, *Oxford Journal of Legal Studies*, 28 (3), 409–441.

King, J. (2012). *Judging Social Rights*, Cambridge: Cambridge University Press.

King, J. (2013). Constitutions as Mission Statements. In D. Galligan, & M. Versteeg, eds., *Social and Political Foundations of Constitutions*. Cambridge: Cambridge University Press, pp. 73–102.

King, J. (2015). Parliament's Role following Declarations of Incompatibility under the Human Rights Act. In H. Hooper, M. Hunt & P. Yowell, eds., *Parliaments and Human Rights*. Oxford: Hart Publishing, pp. 165–192.

King, J. (2018). Social Rights in Comparative Constitutional Theory. In G. Jacobson, & M. Schor, eds., *Comparative Constitutional Theory*. Cheltenham: Elgar.

King, J. (2019a). Martin Krygier and the Tempering of Power. *Hague Journal of the Rule of Law*, 11 (2–3), 363–370.

King, J. (2019b) The Democratic Case for a Written Constitution, *Current Legal Problems*, 72 (1), 1–36.

King, J. (2022). Effective Governance and the Social Dimension of the Rule of Law. In V. Jackson, & Y. Dawood, eds., *Constitutionalism and a Right to Effective Government?* Cambridge: Cambridge University Press, pp. 34–46.

King, J. (2024). *The Social Dimension of the Rule of Law*. In: Cambridge UK: Cambridge Handbook for Constitutional Theory.

King, Jr., M. L. (1963). Letter from a Birmingham jail. Available from: www.africa.upenn.edu/Articles_Gen/Letter_Birmingham.html

King, P. (1982). *Federalism and Federation*, London: Croom Helm.

Kingsbury, B., Krisch, N., & Stewart, R. B. (2005). The Emergence of Global Administrative Law. *Law and Contemporary Problems*, 68 (3/4), 15–61.

Kingston, L. N. (2019). *Fully Human: Personhood, Citizenship, and Rights*, New York: Oxford University Press.

Kirchheimer, O., & Neumann, F. (1987). *Social Democracy and the Rule of Law*. Translated by L. Turner. Edited by K. Tribe. Translated by L. Tanner and K. Tribe. London: Allen and Unwin.

Kishlansky, M. (1986). *Parliamentary Selection: Social and Political Choice in Early Modern England*, Cambridge: Cambridge University Press.

Kissinger, H., (2001). The Pitfalls of Universal Jurisdiction. *Foreign Affairs*, 80 (4), 86–96.

Klabbers, J. (2009). *An Introduction to International Institutional Law*, 2nd edn, Cambridge: Cambridge University Press.

Klabbers, J. (2015). The EJIL Foreword: The Transformation of International Organizations Law. *European Journal of International Law*, 26 (1), 9–82.

Klabbers, J., Peters, A., & Ulfstein, G. (2009). *The Constitutionalization of International Law*, Oxford: Oxford University Press.

Klare, K. (1998). Legal Culture and Tranformative Constitutionalim. *South African Journal on Human Rights*, 14 (1), 146–188.

Klarman, M. (2016). *The Framers' Coup: The Making of the United States Constitution*, New York: Oxford University Press.

Klein, C., & Sajó, A. (2012). Constitution-Making: Process and Substance. In M. Rosenfeld, & A. Sajó, eds., *The Oxford Handbook of Comparative Constitutional Law*. Oxford: Oxford University Press, pp. 419–438.

Klein, S. (2020a). *A Good War: Mobilizing Canada for the Climate Emergency*, Toronto: ECW Press.

Klein, S. (2020b). *The Work of Politics: Making a Democratic Welfare*, Cambridge, UK: Cambrige University Press.

Klein, S. (2021). Democracy Requires Organized Collective Power. *Journal of Political Philosophy*. Online first.

Klein, S., & Lee, C.-S. (2019). Towards a Dynamic Theory of Civil Society: The Politics of Forward and Backward Infiltration. *Sociological Theory*, 37 (1), 62–68.

Kleinig, J. (2014). *On Loyalty and Loyalties: The Contours of a Problematic Virtue*, Oxford: Oxford University Press.

Kleinlein, T., & Peters, A. (2018). International Constitutional Law. In *Oxford Bibliographies*. Available from: www.oxfordbibliographies.com/view/document/obo-9780199796953/obo-9780199796953-0039.xml.

Kloppenberg, J. T. (1986). *Uncertain Victory: Social Democracy and Progressivism in European and American thought, 1870–1920*, New York: Oxford University Press.

Knorr, K, (1944). *British Colonial Theories 1570–1850*, Toronto: University of Toronto Press.

Knox, J. H. (2009). Climate Change and Human Rights Law. *Virginia Journal of International Law*, 50 (1), 163–218.

Knudsen, C., & Tsoukas, H. (2009). *The Oxford Handbook of Organization Theory*, Oxford: Oxford University Press.

Koch, C. M. (2020). Varieties of populism and the challenges to Global Constitutionalism: Dangers, promises and implications, *Global Constitutionalism*, Online first, 1–39.

Kochi, T. (2020). *Global Justice and Social Conflict: The Foundations of Liberal Order and International Law*, Abingdon, Oxon: Routledge.

Kolodny, N. (2014). Rule Over None II: Social Equality and the Justification of Democracy. *Philosophy and Public Affairs*, 42 (4), 287–336.

Kommers, D. (2001). Autonomy versus Accountability: The German Judiciary. In P. H. Russel, & D. M. O'Brien, eds. *Judicial Independence in the Age of Democracy*. Charlottesville: University Press of Virginia, pp. 131–154.

Kommers, D., & Miller, R., eds. (1997). *The Constitutional Jurisprudence of the Federal Republic of Germany*, Durham: Duke University Press.

Kong, H. (2015). Election Law and Deliberative Democracy: Against Deflation. *Journal of Parliamentary and Political Law*, 9, 35–58.

Kong, H., & Levy, R. (2018). Deliberative Constitutionalism. In A. Bächtiger, J. Dryzek, J. Mansbridge, & M. Warren, eds., *The Oxford Handbook of Deliberative Democracy*. Oxford: Oxford University Press, pp. 625–639.

Koop, C., & Lodge, M. (2017). What Is Regulation? An Inter-Disciplinary Concept Analysis. *Regulation and Governance*, 11 (1), 95–108.

Kornhauser, A. M. (2015). *Debating the American State: Liberal Anxieties and the New Leviathan, 1930–1970*, Philadelphia: University of Pennsylvania Press.

Kornhauser, L. A. (2002). Is Judicial Independence a Useful Concept? In S. B. Burbank, & B. Friedman, eds., *Judicial Independence at the Crossroads*. Thousand Oaks: Sage Publications, pp. 45–55.

Korsch, K. (2013). *Revolutionary Theory*. Edited by D. Kellner. Austin: University of Texas Press.
Kosař, D. (2016). *Perils of Judicial Self-Fovernment in Transitional Societies: Holding the Least Accountable Branch to Account*, Cambridge: Cambridge University Press.
Kosař, D., & Šipulová, K. (2023). Comparative Court-Packing. *International Journal of Constitutional Law*, 21 (1), 80–126.
Koselleck, R. (1989 [1967]). *Preußen zwischen Reform und Revolution: Politische Reform in Preußen und in Süddeutschen Staaten, 1800–1820*, München: Deutschen Taschenbuch Verlag.
Koselleck, R. (1992). Verwaltung, Amt, Beamter. Einleitung. In O. Brunner, W. Conze, & R. Koselleck, eds., *Geschichtliche Grundbegriffe*, Stuttgart: Klett-Cotta, pp. 1–7.
Koskenniemi, M. (2001). *The Gentle Civilizer of Nations. The Rise and Fall of International Law 1870–1960*, Cambridge: Cambridge University Press.
Kostal, R. (2005). *A Jurisprudence of Power: Victorian Empire and the Rule of Law*, Oxford: Oxford University Press.
Kotzé, L. (2012). Arguing Global Environmental Constitutionalism. *Transnational Environmental Law*, 1 (1), 199–233.
Kotzé, L. (2016). *Global Environmental Constitutionalism in the Anthropocene*, Oxford: Hart Publishing.
Kotzé, L. (2018). Six Constitutional Elements for Implementing Environmental Constitutionalism in the Anthropocene. In Daly, E., & May, J. R., eds, *Implementing Environmental Constitutionalism: Current Global Challenges*. Cambridge: Cambridge University Press, pp. 13–33.
Kouvelakis S. (2003). *Philosophy and Revolution: From Kant to Marx*, New York: Verso.
Krajewski, M. (2019). International Organizations or Institutions, Democratic Legitimacy. In A. Peters, & R. Wolfrum, eds., *Max Planck Encyclopedia of Public International Law*. Oxford: Oxford University Press.
Kramer, L. (2004). *The People Themselves: Popular Constitutional and Judicial Review*, Oxford: Oxford University Press.
Kramer, M. (1998). Rights without Trimmings. In M. Kramer, N. E. Simmonds, & H. Steiner, *A Debate Over Rights: Philosophical Enquiries*. Oxford: Oxford University Press, pp. 7–111.
Kramer, M. (2003). *The Quality of Freedom*, Oxford: Oxford University Press.
Kramer, M. (2007). *Objectivity and the Rule of Law*, Cambridge: Cambridge University Press.
Kramer, M. (2010). Refining the Interest Theory of Rights. *American Journal of Jurisprudence*, 55 (1), 31–39.
Kramer, M. (2017). *Liberalism with Excellence*, Oxford: Oxford University Press.
Kramer, M. (2021). *Freedom of Expression as Self-Restraint*, Oxford: Oxford University Press.
Kranenpohl, U. (2010). *Hinter dem Schleier des Beratungsgeheimnisses*, Wiesbaden: VS Verlag für Sozialwissenschaften.
Krisch, N. (2011). *Beyond Constitutionalism*, Oxford: Oxford University Press.
Krisch, N. (2016). *Pouvoir constituant* and *pouvoir irritant* in the postnational order. *International Journal of Constitutional Law*, 14 (3), 637–679.
Krishnaswamy, S. (2009). *Democracy and Constitutionalism in India*, Oxford: Oxford University Press.
Krygier, M. (2011). Four Puzzles about the Rule of Law: Why? What? Where? And Who Cares? In J. Fleming, ed., *Getting to the Rule of Law: NOMOS L*. New York: New York University Press, pp. 64–104.
Krygier, M. (2012a). *Philip Selznick: Ideals in the World*, Stanford: Stanford University Press.
Krygier, M. (2012b). The Rule of Law. In A. Sajó, & M. Rosenfeld, eds., *The Oxford Handbook of Comparative Constitutional Law*. Oxford University Press, pp. 233–249.
Krygier, M. (2014). Inside the Rule of Law. *Rivista di Filosofia del Diritto*, 3 (1), pp. 77–98.

Krygier, M. (2017). Tempering Power. In M. Adams et al., eds, *Constitutionalism and the Rule of Law: Bridging Ideas and Realism*. Cambridge: Cambridge University Press, pp. 34–59.

Kühn, Z. (2012). Judicial Administration Reforms in Central-Eastern Europe: Lessons to be Learned. In A. Seibert-Fohr, ed. *Judicial Independence in Transition*. Dodrecht: Springer, pp. 603–618.

Kumar, V. (2016). International Law, Kelsen and the Aberrant Revolution: Excavating the Politics and Practices of Revolutionary Legality in Rhodesia and Beyond. In N. M. Rajkovic, T. E. Aalberts, & T. Gammeltoft-Hansen, eds., *The Power of Legality: Practices of International Law and Their Politics*. Cambridge: Cambridge University Press, pp. 157–187.

Kumhof, M., & Benes, J. (2012). *The Chicago Plan Revisited*. IMF Working Paper 12/202. Washington, DC: International Monetary Fund.

Kumm, M. (1999). Who Is the Final Arbiter of Constitutionality in Europe? Three Conceptions of the Relationship between the German Federal Constitutional Court and the European Court of Justice. *Common Market Law Review*, 36 (2), 351–386.

Kumm, M. (2005). The Jurisprudence of Constitutional Conflict: Constitutional Supremacy in Europe before and after the Constitutional Treaty. *European Law Journal*, 11 (3), 262–307.

Kumm, M. (2009). The Cosmopolitan Turn in Constitutionalism: On the Relationship Between Constitutionalism in and Beyond the State. In J. L. Dunoff, & J. P. Trachtman, eds., *Ruling the World? International Law, Global Governance, Constitutionalism*. Cambridge: Cambridge University Press, pp. 258–326.

Kumm, M. (2010a). The Best of Times and the Worst of Times: Between Constitutional Triumphalism and Nostalgia. In P. Dobner, & M. Loughlin, eds., *The Twilight of Constitutionalism*. Oxford: Oxford University Press.

Kumm, M., (2010b). The Idea of Socratic Contestation and the Right to Justification: The Point of Rights-Based Proportionality Review. *Law and Ethics of Human Rights*, 4 (2), 142–175.

Kumm, M. (2013). The Cosmopolitan Turn in Constitutionalism: An Integrated Conception of Public Law. *Indiana Journal of Global Legal Studies*, 20 (2), 605–628.

Kumm, M. (2016). Constituent Power, Cosmopolitan Constitutionalism, and Post-Positivist Law. *International Journal of Constitutional Law*, 14 (3), 697–711.

Kumm, M., & Walen, A., (2014). Human Dignity and Proportionality. In G. Huscroft, B. Miller, & G. Webber, eds., *Proportionality and the Rule of Law*. Cambridge: Cambridge University Press, pp. 67–89.

Kumm, M., Lang, A., Tully, J., & Wiener, A. (2014). How Large Is the World of Global Constitutionalism? *Global Constitutionalism*, 3 (1), 1–8.

Kurian, J., (2016). Expanding the idea of India. *The Hindu*. 15 July. Available from: https://web.archive.org/web/20190106042838/ www.thehindu.com/opinion/op-ed/Expanding-the-Idea-of-India/article14488980.ece. [Viewed 6 January 2019].

Kydland, F., & Prescott, E. (1977). Rules Rather than Discretion: The Inconsistency of Optimal Plans. *Journal of Political Economy*, 85 (3), 473–491.

Kymlicka, W. (1995). *Multicultural Citizenship: A Liberal Theory of Minority Rights*, Oxford: Clarendon Press.

Kymlicka, W. (2001). *Politics in the Vernacular*, Oxford: Oxford University Press.

Kyritsis, D. (2014). Whatever Works: Proportionality as a Constitutional Doctrine. *Oxford Journal of Legal Studies*, 34 (2), 395–415.

Laborde, C. (2000). *Pluralist Thought and the State in Britain and France, 1900–25*. Basingstoke: Macmillan.

Laborde, C. (2008). *Critical Republicanism. The Hijab Controversy and Political Philosophy*. Oxford: Oxford University Press.

Laborde, C. (2013). Political Liberalism and Religion: On Separation and Establishment. *Journal of Political Philosophy*, 21 (1), 67–86.
Laborde, C. (2014). Equal Liberty, Non-Establishment and Religious Freedom. *Legal Theory*, 20 (1), pp. 52–77.
Laborde, C. (2017a). *Liberalism's Religion*, Cambridge, MA: Harvard University Press.
Laborde, C. (2017b). The Evanescence of Neutrality. *Political Theory*, 46 (1), 99–105.
Laborde, C., & Maynor, J., eds. (2007). *Republicanism and Political Theory*, Oxford: Blackwell.
Lacerda, A. D. F. (2020). The Normative Bases of Semi-Presidentialism: Max Weber and the Mitigation of Caesarism. *Brazilian Political Science Review*, 14 (1), 1–32.
Lacey, J. (2017). *Centripetal Democracy: Democratic Legitimacy and Political Identity in Belgium, Switzerland and the European Union*, Oxford: Oxford University Press.
Laclau, E. (2005). *On Populist Reason*, London: Verso.
LaCroix, A. (2011). *The Ideological Origins of American Federalism*, Cambridge, MA: Harvard University Press.
Ladeur, K-H. (2012). The Emergence of Global Administrative Law and Transnational Regulation. *Transnational Legal Theory*, (3) 3, 243–267.
Lafont, C. (2012). *Global Governance and Human Rights*, Amsterdam: Van Gorcum.
Lafont, C. (2015). Deliberation, Participation and Democratic Legitimacy: Should Deliberative Minipublics Shape Public Policy? *The Journal of Political Philosophy*, 23 (1), 40–63.
Lafont, C. (2016). Philosophical Foundations of Judicial Review. In D. Dyzenhaus, & M. Thorburn, eds., *Philosophical Foundations of Constitutional Law*. Oxford: Oxford University Press, pp. 265–280.
Lafont, C. (2017). Can Democracy be Deliberative and Participatory? The Democratic Case for Political Uses of Minipublics. *Daedalus, the Journal of the American Academy of Arts and Sciences*, 146 (3), 85–105.
Lafont, C. (2020). *Democracy without Shortcuts. A Participatory Conception of Deliberative Democracy*, Oxford: Oxford University Press.
Lafont, C. (2023). A Democracy, If We Can Keep It. Remarks on J. Habermas's *The New Structural Transformation of the Public Sphere*. *Constellations*.
Laing, M., & McCaffrie, B. (2013). The Politics Prime Ministers Make: Political Time and Executive Leadership in Westminster Systems. In P. Strangio, P. Hart, & J. Walter, eds., *Understanding Prime Ministerial Performance: Comparative Perspectives*. Oxford: Oxford University Press, pp. 79–101.
Lake, D., Martin, L., & Risse, T. (2021). Challenges to the Liberal Order: Reflections on International Organization. *International Organization*, 75 (2), 225–257.
Landa, D., & Pevnik, R. (2021). Is Random Selection a Cure for the Ills of Electoral Representation? *Journal of Political Philosophy*, 29 (1), 46–72.
Landau, D. (2018). Populist Constitutions. *University of Chicago Law Review*, 85 (2), 521–544.
Landau, R. S. (1995). Specifying Absolute Rights. *Arizona Law Review*, 37 (1), 209–225.
Landemore, H. (2012). *Democratic Reason: Politics, Collective Intelligence, and the Rule of the Many*. Princeton, NJ: Princeton University Press.
Landemore, H. (2013). *Democratic Reason: Politics, Collective Intelligence, and the Rule of the Many*, Princeton: Princeton University Press.
Landemore, H. (2019). The Principles of Open Democracy. In N. Urbinati, ed., *Thinking Democracy Now: Between Innovation and Regression*. Milan: Feltrinelli, pp. 97–116.
Landemore, H. (2020). *Open Democracy. Reinventing Popular Rule for the Twenty-First Century*, Princeton: Princeton University Press.

Landemore, H., & Page, S. (2015). Deliberation and Disagreement: Problem Solving, Prediction, and Positive Dissensus. *Politics, Philosophy and Economics*, 14 (3), 229–254.
Landes, W. M., & Posner, R. (1975). The Independent Judiciary in an Interest Group Perspective. *Journal of Law and Economics* 18 (3), 875–901.
Landfried, C. (1994). The Judicialization of Politics in Germany. *International Political Science Review*, 15 (2), 113–124.
Landfried, C. (2019). Introduction. In C. Landfried, ed., *Judicial Power. How Constitutional Courts Affect Political Transformations*. Cambridge, UK: Cambridge University Press, pp. 1–17.
Landfried, C. (2023). Constitutional Review in the European Legal Space: A Political Science Perspective. In: A. v. Bogdandy, P. M. Huber, & C. Grabenwarter, eds., *Constitutional Adjudication: Common Themes and Challenges. Volume IV of Max Planck Handbooks in European Public Law*. Oxford: Oxford University Press, pp. 591–612.
Landis, J. M. (1938). *The Administrative Process*, New Haven: Yale University Press.
Landis, J. M. (2018). Whither Parties? Hume on Partisanship and Political Legitimacy. *American Political Science Review*, 112 (2), 219–230.
Lang, A. (2011). *World Trade Law after Neoliberalism*, Oxford: Oxford University Press.
Langford, M. (2009). *Social Rights Jurisprudence: Emerging Trends in International and Comparative Law*, Cambridge: Cambridge University Press.
Lara, M. P. (2002a). Cultural Citizenship. In E. F. Isin, & B. S. Turner, eds., *Handbook of Citizenship Studies*. London: Sage, pp. 232–243.
Lara, M. P. (2002b). Democracy and Cultural Rights: Is there a New State of Citizenship? *Constellations*, 9 (2), 207–220.
Larkins, C. M. (1996). Judicial Independence and Democratization: A Theoretical and Conceptual Analysis. *American Journal of Comparative Law*, 44 (4), 605–626.
Larsen, S. R. (2021). *The Constitutional Theory of the Federation and the European Union*, Oxford: Oxford University Press.
Lassalle, F. (1942). On the Essence of Constitutions. *Marxist Archive*. Available from: www.marxists.org/history/etol/newspape/fi/vol03/n001/lassalle.htm.
La Serna, M. (2012). *The Corner of the Living: Ayacucho on the Eve of the Shining Path Insurgency*, Chapel Hill: University of North Carolina Press.
Lastra, R. (2015). *International Financial and Monetary Law*, 2nd edn, Oxford: Oxford University Press.
Latham, R. T. E. (1949). *The Law and the Commonwealth*, London: Oxford University Press.
La Torre, M. (2010). *Law as Institution*, Dordercht: Springer.
Latour, B. (1993). *We Have Never Been Modern*, New York, London: Harvester Wheatsheaf.
Law, S. (1984). Rethinking Sex and the Constitution. *University of Pennsylvania Law Review*, 132 (5), 955–1040.
Lawless, J. (2018). Gruesome Freedom: The Moral Limits of Non-constraint. *Philosopher's Imprint*, 18 (3), 1–19.
Laws, S. (2020). Parliamentary Sovereignty, Statutory Interpretation and the UK Supreme Court. In D. Clarry, ed., *The UK Supreme Court Yearbook, Volume 10: 2018–2019 Legal Year*. London: Appellate Press, pp. 160–206.
Lawson, G. (1992 [1678]). *Politica sacra et civilis*. Edited by C. Condren. Cambridge: Cambridge University Press.
Lawson, G. (1994). The Rise and Rise of the Administrative State. *Harvard Law Review*, 107 (6), 1231–1254.
Lazar, N. C. (2009). *States of Emergency in Liberal Democracies*, Cambridge: Cambridge University Press.
Lazar, N. C. (2019). *Out of Joint: Power, Crisis and the Rhetoric of Time*, New Haven: Yale University Press.

Ledeneva, A. (2008). Telephone Justice in Russia. *Post-Soviet Affairs*, 14 (4), 324–350.
LeDuc, L. (2015). Referendums and Deliberative Democracy. *Electoral Studies*, 38, 139–148.
Lee, C., ed. (2010). *Making a World After Empire: The Bandung Moment and Its Political Afterlives*. Ohio: Ohio University Press.
Lee, D. (2008). The Legacy of Medieval Constitutionalism in the Philosophy of Right: Hegel and the Prussian Reform Movement. *History of Political Thought*, 29 (4), 601–634.
Lee, D. (2013). "Office Is a Thing Borrowed": Jean Bodin on Offices and Seigneurial Government. *Political Theory*, 41 (3), 409–440.
Lee, D. (2016). *Popular Sovereignty in the Early Modern Constitutional Thought*, Oxford: Oxford University Press.
Lee, S. Z. (2010). Race, Sex, and Rulemaking: Administrative Constitutionalism and the Workplace, 1960 to the Present. *Virginia Law Review*, 96 (4), 799–886.
Lefkowitz, D. (2007). On a Moral Right to Civil Disobedience. *Ethics*, 117 (2), 202–233.
Lefort, C. (2007). *Complications: Communism and the Dilemmas of Democracy*. Translated by J. Bourg. New York: Columbia University Press.
Lehmbruch, G. (1984). Concertation and the Structure of Corporatist Networks. In J. Goldthorpe, ed., *Order and Conflict in Contemporary Capitalism*. Oxford: Oxford University Press, pp. 60–80.
Leib, E. J. (2004). *Deliberative Democracy in America: A Proposal for a Popular Branch of Government*, University Park: Pennsylvania State University Press.
Leib, E. J., Ponet, D., & Serota, M. (2014). Mapping Public Fiduciary Relationships. In A. Gold, & P. Miller, eds., *Philosophical Foundations of Fiduciary Law*. Oxford: Oxford University Press, pp. 388–403.
Leibholz, G. (2007). *Il diritto costituzionale fascista*, Naples: Guida.
Leiter, B. (2013). *Why Tolerate Religion?* Cambridge, MA: Harvard University Press.
Leiter, B. (2014). *Why Tolerate Religion?* Cambridge, MA: Harvard University Press.
Lenard, P., (2016). Democracies and the Power to Revoke Citizenship. *Ethics & International Affairs*, 30 (1), 73–91.
Lenton, T. M. et al. (2019). Climate Tipping Points – Too Risky to Bet Against. *Nature Comment*, 575, 592.
Leow, R. (2019). Understanding Agency: A Proxy Power Definition. *Cambridge Law Journal*, 78 (1), 99–123.
Lessig, L. (2009). *Code and Other Laws of Cyberspace, Version 2.0*, Google Books.
Letsas, G. (2006). Two Concepts of the Margin of Appreciation. *Oxford Journal of Legal Studies*, 26 (4), 705–732.
Letsas, G. (2007). *A Theory of Interpretation of the European Convention on Human Rights*, Oxford: Oxford University Press.
Letsas, G. (2015a). Rescuing Proportionality. In: R. Cruft, S. Liao, & M. Renzo, eds., *Philosophical Foundations of Human Rights*. Oxford: Oxford University Press, pp. 316–340.
Letsas, G. (2015b). The Scope and Balancing of Rights: Diagnostic or Constitutive? In E. Brems, & J. Gerards, eds., *Shaping Rights in the ECHR*. Cambridge: Cambridge University Press, pp. 38–64.
Letsas, G. (2017). Reclaiming Proportionality. A Reply to Ripstein. *Journal of Applied Philosophy*, 34 (1), 24–31.
Letsas, G. (2018a). Proportionality as Fittingness. *Current Legal Problems*, 71 (1), 53–86.
Letsas, G. (2018b). The Margin of Appreciation Revisited: A Response to Follesdal. In A. Etinson, ed., *Human Rights: Moral or Political?* Oxford: Oxford University Press.
Lettanie, U. (2019). The ECB's Performance Under the ESM Treaty on a Sliding Scale of Delegation. *European Law Journal*, 25 (3), 317–332.

Lev, A. (2019). Introduction: Federalism and Public Law Theory. In A. Lev, ed., *The Federal Idea: Public Law between Governance and Political Life*. Oxford: Hart Publishing, pp. 1–26.

Levellers. (1967). A Remonstrance of Many Thousand Citizens, and Other Free-born People of England, to their Own House of Commons. In D. M. Wolfe, ed., *Leveller Manifestoes of the Puritan Revolution*. New York: Humanities Press, pp. 112–134.

Lever, A. (2005). Why Racial Profiling Is Hard to Justify. *Philosophy and Public Affairs*, 33 (1), 94–110.

Lever, A. (2009). Democracy and Judicial Review: Are They Really Incompatible? *Perspectives on Politics*, 7 (4), 805–822.

Lever, A. (2017). Democracy, Epistemology and the Problem of All-White Juries. *Journal of Applied Philosophy*, 34 (4), 541–556.

Lever, A. (2020). A Sense of Proportion: Some Thoughts on Equality, Security and Justice. *Res Publica*, 26 (3), 357–371.

Levey, G. B., & Modood, T., eds., (2009). *Secularism, Religion and Multicultural Citizenship*, Cambridge: Cambridge University Press.

Levine, M. E., & Forrence, J. L. (1990). Regulatory capture, public interest, and the public agenda: Toward a synthesis. *JL Econ & Org*. 6.

Levinson, D. (2011). Parchment and Politics: The Positive Puzzle of Constitutional Commitment. *Harvard Law Review*, 124 (3), 657–746.

Levinson, D., & Pildes, R. (2006). Separation of Parties, Not Powers. *Harvard Law Review* 119 (8), 2312–2386.

Levinson, S. (2008). *Our Undemocratic Constitution. Where the Constitution Goes Wrong (and How We the People can Correct It)*, Oxford: Oxford University Press.

Levinson, S. (2011). Do Constitutions Have a Point? Reflections on Parchment Barriers and Preambles. *Social Philosophy and Policy*, 28 (1), 150–178.

Levitsky, S., & Ziblatt, D. (2018). *How Democracies Die*, New York: Crown.

Levy, J. T. (2000). *The Multiculturalism of Fear*, Oxford: University Press.

Levy, J. T. (2007). Federalism, Liberalism, and the Separation of Loyalties. *American Political Science Review*, 101 (3), 459–477.

Levy, J. T. (2015). *Rationalism, Pluralism, and Freedom*, Oxford: Oxford University Press.

Levy, J. T. (2016). There Is No Such Thing as Ideal Theory. *Social Philosophy and Policy*, 33 (1–2), 312–333.

Levy, J. T. (2021). The Separation of Powers and the Challenge to Constitutional Democracy. *Review of Constitutional Studies*, 25 (1), 1–18.

Levy, R., & Orr, G. (2017). *The Law of Deliberative Democracy*, London: Routledge.

Levy, R., Kong, H., Orr. G., & King, eds. (2018). *The Cambridge Handbook of Deliberative Constitutionalism*. Cambridge: Cambridge University Press.

Levy, R., O'Flynn, I., & Kong, H. (2021). *Deliberative Peace Referendums*, Oxford: Oxford University Press.

Levy, J. D., Leibfried, S., & Nullmeier, F. (2015). Changing Perspectives on the State, In S. Leibfried, E. Huber, & M. Lange et al., eds., *The Oxford Handbook of Transformations of the State*. Oxford: Oxford University Press, pp. 33–58.

Lewis, B. (2018). *Environmental Human Rights and Climate Change Current Status and Future Prospects*, Singapore: Springer.

Lewis, D. (1969). *Convention. A Philosophical Study*, Cambridge, MA: Harvard University Press.

Lewis, D. (2012). *Direct Democracy and Minority Rights: A Critical Assessment of the Tyranny of the Majority in the American States*, London: Routledge.

Lewis, M. (2018). *The Fifth Risk: Undoing Democracy*, Penguin.

Ley, I. (2015). Opposition in International Law: Alternativity and Revisibility as Elements of a Legitimacy Concept for Public International Law. *Leiden Journal of International Law*, 28 (4), 717–742.
Liebenberg, S. (2012). Engaging the Paradoxes of the Universal and Particular in Human Rights Adjudication. The Possibilities and Pitfalls of 'Meaningful Engagement. *African Human Rights Law Journal*, 12 (1), 1–29.
Liebenberg, S. (2015). Toward an Equality-Promoting Interpretation Interpretation of Socio-economic Rights in South Africa. Insights from the Egalitarian Liberal Tradition. *The South African Law Journal*, 132 (2), 411–437.
Lijphart, A. (1968). Typologies of Democratic Systems. *Comparative Political Studies* 1 (1), 3–44.
Lijphart, A. (1969). Consociational Democracy. *World Politics*, 21 (2), 207–225.
Lijphart, A. (1975). *The Politics of Accommodation: Pluralism and Democracy in the Netherlands*, 2nd edn, Berkeley: University of California Press.
Lijphart, A. (1977). *Democracy in Plural Societies*, New Haven: Yale University Press.
Lijphart, A. (1986). Proportionality by Non-PR Methods: Ethnic Representation in Belgium, Cyprus, Lebanon, New Zealand, West Germany and Zimbabwe. In B. Grofman, & A. Lijphart, eds., *Electoral Laws and their Political Consequences*. New York: Agathon Press, pp. 113–123.
Lijphart, A. (1992). Introduction. In A. Lijphart, ed., *Parliamentary versus Presidential Government*. Oxford: Oxford University Press, pp. 1–27.
Lijphart, A. (1996). The Puzzle of Indian Democracy: A Consociational Interpretation. *American Political Science Review*, 90 (2), 258–268.
Lijphart, A. (2008). Self-determination versus Pre-determination of Ethnic Minorities in Power-Sharing Systems. In A. Lijphart, *Thinking About Democracy: Power-Sharing and Majority Rule in Theory and Practice*. New York: Routledge, pp. 66–74.
Lijphart, A. (2012). *Patterns of Democracy*, 2nd edn, New Haven: Yale University Press.
Lin, A. C. (2019). President Trump's War on Regulatory Science. *Harvard Environmental Law Review*, 43 (2), 247–306.
Lin, J. (2012). Climate Change and the Courts. *Legal Studies*, 32 (1), 35–57.
Lincoln, A. (1861 [1953]). First Inaugural Address. In R. Basler et al, eds., *Collected Works of Abraham Lincoln*, vol. IV. New Brunswick: Rutgers University Press, pp. 263–271.
Lindahl, H. (2008). Constituent Power and Reflexive Identity: Towards an Ontology of Collective Selfhood. In M. Loughlin, & N. Walker, eds., *The Paradox of Constitutionalism*. Oxford: Oxford University Press, pp. 9–24.
Lindahl, H. (2013). *Fault Lines of Globalisation*, Oxford: Oxford University Press.
Lindahl, H. (2015). Law as Concrete Order. In D. Dyzenhaus, & T. Poole, eds., *Law, Liberty and the State*. Cambridge: Cambridge University Press, pp. 38–46.
Linder, W., & Mueller, S. (2021). *Swiss Democracy: Possible Solutions to Conflict in Multicultural Societies*, 4th edn, London: Palgrave Macmillan.
Lindseth, P. (2004). The Paradox of Parliamentary Supremacy: Delegation, Democracy, and Dictatorship in Germany and France, 1920s–1950s. *Yale Law Journal*, 113 (7), 1341–1415.
Lindseth, P. (2010). *Power and Legitimacy: Reconciling Europe and the Nation-State*, Oxford: Oxford University Press.
Linz, J. (1990). The Perils of Presidentialism. *Journal of Democracy*, 1 (1), 51–69.
Linz, J. (1994). Presidential or Parliamentary Democracy: Does It Make a Difference? In J. Linz, & A. Valenzuela, eds., *The Failure of Presidential Democracy: The Case of Latin America*. Baltimore: Johns Hopkins University Press, pp. 3–90.

Lippman, M. (1994). Liberating the Law: The Jurisprudence of Civil Disobedience and Resistance. *San Diego Justice Journal*, 2 (2), 299–394.
Lippert-Rasmussen, K. (2018). *Relational Egalitarianism: Living as Equals*. Cambridge: Cambridge University Press.
List, C., & Goodin, R. (2001). Epistemic Democracy: Generalizing the Condorcet Jury Theorem. *Journal of Political Philosophy*, 9 (3), 277–306.
Lister, R. (2003). *Citizenship: Feminist Perspectives*, 2nd edn, New York: NYU Press.
Livingston, W. S. (1956). *Federalism and Constitutional Change*, Oxford: Clarendon Press.
Lobel, J. (1989). Emergency Power and the Decline of Liberalism. *Yale Law Journal*, 98 (7), 1385–1433.
Locke, J. (1764). *Two Treatises of Government*, London.
Locke, J. (1980 [1689]). *Second Treatise of Government*. Edited by C. B. Macpherson. Indianapolis and Cambridge: Hackett Publishing Company.
Locke, J. (1988 [1689]). *Two Treatises of Government*. Edited by P. Laslett. Cambridge: Cambridge University Press.
Locke, J. (1991). *A Letter Concerning Toleration*, London: Routledge.
Loevy, K. (2016). *Emergencies in Public Law: The Legal Politics of Containment*, Cambridge: Cambridge University Press.
Lokdam, H. (2020). "We Serve the People of Europe": Reimagining the ECB's Political Master in the Wake of Its Emergency Politics. *JCMS: Journal of Common Market Studies*, 58 (4), 978–998.
Lombaerde, P., Söderbaum, F., van Langenhove, L., & Baert, F. (2010). Problems and Divides in Comparative Regionalism. In F. Laursen, ed., *Comparative Regional Integration: Europe and Beyond*. Farnham: Routledge.
Lopez-Guerra, C. (2011). The Enfranchisement Lottery. *Politics, Philosophy, and Economics*, 10 (2), 211–233.
Lopez-Guerra, C. (2014). *Democracy and Disenfranchisement. The Morality of Electoral Exclusions*, Oxford: Oxford University Press.
Losurdo, D. (2020). *War and Revolution: Rethinking the Twentieth Century*. Translated by Gregory Elliott. New York: Verso.
Loughlin, M. (1992). *Public Law and Political Theory*, Oxford: Oxford University Press.
Loughlin, M. (1999). The State, the Crown and the Law. In M. Sunkin, & S. Payne, eds., *The Nature of the Crown*. Oxford: Oxford University Press, pp. 33–76.
Loughlin, M. (2003). *The Idea of Public Law*, Oxford: Oxford University Press.
Loughlin, M. (2005). Constitutional Theory: A 25th Anniversary Essay. *Oxford Journal of Legal Studies*, 25 (2), pp. 183–202.
Loughlin, M. (2007). Constituent Power Subverted: From Constitutional Argument to British Constitutional Practice. In M. Loughlin, & N. Walker, eds., *The Paradox of Constitutionalism*. Oxford: Oxford University Press, pp. 27–48.
Loughlin, M. (2009). In Defence of *Staatslehre*. *Der Staat*, 48 (1), 1–27.
Loughlin, M. (2010). *Foundations of Public Law*, Oxford: Oxford University Press.
Loughlin, M. (2013). *The British Constitution: A Very Short Introduction*, Oxford: Oxford University Press.
Loughlin, M. (2014). Constitutional Pluralism: An Oxymoron? *Global Constitutionalism*, 3 (1), 9–30.
Loughlin, M. (2015). Nomos. In D. Dyzenhaus, & T. Poole, eds., *Law, Liberty and the State*. Cambridge: Cambridge University Press, pp. 65–95.
Loughlin, M. (2017). *Political Jurisprudence*, Oxford: Oxford University Press.
Loughlin, M. (2022). *Against Constitutionalism*, Cambridge, MA: Harvard University Press.

Lovett, F. (2010). *A General Theory of Domination and Justice*, Oxford: Oxford University Press.
Lovett, F. (2016). *A Republic of Law*, Cambridge: Cambridge University Press.
Lowell, A. L. (1920). *The Government of England*, new edn, vol. I, New York: Macmillan Company.
Lübbe-Wolff, G. (1981). Hegels Staatsrecht als Stellungsnahme im ersten preußischen Verfassungskampf. *Zeitschrift für philosophische Forschung*, 35 (3/4), 476–501.
Lübbe-Wolff, G. (2016). Cultures of Deliberation in Constitutional Courts. In P. Maraniello, ed., *Justicia Constitucional*, vol. I. Resistencia – Chaco: ConTexto Libreria, pp. 37–52.
Lübbe-Wolff, G. (2020a). Das dysfunktionale Gericht. *Frankfurter Allgemeine Zeitung*, 6 October, 11.
Lübbe-Wolff, G. (2020b). Why Is the German Federal Constitutional Court a Deliberative Court, and Why Is that a Good Thing? In B. Häcker, & W. Ernst, eds., *Collective Judging in Comparative Perspective*. Cambridge: Intersentia 2020, pp. 157–179.
Lübbe-Wolff, G. (2022). *Beratungskulturen. Wie Verfassungsgerichte arbeiten, und wovon es abhängt, ob sie integrieren oder polarisieren*. Berlin: Konrad-Adenauer-Stiftung.
Luce, R. and Raiffa, H. (1957). *Games and Decisions*, New York: Wiley.
Lucy, W. (2014). The Rule of Law and Private Law. In L. Austin, & D. Klimchuk, eds., *The Rule of Law and Private Law*. Oxford: Oxford University Press, pp. 41–66.
Luhmann, N. (1998). Der Staat des politischen Systems. In U. Beck, ed., *Perspektiven der Weltgesellschaft*, Frankfurt-am-Main: Suhrkamp, pp. 345–380.
Lukács, G. (1968). *History and Class Consciousness: Studies in Marxist Dialectics*. Translated by Rodney Livingstone. Cambridge, MA: MIT Press.
Lukes, S. (2005). *Power. A Radical View*, 2nd edn, Houndsmills and New York: Palgrave Macmillan.
Lupia, A. (2016). *Uninformed: Why People Seem to Know So Little about Politics and What we Can Do about It*, Oxford: Oxford University Press.
Luxemburg, R. (2006). *Reform or Revolution and Other Writings*, Mineola: Dover Publications.
Lyons, D. (2013). *Confronting Injustice: Moral History and Political Theory*, Oxford: Oxford University Press.
Maas, W. (2017). Multilevel Citizenship. In A. Shachar et al., eds., *The Oxford Handbook of Citizenship*. Oxford: Oxford University Press, pp. 644–668.
Mac Amhlaigh, C. (2016). Putting Political Constitutionalism in Its Place. *International Journal of Constitutional Law*, 14 (1), 175–197.
Macaulay, M. (2018). Bernie and the Donald: A Comparison of Left- and Right-Wing Populist Discourse. In M. Macaulay, ed., *Populist Discourse: International Perspectives*. Cham, Switzerland: Palgrave Macmillan, pp. 165–196.
MacCormick, N. (1982). *Legal Rights and Social Democracy: Essays in Legal and Political Philosophy*, Oxford: Clarendon.
MacCormick, N. (1984). Der Rechtsstaat und die rule of law, *Juristenzeitung*, 39 (2), 65–70.
MacCormick, N. (1989). Spontaneous Order and the Rule of Law: Some Problems. *Ratio Juris*, 2 (1), 41–54.
Macdonald, R. (2000). The Charter of the United Nations as a World Constitution. *International Law Studies* 75 (1), 263–300.
Macfarlane, E. (2016). Constitutional Constraints on Electoral Reform in Canada: Why Parliament Is (Mostly) Free to Implement a New Voting System. *Supreme Court Law Review*, 76, 400–416.
Macfarquhar, N., & Shadid, A. (2012). Russia and China Block U.N. Action on Syrian Crisis. *The New York Times*, February 4.

Machiavelli. (1965 [1517]). Discourses on the First Decade of Titus Livius. In *Machiavelli: The Chief Works and Others*. Volume 1. Translated by A. Gilbert. Durham: Duke University Press, pp. 175–532.
Machiavelli, N. (2005). 'A Discourse or Dialogue Concerning Our Language' (ed. and tr.W. J. Landon), In. Landon, W. J., Politics, Patriotism, and Language : Niccolò Machiavelli's "secular patria" and the Creation of an Italian National Identity. New York: Peter Lang, pp. 129–142.
MacKenzie, M. K., & Warren, M. E. (2012). Two Trust-Based Uses of Minipublics in Democratic Systems. In J. Parkinson, & J. Mansbridge, eds., *Deliberative Systems: Deliberative Democracy at the Large Scale*. New York: Cambridge University Press, pp. 95–124.
Mackie, G. (2004). *Democracy Defended*, Cambridge: Cambridge University Press.
Mackie, G. (2012). Rational Ignorance and Beyond. In H. Landemore, & J. Elster, eds., *Collective Wisdom: Principles of Mechanisms*. Cambridge: Cambridge University Press, pp. 290–318.
MacKinnon, C. A. (1988). *Feminism Unmodified: Discourses on Life and Law*, Cambridge, MA: Harvard University Press, pp. 290–318.
MacKinnon, C. A. (1979). *The Sexual Harassment of Working Women: A Case of Sex Discrimination*, New Jersey: Yale University Press.
Macklin, R. (2003). Dignity Is a Useless Concept. *British Medical Journal*, 327 (7429), 1419–1420.
Maclure, J., & Taylor, C. (2011). *Secularism and Freedom of Conscience*. Translated by J. M. Todd. Cambridge, MA: Harvard University Press.
Madison, J. (1787). *Vices of the Political System*. Available from: https://sls-ushistory11.wikispaces.com/file/view/Vices+of+the+Political+System.PDF
Madison, J. (1961). Federalist No. 51: The Structure of the Government Must Furnish the Proper Checks and Balances Between the Different Departments. In *The Federalist Papers*. Edited by Clinton Rossiter. New York: New American Library.
Maduro, M. (2003). Contrapunctual Law: Europe's Constitutional Pluralism in Action. In N. Walker, ed., *Sovereignty in Transition*, Oxford: Hart.
Maduro, M. (2005a). The Importance of Being Called a Constitution: Constitutional Authority and the Problem of Constitutionalism. *International Journal of Constitutional Law*, 3 (3), 332–356.
Maduro, M. (2005b). Sovereignty in Europe: The European Court of Justice and the Creation of a European Political Community. In M. Volcansek, & J. Stack, eds., *Courts Crossing Borders: Blurring the Lines of Sovereignty*. Durham: Carolina Academic Press.
Maeda, Ko (2010). Two Modes of Democratic Breakdown: A Competing Risks Analysis of Democratic Durability. *The Journal of Politics*, 72 (4), 1129–1143.
Magnetter, P. (2003). Between Parliamentary Control and the Rule of Law: The Political Role of the Ombudsman in the European Union. *Journal of European Public Policy*, 10 (5), 677–694.
Mahmood, S. (2005). *Politics of Piety: The Islamic Revival and the Feminist Subject*, Princeton: Princeton University Press.
Mahmood, S. (2009). Religious Reason and Secular Affect. *Critical Inquiry* 35 (4), 836–862.
Mahmud, T. (1994). Jurisprudence of Successful Treason: Coup d'Etat and Common Law. *Cornell International Law Journal*, 27 (1), 49–140.
Mainwaring, S., & Shugart, M. (1997). Juan Linz, Presidentialism, and Democracy. *Comparative Politics*, 29 (4), 449–471.
Mair, P. (2013). *Ruling the Void: The Hollowing of Western Democracy*, London: Verso.
Maistre, J. D. (1994). *Considerations on France*. Edited by Richard A. Lebrun. Cambridge: Cambridge University Press.

Majone, G. (1994). The Rise of the Regulatory State in Europe. *West European Politics*, 17 (3), 77–101.
Majone, G. (2001). Two Logics of Delegation: Agency and Fiduciary Relations. *European Union Politics*, 2 (1), 103–122.
Majone, G. (2005). *Dilemmas of European Integration. The ambiguities and pitfalls of integration by stealth*, Oxford: Oxford University Press.
Maldonado, D. B. (2013). Introduction: Toward a Constitutionalism of the Global South. In D. B. Maldonado, ed., *Constitutionalism of the Global South: The Activist Tribunals of India, South Africa, and Colombia*, Cambridge: Cambridge University Press, pp. 1–38.
Malleson, K. (2002). Safeguarding Judicial Impartiality. *Legal Studies*, 22 (1), 53–70.
Mamdani, M. (1996). *Citizen and Subject: Contemporary Africa and the Legacy of Late Colonialism*, Princeton: Princeton University Press.
Manin, B. (1987). On Legitimacy and Political Deliberation. *Political Theory*, 15 (3), 338–368.
Manin, B. (1995). *Principes du gouvernement représentatif*, Paris: Gallimard.
Manin, B. (1997). *The Principles of Representative Government*, Cambridge: Cambridge University Press.
Manin, B. (2008). The Emergency Paradigm and the New Terrorism: What If the End of Terrorism Was Not in Sight? In S. Baume, & B. Fontana, eds., *Les usages de la séparation des pouvoirs*. Paris: Michel Houdiard, pp. 136–171 (also available at http://as.nyu.edu/docs/IO/2792/emerg.pdf).
Mann, M. (1993). *The Sources of Social Power: Volume II*, Cambridge, UK: Cambridge University Press.
Mann, M. (1997). Has Globalization Ended the Rise and Rise of the Nation-State? *Review of International Political Economy*, 4 (3), pp. 472–496.
Mann, G., & Wainwright, J. (2018). *Climate Leviathan: A Political Theory of Our Planetary Future*, London: Verso.
Manning, J (2003). The Absurdity Doctrine. *Harvard Law Review*, 116 (8), 2387–2486.
Manning, J. (2005). Textualism and Legislative Intent. *Virginia Law Review*, 91 (2), 419–450.
Manning, J. (2006). What Divides Textualists From Purposivists. *Columbia Law Review*, 106 (1), 70–111.
Mansbridge, J. ed. (1990). *Beyond Self-Interest*, Chicago: University of Chicago Press.
Mansbridge, J. (1999). Should Blacks Represent Blacks and Women Represent Women? A Contingent "Yes." *Journal of Politics*, 61 (3), 628–657.
Mansbridge, J. (2003). Rethinking Representation. *American Political Science Review*, 97 (4), 515–526.
Mansbridge, J., et al. (2010). The Place of Self-interest and the Role of Power in Deliberative Democracy. *Journal of Political Philosophy*, 18 (1), 64–100.
Mansbridge, J., et al. (2012). A Systemic Approach to Deliberative Democracy. In J. Parkinson, & J. Mansbridge, eds., *Deliberative Systems: Deliberative Democracy at the Large Scale*. Cambridge: Cambridge University Press, pp. 1–26.
Mansbridge, J. (2020). Representation Failure. In M. Schwartzberg, & D. Viehoff, eds., *NOMOS LXIII: Democratic Failure*. New York: New York University Press, pp. 101–140.
Mansfield, H. (1989). *Taming the Prince: The Ambivalence of Modern Executive Power*, New York: Free Press; London: Macmillan.
Marceau, G. (2011). IGOs in Crisis? or New Opportunities to Demonstrate Responsibility? *International Organizations Law Review*, 8 (1), 1–13.
Marcussen, M. (2009). Scientization of Central Banking: The Politics of A-Politicization. In K. H. F. Dyson, & M. Marcussen, eds., *Central Banks in the Age of the Euro: Europeanization, Convergence, and Power*. Oxford: Oxford University Press, pp. 373–390.
Margalit, A. (1996). *The Decent Society*, Cambridge, MA: Harvard University Press.

Marglos, E., & Laurence, S. (2019). Concepts. In E. Zalta, ed., *Stanford Encyclopaedia of Philosophy*. Available from: https://plato.stanford.edu/entries/concepts/
Markesinis, B. S., Unberath, H., & Johnston, A. (2010). *The German Law of Contract*, Oxford: Hart Publishing.
Markovits, I. (1996). Children of a Lesser God: GDR Lawyers in Post-Socialist Germany. *Michigan Law Review*, 94 (7), 2270–2308.
Marmor, A. (2001). *Positive Law and Objective Values*, Oxford: Oxford University Press.
Marmor, A. (2004). The Rule of Law and Its Limits. *Law and Philosophy*, 23 (1), 1–43.
Marmor, A. (2008). *Social Conventions*, Princeton: Princeton University Press.
Marshall, G. (1986). *Constitutional Conventions*, Oxford: Oxford University Press.
Marshall, T. H., & Bottomore, T. (1987). *Citizenship and Social Class*, London: Pluto Press.
Marten, K. (2007). Warlordism in Comparative Perspective. *International Security*, 31 (3), 41–73.
Martinez, J. (2012). Horizontal Structuring. In M. Rosenfeld, & A. Sajó, eds., *The Oxford Handbook of Comparative Constitutional Law*. Oxford: Oxford University Press, pp. 547–575.
Marx, F. M. (1957). *The Administrative State: An Introduction to Bureaucracy*, Chicago: University of Chicago Press.
Marx, K. (1849). The Trial of the Rhenish District Committee of Democrats. *Neue Rheinische Zeitung*, No. 231 and 232, February 1849.
Marx, K. (1978a). The Civil War in France. In R. Tucker ed. *The Marx-Engels Reader*, 2nd edn, New York: W.W. Norton & Company, p. 618.
Marx, K. (1978b). Critical Marginal Notes on the Article "The King of Prussia and Social Reform". In R. Tucker ed. *The Marx-Engels Reader*, 2nd edn. W.W. Norton & Company. p. 126.
Marx, K. (1978c). On the Jewish Question. In R. Tucker ed. *The Marx-Engels Reader*, 2nd edn. W.W. Norton & Company. p. 26.
Marx, K. (1978d). The Class Struggles in France, 1848–1850. In R. Tucker ed. *The Marx-Engels Reader*, 2nd edn. W.W. Norton & Company. p. 586.
Marx, K. (1978e). The Eighteenth Brumaire of Louis Bonaparte. In R. Tucker ed. *The Marx-Engels Reader*, 2nd edn. W.W. Norton & Company. p. 594.
Marx, K. (1990). *Capital Volume I*, London: Penguin Classics.
Marx, K. (1996). *Early Writings*, London: Penguin.
Marx, K. (2000). On the Jewish Question. In D. McLellan, ed., *Karl Marx: Selected Writings*, 2nd edn. Oxford: Oxford University Press, pp. 46–70.
Maskikiver, J. (2020). *The Duty to Vote*, Oxford: Oxford University Press.
Masri M. (2017). *The Dynamics of Exclusionary Constitutionalism: Israel as a Jewish and Democratic State*, Oxford: Hart.
Massey, I. P. (2012). *Administrative Law*, Lucknow: Eastern Book Company.
Masur, J., & Posner, E. (2018). Cost-Benefit Analysis and the Judicial Role. *University of Chicago Law Review*, 85 (4), 935–986.
Matikainen, S., Campiglio, E., & Zenghelis, D. (2017). *The Climate Impact of Quantitative Easing*, London: Grantham Research Institute on Climate Change and the Environment.
Matsuda, M. J. (1987). Looking to the Bottom: Critical Legal Studies and Reparations. *Harvard Civil Rights–Civil Liberties Law Review*, 22 (2), pp. 323–399.
Matsusaka, J. D. (2020). *Let the People Rule. How Direct Democracy Can Meet the Populist Challenge*, Princeton: Princeton University Press.
Matthes, C.-Y. (2022). Judges as Activists: How Polish Judges Mobilise to Defend the Rule of Law. *East European Politics*, 38 (3), pp. 468–487.
Mattli, W. (1991). *The Logic of Regional Integration. Europe and Beyond*, Cambridge: Cambridge University Press.

May, E. (2019 [1844]). *A Treatise on the Law, Privileges, Proceedings, and Usage of Parliament.* 25th edn. Available from: https://erskinemay.parliament.uk/

May, J. R., & Daly, E. (2019). Global Climate Constitutionalism and Justice in the Courts. In J. Jaria-Manzano, & S. Borras, eds., *Research Handbook on Global Climate Constitutionalism.* Cheltenham, UK: Edward Edgar Publishing, pp. 235–245.

May, K. (1952). A Set of Independent Necessary and Sufficient Conditions for Simple Majority Decision. *Econometrica,* 20 (4), 680–684.

May, L. (2019). *Ancient Legal Thought: Equity, Justice, and Humaneness from Hammurabi and the Pharaohs to Justinian and the Talmud,* New York: Cambridge University Press.

Mayhew, D. (1974). *Congress: The Electoral Connection,* New Haven: Yale University Press.

Mashaw, J. L. (1983). *Bureaucratic Justice: Managing Social Security Disability Claims,* New Haven: Yale University Press.

Mashaw, J. L. (2012). *Creating the Administrative Constitution: The Lost One Hundred Years of American Administrative Law,* New Haven: Yale University Press.

Mashaw, J. L. (2018). *Reasoned Administration and Democratic Legitimacy: How Administrative Law Supports Democratic Self-government,* Cambridge: Cambridge University Press.

Mayer, A. (2000). *The Furies: Violence and Terror in the French and Russian Revolutions,* Princeton: Princeton University Press.

Mayer, O. (1924). *Deutsches Verwaltungsrecht,* 3rd edn, München: Verlag von Duncker & Humblot.

Mbiti, J. (1970). *African Religions and Philosophy,* New York: Doubleday.

McBride, M. (2021). The Tracking Theory of Claim-Rights. *Analytic Philosophy.* Forthcoming.

McCall Rosenbluth, F., & Shapiro, I. (2018). *Responsible Parties: Saving Democracy from Itself,* New Haven: Yale University Press.

McCarthy, T. (2009). *Race, Empire, and the Idea of Human Development,* Cambridge: Cambridge University Press.

McConnell, M. W. (2013–2014). Reconsidering *Citizens United* as a Press Clause Case. *Yale Law Journal,* 123 (2), pp. 412–458.

McCormick, J. (2008). People and Elites in Republican Constitutions, Traditional and Modern. In M. Loughlin, & N. Walker, eds., *The Paradox of Constitutionalism: Constituent Power and Constitutional Form.* Oxford: Oxford University Press, pp. 107–126.

McCormick, J. (2011). *Machiavellian Democracy,* Cambridge: Cambridge University Press.

McCrudden, C. (2008). Human Dignity in Human Rights Interpretation. *European Journal of International Law,* 19 (4), 655–724.

McCubbins, M. D., & Schwartz, T. (1984). Congressional Oversight Overlooked: Police Patrols and Fire Alarms. *American Journal of Political Science,* 28 (1), 165–179.

McCubbins, M. D., Noll, R. G., & Weingast, B. R. (1989). Structure and Process, Politics and Policy: Administrative Arrangements and the Political Control of Agencies. *Virginia Law Review,* 75 (2), 431–482.

McCulloch, A. (2014). Consociational Settlements in Deeply Divided Societies: The Liberal-Corporate Distinction. *Democratization,* 21 (3), 501–518.

McGann, A. (2006). *The Logic of Democracy. Reconciling Equality, Deliberation, and Minority Protection,* Ann Arbor: University of Michigan Press.

McGarry, J. (2019). Classical Consociational Theory and Recent Consociational Performance. *Swiss Political Science Review,* 25 (4), 538–555.

McGarry J., & O'Leary, B. (2009). Power Shared After Death of Thousands. In R. Taylor, ed., *Consociational Theory. McGarry and O'Leary and the Northern Ireland Conflict.* Abingdon: Routledge, pp. 15–84.

McGinnis, J., & Movsesian, M. (2000). The World Trade Constitution. *Harvard Law Review* 114 (2), 511–605.
McIlwain, C. H. (1940). *Constitutionalism Ancient and Modern*, Ithaca, NY: Cornell University Press.
McIlwain, C. H. (2008). *Constitutionalism: Ancient and Modern*, rev. edn, Indianapolis, IN: Liberty Fund Inc.
McKerrell, N. (2019). Explainer: What Scotland's new citizen assemblies could mean for democracy. *The Conversation*, July 3. Available from: https://theconversation.com/explainer-what-scotlands-new-citizen-assemblies-could-mean-for-democracy-119793
McKie, R. (2017). How Sea Shepherd lost battle against Japan's whale hunters in Antarctic. *The Guardian*. 23 December. Available from: www.theguardian.com/environment/2017/dec/23/sea-shepherd-loses-antarctic-battle-japan-whale-hunters (Accessed: 15 November 2019).
McKinnon, J. (2012). Tax history: why U.S. pursues citizens overseas. *The Wall Street Journal*. 18 May. Available from: www.wsj.com/articles/BL-WB-34630 [Viewed 29 November 2020].
McLachlan, C. (2020). The Double-facing Foreign Relations Function of the Executive and Its Self-enforcing Obligation to Comply with International Law. In J. Bomhoff, D. Dyzenhaus, & T. Poole, eds., *The Double-Facing Constitution*. Cambridge: Cambridge University Press, pp. 376–412.
McLean, J. (2012). *Searching for the State in British Legal Thought. Competing Conceptions of the Public Sphere*, Cambridge: Cambridge University Press.
McLean, J. (2020). Between Sovereign and Subject: The Constitutional Position of the Official. *University of Toronto Law Journal*, 70 (supp. 2), 167–182.
McMahan, J., (2005). Just Cause in War. *Ethics and International Affairs*, 19 (3), 1–21.
McPherson, L. K., & Shelby, T. (2004). Blackness and Blood: Interpreting African American Identity. *Philosophy & Public Affairs*, 32 (2), 171–192.
Medina, V. (2002). Locke's Militant Liberalism. *History of Philosophy Quarterly*, 19 (4), 345–365.
Mee, S. (2019). *Central Bank Independence and the Legacy of the German Past*, Cambridge: Cambridge University Press.
Mehrling, P. (2010). *The New Lombard Street: How the Fed Became the Dealer of Last Resort*. Princeton: Princeton University Press.
Mehta, L. et al. (2019). Climate Change and Uncertainty from "above" and "below": Perspectives from India. *Regional Environmental Change*, 19 (6), 1533–1547.
Meierhenrich, J. (2018). *The Remnants of the Rechtsstaat: An Ethnography of Nazi law*, Oxford: Oxford University Press.
Meierhenrich, J. (2021). *Rechtsstaat* versus the Rule of Law. In J. Meierhenrich, & M. Loughlin, eds., *The Cambridge Companion to the Rule of Law*. Cambridge: Cambridge University Press, pp. 39–67.
Meierhenrich, J., & Loughlin, M., eds. (2021). *The Cambridge Companion to the Rule of Law*. Cambridge: Cambridge University Press.
Meinecke, F. (1957). *Machiavellism: The Doctrine of Raison d'État and its Place in Modern History*. Translated by D. Scott. Introduction by W. Stark. London: Routledge.
Meinel, F. (2021). *Germany's Dual Constitution: Parliamentary Democracy in the Federal Republic*, Oxford: Hart Publishing.
Melton, J., & Ginsburg, T. (2014). Does De Jure Judicial Independence Really Matter?: A Reevaluation of Explanations for Judicial Independence. *Journal of Law and Courts*, 2 (2), 187–217.
Mendes, C. H. (2013). *Constitutional Courts and Deliberative Democracy*, Oxford: Oxford University Press.

Mendes, J. (2011). *Participation in EU Rule-Making: A Rights-Based Approach*, Oxford: Oxford University Press.
Menkiti, I. (1984). Person and Community in African Traditional Thought. In R. Wright, ed., *African Philosophy: An Introduction*. Lanham University Press of America, pp. 171–182.
Menzies, J., & Tiernan, A. (2015). Caretaker Conventions. In B. Galligan, & S. Brenton, eds., *Constitutional Conventions in Westminster Systems*. Cambridge: Cambridge University Press, pp. 91–115.
Mercat-Bruns, M. (2015). Les Discriminations Multiples et l'identité Au Travail Au Croisement Des Questions de Libertés et d'égalité. *Revue de Droit du Travail*, 1, 28–38.
Mercat-Bruns, M. (2016). *Discrimination at Work: Comparing European, French, and American Law*, Oakland: University of California Press.
Mercat-Bruns, M. (2018). Multiple Discrimination and Intersectionality: Issues of Equality and Liberty. *International Social Science Journal*, 67 (223–224), 43–54.
Mercat-Bruns, M. (2021). Discrimination Intersectionnelle: Une Notion Émergente En Droit Du Travail. *Bulletin Joly Travail*, 4, 52.
Mérieau, E. (2019). French Authoritarian Constitutionalism and Its Legacy. In H. A. Garcia, & G. Frankenberg, eds., *Authoritarian Constitutionalism: Comparative Analysis and Critique*. Northampton: Edward Elgar, pp. 185–208.
Merkel, W. (2014). Is There a Crisis of Democracy? *Democratic Theory*, 1 (2), 11–25.
Merker, N. (2009). *Filosofie del populismo*, Rome: Laterza.
Merkl, A. (1927). *Allgemeines Verwaltungsrecht*, Wien/Berlin: Verlag Österreich.
Merton, K. (1938). Social Structure and Anomie. *American Sociological Review*, 3 (5), 672–682.
Metzger, G. E. (2010). Ordinary Administrative Law as Constitutional Common Law. *Columbia Law Review*, 110 (2), 479–536.
Metzger, G. E. (2015). The Constitutional Duty to Supervise. *Yale Law Journal*, 126 (6), 1836–2201.
Meyer, D. S. (2007). *The Politics of Protest: Social Movements in America*, New York: Oxford University Press.
Meyer, M. (2018a). The Ethics of Consumer Credit: Balancing Wrongful Inclusion and Wrongful Exclusion. *Midwest Studies In Philosophy*, 42 (1), 294–313.
Meyer, M. (2018b). The Right to Credit. *Journal of Political Philosophy*, 26 (3), 304–326.
Michaels, J. D. (2018). *Constitutional Coup: Privatization's Threat to the American Republic*, Cambridge, MA: Harvard University Press.
Michelman, F. (1969). Foreword: On Protecting the Poor through the Fourteenth Amendment. *Harvard Law Review*, 83 (1), 7–59.
Michelman, F. (1979). Welfare Rights in a Constitutional Democracy. *Washington University Law Quarterly*, 1979 (3), 659–693.
Michelman, F. (1988). Law's Republic. *Yale Law Journal*, 97 (8), 1493–1537.
Michelman, F. (1999). Constitutional Authorship by the People. *Notre Dame Law Review*, 74 (5), 1605–1630.
Michelman F. (2000). Human Rights and the Limits of Constitutional Theory. *Ratio Juris*, 13, 63.
Michelman, F. I. (2003a). Ida's Way: Constructing the Respect-Worthy Governmental System. *Fordham Law Review*, 72 (2), 345–365.
Michelman F. I. (2003b). Is the Constitution a Contract for Legitimacy? *Review of Constitutional Studies*, 8 (2), 101–128.
Michelman, F. I. (2004). Is the Constitution a Contract for Legitimacy? *Review of Constitutional Studies*, 8 (2), 101.

Michelman, F. (2011). The Interplay of Constitutional and Ordinary Jurisdiction. In T. Ginsburg, & R. Dixon, eds., *Comparative Constitutional Law*. Cheltenham: Edward Elgar, pp. 278–297.

Michelman, F. (2018). Human Rights and Constitutional Rights: A Proceduralizing Function for Substantive Constitutional Law? In S. Voeneky, & G. Neuman, eds., *Human Rights, Democracy, and Legitimacy in a World of Disorder*. Cambridge: Cambridge University Press, pp. 73–96.

Michelman, F. (2019). Political-Liberal Legitimacy and the Question of Judicial Restraint. *Jus Cogens*, 1 (1), 59–75.

Michelmann, H., ed. (2005). *A Global Dialogue on Federalism: Legislative, Executive, and Judicial Governance in Federal Countries*, Kingston/Montreal: McGill-Queen's University Press.

Michels, R. (1962 [1911]). *Political Parties: A Sociological Study of the Oligarchic Tendencies of Modern Democracy*. Translated by E. Paul and C. Paul. Introduction by S. Martin Lipset. New York: Free Press.

Miles, D. (2020). *Democracy, the Courts, and the Liberal State: A Comparative Analysis of American and German Constitutionalism*, Abingdon: Routledge.

Mill, J. S. (1969). *The Subjection of Women*, London: Longmans, Green, and Co.

Mill, J. S. (1977 [1861]). *Considerations on Representative Government, in Collected Works*, vol. XIX. Edited by J. M. Robson. Toronto: University of Toronto Press; London: Routledge and Kegan Paul, pp. 371–577.

Miller, D. (1995). *On Nationality*, Oxford: Oxford University Press.

Miller, D. (2001). Nationality in Divided Societies. In A.-G. Gagnon, & J. Tully, eds., *Multinational Democracies*. Cambridge: Cambridge University Press, pp. 299–318.

Miller, D. (2014). Immigration: The Case for Limits. In A. I. Cohen, & C. Heath Wellman, eds., *Contemporary Debates in Applied Ethics*. Malden: Wiley-Blackwell, pp. 193–206.

Miller, D. (2016). *Strangers in Our Midst: The Political Philosophy of Immigration*, Cambridge, MA: Harvard University Press.

Miller, D. (2018). What Makes a Democratic People? In D. Owen, ed., *Democratic Inclusion: Rainer Bauböck in Dialogue*. Manchester: Manchester University Press, pp. 125–142.

Miller, D. (2020). *Is Self-Determination a Dangerous Illusion?* Cambridge: Polity Press.

Miller, F. (1995). *Nature, Justice, and Rights in Aristotle's Politics*, Oxford: Oxford University Press.

Miller, P. (2001). Governing by Numbers: Why Calculative Practices Matter. *Social Research*, 68 (2), 379–396.

Miller, P. (2018). Fiduciary Representation. In E. Criddle et al. pp. 21–48.

Milligan, T. (2013). *Civil Disobedience: Protest, Justification and the Law*, New York, London: Bloomsbury Acadeemic.

Minority Rights Group International. (2021). Peoples under Threat Data. Available from: https://peoplesunderthreat.org/data/ (Accessed: 13 February 2022).

Minow, M. (1990). *Making All the Difference: Inclusion, Exclusion, and American Law*, Ithaca: Cornell University Press.

Minow, M. (2017). Alternatives to the State Action Doctrine in the Era of Privatization, Mandatory Arbitration, and the Internet: Directing Law to Serve Human Needs. *Harvard Civil Rights – Civil Liberties Law Review*, 52 (1), 145–167.

Mitchell, P., Evans, G., & O'Leary, B. (2009). Extremist Outbidding in Ethnic Party Systems Is Not Inevitable: Tribune Parties in Northern Ireland. *Political Studies* 57 (2), 397–421.

Mitchell, R. B. (2018). Climate Law: Accomplishments and Areas for Growth. *Climate Law*, 8 (3–4), 135–150.

Modood, T. (2016). State-Religion Connections and Multicultural Citizenship. In J. Cohen, & C. Laborde, eds., *Religion, Secularism, and Constitutional Democracy.* New York: Columbia University Press, pp. 182–203.

Moeckli, D. (2011). Of Minarets and Foreign Criminals: Swiss Direct Democracy and Human Rights. *Human Rights Law Review,* 11 (4), 774–794.

Moeckli, D. (2018). Referendums: Tyranny of the Majority? *Swiss Political Science Review,* 24 (3), 335–341.

Moellendorf, D. (2002). *Cosmopolitan Justice,* Boulder: Westview Press.

Moffitt, B. (2017). Transnational Populism? Representative Claims, Media and the Difficulty of Constructing a Transnational "People", *Javnost-The Public,* 24 (2), 409–425.

Molina, O., & Rhodes, M. (2002). Corporatism: The Past, Present, and Future of a Concept. *Annual Review of Political Science,* 5, 305–331.

Møller, J., & Skaaning, S.-E. (2010). Beyond the Radial Delusion: Conceptualizing and Measuring Democracy and Non-democracy. *International Political Science Review,* 31 (3), 261–283.

Møller, J., & Skanning, S.-E. (2014). *The Rule of Law: Definitions, Measures, Patterns and Causes,* Basingstoke: Palgrave Macmillan.

Möller, K. (2018). Popular Sovereignty, Populism and Deliberative Democracy. *Philosophical Inquiry,* 42 (1/2), 14–36.

Moller, K. (2019). Justifying the Culture of Justification. *International Journal of Constitutional Law,* 17 (4), 1078–1097.

Möllers, C. (2011a). Multi-Level Democracy. *Ratio Juris,* 24 (3), 247–266.

Möllers, C. (2011b). Pouvoir Constituant-Constitution-Constitutionalisation. In A. von Bogdandy, & J. Bast, eds., *Principles of European Constitutional Law.* Oxford: Hart, pp. 169–204.

Möllers, C. (2011c). *Staat als Argument,* 2nd edn, Tübingen: Mohr Siebeck.

Möllers, C. (2013). *The Three Branches: A Comparative Model of Separation of Powers,* Oxford: Oxford University Press.

Möllers, C. (2014). Scope and Legitimacy of Judicial Review in German Constitutional Law – the Court versus the Political Process. In H. Pünder, & C. Waldhoff, eds., *Debates in German Public Law.* Oxford: Hart, pp. 3–25.

Mommsen, T. (1952). *Römisches Staatsrecht, Zweiter Band,* 1. Teil, Akademissche Druck-u Verlagsansstalt.

Monnet, E. (2018). *Controlling Credit: Central Banking and the Planned Economy in Postwar France, 1948–1973,* Cambridge: Cambridge University Press.

Monnet, E. (2021). *La Banque Providence: Démocratiser les banques centrales et la monnaie,* Paris: Seuil.

Montesquieu. (1989 [1748]). *The Spirit of the Laws.* Edited by A. Cohler, B. C. Miller, & H. S. Stone. Cambridge: Cambridge University Press.

Moore, A., & O'Doherty, K. (2014). Deliberative Voting: Clarifying Consent in a Consensus Process. *Journal of Political Philosophy,* 22 (3), pp. 302–319.

Moore, B. J. (1988). *Horizontalists and Verticalists: The Macroeconomics of Credit Money,* Cambridge and New York: Cambridge University Press.

Moore, G., Loizides, N., Sandal, N. A., & Lordos, A. (2014). Winning Peace Frames: Intra-Ethnic Outbidding in Northern Ireland and Cyprus. *West European Politics,* 37 (1), 159–181.

Moore, M. (2015). *A Political Theory of Territory,* Oxford: Oxford University Press.

Morales-Gálvez, S. (2017). Living Together as Equals: Linguistic Justice and Sharing the Public Sphere in Multilingual Settings. *Ethnicities,* 17 (5), 646–666.

Morell, M. (2016). I Ran the C.I.A. Now I'm Endorsing Hillary Clinton. *New York Times*, 5 August. Available at: www.nytimes.com/2016/08/05/opinion/campaign-stops/i-ran-the-cia-now-im-endorsing-hillary-clinton.html

Moretti, F. (2015). *Quantitative Formalism: An Experiment*, Stanford Literary Lab Pamphlet 1. Available from: https://litlab.stanford.edu/LiteraryLabPamphlet1.pdf.

Morgan, D. (2007). *The Mongols*, Oxford: Blackwell.

Morgan, E. S. (1988). *Inventing the People: The Rise of Popular Sovereignty in England and America*, New York: W.W. Norton & Company.

Morgan, I., & Davies, P., eds. (2008). *The Federal Nation: Perspectives on American Federalism*, Palgrave Macmillan.

Morgenbesser, L. (2017). The Autocratic Mandate: Elections, Legitimacy and Regime Stability in Singapore. *Pacific Review*, 30 (2), 205–231.

Morris, B. (1946). The Dignity of Man. *Ethics*, 57 (1), 57–64.

Morris, B. (2004). *The Birth of the Palestinian Refugee Problem Revisited*, 2nd edn, Cambridge: Cambridge University Press.

Morris, D. (2020). *Legal Sabotage: Ernst Fraenkel in Hitler's Germany*, Cambridge: Cambridge University Press.

Morrison, T. (2011). Libya, "Hostilities," the Office of Legal Counsel, and the Process of Executive Branch Legal Interpretation. *Harvard Law Review Forum*, 124 (42), 62–74.

Morrison, T., Weiler, J. H. H. (2009). *Introduction to the Art Collection of 22*, Washington Square North, New York.

Mortati, C. (2001). *L'ordinamento del governo*, Milan: Giuffrè.

Mortati, C. (2020). *La teoria del potere costituente*, Rome: Quodlibet.

Mortati, C. (2025). *The Constitution in the Material Sense*, Abingdon: Routledge.

Morton, P. A. (1991–1992). Conventions of the British Constitution. *Holdsworth Law Review*, 15, 114–180.

Moschella, M. (2015). Currency Wars in the Advanced World: Resisting Appreciation at a Time of Change in Central Banking Monetary Consensus. *Review of International Political Economy*, 22 (1), 134–161.

Motomura, H. (2006). *Americans in Waiting: The Lost Story of Immigration and Citizenship in the United States*, New York: Oxford University Press.

Mouffe, C. (2018). *For a left populism*, London: Verso Books.

Mudde, C. (2013). Are Populists Friends or Foes of Constitutionalism? The Foundation for Law, Justice and Society Policy Brief.

Mudde, C., & Kaltwasser, C. R. (2013). Exclusionary vs. Inclusionary Populism: Comparing Contemporary Europe and Latin America. *Government and Opposition*, 48 (2), 147–174.

Mudge, S. L., & Vauchez, A. (2018). Too Embedded to Fail: The ECB and the Necessity of Calculating Europe. *Historical Social Research / Historische Sozialforschung*, 43 (3), 248–273.

Mueller, D. C. (2003). *Public Choice III*, Cambridge: Cambridge University Press.

Mügge, D. (2016). Studying Macroeconomic Indicators as Powerful Ideas. *Journal of European Public Policy*, 23 (3), 410–427.

Muirhead, R. (2006). A Defence of Party Spirit. *Perspectives on Politics*, 4 (4), 713–727.

Muirhead, R. (2014). *The Promise of Party in a Polarized Age*, Cambridge, MA: Harvard University Press.

Muirhead, R., & Rosenblum, N. (2006). Political Liberalism vs. "The Great Game of Politics": The Politics of Political Liberalism. *Perspectives on Politics*, 4 (1), 99–108.

Muirhead, R., & Rosenblum, N. (2015). The Uneasy Place of Parties in the Constitutional Order. In M. Tushnet, M. Graber, & S. Levinson, eds., *The Oxford Handbook of the U.S. Constitution*. Oxford: Oxford University Press, pp. 217–240.

Muirhead, R., & Rosenblum, N. (2020). The Political Theory of Parties and Partisanship: Catching Up. *Annual Review of Political Science*, 23 (1), 95–110.
Müller, J.-W. (2012). Militant Democracy. In M. Rosenfeld, & A. Sajó, eds., *Oxford Handbook of Comparative Constitutional Law*. Oxford: Oxford University Press, pp. 1253–69.
Müller, J.-W. (2016). *What Is Populism?* Philadelphia: University of Pennsylvania.
Müller, J.-W. (2018). Populism and Constitutionalism. In C. R. Kaltwasser et al., eds., *The Oxford Handbook of Populism*. Oxford: Oxford University Press, pp. 590–606.
Munday, R. (2016). *Agency: Law and Principles*, 3rd edn, Oxford: Oxford University Press.
Munro, C. (1975). Laws and conventions distinguished. *Law Quarterly*, 91, 208–235.
Munro, C. (1994). Review of Law, Liberty and Justice: The Legal Foundations of British Constitutionalism. *Legal Studies*, 14 (3), 456–458.
Munro, C. (2005). *Studies in Constitutional Law*, 2nd edn, Oxford: Oxford University Press.
Murau, S. (2017). Shadow Money and the Public Money Supply: The Impact of the 2007–2009 Financial Crisis on the Monetary System. *Review of International Political Economy*, 24 (3), 802–838.
Murdoch, Z., Connolly, S., & Kassim, H. (2018). Administrative Legitimacy and the Democratic Deficit of the European Union, *Journal of European Public Policy*, 25 (3), 389–408.
Mureinik, E. (1992). Beyond a Charter of Luxuries: Economic Rights in the Constitution. *South African Journal on Human Rights*, 8 (4), 464–474.
Murkens, J. E. K. (2013). *From Empire to Union. Conceptions of German Constitutional Law Since 1871*, Oxford: Oxford University Press.
Murphy, W. (1993). Constitutions, Constitutionalism, and Democracy. In Greenberg, D., et. al., eds., *Constitutionalism & Democracy: Transitions in the Contemporary World*. Oxford: Oxford University Press.
Murphy, W. (2007). *Constitutional Democracy*, Oxford: Oxford University Press.
Nabulsi, K. (1999). *Traditions of War: Occupation, Resistance, and the Law*, Oxford: Oxford University Press.
Nabulsi, K., & Takriti, A. R., eds. (2016). *The Palestinian Revolution Website*. Available from: learnpalestine.politics.ox.ac.uk
Nadakavukaren Schefer, K. (2021). Introduction. In S. Baume, V. Boillet, & V. Martenet, eds. *Misinformation in Referenda*, London: Routledge, pp. 1–12.
Nader, L., & Mattei, U. (2008). *Plunder: When the Rule of Law Is Illegal*, Oxford: Blackwell.
Nagel, R. (2002). *The Implosion of American Federalism*, Oxford: Oxford University Press.
Nagel, T. (1995). Personal Rights and Public Space. *Philosophy and Public Affairs*, 24 (2), 83–107.
Nakamoto, S. (2008). Bitcoin: A Peer-to-Peer Electronic Cash System. *Decentralized Business Review*, 21260. https://bitcoin.org/bitcoin.pdf
Napoleon, V. (1910 [1804]). *The Corsican: A Diary of Napoleon's Life in His Own Words*. Edited by R. M. Johnston. Boston: Houghton Mifflin Co.
Napoleon, V., & Friedland, H. (2014). Indigenous Legal Traditions: Roots to Renaissance. In M. D. Dubber, & T. Hörnle, eds., *Oxford Handbook on Criminal Law*. Oxford: Oxford University Press, pp. 225–247.
Napoli, P. (2018). What If More Speech Is No Longer the Solution? First Amendment Theory Meets Fake News and the Filter Bubble. *Federal Communications Law Journal*, 70 (1), 55–104.
Nash, K. (2016). Politicising Human Rights in Europe: Challenges to Legal Constitutionalism from the Left and the Right. *International Journal of Human Rights*, 20 (8), 1295–1308.
Nason, S. (2016). *Reconstructing Judicial Review*, Oxford: Hart.

Näsströom, S. (2015). Democratic Representation Beyond Elections. *Constellations*, 22 (1), 1–12.
Natarajan, U. (2015). Human rights – help or hindrance to combatting climate change? *Open Democracy*. Available from: www.opendemocracy.net/en/openglobalrights-openpage-blog/human-rights-help-or-hindrance-to-combatting-climate-change/
Natarajan, U., & Khoday, K. (2014). Locating Nature: Making and Unmaking International Law. *Leiden Journal of International Law*, 27 (3), 573–593.
Naudé, G. (2020). *Political Considerations upon Refin'd Politicks, and the Master-Strokes of State*. Translated by W. King. Edited by K. Watson. Independently Published.
Neblo, M. (2007). Family Disputes: Diversity in Defining and Measuring Deliberation. *Swiss Political Science Review* 13 (4), pp. 527–557.
Neblo, M. (2015). *Deliberative Democracy between Theory and Practice*, Cambridge: Cambridge University Press.
Neblo, M., & Sterling, K. (2018). *Politics with the People: Building a Directly Representative Democracy*, Cambridge: Cambridge University Press.
Necker, J. (2020). *On Executive Power in Great States*. Edited by A. Craiutu. Indianapolis: Liberty Fund.
Negri, A. (2009). *Insurgencies: Constituent Power and the Modern State*. Translated by Maurizia Boscagli. 2nd edn, Minneapolis: University of Minnesota Press.
Nelson, E. (2014). *The Royalist Revolution: Monarchy and the American Founding*, Harvard: Harvard University Press.
Nemacheck, C. (2017). Appointing Supreme Court Justices. In L. Epstein, & S. Lindquist, eds., *The Oxford Handbook of U.S. Judicial Behavior*. Oxford: Oxford University Press, pp. 29–47.
Nethercote, J. R. (2015). Parliament. In B. Galligan, & S. Brenton, eds., *Constitutional Conventions in Westminster Systems*. Cambridge: Cambridge University Press, pp. 137–156.
Neufeld, B. (2015). Public Reason. In J. Mandle, & D. A. Reidy, eds., *The Cambridge Rawls Lexicon*. Cambridge: Cambridge University Press, pp. 666–673.
Neuman, G. (2000). Human Dignity in United States Constitutional Law. In Dieter Simon and Manfred Weiss, eds., *Zur Autonomie des Individuums: Liber Amicorum Spiros Simitis*. Baden-Baden: Nomos Verlagsgesellschaft, pp. 249–271.
Neuman, G. (2003). Human Rights and Constitutional Rights: Harmony and Dissonance. *Stanford Law Review*, 55 (5), 1863–1900.
Neumann, F. (1944). *Behemoth: The Structure and Practice of National Socialism, 1933–44*, Oxford: Oxford University Press.
Neumann, F. (1978). Rechtsstaat, Gewaltenteilung, und Demokratie. In A. Söllner, ed., *Wirtschaft, Staat, Demokratie, Aufsätze*. Frankfurt-am-Main: Suhrkamp, pp. 1930–1954.
Neumann, F. (1987 [1934]). Rechstaat, the Division of Powers and Socialism'. In O. Kirchheimer and F. Neumann, eds., *Social Democracy and the Rule of Law*. Edited by K. Tribe. Translated by L. Tanner and K. Tribe. London: Allen and Unwin.
Neves, M. (2013). *Transconstitutionalism*. Oxford: Hart.
Ngai, M. (2004). *Impossible Subjects: Illegal Aliens and the Making of Modern America*, Princeton: Princeton University Press.
Nicholas, B. (1970). Loi, Règlement and Judicial Review in the Fifth Republic. *Public Law*, 1970, 251–276.
Nickel, J. (2005). Who Needs Freedom of Religion? *University of Colorado Law Review*, 76 (4), 941–964.
Nickel, J. (2007). *Making Sense of Human Rights*, 2nd edn, Oxford: Blackwell.

Nickel, J. (2013). Goals and Rights: Working Together? In M. Langford et al., eds., *The MDGs and Human Rights: Past, Present, and Future.* Cambridge: Cambridge University Press, pp. 38–48.

Nicolaïdis, K. (2012). The Idea of European Demoi-cracy. In J. Dickson, & P. Eleftheriadis, eds., *Philosophical Foundations of European Union Law.* Oxford: Oxford University Press, pp. 247–274.

Niemeyer, S. (2014). Scaling Up Deliberation to Mass Publics: Harnessing Mini-Publics in a Deliberative System. In K. Grönlund, A. Bächtiger, & M. Setälä, eds., *Deliberative Mini-Publics: Involving Citizens in the Democratic Process.* Colchester: ECPR Press, pp. 177–201.

Nino, C. (1997). *The Constitution of Deliberative Democracy*, New Haven: Yale University Press.

Nkrumah, K. (1996). *Consciencism: Philosophy and Ideology for De-Colonization*, 2nd edn, New York: Monthly Review Press.

Nolte, D., & Schilling-Vacaflor, A., eds. (2012). *New Constitutionalism in Latin America: Promises and Practices*, London, New York: Routledge.

Norman, W. (2006). *Negotiating Nationalism: Nation-Building, Federalism, and Secession in the Multinational State*, Oxford: Oxford University Press.

Norocel, O. C., & Baluta, I. (2021). Retrogressive Mobilization in the 2018 "Referendum for Family" in Romania. *Problems of Postcommunism*, 70 (2), 1–10.

North, D. (1993). Institutions and Credible Commitment. *Journal of Institutional and Theoretical Economics (JITE) / Zeitschrift Für Die Gesamte Staatswissenschaft*, 149 (1), 11–23.

North, D., & Weingast, B. (1989). Constitutions and Commitment: The Evolution of Institutions Governing Public Choice in Seventeenth-Century England. *The Journal of Economic History*, 49 (4), 803–832.

North, D., Wallis, J., & Weingast, B. (2009). *Violence and Social Orders*, Cambridge: Cambridge University Press.

Nosek, G. (2018). Climate Change Litigation and Narrative: How to Use Litigation to Tell Compelling Climate Stories. *William & Mary Environmental Law and Policy Review*, 42 (3), 733–804.

Novak, W. N. (2018). The Progressive Idea of Democratic Administration. *University of Pennsylvania Law Review*, 167 (7), 1823–1848.

Nozick, R. (1974). *Anarchy, State, and Utopia*, New York: Basic Books.

Nuffield Council on Bioethics. (2016). *Genome Editing: An Ethical Review.* London: Nuffield Council on Bioethics.

Nussbaum, M. (1990). Aristotelian Social Democracy. In R. B. Douglass, G. M. Mara, & H. S. Richardson, eds., *Liberalism and the Good.* New York: Routledge. pp. 203–252.

Nussbaum, M. (1995). *Poetic Justice*, Boston: Beacon Press.

Nussbaum, M. (2006). *Frontiers of Justice. Disability, Nationality, Species Membership*, Cambridge, MA: Harvard University Press.

Nussbaum, M. (2011). *Creating Capabilities: The Human Development Approach*, Cambridge, MA: Harvard University Press.

Nussbaum, M. (2019). Civil Disobedience and Free Speech. In J. Lackey, ed., *Academic Freedom.* Oxford: Oxford University Press, pp. 170–185.

Nye, J. (1990). Soft Power. *Foreign Policy*, 80, 153–171.

Oakeshott, M. (1996). *The Politics of Faith and the Politics of Scepticism*, New Haven, London: Yale University Press.

Oberman, K. (2016). Immigration as a Human Right. In S. Fine and L. Ypi, eds., *Migration in Political Theory: The Ethics of Movement and Membership.* Oxford: Oxford University Press, pp. 32–56.

Ochoa Espejo, P. (2011). *The Time of Popular Sovereignty: Process and the Democratic State*, University Park: Penn State University Press.
O'Donnell, G. (2004). Why the Rule of Law Matters. *Journal of Democracy*, 15 (4), 32–46.
O'Donoghue, A. (2014). *Constitutionalism in Global Constitutionalisation*, Cambridge: Cambridge University Press.
O'Donovan, O. (2007). *The Ways of Judgment*, Grand Rapids: Eerdmans Publishing.
OECD. (2017). *Behavioural Insights and Public Policy: Lessons from Around the World*, Paris: OECD.
OECD. (2018). *Regulatory Policy Review*, Paris: OECD.
O'Flynn, I. (2017). Pulling Together: Shared Intentions, Deliberative Democracy and Deeply Divided Societies. *British Journal of Political Science*, 47 (1), 187–202.
Ogien, A. (2015). La désobéissance civile peut-elle être un droit? *Droit et société*, 3 (91), 579–592.
Okin, S. (1989). *Justice, Gender and the Family*, New York: Basic Books.
Oklopcic, Z. (2019). Imagined Ideologies: Populist Figures, Liberalist Projections, and the Horizons of Constitutionalism. *German Law Journal*, 20 (2), 201–224.
O'Leary, B. (2019). Consociation in the Present. *Swiss Political Science Review* 25 (4), 556–574.
O'Leary, K. (2006). *Saving Democracy: A Plan for Real Representation in America*, Stanford: Stanford University Press.
Oliver, D. (1999). *Common Values and the Public-Private Divide*, Cambridge: Cambridge University Press.
Olsen, F. (1995). *Feminist Legal Theory*. 2 vols. New York: New York University Press.
Olsen, F. (2005). Civil Disobedience for Social Change. *Griffith Law Review*, 14 (2), 213–226.
O'Neill, O. (1989). *Constructions of Reason. Explorations of Kant's Practical Philosophy*, Cambridge: Cambridge University Press.
O'Neill, M. 2016. What We Owe Each Other: T.M. Scanlon's Egalitarian Philosophy. *Boston Review*, June 2. Available from: www.bostonreview.net/articles/martin-oneill-tm-scanlon-inequality/.
O'Neill, M., & White, S. (2018). Trade Unions and Political Equality. In H. Collins, G. Lester, & V. Mantouvalou, eds., *Philosophical Foundations of Labour Law*. Oxford: Oxford University Press, pp. 252–268.
Ongena, S., & Popov, A. (2016). Gender Bias and Credit Access. *Journal of Money, Credit and Banking*, 48 (8), 1691–1724.
O'Regan, K. (2017). The Constitution and Administrative Law: Insights from South Africa's Constitutional Journey. *Admin Law Blog*. Available from: adminlawblog.org/2017/04/12
Orphanides, A. (2017). *ECB Monetary Policy and Euro Area Governance: Collateral Eligibility Criteria for Sovereign Debt*. Working Paper No. 5258–17. Cambridge, MA: MIT Sloan School.
Orren, K., & Skowronek, S. (2004). *The Search for American Political Development*, New York: Cambridge University Press.
Osofsky, H. M. (2007). The Inuit Petition as a Bridge? Beyond Dialectics of Climate Change and Indigenous Peoples' Rights. *American Indian Law Review*, 31 (2), 675–697.
Osofsky, H. M. (2011). Diagonal Federalism and Climate Change Implications for the Obama Administration. *Alabama Law Review*, 62 (2), 237–303.
Osterkamp, J. (2009). *Verfassungsgerichtsbarkeit in der Tschechoslowakei (1920–1939): Verfassungsidee, Demokratieverständnis, Nationalitätenproblem*, Frankfurt-am-Main: Vittorio Klostermann.
Ostler J. (2019). *Surviving Genocide: Native Nations and the United States from the American Revolution to Bleeding Kansas*, New Haven: Yale University Press.

Ostrogorski, M. (1902). *Democracy and the Organization of Political Parties*, 2 vols. Translated by F. Clarke. Preface by James Bryce. London: Macmillan and Co.

Ottolenghi, E. (2001). Why Direct Election Failed in Israel. *Journal of Democracy*, 12 (4), 109–122.

Owen, D., & Smith, G. (2018). Sortition, Rotation, and Mandate: Conditions for Political Equality and Deliberative Reasoning. *Politics & Society*, 46 (3), 419–434.

Ozouf, M. (1989). Revolution. In F. Furet, & M. Ozouf, eds., *A Critical Dictionary of the French Revolution*. Translated by Arthur Goldhammer. Cambridge, MA: Harvard University Press, pp. 806–817.

Pacheco, J. F. (1845). Lecciones de Derecho Político Constitucional, Madrid: [s.n.].

Paddock, R. (2020). U.N. Court Orders Myanmar to Protect Rohingya Muslims. *The New York Times*, January 23, sec. World. Available from: www.nytimes.com/2020/01/23/world/asia/myanmar-rohingya-genocide.html.

Page, E. (2001). *Governing by Numbers: Delegated Legislation and Everyday Policymaking*, Oxford: Hart Publishing.

Paine, T. (1995 [1791]). *Rights of Man, Common Sense, and Other Political Writings*. Edited by Mark Philp. Oxford: Oxford University Press.

Pal, M. (2016). Electoral Management Bodies as a Fourth Branch of Government. *Review of Constitutional Studies*, 21 (1), 85–113.

Pal, M. (2020). Social Media and Democracy: Challenges for Election Law and Administration in Canada.*Election Law Journal*, 19 (2), 111–261.

Pal, M., & Choudhry, S. (2014). Still Not Equal? Visible Minority Vote Dilution in Canada. *Canadian Political Science Review*, 8 (1), 85–101.

Palermo, F., & Kössler, K. (2017). *Comparative Federalism: Constitutional Arrangements and Case Law*, Oxford: Hart Publishing.

Paley, W. (2002). *The Principles of Moral and Political Philosophy*, Indianapolis: Liberty Fund.

Palladin, L. (2008). *Saggi di storia costituzionale*, Bologna: Il Mulino.

Palmer R. R. (2014). *The Age of the Democratic Revolution: A Political History of Europe and America, 1760–1800*, Princeton: Princeton University Press.

Panayotu, P. (2017). Towards a Transnational Populism: A Chance for European Democracy (?) The Case of DiEM25. *Populismus* Working Paper No. 5.

Pappe, I. (2006). *The Ethnic Cleansing of Palestine*, Oxford: OneWorld Publications.

Parau, C. E. (2018). *Transnational Networking and Elite Self-Empowerment: The Making of the Judiciary in Contemporary Europe and Beyond*, Oxford: Oxford University Press.

Parekh, B. (1981). *Hannah Arendt and the Search for a New Political Philosophy*, London: Palgrave Macmillan.

Parekh, B. (2004). *Rethinking Multiculturalism: Cultural Diversity and Political Theory*, Basingstoke: Palgrave.

Parfit, D. (1997). Equality and Priority. *Ratio*, 10 (3), 202–221.

Parrillo, N. (2014). *Against the Profit Motive: The Salary Revolution in American Government, 1780–1940*, New Haven: Yale University Press.

Parkinson, J. (2006). *Deliberating in the Real World: Problems of Legitimacy in Deliberative Democracy*, Oxford: Oxford University Press.

Parkinson, J. (2020). The Roles of Referendums in Deliberative Systems. *Representation: Journal of Representative Democracy*, 56 (4), 485–500.

Parra, O. (2016). The Protection of Social Rights. In J. Bertomeu, & R. Gargarella, eds., *The Latin American Casebook*. London: Routledge, pp. 147–171.

Pasquino, P. (1998). Locke on King's Prerogative. *Political Theory*, 26 (2), 198–208.

Pateman, C. (1970). *Participation and Democratic Theory*, Cambridge: Cambridge University Press.
Pateman, C. (1988). The Patriarchal Welfare State. In Amy Gutmann, ed., *Democracy and the Welfare State*. Princeton: Princeton University Press.
Pateman, C. (2018). *The Sexual Contract*, Palo Alto: Stanford University Press.
Patberg, M. (2016). Against Democratic Intergovernmentalism: The Case for a Theory of Constituent Power in the Global Realm. *International Journal of Constitutional Law*, 14 (3), 622–638.
Patten, A. (2002). Democratic Secession from a Multinational State. *Ethics*, 112 (3), 558–586.
Patten, A. (2006). The Humanist Roots of Linguistic Nationalism. *History of Political Thought*, 27 (2), 223–262.
Patten, A. (2014). *Equal Recognition: The Moral Foundations of Minority Rights*, Princeton: Princeton University Press.
Patterson, D. (2021). Dworkin's Critique of Hart's Positivism. In T. Spaak, & P. Mendus, eds., *The Cambridge Companion to Legal Positivism*. Cambridge: Cambridge University Press, pp. 675–594.
Pavel, C. (2015). *Divided Sovereignty: International Institutions and the Limits of State Authority*, Oxford: Oxford University Press.
Pavel, C. (2021a). *Law Beyond the State: Dynamic Coordination, State Consent, and Binding International Law*, New York: Oxford University Press.
Pavel, C. (2021b). The Rule of Law and the Limits of Anarchism. *Legal Theory*, 27 (1), 70–95.
Peake, G. (2003). From Warlords to Peacelords? *Journal of International Affairs*, 56 (2), 181–191.
Pedersen, J. (2008). Habermas' Method: Rational Reconstruction. *Philosophy of Social Sciences*, 38 (4), pp. 457–485.
Peel, J., & Lin, J. (2019). Transnational Climate Litigation: The Contribution of the Global South. *The American Journal of International Law*, 113 (4), 679–726.
Peel, J., & Osofsky, H. M. (2015). *Climate Change Litigation: Regulatory pathways to cleaner energy*, Cambridge: Cambridge University Press.
Peel, J., & Osofsky, H. M. (2018). A Rights Turn in Climate Litigation? *Transnational Environmental Law*, 7 (1), 37–67.
Peer, N. O. (2019). Negotiating the Lender of Last Resort: The 1913 Federal Reserve Act as a Debate Over Credit Distribution. *New York University Journal of Law & Business*, 15 (2), 367–452.
Peled, Y. (2018). Language Barriers and Epistemic Injustice in Healthcare Settings. *Bioethics*, 32 (6), 360–367.
Pennington, K. (1993). *The Prince and the Law 1200–1600: Sovereignty and Rights in the Western Legal Tradition*, Berkeley: University of California Press.
Pérez-Liñán, A. (2020). Narratives of Executive Downfall: Recall, Impeachment, or Coup? In Y. Welp and L. Whitehead, eds., *The Politics of Recall Elections*. Basingstoke: Palgrave Macmillan, pp. 201–228.
Perreau, B. (2021). Les Analogies Du Genre: Différance, Intrasectionallité et Droit. In C. Bosvieux-Onyekwelu and V. Mottier, eds., *Genre, Droit et Politique*. Paris: LGDJ.
Perry, A. (2015). The Crown's Administrative Powers. *Law Quarterly Review* 131, 652–672.
Perry, A. (2017). Plan B: A Theory of Judicial Review. *Oxford Legal Studies Research Paper*, No. 66/2017, 22. Available at: https://papers.ssrn.com/sol3/papers.cfm?abstract_id=3075886 (Accessed: 31 August 2019).
Perry, A., & Ahmed, F. (2014). The Coherence of the Doctrine of Legitimate Expectations. *Cambridge Law Journal* 73 (1), 61–85.

Perry, A., & Tucker, P. (2018). Top-Down Constitutional Conventions. *Modern Law Review*, 81 (5), 765–789.
Perse, H., & Warren, M., eds. (2007). *Designing Deliberative Democracy: The British Columbia Citizens' Assembly*, Cambridge: Cambridge University Press.
Pescatore, P. (1983). The Doctrine of "Direct Effect": An Infant Disease of Community Law. *European Law Review*, 8, 155–177.
Peter, F. (2009). *Democratic Legitimacy*, New York: Routledge.
Peters, A. (2006). Compensatory Constitutionalism: The Function and Potential of Fundamental International Norms and Structures. *Leiden Journal of International Law*, 19 (3), 579–610.
Peters, A. (2009a). Dual Democracy. In J. Klabbers, A. Peters, & G. Ulfstein, *The Constitutionalization of International Law*. Oxford: Oxford University Press, pp. 263–341.
Peters, A. (2009b). Membership in the Global Constitutional Community. In J. Klabbers, A. Peters, & G. Ulfstein, eds., *Constitutionalization of International Law*, Oxford: Oxford University Press, pp. 153–262.
Peters, A. (2011). The Constitutionalisation of International Organisations. In N. Walker, J. Shaw, & S. Tierney, eds., *Europe's Constitutional Mosaic*. Oxford: Hart, pp. 264–266.
Peters, A. (2013). Das Gründungsdokument internationaler Organisationen als Verfassungsvertrag. *Zeitschrift für öffentliches Recht*, 68 (1), 1–57.
Peters, A. (2016). International Organizations and International Law. In J. K. Cogan, I. Hurd, & I. Johnstone, eds., *The Oxford Handbook of International Organizations*. Oxford: Oxford University Press, pp. 33–59.
Peters, A. (2018). Global Constitutionalism: The Social Dimension. In T. Suami, A. Peters, D. Vanoverbeke, & M. Kumm, eds., *Global Constitutionalism from European and East Asian Perspectives*. Cambridge: Cambridge University Press, pp. 277–350.
Petersmann, E.-U. (2007). Multilevel Judicial Governance of International Trade Requires a Common Conception of Rule of Law and Justice. *Journal of International Economic Law*, 10 (3), 529–552.
Pettit, P. (1996). Freedom and Antipower. *Ethics*, 106 (3), 76–604.
Pettit, P. (1997). *Republicanism: A Theory of Freedom and Government*, Oxford: Oxford University Press.
Pettit, P. (2008). Freedom and Probability: A Comment on Goodin and Jackson. *Philosophy and Public Affairs*, 36 (2), 206–220.
Pettit, P. (2012). *On the People's Terms: A Republican Theory and Model of Democracy*, Cambridge: Cambridge University Press.
Pettit, P. (2014). *Just Freedom: A Moral Compass for a Complex World*, New York: W.W. Norton & Company.
Pettit, P. (2015). Justice, Social and Political. In D. Sobel, P. Vallentyne, & S. Wall, eds., *Oxford Studies in Political Philosophy*, vol. I. Oxford: Oxford University Press, pp. 9–35.
Pettit, P. (2019). Analyzing Concepts and Allocating Referents. In A. Burgess, H. Cappelen, & D. Plunkett, eds., *Conceptual Engineering and Conceptual Ethics*. Oxford: Oxford University Press, pp. 333–357.
Pettit, P. (2023). *The State*, Princeton: Princeton University Press.
Pevnick, R. (2011). *Immigration and the Constraints of Justice: Between Open Borders and Absolute Sovereignty*, Cambridge: Cambridge University Press.
Peyrefitte, A. (1997). *C'était de Gaulle*, vol. 1, Paris: Fayard.
Philippopoulos-Mihalopoulos, A. 2011. Towards a Critical Environmental Law. In Philippopoulos-Mihalopoulos, Andreas, ed., *Law and Ecology: New Environmental Foundations*. London: Routledge, pp. 18–38.

Phillips, A. (1995). *The Politics of Presence*, Oxford: Oxford University Press.
Phillips, T., Holmes, O., & Bowcott, O. (2016). Beijing Rejects Tribunal's Ruling in South China Sea Case. *The Guardian*, July 12, sec. World news. Available from: www.theguardian.com/world/2016/jul/12/philippines-wins-south-china-sea-case-against-china.
Phillipson, G. (2019). Indeterminate, inaccessible, illegitimate: Three weaknesses constitutional conventions bring to the unwritten constitution. Working Paper. Bristol University.
Piana, D. (2010). *Judicial Accountabilities in New Europe: From Rule of Law to Quality of Justice*, London: Routledge.
Pierce, R. J. (1985). The Role of Constitutional and Political Theory in Administrative Law. *Texas Law Review*, 64 (3), 469–529.
Pierce, Jr., R., Shapiro, S., & Verkuil, P. (2014). *Administrative Law and Process*, 6th edn, St. Paul: West Academic.
Pierson, P. (2011). *Politics in Time*, Princeton: Princeton University Press.
Piketty, T. (2018). Brahmin Left vs, Merchant Right: Rising Inequality & the Changing Structure of Political Conflict (Evidence from France, Britain and the US, 1948–2017). *WID.world WORKING PAPER SERIES* N° 2018/7 (Accessed: 1 March 2020).
Pillay, A. (2019). The Constitution of the Republic of India. In R. Masterman, & R. Schütze, eds., *The Cambridge Companion to Comparative Constitutional Law*. Cambridge: Cambridge University Press, pp. 141–170.
Pincock, H. (2018). Can Democratic States Justify Restricting the Rights of Persons with Mental Illness? Presumption of Competence, Voting, and Voting Rights. *Politics, Groups, and Identities*, 6 (1), 20–38.
Pincus, S. (2009). *1688: The First Modern Revolution*, New Haven: Yale University Press.
Pinelli, C. (2011). The Populist Challenge to Constitutional Democracy. *European Constitutional Law Review*, 7 (1), 5–6.
Pinker, S. (2008). The Stupidity of Dignity. *The New Republic*, May 28.
Pinnow, C. (2022). Monetary-Policy Delegation for Democrats. Critical Review of International Social and Political Philosophy. Online Ahead of Print. DOI: 10.1080/13698230.2022.2108228
Pinto, A. C. (2017). *Corporatism and Fascism: The Corporatist Wave in Europe*, London: Routledge.
Pisarello, G: (2007). *Los derechos sociales y sus garantías*, Madrid: Trotta.
Pistor, K. (2013). A Legal Theory of Finance. *Journal of Comparative Economics*, 41 (2), 315–330.
Pitkin, H. F. (1967). *The Concept of Representation*, Berkeley: University of California Press.
Pitkin, H. F. (2004). Representation and Democracy: Uneasy Alliance. *Scandinavian Political Studies*, 27 (3), 335–342.
Plant, R. (2010). *The Neoliberal State*, Oxford: Oxford University Press.
Plato. (1992). *Statesman*. Translated by J.B. Skemp. Edited by M. Ostwald. Indianapolis and Cambridge: Hackett Publishing.
Plato. (1997). Gorgias. In J. M. Cooper ed., *Plato: Complete Works*. Indianapolis and Cambridge: Hackett Publishing, pp. 791–869.
Plato. (2000). *The Republic*. Edited by G. R. F. Ferrari. Translated by Tom Griffith. Cambridge: Cambridge University Press.
Plotke, D. (1997). Representation Is Democracy. *Constellations*, 4 (1), 19–34.
Pochet, Philippe (2019). *À la recherche de l'Europe sociale*, Paris: Presses Universitaires de France.
Pocock, J. G. A. (1987). *The Ancient Constitution and the Feudal Law: A Study of English Historical Thought in the Seventeeth Century*, Cambridge: Cambridge University Press.
Pocock, J. G. A. (1995). The Ideal of Citizenship Since Classical Times. In R. Beiner, ed., *Theorizing Citizenship*. Albany: State University of New York Press, pp. 29–52.

Poguntke, T., & Webb, P., (2005) eds. *The Presidentialization of Politics: A Comparative Study of Modern Democracies.* Oxford University Press.

Pogge, T. (2003). Accommodation Rights for Hispanics in the U.S. In W. Kymlicka, & A. Patten, eds., *Language Rights and Political Theory.* Oxford: Oxford University Press, pp. 105–122.

Poggi, G. (1990). *The State. Its Nature, Development and Prospects,* Cambridge: Polity Press.

Polanyi, K. (2001 [1944]). *The Great Transformation: The Political and Economic Origins of Our Time,* Boston: Beacon Press.

Polsby, N. W. (1997). Political Opposition in the United States. *Government and Opposition,* 32 (4), 511–527.

Poole, T. (2003). Back to the Future? Unearthing the Theory of Common Law Constitutionalism. *Oxford Journal of Legal Studies,* 23 (3), 435–454.

Poole, T. (2005). Questioning Common Law Constitutionalism. *Legal Studies,* 25 (1), 142–163.

Poole, T. (2010). Proportionality in Perspective. *New Zealand Law Review,* 2010 (2), 369–391.

Poole, T. (2015). *Reason of State: Law, Prerogative and Empire,* Cambridge: Cambridge University Press.

Poole, T. (2019). The Executive Power Project. Available from: www.lrb.co.uk/blog/2019/april/the-executive-power-project

Poole, T. (2020). The Idea of the Federative. In J. Bomhoff, D. Dyzenhaus, & T. Poole, eds., *The Double-Facing Constitution.* Cambridge: Cambridge University Press, pp. 54–93.

Popova, M. (2012). *Politicized Justice in Emerging Democracies: A study of Courts in Russia and Ukraine,* New York: Cambridge University Press.

Popper, K. (2011 [1945]), *The Open Society and Its Enemies,* London: Routledge.

Porter, T. (2019). Donald Trump Is Not "Unwitting Agent" to Russia, "Knows Exactly What He Is Doing" Says House Intelligence Democrat. *Newsweek,* 16 January. Available at: www.newsweek.com/donald-trump-not-unwitting-agent-russia-knows-exactly-what-he-doing-says-1293373

Portes A, & Hao L. (2002). The Price of Uniformity: Language, Family, and Personality Adjustment in the Immigrant Second Generation. *Ethnic and Racial Studies,* 25 (6), 889–912.

Posner, R. (1974). Theories of Economic Regulation. *Bell Journal of Econmics and Management Science,* 5 (2), 335–358.

Posner, R. (2003). *Law, Pragmatism, and Democracy,* Cambridge, MA: Harvard University Press.

Posner, R. (2006). *Not a Suicide Pact: The Constitution in Times of Emergency,* New York: Oxford University Press.

Posner, E., & Vermeule, A. (2002). Legislative Entrenchment: A Reappraisal. *Yale Law Journal,* 111 (7), 1165–1706.

Posner, E., & Vermeule, A. (2005). Accommodating Emergencies. In M. Tushnet, ed., *The Constitution in Wartime: Beyond Alarmism and Complacency,* Durham: Duke University Press, pp. 55–93.

Posner, E., & Vermeuele, A. (2010). *The Executive Unbound: After the Madisonian Republic,* Oxford: Oxford University Press.

Post, G. (1964). *Studies in Medieval Legal Thought: Public Law and the State 1100–1322,* Princeton: Princeton University Press.

Post, R. (2023). The Taft Court: Making Law for a Divided Nation, 1921–1930, Volume X of *the Oliver Wendell Holmes Devise History of the Supreme Court of the United States,* Cambridge: Cambridge University Press.

Postema, G. (2014). Fidelity in Law's Commonwealth. In L. Austin, & D. Klimchuk, eds., *The Rule of Law and Private Law*. Oxford: Oxford University Press, pp. 17–40.
Postema, G. (2022). *Law's Rule: The Nature, Value, and Viability of the Rule of Law*, Oxford: Oxford University Press.
Pottage, A. (2012). The Materiality of What? *Journal of Law and Society*, 39 (1), 167–183.
Potter, A. (1966). Great Britain: Opposition with a Capital "O". In R. Dahl, ed., *Political Oppositions in Western Democracies*. New Haven: Yale University Press.
Powell, B. (2000). *Elections as Instruments of Democracy. Majoritarian and Proportional Visions*, New Haven: Yale University Press.
Powell, W. W. (1990). Neither Markets nor Hierarchies: Network Forms of Organization. *Research in Oragnizational Behaviour*, 12, 295–336.
Powell, W. W., & di Maggio, P. J. (1992). *The New Institutionalism in Organizational Analysis*, Chicago: University of Chicago Press.
Power, M. (1997). *The Audit Society: Rituals of Verification*. Oxford: Oxford University Press.
Pozas-Loyo, A., & Rios-Figueroa, J. (2018). Anatomy of an Informal Institution: The "Gentlemen's Pact" and Judicial Selection in Mexico, 1917–1994. *International Political Science Review*, 39 (5), 647–661.
Pozas-Loyo, A., & Rios-Figueroa, J. (2022). Instituciones informales e independencia judicial de facto. El eslabón olvidado en el camino hacia la eficacia institucional. *Política y gobierno*, 29 (2), 1–27.
Pozen, D. E. (2019). Hardball and/as Anti-Hardball. *New York University Journal of Legislation & Public Policy*, 21 (4), 949–955.
Prakash, S. B. (2020). *The Living Presidency: An Originalist Argument against Its Ever-Expanding Powers*, Cambridge: The Belknap Press of Harvard University Press.
President's Committee on Administrative Management (PCAM). (1937). *Administrative Management in the Government of the United States*, Washington, DC: United States Government Printing Office.
Presidential executive order on restoring state, tribal, and local law enforcement's access to life-saving equipment and resources. *Federal Register* 82, 168, Executive Order 13809 of August 28 (2017).
Preuss, U. K. (1994). Constitutional Powermaking for the New Polity: Some Deliberations on the Relations Between Constituent Power and the Constitution. In M. Rosenfeld, ed., *Constitutionalism, Identity, Difference, and Legitimacy: Theoretical Perspectives*. Duke University Press, pp. 143–164.
Prins, N. (2018). *Collusion: How Central Bankers Rigged the World*, New York: Nation Books.
Pritchard, M. (1972). Human Dignity and Justice. *Ethics*, 82 (4), 299–313.
Przeworski, A. (2010). *Democracy and the Limits of Self-Government*, Cambridge: Cambridge University Press.
Przeworski, A. (2018). *Why Bother with Elections?* Medford: Polity Press.
Przeworski, A. (2019). *Crises of Democracy*, Cambridge: Cambridge University Press.
Psygkas, A. (2017). *From the "emocratic Deficit" to a "Democratic Surplus": Constructing Administrative Democracy in Europe*, Oxford: Oxford University Press.
Puetter, U. (2014). *European Council and the Council*, Oxford: Oxford University Press.
Pünder, H. (2014). Administrative Procedure – Mere Facilitator of Material Law versus Cooperative Realization of Common Welfare. In H. Pünder, & C. Waldhoff, eds., *Debates in German Public Law*. Oxford: Hart Publishing, pp. 239–260.
Pünder, H. (2015). More Government with the People: The Crisis of Representative Democracy and Options for Reform in Germany. *German Law Journal*, 16, 713–740.

Punnett, R. M. (1973). *Front-Bench Opposition: The Role of the Leader of the Opposition, the Shadow Cabinet and the Shadow Government in British Politics*, New York: St. Martin's Press.
Quah, J. (2011). *Curbing Corruption in Asian Countries; An Impossible Dream?* Portland: Emerald Group Publishing.
Quinn, S. L. (2019). *American Bonds: How Credit Markets Shaped a Nation*, Princeton: Princeton University Press.
Quong, J. (2011). *Liberalism without Perfection*, Oxford: Oxford University Press.
Quong, J. (2017). Public Reason. In E. Zalta, *Stanford Encyclopaedia of Philosophy*. Available from: https://plato.stanford.edu/entries/public-reason/
Qvortrup, M. (2006). Democracy by Delegation: The Decision to Hold Referendums in the United Kingdom. *Representation* 42 (1), 59–72.
Qvortrup, M. (2014). *Referendums and Ethnic Conflict*, Philadelphia: Pennsylvania University Press.
Rabe, B. (2011). Contested Federalism and American Climate Policy. *The Journal of Federalism*, 41 (3), 494–521.
Rabushka, A., & Shepsle, K. (1971). Political Entrepreneurship and Patterns of Democratic Instability in Plural Societies. *Race and Class* 12 (4), 461–476.
Radin, M. (1942). Martial Law and the State of Siege, *California Law Review*, 30 (6), 634–647.
Rahman, K. S. (2016). *Democracy Against Domination*, New York: Oxford University Press.
Ramakrishnan, K., & Colbern, A. (2019). *Progressive State Citizenship*, New York: Cambridge University Press.
Ramseyer, J. M. (1994). The Puzzling (In)dependence of Courts: A Comparative Approach. *Journal of Legal Studies*, 23 (2), 721–747.
Ramseyer, J. M., & Rasmusen, E. B. (1997). Judicial Independence in a Civil Law Regime: The Evidence From Japan. *The Journal of Law, Economics, & Organization*, 13 (2), 259–286.
Rao, N. (2008). On the Use and Abuse of Dignity in Constitutional Law. *Columbia Journal of European Law*, 14 (2), 201–255.
Raskin, J. B. (1993). Legal Aliens, Local Citizens: The Historical, Constitutional and Theoretical Meanings of Alien Suffrage. *University of Pennsylvania Law Review*, 141 (4), 1391–1470.
Rathja, J. (2012). *Authoritarian Rule of Law: Legislation, Discourse and Legitimacy in Singapore*, Cambridge: Cambridge University Press.
Ratner, S. (2015). *The Thin Justice of International Law: A Moral Reckoning of the Law of Nations*, Oxford: Oxford University Press.
Rave, D. (2018). Two Problems of Fiduciary Government. In Criddle et al. pp.
Rawlings, R. (2008). Modelling Judicial Review. *Current Legal Problems*, 61 (1), 95–123.
Rawls, J. (1971). *A Theory of Justice*, Oxford: Oxford University Press.
Rawls, J. (1993). *Political Liberalism*, New York: Columbia University Press.
Rawls, J. (1996). *Political Liberalism*. Columbia University Press
Rawls, J. (1999a). *A Theory of Justice*, rev. edn, Cambridge, MA: Harvard University Press.
Rawls, J. (1999b). *The Law of Peoples*, Cambridge, MA: Harvard University Press.
Rawls, J. (2001). *Justice as Fairness: A Restatement*, Cambridge, MA: Belknap Press of Harvard University Press.
Rawls, J. (2005). *Political Liberalism*, expanded edn, New York: Columbia University Press.
Raz, J. (1972). Legal Principles and the Limits of the Law. *Yale Law Journal*, 81 (5), 823–854.
Raz, J. (1979a). *The Authority of Law: Essays on Law and Morality*, Oxford: Clarendon Press.

Raz, J. (1979b). The Rule of Law and Its Virtue. In J. Raz ed., *The Authority of Law: Essays in Legal Philosophy*. Oxford: Clarendon Press, pp. 210–229.
Raz, J. (1986). *The Morality of Freedom*, Oxford: Oxford University Press.
Raz, J. (1992). The Relevance of Coherence. *Boston University Law Review*, 72 (2), 273–321.
Raz, J. (1994). Rights and Individual Well-Being. In *Ethics in the Public Domain*. Oxford: Oxford University Press, pp. 43–59.
Raz, J. (1998). On the Authority and Interpretation of Constitutions: Some Preliminaries. In L. Alexander, ed., *Constitutionalism: Philosophical Foundations*. Cambridge: Cambridge University Press, pp. 152–193.
Raz, J. (2009). Intentions in Interpretation. In J. Raz ed., *Between Authority and Interpretation: On the Theory of Law and Practical Reason*. Oxford: Oxford University Press, pp. 265–298.
Raz, J. (2015). Human Rights in the Emerging World Order. In R. Cruft, M. Liao, & M. Renzo, eds., *Philosophical Foundations of Human Rights*. Oxford: Oxford University Press, pp. 217–231.
Raz, J. (2019). The Law's Own Virtue. *Oxford Journal of Legal Studies*, 39 (1), 1–15.
Redslob, R. (1912). *Staatstheories der französischen Nationalversammlung von 1789*, Leipzig: von Veit.
Reed, R. (2020). Collective Judging in the UK Supreme Court. In B. Häcker, & W. Ernst, eds., *Collective Judging in Comparative Perspective*, Cambridge: Intersentia, pp. 21–35.
Rehfeld, A. (2005). *The Concept of Constituency*, Cambridge: Cambridge University Press.
Rehnquist, W. H. (1976). The Notion of a Living Constitution. *Texas Law Review*, 54 (4), 693–706.
Reilly, B. (2001). *Democracy in Divided Societies: Electoral Engineering for Conflict Management*, Cambridge: Cambridge University Press.
Reilly, B. (2012). Institutional Designs for Diverse Democracies: Consociationalism, Centripetalism and Communalism Compared. *European Political Science*, 11 (2), 259–270.
Reilly, B. (2020). Cross-ethnic Voting: An Index of Centripetal Electoral Systems. *Government and Opposition*. First view. Available from: https://doi.org/10.1017/gov.2019.36
Reinach, T. (1885). *De l'état de siège*, Paris: François Pichon.
Reitz, J. C. (2006). Political Economy and Separation of Powers. *Transnational Law & Contemporary Problems*, 15 (2), 579–625.
Renan, E. (2018). *What Is a Nation? and Other Political Writings*, New York: Columbia University Press.
Renda, A. (2011). *Law and Economics in the RIA World: Improving the Use of Economic Analysis in Public Policy and Legislation*, Cambridge: Intersentia.
Renwick, A., Palese, M., & Sargeant, J. (2020). Information in Referendum Campaigns: How Can It Be Improved? *Representation*, 56 (4), 521–537.
Resnik, J. (2005). Judicial Selection and Democratic Theory: Demand, Supply, and Life Tenure. *Cardozo Law Review*, 26 (2), 579–658.
Reuchamps, M., & Suiter, J. eds. (2016). *Constitutional Deliberative Democracy in Europe*, Colchester: ECPR Press.
Revkin, A. C. (2012). Beyond Rio: Pursuing "Ecological Citizenship." *The New York Times*. 25 June.
Rhode, D. (1991). *Justice and Gender: Sex Discrimination and the Law*, revised edn, Cambridge, MA: Harvard University Press.
Rice, C. (2013). Defending the Objective List Theory of Well-Being. *Ratio*, 26 (2), 196–211.
Rich, A. (1980). Compulsory Heterosexuality and Lesbian Existence. *Signs* 5 (4), 631–660.
Richardson, H. S. (2002). *Democratic Autonomy: Public Reasoning about the Ends of Policy*, New York: Oxford University Press.

Ricks, M. (2016). *The Money Problem: Rethinking Financial Regulation*, Chicago: University of Chicago Press.
Riker, W. H. (1964). *Federalism: Origin, Operation, Significance*, Boston: Little, Brown.
Riker, W. H. (1982). *Liberalism Against Populism: A Confrontation Between the Theory of Democracy and the Theory of Social Choice*, San Francisco: Waveland Press.
Rios-Figueroa, J., 2006. Judicial Independence and Corruption: An Analysis of Latin America. SSRN. Available from: http://papers.ssrn.com/sol3/papers.cfm?abstract_id=912924
Ripley, R. B. (1967). *Party Leaders in the House of Representatives*, Washington, DC: The Brookings Institution.
Ripple, W. J. et al. (2020). World Scientists' Warning of a Climate Emergency. *BioScience*, 70 (1), 8–12.
Ripstein, A. (2009). *Force and Freedom: Kant's Legal and Political Philosophy*, Cambridge, MA: Harvard University Press.
Ripstein, A., (2016). Reclaiming Proportionality. *Journal of Applied Philosophy*, 22 (2), 24–31.
Ritter J. (1984). *Hegel and the French Revolution: Essays on The Philosophy of Right*. Translated by Richard Dien Winfield. Cambridge, MA: MIT Press.
Roberts, A. (2020). Should We Defend the Administrative State? *Public Administration Review*, 80 (3), 391–401.
Roberts, D. (1997). *Killing the Black Body: Race, Reproduction and the Meaning of Liberty*, New York: Pantheon Books.
Roberts, J. C., & Chemerinsky, E. (2003). Entrenchment of Ordinary Legislation: A Reply to Professors Posner and Vermeule. *California Law Review* 91 (6), 1773–1820.
Roberts, T. M. (2009). *Distant Revolutions: 1848 and the Challenge to American Exceptionalism*, Charlottesville: University of Virginia Press.
Robertson, D. (2010). *The Judge as Political Theorist. Contemporary Constitutional Review*, Princeton: Princeton University Press.
Robertson, D. (2018). The Counter-Majoritan Thesis. In G. Jacobson, & M. Schor, eds., *Comparative Constitutional Theory*. Cheltenham: Edward Elgar, pp. 189–207.
Robinson, M. (2014). Social and Legal Aspects of Climate Change. *Journal of Human Rights and the Environment*, 5, 15–17.
Rodgers, D. T. (1998). *Atlantic Crossings: Social Politics in a Progressive Agency*, Cambridge, MA: Harvard University Press.
Rodgers, D. T. (2000). *Atlantic Crossings: Social Politics in a Progressive Age*. Cambridge, MA: Harvard University Press.
Rodrik, D. (2011). *The Globalization Paradox: Democracy and the Future of the World Economy*, New York, London: W.W. Norton & Company.
Rodríguez-Garavito, C. A., & Arenas, L. (2005). Indigenous Rights, Transnational Activism, and Legal Mobilization: The Struggle of the U'wa People in Colombia. In B. de Sousa Santos, & C. A. Rodríguez-Garavito, eds., *Law and Globalization from Below*. Cambridge: Cambridge University Press, pp. 241–266.
Rolfe, J. (2010). Combating Climate Change with Words: The Effect of Incorporating "Climate Change" into Development-Regulating Laws. *Queensland Environmental Practice Reporter* 15, (70), 164–179.
Romain, P. (1918). *L'état de siège politique*, Albi: Librairie des Orphelins-Apprentis.
Romano, S. (2017). *The Legal Order*, Abingdon: Routledge.
Ronkainen, A., & Sorsa, V.-P. (2018). Quantitative Easing Forever? Financialisation and the Institutional Legitimacy of the Federal Reserve's Unconventional Monetary Policy. *New Political Economy*, 23 (6), 711–727.
Root, H. (1989). Tying the King's Hands. *Rationality and Society*, 1 (2), 240–258.

Rorty, R. (1979). *Philosophy and the Mirror of Nature*, Princeton: Princeton University Press.
Rorty, R. (2012). The Priority of Democracy to Philosophy. In R. Rorty, ed., *Objectivism, Relativism, and Truth*. Cambridge: Cambridge University Press, pp. 175–196.
Rosanvallon, P. (2006). *La contre-démocratie. La politique à l'âge de la défiance*, Paris: Seuil.
Rosanvallon, P. (2011a). *Democratic Legitimacy: Impartiality, Reflexivity, Proximity*. Translated by A. Goldhammer. Princeton: Princeton University Press.
Rosanvallon, P. (2011b). Penser le populisme. *La vie des idees*, January 27. Available from: www.laviedesidees.fr/Penser-le-populisme.html.
Rosanvallon, P. (2018). *Good Government*. Translated by A. Goldhammer. Cambridge, MA: Harvard University Press.
Rose, R., (1984). *Do Parties Make a Difference?* 2nd edn, London: The Macmillan Press.
Rose-Ackerman, S. (1992). *Rethinking the Progressive Agenda: The Reform of the American Regulatory State*, New York: The Free Press.
Rose-Ackerman, S. (1995). *Controlling Environmental Policy; the Limits of Public Law in Germany and the United States*, New Haven: Yale University Press.
Rose-Ackerman, S. (2017). Citizens and Technocrats: An Essay on Trust, Public Participation, and Government Legitimacy. In S. Rose-Ackerman, P. Lindseth, & B. Emerson, eds., *Comparative Administrative Law*. Cheltenham: Elgar, pp. 251–267.
Rose-Ackerman, S. (2021). *Democracy and Executive Power: Policymaking Accountability in the US, the UK, France, and Germany*, New Haven: Yale University Press.
Rose-Ackerman, S., Egidy, S., & Fowkes, J. (2015). *Due Process of Lawmaking: The United States, South Africa, Germany, and the European Union*, Cambridge, UK: Cambridge University Press.
Rose-Ackerman, S., & Palifka, B. (2016). *Corruption and Government: Causes, Consequences, and Reform*, 2nd edn, Cambridge: Cambridge University Press.
Rose-Ackerman, S., & Perroud, T. (2014). Policymaking and Public Law in France: Public Participation, Agency Independence, and Impact Assessment. *The Columbia Journal of European Law*, 19 (2), 225–312.
Rosemont, H. (2004). Whose Democracy? Which Rights? A Confucian Critique of Modern Western Liberalism. In K.-L. Shung, & D. Wong, eds., *Confucian Ethics: A Comparative Study of Self, Autonomy, and Community*. pp. 49–71.
Rosen, M. (2012). *Dignity: Its History and Meaning*, Cambridge, MA: Harvard University Press.
Rosenberg, A. (2004). On the Priority of Intellectual Property Rights, Especially in Biotechnology. *Politics, Philosophy and Economics*, 3 (1), 77–95.
Rosenblum, N. (2008). *On the Side of the Angels: An Appreciation of Parties and Partisanship*, Princeton: Princeton University Press.
Rosenblum, N. (2022). The Anti-fascist Roots of Presidential Administration. *Columbia Law Review*, 122 (1), 1–85.
Rosenbluth, F. M., & Shapiro, I. (2018). *Responsible Parties: Saving Democracy from Itself*, New Haven: Yale University Press.
Rosenne, S. (1966). Is the Constitution of an International Organization an International Treaty? – Reflections on the Codification of the Law of Treaties. *Comunicazioni e studi*, 12 (1), 21–89.
Ross, A. (2018). Post-Revolutionary Politics: The Case of the Prussian Ministry of State. In D. Moggach, & G. Stedman Jones, eds., *The 1848 Revolutions and European Political Thought*. Cambridge: Cambridge University Press, pp. 276–292.
Ross, B. L. (2019). Administrative Constitutionalism as Popular Constitutionalism. *University of Pennsylvania Law Review*, 167 (7), 1783–1823.

Rossiter, C., ed. (1961). *The Federalist Papers*, New York: New American Library.
Rossiter, C. (1982). *Conservatism in America*, Cambridge, MA: Harvard University Press.
Rossiter, C. (2002 [1948]). *Constitutional Dictatorship: Crisis Government in the Modern Democracies*, New Brunswick: Transaction Publishers.
Roszkowski, T., & Goldsworthy, J. (2012). Symmetric Entrenchment of Manner and Form Requirements. *Public Law Review* 23 (3), 216–222.
Roth, B. (2011). *Sovereign Equality and Moral Disagreement: Premises of a Pluralist International Legal Order*, Oxford: Oxford University Press.
Roth, K. (2001). The Case for Universal Jurisdiction. *Foreign Affairs*, 80 (5), 150–154.
Rothstein, B. (2004). Social Trust and Honesty in Government: A Causal Mechanism Approach. In: J. Kornai, B. Rothstein, & S. Rose-Ackerman, eds., *Creating Social Trust in Post-Socialist Societies*. New York: Palgrave, pp. 13–30.
Rothstein, R. (2017). *The Color of Law: A Forgotten History of How Our Government Segregated America*, W.W. Norton & Company.
Roubier, P. (1929). *Les conflicts de lois dans le temps – Théorie dite de la non-rétroactivité des lois*, vol. I, 2nd edn, Paris: Sirey.
Roughan, N. (2018). The Official Point of View and the Official Claim to Authority. *Oxford Journal of Legal Studies*, 38 (2), 191–216.
Rousseau, D., Gahdoun P.-Y., & Bonnet, J. (2016). *Droit du contentieux constitutionnel*, 11th edn, Paris: LGDJ.
Rousseau, J.-J. (1973). *The Social Contract*. Translated by G. D. H. Cole. London: J. M. Dent & Sons.
Rousseau, J.-J. (1987). The Social Contract. In D. A. Cress ed., *Basic Political Writings*. Indianapolis: Hackett Publishing.
Rousseau, J.-J. (1997 [1762]). The Social Contract. In V. Gourevitch ed., *The Social Contract and Other Later Political Writings*. Cambridge: Cambridge University Press.
Rousseau, J.-J. (2003 [1762]). *On the Social Contract*. Translated by G.D.H. Cole. Mineola: Dover Publications.
Rousseau, J. J. (2004). Letter to Mirabeau. In J. J. Rousseau ed., *The Social Contract and Other Later Political Writings*. Cambridge: Cambridge University Press, pp. 268–271.
Roux, T. (2015). *In Defence of Empirical Entanglement: The Methodological Flaw in Waldron's Case against Judicial Review*, University of New South Wales Working Paper No. 2015–73.
Rowlands, M. (2013). *Animal Rights: All That Matters*, London: Hodder Stoughton.
Roy, S. (2011). *Hamas and Civil Society in Gaza: Engaging the Islamist Social Sector*, Princeton: Princeton University Press.
Roznai, Y. (2017). *Unconstitutional Constitutional Amendments*, Oxford: Oxford University Press.
Rubenfeld, J. (1998). The Moment and the Millennium. *George Washington Law Journal*, 66 (5/6), 1085–1111.
Rubenfeld, J. (2001). *Freedom and Time*, New Haven: Yale University Press.
Rubenstein, K. (1995). Citizenship in Australia: Unscrambling Its Meaning. *Melbourne University Law Review*, 20 (2), 503–527.
Rubin, E. (2005). *Beyond Camelot: Rethinking Politics and Law for the Modern State*, Princeton: Princeton University Press.
Rubinelli, L. (2018). Taming Sovereignty: Constituent Power in Nineteenth Century French Political Thought. *History of European Ideas*, 44 (1), 60–74.
Rubinelli, L. (2019a). Constantion Mortati and the Idea of Material Constitution. *History of Political Thought*, 40 (3), 515–547.

Rubinelli, L. (2019b). How to Think Beyond Sovereignty: One Sieyès and Constituent Power. *European Journal of Political Theory*, 18 (1), 47–67.
Rubinelli, L. (2020). *Constituent Power: A History*, Cambridge: Cambridge University Press.
Rudd, J. B. (2021). Why Do We Think That Inflation Expectations Matter for Inflation? (And Should We?). In *Finance and Economics Discussion Series* (No. 2021–062). Board of Governors of the Federal Reserve System (U.S.).
Rufus Davis, S. (1956). The "Federal Principle" Reconsidered, Part 2. *Australian Journal of Politics and History*, 1 (2), 59–85.
Ruggie, J. G. (1982). International Regimes, Transactions, and Change: Embedded Liberalism in the Postwar Economic Order. *International Organization*, 36 (2), 379–415.
Ruggie, J. (1998). Globalisation and the Embedded Liberalism Compromise, The End of an Era? In W. Streeck, ed., *Internationale Wirtschaft, nationale Demokratie: Herausforderungen für die Demokratietheorie*. Frankfurt-am-Main: Campus, pp. 79–97.
Runciman, D. (1997). *Pluralism and the Personality of the State*, Cambridge: Cambridge University Press.
Rundle, K. (2012). *Forms Liberate: Reclaiming the Jurisprudence of Lon L Fuller*, Oxford and Portland: Hart Publishing.
Russell, M., & Gover, D. (2017). *Legislation at Westminster*, Oxford: Oxford University Press.
Russell, P. H. (2001). Toward a General Theory of Judicial Independence. In P. H. Russell, & D. M. O'Brien, eds., *Judicial Independence in the Age of Democracy: Critical Perspectives from around the World*. Charlottesville: University Press of Virginia, pp. 1–24.
Russell, P. H. (2015). Codifying Conventions. In B. Galligan, & S. Brenton, eds., *Constitutional Conventions in Westminster Systems*. Cambridge: Cambridge University Press, pp. 233–248.
Russell-Brown, K. (2009). *The Color of Crime*, New York: New York University Press.
Ryan, A. (1982). *John Dewey and the High Tide of American Liberalism*, New York: W.W. Norton & Company.
Ryan-Collins, J. (2017). Breaking the Taboo: A History of Monetary Financing in Canada, 1930–1975: Monetary Financing. *The British Journal of Sociology*, 68 (4), 643–669.
Sábato, H. (2010). *Pueblo y política. La construcción de la Argentina moderna*, Buenos Aires: Capital Intelectual.
Sábato, H., & Lettieri, A. (2003). *La vida política en la Argentina del siglo XIX. Armas, votos y voces*, Buenos Aires: Fondo de Cultura Económica.
Sabel, C. F., & Simon, W. H. (2017). Democratic Experimentalism. In J. Desautels-Stein, & C. Tomlins, eds., *Searching for Contemporary Legal Thought*. Cambridge and New York, Cambridge University Press, pp. 477–498.
Sabel, C. F., & Zeitlin, J. (2008). Learning from Difference: The New Architecture of Experimentalist Governance in the EU. *European Law Journal*, 14 (3), 271–327.
Sabl, A. (2002). *Ruling Passions: Political Offices and Democratic Ethics*, Princeton: Princeton University Press.
Sadurski, W. (2019). *Poland's Constitutional Breakdown*, Oxford: Oxford University Press.
Sadurski, W. (2020). Majority Rule, Democracy, and Populism: Theoretical Considerations. Sydney Law School Research Paper 20/01.
Said, E. W. (1993). *Culture & Imperialism*, New York: Vintage Books.
Sajó, A. (1999). *Limiting Government: An Introduction to Constitutionalism*, Budapest: Central European Press.
Sajó, A. (2021). *Ruling by Cheating: Governance in Illiberal Democracy*, Cambridge: Cambridge University Press.
Sajó, A., & Uitz, R. (2017). *The Constitution of Freedom: An Introduction to Legal Constitutionalism*, Oxford: Oxford University Press.

Sampford, C. J. G. (1987). "Recognize and Declare": An Australian Experiment in Codifying Constitutional Conventions. *Oxford Journal of Legal Studies*, 7 (3), 369–420.

Sample, I. (2010). Deep-Sea Trawling Is Destroying Coral Reefs and Pristine Marine Habitats. *The Guardian*. February 18. Available from: www.theguardian.com/environment/2010/feb/18/deep-sea-trawling-coral-reefs.

Samuels, D., & Shugart, M. (2010). *Presidents, Parties, and Prime Ministers – How the Separation of Powers Affects Party Organization and Behavior*, Cambridge: Cambridge University Press.

Sanchez-Sibony, O. (2018). Competitive Authoritarianism in Ecuador under Correa. *Taiwan Journal of Democracy*, 14 (2), 97–120.

Sandalow, T. (1969). Review of *Concerning Dissent and Civil Disobedience*, by A. Fortas. *Michigan Law Review*, 67 (3), 599–612.

Sandel, M. (1996). *Democracy's Discontent: America in Search of a Public Philosophy*, Cambridge, MA: Belknap Press.

Sandel, M. (1998). Religious Liberty: Freedom of Choice or Freedom of Conscience? In R. Bhargava, ed., *Secularism and Its Critics*. Oxford: Oxford University Press.

Santiago Nino, C. (1996). *The Constitution of Deliberative Democracy*, New Haven: Yale University Press.

Sarat, A., Douglas L., & Umphrey M., eds. (2005). *The Limits of Law*, Stanford: Stanford University Press.

Sartori, G. (1962). Constitutionalism: A Preliminary Discussion. *American Political Science Review*, 56 (4). 853–864.

Sartori, G. (1997). *Comparative Constitutional Engineering*, 2nd edn, New York: New York University Press.

Sassen, S. (2002). Towards Post-national and Denationalized Citizenship. In E. F. Isin, & B. S. Turner, eds. *Handbook of Citizenship Studies*. London: Sage. pp. 279–280.

Saunders, C. (2011). *The Constitution of Australia*, Oxford: Hart Publishing.

Saunders, C. (2017). Constitutional Review in Asia: A Comparative Perspective. In A. H. Y. Chen, & A. Harding, eds., *Constitutional Courts in Asia: A Comparative Perspective*. Cambridge: Cambridge University Press, pp. 32–59.

Saunders, C. (2018). Theoretical Underpinnings of Separation of Powers. In G. Jacobson, & M. Schor, eds., *Comparative Constitutional Theory*. Cheltenham: Edward Elgar, pp. 66–85.

Saunders, C. (2019). Global Constitutionalism – Myth and Reality. In J. Varuhas, & S. Stark, eds., *The Frontiers of Public Law*. Oxford: Hart, pp. 19–40.

Saward, M. (2010). *The Representative Claim*, Cambridge: Cambridge University Press.

Sayigh, R. (2007). *The Palestinians: From Peasants to Revolutionaries*, 2nd edn, London & New York: Zed Books.

Sbragia, A. (2008). Comparative Regionalism: What Might It Be? *Journal of Common Market Studies*, 40 (1), 29–49.

Scalia, A (1997). *A Matter of Interpretation: Federal Courts and the Law*, Princeton: Princeton University Press.

Scalia, A., & Garner, B. (2012). *Reading Law: The Interpretation of Legal Texts*, St Paul: Thomson West.

Scanlon, T. (1972). A Theory of Freedom of Expression. *Philosophy and Public Affairs*, 1 (2), 204–226.

Scanlon, T. (1998). *What We Owe to Each Other*, Cambridge, MA: Harvard University Press.

Scanlon, T. (2003). *The Difficult of Tolerance: Essays in Political Philosophy*, Cambridge: Cambridge University Press.

Scanlon, T. (2018). *Why Does Inequality Matter?* Oxford: Oxford University Press.

Schachter, O. (1983). Human Dignity as a Normative Concept. *American Journal of International Law*, 77 (4), 848–854.
Scharpf, F. (1970). *Die politischen Kosten des Rechtsstaats*, Tübingen: J.C.B. Mohr.
Scharpf, F. (1999). *Governing in Europe: Effective or Democratic?* Oxford: Oxford University Press.
Scharpf, F. (2010). The Asymmetry of European Integration, or Why the EU Cannot be a Social Market Economy. *Socio-Economic Review*, 8 (2), 211–250.
Schattschneider, E. E. (1988). *The Semisovereign People: A Realist's View of Democracy in America*, South Melbourne, Victoria: Wadsworth Thomson Learning.
Schattschneider, E. E. (2009). *Party Government*. Introduction by Sidney A. Pearsons. Jr. New Brunswick and London: Transaction Publishers.
Schauer, F. (2006). Legislatures as Rule-Followers. In R. Bauman, & T. Kahana, eds., *The Least Examined Branch: The Role of Legislatures in the Constitutional State*. Cambridge: Cambridge University Press, pp. 468–479.
Schauer, F. (2009–10). When and How (If At All) Does Law Constrain Official Action? *Georgia Law Review*, 44 (3), 769–801.
Scheingold, S. (2004). *The Politics of Rights*, Ann Arbor: University of Michigan Press.
Scheppele, K. L. (2000). The Constitutional Basis of Hungarian Conservatism. *East European Constitutional Review*, 9 (4), 51–57.
Scheppele, K. L. (2005). Small Emergencies. *Georgia Law Review*, 40 (3), 835–862.
Scheppele, K. L. (2008). Legal and Extralegal Emergencies, In K. E. Whittington, R. D. Kelemen, & G. A. Caldeira, eds., *The Oxford Handbook of Law and Politics*. Oxford: Oxford University Press, pp. 164–188.
Scheppele, K. L. (2018). Autocratic Legalism. *University of Chicago Law Review*, 85 (2), 545–583.
Scheppele, K. L. (2019). The Opportunism of Populists and the Defense of Constitutional Liberalism. *German Law Journal*, 20 (3), 314–331.
Schermers, H., & Blokker, N. (2018). *International Institutional Law: Unity within Diversity*, Leiden: Brill.
Scheuerman, W. E. (1994). *Between the Norm and the Exception: The Frankfurt School and the Rule of Law*, Cambridge, MA: MIT Press.
Scheuerman, W. E. (2005). American Kingship? Monarchical Origins of Modern Presidentialism. *Polity*, 37 (1), 24–53.
Scheuerman, W. E. (2006). Survey Article: Emergency Powers and the Rule of Law After 9/11. *The Journal of Political Philosophy*, 14 (1), 61–84.
Scheuerman, W. E. (2018). *Civil Disobedience*, Cambridge, UK, Medford: Polity Press.
Schielke, S. (2015). *Egypt in the Future Tense: Hope, Frustration, and Ambivalence before and after 2011*, Bloomington: Indiana University Press.
Schiller, R. E. (2007). The Era of Deference: Courts, Expertise, and the Emergence of New Deal Administrative Law. *Michigan Law Review*, 106 (3), 399–442.
Schirazi, A. (1997). *The Constitution of Iran: Politics and the State in the Islamic Republic*. Translated by John O'Kane. I.B. London: Tauris Publishers.
Schlesinger, A. (1973). *The Imperial Presidency*, Boston: Houghton Mifflin.
Schlozman, K. L., Brady, H., & Verba, S. (2018). *Unequal and Unrepresented: Political Inequality in the New Gilded Age*, Princeton: Princeton University Press.
Schlozman, K. L., Page B., Verba, S., & Fiorina, M. (2005). Inequality of Political Voice. In L. R. Jacobs, & T. Skocpol, eds., *Inequality and American Democracy*. New York: Russell Sage Foundation, pp. 19–87.
Schmidt, S., & Kelemen, D. (2013). *The Power of the European Court of Justice*, London: Routledge.

Schmidt-Aßmann, E. (1991). Verwaltungslegitimation als Rechtsbegriff. *Archiv des öffentliches Rechts*, 116 (3), 329–390.
Schmidt-Assmann, E. (2004). Der Rechtsstaat. In J. Isensee, & P. Kirchhof, eds, *Handbuch des Staatsrecht der Bundesrepublik Deutschland*. CF Müller 2004.
Schmitt, C. (1928). *Verfassungslehre*, München und Leipzig: Duncker & Humblot.
Schmitt, C. (1958 [1941]). Staat als ein konkreter, an eine geschichtliche Epoche gebundener Begriff. In C. Schmitt ed., *Verfassungsrechtliche Aufsätze aus den Jahren 1924–1954. Materialien zu einer Verfassungslehre*, 4th edn, Berlin: Duncker & Humblot, pp. 375–385.
Schmitt, C. (1963 [1932]). *Der Begriff des Politischen. Text von 1932 mit einem Vorwort und drei Corollarien*, 2nd edn, Berlin: Duncker & Humblot.
Schmitt, C. (1985 [1922]). *Political Theology: Four Chapters on the Concept of Sovereignty*. Translated by G Schwab. Cambridge, MA: MIT Press.
Schmitt, C. (1985 [1926]). *The Crisis of Parliamentary Democracy*. Translated by E. Kennedy. Cambridge, MA: MIT Press.
Schmitt, C. (1991 [1919]). *Political Romanticism*. Translated by G. Oakes. Cambridge, MA: MIT Press.
Schmitt, C. (1996 [1932]). *The Concept of the Political*. Translated by G. Schwab. Chicago: University of Chicago Press.
Schmitt, C. (2004 [1932]). *Legality and Legitimacy*. Translated by J. Seitzer., ed. Durham, Durham, NC: Duke University Press.
Schmitt, C. (2005 [1922]). *Political Theology: Four Chapters on the Concept of Sovereignty*. Translated by G Schwab. Chicago: University of Chicago Press.
Schmitt, C. (2008 [1928]). *Constitutional Theory*. Translated by J. Seitzer. Durham: Duke University Press.
Schmitt, C. (2014 [1921]). *Dictatorship: From the Origin of the Modern Concept of Sovereignty to Proletarian Class Struggle*. Translated by M. Hoelzl and G. Ward. Cambridge: Polity Press.
Schmitt, C. (2015). The Guardian of the Constitution. In L. Vinx ed., *The Guardian of the Constitution: Hans Kelsen and Carl Schmitt on the Limits of Constitutional Law*. Cambridge: Cambridge University Press, pp. 79–173.
Schmitter, P. (1974). Still the Century of Corporatism? *Review of Politics*, 36 (1), 85–131.
Schnapper, D. (2010). *Une Sociologue au Conseil Constitutionnel*, Paris: Gallimard.
Schneider, J. (2007). Regulation and Europeanisation as Key Patterns of Change in Administrative Law. In M. Ruffert, ed., *The Transformation of Administrative Law in Europe*. Munich: Sellier, pp. 309–323.
Schönberger, C. (1999). Der "Staat" der Allgemeinen Staatslehre: Anmerkungen zu einer eigenwilligen deutschen Disziplin im Vergleich mit Frankreich. In O. Beaud, & E. V. Heyen, eds., *Eine deutsch-französische Rechtswissenschaft? Une science juridique franco-allemande?* Baden-Baden: Nomos, pp. 111–137.
Schönberger, C. (2011). Vorrang der Verfassung. In: I. Appel, G. Hermes, & C. Schönberger, eds., *Öffentliches Recht im offenen Staat. Festschrift für Rainer Wahl zum 70. Geburtstag*. Berlin: Duncker & Humblot, pp. 385–403.
Schreurs, M. A. (2008). From the Bottom Up: Local and Subnational Climate Change Politics. *The Journal of Environment and Development*, 17 (4), 343–355.
Schuck, P. (1998). *Citizens, Strangers, and In-Betweens: Essays on Immigration and Citizenship*, Boulder: Westview Press.
Schumpeter, J. (1958). *Capitalism, Socialism and Democracy*, New York: Harper and Row.
Schumpeter, J. (1984). *Capitalism, Socialism, and Democracy*, New York: Harper Torchbooks.
Schuppert, G. F. (2003). *Staatswissenschaft*, Baden-Baden: Nomos.

Schütze, R. (2009). *From Dual to Cooperative Federalism: The Changing Structure of European Law*, Oxford: Oxford University Press.
Schwartz, M. (2020). Criminalizing A Constitutional Right. *New York Review of Books*, December 3. Available from: www.nybooks.com/articles/2020/12/03/criminalizing-abortion- constitutional-right/.
Schwartzberg, M. (2007). *Democracy and Legal Change*, Cambridge: Cambridge University Press.
Schwartzberg, M. (2013). *Counting the Many: The Origins and Limits of the Supermajority Rule*, Cambridge: Cambridge University Press.
Schwartzberg, M. (2018). Justifying the Jury: Reconciling Justice, Equality and Democracy. *American Political Science Review*, 112 (3), 446–458.
Schwartzman, M. (2012). What if Religion Is Not Special? *University of Chicago Law Review* 79 (4), 1351–1427.
Schwindt-Bayer, L., & Tavits, M. (2016). *Clarity of Responsibility, Accountability, and Corruption*, New York: Cambridge University Press.
Scott, C. (2001). Analysing Regulatory Space: Fragmented Resources and Institutional Design. *Public Law*, 283–305.
Scott, J. C. (1999). *Seeing Like a State: How Certain Schemes to Improve the Human Condition Have Failed*, New Haven: Yale University Press.
Scott, K. (2011). *Federalism: A Normative Theory and its Practical Relevance*, New York: Continuum.
Scott, W. R. (2001). *Institutions and Organizations*, 2nd edn, Thousand Oaks; London: Sage.
Sea Shepherd. (2018). *Sea Shepherd's Statement on Japan's Decision to Commercially Slaughter Whales*, 26 December. Available from: https://seashepherd.org/2018/12/26/sea-shepherd-welcomes-the-end-of-whaling-in-the-southern-ocean/ (Accessed: 3 October 2019).
Segal, J, & Cover, A. (1989). Ideological Values and the Votes of U.S. Supreme Court Justices. *American Political Science Review*, 83 (2), 557–565.
Seidman, L. M. (2013). *On Constitutional Disobedience*, Oxford: Oxford University Press.
Sejersted. F. (2002). *Konstitusjon og Kontroll*, Oslo: Cappelen.
Selgin, G. A. (1988). *The Theory of Free Banking: Money Supply under Competitive Note Issue*, New Jersey: Rowman & Littlefield.
Selinger, W. (2019). *Parliamentarism: From Burke to Weber*, Cambridge: Cambridge University Press.
Sempill, J. (2017). The Lions and the Greatest Part: The Rule of Law and the Constitution of Employer Power. *Hague Journal on the Rule of Law*, 9 (2), 283–314.
Sempill, J. (2018a). Ruler's Sword, Citizen's Shield: The Rule of Law and the Constitution of Power. *Journal of Law & Politics*, 31 (3), 333–415.
Sempill, J. (2018b). What Rendered Ancient Tyrants Detestable: The Rule of Law and the Constitution of Corporate Power. *Hague Journal on the Rule of Law*, 10 (2), 219–253.
Sen, A. (1993). Capability and Well-Being. In M. Nussbaum, & A. Sen, eds., *The Quality of Life*. Oxford: Oxford University Press.
Senellart, M. (1989). *Machiavellisme et raison d'État*, Paris: Presses Universitaires de France.
Sengupta, A. (2019). *Independence and Accountability of the Indian Higher Judiciary*, Cambridge: Cambridge University Press.
Serres M., & Polacco, M. (2018). *Défense et illustration de la langue française aujourd'hui*, Paris: Le Pommier.
Setzer J., & Vanhala, L. (2019). Climate Change Litigation: A Review of Research on Courts and Litigants in Climate Governance. *Wiley Interdisciplinary Reviews: Climate Change*, 10 (3), e580.

Sewell, Jr, W. H. (1994). *A Rhetoric of Bourgeois Revolution: The Abbé Sieyès and What Is the Third Estate?* Durham: Duke University Press.
Sewell, W. H. (1996). Historical Events as Transformations of Structures: Inventing Revolution at the Bastille. *Theory and Society*, 25 (6), 841–881.
Shaafqat, S. (2018). Civil Society and the Lawyers' Movement of Pakistan. *Law and Social Inquiry*, 43 (3), 889–914.
Shachar, A. (2006). The Race for Talent: Highly Skilled Migrants and Competitive Immigration Regimes. *NYU Law Review*, 81 (1), 148–206.
Shachar, A. (2009). *The Birthright Lottery: Citizenship and Global Inequality*, Cambridge, MA: Harvard University Press.
Shachar, A. (2017). Citizenship for Sale? In A. Shachar et al., eds., *The Oxford Handbook of Citizenship*. Oxford: Oxford University Press, pp. 789–816.
Shachar, A., & Hirschl, R. (2014). On Citizenship, States, and Markets. *Journal of Political Philosophy*, 22 (2), 231–257.
Shaffer, G. (2009). Developing Country Use of the WTO Dispute Settlement System: Why It Matters, the Barriers Posed. In J. Hartigan, ed., *Trade Disputes and the Dispute Settlement Understanding of the WTO: An Interdisciplinary Assessment. Volume 6 of Frontiers of Economics and Globalization*. Leeds, UK: Emerald Group Publishing Limited, pp. 167–190.
Shah, R. (2021). *Top upper caste judges in India "biased" against Dalit colleagues: US Bar Association report.* Available from: https://theleaflet.in/top-upper-caste-judges-in-india-biased-towards-dalit-colleagues-us-bar-association-report/
Shakman Hurd, E. (2015). *Beyond Religious Freedom: The New Global Politics of Religion*, Princeton: Princeton University Press, 2015.
Shane, P. M. (2009). *Madison's Nightmare: How Executive Power Threatens American Democracy*, Chicago: Univesity of Chicago Press.
Shapiro, I. (1994). *The Rule of Law: NOMOS XXXVI*, New York: New York University Press.
Shapiro, I. (2016). *Politics against Domination*, Cambridge, MA: Harvard University Press.
Shapiro, M. (2010). A Comparison of US and European Independent Agencies. In S. Rose-Ackerman, & P. Lindseth, eds., *Comparative Administrative Law, Research Handbooks in Comparative Law*. Cheltenham: Edward Elgar, pp. 293–308.
Shapiro, M. (2019). Judicial Power and Democracy. In C. Landfried, ed., *Judicial Power. How Constitutional Courts Affect Political Transformations*. Cambridge: Cambridge University Press, pp. 21–35.
Shapiro, S. (2011). *Legality*, Cambridge: Harvard University Press.
Sharlet, R. (1993). The Russian Constitutional Court: The First Term. *Post-Soviet Affairs*, 9 (1), 1–39.
Sharman, C. (2015). Upper Houses. In B. Galligan, & S. Brenton, eds., *Constitutional Conventions in Westminster Systems*. Cambridge: Cambridge University Press, pp. 157–172.
Shaw, C. K. (1992). Hegel's Theory of Modern Bureaucracy, *American Political Science Review*, 86 (2), 381–389.
Shaw, J. (2020). *The People in Question: Citizens and Constitutions in Uncertain Times*, Bristol: Bristol University Press.
Shepsle, K. (1991). Discretion, Institutions and the Problem of Government Commitment. In P. Bourdieu, & J. Coleman, ed., *Social Theory for a Changing Society*. New York: Russell Sage.
Shepsle, K. (1992). Congress Is a "They," Not an "It": Legislative Intent as an Oxymoron. *International Review of Law & Economics*, 12 (2), 239–256.
Sheridan, J. E. (1975). *China in Disintegration: The Republican Era in Chinese History, 1912–1949*, New York: Free Press.

Shetreet, S. (2011). Judicial Independence and Accountability: Core Values in Liberal Democracies. In H. Lee, ed. *Judiciaries in Comparative Perspective*. Cambridge: Cambridge University Press, pp. 3–24.
Shiffrin, S. (2021). *Democratic Law*. Edited by H. Ginsborg. New York: Oxford University Press.
Shihata, I. (2000). The Dynamic Evolution of International Organizations: The Case of the World Bank. *Journal of the History of International Law*, 2 (2), 217–249.
Shklar, J. (1987). Political Theory and the Rule of Law. In A. Hutchinson, & P. Monahan, eds., *The Rule of Law: Ideal or Ideology?* Toronto: Carswell.
Shklar, J. (1989). The Liberalism of Fear. In N. Rosenblum, ed., *Liberalism and the Moral Life*. Cambridge, MA: Harvard University Press.
Shonfield, A. (1965). *Modern Capitalism: The Changing Balance of Public and Private Power*, Oxford: Oxford University Press.
Shu, M. (2008). Referendums and the Political Constitution of the EU. *European Law Journal* 14 (4), 423–445.
Shugart, M. S., & Carey, J. (1992). *Presidents and Assemblies. Constitutional Design and Electoral Dynamics*, New York: Cambridge University Press.
Shugart, M. S., & Wattenberg, M. P. (2001). *Mixed-Member Electoral Systems. The Best of Both Worlds?* Cambridge: Cambridge University Press.
Shugerman, J. (2002–2003). A Six-Three Rule: Reviving Consensus and Deference on the Supreme Court. *Georgia Law Review* 37 (3), 893–1020.
Sidney, A. (1990). *Discourses Concerning Government*, Indianapolis: Liberty Classics.
Sieder, R. (2016). Legal Pluralism and Indigenous Women's Rights in Mexico: The Ambiguities of Recognition. *New York University Journal of International Law and Politics*, 48 (4), 1125–1150.
Siegel, R. (1997). Why Equal Protection No Longer Protects: The Evolving Forms of Status-Enhancing State Action. *Stanford Law Review*, 49 (5), 1111–1148.
Siep, L. (2017). Hegel's Liberal, Social, and "Ethical" State. In D. Moyar, ed., *The Oxford Handbook of Hegel*. Oxford: Oxford University Press, pp. 515–534.
Siéyès, E.-J. (1795). *Opinion sur les attributions et l'organisation du jury constitutionnaire*, Paris.
Sieyès, E.-J. (2003 [1789]). What Is the Third Estate? In *Political Writings*. Translated by M. Sonenscher. Indianapolis: Hackett, pp. 92–162.
Sieyès, E.-J. (2014 [1789]). What Is the Third Estate? In *Emmanuel Joseph Sieyès: The Essential Political Writings*. Edited by O. W. Lembcke and F. Weber. Leiden: Brill.
Sillen, J. (2019). The Concept of "Internal Judicial Independence" in the Case Law of the European Court of Human Rights. *European Constitutional Law Review*, 15 (1), 104–133.
Silverstein, G. (2008). Singapore: The Exception That Proves Rules Matter. In T. Ginsburg and T. Moustafa, eds. *Rule of Law: The Politics of Courts in Authoritarian Regimes*. New York: Cambridge University Press, pp. 73–102.
Simmons, A. J. (1992). *The Lockean Theory of Rights*, Princeton: Princeton University Press.
Simmons, B. (2002). Capacity, Commitment, and Compliance: International Institutions and Territorial Disputes. *Journal of Conflict Resolution* 46 (6), 829–856.
Simmons, B. (2012). *Mobilizing for Human Rights: International Law in Domestic Politics*, Oxford: Oxford University Press.
Simon, D. (1981). *L'interprétation judiciaire des traités d'organisations internationales*, Paris: Editions A. Pedone.
Simpson, R. M. (2013). Intellectual Agency and Responsibility for Belief in Free-Speech Theory. *Legal Theory*, 19 (3), 307–330.

Sinclair, G. F. (2017). *To Reform the World: International Organizations and the Making of Modern States*, Oxford: Oxford University Press.
Sinden, A. (2019). A Human Rights Framework for the Anthropocene. In J. Jaria-Manzano, & S. Borras, eds., *Research Handbook on Global Climate Constitutionalism*. Cheltenham, UK: Edward Elgar Publishing, pp. 132–152.
Singer, P. (1973). *Democracy and Disobedience*, Oxford: Oxford University Press.
Singer, P. (1990). *Animal Liberation*, 2nd edn, New York: New York Review of Books.
Singer, P. (1991). Disobedience as a Plea for Reconsideration. In H. A. Bedau, ed., *Civil Disobedience in Focus*. London: Routledge, pp. 122–129.
Sintomer. Y. (2013). The Meanings of Political Representation: Uses and Misuses of a Notion. *Raisons Politiques*, 50 (2), 13–34.
Šipulová, K. (2021). Under Pressure: Building Judicial Resistance to Political Inference. In D. J. Galligan, ed., *The Courts and the People: Friend or Foe? The Putney Debates 2019*. Oxford: Hart Publishing, pp. 153–170.
Šipulová, K. et al. (2023). Judicial Self-Governance Index: Towards better understanding of the role of judges in governing the judiciary. *Regulation & Governance*, 17(1), pp. 22–42.
Skinner, C. (2021). Central Bank Activism. *Duke Law Journal*, 71 (2), 247–328.
Skinner, Q. (1965). History and Ideology in the English Revolution. *The Historical Journal*, 8 (2), 151–178.
Skinner, Q. (1978). *The Foundations of Modern Political Thought, Volume 2: The Age of Reformation*, Cambridge: Cambridge University Press.
Skinner, Q. (1989). The State. In T. Ball, J. Farr, & R. L. Hanson, eds., *Political Innovation and Conceptual Change*. Cambridge: Cambridge University Press, pp. 90–131.
Skinner, Q. (1998). *Liberty Before Liberalism*, Cambridge: Cambridge University Press.
Skinner, Q. (2002). *Hobbes and Civil Science. Volume III of Visions of Politics*, Cambridge: Cambridge University Press.
Skinner, Q. (2009). A Genealogy of the Modern State, *Proceedings of the British Academy*, 162, pp. 325–370.
Skocpol, T. (1979). *States and Social Revolutions: A Comparative Analysis of France, Russia, and China*, Cambridge: Cambridge University Press.
Skowronek, S. (1982). *Building a New American State: The Expansion of National Administrative Capacities, 1877–1920*, Cambridge: Cambridge University Press.
Skowronek, S. (1997). *The Politics Presidents Make: Leadership from John Adams to Bill Clinton*, Cambridge, MA: Harvard University Press.
Skowronek, S., Dearborn, J. A., & King, D. (2021). *Phantoms of a Beleaguered Republic: The Deep State and the Unitary Executive*, New York: Oxford University Press.
Slaughter, A.-M., Stone Sweet, A., & Weiler, J., eds (1998). *The ECJ and National Courts: Doctrine and Jurisprudence*, Oxford: Hart.
Sloan, B. (1989). The United Nations Charter as a Constitution. *Pace International Law Review* 1 (1), 61–126.
Smend, R. (1955 [1923]). Die politische Gewalt im Verfassungsstaat. In Verfassung und Verfassungsrecht, *Staatsrechtliche Abhandlungen*, 2nd edn, Berlin: Dunkner & Humbolt, pp. 69–88.
Smith, A. (1976 [1776]). *An Inquiry into the Nature and Causes of the Wealth of Nations*. Edited by E. Cannan. Chicago: University of Chicago Press.
Smith, A. (1985[1762–63]). *Lectures on Rhetoric and Belles Lettres*. Edited by J. C. Bryce. Indianapolis: Liberty Fund.
Smith, A. (1981 [1776]). *An Inquiry into the Nature and Causes of the Wealth of Nations*. Edited by R. H. Campbell, A. Skinner, & W. Todd. Indianapolis: Liberty Fund.

Smith, D. E. (2013). *Across the Aisle: Opposition in Canadian Politics*, Toronto: University of Toronto Press.
Smith, G. (2009). *Democratic Innovations: Designing Institutions for Citizen Participation*, Cambridge: Cambridge University Press.
Smith, H. (2016). Equity and Administrative Behaviour. In P. G. Turner, ed., *Equity and Administration*. Cambridge: Cambridge University Press, pp. 326–366.
Smith, G., & Setälä, M. (2019). Mini-Publics and Deliberative Democracy. In Bächtiger, A., Dryzek, J. S., Mansbridge, J., & Warren, M., eds., *The Oxford Handbook of Deliberative Democracy*. Oxford: Oxford University Press, pp. 300–314.
Smith, M. N. (2008). Rethinking Sovereignty, Rethinking Revolution. *Philosophy & Public Affairs*, 36 (4), 405–440.
Smith, R. (1997). *Civic Ideals: Conficting Visions of Citizenship in U.S. History*, New Haven: Yale University Press.
Smith, R. (2018). New South Wales: An Accidental Case of Semi-Parliamentarism? *Australian Journal of Political Science*, 53 (2), 256–263.
Smith, S. (2004). *Contract Theory*, Oxford: Oxford University Press.
Smith, W. (2013). *Civil Disobedience and Deliberative Democracy*, Cambridge: Cambridge University Press.
Smoleńska, A., & van 't Klooster, J. (2022). A Risky Bet: Climate Change and the EU's Microprudential Framework for Banks. *Journal of Financial Regulation*, 8 (1), 51–74.
Snowden, E. (2019). *Permanent Record*, Metropolitan Books/Henry Holt & Company.
Sokol, M., & Pataccini, L. (2021). Financialisation, regional economic development and the coronavirus crisis: A time for spatial monetary policy? *Cambridge Journal of Regions, Economy and Society*, rsab033.
Solt, F. (2008). Economic Inequality and Democratic Political Engagement. *American Journal of Political Science*, 52 (1), 48–60.
Solum, L. B. (2008). *Semantic Originalism*. Illinois Public Law Research Paper, 7–24.
Somek, A. (2003). Authoritarian Constitutionalism: Austrian Constitutional Doctrine 1933 to 1938 and Its Legacy. In C. Joerges, & N. Singh Ghaleigh, eds., *Darker Legacies of Law in Europe*, Oxford: Hart.
Somek, A. (2006). Stateless Law: Kelsen's Conception and Its Limits. *Oxford Journal of Legal Studies*, 26 (4), 753–774.
Somin, I. (2014). *Democracy and Political Ignorance: Why Smaller Government is Smarter* (Stanford, CA: Stanford University Press).
Sommermann, K.-P. (1997). *Staatsziele und Staatszielbestimmungen*, Tübingen: Mohr Siebeck.
Song, S. (2017). Why Does the State Have the Right to Control Immigration? In J. Knight, ed., *NOMOS LVII: Migration, Emigration, and Immigration*. New York: New York University Press, pp. 3–50.
Song, S. (2018). *Immigration and the Limits of Democracy*, Oxford: Oxford University Press.
Sordi, B. (2017). Révolution, Rechtsstaat, and the Rule of Law: Historical Reflections on the Emergence of Administrative Law. In S. Rose-Ackerman, P. Lindseth, & B. Emerson, eds., *Comparative Administrative Law*, 2nd edn. Cheltenham, UK; Edward Elgar, pp. 23–37.
Sørensen, M. (1983). Autonomous Legal Orders: Some Considerations Relating to a Systems Analysis of International Organisations in the World Legal Order. *International & Comparative Law Quarterly*, 32 (3), 559–576.
Sossin, L. (2003). Public Fiduciary Obligations, Political Trusts, and the Equitable Duty of Reasonableness in Administrative Law. *Saskatchewan Law Review*, 66 (1), 129–182.

Sossin, L. (2004). The Quasi-Revival of the Canadian Bill of Rights and Its Implications for Administrative Law. *Supreme Court Law Review*, 2nd series, 25, 191–212.

Souter, J. (2014). Towards a Theory of Asylum as Reparation for Past Injustice. *Political Studies*, 62 (2), 326–342.

Soysal, Y. (2012). Postnational Citizenship: Rights and Obligations of Individuality. In K. Nash, & A. Scott, eds., *The Wiley-Blackwell Companion to Political Sociology*. Hoboken: Wiley Blackwell. pp. 383–393.

Spáč, S. (2018). Recruiting European Judges in the Age of Judicial Self-Government. *German Law Journal*, 19 (7), 2077–2104.

Spáč, S. (2022). The Illusion of Merit-Based Judicial Selection in Post-Communist Judiciary: Evidence from Slovakia. *Problems of Post-Communism*, 69 (6), 528–538.

Spector, H. (2009). The Right to a Constitutional Jury. *Legisprudence*, 3 (1), 111–123.

Spencer, M. (2002). Hume and Madison on Faction. *The William and Mary Quarterly*, 59 (4), 869–896.

Spiegel, S. (2021). Climate Injustice, Criminalisation of Land Protection and Anti-colonial Solidarity: Courtroom Ethnography in an Age of Fossil Fuel Violence. *Political Geography*, 84. www.sciencedirect.com/science/article/pii/S0962629820303619?via%3Dihub

Spieler, M. F. (2009). The Legal Structure of Colonial Rule during the French Revolution. *William and Mary Quarterly*, 66 (2), 365–408.

Spinelli, A., & Rossi, E. (1941). The Manifesto of Ventotene for a Free and United Europe. Available from: www.ena.lu/manifesto-ventotene-1941-020000007.html.

Spinner-Halev, J. (2005). Hinduism, Christianity and Liberal Religious Toleration. *Political Theory*, 33 (1), 28–57.

Spiro, P. (2013). The (Dwindling) Rights and Obligations of Citizenship. *William & Mary Bill of Rights Journal*, 21 (3), 899–923.

Spiro, P. (2016). *At Home in Two Countries: The Past and Future of Dual Citizenship*, New York: New York University Press.

Sreenivasan, G. (2005). A Hybrid Theory of Claim-Rights. *Oxford Journal of Legal Studies*, 25 (2). 257–274.

Stacey, J. (2018). *The Constitution of the Environmental Emergency*, Oxford: Hart Publishing.

Stacey, J. (2022). The Public Law Paradoxes of Climate Emergency Declarations. *Transnational Environmental Law*, 11 (2), 291–323.

Staughton, L. (1967). *Class Conflict, Slavery, and the United States Constitution: Ten Essays*, Indianapolis: The Bobbs-Merill Company, Inc.

Stears, M. (2002). *Progressives, Pluralists, and the Problems of the State: Ideologies of Reform in the United States and Britain, 1909–1926*, New York: Oxford University Press.

Stein, E. (1981). Lawyers, Judges, and the Making of a Transnational Constitution. *American Journal of International Law*, 75 (1), 1–27.

Steinberg, R. (1994). Untergesetzliche Regelwerke und Gremien. In R. Steinberg, ed., *Reform des Atomrechts*. Baden-Baden: Nomos, pp. 82–100.

Steinberg, R. (2002). In the Shadow of Law or Power? Consensus-Based Bargaining and Outcomes in the GATT/WTO. *International Organization* 56 (2), 339–374.

Steiner, H. (1992). Libertarianism and the Transnational Migration of People. In B. Barry, & R. E. Goodin, eds., *Free Movement: Ethical Issues in the Transnational Migration of People and of Money*. University Park: Pennsylvania State University Press, pp. 87–94.

Steiner, H. (1994). *An Essay on Rights*, Oxford: Blackwell.

Stepan, A. (1999). Federalism and Democracy: Beyond the U.S. Model. *Journal of Democracy*, 10 (4), 19–33.

Stephens, T. (2019). What Is the Point of International Environmental Law Scholarship in the Anthropocene? In Ole W. Pedersen, ed., *Perspectives on Environmental Law Scholarship*. Cambridge: Cambridge University Press, pp. 121–139.

Stephenson, M. (2003). "When the Devil Turns…": The Political Foundations of Independent Judicial Review. *Journal of Legal Studies*, 32 (1), 59–89.

Stephenson, M. (2006). A Costly Signaling Theory of Hard Look Judicial Review. *Administrative Law Review*, 58 (4), 753–814.

Stephenson, S. (2021). Constitutional Conventions and the Judiciary. *Oxford Journal of Legal Studies*, 41 (3), 750–775.

Steurer, R., Clar, C., & Casado-Asensio, J. (2020). Climate Change Mitigation in Austria and Switzerland: The Pitfalls of Federalism in Greening Decentralized Building Policies. *Natural Resources Forum*, 44 (1), 89–108.

Stevin, S. (1955 [1586]). *General Introduction Mechanics. Vol. I of The Principal Works of Simon Stevin*. Edited by E. J. Dijksterhuis. Amsterdam: C.V. Swets & Zeitlinger.

Stewart, R. B. (1975). The Reformation of Administrative Law. *Harvard Law Review*, 88 (8), 1667–1813.

Stewart, R. B. (1977). Pyramids of Sacrifice? Problems of Federalism in Mandating State Implementation of National Environmental Policy. *The Yale Law Journal*, 86 (6), 1196–1272.

Stich, S. G. W. (2014). When Democracy Meets Pluralism: Landemore's Epistemic Argument for Democracy and the Problem of Value Diversity. *Critical Review*, 26 (1–2), 170–183.

Stigler, G. (1971). The Theory of Economic Regulation. *Bell Journal of Economics and Management Science*, 2 (1), 3–21.

Stiglitz, J. (2019). The Climate Crisis Is Our Third World War. It Needs a Bold Response. *The Guardian*. 4 June.

Stilz, A. (2013). Occupancy Rights and the Wrong of Removal, *Philosophy & Public Affairs*, 41 (4), 324–356.

Stilz, A. (2015). Language, Dignity, and Territory. *Critical Review of International Social and Political Philosophy*, 18 (2), 178–190.

Stolleis, M. (1992). *Staatsrechtslehre und Verwaltungswissenschaft 1800–1914*. Vol. II of *Geschichte des öffentlichen Rechts in Deutschland*. München: C. H. Beck.

Stone, B. (2008). State Legislative Councils: Designing for Accountability. In N. Aroney, S. Prasser, & J. Nethercote, eds., *Restraining Elective Dictatorship: The Upper House Solution?* Perth: University of West Australia Press, 175–195.

Stojanović, N. (2006). Do Multicultural Democracies Really Require PR? Counterevidence from Switzerland. *Swiss Political Science Review*, 12 (4), 131–157.

Stojanović, N. (2011). Limits of Consociationalism and Possible Alternatives. Centripetal Effects of Direct Democracy in a Multiethnic Society. *Transitions* 51 (1–2), 99–114.

Stojanović, N. (2016). Party, Regional and Linguistic Proportionality Under Majoritarian Rules: Swiss Federal Council Elections. *Swiss Political Science Review*, 22 (1), 41–58.

Stojanović, N. (2020). Democracy, Ethnoicracy and Consociational Demoicracy. *International Political Science Review*, 41 (1), 30–43.

Stolleis, M. (2001). Konstitution und Intervention. Studien zur Geschichte des oeffentliches Rechts im 19. Jahrhundert, Frankfurt-am-Main: Suhrkamp.

Stolleis, M. (2004). *A History of Public Law in Germany, 1914–1945*. Translated by M. Dunlap. Oxford: Oxford University Press.

Stone Sweet, A. (2004). *The Judicial Construction of Europe*, Oxford: Oxford University Press.

Stone Sweet, A., & Mathews, J. (2019). *Proportionality Balancing and Constitutional Governance: A Comparative and Global Approach*, Oxford: Oxford University Press.

Stone Sweet, A., & Shapiro, M. (2002). Abstract and Concrete Review in the United States. In M. Shapiro, & A. Stone Sweet eds., *On Law, Politics, and Judicialization*. Oxford: Oxford University Press, pp. 347–375.
Strauss, D. (1999). What Is Constitutional Theory. *California Law Review*, 87 (3), 581–592.
Strauss, D. (2010). *The Living Constitution*, Oxford: Oxford University Press.
Strauss, D. (2011). Do We Have a Living Constitution? *Drake Law Review*, 59 (4), 973–984.
Strauss, P. L. (2007). Overseer or "the Decider"? The President in Administrative Law. *George Washington Law Review*, 75 (4), 696–760.
Strauss, P. L. (2013–2014). Private Standards Organizations and Public Law. *William & Mary Bill of Rights Law Journal*, 22 (2), 497–562.
Strawson, P. (1962). *Freedom and Resentment and Other Essays*, London: Methuen.
Streeck, W., & Thelen, K. (2005). *Beyond Continuity: Institutional Change in Advanced Political Economies*, Oxford: Oxford University Press.
Streeck, W. (2015). German Hegemony: Unintended and Unwanted. 15 May. Available from: https://wolfgangstreeck.com/2015/05/15/german-hegemony-unintended-and-unwanted/.
Strøm, K., Müller, W., & Bergman, T., eds. (2003). *Delegation and Accountability in Parliamentary Democracies*, New York: Oxford University Press.
Stubbs, P., & Lendvai-Bainton, N. (2020). Authoritarian Neoliberalism, Radical Conservatism and Social Policy within the European Union: Croatia, Hungary and Poland. *Development and Change*, 51 (2), 540–560.
Stykow, P. (2019). The Devil in the Details: Constitutional Regime Types in Post-Soviet Eurasia. *Post-Soviet Affairs*, 35 (2), 122–139.
Suchman, M (1995). Managing Legitimacy: Strategic and Institutional Approaches, *Academy of Management Review*, 20 (3), 571–610.
Suiter, J., Farrell D., & Harris, C. (2016). The Irish Constitutional Convention: A Case of "High Legitimacy"? In M. Reuchamps, & J. Suiter, eds., *Constitutional Deliberative Democracy in Europe*. Colchester: ECPR Press, pp. 33–54.
Suiter, J., & Reidy, T. (2020). Does Deliberation Help Deliver Informed Electorates: Evidence from Irish Referendum Votes. *Representation*, 56 (4), 539–557.
Suleiman, E., & Courty, G. (1997). *L'Âge d'Or de l'État: Une métamorphose annoncée*, Paris: Seuil.
Sullivan, T., & Frase, F. (2008). *Proportionality Principles in American Law: Controlling Excessive Government Actions*, Oxford: Oxford University Press.
Sullivan, W. F. (2005). *The Impossibility of Religious Freedom*, Princeton: Princeton University Press.
Sullivan, W. F., Shakman Hurd, E., Mahmood, S., & Danchin, P. G., eds., (2015). *The Politics of Religious Freedom*, Chicago: University of Chicago Press.
Sultany, N. (2012). The State of Progressive Constitutional Theory: The Paradox of Constitutional Democracy and the Project of Political Justification. *Harvard Civil Rights–Civil Liberties Law Review*, 47 (2), 371–455.
Sultany, N. (2017a). *Law and Revolution: Legitimacy and Constitutionalism After the Arab Spring*, Oxford: Oxford University Press.
Sultany, N. (2017b). The Legal Structures of Subordination: The Palestinian Minority and Israeli Law. In N. N. Rouhana, & S. N. Huneidi, eds., *Ethnic Privileges in the Jewish State: Israel and its Palestinian Citizens*. Cambridge: Cambridge University Press, pp. 191–237.
Sultany, N. (2019). What Good Is Abstraction? From Liberal Legitimacy to Social Justice. *Buffalo Law Review*, 67 (3), 823–887.
Sultany, N. (2021). Marx and Critical Constitutional Theory. In P. O'Connell, & U. Özsu, eds., *Research Handbook on Law and Marxism*. Cheltenham: Edward Elgar, pp. 209–241.

Sunstein, C. (1990). *After the Rights Revolution: Reconceiving the Regulatory State*, Cambridge, MA: Harvard University Press.
Sunstein, C. (1991). Constitutionalism and Secession. *University of Chicago Law Review* 58 (2), 633–670.
Sunstein, C. (1993a). Against Positive Rights. *East European Constitutional Review*, 2 (1), 35–38.
Sunstein, C. (1993b). Democracy and Shifting Preferences. In D. Copp, J. Hampton, & J. Roemer, eds., *The Idea of Democracy*. Cambridge: Cambridge University Press, pp. 196–230.
Sunstein, C. (1993c). The Anticaste Principle. *Michigan Law Review*, 92 (8), 2410–2455.
Sunstein, C. (1993d). *The Partial Constitution*, Cambridge, MA: Harvard University Press.
Sunstein, C. (1996). On the Expressive Function of Law. *University of Pennsylvania Law Review*, 144 (5), 2021–2054.
Sunstein, C. (1999). *One Case at a Time*, Cambridge, MA: Harvard University Press.
Sunstein, C. (2000/2001). Social and Economic Rights? Lessons from South Africa. *Constitutional Forum*, 11 (4), 123–132.
Sunstein, C. (2001). *Designing Democracy: What Constitutions Do*, New York: Oxford University Press.
Sunstein, C. (2006). *The Second Bill of Rights*, New York: Basic Books.
Sunstein, C. (2007). *Republic 2.0*, Princeton: Princeton University Press.
Sunstein, C. (2009). *A Constitution of Many Minds*, Princeton: Princeton University Press.
Sunstein, C. (2017). Cost-Benefit Analysis and Arbitrariness Review. *Harvard Environmental Law Review* 41 (1), 1–41.
Sunstein, C. ed. (2018a). *Can it happen here? Authoritarianism in America*, New York: Dey Street/Harper Collins.
Sunstein, C. (2018b). *The Cost-Benefit Revolution*, Cambridge, MA: MIT Press.
Sunstein, C. (2020). Falsehoods and the First Amendment. *Harvard Journal of Law & Technology*, 33 (2), 387–426.
Sunstein, C., & Barnett, R. (2005). Constitutive Commitments and Roosevelt's Second Bill of Rights: A Dialogue. *Drake Law Review*, 53 (2), 205–230.
Sunstein, C., & Vermeule, A. (2017). The Morality of Administrative Law. *Harvard Law Review*, 131 (7), 1924–1978.
Sunstein, C., & Vermeule, A. (2020). *Law and Leviathan: Redeeming the Administrative State*, Cambridge, MA: The Belknap Press of Harvard University Press.
Surowiecki, J. (2004). *The Wisdom of Crowds*, New York: Anchor Books.
Suteu, S. (2015). Constitutional Conventions in the Digital Era: Lessons from Iceland and Ireland. *Boston College International & Comparative Law Review*, 38 (2), 251–276.
Suteu, S. (2019). Recourse to the People in Semi-presidential Systems: Lessons from Romanian Referendum Practice during Periods of Divided Government. *Romanian Journal of Comparative Law*, 10 (2), 264–300.
Suteu, S. (2022a). The View from Nowhere in Constitutional Theory: A Methodological Inquiry. In D. Kyritsis, & S. Lakin, eds., *The Methodology of Constitutional Theory*. London: Hart, pp. 341–358.
Suteu, S. (2022b). Scotland's Political and Constitutional Process: Negotiating Independence under a Flexible Constitution. In J. Vidmar, S. McGibbon, & L. Raible, eds., *Research Handbook on Secession*. Cheltenham: Edward Elgar, pp. 128–147.
Suteu, S., & Tierney, S. (2018). Squaring the Circle? Bringing Deliberation and Participation Together in Processes of Constitution-Making. In R. Levy, H. Kong, & J. King, eds., *The Cambridge Handbook of Deliberative Constitutionalism*. Cambridge: Cambridge University Press, pp. 282–294.

Svensen, A., & McCarthy, C. (1998). *The International Law of Human Rights and States of Exception*, The Hague: Martinus Nijhoff.
Svolik, M. (2015). Which Democracies Will Last? Coups, Incumbent Takeovers, and the Dynamic of Democratic Consolidation. *British Journal of Political Science*, 45 (4), 715–738.
Swain, C., ed. (2007). *Debating Immigration*, Cambridge: Cambridge University Press.
Swenden, W. (2015). Belgium and the Crisis of Governability 2007–2011. Rebooting Territorial Pluralism? In K. Basta, J. McGarry, & R. Simeon, eds., *Territorial Pluralism. Managing Difference in Multinational States*. Vancouver: University of British Columbia Press, pp. 196–219.
Swyngedouw, M., Abts, K., Baute, S. Galle, J., & B. Meuleman (2015). *Het communautaire in de verkiezingen van 25 mei 2014*. CeSO/ISPO/2015–1.
Szpiro, G. (2010). *Numbers Rule. The Vexing Mathematics of Democracy, From Plato to the Present*, Princeton: Princeton University Press.
Taflaga, M. (2018). What's in a Name? Semi-Parliamentarism and Australian Commonwealth Executive-Legislative Relations. *Australian Journal of Political Science*, 53 (2), 248–255.
Takayasu, K. (2015). Is The Japanese Prime Minister Too Weak or Too Strong?: An Institutional Analysis. 成蹊法学, (83), 147–169.
Takriti, A. R. (2013). *Monsoon Revolution: Republicans, Sultans, and Empires in Oman, 1965–1976*, Oxford: Oxford University Press.
Takriti, A. R. (2019a). Colonial Coups and the War on Popular Sovereignty. *The American Historical Review*, 124 (3), 878–909.
Takriti, A. R. (2019b). Before BDS: Lineages of Boycott in Palestine. *Radical History Review*, 134, 58–95.
Tallberg, J., Sommerer, T., Squatrito, T., & Jönsson, C. (2013). *The Opening up of International Organizations: Transnational Access in Global Governance*, Cambridge: Cambridge University Press.
Talleyrand, C. M. de (1967). *Mémoires*, Paris: Jean Bonnot.
Talmon, S. (2005). The Security Council as World Legislature. *The American Journal of International Law*, 99 (1), 175–193.
Tamanaha, B. (2004). *On the Rule of Law: History, Politics, Theory*, Cambridge: Cambridge University Press.
Tamir, Y. (2019), *Why Nationalism*. Princeton: Princeton University Press.
Tan, K. C. (2017). Cosmopolitan Citizenship. In A. Shachar et al., eds. *The Oxford Handbook of Citizenship*. Oxford: Oxford University Press, pp. 694–713.
Tani, K. (2014). Administrative Equal Protection: Federalism, The Fourteenth Amendment, and the Rights of the Poor. *Cornell Law Review*, 100 (4), 825–900.
Tani, K. (2019). Administrative Constitutionalism at the "Borders of Belonging": Drawing on History to Expand the Archive and Change the Lens. *University of Pennsylvania Law Review*, 167 (7), 1603–1630.
Tarullo, D. K. (2017). *Monetary policy without a working theory of inflation* (Hutchins Center Working Paper No. 33). Washington: Brookings Institution.
Tasioulas, J. (2015). On the Foundations of Human Rights. In R. Cruft, S. M. Liao, & M. Renzo, eds., *Philosophical Foundations of Human Rights*. Oxford: Oxford University Press, pp. 47–70.
Taub, N., & Schneider, E. (1990). Women's Subordination and the Role of Law. In D. Kairys, ed., *The Politics of Law: A Progressive Critique*. New York: Pantheon Books, pp. 152–176.
Tavits, M. (2009). *Presidents with Prime Ministers. Do Direct Elections Matter?* New York: Oxford University Press.
Taylor, C. (1979). *Hegel and Modern Society*, Cambridge: Cambridge University Press.

Taylor, C. (1985). Atomism. In *Philosophy and the Human Sciences: Philosophical Papers*, vol. II. Cambridge: Cambridge University Press.
Taylor, C. (1989). *Sources of the Self: The Making of the Modern Identity*, Cambridge, MA: Harvard University Press.
Taylor, C. (1995). *Philosophical Arguments*, Cambridge, MA: Harvard University Press.
Taylor, C. (2006). What's Wrong with Negative Liberty? In David Miller, ed., *The Liberty Reader*. London: Routledge, pp. 141–162.
Taylor, C. (2017). *A Secular Age*, Cambridge, MA: Harvard University Press.
Taylor, C., Nanz, P., & Beaubien Taylor, M. (2020). *Reconstructing Democracy: How Citizens Are Building from the Ground Up*, Cambridge, MA: Harvard University Press.
Taylor, M. M. (2014). The Limits of Judicial Independence: A Model with Illustration from Venezuela under Chávez. *Journal of Latin American Studies*, 46 (2), 229–259.
Ternavasio, M. (2002). *La revolución del voto. Política y elecciones en Buenos Aires, 1810–1852*, Buenos Aires: Siglo XXI.
Tetley, W. (2014). *October Crisis 1970: An Insider's View*, Montreal: McGill-Queen's University Press.
Teubner, G. (1993). *Law as an Autopoietic System*, Oxford: Blackwell.
Teubner, G., (2000). Ein Fall von struktureller Korruption? Die Familienbürgschaft in der Kollision unverträglicher Handlungslogiken (BVerfGE 89, 214 ff.). *Kritische Vierteljahreszeitschrift für Gesetzgebung und Rechtswissenschaft (Krit V)*, 83 (3/4), 388–404.
Teubner, G. (2012). *Constitutional Fragments: Societal Constitutionalism in the Globalization*, Oxford: Oxford University Press.
Teubner, G. (2018). Quod Omnes Tangit: Transnational Constitutions Without Democracy? *Journal of Law and Society*, 45 (1), 5–29.
Thaler, R. H., & Sunstein, C. R. (2021). *Nudge: The Final Edition*, London: Penguin Books.
Thatcher, M. (2002). Regulation after Delegation: Independent Regulatory Agencies in Europe. *Journal of European Public Policy*, 9 (6), 954–972.
The Associated Press. 2020. AP Interview: Egypt Wants UN to Avert Unilateral Fill of Dam. *The New York Times*, June 21, sec. World. Available from: www.nytimes.com/aponline/2020/06/21/world/middleeast/ap-ml-egypt-ethiopia-dam-dispute.html.
Thelen, K. (2014). *Varieties of Liberalization and the New Politics of Social Solidarity*, New York: Cambridge University Press.
Thiemann, M. (2019). Is Resilience Enough? The Macroprudential Reform Agenda and the Lack of Smoothing of the Cycle. *Public Administration*, 97 (3), 561–575.
Thies, M., & Yanai, Y. (2014). Bicameralism vs. Parliamentarism: Lessons from Japan's Twisted Diet. *Japanese Journal of Electoral Studies*, 30 (2), 60–74.
Thio, L.-A. (2012). Constitutionalism in Illiberal Polities. In M. Rosenfeld, & A. Sajó, eds., *The Oxford Handbook of Comparative Constitutional Law*. Oxford: Oxford University Press, pp. 133–152.
Thiruvengadam, A. K. (2019). Evaluating Bruce Ackerman's "Pathways to Constitutionalism" and India as an Exemplar of "Revolutionary Constitutionalism on a Human Scale". *International Journal of Constitutional Law*, 17 (2), 682–689.
Thoma, R. (1953/2008). Rechtsgutachten betreffend die Stellung des Bundesverfassungsgerichts. In H. Dreier, ed., *Rechtsstaat – Demokratie – Grundrechte: ausgewählte Abhandlungen aus fünf Jahrzehnten*. Tübingen: Mohr Siebeck, pp. 511–554.
Thomas, C. (1902). *The Bastille. Vol. I of The French Revolution: A History*, London: Chiswick Press.
Thomassen, L. (2007). Within the Limits of Deliberative Reason Alone: Habermas, Civil Disobedience and Constitutional Democracy. *European Journal of Political Theory* 6 (2), 200–218.

Thompson, D. (2002). *Just Elections. Creating a Fair Electoral Process in the United States*, Chicago: University of Chicago Press.
Thompson, D. (2022). Why Representative Democracy Requires Referendums. In James A. Gardener, ed., *Comparative Electoral Law*. Cheltenham: Edward Elgar, pp. 193–211.
Thompson, M. (2004). What Is It to Wrong Someone? A Puzzle about Justice. In R. Wallace, P. Pettit, S. Scheffler, & M. Smith, eds., *Reason and Value: Themes from the Moral Philosophy of Joseph Raz*. Oxford: Oxford University Press.
Thomson, V. E., & Arroyo, V. (2011). Upside-Down Cooperative Federalism: Climate Change Policymaking and the States. *Virginia Environmental Law Journal*, 29 (1), 1–62.
Thoreau, H. D. (1974). *The Writings of Henry David Thoreau: Reform Papers*. Edited by T. F. Glick. Princeton: Princeton University Press.
Thornhill, C. (2011). *A Sociology of Constitutions*, Cambridge: Cambridge University Press.
Thornhill, C. (2012). Contemporary Constitutionalism and the Dialectic of Constituent Power. *Global Constitutionalism*, 1 (3), 369–404.
Thornhill, C. (2013). A Sociology of Constituent Power: The Political Code of Transnational Societal Constitutions. *Indiana Journal of Global Legal Studies*, 20 (2), 551–603.
Thornhill, C. (2017). The Rise and Fall of Corporatist Constitutionalism: A Sociological Thesis. In A. C. Pinto, ed., *Corporatism and Fascism: The Corporatist Wave in Europe*. London: Routledge.
Thornhill, C. (2020). Constitutionalism and Populism: National Political Integration and Global Legal Integration. *International Theory*, 12 (1), 1–32.
Thrush, A., & Ferris, J. P., eds. (2010). *The House of Commons 1604–1629*, vol. I, Cambridge: Cambridge University Press for The History of Parliament Trust.
Tiebout, C. (1956). A Pure Theory of Local Expenditures. *Journal of Political Economy*, 64 (5), 416–424.
Tiede, L. B. (2006). Judicial Independence: Often Cited, Rarely Understood. *Journal of Contemporary Legal Issues*, 15 (1), 129–161.
Tierney, B. (1997). *The Idea of Natural Rights*, Grand Rapids: Emory University Press.
Tierney, S. (2004). *Constitutional Law and National Pluralism*, Oxford: Oxford University Press.
Tierney, S. (2012). *Constitutional Referendums: The Theory and Practice of Republican Deliberation*, Oxford: Oxford University Press.
Tierney, S. (2018). Federalism and Constitutional Theory. In G. Jacobsohn, & M. Schor, eds, *Comparative Constitutional Theory*. Cheltenham: Edward Elgar Publishing, pp. 45–65.
Tilly, C. (1978). *From Mobilization to Revolution*, Reading, MA: Random House.
Tilly, C. (1990). *Coercion, Capital, and European States AD 990–1992*, Oxford: Blackwell.
Tilly, C. (1995). *European Revolutions, 1492–1992*, Oxford: Blackwell.
Tobin, B. (2016). Marriage Equality in Ireland: The Politico-Legal Context. *International Journal of Law, Policy and the Family*, 30 (2), 115–130.
Tocqueville, A. (1835). *Democracy in America*, vol. I. Translated by H. Reeve. London: Saunders and Otley, Conduit Street.
Tocqueville, A. (1956). *Democracy in America*, New York: New America Library.
Tocqueville, A. (2008). *The Ancien Régime and the Revolution*. Translated by Gerald Bevan. London: Penguin Classics.
Toharia, J. J. (1975). Judicial Independence in an Authoritarian Regime: The Case of Contemporary Spain. *Law and Society Review*, 9 (3), 475–496.
Tollison, R. (1988). Public Choice and Legislation. *Virginia Law Review* 74 (2), 339–371.
Tomkins, A. (2005). *Our Republican Constitution*, Oxford: Hart Publishing.

Tomkins, A. (2006). The Struggle to Delimit Executive Power in Britain. In P. Craig, & A. Tomkins, eds., *The Executive and Public Law*. Oxford: Oxford University Press, pp. 16–51.

Tomkins, A. (2010). The Role of the Courts in the Political Constitution. *University of Toronto Law Journal*, 60 (1), 1–22.

Tomlinson, J. (2019a). *Justice in the Digital State: Assessing the Next Revolution in Administrative Justice*, Bristol: Policy Press.

Tomlinson, J. (2019b). Quick and Uneasy Justice: An Administrative Analysis of the EU Settlement Scheme. *Public Law Project*. Available from: https://publiclawproject.org.uk/resources/quick-and-uneasy-justice/

Tormey, S. (2014). The Contemporary Crisis of Representative Democracy. *Democratic Theory* 1 (2), 104–112.

Traverso E. (2021). *Revolution: An Intellectual History*, New York: Verso.

Tribe, L. H., & Gudridge, P. O. (2004). The Anti-Emergency Constitution. *Yale Law Journal*, 113 (8), 1801–1870.

Trochev, A., & Ellett, R. (2014). Judges and Their Allies: Rethinking Judicial Autonomy Through the Prism of Off-Bench Resistance. *Journal of Law and Courts*, 2 (1), 67–91.

Troper, M. (1973). *La séparation des pouvoirs et l'histoire constitutionelle française*, Paris: LGDJ.

Troper, M. (1994). *Pour une théorie juridique de l'Etat*, Paris: Presses Universitaires de France.

Troper, M. (2008). *Comment décident les juges : la constitution, les collectivités locales et l'éducation*, Paris: Economica.

Trotsky, L. (2017). *The History of the Russian Revolution*, Chicago, IL: Penguin Classics.

Trouillot, M. R. (1997). *Silencing the Past: Power and the Production of History*, Boston: Beacon Press.

Trudeau, P. E. (1993). *Memoirs*, Toronto: McClelland and Stewart.

Trueblood, L. (2020). Are Referendums Directly Democratic? *Oxford Journal of Legal Studies*, 40 (3), 425–448.

Trueblood, L. (2022). Brexit and Two Roles for Referendums in the United Kingdom. In R. Albert, & R. Stacey, eds., *The Limits and Legitimacy of Referendums*. Oxford: Oxford University Press, pp. 183–201.

Truman, B. (1962). Federalism and the Party System. In A. B. Wildavsky, ed., *American Federalism in Perspective*. Boston: Little, Brown.

Tsakyrakis, S. (2009). Proportionality: An Assault on Human Rights? *International Journal of Constitutional Law*, 7 (3), 468–493.

Tsebelis, G. (2002). *Veto Players: How Political Institutions Work*, Princeton: Princeton University Press.

Tuck, R. (2016). *The Sleeping Sovereign*, Cambridge: Cambridge University.

Tuck, R. (2019). Active and Passive Citizens. The Yeoh Tiong Lay Centre for Politics, Philosophy & Law annual lecture. London: King's College.

Tuck, R. (2020). *The Left Case for Brexit*, London: Polity Books.

Tucker, P. (2018). *Unelected Power: The Quest for Legitimacy in Central Banking and the Regulatory State*, Cambridge, MA: Harvard University Press.

Tully, J. (1995). *Strange Multiplicity: Constitutionalism in an Age of Diversity*, Cambridge: Cambridge University Press.

Tuori, K. (2020). Constitutional Review in Finland. In A. v. Bogdandy, P. M. Huber, & C. Grabenwarter, eds., *Constitutional Adjudication: Institutions. Vol. III of The Max Planck Handbooks in European Public Law*. Oxford: Oxford University Press, pp. 183–221.

Turner, A. (2015). *The Case for Monetary Finance – An Essentially Political Issue*, Washington, DC: International Monetary Fund.

Turpin, C. (2002). *British Government and the Constitution*, 5th edn, Colchester: Butterworths.
Turner, B. (2001). The Erosion of Citizenship. *British Journal of Sociology*, 52 (2), 189–209.
Turner, P. G., ed. (2016). *Equity and Administration*, Cambridge: Cambridge University Press.
Tushnet, M. (1999). *Taking the Constitution Away from the Courts*, Princeton: Princeton University Press.
Tushnet, M. (2004). Constitutional Hardball. *John Marshall Law Review*, 37 (2), 523–553.
Tushnet, M. (2005a). Emergencies and the Idea of Constitutionalism. In M. Tushnet ed., *The Constitution in Wartime: Beyond Alarmism and Complacency*. Durham: Duke University Press, pp. 39–54.
Tushnet, M. (2005b). The Relationship between Judicial Review of Legislation and the Interpretation of Non-Constitutional Law, with Reference to Third Party Effect. In A. Sajó, & R. Uitz, eds., *The Constitution in Private Law Relations. Expanding Constitutionalism*. Utrecht: Eleven International Publishing, pp. 167–182.
Tushnet, M. (2006). Weak-Form Judicial Review and "Core" Civil Liberties, *Harvard Civil Rights-Civil Liberties Law Review*, 41 (1), 1–22.
Tushnet, M. (2008a). The Political Constitution of Emergency Powers: Some Conceptual Issues. In V. V. Ramraj, ed., *Emergencies and the Limits of Legality*. Cambridge, UK: Cambridge University Press, pp. 145–155.
Tushnet, M. (2008b). *Weak Courts, Strong Rights. Judicial Review and Social Welfare Rights in Comparative Constitutional Law*, Princeton: Princeton University Press.
Tushnet, M. (2011). Administrative Law in the 1930s: The Supreme Court's Accommodation of Progressive Legal Theory. *Duke Law Journal*, 60 (7), 1565–1638.
Tushnet, M. (2015). Authoritarian Constitutionalism. *Cornell Law Review*, 100 (2), 2015, 391–463.
Tushnet, M. (2017a). Making Easy Cases Harder. In V. Jackson, & M. Tushnet, eds., *Proportionality: New Frontiers, New Challenges*. Cambridge: Cambridge University Press, pp. 303–321.
Tushnet, M. (2017b). Review of Böckenförde, *Constitutional and Political Theory: Selected Writings*. *Constellations*, 24 (3), 480–488.
Tushnet, M. (2018a). *Advanced Introduction to Comparative Constitutional Law*. 2nd revised edn, Cheltenham: Edward Elgar Publishing Ltd.
Tushnet, M. (2018b). Amendment Theory and Constituent Power. In G. Jacobson, & M. Schor, eds., *Comparative Constitutional Theory*. Cheltenham: Edward Elgar, pp. 317–333.
Tushnet, M. (2018c). Comparing Right-wing and Left-wing Populism. In M. Graber, S. Levinson, & M. Tushnet, eds., *Constitutional Democracy in Crisis*. Oxford: Oxford University Press, pp. 639–650.
Tushnet, M. (2019). Institutions Supporting Constitutional Democracy: Some Thoughts About Anti-Corruption (and Other) Agencies. *Singapore Journal of Legal Studies*, 2019, 440–455.
Tushnet, M. (2020). *Taking Back the Constitution: Activist Judges and the Next Age of American Law*, New Haven: Yale University Press.
Tushnet, M. (2021). *The New Fourth Branch: Institutions for Protecting Constitutional Democracy*, Cambridge: Cambridge University Press.
Tymoigne, E. (2009). *Central Banking, Asset Prices and Financial Fragility*, London: Routledge.
Uitz, R. (2015). Can You Tell When an Illiberal Democracy Is in the Making? An Appeal to Comparative Constitutional Scholarship from Hungary. *International Journal of Constitutional Law*, 13 (1), 279–300.

Umbach, M., ed. (2002). *German Federalism: Past, Present and Future*, London: Palgrave Macmillan.
Underdal, A. (2010). Complexity and Challenges of Long-Term Environmental Governance. *Global Environmental Change*, 20 (3), 386–393.
Unger, R. M. (1976). *Law in Modern Society*, New York: Free Press.
United Nations Environment Programme. (2019a). *Emissions Gap Report 2019*, Nairobi: UNEP.
United Nations Environment Programme. (2019b). *Environmental Rule of Law: First Global Report*, Nairobi: UNEP.
United States v. Cullen, 454 F.2d 386, 392 (7th Cir. 1971).
United States v. O'Brien, 391 U.S. 367, 382 (1968).
Urbániková, M., & Šipulová, K. (2018). Failed Expectations: Does the Establishment of Judicial Councils Enhance Confidence in Courts? *German Law Journal*, 19 (7), 2105–2136.
Urbina, F. (2017). *A Critique of Proportionality and Balancing*, Cambridge: Cambridge University Press.
Urbinati, N. (1998). Democracy and Populism. *Constellations*, 5 (1), 110–124.
Urbinati, N. (2006). *Representative Democracy: Principles and Genealogy*, Chicago: University of Chicago Press.
Urbinati, N. (2014). *Democracy Disfigured: Opinion, Truth and The People*, Cambridge, MA: Harvard University Press.
Urbinati, N. (2019). *Me The People: How Populism Transforms Democracy*, Cambridge, MA: Harvard University Press.
Urbinati, N., & Warren, M. (2008). The Concept of Representation in Contemporary Political Theory. *Annual Review of Political Science*, 11 (1), 387–412.
U.S. Congress. (ca. 2020). Majority and Minority Leaders. *United States Senate*. Available from: www.senate.gov/artandhistory/history/common/briefing/Majority_Minority_Leaders.htm (Accessed: 22 September 2020).
Vallier, K. (2015). Public Justification Versus Public Deliberation: The Case for Divorce. *Canadian Journal of Philosophy*, 45 (2), 139–158.
van Caenegem, R. C. (2012). *An Historical Introduction to Western Constitutional Law*, Cambridge: Cambridge University Press.
van Dijk, F. (2024). Conceptualizing and Measuring Judicial Independence. In Lee Epstein and others (eds.), *The Oxford Handbook of Judicial Behaviour*. Oxford: Oxford University Press, pp. 775–800.
Van Doorslaer, H., & Vermeiren, M. (2021). Pushing on a String: Monetary Policy, Growth Models and the Persistence of Low Inflation in Advanced Capitalism. *New Political Economy*, 26 (5), 797–816.
van Parijs, P. (1995). *Real Freedom for All*, Oxford: Oxford University Press.
van Parijs, P. (2008). Linguistic Justice for Europe, Belgium, and the World. In B. Raymaekers, ed., *Lectures for the XXIst Century*. Leuven: Leuven University Press, pp. 13–36.
van Parijs, P. (2011). *Linguistic Justice for Europe and for the World*, Oxford: Oxford University Press.
van Reybrouck, D. (2014). *Contre les élections*, Paris: Actes Sud.
van Reybrouck, D. (2016). *Against Elections: The Case for Democracy*, London: Random House.
van Steenbergen, B. (1994). *The Condition of Citizenship*, New York: Sage.
van 't Klooster, J. (2018). *How to make money: Distributive justice, finance, and monetary constitutions*. PhD thesis. Cambridge University.
van 't Klooster, J. (2019). Central Banking in Rawls's Property-Owning Democracy. *Political Theory*, 47 (5), 674–698.

van 't Klooster, J. (2020). The Ethics of Delegating Monetary Policy. *Journal of Politics*, 82 (2), 587–599.

van 't Klooster, J., & Fontan, C. (2020). The Myth of Market Neutrality: A Comparative Study of the European Central Bank's and the Swiss National Bank's Corporate Security Purchases. *New Political Economy*, 25 (6), 865–879.

van 't Klooster, J., & van Tilburg, R. (2020). *Targeting a sustainable recovery with Green TLTROs*. Positive Money Europe & Sustainable Finance Lab.

Vargova, M. (2005). Democratic Deficit of a Dualist Deliberative Constitutionalism: Bruce Ackerman and Jürgen Habermas, *Ratio Juris*, 18 (3), 365–386.

Varol, O. O., Dalla Peregrina, L., & Groupa, N. (2017). An Empirical Analysis of Judicial Transformation in Turkey. *American Journal of Comparative Law*, 65 (1), 187–216.

Varuhas, J. (2013). The Reformation of English Administrative Law? "Rights", Rhetoric and Reality. *Cambridge Law Journal*, 72 (2), 369–413.

Varuhas, J. (2018). Taxonomy and Public Law. In M. Elliott, J. Varuhas, & S. Stark, eds., *The Unity of Public Law? Doctrinal, Theoretical and Comparative Perspectives*. Oxford: Hart Publishing, pp. 39–78.

Vedel, G. (1985). Rétrodictions: Si de Gaulle avait perdu en 1962, si Alain Poher avait gagné en 1969. In O. Duhamel, & J.-L. Parodi, eds., *La Constitution de la cinquième République*. Paris: Presses de la Fondation Nationale des Sciences Politiques, pp. 133–165.

Vermeule, A. (2007). *Mechanisms of Democracy. Institutional Design Writ Small*, Oxford: Oxford University Press.

Vermeule, A. (2016). *Law's Abnegation: From Law's Empire to the Administrative State*, Cambridge, MA: Harvard University Press.

Vermeule, A. (2022). *Common Good Constitutionalism*, Boston: Polity.

Versteeg, M., & Ginsburg, T. (2016). Measuring the Rule of Law: A Comparison of Indicators. *Law and Social Inquiry*, 42 (1), 100–137.

Versteeg, M., & Zackin, E. (2016). Constitutions Unentrenched: Toward an Alternative Theory of Constitutional Design. *American Political Science Review*, 110 (4), 657–674.

Viehoff, D. (2014). Democratic Equality and Political Authority. *Philosophy and Public Affairs*, 42 (4), 337–375.

Vile, M. J. C. (1967). *Constitutionalism and the Separation of Powers*, Oxford: Clarendon Press.

Vinx, L. (2007). *Legality and Legitimacy*, Oxford: Oxford University Press.

Vinx, L., ed., trans. (2015). *The Guardian of the Constitution: Hans Kelsen and Carl Schmitt on the Limits of Constitutional Law*, Cambridge: Cambridge University Press.

Viola, L. (2020). *The Closure of the International System: How Institutions Create Political Equalities and Hierarchies*, New York: Cambridge University Press.

Voigt, C. ed. (2013). *Rule of Law for Nature*, Cambridge: Cambridge University Press.

Voigt, S., Gutmann, J., & Feld, L. P. (2015). Economic Growth and Judicial Independence, a Dozen Years On: Cross-country Evidence Using and Updated Set of Indicators. *European Journal of Political Economy*, 38 (C), 197–211.

Volk, C. (2012). Why Global Constitutionalism Does not Live up to Its Promises. *Goettingen Journal of International Law*, 4 (2), 551–574.

Volpp, L. (2017). Feminist, Sexual, and Queer Citizenship. In A. Shachar et al., eds. *The Oxford Handbook of Citizenship*. Oxford: Oxford University Press, pp. 153–177.

von Haldenwang, C. (2016). *Measuring Legitimacy – New Trends, Old Shortcomings?* Bonn: Deutsches Institut fur Entwicklungspolitik.

von Mohl, R. (1866). *Die Polizeiwissenschaft nach den Grundsaetzen des Rechtsstaates*, 3rd edn, Tuebingen: Verlag H. Laupp'schen.

von Stein, L. (2010 [1870]). *Handbuch der Verwaltungslehre und des Verwaltungsrechts.* Edited by Utz Schliesky. Tübingen: Mohr Siebeck.
Voßkuhle, A. (2004). Die Renaissance der Allgemeinen Staatslehre im Zeitalter der Europäisierung und Internationalisierung, *Juristische Schulung,* 1 (44), 2–7.
Voßkuhle, A. (2013). Die Staatstheorie des Bundesverfassungsgerichts, *Der Staat,* Beiheft 21, 371–383.
Wade, W. (1955). The Basis of Legal Sovereignty. *Cambridge Law Journal,* 13 (2), 172–197.
Wadsworth, T., & Kubrin, C. E. (2007). Hispanic Suicide in U.S. Metropolitan Areas: Examining the Effects of Immigration, Assimilation, Affluence, and Disadvantage. *American Journal of Sociology,* 112 (6), 1848–1885.
Wagner, W. (2010). Administrative Law, Filter Failure, and Information Capture. *Duke Law Journal,* 59 (7), 1321–1432.
Wahl, R. (1981). Der Vorrang der Verfassung. *Der Staat,* 20, 485–516.
Wahl, R. (2006). *Herausforderungen und Antworten: Das Öffentliches Recht der letzten fünf Jahrzehnte,* Berlin: de Gruyter.
Wahnich S. (2012). *In Defence of the Terror: Liberty or Death in the French Revolution,* New York: Verso.
Waldo, D. (1948). *The Administrative State: A Study of the Political Theory of American Public Administration,* New York: Ronald Press.
Waldron, J. (1989a). Democratic Theory and the Public Interest. *American Political Science Review,* 83, (4), 1322–1328.
Waldron, J. (1989b). The Rule of Law in Contemporary Liberal Theory. *Ratio Juris* 2 (1), 79–96.
Waldron, J. (1992). Superseding Historic Injustice. *Ethics,* 103 (1), 4–28.
Waldron, J. (1993a). *Liberal Rights,* Cambridge: Cambridge University Press.
Waldron, J. (1993b). Rights. In R. Goodin, & P. Pettit, eds., *A Companion to Contemporary Political Philosophy,* Oxford: Blackwell.
Waldron, J. (1993c). A Rights-Based Critique of Constitutional Rights Review. *Oxford Journal Law Review,* 13 (1), 18–51.
Waldron, J. (1999a). *Law and Disagreement,* Oxford: Oxford University Press.
Waldron, J. (1999b). *The Dignity of Legislation,* Cambridge: Cambridge University Press.
Waldron, J. (2000). Legislation by Assembly. *Loyola Law Review,* 46 (3), 507–534.
Waldron, J. (2002). Is the Rule of Law an Essentially Contested Concept (in Florida)? *Law & Philosophy,* 21 (2), 137–164.
Waldron, J. (2003). Legislating with Integrity. *Fordham Law Review,* 72 (2), 373–394.
Waldron, J. (2004). Liberalism, Political and Comprehensive. In G. Gaus, & C. Kukathas, eds., *Handbook of Political Theory.* London: Sage Publications.
Waldron, J. (2005). Compared to What? Judicial Activism and the New Zealand Parliament. *New Zealand Law Journal,* 2005 (11), 441–445.
Waldron, J. (2006). The Core of the Case Against Judicial Review. *The Yale Law Journal,* 115 (6), 1346–1406.
Waldron, J. (2007). Dignity and Rank. *European Journal of Sociology,* 48 (2), 201–237.
Waldron, J. (2008). Did Dworkin Ever Answer the Crits? In S. Hershovitz, ed., *Exploring Law's Empire: The Jurisprudence of Ronald Dworkin.* Oxford: Oxford University Press, pp. 155–182.
Waldron, J. (2008–2009). The Concept and the Rule of Law. *Georgia Law Review,* 43 (1), 1–61.
Waldron, J. (2011a). Are Sovereigns Entitled to the Benefit of the International Rule of Law? *European Journal of International Law,* 22 (2), 315–343.

Waldron, J. (2011b). The Rule of Law and the Importance of Procedure. In J. Flemming, ed., *Getting to the Rule of Law: NOMOS L*. New York: New York University Press, pp. 3–31.

Waldron, J. (2011c). Thoughtfulness and the Rule of Law. *British Academy Review*, 18, 1–8.

Waldron, J. (2012a). Bicameralism and the Separation of Powers. *Current Legal Problems*, 65 (1), 31–57.

Waldron, J. (2012b). *Dignity, Rank and Rights*, New York: Oxford University Press.

Waldron, J. (2012c). How Law Protects Dignity. *Cambridge Law Journal*, 71 (1), 200–222.

Waldron, J. (2012d). *The Rule of Law and the Measure of Property*, Cambridge: Cambridge University Press.

Waldron, J. (2013). Citizenship and Dignity. In C. McCrudden, ed., *Understanding Human Dignity*. London: The British Academy, pp. 327–343.

Waldron, J. (2014a). Five to Four: Why Do Bare Majorities Rule on Courts? *Yale Law Journal*, 123 (6), 1692–1731.

Waldron, J. (2014b). Never Mind the Constitution. *Harvard Law Review*, 127 (4), 1147–1172.

Waldron, J. (2015). Is Dignity the Foundation of Human Rights? In M. Liao, M. Renzo, & R. Cruft, eds., *The Philosophical Foundations of Human Rights*. Oxford: Oxford University Press, pp. 117–137.

Waldron, J. (2016a). Accountability and Insolence. In J. Waldron, *Political Political Theory: Essays on Institutions*. Cambridge, MA: Harvard University Press, pp. 167–194.

Waldron, J. (2016b). Constitutionalism: A Skeptical View. In J. Waldron, *Political Political Theory: Essays on Institutions*. Cambridge, MA: Harvard University Press, pp. 23–44.

Waldron, J. (2016c). Political Political Theory. In J. Waldron, *Political Political Theory. Essays on Institutions*. Cambridge, MA: Harvard University Press, pp. 1–22.

Waldron, J. (2016d). *Political Political Theory: Essays on Institutions*, Cambridge, M: Harvard University Press.

Waldron, J. (2016e). Representative Lawmaking. In J. Waldron, *Political Political Theory. Essays on Institutions*. Cambridge, MA: Harvard University Press, pp. 125–144.

Waldron, J. (2016f). Separation of Powers in Thought and Practice. In J. Waldron, *Political Political Theory. Essays on Institutions*. Cambridge, MA: Harvard University Press, pp. 45–71.

Waldron, J. (2017). *One Another's Equals. The Basis of Human Equality*, Cambridge, MA: Harvard University Press.

Waldron, J. (2018). All Kings in the Kingdom of Ends. NYU School of Law, Public Law Research Paper No. 13–39. Available from: https://ssrn.com/abstract=3207754

Waldron J. (2019). Quibbling, Wrangling. *London Review of Books*. 12 September.

Waldstreicher, D. (2010). *Slavery's Constitution: From Revolution to Ratification*, New York: Hill & Wang Inc.

Walen, A. (2009). Judicial Review in Review: A Four-Part Defense of Legal Constitutionalism. A Review Essay on Political Constitutionalism. *International Journal of Constitutional Law*, 7 (2), 329–354.

Walker, N. (2002). The Idea of Constitutional Pluralism. *Modern Law Review*, 65 (3), 317–359.

Walker, N. (2003). Postnational Constitutionalism and the Problem of Translation. In J. Weiler, & M. Wind, eds., *European Constitutionalism beyond the State*. Cambridge: Cambridge University Press.

Walker, N. (2016). The Return of Constituent Power: A Reply to Mattias Kumm. *International Journal of Constitutional Law*, 14 (4), 906–913.

Walker, N. (2019). Populism and Constitutional Tension, *International Journal of Constitutional Law*, 17 (2), 515–535.

Wall Street Journal. (1984). In Praise of Huddled Masses. Editorial, 3 July.
Waluchow, W. J. (2007). A Common Law Theory of Judicial Review. *The American Journal of Jurisprudence*, 52 (1), 297–312.
Waluchow, W. J. (2014). Constitutional Interpretation. In A. Marmor, ed., *The Routledge Companion to Philosophy of Law*. New York: Routledge, pp. 417–433.
Waluchow, W. J. & Kyritsis, D. (2023). Constitutionalism. In E. Zalta, ed., *The Stanford Encyclopedia of Philosophy* (Summer 2023 Edition). Available from: https://plato.stanford.edu/archives/sum2023/entries/constitutionalism/.
Walzer, M. (1967). The Obligation to Disobey. *Ethics*, 77 (3), 163–175.
Walzer, M. (1970). *Obligations: Essays on Disobedience, War, and Citizenship*, Cambridge, MA: Harvard University Press.
Walzer, M. (1983). *Spheres of Justice: A Defense of Pluralism and Equality*, New York: Basic Books.
Ward, H., & Weale, A. (2010). Is Rule by Majorities Special? *Political Studies*, 58 (1), 26–46.
Warren, M. E. (2017). A Problem-based Approach to Democratic Theory. *American Political Science Review*, 111 (1), 39–53.
Warren, M. E. (2018). How Representation Enables Democratic Citizenship. In D. Castiglione, & J. Pollack, eds., *Creating Political Presence: The New Politics of Democratic Representation*. Chicago: University of Chicago Press, pp. 39–60.
Warren, M. E., & Pearse, H., eds. (2008). *Designing Deliberative Democracy: The British Columbia Citizen's Assembly*, Cambridge: Cambridge University Press.
Watkins, D., & Lemieux, S. (2015). Compared to What? Judicial Review and Other Veto Points in Contemporary Democratic Theory. *Perspectives on Politics*, 13 (2), 312–326.
Watts, R. L. (2008). *Comparing Federal Systems*, 3rd edn, Kingston/Montreal: McGill-Queens University Press.
Watts, R. L. (1998). Federalism, Federal Political Systems, and Federations. *Annual Review of Political Science*, 1 (1), 117–137.
Watts, V. (2013). Indigenous Place-Thought & Agency Amongst Humans and Non-humans (First Woman and Sky Woman go on a European World Tour!). *Decolonization: Indigeneity, Education & Society*, 2 (1), 20–34.
Weaver, R. H., & Kysar, D. A. (2017). Courting Disaster: Climate Change and the Adjudication of Catastrophe. *Notre Dame Law Journal*, 93 (1), 295–356.
Webb, P. (2013). *International Judicial Integration and Fragmentation*, Oxford: Oxford University Press.
Webb Yackee, J., & Webb Yackee, S. (2006). A Bias toward Business? Assessing Interest Group Influence on the U.S. Bureaucracy. *Journal of Politics* 68 (1), 128–139.
Webber, G. (2014). On the Loss of Rights. In G. Huscroft, B. Miller, & G. Webber, eds., *Proportionality and the Rule of Law*. Cambridge: Cambridge University Press, pp. 123–154.
Webber, G. (2017). Loyal Opposition and the Political Constitution, *Oxford Journal of Legal Studies*, 37 (2), 357–382.
Webber, G., Yowell, P., Ekins, R.; Köpcke, M., Miller, B. W., & Urbina, F. J. (2018). *Legislated Rights: Securing Human Rights through Legislation*, Cambridge: Cambridge University Press.
Webber, G., & Yowell, P. (2020). *Legislated Rights* in the real world. *Jerusalem Review of Legal Studies*, 20 (1), 145–170.
Weber, B. (2018). *Democratizing Money?* Cambridge: Cambridge University Press.
Weber, M. (1946). Bureaucracy. In H.H. Gerth & C. Wright Mills, eds., *From Max Weber: Essays in Sociology*. New York: Oxford, 196–245.
Weber, M. (1964). *Wirtschaft und Gesellschaft*. Edited by J. Winckelmann. Vol. II. Köln, Berlin: Kiepenheuer & Witsch.

Weber, M. (1978). *Economy and Society: An Outline of Interpretive Sociology*. Edited by G. Roth, & C. Wittich. Berkeley: University of California Press.

Weber, M. (1994 [1919]). Parliament and Government in Germany under a New Political Order. In P. Lassman, & R. Speirs eds., *Political Writings*. Cambridge: Cambridge University Press, pp. 130–217.

Weil, P. (2012). *The Sovereign Citizen*, Philadelphia: University of Pennsylvania Press.

Weil, S. (2013 [1950]). *On the Abolition of Parties*. Translated by S. Leys. New York: New York Review of Books.

Weiler, J. (1981). The Community System: The Dual Character of Supranationalism, *Yearbook of European Law*, 1, 268–306.

Weiler, J. H. H. (1991). The Transformation of Europe. *Yale Law Journal*, 100 (8), 2403–2483.

Weiler, J. H. H. (2003). In Defense of the Status Quo, Europe's Constitutional Sonderweg. In J. H. H. Weiler, & M. Wind, eds., *European Constitutionalism beyond the State*. Cambridge: Cambridge University Press, pp. 7–25.

Weiler, J. H. H., Haltern, U. R., & Mayer, F. C. (1995). European Democracy and Its Critique, *West European Politics*, 18 (3), 4–39.

Weiler, J. H. H., & Wind, M., eds. (2003). *European Constitutionalism beyond the State*, Cambridge: Cambridge University Press.

Weiler, P. (1982). *The New Liberalism: Liberal Social Theory in Great Britain, 1889–1914*, London: Routledge.

Weill, R. (2012). Reconciling Parliamentary Sovereignty and Judicial Review: On the Theoretical and Historical Origins of the Israeli Legislative Override Power. *Hastings Constitutional Law Quarterly*, 39 (2), 457–512.

Weill, R. (2014). The New Commonwealth Model of Constitutionalism Notwithstanding: On Judicial Review and Constitution-Making. *American Journal of Comparative Law*, 62, 127.

Weinberg, J. (2018). The View from the Oval Office: Understanding the Legislative Presidency. *The Journal of Legislative Studies*, 24 (4), 1–18.

Weinrib, J. (2016). *Dimensions of Dignity: The Theory and Practice of Modern Constitutional Law*, Cambridge: Cambridge University Press.

Weinstein, J. (2018). Climate Change Disinformation, Citizen Competence, and the First Amendment. *University of Colorado Law Review*, 89 (2), 341–376.

Weinstock, D. (2001). Towards a Normative Theory of Federalism. *International Social Science Journal*, 53 (167), 75–83.

Weinstock, D. (2003). The Antinomy of Language Rights. In W. Kymlicka, & A. Patten, eds., *Language Rights and Political Theory*. Oxford: University Press, pp. 250–270.

Weinstock, D. (2010). On Voting Ethics for Dual Nationals. In K. Breen, ed., *After the Nation-State*. London: Palgrave Macmillan, pp. 177–195.

Weinstock, D. (2015a). In Praise of Some Unfashionable Democratic Institutions: Political Parties, Party Discipline, and "First Past the Post". *Journal of Parliamentary and Political Law*, 9, 291–306.

Weinstock, D. (2015b). Health Justice after the Social Determinants of Health Revolution. *Social Theory and Health*, 13 (3–4), 437–453.

Weinstock, D. (2015c). Integrating Intermediate Goods to Theories of Distributive Justice: The Importance of Platforms. *Res Publica*, 21 (2), 171–183.

Weinstock, D. (2016). How Democratic Is Civil Disobedience? *Criminal Law and Philosophy*, 10 (4), 707–720.

Weinstock, D. (2017). The Complex Normative Landscape of Electoral Systems. In P. Loewen, A. Potter, & D. Weinstock, eds., *Should We Change How We Vote?* Montreal: McGill-Queens Press, pp. 14–22.

Weinstock, D. (2019). On Partisan Compromise. *Political Theory*, 47 (1), 90–96.
Weinstock, D. (2020). What's So Funny About Voting Rights For Children? *Georgetown Journal of Law and Public Policy*, 18 (2), 751–771.
Weis, L. (2017). Constitutional Directive Principles. *Oxford Journal of Legal Studies*, 37 (4), 916–945.
Wellens, K. (2010). Revisiting Solidarity as a (Re-) Emerging Constitutional Principle: Some Further Reflections. In R. Wolfrum, & C. Kojima, eds., *Solidarity: A Structural Principle of International Law*. Springer: Berlin, Heidelberg, pp. 3–54.
Weller, P. (2015). Cabinet Government. In B. Galligan, & S. Brenton, eds., *Constitutional Conventions in Westminster Systems*. Cambridge: Cambridge University Press, pp. 72–90.
Wellman, C. H. (2008). Immigration and Freedom of Association. *Ethics*, 119 (1), 109–141.
Wellman, C. H. (2011). In Defense of the Right to Exclude. In G. Brock, & C. H. Wellman, *Debating the Ethics of Immigration: Is There a Right to Exclude?* Oxford: Oxford University Press, pp. 13–56.
Welp, Y., & Whitehead, L. (2020). Recall: Democratic Advance, Safety Valve or Risky Adventure? In Y. Welp and L. Whitehead, eds., *The Politics of Recall Elections*. Basingstoke: Palgrave Macmillan, pp. 9–27.
Wenar, L. (2013). The Nature of Claim-Rights. *Ethics*, 123 (2), 202–229.
Wenar, L. (2017). John Rawls. In E. Zalta, ed., *The Stanford Encyclopedia of Philosophy* (Spring 2017 Edition). Available from: https://plato.stanford.edu/archives/spr2017/entries/rawls/
Wenar, L. (2020). Rights. In E. Zalta, ed., *The Stanford Encyclopaedia of Philosophy* (Spring 2020 Edition). Available from: https://plato.stanford.edu/archives/spr2020/entries/rights/
Wendenburg, H. (1984). *Die Debatte um die Verfassungsgerichtsbarkeit und der Methodenstreit der Staatsrechtslehre in der Weimarer Republik*, Göttingen: Schwartz.
Werner, F. (1959). Verwaltungsrecht als konkretisiertes Verfassungsrecht, *Deutsches Verwaltungsblatt*, 74, 527–533.
Wertheimer, A. (1996). *Exploitation*, Princeton: Princeton University Press.
West, R. (2003). *Re-Imagining Justice: Progressive Interpretations of Formal Equality, Rights, and The Rule of Law*, Aldershot: Ashgate.
West, R. (2011). The Limits of Process. In J. Fleming, ed., *Getting to the Rule of Law: NOMOS L*. New York: New York University Press, pp. 32–51.
Weyland, K. (2020). Populism's Threat to Democracy: Comparative Lessons for the United States. *Perspectives on Politics*, 18 (2), 389–406.
Whalen, C., & Whalen, B. (1989). *The Longest Debate: A Legislative History of the 1964 Civil Rights Act*, Cabin John; Washington, DC: Seven Locks Press.
Wheare, K. C. (1946). *Federal Government*, Oxford: Oxford University Press.
Wheare, K. C. (1951). *Modern Constitutions*, Oxford: Oxford University Pres.
Wheare, K. C. (1967). *Legislatures*, 2nd edn, Oxford: Oxford University Press.
Wheatley, S. (2010). *The Democratic Legitimacy of International Law*, Oxford: Hart.
White, J. (1998). Talking about Religion in the Language of the Law: Impossible but Necessary. *Marquette Law Review*, 81 (2), 177–202.
White, J. (2018). The British Academy Brian Barry Prize Essay: The Ethics of Political Alliance. *British Journal of Political Science*, 48 (3), 593–609.
White, J. (2021). What Kind of Electoral System Sustains a Politics of Firm Commitments? *Representation*, 57 (3), 329–345.
White, J., & Ypi, L. (2010). Rethinking the Modern Prince: Partisanship and the Democratic Ethos. *Political Studies*, 58 (4), 809–828.
White, J., & Ypi, L. (2016). *The Meaning of Partisanship*, Oxford: Oxford University Press.

White, J., & Ypi, L. (2020a). Reselection and Deselection in the Political Party. In Y. Welp, & L. Whitehead, eds., *The Politics of Recall Elections*. Basingstoke: Palgrave Macmillan, pp. 179–199.

White, J., & Ypi, L. (2020b). Recalling Representatives. In N. Urbinati, eds., *Thinking Democracy Now: Between Innovation and Regression*. Milan: Feltrinelli, pp. 135–150.

White, S. (1997). Freedom of Association and the Right to Exclude. *Journal of Political Philosophy*, 5 (4), 373–391.

White, S. (2020). Citizens' Assemblies and Radical Democracy. In B. Leipold, K. Nabulsi, & S. White, eds., *Radical Republicanism: Recovering the Tradition's Popular Heritage*. Oxford: Oxford University Press, pp. 81–102.

White, S. K. (2017). *A Democratic Bearing: Admirable Citizens, Uneven Injustice, and Critical Theory*, Cambridge, UK: Cambridge University Press.

Whyte, K. (2017). Indigenous Climate Change Studies: Indigenizing Futures, Decolonizing the Anthropocene. *English Language Notes*, 55 (1–2), 153–162.

Widner, J. (1999). Building Judicial Independence in Common Law Africa. In A. Schedler, L. Diamond, & M. Plattner, eds., *The Self-Restraining State: Power and Accountability in New Democracies*. Boulder: Lynne Rienner, pp. 177–194.

Wiener, A. (2018). *Contestation and Constitution of Norms in Global International Relations*, New York: Cambridge University Press.

Williams, B. (2005). Realism and Moralism in Political Theory. In B. Williams ed., *In the Beginning Was the Deed. Realism and Moralism in Political Argument*. Princeton: Princeton University Press, pp. 1–17.

Williams, G, Brennan, S, & Lynch, A. (2014). *Blackshield and Williams: Australian Constitutional Law and Theory*, 6th edn, Sydney: Federation Press.

Williams, I. (2021). James VI and I, *rex et iudex*: One King as Judge in Two Kingdoms. In W. Eves, J. Hudson, I. Ivarsen, & S. B. White, eds., *Common Law, Civil Law and Colonial Law: Essays in Comparative Legal History from the Twelfth to the Twentieth Centuries*. Cambridge: Cambridge University Press, pp. 86–119.

Williams, M. (2000). *Voice, Trust and Memory*, Princeton U.P.

Williams, M. S. (1998). *Voice, Trust, and Memory: Marginalized Groups and the Failings of Liberal Representation*, Princeton: Princeton University Press.

Williamson, J. (1990). What Washington Means by Policy Reform. In J. Williamson, ed., *Latin American Adjustment: How Much Has Happened?* Washington, DC: Institute for International Economics, pp. 5–38.

Willoughby, W. W. (1992 [1896]). *An Examination of the Nature of the State: A Study in Political Philosophy*, New York: Macmillan.

Wilson, J. (1992). American Constitutional Conventions. *Buffalo Law Review*, 40 (3), 645–738.

Wilson, J. L. (2019). *Democratic Equality*, Princeton: Princeton University Press.

Winkler, H. (2006). *Germany: The Long Road West. Volume 1: 1789–1933*, Oxford: Oxford University Press.

Winters, J. A. (2011). *Oligarchy*, Cambridge: Cambridge University Press.

Winterton, G. (1980). Can the Commonwealth Parliament Enact "Manner and Form" Legislation? *Federal Law Review*, 11 (2), 167–182.

Witt, J. F. (2007). Anglo-American Empire and the Crisis of the Legal Frame (Will the Real British Empire Please Stand Up?). *Harvard Law Review*, 120 (3), 754–796.

Wong, D. (2004). Rights and Community in Confucianism. In K.-L. Shun, & D. B. Wong, eds., *Confucian Ethics: A Comparative Study of Self, Autonomy, and Community*. Cambridge: Cambridge University Press, pp. 31–48.

Wolf, S. (1997). Happiness and Meaning: Two Aspects of the Good Life. *Social Philosophy and Policy*, 14 (1), 207–225.
Wolff, J., & de-Shalit, A. (2007). *Disadvantage*, Oxford: Oxford University Press.
Wolff, R. P. (1998). *In Defense of Anarchism*, Berkeley: University of California Press.
Wolfrum, R. (2006). Solidarity Amongst States: An Emerging Structural Principle of International Law. In: P.-M. Dupuy, B. Fassbender, M. Shaw, & K. Sommermann, eds., *Common Values in International Law: Essays in Honour of Christian Tomuschat*. Kehl: Engel, pp. 1087–1101.
Wolkestein, F. (2019). *Rethinking Party Reform*, Oxford: Oxford University Press.
Wolkenstein, F. (2020). *Rethinking Party Reform*, Oxford: Oxford University Press.
Wood, G. S. (1969). *The Creation of the American Republic, 1776–1787*, Chapel Hill: University of North Carolina Press.
Wood, G. S. (1993). *The Radicalism of the American Revolution*, New York: Vintage Books.
Wood, S., Eberlein, B., Meidinger, E., Schmidt, R., & Abbott, K. W. (2019). Transnational Business Governance Interactions, Regulatory Quality and Marginalized Actors: An Introduction. In S. Wood et al., eds., *Transnational Business Governance Interactions*. Cheltenham: Edward Elgar Publishing, pp. 1–26.
Wood, S., Tanner, G., & Richardson, B. J. (2010). What Ever Happened to Canadian Environmental Law? *Ecology Law Quarterly*, 37 (4), 981–1040.
Wright, G. (2013). *Sharing the Prize: The Economics of the Civil Rights Revolution in the American South*, Cambridge, MA: Harvard University Press.
Wright, J. (2019). *Pluralism and social epistemology in economics*. PhD thesis. Cambridge: University of Cambridge.
Yamin, A., & Parra, O. (2009). The role of courts in Refining Health policy: The case of the Colombian Court. Manuscript in file with R. Gargarella.
Yamin, A., & Gloppen, S. (2011). *Litigating Health Rights: Can Courts Bring More Justice to Health?* Cambridge: Harvard University Press.
Yeager, L. (1962). *In Search of a Monetary Constitution*, Cambridge, MA: Harvard University Press.
Yeung, K. (2010). The Regulatory State. In Baldwin, R., & Lodge, M., eds., *The Oxford Handbook of Regulation*. Oxford: Oxford University Press, pp. 64–84.
Yeung, K. (2018). Algorithmic Regulation: A Critical Interrogation. *Regulation & Governance*, 12 (4), 505–523.
Young, A. (2008). *Parliamentary Sovereignty and the Human Rights Act*, Oxford: Hart Publishing.
Young, I. M. (1990). *Justice and the Politics of Difference*, Princeton: Princeton University Press.
Young, I. M. (2011). *Responsibility for Justice*, Oxford: Oxford University Press.
Young, J. (1986). *The Washington Community 1800–1828*, New York: Columbia University Press.
Young, K. (2012). *Constituting Economic and Social Rights*, Oxford: Oxford University Press.
Yowell, P. (2018). *Constitutional Rights and Constitutional Design: Moral and Empirical Reasoning in Judicial Review*, Oxford: Hart Publishing.
Zack, N. (2015). *White Privilege and Black Rights: The Injustice of U.S. Police Racial Profiling and Homicide*, New York: Rowman and Littlefield.
Zacklin, R. (1968). *The Amendment of the Constitutive Instruments of the United Nations and Specialised Agencies*, Leyden: Sijthoff (reprint 2005 Brill).
Zahra, T. (2016). *The Great Departure: Mass Migration from Eastern Europe and the Making of the Free World*, New York: W.W. Norton & Company.

Zeisberg, M. (2013). *War Powers*, Princeton: Princeton University Press.
Zhang, Q. (2012). *The Constitution of China: A Contextual Analysis*, Oxford: Hart Publishing.
Zhao, D. (2009). The Mandate of Heaven and Performance Legitimacy in Historical and Contemporary China. *American Behavioral Scientist*, 53 (3), 416–433.
Ziller, J. (2008). Political Accountability in France. In H. Broeksteeg, L. Verhey, & I. Van den Driessche, eds., *Political Accountability in Europe: Which Way Forward?* Groningen: Europa Law Publishing, pp. 81–98.
Zinn, H. (2002 [1968]). *Disobedience and Democracy: Nine Fallacies of Law and Order*, Cambridge, MA: South End Press.
Zreik R. (2018). Kant on Time and Revolution. *Graduate Faculty Philosophy Journal*, 39 (1), 197–225.
Zuber, Christina I., & Szöcsik, E. (2015). Ethnic Outbidding and Nested Competition: Explaining the Extremism of Ethnonational Minority Parties in Europe. *European Journal of Political Research*, 54 (4), 784–801.
Zuckerman, I. (2006). One Law for War and Peace? Judicial Review and Emergency Powers between the Norm and the Exception. *Constellations*, 13 (4), 522–545.
Zurn, C. (2007). *Deliberative Democracy and the Institutions of Judicial Review*, Cambridge: Cambridge University Press.
Zurn, C. (2010). The Logic of Legitimacy: Bootstrapping Paradoxes of Constitutional Democracy. *Legal Theory*, 16 (3), 191–227.
Zurn, C. (2011). Judicial Review, Constitutional Juries and Civic Constitutional Fora: Rights, Democracy and Law. *Theoria*, 58 (2), 63–94.
Zurn, C. F. (2020). Constitutional Interpretation and Public Reason: Seductive Disanalogies. In S. A. Langvatn, M. Kumm, & W. Sadurski, eds., *Public Reason and the Courts*. Cambridge: Cambridge University Press, pp. 323–349.
Zweifel, T. (2006). *International Organizations and Democracy: Accountability, Politics, and Power*, Boulder: Lynne Rienner.
Zweig, E. (1909). *Die Lehre vom Pouvoir Constituant: Ein Beitrag zum Staatrecht der französischen Revolution*, Tübingen: JCB Mohr.

Index

9/11 terrorist attacks, 1042

Abdel Nasser, G., 512, 517
Abebe, A., 617
Abendroth, W., 690
Abizadeh, A., 772, 773, 1059
Ablavsky, G., 510
Abrams, S., 788
abstract review, 857–859
accountability
  performance, 701–702
  policymaking, 703
  principle of, 17
  rights-based, 702
Achen, C., 760
Ackerman, B., 250, 252, 497, 500, 505, 510, 647, 898
  Bills of Rights, 898–900
  Revolutionary Constitutions, 499
  We the People, 3
Act of Settlement 1701, 13
Acton, L., 139
Addressive Theory, 42, 44
administrative constitutionalism, 686
administrative law, 903–906
  de facto powers, 907
  the Crown, 903, 904
  theory, 909
  with delegation, 909–915
Administrative Procedure Act (APA), 420, 690, 715
administrative state, 292–293
  administrative law, 687
  bureaucracy, 680
  concept of, 679–680
  constitutional displacement, 687–691
  delegation, 688
  democratic principles, 691–693
  democratic-constitutional rules, 691
  executive power, 680
  generative conceptions, 683–687
  implementation, 680–683
  regulation, 685
Adolph, C., 636
Affolder, N., 1036
African Americans, 109
Alexy, R., 386
"all affected" principle, 747
Allan, T.R.S., 300
  The Sovereignty of Law, 197
altera pars of government, 271–275
Alternative Vote system, 573
Althusius, J., 208, 559
  Politica, 674
Alvarez, J., 976
American Civil War, 692
American political development (APD), 1077
American Political Science Association (APSA), 782
American Revolution, 492, 501, 502, 503, 504, 506, 507, 508, 509, 516, 517
amnesty, 743
analytic philosophy, 62–64
Anderson, E., 97
  Private Government, 311
anti-populism, 1016–1018
Arab Spring, 491, 501, 502, 519
Arato, A., 220, 221, 223, 250, 645, 724, 725, 1023, 1025
arbitrary power
  definition of, 306
  of public officials, 305
  reduction of, 306
arbitrary rule, 127
Arendt, H., 410, 499, 504–509, 511, 512, 739
Argentina, 999, 1002
aristocracy, 104, 138, 210, 212, 222, 272, 290, 504, 594, 601, 947

Aristotle, 247, 260, 266, 283, 305, 378, 737, 776, 777, 781, 782
   Nichomachean Ethics, 777
Arizona Independent Redistricting Commission, 612
assembly-independent government, 643, 644, 652–653
Austin, J., 193–196, 200, 203
   Lectures on Jurisprudence, or The Philosophy of Positive Law, 193
Australia, 749, 851
Austria, 767, 855, 858, 1005
authoritarian democracy, 238
authoritarian system, 7, 56
authority of justice, 127–129
authorization, form of, 238
Aydın, A., 874

bad revolution, 502–505
balanced multi-partisanship, 616
Banfield, A., 329
Bank of England, 625, 628, 630, 634, 637
Bank of Japan Act, 627
Barak, A., 26, 385
Barber, N., 282
Barère, B., 138
Barroso, R., 35
Barry, B., 138
Bartels, L., 760
Basel Committee for Banking Supervision, 626
Beard, C., 508
Beaud, O., 550
Bedau, H., 401
Beetham, D., 184
Belgium, 140, 145, 150, 569
Belize Constitution, 616
Bellamy, R., 38, 129, 131, 134, 349, 739, 745, 815, 947
   Bills of Rights, 893–898
Benhabib, S., 740
Benjamin, W., 519
Bentham, J., 28, 77, 238, 327, 328, 350
Berlin, I., 74–77, 121, 972
   Two Concepts of Liberty, 75
Bernal, A. M., 516
bespoke/general personnel panels, 615
bicameralism, 654, 773
Bickel, A., 354
   The Least Dangerous Branch: The Supreme Court at the Bar of Politics, 1010
Bill of Rights 1689, 262
Bills of Rights
   Ackerman's view, 898–900
   Bellamy's view, 893–898

constitutional Court, 895
   democracy, 884
   democratic enactment of, 898–900
   Dworkin's view, 885–890
   Ely's view, 890–893
   judicial review, 885
   King's view, 898–900
   legislative, 893–900
   procedural case for, 890–893
   substantive case for, 885–890
   Tushnet's view, 893–898
   Waldron's view, 893–898
birthright citizenship, 748
Black Lives Matter, 519
Blackstone, W., 440, 442, 445–447, 665
   Commentaries on the Laws of England, 665
Blackwell, J., 710
Blake, M., 1059, 1067
Blick, A., 323, 329, 331
Böckenförde, E.-W., 213, 682, 923
Bodin, J., 192, 193, 216, 218, 525, 559, 683
   Les six livres de la république, 208
Bolívar, S., 998, 1009
Bolivia, 1002
Bork, R., 1075
Bostock v. Clayton County, 182
Bradley, J., 1035
Brandenburg v Ohio case, 170
Brazil, 1002
Brennan, J., 758
broad model, public law, 703–704
Brown, H., 401
Brown, W., 1048
Brownlee, K., 407–409
   Conscience and Conviction, 408
Brubaker, R., 1024
Bryce, J., 238
   The American Commonwealth, 321
Buchanan, J., 139, 944
Bugaric, B., 1018, 1019, 1025
Bundesbank, 636
burdens of judgment, 164, 264
burdens of taxation, 158
bureaucratic delegation, 622, 623, 629, 633, 634, 637
Burgess, M., 555, 561, 562, 564
Burke, E., 239, 502, 516, 797, 997
Butterfield, H., 4

Cabral, A., 495
Calabresi, S., 645
Calvert, G., 495
Canada, 24, 137, 140, 150, 569, 748, 772, 851, 1005
Canadian Bill of Rights 1960, 420

Canadian Charter of Rights and Freedoms, 24, 183, 188
Carens, J., 1056–1058, 1059
caretaker constitutional conventions (CCs), 319, 320
Carey, J. M., 648
Carlyle, T., 516
Carré de Malberg, R., 213, 530
Carreras, M., 647
Carter, I., 45
cash-for-passport programs, 749
caveats
  instrumental value, 100
  slippery slope of constitutionalisation, 99–100
Center for Reproductive Rights, 1006
central banks
  bureaucratic delegation, 622, 623
  competition, 625
  constitutionalism, 622
  democracy, 626
  democratic objections, 632–633
  Financial Crisis, 626
  independence, 634–637
  inflation, 629
  interpretation of, 627
  monetary constitution, 623, 624
  monetary policy, 626–631
  permissibility of, 632
  public money, 625
  quantitative easing (QE) operations, 630, 631, 635, 636
  sovereignty, 634
  trade, 625
centripetal democracy, 582–583
Chambers, S., 817
Chapman, E. B., 768
Charles I, 262, 263
Charter of Fundamental Rights of the EU (CFREU), 922
Charter of the German Institute for Human Rights, 612
Charter of the United Nations, 23
Cheibub, J., 650, 652
Chile, 816, 1009
Chilean Constitutional Convention of 2021, 734
Chinese Exclusion Act, 1061
Choudhry, S., 755
Christianity, 336
Christiano, T., 756
Cicero, M. T., 111, 445
citizenship
  boundaries, 737
  civic republicanism, 737, 739, 740. *See also* republicanism
  cultural, 739
  definition of, 742–744
  deliberation, 255–258
  demos, 746, 747
  dignity of, 32
  discursive models of, 739
  economic, 739
  ideal theory of, 740
  jury service to, 745
  jus sanguinis, 748
  jus soli, 748
  liberal, 740
  liberalism, 737
  model of, 114–118
  nation-state, 742
  non-Muslim, 743
  participation of, 112–114
  personal incomes of, 746
  queer theoretic interrogations of, 741
  rights, 738, 741, 744
  state-centric approach, 741
  voting rights, 745, 745
  women's experiences of rights, 740
civil disobedience
  accommodation, 406–411
  conscience, 404
  constitutional protections, 414
  costs and limits, 411–415
  covertness and evasion, 413
  freedom of expression, 397
  integrity-based, 404
  justice-based, 404
  justification of, 402
  leniency, 401–406
  in principle of humanism, 407
  punishment, 397–400
  resistance, 413
  speech, 407
Civil Rights Act of 1866, 1000
Civil Rights Act of 1964, 694
Civil Rights Movement, 403
Civil War, 891, 893, 898, 1000
claim-rights, 42, 43, 47–49
Clark, T. S., 873, 874
Clemens, M., 1058
climate change, 2, 1041–1044
  federalism, 1040–1041, 1049–1051
  responsible agency, 1045–1047
  rights, 1038–1040, 1048–1049
  rule of law, 1036–1038, 1047–1048
climate justice, 1037, 1044, 1047
climate litigation, 1038, 1039, 1040
Cohen, C., 401, 405
Cohen, G. A., 126

Cohen, J., 1025
Coke, E., 284, 286
Cole, G. D. H., 590, 597, 600
Cole, P., 1058
collective agency, 494–498
Collins, H., 608
Colombian Constituent Assembly of 1990, 727–730
colonialism, 506–511, 547
Colón-Ríos, J., 1020
Commonwealth constitutional law, 4, 496
communication-neutrality, 169–171
communicative action, 739
comparative constitutionalis, 342
concentrated constitutional review, 851–852
Concept of Law (Hart), 3, 196, 550
concretized constitutional law, 687
Condorcet Jury Theorem, 103, 758
conflict of interest, 84, 110, 612
Confucian systems, 39, 42
Congress of Racial Equality (CORE), 401
conscience-centered model, 412
consociationalism
   achievement of, 578
   centripetal democracy, 582–583
   constitutional theory, 569
   corporate *vs.* liberal, 571
   deep diversity, 568
   definition of, 570–573
   democratic deficits, 574, 579
   exiting, 577
   instability of, 578–582
   joining, 576
   modus vivendi, 579, 580, 581, 582
   non-majoritarian principles, 580
   overlapping consensus, 578, 579
   political stability, 569
   recognition, 574
   resisting, 576–577
   voting, 577
constituency principle, 763
constituent assembly
   Article 374, 731
   Article 376, 731
   Colombian Constituent Assembly of 1990, 727–730
   constitution-making, 722, 723
   formal, 722
   function, 722–723
   power, 723–724
   and sovereignty, 724–727
constituent power
   assemblies, 731–734
   and constitutionalism, 212–213
   concept of, 208, 211, 212
   federalism, 558
   formulated by representatives, 210–212
   origin of, 208–209
   popular sovereignty, 209
   populism, 1023
   post-sovereign, 220–222
   and sovereignty, 215–219
   as sovereign power, 214–215
constitution
   bills of rights, 885
   conventions. *See* constitutional conventions (CCs)
   definition of, 5–10
   interpretation, 182
   and justice, 122
   unwritten constitution, 320
   unwritten law, 10–16, 177, 194, 374, 354, 674
   written constitutions, 10–16
Constitution of Dominica, 612
Constitution of Finland, 23
Constitution of Ghana, 620
Constitution of India, 361
Constitution of Seychelles, 616
Constitution of South Africa (CSA), 25, 50
Constitution, US Federal of 1787, 209
constitutional community, 25
constitutional conventions (CCs)
   breakdown of, 327
   causal efficacy of, 323–332
   characterizing of, 317–318
   as cooperation equilibria, 324–327
   as coordination equilibria, 323–324
   emergence of, 320–323
   evolution of, 321
   existence of, 319–320
   inter-legislature, 325
   intra-legislature, 324
   maintained by fear of sanctions, 327–329
   modal nature of, 317
   as self-denying ordinances, 329–331
   unwritten norms, 325
   violation of, 318, 328
   in Westminster systems, 317
   written constitution, 317
constitutional deliberation. *See also* deliberation
   concept of, 250–253
   democratic self-determination, 250
   liberal rights, 250
   and public reason, 253–255
constitutional design, 130, 199, 206, 244, 271, 275, 277, 510, 570, 584, 601, 640, 644, 655, 661, 676, 825, 953, 957, 968
   constitution-making processes, 258–260

constitutional governance, regulators
   behaviours, 467–468
   cognitive frameworks, 462–465
   epistemologies, 462–465
   goals, purposes and values, 461–462
   methods/techniques, 465–466
   organisations, 465–467
   trust and legitimacy, 468–469
constitutional hardball
   civil society, 1085–1086
   definition of, 1071–1074
   democratic backsliding, 1071
   informal game-theoretic analysis, 1082–1085
   militant democracy, 1081
   norms, 1071
   party competition, 1078
   political development, 1077
   political regimes, 1077
   practices of, 1074–1077
   public institutions, 1081
   regime-centered analysis, 1077–1080
   self-help/anti-hardball, 1081–1082
constitutional interpretation
   adjudication, 371–373
   concept of, 362
   courts, 374–375
   evolutive, 366
   judicial change, 370–371
   judicial creativity, 362
   justice, 368–370
   living tree, 366, 367, 377
   objects of, 373–374
   rational basis review (RBR), 475, 477
      vs. heightened scrutiny in rights doctrine, 483
   rule of law, 366–368
   significance, 363–366
   signification, 363–366
constitutional juries, 832
constitutional law, 903–906
   cost-benefit analysis, 470
   domestic, 201
   human dignity in, 23–25
   proportionality, 385
constitutional legitimacy. *See* legitimacy
   consent, 179
   as currency, 184–191
   empirical approach, 177–184
   interpretation of, 182
   normative approach, 177–184
   order- and performance-based criteria, 178
   performance of, 178
   performance- or order-based, 178
   power, 185, 187
   procedural legitimacy, 177
   symbolic communication, 183
constitutional mini-publics, 1473. *See also* deliberation
   anticipatory uses of, 843–844
   constitutional, 844–845
   constitutional amendments, 844
   constitutional review, 832
   contestatory uses of, 839–841
   empowered uses of, 838–839
   political uses of, 831–834
   public opinion, 835–838
   vigilant uses of, 841–843
constitutional norms, 10–16
constitutional review. *See also* rule of law
   cases, 353–354
   concept of, 343–344
   constitutionalism, 348–349
   constitutionalism vs democracy, 849–850
   courts, 353
   decision-making, 354
   deliberation, 354–355
   diffuse, concept of, 851–855
   European practice, 344–345
   federalism, 355–357
   functional democratic systems, 357–358
   jurisprudential arguments, 350
   legal reasoning, 354–355
   legitimacy of, 358–359
   normative claim of justificatory argument, 351–352
   political vs. legal constitutionalism, 359
   post-war developments, 346–347
   rights, 348–349
   separation of powers, 348–349, 355–357
   settlements, 353–354
   U.S. Supreme Court, 347–348
constitutional rights. *See also* human rights
   claim-rights, 47
   and constitutionalism, 49–54
   democracy, 47–49
   human rights, 44–47
   and individualism, 49–54
   natural rights, 44–47
   nature of, 38–44
   reason-based theories of, 389–392
constitutional theory, 553
   concept and conceptions, 2
   definition of, 2–5
   federalism, 560–564
   normative constitutional theory, 2
   norms and principles, 2
   rational reconstruction, 122

constitutionalisation, critique of, 920–924
  democratic deliberation, 928
  legislatures, 929
  ordinary courts, 929
  private autonomy, 921
  private law, 930–934
  progressive/democratic-minded critique, 924–927
  reviewing constitutional courts, 922
constitutionalism, 16–19, 49–54, 118–119, 348–349
  beyond state, 957–959
  and constituent power, 212–213
  corporatism, 585
  deliberation, 250–253
  and democracy, 849–850
  essential contestability, 16
  modern constitutionalism, 493
  national constitutionalism
    against commitment devices, 947–948
    human rights, 941
    paradox of commitment, 944
    as pre-commitment devices, 944–947
    state consent, 941–944
    societal, 542–544
    supranational, 547–550
  political constitution, 10–16
  political constitutionalism, 129, 199, 257
  and populism, 1019–1020
constitutionality, 64–68
constitutive theory, 204
conventions, 11
The Convention on International Civil Aviation (1944), 941
Cook, B., 686
Cornell, D., 496, 498
corporatism
  concept of, 586–591
  constitutionalism, 585
  democratic challenges, 595
  and democracy, 597–601
  and economic constitutionalism, 596–597
  economic form of, 591
  embedded liberalism, 592
  fascism, 587
  industrial democracies, 593
  labour rights, 592
  pluralism, 593
  power over, 598
  power with, 599
  social rights, 601
  and societal self-legislation, 1057–1059
  system of consultation, 594–596
  welfare state, 592
Correa, R., 649

Corsican Revolution, 516
cost-benefit analysis (CBA)
  constitutional rights, 477
  constitutional structures, 555
  democratic legitimacy, 486–487
  first-order vs. second-order, 487–488
  judicial expertise, 488–489. *See also* expertise model
  justification, 481–484
  money-metric, 472
  qualitative, 472–473
  quantitative, 471–472
  rational basis review vs. heightened scrutiny, 483
  structural doctrines, 483
  text of Constitution, 484–485
  tiers of scrutiny, 477
  U.S. public law. *See* U.S. administrative law
  welfarism, 470–471
counter-majoritarian difficulty, 347–348
Court of Justice of the European Union (CJEU), 940, 960
court deliberations, 255–258
COVID-19 pandemic, 433, 455, 458, 634, 989, 1042
Craiutu, A., 779
Crenshaw, K., 61, 62
crisis of democracy, 228, 238–242, 770
critical theory, 62, 124, 126, 128, 435
Cuba, 1002
cultural citizenship, 739
currency, 184–191
Czechoslovakia, 1005

Dahl, R., 65, 533, 747
Daly, E., 814
Darwall, S., 26
Dawood, Y., 754
de facto institutional independence, courts 882, 868, 876–879
de jure institutional independence, courts 868, 875–876, 882
De Wet, E., 939
decision rule, 248
decisional independence, 868, 875, 879–882
declaratory theory, 204
deep diversity, 568
deflationary accounts, self-government, 106–107
delegation, 230–238
deliberation, 575–576
  citizens, 255–258
  conceptions of, 247–249
  constitutional referendums, 258
  constitutionalism, 250–253

constitution-making, 258–260
courts, 255–258
democracy, 248, 739, 811
minipublics, 829
parliaments, 255–258
and public health, 253–255
demand theory, 41
democracy, 64–68, 109, 138
corporatism and, 597–601
deficits, 574
Democracy and Distrust (Ely), 4
legitimacy, 486–487
mass, 238
modern constitutional democracy, 212
principles, 691–693
processes, 641
representation, 228–229. *See also* representation
revolution, 494–498
self-government, 47–49
theory, 753, 811
democratic accountability, 12
democratic constitution
administrative development of, 693–696
rules, 691–693
Denninger, E., 712
Department of Health Education and Welfare, 693–695
depoliticization
issues of, 575
process of, 635
desire-satisfaction theory, 92–94
Dhufar Revolution in Oman, 498
dialogic constitutionalism
and equality, 1012–1014
Dicey, A. V., 14, 15, 195, 674, 675, 446
The Law of the Constitution, 193, 674
Dicke, K., 29
diffuse review, 851–855
dignity, 11. *See* human dignity
skepticism, human dignity, 34–35
direct protection of people, 80
disability, 65
Disch, L., 233
discourse theory, 125, 250, 251
discrimination, 58, 59. *See also* equality
non-discrimination, 132
religious, 64
sex, 62, 64
status-based argument, 132
divergence, modes of, 73–74
division of labor, 116–119
Dixon, R., 1011
Dodik, M., 580
dogmatic separation, 334

neutralist secularism, 336–337
public justifications, 341
domination. *See also* non-domination
arbitrary rule, 127
colonial and imperial, 502
guarding people against private, 79–81
guarding people against public, 81–84
interpersonal, 63
populism, 807
private, 79–81
public, 81–84
religious, 130
self-government, 110
social, 128
type of legitimacy, 177
double sovereignty, 208. *See also* sovereignty
Downs, A., 116
dual legitimacy, 649, 650
dualism, 203
Duguit, L., 530, 589
Dummett, M., 765
Dunoff, J., 959
Durkheim, E., 589
Duverger, M., 762
Dworkin, G., 95
Dworkin, R, 4, 11, 29, 162, 165, 167, 202, 300, 338, 350, 391, 392, 401–406, 411, 412, 514, 556, 756, 793, 796, 804, 806, 884, 890, 891, 894, 895, 897
Bills of Rights, 885–890
interpretive theory, 199
Law's Empire, 35
legal theory, 197
Dyzenhaus, D., 221, 222, 434, 436, 905, 906, 1045, 1046, 1049
Dzur, A. W., 67

Eagleton, T., 505
eco-fascism, 1044
economic and social rights (ESR), 133, 1004
economic citizenship, 739
economic constitutionalism, 594, 596–597
economic growth, 108, 326, 465, 526, 873, 878
economic inequality, 108. *See also* inequality
inverse per-capita distribution, 149
economic realism, 508
egalitarian democracy, 110
egalitarian theory of religious freedom, 337
Eisgruber, C., 256, 802
Religious Freedom and the Constitution, 338
Ekins, R., 366
Elazar, D., 561

elections
  boundaries, 754
  centrality of, 753
  epistocracy, 758
  first past the post systems, 761
  franchise, 757
  justification of democracy, 756
  proportional multi-partisanship, 616
  proportional representation (PR) systems, 763, 764
  voters, 760–766
Elgie, R., 651
Eliot, J., 262, 263, 265
elite polarisation, 788
Elkins, Z., 188
Elster, J., 430, 723
Ely, J. H., 4, 65, 347
  Bills of Rights, 890–893
embedded liberalism, 592
embodiment, 230–238
emergencies, 433
emergency powers
  authorization, 434, 448
  dictatorship, 441
  exception, 433
  French state of siege, 442–443
  German state of exception, 443–444
  jurisdiction, 449
  law's authority, 438–439
  legal politics of containment, 447–449
  martial law and suspension acts, 441–442
  neo-Roman model of dictatorship, 439–441
  norm, 433
  post 9/11 emergency, 435–437
  prerogative power, 438
  problem of definitions, 434, 447
  problem of jurisdiction, 434
  rule of law, 439
  temporality, 434, 448–449
  theory and practice of, 444–445
empirical legal research, 358
England, 33, 196, 228, 287, 288, 307, 326, 508, 511, 523, 524, 833
  modern state in, 524–527
English-First principle, 139
Enlightenment, 23, 29, 738
entrenchment
  alteration of law, 426–427
  constitutional amendment, 453
  courts, 419
  form, 419–420
  identity, 425–426
  inflexibility in law, 430
  institutions, protection of, 428

  legal stability, 424
  legislative amendment, 420
  legislatures, 419
  moral panics, protection of, 429
  political stability, 424
  regions, protection of, 428
  rules, 423
  self-imposed, 422
  stability, 424–425
  statutory drafting, 699
  tension between institutions, 431
  time, 420–421
  voting units, 412–422
Environmental Protection Agency (EPA), 474
environmental rights, 1039
epistemic reliability, 161
equal dignity, 143
Equal Employment Opportunity Commission, 693
equal per capita principle, 148, 149
Equal Protection Clause, 686
equal recognition of national cultures, 151
equal services approach, 148, 149
equality, 11, 25, 997–999. *See also* political equality
  'subordination' approach, 61
  analytic philosophy, 62–64
  constitutionality, 64–68
  democracy, 64–68
  dialogic constitutionalism and, 1012–1014
  dimensions of, 62–64
  epistemic injustice, 61
  historical injustice, 56
  monorecognition, 144–147
  principal of, 694
  principle of, 205
  sex discrimination, 62, 64
  sexual equality, 59, 60
  sexual harassment, 59, 61
  sexual inequality, 60, 64
    causes of, 61
  substantive equality, 1001
  substantive inequality, 1000–1002
  treat people as, 57–62
equality of opportunity, 61, 108, 138, 139, 1057
ethical pluralism, 335
ethical reliability, 161
ethical secularism, 333. *See also* secularism
ethnic voting, 577
ethnicity, 158
ethnocentrism, 333

European Convention on Human Rights
    (ECHR), 43, 702, 922, 933
European Central Bank, 631
European constitutionalism, 344–345
European Court of Human Rights (ECtHR),
    922, 933
European Court of Justice, 347
European Medicines Agency, 94
European Union (EU), 550, 787
    anti-constitutional, 967
    anti-democratic, 967–970
    as constitutional regime, 970–972
    constitutional elements of, 959–963
    constitutional legitimacy, 965
    constitutional system, 965–967
    effective government, 965
    functional constitutionalism in, 963–965
    horizontal effect, 922
    legitimacy, 178
    as regional integration, 955–957
    supranationalism, 958
European Union Rule of Law Mission in Kosovo
    (EULEX), 981
Evans, P. B., 533
Evans, R., 608
evolutive interpretation, 366
executive. *See also* administrative state;
        prerogative; government
    advantages of, 646–647
    hyper-presidentialism, 1009
    perils of presidentialism, 647–648, 1141
    personalism, 641, 644
    policymaking authority, 713
    power, 286, 287
    premier-presidential, 643
    presidential government, 643
    presidential systems, 271, 273–275
    presidentialism, 712–714
        separation of powers, 714–716
    presidentialism embraces, 644
    presidentialism vs. parliamentarism,
        646–651
    president-parliamentary, 643
    prime-ministerial government, 644, 651
    rights as bribes, 1011
    rulemaking, 704
exercise of authority, 9, 1050, 1051
expertise model, policymaking accountability,
    705–706
    contributory expertise, 608
exploitation, 61, 62
external sovereign, 200–203
Extinction Rebellion, 519
extralegal model, emergency powers, 436

Fallon, R., 486
Fanon, F., 495, 517
Fascism, 23, 238, 541, 673, 679, 852, 1025. *See also*
    eco-fascism
federal government, 553, 555, 562
Federal Reserve System, 627, 635
federalism, 554
    climate change, 1040–1041
    climate emergency, 1049–1051
    concept of, 553–555
    constituent power, 555
    as constitutional idea, 564–567
    constitutional law, 553
    constitutional review, 355–357
    constitutional theory of, 560–564
    functional normativity, 563
    modernity, 558–560
    proliferation of, 555
    scope of federal power, 479–481
    scope of state power, 481
    theory deficit, 555–558
federative power, 286
Feeley, M., 556
Feinberg, J., 39, 42, 43, 312
Feld, L. P., 873
feminism
    poverty, 61
    sameness feminism, 60
    Second Wave Feminism, 56, 57
Ferejohn, J., 255, 256, 870, 945, 946
feudalism, 56, 210, 222, 1056
Figgis, J., 527, 590
Fiji, 580
Finland, 850
Finnis, J., 5, 299, 300, 305
Fiorina, M., 788
First World War, 173, 214
first-order *vs.* second-order cost-benefit analysis
    (CBA), 487–488
Fish, S., 335
Fisher, E., 687
Fiss, O., 872
Food and Drug Administration, 94
foreign policy, 264, 504, 665, 788, 1078
formal equality, 999–1000
Forsthoff, E., 533, 690
Fortas, A., 401
    *Concerning Dissent and Civil
        Disobedience*, 399
fourth branch. *See* guarantor institutions
Fox, R., 710
Fraenkel, E., 690
    *The Dual State: A Contribution to the Theory
        of Dictatorship*, 671, 673

France, 288, 317, 328, 337, 346, 505, 506, 511, 855, 858
  French Constitution, 712
    in state of siege, 442–443
  French constitutional development, 213
  French Revolution, 210, 211, 214, 501–504, 506–508, 512, 516, 519, 588, 589
  French Revolution of 1789, 492
  modern state in, 524–527
  presidentialism, 712–714
Franklin, J. H., 209
free previous and informed consultation (FPIC), 1007, 1008
Freeden, M., 1021
freedom, 90, 98, 266. *See also* non-domination
  constitution, 85
  contestation, 83
  democracy, 77
  divergence, 73–74
  freedom of choice, 71–72
  interference, 75
  as non-domination, 77–79
  as non-frustration, 74–75
  as non-interference, 75–77
freedom of expression, 132, 174
  communication-neutrality, 169–171
  content-neutrality, 171–172
  speaker-neutrality, 172–173
  upshot of neutrality, 173–175
freedom of religion, 63, 130, 132, 251, 389
Frega, R., 1026
Friedman, M., 624, 635
Front de libération du Québec (FLQ), 269
Fugitive Slave Act, 400
Fuller, L. L., 281, 298, 299, 305
fundamental rights, roles of, 917–919

Gadamer, H., 142
Gallie, W.B., 16, 19
Gandhi, M., 412
Ganghof, S., 643, 646, 649, 650, 653, 654
Gardbaum, S., 654
Gardner, J., 14, 38, 48, 796, 903, 1070
Garlicki, L., 923
gender equality, 132
gender inequality, 1005–1006
general protection of people, 80
Germany, 214, 345, 346, 351, 368, 443, 462, 529, 532–534, 589, 591, 672, 692, 699, 702, 825, 852, 855, 856–858, 959, 1003
  German Basic Law, 133
  German Bundesbank, 628
  German constitutional law, 524
  German legal theory, 195
  German Revolution, 214, 592

German Romanticism, 141
German state of exception, 443–444
parliamentarianism, 708–712
Ginsburg, T., 188, 873, 1003
Glendon, M. A., 889
global constitutionalism, 4, 939, 940, 948, 951, 989, 990, 992, 1037
Glorious Revolution, 228, 328, 367, 502, 503, 506, 511. *See also* United Kingdom and England
Goldsworthy, J.
  The Sovereignty of Parliament, 197
Goodin, R., 103, 312
Goodman, S. W., 748
Goodnow, F. J., 681
Gordon, S., 280–283
Gorsuch, N., 181
Gosepath, S., 134
government
  accountability, 700
  administration, 678
  attributes of bureaucracy, 665
  authentic power of, 672
  birth of, 662–663
  bureaucratic, growth of, 679
  challenges to, 701
  elected prime-ministerial government, 643
  federalism, 1040
  judges, appointment of, 855
  laws and acts of, 850
  law and legislation, 668
  legislatures, 799–801
  liberal theory of, 795
  machinery of government, 317
  military, 722
  political structure, 684
  powers, 284–285, 684, 698
  principle of, 669
  representation, people, 801–804
  responsibility, separation of powers, 292
  Second Treatise of, 668
  semi-parliamentary government, 643, 644, 653–654
  semi-presidential government, 643, 651–652
  semi-presidentialism embraces, 644
Gramsci, A., 240, 539
Great Depression, 898
Grégoire, H., 138, 139, 141
Griffin, J., 4, 9, 98
Grimm, D., 962
Griswold, E., 400
Gross, O., 435
Grotius, H., 178
guarantor institutions

accountability, 605, 619
  bespoke/general personnel panels, 615
  constitutional theory, 606
  constitutionalism, 609
  contributory expertise, 608
  democracy, 606
  design of, 620
  ex ante disqualifications, 611–613
  ex post disqualifications, 611–613
  expertise, 605
  incompetent, 608–611
  independence, 604, 605
  integrity institutions, 604
  interactional expertise, 608
  maladministration, risk of, 618–620
  nature of, 608
  non-partisan members, 617–618
  operational dimension, 618–620
  partisan capture of, 611
  partisan character, 615–617
  personnel panels, 613–615
  political accountability of, 619
  removal of leaders, 618
  separation of power, 604
  structural dimension of, 608–611
  as trustees, 605–608
Guatemala, 1002
Guerrero, A., 771, 772
Gutmann, J., 873
Guzman, A., 942

Habermas, J. 4, 122, 129, 184, 222, 250–254, 257, 401–403, 406, 410, 556, 593, 600, 739
Haitian Revolution, 492, 499, 503, 508
Halmai, G., 1016
Hamilton, A., 510, 647, 680, 850, 1010
Hampshire, S., 123
Hand, L., 888, 889, 896
harassment, 59, 62, 64
Hardin, R., 187
Harrington, J., 305, 674
  The Commonwealth of Oceana, 673
Hart, H. L. A., 3, 7, 196, 197, 202, 203, 485
  The Concept of Law, 193, 196, 550
Hayek, F. A., 7, 300, 302, 304, 305, 310, 920
  The Constitution of Liberty, 308
  Law, Legislation and Liberty, 303, 308
Hazell, R., 330
hedonism, 88
Hegel, G. W. F., 232, 512, 519, 589, 590, 684, 686
  concept of the state, 527–528
  Philosophy of Right, 527
  The Philosophy of Right, 588, 683
Heller, H., 204–206, 215, 689

Helmke, G., 648
Henkin, L., 938
Herron, E. S., 874
Higonnet, P., 507
Hill, L., 768
Hinduism, 336
Hirshl, R., 342
Hobbes, T., 74, 192, 193, 197, 206, 225, 247, 284, 307, 526, 529, 559, 587
Hobsbawm, E., 499, 501
Hohfeld, W. N., 40
Holmes, O. W., 169
Holmes, S., 1003
Hong, L., 103
Honneth, A., 152
horizontal inequality, 645
Howse, R., 1021
human dignity
  in constitutional law, 23–25
  constitutional provisions, 31–34
  constitutional value, 31
  democracy, 25, 32
  equality, 25
  foundation, 26
  in human rights law, 23–25
  non-racialism, 25
  non-sexism, 25
  redundant, 30–31
  as right, 31
  rule of law, 25
  sacredness of, 29–30
  use of, 27
human rights, 938
  democracy, 314–315
  law, 23–25
  natural rights and, 44–47
  and remedies, 981–982
  rule of law, 309–310
Human Rights Act 1998
  Human Rights Advisory Panel (HRAP), 981
  Human Rights Committee, 618
  Human Rights Review Panel (HRRP), 981
human welfare. *See* welfare
Humboldt, W. v., 142
Hume, D., 322, 324, 328, 778
  History of England, 778
Hungary, 820, 821, 867, 1012, 1018
Hunt, M., 504
Huq, A., 1011
Hybrid Theory, rights, 41

Iceland, 329, 368
illiberal democracy, 238

impartiality
  absence of, 161
  constitutionalism, 167
  decision-maker, 158
  decision-making procedure, 161
  in detachedness, 159
  disinterestedness, 157, 158
  epistemic reliability of, 160
  ethical reason for, 161
  freedom of expression, 169, 171
  good, conceptions of, 162–164
  ideal of, 161
  liberal democracy, 162
  liberal-democratic systems of governance, 160
  neutrality, 162–168
  objectivity, 157
  of rule of law, 157–162
  open-mindedness, 158, 159
  personal stake, avoidance, 158
impoverishment, 61
income support, 66
independence of the administrative staff, 618
India, 851, 959
Indian Citizenship (Amendment) Act of 2019, 743
Indian Citizenship Act of 1955, 743
indigenous rights, 1007–1008, 1011
indirect protection of people, 80
individualism, 49–54
industrial capitalism, 591
inequality, 2, 56, 57, 97. *See also* racial inequality; sexual inequality
  horizontal, 645
  income, 1026
  organization of powers, 1008–1010
  problems of, 65
  vertical, 645
inflation, 629, 630, 633, 635–637
institutional separation, 334
institutions, 112–114
integrity-based civil disobedience, 403, 405
interactional expertise, 608
interest-protecting trustees, 607
intergroup misrecognition, 145, 151
Int'l Convention on Economic, Social and Cultural Rights (ICESCR), 741
International Covenant on Civil and Political Rights (ICCPR), 25, 27, 741, 1064
International Human Rights Law, 1006
international law monism, 201
international law
  ICCPR, 25, 27, 741, 1064
  ICESCR, 741
  international law monism, 201

Universal Declaration of Human Rights (UDHR), 24–27, 30
International Monetary Funds (IMF), 979, 982, 988
international organisations
  concept of, 974–975
  constituting and enabling, 976–978
  containment and accountability, 979–980
  critiques, 978
  democracy, 982–984, 986–988
  human rights and remedies, 981–982
  human welfare, 988–989
  individualism, 985–986
  institutional balance, 980–981
  Inter-American Commission on Human Rights, 1038
  Intergovernmental Panel on Climate Change (IPCC), 103
  International Criminal Court (ICC), 1038, 1039
  International Labor Organization (ILO), 979
  International Monetary Funds (IMF), 979, 982, 988
  liberalism, 984
  post colonialism, 991
  postcolonial sensibility, 989–991
  regional integration organization, 955–957
  rule of law, 980–981
interpretive theory, 199, 911–913
intragroup misrecognition, 145, 146, 151
Inuit Circumpolar Conference (ICC), 1038, 1039
Ipsen, H.P., 977
Iranian Revolution 1979, 501
Iraq, 499, 580
Ireland, 818, 822, 900, 1014
Irish Constitution of 1937, 23
irregular migrants, 1068
Islam, 336
Israel, 953
Italy, 462, 852, 855, 1033
  Five Star Movement, 1024, 1028, 1029

Jackson, A., 560
Jaconelli, J., 318
Japan, 462, 643, 654, 851
Jefferson, T., 503
Jellinek, G., 195
  state, concept of, 528–530
Jennings, I. W., 266, 321
Jessop, B., 539
Johnson, B., 15
Jordan, W., 504
Jubb, R., 412
Judaism, 336

judicial independence
  capacity, 870
  concrete review, 857–859
  corruption, 880
  courts, 868
  de facto institutional independence, 876–879
  de jure institutional independence, 875–876
  decisional independence, 879–882
  decision-making, 867
  definition of, 869–871
  impartiality, 869
  institutional approaches to, 871–873
  judges, 871
  judicial governance, 867
  output-oriented approaches to, 873–874
  rule of law, 870
  separation of powers, 875
  willingness, 870
judicial review
  weak form, 699
  string form, 348–349
justice
  authority of, 127–129
  basic rights, 127, 129, 132
  concept of, 127–129
  and constitution, 122
  freestanding conception of, 123
  as justification, 127–129
  normative power, 133
  political, 124
  political autonomy, 133
  priority of, 121–122
  procedural justice, 123
  and rights, 131–134
  right to justification, 129
  social and political justice, 124, 127

Kaczyński, J., 871
Kahana, T., 806
Kaltwasser, C. R., 1025
Kant, I., 26, 32, 128, 233, 234, 265, 270, 683, 970
  Doctrine of Right (Rechtslehre), 302
Karenina, A., 881
Karlan, P. S., 880
Karmis, D., 557
Kateb, G., 29
Kelle, S., 92
Kelsen, H., 3, 6, 196–198, 200–202, 204, 214, 215, 233, 345–346, 494, 514, 534, 548, 685, 851, 852, 939
  state, concept of, 531–532
Kennedy, D., 926–928
Kenya, 580
Khaitan, T., 603, 653, 654

Kind-Desire Theory, 42
King, A., 6–9, 13
King, J., 134, 412
  Bills of Rights, 898–900
King, P., 1059
Klabbers, J., 939
Klarman, M., 508
Kornhauser, A.M., 873
Korsch, K., 491
Kosař, D., 878
Kramer, M., 873
Krygier, M., 304, 306
Kumm, M., 134, 222, 382
Kymlicka, W., 142

lack of partiality.
  See impartiality
LaCroix, A., 559, 563
Lafont, C., 257, 770
Landemore, H., 770
Landis, J., 685
language knowledge, 140
language policy, 147, 149, 150
Larkins, C. M., 872, 873
Laski, H., 527, 590
Lassalle, F., 539
Latham, R.T.E, 196
law, 84–85
  constitutionalized, 85–86
  property laws, 80
  unwritten law, 10–16
Lawson, G., 208
Ledeneva, A., 880
Lee, D., 589
Lee, S., 686
Lefkowitz, D., 407, 408
Lefort, C., 229
left-wing populism, 1025–1032
legal constitutionalism, 352, 359. *See also* constitutionalism
legal institutionalism, 540–542
legal politics of containment, 447–449
legal theory, 197, 199
legislatures
  agency, 795–799
  democracy, 803
  freedom, 805–807
  from prince to parliament, 793–795
  government, 799–801
  intentions, 796
  lawmaking, 804–805
  opposition, 800
  representation, 792
  representation, people, 801–804

legislatures (cont.)
    self-government, 795
    statutory interpretation, 804–805
legitimacy, 458–459. *See also* constitutional legitimacy
    empirical constitutional, 177–184
    normative constitutional legitimacy, 177–184
    principle of, 124
Lehmbruch, G., 599
Leibholz, G., 549
Levinson, S., 180
Levitsky, S., 468, 1072, 1081
Levy, J., 139
Levy, R., 1049
Lewis, D., 323
Lewis, M., 465
liberalism, 56, 334
    justice and neutrality, 336–339
    "liberal consensus" approach, 740
    liberal-democratic systems of governance, 160
    market, 308
    neutralism, 164–168
liberty, 84–85. *See also* freedom
Lijphart, A., 569, 580, 645, 650
Lincoln, A., 802
Lindahl, H., 566
Linz, J., 640, 646, 647, 649, 650
Lippman, M., 400
living constitution, 182
Locke, J., 208, 209, 217, 285–287, 289, 294, 334, 434, 448, 558, 656, 663, 664, 666–669, 672–674, 680, 1041
    prerogative power, 438
    Second Treatise of Government, 209, 307
Loughlin, M., 3, 463, 530, 656
Louis XIV, 288, 525
Loyal Opposition, 263, 271, 272, 276. *See also* parliaments
    government, 266–268, 275–277
    measures, 264–266
Luhmann, N., 543
Lukács, G., 514

Maastricht Agreement, 744
Mac Amhlaigh, C., 1019
Macchiavelli, 525
MacDonald, R., 783
Machiavelli, 143, 434, 440, 441
Mackie, G., 105
MacKinnon, C., 60, 61
Madison, J., 239, 240, 681, 776, 778, 875, 998
Maeda, K., 650
Mahmood, S., 336
Maistre, J. D., 502

Maitland, F., 590
maladministration, 618–620
Mamdani, M., 497, 498
Manin, B., 434, 444, 445
Manning, J., 804
Mansbridge, J., 577
marginalization, 61
market integration, 955, 964, 969, 971
market neutrality, 630
Marmor, A., 551
marriage, 58, 59, 249, 259, 353, 741, 819
Marshall, G., 328
Marshall, T. H., 596, 738
Martinez, J., 640
Marx, K., 511, 512, 517, 519
Marxism, 56, 542
Mashaw, J., 687
Maskikver, J., 768
master-strokes of State, 663–666
material constitution
    change, 547–550
    definition of, 537–538
    development of, 539
    identity, 547–550
    legal institutionalism, 540–542
    orders, 544–547
    organisation, 547–550
    political thought, 538
    rule of recognition, 196–200, 485, 550–552
    societal constitutionalism, 542–544
    supranational constitutionalism, 547–550
    system of production, 538
Matsuda, M., 415
Mattli, W., 955
Mayer, O., 688
Mayhew, D., 716
McCrudden, C., 29, 30
McGann, A., 644, 645
McIlwain, C. H., 280–283
Medicine and Healthcare Products Regulatory Agency, 94
Meinel, F., 646
Melton, J., 188, 873
Mexican Revolution (1910–1919), 501
Michaels, J. D., 686
Michelman, F., 250, 518, 924, 925, 928
Michels, R., 241
migration, 2
    immigration control, 1060–1068
    open borders, 1056–1060
    right to control, 1054
Mill, J. S., 162, 170, 238, 568, 759, 895
    Considerations on Representative Government, 239

Miller, D., 1059–1061
moderate welfarism. *See* welfarism
modernity, 558–560
modus vivendi approach, 579–582
Moellendorf, D., 1057
Möller, K., 1023
Möllers, C., 685
Mommsen, T., 237
Montesquieu, 279, 284
  The Spirit of the Laws, 287–290
Moore, G., 575
Moore, M., 556
Morris, B., 34
Mortati, C., 541, 543
Morton, P. A., 329
Mosca, G., 238
Mudde, C., 1025
Mulford Act (1967), 414
Müller, J.-W., 1016, 1070
multi-criterial theory, 342
murder, 62
Murphy, W., 280

Napoleon, 213
narrow model, public law, 703–704
Nash, K., 1022
National (Constituent) Assembly, 210, 725, 727
national law monism, 201, 203
natural rights, 44–47. *See also* human rights
Naudé, G., 664–666, 669, 675
  Considérations politiques sur les coups d'état, 663
Nazi legal system, 671
Nazi totalitarianism, 690
Nazism, 23, 238
Negri, A., 219
neo-Roman model of dictatorship, 437, 439–441
Nepali Constitution, 610, 612, 615, 619
Nethercote, J.R., 330
Netherlands, 570, 576, 580, 581, 594, 889, 1005, 1024, 1030
Network for Greening the Financial System (NGFS), 634
Neuman, G., 32
Neumann, F., 303, 689
neutrality
  communication, 169–171
  content, 171–172
  justification, 166, 167
  speaker, 172–173
  subject matter, 171
  upshot of, 173–175
  viewpoint, 171, 172
New Deal-Civil Rights, 898

New Left social movements, 594
New Zealand, 749, 889, 953
Nino, C. S., 250, 252, 1009
non-domination. *See also* domination
  freedom as, 77–79
  linguistic, 143
  political and social, 133
  private domination, 79–81
  rule of law, 304
non-frustration theory, 74–75
nongovernmental organizations (NGOs), 1085
non-racialism, 25
non-rights constitutions, 38–44
non-sexism, 25
Norman, W., 556, 557
North, D., 280
Norway, 851
Nozick, R., 556
Nussbaum, M., 124, 130, 397, 404

O'Donoghue, A., 939
O'Neill, M., 63
Oberman, K., 1060
Occupy Wall Street movement, 501, 519
October Crisis, 269
Ogien, A., 407, 410
Olsen, F., 411
open borders, 1056–1059
  critique of, 1059–1060
open-mindedness, 158, 159
opposition
  altera pars of government, 271–275
  formation in, 263
  government, 266–268, 275–277
  idea of, 263
  legislature, 277
  loyal opposition, 270
  measures, 264–266
  modalities of, 263–266
  opposition (parliamentary), 273, 274
  reciprocity, 269–271
  responsibility, 269–271
Orr, G., 1049
Ostler, J., 510
over-constitutionalization, 927–928

Page, S., 103
Paine, T., 13, 16
Pal, M., 755
Palestinian Revolution, 495, 499
Paley, W., 77
Palmer R.R., 504, 505, 507
Paris Agreement, 634
Paris Commune of 1871, 511

parity of esteem, 143
Parkinson, J., 833
parliaments, 238–242, 255–258
   democracy, 198, 270, 591, 592, 689, 806
   in Germany, 708–712
   government, 263, 271, 643
   vs. presidentialism, 646–654
   privileges of, 262
   rejects, 644
   sovereignty, 15, 194, 526, 710, 815, 915
   in UK, 708–712
Parti Québécois (political party), 269
participation of citizens, 112–114
parties and partisanship, 292, 787. *See also* political parties
   claim-rights, 47
   separation of powers, 292
partisan-balance model, 706–707
'party-divided' separation of powers, 274, 275
'party-united' separation of powers, 274, 275
Pasquino, P., 255
Patten, A., 140, 147
performance accountability, 701–702
Perry, A., 140, 147
personnel dimension of guarantor, 611
personnel panels, guarantor, 613
'personal' sovereignty, 613
Peru, 1009
Peters, A., 939
Pettit, P., 307
Pevnick, R., 1062
Philadelphia Convention, 510
Philippopoulos-Mihalopoulos, A., 1046
Phillipson, G., 321
Pincus, S., 328
Pitkin, H., 232
Placatian policy, 166
Plato, 660–662
   Statesman, 659
pluralism, 236, 238, 247
   recognition of, 147–152
plurinational theory, 555
Pocock, J.G.A., 738
Pogge, T., 139
Poland, 848, 867, 871, 876, 1005, 1012, 1018
policymaking accountability, 703
   chain-of-legitimacy model, 704
   executive rulemaking, 707
   expertise model, 705–706
   partisan-balance model, 706–707
   privatization model, 707
   public, 701–703
political attitudes, 555
political culture, 10–16
political equality, 108–112, 110, 236, 785

political friendship, 266–271, 277
political identities, 555
political legal theory, 206
political legitimacy, 184
Political Liberalism (Rawls), 163, 168
political mandate, 230–238
political opposition, 269, 272, 276
political parties, 238–242
   constitutions, 777–783
   contemporary form, 787–790
   definition of, 776–777
   moderation, 777–783
   partisanship, 783–487
   polarization, fear of, 787–790
   political conflict, 776, 778
   role of, 546
political power, 109, 112, 553, 554
political representation, 225, 236
political secularism, 334
political theory, 2, 556
political unity, 544
polycentric model, regulatory governance, 452–453
Popova, M., 870, 874, 881
popular sovereignty, 32, 179, 209, 211, 213, 217, 218, 220, 258, 260, 693, 732, 785
   of constituent authority, 258
   popular will approach, 102–105
populism, 2
   anti-populist thesis, 1016–1018
   comparative analysis, 1021
   inclusion vs. exclusion, 1021–1022
   leftwing vs. rightwing, 1025–1032
   national, 1024–1025
   past vs. future, 1022–1023
   reformist vs. constituent politics, 1023–1024
   transnational, 1024–1025
Portugal, 591, 855
Posner, E., 418
Postema, G., 306, 307, 310, 311
   Laws' Rule, 312
Poulantzas, N., 539
poverty, 66, 188
Powell, B., 650
powers-separation, presidential government, 644
   perils of, 649–650
   promise of, 650–651
Pozen, D., 1082
prerogative
   birth of government, 662–663
   concept of, 656–658
   constitutionalism, 674–676
   disposition, 658, 676
   the exception, 665

King power, 666–668
law, 668–671
legislation, 668–671
master-strokes of State, 663–666
original power, 657
past and present constitution, 658
powers, 658, 658
princely model, 661–662
republican constitution, 672–674
sovereign violence, 675
state, 671–672
statecraft, 658, 661
Statesman, 659–661
princely model, 661–662
principal/agent relationship, 235
principles of justice, 163
private coercion, 312
procedural justice, conception of, 123
Progressives' theory, 688
property of reasonableness, 163
proportionality
balancing, 388–389
balancing of, 385
bottom-up accounts of, 380
concept of, 378–380
consequentialism, 388
deontology, 387
equal respect and concern, 381
equality-based arguments, 381
externalism, 382
fundamental rights, 379, 380
incommensurability, 388–389
institutional approaches, 382–385
internalism, 382
non-institutional approaches, 385
optimization requirements, 386
reason/justification, 389–392
specificationism, 378
top-down approach, 381
use of, 378
without balancing, 392–395
protection, types of, 80
Przeworski, A., 760
public accountability, 12
types of, 701–703
public coercion, 312
public justification, 1035, 1041, 1044–1052
public law theory, 703–704
public reason, 253–254. *See also* Rawls, J.
Publius, 291
Pünder, H., 712

quantitative formalism, 358
Quong, J., 168
Liberalism without Perfection, 168

Rabushka, A., 583
race, 158. *See also* discrimination; equality
discrimination, 59, 62, 64
equality, 56–58
inequality, 58, 64
radical constitutionalism, 415
Rahman, S., 311
Randazzo, K. A., 874
rape, 62
rational discourse, 250
Rawls, J., 6, 7, 53, 63, 68, 72, 83, 89, 121, 123, 125,
    126, 130, 133, 134, 162–168, 173, 180, 249,
    253, 255, 264, 270, 298, 309, 334, 337, 338,
    349, 401–403, 405, 406, 411, 578, 579, 756,
    779, 925, 1054, 1056
A Theory of Justice, 556
Raz, J., 1, 7, 8, 10, 298–301, 303–308, 398,
    796, 804
Raz, T., 16, 33, 46
realism, 123–124
reasonable disagreement, 122–123
reciprocity, 269–271
reciprocity-based argument, 132
recognition
cultural rights, 137
dignity, 142
equal identity, 147–152
equal interest, 149, 151
equal language, 151
federalism, 150
group-specific, 147
interests in, 137–144
language rights, 145
life-world, 140
life-world access interest, 141
linguistic territoriality principle (LTP), 145,
    146, 149
misrecognition, 145
monorecognition, 144–147
multiculturalism, 139
national-cultural identity, 150, 151
national-cultural-linguistic
    group, 150
nonrecognitionalism, 137–144
pluralism, 147–152
value of, 574
Reed, R., 862
referendums
anti-LGBTQ, 815, 820
definition of, 810–812
disinformation, 811
informed voting, 821–826
and minority rights, 816–820
representative democracy, 812–816
vote, 819

refugees, 1056, 1060, 1067, 1068. *See also* migration
regime-centered analysis, 1077–1078
regulation
  accountability, 458
  behaviours, 457–458
  constitutional governance, 461–469
  constitutional systems, 469–461
  legitimacy, 458–459
  organisational dynamics, 456–457
  polycentric model, 452–453
  processes, 456–457
  self-regulatory bodies, 451
  structures, 456–457
  techniques, 455–456
  transnational regulatory bodies, 451
  trust, 458–459
regulatory governance systems
  goals, purposes and values, 453–454
  knowledge and understandings, 454–455
Rehnquist, W., 181
Reilly, B., 583
relation of equality, 251
religion, 158
  belief and thought, 335, 338–339
  church and state, separation of, 336, 342
  concepts of, 339
  discrimination, 64
  disestablishment of, 340
  ethical salience of, 340
  problem of, 336
  protection of, 334
  in public discourse, 340
  salience of, 339
religious freedom, 337
religious persecution, 56
Renan, E., 1065
Renwick, A., 822
representation, 575
  in constituent power, 226
  crisis of democracy, 238–242
  delegation, 230–238
  democracy, 226, 242–245
  democratic implications of, 228–229
  direct *vs.* political mandate, 244
  electoral representation, 242
  embodiment, 230–238
  media, 240
  parliament, 238–242
  political, 225
  political equality, 236
  political mandate, 230–238
  political parties, 238
  private, 225

  public opinion, 241
  public usage of, 225
  voting right, 226
republicanism
  freedom as non-domination, 77–79
  republican tradition, 344–345
  prerogative, 672–674
  republican constitution, 672–674
republican prerogative, 672–674
Reserve Bank of New Zealand, 627
responsibility, 269–271
revolution
  abstract theory of, 491
  assessment of, 492
  collective agency, 494–498
  colonialism, 506–511
  consciousness, 495
  constituent power, 514–518
  contestability of, 491
  de-contextualisation, 499–502
  democracy, 494–498
  exclusion, 499–502
  good and bad, 502–505
  good revolution, 502–505
  importance of, 491
  inclusion, 499–502
  legality, 514–518
  political and social, 492, 511–513
  reforms, 505
  Revolutionary War, 512
  slavery, 506–511
  violence, 506–511
Rice, C., 94
right to justification, 129, 132, 134
right to political participation, 133, 407
rights. *See also* constitutional rights
  Canadian Charter of Rights and Freedoms, 183
  Charter of Rights and Freedoms, 188
  Civil Rights Act of 1964, 401
  claim, 42
  climate change, 1038–1040
  climate emergency, 1048–1049
  constitutional review, 348–349
  federalism, 355–357
  interest/benefit theory, 41
  and justice, 131–134
  power-rights, 40–42
  powers *vs.* expansion, 1010–1012
  reason-based theories of, 389–392
  reason-blocking theory, 392
  separation of powers, 355–357
  social rights, 133
  U.S. constitutional law, 475–479

Universal Declaration of Human Rights
  (UDHR), 27, 30
 will/control theory, 41
rights-based accountability, 702
rightwing populism, 1025–1032
Riker, W. H., 105
Rios-Figueroa, J., 872, 880
Ripstein, A., 381
role of law, 80
Roman Republic, 104
Romano, S., 543
Roosevelt, F. D., 685, 1028, 1072, 1076
Rose-Ackerman, S.
  Democracy and Executive Power: Policymaking Accountability in the US, the UK, Germany, and France, 699
Rousseau, J.-J., 103, 193, 203, 211, 217, 233, 665, 738, 758, 795
  Du Contrat Social, 217
  Social Contract, 516
Roznai, Y., 422
Rubin, E., 556, 689
Rueschemeyer, D., 533
rule of law, 12, 25, 281
  arbitrary power, 305–307
  climate change, 1036–1037
  climate emergency, 1047–1048
  concept of, 297–298
  constitutional interpretation, 366–368
  essence of legality, 398–300, 398–305
  formal conceptions, 298–300
  human rights, 309–310
  international law, 949–951
  impartiality, 949–951
  liberal and republican traditions, 307–309
  limited government approach, 310–311
  policymaking accountability, 701
  protection of, 313
  separation anxiety, 300–303
  separation of powers, 283–284
  social dimension of, 311–314
  substantive conceptions, 314
  welfare state, 298, 310
rule of recognition, 196–200, 485, 550–552
  material constitution, 550–552
rulemaking
  in France, 702, 712–714
  in Germany, 702, 708–712
  parliamentarianism, 708–712
  policymaking accountability, 701
  presidentialism, 712–714
  separation of powers presidentialism, 714–716
  in UK, 699, 702, 708–712
  in US, 699, 714–716
Russell, M., 319
Russell, P. H., 870, 872, 874, 878
Russia, 880, 953
Russian Revolution, 501, 517

Sadurski, W., 1016
Sager, L., 945, 946
  Religious Freedom and the Constitution, 338
Sajó, A., 1017
same-sex marriage, 485, 486, 815, 818, 820, 822
Samuels, D., 642, 648
Sandalow, T., 399
Sanders, B., 1026
Sartori, G., 6, 9, 15, 18, 958
Saudi Arabia constitution, 548
Sayigh, R., 495
Sbragia, A., 956
Scalia, A., 181
Scanlon, T., 63, 390
scepticism, 5
Schachter, O., 34
Scharpf, F., 178
Schattschneider, E. E., 242
Schauer, F., 322, 806
Schmitt, C., 3, 198–200, 203, 204, 206, 214–216, 218–220, 223, 237, 240, 263, 302, 435, 540, 669, 675, 689, 690, 730, 795, 797, 1042, 1045, 1046
  Constitutional Theory, 670
  Political Theology: Four Chapters on the Concept of Sovereignty, 216, 670
  state, concept of, 530–531
Schmitter, P., 593, 594, 600
Scotland, 260, 506, 813
Second World War, 23, 57, 553, 561
secularism
  arbitrary singling out, 335
  church and state, separation of, 333
  citizens, equal inclusion, 340
  criticisms of, 334–336
  definition of, 333–334
  dogmatic separation, 334
  ethical, 333
  liberal justice, 336–339
  neutralist secularism
    arbitrary singling out, 337–338
    dogmatic separation, 336–337
    protestantised belief, 338–339
    personal liberty, 339–340
  political, 334
  protestantised religion, 335–336
  public justifications, 340–342

secularism (cont.)
  state neutrality, 341
  transnational constitutionalism, 342
Selective Service System, 746
self-embracing entrenchment rules, 422–423
self-government
  conceptions of, 102
  and constitutionalism, 118–119
  deflationary accounts of, 106–107
  and division of labor, 118–119
  economic democracy, 116
  egalitarian conception of, 110
  information, 112
  participation, 104
  popular will conceptions of, 102–105
self-regulation, 707
semi-citizenship, 749–751
Sempill, J., 305, 312
Sen, A., 75
separation anxiety, 300–303
separation of powers, 12, 291–295, 641
  administrative state, 292–293
  checks and balances, 280, 284
  concept of, 279–283
  constitutional review, 348–349, 355–357
  executive power, 286
  governing powers, 284–285
  mixed constitution, 285
  parties, 292
  presidentialism, 714–716
  responsible government, 292
  rule of law, 283–284
Seychelles Constitution, 616
Shepsle, K., 583
Shetreet, S., 872
Shihata, I., 977
Shklar, J., 308
Shugart, M., 642, 648
Sieyès, A., 516
Sieyès, E.-J., 210–213, 215, 219, 220, 233, 517
  What is the Third Estate?, 210
Simmons, A. J., 1061
Singapore, 148, 178, 745, 826
Singer, P., 401, 402
single-party political system, 761, 762, 764, 766
Sinzheimer, H., 592, 593, 597
Skinner, Q., 503
Skocpol, T., 533
slavery, 506–511
Slovakia, 871, 876
Smend, R., 591, 685
Smith, A.
  Wealth of Nations, 289
Smith, M.N., 497

Smith, R., 740
Smith, W., 407, 409
social revolution, 511–513
social rights, 133, 1002–1005
social welfare function (SWF), 472
societal constitutionalism, 542–544
societal self-legislation, 594–596
Socrates, 265
South Africa, 140, 580
South African Reserve Bank, 613
South-Africa, 851
sovereignty, 13, 187
  authority, 192
  basic norm, 196–200
  concept of, 206
  and constituent assembly, 724–727
  and constituent power, 215–219
  external, 200–203
  internal, 200
  legal definition of, 195
  personal, 208
  political definition of, 195
  political legal theory, 206
  power, 214–215
  primacy of political conception of, 203–205
  real, 209
  rule of law, 205
  rule of recognition, 196–200
  ruler, 216
  theory of, 193
  two-sided theory of state, 193–196
Spain, 150, 852, 855
specific protection of people, 80
Spring of Nations, 501
state interference, 90–91
  and desire-satisfaction, 92–94
  and pleasure, 90–91
  and welfare, 94–99
state sovereignty, 494, 560, 588, 590
state, concept of
  administrative state, 531
  in constitutional theory, 535
  in England, 524–527
  in France, 524–527
  general theory of the state, 529, 530
  constitution, 534–535
  death of, 532–534
  demystifying, 531–532
  European conceptual tradition of, 523
  executive strength, 530–531
  juristic, 528–530
  in nineteenth and twentieth century, 527
  non-universal concept, 523–524

sacralising, 527–528
as time sensitive, 523–524
state-based regulators, 458
status quo neutrality, 999–1000
statutory instruments (SIs), 710
Staughton, L., 508
Steinberg, R., 712
Steiner, H., 1058, 1060, 1062
Stephens, T., 1038
Stevin, S., 143
subordinate recognition, 151
substantive proceduralism, 129–131
Sudan, 580
Sunstein, C., 89, 424, 1003
supranational constitutionalism, 547–550
Supreme Court of Israel, 347
supreme courts and constitutional courts
   abstract and concrete review, 857–859
   differences, 861
   gradual convergence and persistent differences, 861–862
   judges, appointment of, 855–857
   judicial decision-making, 859–860
   judicial *vs* political decision-making, 853
   judicialization of politics, 864
   partial convergence, 861
   social integration, 852
Svolik, M., 650
Sweden, 326, 1005
Swift, A., 134
Swiss constitution, 548, 652
Switzerland, 57, 145, 816, 817, 1005

Takriti, A.R., 497
talent for citizenship, 749
Talleyrand, C. M. de
   Memoirs, 324
Tamanaha, B., 305
Taylor, C., 142, 146, 147, 340
technologies of regulation, 456
territorial pluralism, 553, 554
Teubner, G., 543
Thai Constitution, 616–618
Thiruvengadam, A.K., 500, 505
Thoreau, H. D., 412
Thornhill, C., 1017
Tiebout, C., 480
Tiede, L. B., 874
Tierney, S., 813, 814
Tilly, C., 497, 525
tobacco policy, 93
Tocqueville, A., 503, 558, 683
token multi-partisanship, 615
totalitarian democracy, 238

Trachtman, J., 959
transnational populism, 1024–1025. *See also* populism
Treasury and the House of Commons Public Accounts, 330
Treaty of Rome, 960, 969
Troper, M., 532
Trotsky, L., 517
Trueblood, L., 814, 815
Trump, D., 437, 634
trust, 458–459
trustees
   duty of loyalty, 605
   interest-protecting, 607
Tucker, P., 316, 330, 331
   Unelected Power, 622
Turkey, 821, 1012
Tushnet, M., 436, 921–923, 928, 931, 1018, 1019, 1025, 1026
   Bills of Rights, 893–898
two-sided theory of state, 193–196

U.K. Equality Commission, 618
U.S. constitutional law
   District of Columbia v. Heller, 477
   Dobbs v. Jackson Women's Health Organization, 477
   Entergy v. Riverkeeper, 474
   EPA v. EME Home City Generation, 474
   federal government institutions, 479
   federalism, 479–481
   Gonzales v. Raich, 480
   Mathews v. Eldridge, 476
   Michigan v. EPA, 474
   Morrison v. Olson, 479
   NFIB v. Sebelius, 480
   Obergefell v Hodges, 485
   Pike v. Bruce Church, 481
   Planned Parenthood v. Casey, 476
   rights, 475–479
   Roe v. Wade, 477
   Whitman v. American Trucking Associations, 474
   Whole Woman's Health v. Hellerstedt, 476
U.S. Supreme Court., review powers of, 347–348
Uitz, R., 1017
UK Human Rights Act, 894, 896
Ulfstein, G., 939
UN Charter, 939, 942, 949, 951
uncivil disobedience, 413, 414
uni-partisanship, 615
United Kingdom (UK), 172, 182, 188, 190, 271, 276, 316, 322, 368, 612, 615, 754, 761, 855, 859, 893, 912, 953

United Kingdom (UK) (cont.)
  Fixed Term Parliament Act (FTPA), 708
  Human Rights Act 1998, 13
  King Charles, 277
  King Charles I, 270
  parliamentarianism, 708–712
  Political Parties, Elections and Referendums Act, 754
  Representation of the People Act, 754
  single issue lottery-selected legislatures (SILL), 771
  single transferable vote (STV) systems, 763, 764
  Queen Victoria, 263, 270, 277
United Kingdom's Labour Party, 172
United Nations Convention on the Law of the Sea (UNCLOS), 941
United Nations Mission in Kosovo (UNMIK), 981
United States (US), 105, 108, 183, 188, 190, 228, 769, 801, 856, 857, 889, 1000, 1001, 1003, 1012, 1080
  Administrative Procedure Act (APA), 715
  separation-of-powers presidentialism, 714–716
  United States Congress, 273, 274, 681
    majority leadership in, 275
    power limit, 327
    representation in, 347
  United States Congress of 1789, 681
  US Constitution, 4, 14, 17, 36, 39, 85, 183, 273, 275, 293, 391, 504, 508, 518, 647, 738, 890, 892, 903
    dormant Commerce Clause, 481
  US Federal Constitution of 1787, 209
Universal Declaration of Human Rights, 741, 1058
Uruguay, 816, 1002

Van Parijs, P., 143, 145
Van Reybrouck, D., 770
Vermeule, A., 418, 686
Versteeg, M., 957, 967
vertical inequality, 645
Vienna Convention on the Law of Treaties (VCLT), 942, 943, 949
violence, 57, 59
  revolution, 506–511
Voigt, S., 873
von Gierke, O., 589, 590, 592, 595
von Stein, L., 681, 686
voting and voting systems, 36, 42, 54, 58, 574, 577, 226, 744
  children right, 767
  Mixed-Member Electoral systems, 763
  MMP systems, 764
  Parliamentary representation, 762
  Representation of the People Acts 1832–1928, 13

right to, 766–769
simple plurality system, 761, 762, 764, 766
single transferrable vote systems, 763
Voting Rights Act (1964), 888
Voting Rights Act of 1965, 109

Wade, W., 196
Wahnich, S., 507, 512
Waldron, J., 18, 50, 123, 131, 143, 280, 281, 288, 299–302, 305, 311, 348–351, 353, 360, 757, 793, 794, 796, 798, 804, 947, 950, 1010
  Bills of Rights, 893–898
  Core Of The Critique, 348
Walker, N., 222
Wallis, J., 280
Walzer, M., 1054–1056, 1060, 1062
war and peace, 105, 675
Warren, M. E., 72, 574, 575, 578
Washington, G., 509
Watt-Cloutier, S., 1039
Watts, R., 561
Webb, P., 941
Webb Yackee, J. W., 716
Webb Yackee, S. W., 716
Weber, M., 177, 186, 232, 237–239, 559, 681, 920
weighted multi-partisanship, 616–617
Weimar Constitution, 199
Weingast, B., 280
Weinrib, J., 368, 806
Weinstock, D., 138
Weithman, P., 134
welfare, 66, 94–99
welfarism, 470–471
well-being
  autonomy, 95
  desire-satisfaction, 88, 92–94
  freedom, 98
  hedonism, 88
  individual achievement of, 88
  liberty, 88
  objective list theories, 88
  pleasure, 90–91
  state control, 96
  state interference, 90–99
  welfare, 94–99
Wellman, C. H., 1062, 1063
Wenar, L, 40
Werner, F., 687
Wertheimer, A., 312
West, R., 311
Western Civilisation, 492, 50
Westminster parliamentary systems, 761, 768
Westminster system, 285, 316, 317, 321
Wheare, K., 6, 7, 10, 12

White, S., 983
Williams, B., 123, 124, 128, 176
Willoughby, W.W., 688
Wilson, J., 647
Wood, G., 503, 507
World Bank, 979, 981, 982
World Health Organization (WHO), 983, 1006
World Trade Organization (WTO), 939, 941, 950, 955, 977, 979, 982
World War I, 592

World War II, 193, 592, 597
Wright, G., 109

Young, I. M., 64

Zackin, E., 957, 967
Ziblatt, D., 468, 1072, 1081
Zimbabwe, 499, 816
Zionist revolution, 500, 510
Zurn, C., 256